U.S. Congress
on the
Sikh Struggle for Khalistan

VOLUME TWO
1999 - 2007

compiled and published by

International Sikh Organization

U.S. Congress on the Sikh Struggle for Khalistan

ISBN 978-0-9889370-1-7

Published in the United States of America

All spelling and grammar errors found in the documents are are part of the official record.

Dedications

Dedicated to the memory

of

In honor and remembrance of Sant Jarnail Singh Bhindrawale, Maj.General Shahbeg Singh, Bhai Amrik Singh, Sardar Satwant Singh, Sardar Beant Singh, Sardar Sukhjinder Singh (Sukha), Sardar Harjinder Singh (Jinda), Sardar Dilawar Singh and all the great Sikh martyrs, men, women, children who sacrificed their lives to protect their Faith, against the tyranny of the Indian government.

Foreword

Dr. Gurmit Singh Aulakh gave up a secure and prestigious position as a research scientist with the Harvard Medical School, Boston, MA, to serve the Sikh Nation. It is rare to find an individual who is so committed, dedicated and with single minded determination who forged ahead in trying to lobby the US Government for the freedom of the Sikhs and their Nation, Khalistan. The trials and tribulations of a political cause are never easy and the road to freedom is paved with untold difficulties. In spite of the financial constraints, Dr. G.S.Aulakh made the best of the situation, by doing an outstanding job of lobbying the US Congress and government for over two decades. Dr. G.S.Aulakh made sure, that the United States government knew and understood the untold miseries perpetuated against the Sikhs, a less than two percent, religious minority in majority ruled Hindu India. Due to his tireless efforts the, "Congressional Records" have been placed in permanent record. These records preserve the sustained ethnic cleansing, a history of continuous, gross human rights violations propagated against the Sikhs in Punjab and elsewhere in India, starting from 1984 till 2007.

India, the largest democracy in the world does not want the West to know its dark side, especially the hundreds of thousands of skeletons in its closet - literally. Hindu terrorism against Sikhs (Punjab), Kashmiri Muslims (Kashmir), Nagas (Nagaland), Manipuris (Manipur), Mizos (Mizoram), Dalits (the indigenous people), tribals (also indigenous people) across the swath of central India goes on unabated as the United States of America instead turns a blind eye on the highly profitable bilateral economic trade relations with India which seem to override gross human rights violations and justice. Real democracies listen to the genuine grievances of its aggrieved citizenry but does not beat them into submission and murder them. When multitude voices of liberty are muted by force for decades, the only option left for the discontented is to defy and defend themselves, against tyrannical oppression - peacefully. Unfortunately, even peaceful protest is violently curbed by the Indian-Hindu regime, all under the guise of national security and so-called terrorism. This two volume book is to remind and enlighten American citizens about the plight of the Sikhs in Punjab, India.

It has taken hundreds of hours to compile, format and finally finish this book. I would like to thank my wonderful family for their patience and support in this noble endeavor. I also would like to thank all the advisors of the "International Sikh Organization," volunteers, and many genuine well-wishers to bring this two volume book, "U.S. Congress on the Sikh Struggle for Khalistan 1985 – 2007," to fruition.

The Sikh Education Trust
USA

Introduction

We welcome the publication of *U.S. Congress on the Sikh Struggle for Khalistan*. This book is invaluable for all who seek to understand the truth about India's repression of Sikhs and other minorities. The statements in the *Congressional Record*, dating back to 1984, have been a very effective counter against the Indian government's efforts to rewrite history and erase their own brutal repression and their culpability in numerous tyrannical, violent, and even terrorist acts. I would like to thank all the Members of Congress, Republican and Democrat, past and present, who have spoken out against Indian repression. They have helped to keep the effort to liberate the Sikh Nation and the other nations of South Asia alive.

The Sikh Nation has been challenged many times since it came into existence. It has always risen to the challenge and has managed to preserve and protect its culture, heritage, and religion in the face of the most brutal repression. Its freedom and its very existence have been threatened. Each time, those who threatened the Sikh Nation have been destroyed. Today, the Indian government threatens the existence of the Sikh Nation and the Sikh religion. It will meet the same fate as all who have threatened us.

Since 1947, the Indian government has been enslaving the Sikh Nation. Under Indian rule, Sikhs are slaves. They are exploited, tortured, and killed for the convenience of the rulers. Despite India's repression of the Sikhs 'symbolized by half a million troops enforcing the peace of the bayonet' the Sikhs are reclaiming the freedom that is our birthright. The record of India's treatment of the Sikhs makes it clear that there is no place for the Sikhs in India's "democracy".

In June 1984, India undertook Operation Bluestar, a vicious military attack on the Golden Temple, the center and seat of Sikhism. The objective was to muzzle the voice of the Sikhs and to shut down the Sikh freedom movement that was emerging. India had been engaging in a pattern of abuse and deceit going back to the time of independence. But they forgot Sikhs do not submit to oppression. What the attack accomplished was to wake up the Sikh Nation to the necessity for its own independence in a sovereign Khalistan. Only through Khalistan can Sikhs be masters of their own destiny.

At the time that India became independent, Sikhs were to receive a sovereign state as Hindus and Muslims had. But Master Tara Singh and the Sikh leaders of the time were deceived into taking their share with India on the solemn promise that Sikhs would enjoy "the glow of freedom" in Punjab. That promise was broken almost immediately, with Home Minister Patel issuing a memorandum calling Sikhs "a criminal tribe" that was to be put under special watch. That memo justified the brutal repression of the Sikh Nation.

This repression has been bloody. Former Speaker of the Indian Parliament Balram Jakhar said, `If we have to kill a million Sikhs to preserve India's territorial integrity, so be it."

Guru Gobind Singh, the last of the Sikh Gurus, bestowed sovereignty on the Sikhs. Every morning and evening Sikhs pray, "Raj Kare Ga Khalsa," meaning "the Khalsa shall rule." Do we mean it?

It was out of this background that a Sikh freedom movement began to emerge. One of the leading spokesmen was Sant Jarnail Singh Bhindranwale. India labels Bhindranwale a terrorist, but that is the word they use for any Sikh who speaks out for freedom and sovereignty. One of the objectives of Operation Bluestar was to kill Bhindranwale and other Sikh leaders such as General Shabeg Singh, Bhai Amrik Singh, and others, in order to shut down the Sikh freedom movement. A former officer of the Research and Analysis Wing (RAW), Gurdev Singh Garewal, writes in his book *Secret Eye* that Sant Bhindranwale was shot at point-blank range by the Indian forces. Sant Bhindranwale said that such an attack would "lay the foundation stone for Khalistan," and that prediction turned out to be accurate. But the Indian forces thought it would end the movement.

In that attack and the simultaneous attack on 37 other Gurdwaras throughout Punjab, over 20,000 Sikhs were killed. The Indian forces shot bullets into the *Guru Granth Sahib*, the Sikh holy scriptures. They took young boys ages 8 to 13 outside and asked them if they supported Khalistan. When the young boys responded *"Bole So Nihal"*, they were shot to death.

Operation Bluestar was carried out with the cooperation of Sikhs who were opposed to Sant Bhindranwale such as the late Gurcharan Singh Tohra. Gurtej Singh, IAS, Professor of Sikhism, prints their letters and other documents in his book *Chakravyuh: Web of Indian Secularism*. After the attack, the Indian government sent their agents such as General Jaswant Singh Bhullar, Manjit Singh Sidhu, and others out to North America and other places to mislead the Sikhs and destroy the Sikh struggle for freedom. They formed organizations such as the World Sikh Organization for this purpose. They infiltrated Sikh organizations to neutralize them. They have sent 2,600 agents to America and Canada.

In the wake of Operation Bluestar, two Sikhs assassinated Prime Minister Indira Gandhi. Then they laid down their arms and surrendered. This led to the Delhi Massacre, which claimed another 20,000 Sikh lives. As the state-run radio and television cried "Blood for blood", Sikh police officers were locked in their barracks to keep them from interfering. Meanwhile, the government's carnage of Sikhs continued. Like Operation Bluestar, the Delhi massacres were designed to end the effort to liberate the Sikh homeland; like Operation Bluestar, they failed. Instead, the Delhi massacres served to remind Sikhs of the need to liberate Khalistan.

On October 7, 1987, the Sikh Nation declared its independence from India, naming its new country Khalistan. India responded by sending over half a million troops to Punjab to continue and expand the repression there. India does not seem to get the message that the Sikhs will not submit to their brutal repression. There are over 70,000 paramilitary forces, known as Black Cats, who have free rein to do as they please. Extrajudicial killings are routine in Punjab, even now when the violence is considered to have subsided. Sfor Khalistan continues to rise, with such leading figures as Jathedar Joginder Singh Vedanti and others overtly supporting it. (Jathedar Vedanti was recently forced out as Jathedar of the Akal Takht due to his support for Khalistan.) As former Jathedar of the Akal Takht Darshan Singh said, "*If a Sikh is not a Khalistani, he is not a Sikh.*" This book will show you many of the reasons why that is true. To this day, no sikh representative has ever signed the Indian constitution.

In 1994, the U.S. State Department reported that between 1992 and 1994, more than 41,000 cash bounties were paid to police officers for killing Sikhs. One of these was paid to a policeman who killed a three-year-old toddler. Another was paid to a police officer who killed a supposed "militant" who turned out to be alive and sued the Indian government, according to the *New York Post*. Militancy is the excuse that the Indian regime used for its mass killing of Sikhs.

India has murdered over 250,000 Sikhs since 1984, according to figures compiled by the Punjab State Magistracy and human-rights groups and reported in the book *The Politics of Genocide* by Inderjeet Singh Jaijee. It has also killed over 90,000 Kashmiri Muslims since 1988, 2,000 to 5,000 Muslims in Gujarat, more than 300,000 Christians in Nagaland since 1947, and thousands of Christians and Muslims elsewhere in the country, as well as tens of thousands of Assamese, Bodos, Dalits ("Untouchables," the dark-skinned aboriginal people of South Asia), Manipuris, Tamils, and other minorities. The Indian Supreme Court called the Indian government's murders of Sikhs **"worse than a genocide."**

According to a report by the Movement Against State Repression (MASR), 52,268 Sikhs are being held as political prisoners in India without charge or trial. Some have been in illegal custody since 1984! Amnesty International reported that tens of thousands of other minorities are also being held as political prisoners.

A human-rights activist named Jaswant Singh Khalra, Secretary General of the Human Rights Wing (SAD), was arrested after he exposed their policy of mass cremation of Sikhs, in which over 50,000 Sikhs have been arrested, tortured, and murdered, then their bodies were declared unidentified and secretly cremated. He studied three secret cremation grounds in Punjab to expose this brutal policy. Khalra was murdered in police custody. His body was not given to his family. No one has been brought to justice for the kidnapping and murder of Jaswant Singh Khalra.

The only witness to the Kahlra kidnapping, Rajiv Singh Randhawa, has been repeatedly harassed by the Punjab police, subjected to arrest for all sorts of pretended offenses, including trying to hand a petition to the British Home Minister in front of the Golden Temple. The late Sukhbir Singh Osan, proprietor of Burning Punjab, was repeatedly harassed and threatened for exposing Indian repression against the

Sikhs. In one typicakl phone call, he was warned by a hushed, secretive voice that "it is dangerous to write against the government."

The year after the Golden Temple attack, the Indian government tried to destroy the Sikhs by carrying out the worst act of aerial terrorism prior to the September 11, 2001 attacks on New York and Washington. That was the infamous 1985 bombing of Air India flight 182, which killed 329 innocent people. The definitive book on the subject is *Soft Target* by Zuhair Kashmeri and Brian McAndrew, which you will see referred to in some of these statements.

Soft Target proves that the Indian government itself carried out the bombing. This finding is confirmed in a book by former Member of Parliament David Kilgour entitled Betrayal: The Spy Canada Abandoned.

Soft Target shows how the Indian regime bombed its own airliner in 1985, killing 329 innocent people, to justify further repression against the Sikhs. The book quotes an investigator from the Canadian Security Investigation Service as saying, "If you really want to clear the incidents quickly, take vans down to the Indian High Commission and the consulates in Toronto and Vancouver, load up everybody and take them down for questioning. We know it and they know it that they are involved."

Among many other things, they note that the Indian Consul General in Toronto, Mr. Surinder Malik called in a detailed description of the disaster just hours later when it took the Canadian investigators weeks to find that information. He told them that they should check the passenger manifest for an "L.Singh" because he was responsible -- before there was any public knowledge of the bombing!

According to Wikipedia, on June 20, 1985, two days before the flight, "at 1910 GMT, a man paid for the two tickets with $3,005 in cash at a CP ticket office in Vancouver. The names on the reservations were changed; 'Jaswand Singh' became 'M. Singh' and 'Mohinderbel Singh' became 'L. Singh.'". Note that this is the same name that Consul General Malik told investigators to look for – "L. Singh."

It would later come out in newspaper reports that a Sikh named Lal Singh told the press that he was offered "two million dollars and settlement in a nice country" by the Indian regime to give false testimony in the case.

Malik had also pulled his wife and daughter off the flight suddenly at the last minute, on the feeble excuse that the daughter had a paper for school. A friend of Consul General Malik's who was a car dealer also cancelled at the last minute.

According to Kashmeri and McAndrew, "Curiously, [Consul General] Malik knew more details about the two blasts than did the police investigators....Malik said that while one of the suspects was booked to Japan, the other was booked to Toronto and onwards to Bombay. He also said that the two checked their bomb-laden bags but did not board the flight themselves. In sum, Malik had painted a scenario of the double sabotage operation that was a near perfect account of what the Mounties would take weeks to fathom.

[Consul General] Malik continually fed the Globe information pointing to Sikh terrorists as the source of the bombs. He was behind another story six days after the crash, this one headlined 'Air-India pilot reported given parcel by Sikh.'" Kashmeri and McAndrew also wrote, "Malik pressured the *Globe* to publish this story, adding that it could be used to make a stronger case for blaming the Air-India and Narita bombings on the Babbar Khalsa leader. Malik also decried the Canadian system of justice for failing to come up with a quick solution to the bombings. 'In India we would have had a confession by now. You people have too many civil and human-rights laws,' he complained."

The Sikh organization that the Indian government said was responsible, Babbar Khalsa, is and was then heavily infiltrated by Indian government operatives at very high levels of the organization. The main backer of the group had received a $2 million loan from the State Bank of India just before the plane was attacked, according to *Soft Target*. The year after the bombing, three Indian consuls general were asked to leave the country.

In his book, Kilgour wrote that Canadian-Polish double agent Ryszard Paszkowski was approached to join a plot to carry out a second bombing. The people who approached Paszkowski were connected to the Indian government.

Yet the Indian government continues to apply pressure to find some Sikhs guilty of the bombing despite the acquittal of the two Sikhs accused of carrying it out, Ripudaman Singh Malik and Ajaib Singh Bagri, who were acquitted by a Canadian judge, who said that the witnesses against them were "not credible."

These atrocities were unfortunately just two of the more egregious examples of the Indian government's terrorism against the Sikh Nation and the other minorities living within India's borders. There are such incidents as the planting of RDX explosives in the vehicle of a Sikh businessman from Sacramento who was in Punjab for a visit.

When the former Governor of Punjab, Surendra Malik, died, it was reported by an Indian newspaper that he had received $1.5 billion from the Indian government to foment and support covert state terrorism in Punjab and Kashmir.

Jathedar Gurdev Singh Kaunke was murdered by a police official; no one has ever been brought to justice. The driver for Sikh religious leader Baba Charan Singh had his legs tied to jeeps, which then drove off in opposite directions, tearing him apart. Where is the punishment of Swaran Singh Ghotna, who murdered Jathedar Gurdev Singh Kaunke? Where is the punishment of the police officers who kidnapped and murdered Sardar Jaswant Singh Khalra?

Professor Devinderpal Singh was deported to India from Germany, which claimed he had nothing to fear if he was sent back. He was immediately arrested and put in prison as soon as he landed in Delhi, tortured to obtain a false confession, charged and sentenced to death by hanging for a crime he did not commit.

Torture is routine in India, including such practices as stretching people, putting hot irons on their genitals, running heavy rods over their legs, and other such brutal practices. Yet India continues to proclaim itself "the world's largest democracy." In fact, as Representative Dana Rohrabacher (R-Cal.) pointed out, for minorities "India might as well be Nazi Germany." As Representative Edolphus Towns (D-NY) has said, "the mere fact that they have the right to choose their oppressors does not mean they live in a democracy." A spokesman for the Golden Temple told National Public Radio, "The Indian government, they are always boasting that they are democratic, that they are secular. They have nothing to do with a secularism, nothing to do with a democracy. They just kill Sikhs just to please the majority."

On Republic Day a few years ago, 35 Sikhs were arrested for marching, making speeches, and raising the flag of Khalistan. These are not crimes in a democratic country, but it shows just how desperate the Indain regime is to maintain its brutal control over Punjab, Khalistan.

As recently as late this past June, a Sikh was killed in Mumbai while protesting the Dera Sacha Sauda leader Ram Rahim Singh, who is a creation and operative of the Indian government.

India will not even accede to simple requests like returning Chandigarh to Punjab, allowing the Sikh farmers to make a decent living, or ending the diversion of Punjab's water to nonriparian states. Sikh farmers are forced to buy supplies at grossly inflated rates and forced to sell their crops at below-market rates. This has led to a massive number of suicides among Punjabi farmers. Sikhs are not allowed to buy land in the states outside Punjab, but Hindus are allowed – and encouraged -- to buy land in Punjab as part of the Hindu Raj's ongoing attempt to subsume Sikh culture and the Sikh religion into Hinduism.

In 2000, just before then-President Bill Clinton was due to visit India, 35 Sikhs were murdered in the village of Chithisinghpora. His own book, as well as the investigations of New York Times Magazine reporter Barry Bearak, and both the International Human Rights Organization and a joint effort of the Movement Against State Repression and the Punjab Human rights Organization found that Indian forces were responsible. Indian forces were caught red-handed in another village trying to set fire to Sikh homes and a Gurdwara to set the Sikh and Muslim residents against each other. The Sikhs and Muslims in the village worked together to detain the soldiers and capture their jeep.

On April 13, 1978, thirteen Sikhs were killed in cold-blood by the pseudo-Nirankaris in the heart of Amritsar who had been given permission to voice anti-Sikh sermons in the holy city of Amritsar by the Punjab government. In the same year, 4 Nihang Sikhs were killed at Pundri, Haryana, by police of the Akali Dal supported Haryana Government under the chief ministership of Chaudhary Devi Lal. In the same year Sikh protestors were fired at in Kanpur and Delhi leading to death of some activists.

On April 3, 1992, former judge of the Punjab and Haryana High Court and chairman of the Punjab Human Rights Organization, Justice Ajit Singh Bains was arrested under the anti-people legislation, TADA. In spite of massive protests by human rights activists, lawyers and political activists, the Punjab and Haryana High Court did not intervene.

In June 2005, the leaders of the Dal Khalsa and Shiromani Akali Dal (Amritsar) were implicated in false cases under sedition charges when they participated in a function to observe the anniversary of the attack on Darbar Sahib.

Foreign media and human-rights groups such as Amnesty International have been banned from Punjab. Amnesty International was banned in 1987. Even Castro's Cuba, one of the worst regimes on Earth, has allowed them in more recently than India.

As the late General Narinder Singh said, "Punjab is a police state."

These are but a few of the incidents of India's repression of the Sikhs and other minorities, which are discussed in detail in this volume. In addition, you will read about India's longtime alliance with the Soviet Union, its efforts to build a security alliance against the United States, its support of cross-border terrorism, and its long record of hostility to America and the democratic world.

The time has come for Sikhs to break free of the repressive Indian regime. This is the only way that their human rights will ever be respected. And the world is beginning to notice. In the United States Congress, the *Congressional Record* is serving as a vehicle to keep an accurate record of the repression and to defeat India's effort to whitewash the situation and the history of the Sikhs and other minorities.

Democracies don't commit genocide. Only in a free and sovereign Khalistan will the Sikh Nation prosper. In a democracy, the right to self-determination is the *sine qua non* and India should allow a plebiscite for the freedom of the Sikh Nation. Without political power, religions cannot flourish and nations perish. In this hour of supreme challenge, every Sikh, wherever he or she may be, must work for a free Khalistan. Let every Sikh work towards that end as if on him or her alone depends the survival of our nation.

Dr. Gurmit Singh Aulakh
President
Council of Khalistan
January 1, 2009

Table of Contents

MAP OF PUNJAB

(SHOWING DISTRICTS AND IMPORTANT CITIES AND TOWNS)

Document

CONGRESSIONAL RECORD -- EXTENSIONS

Friday, December 14, 2007
110th Congress, 1st Session
153 Cong Rec E 2585

REFERENCE: Vol. 153, No. 192
SECTION: Extension of Remarks
TITLE: INDIAN INTELLIGENCE PLANS TO ASSASSINATE SIKH LEADERS

Speech of
HON. EDOLPHUS TOWNS
of New York
in the House of Representatives
Thursday, December 13, 2007

Mr. TOWNS . Madam Speaker, while Dr. Gurmit Singh Aulakh, President of the Council of Khalistan, was visiting Belgium, he was informed of a very sinister plan by the Research and Analysis Wing (RAW), the intelligence service of the Indian government. RAW is the agency behind the Golden Temple attack and also, according to the excellent and well-documented book Soft Target, the agency behind the Air India bombing, which was the largest aviation terror attack prior to September 11.

According to sources in Belgium, which is the European headquarters of RAW, RAW is planning to assassinate Sikh leaders using Sikh operatives here in the United States. This sounds very much like their strategy in the Air India attack. Apparently, they haven't been able to come up with new terror tactics in 22 years.

One of the targets is a former Jathedar of the Akal Takht, which is the highest office in the Sikh religion. The Sikh leaders who are being targeted have one thing in common: they are supporters of freedom and sovereignty for Khalistan, the Sikh homeland that declared its independence from India in 1987.

You might also remember, Madam Speaker, that the Washington Times reported on January 2, 2002 that India was sponsoring cross-border terrorism in the Pakistani province of Sindh.

Given this terrorist record, why are American taxpayers being asked to support such a country? Although India proclaims itself democratic, the real India is the one that plans to assassinate Sikh leaders for seeking freedom, bombs its own airplanes to create an excuse to kill its Sikh minority, sponsors cross-border terror, and carries out other such reprehensible acts. Yet many in this country are blinded by India's democratic claims.

The time has come to say no more, Madam Speaker. We must stop our aid to this regime until every citizen within its borders and those outside can live securely in freedom, comfortable that no oppression, torture, or assassination plots will be aimed at them. We must demand a free and fair vote for all the people seeking their freedom from this brutal regime. And someone should call the FBI.

Plotting to assassinate Americans and others, no matter the circumstances, is an attack on us all, Madam Speaker. I hope that all my colleagues will join me in condemning it.

I would like to place the Council of Khalistan's news release on the RAW assassination plot into the Record for the information of my colleagues.

RAW Planning To Assassinate Sikh Leaders

Washington, D.C., December 6, 2007_During his recent visit to Belgium, Dr. Gurmit Singh Aulakh, President of the Council of Khalistan, was informed that agents of the Research and Analysis Wing (RAW), the intelligence agency of the Indian government, plan to assassinate prominent Sikh leaders, including a former Jathedar of the Akal Takht. Belgium is the European headquarters of RAW.

A very reliable Sikh source, who intervened to stop the assassination of a prominent Sikh leader, told Dr. Aulakh about the plot The RAW plot seeks to use Sikhs in the United States as their operatives.

India is determined to destroy the Sikh Nation and the Sikh religion, both inside and outside India. They are determined to eliminate the pro-Khalistan Sikh leadership worldwide so they can continue to carry out their violent rule over the Sikhs and absorb the Sikh religion into Hinduism. Indian intelligence is using every trick available to them to achieve this goal.

According to the book Soft Target by Zuhair Kashmeri of the Toronto Globe and Mail and Brian McAndrew of the Toronto Star, it was RAW that was responsible for the bombing of an Air India flight in 1985 that killed 329 people. Two Canadian Sikhs were acquitted on charges related to the bombing by a Canadian judge who said the evidence against them was "not credible." It was RAW that was responsible for the attack on the Golden Temple, the seat of the Sikh religion, and 38 other Gurdwaras in June 1984, an operation that killed more than 20,000 Sikhs.

The Indian government has murdered over 250,000 Sikhs since 1984, more than 300,000 Christians since 1948, over 90,000 Muslims in Kashmir since 1988, and tens of thousands of Tamils, Assamese, Manipuris, Dalits, and others. The Indian Supreme Court called the Indian government's murders of Sikhs "worse than a genocide."

Indian police arrested human-rights activist Jaswant Singh Khalra after he exposed their policy of mass cremation of Sikhs, in which over 50,000 Sikhs have been arrested, tortured, and murdered, and then their bodies were declared unidentified and secretly cremated. He was murdered in police custody. His body was not given to his family.

The police never released the body of former Jathedar of the Akal Takht Sardar Gurdev Singh Kaunke after SSP Swaran Singh Ghotna murdered him. Ghotna has never been brought to trial for Jathedar Kaunke's murder. No one has been brought to justice for the kidnapping and murder of Jaswant Singh Khalra.

According to a report by the Movement Against State Repression (MASR), 52,268 Sikhs are being held as political prisoners in India without charge or trial. Some have been in illegal custody since 1984! Tens of thousands of other minorities are also being held as political prisoners, according to Amnesty International. We demand the immediate release of all these political prisoners.

History shows that multinational states such as India are doomed to failure. Countries like Austria-Hungary, India's longtime friend the Soviet Union, Yugoslavia, Czechoslovakia, and others prove this point. India is not one country; it is a polyglot like those countries, thrown together for the convenience of the British colonialists. It is doomed to break up as they did.

"The flame of freedom burns brightly in the hearts of Sikhs," said Dr. Aulakh. "As Professor Darshan Singh, a former Jathedar of the Akal Takht, said, 'If a Sikh is not for Khalistan, he is not a Sikh'," Dr. Aulakh noted. "Liberating Khalistan is the only way to let the Sikh Nation live in freedom and dignity."

***

Document

CONGRESSIONAL RECORD -- EXTENSIONS

Thursday, December 13, 2007
110th Congress, 1st Session
153 Cong Rec E 2581

REFERENCE: Vol. 153, No. 191
SECTION: Extension of Remarks
TITLE: PAKISTANI GOVERNMENT RECOGNIZES ANAND MARRIAGE ACT

Speech of
HON. EDOLPHUS TOWNS
of New York
in the House of Representatives
Thursday, December 13, 2007

Mr. TOWNS . Madam Speaker, the government of Pakistan has recognized the Anand Marriage Act of 1909. This act covers Sikh marriages. I commend the Pakistani government for this show of tolerance and religious freedom.

There are only about 15,000 Sikhs in Pakistan. When is India, with its 22 million Sikhs, going to recognize the same act? It has been on the books for almost a century.

India refuses to enforce or even recognize the Anand Marriage Act. Instead, it records all Sikh marriages as Hindu marriages under the Hindu Marriage Act. This constitutes a refusal of "secular", "democratic"

India to recognize Sikhism as a separate religion. Instead, they seek to subsume it under Hinduism.

The fact that Guru Nanak, who began the Sikh religion, was born Hindu no more makes Sikhism a part of Hinduism than the fact that Jesus was Jewish makes Christianity part of Judaism. The Indian government is simply trying to eliminate the Sikh religion by subverting it and forcing Sikhs into Hinduism. Where is the freedom of religion in India?

Madam Speaker, this is unacceptable! America can and must do something to protect the rights and freedoms of all people in South Asia. We can start by stopping our aid to India and our trade until such time as it learns to respect the rights of all people regardless of ethnicity, religion, or social status. And we should put this Congress on record in support of self-determination for the Sikhs of Punjab, Khalistan, the Muslims of Kashmir, the Christians of Nagaland, and all the others who seek freedom. India will not allow such free and fair votes, belying its self-proclaimed democratic principles. The essence of democracy is the right to self-determination.

Madam Speaker, I would like to insert the Council of Khalistan's press release on the Anand Marriage Act into the Record.

Pakistan Recognizes Anand Marriage Act

Washington, D.C., December 6, 2007._The government of Pakistan has formally recognized the Anand Marriage Act, which governs Sikh marriages. The act was adopted in 1909.

Even though there are only about 15,000 Sikhs in Pakistan and there are millions of Sikhs in India, India still refuses to recognize the act. While Sikhs conduct marriages in accord with the Anand Marriage Act, the Indian government will not certify them under the act. Instead, they are recorded under the Hindu Marriage Act. The Indian government is trying to destroy the Sikh religion. Its failure to recognize the Anand Marriage Act is one more way that it is carrying out this effort. Sikh marriages are different from Hindu marriages. Hindu couples circle around a fire. Sikh couples circle around the Guru Granth Sahib, the Sikh holy scripture, four times.

"I would like to thank the Pakistani government for its recognition of the Anand Marriage Act, which is almost a hundred years old," said Dr. Gurmit Singh Aulakh, President of the Council of Khalistan, which leads the Sikh struggle for freedom. "Pakistan's action has shown a level of tolerance that supposedly secular, supposedly democratic India has never shown," he said. "That is very telling. It shows the true face of India," he said. "There is no place for Sikhs, Muslims, Christians, or other minorities there."

The Indian government has murdered over 250,000 Sikhs since 1984, more than 300,000 Christians since 1948, over 90,000 Muslims in Kashmir since 1988, and tens of thousands of Tamils, Assamese, Manipuris, Dalits, and others. The Indian Supreme Court called the Indian government's murders of Sikhs "worse than a genocide."

Indian police arrested human-rights activist Jaswant Singh Khalra after he exposed their policy of mass cremation of Sikhs, in which over 50,000 Sikhs have been arrested, tortured, and murdered, and then their bodies were declared unidentified and secretly cremated. He was murdered in police custody. His body was not given to his family.

The police never released the body of former Jathedar of the Akal Takht Sardar Gurdev Singh Kaunke after SSP Swaran Singh Ghotna murdered him. Ghotna has never been brought to trial for the Jathedar Kaunke murder. No one has been brought to justice for the kidnapping and murder of Jaswant Singh Khalra.

According to a report by the Movement Against State Repression (MASR), 52,268 Sikhs are being held as political prisoners in India without charge or trial. Some have been in illegal custody since 1984! Tens of thousands of other minorities are also being held as political prisoners, according to Amnesty International. We demand the immediate release of all these political prisoners.

History shows that multinational states such as India are doomed to failure. Countries like Austria-Hungary, India's longtime friend the Soviet Union, Yugoslavia, Czechoslovakia, and others prove this point. India is not one country; it is a polyglot like those countries, thrown together for the convenience of the British colonialists. It is doomed to break up as they did.

"Only a sovereign, independent Khalistan will allow the Sikhs of Punjab and the other people of the subcontinent to live in freedom, dignity, and prosperity," said Dr. Aulakh. "As Professor Darshan Singh, a former Jathedar of the Akal Takht, said, 'If a Sikh is not for Khalistan, he is not a Sikh'," Dr. Aulakh noted. "We must continue to press for our God-given birthright of freedom," he said. "Without political power, religions cannot flourish and nations perish. Let us join together and free Khalistan."

***

Document

CONGRESSIONAL RECORD -- EXTENSIONS

Thursday, December 13, 2007
110th Congress, 1st Session
153 Cong Rec E 2583

REFERENCE: Vol. 153, No. 191
SECTION: Extension of Remarks
TITLE: DR. AULAKH, PRESIDENT OF COUNCIL OF KHALISTAN, HAS SUCCESSFUL TRIP TO EUROPE

Speech of
HON. EDOLPHUS TOWNS
of New York
in the House of Representatives
Thursday, December 13, 2007

Mr. TOWNS . Madam Speaker, recently, Dr. Gurmit Singh Aulakh, President of the Council of Khalistan, made a very successful trip to Great Britain and Belgium. Belgium is the European headquarters of the Research and Analysis Wing (RAW), India's shadowy "intelligence service."

Dr. Aulakh spoke at three Gurdwaras and the crowds responded enthusiastically. They chanted pro-Khalistan slogans and they overwhelmingly supported the message of freedom for Khalistan, the Sikh homeland. This was a blow to the Indian occupation and oppression in Punjab, Khalistan.

Their support should be rewarded, Madam Speaker. We should go on record supporting a free and fair vote on the matter. And we should stop our aid to India until such time as they recognize basic human rights.

Madam Speaker, I would like to add the Council of Khalistan's recent release on Dr. Aulakh's European visit to the Record at this time.

Dr. Aulakh's Visit to Europe Very Successful

Washington, DC, Dec. 6._Dr. Gurmit Singh Aulakh, President of the Council of Khalistan, has recently returned from a very successful trip to Europe. He traveled to Gurdwaras in Belgium and Great Britain. He spoke at the Gurdwaras in Sint-Truiden in Belgium and in Slough and Birmingham in the United Kingdom. Belgium is the European headquarters of India's Research and Analysis Wing (RAW).

At every stop, slogans of "Khalistan Zindabad" filled the air. Enthusiastic crowds greeted Dr. Aulakh's message of freedom for Khalistan, the Sikh homeland that declared its independence from India on October 7, 1987.

"I would like to thank my hosts in Europe for helping to make the trip so successful," Dr. Aulakh said. The show of support for liberating the Sikh Nation, Khalistan, from Indian occupation shows that the flame of freedom burns brightly in the hearts of the Sikh Nation despite India's many years of oppression."

India has refused to allow so much as a vote on the matter of independence for Khalistan. It has refused to grant the people of Kashmir the plebiscite on their status that they were promised in 1948. It continues to kill and harass Sikhs and other minorities.

The Indian government has murdered over 250,000 Sikhs since 1984, more than 300,000 Christians since 1948, over 90,000 Muslims in Kashmir since 1988, and tens of thousands of Tamils, Assamese, Manipuris, Dalits, and others. The Indian Supreme Court called the Indian government's murders of Sikhs "worse than a genocide."

Indian police arrested human-rights activist Jaswant Singh Khalra after he exposed their policy of mass cremation of Sikhs, in which over

50,000 Sikhs have been arrested, tortured, and murdered, and then their bodies were declared unidentified and secretly cremated. He was murdered in police custody. His body was not given to his family.

The police never released the body of former Jathedar of the Akal Takht Sardar Gurdev Singh Kaunke after SSP Swaran Singh Ghotna murdered him. Ghotna has never been brought to trial for Jathedar Kaunke's murder. No one has been brought to justice for the kidnapping and murder of Jaswant Singh Khalra.

According to a report by the Movement Against State Repression (MASR), 52,268 Sikhs are being held as political prisoners in India without charge or trial. Some have been in illegal custody since 1984! Tens of thousands of other minorities are also being held as political prisoners, according to Amnesty International. We demand the immediate release of all these political prisoners.

History shows that multinational states such as India are doomed to failure. Countries like Austria-Hungary, India's longtime friend the Soviet Union, Yugoslavia, Czechoslovakia, and others prove this point. India is not one country; it is a polyglot like those countries, thrown together for the convenience of the British colonialists. It is doomed to break up as they did.

"The desire to reclaim the sovereignty that Guru Gobind Singh declared for us still resides in every Sikh heart," said Dr. Aulakh. "As Professor Darshan Singh, a former Jathedar of the Akal Takht, said, 'If a Sikh is not for Khalistan, he is not a Sikh'," Dr. Aulakh noted. *"We must continue to press for our God-given birthright of freedom," he said. "Khalistan must and will be free soon."*

***

Document

CONGRESSIONAL RECORD -- EXTENSIONS

Wednesday, November 14, 2007
110th Congress, 1st Session
153 Cong Rec E 2405

REFERENCE: Vol. 153, No. 176
SECTION: Extension of Remarks
TITLE: SIKHS OBSERVE ANNIVERSARY OF DELHI MASSACRES

Speech of
HON. EDOLPHUS TOWNS
of New York
in the House of Representatives
Tuesday, November 13, 2007

Mr. TOWNS . Madam Speaker, on November 3, Sikhs from up and down the East Coast gathered here in Washington to protest the 23rd anniversary of the Delhi massacres. Over 20,000 Sikhs were killed in that massacre, which followed the assassination of Indira Gandhi. Sikh police officers were locked in their barracks to keep them from interfering with the massacre. State TV and radio called for "blood for blood," inciting the people to kill more Sikhs.

This was a massive atrocity by the Indian regime against the Sikhs. It made it clear that the Indian government had no intention of treating the Sikhs like people in a free and democratic country ought to be treated. Instead, they chose to inflict mass terror on their Sikh citizens. This is not the way a democratic government acts, Madam Speaker. It is the action of a terrorist regime. India should be declared a terrorist regime for acts like this, for creating the Liberation Tigers of Tamil Eelam, and for its ongoing subversion of Pakistan by sponsoring cross-border terrorism in Sindh, as reported in the January 2, 2002 Washington Times.

Sikhs in attendance at the demonstration raised slogans in support of Khalistan as well as slogans in opposition to the massacre. As you know, the Sikhs declared their independence from India on October 7, 1987. Khalistan is their country, but it remains occupied by over half a million Indian forces. I would like to know why "the world's largest democracy" insists on maintaining authoritarian control of Khalistan instead of allowing the people there to have a free and fair vote on its status. This congress should put itself on record in support of such a vote, as well as the plebiscite that was promised to the Kashmiri people in 1948 and has never occurred. Nagalim, too, seeks its independence from India. The Nagas should also be granted the right to vote on their status. What would be wrong with that, if India is the democracy it says it is? And if India is the democracy it says it is, then why are so many peoples trying to get out from under its rule?

In addition to demanding that India allow the right to self-determination (which is the essence of democracy), we should demand that basic human rights be observed in "the world's largest democracy." The Delhi massacre is just one example of how basic human rights are ignored there. The murders of over 250,000 Sikhs, over 90,000 Kashmiri Muslims, more 2,000 to 5,000 Muslims in Gujarat, more than 300,000 Christians in Nagaland, and tens of thousands of other minorities, including Assamese, Bodos, Dalits, Manipuris, Tamils, and others speak loudly on the lack of human rights in India. So does the fact that Amnesty International has not been allowed into Punjab since 1984. This situation cannot continue.

We should cut off our aid and trade with India until it allows basic human rights, including but not limited to the right to self-determination, to all people under its rule.

Madam Speaker, the Council of Khalistan issued an excellent and informative press release on the Delhi massacres and the demonstration that was held this month. I recommend it to all my colleagues and I would like to place it in the Record at this time.

Sikhs Remember Delhi Massacres
With Very Successful Demonstration

Washington, D.C., November 13, 2007. *Sikhs from around the East Coast gathered by the Gandhi statue at the Indian Embassy in Washington, DC on November 3 to commemorate the Delhi massacres of November 1984 in which over 20,000 Sikhs were murdered while the police were locked in their barracks and the state-run television and radio called for more Sikh blood.*

The rally was attended by Sikhs from Philadelphia, including Dr. Bakhshish Singh Sandhu, S. Karj Singh, and S. Dharam Singh, as well as Sikhs from New Jersey, Baltimore, Maryland, Virginia, Washington DC, and other locations. New York Sikhs led by Sardar Avtar Singh Pannu also participated. The attendees spoke, carried signs, and chanted slogans. Slogans included "Khalistan Zindabad" ("Long live Khalistan"), "India free Khalistan", "India stop killing minorities", "India free Kashmir", "India free Christian Nagaland", and others.

The Delhi massacres were a brutal chapter in India's repression of the Sikhs, according to Dr. Gurmit Singh Aulakh, President of the Council of Khalistan, which is leading the demonstration. "This brutal, government-inspired massacre clarified that there is no place in India for Sikhs," Dr. Aulakh said. On October 7, 1987, the Sikh Nation declared its independence from India, naming its new country Khalistan. In the twenty years since then, India has continued its illegal occupation of Khalistan and stepped up the repression of the Sikhs while the Sikh Nation has continued to work to achieve its birthright.

History shows that multinational states such as India are doomed to failure. Countries like Austria-Hungary, India's longtime friend the Soviet Union, Yugoslavia, Czechoslovakia, and others prove this point. India is not one country; it is a polyglot like those countries, thrown together for the convenience of the British colonialists. It is doomed to break up as they did.

The Indian government has murdered over 250,000 Sikhs since 1984, more than 300,000 Christians since 1948, over 89,000 Muslims in Kashmir since 1988, and tens of thousands of Tamils, Assamese, Manipuris, Dalits, and others. The Indian Supreme Court called the Indian government's murders of Sikhs "worse than a genocide."

Indian police arrested human-rights activist Jaswant Singh Khalra after he exposed their policy of mass cremation of Sikhs, in which over 50,000 Sikhs have been arrested, tortured, and murdered, and then their bodies were declared unidentified and secretly cremated. He was murdered in police custody. His body was not given to his family.

The police never released the body of former Jathedar of the Akal Takht Gurdev Singh Kaunke after SSP Swaran Singh Ghotna murdered him. Ghotna has never been brought to trial for the Jathedar Kaunke murder. No one has been brought to justice for the kidnapping and murder of Jaswant Singh Khalra.

According to a report by the Movement Against State Repression (MASR), 52,268 Sikhs are being held as political prisoners in India without charge or trial. Some have been in illegal custody since 1984! Tens of thousands of other minorities are also being held as political prisoners, according to Amnesty International. We demand the immediate release of all these political prisoners.

"Only a sovereign, independent Khalistan will end the repression and lift the standard of living for the people of Punjab," said Dr. Gurmit Singh Aulakh, President of the Council of Khalistan. "Democracies don't commit genocide. As Professor Darshan Singh, a former Jathedar of the Akal Takht, said, 'If a Sikh is not for Khalistan, he is not a Sikh'," Dr. Aulakh noted. "We must continue to press for our God-given birthright of freedom," he said. "Without political power, religions cannot flourish and nations perish."

***

Document

CONGRESSIONAL RECORD -- EXTENSIONS

Wednesday, November 14, 2007
110th Congress, 1st Session
153 Cong Rec E 2406

REFERENCE: Vol. 153, No. 176
SECTION: Extension of Remarks
TITLE: BIRTHDAY OF GURU NANAK, FOUNDER OF SIKHISM

Speech of
HON. EDOLPHUS TOWNS
of New York
in the House of Representatives
Tuesday, November 13, 2007

Mr. TOWNS . Madam Speaker, this month marks the 538th birthday of Guru Nanak, the founder of the Sikh religion. As you may know, Guru Nanak was born in 1469 in what is now West Punjab. Every year, Sikhs from around the world gather in Nankana Sahib, where Guru Nanak was born, to honor him. Let me take this opportunity to honor Guru Nanak also and to congratulate the Sikhs of the world on this important occasion.

Guru Nanak stood up to tyranny. He worked to liberate his people from the tyranny of the Moghul ruler Babar. Today, Sikhs suffer under oppression from Hindu rulers who have murdered over a quarter of a million of them and hold more than 52,000 as political prisoners. They also killed over 300,000 Christians in Nagaland, over 90,000 Muslims in Kashmir, and tens of thousands of Assamese, Bodos, Dalits, Manipuris, Tamils, and other minorities. This oppression is no more acceptable than the oppression of Guru Nanak's time.

Sikhs can honor Guru Nanak by standing up to India to secure their own freedom and helping the other minorities secure theirs too. Freedom is the longing of every human heart. God intends for everyone to be free.

We are the primary power in today's world, Madam Speaker. We can use our influence to support the cause of freedom in South Asia. By doing so, we can honor Guru Nanak and all those who have worked for freedom around the world.

The time has come to let India know that if it is going to proclaim itself a democracy, it must act like one. That means allowing everyone, including minorities, to exercise their most basic human rights. Freedom is the birthright of all people. If India will not do so, it should be placed back on the list of nations that do not respect religious freedom, as it was at one time, and the appropriate sanctions should be imposed. In addition, unless India is willing to live up to its democratic principles, we should stop our aid to India in all forms.

Acting like a democracy also means recognizing the right of self-determination. Self-determination is the essence of democracy. Where is the vote on the status of Kashmir that India promised a mere 59 years ago? Does it take 59 years to set up a free and fair vote? Khalistan, the Sikh homeland, declared itself independent 20 years ago. Where is the vote on its status? And what of the Nagas and all the people simply seeking the freedom to rule themselves? The United States carries a lot of weight in the world. If we are serious about spreading democracy, we should work to bring about self-determination for all the peoples and nations of the subcontinent. That would help all people shake off oppression and live in dignity and prosperity, and it is the right thing to do.

Madam Speaker, I would like to place the Council of Khalistan's open letter regarding the birthday of Guru Nanak into the Record.

Congratulations to the Khalsa Panth on the Parkash Devas of Guru Nanak

Dear Khalsa Panth: As you know, this month marks the birthday (Parkash Devas) of the first Sikh Guru; Guru Nanak, founder of the Sikh religion. Congratulations to the Sikh Nation on this momentous occasion.

This year marks the 538th anniversary of the birth of Guru Nanak. He was born in 1469 and departed this world for his heavenly abode in 1539. Guru Nanak was the founder of the Sikh religion. ("Mary Sikha Jagat Witch Nanak Nirmal Panth Chalaya.") On November 24 in Nankana Sahib, now in West Punjab, Sikhs from around the world will celebrate this occasion. Last year, over 10,000 showed up for the celebration. Crowds enthusiastically raised slogans of "Khalistan Zindabad!" The Sangat showed great devotion and reverence on this pious occasion.

Guru Nanak confronted Babar, the Moghul ruler of the time and called him a Jabbar (oppressor) and spoke out against the tyranny of the rulers of that time. He was even imprisoned by Babar, along with his followers. Today, Sikhs face similar oppression by the Hindu rulers of India.

Just as Guru Nanak spoke out against the Moghul tyrant Babar, we must work to free our Sikh brothers and sisters from the oppression of the Brahmins. It is incumbent on us to achieve freedom for Khalistan, as is our birthright. As former Jathedar of the Akal Takht Professor Darshan Singh has said, "If a Sikh is not a Khalistani, he is not a Sikh."

India has murdered over 250,000 of our Sikh brothers and sisters, as well as more than 300,000 Christians in Nagaland, over 90,000 Kashmiri Muslims, and tens of thousands of other minorities. More than 52,000 Sikhs (and tens of thousands of other minorities) are being held as political prisoners. In 1994, the U.S. State Department reported that the Indian government had paid over 41,000 cash bounties for killing Sikhs.

A MASR report quotes the Punjab Civil Magistracy as writing "if we add up the figures of the last few years the number of innocent persons killed would run into lakhs [hundreds of thousands.]" The Indian Supreme Court called the Indian government's murders of Sikhs "worse than a genocide." Guru Nanak did not tolerate oppression; he struggled against it wherever it reared its ugly head. We must be good followers of Guru Nanak by doing the same today.India is also destroying Sikhs economically. The Indian government fixes the price for fertilizer very high and the price for produce very low so Sikh farmers can't even get the cost of production for their crops. This year it fixed the wheat price at Rs 750 per quintal. Even Badal demanded Rs 1000 per quintal. If Punjab farmers could sell their produce across the border in Pakistan and the Middle East, they could easily get close to Rs 1,500 per quintal and would be able to make a living.

India diverts Punajb's river water, its natural resource, to neighboring Haryana and Rajasthan without any compensation. India seeks to destroy the Sikh Nation religiously, economically, and politically. Guru Nanak would not permit them to do so. We must show the spirit of Guru Nanak and reclaim our sovereignty.

Guru Nanak travelled extensively, to the Middle East, where he visited Baghdad, and throughout India, along with his two companions, one Hindu, one Muslim. He spread his message of truthfulness, respect for the rights of individuals, earning an honest living, sharing with the needy, and praying to Almighty God. He was revered by Hindus and Muslims alike. When he left this world, his body was not found. The sheet covering his body was torn in two. The Hindus cremated it and the Muslims buried it, each according to their customs. Overcoming oppression in today's world will earn the Sikhs of today similar respect. We must not accept India's tyrannical rule over our homeland.

Guru Nanak is remembered as Baba Nanak Shah Faqir, Hindu Da Guru, Mussleman Da Pir. He preached the equality of the entire human race, including gender equality. To this day, these are cornerstones of the Sikh religion. But our Sikh brethren in Punjab, Khalistan do not get to experience equality. Instead, they are subjected to the worst kind of oppression by the Indian regime.

India is on the verge of disintegration. Kashmir is about to separate from India. As L.K. Advani said, "If Kashmir goes, India goes." History shows that multinational states such as India are doomed to failure. Countries like Austria-Hungary, India's longtime friend the Soviet Union, Yugoslavia, Czechoslovakia, and others prove this point. India is not one country; it is a polyglot like those countries, thrown together for the convenience of the British colonialists. It is doomed to break up as they did. Currently, there are 17 freedom movements within India's borders. It has 18 official languages. Montenegro, which has less than a million people, has become a sovereign country and a member of the United Nations. Now it is the time for the Sikh Nation of Punjab, Khalistan to become independent. The sooner the better.

Guru Nanak gave the Sikhs our identity. We can honor him by re-claiming the freedom that is our birthright: "Raj Bina Na Dharam Chaley Hain, Dharam Bina Sab Dale Male Hain." ("Without political power, a religion cannot flourish and without religion, people are oppressed and persecuted.") Let us stand up for the ideals of Guru Nanak and defend the integrity of the Sikh religion and the Sikh Nation.

> *Sincerely,*
> *Dr. Gurmit Singh Aulakh*
> *President, Council of Khalistan.*

***

Document 10

CONGRESSIONAL RECORD -- EXTENSIONS

Tuesday, October 23, 2007
110th Congress, 1st Session
153 Cong Rec E 2211

REFERENCE: Vol. 153, No. 161
SECTION: Extension of Remarks
TITLE: INDIA'S JEWISH COMMUNITY OUTRAGED OVER "NAZI COLLECTION"

Speech of
HON. EDOLPHUS TOWNS
of New York
in the House of Representatives
Tuesday, October 23, 2007

Mr. TOWNS . Madam Speaker, on September 30, Fox News reported an outrageous story. India has a small Jewish community and they are outraged at the emergence in Mumbai (formerly Bombay) of a new line of bedspreads called the "Nazi Collection." The proprietor, one Kapil Kumar Todi, claimed that it stands for "New Arrival Zone for India," but nobody takes that claim seriously. Mr. Todi pretends not to understand the outrage of the Jewish community, saying "It really does not matter to me who feels bad about it."

This collection is an outrage, not only against Jews, but against all people who believe in decency and tolerance. India should shut it down.

A restaurant in Mumbai used swastikas on its menus and called itself Hitler's Cross. After the Jewish community protested, the restaurant was forced to change its name. This shows the tolerance for Nazi ideas in India, and yet it considers itself the ally of Israel and the Jewish people.

As you know, Madam Speaker, India has been plagued by Hindu fundamentalism and many instances of religious intolerance. Christians, Muslims, Sikhs, and others have suffered religious violence that has claimed hundreds of thousands of lives. There has been destruction and laws have been enacted to prevent a Hindu from converting to another religion. A booklet was published telling people how to implicate Christians and others in false criminal cases. This is merely the latest outrage. But it is one more example of the lack of religious freedom in India. That is one reason that there are 17 freedom movements inside India.

This is unacceptable, Madam Speaker. It is one more reason why we should cut off our aid to India and our trade with that country and put the U.S. Congress on record in support of self-determination and freedom for the many nations seeking their freedom from India.

[From Fox News, Sept. 30, 2007]
Indian Jews Outraged Over "The Nazi Collection" Line of Bedspreads

Mumbai, India_Leaders of India's Jewish community expressed outrage Sunday over a new line of bedspreads called "The Nazi Collection" from a Mumbai-based home furnishing company that used swastikas in its promotional material.

The furnishing dealer said the name stands for "New Arrival Zone for India" and was not meant to be anti-Semitic.

But Jewish groups said they would file a lawsuit against the company.

"This is an enormous insult to Jews and all right-thinking people and must be retracted," said Jonathan Solomon, chairman of the Indian Jewish Federation.

There are about 5,500 Jews living in India, a predominantly Hindu nation of 1.1 billion people.

The bedspread line is not yet on sale, but brochures were handed out in a mall in a northern Mumbai suburb, the Times of India newspaper reported Sunday.

Furnishing dealer Kapil Kumar Todi said he chose the name because "that's what came to my mind," according to the paper.

"It really does not matter to me who feels bad about it," he said.

Some Indians regard Hitler as just another historical figure and have little knowledge about the Holocaust in which 6 million Jews were killed during World War II.

The swastika symbol, which was appropriated by the Nazis, was originally an ancient symbol used in Hinduism, Buddhism and other religions, and is still displayed all over India in hopes of bringing luck.

Last year, a restaurant in Mumbai, India's financial and entertainment capital, changed its name from Hitler's Cross after the city's Jewish community protested. The restaurant used swastikas on its signs and menus.

***

Document

CONGRESSIONAL RECORD -- EXTENSIONS

Tuesday, October 23, 2007
110th Congress, 1st Session
153 Cong Rec E 2212

REFERENCE: Vol. 153, No. 161
SECTION: Extension of Remarks
TITLE: K.P.S. GILL SHOULD NOT TESTIFY IN AIR INDIA INQUIRY

Speech of
HON. EDOLPHUS TOWNS
of New York
in the House of Representatives
Tuesday, October 23, 2007

Mr. TOWNS . Madam Speaker, K.P.S. Gill, the former Director General of Police in Punjab, has requested the opportunity to testify before the Major Commission, which is investigating the 1985 Air India bombing. The request comes in response to the testimony of officials from the Punjab Human Rights Organization who had valuable new information to impart. Mr. Gill should not testify.

Gill was part of the same machinery of Indian repression that led to the bombing. He was responsible for the murders of tens of thousands of Sikhs while he was DGP in Punjab. Mr. Gill was quoted as endorsing extrajudicial killings, saying that they "should happen." These are incidents where the police kill innocent people, then report it as an "encounter" to justify their actions. He was denied passage to the 1996 Olympics in Atlanta by every airline because of his terrorism and he had to leave the country immediately after India's field hockey games. He serves as president of the Indian Field Hockey Association. Almost 50 Members of Congress wrote to the State Department urging them to deny Mr. Gill a visa. He stands convicted of sexually harassing a high-level female Indian Administrative Service employee. He is not fit to be a witness in any civilized country. He ought to be in prison.

Gill has no information on the Air India incident. Why doesn't the Major Commission call Zuhair Kashmeri and Brian McAndrew, who wrote the book Soft Target, which details the Indian government's involvement in this terrorist act, or former Member of Parliament David Kilgour, who exposed the story of Ryszard Paskowski? Paszkowski was a

Canadian-Polish double agent who was approached by representatives of the Indian government who asked him to be involved in a second bombing. They said, "the first one worked so well." For For that matter, why not just call Mr. Paszkowski himself?

Gill's involvement in genocide is well known. Why should the Major Commission accept him as a witness?

Gill Should Not Testify Before Major Commission

Washington, DC, October 3, 2007._Former Punjab Director General of Police K.P.S. Gill is seeking to testify before the Major Commission, which is investigating the 1985 Air India disaster. His request comes in response to testimony from two officials of the Punjab Human Rights Organization (PHRO.)

Gill should not testify because he is a terrorist," said Dr. Gurmit Singh Aulakh, President of the Council of Khalistan. "He is responsible for the murders of tens of thousands of Sikhs. Now he is portraying himself as some sort of expert on the Air India bombing. The Council of Khalistan, the government pro tempore of Khalistan, leads the struggle to liberate Khalistan from India.

Gill was denied passage to the Atlanta Olympics by every airline in 1996 because of his terrorism. He had to be sent to Atlanta in a special train and he was sent out as soon as the hockey game was over. 49 Members of the U.S. Congress wrote to the State Department, urging them not to give Gill a visa. In that same year, he was convicted of sexually harassing a senior IAS official. A few years ago when Gill was visiting Belgium, his turban was removed from him by Sikh activists, who then chased him down to his hotel. In 1999, he was quoted as saying that fake encounters "should occur" if they are "necessary." Many innocent people, including a three-year-old child, have been killed in such encounters. In 1994, the U.S. State Department reported that the Indian government paid out over 41,000 cash bounties to police officers for such killings.

Gill presided over more than 50,000 extrajudicial killings, which were exposed by the PHRO in a study begun by Sardar Jaswant Singh Khalra, who was picked up by the police in September 1995 and murdered in police custody in October of that year. Many of these were secret cremations, in which Sikhs were arrested, tortured, and murdered, then their bodies were secretly cremated and declared "unidentified." Their remains were never even given to their families. It was for exposing this brutal policy that Gill's police arrested and murdered Sardar Khalra.

Gill serves as head of the Anti-Terrorist Institute of India, which has so far received $95 million in taxpayer funding from the government of Canada, and of the Institute for Conflict Management, which has received $65,000. "It is ironic that Gill heads an antiterrorism institute and he is a terrorist himself," said Dr. Aulakh. "Like most police officials, he has escaped any consequences of his actions. Gill should be tried for genocide."

Information recently released to Tehelka by the PHRO showed that Talwinder Singh Parmar, the leader of Babbar Khalsa (an organization significantly infiltrated and controlled by the Indian government) had identified Lakhbir Singh Brar (Rode), leader of the International Sikh Youth Federation (ISYF), as the main culprit behind the bombing and as an Indian government agent. A police official, Harmail Singh Chandi, showing documents that were supposed to have been destroyed, reported that Parmar was murdered in police custody. It is clear that Parmar was killed to keep him from talking about Rode's involvement. As a Canadian Security Investigative Service agent who was quoted in Zuhair Kashmeri and Brian McAndrew's book Soft Target said. "If you really want to clear up the incidents quickly, take vans down to the Indian High Commission and the consulates in Toronto and Vancouver. We know it and they know it that they are involved."

"If Gill can testify, why not call Kashmeri and McAndrew? Former Member of Parliament David Kilgour, who wrote Betrayal: The Spy That Canada Abandoned, should also be invited to testify," Dr. Aulakh said. In his book Kilgour reports on a Canadian-Polish double agent named Ryszard Paszkowski, who was approached by representatives of the Indian regime, who asked him to participate in a second bombing because "the first one worked so well." Paszkowski should also be invited to testify.

A report issued by the Movement Against State Repression (MASR) shows that India admitted that it held 52,268 political prisoners under the repressive "Terrorist and Disruptive Activities Act" (TADA), which expired in 1995. Many have been in illegal custody since 1984. According to Amnesty International, there are tens of thousands of other minorities being held as political prisoners in India. The Indian government has murdered over 250,000 Sikhs since 1984, more than 300,000 Christians in Nagaland, over 90,000 Muslims in Kashmir, tens of thousands of Christians and Muslims throughout the country, and tens of thousands of Tamils, Assamese, Manipuris, Dalits, Bodos, and others. The Indian Supreme Court called the Indian government's murders of Sikhs "worse than a genocide."

"How can anyone accept testimony of the representative of this bloody regime?" Dr. Aulakh asked. "In a free Khalistan, no one would accept those who carry out genocide against the Sikh religion and the Sikh Nation or against any other people," he said. "The Sikh Nation and the Sikh religion cannot flourish without political power. We must free Khalistan now.'

***

Document
CONGRESSIONAL RECORD -- EXTENSIONS

Tuesday, October 23, 2007
110th Congress, 1st Session
153 Cong Rec E 2213

REFERENCE: Vol. 153, No. 161
SECTION: Extension of Remarks
TITLE: BIRTHDAY OF GURU NANAK, FOUNDER OF SIKH RELIGION

Speech of
HON. EDOLPHUS TOWNS
of New York
in the House of Representatives
Tuesday, October 23, 2007

Mr. TOWNS . Madam Speaker, on October 20, Sikhs around the world will celebrate the birthday of Guru Nanak Dev Ji, the founder of the Sikh religion, who was born in 1469. There are about 25 million Sikhs worldwide. I would like to take this opportunity to congratulate Sikhs around the world on this important occasion.

Guru Nanak had a spiritual experience in 1499 while bathing in the Bein river. He received revelations for 3 days, then became a travelling preacher, preaching a philosophy of inclusion, tolerance, and univeralism. "There is neither Hindu nor Muslim," he said, and he used both Hindu and Muslim titles for God. Guru Nanak met with both Hindu and Muslim leaders.

His following continued to grow. He eventually settled in Kartarpur, Punjab.

Guru Nanak taught that humans could approach God directly, that God is a formless, unified being. He taught that we could do this by many means including meditation, purification, spiritual purity, and achieving detachment. He encouraged charity. He taught that caste didn't matter. All that mattered was following the spiritual path. He admonished his followers to oppose tyranny and repression.

The teachings of Guru Nanak and his successors are recorded in the Adi Granth, the holy scripture of the Sikh religion, also called the Guru Granth Sahib. It is written in Punjabi, the language of the Sikhs, which was not considered acceptable by the other religious leaders of the time, but which shows that God favors no caste or group.

Guru Nanak's birthday is a major occasion for the Sikh Nation and I congratulate Sikhs worldwide on the celebration of his birth, which gave rise to their religion.

***

Document

CONGRESSIONAL RECORD -- EXTENSIONS

Thursday, October 18, 2007
110th Congress, 1st Session
153 Cong Rec E 2178

REFERENCE: Vol. 153, No. 158
SECTION: Extension of Remarks
TITLE: INDIA IS A DEFICIENT DEMOCRACY

Speech of
HON. DAN BURTON
of Indiana
in the House of Representatives
Thursday, October 18, 2007

Mr. BURTON of Indiana . Madam Speaker, I was extremely disappointed today to see the Human Rights Watch had to issue a statement calling on the Government of India to finally take concrete steps to hold accountable members of its security forces who killed, "disappeared," and tortured thousands of Sikhs during its military campaign in the Punjab. I was disappointed because India should already be doing this. I was disappointed because this call to action is simply further proof that India_which prides itself on being the world's most populous democracy_is in reality a highly deficient democracy; and that it has yet to do what it legally and morally must do; which is to clean up its atrocious human rights record.

The massive human rights violations of the Indian Government have been well documented. In fact, according to the Department of State's 2006 Human Rights Report for India: "Major problems included extrajudicial killings of persons in custody, disappearances, torture and rape by police and security forces. The lack of accountability permeated the government and security forces, creating an atmosphere in which human rights violations often went unpunished. Although the country has numerous laws protecting human rights, enforcement was lax and convictions were rare." Again, these are not my words; this is from the State Department's official report on Human Rights.

Although relations between India and the United States have been rocky in the past, since 2004 Washington and New Delhi have been pursuing a "strategic partnership" based on shared values such as democracy, multi-culturalism, and rule of law. In addition, numerous economic, security and globally focused initiatives, including plans for "full civilian nuclear energy cooperation," are currently underway. I support these initiatives but I remain deeply concerned about the numerous serious problems that remain when it comes to India's respect for the rights of all of her citizens.

Madam Speaker, I ask unanimous consent to place a copy of the Human Rights press release into the Record at this time. I urge my colleagues to read it and remember it and as the United States and India move towards greater cooperation in numerous endeavors to insist that India live up to its moniker and adhere to the full expression of democracy and basic human rights; especially for members of ethnic or religious minorities.

India: Time To Deliver Justice for Atrocities in Punjab

Delhi._The Indian government must take concrete steps to hold accountable members of its security forces who killed, "disappeared," and tortured thousands of Sikhs during its counterinsurgency campaign in the Punjab, Human Rights Watch and Ensaaf said in a new report released today.

In order to end the institutional defects that foster impunity in Punjab and elsewhere in the country, the government should take new legal and practical steps, including the establishment of a commission of inquiry, a special prosecutor's office, and an extensive reparations program.

The 123-page report, "Protecting the Killers: A Policy of Impunity in Punjab, India," examines the challenges faced by victims and their relatives in pursuing legal avenues for accountability for the human rights abuses perpetrated during the government's counterinsurgency campaign. The report describes the impunity enjoyed by officials responsible for violations and the near total failure of India's judicial and state institutions, from the National Human Rights Commission to the Central Bureau of Investigation (CBI), to provide justice for victims' families.

Beginning in the 1980s, Sikh separatists in Punjab committed serious human rights abuses, including the massacre of civilians, attacks upon Hindu minorities in the state, and indiscriminate bomb attacks in crowded places. In its counterinsurgency operations in Punjab from 1984 to 1995. Indian security forces committed serious human rights abuses against tens of thousands of Sikhs. None of the key architects of this counterinsurgency strategy who bear substantial responsibility for these atrocities have been brought to justice.

"Impunity in India has been rampant in Punjab, where security forces committed large-scale human rights violations without any accountability," said Brad Adams, Asia director at Human Rights Watch. "No one disputes that the militants were guilty of numerous human rights abuses, but the government should have acted within the law instead of sanctioning the killing, 'disappearance,' and torture of individuals accused of supporting the militants."

A key case discussed in detail in the report is the Punjab "mass cremations case," in which the security services are implicated in thousands of killings and secret cremations throughout Punjab to hide the evidence of wrongdoing. The case is currently before the National Human Rights Commission, a body specially empowered by the Supreme Court to address this case. However, the commission has narrowed its efforts to merely establishing the identity of the individuals who were secretly cremated in three crematoria in just one district of Punjab. It has rejected cases from other districts and has ignored the intentional violations of human rights perpetrated by India's security forces. For more than a decade, the commission has failed to independently investigate a single case and explicitly refuses to identify any responsible officials.

"The National Human Rights Commission has inexplicably failed in its duties to investigate and establish exactly what happened in Punjab,"

said Adams. "We still hold out hope that it will change course and bring justice to victims and their families."

The report discusses the case of Jaswant Singh Khalra, a leading human rights defender in Punjab who was abducted and then murdered in October 1995 by government officials after being held in illegal detention for almost two months. Despite credible eyewitness testimony that police chief KPS Gill was directly involved in interrogating Khalra in illegal detention just days prior to Khalra's murder, the Central Bureau of Investigation has thus far refused to investigate or prosecute Gill. In September 2006, Khalra's widow, Paramjit Kaur, filed a petition in the Punjab & Haryana High Court calling on the CBI to take action against Gill. More than a year later, she is still waiting for a hearing on the merits.

"Delivering justice in Punjab could set precedents throughout India for the redress of mass state crimes and superior responsibility," said Jaskaran Kaur, co-director of Ensaaf. "Indians and the rest of the world are watching to see if the current Indian government can muster the political will to do the right thing. It if fails, then the only conclusion that can be reached is that the state's institutions cannot or will not take on the security establishment. This has grave implications for Indian democracy."

Victims and their families seeking justice face severe challenges, including prolonged trials, biased prosecutors, an unresponsive judiciary, police intimidation and harassment of witnesses, and the failure to charge senior government officials despite evidence of their role in the abuses.

Tarloehan Singh described the hurdles he has faced in his now 18-year struggle before Indian courts for justice for the killing of his son, Kulwinder Singh:

"I used to receive threatening phone calls. The caller would say that they had killed thousands of boys and thrown them into canals, and they would also do that to Kulwinder Singh's wife, kid, or me and my wife . . .

"The trial has been proceeding . . . with very little evidence being recorded at each hearing, and with two to three months between hearings. During this time, key witnesses have died."

After Mohinder Singh's son Jugraj Singh was killed in an alleged faked armed encounter between security forces and separatists in January 1995, he pursued numerous avenues of justice. He brought his case before the Punjab & Haryana High Court and the CBI Special Court, but no police officer was charged. A CBI investigation found that Jugraj Singh had been killed and cremated by the police. However, 11 years and a few inquiry reports later, the CBI court ended Mohinder Singh's pursuit for accountability by dismissing his case in 2006. Mohinder Singh describes his interactions with the CBI:

"On one occasion when [the officer] from the CBI came to my house, he told me that I wasn't going to get anything out of this. Not justice and not even compensation. He further said that: 'I see you running around pursuing your case. But you shouldn't get into a confrontation with the police. *You have to live here and they can pick you up at any time.' He was indirectly threatening me."*

Human Rights Watch and Ensaaf expressed concern that the Indian government continues to cite the counterinsurgency operations in Punjab as a model for preserving national integrity.

"The government's illegal and inhuman policies in the name of security have allowed a culture of impunity to prevail that has brutalized its police and security forces," said Kaur.

The report suggests a comprehensive framework to address the institutionalized impunity that has prevented accountability in Punjab. The detailed recommendations include establishing a commission of inquiry, a special prosecutor's office, and an extensive reparations program.

"The Indian government needs to send a clear message to its security services, courts, prosecutors, and civil servants that it neither tolerates nor condones gross human rights violations under any circumstances," said Adams. "This requires a comprehensive and credible process of accountability that delivers truth, justice, and reparations to its victims, who demand nothing more than their rights guaranteed by India's constitution and international law."

***

Document

CONGRESSIONAL RECORD -- EXTENSIONS

Wednesday, October 03, 2007
110th Congress, 1st Session
153 Cong Rec E 2053

REFERENCE: Vol. 153, No. 149
SECTION: Extension of Remarks
TITLE: INDIA BUGGED BLAIR'S HOTEL ROOM

Speech of
HON. EDOLPHUS TOWNS
of New York
in the House of Representatives
Wednesday, October 3, 2007

Mr. TOWNS . Madam Speaker, on August 3, India-West reported that during former British Prime Minister Tony Blair's visit to India shortly after the 9/11 attacks, the Indian regime bugged Prime Minister Blair's hotel room. According to the article, they didn't do a very good job of it, either.

India-West reported that Prime Minister Blair's associate, Alistair Campbell, wrote in his book that Blair's people found the bugs but decided not to make a fuss about them. According to India-West, Campbell writes that "On his way to the hotel, Blair asked the then British

High Commissioner in India if the car was bugged only to receive a 'kind of noncommittal no.'" Campbell also describes the discovery of two listening devices in Prime Minister Blair's hotel room. Campbell reported that the bugs couldn't be removed "without drilling the wall," so Mr. Blair simply used a different room. He also writes about a valet named Sunil who was there wherever Campbell went. "I was beginning to wonder whether he had been put there either by spooks or by a paper," Campbell wrote.

Madam Speaker, this is an outrage. The fact that India feels the need to spy on a democratic leader who is fighting the same war on terror that India claims to support shows that India's sympathies do not lie on the side of the Free World. It also shows that India's claims to be a democracy ring hollow. Perhaps they can hear their claims ring hollow in one of their listening devices.

Those claims are further belied by India's ongoing repression against Sikhs, Christians, Muslims, and other minorities. We all know that India has murdered more than a quarter of a million Sikhs, over 300,000 Christians in Nagaland, more than 90,000 Muslims in Kashmir, 2,000 to 5,000 Muslims in Gujarat, and tens of thousands of other minorities such as manipuris, Tamils, Bodos, Assamese, Bengalis, Dalits, et cetera. We all know of the tens of thousands of political prisoners. Harassment and false arrest are common. Some Sikh activists were arrested for making speeches and raising a flag! Does that sound like democracy to you, Madam Speaker?

Why do we accept this? America is founded on the idea of freedom for all. There is something we can do about the tyranny in India. We owe it to the oppressed people there to stop our aid and trade with India (especially since more than 836 million people there live on less than 40 cents per day) and we should demand self-determination for the people of Punjab, Khalsitan, Nagalim, Kashmir, and all people seeking their freedom. Self-determination is the essence of democracy. Our actions can help bring real freedom and prosperity to all the people of the subcontinent. Let us do whatever we can.

[From the Times of India, Aug. 3, 2007]
Delhi Clumsily Bugged Tony Blair's Room During 2001 Visit
(By Rashmee Roshan Lall)

London._Indian intelligence clumsily bugged Tony Blair's hotel room in Delhi during the British prime minister's visit to India one month after the 9/11 attacks, his chief spin doctor Alastair Campbell has said.

In his newly published diaries released in India July 25. Campbell said Blair's entourage found the bugs but decided not to make a fuss. On his way to the hotel, Blair asked the then British High Commissioner in Delhi if the car was bugged, only to receive a "kind of noncommittal no." Campbell writes about Blair's passage to India on Oct. 5, 2001.

Later, he describes an "incriminating" discovery of two bugs in the British prime minister's hotel room.

"At the hotel, our security service guys had found two bugs in TB's bedroom and said they wouldn't be able to move them without drilling the wall, so TB used a different room," he wrote.

Campbell's revelations are probably the first time someone within the innermost circle of a British prime minister has openly accused the Indian authorities of bugging and dirty tricks. Campbell also claims in the diaries, titled "The Blair Years," that he too was probably spied upon by Indian intelligence, via the services of a "valet" named Sunil.

The "valet," says Campbell drove him "bananas everywhere I went, he was there. I was beginning to wonder whether he had been put there either by the spooks or a paper."

***

Document

CONGRESSIONAL RECORD -- EXTENSIONS

Wednesday, October 03, 2007
110th Congress, 1st Session
153 Cong Rec E 2054

REFERENCE: Vol. 153, No. 149
SECTION: Extension of Remarks
TITLE: TOP POLICE OFFICIAL ARRESTED IN PUNJAB

Speech of
HON. EDOLPHUS TOWNS
of New York
in the House of Representatives
Wednesday, October 3, 2007

Mr. TOWNS . Madam Speaker, recently, the former Director General of Police of Punjab, S.S. Virk, was arrested on September 9 on corruption charges. Ironically, he was arrested by the government of Chief Minister Parkash Singh Badal, who in his previous tenure redefined corruption as "fee for service"_no fee, no service.

Apparently, Mr. Virk managed to collect the equivalent of a billion dollars in assets on a meager police official's salary. I salute the arrest of Mr. Virk and hope he does serious jail time. But Mr. Virk should be arrested for more than corruption.

Mr. Virk was Director General when tens of thousands of Sikhs were murdered by the Indian regime in Punjab, Khalistan. Nobody has been brought to justice for these murders nor for the murders of other minorities, such as Christians, Muslims, and others.

I call on the Indian government to bring to justice the likes of Mr. Virk, K.P.S. Gill, and the others who were responsible for the atrocities against the Sikhs and other minorities. Until they do so, we should stop our aid to India and our trade with that country. And we should put the

U.S. Congress on record in support of freedom for Khalistan, Kashmir, Nagalim, and the other nations seeking to be free in south Asia by means of a free and fair plebiscite on their status.

The Indian newspapers gave some good coverage to Mr. Virk's arrest and the Council of Khalistan published an excellent press release about the situation.

Former DGP Virk Arrested for Corruption

Washington, DC, Sept. 12, 2007._Former Punjab Director General of Police S.S. Virk was arrested Sunday by the Vigilance Bureau (a state agency of Punjab) for corruption. He had amassed wealth in excess of 100 crore (100 million) rupees. This was far in excess of what he received from his position as DGP. He was also charged with misuse of his official position, making private business deals as a public servant. Virk had arrangements with "Cats," former "militants" who turned to working for the Indian regime, to kill Sikhs throughout Punjab. While Virk was amassing this wealth, half of the population of India continues to subsist on less than two dollars per day.

Hours after his arrest, he was hospitalized with high blood pressure and gallstones. A case was registered against him under the Prevention of Corruption Act. Virk had been removed as DGP shortly before the Punjab elections earlier this year. He had been suspended by the Badal government shortly after it came to power in February. Former Chief Minister Amarinder Singh has openly supported Virk. "We are amazed that someone of the stature of Captain Amarinder Singh supports the corruption and the killing of Sikhs under S.S. Virk's regime," said Dr. Gurmit Singh Aulakh, President of the Council of Khalistan. Virk was quoted as saying that "everyone in the world" keeps agents like the "Cats." "Even if that were true, that does not relieve him of his responsibility," Dr. Aulakh said. "No law enforcement agency should be allowed to murder ordinary citizens. If they break the law, they should be tried in the court and punishment should be determined by the courts, not by police officials."

Virk claimed that his arrest was a "political victimization and vendetta." The Badal family, during their prior term in office, ran the most corrupt government in Punjab's history. They practiced corruption on a grand scale. Unless they were paid a bribe (which they renamed "fee for service"), no service was provided. Former DGP K.P.S. Gill presided over the murders of more than 50,000 extrajudicial killings, which were exposed by the Punjab Human Rights Organization (PHRO) in a study begun by Sardar Jaswant Singh Khalra, who was picked up by the police in September 1995 and murdered in police custody in October of that year.

"We salute the arrest of S.S. Virk," said Dr. Gurmit Singh Aulakh, President of the Council of Khalistan. "We are glad that he is under arrest. There shouldn't be any corruption in high places," Dr. Aulakh said. "When will Badal, Gill, and the others responsible for high-level corruption and atrocities against the Sikh nation be arrested?" he asked.

"In a free Khalistan, no one would accept those who carry out geno-cide against the Sikh religion and the Sikh Nation or against any other people. They would all be arrested, not just selectively arrested to cover the corruption of the leaders ordering the arrest" said Dr. Aulakh.

Dr. Aulakh also cited the case of Sukhwinder Singh Sukhi, a "Cat," who was reported as killed. Someone was killed in his place, his identity was changed, and he was used by the police to kill Sikhs. "Who was killed in Sukhi's place?" asked Dr. Aulakh. Several years ago, a Sikh man who had been reported as killed by the police went to court to force the government to declare him alive.

A report issued by the Movement Against State Repression (MASR) shows that India admitted that it held 52,268 political prisoners under the repressive "Terrorist and Disruptive Activities Act" (TADA), which expired in 1995. Many have been in illegal custody since 1984. According to Amnesty International, there are tens of thousands of other minorities being held as political prisoners in India. The Indian government has murdered over 250,000 Sikhs since 1984, more than 300,000 Christians in Nagaland, over 90,000 Muslims in Kashmir, tens of thousands of Christians and Muslims throughout the country, and tens of thousands of Tamils, Assamese, Manipuris, Dalits, Bodos, and others. The Indian Supreme Court called the Indian government's murders of Sikhs "worse than a genocide."

"The time is now to launch a Shantmai Morcha to free Khalistan," Dr. Aulakh said. "That is the only way to prevent this kind of corruption and allow the Sikh Nation to live in freedom, peace, dignity, and prosperity. The time has come for some pro-Sikh organizations such as Dal Khalsa and others to step forward in Punjab and accelerate our struggle for the liberation of Khalistan," he said. "Religions cannot flourish without political power. We must free Khalistan now."

- - - - - - - - -

[From the Times of India, Sept. 9, 2007.]
Former Punjab DGP S S Virk Arrested

New Delhi_Former Punjab DGP S S Virk was arrested here on Sunday by Punjab Vigilance Bureau in connection with a case registered against him for allegedly possessing assets disproportionate to his known sources of income. Virk, who was removed as DGP shortly before the assembly elections in Punjab this year, was arrested from Maharashtra Sadan by a team of vigilance officials, senior Bureau officials said. The senior IPS officer of the Maharashtra cadre, who was repatriated from Punjab by the Centre after the Punjab elections, was also charged with having misused his authority by indulging in private business as a public servant in violation of service rules, the sources said.

The case was registered against Virk on Saturday under the Prevention of Corruption Act after investigations for the last few months, the sources said, adding the former DGP did not offer any resistance at the time of his arrest.

- - - - - - - - -

[From Rediff India Abroad, Sept. 9, 2007]
Former Punjab DGP S S Virk Arrested

Former Punjab Director General of Police S S Virk, who was removed shortly before the assembly poll in the state, was arrested on Sunday on charges of possessing assets disproportionate to his known sources of income and misuse of official position.

Virk, a senior IPS officer of the Maharashtra cadre, who was arrested in Delhi by a team of Punjab Vigilance Bureau officials, described the charges against him as 'false and fabricated.'

A case was registered against Virk under the Prevention of Corruption Act on Saturday, Vigilance Bureau Sources said, adding that he did not offer any resistance at the time of his arrest.

Soon after his arrest from Maharashtra Sadan in New Delhi on Sunday morning, the former Punjab Police chief was taken by road to Mohali near Chandigarh where he was quizzed by vigilance sleuths.

He was also medically examined, the sources said, adding that searches were also conducted at a number of places in Punjab in connection with properties owned by the former DGP.

The team that arrested Virk included four officers of the rank of Superintendent of Police.

Besides allegedly possessing assets disproportionate to his known sources of income, the ex-DGP was charged with misusing his authority by indulging in private business as a public servant in violation of service rules.

A visibly tired Virk, who was repatriated by the Centre from Punjab after the assembly election, told media persons at a police station in Mohali that all the cases registered against him were false and fabricated. "It is political victimisation and vendetta," said the IPS officer.

Virk, the first DGP from the state to be arrested, was suspended by the SAD-BJP government, led by Parkash Singh Badal, soon after it came to power in February this year.

He was removed as DGP shortly before the assembly poll by the Election Commission after the opposition SAD leveled allegations of corruption against him.

It also charged Virk with helping the then ruling Congress at former Chief Minister Amarinder Singh's behest After his removal as DGP, Virk was initially posted as DGP-cum-Chairman Punjab Police Housing Corporation on January 22 and suspended in April.

R S Gill, a 1973 batch IPS officer, was appointed DGP Punjab on January 22 after Virk was removed by the Election Commission.

***

Document

CONGRESSIONAL RECORD -- EXTENSIONS

Thursday, September 27, 2007
110th Congress, 1st Session
153 Cong Rec E 1999

REFERENCE: Vol. 153, No. 145
SECTION: Extension of Remarks
TITLE: OPERATION SILENCE: SHIFTING BLAME ON AIR INDIA
BOMBING

Speech of
HON. EDOLPHUS TOWNS
of New York
in the House of Representatives
Thursday, September 27, 2007

Mr. TOWNS . Madam Speaker, on August 4, the Indian newspaper and website Tehelka, which has done significant work exposing corruption in India, published a report on the 1985 Air India bombing, which was the worst terrorist incident involving aircraft until September 11, 2001. In the report, they produce new evidence that the Indian Government was responsible for the attack, which killed 329 innocent people.

The new report discusses the interrogation of the late Babbar Khalsa leader Talwinder Singh Parmar, who was considered by the Indians to be one of the masterminds of the attack. It should be noted that Babbar Khalsa was and is heavily infiltrated by the Indian Government and has been pretty much under its control

In his interrogation, Parmar points the finger of responsibility straight at the Indian Government. The documents, obtained from the Punjab Human Rights Organization, PHRO, which conducted a 7-year investigation, were supposed to have been destroyed by the interrogating officer, but he secretly kept them all this time.

Parmar identifies Lakhbir Singh Rode as a mastermind of the bombing. Rode is head of the International Sikh Youth Federation. According to PHRO, Rode is an agent of the Indian Government. Sarabjit Singh, chief investigator for the PHRO, reports that Parmar was ordered killed to cover up Rode's involvement.

Parmar was supposed to have been killed in an encounter with police, but the PHRO pointed out that he had been in police custody for some time at the time he was killed. PHRO reports that there is "conclusive evidence" that Parmar was killed in police custody.

With this information coming on top of the mountain of evidence produced by Zuhair Kashmeri and Brian McAndrew in their book Soft Target and the report by former Member of Parliament David Kilgour in his book Betrayed: The Spy Canada Abandoned, in which he reports that a Canadian-Polish double agent was approached by representatives of the Indian Government asking him to become involved in a second bombing because "the first one worked so well," there can be no doubt that the Indian Government itself is the real culprit behind this act of terrorism. The links are just too strong.

State terrorism is unacceptable whether it is carried out by the Taliban in Afghanistan, by Mr. Ahmadinejad in Iran, by some tinhorn dictator in Latin America, or by the "world's largest democracy." We cannot let this stand. The time has come to stop our aid to India, end our trade, and speak out strongly for self-determination, the cornerstone of democracy, throughout South Asia. Only then will these kinds of abuses, designed to set up one ethnic or religious group as "terrorists" so they can be killed, come to an end.

I request the permission of the House to place the Tehelka article in the Record for the information of my colleagues and the public.

Kanishka Tragedy_Operation Silence
(By Vikram Jit Singh)

Fifteen years after Babbar Khalsa International leader Talwinder Singh Parmar, one of the two alleged masterminds of the mid-air bombing of Air India's Kanishka airplane, was shown as having being killed in an encounter in Punjab, retired Punjab Police DSP Harmail Singh Chandi, who nabbed Parmar from Jammu in September 1992 and interrogated him for five days before he was killed along with five others, has come forward with the claim that Parmar was killed in police custody on the orders of senior police officers, who also asked his confession record to be destroyed. In his confession, Parmar had named Lakhbir Singh Brar "Rode", nephew of the late Bhindranwale and head of the banned International Sikh Youth Federation, as the mastermind of the bombing. Rode, who is now said to be holed up in Lahore, has never figured in the investigations of either the CBI or the Canadian authorities.

Chandi has brought forward the entire record of Parmar's confession, including audio tapes and statements, before the Royal Canadian Mounted Police (RCMP) and the John Major Commission of Inquiry that is reinvestigating the June 23, 1985 blast that claimed 331 lives off the Irish coast. Chandi had been ordered by senior officers to destroy the records but he retained them secretly. The record was brought before the Major Commission due to seven-year-long investigations by the Punjab Human Rights Organisation (PHRO), a Chandigarh-based ngo that conducted interviews of Parmar's associates in India and Canada and pieced together a comprehensive report. The PHRO's Principal Investigator Sarbjit Singh and lawyer Rajvinder Singh Bains flew to Canada along with Harmail in June and produced their findings before the Commission's counsels.

A Canadian citizen, Parmar was shown as having been killed in an exchange of fire between police and six militants in the wee hours of October 15, 1992, near village Kang Arian in Phillar sub-division. However, evidence brought forward by Harmail (who was then DSP, Phillaur) shows that Parmar was interrogated between October 9 and 14 by senior police officers, where he revealed that the blasts were instigated by Lakhbir Singh Brar Rode.

Parmar's confession reads: "Around May 1985, a functionary of the International Sikh Youth Federation came to me and introduced himself as Lakhbir Singh and asked me for help in conducting some violent activities to express the resentment of the Sikhs. I told him to come after a few days so that I could arrange for dynamite and battery etc. He told me that he would first like to see a trial of the blast . . . After about four days, Lakhbir Singh and another youth, Inderjit Singh Reyat, both came to me. We went into the jungle (of British Columbia). There we joined a dynamite stick with a battery and triggered off a blast. Lakhbir and Inderjit, even at that time, had in their minds a plan to blast an aeroplane. I was not too keen on this plan but agreed to arrange for the dynamite sticks. Inderjit wanted to use for this purpose a transistor fitted with a battery . . . That very day, they took dynamite sticks from me and left.

"Then Lakhbir Singh, Inderjit Singh and their accomplice, Manjit Singh, made a plan to plant bombs in an Air India (AI) plane leaving from Toronto via London for Delhi and another flight that was to leave Tokyo for Bangkok. Lakhbir Singh got the seat booking done from Vancouver to Tokyo and then onwards to Bangkok, while Manjit Singh got it done from Vancouver to Toronto and then from Toronto to Delhi. Inderjit prepared the bags for the flights, which were loaded with dynamite bombs fitted with a battery and transistor. They decided that the suitcases will be booked but they themselves will not travel by the same flights although they will take the boarding passes. After preparing these bombs, the plan was ready for execution by June 21 or 22, 1985. However, the bomb to be kept in the flight from Tokyo to Delhi via Bangkok exploded at the Narita airport on the conveyor belt. The second suitcase that was loaded on the Toronto-Delhi ai flight exploded in the air."

Sarabjit said the PHRO's probe has shown that Parmar was killed to hide the name of Lakhbir, who was an Indian agent. "After the Khalistan movement gained in sympathy in the West, especially in Canada, after the 1984 Blue Star operation and the killing of Sikhs in Delhi, a plot was hatched to discredit the Sikh movement. Parmar was roped in by Lakhbir at the behest of his masters. The Punjab Police got orders to finish off Parmar as he knew too much about the main perpetrators. On the day of the Kanishka blast, an explosion took place at Japan's Narita airport, where two Japanese baggage handlers were killed. The plot was to trigger blasts when the two aircraft had de-embarked their passengers but the 1 hour 40 minute delay in Kanishka's takeoff led to the bomb exploding mid-air," Sarbjit said.

What gives credence to Sarabjit's charge is the Source Report (in Tehelka's possession) prepared by the Jalandhar Police soon after Parmar was killed. Based on information provided by Parmar_though not attributing it to his interrogation_the report makes no reference to Lakhbir. Interestingly, Lakhbir, accused in many acts of terrorist violence, is wanted by the Indian Government in only a minor case registered in Moga, Punjab. The Red Corner Interpol notice, A-23/1-1997, put out by the CBI against Lakhbir states: "OFFENCES: House breaking, theft, damage by fire."

The PHRO told Canadian authorities that conclusive evidence existed of Parmar being killed in police custody and not in the "encounter" shown in FIR No 105 registered at Phillaur police station on October 15, 1992. The PHRO report, AI Flight 182 Case, states "On October 14, 1992, a high-level decision was conveyed to the police that Parmar had to be killed . . . The contradiction in the FIR and post-mortem report (PMR) is too obvious. As per the FIR, Parmar was killed by AK-47 fire by SSP Satish K Sharma from a rooftop. The PMR shows the line of fire of the three bullets is different. It cannot be if one person is firing from a fixed position. The PMR is very sketchy and no chemical analysis was done. Moreover, the time of death is between 12am and 2am according to the PMR, whereas the FIR records the time of death at 5.30am." Then Jalandhar SSP and now IGP, Satish K Sharma, denied the charge. "It was a clean encounter. The RCMP is bringing this up because they botched their investigations and failed to get convictions," he said.

***

Document

CONGRESSIONAL RECORD -- EXTENSIONS

Thursday, September 27, 2007
110th Congress, 1st Session
153 Cong Rec E 2002

REFERENCE: Vol. 153, No. 145
SECTION: Extension of Remarks
TITLE: ANOTHER POLICE MURDER BY POLICE IN INDIA

Speech of
HON. EDOLPHUS TOWNS
of New York
in the House of Representatives
Thursday, September 27, 2007

Mr. TOWNS . Madam Speaker, on September 22, the Tribune newspaper of Chandigarh reported that a Sikh woman by the name of Lakhbir Kaur held a press conference to expose the murder of her brother, Kinder Singh, by the Indian police. Kinder Singh was an innocent truck driver. He was killed in one of the fake encounters that continue to plague Punjab and other minority areas of India. Kinder Singh was just 20 years old when "the world's largest democracy" snuffed out his life.

Apparently, Kinder Singh was a victim of India's policy of paying bounties to police officers for killing "militants." When he was killed, the police claimed that they had killed a man named Jaspal Singh, who had a bounty of Rs. 5 lakh, 500,000 rupees, or about $13,000, on his head. In a country where two-thirds of the populace lives on 40 cents per day, $13,000 is a massive amount of money.

Jaspal Singh. the person who was allegedly killed in the encounter, sat right next to Ms. Kaur during her announcement. He is not the first person to have been proclaimed dead by the Indian government who has turned up alive. Several years ago, the New York Post reported on another man who had to sue the government to have himself declared alive. This is not uncommon in India.

Also there was Colonel G.S. Sandhu of the Majha Ex-Servicemen Human Rights Front. He detailed how Kinder Singh was pulled out of his truck by the police and killed for no apparent reason except to collect the bounty. This is one of over 41,000 cash bounties that our State Department says the Indian Government paid to police for killing Sikhs. One policeman got a cash bounty for killing a three-year-old boy.

Colonel Sandhu demanded that a retired High Court judge conduct a probe into the massive atrocities of the police. He has set up a hotline to report terrorist incidents. We salute Lakhbir Kaur for her courage and we salute Colonel Sandhu for his efforts. I second his call for an impartial probe of the atrocities committed in Punjab.

Unfortunately, the repression is ongoing. Even today, people get arrested for acts such as marching, making speeches, and raising a flag. We cannot accept this, Madam Speaker. We need to stop providing financial support for the Indian regime by stopping our aid and trade, and we need to put the U.S. Congress on record in support of self-determination for the Sikhs of Khalistan, the Christians of Nagalim, the Muslims of Kashmir, and all the oppressed minorities of South Asia. Until the people have their freedom and self-determination, atrocities like the one that happened to Lakhbir Kaur's family will sadly continue.

I would like to place the Tribune article on Lakhbir Kaur into the Record at this time.

Mistaken Identity or Fake Encounter?

Amritsar, September 21, 2007: In what could be yet another case of mistaken identity or a planned fake encounter, the sister of a victim here today claimed that the actual "militant" the police claimed to have killed was still alive.

Lakhbir Kaur alleged that the police killed her brother, Kinder Singh, who was an innocent truck driver, on August 13, 1993, for no reason. Interestingly, Jaspal Singh, who had an award of Rs 5 lakh on his head and was shown killed in police files, was still alive. He was present with Lakhbir Kaur here today.

Addressing a press conference, Col G.S. Sandhu, chairman of the Majha ExServicemen Human Rights Front & NGO Aapna Punjab, demanded a probe by a retired high court judge to bring out the truth of fake encounters so that compensation could be given to the families of the victims.

"Kinder Singh of Nagoke (20) was pulled out of a truck in Shivpuri, Madhya Pradesh, and shot dead. The story planted was that militant

Jaspal Singh of Nangli, carrying a reward of Rs 5 lakh, was shot in a police encounter. Kunan Singh, father of Kinder Singh, sold his 3 acres of land and shifted to UP and the family is now living in abject poverty," said Colonel Sandhu.

"Already, leaks from police sources suggest that Kinder Singh and Sukhpal Singh of Kala Afghana were killed as a result of mistaken identity as no reward money was claimed and the records being old have been destroyed as per laid down rules and now it is difficult to pinpoint responsibility at this stage. The issue is why the families of the two victims were not informed about their deaths," he questioned.

Colonel Sandhu demanded "the state should not shy away from admitting past mistakes, render apology, provide compensation and bring the guilty to the book." He also sought downsizing of the top-heavy police in Punjab. He has also started a terror help line in Tarn Taran.

***

Document

CONGRESSIONAL RECORD -- EXTENSIONS

Thursday, September 27, 2007
110th Congress, 1st Session
153 Cong Rec E 2004

REFERENCE: Vol. 153, No. 145
SECTION: Extension of Remarks
TITLE: OTHER MINORITIES SUFFER MAJOR PERSECUTION AS WELL

Speech of
HON. EDOLPHUS TOWNS
of New York
in the House of Representatives
Thursday, September 27, 2007

Mr. TOWNS . Madam Speaker, recently, Dr. Awatar Singh Sekhon, Chairman of the Sikh Educational Trust and Managing Editor of the international Journal of Sikh Affairs, wrote to President Bush. He noted that "Sikhs live in peace and harmony in every democracy in the world; India is the only exception."

In his excellent letter, Dr. Sekhon outlines the tyranny and abuse the Sikhs have been subjected to in India. While India talks and talks about being "the world's largest democracy," it continues to commit atrocities against the Sikhs, Christians, Muslims, and other minorities. Madam Speaker, the essence of democracy is self-determination.

As if the murders of 250,000 Sikhs by the Indian government (the number comes from the Punjab State Magistracy and human-rights groups) wasn't enough, Sikhs from outside India must get the formal permission of the Indian government to visit the Golden Temple in

Amritsar, the seat of Sikhism, equivalent to the Vatican of the Sikhs. Suppose that Catholics were barred from Vatican City without permission of the Italian government. Do you think the world would be up in arms about that? Yet, the equivalent condition is imposed upon the Sikhs and nobody says a word. That is how deeply India's propaganda about being "the world's largest democracy" has permeated the world's perceptions, thanks to massive amounts of money spent to propagate this viewpoint through lobbying and media manipulation. It is time to wake up. Madam Speaker. It is time to call India on the carpet for its persecution of minorities.

If the tyranny against the Sikhs were all that India was doing, that would be bad enough. But it is compounded by the persecution of Christians and Muslims, as well as other minorities such as Assamese, Bodos, Dalits, Manipuris, Tamils, and others.

In Gujarat, 2,000 to 5,000 Muslims were killed in riots that a policeman told the newspapers were planned and organized by the Indian government. It has killed over 90,000 Muslims in Kashmir while refusing to give the Kashmiris self-determination via a free and fair plebiscite on their status, as India promised the United Nations in 1948.

Christians have been prime targets of Indian persecution. Churches have been burned. Nuns have been raped and forced to drink their own urine, to the cheers of militant Hindu organizations such as the pro-Fascist Rashtriya Swayamsewak Sangh (RSS), which produced a booklet on how to implicate Christians and other minorities in false criminal cases. Priests have been murdered, schools and prayer halls have been vandalized, and more than 300,000 Christians have been killed in Nagaland at the hands of the Indian government. Missionary Graham Staines was killed by a mob of Hindu militants along with his eight-year-old son. The killers poured gasoline over their jeep, set it on fire, and chanted "Victory to Hannuman." Missionary Joseph Cooper, an American, was expelled from the country after he was beaten up so badly that he had to spend a week in an Indian hospital. A Christian religious festival on the theme "Jesus is the Answer" was broken up by police gunfire after people there distributed religious literature.

In several Indian states, there are laws prohibiting anyone from converting to any religion but Hinduism.

Madam Speaker, this is unacceptable. We must support the rights of these minorities by stopping American aid to India and stopping our trade with India as well. It's clearly not benefitting the Indian people. Two thirds of the population lives on less than half a dollar a day. We must also demand a free and fair vote on independence for the Sikhs of Khalistan, the Christians of Nagalim, the Muslims of Kashmir, and all the various peoples seeking their freedom from India.

Madam Speaker, I would like to add Dr. Sekhon's excellent letter to the Record at this time.

The Sikh Educational Trust,
Edmonton, Alberta, Canada, July 30, 2007.
Re: *violation of religious and political rights of Sikhs in India.*
Hon. *George W. Bush, President, United States of America,*
The White House, Washington, DC.

Honourable President, I am writing this letter to seek your interven-tion in the religious affairs of the Sikhs, especially the Diaspora Sikhs in North America, Europe and other continents.

The Sikhs live in peace and harmony in every democracy in the world; India is the only exception. In fact, the Sikhs are treated as slaves even in the Punjab, which is the holy and historic homeland of the Sikhs. This is because the ruling class consists of Brahmins_who are only 4 percent of the population along with 10-11 percent of Hindus of other castes. Although a majority in the Punjab, the Sikhs are 2.5 percent of the huge population of India that is approximately 1.1 billion. It is because of the denial of the right of self-determination in our land that India is able to marginalized the Sikhs as a small minority. The Hindu-Brahmin rulers have pursued their anti-human agenda: (i) practice of unsociability against the native majority who are 65 percent of the population, and (ii) persecution of mono-theistic faiths_the Sikhs, the Christians and the Muslims, by maintaining an environment of fear and of crushing poverty.

In June 1984, even the facade of Secular Tolerance was discarded when the Indian Army assaulted the holiest shrine of the Sikhs_the Darbar Sahib (also known as the Golden Temple) including the Supreme Seat of Sikh Polity, the Akal Takht Sahib, killing tens of thousands of devotees inside the Temple. The Indian administration has ever since maintained heavy presence of its intelligence and armed personnel in the state. No Sikh from outside India can visit his/her holy place and the seat of Sikhs' polity without having a formal 'visa' endorsement in their passport from the Indian Embassy or Consulate. Mr President, this constitutes a violation of the Sikhs' religious rights. Pilgrimage to pay respect to Gurus is a right that should not depend on the caprice of a government. It certainly should not depend on the goodwill of a state that has not just failed to protect but has actually been an instrument of our persecution and destruction of our holy sites by wanton bombardment.

Mr. President, India is interfering in my religious affairs. As a free citizen of a free country. I cannot approve of the way the Sikhs are treated in India; I cannot condone the assault of the Indian Army on Darbar Sahib in June 1984; I cannot support that the Sikhs relinquish their right to self-determination. I am required to do all this in order to get a visa. And if I did any of these things, I would not be a Sikh. That means, in order to get an Indian visa, I am required to renounce my faith. That cannot be acceptable.

Mr. President, no Roman Catholic needs a visa to visit the Vatican, no Jew is prevented from visiting Jerusalem, a visa cannot be denied to a Muslim to go to Mecca, why do the Sikhs need to have India's Hin-du/Brahmins (neither a religion nor a culture), permission to visit their holiest shrine? Indian administration's control of the Sikhs' shrines constitutes an intervention into their religious affairs. That's why, Honourable President, none of the elected representatives of the Sikhs accepted/initiated/endorsed the Indian Constitution of 1950. Under Article 25 of that Constitution, the Sikh faith and national identity was 'de-recognized'. The Sikhs were constitutionally 'exterminated'. Because of this blatant injustice, the Sikhs, elected representatives_Sardar Hukam Singh, MP; Sardar Bhupinder Singh Maan, MP; and Sirdar Kapur Singh, ICS, MP, MLA and National Professor of Sikhism_'Rejected' the Indian Constitution of 1950 and its Article 25, in its draft and final forms, every time it was put to vote in the Indian parliament_in 1948, on 26th November, 1949, in 1950 and on 6thSeptember, 1966.

Honourable President, the question is why we, the Sikh citizens of the United States and Canada, of Europe, Far East, and other continents should need a 'Visa' or the permission of the predominantly Hindu-Brahmin administration. Especially after the June, 1984 assault on Darbar Sahib Complex_which is the Sikh Vatican_and an 'undeclared' war on the Sikhs ever since. This undeclared war has taken a heavy toll. The "Operation Bluestar" of June, 1984 was blessed by the government of a so-called 'democratic' state. The desecration of their holy places and wanton massacre of the Sikhs was carried out for no reason other than their demanding the right of self-determination honouring the pledges made to the Sikhs by Mahatma Gandhi and Prime Minister Jawahar Lal Nehru. More than 250,000 innocent Sikh (majority of whom were infants, children, youth, females and the elderly have been killed by Indian security forces. This is the hallmark of a fascist oligarchy, not a democracy.

In recent months, the arrests of Simranjit Singh Mann, Chief of Akali Dal Amritsar, Mann's vice president, Daljit Singh Dittu and the arrest warrants of an Editor and academic, Dr Sukhpreet Singh Udhoke, provide further evidence that repression of the Sikhs continues even in the Sikh majority state of the Punjab, the administration of which is headed by a Sikh, Prakash Badal. The former two are being tried, along with 30 other Sikhs, on charges of 'treason'. Treason against who? How does the Indian Constitution apply to the Sikhs when the Sikhs' elected representatives 'rejected' it repeatedly?

Mr. President, there is great anxiety among the Sikhs in Diaspora over the denial of their religious and political rights and repression of dissent. If India is not restrained by the international community and its leader_the USA_peace and security in the whole region would be undermined. In retrospect and historically, India was never a country; it was an empire (the British Empire). In its belly there are many peoples with legitimate right to self-determination_in Kashmir (mainly Muslim) in the Punjab (mainly Sikhs) in the states of Assam (mainly Christian) who are not a part of the Indian nation. The issues relating to the native majority_the children of lesser gods_encompass a huge section of humanity, as many as 700 million people. All this cannot be swept under the carpet or buried under slogans like 'India Shining'. The Sikhs want their own

sovereign state_as they had been (1799 to 14th March, 1849, under a Sikh monarch Ranjit Singh) before the British take over, as an "annexed" state, of the Punjab in 1849. Until then, we want unrestricted access to our holy places. No Sikh should need a visa to go to the Punjab. And peaceful dissent should not just be tolerated; it should be respected and honoured. Is dissent not the hall mark of democracy?
   I shall look forward to hearing from you.

   With regards,
   Respectfully submitted,
   Awatar Singh Sekhon.

                              ***

                            Document

CONGRESSIONAL RECORD -- EXTENSIONS

                   Tuesday, September 18, 2007
                    110th Congress, 1st Session
                       153 Cong Rec E 1905

REFERENCE: Vol. 153, No. 138
SECTION: Extension of Remarks
TITLE: SIKHS SHOULD NOT BE FORCED TO REMOVE TURBANS AT AIRPORTS

                           Speech of
                     HON. EDOLPHUS TOWNS
                          of New York
                 in the House of Representatives
                   Tuesday, September 18, 2007

   Mr. TOWNS . Madam Speaker, recently a Sikh named Dr. Ranbir Singh Sandhu was stopped at the San Francisco airport as he tried to board a flight and forced by agents of the Transportation Security Administration to take off his turban. Dr. Sandhu, who is around 80, was on his way to a funeral in Vancouver. He refused to take off his turban and was barred from the flight, forcing him to make a 20-hour drive to get to the funeral.
   This is unacceptable. I certainly understand and support wanding the turban for security reasons in this day and age, but forcing a Sikh to remove his turban is an insult to his religious identity. TSA does not make Jewish passengers take off their yarmulkes and that is right. They shouldn't. But they require Sikhs to take off their turbans. That is unfair, discriminatory, and wrong.
   Airport security is important. We were just reminded of that again by the passing of another anniversary of the September 11 attacks. But we must not let that be used as an excuse to violate the religious liberties or

the civil rights of anyone. We should stop asking Sikhs to remove their turbans.

The Council of Khalistan recently wrote to President Bush, Homeland Security Secretary Chertoff, and the TSA Administrator, Kip Hawley, asking that this policy be changed.

September 12, 2007.
Hon. Michael Chertoff,
Secretary of Homeland Security,
Washington, DC.

Dear Secretary Chertoff: I am writing to you today about the Transportation Safety Administration's practice of making Sikhs remove their turbans in order to travel. Recently, Dr. Ranbir Singh Sandhu of California, a retired engineering professor who is around 80 years old, was stopped at San Francisco International Airport on his way to Vancouver for a funeral. He was ordered by TSA security workers to remove his turban. When he refused he was not allowed to board his flight and he wound up having to drive 20 hours to Vancouver to get to the funeral.

Asking a Sikh to remove his turban in public is worse than asking someone to remove his pants in public. No one would even think of making such a request, yet the TSA thinks nothing of asking Sikhs to remove their turbans in public.

I salute TSA for not asking Jewish people to remove their yarmulkes in public. This is because they are religious symbols. Jewish people are required to wear them in public. By the same principle, Sikhs are required to wear their turbans. Wanding the turban should be enough and would be understandable in light of security concerns, but forcing a Sikh to remove his turban is unacceptable. It is a strike against his Sikh religion and his Sikh identity.

I respectfully but strongly urge you to take action to prevent what happened to Dr. Sandhu from happening to any other Sikh traveller. Please order the TSA workers to respect the religion and identity of Sikhs and not to force them to remove their turbans. Thank you for your attention to this matter.

> *Sincerely,*
> *Dr. Gurmit Singh Aulakh*
> *President, Council of Khalistan.*

***

Document

CONGRESSIONAL RECORD -- EXTENSIONS

Tuesday, September 18, 2007
110th Congress, 1st Session
153 Cong Rec E 1906

REFERENCE: Vol. 153, No. 138
SECTION: Extension of Remarks
TITLE: SONIA GANDHI SHOULD NOT SPEAK ON NONVIOLENCE

Speech of
HON. EDOLPHUS TOWNS
of New York
in the House of Representatives
Tuesday, September 18, 2007

Mr. TOWNS . Madam Speaker, I was distressed to learn that the United Nations invited Sonia Gandhi to speak on nonviolence next month. She is the leader of the Congress Party, which has presided over massive atrocities against Christians, Sikhs, Muslims, and other minorities.

Mrs. Gandhi is Catholic. How can she speak on nonviolence when her party presides over a country in which nuns have been raped and forced to drink their own urine, priests have been murdered, Christian schools have been burned to the ground, and prayer halls have been vandalized?

It was Mrs. Gandhi's party that carried out the Golden Temple massacre that killed so many thousands of innocent Sikhs, including young boys ages 8 to 13. Her party presided over the Delhi massacres in which over 20,000 Sikhs were murdered while the Sikh police were locked in their barracks.

It was Beant Singh, a Congress Party Chief Minister, who presided over the murders of over 50,000 Sikhs while he was in office. No one from that party has the moral authority to speak on nonviolence, especially when there are so many better spokespersons, such as the Dalai Lama, who will be in America to receive an award right after Mrs. Gandhi's speech.

Madam Speaker, the Council of Khalistan wrote an excellent letter to UN Secretary General Ban Ki-moon, which follows.

Council of Khalistan,
September 12, 2007.
Hon. Ban Ki-moon
Secretary-General of the United Nations
Dag Hammerskjold Plaza
New York, NY.

Dear Secretary General Ban: It has come to my attention that you are having Sonia Gandhi speak to the United Nations on nonviolence on October 2. Mrs. Gandhi has no moral standing to be discussing this subject. I urge you to find someone else. Perhaps the Dalai Lama, who will be in the United States the following weekend to receive an award, would be a good choice. There are other people more qualified than Mrs. Gandhi, as well.

How could you pick the head of India's Congress Party for this talk? India is one of the most violent countries in the world. According to the

Punjab State Magistracy, over 250,000 Sikhs have been murdered at the hands of the Indian government. Between 1993 and 1995, according to the United States Department of State, the Indian government paid out over 41,000 cash bounties to police officers for killing Sikhs. A report by the Movement Against State Repression (MASR) reveals that over 52,000 Sikhs are being held as political prisoners without charge or trial. Some have been in illegal custody since 1984!

Amnesty International reports that tens of thousands of other minorities are being held as political prisoners as well. In addition, the regime has killed 300,000 Christians in Nagaland, more than 90,000 Kashmiri Muslims and tens of thousands of Muslims and Christians in the rest of the country, and tens of thousands of Assamese, Bodos, Dalits (the dark-skinned aboriginal people of South Asia, referred to as "Untouchables"), Manipuris, Tamils, and others.

The Gandhi family were perhaps the most cruel of Indian rulers; it was Mrs. Gandhi's mother-in-law, Indira Gandhi, who suspended democracy and imposed martial law (dictatorship) on the country. It was the Congress Party under Indira Gandhi, then under Mrs. Gandhi's husband, Rajiv Gandhi, who succeeded Indira Gandhi as Prime Minister, that the government carried out the brutal attack on the Golden Temple in Amritsar, the center and seat of the Sikh religion, in June 1984, as well as 224 other Gurdwaras (Sikh places of worship) throughout Punjab. Sikh leaders Sant Jarnail Singh Bhindranwale, General Shabeg Singh, and others, as well as over 20,000 Sikhs were killed in these attacks. The Sikh holy scripture, the Guru Granth Sahib, written in the time of the Sikh Gurus, was shot full of bullet holes by the Indian Army. Over 100 young Sikh boys ages 8 to 13 were taken out into the courtyard and asked if they supported Khalistan, the independent Sikh state. When they answered with the Sikh religious incantation "Bole So Nihal" they were summarily shot to death.

After Indira Gandhi was killed, Rajiv Gandhi said, "When a tree falls, the Earth shakes." Then he locked the Sikh Police in their barracks while the government murdered another 20,000 Sikhs in Delhi and the surrounding areas in the massacres of November 1984. Sikhs were burned alive, Sikh businesses were burned, Sikhs were chained to trucks. The driver for Baba Charam Singh, a Sikh religious leader, was killed by tying his legs to jeeps which then drove off in different directions.

Sardar Jaswant Singh Khalra looked at the records of the cremation grounds at Patti, Tarn Taran, and Durgiana Mandar and documented at least 6,018 secret cremations of young Sikh men ages 20-30. These young Sikhs were arrested by the police, tortured, murdered, then declared unidentified and secretly cremated. Their bodies were not even returned to their families. They have never officially been accounted for. The Punjab Human Right Commission estimates that about 50,000 such secret cremations have occurred.

For exposing this horrendous atrocity, Sardar Khalra was abducted by the police on September 6, 1995 while he was washing his car, then murdered in police custody. The only witness to his kidnapping, Rajiv

Singh Randhawa, has been repeatedly harassed by the police. Once he was arrested for trying to hand a petition to the then-British Home Minister, Jack Straw, in front of the Golden Temple in Amritsar.

Police SSP Swaran Singh Ghotna tortured and murdered Akal Takht Jathedar Gurdev Singh Kaunke and has never been punished for doing so. K.P.S. Gill, who was responsible for the murders of over 150,000 Sikhs in his time as Director General of Police, is still walking around scot-free. He was even involved in leading the Indian Olympic field hockey team. His trip to the Atlanta Olympics in 1996 was protested by the Sikh community in the United States, which is over half a million strong, but he was allowed to come to the Olympics on an Olympic Committee visa. Immediately after the Olympic hockey game, he was shipped back to Punjab as a threat to peace and an affront to the Sikh community. 50 members of the U.S. Congress from both parties wrote to the President protesting his appearance in the United States.

Unfortunately, other minorities have also suffered greatly under the boot of Indian repression. In March 2002, 5,000 Muslims were killed in Gujarat while police were ordered to stand by and let the carnage happen, in an eerie parallel to the Delhi massacre of Sikhs in November 1984 in which Sikh police officers were locked in their barracks while the state-run television and radio called for more Sikh blood.

Christians have suffered under a wave of repression since Christmas 1998. An Australian missionary, Graham Staines, and his two young sons, ages 8 and 10, were burned to death while they slept in their jeep by a mob of Hindu militants connected with the Rashtriya Swayamsewak Sangh (RSS), an organization formed in support of the Fascists. The mob surrounded the burning jeep and chanted "Victory to Hannuman," a Hindu god. None of the mob has ever been brought to justice; instead the crime has been blamed on one scapegoat. Mr. Staines's widow was thrown out of the country after the incident. An American missionary, Joseph Cooper of Pennsylvania, was expelled from India after being beaten so severely that he had to spend a week in the hospital. None of the persons responsible for beating Mr. Cooper has been prosecuted. Churches have been burned. Christian schools and prayer halls have been attacked and vandalized, priests have been murdered, nuns have been raped, all with impunity. Police broke up a Christian religious festival with gunfire.

Amnesty International has not been allowed into Punjab since 1978. Even Castro's Cuba has allowed Amnesty into the country more recently. What is India hiding?

My organization, the Council of Khalistan, is leading the Sikh struggle for freedom and sovereignty. Working with the Congress of the United States, we have internationalized the struggle for freedom for Sikhs and all the people of South Asia since the Council of Khalistan's inception on October 7, 1987, the day that the Sikh Nation declared its independence from India. We have worked to preserve the accurate history of the Sikhs and the repression of minorities by India by preserving the information in the Congressional Record. We continue to work for freedom for the Sikh Nation. Self-determination is the essence of democracy.

We cannot accept the leader of the Congress Party, the party that carried out the bulk of these atrocities, speaking to an organization like the United Nations on a subject like non-violence, especially when there are much better spokespersons available. I cannot urge you strongly enough to cancel this appearance.

Thank you in advance for your attention to this situation and helping the people of South Asia.

> *Sincerely,*
> *Dr. Gurmit, Singh Aulakh*
> *President, Council of Khalistan.*

***

Document

CONGRESSIONAL RECORD -- EXTENSIONS

Wednesday, August 01, 2007
110th Congress, 1st Session
153 Cong Rec E 1674

REFERENCE: Vol. 153, No. 125
SECTION: Extension of Remarks
TITLE: COUNCIL OF KHALISTAN WRITES TO CHIEF MINISTER TO DEMAND WITHDRAWAL OF WARRANT AGAINST DR. UDHOKE AND RELEASE OF MANN

Speech of
HON. EDOLPHUS TOWNS
of New York
in the House of Representatives
Tuesday, July 31, 2007

Mr. TOWNS . Madam Speaker, as I have discussed recently, the Punjab Government has issued an arrest warrant against Dr. Sukhpreet Singh Udhoke for the crime of writing about Sikh freedom and criticizing the chief minister. Mr. Mann's crime was placing a picture at the statue of the brutal late chief minister, Beant Singh.

The Council of Khalistan has recently written to Chief Minister Parkash Singh Badal to demand the withdrawal of the warrant against Dr. Udhoke and the release of Mr. Mann. We should join in that demand, Madam Speaker. We should stop aid and trade with India to support rights for everyone and we should demand a free and fair vote on freedom for Khalistan, the Sikh homeland, for Nagalim, for Kashmir, and for the other nations seeking their freedom.

I would like to add that letter to the Record, Madam Speaker.

Council of Khalistan,
Washington, DC, June 28, 2007.
Hon. Parkash Singh Badal,
Chief Minister of Punjab,
Chandigarh, Punjab, India.

Dear Chief Minister Badal: I am writing to you regarding the recent arrest warrant for Dr. Sukhpreet Singh Udhoke and the arrests of Sardar Simranjit Singh Mann and his associates. As you know, both were involved in peaceful political action, which is protected under the Indian constitution, at the time the warrants for their arrests were issued by your government. Dr. Udhoke's offense was publishing articles critical of you. Sardar Mann's was protesting and placing a picture of a Sikh martyr at the statue of the brutal, genocidal Beant Singh, who presided over the murders of over 50,000 Sikhs. Mann had previously been arrested for the dangerous crimes of making a speech and raising a flag.

You have been in opposition. You have engaged in political activities while in opposition. What would you think if you were arrested for those activities? That is exactly what your government is doing to S.S. Mann and proposes to do to Dr. Udhoke as soon as you can find him.

When did the right to protest peacefully disappear in Punjab, Khalistan? Are you determined to prove the late General Narinder Singh right that "Punjab is a police state"?

On behalf of the 25 million strong Sikh Nation in Punjab, in India, and around the world, I am writing to demand the withdrawal of the arrest order against Dr. Udhoke and his associates and the immediate release of Simranjit Singh Mann and his associates. I do not do this for political reasons; Mann has been a vocal critic of this office and has cooperated with the Indian government. But if you truly believe in democracy_the system that put you back in power earlier this year_then you cannot in good conscience arrest people for dissent.

Indeed, Mann's arrest shows what can happen to a Sikh even if he cooperates with the Indian government, as you have done throughout your political career to the detriment of the Sikh Nation. One day, your utility to them will be exhausted and they may then have you thrown in jail for a peaceful political activity_simply because you are a Sikh. Who will you turn to defend you then? To this office?

Yet while you seem intent on prosecuting peaceful dissent, you are unwilling to take action against those who commit murder and other serious crimes. Is that because of your alliance with the BJP, which is the political arm of the pro-Fascist, militant Hindu nationalist, anti-Sikh RSS?

When you were elected in 1997, you promised the Sikhs of Punjab that you would appoint a commission to inquire into the atrocities in Punjab and prosecute the police officers who murdered Sikhs. Instead, you protected SSP Swaran Singh Ghotna, who murdered Akal Takht Jathedar Gurdev Singh Kaunke.

Just recently, Gurmit Ram Rahim Singh was fraudulently dressing as Guru Gobind Singh, performing baptisms that are reserved for the Panj

Piaras, and advertising it in the newspaper. This was a desecration of the Sikh religion and a fraud. Yet you met with Ram Rahim to ask for his political support. But you couldn't even succeed in persuading this corrupt baba to support you! Yet when he perpetrated this fraud, you protected him until the political pressure to prosecute him got too intense. He still has not been arrested, nor has an arrest warrant been issued. I guess the jails are too crowded from holding the likes of Dr. Sukhbir Singh Udhoke and Simranjit Singh Mann.

In 1978, during your Chief Ministership, the Nirankari cult had a meeting and desecrated the Guru Granth Sahib. Sant Jarnail Singh Bhindranwale and his supporters peacefully protested outside. Your police fired on the protestors, killing 13 of them, then your police escorted the Nirankari leader, Gurbachan Singh, safely out of Punjab.

Apparently, you were not through trying to destroy Sant Bhindranwale. According to letters reprinted in the book Chakravyuh: Web of Indian Secularism, you, along with Harcharan Singh Longowal and the late Gurcharan Singh Tohra, invited the Indian government to attack the Golden Temple in June 1984 to kill Sant Bhindranwale. 37 other Gurdwaras were attacked simultaneously. Over 20,000 Sikhs were killed in those attacks. Their blood is on your hands, Mr. Chief Minister.

Furthermore, your government in your previous term was the most corrupt in Punjab's history. You creatively invented a new term for bribery; "fee for service." No fee, no service. The sale of government offices was standard operating procedure. Your wife even developed the handy skill of being able to tell how much money was in a bag just picking it up.

Furthermore, your operatives are calling this office repeatedly and harassing me about my website because it exposes you. You may be able to suppress the freedom of Sikhs in Punjab, but you cannot stop the Sikh diaspora from exposing your brutal and corrupt acts. Remember that Sikhs have a long memory of those who are traitors and murderers and who cooperate with the oppressors of the Sikh Nation. K.P.S. Gill's turban is still preserved in Belgium. When Khalsitan is free, it will be on display so that the Sikh Nation will never forget those who committed atrocities against us.

Punjab's water is being taken away by non-riparian states without compensation. At least your predecessor, who is from the Congress Party, the enemy of all Sikhs, tried to do something about it. He cancelled the water agreements. The bill passed by the Legislative Assembly expressly affirmed the sovereignty of Punjab.

Under your rule, the economy of Punjab is deteriorating. Sikh farmers are committing suicide because they cannot make a living, due to the fact that your friends in Delhi force them to pay exorbitant prices for fertilizer and seeds, but forces them to sell their crop at substandard prices. And you, who as Chief Minister and head of the Akali Dal are supposed to protect the interests of the Sikhs, sit there and kowtow to these criminals.

Even though the government of Pakistan said it would build a road to Kartapur, where Guru Nanak went to his heavenly abode, with no visas, your government has refused to build the Punjab side of the road so that Sikhs can go freely to this sacred site.

From these actions, it is clear where your loyalties lie, and they are not with the Sikh Nation or with the Sikh religion or with the people of Punjab, but with the violent, pro-Fascist, murderous Hinducrat thugs from Delhi who sponsor you and your career. But remember the warning I gave you earlier; when they are through with you, when you no longer have any usefulness to them, they will dispense with you as they have dispensed with so many other Sikhs who have served them.

That is why it is incumbent on every Sikh to engage in the "long struggle" to free Khalistan. Only then will Sikhs such as Dr. Udhoke, Sardar Mann, and even the likes of you be protected from the violent and brutal whims of the oppressive Hindustani regime. It is crucial to protect the Sikh religion and the Sikh Nation from this oppression by liberating Khalistan today, in accord with our declaration of October 7, 1987. For your good, Mr. Badal, I urge you to get on the right side of history today. Or would you rather be remembered as an enemy of the Sikh Nation?

> *Sincerely,*
> *Gurmit Singh Aulakh*
> *President, Council of Khalistan.*

***

Document

CONGRESSIONAL RECORD -- EXTENSIONS

Monday, July 23, 2007
110th Congress, 1st Session
153 Cong Rec E 1598

REFERENCE: Vol. 153, No. 118
SECTION: Extension of Remarks
TITLE: DEMOCRACY IN INDIA

Speech of
HON. DAN BURTON
of Indiana
in the House of Representatives
Monday, July 23, 2007

Mr. BURTON of Indiana . Madam Speaker, as many of our colleagues in this House know, India prides itself on being the world's most populous democracy. Although relations between India and the United States have been rocky in the past, since 2004 Washington and New Delhi have been pursuing a "strategic partnership" based on shared values such as democracy, multiculturalism, and rule of law. In addition, numerous economic, security and globally focused initiatives, including plans for "full civilian nuclear energy cooperation," are currently underway. I support these initiatives but I remain deeply concerned about the numerous serious problems that remain when it comes to India's respect for the rights of all of her citizens.

In fact, according to the Department of State's 2006 Human Rights Report for India: "Major problems included extrajudicial killings of persons in custody, disappearances, torture and rape by police and security forces. The lack of accountability permeated the government and security forces, creating an atmosphere in which human rights violations often went unpunished. Although the country has numerous laws protecting human rights, enforcement was lax and convictions were rare."

Again, these are not my words; this is from the State Department's official report on Human Rights. I firmly believe that as the United States and India move towards greater cooperation in numerous endeavors we must at the same time continue to insist that India adhere to the full expression of democracy and basic human rights; especially for members of ethnic or religious minorities.

For example, according to reports, on April 20, 2006, Sikh activist Daljit Singh Bittu was arrested after making a speech. He was charged with sedition and "making inflammatory speeches." Mr. Bittu's crime was to speak out against the acquisition of the land of poor farmers by the State of Punjab on behalf of private business firms. Fortunately, Mr. Bittu was ultimately released on bail. The issue of government taking land by eminent domainfor private usage is also extremely controversial in this country, but to the best of my knowledge no one has ever been charged with sedition for speaking out about it. On June 2nd of this year, Daljit Singh Bittu, was again arrested and charged with sedition. What did Mr. Bittu do this time? He participated in a peaceful march protesting government inaction on several issues where some of the marchers_and by all accounts not Mr. Bittu_allegedly expressed their desire_unrelated to the topic of the march_for an independent Sikh nation of Khalistan by shouting "Khalistan Zindabad."

As I understand it, according to the Indian Supreme Court in the case Balwant Singh vs. State of Punjab, the mere public use of the slogan "Khalistan Zinabad" is not illegal; and as the march itself was peaceful, it is difficult to understand how the Indian Government believes Mr. Bittu did anything that can, to the best of my knowledge, be legitimately considered a crime_much less sedition_under United States, International, or Indian law.

What is really at issue here, Madam Speaker, is the fact that India is a nation comprised of a hodgepodge of ethnicities, some of whom do not wish to be a part of Hindu-dominated India. The conflict over the Muslim-majority region of Jammu and Kashmir is perhaps most familiar to Americans as it has sparked three major wars between India and Pakistan, but it is by no means the only ethnic or religious conflict roiling India. In 1948, India promised a free and fair plebiscite on the status of Kashmir. No such vote has ever been held. As our Nation fights to spread democracy to oppressed people across the globe, why don't we insist on a simple democratic vote, with international monitors, in

Kashmir, in Punjab, Khalistan, in predominantly Christian Nagalim, and wherever people seek their freedom from India? The answer tragically is all too obvious, in the world of international diplomacy and geopolitics, sometimes expedience and "good relations" trump freedom and human rights.

I do not know whether the plebiscite promised to the people of Kashmir will ever happen, and I do not know whether a Sikh nation of Khalistan or a Christian nation of Nagalim will ever come into existence; but I do know that the Muslims of Kashmir, the Sikhs of Punjab/Khalistan and the Christians of Nagalim should never have to live in fear for freely and peacefully expressing their opinions.

***

Document

CONGRESSIONAL RECORD -- EXTENSIONS

Thursday, June 28, 2007
110th Congress, 1st Session
153 Cong Rec E 1440

REFERENCE: Vol. 153, No. 106
SECTION: Extension of Remarks
TITLE: NEW THREAT TO FREEDOM OF SPEECH AND PRESS IN INDIA
AS WARRANT IS ISSUED FOR SIKH EDITOR

Speech of
HON. EDOLPHUS TOWNS
of New York
in the House of Representatives
Thursday, June 28, 2007

Mr. TOWNS . Madam Speaker, recently an arrest warrant was issued by the government of Punjab for Dr. Sukhpreet Singh Udhoke, a practicing physician, International Secretary General of Dal Khalsa USA, and Editor-in-Chief of the Sikh publication Shamshir-e-Qaum. Warrants were also issued for two of his associates. This is a blatant violation of the basic rights of freedom of speech and freedom of the press. Freedom of speech and freedom of the press are two of the rights that are basic to democracy, yet they can be suppressed at will in "the world's largest democracy."

Dr. Udhoke's crime was to publish articles in his magazine that criticized the Chief Minister of Punjab, Parkash Singh Badal, and advocated freedom for the Sikhs. For this, he is under the cloud of an arrest warrant. He has had to go underground to avoid arrest.

Madam Speaker, this is frighteningly familiar. It is reminiscent of the tactics of the Soviet Union, Nazi Germany, or any of the other totalitarian police states around the world which America has always opposed. How can any Member of Congress support such a blatantly authoritarian country?

I would strongly advise the Indian government to withdraw the arrest warrant against Dr. Udhoke. If it does not, it will confirm that it is the tyrannical, authoritarian, repressive regime that the minorities charge that it is, rather than the democracy it proclaims itself to be.

This is unfortunately just the latest chapter in a long line of repression against minorities. We have detailed for many years the tens of thousands of Christians, Sikhs, Muslims, Dalits, and other minorities who have been murdered at the hands of the Indian government, as well as the tens of thousands of political prisoners who are held in India, according to Amnesty International. Laws have been passed that prohibit anyone from converting from Hinduism to any other religion. Booklets have been published on how to implicate Christians and other minorities in false criminal cases. Sikhs have been arrested for marches and speeches. A Christian priest was forced to drink his own urine. And the arrest warrant for Dr. Udhoke shows that the repression goes on.

Madam Speaker, India's Constitution, like ours, guarantees freedom of speech and the Indian courts have ruled that peacefully advocating independence for Khalistan (or any other minority nation) is not a crime. So what was the basis for Dr. Udhoke's arrest?

I thank Dr. Gurmit Singh Aulakh, President of the Council of Khalistan, for bringing the Udhoke case to my attention. The Council of Khalistan has issued a press release condemning the arrest warrant against Udhoke. I recommend it strongly to my colleagues. It shows the truth about how democracy is really practiced in India. The need for the Sikhs of Khalistan, the Christians of Nagaland, the Muslims of Kashmir, and the other minorities within India's artificial borders to claim their God-given right to be free could not be clearer. If they can be arrested for articles they publish, how can they count on the government to protect any of their rights?

It is time for us to speak up and take action. We can help by stopping aid and trade with India until the basic human rights and civil rights of all people are observed. India can start by withdrawing the arrest warrant for Dr. Udhoke and his associates. We should also put the United States Congress on record publicly in support of self-determination for the Sikhs of Punjab, Khalistan, the Muslims of Kashmir, the Christians of Nagalim, and all the people seeking freedom in South Asia in the form of a free and fair vote on their status. Isn't that the democratic way?

Arrest Warrant for Udhoke Must Be Withdrawn

Washington, DC, June 28, 2007._The Council of Khalistan today demanded that the arrest warrant for Dr. Sukhpreet Singh Udhoke, International Secretary General of Dal Khalsa USA and Editor-in-Chief of the periodical Shamshir-e-Qaum, and two of his associates be withdrawn. The arrest warrant was issued by the government of Punjab after Dr. Udhoke printed articles about the persecution of the Sikh Nation and how the Sikh religion is being attacked by the RSS and its political arm, the

BJP. He criticized Chief Minister Parkash Singh Badal in his articles. The Akali Dal government of Badal is in a political alliance with the BJP. Dr. Udhoke and his associates' persecution has been condemned recently by the World Peace Forum.

Dr. Udhoke is a medical doctor who takes care of the sick as well as being an activist for the interests of the Sikh religion and the Sikh Nation. Dr. Udhoke, a resident of the Amritsar district, has been forced underground. He is charged with treason and antinational activities. His magazine, which was on the stands for sale, was removed by the Badal government. This action is a threat to freedom of speech, of the press, and of religion, which are basic democratic and civil rights.

Badal is the Chief Minister. As such, he is responsible for law and order. Yet he was quick to put out an arrest warrant for Dr. Udhoke for exercising his freedom of speech, but he had to be pressured into prosecuting Ram Rahim, the fraudulent baba who was impersonating Guru Gobind Singh, and he has not yet arrested him. This shows what the Badal government's priorities and allegiances are. He is more concerned with arresting those who defend the interests of the Sikh Nation and the Sikh religion than those who violate it. Ironically, despite Badal's begging and pleading, Ram Rahim supported the Congress Party in the recent elections in Punjab.

"The arrest warrant against Dr. Udhoke shows that there is no freedom of speech in Punjab or in India," said Dr. Gurmit Singh Aulakh, President of the Council of Khalistan. "As the late General Narinder Singh said, 'Punjab is a police state.' Only a free Khalistan will allow Dr. Udhoke and all Sikhs to enjoy freedom of speech, freedom of the press, freedom of religion, and all the rights of free people, rights that are the birthright of all people," he said.

"Badal's conduct is shameful for a Sikh leader," said Dr. Gurmit Singh Aulakh, President of the Council of Khalistan. "He is the leader of a government of the Akali Dal, which was organized to protect the interests of the Sikh Nation, yet he is in bed with the Indian government that is oppressing the Sikhs. Badal is under the complete control of the Indian government, rather than working for the Sikhs. We must free ourselves of corrupt, anti-Sikh leaders like Badal and his friends by liberating Khalistan." he said. "As former Akal Takht Jathedar Professor Darshan Singh said: 'If a Sikh is not a Khalistani, he is not a Sikh.'"

A report issued by the Movement Against State Repression (MASR) shows that India admitted that it held 52,268 political prisoners under the repressive "Terrorist and Disruptive Activities Act" (TADA) even though it expired in 1995. Many have been in illegal custody since 1984. There has been no list published of those who were acquitted under TADA and those who are still rotting in Indian jails. Additionally, according to Amnesty International, there are tens of thousands of other minorities being held as political prisoners in India.

The MASR report quotes the Punjab Civil Magistracy as writing "if we add up the figures of the last few years the number of innocent persons killed would run into lakhs [hundreds of thousands.]" The Indian government has murdered over 250,000 Sikhs since 1984, more than 300,000 Christians in Nagaland, over 90,000 Muslims in Kashmir, tens of thousands of Christians and Muslims throughout the country, and tens of thousands of Tamils, Assamese, Manipuris, Dalits, Bodos, and others. The Indian Supreme Court called the Indian government's murders of Sikhs "worse than a genocide."

"The Sikh masses and the Akali Dal must rise to the occasion and establish new leadership that works for the interest of the Khalsa Panth and abides by Sikh tradition," said Dr. Aulakh. "Badal and his government have betrayed the Sikh Rehat Maryada, Sikh principles, and Sikh tradition. Their leadership must be rejected for the interests of the Khalsa Panth," he said. "Remember Guru Gobind Singh's words: 'In grieb Sikhin ko deon patshahi.' It is time to realize Guru Sahib's blessing. Only a free Khalistan will put a stop to occurrences like the arrest of Dr. Udhoke," he said. "Without political power, religions cannot flourish and nations perish. The time is now to launch a Shantmai Morcha to free Khalistan."

***

Document

CONGRESSIONAL RECORD -- EXTENSIONS

Thursday, June 28, 2007
110th Congress, 1st Session
153 Cong Rec E 1443

REFERENCE: Vol. 153, No. 106
SECTION: Extension of Remarks
TITLE: FORMER MEMBER OF PARLIAMENT ARRESTED AGAIN

Speech of
HON. EDOLPHUS TOWNS
of New York
in the House of Representatives
Thursday, June 28, 2007

Mr. TOWNS . Madam Speaker, recently the government of Punjab erected a statue to honor Beant Singh, the late Chief Minister of Punjab, who presided over the murders of over 50,000 Sikhs and the secret cremations of Sikhs in Punjab at the behest of the Indian government. Longtime Sikh activist and former member of Parliament Simranjit Singh Mann showed up with some associates to protest the honor given to this brutal, barbaric ruler. During the protest, they tried to hang a picture of Dilawar Singh, who killed Beant Singh, on the statue. Dilawar Singh is considered by the Sikhs to be a martyr. For this act of protest, they were arrested.

Mr. Mann is also one of the people who was arrested in 2005 for the crime of making speeches in support of Khalistan, the independent Sikh homeland, and raising the flag of Khalistan. I fail to see what crime was committed in any of these acts.

Coupled with the recent arrest of Dr. Sukhpreet Singh Udhoke for publishing articles critical of the Chief Minister, Mann's arrest makes it clear that for minorities such as the Sikhs, free speech, free assembly, and a free press do not exist in India. For minorities such as Christians, Sikhs, Muslims, and others, India is far from the democracy it claims to be. For them, it's a police state just like the Soviet Union or Nazi Germany.

Mann's arrest and Udhoke's arrest violate India's constitution as well as all the principles of freedom and democracy. We cannot stand idly by and let these arrests go by without taking any action.

What can we do? We can and should cut off our aid and trade with India until all people there are allowed to enjoy basic human rights and civil rights. We can and should publicly demand self-determination for the Sikhs of Punjab, Khalistan, the Muslims of Kashmir, the Christians of Nagalim, and all the people seeking freedom in South Asia in the form of a free and fair vote on their status. Self-determination is the essence of democracy. Unfortunately, "the world's largest democracy" denies this essential right to its minority citizens. We have a strong voice. Let us raise it in support of these minorities.

The Council of Khalistan has issued a very informative press release on the arrest of Mr. Mann and his associates.

Simranjit Singh Mann Must Be Released

Washington, DC, June 28, 2007._The Council of Khalistan today demanded the immediate release of former Member of Parliament Sardar Simranjit Singh Mann and his associates who tried to hang a picture of Beant Singh's assassin on the late_Chief Minister's statue in Jalandhar. Beant Singh, who received less than 7 percent of the vote, was installed as Chief Minister by the Indian government. He presided over the murders of more than 50,000 Sikhs. He was the person who instituted the policy of secret cremation, in which young Sikhs were arrested, murdered in police custody, then declared unidentified" and secretly cremated and the families never received their bodies. This barbaric policy was exposed by human-rights activist Sardar Jaswant Singh Khalra. As a result of his report, Khalra was arrested and murdered while in police custody. His body was also secretly cremated and was never given to his family.

Recently, the Punjab government under Parkash Singh Badal erected a statue of Beant Singh in Jalandhar. Sardar Mann and his associates were arrested when they tried to hang a picture of his assassin, Dilawar Singh, on it.

"The arrest of Simranjit Singh Mann and his associates is another blow to freedom of speech and freedom of assembly in India. basic rights of free people," said Dr. Gurmit Singh Aulakh, President of the Council of Khalistan. "If a group of people can't even hold a peaceful demonstration without being arrested, then what rights do they really have? Where is India's often and loudly proclaimed commitment to democracy? Mann and his associates must be released immediately."

Mann was previously arrested in 2005, along with other Sikh activists, for making speeches in support of Khalistan and raising the Khalistani flag. He came to prominence after the Indian government's military attack on the Golden Temple and 37 other Gurdwaras in June 1984, in which over 20,000 Sikhs were killed, including Sant Jarnail Singh Bhindranwale. Mann resigned from the police, saying that he could not serve a government that would attack the Golden Temple. In 1989, Mann wrote to the chief Justice of India, "reiterating my allegiance to the Constitution and territorial integrity of India," according to Chakravyuh: Web of Indian Secularism by Professor Gurtej Singh IAS, which reprints the letter. He also served as a Member of parliament from Punjab around that time. In the mid-1990s, Mann was arrested for peaceful political activities by the Indian government and the Council of Khalistan secured his release. In 2000, Mann came to the United States with the blessing of the Indian government, escorted through the United States and Canada by Amarjit Singh of the Khalistan Affairs Center. He spoke to a group on Capitol Hill in Washington DC and while speaking in New York, he said that the office of the Council of Khalsitan in Washington, DC should be closed. Since then, he has continued his political activism in Punjab, Khalistan. Neither Amarjit Singh nor the Khalistan Affairs Center has uttered a word of protest against Mann's arrest. Mann's grandfather gave a siropa to General Dyer, the British general who was in charge of the army that massacred over 1,300 Sikhs at Jalianwalia Bagh. A few years ago, Queen Elizabeth apologized to the Sikhs for the massacre during her visit to Punjab.

"The arrest of Simranjit Singh Mann and his associates shows that there is no freedom of speech in Punjab or in India," said Dr. Aulakh. "This underlines the need for a free, sovereign, independent Khalistan. In a free Khalistan, no one would be arrested for peaceful political activity," he said. "In a free Khalistan, no one would erect a statue to honor those who carry out genocide against the Sikh religion and the Sikh Nation. These arrests should make it clear to Sikhs that even if you cooperate with India. they will use you and throw you away," said Dr. Aulakh.

A report issued by the Movement Against State Repression (MASR) shows that India admitted that it held 52,268 political prisoners under the repressive "Terrorist and Disruptive Activities Act" (TADA), which expired in 1995. Many have been in illegal custody since 1984. According to Amnesty International, there are tens of thousands of other minorities being held as political prisoners in India. The Indian government has murdered over 250,000 Sikhs since 1984, more than 300,000 Christians in Nagaland, over 90,000 Muslims in Kashmir, tens of thousands of Christians and Muslims throughout the country, and tens of thousands of Tamils, Assamese, Manipuris, Dalits, Bodos, and others. The Indian Supreme Court called the Indian government's murders of Sikhs "worse than a genocide."

"The arrests of Simranjit Singh Mann and Dr. Sukhpreet Singh Udhoke show that it is urgent to liberate Khalistan from Indian rule as

soon as possible," said Dr. Aulakh. "The time is now to launch a Shantmai Morcha to free Khalistan."

***

Document

CONGRESSIONAL RECORD -- EXTENSIONS

Wednesday, May 23, 2007
110th Congress, 1st Session
153 Cong Rec E 1125

REFERENCE: Vol. 153, No. 85
SECTION: Extension of Remarks
TITLE: AIR INDIA INQUIRY QUESTIONED

Speech of
HON. EDOLPHUS TOWNS
of New York
in the House of Representatives
Tuesday, May 22, 2007

Mr. TOWNS . Madam Speaker, recently a Canadian writer and editor named Dr. Awatar Singh Sekhon, Managing Editor of the International Journal of Sikh Affairs, wrote a detailed response to an article about the 1985 Air India bombings. As you know, those bombings continue to be controversial more than 20 years later and the Canadian government is launching yet another inquiry into the matter.

Dr. Sekhon's quite comprehensive letter, which was written in response to an Edmonton Sun article, is very detailed. It makes a very strong argument and brings up a lot of very important information on the case. Before I put it into the Record, I will attempt to summarize the highlights.

Dr. Sekhon points out that Indian diplomat Mani Shankar says that in 1984, the year before the bombing, the Indira Gandhi government in India commissioned him "to portray Sikhs as terrorists." This directive occurred before Operation Bluestar, the June 1984 attack on the Golden Temple in amritsar (the seat of Sikhism) and several other Sikh Gurdwaras around Punjab, in which 20,000 Sikhs, including over 100 Sikh youth ages 8 to 13, were killed and the Sikh holy scripture, the Guru Granth Sahib, was desecrated by being shot with Indian Army bullets. The orders for that operation were given in January 1984, according to the Sikh Bulletin, October-November 1985. The Air India operation was part of that campaign. In addition, the newspaper Hitavada reported that the Indian government paid the late governor of Punajb, Surendra Nath, the equivalent of $1.5 billion to foment terrorist activity in Punjab and Kashmir.

Dr. Sekhon refers to the first hijacking of an Air India plane by two Brahmin brothers named Pandey to secure Indira Gandhi's release from jail. He notes the penetration of Canada by Indian intelligence in the 1980s.

The letter cites both Zuhajr Kashmeri and Brian McAndrew's excellent book Soft Target and former Canadian Member of Parliament David Kilgour's book Betrayal: The Spy That Canada Forgot. Both show India's responsibility for the bombing. Kashmeri and McAndrew cite the Canadian Security Intelligence Service (CSIS), which said, "if you really want to clear the incidents quickly, take vans to the Indian High Commission and the consulates in Toronto and Vancouver, load up everybody and take them down for questioning. We know it and they know it that they are involved."

Kilgour writes that a Canadian-Polish double agent was approached by an East German named Udo Ulbrecht, who was working with people affiliated with the Indian government, to participate in a second bombing, but he declined to be part of it and the plot never came off. Dr. Sekhon rightly asks why neither Kashmeri, McAndrew, nor Kilgour has been asked to testify in the current inquiry. He also requests that the Indian diplomatic and intelligence personnel who were declared persona non grata in Canada in the wake of the Air India bombing be summoned back to testify before the inquiry.

He notes the mass killings of Sikhs, Christians, Muslims, Assamese, Tamils, and other non-Brahmin minorities by the Indian government Their effort to portray the Sikhs, especially those who speak out peacefully and democratically for an independent Khalistan, as terrorists is a pretext for this "ethnic cleansing."

He quotes my colleague, the gentleman from California, who said in this chamber that for Sikhs and Kashmiris, "India might as well be Nazi Germany." The late General Narinder Singh said that Punjab was a police state. This has been an extension of the India government's strategy that was outlined in a memo in 1947 in which India's first Home Minister V.B. Patel described the Sikhs as "a lawless people" and "a criminal tribe." In other words, the Indian government was trying to discredit and destroy the Sikhs almost from the moment of independence.

Madam Speaker, the time has come to stop our aid and trade with this repressive regime and to demand self-determination for the Sikhs of Punjab, Khalistan, the Muslims of Kashmir, the Christians of Nagalim, and all the people seeking freedom in South Asia. The essence of democracy is the right to self-determination, not an ongoing half-century effort to kill your minority citizens.

I would like to place Dr. Sekhon's letter into the Record at this time for the information of my colleagues.

The Sikh Educational Trust, International Journal of Sikh Affairs, Edmonton, Alberta, Canada, May 9, 2007.
Ret Air India Flight 182 (Toronto_Montreal_London_Delhi), June, 23 1985: Enquiry of Justice John Major

Dear Sir, My writing to you relates with some minor and major comments related to the subject, and also on "Air India's Shared Tragedy Lost in the 'SILOS' between two nations by George Abraham (The Edmonton Journal, 8th May, 2007)."

I would like to comment on Abraham's writing "Prime Minister (Brian) Mulroney had telephoned his condolences to his Indian counterpart, Rajiv Gandhi_an act that was based on a fundamental misunderstanding of who, exactly, had been victimized, and who, in fact, was to blame." Mr. Abraham seems to be in the grip of part of the problem. As a Canadian national and belonging to the Canadian Sikh community, it appears to me that 'telephoning to the prime minister of a country, which had betrayed Canada and the international community in 1974 (explosion of a nuclear device prepared from the by-product of a Candu reactor technology for peaceful and medical purposes) by the Right Hon. Prime Minister of Canada' was far more important than about 90 percent of the Canadian passengers of the ill-fated aircraft. It, certainly, is new information that has come out in Justice Major's enquiry. What a pity our Canadian prime minister, who put Rajiv Gandhi first rather than thinking and offering his condolences to the Canadian Sikhs and the victimized families. This act of Prime Minister Mulroney will never be forgotten by the Canadian Sikhs. Earlier, his predecessor, Charles Joseph Clark, had said to the journalists that "if you want more information about Sikhs, go and call these numbers (of the Indian Consulate Toronto and High Commission in Ottawa):" What an unacceptable act of the prime minister, who hands out the telephone numbers of a foreign mission to get information about Canadian Sikhs. Should we, the Canadian Sikhs who have been in Canada over a century, imply that our Canadian administration has no idea of its Sikh Canadians; or, a foreign mission in Canada has more information about the Canadian Sikhs, especially when the Indian Constitution 1950, Article 25, has eliminated the 'Sikh Identity and Sikh Faith'. The latter is one of the six major faiths of our world.

Does George Abraham know that Mani Shanker Iyer, an Indian diplomat, said, "In early 1984, to the hearing of all, mentioned that at the instance of Indira Gandhi, he was given an unpleasant job of portraying Sikhs as terrorists." A few days later, Iyer stated that, "against his wishes he had done the job?" This was before "Operation Bluestar, the orders for which had been delivered in January 1984" (The Sikh Bulletin, October-November 2005, p. 11; editor@sikhbulletin.com).

Based on the two previous enquiries and the present one which is going on, it appears to me that nothing extraordinary will come from these enquiries, because the major things which might yield substantial information and which might reveal the real cause of the 'Air India Explosion of Flight 182' will never find a place in the enquiry that is going on. Some of the points that, as I believe, have not been discussed so far, are summarized below:

1. *Why Mr. Zuhaire Kashmeri and Mr. Brian McAndrew, two Canadian journalists, who gave their views in their title, Soft Target India's Intelligence Service and its Role in The Air India Disaster 1989 first ed. and 2005 second ed. ISBN 10:1-55028-904-7 and 13: 978-1-55028-904-6, have not been called to testify before the enquiry commission?*

2. *Why Hon. David Kilgour, former member of parliament, Speaker of the House of Commons, former Secretary of State for Asia and Africa, and the author of the title BETRAYAL THE SPY CANADA ABANDONED 1994 Prentice Hall Canada Inc., Scarborough, ON ISBNO-13-325697-9, the title that contained Chapter 9 and 10, A Bizarre Episode in Rome and A Battle For Canada, pp.129-163, has not been asked to testify? Hon. Kilgour writes "One day, while reading a German newspaper, I spotted the photograph and description of a wanted terrorist. I would have known that face anywhere. It was the man who had conducted the meeting in Rome, plotting to bomb some Air India flight. I was quite positive it was him; his name was Udo Ulbrecht or Albrecht, wanted for many terrorist attacks and kidnappings in West Germany and Western Europe. I was upset by the whole thing and decided I wanted out of West Germany as soon as I had done my time." In Hon. Kilgour's title, he further writes "He was greeted in English, heavily accented with German, and led into a larger room where a number of men were already seated and smoking. There were two Sikhs wearing traditional turbans, another pair who looked Italian, Paszkowski and the German, who chaired and greeted them in English as all of them spoke the language with differing levels of fluency. The German spoke of the need for international cooperation and how important the mission was for each of their respective governments. He stressed that the group must work closely together. "Some of the tasks," he said, "might appear strange or even incomprehensible to you. Don't worry about that. Let it be the concern of those who sent you here. Your role is to carry out orders to the letter without asking questions." Everyone sat quietly and listened intently. "The job at hand is, with the use of explosives, to blow up an Air India plane in Europe. Lives will be lost but we must not think about it . . . Each of you will be supplied with documents allowing you to move freely in Europe, weapons, explosives, money and detailed instructions. I will meet with each of you personally to supply you with all these. Wait for me and be prepared for action at any time."*

3. *Under the guise of 'Democracy', the Indian administrations of post-15th of August, 1947 era ((JL Nehru to Manmohan Sinh) and before becoming the political masters of the British Empire later known as the British India Empire, the Brahmins/Hindus (neither a religion nor a culture; see Dalit Voice, Dalit Sahitya Akademy, Bangore, and other Sikh and non-Sikh academics), betrayed the international community and the Sikhs of Punjab, now the State of Punjab (under the occupation of the alleged Indian democracy, since the 15th of August, 1947). It must be*

noted that the Sikh Raj of monarch Ranjit Singh, 1799 to 14th March, 1849, was the first Secular and Sovereign country of South Asia. The Sikhs lost to the British Empire's forces led by General Gilbert on the 14th of March, 1849. As such, the "Struggle To Regain Their Lost Sovereignty, Independence and Political Power of the Sikhs began, by peaceful means taught by their 10 Masters/Gurus (from Guru Nanak Sahib to Guru Gobind Singh ji) right on the day they lost to the British Empire's forces." "The new territory of the British Empire remained 'status less' but on the 29th of March, 1849, the British agent made a proclamation that the newly conquered 'Sikh Raj' is "annexed" but not "amalgamated" to the British Empire for the 'administration purpose only'. It should be noted that the status of the Sovereign and Secular Sikh Raj of Monarch Ranjit Singh remained as "annexed" territory and 'not' the art of India under British Empire or the time British exit from India on the 15th of August, 1947. It should also be noted that there did not exist the word 'India' in any dictionary or Encyclopedia of the English language until the British agent made the annexation of The Sikh Raj to the British Empire on the 29th of March, 1849. As such, the existence of the 'Indian nationality' until the 29th of March, 1849, was out of question. The Sikhs were 'never' Indian nationals, as evident from the Indian Constitution 1950, Article 25. The Constitution which Sikhs' elected representatives 'rejected' in its draft and final forms in the Indian parliament in 1948, the 26th of November, 1949, 1950 and more recently on the 6th of September, 1966. The Canadian news media, along with the international news media and major democratic administrations like the United Kingdom., Canada, United States, Australia, etc., never paid any attention on the "Sikhs" Struggle for Independence" for the reason only known to themselves. Volumes of books and tens of tons news dispatches have been made by the journalists virtually 'devoid' of the Sikhs' Struggle for Sovereignty and Sikhs' status in the Indian Constitution 1950 Article 25. which proclaimed the alleged Indian state as the Republic of India.

Under the umbrella of democracy (or Brahmins autocracy), India has killed more than 2.3 to 3.2 million Sikhs; over 500,000 Muslims in general; more than 100,000 Muslims of the Internationally Disputed Areas of Jammu and Kashmir; over 300,000 Christians; tens of thousands of Dalits; 15,000 Tamils, thousands of Assamese and other non-Brahmin, non-Hindu minorities, since 15th August, 1947. What kind of democracy in India is this which kills its own citizens? There are other democracies in our world, like the United States, Canada, United Kingdom, Australia and others. Has anyone of these countries killed its own citizen(s)? How many Brahmins, Hindus or pro-Brahmins India and its armed forces killed since its inception?

I would like to hear from the journalists like Madam Kim Bolan on the genocides of the Sikhs, Muslims, Christians, Kashmiris and other non-Brahmin and non-Hindu minorities carried out by the Indian democracy? Does she have any information or has she written even a single word on India carrying out genocides of non-Brahmin and non-Hindus since the 15th of August, 1947? Or, else she loves writing against the Sikhs.

*For Madam Kim Bolan and her national and international col-
leagues written specifically or generally on the 'fake hijacking' carried
out by the RAW of India (they must examine the archives of the All India
Radio, if they pretend to be unaware of the activities of the Indian
personnel of RAW and other agencies).*

*The author was wondering if Madam Kim Bolan and her journalistic
colleagues know that the 'first hijacking' of South Asia' was carried out
by two 'Brahmin' brothers (the Pandey brothers), to secure the release of
their Congress leader Indira Gandhi from a jail. Indira Gandhi awarded
them, the Brahmins, with her Congress' nominations to the UP Legislative
Assembly. These criminals were made the 'law makers'. When criminals
are made the law makers intentionally, then what could be expected in a
democratic country, so to speak?*

*Madam Kim Bolan and other journalists must read Congressman
Dan Rohrabacher of California's remarks appeared in the United States
Congressional Records of the House of Representatives that "For the Sikhs,
Christians, Muslims and other non-Hindu minorities, India might as well
be a Nazi Germany."*

4. A community, which is less than 15 percent of the total population of
India, i.e., the Brahmins, Hindus and pro-Brahmins (3+12=15 percent),
deceived and betrayed the Sikhs of the Sikh Raj of monarch Ranjit Singh,
robbed them from their land (partitioned on the 15th of August, 1947) in
the day light, along with the Sovereign people of states like Assam, Jammu
and Kashmir, Hyderabad, Faridkot (now in Punjab), Bikaner (now in
Rajasthan), Dalits (who are still used to remove the human waste from
the households and public places of India), Adivaasis, etc.

5. The journalists and writers like Kim Bolan, George Abraham, Martin
Collacott, Ian Mulgrew, Bharti Mukeherjee, Clark Blaise, Bill Moyer, etc.,
are virtually devoid of the 'Sikhs' history from the Sikhs' point of view'.
They are known as staunchly anti-Sikh writers and do not get along with
the Canadian and/or American Sikhs, simply because they are 'devoid' of
the Sikh history. Indeed, they are well known anti-Sikh writers. Why are
they anti-Sikhs and write against the Sikhs, it is only known to them. They
cannot exonerate themselves from the 'anti-Sikh' renowned journalists or
writers for the reasons only known to them.

6. Madam Kim Bolan and other Canadian journalists, with the exception
of well respected Zuhaire Kashmeri and Brian McAndrew, never understood the Canadian Sikh psyche. Why is it so? Only Madam Kim Bolan,
other journalists and one Narula of the Asia Watch may explain their
position, if they so desire.

7. It goes without doubt that Indian intelligence penetrated Canada in
1980s. This was done to provide cover for the Indian administration's
intended 'attack on the Sikhs' Darbar Sahib Complex (mistakenly known
as the Golden Temple Complex), which includes the Supreme Seat of Sikh
Polity, The Akal Takht Sahib, Amritsar, in the name of a brutal Indian
military "Operation Bluestar" of June, 1984. This was not only an

'undeclared' war on the Sikh Nation, Punjab, but it was carried out to 'Exterminate The Sikh Identity and The Sikh Faith'. One may ask the question did Indian administration succeed? The answer is 'No'; it failed miserably. Their penetration made the life of the Sikhs of Canada no less than a hell. Did anybody, especially the Canadian journalists, with two exceptions, pay any attention to Sikh nationals of Canada? Every Sikh, who is the follower of the Sikh religion, believes in the Canadian way of life, Canadian law, Canadian policy of multiculturalism provided by the administration of the Right Honourable Pierre Elliot Trudeau and Canadian values. Whereas, the Indian administration deliberately made the Sikhs as 'terrorists'; on the 10th of October, 1947, just 7-weeks post of the 15th of August, 1947; the Indian administration of JL Nehu and VB Patel and their man, Chandulal Trivedi in Punjab 'declared' the "Sikhs as lawless people" in a secret memo. The writer is citing only a few major points out of numerous.

8. Considering the penetration of Indian intelligence in 1980s, not only the RAW personnel (Research and Analysis Wing), but the Indian administration made use of Sikhs, especially Akalis like Gurcharan Singh Tohra, Harchand Longowal, Balwant Ramoowalia, Prakash Singh Badal, Balwant Singh, Dr Jagjit Singh Chohan (now deceased), Maj-Gen Jaswant Bhullar, M S Sidhu, Didar Singh Bains of the United States, Prabhu Dayal Singh, Harjinderpal Singh Nagra and Akalis (correspondence between R K Dhawan of 1, Safdarjang Road, New Delhi; the 30th of January_April 25, 1984; please see Chakravyuh Web of Indian Secularism by Gurtej Singh 2000 ISBN81-85815-14-3).

When democratic administrations employ their 'state intelligence' against their own citizens, then what is the guarantee that any individual or state appointed commission will find a way to deliver its 'just' judgment?

I could write more but I should conclude my writing by elaborating that (i) the Indian missions' employees/intelligence workers, who have since been declared persona non grata or left Canada should be summoned back by the commission to question them. I have my doubts that the 'Diplomatic Immunity' may play its stumbling block's role and nothing constructive will come out from any commission; (ii) the Indian administrations' notoriousness is responsible for the Air India disaster of 1985; (iii) in fact, there should be an International Commission to explore and examine the terrorism, persecution, atrocities, human rights violations, and genocides committed by the democratic India. I am of the opinion that Sirdar Gurtej Singh, IAS & IPS (formerly), Professor of Sikhism and Editorial Advisor of the International Journal of Sikh Affairs ISSN 1481-5435 may shed much needed light to the Commission of Justice John Major. All in all, Indian administrations have been responsible not only of the Air India Flight 182, but also of other humanitarian problems, such as Manorama of Assam, who was raped by the Indian Armed

personnel in Assam (Assam situation discussed at the 5th United Nations Human Rights Council, Geneva, Switzerland in March 2007).
   Best wishes and warmest regards.

   Sincerely,
   Awater Singh Sekhon
   Managing Editor and Acting Editor in Chief.

∗∗∗

Document

CONGRESSIONAL RECORD -- EXTENSIONS

Wednesday, May 23, 2007
110th Congress, 1st Session
153 Cong Rec E 1127

REFERENCE: Vol. 153, No. 85
SECTION: Extension of Remarks
TITLE: INDIAN POLICEMAN IN GOLDEN TEMPLE WITH A REVOLVER

Speech of
HON. EDOLPHUS TOWNS
of New York
in the House of Representatives
Wednesday, May 23, 2007

   Mr. TOWNS . Madam Speaker, Indian policeman in Temple with revolver is not the solution to a game of Clue, it's the latest outrage out of India. As we approach the 23rd anniversary of India's brutal military attack on the Golden Temple, the center of the Sikh culture and religion, an undercover Indian policeman was found carrying a revolver into the Golden Temple, where these kinds of weapons are prohibited. It was discovered when the gun fell out of his pocket. I shudder to think what he may have been intending to do with it.

   The chief minister of Punjab, Paraksh Singh Badal, did nothing about this outrage because he is in bed with the Indian Government and in opposition to his Sikh constituents. This desecration of the Golden Temple is outrageous and a reminder that India remains an occupying power in the Sikh homeland, Punjab, Khalistan, which declared its independence on October 7, 1987.

   The Council of Khalistan has published an open letter deploring this desecration of the Sikh nation's most sacred site. It notes that this is part of the Indian Government's ongoing effort to destroy the Sikh religion and demands that the jathedar of the Akal Takht, Joginder Singh Vedanti, censure chief Minister Badal for his part in allowing this to occur.

   We cannot continue to support such actions. They violate the fundamental religious freedom that all free people enjoy. We must take strong action. Cutting off aid and trade until these kinds of atrocities end would be a good first step. And we should demand a free and fair vote in Khalistan, in Kashmir, in Nagaland, and wherever the people seek freedom on the subject of independence. Self-determination is the essence of democracy.

Indian Policeman Caught at Akal Takht Sahib With Revolver

Just a few days ago, the Tribune of Chandigarh reported that an Indian policeman was caught with a revolver at the Akal Takht Sahib. His revolver fell on the ground. He was manhandled by the Sikhs there.

No one is allowed to take firearms inside the Golden Temple. By doing so, this policeman violated the Maryada of the Golden Temple. The shameful Akali government has allowed undercover policemen to desecrate the Golden Temple. The Khalsa Panth condemns this with full force.

Chief Minister Parkash Singh Badal should be removed from his position and the Akal Takht Jathedar should censure him for his sacrilege and violating the Rehat Maryada of the Akal Takht.

The Indan government is determined to destroy the Sikh religion by any and all means. They are trying to create sects in the Sikh religion, such as Dera Sucha (Jhutha) Sauda, Nirankari, Radswami, and other such cults. After Guru Gobind Singh there is no living guru, as the heads of these sects claim to be. That is contrary to the Sikh religion. It is blasphemous. These Deras are a cancer on the Sikh religion. They must not be allowed to spread their cancer and the violence that they bring among the Sikhs.

Guru Gobind Singh Sahib bestowed the guruship on the Guru Granth Sahib and for political decisions transferred power to the Panj Piaras (the Five Chosen Ones.) This desecration of Sikhism cannot be allowed to continue. It will only stop when we free Khalistan from Indian occupation.

Badal blames Captain Amarinder Singh for this situation. He cannot shirk his own responsibility. As Chief Minister, he is responsible for law and order. He should prosecute this baba and such cult leaders and close all Deras in Punjab. If he won't do it, the Khalsa Panth will and we will find new leaders who can serve the interests of the Khalsa Panth, not the Indian government.

Sikhs should have known better. In 1984, it was this Akali party and this Akali leadership of Badal, Tohra, and Longowal who invited the Indian army into the Golden Temple. If anyone attacks the Golden Temple, Sikhs can never forgive or forget it. The Congress Party attacked the Golden Temple; they should not be supported by the Khalsa Panth. It was the Akalis who invited them in. They should also be rejected. We need new Sikh leadership which can deliver a sovereign, independent Khalistan to the Sikh Nation.

Power resides in the Khalsa Panth. Sikhs in Punjab must shoulder their responsibility. Get rid of the present Akali leadership and establish a new Sikh leadership. If we do not, if we let this leadership linger, our misery is prolonged and the Sikh Nation suffers more. It is time to stand up and free the Sikh homeland, Punjab, Khalistan.

In 1986, the Sarbat Khalsa was called. The Sarbat Khalsa formed the Panthic Committee under the leadership of Baba Gurcharan Singh Manochabal (who was later murdered by the Indian government.) It passed a resolution for Khalistan on April 29, 1986. The Panthic Committee formally declared independence on October 7, 1987. It established the Council of Khalistan at that time to serve as the government pro tempore of Khalistan and appointed this humble sewadar as President of the Council of Khalistan.

For the past 20 years, I have worked very hard, along with all the advisors and supporters of the Council of Khalistan, to achieve our objective of sovereignty for Khalistan. Any major event in Punjab since 1984 has been documented in the Congressional Record in statements by various Members of Congress. We thank them for their support for the independence of Khalistan. Congressional hearings were held in the U.S. Congress by Rep. Ben Blaz, Rep. Dan Burton and others on human-rights violations and the independence of Khalistan. Special orders of the U.S. Congress on human-rights violations and the independence of Khalistan have been conducted. The Indian government is trying to alter the Sikh history in Punjab since 1984. They will not succeed because it is preserved in the library of the U.S. Congress. It will lie there safely for a long time. Students of history will find the true story of what happened to the Sikh Nation since 1984.

Khalsa Ji, the time has come for Sikhs to unite and free Khalistan. Remember the words of Guru Gobind Singh, "I grant sovereignty to the humble Sikhs." Freedom is the birthright of all people and nations. It is also granted by our Gurus. The Indian government is so afraid that it is planting agents in Gurdwara committees and organizations that fight for Khalistan. It is creating Deras and planting agents in the Golden Temple to try to stoke violence. It is arresting Sikh activists for protesting a statue of the repressive, murderous Beant Singh, who was responsible for the murder of over 50,000 Sikhs and the secret cremation of their bodies by declaring them "unidentified", as well as the murders of Sardar Jaswant Singh Khalra, who exposed that brutal policy, and Jathedar Gurdev Singh Kaunke, or for making pro-Khalistani speeches and raising the flag of Khalistan. Beware of Sikh leaders who do the bidding of the Indian government.

Just the other day in the Southall Gurdwara in the United Kingdom, Sikh youth took control of the stage when the present management, which is under the control of the Indian Embassy, refused to do Ardas for Shaheed Bhai Kanwaljit Singh, who was killed by followers of the cult leader Ram Rahim when he went to confront them. We must replace these management committees with pro-Sikh, pro-Khalistani managements.

Khalsa Ji, the time has come. Take responsibility and rise to the occasion. Work for the freedom of Khalistan so that the Sikh religion can flourish and the Sikh Nation can live with honor and dignity. Only then can the future of the Khalsa Panth be bright. Remember the words of the former Jathedar of the Akal Takht Sahib, Professor Darshan Singh, that

"If a Sikh is not a Khalistani, he is not a Sikh." Let us show true Sikh spirit. We must rise up and free Khalistan now.

***

Document

CONGRESSIONAL RECORD -- EXTENSIONS

Wednesday, May 23, 2007
110th Congress, 1st Session
153 Cong Rec E 1128

REFERENCE: Vol. 153, No. 85
SECTION: Extension of Remarks
TITLE: 23RD ANNIVERSARY OF GOLDEN TEMPLE ATTACK

Speech of
HON. EDOLPHUS TOWNS
of New York
in the House of Representatives
Wednesday, May 23, 2007

Mr. TOWNS . Madam Speaker, the beginning of June marks the 23rd anniversary of India's military attack on the Golden Temple in Amritsar, which is the seat of the Sikh religion. It occurred from June 3 through June 6, 1984. Many other Sikh Gurdwaras were attacked at the same time in what was known as Operation Bluestar, which killed over 20,000 Sikhs. That was the beginning of a genocide in which over 250,000 Sikhs were killed.

During the attack, young Sikh boys, ranging in age from 8 to 13 years old, were taken outside and shot to death. Other soldiers bravely shot bullets into the Sikh holy scriptures. As Sant Jarnail Singh Bhindranwale, who was killed in the attack, predicted, it laid the foundation for the liberation of the Sikh homeland, Khalistan.

This brutal attack was a desecration of the Sikh religion and culture and a bitter reminder that there is no place for Sikhs or other minorities in Hindu India. They are simply used for the greater glory of the Brahmins.

The Council of Khalistan, which will be leading a commemorative demonstration across from the White House on June 2, has published an excellent open letter on the massacre.

If we want to put an end to ongoing repression, Madam Speaker, we should support independence for all the nations of South Asia. We should go on record in support of a free and fair plebiscite, monitored, on the question of independence for Khalistan, Kashmir, Nagaland, and all the nations of the subcontinent. We should stop trading with India and providing it aid until it respects the basic right to self-determination and all human rights for all its people, whether Brahmin or Dalit, whether Hindu, Sikh, Christian, Muslim, or whatever. We send India development aid, Madam Speaker, and it puts just 2 percent of its development budget to education and just 2 percent to health, but 25 percent to nuclear development! Remember that India began the nuclear escalation in South Asia.

23rd Anniversary of Golden Temple Attack

Dear Khalsa Panth: Next month marks the 23rd anniversary of the Indian government's brutal attack and desecration of Darbar Sahib, the Golden Temple complex in Amritsar. Sikhs must never forget or forgive this atrocity. Remember that the Indian troops shot bullet holes into an original copy of the Guru Granth Sahib, written in the time of the Gurus. They took over 100 young Sikh boys, ages 8 to 13, out into the courtyard of the complex and asked them if they supported Khalistan. When they answered "Bole So Nihar", they were shot to death. Thirty seven (37) other Gurdwaras were simultaneously attacked. In all, more than 20,000 Sikhs were killed in that operation. This kind of brutality makes it clear that there is no place for Sikhs in India.

Since that horrible four-day operation, which took place from June 3 through 6, 1984, over a quarter of a million Sikhs have been murdered at the hands of the Indian government, according to figures compiled by the Punjab State magistracy and human-rights groups. More than 52,000 are being held as political prisoners, according to a report by the Movement Against State Repression. They are held without charge or trail, many since 1984. We demand the immediate release of all political prisoners and a full accounting for those who may have died in custody.

Instead, our highest institutions_the Golden Temple, the Punjab government, the Akali Dal, and others_remain under Indian control. Our homeland, Khalistan, remains under Indian occupation 20 years after declaring its independence from India. Half a million Indian troops continue to enforce the peace of the bayonet in Punjab, Khalistan.

Remember the words of Narinder Singh, a spokesman for the Golden Temple, to America's National Public Radio: "The Indian government, all the time they boast that they are democratic, that they are secular, that they have nothing to do with a democracy, nothing to do with a secularism. They just kill Sikhs just to please the majority."

Sant Bhindranwale told us that the attack would "lay the foundation of Khalistan." Indeed, it did. On October 7, 1987, Khalistan declared its independence. We must use this anniversary to rededicate ourselves to reclaiming that freedom that is our birthright.

In 1986, Harcharan Singh Longowal struck the Rajiv-Longowal Accord, in which India promised to return the capital city of Chandigarh, which Sikhs built, and the Punjabi-speaking areas of Himachal Pradesh and Haryana, which were kept out of Punjab in 1965. Twenty-one years later, India has not kept that promise.

India has a long history of not keeping its promises. It promised the people of Kashmir a plebiscite on their status in 1948 and the vote has never been held. Nor has it kept its promises to the people of Nagaland.

Instead, Nehru said that even if he had to put a soldier under every tree, he would never allow a free Nagaland. The Indian government has killed over 90,000 Kashmiri Muslims, over 300,000 Christians in Nagaland, tens of thousands of Muslims and Christians elsewhere in the country, and tens of thousands of Assamese, Bodos, Dalits, Manipuris, Tamils, and other minorities. Tens of thousands more of them continue to be held as political prisoners, according to Amnesty International. Is that a democracy? These facts underline the necessity to free our homeland, Khalistan, now, and to support freedom for all the people of South Asia.

Remember the words of Guru Gobind Singh, "In grieb Sikhin ko deon Patshahi." ("I grant sovereignty to the humble Sikhs.") Freedom is the birthright of all people and nations. It is also granted by our Gurus.

When I visited Pakistan in November for Guru Nanak's birthday, the Prime Minister of Pakistan, Shaukat Aziz, offered to build a road from Kartarpur (where Guru Nanak left this world) to the border if India will build their portion. They even offered to build a fence if India wants one. With this road, Sikhs could go, and visit this holy site with no visa. The Akalis could build this road themselves, but they have not done it so far. The spineless Akalis continue to be lapdogs of Delhi. How could the Akalis join with the BJP (the political arm of the RSS) to form a government when the BJP is determined to destroy the Sikh religion by any and all means at their disposal? We must end Indian control of our government, society, and institutions. That control is what the Golden Temple attack was designed to cement. We must stand up and say no. Remember Maharajah Ranjit Singh, who led a powerful, secular Sikh state that was independent from 1765 to 1849. Let us have a new birth of freedom, in our homeland, Khalistan.

The Indian government is scared of the Sikh Nation's aspiration for freedom. Recently, it set off an incident in which Baba Gurmit Ram Rahim Singh dressed up as Guru Gobind Singh and advertised in the newspaper, offering to give Amrit to anyone, a function reserved for the Panj Piaras after Guru Gobind Singh baptized them. In addition, it recently put up a statue of Beant Singh, former Chief Minister of Punjab, who presided over the killing of a majority of the 250,000-plus Sikhs who have been murdered. Simranjit Singh Mann and Wassan Singh Zaffarwal were arrested for peacefully protesting the statue. In 2005, 35 Sikhs were arrested for making speeches and raising the flag of Khalistan. All these repressive acts are in the spirit of the Golden Temple attack and continue the repression. They are evidence that we must free Khalistan now.

Let us remind the Indian government that we have not forgotten the atrocities committed against the Khalsa panth at the Golden Temple and from then on. It is time to reclaim our freedom. India must act like the democracy it claims to be and grant a free and fair plebiscite on the issue of Khalistan under international supervision. It must stop arresting Sikh activists for peaceful political activity. And we must honor the spirits of Bhindranwale and all the others killed at the Golden Temple and the 37 other Gurdwaras by launching a Shantmai Morcha to liberate our homeland, Khalistan, once and for all. Until then, we will continue to suffer under India's brutal repression. Let's see to it that our Sikh brothers and sisters finally enjoy the glow of freedom. I ask Sikhs of all shades and political affiliations to join hands to free Khalistan. Remember the words of the former Jathedar of the Akal Takht Sahib, Professor Darshan Singh, that "If a Sikh is not a Khalistani, he is not a Sikh."

> *Sincerely,*
> *Dr. Gurmit Singh Aulakh,*
> *President, Council of Khalistan.*

***

Document

CONGRESSIONAL RECORD -- EXTENSIONS

Wednesday, May 23, 2007
110th Congress, 1st Session
153 Cong Rec E 1129

REFERENCE: Vol. 153, No. 85
SECTION: Extension of Remarks
TITLE: INDIA MUST STOP PROMOTING SECTARIAN VIOLENCE

Speech of
HON. EDOLPHUS TOWNS
of New York
in the House of Representatives
Wednesday, May 23, 2007

Mr. TOWNS . Madam Speaker, India is again promoting sectarian violence in pursuit of its continued control of the Sikhs and other minorities. A fake baba named Baba Gurmit Ram Rahim Singh, who is sponsored by the Indian government, created a sect called Dera Sacha Sauda, one of many sects set up to divide the Sikh people. He took out a newspaper ad in which he dressed up as Guru Gobind Singh and offered to perform the rite of Amrit, which not anyone can perform, for anyone who contacted him. Performing this rite is reserved for specific religious leaders.

This ad caused massive protests, as it was an insult to the Sikh religion. Those demonstrations turned violent. A man named Kanwaljit Singh was murdered by the followers of the Dera when he went there to confront them about Ram Rahim's behavior.

This marks an ongoing practice of promoting violence in the minority communities so as to divide and rule them. As they did in Gujarat a few years ago, the Hindu government set in motion bloodshed to keep the minority community_Muslims then, Sikhs now_divided.

Madam Speaker, this is reprehensible, unacceptable, and undemocratic. It is outrageous behavior for any government and it should not be supported by countries like ours. We must stop aid and trade with India and we must support freedom for Khalistan and the other nations seeking their freedom from Indian rule.

The Council of Khalistan put out a good press release condemning the Indian government's incitement of sectarian violence.

Council of Khalistan Condemns Promotion of Sectarian Violence by India

Washington, DC, May 16, 2007._The Council of Khalistan condemned the recent violence in Punjab, sparked by an advertisement in the newspaper by Baba Gurmit Ram Rahim Singh, the head of Dera Sacha Sauda, in which Baba Gurmit Ram Rahim Singh dressed as Guru Gobind Singh and advertised that he would give Amrit to anyone who asked. This is reserved only for the Panj Plaras. This is an insult to the Sikh religion and clearly backed by the Indian government, said Dr. Gurmit Singh Aulakh, President of the Council of Khalistan, the government pro tempore of Khalistan, which leads the struggle for Khalistan's independence.

"There are no Deras or sects in the Sikh religion. There is only one Sikh religion and Sikh Nation," said Dr. Aulakh. "Fake Babas like Baba Gurmit Ram Rahim Singh are part of the Indian government's ongoing effort to weaken the Sikh religion and prevent Sikhs from achieving freedom," he said,

Next month marks the anniversary of the Golden Temple massacre, Dr. Aulakh noted. During that attack, young boys ages 8 to 13 were taken outside and asked if they supported Khalistan, the independent Sikh country. When they answered with the Sikh religious phrase "Bole So Nihal," they were shot to death. The Guru Granth Sahib, the Sikh holy scriptures, written in the time of the Sikh Gurus, were shot full of bullet holes and burned by the Indian forces.

Former President Bill Clinton wrote in the foreword to Madeleine Albright's book that Indian forces were responsible for the massacre of 38 Sikhs in 2000 in the village of Chithisinghpora. Recently, two leading Sikh activists were arrested for peacefully protesting the construction of a statue to honor Beant Singh, the late Chief Minister who presided over the murder of tens of thousands of Sikhs. In 2005, 35 Sikhs were arrested for making speeches and raising the flag of Khalistan. Sikh farmers are forced by the government to buy supplies and seeds for unaffordably high prices and forced to sell their crops well below market prices.

"These incidents show that we need to free our homeland, Khalistan," said Dr. Aulakh. "Remember what former Akal Takht Jathedar Professor Darshan Singh said: 'If a Sikh is not a Khalistani, he is not a Sikh.'"

A report issued by the Movement Against State Repression (MASR) shows that India admitted that it held 52,268 political prisoners under the repressive "Terrorist and Disruptive Activities Act" (TADA) even though it expired in 1995. Many have been in illegal custody since 1984. There has been no list published of those who were acquitted under TADA and those who are still rotting in Indian jails. Additionally, according to

Amnesty International, there are tens of thousands of other minorities being held as political prisoners. MASR report quotes the Punjab Civil Magistracy as writing "if we add up the figures of the last few years the number of innocent persons killed would run into lakhs [hundreds of thousands.]" The Indian government has murdered over 250,000 Sikhs since 1984. more than 300,000 Christians in Nagaland, over 90,000 Muslims in Kashmir, tens of thousands of Christians and Muslims throughout the country, and tens of thousands of Tamils, Assamese, Manipuris, and others. The Indian Supreme Court called the Indian government's murders of Sikhs "worse than a genocide."

"Only in a free Khalistan will the Sikh Nation prosper and get justice," said Dr. Aulakh. "When Khalistan is free, we will have our own Ambassadors, our own representation in the UN and other international bodies, and our own leaders to keep this sort of thing from happening. We won't be at the mercy of the brutal Indian regime and its Hindu militant allies," he said. "Democracies don't commit genocide. India should act like a democracy and allow a plebiscite on independence for Khalistan and all the nations of South Asia," Dr. Aulakh said. "We must continue to pray for and work for our God-given birthright of freedom," he said. "Without political power, religions cannot flourish and nations perish."

***

Document

CONGRESSIONAL RECORD -- EXTENSIONS

Wednesday, May 23, 2007
110th Congress, 1st Session
153 Cong Rec E 1130

REFERENCE: Vol. 153, No. 85
SECTION: Extension of Remarks
TITLE: COUNCIL OF KHALISTAN WRITES TO CANADIAN JUSTICE MINISTER ABOUT AIR INDIA INVESTIGATION

Speech of
HON. EDOLPHUS TOWNS
of New York
in the House of Representatives
Wednesday, May 23, 2007

Mr. TOWNS . Madam Speaker, as you mow, the government of Canada has undertaken another investigation into the 1985 Air India bombing. Recently, the Council of Khalistan wrote to the Canadian Justice Minister about that investigation.

The letter states that "the Indian government continues to try to blame Sikhs for this atrocity, despite the fact that Ripudaman Singh Malik and Ajaib Singh Bagri were acquitted by a Canadian judge, who said that the witnesses against them were not credible." In the letter, Dr. Gurmit Singh Aulakh, President of the Council of Khalistan, notes that the Canadian Security Investigation Service (CSIS) said at the time, "if you really want to clear the incidents quickly, take vans down to the Indian High Commission and the consulates in Toronto and Vancouver, load up everybody and take them down for questioning. We know it and they know it that they were involved."

The Indian Consul General in Toronto, Mr. Surinder Malik, pulled his wife and daughter off the flight at the last minute. A friend of his who was a car dealer also cancelled his reservation suddenly. Mr. Malik called in a lot of information about the case before the incident was even public knowledge, including a tip to look for an "L. Singh" on the passenger manifest. "L. Singh" was the name under which one of the bombers held his tickets. The other was "M. Singh." Later, a man named Lal Singh told the press that he was offered "two million dollars and settlement in a nice country" to give false testimony in the case_an offer that Mr. Singh declined. It seems that, as Zuhair Kashmeri and Brian McAndrew, the Canadian journalists who wrote the definitive book on the case, Soft Target, noted, "[Consul General] Malik knew more details about the two blasts than did the police investigators." How did this Indian government official know so much so soon?

He also admitted that he fed information to the Toronto Globe and Mail to make a stronger case to blame the Sikhs for the bombing. This was part of a coordinated Indian government effort to paint the Sikh community as terrorists.

It is also worth noting that the Sikh group on whom India has placed the blame all these years is a group called Babbar Khalsa. It is heavily infiltrated by the Indian government. So by trying to blame Babbar Khalsa, the government is essentially taking the blame itself.

I recommend to all my colleagues that they read this informative letter.

This is just further proof, if any is needed, that India is a regime that will carry out acts of terror to promote its own political objectives. Remember that India has killed more than a quarter of a million Sikhs, according to the Punjab State Magistracy, and hold over 52,000 of them as political prisoners, according to the Movement Against State Repression. As I have asked before, why does a democracy need a Movement Against State Repression anyway? Amnesty International reports that tens of thousands of other minorities are held as political prisoners in India, and it has killed over 90,000 Kashmiri Muslims, over 300,000 Christians in Nagaland, and tens of thousands of other minorities as well.

Why should the American people and government support such a government, especially at a time when we are putting our young people on the front lines to fight against terrorism? The time has come to cut off our aid to Indian, end our trade with them, and put Congress on record in support of the freedom movements there. This is the way to peace, freedom, prosperity, and stability in South Asia, Madam Speaker.

Council of Khalistan,
Washington, DC, May 16, 2007.
Hon. Robert Douglas Nicholson,
Justice Minister of Canada,
House of Commons, Ottawa, Canada.

Dear Minister Nicholson: I am writing in regard to your new inquiry into the Air India Flight 182 bombing of 1985. I see no purpose for this ongoing inquiry. As you know, the Indian government continues to try to blame Sikhs for this atrocity, despite the fact that Ripudaman Singh Malik and Ajaib Singh Bagri were acquitted by a Canadian judge, who said that the witnesses against them were "not credible."

Shortly after the bombing occurred, two Canadian journalists, Zuhair Kashmeri of the Toronto Globe and Mail and Brian McAndrew of the Toronto Star, wrote an excellent book on the case entitled Soft Target, which proves that the Indian government itself carried out the bombing. This finding is confirmed in a book by former Member of Parliament David Kilgour entitled Betrayal: The Spy Canada Abandoned. I urge you to call Mr. Kashmeri and Mr. Mcandrew as witnesses in the inquiry.

Soft Target shows how the Indian regime bombed its own airliner in 1985, killing 329 innocent people, to justify further repression against the Sikhs. The book quotes an investigator from the Canadian Security Investigation Service as saying, "If you really want to clear the incidents quickly, take vans down to the Indian High Commission and the consulates in Toronto and Vancouver, load up everybody and take them down for questioning. We know it and they know it that they are involved."

Among many other things, they note that the Indian Consul General in Toronto, Mr. Surinder Malik (no relation to Ripudaman Singh Malik), called in a detailed description of the disaster just hours later when it took the Canadian investigators weeks to find that information. He told them that they should check the passenger manifest for an "L. Singh" because he was responsible_before there was any public knowledge of the bombing!

According to Wikipedia, on June 20, 1985, two days before the flight, "at 1910 GMT, a man paid for the two tickets with $3,005 in cash at a CP ticket office in Vancouver. The names on the reservations were changed; 'Jaswand Singh' became 'M. Singh' and 'Mohinderbel Singh' became 'L. Singh.'". Note that this is the same name that Consul General Malik told investigators to look for_"L. Singh."

It would later come out in newspaper reports that a Sikh named Lal Singh told the press that he was offered "two m111ion dollars and settlement in a nice country" by the Indian regime to give false testimony in the case.

Consul General Malik had also pulled his wife and daughter off the flight suddenly at the last minute, on the feeble excuse that the daughter had a paper for school. A friend of Consul General Malik's who was a Car dealer also cancelled at the last minute.

According to Kashmeri and McAndrew, "Curiously, [Consul General] Malik knew more details about the two blasts than did the police investi-

gators. . . . Malik said that while one of the suspects was booked to Japan, the other was booked to Toronto and onwards to Bombay. He also said that the two checked their bomb-laden bags but did not board the flight themselves. In sum, Malik had painted a scenario of the double sabotage operation that was a near perfect account of what the Mounties would take weeks to fathom.

[Consul General] Malik continually fed the Globe information pointing to Sikh terrorists as the source of the bombs. He was behind another story six days after the crash, this one headlined 'Air-India pilot reported given parcel by Sikh.'." Kashmeri and McAndrew also wrote, "Malik pressured the Globe to publish this story, adding that it could be used to make a stronger case for blaming the Air-India and Narita bombings on the Babbar Khalsa leader. Malik also decried the Canadian system of justice for failing to come up with a quick solution to the bombings. 'In India we would have had a confession by now. You people have too many civil and human-rights laws,' he complained."

The Sikh organization that the Indian government said was responsible, Babbar Kahlsa, is and was then heavily infiltrated by Indian government operatives at very high levels of the organization. The main backer of the group had received a $2 million loan from the State Bank of India just before the plane was attacked, according to Soft Target. The year after the bombing, three Indian consuls general were asked to leave the country.

In his book, Kilgour wrote that Canadian-Polish double agent Ryszard Paszkowski was approached to join a plot to carry out a second bombing. The people who approached Paszkowski were connected to the Indian government.

Yet the Indian government continues to apply pressure to find some Sikhs guilty of the bombing. I am sure that your inquiry will be conducted with fairness and justice. I hope that you will find the real culprits and put this matter to rest. The bombing was an Indian government operation from the beginning.

If there is anything I can do to assist you, please feel free to contact me.

Sincerely,
Dr. Gurmit Singh Aulakh,
President, Council of Khalistan.

***

Document

CONGRESSIONAL RECORD -- EXTENSIONS

Wednesday, May 23, 2007
110th Congress, 1st Session
153 Cong Rec E 1132

REFERENCE: Vol. 153, No. 85
SECTION: Extension of Remarks
TITLE: PUNJAB CHIEF MINISTER ATTACKED FOR ANTI-SIKH
BEHAVIOR

Speech of
HON. EDOLPHUS TOWNS
of New York
in the House of Representatives
Wednesday, May 23, 2007

Mr. TOWNS . Madam Speaker, recently it has been discovered that the Chief Minister of Punjab, Parkash Singh Badal, went and met with a Punjabi cult leader named Gurmit Ram Rahim Singh, who claimed to be a baba and was recently in the news for dressing up as the last Sikh guru, Guru Gobind Singh, and offering Amrit to anyone who called. Amrit is a very sacred ceremony in the Sikh religion and it cannot be done by just anyone. Ram Rahim also has murder and rape charges pending against him. Yet Mr. Badal went to him and bowed, seeking votes. Ironically, Ram Rahim came out for Mr. Badal's political opponents, the Congress Party.

As Chief Minister, one of Mr. Badal's chief responsibilities is maintaining law and order. Yet he seeks support from this fake religious leader instead of prosecuting him for the damage he has done to the Sikh community and to Punjab.

Dr. Gurmit Singh Aulakh, President of the Council of Khalistan, has issued a press release condenming Badal's activities. It shows that chief Minister is allied with the Indian government against the Sikh people. Remember that when Badal was chief Minister before, he presided over the most corrupt government in Punjab's history. They even renamed bribery "fee for service." His wife could tell the amount of money in a bag just by picking it up.

Only by freeing themselves of Indian rule will the Sikhs be able to rid themselves of this kind of anti-Sikh leadership. The U.S. government can help by stopping aid and trade with India until criminals such as Ram Rahim are prosecuted and all human rights are observed and by putting ourselves on record publicly in support of self-determination for the Sikhs of Punjab, Khalistan, the Muslims of Kashmir, the Christians of Nagalim, and all the people seeking freedom in South Asia in the form of a free and fair vote. Isn't that the democratic way? The people of Kashmir were promised a vote on their status in 1948. They're still waiting.

Council of Khalistan Deplores Anti-Sikh Behavior of Paraksh Singh Badal

Washington, DC, May 22, 2007._The Council of Khalistan condemned the behavior of Punjab Chief Minister Parkash Singh Badal. It has recently surfaced that before the Punjab elections, Badal and his son Sukhbir went to meet with Baba Gurmit Ram Rahim Singh, leader of the

Dera Sacha Sauda cult which has brought about so much strife in Punjab. While there, they bowed their heads to Ram Rahim. A Sikh is not supposed to bow except to the Guru Granth Sahib. This is the moral degeneration of the Akali leadership.

Ironically, despite Badal's begging and pleading, Ram Rahim supported the Congress Party in the recent elections in Punjab. Now Badal is blaming his predecessor, Captain Amarinder Singh, for the problem. Badal didn't even get votes out of his shameful actions. Perhaps it's time he paid attention to the Sikhs who elected him rather than the anti-Sikh BJP, his coalition partner, and the leaders in Delhi.

Badal is the Chief Minister. As such, he is responsible for law and order. Yet he refused to prosecute this fraudulent baba pretending to be Guru Gobind Singh. There are pending charges of murder and rape against Ram Rahim. Why does Badal kowtow to him?

"There are no Deras or sects in the Sikh religion. There is only one Sikh religion and Sikh Nation," said Dr. Gurmit Singh Aulakh, President of the Council of Khalistan. "Fake Babas like Baba Gurmit Ram Rahim Singh are part of the Indian government's ongoing effort to weaken the Sikh religion and prevent Sikhs from achieving freedom," he said. "Sikh leaders should not be dignifying them. Badal should be prosecuting this fraudulent baba for these despicable acts."

"Badal's conduct is shameful for a Sikh leader," said Dr. Gurmit Singh Aulakh, President of the Council of Khalistan. "This shameful conduct shows that Badal is under the complete control of the Indian government, rather than working for the Sikhs. We must free ourselves of corrupt, anti-Sikh leaders like Badal and his friends by liberating Khalistan," he said. "Remember what former Akal Takht Jathedar Professor Darshan Singh said: 'If a Sikh is not a Khalistani, he is not a Sikh.'"

A report issued by the Movement Against State Repression (MASR) shows that India admitted that it held 52,268 political prisoners under the repressive "Terrorist and Disruptive Activities Act" (TADA) even though it expired in 1995. Many have been in illegal custody since 1984. There has been no list published of those who were acquitted under TADA and those who are still rotting in Indian jails. Additionally, according to Amnesty International, there are tens of thousands of other minorities being held as political prisoners. MASR report quotes the Punjab Civil Magistracy as writing "if we add up the figures of the last few years the number of innocent persons killed would run into lakhs [hundreds of thousands.]" The Indian government has murdered over 250,000 Sikhs since 1984, more than 300,000 Christians in Nagaland, over 90,000 Muslims in Kashmir, tens of thousands of Christians and Muslims throughout the country, and tens of thousands of Tamils, Assamese, Manipuris. and others. The Indian Supreme Court called the Indian government's murders of Sikhs "worse than a genocide."

"The Sikh masses must rise to the occasion and establish new leadership that works for the interest of the Khalsa Panth and abides by Sikh tradition," said Dr. Aulakh. "Badal and his son have betrayed the Sikh

Rehat Maryada, Sikh principles, and Sikh tradition. Their leadership must be rejected for the interests of the Khalsa Panth. The Jathedar of the Akal Takht must censure him for violating the Sikh Rahat Maryada, betraying the Sikh Nation, and defaming the Sikh religion," he said. *"Incidents like this test the resolve of the Sikh Nation. The Khalsa Panth will never allow the cult babas to dare to compare themselves with our revered Guru Gobind Singh Sahib. who sacrificed his whole family for the Chardi Kala of the Khalsa Panth,"* said Dr. Aulakh. *"Remember Guru Gobind Singh's words: 'Sava lath se ek laraon, tabe nam Gobind Singh kahaon.' Also remember Guru's blessing, 'In grieb Sikh in ko deon patshahi.' Only a free* Khalistan will put a stop to occurrences like this. We must continue to pray for and work for our God-given birthright of freedom," he said. "Without political power, religions cannot flourish and nations perish. The time is now to free Khalistan."

- - - - - - - - -

[From the Panthic Weekly, May 17, 2007]
Badal and Family are Sacha Sauda Premis: Cult Spokesman

Amritsar Sahib (KP)_At a news conference organized by the Sacha Sauda Cult, photographic evidence was released indicating that as recent as January of 2007, Shiromani Akali Dal's president Parkash Badal, his son Sukhbir Badal, and other Akalis met with the dehdahri-cult guru Ram-Rahim and asked for his blessings.

This announcement was made after a large Sikh conclave held at Takht Sri Damdama Sahib called upon the Sikh Nation to socially boycott the entire Sirsa cult, and demanded the Punjab and Haryana Governments to take stern action against the cult leader.

Panthic observers doubt any action would be taken by the Akal Takht Jathedars against the Badals, nor will the Punjab Government take action against the cult. Parkash Badal's cozy relationship between the Sauda leader and other similar cults is now a widely accepted fact.

The recent softening of the tone by Jathedar Joginder Singh Vedanti is an indication that he does not want to ruffle the feathers of his Akali bosses. The recent call for a boycott was not what Vedanti wanted_as evidenced by his silence at the meeting_instead pressure from Jathedar Balwant Singh Nandgarh and the Sikh Sangat left him no other option. Observers predict ultimately it would be the Sikh Sangat that will rise up against the onslaught of derawaad that has been flourishing in Punjab under the Akali administration. Photos such as the above should be ample proof for the agitating Sikh Sangat which side of the fence the Akalis and their puppet Jathedars are really standing on.

***

Document

CONGRESSIONAL RECORD -- EXTENSIONS

Tuesday, April 17, 2007
110th Congress, 1st Session
153 Cong Rec E 760

REFERENCE: Vol. 153, No. 61
SECTION: Extension of Remarks
TITLE: VAISAKHI DAY CELEBRATED AROUND THE WORLD

Speech of
HON. EDOLPHUS TOWNS
of New York
in the House of Representatives

Mr. TOWNS . Madam Speaker, on April 13 and 14, the Sikhs community celebrated Vaisakhi Day with events in Washington, New York, London, Canada, Australia, and wherever Sikhs live. It was a very proud day for them. The Washington, DC, event was led by Dr. Paramjit Singh Ajrawat, a well-known Sikh activist and supporter of a free Khalistan.

Large numbers of Sikhs showed up in these locations to celebrate the day. They called for freedom for the Sikh nation. They raised slogans in support of Khalistan, the Sikh homeland. Freedom is the birthright of all peoples and nations.

When America became independent, Punjab was already independent. Dr. Gunnit Singh Aulakh, president of the Council of Khalistan, has called on Sikhs to celebrate Vaisakhi Day by rededicating themselves to achieving the freedom that is their birthright.

Madam Speaker, we should put this Congress on record with a resolution in support of self-determination for Khalistan and throughout the subcontinent. Why is India opposed to a free and fair vote on the matter, in the democratic way? We should end our aid and trade with India until I the basic rights of all are allowed to be enjoyed, the way that democratic countries behave.

Vaisakhi Day Celebrated With Parades, Events

Washington, DC, Apr. 14, 2007._Vaisakhi Day, the 308th anniversary of the creation and consecration of the Khalsa Panth by Guru Gobind Singh, is being celebrated with parades and events in Washington, London, New York, Canada, England, Australia, and around the world.

The Washington parade occurs on April 14 under the leadership of Dr. Paramjit Singh Ajrawat with the cooperation of the local Sikh Gurdwaras. Later in April, the annual Sikh Day Parade in New York will be held.

Guru Gobind baptized the first five baptized Sikhs, known as the Panj Piaras, on Vaisakhi Day in 1699, then asked them to baptize him. He declared, "In grieb Sikhin ko deon Patshahi ("I give sovereignty to the humble Sikhs") Just two years after his departure from this earthly plane in 1708, the Sikhs established their own independent state in Punjab.

At the time that America became independent, Punjab was an independent country already. It was independent from 1710 to 1716 and again from 1765 to 1849, when the British conquered South Asia. Today Sikhs struggle to regain the sovereignty that Guru Gobind Singh bestowed upon them over 300 years ago.

Vaisakhi Day is the anniversary of the founding of the Khalsa. On Vaisakhi Day in 1699, Guru Gobind Singh baptized the Sikhs and required them to keep the five Ks. He made the Sikhs into saints and soldiers. That memory is celebrated on Vaisakhi Day each year.

"I send Vaisakhi Day greetings to all Sikhs and I urge all Sikhs to take this occasion to fulfill Guru Gobind Singh's vision by working to liberate our homeland, Khalistan, from Indian oppression," said Dr. Gurmit Singh Aulakh, President of the Council of Khalistan, which leads the struggle to achieve independence for Khalistan. Khalistan declared itself independent on October 7, 1987. Over 250,000 Sikhs have been killed since the Indian government attacked the Golden Temple in Amritsar in June 1984. More than 52,000 are being held as political prisoners, some for over 20 years.

"Vaisakhi Day should be a time to renew our commitment to freedom for our Sikh brothers and sisters in Punjab, Khalistan so they can live in prosperity, dignity, and security. Only a free Khalistan can end the repression of the Sikh Nation," Dr. Aulakh said. "Always remember our heritage: Raj Kare Ga Khalsa; Khalsa Bagi Van Badshah. Freedom for Khalistan is closer than ever. Now is the time to claim it"

***

Document

CONGRESSIONAL RECORD -- EXTENSIONS

Tuesday, April 17, 2007
110th Congress, 1st Session
153 Cong Rec E 762

REFERENCE: Vol. 153, No. 61
SECTION: Extension of Remarks
TITLE: COUNCIL OF KHALISTAN SENDS VAISAKHI GREETINGS TO SIKH NATION

Speech of
HON. EDOLPHUS TOWNS
of New York
in the House of Representatives
Tuesday, April 17, 2007

Mr. TOWNS . Madam Speaker, April 13 is a very important day in the Sikh community. It is called Vaisakhi Day, the anniversary of the consecration or the Khalsa Panth in 1699 by Guru Gobind Singh. It is celebrated in Sikh families around the world. There is a parade here in DC and later one in New York. I rise today to offer Vaisakhi Day greetings to the Sikh community.

Recently, the Council of Khalistan issued Vaisakhi greetings to the Sikh Nation. In the letter, Dr. Gurmit Singh Aulakh, President of the Council of Khalistan urges the Sikh nation to work for the liberation of Khalistan, the Sikh homeland that declared its independence from India on October 7, 1987. The Indian government has subjected the Sikhs and other minorities, such as Christians, Muslims, and others, to major atrocities. Over a quarter of a million Sikhs have been murdered by the government since 1984. More than 90,000 Kashmiri Muslims, over 300,000 Christians in Nagaland, and lens of thousands of other minorities have lost their lives at the hands of the regime and its operatives. The Movement Against State Repression reports that more than 52,000 Sikhs are being held as political prisoners without charge or trial, as well as tens of thousands of other minorities.

Freedom is the birthright of all peoples and nations, and Dr. Aulakh points out that Guru Gobind Singh conferred sovereignty on the Sikh Nation. That birthright has been suppressed.

Dr. Aulakh also pointed out the ongoing activities in support of Khalistan in Punjab and elsewhere. On behalf of the Sikh nation, Dr. Awatar Singh Sekhon recently submitted a memorandum on the oppression of the Sikhs and the need for independence to the United Nations Human rights Commission in Geneva. Former Member of Parliament Atinder Pal Singh ran in the recent Punjab elections on a platform supporting Khalistan. He also organized a seminar on Khalistan. Sikh leaders were arrested on two separate occasions just for making speeches in support of Khalistan and raising the Khalistani flag. Jagjit Singh, President of Dal Khalsa, was quoted in the Deccan Herald as saying that "the Indian government can never suppress the movement. Sikh aspirations can only be met when they have a separate state." Yet India prefers to continue its repression, stationing half a million troops in Punjab alone.

Only independence will allow the Sikhs and the other oppressed minorities to live in freedom, prosperity, security, and dignity, which is their birthright. It is clear that as long as they remain under India's rule, they cannot get just and fair treatment. The atrocities will continue. This is unacceptable, Madam Speaker.

We should be on record in support of self-determination for Khalistan and throughout the subcontinent. We should also stop our aid and trade with India until it learns to respect the human rights of all people.

This is in accord with American principles and these are practical steps we can take to bring real freedom to South Asia.

[April 4, 2007]
Vaisakhi Day Message to the Sikh Nation

Dear Khalsa Ji: WAHEGURU JI KA KHALSA, WAHEGURU JI KI FATEH!

On April 13, the Sikh Nation will celebrate Vaisakhi Day, observing the 308th anniversary of the day Guru Gobind Singh established the Khalsa Panth. I would like to take this opportunity to wish you and your family and friends and all Sikhs a Happy Vaisakhi Day. As you know, Vaisakhi Day is the anniversary of the founding of the Khalsa. On Vaisakhi Day in 1699, Guru Gobind Singh baptized the Sikhs and required them to keep the five Ks. He made the Sikhs into saints and soldiers, giving the blessing "In grieb Sikhin ko deon Patshani" ("I give sovereignty to the humble Sikhs.") Just two years after his departure from this earthly plane in 1708, the Sikhs established their own independent state in Punjab. Today we struggle to regain the sovereignty that Guru Gobind Singh bestowed upon us over 300 years ago.

We must remind ourselves of our heritage by raising slogans of "Khalistan Zindabad" and beginning a Shantmai Morcha to liberate our homeland, Khalistan. Every morning and evening we recite, "Raj Kare Ga Khalsa." Now is the time to act on it. Do we mean what we say every morning and evening?

Last week, Dr. Awatar Singh Sekhon, Managing Editor of the International Journal of Sikh Affairs, representing the Council of Khalistan, presented a memorandum on Sikh sovereignty and the release of the Sikh political and non-political prisoners in India to the United Nations Human Rights Commission in Geneva. The memorandum discussed the Human Rights Violations, persecution, torture, genocide of Sikhs since 1984 as well as the current situation in Punjab, Khalistan. The ongoing effort to reclaim the freedom that is our birthright took another step forward with this delivery.

The Sikhs in Punjab have suffered enormous repression at the hands of the Indian regime in the last 23 years. The Indian government has murdered over 250,000 Sikhs since 1984. In addition, over 50,000 Sikh youth were picked up from their houses, tortured, murdered in police Custody, then secretly cremated as "unidentified bodies." Their remains were never even given to their families! Over 52,000 Sikhs sit in Indian jails as political prisoners without charge or trial, according to a report by the Movement Against State Repression (MASR.) Some of them have been in illegal custody for over 20 years! Repression and genocide of this magnitude at the hands of the Indian government is unparallelled in the late part of the 20th century. India should be ashamed of the genocide it has committed against Sikhs, Christians, Muslims, and other minorities.

Recently, Chief Minister Badal backed off his promise to repeal Section 5 of the Punjab Termination of Agreement Act, the section that allowed the free transfer of Punjab's river water to Haryana and Rajasthan to continue. This promise was essential to getting him elected.

Although he is the leader of the Akali Dal, Badal has again shown that he is under the control of the Hindutva movement. It is time for the Sikh leadership to stop kowtowing to the Indian government and start protecting the interests of the Sikh Nation. He should immediately sever his alliance with the BJP. As every Sikh knows, the BJP is determined to destroy the Sikh religion and the Sikh Nation.

Dr. K.S. Aulakh (no relation) recently resigned as Vice Chancellor of Punjab Agricultural University after Mr. Badal ordered him to open the University gate, which had been closed because of robberies and a murder, something that he could not do. Dr. G.S. Kalkat, former Vice chancellor of PAU and chairman of the Punjab Farmers Commission, described this resignation as unfortunate and said there should be no political interference in the workings of the University could not be tolerated. Dr. Darshan Singh, former Dean of Postgraduate Studies at PAU; Dr. D.R. Bhumbla, former Vice Chancellor of Haryana AgriculturaUniversity; Prof. Pritpal Singh Kapur, former pro-Vice Chancellor of Guru Nanak Dev University; Dr. Darshan Singh, former Dean of Postgraduate Studies at PAU; and Lt. Col. Chanan Singh Dhillon, retired President of the Indian Ex-Services League; among others, were also critical of Badal's political interference. Dr. K.S. Aulakh was appointed by Mr. Badal several years ago when Badal was Chief Minister before, so this was an unusually courageous act on his part and he is to be saluted for it. Mr. Badal is Chief Minister of Punjab. Why doesn't he even want to protect the students, faculty, and staff at PAU from robberies and murders?

Jathedar Joginder Singh Vedanti is another who is under Indian government control. A couple of years ago, he was quoted as saying, "We don't want separate territory." Apparently, Vedanti would rather maintain the oppression and the atrocities against the Sikh Nation than enjoy the glow of freedom, as promised to us at the time of independence. Has he forgotten our heritage of freedom? How can the spiritual leader of the Sikh religion deny the Sikh Nation's legitimate aspiration for freedom and sovereignty? Is he not stung by the words of one of his predecessors, former AkalTakht Jathedar Professor Darshan Singh, who said, "If a Sikh is not a Khalistani, he is not a Sikh"? Is Akal Takht occupied by a person who does not believe in Sikh values and Sikh aspirations?

Sikhs can never forgive or forget the Indian government's military attack on the Golden Temple and 125 other Gurdwaras throughout Punjab. Over 20,000 Sikhs were murdered in those attacks as Operation Bluestar, including Sant Jarnail Singh Bhindranwale, General Shabeg Singh, Bhai Amrik Singh, and over 100 Sikh religious students ages 8-13 who were taken out into the courtyard and shot. These attacks accelerated the Sikh independence movement and deepened the desire for independence in the hearts of Sikhs, a fire that burns brightly in the hearts of the Sikh Nation to this day. Sant Bhindranwale said that the attack on the Golden Temple would "lay the foundation stone of Khalistan" and he was right.

Khalsa Ji, at this time of Vaisakhi, the whole Khalsa Panth must be energized to reestablish a sovereign, independent Khalsa Raj by freeing our homeland, Khalistan. It is time for Sikhs to look back at our history of persecution and suffering over the past two decades. The Hindu government of India, whether run by the Congress Party of by the BJP, wants minorities either subservient to Hinduism or completely wiped out. In spite of the fact that the religions believe completely opposite things, Hindus desire to engulf Sikhism just as they did with Jainism and Buddhism in India. They think that Buddhism is part of Hinduism because Siddhartha Gautama, the Buddha, was born in India. Similarly, Guru Nanak was born Hindu, so they proclaim Sikhism to be part of Hinduism. Yet Guru Nanak said that he was "neither Hindu nor Muslim." Jesus was born Jewish. Does that mean that Christianity is merely part of Judaism?

On this auspicious occasion celebrating the birth of the Khalsa Panth, we must bring back our Khalsa spirit. We must remember our heritage and tradition of "Khalsa Bagi Yan Badshah" by committing ourselves to freeing our homeland, Punjab, Khalistan, from Indian Occupation. We need a new Sikh political party which has a dedication to the interests of the Sikh Nation as its sole objective, to establish Khalsa Raj by liberating Khalistan, severing all political ties with India.

The Indian government wants to break the will of the Sikh Nation and enslave them forever, making Sikhism a part of Hinduism. This can only be stopped if we free Punjab from Delhi's control and reestablish a sovereign, independent country, as declared on October 7, 1987. We must recommit ourselves to freeing our homeland, Punjab, Khalistan. Raise slogans of "Khalsa Bagi Yan Badshah," "Raj Kare Ga Khalsa," "Khalistan Zindabad," and "India out of Khalistan." Use this vaisakhi to launch a Shantmai Morcha to liberate Khalistan. In spite of India's best efforts, they cannot arrest all of us. Their jails are overflowing as it is. We must keep the pressure on every day to force India to withdraw from our homeland and allow the glow of freedom in Khalistan.

The flame of freedom still burns brightly in Punjab in spite of the Indian government's brutal repression. Perhaps this is why India is afraid to hold a free and fair vote on the subject of independence. The essence of democracy is the right to self-determination. The time to achieve our independence is now. Always remember our heritage: Raj Kare Ga Khalsa; Khalsa Bagi Yan Badshah. Freedom for Khalistan is closer than ever. We must rededicate ourselves to achieving it.

Pantha Da Sewadar,
Dr. Gurmit Singh Aulakh
President, Council of Khalistan.

***

Document

CONGRESSIONAL RECORD -- EXTENSIONS

Tuesday, April 17, 2007
110th Congress, 1st Session
153 Cong Rec E 766

REFERENCE: Vol. 153, No. 61
SECTION: Extension of Remarks
TITLE: IN MEMORY OF DR. GURCHARAN SINGH, HUMANITARIAN AND
FREEDOM ACTIVIST

Speech of
HON. EDOLPHUS TOWNS
of New York
in the House of Representatives
Tuesday, April 17, 2007

Mr. TOWNS . Madam Speaker, I was distressed to learn that Dr. Gurcharan Singh, a Sikh scholar from Long lsland, was killed March 31 in a hit-and-run traffic accident. Professor Singh was on his way to the Gurdwara (the Sikh place of worship) at the time. The driver has not yet been found.

Professor Singh was a professor at Marymount Manhattan College and a leader In the Sikh community in New York. He was a father and grandfather. According to WNBC-TV, he was "a counselor to New York's Sikh community and a philanthropist devoted to bringing people of different faiths and nationalities together." He was also an activist in support of Sikh freedom, serving as an advisor to the Council of Khalistan, which leads the effort to free the Sikh homeland, Khalistan, from Indian occupation. In that capacity, he would accompany the Council's President, Dr. Gurmit Singh Aulakh, when he would go to the U.N. Human Rights Commission.

Prior to teaching at Marymount, Dr. Singh had been a professor at Columbia University. He taught political science and international studies.

The Council of Khalistan issued a press release about Dr. Singh's passing. It was also reported on WNBC Channel 4 in New York, on Yahoo News, on several Sikh and South Asian news outlets, and around the Internet.

On behalf of all my colleagues, I wish to extend the sympathies of the U.S. Congress to Dr. Singh's family, friends, and students. I'm sure that everyone joins me in this. I know that he will leave a void that will be very difficult to fill.

Madam Speaker, the best tribute we could pay to Dr. Singh is to continue his work, as Dr. Aulakh points out. This Congress can help by stopping aid to India and trade with that country until all people there enjoy human rights and by going on record in support of self-determination for Dr. Singh's Sikh Nation and for the Nagas, Kashmiris, and all the people seeking freedom in India. Self-determination is the essence of democracy.

Plainview Scholar, Leader Mourned After Hit-And-Run Death Gurcharan Singh, 77, Taught at Columbia, Marymount Manhattan College

Plainview, N.Y._A family and a community were mourning Saturday night the death of beloved professor and role model killed by a hit-and-run driver on Long Island, NewsChannel 4's Aimee Nuzzo reported.

Gurcharan Singh, 77, a scholar and a professor, was also a counselor to New York's Sikh community and a philanthropist devoted to bringing people of different faiths and nationalities together, according to family and friends.

"He is the gem of our community," said friend Paul Kandhari. "If there was a family problem, he'll be there. If the father and son have a problem, he'll be there."

The Plainview father of three and grandfather was struck and killed by a hit-and-run driver while walking from his home to church Friday night.

Dr. Singh was crossing Old Country Road in Plainview just after 8 p.m. headed for the Sikh Temple, when a red or maroon car traveling westbound ran a red light, struck him and kept going, police told Nuzzo.

Singh was airlifted to Nassau University Medical Center with multiple fractures and head trauma, but he did not survive.

"My father was a very selfless man who served his community and society with all his heart, and we'd really love any assistance in finding the individual who did this," said Surinder Singh, the victim's son.

Anyone with information about the mishap was asked to call Nassau County Crime Stoppers at 1-800-244-TIPS.

Once a professor at Columbia University, Singh taught political science and international studies at Marymount Manhattan College for more than three decades and continued to teach part-time, Nuzzo said.

A statement from Marymount Manhattan College said the "community is deeply saddened by the news of Professor Singh's death. He served as a devoted teacher at the college for many years, and his loss will be felt by all of our faculty, staff, students and alumni. Our thoughts are with his family during this difficult time." Dr. Singh's friends said they have no doubt the selfless humanitarian would have forgiven the hit-and-run driver who took his life. They said they hoped that would help whoever is responsible to come forward.

- - - - - - - - -

[Council of Khalistan Press Release]
Dr. Gurcharan Singh, Advisor to Council of Khalistan, Killed in
Hit-and-Run Traffic Accident
Leading Sikh Scholar, Teacher, Humanitarian

Washington, DC, Apr. 4, 2007_Dr. Gurmit Singh Aulakh, President of the Council of Khalistan, today expressed "deepest sympathies" to the family and friends of Professor Gurcharan Singh, a leading Sikh scholar and a teacher at Marymount Manhattan College. Professor Gurcharan Singh was killed by a hit-and-run driver about 8:00 p.m. on the evening of March 31 as he was heading to the Gurdwara.

"Professor Gurcharan Singh leaves a vacuum that will be hard to fill, not only within the Sikh community and Nassau County, but for his family, friends, students, and the many whose lives he touched," said Dr. Aulakh, "He will be greatly missed. I am proud that he was my friend."

"Only God gives life and takes life. As human beings, we are helpless. 'Ghale Aawe Nanka Sadhe Uthin Jai.' We can only mourn his loss but the best tribute to Dr. Gurcharan Singh will be to continue his mission which he worked for, that is serving humanity and working hard to liberate Khalistan from Indian occupation. Only in a free Khalistan will the Sikh religion flourish and the Sikh Nation prosper."

Professor Gurcharan Singh was well known as a humanitarian on Long Island. "My father was a very selfless man who served his community and society with all his heart," said his son Surinder Singh, He served as a counselor to the New York Sikh community and was a philanthropist.

Professor Gurcharan Singh was also a strong supporter of Khalistan, the independent Sikh homeland that declared its independence from India on October 7, 1987. In that effort, he served as an advisor to the President of the Council of Khalistan, which leads the peaceful, democratic, nonviolent effort to liberate Khalistan. He accompanied Dr. Aulakh whenever he went to talk to the United Nations Human Rights Commission.

His death was reported on WNBC-TV New York and on its website; on Indo-Asian News Service; on Sikh media outlets; on a variety of websites; and on other media outlets.

"Professor Gurcharan Singh's passing is a loss to the Sikh Nation, to the people of Long Island and America, to his family and friends, and to friends of freedom," said Dr. Aulakh. "May God bless this departed soul."

***

Document

CONGRESSIONAL RECORD -- EXTENSIONS

Thursday, March 01, 2007
110th Congress, 1st Session
153 Cong Rec E 432

REFERENCE: Vol. 153, No. 35
SECTION: Extension of Remarks
TITLE: NEW PUNJAB CHIEF MINISTER URGED TO WORK FOR SIKH
SOVEREIGNTY

Speech of
HON. EDOLPHUS TOWNS
of New York
in the House of Representatives
Thursday, March 1, 2007

Mr. TOWNS . Madam Speaker, recently elections were held in Punjab. The voters turned out the Congress Party government and restored the Shiromani Akali Dal to power. This means that Parkash Singh Badal returns as Chief Minister.

The Congress Party claims to be secular, but the fact is that it presided over the massacre of Sikhs that took the lives of over a quarter of a million Sikhs. It was the party that carried out the military attack on the Golden Temple in Amritsar, the center and seat of the Sikh religion. On the other hand, the Akali Dal has historically been the pro-Sikh party. However, during the tenure of Chief Minister Amarinder Singh, Punjab did reclaim its water rights and cancel the agreements that allowed diversion of that water to other states. The bill implementing the cancellation explicitly declared the sovereignty of Punjab.

As you know, Madam Speaker, Punjab, Khalistan declared its independence on October 7, 1987.

Dr. Gurmit Singh Aulakh, President of the Council of Khalistan, has written to Chief Minister Badal urging him to keep his campaign promises of a better economic life for Punjab fanners, of clean government, and to reclaim the capital city of Chandigarh for Punjab. He also urged Mr. Badal to declare again the independence of Punjab, Khalistan and to work for a free and fair vote.

The essence of democracy is the right to self-determination. As such, a free and fair vote on the issue of independence is called for if India still wishes to be looked upon as the democracy it claims to be. The Indian government is sending out its sycophants to spin the Punjab elections as having "debunked" the Khalistan movement, but in fact, quite the opposite is the truth of the matter.

I call on this Congress to stand up for freedom and join in urging the Punjab Legislative Assembly to declare independence again, and to urge India to allow a free and fair plebiscite on the matter of independence for Khalistan, for the Christians of Nagaland, and for Kaslunir, as promised in 1948, as well as all others who seek their freedom. I also call for a stop to American aid and trade with India until basic human lights are respected and everyone there is allowed to live in freedom, dignity, prosperity, and security.

Madam Speaker, I would like to place the Council of Khalistan's letter to Chief Minister Badal into the Record at this time with the permission of the House.

Council of Khalistan,
Washington, DC, February 28, 2007.
Hon. Paraksh Singh Badal,
Chief Minister of Punjab, Chandigarh, Punjab, India.

Dear Chief Minister Badal: Congratulations on your victory in the Punjab elections and your return as Chief Minister. You promised the return of clean government to Punjab. That would be a welcome relief for the people of Punjab. You also promised free electricity and Rs4 per kilo for wheat flour and Rs20 per kilo for lentils for the poor. We welcome these promises and urge you to implement them as soon as possible.

I call upon you to get Chandigarh back for Punjab. As you know, Punjab built Chandigarh to be its capital and it rightfully belongs to Punjab. It is time to get it back.

We also urge you to maintain. Captain Amarinder Singh's water policy. His government cancelled the unfair agreements that allowed the diversion of Punjab's water to nonriparian states. In that bill, the Legislative Assembly explicitly declared the sovereignty of Punjab. Unfortunately, the Congress Party, which presided over the massacre of Sikhs, is an anti-Sikh party. The Akali Dal has historically been the pro-Sikh party. Yours is the party that called on the Sikh Nation to prepare ourselves for "the long struggle to liberate Khalistan." You are presiding over a Sikh political and religious institution that controls the gurdwaras in Punjab. Remember that Professor Darshan Singh, an Akali and former Jathedar of the Akal Takht, has said, "If a Sikh is not for Khalistan, he is not a Sikh."

Each morning and evening, we pray, "Raj Kare Ga Khalsa," the Khalsa shall rule. Do you say this prayer sincerely? Will Delhi let you implement the new price structure you promised? They have done everything in their power to keep the Sikhs oppressed, including imposing President's rule on Punjab nine times. They have been responsible for the murders of a quarter of a million Sikhs, according to figures compiled by the Punjab State Magistracy and published in The Politics of Genocide by Inderjit Singh Jaijee. The Movement Against State Repression reports that over 52,000 Sikhs are being held as political prisoners without charge or trial, some since 1984! The late General Narinder Singh said that "Punjab is a police state."

You have promised to end "the dark and corrupt legacy of despotic dictatorship." There is only one way to do so. That is to declare the sovereign independence of Khalistan. The Legislative Assembly can do this and should do it. This would elevate you immediately from Chief Minister to Prime Minister. Self-determination is the essence of democracy. Why can't India do the democratic thing and allow the people of Punjab, Khalistan to vote in a free and fair plebiscite on the question of independence? What are they afraid of?

Again I congratulate you and urge you to work to end the oppression of Sikhs and keep the interests of the Sikh Nation foremost in your mind as you embark upon your term as Chief Minister. I urge you to work to regain the sovereignty that is our birthright.

Sincerely,
Dr. Gurmit Singh Aulakh,
President, Council of Khalistan.

***

Document

CONGRESSIONAL RECORD -- EXTENSIONS

Thursday, March 01, 2007
110th Congress, 1st Session
153 Cong Rec E 435

REFERENCE: Vol. 153, No. 35
SECTION: Extension of Remarks
TITLE: COUNCIL OF KHALISTAN COMMENTS ON PUNJAB ELECTIONS

Speech of
HON. EDOLPHUS TOWNS
of New York
in the House of Representatives
Thursday, March 1, 2007

Mr. TOWNS . Madam Speaker, the Council of Khalistan recently issued a press release on the elections in Punjab and the victory of the Shiromani Akali Dal. Dr. Gurmit Singh Aulakh, President of the Council of Khalistan, noted the unfortunate cycle between the Congress party, which was primarily responsible for the genocide against Sikhs, and the Shiromani Akali Dal, which is in coalition with the Hindu nationalist Bharatiya Janata Party (BJP), which is the political arm of the Rashtriya Swayamsewak Singh (RSS), an organization formed in support of the Fascists of Europe which has been responsible for acts of violence against minorities. The RSS also published a booklet on how to implicate minorities such as Sikhs, Christians, and others in false criminal cases. An alternative to these two parties is sorely needed. The Sikh nation needs leaders who are committed to protecting their interests.

As you know, Madam Speaker, former President Bill Clinton, in his foreword to Madeline Albright's book, wrote that 38 Sikhs in Chithisinghpora were murdered while he was visiting by Hindu militants. New York Times reporter Barry Bearak has concluded that the Indian government's forces were responsible. Although the killers dressed as "militants," they spoke to each other in the language of the Indian army. It appears that this is just another of the many incidents where either the Indian military or its paid "Black Cats" paramilitary units have been caught carrying out terrorist incidents in the guise of alleged "militants."

Remember that according to India Today, India's leading news magazine, it was the Indian government itself that created the Liberation

Tigers of Tamil Eelam, identified by the U.S. government as a terrorist organization.

Madam Speaker, the essence of democracy is the right to self-determination. It is time for India to end the repression of its minorities and allow them to exercise their basic democratic right to a free and fair vote on the question of independence. This Congress should put itself on record demanding that India do so. Further, we should cut off our aid to India and our trade with that country until full human rights, including the right to self-determination, are enjoyed by all the people there.

Madam Speaker, I request permission to place the Council of Khalistan's press release on the Punjab ejections into the Record at this time.

[From the Council of Khalistan_Press Release]
Akali Dal Wins Punjab Elections_Must Put Interests of Sikh Nation First_Khalistan Is the Only Solution

Washington, DC., Feb. 28, 2007._The Shlromani Akali Dal, under the leadership of Parkash Singh Badal, won the state elections for the Punjab Legislative Assembly, winning 48 of 117 seats to 44 for the Congress party, 19 for the Bharatiya Janata Party, 5 Independents. and one seat still to be elected. Since the Akalls and the BJP are coalition partners, this puts the Akall coalition back in charge with a 67-seat majority. As a reward, the BJP got the position of Deputy Chief Minister.

"It is sad that the people of Punjab are re-enacting the cycle of choosing between the Congress Party, which presided over the massacre of Sikhs and the Akalis, whose coalition partner, the BJP, wants to wipe out the Sikhs and all minorities," said Dr. Gurmit Singh Aulakh, President of the Council of Khalistan. "Captain Amarinder Singh is to be given credit for doing some pro-Sikh things like cancelling the water agreements that permitted the diversion of Punjab's water to non-riparian states," said Dr. Aulakh. "But he is still trapped by the Congress Party. Badal, who presided over the most corrupt government in Punjab's history, has pledged clean government. He has promised free electricity for Punjab farmers and Rs4 per kilo for wheat flour and Rs20 per kilo for lentils to the poor. Let's see if he keeps his word, Dr. Aulakh said.

"Radal is the head of a Sikh religious and political body. His party controls the Gurdwaras in Punjab. That's where he got the money to buy the alcohol for his election," Dr. Aulakh said. He noted that the BJP, the Akalls' coalition partner, is the political arm of the Rashtriya Swayamsewak Sangh (RSS). a pro-Fascist organization that has worked to eliminate minorities from India. "Is Badal on the side of the Sikhs or the RSS?" Dr. Aulakh asked. He called on the Badal government to get Chandigarh back for Punjab. "Punjab built Chandigarh to be its capital. It properly belongs to us. The government of Punjab should be pressing to get our capital back," he said.

"Remember that the Akalls once called on the Sikh Nation to carry out 'the long struggle to liberate Khalistan,'" Dr. Aulakh said. "These elections show why we must liberate Khalistan from Indian occupation and oppression," said Dr. Aulakh. "That is the only way for Sikhs to protect

ourselves from India's brutality. Elections under the Indian constitution will only perpetuate it. The only way that the repression will stop and Sikhs will live in freedom, dignity, and prosperity is to liberate Khalistan," said Dr. Aulakh. "As Professor Darshan Singh, former Jathedar of the Akal Takht, said, 'If a Sikh is not a Khalistani, he is not a Sikh.'," Dr. Aulakh said.

After human-rights activist Jaswant Singh Khalra exposed the Indian government's policy of mass cremation of Sikhs, in which over 50,000 Sikhs have been arrested, tortured, and murdered, then their bodies were declared unidentified and secretly cremated, the police kidnapped him. Khalra was murdered in police custody. No one has been brought to justice for the kidnapping and murder of Jaswant Singh Khalra. Rajiv Singh Randhawa, who was the only witness to the Khalra kidnapping, has been repeatedly subjected to police harassment. This includes being arrested for trying to hand a piece of paper to then-British Home Secretary Jack Straw in front of the Golden Temple. The police never released the body of former Jathedar of the Akal Takht Gurdev Singh Kaunke after SSP Swaran Singh Ghotna murdered him. He was never punished for this crime.

In 1994, the U.S. State Department reported that the Indian government had paid over 41,000 cash bounties for killing Sikhs. A report by the Movement Against State Repression (MASR) quotes the Punjab Civil Magistracy as writing "if we add up the figures of the last few years the number of innocent persons killed would run into lakhs [hundreds of thousands.]" The Indian Supreme Court called the Indian government's murders of Sikhs "worse than a genocide." The MASR report states that 52,268 Sikhs are being held as political prisoners in India without charge or trial, mostly under a repressive law known as the "Terrorist and Disruptive Activities Act" (TADA), which expired in 1995. Many have been in illegal custody since 1984. There has been no list published of those who were acquitted under TADA and those who are still rotting in Indian jails. Tens of thousands of other minorities are also being held as political prisoners, according to Amnesty International. Last year, 35 Sikhs were charged and arrested in Punjab for making speeches in support of Khalistan and raising the Khalistani flag. "How can making speeches and raising a flag be considered crimes in a democratic society?" asked Dr. Aulakh.

India is on the verge of disintegration. Kashmir is about to separate from India. As L.K. Advani said, "If Kashmir goes, India goes." History shows that multinational states such as India are doomed to failure. "Countries like Austria-Hungary, India's longtime friend the Soviet Union, Yugoslavia, Czechoslovakia, and others prove this point. India is not one country; it is a polyglot like those countries, thrown together for the convenience of the British colonialists. It is doomed to break up as they did. There is nothing in common in the culture of a Hindu living in Bengal and one in Tamil Nadu, let alone between them and the minority nations of South Asia," Dr. Aulakh said.

"Freedom is the God-given right of every nation and every human being," said Dr. Aulakh. He noted that the Indian government was already spinning the results. "Their wholly-owned U.S. Congressman, Frank Pallone (D-New Jersey) has already portrayed the elections as a rejection of Khalistan, even though the voters defeated the Congress Party, which is against Khalistan,' Dr. Aulakh said. "Congressman Pallone sounds like he is being compensated by the Indian regime," Dr. Aulakh noted. "Sikhs must be allowed to have a free and fair plebiscite on the issue of Khalistan. In a democracy, you cannot continue to rule against the wishes of the people," he said. "The essence of democracy is the right to self-determination. Currently, there are 17 freedom movements within India's borders. It has 16 official languages. It cannot hold together for very long," he said. "We hope that India's breakup will be peaceful like Czechoslovakia's, not violent like Yugoslavia's," Dr. Aulakh said. "Earlier this year, Montenegro, which is less than a million people, became a sovereign country and a member of the United Nations," he said. "Now it is the time for the Sikh Nation of Punjab, Khalistan to become independent. We must free Khalistan now."

***

Document

CONGRESSIONAL RECORD -- EXTENSIONS

Thursday, March 01, 2007
110th Congress, 1st Session
153 Cong Rec E 437

REFERENCE: Vol. 153, No. 35
SECTION: Extension of Remarks
TITLE: SIKH EDITOR WRITES TO PRESIDENT BUSH, URGES SUPPORT
FOR SIKH FREEDOM

Speech of
HON. EDOLPHUS TOWNS
of New York
in the House of Representatives
Thursday, March 1, 2007

Mr. TOWNS . Madam Speaker, recently, Dr. Awatar Singh Sekhon, Managing Editor of the International Journal of Sikh Affairs, wrote to President Bush about the dangerous situation in India, where democratic rights for minorities are under continuing threat. He also published the letter in his magazine.

Dr. Sekhon noted that the interests of the United States and its allies, such as Canada, are likely to be damaged by continuing close cooperation with India. As he observed, although India proudly portrays itself as "the world's largest democracy," it is a country where, as he writes, "democracy has been used to deny freedom, national and human rights, and basic human dignity to the majority." That majority includes Christians, Sikhs, Muslims, Dalits, and other minorities.

He notes that in India, the Brahmin class, which is 15 percent of the population, uses the most brutal oppression to suppress and rule the minorities. The caste system is still rigorously enforced, despite being made illegal in 1950. It is used to keep the people down, backed by violent repression. He notes that in 1948, the Indian government promised the people of Kashmir a plebiscite on their status. Punjab was promised sovereignty at the time of Indian independence. Those promises have not been kept and any effort to claim what was promised has been met with brutality that has resulted in the murders of over 250,000 Sikhs, over 300,000 Christian Nagas, over 90,000 Kashmiri Muslims, Muslims and Christians elsewhere in the country, and tens of thousands of other minorities. Yet our policymakers insist on treating India both as a democratic country and as an ally, despite its longstanding and still current friendship with Russia, as well as its coziness with the mullahs of Iran, to whom it has sold heavy water and other components.

Dr. Sekhon cites the attack on the Golden Temple as another example of India's effort to eliminate the minorities and subsume them into a Hindu state.

Madam Speaker, I call on all my colleagues, especially those who are promoters of India, to read this devastating letter. It is quite damaging to India and it is right on target. It will give you essential information on the lack of basic liberties in that country.

We can makce a difference, Madam Speaker. Instead of cozying up to India and trying to cut deals with them in the name of stability, it is time to stop our aid and our trade to pressure India to allow all its people to enjoy basic human rights. And it is time to put the U.S. Congress on record in support of self-determination for all the peoples and nations of the subcontinent through a free and fair plebiscite on their status. Isn't that the fair and responsible way to handle questions like this? Isn't that the way democracies do it? Why is India afraid of real democracy?

Madam Speaker, I would like to insert Dr. Sekhon's excellent letter into the record. Again, I urge eveyone to read it. It will prove very informative.

International Journal of Sikh Affairs
January 24, 2007.
Hon. George W. Bush,
President, United States of America,
The White House, Washington, DC.

South Asia: interests, permanent allies, world peace and the role of the United States in the region
I am a citizen of Canada and a member of the Canadian Sikh community. I retired from service in public health as a microbiologist, research scientist, administrator and academic a few years ago. I am now active in work for human rights. These rights are not peculiar to a

people or country; they protect the entire human race. I am expressing below my concerns over the likelihood of damage to long-term interests of the United States of America, its allies, the NATO forces, Canada in particular. The pain of sufferings families of North America, in Europe, the Middle East and South Asia is hard to ignore. The irony is that the more the U.S. tried to ameliorate conditions, the worse they have become.

The people of North America know very well the objectives of the United States (U.S.) and the hurdles faced in leading the world during much of the 20th and in the current 21st centuries. The people of the U.S. and their elected leaders have devoted a lot of time, money and precious resources in manpower and management for the good of the mankind to make the world better and safer. Despite all the good intentions of the democratic world it has been struggling to find a basis for lasting world peace. I believe that the long-term interests of the United States and the world at large are complementary. The U.S. leadership is good for the world. Yet, increasingly fewer people believe that to be true. Is there anything amiss?

I firmly believe that the United States and its allies eagerly want to prevent the sufferings of friendly peoples whose governments they have influence over. While we find the stern hand of the U.S. military operating against enemies, there is little effort to impose the same principles of human freedom and dignity on "friends". Much of South Asia is democratic; India boasts of being the largest democracy in the world. Yet it is in India_more than anywhere else_where democracy has been used to deny freedom, national and human rights, and basic human dignity to the majority. As the Hon. Dana Rohrabacher, (R-Cal) had said as far as the minorities (the Sikhs, Muslims in general, Muslims of the Internationally Disputed Areas of Jammu and Kashmir, Christians, Dalits, Adivasasis or the indigenous native people, and other non-Hindu, non-Brahmin) are concerned, India is a Nazi Germany for them (Tim Phares 2006 Int J Sikh Affairs 16(1),40-42 ISSN 1481-5435).

Congressman Rohrabacher's assessment is accurate and well justified; it can be the focal point of a new beginning with India. The question is: how could a country, which is the world's largest democracy, sustain caste apartheid and pogroms against minorities without facing recrimination? It is done by mis-definition and misrepresentation the world is too busy to try and unravel. India is not a nation and has not even tried to become a nation during the 60 years that it has been "free". It has relied entirely on brute military force to crush any people that demanded its rights. The fact is the Muslims are a majority in Jammu and Kashmir, the Sikhs are a majority in the Punjab and Hill tribes of Assam are mostly Christian. The People of Jammu and Kashmir were promised a plebiscite that was endorsed by the United Nations. The Sikhs were promised their separate state Khalistan by the Congress leaders in exchange for rejecting Pakistan's offer of the same. The Tribal peoples of Assam were also promised "freedom" if they sided with the Congress Party against the British. Now that these peoples demand what was promised, India has unleashed the most diabolical genocide and an international campaign to demonize their stuggle. The British Raj lasted as long as it did because it was founded on recognition of India as multiple nations. How can a country call itself a democracy when it discards its very foundation_the right of national self-determination?

India aspires for its leaders_M.K. Ghandi and J.L. Nehru_to be recognized with other great leaders of the democratic world like George Washington, Franklin D Roosevelt, Abraham Lincoln, J.F. Kennedy, Jimmy Carter, and William Jefferson Clinton. But it cannot even begin to secure that position until it can show that they stood up for the oppressed within the country and without. India has invaded each one its neighbours, overtly or covertly; if it gave in to any demand, it sought to hurt twice as much elsewhere. The Untouchables or Dalits_who are a majority in several states of India and constitute 65 % of its population_were promised "reservation" of seats in the parliament, in education and jobs. Even after 60 years, it is still denied to backward castes and to Muslims. India uses "democracy" as means to fudge issues and deny rights by never ending arguments in circles. That is the experience of the people in the country and neighbours who live in dread of roads being closed or rivers being diverted.

The devious policies and broken promises is the hallmark of India today. The Sikhs have been the worst victims. They founded the first secular and sovereign state in South Asia by Sikh monarch Ranjit Singh in 1799 that was "annexed" by treaty to the British Empire on 14th March, 1849. In June 1984, the Darbar Sahib Complex which includes the Supreme Seat of Sikh Polity, The Akal Takht Sahib, Amritsar (mistakenly known as Golden Temple of Amritsar), which is the Vatican of the Sikh faith, was assaulted by the Indian Army killing 20,000 devotees who were inside the Temple and their leader Sant Jarnail Singh Bhindranwale was martyred. When the Sikh guards of Prime Minister Indira Gandhi avenged the assault assassinating her, the worst pogrom was unleashed upon the Sikhs all over India that resulted in 250,000 Sikhs_mostly young men and their families_who were mercilessly killed, Indian diplomats talk about the tradition of non-violence in India of which Mahatma Gandhi is considered to be a universal symbol. But the truth is that India is violent but only to the weak; when confronted with strong and powerful the Brahmin response is obsequious folding of hands. This manner of greeting appears to be show of humillty. But it is actually a statement that the person being greeted is of low birth and is untouchable.

On 15th of August 1947, the British handed over political power to the "unelected" Hindu leadership. But the Hindus/Brahmins (neither a religion nor a culture) were only 15 % of the population; how could they be the successors of the British Empire in India. Once installed in power, they have relied on a combination of hate (for people of foreign faiths or of low birth), guile and stratagem far mor complex than any Machiavelli. The record of their rule over India speaks eloquently how Hindus/Brahmins have been master-mind in persecution of faith minorities and the low caste majority of native peoples who are deemed to be inferior by birth in their unique faith. Through Article 25 of the Indian

*Constitution 1950, the Sikh, the Buddhists and Jains and all the Un-
touchables, all of who are victims of oppression and apartheid, are
denied their separate identity and deemed to be Hindus. The Sikh faith
founded by Guru Nanak Sahib was a rebellion to reject the caste "apartheid" enforced by the Hindus of Brahmin caste. The irony is that when
freedom came, the Sikhs were declared to be Hindus (long haired Hindus) albeit of the renegade variety, against the teachings of its founder,
Guru Nanak Sahib, and the Sikhs' Holy Scripture, Adi Guru Granth
Sahib. It is difficult to portray the anger, revulsion and frustration felt by
the Sikhs in this unwelcome embrace of Hinduism (which is neither a
religion nor a culture according to the verdict of Punjab and Haryana
High Court, 1984). Brahmin rule in post-15th August, 1947, India has
interest only in maintaining the apartheid system; its objective is the
prosperity of urban dwelling upper castes_the so called 200 million
middle class.*

*Suave Indian diplomats routinely underlines that the USA and India
are natural allies. Even American politicians and diplomats have started
to harp on the same theme. It is time, this was questioned. What makes
them natural allies? During the years of the Cold War, India was the
friend of The Soviet Union, not of America. Why? It is because both were
internally and internationlly imperialist. Now, India needs an imperial
patron to underpin its own imperious. It needs the U.S. Is that the role the
USA sees for itself in the world? As supporter of local imperialists? Surely
the power and prestige of the USA is such that it must aim higher: obtain
lasting universal peace and harmony; amity between faiths; unfettered
democracy; free trade. Tied to apron strings of India, the USA is bound to
drift into petty machinations to deny freedom to some and equality to all.
India's imperialism is founded on delaying tactics and betrayal. All the
problems in the South Asian region are product of Brahmin spin or
stratagem. The media makes wild forecasts of India of the future. It is
supposed to be a huge market for consumer goods. Whose? Peoples'
Republic of China?*

*Some people have become very rich in India. Diaspora Indians are
clever and are also becoming rich. But for the majority, India is a
hellhole and will always remain so. Caste based India has structural,
infrastructual and social problems that it cannot overcome until it
abandons its "poverty imperialism". However, India is country of 1.1
billion people who deserve better. If India allowed the right of self-
determination to the Sikhs, to the peoples of Jammu and Kashmir and
Assam, it would still be the second largest country with population more
than all of Europe. However, it would no longer need to maintain
hostility with neighbouring states and would be in a position to remove
strife, tension and hate from its social scene. India must give the native
peoples their national rights and create autonomous states of India that
would facilitate a compact of states within each the interplay of diverse
ethnic and caste interests would create grass root harmony.*

*For the United States to articulate its interests in far off lands and
develop mechanisms to secure those interests, its diplomats and politi-*

cians have to be conversant with the history and customs of those lands. Historically, the Sikhs of Punjab and the people of Afghanistan have never been "subservient" to any foreign ruler. That was true in the 19th Century as it is today. There are nearly 20 nations within the "Indian union", which are struggling to regain their lost sovereignty and independence ever since the British Indian Empire was hurriedly partitioned in 1947. The end of the British Empire marked the end of the imperial era in the whole world. India's efforts to build and expand its empire are the biggest threat to peace and stability of Asia. Consider Mr. President, if 20 or so nations, including the Sikhs of Punjab, Christians of Nagaland, the tribal people of Assam and Manipur, the south Indian states most notably Tamil Nadu, were to become "sovereign" states, what a huge change for the better it would be for the region and the world. That is the only way to replace the polity of hate and oppression with polities of peace and harmony underpinned by secure undefended borders. Large is not fashionable; not just for women.

I hope I have given some points to ponder. The USA can lead the world with a global vision. There are not many regions where so much is old and archaic ready to crumble and hit dust. Many Americans are fond of India but they do not know why? The present rulers of India would like your help in building their empire. But that is not the best interest of the people of India. India is one country that needs benign intervention to dismantle the social and political structures to be replaced by structures founded on national self-determination. That would be good for business; that would be good for world peace; that is the calling of greatness.

Best wishes and warmest regards.

Sincerely,
Awatar Singh Sekhon,
Ph.D, FIBA, RM (CCM), Associate Professor (Retired), Medical Microbiology and Immunology; Director (Former), National Centre for Human Mycotic Diseases Canada; Managing Editor and Acting Editor in Chief.

***

Document

CONGRESSIONAL RECORD -- EXTENSIONS

Friday, January 12, 2007
110th Congress, 1st Session
153 Cong Rec E 96

REFERENCE: Vol. 153, No. 7
SECTION: Extension of Remarks
TITLE: CHRISTIANS CONTINUE TO SUFFER IN INDIA

HON. EDOLPHUS TOWNS
of New York
in the House of Representatives
Friday, January 12, 2007

Mr. TOWNS . Madam Speaker, just before the new Congress convened, many of us celebrated Christmas with families and friends. I hope that every one of my colleagues, old and new, had a very happy Christmas and holiday season. But Christmas is another anniversary also for the Christians of India. Since Christmas 1998, 8 years now, India has been focusing its persecution in large measure on Christians.

In September, the convent and school of Loreto were violently attacked by the violent Hindu organization the Bharatiya Janata Yuva, a youth arm of the BJP, which is the political arm of the RSS, a Fascist organization that published a book on how to get minorities, including Christians, falsely implicated in criminal cases. A BJP spokesman demanded a high-level inquiry into the school, according to the Tribune newspaper of Chandigarh, saying it engaged in "irrational behavior." As I noted at the time of the attack, apparently, being a Catholic is irrational behavior and "unscientific activity" in the world of Hindu militants.

Over 300,000 Christians in Nagaland have been murdered in India. Nuns have been raped, priests have been murdered, Christian schools and prayer halls have been attacked. Laws have been passed requiring the permission of the Hindu regime before one may be baptized. Christians have faced jail time, as well as threats and physical violence, just for sharing their faith.

Missionary Graham Staines was sleeping in his jeep with his two young sons when they were surrounded by a mob chanting "Victory to Hannuman," a Hindu god. The mob then burned Staines and his sons to death. Missionary Joseph Cooper of Pennsylvania was beaten so severely that he had to spend a week in an Indian hospital. Then the Indian government threw him out of the country. Police gunfire broke up a Christian religious festival on the theme "Jesus is the answer." Is this the secularism that India is so proud of?

It would be bad enough if Christians were the only ones suffering. But they are not. Sikhs, Muslims, Dalits, and others have also felt the lash of Indian repression. The time has come for freedom in the subcontinent. The time has come for the persecution to end.

Madam Speaker, there is a way to help bring freedom and secularism to the people of south Asia. We should end all U.S. aid and trade with India until everyone within its jurisdiction enjoys full human rights there. And now that we have a new Congress, we should go on record in support of freedom everywhere in South Asia. There is no better time than now. If we can help to stop the persecution we have a duty to do so.

I would like to place an article from the website of the Bible League into the Record at this time, Madame Speaker. It has further details about the persecution of Christians.

"He Heard Our Fears and Prayers"

Nearly two years after the establishment of anti-conversion laws, Indian Christians are celebrating the effects of their repeal. Only time will tell the long-term blessings of this legal change, but several resulting miracles have already taken place. In the first month alone, a group of 50 Indian church planters reports having baptized over 1,200 new Christians!

Christians throughout India were stunned when the pro-Hindu government was overturned in the Spring 2004 national election, and several state governments annulled local anti-conversion laws.

Said one local Bible League-trained Christian, "I praise God for enabling us to spread the Gospel in our country. He heard our fears and prayers regarding the election. God gave us an extra bonus when He made our state government remove the anti-conversion law which was in force until now. Hallelujah!"

Undeterred by fear

Indian Christians have faced many hardships in sharing the Gospel. Bible League-trained Christians in India report that they or fellow believers have faced threats, physical attacks, and jail time for sharing their faith.

Baptisms, in particular, became a significant challenge for local churches. Under the anti-conversion laws, anyone who chose to become baptized was legally obligated to seek permission from the government, as well as provide them with the name of the person performing the baptism. Fearing repercussions, many new Christians did not make this outward profession of faith until after the laws were repealed.

Still, thousands of Indians were undeterred in their faith. A local Bible League-trained Christian, while under the anti-conversion law, wrote, "We continue to encourage Christians through the Word of God. We remind them of the promises (Matthew 28:20) and the testimonies of the great martyrs. We are encouraged to fulfill the Great Commission of Christ, regardless of what happens to us. We are prepared for imprisonment, punishment, and even death for the sake of Christ."

Relying on God's faithfulness

Continue to pray for the Church in India. The repeal of state anti-conversion laws has been a tremendous miracle_but challenges still remain. One state continues to uphold anti-conversion laws, and persecution persists throughout the country.

Yet God has been faithful to His children in India, and they are recognizing Him as their Savior by the thousands. Praise God for increasing opportunities to share His Word with the lost.

The great commission_Matthew 28:19-20

19 Therefore go and make disciples of all nations, baptizing them in the name of the Father and of the Son and of the Holy Spirit, 20 and teaching them to obey everything I have commanded you. And surely I am with you always, to the very end of the age.

***

Document

CONGRESSIONAL RECORD -- EXTENSIONS

Thursday, January 11, 2007
110th Congress, 1st Session
153 Cong Rec E 73

REFERENCE: Vol. 153, No. 6
SECTION: Extension of Remarks
TITLE: HIGHEST SIKH RELIGIOUS AUTHORITY SEEMS TO BE UNDER HINDUTVA CONTROL

Speech of
HON. EDOLPHUS TOWNS
of New York
in the House of Representatives
Thursday, January 11, 2007

Mr. TOWNS . Madam Speaker, the Council of Khalistan recently sent a letter to Joginder Singh Vedanti, the Jathedar of the Akal Takht, who has been promoting a piece of flim-flam known as the Dasam Granth, in which several writers took a snippet of the writing of the last Sikh guru, Guru Gobind Singh, and added other items, some pornographlc, trying to pass it off as the genuine work of Guru Gobind Singh in order to damage the Sikh religion. Jathedar Vedanti's endorsement of the Dasam Granth makes him a particpant in this effort to undermine the Sikh culture and religion.

The Council of Khalistan urged the Jathedar to stop diverting the attention of the Sikhs to this severely altered book and instead to focus on the issue of freedom for Khalistan. He noted that on the two occasions last year when Slkh leaders were arrested for making speeches in support of Khalistan and raising a Khalistani flag, there was no protest from Jathedar Vedanti.

It is time for us to support the legitimate aspirations of the Sikhs and all the minorities of India who are seeking their freedom by stopping our aid to India) suspending our trade with that country and by supporting the right to self-determination for all the minority nations of the subcontinent. Self-determination is the essence of democracy. Why can't "the world's largest democracy" hold a simple vote on this fundamental question?

Madam Speaker, I would like to insert the Council of Khalistan's letter to Jathedar Vedanti into the Record at this time for the information of the American people.

January 9, 2007.

Dear Jathedar Vedanti: I am writing to you about the Dasam Granth, which you have been promoting as the genuine writing of Guru Gobind Singh. The issue of its authorship was settled long ago. As you know, the authors of the Dasam Granth identify themselves within the text and only a small part is written by Guru Gobind Singh. The rest was appended by Hindu writers looking to harm the Sikh religion. Much of it is pornographic. For a jathedar of the Akal Takht to promote it as genuine Sikh scripture, especially since Guru Gobind Singh left the Guruship in the Guru Granth Sahib, is harmful to the Sikh religion and the Sikh Nation. Sikhs should bow only to the Guru Granth Sahib, nothing else.

The Dasam Granth is not the real issue. Do not get sidetracked, and do not sidetrack the Sikh Nation from the real issue, freedom and sovereignty for Khalistan. Do not let this controversy divert and waste the resources of the Sikh Nation from the preservation of our religion and culture.

It is vitally important that the Akal Takht Jathedar, the spiritual leader of the Sikh religion, be committed to the well-being of the Sikh Nation. Preserving its history, religion, culture, and scripture is essential to that well-being, especially when it is under assault from Hindus who are trying to subsume the Sikh religion and culture into those of the Hindus as part of Hindutva. Remember that a former Cabinet minister said that everyone who lives in India must either be a Hindu or be subservient to Hindus. But also remember the words of your predecessor, Professor Darshan Singh, who said, "If a Sikh is not a Khalistani, he is not a Sikh."

Jathedar Vedanti, the duty of the Jathedar of the Akal Takht is to protect, promote, and disseminate the Sikh religion. How can we do that within the framework of India when India is working to destroy the Sikh religion? The experience or the Jewish people shows that when a nation has sovereignty, it flourishes, but when it does not it perishes.

The only way to preserve, promote, and disseminate the Sikh religion and culture is in a free and sovereign Khalistan. Yet when Sikh leaders in Punjab were arrested last year simply for making speeches and raising the Khalistani flag, we did not hear a word of protest from the Akal Takht. Nor did we hear a protest of the actions of the Badal government in Punjab, the most corrupt in Punjab's history. The Badal government even sold jobs_they called it "fee for service" and Mrs. Badal was able to tell how moch money was in a bag just by picking it up.

Please do not let your energy be diverted to issues like the Dasam Granth, which has long been known to be altered. We need every Sikh to help bring freedom, dignity, prosperity, and security is in a free, sovereign, independent Khalistan. Discussion of issues like the Dasam Granth merely diverts the Khalsa Panth from freedom and sets back the cause of protecting the Khalsa Panth.

Panth Da Sewadar,
Dr. Gurmit Singh Aulakh,
President, Council of Khalistan.

***

Document

CONGRESSIONAL RECORD -- EXTENSIONS

Tuesday, January 09, 2007
110th Congress, 1st Session
153 Cong Rec E 48

REFERENCE: Vol. 153, No. 4
SECTION: Extension of Remarks
ITLE: COUNCIL OF KHALISTAN SENDS NEW YEAR GREETING TO THE
SIKH NATION

Speech of
HON. EDOLPHUS TOWNS
of New York
in the House of Representatives
Tuesday, January 9, 2007

Mr. TOWNS . Madam Speaker, the Council of Khalistan, which leads the peaceful, democratic, nonviolent effort to free Khalistan, the Sikh homeland, from India, has sent New Year's greetings to the Sikhs from the council and its president, Dr. Gurmit Singh Aulakh.

In the letter, Dr. Aulakh calls On Sikh political leaders to stand up for the interests of their people, which is what all of us in public office anywhere should be doing. He notes that without sovereignty, nations perish, and he cites the situation of the Jewish people before World War II as compared to their situation now. That is a good example of what sovereignty can do for a people. He calls on the Punjab Legislative Assembly that is about to be elected next month to pass a resolution again declaring Khalistan's independence.

Dr. Aulakh calls for the return of the state capital, Chandigarh, to Punjab, along with the Punjabi areas of neighboring states Himachal Pradesh and Haryana. He urges an end to the diversion of Punjab's water without compensation. He notes that the fanners are being oppressed by being forced to buy fertilizer at exorbitantly high rates but being forced to sell their crops at ridiculously low prices. He notes the insults and repression that India has inflicted on the Sikhs, including the Golden Temple attack, the murder of over 250,000 Sikhs since 1984, the fact that more than 52,000 Sikhs are being held as political prisoners, and so many other violations. The letter notes that in an independent Khalistan, India would not be able to inflict such insults and repression on the Sikh Nation.

In addition to the quarter of a million Sikhs it has murdered, the Indian regime has killed over 300,000 Christians in Nagaland, more than 90,000 Muslims in Kashmir and 2,000 to 5,000 in Gujarat, as well as Christians and Muslims elsewhere in the country and Tamils, Manipuris, Dalits, Bodos, Assamese, and other minorities. Tens of thousands of people are held as political prisoners, according to Amnesty International. Congress should demand the release of all political prisoners and the prosecution of those who have violated the rights of Sikhs, Muslims, Christians, and other minorities.

Madam Speaker, the time has come for the glow of freedom to be enjoyed by everyone. It is time to cut off American aid and trade with India until all people enjoy full human rights there. In addition, we should put the U.S. Congress on record in support of freedom everywhere in South Asia. Now that a new Congress has taken office, it is an ideal time to pass a resolution calling for a free and fair plebiscite on the subject of independence. That is the democratic way to do things and it's time that India started behaving like a democracy.

Madam Speaker, I would like to put the Council of Khalistan's New Year message into the Record at this time.

Council of Khalistan, Washington, DC, January 9, 2007.

Dear Khalsa Ji:

Waheguru Ji Ka Khalsa, Waheguru Ji Ki Fateh!

The New Year has already arrived. Happy New Year to you and your family and the Khalsa Panth. May 2007 be your best year ever. I wish you health, joy, and prosperity in the new year.

The flame of freedom continues to burn brightly in the heart of the Sikh Nation. No force can suppress it. Guru Gobind Singh blessed the Khalsa Panth, saying "in grieb Sikhin ko deom Patshahi." ("I bless the humble Sikhs with sovereignty.") The Sikh Nation must dedicate this year to working hard to achieve that goal. Self-determination is the right of all peoples and nations and the essence of democracy. Without sovereignty, religions perish. With sovereignty, they flourish. Compare the situation of the Jewish people in Europe before World War II to their situation now. There is no reason Sikhs cannot achieve a similar change of fortune.

It has been said that "without vision, the people perish," but with vision, the people flourish. It is time for the Sikh Nation to flourish. Sikhs have suffered too much already under the yoke of Indian persecution since independence, especially over the past 25 years. We have seen the attack on the Golden Temple, over 250,000 Sikhs murdered and over 52,000 held as political prisoners, the murder of the Akal Takht Jathedar, more than 50,000 Sikh youth tortured, murdered, then declared unidentified and secretly cremated, their bodies never returned to their families. Their families continue to suffer. We must help their widows and orphans. Let us find the vision to throw off this repression. With that vision, the Sikh Nation will flourish; without it, we will perish and India's effort to eliminate Sikhism will succeed. This is the reason that Guru Gobind

Singh sent Sikhs to learn Sanskrit and to gain knowledge of other religions, so that the Khalsa Panth might be more enlightened and be aware of the qualities of its own religion and culture.

The Indian government is reacting to the rising tide of freedom for the Sikh Nation. It has stepped up its efforts to destroy the Sikh religion and deny Sikhs an environment to flourish. They have kept Punjabi-speaking areas out of Punjab while supporting an influx of Hindus into Punjab. Sikhs are prohibited from buying land in Rajasthan, Himachal Pradesh, and Uttaranchal Pradesh, yet there are no restrictions on land ownership in Punjab by non-Sikhs. People from anywhere can buy land in Punjab, including people from Rajasthan and Himachal Pradesh. India is trying to subvert Khalistan's independence by overrunning Punjab with non-Sikhs while keeping Sikhs from escaping the brutal repression in Punjab. I ask Captain Amarinder Singh and Badal to get the Punjabi-speaking areas back from Haryana and Himachal Pradesh. These areas rightfully belong to Punjab. When will the political leaders of Punjab stand up for the Sikhs?

In Punjab, the Sikh population is 75 percent rural. Sikhs are dependent on agriculture. The lifeline of farmers is water. We must stop the diversion of Punjab's water to Rajasthan and Haryana without compensation. That is a natural resource of Punjab. A couple of years ago, Captain Amarinder Singh's government cancelled the water agreements. I call on Chief Minister Amarinder Singh to use his power to receive payments for this water. As we pay the price for the coal we get from the Indian government, then why can't we get paid for the water we give? Sikh leaders in Punjab must take a strong stand on this issue.

The Indian government squeezes Sikh farmers by all available means. They sell fertilizer and seeds at very high cost but when it comes time to sell produce, the government sets the price very low. This leads to thousands of farmers committing suicide because of their colossal financial indebtedness to the Indian government.

It is time to take control of the Bhakra Dam and the Nangal hydroelectric project. These belong to Punjab but are controlled by the Delhi regime. Punjab must take complete control of these projects and sell electricity at market rates. The Gobindgarah Fort, which was built by the Sikh missal Bhangian, was recently returned to Punjab by the Indian government. That is a good first step. Now all that is the Khalsa Panth's, including the sovereignty that is our birthright, must also be returned so that Sikhs can flourish in the glow of freedom promised by the Indian National Congress during the independence struggle.

The capital of Chandigarh was built by Punjab. Punjab must get it back from the Indian government. It is the height of highhandedness to make Chandigarh a Union Territory. I ask Chief Minister Amarinder Singh to take this good opportunity to regain, control of Chandigarh. This will help him politically as well. Haryana is a wealthy state; let Haryana build its own capital.

In November we met with Pakistani Prime Minister Shaukat Aziz. He said he would build a road from Kartapur Sahib to the Indian border,

*provided that the Punjab government builds its portion as well. I have
visited Kartapur. There is only a mile or so of the road and the Ravi River
is completely dried up. The bridge, which is on the Indian side, needs
minor repairs. This road would be good for the people on both sides of the
border. It would help build good relations between India and Pakistan,
particularly between Pakistan and the Sikhs of Punjab. I urge Captain
Amarinder Singh to build the road immediately so that Sikhs from
Punjab can visit Kartapur Sahib where Guru Nanak departed this Earth
for his heavenly abode. It is a serene place.*

*The RSS and its political arm, the BJP, want to divide the Sikh Nation.
The Dasam Granth is RSS mischief. The issue of its authorship has been
settled long ago, despite what any Indian-controlled Sikh leader may say
now. I urge Akal Takht Jathedar Jogincder Singh Vedanti to stop the
discussion of the Dasam Granth completely and concentrate his efforts on
achieving freedom for Khalistan and stopping the vices that have perco-
lated in the Sikh religion, including abortion of female fetuses, drinking
liquor, and the caste system. Guru Gobind Singh created the Khalsa as
equals. Mazhabi Sikhs are as good Sikhs as anyone else. They are our
brothers and sisters and we must treat them as equals. Remember what
Guru Gobind Singh said: "Ragrete Guru ke Bete." ("The Mazhabi Sikhs
are the sons of the guru.") Guru Gobind Singh lifted them up and Sikhs
established Sikh rule from 1710 to 1716 and from 1765 to 1849. When
America declared its independence in 1776, Punjab was already ruled
independently by the Sikh missals.*

*Twice last year, Sikhs were arrested for making speeches in support of
Khalistan and raising the Khalistani flag. The Indian regime is clearly
worried about the rising tide in support of Sikh sovereignty. Let us
dedicate our energy this year to achieving the establishment of Khalistan.
Any organization that sincerely supports Khalistan deserves the support
of the Sikh Nation. When Khalistan is free, the Sikhs can resolve these
issues in a way that benefits the Khalsa Panth, not the forces of Hindutva.*

*However, the Sikh Nation needs leadership that is honest, sincere,
consistent, and dedicated to the cause of Sikh freedom if we are to
continue to move the cause of freedom for Khalistan forward in 2007 as
we did in 2006. Remember the words former Jathedar of the Akal Takht
Professor Darshan Singh: "If a Sikh is not a Khalistani, he is not a Sikh."
Khalistan is the only way that Sikhs will be able to live in freedom, peace,
prosperity, and dignity. It is time to start a Shantmai Morcha to liberate
Khalistan from Indian occupation. We must achieve our freedom by
peaceful, democratic, nonviolent means. Let that be the mission of 2007.*

*Elections for the Punjab Legislative Assembly will be held on February
13. Vote only for candidates who are committed to establishing Khalistan
and will work to make it a reality. Every morning and evening the Khalsa
Panth recites "Raj Kare Ga Khalsa." We must dedicate ourselves to
realizing this. The time is now. We can do it by the ballot. I ask Sikhs of
every political shade not to miss this opportunity. We must realize it now.
When the Punjab Legislative Assembly reconvenes it must pass a resolution for the independence of Khalistan. As soon as that resolution passes,*

India will no longer be able to repress the Sikhs. Three million Sikhs living outside India will make sure that Khalistan is free without any further loss of human life. In a democracy, you can't rule the people against their wishes.

Sikhs will never get any justice from Delhi. Ever since independence, India has mistreated the Sikh Nation, starting with Patel's shameful memo labeling Sikhs "a criminal tribe" even though the Sikh Nation gave over 80 percent of the sacrifices to free India. How can Sikhs continue to live in such a country? There is no place for Sikhs in supposedly secular, supposedly democratic India.

Let us make certain that 2007 is the Sikh Nation's most blessed year by making it the year that we shake ourselves loose from Indian oppression and liberate our homeland, Khalistan, so that all Sikhs may live lives of prosperity, freedom, and dignity. Now it is up to us. Do not waste this opportunity.

May Guru bless the Khalsa Panth in 2007 and always.

> *Sincerely,*
> *Dr. Gurmit Singh Aulakh,*
> *President, Council of Khalistan.*

***

Document

CONGRESSIONAL RECORD -- EXTENSIONS

Friday, December 08, 2006
109th Congress, 2nd Session
152 Cong Rec E 2146

REFERENCE: Vol. 152, No. 135
SECTION: Extension of Remarks
TITLE: COUNCIL OF KHALISTAN URGES SIKHS TO WORK TO FREE KHALISTAN SEES DISINTEGRATION OF INDIA

Speech of
HON. EDOLPHUS TOWNS
of New York
in the House of Representatives
Thursday, December 7, 2006

Mr. TOWNS . Mr. Speaker, last month, Dr. Gurmit Singh Aulakh, President of the Council of Khalistan, spoke at the Press Club in Lahore, Pakistan. In that speech, he predicted disintegration of India, according to the newspaper Dawn from Lahore. "There is nothing common in the culture of the Hindu living in Bengal and the one in Tamil area," the paper quotes Dr. Aulakh as saying. "A country having 18 official languages cannot hold its people together for a long time, especially when there is state sponsored suppression against minorities," he went on to say.

Dr. Aulakh cited the BJP's statement that if you want to live in Hindustan, you must be a Hindu. He discussed India's long record of violence against the minorities within its borders, including the murders of over a quarter of a million Sikhs, more than 90,000 Kashmiri Muslims, over 300,000 Christians in Nagaland, 2,000 to 5,000 Muslims in Gujarat, tens of thousands of Christians and Muslims around the rest of the country, and tens of thousands of Assamese, Bodos, Dalit "untouchables", Manipuris, Tamils, and other minorities. He cited numerous other incidents, including the murder of former Jathedar of the Akal Takht Gurdev Singh Kaunke, the kidnapping and murder by the police of human-rights activist Jaswant Singh Khalra, the recent attack on the Convent of Loreto, the attack on the Babri mosque, and many other such events.

Dr. Aulakh said that the only solution to this situation is a free, sovereign, independent Khalistan, which was declared on October 7, 1987. It is time for the United States to help protect the dignity of all people in South Asia by helping them to live in freedom. There should be a free and fair plebiscite in Punjab on the independence of Khalistan, as well as a plebiscite in Kashmir, as promised to the United Nations in 1948, in Nagaland, and wherever people are seeking freedom from India. The essence of democracy is the right to self-determination. The United States Congress should be on record in support of that. In addition, we should stop our aid and trade with India until such time as the tyranny stops and all people there enjoy full human rights.

We seek good relations with India, but not at the expense of our principles. India must spread the blessings of freedom and democracy to all its people, not just the ruling elite and its friends.

Mr. Speaker, I would like to insert the Dawn article and an article from The News concerning Dr. Aulakh's statement into the Record.

[From Dawn Lahore, Nov. 7, 2006]
Khalistan Council Sees India's Disintegration
(By Our Staff Reporter)

Lahore, Nov. 6: India will break up in many states like the former USSR, says Council of Khalistan president Dr. Gurmit Singh Aulakh.

"There is nothing common in the culture of the Hindu living in Bengal and the one in Tamil area. A country having 18 official languages cannot hold its people together for a long time, especially when there is state-sponsored suppression against minorities," Dr. Aulakh said at a press conference at the Lahore Press Club on Monday.

The BJP had conveyed to all the minorities in the strongest terms that if they wanted to live in 'Hindustan', they have to become Hindus. Over a million people have been killed since independence merely because they were not Hindus. The Indian government has committed terrorism against its own minorities. More than 250,000 Sikh infants, children, youth, men, women and elderly had been murdered since 1984, in addition to more than 300,000 Christians in Nagaland, over 90,000 Muslims in Kashmir, tens of thousands of Christians and Muslims throughout the country besides tens of thousands of Assameese, Bodos, Dalits, Manipuris, Tamils and other minorities.

Indian police arrested human rights activist Jaswant Singh Khalra after he exposed their policy of mass cremation of Sikhs. Over 50,000 Sikhs were arrested, tortured, murdered and then their bodies were declared unidentified and secretly cremated, said Dr. Aulakh.

Mr. Khalra was murdered in police custody and his body was not handed over to his family. No one was brought to justice for his kidnap and murder. The only witness to the Khalra kidnapping, Rajiv Singh Randhawa, had been repeatedly harassed by the police, including having been arrested for trying to hand a note to the then British home secretary Jack Straw.

The Khalistan Council chief said 35 Sikhs were arrested in Punjab last year for delivering speeches in support of Khalistan and raising its flag. How can delivering speeches and raising a flag be considered crimes in a democratic society?

The police never released the body of Gurdeve Singh Kaunke, the former Jathedar of the Akal Takht, after SSP Swaran Singh Ghotna murdered him. The police officer had never been tried for the murder.

Mr. Graham Stains, missionary, was murdered along with his two sons, ages 8 and 10, by a mob of militant, fundamentalist Hindu nationalists who set fire to the jeep, surrounded it, and chanted Hannuman ki jay (Victory to Hannuman). Another missionary, Joseph cope, was beaten so badly that he had to remain in an Indian hospital for a week. Later, the Indian government threw him out of the country and none of the people involved had been tried.

"Police broke up a Christian religious festival with gunfire but the people who murdered priests, raped nuns and burnt churches had yet to be charged or tried. Recently, militants from the Bharatiya Januata Yuva, the youth movement affiliated with the BJP and the fascist RSS, attacked the Convent of Loreto.

"The murderers of 2,000 to 5,000 Muslims in Gujarat have never been brought to trial. An Indian newspaper reported that the police were ordered not to get involved in that massacre, a frightening parallel to the Delhi massacre of Sikhs in 1984. Militant Hindu fundamentalists destroyed the most important mosque in India, the Babri Masjid, but no one had ever been held responsible," said Dr. Aulakh.

"What good it did to the Sikh nation if the Indian government apologized for the Delhi massacres, in which over 20,000 Sikhs were killed? Where are the apologies for the Golden Temple attack, the destruction of the Akal Takht, the desecration of Darbar Sahib and the other atrocities? Where is the compensation for the victims' families?" asked a charged Khalistan Council chief.

Sikh farmers were expelled from Uttaranchal last year and their land was seized, police thrashed them, their homes that were built out of their life savings and by their own hands, were bulldozed by paratroopers. "We condemn this act of state terrorism by the government of Uttaranchal," he said.

Sikhs could not buy land in Rajasthan and Himachal Pradesh and now Uttaranchal had been added to the list while there were no restrictions on land ownership in Punjab by non-Sikhs.

India was trying to subvert Khalistan's independence by overrunning Punjab with non-Sikhs while keeping Sikhs from escaping the brutal repression in Punjab. "It is now incumbent on the Sikh diaspora to free Khalistan. We must redouble our efforts. That is the only way to keep these atrocities from continuing and to protect the Sikh nation and the religion."

The Akali Dal, Dr. Aulakh alleged, conspired with the Indian government in 1984 to invade the Golden Temple to murder Sant Bhindranwale and 20,000 other Sikhs in June 1984 in Punjab.

In response to a question, he said the Indian prime minister was a puppet. "Mr. Manmohan Singh lied before the Geneva Commission in 1992 that there were no atrocities against Sikhs in India in spite of the fact that there were 52,000 Sikhs in Indian jails under the notorious TADA. He lacks the true Sikh spirit, if a Sikh is not Khalistani, he is not a Sikh," declared Dr. Aulakh.

Sikhs would never get any justice from Delhi. Ever since independence, India had mistreated the Sikh nation, starting with Patel's memo calling Sikhs 'a criminal tribe.'

"What a shame for Home Minister Patel and the Indian government to issue this memorandom when the Sikh nation gave over 80 percent of the sacrifices to free India. There is no place for Sikhs in supposedly secular, democratic India. Our moment of freedom is closer than ever. Sikhs will continue to work to make certain that we shake ourselves loose from the yoke of Indian oppression and liberate our homeland, Khalistan, so that all Sikhs may live lives of prosperity, freedom and dignity.

"The flame of freedom continues to burn brightly in the heart of every Sikh and no force can suppress it. Recently, Dal Khalsa and the Shiromment Khalsa Dal announced that they are uniting for sovereignty for Khalistan. The Punjab legislative assembly proclaimed the sovereignty of Punjab when it cancelled the water agreements. Only by liberating Khalistan can we put an end to the repression and terrorism against the Sikh nation by the Indian regime. Now is the time to rededicate ourselves to the liberation of Khalistan.

"The Sikhs are a free nation and they would neither compromise on their freedom nor they could be subjugated. Freedom is the right of every nation. We have been struggling for the independence of our homeland from the day when the Golden Temple was attacked. We have been exposing the indian atrocities worldwide since then," the Khalistan Council chief said.

- - - - - - - - -

[From The News International, Nov. 7, 2006]
Sikhs Urged to Work for Homeland

Sardar Gurmeet Singh Aulak, president of Council of Khalistan, has said that it is the moral duty of Sikhs to establish free homeland and get freedom from India.

While addressing a press conference here Monday at Lahore Press Club, he said Sikhs had to come forward to get free homeland for the Sikhs living around the world. He said the foundation of Khalistan was laid after the attack on Golden Temple in 1984 adding that now the Sikhs were fighting for their birth right though the war was long but it has to meet logical end.

He said the biggest mistake which the Sikh nation had committed was that they did not accept the offer of Quaid-e-Azam Muhammad Ali Jinnah and for that they have to pay for few more decades.

He said their struggle was peaceful and political but India turned into violent by killing innocent Sikhs in East Punjab and tagged them as terrorists.

He said in India, 18 different languages were being spoken and when there was no commonality in cultures, the country was bound to be divided into parts like the USSR. He said on October 17, 1987, the resolution was passed by Council of Khalistan for free homeland and from that date the Sikhs were struggling to get their homeland.

He said Sikhs has no claim on that piece of land where they did not have any population but they want homeland on areas of East Punjab, Himachal and Haryana, where the Sikhs were in majority. About Kashmir issue, he said he was surprised to note that with so many Muslim countries around the world, the state was not freed yet as if the Sikhs have the same number of countries, they had freed their land from the cruel clutches of India.

About Prime Minister Manmohan Singh, he said he was a puppet PM and dance to the tunes of Sonia Gandhi and lacks confidence of Sikh nation.

***

Document

CONGRESSIONAL RECORD -- EXTENSIONS

Friday, December 08, 2006
109th Congress, 2nd Session
152 Cong Rec E 2189

REFERENCE: Vol. 152, No. 135
SECTION: Extension of Remarks
TITLE: SUPPORTERS OF S.S. MANN BEATEN UP IN TARN TARAN

HON. EDOLPHUS TOWNS
of New York
in the House of Representatives
Friday, December 8, 2006

Mr. TOWNS . Mr. Speaker, on December 3, supporters of the former member of India's Parliament, Simranjit Singh Mann, were beaten up in the town of Tarn Taran in Punjab, which Mr. Mann used to represent in parliament.

Mr. Mann was burned in effigy. He has blamed former Chief Minister Parkash Singh Badal for the incident. Badal's party is aligned with the Bharatiya Janata Party, BJP, the former ruling party, which is under the umbrella of the fascist, Hindu militant Rashtriya Swayamsewak Sangh, RSS.

The Hindu extremists attacked Mr. Mann's supporters and Mann's supporters were the ones who got arrested.

Tarn Taran is a central place in Sikhism, built by the fifth of the Sikh gurus, Guru Arjun Dev, and there is a historic Gurdwara_Sikh place of worship_in the town. The fact that supporters of the RSS are able to beat Sikhs in Tarn Taran is distressing. It shows the need for Sikh independence in a sovereign Khalistan.

According to SS News online, at least six people were injured in the clash, which broke out after one of Mann's supporters wrote an article critical of Shiv Sena, one of the militant branches of the RSS.

Mr. Speaker, Dr. Gurmit Singh Aulakh, president of the Council of Khalistan, has issued an excellent press release on tbe incident. He notes that a free, sovereign Khalistan, the Sikh homeland that declared its independence from India on October 7, 1987, would help put an end to incidents like this. As long as Sikhs are under Indian subjugation, the RSS and its allies are going to be able to run roughshod over Sikhs and other minorities. Remember that last year, 35 Sikhs were arrested simply for making pro-Khalistan speeches and raising the Khalistani flag. Since when are making speeches and raising a flag crimes in a democracy?

India has kllled more than a quarter of a million Sikhs, over 90,000 Kashmiri Muslims, 2,000 to 5,000 Muslims in Gujarat, over 300,000 Christians in Nagaland and tens of thousands of other minorities such as Assamese, Bodos, Dalits, Manipuris, Tamils, and others. If India is the democracy that it claims to be, how can it do such things?

America is the beacon of freedom, Mr. Speaker. That is why we need to act. Incidents like this must not be allowed to continue. We should stop our aid to India and end our trade with that country until human rights are respected for all people there. And we should put the Congress on record in support of a free and fair plebiscite on independence in Khalistan, Kashmir, Nagalim, and wherever else it is sought. That is the best way to help bring freedom, security, safety, dignity, and prosperity to all the people of South Asia.

Mr. Speaker, I would like to put the Council of Khalistan's press release on the beating of Mann supporters in the Record at this time.

Washington, DC, Dec. 7, 2006. Supporters of former Member of Parliament Simranjit Singh Mann were beaten up in Tarn Taran by members of the Bharatiya Janata Party (BJP) and Mr, Mann's effigy was burned. Mann has publicly blamed former Chief Minister Parkash Singh Badal, who is allied with the BJP, a branch of the fascist Rashtriya Swayamsewak Sangh (RSS), for the beating. Mann was elected to represent Tarn Taran in the Indian Parliament with 95 percent of the vote while he was in jail in 1989.

Tarn Taran is the center of the Sikh religion. Guru Arjun Dev Ji, the fifth Sikh Guru, established Tarn Taran and there is a historic Gurdwara there. Captain Amarinder Singh, the chief minister of Punjab, is establishing a Guru Arjun Dev Ji University there.

"It is outrageous that supporters of Mann could be beaten up and his effigy burned in a place so central for the Sikh Nation as Tarn Taran," said Dr. Gurmit Singh Aulakh, President of the Council of Khalistan. "We hope that Badal is not behind the incident," said Dr, Aulakh. "If he is, shame on him. Ultimately, the Indian government is behind this act and both Badal and Mann are under the control of the Indian government, as their letters published in Chakravyuh: Web of Indian Secularism demonstrate," said Dr. Aulakh. In one letter, Mann pledges, "I reiterate my allegiance to the Constitution and I stand by the integrity of the country." On his trip to the United States in 2000, Mann attended a Sikh event and said, "Close the offices of the Council of Khalistan, headed by Dr. Gurmit Singh Aulakh in Washington DC."

"If the BJP can carry out its nefarious activities in a place as central to the Sikh Nation as Tarn Taran, then the handwriting is on the wall for the future of the Sikh Nation. They cannot protect their respect and honor and they are salves in India. This shows why we must liberate Khalistan from Indian occupation and oppression," said Dr. Aulakh. "That is the only way for Sikhs to protect ourselves from India's brutality."

After human-rights activist Jaswant Singh Khalra exposed the Indian government's policy of mass cremation of Sikhs, in which over 50,000 Sikhs have been arrested, tortured, and murdered, then their bodies were declared unidentified and secretly cremated, the police kidnapped him. Khalra was murdered in police custody. No one has been brought to justice for the kidnapping and murder of Jaswant Singh Khalra. Rajiv Singh Randhawa, who was the only witness to the Khalra kidnapping, has been repeatedly subjected to police harassment. This includes being arrested for trying to hand a piece of paper to then-British Home Secretary Jack Straw in front of the Golden Temple. The police never released the body of former Jathedar of the Akal Takht Gurdev Singh Kaunke after SSP Swaran Singh Ghotna murdered him.

In 1994, the U.S. State Department reported that the Indian government had paid over 41,000 cash bounties for killing Sikhs. A report by the Movement Against State Repression (MASR) quotes the Punjab Civil Magistracy as writing "if we add up the figures of the last few years the number of innocent persons killed would run into lakhs [hundreds of thousands.]" The Indian Supreme Court called the Indian government's murders of Sikhs "worse than a genocide."

The MASR report states that 52,268 Sikhs are being held as political prisoners in India without charge or trial, mostly under a repressive law known as the "Terrorist and Disruptive Activities Act" (TADA), which expired in 1995. Many have been in illegal custody since 1984! There has been no list published of those who were acquitted under TADA and those who are still rotting in Indian jails. Tens of thousands of other minorities are also being held as political prisoners, according to Amnesty International. Last year, 35 Sikhs were charged and arrested in Punjab for making speeches in support of Khalistan and raising the Khalistani flag. "How can making speeches and raising a flag be considered crimes in a democratic society?" asked Dr. Aulakh.

India is on the verge of disintegration. Kashmir is about to separate from India. As L.K. Advani said, "if Kashmir goes, India goes." History shows that multinational states such as India are doomed to failure. "Countries like Austria-Hungary, India's longtime friend the Soviet Union, Yugoslavia, Czechoslovakia, and others prove this point. India is not one country; it is a polyglot like those countries, thrown together for the convenience of the British colonialists. It is doomed to break up as they did. There is nothing in common in the culture of a Hindu living in Bengal and one in Tamil Nadu, let alone between them and the minority nations of South Asia," Dr. Aulakh said.

"Freedom is the God-given right of every nation and every human being," said Dr. Aulakh. Sikhs must be allowed to have a free and fair plebiscite on the issue of Khalistan. In a democracy, you cannot continue to rule against the wishes of the people. As former Senator George Mitchell said about the Palestinians, 'the essence of democracy is the right to self-determination.' We must reclaim the sovereignty of the Sikh Nation," Dr. Aulakh said. "Currently, there are 17 freedom movements within India's borders. It has 18 official languages. A country having 18 official languages cannot hold its people together for very long," he said. "We hope that India's breakup will be peaceful like Czechoslovakia's, not violent like Yugoslavia's," Dr. Aulakh said. "Earlier this year, Montenegro, which has less than a million people, became a sovereign country and a member of the United Nations," he said. "Now it is the time for the Sikh Nation of Punjab, Khalistan to become independent."

Dr. Aulakh stressed his commitment to the peaceful, democratic, non-violent struggle to liberate Khalistan. "The only way that the repression will stop and Sikhs will live in freedom, dignity, and prosperity is to liberate Khalistan," said Dr. Aulakh. "As Professor Darshan Singh, former Jathedar of the Akal Takht, said. 'If a Sikh is not a Khalistani, he is not a Sikh'," Dr. Aulakh said. "We must free Khalistan now."

***

Document

CONGRESSIONAL RECORD -- EXTENSIONS

Friday, December 08, 2006
109th Congress, 2nd Session
152 Cong Rec E 2194

REFERENCE: Vol. 152, No. 135
SECTION: Extension of Remarks
TITLE: PROFESSOR EXPOSES FAKE SIKH SCRIPTURES, HINDU PLAN
TO DESTROY SIKH RELIGION

Speech of
HON. EDOLPHUS TOWNS
of New York
in the House of Representatives
Friday, December 8, 2006

Mr. TOWNS . Mr. Speaker, Professor Gurtej Singh JAS is a Professor of Sikhism and a very widely respected intellectual leader in the Sikh community. Recently, he wrote an article exposing the Dasam Granth, which is alleged by some Hindus to be a Sikh scripture. What apparently was done was to take a few of the writings of Guru Gobind Singh, the last of the Sikh gurus, and combine it with some sexually explicit material from a Hindu sect known as Shakat. The aim is to discredit Guru Gobind Singh and bring the Sikhs into the Hindu fold, according to Professor Gurtej Singh.

The authors of the Dasam Granth identify themselves within the text, yet many insist that the work was written by Guru Gobind Singh and should be equal to the Sikh holy scripture, the Guru Granth Sahib.

Professor Gurtej Singh commented that a leader of the militant Hindu fascist operation known as the Rashtriya Swayamsewak Sangh (RSS), which was formed in support of the Fascists, had commented that all the Sikh "high priests" including Akal Takht Jathedar Joginder Singh Vedanti are on the RSS payroll. Thus, they are cooperating in this effort by the Brahmins to destroy the Sikh religion. Nice trick in a supposedly secular country!

Also cooperating in this effort is former Chief Minister Parkash Singh Badal, who led the most corrupt government in the history of Punjab. These are the kinds of people with whom the Brahins choose to ally themselves.

This kind of control over the leadership of the Sikhs is one reason that they need their independence, to protect their identity and their safety before the Indians wipe them out, as they seek to do. Over a quarter of a million Sikhs killed since 1984 proves that. In addition, the Indian regime has killed over 300,000 Christians in Nagaland, more than 90,000 Muslims in Kashmir and 2,000 to 5,000 in Gujarat, as well as Christians and Muslims elsewhere in the country and Tamils, Manipuris, Dalits, Bodos, Assamese, and other minorities. Tens of thousands of people are held as political prisoners, according to Amnesty International. The Movement Against State Repression reported that India acknowledged holding 52,268 Sikhs as political prisoners. Many of these have been in illegal detention since 1984.

These political prisoners must be released at once and those who violate human rights must be brought to justice or we should stop all of our aid and trade with India. And we should put the U.S. Congress on record in support of freedom everywhere in South Asia in the form of a plebiscite on the subject of independence, under international supervision to ensure its fairness. Isn't that the democratic way to do things?

While Professor Gurtej Singh's article is too long to put in the Record, the Council of Khalistan did an excellent press release on it. Mr. Speaker, I would like to add that press release on the Dasam Granth fraud to the Record at this time for the information of my colleagues.

Professor Gurtej Singh Exposes Dasam Granth Fraud

Washington, DC, December 7, 2006_Professor Gurtej Singh, a leading Sikh scholar, Professor of Sikhism, and an advisor to the International Journal of Sikh Affairs, has published an extensive article exposing how Hindu fundamentalists have promoted the Dasam Granth, which contains very little of the work of Guru Gobind Singh, as his writing and as genuine Sikh scripture, parallel to the Guru Granth Sahib. He exposes the fact that "the Hindu plan to drag the Sikhs back to the Hindu fold" requires promoting the Dasam Granth and that this plan has received the support of such allegedly Sikh leaders as former Punjab Chief Minister Parkash Singh Badal and the high Sikh "high priests" led by Jathedar Joginder Singh Vedanti. Badal led the most corrupt government in Punjab's history, selling jobs for money, and regularly visits Hindu and other anti-Sikh places of worship, according to Professor Gurtej Singh.

Professor Gurtej Singh writes that Jathedar Vedanti "was given the task of actually dragging the Sikh panth into the fold of Hinduism." He notes that Jathedar Vedanti, like Mr. Badal, succumbed to the temptations of money. In order to carry out this nefarious plan, Professor Gurtej Singh writes, Vedanti embraced the Dasam Granth as genuine Sikh scripture, claiming that it was written by Guru Gobind Singh and was to be treated as scripture and canon. The Dasam Granth includes vivid, lewd descriptions of sex acts and other pornographic and obscene references that were added to Guru Gobind Singh's writing to make him look bad.

Professor Gurtej Singh notes that the authors of the Dasam Granth identified themselves in the text. Yet the Hindus insist that Guru Gobind Singh is the author and that the book is Sikh scripture. According to Professor Gurtej Singh, it is a scripture of the Shakat sect, who are worshippers of the Hindu goddess Shiva, as it reflects their mode of worship and their practices. "It has been a long standing Hindu desire to bring the Sikhs under the umbrella of the Shakat sect," he writes. "This involves getting them to accept some of the rituals of that sect as modes of worship." He goes on to write, "To propagate the dasam granth as Sikh scripture at par with Guru Granth, has been the aim of a section of the Hindu zealots and a section of the Media mostly controlled by such Hindus,"

According to Professor Gurtej Singh, Mr. Sudarshan of the fascist, Hindu militant Rashtriya Swayamsewak Sangh (RSS), parent organization of the Hindu fundamentalist BJP, stated that all of the Sikh "high priests" including Vedanti are on the payroll of his organization.

"We appreciate and commend Professor Gurtej Singh for doing this outstanding work for the Sikh Nation," said Dr. Gurmit Singh Aulakh, President of the Council of Khalistan. "He is doing his job as Professor of Sikhism. The Sikh Nation commends him," Dr. Aulakh said. "Only about 60 pages of the Dasam Granth is the writing of Guru Gobind Singh," he noted. "The rest is later writings that were added and changed. Guru Gobind Singh gave guruship to the Guru Granth Sahib and ordered Sikhs to consider the Guru Granth Sahib as the living Guru," Dr. Aulakh noted. "The Guru Granth Sahib is the living Guru which Sikhs accept with reverence and respect. Recitation of the Dasam Granth should not take place in any Gurdwara," he said. "Sikhs should practice Rehat Maryada which was published in the 1940s by the SGPC after a long review and discussion by the Khalsa Panth."

Dr. Aulakh said that it is very disturbing that most of the Sikh leadership is under the control of the Indian government. "This campaign to destroy Sikhism by means of the Dasam Granth could not be taking place if we had our own homeland. We could more effectively stand up to India's ongoing effort to destroy the Sikh religion," he said. "Without political power, nations perish and religions are destroyed," he said.

India is on the verge of disintegration. Kashmir is about to separate from India. As L.K. Advani said, "if Kashmir goes, India goes." History shows that multinational states such as India are doomed to failure. "Countries like Austria-Hungary, India's longtime friend the Soviet Union, Yugoslavia, Czechoslovakia, and others prove this point. India is not one country; it is a polyglot like those countries, thrown together for the convenience of the British colonialists. It is doomed to break up as they did. There is nothing in common in the culture of a Hindu living in Bengal and one in Tamil Nadu, let alone between them and the minority nations of South Asia," Dr. Aulakh said.

"Freedom is the God-given right of every nation and every human being," said Dr. Aulakh. Sikhs must be allowed to have a free and fair plebiscite on the issue of Khalistan. In a democracy, you cannot continue to rule against the wishes of the people. As former Senator George Mitchell said about the Palestinians, 'the essence of democracy is the right to self-determination,' We must reclaim the sovereignty of the Sikh Nation," Dr. Aulakh said. "Currently, there are 17 freedom movements within India's borders. It has 18 official languages, A country having 18 official languages cannot hold its people together for very long," he said. "We hope that India's breakup will be peaceful like Czechoslovakia's, not violent like Yugoslavia's," Dr. Aulakh said. "Earlier this year, Montenegro, which has less than a million people, became a sovereign country and a

member of the United Nations," he said. "Now it is the time for the Sikh Nation of Punjab, Khalistan to become independent."

Dr. Aulakh stressed his commitment to the peaceful, democratic, non-violent struggle to liberate Khalistan. "The only way that the repression will stop and Sikhs will live in freedom, dignity, and prosperity is to liberate Khalistan," said Dr. Aulakh, "As Professor Darshan Singh, former Jathedar of the Akal Takht, said, 'If a Sikh is not a Khalistani, he is not a Sikh.',"Dr. Aulakh said. "We must free Khalistan now."

***

Document

CONGRESSIONAL RECORD -- EXTENSIONS

Thursday, December 07, 2006
109th Congress, 2nd Session
152 Cong Rec E 2108

REFERENCE: Vol. 152, No. 134
SECTION: Extension of Remarks
TITLE: SIKHS CELEBRATE BIRTHDAY OF GURU NANAK, FIRST SIKH GURU

HON. EDOLPHUS TOWNS
of New York
in the House of Representatives
Wednesday, December 6, 2006

Mr. TOWNS . Mr. Speaker, I rise today because earlier this month, about 15,000 Sikhs from all over the world celebrated the birth of the first Sikh guru, Guru Nanak, in his birthplace, Nankana Sahib, which is now in Pakistan. The Sikhs in attendance chanted slogans of "Khalsitan Zindabad" calling for the liberation of the Sikh homeland, Khalistan. Over 3,000 Sikhs from Punjab were in attendance and many of them commented on how much better they were treated in Pakistan than in their own country.

A delegation of Sikhs met with Pakistani Prime Minister Shaukat Aziz. He pledged to build a road from Kartarpur, where Guru Nanak died and where there is a shrine to him, to the Indian border if India would build a road to the border also and repair a bridge at the border. This would enable Sikhs to go to Kartarpur and honor Guru Nanak whenever they choose to do so. I call on the governments of Punjab and India to build this road and fix the bridge.

The Pakistani government also issued an open invitation to Sikhs to come and visit Nankana Sahib whenever they wish with no restrictions, although they did express concern that agents of India's Research and Analysis Wing (RAW) would use this to come in and try to undermine Pakistan. That is a very real and legitimate concern.

It is tragic and offensive that the Sikhs who went to Nankana Sahib felt that they were better treated in Pakistan than in their own country. That just shows why the Sikhs in Punjab need to be free of Indian rule. The sovereignty of the Sikhs, recognized in the Indian constitution, was used in cancelling Punjab's water deals with India. It should be used by the Legislative Assembly to declare Punjab's independence, as the Sikhs did on October 7, 1987. Such a declaration from the legislature would carry a lot of weight.

Mr. Speaker, the time has come for the beacon of freedom, America, to take a stand. We can help to stop the tyranny and the repression by stopping our aid and trade to India until full human rights are restored to all people there. And it is time for a free and fair plebiscite in Punjab, Khalistan on the question of independence, as well as Kashmir, Nagalim, and wherever people seek their freedom. India promised Kashmir a plebiscite in 1948 and it has not yet delivered on the promise. When will "the world's largest democracy" decide that it is time for the people to enjoy the most basic of democratic rights, the right to self-determination? If India is the democratic country it says it is, what could be wrong with a simple vote?

I request the permission of the House to insert the Council of Khalistan's press release on the events in Nankana Sahib into the Record at this time.

Sikhs Celebrate Guru Nanak's Birthday With Reverence
Air Filled With Khalistan Zindabad Slogans

Washington, DC, November 16, 2006._More than 15,000 Sikhs came from the United States, Punjab, Thailand, France, the United Kingdom, Germany, and around the world to Nankana Sahib celebrate the 537th anniversary of the birth of their first Guru, Guru Nanak, founder of the Sikh religion. Guru Nanak was born in 1469. This is he highest number of Sikhs who have attended the event since the partition of India. Over 3,000 Sikhs came from Punjab. At the celebration, the air was filled with slogans of "Khalistan Zindabad."

The delegation met with Prime Minister Shaukat Aziz in Islamad on November 4. He welcomed the Sikhs with open arms and offered a road link between Kartarpur and the Indian border if India agrees to build a road on its side and repair the bridge. He said Sikhs were free to visit Kartarpur whenever they want without a visa. The Pakistani government has issued an open invitation to Sikhs from around the world to come and visit Nankana Sahib with no restrictions. Any genuine Sikh who wants to come and visit may do so. There was some concern about agents of India's Research and Analysis Wing (RAW) coming to destabilize Pakistan, however.

The government and people of Pakistan welcomed the Sikhs and treated them so well that Sikhs from Punjab asked why they were treated so well in Pakistan, which is not our country, but in the Sikh homeland, Punjab, Khalistan, the Indian government does not treat them fairly. India attacked the Golden Temple, the center and seat of Sikhism, in June

1984. Since then, the Indian government has murdered over 250,000 Sikhs and another 52,268 are being held as political prisoners, according to a report by the Movement Against State Repression (MASR.) India has killed over 90,000 Muslims in Kashmir as well as 2,000 to 5,000 Muslims in Gujarat, over 300,000 Christians in Nagaland, and tens of thousands of Assamese, Bodos, Dalits (the dark-skinned, aboriginal "Untouchables"), Manipuris, Tamils, and other minorities. In 1994, the U.S. State Department reported that the Indian government had paid over 41,000 cash bounties for killing Sikhs. A MASR report quotes the Punjab Civil Magistracy as writing "if we add up the figures of the last few years the number of innocent persons killed would run into lakhs [hundreds of thousands.]" The Indian Supreme Court called the Indian government's murders of Sikhs "worse than a genocide."

Last year. 35 Sikhs were charged and arrested in Punjab for making speeches in support of Khalistan and raising the Khalistani flag. "How can making speeches and raising a flag be considered crimes in a democratic society?" asked Dr. Gurmit Singh Aulakh. President of the Council of Khalistan, which leads the peaceful, democratic, nonviolent struggle to liberate the Sikh homeland from Indian occupation. The Gujarat massacre was pre-planned, according to a police officer who spoke to Indian newspapers. Nuns have been raped, priests have been murdered, churches have been burned, Christian prayer halls and schools have been attacked, and police broke up a Christian religious festival with gunfire.

India is also destroying Sikhs economically. The Indian government fixes the price for fertilizer very high and the price for produce very low so Sikh farmers can't even get the cost of production for their crops. This year it fixed the wheat price at Rs 750 per quintal. Even Badal demanded Rs 1000 per quintal. If Punjab farmers could sell their produce across the border in Pakistan and the Middle East, they could easily get close to Rs 1,500 per quintal and would be able to make a living. India seeks to destroy the Sikh Nation religiously, economically, and politically.

"Freedom is the God-given right of every nation and every human being," said Dr. Aulakh. Sikhs must be allowed to have a free and fair plebiscite on the issue of Khalistan. In a democracy, you cannot continue to rule against the wishes of the people. As former Senator George Mitchell said about the Palestinians, "the essence of democracy is the right to self-determination." "We must reclaim the sovereignty of the Sikh Nation," Dr. Aulakh said. Dr. Aulakh appealed to the Akali Dal and other Sikh parties in the Punjab Legislative Assembly to pass a resolution documenting all the mistreatment and economic exploitation of the Sikhs by the Indian government since independence. India diverts Punjab's river water, its natural resource, to neighboring Haryana and Rajasthan without any compensation despite Chief Minister Amarinder Singh cancelling Punjab's water agreements with India. We salute Captain Amarinder Singh for this legislation. In the legislation, the Legislative Assembly explicitly affirmed the sovereignty of Punjab as described in the Indian constitution. This same sovereignty can be used by the Assembly to declare

independence. India will be helpless and the Sikh diaspora will help to free Khalistan.

India is on the verge of disintegration. Kashmir is about to separate from India. As L.K. Advani said, "if Kashmir goes, India goes." History shows that multinational states such as India are doomed to failure. Countries like Austria-Hungary, India's longtime friend the Soviet Union, Yugoslavia, Czechoslovakia. and others prove this point. India is not one country; it is a polyglot like those countries, thrown together for the convenience of the British colonialists. It is doomed to break up as they did. Currently, there are 17 freedom movements within India's borders. It has 18 official languages. "We hope that India's breakup will be peaceful like Czechoslovakia's, not violent like Yugoslavia's," Dr. Aulakh said. "Montenegro. which has less than a million people, has become a sovereign country and a member of the United Nations," he said. "Now it is the time for the Sikh Nation of Punjab, Khalistan to become independent. The sooner the better."

"The only way that the Sikh nation can flourish and progress is in a sovereign, independent Khalistan," said Dr. Aulakh. "As Professor Darshan Singh, former Jathedar of the Akal Takht, said, 'If a Sikh is not a Khalistani. he is not a Sikh.'," Dr. Aulakh said. "We must free Khalistan now."

***

Document

CONGRESSIONAL RECORD -- EXTENSIONS

Thursday, December 07, 2006
109th Congress, 2nd Session
152 Cong Rec E 2112

REFERENCE: Vol. 152, No. 134
SECTION: Extension of Remarks
TITLE: INDIA PLAYS THE VICTIM TO COVER UP ITS TERRORIST RECORD

Speech of
HON. EDOLPHUS TOWNS
of New York
in the House of Representatives
Wednesday, December 6, 2006

Mr. TOWNS . Mr. Speaker, last month, Indian Prime Minister Manmohan Singh publicly stated that India is the victim of cross-border terror. The Council of Khalistan under the leadership of Dr. Gurmit Singh Aulakh wrote to Prime Minister Singh and reminded him that India has been sponsoring cross-border terrorism in Sindh, a province of Pakistan, as the Washington Times reported on January 2, 2002 and that according to India Today, which is the leading news magazine in India, the Indian government created the Liberation Tigers of Tamil Eelam, which the U.S. government has identified as a terrorist organization.

It has also sponsored domestic terrorism against the minorities within its borders, including murdering a quarter of a million Sikhs and holding another 52,000 as political prisoners; killing Muslims by the tens of thousands in Kashmir, where more than 90,000 have been killed, Gujarat, where between 2,000 and 5,000 died in a massacre pre-planned by the government, and elsewhere; killing Christians throughout the country, including over 300,000 just in Nagaland; and mass killing many other minorities. Yet India proclaims itself the victim of terrorism and proclaims itself a democracy. Well, Mr. Speaker, it certainly doesn't act that way.

The repression and terrorism must be stopped. We should end all aid and trade with India until such time as the repression ends and people enjoy the most basic human rights, and we should throw our full support behind self-determination in Punjab, Khalistan, in Kashmir, in Nagalim, and wherever people are trying to be free. The essence of democracy is the right to self-determination. In addition, we should designate India a terrorist state and impose the sanctions that that designation brings.

Mr. Speaker, I would like to insert the Council of Khalistan's open letter into the Record. It is a frightening record of Indian terrorism.

India Is a Terrorist State, Not a Victim

Dear Prime Minister Singh: On October 4, you said that India is a victim of cross-border terrorism. India is a terrorist state itself and should be subject to the penalties that are imposed on terrorist states.

On January 2, 2002, the Washington Times reported that India is supporting cross-border terrorism in Sindh, a province of Pakistan, the very same kind of thing that Prime Minister Singh was claiming is victimizing India. In addition, India's leading newsmagazine, India Today, reported that the Indian government created the Liberation Tigers of Tamil Eelam (LTTE), identified by the U.S. government as a terrorist organization, and its leaders were put up by the Indian government in the finest hotel in Delhi. How can you blame Pakistan when India started cross-border terrorism with its own actions?

The Indian government has committed terrorism against its own minorities. It has murdered over 250,000 Sikh infants, children, youth, men, women, and elderly since 1984, as well as more than 300,000 Christians in Nagaland, over 90,000 Muslims in Kashmir, tens of thousands of Christians and Muslims throughout the country, and tens of thousands of Assamese, Bobos, Dalits, Manipuris, Tamils, and other minorities. A report by the Movement Against State Repression (MASR) states that 52,268 Sikhs are being held as political prisoners in India without charge or trial, mostly under a repressive law known as the "Terrorist and Disruptive Activities Act" (TADA), which expired in 1995. Many have been in illegal custody since 1984! There has been no list published of those who were acquitted under TADA and those who are still rotting in Indian jails. Tens of thousands of other minorities are also being held as political prisoners, according to Amnesty International. Tell the families of these innocent Sikhs and others that there is no terrorism in India.

Indian police arrested human-rights activist Jaswant Singh Khalra after he exposed their policy of mass cremation of Sikhs, in which over 50,000 Sikhs have been arrested, tortured, and murdered, then their bodies were declared unidentified and secretly cremated. Khalra was murdered in police custody. His body was not given to his family. No one has been brought to justice for the kidnapping and murder of Jaswant Singh Khalra. The only witness to the Khalra kidnapping, Rajiv Singh Randhawa, has been repeatedly harassed by the police, including having been arrested for trying to hand a note to then-British Home Secretary Jack Straw. Last year, 35 Sikhs were charged and arrested in Punjab for making speeches in support of Khalistan and raising the Khalistani flag. How can making speeches and raising a flag be considered crimes in a democratic society?

The police never released the body of former Jathedar of the Takht Gurdev Singh Kaunke after SSP Swaran Singh Gholna murdered him. He has never been tried for the Jathedar Kaunke murder. In 1994, the U.S. State Department reported that the Indian government had paid over 41,000 cash bounties for killing Sikhs. The MASR report quotes the Punjab Civil Magistracy as writing "if we add up the figures of the last few years the number of innocent persons killed would run into lakhs (hundreds of thousands.)" The Indian Supreme Court called the Indian government's murders of Sikhs "worse than a genocide."

Missionary Graham Staines was murdered along with his two sons, ages 8 and 10, by a mob of militant, fundamentalist Hindu nationalists who set fire to the jeep, surrounded it, and chanted "Victory to Hannuman," a Hindu god. Missionary Joseph Cooper was beaten so badly that he had to spend a week in an Indian hospital. Then the Indian government threw him out of the country. None of the people involved has been tried. The persons who have murdered priests, raped nuns, and burned Christian churches have not been charged or tried. Police broke up a Christian religious festival with gunfire. Recently, militant Hindus from the Bharatiya Janata Yuva (a youth movement affiliated with the BJP and the Fascist RSS) attacked the Convent of Loreto and the school there. A spokesman for the BJP, Mr. H. Dikshit, demanded an investigation of the school!

The murders of 2,000 to 5,000 Muslims in Gujarat have never been brought to trial. An Indian newspaper reported that the police were ordered not to get involved in that massacre, a frightening parallel to the Delhi massacre of Sikhs in 1984. The most important mosque in India, the Babri Mosque, was destroyed by militant Hindu fundamentalists who have never been held responsible for their actions.

It is good that you have admitted the guilt of the Indian government by for the Delhi massacres, in which over 20,000 Sikhs were killed, by apologizing for the massacres, but what good does it do the Sikh Nation? Where are the apologies for the Golden Temple attack, the destruction of the Akal Takht, and the desecration of Darbal Sahib, and the other atrocities? Where is the compensation for the victims' families? That operation was yet another act of Indian domestic terrorism.

The Guru granted sovereignty to the Sikh Nation, saying "In Grieb Sikhin Ko Deon Patshahi." We must remind ourselves of our heritage by raising slogans of "Khalistan Zindabad" and beginning a Shantmai Morcha to liberate our homeland, Khalistan Whoever is honest and dedicated in leading that Shantmai Morcha deserves our support. Every morning and evening we recite, "Raj Kare Ga Khalsa," Now is the time to act on it. Do we mean what we say every morning and evening?

The flame of freedom continues to burn brightly in the heart of the Sikh Nation. No force can suppress it. Recently, Dal Khalsa and the Shiromani Khalsa Dal announced that they are uniting for sovereignty for Khalistan. This was met with chants of "Khalistan Zindabad." The Punjab Legislative Assembly proclaimed the sovereignly of Punjab when it cancelled the water agreements. Only by liberating Khalistan can we put an end to the repression and terrorism against the Sikh Nation by the Indian regime. Now is the time to rededicate ourselves to the liberation of Khalistan,

Last year, Sikh farmers were expelled from Uttaranchal Pradesh and their land was seized. They were beaten up by the police. Their homes were bulldozed by paratroopers, Their homes in many cases were built using their life savings and by their own hands. We condemn this act of state terrorism by the government of Uttaranchal Pradesh. As you know, Sikhs are prohibited from buying land in Rajasthan and Himachal Pradesh. Now Uttaranchal Pradesh joins that list. Yet there are no restrictions on land ownership in Punjab by non-Sikhs. People from anywhere can buy land in Punjab, including people from Rajasthan and Himachal Pradesh. India is trying to subvert Khalistan's independence by overrunning Punjab with non-Sikhs while keeping Sikhs from escaping the brutal repression in Punjab. It is incumbent on the Sikh diaspora to free Khalistan. We must redouble our efforts. That is the only way to keep these atrocities from continuing and to protect the Sikh Nation and the Sikh religion.

The Akali Dal conspired with the Indian government in 1984 to invade the Golden Temple to murder Sant Bhindranwale and 20,000 other Sikhs during June 1984 in Punjab. Among those who conspired with the government, according to Chakravyuh Web of Indian Secularism, were Dr. Chohan, Ganga Singh Dhillon, and Didar Singh Bains. It appears the Indian regime is even willing to arrest its own agents to suppress the movement for Khalistan! Now Badal and Chief Minister Amarinder Singh have been accusing each other of being tied in with "terrorists." These leaders view support for Khalistan as terrorism, as the Indian government does. They have shown where their loyalties lie. How will these so-called Sikh leaders account for themselves? Remember the words of former Jathedar of the Akal Takht Professor Darshan Singh: "If a Sikh is not a Khalistani, he is not a Sikh.

Sikhs will never get any justice from Delhi. Ever since independence, India has mistreated the Sikh Nation, starting with Patel's, memo calling Sikhs "a criminal tribe." What a shame for Home Minister Patel and the Indian government to issue this memorandum when the Sikh Nation gave over 80 percent of the sacrifices to free India. There is no place for Sikhs in supposedly secular, supposedly democratic India. Our moment of freedom is closer than ever. Sikhs will continue to work to make certain that we shake ourselves loose from the yoke of Indian oppression and liberate our homeland, Khalistan, so that all Sikhs may have lives of prosperity, freedom, and dignity.

> *Sincerely,*
> *Dr. Gurmit Singh Aulakh,*
> *President, Council of Khalistan.*

***

Document

CONGRESSIONAL RECORD -- EXTENSIONS

Wednesday, November 15, 2006
109th Congress, 2nd Session
152 Cong Rec E 2040

REFERENCE: Vol. 152, No. 129
SECTION: Extension of Remarks
TITLE: NEW BOOK DETAILS ATROCITIES AGAINST SIKHS

Speech of
HON. EDOLPHUS TOWNS
of New York
in the House of Representatives
Wednesday, November 15, 2006

Mr. TOWNS . Mr. Speaker, in the June issue of the International Journal of Sikh Affairs, Dr. Awatar Singh Sekhon reviews a book entitled "Tabai Ros Jagio," which translates into English as "Details of Fundamentalist Hindus' Attacks on the Sikh Faith," by Dr. Sukhpreet Singh Udhoke. The book details how the fundamentalist Hindus who run India have been attacking Sikhism and other faiths since the very earliest days of the Indian republic. Despite the fact that the Brahmin caste is only 3 percent of the population, they run Indian society, according to Dr. Udhoke.

Dr. Udhoke details those Sikhs who have supported the Hindu fundamentalists in their effort to enforce Hinduism on the entire population of India. He details those who connived with India on the attack on the Golden Temple, the seat of the Sikh religion. He recorded the brutality of the Brahmins and the Hindu fundamentalists. He writes about how their umbrella organization, the Rashtriya Swayamsewak Sangh (RSS), was founded to support the Fascists in Europe. He describes the RSS as a terrorist organization. India claims to be our ally in the War on Terror, but their preeminent ideology is a brand of Fascism that practices violence against minorities and their neighbors.

We should stop aid and trade with India and we should be vocal and active in supporting self-determination for all the people there. That is how we can help bring freedom to all in the subcontinent.

Mr. Speaker, I highly recommend Dr. Sekhon's excellent review of Dr. Udhoke's excellent book to my colleagues, and I would like to place the review in the Record now.

[From the International Journal of Sikh, Affairs, June 2006]
Book Review
(By Awatar Singh Sekhon)

Title: Tabai Ros Jagio, translation in English Details of Fundamental-ist Hindus' Attack on the Sikh Faith 2005, by Dr. Sukhpreet Singh Udhoke, is an eye opener. with regard to the premeditated attacks by the funda-mentalist Hindus, belonging to the Rashtriya Swamsewak Sangh and the members of the "Sangh Parivar/family", on the followers of the Sikh Faith.

It was a great pride and pleasure for the reviewer, who is the Editor in Chief, The International Journal of Sikh Affairs ISSN 1481-5435, pub-lished from Canada, to write a few words on the publication of Dr. Sukhpreet Singh Udhoke. Dr. Udhoke is a medical professional but is devoting most of his precious time in recording the much needed events of the Sikh history of the 20th and 21st centuries. These events pertain to the persecution of the Sikh youth in particular and for the present and coming generations of the Sikh faith, the Guru Khalsa Panth. Dr. Udhoke's first publication, Tabai Ros Jagio, published in July 2004, was an excellent treatise relating to the "Attacks on the Sikh faith, Sikh culture, Sikh heritage, Sikh pride, Sikh esteem, Guru Granth Sahib (Holy Scripture of Sikhs), the Sikh identity, and the Sikh nation, Punjab, Khalistan, struggling for its independence by peaceful means." His book clearly reflects the intimidation of the Sikhs of their holy and historic homeland, Punjab, by their traditional and notorious enemy, the fun-damentalist Hindu organizations as well as the politicians of the preced-ing and present administrations of the Indian democracy, its New Delhi administrations of J.L. Nehru to Manmohan Singh, run primarily by the Brahmins (who are only 3 percent of the total population of India of over a billion hungry mouths) and about 15 percent pro-Brahmins. This group has captured more than 80 percent of the total decision-making jobs of the Indian administration. Dr. Sukhpreet Singh Udhoke's task at hand was not an easy one, especially when his, his forefathers, and the Sikhs' holy and historic homeland is under the occupation of the Sikhs' enemy, the Brahmins, "Butchers of our world", according to the founder of the Sikh faith, Guru Nanak Sahib.

The Indian administration and their international news media's term, the "largest democracy of the world", India, made Dr. Udhoke's task highly difficult in describing the reality and tragedy of the Sikh nation,

Punjab, and beyond the understanding of an ordinary citizen of the Sikhs' holy and historic homeland.

It is amply clear that the Sikh leaders, of Punjab so to speak, and most commonly known as the Dastaardhari (turbaned) Hindus in the Sikh identity, have failed to respond to the psyche and aspirations of the Sikhs of Punjab, the Sikh Diaspora and the Sikh nation. Rather, these Dastaardhari Hindus in the Sikh Identity have fallen into the trap of the Brahmins and pro-Brahmins. The day in and the day out, the Sikhs' Darbar Sahib Complex (Golden Temple Complex), which includes the Supreme Seat of Sikh Polity, Akal Takht Sahib, Amritsar, and other religious and political places of the Sikhs, Gurdwaras (Houses of God), are desecrated, to humiliate the Sikh nation. The saddest moment of the Sikh history of post-15th August, 1947, is that a Dastaardhari Hindu in the Sikh Identity, Prakash Singh Badal, his clan and the Badal faction of Akali Dal were the party for the desecration of Darbar Sahib Complex. So much so the custodian, the so-called jathedar, of Akal Takht Sahib, Vedanti Joginder Singh Saran actively watched the ball game of his employer, the executive of the Shiromani Gurdwara Prabhandhak Committee (SGPC), and SGPC's member as well as the president of the Akali Dal-Badal faction, Prakash Singh Badal himself. What an unfortunate part of the Sikh history!

The present and former custodians of the Akal Takht Sahib, Vedanti Joginder Singh Saran, Puran Singh of Luv and Kush, Manjit of Kesgarh, Kirpal Singh, etc. failed to provide any directions to the Sikh Nation, Guru Khalsa Panth or the Sikhs of Punjab. They however, collaborated with the enemy of the Guru Khalsa Panth.

Dr. Sukhpreet Singh Udhoke, a young Sikh full of energies, recorded in his book, the brutality of the Sikhs' traditional enemies, the Brahmins and pro-Brahmins belonging to the Hindumahasabha (mother of all evils) and its offshoots such as Swam Sevak Sangh, Jansangh, Rashtriya Swamsewak Sangh (RSS), a terrorist organization as declared by the United States administration, Rashtriya Sikh Sangat (formed at the directions of A. B. Vajpayee and his clique in 1990s) the "Sangh family", responsible for anti-non-Brahmin and anti-non-Hindus activities, and other such organizations, as well as the activities of the Saffaronized fundamentalist Hindu organizations Vishwa Hindu Parishad, Hanuman Sena, Shiv Sena, Bajrang Dal, to cite a few. The RSS was formed in support of the Fascists of Europe. Dr. Udhoke has exposed Saffaronization of the Sikh history, disrespect and character assassination of the Sikh Gurus, Guru Nanak Sahib to Sahib Guru Gobind Singhji, by these organizations and their supporters. Finally, I wish Dr. Sukhpreet Singh Udhoke, who is a gifted and prolific writer and speaker all the best. May the the Almighty Lord shower. His blessings on him.

***

Document

CONGRESSIONAL RECORD -- EXTENSIONS

Wednesday, November 15, 2006
109th Congress, 2nd Session
152 Cong Rec E 2045

REFERENCE: Vol. 152, No. 129
SECTION: Extension of Remarks
TITLE: COUNCIL OF KHALISTAN HAS SUCCESSFUL CONVENTION

Speech of
HON. EDOLPHUS TOWNS
of New York
in the House of Representatives
Wednesday, November 15, 2006

Mr. TOWNS . Mr. Speaker, recently, Indian Prime Minister Manmohan Singh publicly stated that India is the victim of cross-border terror. The Council of Khalistan under the leadership of Dr. Gurmit Singh Aulakh wrote to Prime Minister Singh and reminded him that India has been sponsoring cross-border terrorism in Sindh, a province of Pakistan, as the Washington Times reported on January 2, 2002 and that it created the Liberation Tigers of Tamil Eclam, which our government has identified as a terrorist organization, according to Indian Today, which is the leading news magazine in India.

It has also sponsored domestic terrorism against the minorities within its borders, including murdering a quarter of a million Sikhs and holding another 52,000 as political prisoners; killing Muslims by the tens of thousands in Kashmir, where more than 90,000 have been killed, Gujarat, where between 2,000 and 5,000 died in a massacre pre-planned by the government, and elsewhere; killing Christians throughout the country, including over 300,000 just in Nagaland; and mass killing many other minorities. Yet India proclaims itself the victim of terrorism and proclaims itself a democracy. Well, Mr. Speaker, it certainly doesn't act that way.

The repression and terrorism must be stopped. We should end all aid and trade with India until such time as the repression ends and people enjoy the most basic human rights, and we should throw our full support behind self-determination in Punjab, Khalistan, in Kashmir, in Nagalim, and wherever people are trying to be free. In addition, we should designate India a terrorist state and impose the sanctions that that designation brings.

Mr. Speaker, I would like to insert the Council of Khalistan's open letter into the Record. It is a frightening record of Indian terrorism.

Council of Khalistan,
Washington, DC, October 10, 2006.

Open Letter to Indian Prime Minister Manmohan Singh: India Is a Terrorist State, Not a Victim

Dear Prime Minister Singh: On October 4, you said that India is it victim of crossborder terrorism. India is a terrorist state itself and should be subject to the penalties that are imposed on terrorist states.

On January 2, 2002, the Washington Times reported that India is supporting cross-border terrorism in Sindh, a province of Pakistan, the very same kind of thing that Prime Minister Singh was claiming is victimizing India. In addition, India's leading newsmagazine, India Today, reported that the Indan government created the Liberation Tigers of Tamil Eelam (LTTE), identified by the U.S. government as a terrorist organization, and its leaders were put up by the Indian government in the finest hotel in Delhi, How can you blame Pakistan when India started cross-border terrorism with its own actions?

The Indian government has committed terrorism against its own minorities. It has murdered over 250,000 Sikh infants, children, youth, men, women, and elderly since 1984, as well as more than 300,000 Christians in Nagaland, over 90,000 Mulims in Kashmir, tens of thousands of Christians and Muslims throughout the country, and tens of thousands of Assamese, Bodos, Dalits, Manipuris, Tamils, and other minorities. A report by the Movement Against State Repression (MASR) states that 52,268 Sikhs are being held as political prisoners in India without charge or trial, mostly under a repressive law known as the "Terrorist and Disruptive Activities Act" (TADA), which expired in 1995. Many have been in illegal custody since 1984! There has been no list published of those who were acquitted under TADA and those who are still rotting in Indian jails, Tens of thousands of other minorities are also being held as political prisoners, according to Amnesty International. Tell the families of these innocent Sikhs and others that there is no terrorism in India.

Indian police arrested human-rights activist Jaswant Singh Khalra after he exposed their policy of mass cremation of Sikhs, in which over 50,000 Sikhs have been arrested, tortured, and murdered, then their bodies were declared unidentified and secretly cremated. Khalra was murdered in police custody. His body was not given to his family. No one has been brought to justice for the kidnapping and murder of Jaswant Singh Khalra. The only witness to the Khalra kidnapping, Rajiv Singh Randhawa, has been repeatedly harassed by the police, including having been arrested for trying to hand a note to then British Home Secretary Jack Straw. Last year, 35 Sikhs were charged and arrested in Punjab for making speeches in support of Khalistan and raising the Khalistani flag. How can making speeches and raising a flag be considered crimes in a democratic society?

The police never released the body of former Jathedar of the Akal Talkht Gurdev Singh Kaunke after SSP Swaran Singh Ghotna murdered him, He has never been tried for the Jathedar Kaunke murder. In 1994, the U.S. State Department reported that the Indian government had paid over 41,000 cash bounties for killing Sikhs. The MASR report quotes the Punjab Civil Magistracy as writing "if we add up the figures of the last few years the number of innocent persons killed would run into lakhs [hundreds of thousands.]" The Indian Supreme Court called the Indian government's murders of Sikhs "worse than a genocide."

Missionary Graham Staines was murdered along with his two sons, ages 8 and 10, by a mob of militant, fundamentalist Hindu nationalists who set fire to the jeep, surrounded it, and chanted "Victory to Hannuman," a Hindu god. Missionary Joseph Cooper was beaten so badly that he had to spend a week in an Indian hospital. Then the Indian government threw him out of the country. None of the people involved has been tried. The persons who have murdered priests, raped nuns, and burned Christian churches have not been charged or tried. Police broke up a Christian religious festival with gunfire. Recently, militant Hindus from the Bharatiya Janata Yuva (a youth movement affiliated with the BJP and the Fascist RSS) attacked the Convent of Loreto and the school there. A spokesman for the BJP, Mr. H. Dikshit, demanded an investigation of the school!

The murderers of 2,000 to 5,000 Muslims in Gujarat have never been brought to trial. An Indian newspaper reported that the police were ordered not to get involved in that massacre, a frightening parallel to the Delhi massacre of Sikhs in 1984. The most important mosque in India, the Babri Mosque, was destroyed by militant Hindu fundamentalists who have never been held responsible for their actions.

It is good that you have admitted the guilt of the Indian government for the Delhi massacres, in which over 20,000 Sikhs were killed, by apologizing for the massacres, but what good does it do the Sikh Nation? Where are the apologies for the Golden Temple attack, the destruction of the Akal Takht, and the desecration of Darbar Sahib, and the other atrocities? Where is the compensation for the victims' families? That operation was yet another act of Indian domestic terrorism.

The Guru granted sovereignty to the Sikh Nation, saying "In Grieb Sikhin Ko Deon Patshahi." We must remind ourselves of our heritage by raising slogans of "Khalistan Zindabad" and beginning a Shantmai Morcha to liberate our homeland, Khalistan. Whoever is honest and dedicated in leading that Shantmai Morcha deserves our support. Every rooming and evening we recite, "Raj Kare Ga Khalsa." Now is the time to act on it. Do we mean what we say every morning and evening?

The flame of freedom continues to burn blightly in the heart of the Sikh Nation. No force can suppress it. Recently, Dal Khalsa and the Shiromani Khalsa Dal announced that they are uniting for sovereignty for Khalistan. This was met with chants of "Khalistan Zindabad." The Punjab Legislative Assembly proclaimed the sovereignty of Punjab when it cancelled the water agreements. Only by liberating Khalistan can we put an end to the repression and terrorism against the Sikh Nation by the Indian regime. Now is the time to rededicate ourselves to the liberation of Khalistan.

Last year, Sikh farmers were expelled from Uttaranchal Pradesh and their land was seized. They were beaten up by the police. Their homes were bulldozed by paratroopers. Their homes in many cases were built using their life savings and by their own hands. We condemn this act of state terrorism by the government of Uttaranchal Pradesh. As you know, Sikhs are prohibited from buying land in Rajasthan and Himachal Pradesh. Now Uttaranchal Pradesh joins that list. Yet there are no restrictions on land ownership in Punjab by non-Sikhs. People from anywhere can buy land in Punjab, including people from Rajasthan and Himachal Pradesh. India is trying to subvert Khalistan's independence by overrunning Punjab with non-Sikhs while keeping Sikhs from escaping the brutal repression in Punjab. It is incumbent on the Sikh diaspora to free Khalistan. We must redouble our efforts. That is the only way to keep these atrocities from continuing and to protect the Sikh Nation and the Sikh religion.

The Akali Dal conspired with the Indian government in 1984 to invade the Golden Temple to murder Sant Bhindranwale and 20,000 other Sikhs during June 1984 in Punjab. Among those who conspired with the government, according to Chakravyuh: Web of Indian Secularism, were Dr. Chohan, Ganga Singh Dhillon, and Didar Singh Bains.

It appears the Indian regime is even willing to arrest its own agents to suppress the movement for Khalistan! Now Badal and Chief Minister Amarinder Singh have been accusing each other of being tied in with "terrorists." These leaders view support for Khalistan as terrorism, as the Indian government does. They have shown where their loyalties lie. How will these so-called Sikh leaders account for themselves? Remember the words of former Jathedar of the Akal Takht Professor Darshan Singh: "If a Sikh is not a Khalistani, he is not a Sikh."

Sikhs will never get any justice from Delhi. Ever since independence, India has mistreated the Sikh Nation, starting with Patel's memo calling Sikhs "a criminal tribe." What a shame for Home Minister Patel and the Indian government to issue this memorandum when the Sikh Nation gave over 80 percent of the sacrifices to free India. There is no place for Sikhs in supposedly secular, supposedly democratic India. Our moment of freedom is closer than ever. Sikhs will continue to work to make certain that we shake ourselves loose from the yoke of Indian oppression and liberate our homeland, Khalistan, so that all Sikhs may live lives of prosperity, freedom, and dignity.

Sincerely,
Dr. Gurmit Singh Aulakh,
President, Council of Khalistan.

***

Document

CONGRESSIONAL RECORD -- EXTENSIONS

Tuesday, September 19, 2006
109th Congress, 2nd Session
152 Cong Rec E 1747

REFERENCE: Vol. 152, No. 117
SECTION: Extension of Remarks
TITLE: DR. G.S. AULAKH WINS INTERNATIONAL PEACE PRIZE AWARD

Speech of
HON. EDOLPHUS TOWNS
of New York
in the House of Representatives
Tuesday, September 19, 2006

Mr. TOWNS . Mr. Speaker, Dr. Gurmit Singh Aulakh, the President of the Council of Khalistan, whom many of us know, has been awarded the International Peace Prize Award by Dal Khalsa USA. It was awarded for his tireless efforts in support of peace in South Asia and freedom for the Sikh nation. I would like to take this opportunity to congratulate Dr. Aulakh on this prestigious award and congratulate Dal Khalsa on selecting such a worthy honoree. Dr. Aulakh bas worked for over 20 years to free the Sikh nation from oppression that has taken the lives of more than a quarter of a million Sikhs and left over 52,000 as political prisoners. He has worked with many of us here in Congress on both sides of the aisle to expose this repression and free his people.

Mr. Speaker, we should help this struggle by declaring our support for a free and fair plebiscite in Khalistan, Kashmir, Nagaland, and wherever they are seeking the kind of freedom that we enjoy, and we should stop giving aid and trade to India until it stops oppressing its people.

I would like to insert the press release on Dr. Aulakh's award into the Record.

Dr. Aulakh Receives International Peace Award

Washington, D.C., Sept. 12, 2006._Dr. Gurmit Singh Aulakh. President of the Council of Khalistan, received the International Peace Prize Award on August 27 from Dal Khalsa of America, beaded by Sardar Paramjit Singh Sekhon. The award was presented at a ceremony at the Fremont Gurdwara in Fremont, California. He was nominated for this prestigious award by Dr. Awatar Singh Sekhon, Managing Editor of the International Journal of Sikh Affairs. According to a Dal Khalsa USA press release, he was given the award "for his tireless service to preserve peace in South Asia in particular and the world in general." The release cites Dr. Aulakh for "continuing the Sikhs" struggle to regain their lost sovereignty, independence, and political power, by peaceful means."

The award was presented for Dr. Aulakh's continuing efforts to inter-nationalize the peaceful, democratic, nonviolent Sikh struggle for independence and the human rights violations against the Sikhs in India. He has been a tireless worker for the cause of Sikh freedom. Dr. Aulakh has raised awareness of the massive human-rights violations in India.

The Indian government has murdered over 250,000 Sikh infants, children, youth, men, women, and elderly since 1984, more than 300,000 Christians in Nagaland, over 90,000 Muslims in Kashmir, tens of thousands of Christians and Muslims throughout the country, and tens of thousands of Assamese, Bodos, Dalits, Manipuris, Tamils, and others.

Indian police arrested human-rights activist Jaswant Singh Khalra after he exposed their policy of mass cremation of Sikhs, in which over 50,000 Sikhs have been arrested, tortured, and murdered, then their bodies were declared unidentified and secretly cremated, Khalra was murdered in police custody. His body was not given to his family. No one has been brought to justice for the kidnapping and murder of Jaswant Singh Khalra. The police never released the body of former Jathedar of the Akal Takht Gurdev Singh Kaunke after SSP Swaran Singh Ghotna murdered him. He has never been tried for the Jathedar Kaunke murder. In 1994, the U.S. State Department reported that the Indian government had paid over 41,000 cash bounties for killing Sikhs. A report by the Movement Against State Repression (MASR) quotes the Punjab Civil Magistracy as writing "if we add up the figures of the last few years the murder of innocent persons killed would run into lakhs [hundreds of thousands.]" The Indian Supreme Court called the Indian government's murders of Sikhs "worse than a genocide."

The MASR report states that 52,268 Sikhs are being held as political prisoners in India without charge or trial, mostly under a repressive law known as the "Terrorist and Disruptive Activities Act" (TADA), which expired in 1995. Many have been in illegal custody since 1984! There has been no list published of those who were acquitted under TADA and those who are still rotting in Indian jails. Tens of thousands of other minorities are also being held as political prisoners, according to Amnesty International. "We demand the Immediate release of all these political prisoners," said Dr. Aulakh. "Why are there political prisoners in a democracy?"

Missionary Graham Staines was murdered along with his two sons, ages 8 and 10, by a mob of militant, fundamentalist Hindu nationalists who set fire to the jeep, surrounded it, and chanted "Victory to Hannuman," a Hindu god. Missionary Joseph Cooper was beaten so badly that he had to spend a week in an Indian hospital. Then the Indian government threw him out of the country. None of the people involved has been tried. The persons who have murdered priests, raped nuns, and burned Christian churches have not been charged or tried. Police broke up a Christian religious festival with gunfire.

The murderers of 2,000 to 5,000 Muslims in Gujarat have never been brought to trial. An Indian newspaper reported that the police were ordered not to get involved in that massacre, a frightening parallel to the Delhi massacre of Sikhs in 1984.

"Sikhs and other minorities cannot live under Indian rule," said Dr. Aulakh. "The actions of the Indian government have made it clear that there is no place for Sikhs or other minorities such as Christians, Muslims, Dalits, and others in India's Hindu theocracy," he said. Dr. Aulakh took note of the charges filed against 35 Sikhs for making speeches and raising the Khalistani flag. "Clearly India is scared of the peaceful, democratic, nonviolent movement for freedom inside and outside Punjab, Khalistan," he said.

History shows that multinational states such as India are doomed to failure. Countries like Austria-Hungary, India's longtime friend the Soviet Union, Yugoslavia, Czechoslovakia, and others prove this point. India is not one country; it is a polyglot like those countries, thrown together for the convenience of the British colonialists. It is doomed to break up as they did. Currently, there are 17 freedom movements within India's borders. It has 18 official languages.

"Only a sovereign, independent Khalistan will end the repression and raise the standard of living for the people of Punjab," said Dr. Gurmit Aulakh. "As Professor Darshan Singh, former Jathedar of the Akal Takht, said, 'If a Sikh is not a Khallstani, he is not a Sikh.'," Dr. Aulakh said. "We must free Khalistan now."

***

Document

CONGRESSIONAL RECORD -- EXTENSIONS

Tuesday, September 19, 2006
109th Congress, 2nd Session
152 Cong Rec E 1750

REFERENCE: Vol. 152, No. 117
SECTION: Extension of Remarks
TITLE: SIKHS CONTINUE TO FIGHT FOR FREEDOM

Speech of
HON. EDOLPHUS TOWNS
of New York
in the House of Representatives
Tuesday, September 19, 2006

Mr. TOWNS . Mr. Speaker, the Council of Khalistan recently published an open letter showing that the effort to liberate Khalistan from Indian occupation is closer than ever to success. It took note of the speeches and the raising of the flag in support of Khalistan, of the seminar that was given that promoted Khalistan, and numerous other activities that have moved forward the peaceful effort to liberate Khalistan.

The letter argues that Khalistan is the only issue facing the Sikhs. It cites examples of people living in tyranny who put their differences aside to oust the tyrants and urges the Sikh nation to learn from those examples and do the same. It calls on the political leaders in Punjab, Khalistan, to focus their attention on the issue of liberating Khalistan from Indian occupation rather than the lesser issues that so often command their attention.

I recommend this letter highly, Mr. Speaker. It provides an excellent overview of the situation in Punjab, Khalistan.

Mr. Speaker, we must do our part to ensure freedom to the people of Khalistan and all the oppressed people of south Asia and the world. This is critical if we are proclaiming the American values of freedom, democracy, and human rights, which are cornerstones of American foreign policy. In pursuit of that goal, we should end our aid to India and our trade with India until it respects the basic human rights of all people under its control, treating them fairly, equally, and with dignity. And we should actively support democracy for the people of Khalistan and all the occupied nations, such as Kashmir, Nagalim, and others, in the form of democracy and self-determination. They should have a free and fair vote on their status, the democratic way. Does India have a problem with democracy for the people it rules? If so, it is not worthy of our support.

I would like to put the Council of Khalistan's open letter into the Record for the information of my colleagues and the American people.

Sikh Leadership Must Unite to Free Khalistan
August 14, 2006.

Dear Khalsa Ji: As I write this letter, we are again approaching Indian Independence Day. Although it is a celebration for the uppercaste Hindus, it is a black day on the calendar for Sikhs and other minorities suffering under the boot of Indian repression. Over 52,000 of our Sikh brothers and sisters remain in illegal Indian custody as political prisoners without charge or trial. More than a quarter of a million of our fellow Sikhs have been murdered by the Indian government. Similar genocide has been inflicted on Christians, Muslims, and other minorities. Is this what India celebrates? Are they celebrating bloodshed, violence, brutality, and tyranny? Unfortunately, that is the way it looks. How does a democracy justify that kind of celebration?

The flame of freedom continues to burn brightly in the heart of the Sikh Nation. No force can suppress it. The arrests last year and earlier this year of Sikh activists, mostly from Dal Khalsa, merely for raising the Khalistani flag and making pro-Khalistan speeches shows that the movement to free our homeland is on the rise. It has gotten the attention of the world. The seminar organized by former Member of Parliament Sardar Atinder Pal Singh, who has publicly asked why we can't have Khalistan, also moved the cause of freedom for Khalistan forward. We are closer to freedom than ever before, despite the ongoing repression.

Recently, a coalition of Sikh leaders led by Simranjit Singh Mann has come together to oppose both Chief Minister Amarinder Singh and Parkash Singh Badal. While it is good to oppose both of these leaders, who are puppets of the brutal Indian regime, the small, incremental proposals that the Mann-led coalition is making do little to solve the basic problems of the Sikh Nation. The real issue is Khalistan. That is why these 35 Sikhs face charges from the Indian government for raising the Khalistani flag and speaking for Khalistan, not merely for opposition to Badal and Amarinder. As worthwhile as it may be to oppose them, it is diverting the attention of the Sikh Nation from the real issue of Khalistan.

India is trying to subvert Khalistan's independence by overrunning Punjab with non-Sikhs while keeping Sikhs from escaping the brutal repression in Punjab. We must redouble our efforts to free our homeland, Punjab, Khalistan. That is the only way to keep these atrocities from continuing and to protect the Sikh Nation. This is a direct challenge to the Sikh leadership, irrespective of their party affiliation. Yet the new coalition wants to practice politics as usual, within the Indian system. That will never achieve freedom, dignity, security, or prosperity for the Sikhs of Punjab, Khalistan. They must speak out forcefully for Khalistan or their efforts are useless. Please do not waste the Sikh Nation's time on other issues that divert our attention from liberating Khalistan. Those issues can and should be dealt with after Khalistan is free. But until then, no other issue matters to the future of the Khalsa Panth.

Other nations that have faced repression have taught us the lesson that these politicians need to learn. When Nicaragua suffered under a repressive government in the 1980s, the opposition factions put aside their differences and worked together to free the people from the repression of the Ortega regime. A similar thing is happening in other countries around the world today. They know that these differences, as important as they may be, are for a later day. First, they must secure freedom.

Any organization that sincerely supports Khalistan deserves the support of the Sikh Nation. However, the Sikh Nation needs leadership that is honest, sincere, consistent, and dedicated to the cause of Sikh freedom. But we should only support sincere, dedicated, honest leaders. The Council of Khalistan has stood strongly and consistently for liberating our homeland, Khalistan, from Indian occupation. For over 20 years we have led this fight while others were trying to divert the resources and the attention of the Sikh Nation away from the issue of freedom in a sovereign, independent Khalistan.

Mr. Mann is not trustworthy. He is conniving with the Indian government. His letter pledging support for "the constitution and territorial integrity of India" is reproduced on page 185 of Chakravyuh: Web of Indian Secularism. Last year, he was escorted around America by Amarjit Singh. At a Vaisakhi celebration in New York in 2000, he called for the Council of Khalistan office to be closed. He has accused Dr. Awatar Singh Sekhon and me of being Indian government agents!

All factions of the Akali Dal are to be viewed with suspicion. The Akali Dal has lost all its credibility. The Akali Dal conspired with the Indian government in 1984 to invade the Golden Temple to murder Sant Bhindranwale and 20,000 other Sikh during June 1984 in Punjab. If Sikhs will not even protect the sanctity of the Golden Temple, how can the Sikh Nation survive as a nation?

The Akali leaders also walked out when I predicted at a seminar around the celebration of Guru Nanak's birthday that Khalistan will soon be free, a prediction that was greeted with multiple enthusiastic shouts of "Khalistan Zindabad." How will these Akalis account for themselves? Remember the words of former Jathedar of the Akal Takht Professor Darshan Singh: "If a Sikh is not a Khalistani, he is not a Sikh." Khalistan is the only way that Sikhs will be able to live in freedom, peace, prosperity, and dignity. It is time to start a Shantmai Morcha to liberate Khalistan from Indian occupation.

Never forget that the Akal Takht Sahib and Darbar Sahib are under the control of the Indian government, the same Indian government that has murdered over a quarter of a million Sikhs in the past twenty years. These institutions will remain under the control of the Indian regime until we free the Sikh homeland, Punjab, Khalistan, from Indian occupation and oppression and sever our relations with the New Delhi government.

The Sikhs in Punjab have suffered enormous repression at the hands of the Indian regime in the last 25 years. Over 50,000 Sikh youth were picked up from their houses, tortured, murdered in police custody, then secretly cremated as "unidentified bodies." Their remains were never even given to their families! More than a quarter of a million Sikhs have been murdered at the hands of the Indian government. Another 52,268 are being held as political prisoners. Some have been in illegal custody since 1984! Even now, the capital of Punjab, Chandigarh, has not been handed over to Punjab, but remains a Union Territory. How can Sikhs have any freedom living under a government that would do these things?

Sikhs will never get any justice from Delhi. Ever since independence, India has mistreated the Sikh Nation, starting with Patel's memo labelling Sikhs "a criminal tribe." What a shame for Home Minister Patel and the Indian government to issue this memorandum when the Sikh Nation gave over 80 percent of the sacrifices to free India.

How can Sikhs continue to live in such a country? There is no place for Sikhs in supposedly secular, supposedly democratic India. Let us work to make certain that 2006 is the Sikh Nation's most blessed year by making sure it is the year that we shake ourselves loose from the yoke of Indian oppression and liberate our homeland, Khalistan, so that all Sikhs may live lives of prosperity, freedom, and dignity.

> *Sincerely,*
> *Gurmit Singh Aulakh,*
> *President, Council of Khalistan.*

***

Document

CONGRESSIONAL RECORD -- EXTENSIONS

Tuesday, September 19, 2006
109th Congress, 2nd Session
152 Cong Rec E 1752

REFERENCE: Vol. 152, No. 117
SECTION: Extension of Remarks
TITLE: DAL KHALSA USA HOLDS SEMINAR ON KHALISTAN

Speech of
HON. EDOLPHUS TOWNS
of New York
in the House of Representatives
Tuesday, September 19, 2006

Mr. TOWNS . Mr. Speaker, recently, Dal Khalsa USA held a seminar in support of Khalistan, the Sikh homeland. It was a significant demonstration of the continuing support that the Sikh people have for freedom for their homeland. Paramjit Singh Sekhon and Gagandecp Singh, who lead Dal Khalsa USA and organized the seminar, are to be congratulated. Speakers, included Dr. Gurmit Singh Aulakh, Dr. Awatar Singh Sekhon, Dr. Ajit Pal Singh Sandhu, and Dr. Arjinder Singh Sekhorn.

Freedom is a dream that people all over the world share and we should be encouraging it, Mr. Speaker. Both here and in Punjab, support for Khalistan is on the rise and getting more visible.

As the beacon of liberty in the world, it is our duty to encourage people who are reaching for freedom. The essence of democracy is the right to self-determination. But in India, all that elections do for minorities is to change the faces of the oppressors. The time has come to go on record in support of a democratic vote on freedom for Khalistan, Kashmir, Nagaland, and all the minority nations of South Asia. And we should stop our aid to India and our trade until human rights are respected.

Mr. Speaker, the Council of Khalistan issued a press release on the seminar. I would like to add it to the Record.

Dal Khalsa USA Holds Seminar on Khalistan

Washington, D.C._Dal Khalsa USA held a seminar on Khalistan In Fremont, California from August 25 to August 27, The seminar focused on the need to liberate Khalistan, the Sikh homeland, from Indian occupation. Khalistan is the Sikh homeland that declared its independence from India on October 7, 1987. Speakers included Dr. Gurmit Singh aulakh, President of the Council of Khalistan, Dr. Awatar Singh Sekhon, Managing Editor of the International Journal of Sikh Affairs, Dr. Ajit Pal Singh Sandhu, Colonel Arjinderpal Singh Sekhon (US Army Reserve), and others, The seminar was organized by Sardar Paramjit Singh Sekhon,

President of Dal Khalsa USA, and Sardar Gagandeep Singh, General Secretary of Dal Khalsa USA.

The speakers addressed the need for the Sikh Nation to reclaim it lost sovereignty and escape from the oppression of the Indian government, which has murdered over 250,000 Sikh infants, children, youth, men, women, and elderly since 1984, as well as more than 300,000 Christians in Nagaland, over 90,000 Muslims in Kashmir, tens of thousands of Christians and Muslims throughout the country, and tens of thousands of Assamese, Bodos, Dalits, Manipurls, Tamils, and other minorities.

Indian police arrested human-rights activist Jaswant Singh Khalra after he exposed their policy of mass cremation of Sikhs, in which over 50,000 Sikhs have been arrested, tortured, and murdered, then their bodies were declared unidentified and secretly cremated. Khalra was murdered in police custody. His body was not given to his family. No one has been brought to Justice for the kidnapping and murder of Jaswant Singh Khalra. The only witness to the Khalra kidnapping, Rajiv Singh Randhawa, has been repeatedly harassed by the police, including having been arrested for trying to hand a piece of paper to then-British Home Secretary Jack Straw. The police never released the body of former Jathedar of the Akal Takht Gurdev Singh Kaunke after SSP Swaran Singh Ghotna murdered him. He has never been tried for the Jathedar Kaunke murder. In 1994, the U.S. State Department reported that the Indian government had paid over 41,000 cash bounties for killing Sikhs. A report by the Movement Against State Repression (MASR) quotes the Punjab Civil Magistracy as writing "if we add up the figures of the last few years the number of innocent persons killed would run into lakhs [hundreds of thousands.]" The Indian Supreme Court called the Indian governments murders of Sikhs "worse than a genocide."

The MASR report states that 52,268 Sikhs are being held as political prisoners in India without charge or trial, mostly under a repressive law known as the "Terrorist and Disruptive Activities Act" (TADA), which expired in 1995. Many have been in illegal custody since 1984. There has been no list published of those who were acquitted under TADA and those who are still rotting in Indian jails. Tens of thousands of other minorities are also being held as political prisoners, according to Amnesty International. Last year, 35 Sikhs were charged and arrested in Punjab for making speeches in support of Khalistan and raising the Khalistan flag. "How can making speeches and raising a flag be considered crimes in a democratic society?" asked Dr. Aulakh.

Missionary Graham Staines was murdered along with his two sons, ages 8 and 10, by a mob of militant, fundamentalist Hindu nationalists who set fire to the jeep, surrounded it, and chanted "Victory to Hannuman," a Hindu god. Missionary Joseph Cooper was beaten so badly that he had to spend a week in an Indian hospital. Then the Indian government threw him out of the country. None of the people involved has been tried. The persons who have murdered priests, raped nuns, and burned Christian churches have not been charged or tried. Police broke up a Christian religious festival with gunfire. Recently, militant Hindus from the Bharatlya Janata Yuva (a youth movement affiliated with the BJP and the Fascist RSS) attacked the Convent of Loreto and the school there. 13 Catholic schools remain closed and a spokesman for the BJP, Mr. H. Dikshit, demanded an investigation of the school!

The murderers of 2,000 to 5,000 Muslims in Gujarat have never been brought to trial. An Indian newspaper reported that the police were ordered not to get involved in that massacre, a frightening parallel to the Delhi massacre of Sikhs In 1984. The most important mosque in India, the Sabri Mosque, was destroyed by militant Hindu fundamentalists who have never been held responsible for their actions.

"I am honored to be a speaker at this seminar and very pleased that Dal Khalsa USA is holding these activities to focus the attention of America and the world on the plight of the Sikhs in Punjab, Khalistan and the need for a sovereign, Independent Khalistan," said Dr. Aulakh.

History shows that multinational states such as India are doomed to failure. Countries like Austria-Hungary, India's longtime friend the Soviet Union. Yugoslavia. Czechoslovakia, and others prove this point. India is not one country; it is a polyglot like those countries, thrown together for the convenience of the British colonialists. It is doomed to break up as they did. Currently, there are 17 freedom movements within India's borders. It has 18 official languages. "We hope that India's breakup will be peaceful like Czechoslovakia's, not violent like Yugoslavia's," Dr. Aulakh said.

Dr. Aulakh stressed his commitment to the peaceful, democratic, non-violent struggle to liberate Khalistan. "The only way that the repression will stop and Sikhs will live in freedom, dignity and prosperity is to liberate Khalistan," said Dr. Aulakh. "As Professor Darshan Singh, former Jathedar of the Akal Takht, said, 'If a Sikh Is not a Khalistani, he is not a Sikh.'," Dr. Aulakh said. "We must free Khalistan now,"

***

Document

CONGRESSIONAL RECORD -- EXTENSIONS

Tuesday, September 19, 2006
109th Congress, 2nd Session
152 Cong Rec E 1755

REFERENCE: Vol. 152, No. 117
SECTION: Extension of Remarks
TITLE: CONVENT ATTACKED IN INDIA

Speech of
HON. EDOLPHUS TOWNS
of New York
in the House of Representatives
Tuesday, September 19, 2006

Mr. TOWNS . Mr. Speaker, on September 11, while we were observing the anniversary of a horrible terrorist attack on America, 13 Catholic schools were closed in Lucknow, India, after the Convent of Loreto, the school there, and the chapel were attacked by the violent Hindu organization the Bharatiya Janata Yuva, a youth arm of the BJP, which is part of the RSS, a Fascist organization that published a book on how to get minorities, including Christians, falsely implicated in criminal cases.

The spokesman for the BJP demanded a high-level inquiry into the school, according to the Tribune newspaper of Chandigarh, saying it engaged in "irrational behavior." Apparently, being a Catholic is irrational behavior and "unscientific activity" in the world of Hindu militants.

Unforturlately, Mr. Speaker, this is not an isolated incident. There has been a wave of attacks against Christians. According to an article that appeared in the Journal of the London Institute of South Asia, some Christian boys were shot while praying. A mob of Hindus burned a missionary, Graham Staines, and his two sons (ages 8 and 10) to death and they have gotten away with it. Another missionary, Joseph Cooper, was severely beaten and then expelled from India. Christians have been arrested for sharing their religious beliefs. Violent Hindu Fascists have raped nuns, murdered priests, burned churches, and committed other acts of violence against Christians. More than 300,000 Christians have been killed by the Indians in Nagaland alone.

This would be bad enough if it were just Christians, Mr. Speaker, but, sadly, it is not. Sikhs, Muslims, and other minorities, such as Dalits, have been similarly repressed. The Muslims had their most revered mosque in India destroyed. Somewhere between 2,000 to 5,000 Muslims were murdered in one pogrom in Gujarat. More than 90,000 have been killed in Kashmir. The government has murdered over a quarter of a million Sikhs. Their most sacred place of worship, the Golden Temple in Amritsar, which has been called the Sikh equivalent of the Vatican, was attacked in June 1984. Hundreds of people were brutally murdered there, and more than 20,000 were killed in the month of June 1984. More than 52,000 Sikhs are political prisoners in India. They have murdered human-rights activists for exposing their secret cremations, murdered religious leaders, murdered toddlers, and paid out more than 41,000 cash bounties to police officers who killed Sikhs.

I would like to thank Dr. Gurmit Singh Aulakh of the Council of Khalistan for bringing the Loreto attack to my attention.

Mr. Speaker, we are at war right now with Fascists using the cover of Islam. Many of us have criticisms of the war policies, but the recent anniversary of September 11 reminds us that we cannot let terrorists carry out their awful deeds with no consequences. So why do we refuse even to raise our voices against Fascists who use the cover of the Hindu religion and oppress and kill Christians, Muslims, Sikhs. and others? At the very least, Mr. Speaker, we should be willing to stop trading with India and cut off our aid, and we should stand for the principles that America represents by seeking a democratic solution to the repression in the form of a free and fair plebiscite on the status of Christian Nagaland, predominantly Sikh Khalistan, Kashmir, and the others who seek their freedom.

Mr. Speaker, I would like to put the Council of Khalistan's press release on the Loreto attack in the Record.

Catholic Schools in Lucknow Closed After Attack on Convent by Militant Hindus

Washington, D.C._Thirteen Catholic schools were closed today to protest vandalism on the premises of the Loreto Convent, according to the Tribune of Chandigarh. Among the schools that were closed is the Loreto School. Militant Hindus from the Bharatiya Janata Yuva (a youth movement affiliated with the Bharatiya Janata party (BJP) and the Fascist RSS) attacked the Convent of Loreto, Loreto Chapel, and the school there. A spokesman for the BJP, Mr. H. Dikshit, demanded an investigation of the school, saying that it encourages "irrational behavior" and "unscientific activity." Mr. Dlkshit said that the state government is "overreacting to breaking a few flower pots."

The attacks are part of a pattern of violence against Christians that has been going on heavily since Christmas 1998, which is in line with similar tyranny against other minorities. Missionary Graham Staines was murdered along with his two sons, ages a and 10, by a mob of militant, fundamentalist Hindu nationalists who set fire to the jeep, surrounded it. and chanted "Victory to Hannuman," a Hindu god. Missionary Joseph Cooper was beaten so badly that he had to spend a week in an Indian hospital. Then the Indian government threw him out of the country. None of the people involved has been tried. Several states have enacted anti-conversion laws, which in practice prevent anyone from converting to any religion except Hinduism. Such a law is being considered by the Lok Sabha, the national Parliament. Christians report that they have faced threats, physical attacks, and jail time for sharing their beliefs. The Rashtirya Swayamsewak Sangh (RSS), a Hindu Fascist organization that is the parent organization of the BJP, published a booklet on how to implicate Christians and other minorities in false criminal cases. The people who have murdered priests, raped nuns, forced them to drink their own urine, and burned Christian churches have not been charged or tried. In 2002, the Associated Press reported an attack on a Catholic church on the outskirts of Bangalore in which several people were injured. The assailants threw stones at the church, then broke in, breaking furniture and smashing windows before attacking worshippers. Last year, two young Christian boys were shot at while they prayed. Police broke up a Christian religious festival with gunfire.

Sikhs and Muslims know the same repression that Christians have been experiencing lately. In June 1984, Indian forces invaded and desecrated the most sacred center and seat of the Sikh religion, the Golden Temple in Amrltsar, along with 37 other Gurdwaras throughout Punjab. Over 20,00 were killed. Several young Sikh boys were taken into the courtyard of the Darbar Sahib complex and asked if they supported Khalistan (the independent Sikh homeland.) When they answered with the Sikh religious statement. "Bole So Nihal," they were summarily murdered. The Sikh holy scripture, the Guru Granth Sahib, was shot full of bullet holes.

Indian police arrested human-rights activist Jaswant Singh Khalra after he exposed their policy of mass cremation of Sikhs, in which over 50,000 Sikhs have been arrested, tortured, and murdered, then their bodies were declared unidentified and secretly cremated. Khalra was murdered in police custody. His body was not given to his family. No one has been brought to justice for the kidnapping and murder of Jaswant Singh Khaira. The police never released the body of former Jathedar of the Akal Takht Gurdev Singh Kaunke after SSP Swaran Singh Ghotna murdered him. He has never been tried for the Jathedar Kaunke murder. In 1994, the U.S. State Department reported that the Indian government had paid over 41,000 cash bounties for killing Sikhs. A report by the Movement Against State Repression (MASR) quotes the Punjab Civil Magistracy as writing "if we add up the figures of the last few years the number of innocent persons killed would run into lakhs [hundreds of thousands.]" The Indian Supreme Court cal[ed the Indian government's murders of Sikhs "worse than a genocide."

The MASR report states that 52,268 Sikhs are being held as political prisoners in India without charge or trial, mostly under a repressive law known as the "Terrorist and Disruptive Activities Act" (TADA), which expired in 1995. Many have been in illegal custody since 1984! Tens of thousands of other minorities are also being held as political prisoners, according to Amnesty International. Last year, 35 Sikhs were charged and arrested in Punjab for making speeches In support of Khalistan and raising the Khalistani flag.

The murderers of 2,000 to 5,000 Muslims in Gujarat have never been brought to trial. An Indian newspaper reported that the police were ordered not to get involved in that massacre, a frightening parallel to the Delhi massacre of Sikhs in 1984. The most important mosque in India. the Babri Mosque, was destroyed by militant Hindu fundamentalists who have never been held responsible for their actions.

"The attack on the Loreto Convent shows that minorities have no place in India's so-called democracy," said Dr. Gurmit Singh Aulakh, President of the Council of Khalistan, which leads the Sikh struggle for an independent Khalistan. Khalistan declared its independence on October 7, 1987. History shows that multinational states such as India are doomed to failure. Countries like Austria-Hungary, India's longtime friend the Soviet Union, Yugoslavia, Czechoslovakia, and others prove this point. India is not one country; It Is a polyglot like those countries, thrown together for the convenience of the British colonialists. It is doomed to break up as they did. Currently, there are 17 freedom move-

ments within India's borders. It has 18 official languages. "The only way that the repression of Sikhs, Christians. Muslims, and other minorities will end is to liberate our homelands, such as Khalistan, Nagaland, Kashmir. and the rest, said Dr. Aulakh. "As Professor Darshan Singh, former Jathedar of the Akal Takht, said, 'If a Sikh is not a Khalistani, he is not a Sikh.', " Dr. Aulakh said. "We must free Khalistan now."

***

Document

CONGRESSIONAL RECORD -- EXTENSIONS

Thursday, July 27, 2006
109th Congress, 2nd Session
152 Cong Rec E 1556

REFERENCE: Vol. 152, No. 101
SECTION: Extension of Remarks
TITLE: DR. AULAKH, PRESIDENT OF COUNCIL OF KHALISTAN, MAKES
PRESENTATION AT LONDON INSTITUTE OF SOUTH ASIA

Speech of
HON. EDOLPHUS TOWNS
of New York
in the House of Representatives
Thursday, July 27, 2006

Mr. TOWNS . Mr. Speaker, recently the London Institute of South Asia held an event to honor author Professor Gurtej Singh, who has a significant book on the repression in India. In connection with that, they held a seminar on the topic of a separate electorate in India for minorities. Dr. Gunnit Singh Aulakh, President of the Council of Khalistan, spoke at the Institute in connection with the seminar. He spoke about the struggle to liberate Khalistan, the Sikh homeland. As you know, Mr. Speaker, Khalistan declared its independence on October 7, 1987. Yet Indian repression of the Sikh Nation continues to this day.

Dr. Aulakh spoke out against a separate electorate within India for the Sikhs, arguing that only full independence will allow the Sikhs to live in peace, prosperity, dignity, and freedom. He said that independence for Khalistan is inevitable, noting the recent marches, seminars, and other events showing the rising tide of support for freedom for Khalistan. And the politicians in Punjab have noticed and are beginning to speak out for Khalistan. That is a good sign. Even the Congress Party government of Punjab explicitly asserted the sovereignty of Punjab when it cancelled the agreements allowing the transfer of Punjabi water to non-riparian states last year.

He reported on the repression of the Sikhs that continues to show up in the form of the Indian Government destroying Sikh farms with bulldozers, farms that Sikh farmers had worked their lives for, only to see a lifetime of work destroyed by the Indian regime. This repression takes the form of arresting people for raising the flag of Khalistan, even though the Indian courts have ruled that wearing the saffron of Khalistan or raising a flag is not a crime. But the Indian Government apparently believes that it is not bound by the law, a position held not by democratic, but totalitarian governments. As my friend from California has said, for minorities, "India may as well be Nazi Germany."

Mr. Speaker, we cannot sit idly by and let this repression continue. I know that there are many pressing problems on the world stage that require our attention, such as the situation in Lebanon and the continuing fight against terrorism in Iraq and Afghanistan. But we must not let the necessity of attention and action in these important situations allow us to let Indian repression slip under the radar. It is our duty to the principles on which this country was founded to support freedom everywhere in the world, not just in the hot spots. It is time to take action, Mr. Speaker. America should cut off aid and trade with India until all people there are allowed to live in freedom. And we should support real democracy, the kind India claims to believe in, in the form of a free and fair plebiscite in Punjab, Khalistan, in Nagalim, in Kashmir, and wherever people seek their freedom in South Asia.

Mr. Speaker, I would like to place the Council of Khalistan's press release on Dr. Aulakh's visit to the London Institute of South Asia into the Record at this time.

Dr. Aulakh Speaks to London Institute of South Asia
Book Award to Professor Gurtej Singh

Washington, D.C., July 12, 2006. Dr. Gurmit Singh Aulakh, President of the Council of Khalistan, spoke last month at the London Institute of South Asia (LISA.) He went there for a ceremony honoring Professor Gurtej Singh IAS for his book, Tandev of the Centaur, which won the LISA Book Award. The seminar addressed the topic of a separate electorate for Indian. minorities. Dr. Aulakh spoke on the topic of the liberation of Khalistan. He said that the idea of CI separate election could be good for some minorities but was something that would hold back the struggle for freedom of minority nations that are dominant in their areas. He gave four radio interviews on Punjabi stations that are listened to worldwide.

Professor Gurtej Singh said, "As part of my narration [for the book], I found myself suggesting a theory indicating the spurious nature of India's struggle for freedom. I am aware that it renders the main activities of the Congress Party and its leaders to an exercise in collaboration. But I am in good company in coming to that conclusion. Michael Edwards, in his The Myth of the Mahatma. has clearly shown that the British really feared the 'Western style revolutionaries' whom Gandhi effectively neutralized. The Administration considered Gandhi as an ally of the British as a neutralizer of rebellion."

"This book does not clarify everything, but it clarifies a lot," said Brigadier Usman Khalid, Director of LISA. "It lays the foundation for

friendship between two irrepressible nations of the subcontinent_the Muslims and the Sikhs. The national cohesion that exists within the Muslims and the Sikhs cannot be replicated in the caste based Brahminic society," Brigadier Khalid said, "Indian secularism is 'fraudulent; Indian nationalism is a pious hope without foundation or purpose. The book nails those lies. It is a great starting point for the 'freedom for all in South Asia.'"

"Despite the Indian Government's massive efforts over two decades to crush the Khalistani freedom movement and the other freedom movements, there remains strong support for Khalistan in Punjab and the surrounding Sikh areas," Dr. Aulakh said. He noted the anniversary of the attack on the Golden Temple and the atrocities that were committed in Operation Bluestar. He took note of the arrests of Sikh leaders in Punjab for making speeches and hoisting the flag. He noted that Khalistan slogans were raised inside the Golden Temple recently. He noted the seminars organized by Atinder Pal Singh and took note of the atrocities committed by the Indian government. such as the kidnapping and murder of Jaswant Singh Khalra, the murder of Akal Takht Jathedar Gurdev Singh Kaunke, tearing apart the driver of Saba Charan Singh, and the mass cremation of Sikhs. He cited the Chithisinghpora massacre, the bombing of an Indian Airlines flight in 1985, and other atrocities committed by the Indian government.

A report issued by the Movement Against State Repression (MASR) shows that India admitted that it held 52,268 political prisoners under the repressive "Terrorist and Disruptive Activities Act" (TADA) even though it expired in 1995. Many have been in illegal custody since 1984. There as been no list published of those who were acquitted under TADA and those who are still rotting in Indian jails. Additionally, according to Amnesty International, there are tens of thousands of other minorities being held as political prisoners. The MASR report quotes the Punjab Civil Magistracy as writing "if we add up the figures of the last few years the number of innocent persons killed would run into lakhs [hundreds of thousands.]" The Indian government has murdered over 250,000 Sikhs since 1984, more than 300,000 Christians in Nagaland, over 90,000 Muslims in Kashmir. tens of thousands of Christians and Muslims throughout the country, and tens of thousands of Tamils, Assamese, Manipuris, and others. The Indian Supreme Court called the Indian government's murders of Sikhs "worse than a genocide,"

Government-allied Hindu militants have burned down Christian churches and prayer halls, murdered priests, and raped nuns. The Vishwa Hindu Parishad (VHP) described the rapists as "patriotic youth" and called the nuns "antinational elements." Hindu radicals, members of the Bajrang Dal, burned missionary Graham Stewart Staines and his two sons, ages 10 and 8, to death while they surrounded the victims and chanted 'Victory to Hannuman," the Hindu monkey-faced God. The Bajrang Dal is the youth arm of the RSS. The VHP is a militant Hindu Nationalist organization that is under the umbrella of the RSS.

"The genocidal policies of the Indian government are aimed at elimi-nating all these groups," Dr. Aulakh said. "Self-determination must be the standard," he said. "Short of that, it is hard to see how the freedom of all people in South Asia will be protected."

We thank the London Institute of South Asia for including Dr. Aulakh in its presentations. We would like to thank General Khalid, Dr. Awatar Singh Sekhon, V.T. Rajshekar, and all the trustees of the Institute for inviting Dr. Aulakh to make this presentation.

***

Document

CONGRESSIONAL RECORD -- EXTENSIONS

Thursday, July 27, 2006
109th Congress, 2nd Session
152 Cong Rec E 1558

REFERENCE: Vol. 152, No. 101
SECTION: Extension of Remarks
TITLE: COUNCIL OF KHALISTAN PRESIDENT ADDRESSES LONDON
INSTITUTE OF SOUTH ASIA

Speech of
HON. EDOLPHUS TOWNS
of New York
in the House of Representatives
Thursday, July 27, 2006

Mr. TOWNS . Mr. Speaker, Dr. Gurmit Singh Aulakh, President of the Council of Khalistan, recently spoke at the London Institute of South Asia, which was holding a seminar on separate electorate in India. He also contributed an article to the Journal of the London Institute of South Asia. Both presentations were on the same theme: freedom for Khalistan, the sovereign Sikh state that declared its independence from India on October 7, 1987, and has been under Indian occupation ever since then.

Dr. Aulakh stressed that a separate electorate within India, although it might help some of the oppressed minorities there, would not be appropriate for the Sikh nation, which is separate and distinct from India. He said that the achievement of full sovereignty and independence for Khalistan is inevitable. He took note of the Sikh farmers whose farms were bulldozed earlier this year by the Government. He discussed the Sikh activists who were arrested for raising the Khalistani flag. "How can India claim it is a democracy and continue to hold political prisoners?" he asked. "How can a democratic, secular state make it a crime to raise a flag and make speeches? Would America arrest people for raising the Confederate flag? Would the United Kingdom arrest people for speaking in support of Scottish independence?" And the answer is that of course we wouldn't. We may not like these things, but they are not crimes. Yet in India the equivalent act gets you arrested.

Dr. Aulakh noted several other acts of tyranny against the Sikhs, including the kidnapping of human-rights activist Jaswant Singh Khalra, the murder of former Jathedar of the Akal Takht Gurdev Singh Kaunke, the killing of the driver for Sikh religious leader Baba Charan Singh, who was tied to two Jeeps which drove in different directions, tearing this human being apart, and many other atrocities. These things are the mark of a tyrannical, totalitarian regime, Mr. Speaker. Dr. Aulakh writes that in light of these atrocities, "independence for Khalistan is inevitable."

Dr. Aulakh takes note of the rising support for Khalistan in Punjab. He notes the marches being organized, that politicians and other Sikh leaders are speaking out for Khalistan, the seminars held by a former member of Parliament on the subject, and other activities in support of freedom for Khalistan.

Mr. Speaker, the essence of democracy is the right to self-determination. All people and all nations have a right to be free. That is the idea that gave birth to America. As such, we must be active and vigilant in supporting freedom around the world. We should stop our aid and trade with India, which is only propping up the repressive regime. The time has come to put the U.S. Congress on record in support of a free and fair plebiscite in Khalistan and all the minority nations that seek their freedom in South Asia.

Mr. Speaker, I would like to place Dr. Aulakh's article from the Journal of the London Institute of South Asia into the Record at this time.

[From the Journal of the London Institute of South Asia, July, 2006]
Flame of Freedom Burns in Khalistan: Establishment of a Sovereign
Sikh State Is Inevitable
(By Dr. Gurmit Singh Aulakh)

January 2006 was not a good month for the Sikh farmers in Uttaranchal Pradesh, India. Their farms were bulldozed and they were thrown out of the state. They had worked peacefully all their lives, but now everything they had worked for was destroyed. Once again, the government had decided to make Sikhs the victims. This continues a pattern of repression that has kept the Sikh Nation from living in freedom or prosperity. Since 1984, over a quarter of a million Sikhs have been murdered at the hands of the Indian government.

There is no way for these farmers to gain redress within the Indian system. They have lost their life's work with no way of making themselves whole. And they have no means to begin again. They received no compensation for their bulldozed property. This is just a recent example of why Sikhs need their own independent country, Khalistan.

Khalistan, the Sikh homeland, declared its independence from India on October 7, 1987. Since then, India's brutal repression of the Sikh nation has intensified. Last year on Republic Day, 35 Sikhs were arrested for making speeches in support of Khalistan and raising the flag of Khalistan. This past June, even more Sikhs were arrested for hoisting a

*flag and making speeches. They join at least 52,268 Sikh political prison-
ers that India admitted to holding, according to the Movement Against
State Repression (MASR) (as well as tens of thousands of other political
prisoners, according to Amnesty International.)*

*India proclaims itself the world's largest democracy. How can India
claim it is a democracy and continue to hold political prisoners? How
can a democratic, secular state make it a crime to raise a flag and make
speeches? Would America arrest people for raising the Confederate flag?
Would the United Kingdom arrest people for speaking in support of
Scottish independence?*

*The Sikhs are a separate people from India_culturally, linguistically,
and religiously distinct. As such, the Sikh Nation is logically and morally
a separate nation, a separate people. Every day Sikhs pray "Raj Kare Ga
Khalsa," meaning "the Khalsa shall rule." It is part of the Sikh consciousness that we are either rulers or we are in rebellion.*

*Since 1947, the Indian government has been enslaving the Sikh Na-
tion. Under Indian rule, Sikhs are slaves. They are exploited, tortured,
and killed for the convenience of the rulers. Despite India's repression of
the Sikhs 'symbolized by half a million troops enforcing the peace of the
bayonet' the Sikhs are reclaiming the freedom that is our birthright. The
record of India's treatment of the Sikhs makes it clear that there is no
place for the Sikhs in 'India's democracy'.*

*In 1995, human-rights activist Jaswant Singh Khalra published a
report exposing India's policy of secret cremations of Sikhs under which
Sikh men are picked up, tortured, and murdered, then their bodies are
declared 'unidentified' and secretly cremated. Khalra did his work by
studying several cremation grounds in Punjab. He established about
25,000 Sikhs who have been secretly cremated. Follow-up work has
established that the number is around 50,000. Their bodies have never
been given to their families. For his work, Sardar Khalra was murdered
in police custody; no wonder his body also disappeared.*

*The one witness to the Khalra kidnapping, Rajiv Singh Randhawa,
has been consistently harassed by the Indian regime. He even got arrested
for trying to hand information about the repression of the Sikhs to the
British Home Minister outside the Golden Temple.*

*Former Jathedar of the Akal Takht Gurdev Singh Kaunke was mur-
dered by police official Swaran Singh Ghotna. He has never been brought
to justice. The driver for Sikh religious leader Baba Charan Singh was
killed when his legs were tied to two jeeps which then drove in different
directions. The cases of torture by rolling heavy rollers over the legs of
Sikh prisoners are too numerous to mention. In 1994, the U.S. State
Department reported that the Indian government paid out over 41,000
cash bounties to police officers for killing Sikhs.*

*The only way that Sikhs will be able to live in freedom, peace, stabil-
ity, dignity, and prosperity, without constantly fearing for their lives, is by
liberating Khalistan.*

*The establishment of an independent Khalistan is inevitable. Support
for an independent Khalistan is rising in Punjab. Last November,*

Khalistan slogans were raised at Nankana Sahib during the celebration of Guru Nanak's birthday and at a subsequent seminar. More than 25,000 people were in attendance for the birthday celebration. There have been numerous marches demanding freedom for Khalistan in Punjab. Former Member of Parliament Atinder Pal Singh held a seminar on Khalistan. Even when the Punjab Legislative Assembly canceled the agreements that had allowed Punjabi water to be diverted to other states, they openly asserted the sovereignty of the state of Punjab. It seems that the Indian government is aware and afraid of the rising tide of support for Khalistan.

As Steve Forbes wrote in Forbes Magazine in 2002, "India is not a homogeneous state. Neither was the Austro-Hungarian Empire. It attacked Serbia in the summer of 1914 in the hopes of destroying this irritating state after Serbia had committed a spectacular terrorist act against the Hapsburg monarchy. The empire ended up splintering, and the Hapsburgs lost their throne." India is doomed to a similar fate. It is not a single, homogeneous state, but many countries thrown together under one umbrella by the British colonial rulers for their convenience. It has 18 official languages. Such countries historically fall apart. The Soviet Union, Czechoslovakia, and Yugoslavia are other examples from recent history.

Even former Home Minister L.K. Advani has acknowledged the instability of India, saying in Parliament: "if Kashmir goes, India goes." At a seminar in Lahore in November 2005, I predicted that India will break up into five or six different countries. This caused the Akali leaders present to walk out, betraying the interests of the Sikh Nation once again. Sikhs are willing to sit down and negotiate the borders of a free and independent Khalistan. as long as that is the sole subject for negotiation.

The Sikh Nation has a long and distinguished history of freedom and secularism. Guru Gobind Singh Sahib established the Khalsa Nation in 1699 at the historic Vaisakhi Congregation in Anandpur Sahib. This event is celebrated every April on the Sikh holiday of Vaisakhi Day. By his action, Guru Gobind Singh Sahib firmly established a distinct identity for the Khalsa Panth. He gave the Khalsa the blessing of sovereignty and independence: Ain grieh Sikhin ko deon Patshahi. 'Khalsa Bagi Yan Badshah.'

The Gurus laid down the correct way for the Sikh Nation by their example. Guru Nanak Sahib, the first Sikh Guru, confronted the atrocities of the first Mogul ruler Babar against the innocent population. Guru Arun Dev Ji Sahib became a martyr in defense of his principles and acceptance of the will of God. Guru Teg Bahadur Singh Sahib sacrificed his life in defense of the weak and other religions, defending Hindus from forced conversions. Today, it is nationalist Hindus who are carrying out forced conversions, more precisely forced reconversions of those who have converted to another religion.

The tenth and last Guru, Guru Gobind Singh Sahib, completed Guru Nanak Dev Ji Sahib's mission. He infused a new spirit into the Sikh Nation and designed a new road map for the Sikhs. He initiated the

Sacrament of Steel (khande de pahul), ordained the first five Sikhs as Singhs B the Panj Piaras, or Five Beloved Ones B and instituted the Order of the Khalsa. From then on, Guru Gobind Singh Sahib commanded the Sikhs to mark their distinct identity known through five symbols: unshorn hair, symbolizing natural and saintly appearance (worn under a turban); a special comb to keep the hair clean; a steel bracelet symbolizing discipline and gentility; the Kirpan. or sword, a symbol of courage and commitment to justice, truth, freedom, and human dignity; and special knee-length under shorts, symbolizing chastity.

In 1706 Guru Gobind Singh left this world for his heavenly abode. Just two ears later. Banda Singh Bahadur established a Sikh Raj. It lasted from 1710 until 1716. From 1716 to 1765, Sikhs went through horrible persecution by the Mogul ruler Aurang Zeb. During that period, Sikhs experienced the chhota ghalugara (small holocaust) and the wadde ghalugara (large holocaust) In 1762, one third of the Sikh population was killed in three days.

In 1765, Sikhs again established Sikh rule in several Sikh missals (free cantonal republics) as well as the principalities of Patiala, Nabha, Faridkote, Kapurthala, Jind, and Kalsia. This lasted until 1799 when Maharajah Ranjit Singh established Khalsa Raj in Punjab by uniting the missals and principalities. They marched into the capital city of Lahore and hoisted the Sikh flag, manifesting the spirit of liberty reaffirmed at the Vaisakhi of 1699. This Khalsa Raj lasted until 1849 when the British conquered the Sub-continent. This Sikh nation of Punjab was recognized by most of the Western powers of the time. The contemporary struggle to liberate the Sikh homeland, Punjab. Khalistan, is part of the same historical process.

Maharajah Ranjit Singh's rule was the Golden Age for Punjab. Sikhs destroyed Mogul rule and stopped invasions from the Afghan rulers to the west. Under the command of Hari Singh Nerwa, Sikhs defeated the Afghans and occupied Kabul. Nelwa left Kabul after securing the promise from the Afghans that they would not cross east of the Khyber Pass. Maharajah Ranjit Singh and Hari Singh Nerwa invaded Kashmir, which was part of Afghanistan. and annexed it to Punjab in 1819. India and Pakistan owe a debt of gratitude to the Sikhs, as both countries claim Kashmir as their own.

During Maharajah Ranjit Singh's rule, Hindus, Muslims, and Christians all had a share of power alongside the Sikhs. All of them were represented as ministers in his Cabinet. The Faqir brothers, who were Muslims, were trusted ministers in the inner circle of Maharajah Ranjit Singh. General Ventura, a Christian, was in charge of the artillery. The Hindu Dogras (Dhian Singh Dogra and his brother Lal Singh Dogra) wielded enormous power with Maharajah Ranjit Singh.

The Dogras betrayed the Sikhs and connived with the British in the defeat of the Sikh army.

When Hari Singh Nalwa took a lone bullet from an Afghan, he wrote his last letter in blood rather than ink to bid his last fateh to Maharajah Ranjit Singh. Nalwa had previously asked for more troops but those letters

*were intercepted by the Dogra brothers, who kept the requests to them-
selves instead of telling Maharajah Ranjit Singh. They wanted Hari Singh
Nalwa to be killed.*

*Nalwa instructed the messenger to give his letter to Maharajah Ranjit
Singh personally and to no one else. The messenger arrived early in the
morning.*

*Maharajah Ranjit Singh and Dhian Singh Dogra were out for a
morning walk. When the messenger tried to give the letter to Maharajah
Ranjit Singh, Dogra tried to intercept it. The messenger told Maharajah
Ranjit Singh that he was instructed to give the letter to him personally.
When Maharajah Ranjit Singh read the letter, he was so angry with
Dhian Sigh Dogra that he hit Dogra with his water bucket. Then he
instructed the army to get ready to march towards Afghanistan.*

*They arrived at the River Attack. It was flooded. It had overflowed its
banks. The Sikhs wanted to wait until the flood was over, but Maharajah
Ranjit Singh led his horse into the river. The water went down and the
Sikhs crossed the river. Maharajah Ranjit Singh fought the Afghans and
defeated them. That stopped the incursion of the Afghans into the Sikh
territory of Punjab.*

*After the demise of Maharajah Ranjit Singh in 1839, the British infil-
trated their agents like the Dogra brothers and others into the Sikh Raj.
Sikh rulers were murdered, one after the other. The Sikhs gave the British
a tough fight in the Anglo-Sikh wars, but the Sikhs lost the war through
the betrayal of the Dogra brothers and the British annexed Punjab in
1849.*

*The Sikh Nation's desire for sovereignty has not diminished. Sikhs
always recite the couplet 'Raj Kare Ga Khalsa' after their morning and
evening Ardas (prayers.) The Sikhs actively participated in the Indian
struggle for independence from the British. Although Sikhs were just 1.5
percent of the population, they gave over 80 percent of the sacrifices in the
freedom struggle. 2,125 Indians were executed during the freedom
struggle. Of these, more than 1,500 were Sikhs. Out of 2,645 exiled by the
British, 2,147 were Sikhs.*

*At the time of India's independence in 1947, the Hindus of India and
the Muslims of Pakistan received sovereign, independent states. Sikhs
were supposed to be a party to the arrangement and receive their own
state as well. But the Sikh leadership of the time accepted the false promise
of Jawahar Lal Nehru (reaffirmed in resolutions of the Indian National
Congress) that they would have 'the glow of freedom' in Punjab and no
law affecting Sikh rights would be passed without Sikh consent. On this
basis Sikhs took their share with India.*

*However, soon after the independence of India. the Sikhs discovered
that they had been betrayed. The Indian leaders had no intention of
giving them what they had promised. Home Minister Patel shamefully sent
out a memo describing Sikhs as a 'criminal tribe'. The repression of the
Sikh Nation began with that memo and continues to this day.*

*The time has come for Sikhs to break free of the repressive Indian re-
gime. This is the only way that their human rights will ever be respected.*

And the world is beginning to notice. In the United States Congress, the Congressional Record is serving as a vehicle to keep an accurate record of the repression and to defeat India's effort to whitewash the situation and the history of the Sikhs and other minorities. The Congressional Record carries repeated calls for a free and fair plebiscite on the independence of Khalistan and the other nations seeking their freedom from India. There are also repeated calls for a cut off of U.S. aid to India until human rights are respected. The pressure is mounting for human rights and freedom in South Asia. How soon will India collapse under the pressure? It is only a matter of time.

***

Document

CONGRESSIONAL RECORD -- EXTENSIONS

Tuesday, July 25, 2006
109th Congress, 2nd Session
152 Cong Rec E 1519

REFERENCE: Vol. 152, No. 99
SECTION: Extension of Remarks
TITLE: COUNCIL OF KHALISTAN CONDEMNS BOMB BLASTS IN
BOMBAY

Speech of
HON. EDOLPHUS TOWNS
of New York
in the House of Representatives
Tuesday, July 25, 2006

Mr. TOWNS . Mr. Speaker, the Council of Khalistan has condemned the train bombings in Bombay this week. Dr. Gurmit Singh Aulakh, President of the Council of Khalistan, whom most of us know, said that "this is a terrible incident and shameful for whoever carried it out. Terrorism is never acceptable."

The attacks have been attributed to Lashkar-e-Taiba, a Kashmiri organization. One thing you have to say about Lashkar, though: normally, they take responsibility for what they do. But as Dr. Aulakh pointed out, they have not done so in this instance and the attack fits the pattern of the kinds of attacks carried out by the Indian government and its operatives, which the Council of Khalistan details in the release. These include the Air India bombing, the many attacks on Christian groups, the Gujarat massacre, and the fact that as the Washington Times reported, India is sponsoring cross-border terrorism in Sindh. These are not the acts of a responsible democracy.

This kind of activity is the mark of a terrorist state, Mr. Speaker. If we are serious about fighting terrorism, we should stop our aid and trade with India and we should support a free and fair plebiscite in the minority nations that seek their freedom in South Asia.

Council of Khalistan Condemns Train Bombings

Washington, DC., July 12, 2006_Dr. Gurmit Singh Aulakh, President of the Council of Khalistan, today condemned the train bombings in Bombay in which 190 people were killed and over 660 were injured.

"This is a terrible incident and shameful for whoever carried it out," Dr. Aulakh said. "Terrorism is never acceptable." He endorsed the request to donate blood for the victims. "We should join together to take care of the people who were victimized by this brutal attack," he said. The Council of Khalistan leads the peaceful, democratic, nonviolent movement to liberate Khalistan, the Sikh homeland that declared its independence from India on October 7, 1987. Dr. Aulakh was interviewed on WRC-TV Channel 4 news in Washington yesterday about the bombings. Dr. Aulakh noted that the first-class cabins were bombed. "This is where the rich people hid," he said. No one has taken responsibility for the attack, although the Indian government has blamed the Kashmiri organization Lashkar-e-Taiba.

"This is the kind of thing the Indian government is quite capable of carrying out itself," Dr. Aulakh said. He noted that the book Soft Target shows how the Indian regime bombed its own airliner in 1985, killing 329 innocent people, to justify further repression against the Sikhs. The flight was bound for Bombay. The book quotes an investigator from the Canadian Security Investigation Service as saying, "If you really want to clear the incidents quickly, take vans down to the Indian High Commission and the consulates in Toronto and Vancouver, load up everybody and take them down for questioning. We know it and they know it that they are involved." The book shows that within hours after the flight was blown up, the Indian Consul General in Toronto, Surinder Malik (no relation to Ripudaman Singh Malik), called in a detailed description of the bombing and the names of those he said were involved, information that the Canadian government didn't discover until weeks later. Mr. Malik said to look on the passenger manifest for the name "L. Singh." This would turn out to be Lal Singh, who told the press that he was offered "two million dollars and settlement in a nice country" by the Indian regime to give false testimony in the case.

India fomented and pre-planned the massacre of Muslims in Gujarat, according to a police officer who was quoted in the newspapers. Government forces were caught red-handed in a village in Kashmir, trying to burn down the Gurdwara (Sikh place of worship) and some Sikh homes, to blame the Muslims. Two independent investigations, one carried out jointly by the Movement Against State Repression (MASR) and the Punjab Human Rights Organization and the other carried out by the International Human rights Organization of Ludhiana. both concluded that Indian troops carried out the massacre of 38 Sikhs in Chithlsinghpora. Both former President Bill Clinton, in his introduction to Madeleine Albright's book, and New York Times reporter Barry Bearak came to the same conclusion. The killers dressed as "militants" but spoke to each other in the language of the Indian army. This is just one of many incidents where the Indian army or its paid "Black Cats" paramilitary have been caught carrying out terrorist incidents while trying to create the impression that they were alleged "militants."

The Indian newsmagazine India Today *reported that the Indian government created the Liberation Tigers of Tamil Eelam, identified by the U.S. government as a terrorist organization. The January 2, 2002 issue of the* Washington Times *noted that India sponsors cross-border terrorism in Sindh. The Indian newspaper* Hitavada *reported that India paid the late governor of Punjab, Surendra Nath, $1.5 billion to foment and support covert state terrorism in Punjab and Kashmir.*

A report issued by MASR show that India admitted that it held 52,268 political prisoners under the repressive "Terrorist and Disruptive Activities Act" (TADA) even though it expired in 1995. Many have been in illegal custody since 1984. There has been no list published of those who were acquitted under TADA and those who are still rotting in Indian jails. Additionally, according to Amnesty International, there are tens of thousands of other minorities being held as political prisoners. The MASR report quotes the Punjab Civil Magistracy as writing "if we add up the figures of the last few years the number of innocent persons killed would run into lakhs [hundreds of thousands.]" The Indian government has murdered over 250,000 Sikhs since 1984, more than 300,000 Christians in Nagaland, over 90,000 Muslims in Kashmir, tens of thousands of Christians and Muslims throughout the country, and tens of thousands of Tamils, Assamese, Manipuris, and others. The Indian Supreme Court called the Indian government's murders of Sikhs "worse than a genocide."

Government-allied Hindu militants have burned down Christian churches and prayer halls, murdered priests, and raped nuns. The Vishwa Hindu Parishad (VHP) described the rapists as "patriotic youth" and called the nuns "antinational elements." Hindu radicals, members of the Bajrang Dal, burned missionary Graham Stewart Staines and his two sons, ages 10 and 8, to death while they surrounded the victims and chanted "Victory to Hannuman," the Hindu monkey-faced God. The Bajrang Dal is the youth arm of the RSS. The VHP is a militant Hindu Nationalist organization that is under the umbrella of the RSS.

"Only in a free Khalistan will the Sikh Nation prosper and get justice," said Dr. Aulakh. "This is the only issue. India is a terrorist state in which we will never escape from the repression and tyranny." he said. "It is time to liberate Khalistan so that the Sikh Nation can live in freedom, security, prosperity, and dignity," he said. "Remember the words of former Akal Takht Jathedar Professor Darshan Singh: 'If a Sikh is not a Khalistani he is not a Sikh.' The only way we can escape the terrorism and repression is to free Khalistan. Khalistan Zindabad."

***

Document

CONGRESSIONAL RECORD -- EXTENSIONS

Tuesday, July 25, 2006
109th Congress, 2nd Session
152 Cong Rec E 1522

REFERENCE: Vol. 152, No. 99
SECTION: Extension of Remarks
TITLE: REPRESSION IN INDIA EXPOSED

Speech of
HON. EDOLPHUS TOWNS
of New York
in the House of Representatives
Tuesday, July 25, 2006

Mr. TOWNS . Mr. Speaker, the London Institute of South Asia recently published an edition of its Journal. It included many excellent articles on the plight of minorities in India. There were articles about the Sikhs, Dalits, Muslims, and others. A writer named Tim Phares wrote a very comprehensive article on the subject that I would like to share with my colleagues.

He took note of the plight of the Sikhs, the Dalits, the Muslims, the Christians, and other minorities in India. He noted that Christians have become "the targets of choice." He noted that the Indian constitution bans the caste system but it remains in place, a vehicle of oppression of minorities. He reported that India's constitution denies people their fundamental right of self-determination. That is the essence of democracy, Mr. Speaker. I don't know how a country can call itself democratic when it denies people such a fundamental democratic right.

The article takes note of the Rashtriya Swayamsewak Sangh (RSS), formed in support of the fascist movement, publishing a booklet on how to frame Christians and other minorities in fake criminal cases. It comments on anti-conversion laws. It details some of the violence that has come about due to such laws. Shouldn't a person's religion be a fundamental freedom, Mr. Speaker?

The article notes the studies that have been done on the massacre in Chithisinghpora in which at least 35 Sikhs were murdered. It notes that they have come to the common conclusion that the Indian government's forces carried out this massacre. It notes the government's involvement in the Gujarat massacres. The article does an excellent job of detailing incident after. incident of repression against minorities in India.

Mr. Speaker, we must do what we can to support freedom throughout the world. It is time to stop our aid and trade with India until it stops being the repressive regime that it is and starts being the democracy that it says it is. We should declare our support for a free and fair plebiscite in Khalistan, Kashmir, Nagalim, and everywhere people are seeking their freedom in South Asia.

[From the Journal of the London Institute of South Asia, July 2006]
Repression in India
(By Tim Phares)

It is not safe to be a minority in India. As U.S. Congressman Dana Rohrabacher (R-Cal.) pointed out, if you're a Sikh, Muslim, Christian, or other minority, "India might as well be Nazi Germany." While democratic elections occur, they have little effects on minorities except to change the faces.

India has committed or allowed to be committed numerous actions against people (men, women and children) within its borders, actions that, if committed against Americans anywhere would be condemned by us as terrorism.

In India, the overwhelming issues are caste and religion. The caste system defines the rights that people enjoy based on a system of social stratification founded on ancestry and occupation. Unless you are born a Brahmin or other upper-caste Hindu, you are a slave in India. The term Brahmin, for all practical purposes. incorporates all the Hindu upper-castes of India. The Brahmins claim that they were are the "chosen people of God." Brahmins believe that whatever exists belongs to the Brahmin.

Under BJP rule, a new term_Hindutva_came into use that bundled all the peoples of India (except those of foreign faiths_Christians Muslims and Parsis) into the fold of Hinduism. A Cabinet member in the previous government led by BJP was open about it. He said that in India, either you must be a Hindu or you are subservient to Hinduism. Despite the fact that India's constitution bans the caste system, it remains the foundation of Hinduism and the Hindu supremacist system.

India's constitution ignores that India is many nations brought together only under foreign imperial rule and denies its peoples their right to self-determination as recognized under International Law.

The target of choice these days seems to be the Christians. Indian Christians have faced many hardships. Christians in India report that they or fellow believers have faced threats, physical attacks, and jail time for sharing their faith. Baptisms, in particular, became a significant challenge for local churches. Under the anti-conversion laws, anyone who chose to become baptized was legally obligated to seek permission from the government, as well as provide them with the name of the person performing the baptism. Fearing repercussions, many new Christians did not make this outward profession of faith until after the laws were repealed.

Human-rights organizations report that more than 300,000 Christians in Nagaland have been killed by the Indian government. In addition, tens of thousands of Christians have been killed throughout the country. Priests have been killed, nuns have been raped and forced to drink their own urine, churches have been burned, Christian schools and prayer halls have been attacked. No one is ever punished for these activities.

In 2002, the Associated Press reported an attack on a Catholic church on the outskirts of Bangalore in which several people were injured. The assailants threw stones at the church, then broke in, breaking furniture and smashing windows before attacking worshippers. The February 25, 2002 issue of the Washington Times reported another church attack in which 20 people were wounded. Earlier that month, two church workers and a teenage boy were shot at while they prayed. The boy was injured. Two Christian missionaries were beaten with iron rods while they rode their bicycles home. A Christian cemetery in Port Blair was vandalized. Indian police broke up a Christian religious festival with gunfire.

The Hindu militant Rashtriya Swaysmsewak Sangh (RSS), of which all the leaders of the BJP and its various allies and factions are members (founded in support of the Fascists in Italy), published a booklet on how to file false criminal cases against Christians and other religious minorities.

The attacks on Christians continue and the oppression of Christians that has been going on since Christmas 1998 is unabated. In fact, the atrocities have been increasing in the past year. According to Rev. Dave Stravers, President of Mission India, "There is no question that extremists are trying to instill fear in Christians. They want to make Christians afraid to assemble or share their faith." These Hindu militants accuse Christians of forcibly concerting people, then they forcibly reconvert them to Hinduism.

Several Indian states have passed laws forbidding anyone to convert to any religion other than Hinduism. These laws range from requiring a government fee for converting to forcing Dalits to appear before a magistrate and prove a level of education before converting. They often restrict the religious Speech of minority believers as those of a certain income or education level are prohibited from discussing religious matters with uneducated, poor Dalits.

On January 28, 2006, a group of Christians in Madhya Pradesh were engaged in prayer. A mob of Hindu militants stormed the hall, a private facility, and severely beat eight Christians. Five of them are still in the hospital as of this writing. The attack appears to be premeditated. The attackers burst in and knew precisely where to go. They arrived on motorbikes, broke windows, and forced the doors open.

On December 29, 2005 a landmine was planted in the Lengjen (Ngarichan) Committee Hall in Tamenglong District which is a Naga inhabited area in the state of Manipur. The land mine exploded when the children of the village went and played at the hall. One 12-year-old boy died in the hospital. Another boy's limb was ripped off and several others were seriously injured.

On November 4, 2005, a Hindu mob attacked Pastor Feroz Masih of the Believers Church of India. He was threatened with death and arson. After beating Pastor Masih, the Hindu militants told him that unless he and his 60 church members took part in a reconversion, they would be burned to death.

Australian missionary Graham Staines and his two young sons, ages 8 and 10, were burned to death while they slept in their jeep by a mob of Hindus chanting "Victory to Hannuman," a Hindu god with the face of a monkey. Staines's widow was expelled from the country, but only one person was ever brought to trial for the Staines murder.

American missionary Joseph Cooper was beaten so badly that he had to spend a week in an Indian hospital. Then he was expelled from India. No one has ever been brought to justice for Cooper's beating.

The missionaries are having a good deal of success in converting members of the lower castes, especially Dalits, also known as "Untouchables." This removes the lower-caste people from the stratification of the caste system, which is essential to the Hindu religion and its social structure. Recently, in response to the history of caste and its problems, hundreds of thousands of Indians, Dalits particularly, have turned away from Hinduism to join other religions such as Christianity, Buddhism, and Sikhism. This practice created a backlash from a sizeable portion of the Indian population.

Even though they are officially considered Hindus, the Dalits may be the most oppressed people on Earth. The 250 million lower castes include 170 million people called the Scheduled Castes (Untouchables) and 70 million people called the Tribals. Both are looked upon by upper-caste Hindus as less than human and to touch a Dalit renders a person himself "Untouchable." They are called impure, they are shunned, they are banned from Hindu Temples, and they are considered to be so low on India's social scale that they are outside of the caste system.

The Untouchable Dalits and Sudras (another low caste) make up 70 percent of the population of India. Most live in very impoverished conditions. At least half the population of India lives below the international poverty line. Forty percent live on less than two dollars per day.

A few years ago, a Dalit girl was hit across the eyes and blinded by her teacher. Her crime had been to drink from the community water pitcher. A Dalit constable took shelter in a Hindu Temple one day, only to be stoned to death by the upper-caste Hindus there. Discrimination against Dalits includes education inequality, economic disenfranchisement, religious discrimination, a poor system of medical care, and targeted violence against women. Dalit students are often denied the opportunity to receive the public education guaranteed by the Indian constitution. Rape is widespread and massively underreported.

On August 31, 2005, upper-caste villagers in the village of Gohana burned more than 60 Dalit residences, driving over 2,000 Dalit families out of Gohana. In 1998, a judge in Allahabad cleaned the courtroom with blessed water from the Ganges River because it was previously occupied by a judicial officer belonging to a Scheduled Caste.

When Dalits are walking in the presence of a Brahmin, they can be beaten or killed with impunity. Under strict interpretation of the caste system, Dalits are obligated to perform certain manual duties for upper-caste families without compensation. These duties include cleaning latrines, skinning dead animals, and crafting leather shoes, and other menial tasks.

The Sikhs are also highly victimized by the Indian government. Over 250,000 Sikhs have been killed since the military attack on the Golden

Temple in June 1984, according to the book The Politics of Genocide by Inderjit Singh Jaijee. The figures were compiled by the Punjab State Magistracy, which represents the judiciary of Punjab. A report issued by the Movement Against State Repression (MASR) showed that India admitted to holding 52,268 political prisoners. Amnesty International reports that tens of thousands of other minorities are also being held as political prisoners. How can a democracy hold political prisoners?

According to many reports, some of these political prisoners have been in custody for almost two decades. Amnesty International reported last year that tens of thousands of minorities are being held as political prisoners. These prisoners continue to be held under a law called the "Terrorist and Disruptive Activities Act" (TADA), which expired in 1995. It empowered the government to hold people virtually indefinitely for any offence or for no offence at all.

In June 2005, at the observance of the Indian government's 1984 military attack on the Golden Temple, a group of Sikhs marched, then made speeches in support of independence for Khalistan, the Sikh homeland that declared its independence on October 7, 1987, and hoisted the Sikh flag. For this they were arrested. This follows the arrest of 35 Sikhs in January 2005, when they made speeches and raised the Khalistani flag at a Republic Day event. Some of the leaders were held for 50 days without trial.

MASR also co-sponsored with the Punjab Human Rights Organization an investigation of the March 2000 massacre of 35 Sikhs in the village of Chithisinghpora in Indian Kashmir on the eve of the visit of President Clinton to India. It concluded that Indian forces carried out the massacre. The apparent intent was to make use of the presence of the world press to blame Muslims for massacre and vilify the resistance to the occupation of the state by India. A separate investigation conducted by the International Human Rights Organization came to the same conclusion. So did reporter Barry Bearak of the New York Times magazine.

Recently in the state of Uttaranchal Pradesh, Sikh farmers were forced out of their farms, which were bulldozed, and they were thrown out of the state. They received no compensation and have nowhere to go to find roof over their heads or livelihood for their families. The truth is that discrimination against and oppression of minority faiths is so widespread that it draws little attention within or outside India. Although outsiders are allowed to buy land in the Punjab, Sikhs cannot buy land in neighbouring Rajasthan and Himachal Pradesh. This discriminatory policy prevents Sikh farmers from making a living. It has impoverished them forcing many to migrate overseas.

About 50,000 Sikhs were ruthlessly killed by the Punjab Police and their bodies were secretly disposed of to hide the crime. Young Sikhs were abducted, tortured and killed in Police custody. Their bodies were then declared "unidentified" and cremated incinerating all proof of the Indian State's barbarity. Countless bodies were consigned to the canals which abound in the Punjab. The secret cremation policy was exposed by human-rights activist Jaswant Singh Khalra who was arrested for publishing his report and was murdered while in police custody.

Narinder Singh, a spokesman for the Golden Temple, the seat of the Sikh religion, was interviewed in August 1997 by National Public Radio. He told his interviewer, "The Indian government, all the time they boast that they are secular, that they are democratic. But they have nothing to do with a democracy, nothing to do with secularism. They just kill Sikhs to please the majority,"

The Indian government has murdered over 300,000 Muslims in Kashmir. They have sent over 700,000 troops to suppress the people of Kashmir.

On February 27, 2002, a fire on a train in Godhra in Gujarat killed fifty-eight passengers, among them fifteen children. This gave rise to massacres in which 2,000 to 5,000 Muslims were murdered. According to a policeman in Gujarat who was quoted in an Indian newspaper, the government pre-planned the massacre. In an eerie parallel to the Delhi massacre of Sikhs in November 1984, the police were kept from intervening.

In a 70-page report on the massacre, Human Rights Watch reported that not a single person has been convicted in these massacres. More than one hundred Muslims have been charged under India's much-criticized Prevention of Terrorism Act (POTA) for their alleged involvement in the train massacre in Godhra. No Hindus have been charged under POTA in connection with the violence against Muslims.

In Lunawade village in Panchmahal district of Kashmir, during the last week of December 2005, a mass grave was discovered. It contained the bodies of at least 26 victims of the Indian government's pogrom against the Muslims. Their crime? The Kashmiri people were promised a referendum on their status in 1948, but that vote has never been held. In 1989, when all hope of that promise being fulfilled had evaporated, violent resistance began that is being ruthlessly crushed resorting to pogroms and genocide that has led to 100,000 resistance fighters being killed by the Indian military.

The Sikhs were promised their own sovereign state by the leaders of the Congress Party (which rules India today) in exchange for their active support to the freedom movement led by it. The Sikhs have continued to press that the promise be kept. Their representatives did not sign and endorse the Indian constitution for it did not fulfill that promise. Instead of respecting "the glow of freedom" that Nehru and Patel promised to the Sikhs, the government declared them a "criminal class" as soon as the ink was dry on the constitution. It is because of betrayal of such promises that currently there are 17 freedom movements going on within India's borders.

Some Members of the U.S. Congress have called for sanctions against India and for an end to American aid. Some have also endorsed self-determination for the peoples seeking freedom from India through a plebiscite on independence. The Indian government's negotiations with the freedom fighters in predominantly Christian Nagaland have taken a turn for the worse lately, as the ceasefire there has been called off. Former Home Minister L.K. Advani said that once Kashmir achieves freedom. it will cause India to break apart. The truth is India can only survive if it conceded the right of self-determination to those areas where peoples have been betrayed. India must fulfill its promises to the people of Punjab, Khalistan (the Sikh homeland), predominantly Christian Nagaland, predominatly Muslim Kashmir, and the tribal peoples of Assam.

India clearly has a problem with its untouchables who are a majority in many states of India. It has failed to assimilate or integrate them. Since they do not belong to a single race, caste or religion, they are increasingly drawn towards Christian egalitarianism to throw off the yoke of slavery imposed by the caste system. I believe that those who ignore the oppression of the low castes and foreign faiths in India and declare India a 'natural ally' and the friendship of the 'biggest democracy' a state objective of the U.S., do not understand India at all. They help perpetuate systematic oppression and humiliation of a vast segment of humanity_700 million people_who have nothing, not even hope for anything. Even if India continues to make rapid economic rise as it is doing, this segment of humanity would be completely bypassed.

***

Document

CONGRESSIONAL RECORD -- EXTENSIONS

Tuesday, July 25, 2006
109th Congress, 2nd Session
152 Cong Rec E 1525

REFERENCE: Vol. 152, No. 99
SECTION: Extension of Remarks
TITLE: BOOK ON INDIAN FREEDOM STRUGGLE HONORED

Speech of
HON. EDOLPHUS TOWNS
of New York
in the House of Representatives
Tuesday, July 25, 2006

Mr. TOWNS . Mr. Speaker, I was interested to note that the London Institute of South Asia recently held an event to honor Professor Gurtej Singh for his interesting book Tandev of the Centaur. It expounds the theory that the Indian freedom movement was an act of collaboration with the colonialists.

As Professor Gurtej Singh says "As a part of my narration [for the book], I found myself suggesting a theory indicating the spurious nature of India's struggle for freedom. I am aware that it renders the main activities of the Congress Party and its leaders to an exercise in collaboration. But I am in good company in coming to that conclusion. Michael Edwards, in his The Myth of the Mahatma, has clearly shown that the British really feared the 'Western style revolutionaries' whom Gandhi effectively neutralized. The Administration considered Gandhi as an ally of the British as a neutralizer of rebellion."

Professor Gurtej Singh has written previously about the false nature of Indian secularism. His book, Chakravyuh: Web of Indian Secularism, exposes the truth that behind its mask of secularism, India is a repressive, theocratic state where minority rights are not respected.

Mr. Speaker, this is unacceptable. We must take strong action to protect the freedom that is the birthright of all people. Self-determination is the essence of democracy. That is why we should put the Congress on record in support of self-determination for the Sikhs of Punjab, Khalistan, the Muslim people of Kashmir, the Christians of Nagalim, and all the peoples of South Asia. We should also stop our aid and trade with India until basic human rights are respected. India is not a friendly country and it has a long record of anti-American activity. Now it wants to be our partner in fighting terrorism, while it practices terrorism and tyranny against its own people. America should not stand for that.

Seminar and Lisa Book Award_2006

London, June 26, 2006._London Institute of South Asia (lisa) Seminar on the subject of Separate Electorate was held in London on June, 24, 2006 with Dr. Gurmit Singh Aulakh, President Council of Khalistan, in the chair. Separate Electorate was introduced by the British in India in 1905 to give fair representation to all of India's many faiths and castes. Separate Electoral rolls for them provided for effective local government for decades. However, when the same was proposed under the Communal Award in 1932 for state assemblies, the high castes_who constituted only 15 per cent of India's population_saw their dominant position threatened. The Congress party started a campaign against the proposal alleging that the British were playing a game of "divide and rule". The Muslims under the leadership of Mr. Jinnah accepted "Separate Electorate" but Mr. Gandhi was able to persuade the leader of the Untouchables, Dr. Ambedkar, by starting a "fast unto death", to reject the British offer. By a deal signed with the Congress Party (Poona Pact of 1932) the Untouchables accepted Joint Electorate with the Hindus. Mr. Gandhi claimed that India was a Hindu country. With perpetual majority assured, the Hindu leadership of the Congress Party set upon the task of denying all the faith and caste identities and their fair share in power.

In the states where the Muslims were in majority, Joint Electorate suited them better but they took a principled stand for the sake of the minorities. Separate Electorate and the Muslim majority states in the East and the West being grouped into regions were the two Muslim demands. If those had been accepted there would have no partition in 1947 and all the faiths and castes would have had their fair share in power. But that meant the Hindus would have got only 15% in contrast with the Muslims who were 25% of the population and the Bahujan (i.e. native majority who are Untouchables) would have been the largest group in the parliament. The Hindus preferred partition over accepting Separate Electorate to give fair share in power to all faiths and castes. The irony is they have the temerity to blame the Muslims and Mr. Jinnah for the partition and continue to do so. The fact is that the Hindu leaders of the Congress Party forced the partition by rejecting every fair formula for sharing power. After having tricked the Untouchables into accepting Joint Electorate with them, they hoped to rule over India in perpetuity.

The Seminar was addressed by Mr. V.T. Rajshekar, Editor of Dalit Voice, Bangalore, who explained how the dominance of the Brahmin has been challenged by Bahujan. He said that by his thesis that the best way to fight discrimination is to strengthen the caste identity, has helped the castes to consolidate their vote banks to help their own kin to win elections. The result is that the Bahujan parties have won power in several states in India. The rejection of the fair system of Separate Electorate has backfired on the Brahmin. He is looking for new ways to restore its grip over power. The new method is to embrace Communism. They have organized Communist parties and groups all over India. They have captured power in West Bengal and Kerala through elections but in most other areas they operate as terrorist groups under the title of Naxalites or Maoists. The landlords in much of rural India are Thakurs_a caste one level below the Brahmin_and the farm labour is from Untouchable castes. The humiliation of the caste system piled upon exploitation by forced or unpaid labour makes rural India a hell hole. In this charged environment, the Brahmin cadres have started their Naxalite Movement. Given a gun the irate labourers shoot and kill the land lord and end up in prison or on the gallows; the Brahmin secures confirmation as "revolutionary leader". The Brahmin schemes are so complex and diabolical that it is hard to fathom the truth. But the low castes in India are waking up, says Mr. Rajshekar. They can now act wisely and devise a new polity that recognizes rather than denies the multiplicity of India's faiths, castes and states to give them their due and obtain internal harmony and peace with all the neighbours.

Three more papers were read at the Seminar. Brigadier

Dr. Aulakh in his presidential address at the end exposed the truth about India, which practises the worst form of apartheid under minority rule. The Brahmin keeps inventing new gimmicks and tricks to maintain his hold over power. He made a powerful case for a sovereign state for the Sikh nation in the Punjab which has been endorsed by the resolutions of Sarbat Khalsa and reinforced by the massacre of the Sikhs in the Punjab and other parts of India in the wake of the assault and desecration of Durbar Sahib in 1984. He supported the struggle for freedom of the people of Jammu and Kashmir, of Nagas and other peoples of Assam.

The seminar was followed by a ceremony for "Lisa Book Award" given every year to a book by an author from South Asia that has made a difference. The award in 2006 was given to "Tandev of the Centaur_Sikhs and Indian Secularism" by Professor Gurtej Singh. It was presented to him by the winner of the same award last year_Mr. V.T. Rajshekar. The citation read:

"This book shows that the 'freedom struggle' of India was in fact a struggle for succession to hegemony. The British had repeatedly said they were preparing India for self rule and would leave once the job was done. The Muslims took notice and declared that the Brahmin not the British were their main adversary. Since the Muslims were concentrated on the periphery and were sparse in numbers in the rest of India, they wanted autonomous Muslim majority regions and Separate Electorate. This would have protected the rights of all faiths and castes. They demanded Pakistan after failing in every attempt to get their due share in power by constitutional guarantees prior to Independence. The effort of the Hindu leadership was to try and build a majority around the idea of 'Secularism' and 'Joint Electorate'. Under the Poona Pact of 1932, the Bahujan compromised their identity when they agreed to be included on the electoral rolls with the Hindus.

"The Sikhs believed that the British would not leave until thrown out and thus played into the hands of the Hindus to become the vanguard of the armed struggle against the British making thus making the most sacrifices. The Sikhs were promised their separate state; that was a false promise they call 'Raj Neeti'. All those who trusted M.K. Gandhi and relied on Congress 'promises' now feel betrayed. The book reveals that India is founded on a polity of paranoia; it is united only in fear and hate. The Hindu leaders feared the Muslim and wanted the partition even more than the Muslims. After the Muslim majority left and went to Pakistan the Sikhs are seen by them as a threat. The wanton use of force against them for a decade in the wake of the assault on Durbar Sahib in 1984, the Sikh Nation virtually stands expelled from the Indian Union. A sovereign Sikh state is only a matter of time. This has become inevitable due to the clarity of vision of scholar leaders like Sirdar Gurtej Singh.

***

Document

CONGRESSIONAL RECORD -- SENATE

Friday, June 23, 2006
109th Congress, 2nd Session
152 Cong Rec E 1268

REFERENCE: Vol. 152, No. 83
SECTION: Senate
TITLE: COUNCIL OF KHALISTAN COMMEMORATES GOLDEN TEMPLE MASSACRE

Speech of
HON. EDOLPHUS TOWNS
of New York
in the House of Representatives
Thursday, June 22, 2006

Mr. TOWNS . Mr. Speaker, on June 3 Sikhs from around the East Coast gathered here in Washington to commemorate the June 1984 attack on the Golden Temple by the Indian government. That attack occurred simultaneously with attacks on 37 other Gurdwaras in what came to be known as Operation Bluestar. Operation Bluestar took the lives of over 20,000 Sikhs in Punjab.

The demonstration was organized by the Council of Khalistan, which has been leading the peaceful, nonviolent, democratic Sikh struggle for independence for almost 20 years, ever since Khalistan declared its independence from India in 1987.

Mr. Speaker, given the repression of the Sikhs and other minorities, such as Christians, Muslims, and others, I think we would do well for America to support the freedom movement in Khalistan and throughout the subcontinent. This is especially so given that India has a history of anti-American activities.

It is time to press India to pay attention to human rights by stopping our aid and trade with that country and it is time to put the Congress on record in support of self-determination. The essence of democracy is the right to self-determination.

I would like to add the Council of Khalistan's press release on its June 3 demonstration to the Record at this time.

Sikhs Commemorate Golden Temple Attack

Washington, DC, June 3, 2006._Sikhs from Philadelphia, Florida, New Jersey, Maryland, Virginia, and elsewhere on the East Coast gathered in Washington, D.C. on Saturday, June 3 to commemorate the Indian government's brutal military attack on the Golden Temple, the center and seat of the Sikh religion, and 125 other Sikh Gurdwaras throughout Punjab, in June 1984, in which over 20,000 Sikhs were murdered. They chanted slogans such as "India out of Khalistan", "Khalistan Zindabad", and others. In addition, demonstrations were held in several other cities throughout the world.

During the Golden Temple attack, young boys ages 8 to 13 were taken outside and asked if they supported Khalistan, the independent Sikh country. When they answered with the Sikh religious incantation "Bole So Nihaf," they were shot to death. The Guru Granth Sahib, the Sikh holy scriptures, written in the time of the Sikh Gurus, were shot full of bullet holes and burned by the Indian forces.

The Golden Temple attack was a brutal chapter in India's repression of the Sikhs, according to Dr. Gurmit Singh Aulakh, President of the Council of Khalistan, the government pro tempore of Khalistan, which leads the struggle for Khalistan's independence. "Sikhs cannot forgive or

*forget this atrocity against the seat of our religion by the Indian govern-
ment, said Dr. Aulakh "This brutal attack clarified that there is no place
in India for Sikhs," he said. On October 7, 1987, the Sikh Nation declared
its independence from India, naming its new country Khalistan.*

*"Sant Bhindranwale said that attacking the Golden Temple would lay
the foundation stone of Khalistan, and he was right," said Dr. Aulakh.
"Instead of crushing the Sikh movement for Khalistan, as India intended,
the attack strengthened it," he said. "The flame of freedom still burns
bright in the hearts of Sikhs despite the deployment of over half a million
Indian troops to crush it," he said.*

*A report issued by the Movement Against State Repression (MASR)
shows that India admitted that it held 52,268 political prisoners under
the repressive "Terrorist and Disruptive Activities Act" (TADA) even
though it expired in 1995. Many have been in illegal custody since 1984.
There has been no list published of those who were acquitted under TADA
and those who are still rotting in Indian jails. Additionally, according to
Amnesty International, there are tens of thousands of other minorities
being held as political prisoners. MASR report quotes the Punjab Civil
Magistracy as writing "if we add up the figures of the last few years the
number of innocent persons killed would run into lakhs [hundreds of
thousands.]" The Indian government has murdered over 250,000 Sikhs
since 1984, more than 300,000 Christians in Nagaland, over 90,000
Muslims in Kashmir, tens of thousands of Christians and Muslims
throughout the country, and tens of thousands of Tamils, Assamese,
Manipuris, and others. The Indian Supreme Court called the Indian
government's murders of Sikhs "worse than a genocide."*

*In the introduction to former Secretary of State Madeleine Albright's
new book, The Mighty and the Almighty, former U.S. President Bill
Clinton writes that "Hindu militants" are responsible for the massacre of
38 Sikhs at Chithisinghpora in March 2000. This reflects previous
findings by the Punjab Human Rights Organization, the International
Human Rights Organization, the Movement Against State Repression,
and New York Times reporter Barry Bearak. President Clinton writes,
"During my visit to India in 2000, some Hindu militants decided to vent
their outrage by murdering 38 Sikhs in cold blood. If I hadn't made the
trip, the victims would probably still be alive."*

*"Only in a free Khalistan will the Sikh Nation prosper and get jus-
tice," said Dr. Aulakh. "When Khalistan is free, we will have our own
Ambassadors, our own representation in the UN and other international
bodies, and our own leaders to keep this sort of thing from happening. We
won't be at the mercy of the brutal Indian regime and its Hindu militant
allies," he said. "Democracies don't commit genocide. India should act
like a democracy and allow a plebiscite on independence for Khalistan
and all the nations of South Asia," Dr. Aulakh said. "As Professor Darshan Singh, a former Jathedar of the Akal Takht, said, 'If a Sikh is not a
Khalistani, he is not a Sikh'," Dr. Aulakh noted. "We must continue to
pray for and work for our God-given birthright of freedom," he said.
"Without political power, religions cannot flourish and nations perish."*

***

Document

CONGRESSIONAL RECORD -- EXTENSIONS

Friday, June 23, 2006
109th Congress, 2nd Session
152 Cong Rec E 1266

REFERENCE: Vol. 152, No. 83
SECTION: Extension of Remarks
TITLE: SIKHS IN PUNJAB DEMAND INDEPENDENCE WHILE
OBSERVING ANNIVERSARY OF GOLDEN TEMPLE MASSACRE

Speech of
HON. EDOLPHUS TOWNS
of New York
in the House of Representatives
Thursday, June 22, 2006

Mr. TOWNS . Mr. Speaker, June 3 through June 6 marked the anniversary of a very dark chapter in history, the Indian government's military invasion of the Golden Temple, the seat of the Sikh religion, in 1984. That atrocity was commemorated by Sikhs and others all over the world. There were demonstrations here in Washington and in many cities.

At the Golden Temple in Amritsar they had a ceremony to commemorate the occasion. The Jathedar of the Akal Takht, Joginder Singh Vedanti, the highest Sikh religious leader, led the commemoration. During his remarks, he did not mention Saul Jamail Singh Bhindranwale, the leader of the Sikhs who was murdered at the Golden Temple, or General Shabeg Singh or any of the others who were murdered. This displeased the crowd.

The Sikhs in attendance, hundreds of them, chanted slogans of "Khalistan Zindabad," which means "Long live Khalistan," Khalistan is the Sikh homeland which declared itself independent from India on October 7, 1987. These chants show that the movement to liberate Khalistan is still alive in Punjab. Last year, there were speeches and flag-raisings on the Golden Temple anniversary. There were similar events this past January. Those events resulted in arrests and criminal complaints, even though the Indian courts have ruled that speaking out [or Khalistan is not a crime, In spite of these intimidation tactics, the Sikhs spoke out again for Khalistan.

Over 20,000 Sikhs were killed in the Golden Temple attack and the attacks on 37 other Gurdwaras around Punjab, known as Operation Bluestar. During Operation Bluestar, the Indian army shot bullet holes in the Sikh holy scriptures, the Guru Granth Sahib. Young boys were taken outside and summarily shot. The Golden Temple itself was ransacked and severely damaged. Do these sound like the acts of a democracy?

If India were truly committed to democratic values, at the very least, the Indian government would issue a public apology to the Sikhs and pay compensation to the victims' families.

The Golden Temple attacks show that there is no place for Sikhs in India, and other minorities also feel the massive repression of "the world's largest democracy." More than a quarter of a million Sikhs have been killed and over 52,000 continue to be held as political prisoners. India has killed over 300,000 Christians in Nagaland and tens of thousands more in the rest of the country, as well as more than 90,000 Kashmiri Muslims, thousands more Muslims around India, and tens of thousands of Assamese, Bodos, Manipuris, Tamils, and other minorities. For minority peoples and nations, India is one of the world's worst tyrannies. It is a democracy for the Brahmins and a police state for the minorities.

This is not acceptable, Mr. Speaker. I would like to express the sympathy of the Congress to the Sikh Nation for the Golden Temple massacre. In light of this atrocity and the ongoing atrocities of the Indian government, I wonder why the United States continues to fund such a country. The time has come, Mr. Speaker, to stop our aid and trade with India and to support self-determination for all peoples and nations in South Asia. This is the best way to bring about stability, peace, freedom, and prosperity in the subcontinent, to defuse the troubles there, and to make sure that every person's rights are protected.

Mr. Speaker, I would like to place a couple of very good articles on the chanting of Khalistan slogans at the Golden Temple into the Record for the information of my colleagues.

[From the Tribune (Chandigarh), June 7, 2006]
Radicals Raise Khalistan Slogans

Amritsar, June 6._Activists of various radical Sikh organizations raised slogans in favour of Khalistan on Ghallughara divas (genocide day) to mark the 22nd anniversary of Operation Bluestar in front of Akal Takht here today.

Mr. Parkash Singh Badal, president, SAD, distanced himself from it. As soon as Mr. Simranjit Singh Mann, president, SAD (A), came out from Akal Takht after participating in ardas, radicals started raising slogans for an independent Sikh state and showed pages containing statements in favour of Khalistan and posters displaying damaged Akal Takht in the military operation. However, Mr. Badal accused those who indulged in sloganeering of being agents of the Congress, which was responsible for the infamous Army operation. He said Mr. Mann was well aware that Punjab had to suffer greatly because of this.

Mr. Mann said though they were not allowed to continue their peaceful struggle to attain independence, they would contest the next elections democratically.

Commenting on the recent judgments and coverage in newspapers, he claimed that judges and the English media had also saffronised. He asked people to raise their hands if they wanted revival of Anandpur

Sahib's resolution of 1973 and for severing of relations with the Congress and the BJP.

Giani Joginder Singh Vedanti, Jathcdar, Akal Takht, said the real tribute to those killed in the operation would be to protect the Sikh history and culture, and to stop apostasy and addiction among the Sikh youth.

He said the Sikh religion was formed to safeguard human ideal's of truth, righteousness and values. He added at for this reason it had to fight against rulers who forgot their duties towards the masses.

Among those present on the occasion were Mr. Avtar Singh, president, SGPC, Bibi Jagir Kaur, former SGPC president, and senior Akali leaders, including Mr. Gurdev Singh Badal, Mr. Ranjit Singh Brahmpura, Mr. Sewa Singh Sekhwan, Mr. Sucha Singh Langah, Mr. Bikramjit Singh Majithia and Mr. Guljar Singh Ranike.

***

Document

CONGRESSIONAL RECORD -- EXTENSIONS

Friday, June 23, 2006
109th Congress, 2nd Session
152 Cong Rec E 1267

REFERENCE: Vol. 152, No. 83
SECTION: Extension of Remarks
TITLE: ARTICLE EXPOSES REPRESSION OF SIKHS BY INDIA

Speech of
HON. EDOLPHUS TOWNS
of New York
in the House of Representatives
Thursday, June 22, 2006

Mr. TOWNS . Mr. Speaker, a good article appeared in the Argus of Fremont, California on repression of the Sikhs in India. Fremont has a large Sikh population and the article appeared earlier this month in conjunction with the commemoration of the Indian government's June 1984 attack on the Golden Temple, the most sacred Sikh shrine.

The article points out that the abuse at Abu Ghbraib which embarrassed all of us, was a lesser offense than what India did to its Sikh population in June 1984 when it attacked the Golden Temple and 37 other Gurdwaras in Punjab.

The article quotes a Sikh named Jasdeep Singh as saying that "We would have said that was nothing" referring to Abu Ghraib.

Now, Mr. Speaker, since we know how atrocious the Abu Ghraib incidents are, that gives us an indication of the carnage that was inflicted on the Sikh Nation by the Indian regime in June 1984.

The article also discusses the Sikhs' desire for an independent, sovereign Khalistan, which declared its independence from India in 1987. This has been met with many years of bloody repression, including the murders of over 250,000 Sikhs and over 52,000 who are held as political prisoners in "the world's largest democracy."

Mr. Speaker, the time has come to demand self-determination and full human rights for all people in South Asia. We should stop our aid and trade with India and we should demand a free and fair plebiscite not only on the status of Khalistan, but of Kashmir (as India promised in 1948), of Nagalim, and all the nations seeking their freedom in that troubled region. It would be good for the freedom, prosperity, and stability of all concerned.

I would like to insert the Argus article into the Record at this time.

[From the Argus, June 5, 2006]
Fremont Sikhs Recall Oppression
(By Matthew Artz)

Fremont._Jasdeep Singh couldn't help but laugh at the uproar over the torture of prisoners at Abu Ghraib.

"We would have said that was nothing," said Singh, who moved to Fremont in 1992, he said, after Indian authorities detained and tortured him three times because he is Sikh.

Sikh nationalism barely a blip on the international radar, was front and center Sunday at the Fremont Gurdwara Sahib, the local Sikh house of worship, where community leaders reaffirmed support for transforming the Indian state of Punjab into a secular Sikh-majority state of Khalistan.

"We know from our history that Sikhs will never be safe or truly free unless they have a homeland of their own," Singh said.

For the estimated 150,000 Sikhs living in the Bay Area, Tuesday marks the anniversary of two of the most devastating and seminal events in the history of the 500-year-old faith.

In 1984, with Sikhs pressing for an independent Punjab, where they are a majority, the Indian government invaded the Golden Temple_Sikhism's holiest place_and 36 other religious sites where separatists were hiding, killing thousands. The attack came on the 378th anniversary of the torture and death of a Sikh religious leader.

Four months later, when Prime Minister Indira Ghandi was murdered by two of her Sikh bodyguards, rioters murdered thousands more Sikhs, who are easy to identify because the men wore turbans and grow long beards.

The bloodbath and ensuring eight years of repression drove many Sikhs to North America.

Now, 7,500 miles from their ancestral land, leaders of the Fremont gurdwara won't let their brethren forget about what transpired in India.

Photographs of 73 Sikhs murdered by Indian authorities in 1984, including the two men who killed the prime minister, ring the gurdwara's dining room.

On Sunday, the gurdwara installed an exhibit about their faith that included photographs of Sikh men being burned alive or beaten by Indian soldiers. Other pictures commemorated the 400th anniversary of the torture and murder of Guru Arjan Dev Ji, who refused to remove references to Islam and Hinduism from the Sikh's holy book.

"We're trying to make people aware," said Ram Singh, a gurdwara leader who plans to protest outside the Indian Consulate in San Francisco tomorrow. "We don't want our future generations to forget what happened to us."

Jasdeep Singh, an engineer, won't forget the day in 1989 when soldiers raided his graduate school boarding house and detained all the Sikhs in an effort to gain intelligence on separatist leaders.

"First the clothes came off," he said. Later, guards tied his hands behind his back and hung him from the ceiling. "These two shoulders," he said, "felt like they were going to pop out."

Since Singh arrived in Fremont, persecution of Sikhs in India has decreased and the governing Congress Party named a Sikh, Mammohan Singh, to serve as prime minister.

Years of repression followed by some reforms have stifled the independence movement in Punjab and left Sikhs in the Bay Area divided over the nationalist cause, said Ram Singh, who favors an independent Khalistan.

"It's not that simple," said Balraj Gil as he peered at the pictures of torture. "You can't just get an independent state."

***

Document

CONGRESSIONAL RECORD -- EXTENSIONS

Friday, June 16, 2006
109th Congress, 2nd Session
152 Cong Rec E 1178

REFERENCE: Vol. 152, No. 78
SECTION: Extension of Remarks
TITLE: SIKH, CATHOLIC LEADERS MEET

Speech of
HON. EDOLPHUS TOWNS
of New York
in the House of Representatives
Thursday, June 15, 2006

Mr. TOWNS . Mr. Speaker, recently a group of Sikh leaders met in New York with Catholic leaders in an all-day event hosted by an Interfaith organization. Sikh leaders in attendance included Dr. Manohar

Singh, Dr. Tarunjit Singh Butalia, and Dr. Anahat Kaur Sandhu. Monsignor Felix Machado, an official at the Vatican, also attended the meeting.

It is good to see this kind of pluralistic cooperation and I thank Dr. Gurmit Singh Aulakh, President of the Council of Khalistan, for bringing it to my attention.

Contrast this to the situation in India, where Sikhs, Christian, Muslims, and other minorities are subject to brutal and ongoing repression from the government. Perhaps "the world's largest democracy" could learn a thing or two from the meeting in New York.

We should stop our aid to India and we should demand self-determination for all the people of South Asia so that they can live in peace, freedom, harmony, and prosperity, as they do here in America and other Western democracies.

Mr. Speaker, I would like to put the article from India-West into the Record.

[From India-West, June 2, 2006]
Sikh, Catholic Leaders Meet In New York
(By a Staff Reporter)

Representatives of the World Sikh Council-America Region met with Catholic leaders in New York in an all-day event hosted by the Religions for Peace-USA. the Sikh group has said.

Dr. Manohar Singh, the group's chairperson, and Dr. Tarunjit Singh, chair of the group's Interfaith Committee, led the Sikhs.

The U.S. Catholic Conference of Bishops' delegation was headed by Rev. James Massa, executive director of its Secretariat for Ecumenical and Interfaith Affairs.

Monsignor Felix Machado, undersecretary of the Pontifical Council for Inter-religious Dialogue at the Vatican in Rome, was a special guest and adviser.

Two observers of Religions for Peace attended the May 20 meeting.

"The universal message of Sikhism respects pluralism and we welcome our Catholic friends with open arms," Manohar Singh said. "This dialogue is an opportunity for our communities to begin a conversation at the highest level on how we may be able to work with each other in trust and friendship to make this world a more peaceful and just place for all."

Machado responded by saying the Catholic Church appreciates this dialogue with the Sikh community. "Sikhs respect us, not suspect us," he said.

Sikh and Catholic leaders expressed shared concerns over the challenges faced by immigrant communities in the U.S., the curtailment of religious freedom and human rights in South Asia, and the challenges of secularism to both religious communities.

The participants said they would meet again this year with a focus on "Divinity, Humanity and Creation." They also pledged to continue to meet at least once a year through a working committee.

After the meeting, the Catholic and Sikh participants visited the Mata Sahib Kaur Gurdwara Sahib in Glen Cove, N.Y., joined the evening service and partook of langar meal.

***

Document

CONGRESSIONAL RECORD -- EXTENSIONS

Tuesday, June 06, 2006
109th Congress, 2nd Session
152 Cong Rec E 1022

REFERENCE: Vol. 152, No. 70
SECTION: Extension of Remarks
TITLE: HINDU MILITANTS MURDERED 38 SIKHS IN COLD BLOOD

Speech of
HON. EDOLPHUS TOWNS
of New York
in the House of Representatives
Tuesday, June 6, 2006

Mr. TOWNS . Mr. Speaker, recently, former Secretary of State Madeleine Albright wrote a book called The Mighty and the Almighty. The introduction was written by former President Bill Clinton. In his introduction, President Clinton wrote, "During my visit to India in 2000, some Hindu militants decided to vent their outrage by murdering 38 Sikhs in cold blood. If I hadn't made the trip, the victims would probably still be alive. If I hadn't made the trip because I feared what militants might do, I couldn't have done my job as president of the United States."

President Clinton places the blame squarely on Hindu militants, not on the so-called Kashmiri Muslims that the Indian government tried to blame for the massacre. In 2002, the Washington Times reported that the government finally admitted its responsibility and admitted that the evidence that it used to pin the blame on Kashmiris was false.

Reporter Barry Bearak of the New York Times also placed the blame squarely on the Indian government, as did two independent investigations, one by the International Human Rights Organization, which is based in Ludhiana, and the other conducted jointly by the Punjab Human Rights Organization and the Movement Against State Repression. The evidence is overwhelming, yet Indian sycophants continue to deny the government's responsibility.

Unfortunately, this massacre would have been swept under the rug if not for the outstanding efforts of the organizations mentioned above and of the Council of Khalistan, which has painstakingly documented any new developments. I am indebted to them for bringing this to my attention.

The massacre was part of a pattern of repression of minorities that has brought about the murders of over 250,000 Sikhs, more than 300,000 Christians in Nagaland alone, over 90,000 Muslims in Kashmir alone, and Christians and Muslims throughout the country, as well as tens of thousands of Assamese, Bodos, Dalits, Manipuris, Tamils, and other minorities. This is one reason that it is essential to cut off our aid and trade to India and to demand a free and fair plebiscite in Punjab, Khalistan, in Kashmir, in Nagalim, and wherever people are seeking their freedom. This is the only way to bring freedom, peace, stability, and dignity to all the people of south Asia.

I would like to introduce the press release from the Council of Khalistan on Secretary Albright's book into the Record at this time.

"Hindu Militants Murdered 38 Sikhs in Cold Blood"

Washington, DC, May 30, 2006. In the introduction to former Secretary of State Madeleine Albright's new book, The Mighty and the Almighty, former U.S. President Bill Clinton writes that "Hindu militants" are responsible for the massacre of 38 Sikhs at Chithisinghpora in March 2000. This reflects previous findings by the Punjab Human Rights Organization, the International Human Rights Organization, the Movement Against State Repression, and New York Times reporter Barry Bearak.

President Clinton writes, "During my visit to India in 2000, some Hindu militants decided to vent their outrage by murdering 38 Sikhs in cold blood. If I hadn't made the trip, the victims would probably still be alive, If I hadn't made the trip because I feared what militants might do, I couldn't have done my job as president of the United States."

According to Amnesty International, "the attackers wore uniforms of the armed forces and were led by a tall man whom they addressed as Commanding Officer (CO). All Sikh men were rounded up, ostensibly to check their identities, and made to sit on the ground in two groups against the walls of the gurdwaras [Sikh Temples] a few hundred metres from each other; they were shot at point blank range. As the attackers withdrew, they reportedly shouted Hindu slogans." On August 2, 2002, the Washington Times reported that the Indian government admitted that its forces were responsible for the massacre. India finally admitted that the evidence it used to implicate alleged Kashmiri "militants" in the murders was faked.

At the time of the Chithisinghpora massacre, Dr. Gurmit Singh Aulakh, President of the Council of Khalistan, strongly condemned the murders. "What motive would Kashmiri freedom fighters have to kill Sikhs? This would be especially stupid when President Clinton is visiting. The freedom movements in Kashmir, Khalistan, Nagaland, and throughout India need the support of the United States," he said, Khalistan is the Sikh homeland declared independent on October 7, 1987.

The massacres continued a pattern of repression and terrorism against minorities by the Indian government, which it attempts to blame on other minorities to divide and rule the minority peoples within its *artificial borders. The Indian newspaper Hitavada reported that the Indian government paid the late governor of Punjab, Surendra Nath, $1.5 billion to organize and support covert terrorist activity in Punjab, Khalistan, and in neighboring Kashmir.*

A report issued by the Movement Against State Repression (MASR) shows that India admitted that it held 52,268 political prisoners under the repressive "Terrorist and Disruptive Activities Act" (TADA) even though it expired in 1995. Many have been in illegal custody since 1984. There has been no list published of those who were acquitted under TADA and those who are still rotting in Indian jails. Additionally, according to Amnesty International, there are tens of thousands of other minorities being held as political prisoners. MASR report quotes the Punjab Civil Magistracy as writing "if we add up the figures of the last few years the number of innocent persons killed would run into lakhs [hundreds of thousands.]"

The Indian government has murdered over 250,000 Sikhs since 1984, more than 300,000 Christians in Nagaland, over 90,000 Muslims in Kashmir, tens of thousands of Christians and Muslims throughout the country, and tens of thousands of Tamils, Assamese, Manipuris, and others. The Indian Supreme Court called the Indian government's murders of Sikhs "worse than a genocide."

The book Soft Target by Canadian journalists Zuhair Kashmeri and Brian McAndrew shows that the Indian government blew up its own airliner in 1985 to blame Sikhs and justify further repression. It quotes an agent of the Canadian Security Investigation Service. (CSIS) as saying, "If you really want to clear up the incidents quickly, take vans down to the Indian High Commission and the consulates in Toronto and Vancouver. We know it and they know it that they are involved." On January 2, 2002, the Washington Times reported that India sponsors cross-border terrorism in the Pakistani province of Sindh.

"Only in a free Khalistan will the Sikh Nation prosper and get justice," said Dr. Aulakh. "When Khalistan is free, we will have our own Ambassadors, our own representation in the UN and other international bodies, and our own leaders to keep this sort of thing from happening. We won't be at the mercy of the brutal Indian regime and its Hindu militant allies," he said. "Democracies don't commit genocide. India should act like a democracy and allow a plebiscite on independence for Khalistan and all the nations of South Asia," Dr. Aulakh said. "We must free Khalistan now."

***

Document

CONGRESSIONAL RECORD -- EXTENSIONS

Wednesday, April 26, 2006
109th Congress, 2nd Session
152 Cong Rec E 620

REFERENCE: Vol. 152, No. 47
SECTION: Extension of Remarks
TITLE: SIKH ACTIVIST ARRESTED FOR MAKING SPEECH_BETRAYAL OF
DEMOCRATIC PRINCIPLE OF FREEDOM OF SPEECH

Speech of
HON. EDOLPHUS TOWNS
of New York
in the House of Representatives
Wednesday, April 26, 2006

Mr. TOWNS . Mr. Speaker, I was distressed to note that on April 20, Sikh activist Daljit Singh Bittu was arrested after making a speech. He was charged with sedition and "making inflammatory speeches." Mr. Bittu spoke out against the acquisition of the land of poor farmers by Punjab on behalf of private business firms. We have had cases in this country where the government has taken land by eminent domain for private usage, Mr. Speaker, and no one ever gets arrested for speaking out against it. Radio and television commentators across the spectrum have opposed this and they are still on the air. Yet in India, speaking out against this can now get you arrested.

Mr. Bittu is a proponent of freedom for Khalistan, the Sikh homeland that declared its independence from India on October 7, 1987. Recently, Dr. Jagjit Singh Chohan, another Sikh activist, was arrested for predicting on television that Khalistan will be free by 2007. All he did was make a prediction. Is that a crime? If that is a crime, then the jails will overflow with sportscasters, weather reporters, psychics, and others who predict things routinely.

In addition, leaders of Dal Khalsa have been arrested for holding marches, making speeches, and raising a flag. A former member of Parliament was also arrested. It looks like the late General Narinder Singh was right when he said that "Punjab is a police state."

This is unacceptable, Mr. Speaker, especially as the United States and India move towards greater cooperation in numerous endeavors. We must insist on the full expression of democracy and basic human rights there if we are going to do business with India as a normal member of the family of free nations. And the essence of democracy is the right to self-determination.

The time has come to stop our aid and trade with India until it stops arresting people for making speeches, raising flags, and holding marches. The time has come for the U.S. Congress to put itself on record in support of freedom and self-determination for all the nations of South Asia. In 1948, India promised a free and fair plebiscite on the status of Kashmir. No such vote has ever been held in "the world's largest democracy." Why don't we insist on a simple democratic vote, with monitors, in Kashmir, in Punjab, Khalistan, in predominantly Christian Nagalim, and wherever people seek their freedom from India? As long as we turn a blind eye to the repression, the repression will continue. We must be the ones to strike a blow for freedom. Only when all people in the subcontinent enjoy freedom fully will there be stability and peace there.

Mr. Speaker, the Council of Khalistan recently published a press release on the arrest of Daljit Singh Bittu. I would like to place it in the Record at this time.

Daljit Singh Bittu Arrested for Making Speech
Where Is Freedom of Speech in India?

Washington, DC., April 26, 2006._Indian police arrested Daljit Singh Bittu. leader of the Shiromani Khalsa Dal, on charges of sedition and "delivering inflammatory speeches" at Fatehgarh Channa. Sardar Bittu was arrested on April 21 from his home in Ludhiana. He was held by the police, who sought "foreign currency" and a CD of his speeches.

"Where is the freedom of speech in India?" asked Dr. Gurmit Singh Aulakh, President of the Council of Khalistan. "How can a democratic state arrest people for making speeches? This shows us again that there is no place for Sikhs in India."

India proudly bills itself as "the world's largest democracy" and its constitution guarantees freedom of speech. But the arrest of Sardar Bittu is the latest incident in which people have been arrested for making speeches, holding marches, or raising a flag. "The drive for freedom is alive and strong in Punjab," he said. "What kind of democracy arrests people for demanding freedom?" asked Dr. Aulakh.

Leaders of Dal Khalsa have been arrested for sponsoring marches in Punjab in support of a free Khalistan, the Sikh homeland that declared its independence from India on October 7, 1987. In addition, Dr. Jagjit Singh Chohan was arrested for making a statement in which he made the prediction that Khalistan will be free by 2007. "Since when is making a prediction a crime in India?" Dr. Aulakh asked. "Will the weathermen in Delhi now be arrested for predicting rain?"

"The time is now to begin a Shantmai Morcha to liberate Khalistan," said Dr. Aulakh. "India is showing its weakness with these arrests," he said. "As Professor Darshan Singh, a former Jathedar of the Akal Takht Sahib, said, 'If a Sikh is not for Khalistan, he is not a Sikh.'" Every day in prayer Sikhs recite "Raj Kare Ga Khalsa," which means "The khalsa shall rule."

The Indian government has murdered over 250,000 Sikhs since 1984, more than 300,000 Christians since 1948 as well as tens of thousands of Christians throughout the country, over 90,000 Muslims in Kashmir since 1988, 2,000 to 5,000 Muslims in Gujarat, tens of thousands of Muslims elsewhere in India, and tens of thousands of Assamese, Bodos, Dalits, Manipuris, Tamils, and others. An Indian newspaper reported that the police in Gujarat were ordered to stand aside in that massacre and not to get involved, a frightening parallel to the Delhi massacre of Sikhs in 1984. The Indian Supreme Court called the Indian government's murders of Sikhs "worse than a genocide."

Indian police arrested human-rights activist Jaswant Singh Khalra after he exposed their policy of mass cremation of Sikhs, in which over

50,000 Sikhs have been arrested, tortured, and murdered, then their bodies were declared unidentified and secretly cremated. He was murdered in police custody. His body was not given to his family. The police never released the body of former Jathedar of the Akal Takht S. Gurdev Singh Kaunke after SSP Swaran Singh Ghotna murdered him. No one has been brought to justice for the Khalra kidnapping and murder or for the murder of Jathedar Kaunke. Yet according to a report by the Movement Against State Repression (MASR), 52,268 Sikhs are being held as political prisoners in India without charge or trial, some since 1984!

Recently, a new wave of violence has erupted against Christian churches. States are enacting laws prohibiting Hindus from converting to any other religion. Missionary Graham Staines was murdered along with his two sons, ages 8 and 10, by a mob of militant, fundamentalist Hindu nationalists who set fire to the jeep, surrounded it, and chanted "Victory to Hannuman," a Hindu god. None of the people involved has been tried. The persons who have murdered priests, raped nuns, and burned Christian churches have not been charged or tried. The murderers of 2,000 to 5,000 Muslims in Gujarat have never been brought to trial.

"Only in a free Khalistan will the Sikh Nation prosper and get justice," said Dr. Aulakh. "India's illegal occupation of our homeland, Khalistan, must end," he said: "India should act like a democracy and allow a free and fair plebiscite on independence for all the nations of South Asia," Dr. Aulakh said. "We must free Khalistan now."

Sikhs Celebrating 307th Anniversary of Revelation of Khalsa Nation by Guru Gobind Singh Sahib

Washington, D.C., April 26, 2006._Sikhs all over the world have been celebrating Vaisakhi Day, the anniversary of the revelation of the Khalsa Panth by Guru Gobind Singh in 1699. There have been parades in Washington, D.C., Vancouver, Stockton, Seattle, London, and may other cities. There will be an annual Sikh Day parade in New York on April 29. Dr. Gurmit Singh Aulakh, President of the Council of Khalistan, will be speaking at the New York parade. In previous years, Dr. Aulakh's speeches have been punctuated by chants of "Khalistan Zindabad."

Vaisakhi Day is one of the most joyous days in the Sikh calendar. celebrating the emergence of the Khalsa Panth as a distinct people. Sikhs have been celebrating with devotion and reverence. Guru Gobind Singh proclaimed the sovereignty of the Sikh Nation: "In grieb Sikhin ko deon patshahi." Every morning and evening Sikhs recite "Raj Kare Ga Khalsa," meaning "the Khalsa shall rule," and "Khalsa Bagi Yan Badshah," meaning "either the Khalsa is in rebellion or the ruler." Sovereignty is the birthright of all people, and it is the heritage of the Sikh nation. As former Akal Takht Jathedar Professor Darshan Singh has said, "If a Sikh is not a Khalistani, he is not a Sikh."

"We must remind ourselves of our heritage by raising slogans of 'Khalistan Zindabad' and beginning a Shantmai Morcha to liberate our homeland, Khalistan," said Dr. Aulakh. "Whoever is honest and dedicated in leading that Shantmal Morcha deserves our support."

India is stepping up its efforts to repress the Sikh Nation's demand for freedom. Recently, Sardar Daljit Singh Bittu, leader of the Shiromani Khalsa Dal, was arrested for making a speech. Sikh activist Dr. Jagjit Singh Chohan was arrested after he said on India's Zee TV that Khalistan will be free by 2007. Leaders of Dal Khalsa have been arrested for leading marches, making speeches, and raising the Khalistani flag. In January, Sikh farmers were expelled from Ultaranchal Pradesh and their land was seized. They were beaten up by the police. Their homes were bulldozed by paratroopers. Their homes in many cases were built using their life savings and by their own hands.

"It is evident that the Indian government is scared of the increasing amount of peaceful activism in Punjab in support of Khalistan," said Dr. Aulakh. "The Ume of Khalistan's liberation is near. India will fall apart soon," he said. "This office has worked unwaveringly for a sovereign Khalistan for over 20 years," he noted.

History shows that multinational states such as India are doomed to failure. Countries like Austria-Hungary, India's longtime friend the Soviet Union, Yugoslavia, Czechoslovakia, and others prove this point. India is not one country; it is a polyglot like those countries, thrown together for the convenience of the British colonialists. It is doomed to break up as they did. "We only hope that the breakup will be peaceful like that of Czechoslovakia and not violent like that of Yugoslavia," said Dr. Aulakh.

The Indian government has murdered over 250,000 Sikhs since 1984, more than 300,000 Christians in Nagaland, over 90,000 Muslims in Kashmir, tens of thousands of Christians and Muslims throughout the country, and tens of thousands of Tamils, Assamese, Manipuris, and others. The Indian Supreme Court called the Indian government's murders of Sikhs "worse than a genocide."

Indian police arrested human-rights activist Jaswant Singh Khalra after he exposed their policy of mass cremation of Sikhs, in which over 50,000 Sikhs have been arrested, tortured, and murdered, then their bodies were declared unidentified and secretly cremated. He was murdered in police custody. His body was not given to his family. The police never released the body of former Jathedar of the Akal Takht S. Gurdev Singh Kaunke after SSP Swaran Singh Ghotna murdered him. No one has been brought to justice for the Khalra kidnapping and murder. Yet according to a report by the Movement Against State Repression (MASR), 52,268 Sikhs are being held as political prisoners in India without charge or trial, some since 1984!

"Only in a free Khalistan will the Sikh Nation prosper and get justice," said Dr. Aulakh. "India's illegal occupation of our homeland. Khalistan, must end," he said. "India should act like a democracy and allow a free and fair plebiscite on independence for all the nations of South Asia," Dr. Aulakh said. "We must free Khalistan now."

***

Document

CONGRESSIONAL RECORD -- EXTENSIONS

Wednesday, April 26, 2006
109th Congress, 2nd Session
152 Cong Rec E 622

REFERENCE: Vol. 152, No. 47
SECTION: Extension of Remarks
TITLE: SIKHS CELEBRATE VAISAKHI, REVELATION OF SIKH NATION

Speech of
HON. EDOLPHUS TOWNS
of New York
in the House of Representatives
Wednesday, April 26, 2006

Mr. TOWNS . Mr. Speaker, I would like to congratulate the Sikhs on celebrating their important holiday, Vaisakhi Day, around the world. There were marches in Washington, Vancouver, London, and many other cities around the world. There will be a parade April 29 in New York, the annual Sikh Day event.

Vaisakhi Day marks the revelation of the Sikh Nation as a distinct entity by guru Gobind Singh in 1699. At that time, he proclaimed the Sihks sovereign. Today, Sikhs struggle to reclaim this lost birthright as Indian troops occupy their country, Khalistan. As you know, Mr. Speaker, the Sikhs declared themselves independent in 1987, but Indian troops to the tune of half a million continue to occupy Khalistan.

Recently, several Sikh activists have been anested for simply making speeches, raising flags, or holding peaceful marches in support of Khalistan. Is this democracy, Mr. Speaker? Is this how a free country conducts itself?

Mr. Speaker, without the most basic freedoms, such as freedom of speech and self determination, how can the Sikhs hope to survive as a people? In India, it is now iilegal in many parts of the country to join another religion besides Hinduism. The intent to establish a Hindu state is clear.

We can help put an end to these practices as we congratulate the Sikhs on Vaisakhi Day. We must cut off our aid and our trade with India. Although there is a burgeoning middle class, half the country lives under the international poverty line. Losing our dollars would have a significant effect on India. And we must stand up for the principles on which America was founded.

About the same time in the calendar as Vaisakhi Day is the birthday of Thomas Jefferson, who wrote that government is legitimately founded on "the consent of the governed" and that "whenever any form of government becomes destructive of these ends, it is the right of the people to alter or to abolish it and to institute new government, laying its foundation on such principles and organizing its powers in such form, as to them shall seem most likely to effect their safety and happiness."

Clearly, that time has come for too many of the minorities of South Asia_the Sikhs of Khalistan, the Muslims in Kashmir, the predominantly Christian Naga community, and so many others. Let us help them to achieve the basic right of self-determination by putting our Congress on record in support of a free and fair plebiscite in these places on the question of independence. By doing so, we will be helping to achieve freedom, stability, peace, dignity, and prosperity for all the peoples and nations of South Asia.

Mr. Speaker, I request the permission of the House to add the Council of Khalistan's press release and open letter on Vaisakhi to the Record at this time.

Sikhs Will Celebrate Vaisakhi Day April 14

Happy Vaisakhi Day to you and your family and the Khalsa Panth. On April 14, the Sikh Nation will be observing the 307th anniversary of the day Guru Gobind Singh established the Khalsa Panth. The Guru granted sovereignty to the Sikh Nation, saying "In Grieb Sikhin Ko Deon Patshahi." We must remind ourselves of our heritage by raising slogans of "Khalistan Zindabad" and beginning a Shantmai Morcha to liberate our homeland, Khalistan. Whoever is honest and dedicated in leading that Shantmai Morcha deserves our support. Every morning and evening we recite, "Raj Kare Ga Khalsa." Now is the time to act on it. Do we mean what we say every morning and evening?

The flame of freedom continues to burn brightly in the heart of the Sikh Nation. No force can suppress it. Within the past few days, Dal Khalsa and the Shiromani Khalsa Dal announced that they are uniting for sovereignty for Khalistan. This was met with chants of "Khalistan Zindabad." Chief Minister Amarinder Singh, whose own Legislative Assembly proclaimed the sovereignty of Punjab when he cancelled the water agreements, has ordered the leaders of Dal Khalsa and the Shiromani Khalsa Dal placed under police watch for their speeches. Kanwarpal Singh Dhami of the Guru Asra Trust, and Dr. Jagjit Singh Chohan were arrested this month for making speeches in support of Khalistan. Dr. Chohan said, "Khalistan will be free." In January of last year and again in June of last year Sikh activists, mostly from Dal Khalsa, were arrested merely for raising the Khalistani flag and making pro-Khalistan speeches. During his recent visit to India, President George W. Bush walked over to Sukhbir Singh Badal and said, "Give my best wishes and regards to your people from the people of America." Even the President of the United States is aware of our situation. "I wish you could visit Punjab," said Sukhbir Singh. When Khalistan is free, that will happen. President Bush has said, "Freedom is the birthright of every man, woman, and child." These events show that the movement to free our homeland is on the rise. It has gotten the attention of the world. The movement to liberate our homeland is stronger than it has ever been and it has frightened the Indian regime. Now is the time to rededicate ourselves to the liberation of Khalistan.

The Indian government is reacting to the rising tide of freedom for the Sikh Nation. Earlier this year, Prime Minister Manmohan Singh apologized to the Sikh Nation for the Delhi massacres of November 1984 that killed over 20,000 Sikhs. It is good that he apologized and it clearly shows India's responsibility, but what good does it do the Sikh Nation? Where are the apologies for the Golden Temple attack and the other atrocities? Where is the compensation for the victims' families?

In January, Sikh farmers were expelled from Uttaranchal Pradesh and their land was seized. They were beaten up by the police. Their homes were bulldozed by paratroopers. Their homes in many cases were built using their life savings and by their own hands. We condemn this act of state terrorism by the government of Uttaranchal Pradesh. As you know, Sikhs are prohibited from buying land in Rajasthan and Himachal Pradesh. Now Uttaranchal Pradesh joins that list. Yet there are no restrictions on land ownership in Punjab by non-Sikhs. People from anywhere can buy land in Punjab, including people from Rajasthan and Himachal Pradesh. India is trying to subvert Khalistan's independence by overrunning Punjab with non-Sikhs while keeping Sikhs from escaping the brutal repression in Punjab. It is incumbent on the Sikh diaspora to free Khalistan. We must redouble our efforts. That is the only way to keep these atrocities from continuing and to protect the Sikh Nation and the Sikh religion.

Any organization that sincerely supports Kalistan deserves the support of the Sikh Nation. However, the Sikh Nation needs leadership that is honest, sincere, consistent, and dedicated to the cause of Sikh freedom. But we should only support sincere, dedicated, honest leaders. Dal Khalsa deserves the praise of the Sikh nation and I call on every Sikh to support them and every other organization that is working to liberate Khalistan.

The Council of Khalistan has stood strongly and consistently for liberating our homeland, Khalistan, from Indian occupation. For over 18 years we have led this fight while others were trying to divert the resources and the attention of the Sikh Nation away from the issue of freedom in a sovereign, independent Khalistan. Yet Khalistan is the only way that Sikhs will be able to live in freedom, peace, prosperity, and dignity.

The Sikhs in Punjab have suffered enormous repression at the hands of the Indian regime in the last 22 years. The Indian government has murdered over 250,000 Sikhs since 1984. Inderjit Singh Jaijee and Bibi Baljit Kaur of the Movement Against State Repression (MASR) told me that if the Sikhs outside India had not exposed the atrocities of the Indian regime, they could have killed ten times as many Sikhs. Another 52,268 of our brothers and sisters are being held as political prisoners, according to MASR. Some have been in illegal custody since 1984! Over 50,000 Sikh youth were picked up from their houses, tortured, murdered in police custody, then secretly cremated as "unidentified bodies." Their remains were never even given to their families! How can Sikhs have any freedom living under a government that would do these things? India should be ashamed of the genocide it has committed against Sikhs, Christians, Muslims, and other minorities.

Sikhs can never forgive or forget the Indian government's military attack on the Golden Temple and 39 other historic Gurdwaras throughout Punjab. Over 20,000 Sikhs were murdered in those attacks, known as Operation Bluestar, including Sant Jarnail Singh Bhindranwale, General Shabeg Singh. Bhai Amrik Singh, and over 100 Sikh religious students ages 8-13 who were taken out into the courtyard and shot. These attacks accelerated the Sikh independence movement and deepened the desire for independence in the hearts of Sikhs, a fire that burns brightly in the hearts of the Sikh Nation to this day.

The Akali Dal conspired with the Indian government in 1984 to invade the Golden Temple to murder Sant Bhindranwale and 20,000 other Sikhs during June 1984 in Punjab. Among those who conspired with the government, according to Chakravyuh: Web of Indian Secularism, were Dr. Chohan, Ganga Singh Dhillon, and Didar Singh Bains. It appears the Indian regime is even willing to arrest its own agents to suppress the movement for Khalistan! Now Badal and Chief Minister Amarinder Singh have been accusing each other of being tied in with "terrorists." These leaders view support for Khalistan as terrorism, as the Indian government does. They have shown where their loyalties lie. How will these so-called Sikh leaders account for themselves? Remember the words of former Jathedar of tile Akal Takht Professor Darshan Singh: "If a Sikh is not a Khalistani, he is not a Sikh." It seems that Badal and Amarinder are not Sikhs.

Never forget that the Akal Takht Sahib and Darbar Sahib and the present Akali and Congress leadership are under the control of the Indian government, the same Indian government that has murdered over a quarter of a million Sikhs in the past twenty years. These institutions will remain under the control of the Indian regime until we free the Sikh homeland, Punjab, Khalistan, from Indian occupation and oppression and sever our relations with the New Delhi government.

Sikhs will never get any justice from Delhi. Ever since independence, India has mistreated the Sikh Nation, starting with Patel's memo calling Sikhs "a criminal tribe." What a shame for Home Minister Patel and the Indian government to issue this memorandum when the Sikh Nation gave over 80 percent of the sacrifices to free India.

There is no place for Sikhs in supposedly secular, supposedly democratic India. Our moment of freedom is closer than ever. Let us work to make certain that we shake ourselves loose from the yoke of Indian oppression and liberate our homeland, Khalistan, so that all Sikhs may live lives of prosperity, freedom, and dignity.

> *Sincerely,*
> *Gurmit Singh Aulakh,*
> *President, Council of Khalistan.*

***

Document

CONGRESSIONAL RECORD -- EXTENSIONS

Tuesday, March 28, 2006
109th Congress, 2nd Session
152 Cong Rec E 427

REFERENCE: Vol. 152, No. 36
SECTION: Extension of Remarks
TITLE: SIKH ORGANIZATIONS UNITE FOR KHALISTAN

Speech of
HON. EDOLPHUS TOWNS
of New York
in the House of Representatives
Tuesday, March 28, 2006

Mr. TOWNS . Mr. Speaker, the Indian newspaper The Telegraph ran a story on March 21 reporting that two Sikh organizations in Punjab, Dal Khalsa, under the leadership of Satnam Singh, and the Shiromani Khalsa Dal under the leadership of Daljit Singh Bittu, are uniting to promote a sovereign, independent Khalistan. As you know, Mr. Speaker, the Sikhs declared Khalistan independent on October 7, 1987. Ever since then, Sikhs have been struggling against a massive Indian force of over 500,000 troops sent to suppress their drive for freedom.

The announcement from Dal Khalsa and the Shiromani Khalsa Dal was met by shouts of "Khalistan Zindabad," meaning "Long live Khalistan." Now the Chief Minister of Punjab has ordered the police to place the leaders of both organizations under watch. Let me make this clear, Mr. Speaker. They are under police watch in "the world's largest democracy" for peaceful political activities designed to achieve freedom for their people.

These arrests come in short order after the recent arrests of Sikh activists Dr. Jagjit Singh Chohan and Kanwarpal Singh Dhami for speeches they made supporting Khalistan. Dr. Chohan committed the additional crime of flying the Khalistani flag from his residence. Groups of Sikhs were arrested last year in January and June for hoisting the Khalistani flag and making speeches in support of sovereignty for Khalistan. Dal Khalsa organized those events. It has organized numerous events in support of a sovereign Khalistan in Punjab, and the support has been shown to be large. I guess this scares the Indian government.

Mr. Speaker, these actions are unacceptable in any country. We use our influence to put pressure on totalitarian regimes for just these kinds of tactics. They are even more unacceptable when the country using them claims to be democratic. This does not resemble any kind of democracy I know about.

Mr. Speaker, we must take a stand for freedom in South Asia, as we are doing elsewhere in the world. The time has come to cut off our aid and trade with India and until basic human rights for all people are respected there. In addition, we should put the Congress officially on record in support of free and fair plebiscites in Punjab, Khalistan, in Kashmir, in Nagaland, and all the other minority nations seeking their freedom from India. It is time for America to show its active support for freedom, stability, dignity, and human rights.

Mr. Speaker, the Council of Khalistan has published a very good release on the statement by Dal Khalsa and the Shiromani Khalsa Dal. I would like to add it to the Record now for the information of my colleagues.

Sikhs Arrested in India for Speaking for Khalistan

Washington, DC, March 15, 2006._Sardar Kanwarpal Singh Dhami, Chairman of Dal Khalsa, and Dr. Jagjit Singh Chohan were arrested earlier this month for speaking out for an independent Khalistan. They were charged with sedition. These arrests follow the arrests of Sikh leaders last year belonging to Dal Khalsa both in January and June for hoisting the flag of Khalistan. Kanwarpal Singh Dhami was arrested after saying that the Sikh Panth could not live under someone else's rule. He was accused of ". . . sedition, promoting enmity between different groups on grounds of religion, race, doing acts prejudicial to maintenance of harmony, imputations, assertions prejudicial to national integration and statements conducing to public mischief." The government charged that he promoted separatist and 'terrorist' movements.

Dal Khalsa has sponsored numerous marches and conferences in Punjab in support of a free Khalistan, the Sikh homeland that declared its independence from India on October 7, 1987. It was the organizer of the two events at which Sikhs were arrested for making speeches and raising the Khalistani flag. It was announced today that they will be joining forces with the Shiromani Khalsa Dal, headed by Sardar Daljit Singh Bittu, in support of a free Khalistan. The Punjab and Haryana High Court ruled that it is legal to ask for freedom for Khalistan, yet the Indian government continues to treat it as a crime. They do not even live by their own law.

Dr. Chohan said on India's Zee TV that Khalistan will be free by 2007. He has also been flying the Khalistani flag and that of his party, the Khalsa Raj Party, outside his office. According to the book Chakra-vyuh: Web of Indian Secularism (page 183), Dr. Chohan worked with Major General Jaswant Singh Bhullar, Professor Manjit Singh Sidhu, Didar Singh Bains, and others "to stop Sikhs living abroad" from supporting freedom for Khalistan and connived with the Indian government for the June 1984 attack on the Golden Temple.

"It is evident that the Indian government is scared of the increasing amount of peaceful activism in Punjab in support of Khalistan," said Dr. Gurmit Singh Aulakh, President of the Council of Khalistan, which is leading the Sikh struggle for independence. "The time of Khalistan's liberation is near. India will fall apart soon," he said. "We condemn the arrests of Sardar Dhami and Dr. Chohan but remind the Sikh Nation that it must work only with leaders who are honest, sincere, and committed to

the liberation of Khalistan." Dr. Aulakh noted that in New York in 2000, former Member of Parliament Simranjit Singh Mann had called for the Council of Khalistan's office to be closed. "Sikhs must be very careful about the leaders they follow," Dr. Aulakh said. "This office has worked unwaveringly for a sovereign Khalistan for almost 20 years," he noted.

History shows that multinational states such as India are doomed to failure. Countries like Austria-Hungary, India's longtime friend the Soviet Union, Yugoslavia, Czechoslovakia, and others prove this point. India is not one country; it is a polyglot like those countries, thrown together for the convenience of the British colonialists. It is doomed to break up as they did. "We only hope that the breakup will be peaceful," said Dr. Aulakh.

The Indian government has murdered over 250,000 Sikhs since 1984, more than 300,000 Christians in Nagaland, over 90,000 Muslims in Kashmir, tens of thousands of Christians and Muslims throughout the country, and tens of thousands of Tamils, Assamese, Manipuris, and others. The Indian Supreme Court called the Indian government's murders of Sikhs "worse than a genocide."

Indian police arrested human-rights activist Jaswant Singh Khalra after he exposed their policy of mass cremation of Sikhs, in which over 50,000 Sikhs have been arrested, tortured, and murdered, then their bodies were declared unidentified and secretly cremated. He was murdered in police custody. His body was not given to his family. The police never released the body of former Jathedar of the Akal Takht Gurdev Singh Kaunke after SSP Swaran Singh Ghotna murdered him. No one has been brought to justice for the Khalra kidnapping and murder. Yet according to a report by the Movement Against State Repression (MASR), 52,268 Sikhs are being held as political prisoners in India without charge or trial, some since 1984!

Only in a free Khalistan will the Sikh Nation prosper and get justice," said Dr. Aulakh. "India should act like a democracy and allow a plebiscite on independence for Khalistan and all the nations of South Asia," Dr. Aulakh said. "We must free Khalistan now."

***

Document

CONGRESSIONAL RECORD -- EXTENSIONS

Tuesday, March 28, 2006
109th Congress, 2nd Session
152 Cong Rec E 429

REFERENCE: Vol. 152, No. 36
SECTION: Extension of Remarks
TITLE: SIKH ACTIVISTS ARRESTED IN PUNJAB

Speech of
HON. EDOLPHUS TOWNS
of New York
in the House of Representatives
Tuesday, March 28, 2006

Mr. TOWNS . Mr. Speaker, Sikh activists Kanwarpal Singh Dhami and Dr. Jagjit Singh Chohan were recently arrested by the Indian Government on charges of sedition. Their crime was to speak in support of a sovereign Khalistan. Dr. Chohan also flies the Khalistani flag from his residence. When did free speech become a crime in a democracy?

The Sikh homeland of Khalistan declared itself independent from India on October 7, 1987.

These arrests are a follow-up to the arrests of groups of Sikh activists last year on Republic Day in January and again in June on the anniversary of the Golden Temple for making speeches in support of freedom for Khalistan and raising the flag of Khalistan. These events were led by Dal Khalsa. Recently, Dal Khalsa was put under watch by order of the Chief Minister of Punjab after its leader, Satnam Singh, and the leader of the Shiromani Khalsa Dal, Daljit Singh Bittu, announced that they are joining forces to achieve sovereignty for Khalistan.

Mr. Speaker, these are the kinds of tactics that totalitarian governments use, not democratic ones. A real democracy would not arrest people for making speeches. This is underlined by the fact that, according to the Movement Against State Repression, India admitted to holding 52,268 Sikh political prisoners. Tens of thousands of other minorities are also held as political prisoners, according to Amnesty International. How can such things happen in the world's largest democracy?

The time has come to stand up against India's tyranny. We should end our aid to India, especially since India uses 25 percent of its development budget for nuclear development, and we should stop our trade until all people enjoy basic human rights. And we should declare our support for free and fair plebiscites in Kashmir, as India promised in 1948, in Punjab, Khalistan, in Nagaland, and wherever people are seeking freedom. The essence of democracy is the right of self-determination and that basic right is being denied to minorities in India. The best thing we can do to support stability, freedom, and human dignity in the subcontinent is to stop rewarding the tyrants and throw our full support behind those seeking freedom.

Mr. Speaker, the Council of Khalistan has issued a very good release on the arrests of Dr. Chohan and Mr. Dhami. I would like to insert it in the Record at this time. Thank you.

Desire for Khalistan Alive and Well in Punjab

Washington, D.C., Mar. 21, 2006._Slogans of "Khalistan Zindabad" filled the air at the Holla Mohallah festival in Anandpur Sahib, Punjab, led by Dal Khalsa and the Shiromani Khalsa Dal. The two organizations pledged to unite to liberate the Sikh homeland, Khalistan, which declared itself independent from India on October 7, 1987.

Dal Khalsa, led by Satnam Singh, president of Dal Khalsa, and Daljit Singh Bittu, pledged to "provide a fresh platform for the Sikhs who were depressed with the incompetent and incapable leadership of various factions of the Akali Dal," according to The Telegraph, an Indian newspaper. Satnam Singh said the organizations would reach out to people to involve them in "the struggle to uphold our honor and dignity," the newspaper reported. The Punjab government led by Chief Minister Amarinder Singh has directed the police that both groups be put under watch.

Dal Khalsa has sponsored numerous marches in Punjab in support of a free Khalistan, the Sikh homeland that declared its independence from India on October 7, 1987. It was the organizer of the two events at which Sikhs were arrested for making speeches and raising the Khalistani flag.

History shows that multinational states such as India are doomed to failure. Countries like Austria-Hungary, India's longtime friend the Soviet Union. Yugoslavia, Czechoslovakia, and others prove this point. India is not one country; it is a polyglot like those countries. It is doomed to break up as they did.

"The uniting of these two organizations is very good for the Sikh nation and its aspirations," said Dr. Gurmit Singh Aulakh, President of the Council of Khalistan. "The Indian government continues to persecute and kill our Sikh brethren," he said. "Unity is essential for the liberation of Khalistan," he said. "As Professor Darshan Singh, a former Jathedar, said, 'If a Sikh is not for Khalistan, he is not a Sikh'," Dr. Aulakh noted: "This shows that the drive for freedom is still alive in Punjab," he said. "What kind of democracy watches people for demanding freedom? Why don't they watch the Black Cats who have killed thousands of Sikhs with the protection of the Indian government?" he asked.

The Indian government has murdered over 250,000 Sikhs since 1984, more than 300,000 Christians since 1948 as well as tens of thousands of Christians throughout the country, over 90,000 Muslims in Kashmir since 1988, 2,000 to 5,000 Muslims in Gujarat, tens of thousands of Muslims elsewhere in India, and tens of thousands of Assamese, Bodos, Dalits, Manipuris, Tamils, and others. An Indian newspaper reported that the police in Gujarat were ordered to stand aside in that massacre and not to get involved, a frightening parallel to the Delhi massacre of Sikhs in

1984. The Indian Supreme Court called the Indian government's murders of Sikhs "worse than a genocide."

Indian police arrested human-rights activist Jaswant Singh Khalra after he exposed their policy of mass cremation of Sikhs, in which over 50,000 Sikhs have been arrested, tortured, and murdered, then their bodies were declared unidentified and secretly cremated. He was murdered in police custody. His body was not given to his family. The police never released the body of former Jathedar of the Akal Takht Gurdev Singh Kaunke after SSP Swaran Singh Ghotna murdered him. No one has been brought to justice for the Khalra kidnapping and murder or for the murder of Jathedar Kaunke. Yet according to a report by the Movement Against State Repression (MASR), 52,268 Sikhs are being held as political prisoners in India without charge or trial, some since 1984!

Missionary Graham Staines was murdered along with his two sons, ages 8 and 10, by a mob of militant, fundamentalist Hindu nationalists who set fire to the jeep, surrounded it, and chanted "Victory to Hannuman," a Hindu god. None of the people involved has been tried. The persons who have murdered priests, raped nuns, and burned Christian churches have not been charged or tried. The murderers of 2,000 to 5,000 Muslims in Gujarat have never been brought to trial.

"Only in a free Khalistan will the Sikh Nation prosper and get justice," said Dr. Aulakh. "India should act like a democracy and allow a plebiscite on independence for Khalistan and all the nations of South Asia," Dr. Aulakh said. "We must free Khalistan now."

***

Document

CONGRESSIONAL RECORD -- EXTENSIONS

Wednesday, February 15, 2006
109th Congress, 2nd Session
152 Cong Rec E 158

REFERENCE: Vol. 152, No. 19
SECTION: Extension of Remarks
TITLE: COUNCIL OF KHALISTAN SENDS NEW YEAR GREETINGS

Speech of
HON. EDOLPHUS TOWNS
of New York
in the House of Representatives
Wednesday, February 15, 2006

Mr. TOWNS . Mr. Speaker, last month the Council of Khalistan sent out New Year's greetings to the Sikh Nation. In the letter the Council noted that the flame of freedom still burns brightly in Punjab, Khalistan, despite India's ongoing effort to stamp out the freedom movement. In both January and June of 2005, Sikhs were arrested for making speeches in support of freedom Khalistan, the Sikh homeland, and raising the Khalistani flag. When did making speeches and hoisting a flag become crimes in a democracy?

The letter took note of Prime Minister Manmohan Singh's apology to the Sikh Nation for the massacres of November 1984 that killed over 20,000 Sikhs. This clearly admits India's culpability for this horrible massacre. While that apology is a positive step and we applaud it, it was not accompanied by any compensation to the victims' families. Nor was it accompanied by an apology for the military attack on the Golden Temple or any other Indian government atrocity against the Sikhs. Nevertheless, it shows India's awareness of the rising tide of freedom in Punjab, Khalistan.

Last month, the Indian government bulldozed the homes of Sikh farmers in Uttaranchal Pradesh, farms they had worked all their lives for, and expelled them from the state. This is the height of discrimination against the Sikhs. No Sikhs are allowed to own land in Rajasthan and in Himachal Pradesh, but outsiders are allowed to buy land in Punjab. The government encourages Hindus to buy land in Punjab. Is this secularism in action? Is this democracy at work?

Mr. Speaker, these are just the latest acts against the legitimate freedom movement in Punjab, Khalistan. The repression has been ongoing. The Indian government has murdered over 250,000 Sikhs, according to figures compiled by the Punjab State Magistracy and human-rights groups. In addition, the Movement Against State Repression, MASR_an organization that should be unnecessary in a democratic state_reported in one of its studies that the Indian government admitted to holding 52,268 Sikh political prisoners. Some have been held since 1984! These are in addition to tens of thousands of other political prisoners, according to Amnesty International. And the Indian government has killed over 90,000 Kashmiri Muslims, over 300,000 Christians in Nagaland, tens of thousands of Christians and Muslims throughout the country, and tens of thousands of Assamese, Bodos, Dalits, Manipuris, Tamils, and other minorities. And the repression continues, not only in Punjab, Khalistan, but throughout the country.

We can and must do something about it. We can stop our aid and trade with India until it respects full human rights for all people living within its borders. And we can and should declare our support for self-determination in Punjab, Khalistan, in Kashmir, as promised to the UN in 1948, in Nagalim, and wherever the people are seeking freedom. India claims to be democratic and the essence of democracy is the right to self-determination. Democracies also respect the human rights of the minority. Why is India afraid to put this simple question to a free and fair vote? Where is its commitment to democratic principles, Mr. Speaker?

Mr. Speaker, I would like to place the Council of Khalistan's open letter in the Record at this time.

Council of Khalistan,
Washington, DC, January 23, 2006.

May Guru Bless the Khalsa Panth in 2006 With Freedom, Happiness,
Unity, and Prosperity

Dear Khalsa Ji: Waheguru Ji Ka Khalsa, Waherguru Ji Ki Fateh!

Happy New Year to you and your family and the Khalsa Panth. May
2006 be your best year ever. I wish you health, joy, and prosperity in the
new year.

The flame of freedom continues to burn brightly in the heart of the
Sikh Nation. No force can suppress it. The arrests of Sikh activists, mostly
from Dal Khalsa, last January and again in June merely for raising the
Khalistani flag and making pro-Khalistan speeches shows that the
movement to free our homeland is on the rise. It has gotten the attention
of the world.

The Indian government is reacting to the rising tide of freedom for
the Sikh Nation. Prime Minister Manmohan Singh apologized to the Sikh
Nation for the Delhi massacres of November 1984 that killed over 20,000
Sikhs. It is good that he apologized and it clearly shows India's responsi-
bility, but what good does it do the Sikh Nation? Where are the apologies
for the Golden Temple attack and the other atrocities? Where is the
compensation for the victims' families?

Earlier this month, Sikh farmers were expelled from Uttaranchal Pra-
desh and their land was seized. They were beaten up by the police. Their
homes were bulldozed by paratroopers. Their homes in many cases were
built using their life savings and by their own hands. We condemn this
act of state terrorism by the government of Uttaranchal Pradesh. As you
know, Sikhs are prohibited from buying land in Rajasthan and Himachal
Pradesh. Now Uttaranchal Pradesh joins that list. Yet there are no
restrictions on land ownership in Punjab by non-Sikhs. People from
anywhere can buy land in Punjab, including people from Rajasthan and
Himachal Pradesh. India is trying to subvert Khalistan's independence by
overrunning Punjab with non-Sikhs while keeping Sikhs from escaping
the brutal repression in Punjab. We must redouble our efforts to free our
homeland, Punjab, Khalistan. That is the only way to keep these atrocities
from continuing and to protect the Sikh Nation. This is a direct challenge
to the Sikh leadership, irrespective of their party affiliation.

Any organization that sincerely supports Khalistan deserves the sup-
port of the Sikh Nation. However, the Sikh Nation needs leadership that is
honest, sincere, consistent, and dedicated to the cause of Sikh freedom.
But we should only support sincere, dedicated, honest leaders. We must be
careful if we are to continue to move the cause of freedom for Khalistan
forward in 2006 as we did in 2005.

The Akali Dal conspired with the Indian government in 1984 to in-
vade the Golden Temple to murder Sant Bhindranwale and 20,000 other
Sikh during June 1984 in Punjab. If Sikhs will not even protect the
sanctity of the Golden Temple, how can the Sikh Nation survive as a
nation?

The Akali Dal has lost all its credibility. The Badal government was so corrupt openly and no Akali leader would come forward and tell Badal and his wife to stop this unparalleled corruption. Now Badal and his son have accused Chief Minister Amarinder Singh of being tied in with Khalistanis. If this were true, what would be wrong with it? The Akali leaders also walked out when I predicted at a seminar around the celebration of Guru Nanak's birthday that Khalistan will soon be free, a prediction that was greeted with multiple enthusiastic shouts of "Khalistan Zindabad." How will these Akalis, including Badal and his son, account for themselves? Remember the words of former Jathedar of the Akal Takht Professor Darshan Singh: "If a Sikh is not a Khalistani, he is not a Sikh." Badal and his son are not Sikhs.

The corruption of the Badal government was just part of a pattern of corruption in India. Jobs are sold, legislative seats are rigged, judges preside over cases being tried by their family members, and so many other forms of corruption occur. As Dr. M.S. Rahi has pointed out in his excellent new paper on the corruption, this kind of corruption leads to the kind of atrocities that have unfortunately become so routine in India.

The Council of Khalistan has stood strongly and consistently for liberating our homeland, Khalistan, from Indian occupation. For over 18 years we have led this fight while others were trying to divert the resources and the attention of the Sikh Nation away from the issue of freedom in a sovereign, independent Khalistan. Yet Khalistan is the only way that Sikhs will be able to live in freedom, peace, prosperity, and dignity. It is time to start a Shantmai Morcha to liberate Khalistan from Indian occupation.

Never forget that the Akal Takht Sahib and Darbar Sahib are under the control of the Indian government, the same Indian government that has murdered over a quarter of a million Sikhs in the past twenty years. These institutions will remain under the control of the Indian regime until we free the Sikh homeland, Punjab, Khalistan, from Indian occupation and oppression and sever our relations with the New Delhi government.

The Sikhs in Punjab have suffered enormous repression at the hands of the Indian regime in the last 25 years. Over 50,000 Sikh youth were picked up from their houses, tortured, murdered in police custody, then secretly cremated as "unidentified bodies." Their remains were never even given to their families! More than a quarter of a million Sikhs have been murdered at the hands of the Indian government. Another 52,268 are being held as political prisoners. Some have been in illegal custody since 1984! Even now, the capital of Punjab, Chandigarh, has not been handed over to Punjab, but remains a Union Territory. How can Sikhs have any freedom living under a government that would do these things?

Sikhs will never get any justice from Delhi. Ever since independence, India has mistreated the Sikh Nation, starting with Patel's memo labelling Sikhs "a criminal tribe." What a shame for Home Minister Patel and the Indian government to issue this memorandum when the Sikh Nation gave over 80 percent of the sacrifices to free India.

How can Sikhs continue to live in such a country? There is no place for Sikhs in supposedly secular, supposedly democratic India. Let us work to make certain that 2006 is the Sikh Nation's most blessed year by making sure it is the year that we shake ourselves loose from the yoke of Indian oppression and liberate our homeland, Khalistan, so that all Sikhs may live lives of prosperity, freedom, and dignity.

> *Sincerely,*
> *Dr. Gurmit Singh Aulakh,*
> *President, Council of Khalistan.*

***

Document

CONGRESSIONAL RECORD -- EXTENSIONS

Tuesday, January 31, 2006
109th Congress, 2nd Session
152 Cong Rec E 36

REFERENCE: Vol. 152, No. 9
SECTION: Extension of Remarks
TITLE: NEW REPORT SHOWS INDIA ENGULFED BY CORRUPTION

Speech of
HON. EDOLPHUS TOWNS
of New York
in the House of Representatives
Tuesday, January 31, 2006

Mr. TOWNS . Mr. Speaker, I rise today to inform my colleagues about a new report written by Indian writer M.S. Rahi, PhD, entitled "Corruption and Its Effect on Social Life." As you know, we have recently been having some problems with corruption here in Washington as well, so the paper particularly caught my eye at this time.

In it, Dr. Rahi exposes the massive corruption that has engulfed Indian government at all levels. Lately it has even begun to run through the judiciary, which had been the single semi-autonomous branch of government there and the single one that had shown even minimal concern for human rights. This is tragic for the people of India, as Dr. Rahi shows. He notes that India has been plagued with one corruption scandal after another, highlighting the Mundra, Bofors, Security Scam, Kargil Coffin Scam, Tehelka, and Recruitment Scam scandals by name. He notes that many of the lawyers practicing in Indian courts are the family members of the judges before whom they are practicing. He notes how Indian politics have been rigged to ensure dynastic succession, as the sons and daughters of Members of Parliament and of the Legislative Assemblies succeed them.

He does not discuss one of the major Indian corruption scandals of recent times, the selling of government jobs in Punjab by the Badal government (labeled "fee for service"), nor does he discuss the massive human-rights violations in India, except to make the very good and valid point that this kind of endemic corruption inevitably leads to human-rights violations. If the corruption can be cleaned, perhaps the human-rights violations will be reduced, something that we all desire.

The latest scandal is that Sikhs who bought land in the new state of Uttaranchal Pradesh have had their farms taken away and they have been expelled. Sikhs are not permitted to buy property in Rajasthan or in Himachal Pradesh. Yet anyone can buy land in Punjab, the predominantly Sikh state.

As you know, Mr. Speaker, over 250,000 Sikhs have been murdered in India. In addition, over 300,000 Christians in Nagaland, more than 90,000 Muslims in Kashmir, tens of thousands of Muslims and Christians elsewhere in the country, and tens of thousands of Assamese, Bodos, Dalit "untouchables," Manipuris, Tamils, and other minorities have been killed. Recently, the Bodos have threatened to end their truce with the Indian government.

Prime Minister Manmohan Singh made a good first step by apologizing for the Delhi massacre of Sikhs in November 1984, but he has made no move to compensate the families of the victims nor to apologize for any of the Indian government's other atrocities and compensate those victims.

Over 52,000 Sikhs are being held as political prisoners, along with tens of thousands of other minorities. The first step India must take is to release all political prisoners. And it must adopt stricter anti-corruption laws to ensure that corruption will be held to a minimum and when it does occur, it will be punished. As Dr. Rahi reminds us, the impunity of corrupt officials and the impunity of the officials who commit these atrocities go hand in hand. Until basic human rights, including the right to buy property, live free of the threat of violence, and be safe from government corruption, are allowed to be enjoyed by all Indians, we must cut off our aid and trade. And we must put Congress on record in support of a free and fair plebiscite on the subject of independence in Punjab, Khalistan, in Nagaland, in Kashmir (as promised to the United Nations in 1948), and wherever people are seeking their freedom. The essence of democracy is the right to self-determination and the people of these troubled regions will only escape the corruption and brutality when they are allowed to live in freedom.

***

Document

CONGRESSIONAL RECORD -- EXTENSIONS

Tuesday, December 13, 2005
109th Congress, 1st Session
151 Cong Rec E 2506

REFERENCE: Vol. 151, No. 159
SECTION: Extension of Remarks
TITLE: SIKHS ENTHUSIASTICALLY CELEBRATE GURU NANAK'S
BIRTHDAY WITH REVERENCE

Speech of
HON. EDOLPHUS TOWNS
of New York
in the House of Representatives
Tuesday, December 13, 2005

Mr. TOWNS . Mr. Speaker, last month, Sikhs gathered from around the world to celebrate the birthday of Guru Nanak, the founder of Sikhism, with devotion, enthusiasm, and reverence. Over 25,000 Sikhs gathered in Nankana Sahib, in what is now Pakistan, for the celebration.

The celebration included reading of the Sikh holy scripture, the Guru Granth Sahib, the singing of hymns, a procession through the streets, and speeches. One of the speeches was given by Dr. Gunnit Singh Aulakh, President of the Council of Khalistan, the organization that leads the Sikh struggle for independence. Dr. Aulakh's speech was punctuated with slogans of "Khalistan Zindabad," which means "Long live Khalistan." Khalistan is the name of the Sikh state that declared its independence on October 7, 1987.

The celebration was carried live on Pakistani television and on Punjab Radio from London, which is available worldwide.

Guru Nanak had two companions, one Hindu and one Muslim. He was a shining example of acceptance of all. When Guru Nanak passed away, his burial shawl was torn in half and burned by the Hindus, and buried by the Muslims. Both Hindus and Muslims revered him.

Yet today, Hindus persecute the Sikhs, the followers of Guru Nanak. More than 250,000 Sikhs have been murdered at the hands of the Indian government. According to the Movement Against State Repression, MASR, over 52,000 are being held without charge or trial as political prisoners in "the world's largest democracy." Over 50,000 young Sikh men were picked up by the government, tortured, murdered, and then secretly cremated. Their bodies were declared "unidentified" and never returned to their families.

Christians and Muslims throughout the country are also being persecuted. Over 300,000 Christians in Nagaland and over 90,000 Kashmiri Muslims have been killed by the government. In addition, tens of thousands of Assamese, Bodos, Dalits, Manipuris, Tamils, and other minorities have been killed.

Are we going to stand idly by and let this happen? By stopping our aid and trade with India and by declaring our support for the fundamental democratic principle of self-determination, we can help bring real peace, prosperity, freedom, and stability to South Asia.

Mr. Speaker, I would like to insert the Council of Khalistan's very informative press release about the celebration of Guru Nanak's birthday into the Record at this time.

[From the Council of Khalistan, Nov. 22, 2005]
Sikhs Celebrate Guru Nanak's Birthday
With Devotion, Enthusiasm, Reverence

Washington, DC._Over 25,000 Sikhs gathered in Nankana Sahib (now in Pakistan) last week for the celebration of the birthday of Guru Nanak, the first Guru of the Sikh religion. About 15,000 were from Pakistan, about 4,500 were from India, and the rest were from abroad. Slogans of "Khalistan Zindabad" resonated throughout Nankana Sahib during the day's speeches.

The celebration began with the performance of Akand Path, which is the The Guru Granth Sahib, the Sikh holy scripture, was read without interruption for 48 hours leading up to Guru Nanak's birthday. Hymns were sung as midnight struck. In the morning, the Pakistan Gurdwara Prabandhak Committee (PGPC) presented government officials and others with siropas. According to Sikh tradition, the afternoon was marked by a procession led by the Guru Granth Sahib, followed by the Panj Piaras, and then the Sangat, of all the Gurdwaras in Nankana Sahib, ending back at Gurdwara Janam Asthan. The evening program featured speeches given by various Sikh leaders, including Dr. Gurmit Singh Aulakh, President of the Council of Khalistan, which leads the Sikh struggle for independence. When Dr. Aulakh raised slogans of "Khalistan Zindabad," the Sangat responded with great enthusiasm. The Sikh Nation knows that political power is essential for the enhancement of any religion. The Sikh Nation also knows that the gold was added to cover the building of Darbar Sahib when the Sikihs ruled Punjab from 1765 to 1849. Since then, it is also called the Golden Temple. After midnight the celebration concluded with ceremonies according to the Sikh rehat maryada.

The Sang at showed great devotion and reverence on this pious occasion. Guru Nanak was the founder of the Sikh religion. ("Marya Sikha Jagat Sitch Nanak Nirmal Panth Chalaya.") It was an occasion of great happiness for the Khalsa Panth. The events were carried live on Pakistani TV and on Punjab Radio from London, which is heard throughout the world. Sikhs who were able to participate in the celebration were very fortunate.

Guru Nanak confronted Sabar, the Moghul ruler of the time and called him a Jabbar (oppressor) and spoke out against the tyranny of the rulers of that time. He was even imprisoned by Babar, along with his followers. Guru Nanak travelled extensively, to the Middle East, where he visited Baghdad, and throughout India, along with his two companions, one Hindu, one Muslim. He spread his message of truthfulness, respect for the rights of individuals, earning an honest living, sharing with the needy, and praying to Almighty God. He was revered by Hindus and Muslims alike. When he left this world, his body was not found. The sheet covering his body was torn in two. The Hindus cremated it and the Muslims buried it, each according to their customs.

Guru Nanak is remembered as Baba Nanak Shah Faqir, Hindu Da Guru, Mussleman Da Pir. He preached the equality of all the human race, including gender equality.

Sikhism is a divinely revealed, monotheistic, independent religion which has 25 million followers and is the world's fifth largest religion. The Guru Granth Sahib, the Sikh holy scripture, was written by the Gurus themselves as revealed to them by God. Nobody can add or delete anything in the holy scripture, which is considered to be a living Guru after the tenth Nanak, Guru Gobind Singh Sahib.

***

Document

CONGRESSIONAL RECORD -- EXTENSIONS

Tuesday, December 13, 2005
109th Congress, 1st Session
151 Cong Rec E 2508

REFERENCE: Vol. 151, No. 159
SECTION: Extension of Remarks
TITLE: RACISM OF INDIAN FOUNDER EXPOSED

Speech of
HON. EDOLPHUS TOWNS
of New York
in the House of Representatives
Tuesday, December 13, 2005

Mr. TOWNS . Mr. Speaker, the unveiling of a statue of Mohandas K. Gandhi in Johannesburg, South Africa, set off a discussion about the anti-black racism of the founder of India.

When the eight-foot high Gandhi statue was unveiled, portraying him as a young human-rights lawyer, many leaders attacked Gandhi's anti-black statements. "Gandhi had no love for Africans," said one letter in The Citizen, a South African newspaper. "To him, Africans were no better than the 'Untouchables' of India."

As you may know, Mr. Speaker, the dark-skinned aborigines of the subcontinent, known as Dalits or "Untouchables," occupy the lowest rung on the ladder of India's rigid and racist caste system. The caste system exists to protect the privileged position of the Brahmins, the top caste.

Although it was officially banned by India's constitution in 1950, it is still strictly practiced in Hindu India.

Others have pointed out that Gandhi ignored the suffering of black people during the colonial occupation of South Africa. When he was arrested and forced to share a cell with black prisoners, he wrote that they were "only one degree removed from the animal." In other words, Mr. Speaker, he described blacks as less than human. We condemn anyone who says this in our country, such as the Ku Klux Klan and others, as we should. Why is Gandhi venerated for such statements?

In addition, G.B. Singh, a Gandhi biographer, has looked through many pictures of him and never seen one single black person. Gandhi also attacked white Europeans.

Gandhi is honored as the founder of India. These statements and attitudes reveal the racist underpinning behind the secular, democratic facade of India. It explains a worldview that permits a Dalit constable to be stoned to death for entering the Temple on a rainy day, that allows the murders of over 300,000 Christians in Nagaland, over 250,000 Sikhs in Punjab, Khalistan, over 90,000 Muslims in Kashmir, tens of thousands of Christians and Muslims elsewhere in the country, including Graham Staines and his two young sons, and tens of thousands of Assamese, Bodos, Dalits, Manipuris, Tamils, and other minorities. It explains why the pro-Fascist, Hindu militant RSS is a powerful organization in India, in control of one of its two major political parties.

India must abandon its racist attitudes and its exploitation of minorities. It must allow the enjoyment of full human rights by everyone. Until it does so, we should stop our aid and trade with India. Furthermore, Mr. Speaker, the essence of democracy is the right to self-determination. India must allow self-determination for Kashmir, as it promised the United Nations in 1948, in Punjab, Khalistan, in Nagaland, and wherever the people seek to free themselves from the boot of Indian oppression. We should put this Congress on record in support of self-determination for the people of the subcontinent in the form of a free and fair plebiscite on the question of independence. Khalistan declared its independence on October 7, 1987. The people have never been allowed to have a simple, democratic vote on the matter. Instead, India continues to oppress the people there with over half a million troops.

Mr. Speaker, reporter Rory Carroll of The Guardian wrote an excellent article on the controversy about the Gandhi statue. I would like to place it in the Record at this time.

[The Guardian, Friday Oct. 17, 2003]
Gandhi Branded Racist as Johannesburg Honours Freedom Fighter
(By Rory Carroll)

It was supposed to honour his resistance to racism in South Africa, but a new statue of Mahatma Gandhi in Johannesburg has triggered a row over his alleged contempt for black people. The 2.5 metre high (8ft) bronze statue depicting Gandhi as a dashing young human rights lawyer has been welcomed by Nelson Mandela, among others, for recognising the

Indian who launched the fight against white minority rule at the turn of the last century.

But critics have attacked the gesture for overlooking racist statements attributed to Gandhi, which suggest he viewed black people as lazy savages who were barely human.

Newspapers continue to publish letters from indignant readers: "Gandhi had no love for Africans. To [him], Africans were no better than the 'Untouchables' of India," said a correspondent to The Citizen.

Others are harsher, claiming the civil rights icon "hated" black people and ignored their suffering at the hands of colonial masters while championing the cause of Indians.

Unveiled this month, the statue stands in Gandhi Square in central Johannesburg, not far from the office from which he worked during some of his 21 years in South Africa.

The British-trained barrister was supposed to have been on a brief visit in 1893 to represent an Indian company in a legal action, but he stayed to fight racist laws after a conductor kicked him off a train for sitting in a first-class compartment reserved for whites.

Outraged, he started defending Indians charged with failing to register for passes and other political offences, founded a newspaper, and formed South Africa's first organised political resistance movement. His tactics of mobilising people for passive resistance and mass protest inspired black people to organise and some historians credit Gandhi as the progenitor of the African National Congress, which formed in 1912, two years before he returned to India to fight British colonial rule.

However, the new statue has prompted bitter recollections about some of Gandhi's writings.

Forced to share a cell with black people, he wrote: "Many of the native prisoners are only one degree removed from the animal and often created rows and fought among themselves."

He was quoted at a meeting in Bombay in 1896 saying that Europeans sought to degrade Indians to the level of the "raw kaffir, whose occupation is hunting and whose sole ambition is to collect a certain number of cattle to buy a wife with, and then pass his life in indolence and nakedness".

The Johannesburg daily This Day said GB Singh, the author of a critical book about Gandhi, had sifted through photos of Gandhi in South Africa and found not one black person in his vicinity.

The Indian embassy in Pretoria declined to comment, as it prepared for President Thabo Mbeki's visit to India.

Khulekani Ntshangase, a spokesman for the ANC Youth League, defended Gandhi, saying the critics missed the bigger picture of his immense contribution to the liberation struggle.

Gandhi's offending comments were made early in his life when he was influenced by Indians working on the sugar plantations and did not get on with the black people of modern-day KwaZulu-Natal province, said Mr. Ntshangase.

"Later he got more enlightened."

***

Document

CONGRESSIONAL RECORD -- EXTENSIONS

Tuesday, December 13, 2005
109th Congress, 1st Session
151 Cong Rec E 2512

REFERENCE: Vol. 151, No. 159
SECTION: Extension of Remarks
TITLE: AKALI LEADERSHIP BETRAYS SIKH NATION

Speech of
HON. EDOLPHUS TOWNS
of New York
in the House of Representatives
Tuesday, December 13, 2005

Mr. TOWNS . Mr. Speaker, on November 17, leaders of the Akali Dal, the predominant Sikh party, walked out of a seminar in Lahore after Dr. Gurmit Singh Aulakh, Preside: of the Council of Khalistan, predicted that India will break up. The Akali leaders said "We came to unite, not to divide India."

In front of an audience of about 1,500 people, Dr. Aulakh predicted that Kashmir will soon be free and India will break into five or six separate countries, including Khalistan. Former Home Minister L.K. Advani, President of the Bharatiya Janata Party, has said that "if Kashmir goes, India goes." Steve Forbes of Forbes magazine predicted in his magazine that India will break apart as the Austro-Hungarian Empire did.

The Akali leaders who walked out were clearly representing the Research and analysis Wing (RAW), the intelligence operation of the Indian government. Yet as Inderjit Singh Jaijee reported in The Politics of Genocide, more than 250,000 Sikhs were murdered by the Indian government, according to figures compiled by the Punjab State Magistracy. Another 52,268 are being held as political prisoners, according to the Movement Against State Repression (MASR.) Some of these political prisoners have been held since 1984.

Prime Minister Manmohan Singh has apologized for the November 1984 Delhi massacres in which over 20,000 Sikhs were killed. This establishes the guilt of the Indian government beyond any doubt. If he really wants to make amends, he should end India's occupation of Khalistan, the Sikh homeland that declared its independence on October 7, 1987.

India has also killed over 300,000 Christian in Nagaland, over 90,000 Muslims in Kashmir, and tens of thousands of Assamese, Bodos, Dalits, Manipuris, Tamils, and others. Tens of thousands of Muslims and Christians have been killed in other parts of the country. India is not a single country, but a multinational state that cannot hold together. We must do our part to see that this happens peacefully by supporting self-determination for all the people of South Asia. We should also cut off our aid to India and our trade as well until basic human rights are observed fully and enjoyed by all.

Mr. Speaker, the Council of Khalistan's recently issued a press release about the betrayal of the Sikhs by the Akali Dal. I would like to put this release into the Record for the information of my colleagues and the people.

Akalis Again Betray Sikh Nation

Washington, DC, Nov. 22, 2005._On November 17, 2005, the Akali Dal again showed its true colors, as its leaders walked out of a seminar in Lahore after Dr. Gurmit Singh Aulakh, President of the Council of Khalistan, predicted the breakup of India during a speech in support of liberating Khalistan, the Sikh homeland, Khalistan. The Sarbat Khalsa passed a resolution on April 29, 1986 for a free Khalistan and established the Panthic Committee. The Panthic Committee declared Khalistan's independence on October 7, 1987, forming the Council of Khalistan to lead the independence struggle.

About 1,500 people attended the seminar. Dr. Aulakh predicted that Kashmir will soon be free and India will break up into six or seven countries' and Khalistan will be free. The Akali leaders said, "We came to unite, not to divide India." This was a clear indication that those leaders were representing RAW, not those of the Sikh Nation. True Sikhs pray every morning "Raj Kare Ga Khalsa" ("the Khalsa shall rule.") Former Jathedar of the Akal Takht Professor Darshan Singh has said, "If a Sikh is not a Khalistani, he is not a Sikh. "

India has murdered over 250,000 Sikhs since 1984, according to figures compiled by the Punjab State Magistracy and human rights groups and reported in the book The Politics of Genocide by Inderjeet Singh Jaijee. It has also killed more than 90,000 Kashmiri Muslims since 1988, over 300,000 Christians in Nagaland since 1947, and thousands of Christians and Muslims elsewhere in the country, as well as tens of thousands of Assamese, Bodos, Dalits ("Untouchables," the dark-skinned aboriginal people of South Asia), Manipuris, Tamils, and other minorities.

The Indian Supreme Court called the Indian government's murders of Sikhs "worse than a genocide." According to a report by the Movement Against State Repression (MASR), 52,268 Sikhs are being held as political prisoners in India without charge or trial. Some have been in illegal custody since 1984! Amnesty International reported that tens of thousands of other minorities are also being held as political prisoners. We demand the immediate release of all these political prisoners.

Cases were registered against dozens of Sikhs for raising the Sikh flag at the Golden Temple on the anniversary of the Golden Temple attack in the presence of over 30,000 Sikhs. Warrants have been issued for their arrest. The flag of Khalistan was also raised on Republic Day, January

26. 35 Sikhs were arrested at that time. Some of them have been denied bail.

Recently, Indian Prime Minister Manmohan Singh formally apologized to the Sikh Nation for the genocide against the Sikhs in November 1984 in which over 20,000 Sikhs were killed just in Delhi and surrounding areas while Sikh police were locked in their barracks and Indian radio and television called for more Sikh blood. This apology establishes the Indian government's responsibility for the genocide against the Sikh Nation. India must end its occupation of Khalistan, which is the root cause of this genocide. Sikhs are a sovereign nation and they are fighting for their freedom.

Indian police arrested human-rights activist Jaswant Singh Khalra after he exposed their policy of mass cremation of Sikhs, in which over 50,000 Sikhs have been arrested, tortured, and murdered, then their bodies were declared unidentified and secretly cremated. He was murdered in police custody. His body was not given to his family. History shows that multinational states such as India are doomed to failure. Countries like Austria-Hungary, India's longtime friend the Soviet Union, Yugoslavia, Czechoslovakia, and others prove this point. India is not one country; it is a polyglot like those countries. Steve Forbes, writing in Forbes magazine, said that India is doomed to disintegrate like the Austro-Hungarian Empire. "India is not a homogeneous state," Forbes wrote. "Neither was the Austro-Hungarian Empire. It attacked Serbia in the summer of 1914 in the hopes of destroying this irritating state after Serbia had committed a spectacular terrorist act against the Hapsburg monarchy. The empire ended up splintering, and the Hapsburgs lost their throne." India is doomed to fall apart just as Austria-Hungary and the others did.

"We must continue to pray for and work for our God-given birthright of freedom," Dr. Aulakh said. "We must continue to press for the liberation of Khalistan," he said. "Without political power, religions cannot flourish and nations perish. India claims to be a democracy. It is time it recognized the right of self-determination for all people in South Asia."

***

Document

CONGRESSIONAL RECORD -- EXTENSIONS

Wednesday, December 07, 2005
109th Congress, 1st Session
151 Cong Rec E 2469

REFERENCE: Vol. 151, No. 156
SECTION: Extension of Remarks
TITLE: IN MEMORY OF GURDEV SINGH SANDHU

Speech of
HON. EDOLPHUS TOWNS
of New York
in the House of Representatives
Wednesday, December 7, 2005

Mr. TOWNS . Mr. Speaker, I was recently informed of the passing of Gurdev Singh Sandhu at the young age of 62. I would like to extend my sympathies to his family and friends. He is survived by his wife Jaswant Kaur Sandhu, whom he married in 1974, his daughters Samreet and Ramneek, his son Sanmeet, his son-in-law Jason Pavlak, and his grandson London Singh Pavlak.

Gurdev Singh Sandhu was a very passionate supporter of Sikh freedom. He came to this country at age 18 and attended Wayne State University. He worked at many careers, including working as an engineer at Motown Records, working at DEA, employment as an engineer at General Dynamics, and a Quality Manager at Thyssen-Krupp Budd Company. He even had a couple of businesses of his own. He was very involved with his children, helping with homework, coaching Little League Baseball, teaching them to ride a bike, and so many other activities. He designed the house where he and his wife lived.

In his last few years, Gurdev Singh Sandhu had learned to play golf, worked in his garden, was active at a local gym, and worked in his yard and on various home-improvement projects. He had recently built a deck and designed his new garage.

Gurdev Singh Sandhu was a strong supporter of the cause of Sikh freedom and the Sikh homeland, Khalistan. He had hoped to live to see Khalistan free. Hopefully, even though he won't be around to see it, this dream will be achieved in very short order.

Again, Mr. Speaker, I would like to extend my condolences to Mr. Sandhu's family and friends and I know that the Members of this House join me in that. May God bless him.

***

Document

CONGRESSIONAL RECORD -- EXTENSIONS

Thursday, November 03, 2005
109th Congress, 1st Session
151 Cong Rec E 2272

REFERENCE: Vol. 151, No. 144
SECTION: Extension of Remarks
TITLE: PUNJAB ASSEMBLY SHIFTS BLAME ON TERRORISM

Speech of
HON. EDOLPHUS TOWNS
of New York
in the House of Representatives
Thursday, November 3, 2005

Mr. TOWNS . Mr. Speaker, I am glad to hear that the Legislative Assembly in Punjab recently had a discussion on terrorism there. Terrorism
is an important issue which all leaders of the world must address.
However, the debate turned into partisan politics of the type we're too
familiar with here_each side blaming the other for spurring the terrorism
in Punjab, while they ignored the real cause of the problem_the Indian
government.

India has imposed a reign of terror in Punjab, Khalistan for many
years, starting with a memo sent to police by their first Home Minister,
Mr. Patel, describing Sikhs as "a criminal class." This month marks the
anniversary of one particularly brutal chapter in that reign of terror_the
Delhi massacres of November 1984, in which 20,000 Sikhs were murdered. The government locked Sikh police officers in their barracks to
keep them from getting involved and the government's own radio and TV
called for more Sikh blood.

The newspaper Hitavada reported that the Indian government paid
the governor of Punjab, the late Surendra Nath, the equivalent of $1.5
billion to foment terrorism in Punjab and Kashmir. The U.S. State Department reported that the government paid more than 41,000 cash
bounties to police officers for killing Sikhs. One even got a bounty for
killing a three-year-old boy.

Human-rights activist Jaswant Singh Khalra compiled and published
a report showing that India had a policy of picking up young Sikh men,
torturing and killing them, declaring their bodies unidentified, and then
secretly cremating them. Khalra identified over 25,000 such cases at three
cremation grounds in Punjab. Others who have followed up on Khalra's
work found that the number is at least 50,000. For his work, Mr. Khalra
was arrested by the Punjab police and killed while in police custody. The
only witness to the Khalra kidnapping, Rajiv Singh Randhawa, has been
repeatedly arrested and harassed by the police.

Gurdev Singh Kaunke was the Jathedar of the Akal Takht, the highest
Sikh religious leader. He was murdered by a police official named
Swaran Singh Ghotna. No one has ever been punished for this atrocity.
The driver for another religious leader, Baba Charan Singh, had his legs
tied to two jeeps, which then drove off in different directions, tearing the
man in half.

Mr. Speaker, why are such actions tolerated, especially by a government that calls itself democratic? America must take a stand against such
tyranny.

The time has come to stop all our trade with India and all our aid to
that country until such time as basic human rights are fully protected.
And we must put this Congress on record in support of self-
determination for the people of Punjab, Khalistan, and all the other

peoples and nations seeking freedom, such as predominantly Muslim Kashmir and predominantly Christian Nagaland. This is the most effective way to end terrorism in the subcontinent.

Mr. Speaker, I would like to insert the Council of Khalistan's press release into the Record now for the information of my colleagues.

Punjab Assembly Debates Terrorism
Amarinder, Badal should discuss freedom for Sikh nation

Washington, D.C., November 2, 2005_The Punjab Legislative Assembly recently had a session to debate terrorism. Both the Congress Party and the Akali Dal blamed each other for encouraging Sikh youth to carry out the violence.

Amarinder Singh and Parkash Singh Badal are trying to change the history of Punjab. They are fully aware that Punjab, Khalistan has been engaged in a long struggle for independence after the Delhi massacres of November 1984. On April 29, 1986, Sarbat Khalsa passed a resolution for the independence of Khalistan and formed the Panthic Committee. On October 7, 1987, the Panthic Committee declared the independence of Khalistan. The Council of Khalistan was formed at that time to lead the peaceful, democratic, nonviolent struggle to liberate Khalistan.

These leaders are betraying the Sikh Nation. They need to be exposed and removed from their leadership roles. As Professor Darshan Singh, a former Jathedar of the Akal Takht, said, "If a Sikh is not a Khalistani, he is not a Sikh." Recently, Prime Minister Manmohan Singh apologized for the Delhi massacres, in which over 20,000 Sikhs were killed, firmly establishing India's guilt in this atrocity against the Sikh Nation.

The Indian government controls the Sikh leadership. Both Badal's Akali Dal, which claims to be the protector of Sikh interests, and Amarinder Singh's Congress Party, which is the party that carried out the Golden Temple attack, are under Indian government control.

New Sikh leadership is emerging in Dal Khalsa and other organizations. They hoisted the Khalistani flag in front of the Golden Temple on Republic Day in January and again on the anniversary of the Golden Temple attacks. They marched and made speeches for Khalistan. For this, they were charged by the Indian government and 35 were arrested.

History shows that multinational states such as India are doomed to failure. Countries like Austria-Hungary, India's longtime friend the Soviet Union, Yugoslavia, Czechoslovakia, and others prove this point. India is not one country; it is a polyglot like those countries, thrown together for the convenience of the British colonialists. It is doomed to break up as they did. Last year, the Punjab Legislative Assembly passed a bill annulling all water agreements with the Indian government, preventing the government's daylight robbery of Punjab river water. Punjab needs its river water for its crops. In the bill, the Assembly explicitly stated the sovereignty of Punjab.

The Indian government has murdered over 250,000 Sikhs since 1984, more than 300,000 Christians since 1948, over 90,000 Muslims in Kashmir since 1988, and tens of thousands of Tamils, Assamese, Manipu-

ris, Dalits, and others. The Indian Supreme Court called the Indian government's murders of Sikhs "worse than a genocide."

Indian police arrested human-rights activist Jaswant Singh Khalra after he exposed their policy of mass cremation of Sikhs, in which over 50,000 Sikhs have been arrested, tortured, and murdered, then their bodies were declared unidentified and secretly cremated. He was murdered in police custody. His body was not given to his family. No one has been brought to justice for the kidnapping and murder of Jaswant Singh Khalra. The police never released the body of former Jathedar of the Akal Takht Gurdev Singh Kaunke after SSP Swaran Singh Ghotna murdered him. Ghotna has never been brought to trial for the Jathedar Kaunke murder.

According to a report by the Movement Against State Repression (MASR), 52,268 Sikhs are being held as political prisoners in India without charge or trial. Some have been in illegal custody since 1984! Tens of thousands of other minorities are also being held as political prisoners, according to Amnesty International. We demand the immediate release of all these political prisoners.

"It is time to replace Amarinder Singh and Badal with new leadership that is committed to the interests of the Sikh Nation," said Dr. Gurmit Singh Aulakh, President of the Council of Khalistan. "Only a sovereign, independent Khalistan will end the repression and lift the standard of living for the people of Punjab," he said. "We must continue to press for our God-given birthright of freedom," he said. "Without political power, religions cannot flourish and nations perish."

***

Document

CONGRESSIONAL RECORD -- EXTENSIONS

Thursday, November 03, 2005
109th Congress, 1st Session
151 Cong Rec E 2273

REFERENCE: Vol. 151, No. 144
SECTION: Extension of Remarks
TITLE: HUMAN RIGHTS WATCH DEMANDS FULL ACCOUNTING FOR SECRET CREMATIONS IN PUNJAB

Speech of
HON. EDOLPHUS TOWNS
of New York
in the House of Representatives
Thursday, November 3, 2005

Mr. TOWNS . Mr. Speaker, on November 1, Human Rights Watch wrote an excellent letter to the National Human Rights Commission of

India demanding full accounting for the secret cremations of Sikhs in India. The secret cremations were described by India's Supreme Court as "flagrant violation of human rights on a mass scale." The court ordered the Indian government in November 1995, two months after the "disappearance" of Jaswant Singh Khalra, to conduct a full investigation into this brutal policy. Ten years later, that investigation has never taken place. Instead, the commission has chosen to focus on the trivial issue of whether the cremations were conducted in accord with the police rules, a terrible diversion from the real issue, which is that the Indian government is carrying out this genocidal policy against the Sikh minority.

This investigation must proceed, and it must be a full-fledged inquiry into this murderous policy, India must make full restitution to the victims' families.

Mr. Speaker, I will be inserting the letter from Human Rights Watch into the Record at this time.

November 1, 2005.
Re: mass secret cremations in Punjab.

Hon. Dr. Justice A.S. Anand, Chairperson, National Human Rights Commission, Faridkot House, Copernicus Marg, New Delhi, India.

Dear Justice Anand: As the National Human Rights Commission prepares to issue a decision in the Punjab mass secret cremations case, we urge the Commission to order a full accounting of the systematic abuses that occurred in Punjab, determine liability after detailed investigations into the violations, and provide for compensation for surviving family members based on a detailed understanding of the scope of violations suffered by each individual.

In 1994, investigations by human rights activist Jaswant Singh Khalra revealed that security forces had abducted, extrajudicially executed, and secretly cremated thousands of Sikhs in Punjab from 1984 to 1994. Mr. Khalra exposed over 2,000 secret cremations in Amritsar district alone_one of 17 districts in Punjab. Subsequent investigations by human rights groups confirmed that secret cremations had occurred throughout the state, and that cremation was only one form of disposing of victims' bodies. After publicly disclosing his findings, Mr. Khalra was abducted by the Punjab police and "disappeared" in September 1995. In November 1995, the Supreme Court ordered the Central Bureau of Investigation (CBI) to inquire into his abduction and allegations of mass cremations.

On December 12, 1996, the Indian Supreme Court found the inquiry by the CBI into mass cremations in Punjab disclosed a "flagrant violation of human rights on a mass scale" and ordered the National Human Rights Commission (NHRC) to adjudicate these mass crimes and "determine all the issues" (Paramjit Kaur v. State of Punjab). After challenges by the Indian government, the NHRC limited its investigation to illegal cremations in Amritsar district alone. The NHRC has now received 3,500 claims of illegal cremation in Amritsar.

Instead of investigating these secret cremations as unlawful depriva-
tions of life, the Commission has adopted the narrow issue of whether the
victims' bodies were cremated according to police rules. At two hearings
in October 2005, the petitioner Committee for Information and Initiative
on Punjab (CIIP) challenged the Commission's decision to discard
investigations, especially given the failure to identify the vast majority of
victims and establish procedures, standards and mechanisms to adjudi-
cate these cases to capture the full scope of human rights violations.

In almost nine years, the Commission has not heard testimony in a
single case, or held a single security official or agency responsible for
human rights violations. Further, at hearings in recent months, the
Commission has indicated its intention to dispense with investigations
into the violations altogether, and only determine whether the cremations
occurred according to police procedure. This is an odd decision for a
human rights body.

Human Rights Watch strongly urges the Commission to commit itself
to detailed investigations into the rights violations suffered by all victims
of illegal cremations and their family members, including whether
individual deaths were unlawful, the role of state security forces or their
agents in planning or carrying out illegal killings, identifying individual
perpetrators, and determining proper compensation. It is critical that
those cases not addressed by the NHRC's order of November 2004 are also
investigated. Until the facts are determined, "disappearances" remain an
ongoing crime and the NHRC ruling does not close the case.

Such investigations are required by international human rights law.
The International Covenant on Civil and Political Rights, which India
ratified in 1979, provides in article 2 that a victim of a rights violation
shall have an effective remedy and that the right to such a remedy be
determined by a competent authority and be enforced when granted. A
victim's right to an effective remedy imposes an obligation on the state to
undertake investigations to identify the perpetrators of human rights
violations. Indeed, the Commission's August 1997 order concluded that
the Commission must lay the factual foundations of the case in order to
establish liability, but for reasons that are not clear the Commission has
never implemented its own order. Anything less than proper investigations
will be a betrayal of victims and their families.

We note that in the nine years since the Commission took cognizance
of the Punjab mass cremations matter, it has investigated and resolved
numerous other complaints of human rights violations throughout India.
Moreover, the Commission has pursued cases suo motu, without even
receiving a complaint, after violations came to its attention through
media reports. The NHRC has earned a well-deserved reputation for
taking on powerful forces in India, which makes the Commission's
decisions in the Punjab cases even more puzzling.

In this upcoming order, we also urge the Commission to clarify that
the November 2004 order of compensation is interim. This order an-
nounced a total award of 2.5 lakhs rupees (around U.S. $5,500) to 109
families in whose cases police admitted custody of next of kin, without

determining individual responsibility, providing other reparatory measures, or engaging in an inquiry into the facts as directed by the Supreme Court. This grant of compensation is not only paltry, but it does not fulfill the Commission's responsibilities under international human rights law to make an individual determination.

Developing a compensation policy requires extensive investigation to clarify the extent of human rights violations, the potential beneficiaries, and the nature of injuries suffered, among other issues. The expert report submitted at the hearing on October 24, 2005 by Physicians for Human Rights (PHR) and the Bellevue/NYU Program for Survivors of Torture (Bellevue), demonstrates that the deprivation of life occurred within a pattern of violations that included intentional abuse among multiple family members of the "disappeared." The CIIP further called on the Commission to summon the authors of the report to testify. This report should compel the Commission to investigate the deprivation of the right to life of the victim, and the physical and psychological trauma inflicted upon surviving family members. In addition, our brief, submitted to the Commission in December 2003 in conjunction with Harvard Law Student Advocates for Human Rights, demonstrates that human rights bodies have considered evidence from numerous sources to adjudicate "disappearances" and extrajudicial executions, including evidence from international human rights experts. In its upcoming order, we urge the Commission to admit and fully weigh all evidence available, including the PHR/Bellevue report.

To demonstrate its intention to fulfill the mandate of the Supreme Court, the Commission must act to redress the violations of the rights to life and liberty suffered by thousands of families in Punjab. Its failure to do so is contributing to impunity, sending the message that perpetrators of mass crimes are more powerful than the Supreme Court and National Human Rights Commission. The Commission, no doubt, is aware that the prosecution of the officials who "disappeared" Jaswant Singh Khalra, the human rights defender who exposed the mass cremations in Punjab, has not concluded in nine years. The Commission should not allow the Punjab mass cremations case to also stand as an example of the triumph of impunity over the right to justice.

Thank you for your consideration. We look forward to a fruitful dialogue with you and other members of the Commission on this case.

> *Sincerely,*
> *Brad Adams,*
> *Executive Director, Asia Division,*
> *Human Rights Watch.*

***

Document

CONGRESSIONAL RECORD -- EXTENSIONS

Monday, October 17, 2005
109th Congress, 1st Session
151 Cong Rec E 2086

REFERENCE: Vol. 151, No. 131
SECTION: Extension of Remarks
TITLE: COUNCIL OF KHALISTAN CALLS ON ALL SIKHS TO SUPPORT
FREEDOM

Speech of
HON. EDOLPHUS TOWNS
of New York
in the House of Representatives
Monday, October 17, 2005

Mr. TOWNS . Mr. Speaker, recently, the Council of Khalistan issued an open letter in which it called for all Sikhs to work for independence for Khalistan. The letter cites abuses against the Sikh Nation such as the torture of Jagtar Singh Hawara, who had a cigarette forced into his mouth in contravention of a Sikh religious tenet and was forced to desecrate the Sikh holy scripture, the Guru Granth Sahib. This shows that there is no freedom and no tolerance for religious minorities in Hindu-dominated India. And unfortunately, whichever party is in power, the imposition of Hindu theocracy continues. The latest atrocities have occurred under the secular Congress Party, not the openly Hindu nationalist BJP.

It is outrageous that such atrocities against human beings are still occurring in the twenty-first century, Mr. Speaker. The civilized nations of the world must step in to put a stop to this tyrannical brutality.

We must do whatever we can to help all people live in freedom. We can start by ending our aid and our trade with India and by publicly demanding a free and fair vote to settle the question of independence for Khalistan and all the nations of South Asia the democratic way. Separating from India appears to be the only way that the Sikhs of Punjab, Khalistan, the Muslims of Kashmir, the Christians of Nagaland, and so many other minority groups will ever have a chance to live in the freedom that is their birthright as human beings.

I would like to introduce the Council of Khalistan's open letter into the Record for the information of my colleagues. It goes into much more detail than I am able to go into here. I urge my colleagues to read it carefully.

Council of Khalistan,
Washington, DC, October 12, 2005.
All Sikhs Must Work for the Liberation of Khalistan

Dear Khalsa Ji: WAHEGURU JI KA KHALSA, WAHEGURU JI KI FATEH!

Recent events have underlined again the importance of liberating our homeland, Khalistan. All Sikhs must work toward that goal.

Recently, the Council of Khalistan completed its highly successful annual convention. There was great enthusiasm for Khalistan. There have been marches in Punjab demanding a free and sovereign Khalistan. Over 30,000 Sikhs were present at the raising of the Khalistan flag on the anniversary of the Golden Temple attack in June. 35 Sikhs were arrested and many were charged at that time for making speeches and raising the flag. On Republic Day the same thing happened. Sikhs were charged and arrested for raising the Sikh flag and making speeches in support of Khalistan. This blatant attempt to put an end to the Khalistan movement through the use of naked intimidation will not work.

Recently, Prime Minister Manmohan Singh apologized to the Sikh Nation for the Indian government's massacre of Sikhs in Delhi in November 1984. Over 20,000 Sikhs were killed in these massacres while Sikh police were locked in their barracks and the state television and radio issued a call for more Sikh blood. Manmohan Singh's apology squarely establishes India's guilt and it is greatly appreciated. Now we await the apology for Operation Bluestar and the withdrawal of all Indian occupation forces from Punjab, Khalistan.

Captain Amarinder Singh became a hero of the Sikh Nation by asserting Punjab's sovereignty and preserving Punjab's natural resource, its river water, for the use of Punjab farmers by cancelling Punjab's water agreements, This action is saving Punjab from the Hindu regime's plan to make Punjab a desert and eliminate the Sikh Nation, the Sikh people, the Sikh culture, and the Sikh religion from the face of the Earth. The Delhi government, which is always a Hindu majority government whether the BJP or the Congress Party is in power, has never treated Punjab fairly. The government is determined to destroy the Sikh religion and the economy of Punjab.

A recent report issued by ENSAAF entitled Fabricating Terrorism through Illegal Detention and Torture shows that India is still illegally detaining and torturing Sikhs on false charges of "militancy." Yet India claims to have ended the "militancy" years ago. Why are there still Sikhs who are being arrested and tortured on these charges?

Jagtar Singh Hawara is a hero of the Sikh Nation. The Sikh Nation is proud of him. He is a living martyr whose name will be written in Golden letters in Sikh history. According to the Indian Express of July 13, 2005, the Delhi police stuffed cigarettes in his mouth, in violation of the Sikh religion, and forced him to desecrate the Guru Granth Sahib. His attorney, Arvind Thalmr, expressed concern that Sardar Hawara could be eliminated in a fake encounter like so many thousands of Sikhs before him. This treatment is a deliberate affront to the entire Sikh Nation. How would Sardar Hawara's captors feel if they were forced to eat beef (cow meat) prepared by Halall?

Sikhs will never get any justice from Delhi. The leaders in Delhi are only interested in imposing Hindu sovereignty over all the minorities to advance their own careers and their own power. Ever since independence, India has mistreated the Sikh Nation, starting with Patel's memo labelling Sikhs "a criminal tribe." What a shame for Home Minister Patel and the Indian government to issue this memorandum when the Sikh Nation gave over 80 percent of the sacrifices to free India.

The Sikhs in Punjab have suffered enormous repression at the hands of the Indian regime in the last 25 years. Even now, the capital of Punjab, Chandigarh, has not been handed over to Punjab. It was built as Punjab's capital but remains a Union Territory. The Indian government has murdered over 250,000 Sikhs since 1984. Over 50,000 Sikh youth were picked up from their houses, tortured, murdered in police custody, then secretly cremated as "unidentified bodies." Their remains were never even given to their families! 52,268 Sikhs sit in Indian jails as political prisoners without charge or trial, according to the Movement Against State Repression (MASR.) Some of them have been in illegal custody for 20 years! Even those sent to prison for life for murder only serve 16 years. According to Amnesty International, tens of thousands of others are also being held as political prisoners. We call for the immediate release of these Sikh political prisoners and all political prisoners in India. The Indian government must return remains to grieving Sikh families.

The attack on the Golden Temple, the murder of over 20,000 Sikhs in June 1984, diverting Punjab's river water to Hindu states without compensation, giving Punjab farmers lower prices for their produce, and other abuses have left Sikhs with no other choice but to sever all ties with Delhi and finally reclaim our lost sovereignty in a free and independent Sikh state called Khalistan, as declared on October 7, 1987. That is our destiny. Remember that the Guru gave us sovereignty: "In Grieh Sikhin Ko Deon Patshahi."

The time has come for the Sikh Nation to take its seat among the nations of the world at the United Nations and send its ambassadors to almost 200 countries around the world. This will promote the interests of the Sikh Nation and the Sikh religion worldwide. The Sikh diaspora will gain tremendous respect within their host countries when we have our own independent, sovereign country and representatives at the United Nations.

The Sikh Nation must beware of Sikh puppets of the Indian government. Such puppets do not serve our interests. If you want to be remembered as a true Sikh, Mr. Prime Minister, you will fire the Hindu militants from your government, release all political prisoners, and make compensation to the families of the victims of Indian government genocide against the Sikhs.

Nehru promised that Sikhs would have "the glow of freedom" in northwest India, but as soon as independence was achieved, he told Sikh leaders that "things have changed." His Home Minister, Patel, sent out a memo calling Sikhs "a criminal tribe." That is why no Sikh representative has ever signed the Indian constitution.

We must bring back our Khalsa spirit. We must commit ourselves to the greater well being of the Sikhs Nation and to the cause of freedom. We must remember our heritage and tradition of "Khalsa Bagi Yan Badshah" by committing ourselves to the cause of freedom for our Sikh brothers and sisters. Will you commit yourself to this cause, Prime Minister Singh, or will you be a tool of the regime that has unleashed a brutal genocide on our people?

Last year's seminar on Khalistan held in Chandigarh shows that the flame of freedom still burns brightly in Punjab in spite of the Indian government's brutal repression. Always remember our heritage: Raj Kare Ga Khalsa; Khalsa Bagi Yan Badshah. We call on you to take these necessary steps to bring the glow of freedom that was promised to the Sikhs to fruition. That is the only way that you can be considered a good Sikh in alignment with the gurus.

> *Panth Da Sewadar,*
> *Dr. Gurmit Singh Aulakh,*
> *President, Council of Khalistan.*

***

Document

CONGRESSIONAL RECORD -- EXTENSIONS

Monday, October 17, 2005
109th Congress, 1st Session
151 Cong Rec E 2089

REFERENCE: Vol. 151, No. 131
SECTION: Extension of Remarks
TITLE: HONORING GENERAL NARINDER SINGH, A FREEDOM ACTIVIST

Speech of
HON. EDOLPHUS TOWNS
of New York
in the House of Representatives
Monday, October 17, 2005

Mr. TOWNS . Mr. Speaker, it is with great sadness that I note the passing of General Narinder Singh, a leader in the struggle for freedom for the Sikhs in Punjab, Khalistan. General Narinder Singh was an army general who became an activist for his people in his retirement. He frequently spoke out against the atrocities committed against the Sikhs in India. On a visit to the United States, General Narinder Singh said that "Punjab is a police state." Unfortunately, it is still a police state today.

Punjab police recently have arrested numerous Sikhs, held them incommunicado, and tortured them on charges of militancy. This is the same "militancy" that India claimed to have eradicated several years ago! In June, 35 Sikhs were arrested and many more were charged for making speeches in support of freedom for Khalistan, the Sikh homeland, and raising the Sikh flag in front of over 30,000 cheering Sikhs. Even a former Member of Parliament was arrested for making a speech. The same thing happened in January at a protest on India's Republic Day. Mr. Speaker, does this sound like the act of a tyranny or a democracy?

We must not just watch while India forcibly suppresses the freedom of Sikhs and other minorities. The time has come to stop our aid and our trade with India. It is also time to enact a formal resolution calling for a free and fair plebiscite on the question of independence. The essence of democracy is the right of self-determination.

Mr. Speaker, the Council of Khalistan recently published an excellent press release on the passing of General Narinder Singh, which I would like to place in the Record.

Council of Khalistan
In memory of General Narinder Singh

Washington, DC, October 12, 2005_General Narinder Singh, a strong spokesman for an independent Khalistan, died recently. He was 86. He served in the army and became an activist for the Sikh Nation after his retirement. He spoke out for human rights and for freedom for Khalistan, the Sikh homeland that declared its independence on October 7, 1987. General Narinder Singh travelled to countries such as the United States in support of these causes. He participated in political events in Punjab, Khalistan, aimed at securing freedom for the Sikh nation. "General Narinder Singh will be sorely missed," said Dr. Gurmit Singh Aulakh, President of the Council of Khalistan. "We salute his courage and we honor his memory. On behalf of the Sikh Nation, I extend deepest sympathies to his family," Dr. Aulakh said.

General Narinder Singh correctly called Punjab "a police state," and it remains one to this day. India has murdered over 250,000 Sikhs since 1984. In addition, India has also killed more than 90,000 Kashmiri Muslims since 1988, over 300,000 Christians in Nagaland since 1947, and thousands of Christians and Muslims elsewhere in the country, as well as tens of thousands of Assamese, Bodos, Dalits ("Untouchables," the dark-skinned aboriginal people of South Asia), Manipuris, Tamils, and other minorities. The Indian Supreme Court called the Indian government's murders of Sikhs "worse than a genocide." The Movement Against State Repression (MASR) reported that 52,268 Sikhs are being held as political prisoners in India without charge or trial, some since 1984! Amnesty International reported that tens of thousands of other minorities are also being held as political prisoners. We demand the immediate release of all these political prisoners.

Cases were registered against dozens of Sikhs for raising the Sikh flag at the Golden Temple on the anniversary of the Golden Temple attack in the presence of more than 30,000 Sikhs. Warrants have been issued for their arrest. The flag of Khalistan was also raised on Republic Day, January 26. 35 Sikhs were arrested at that time. Some of them have been denied bail.

Recently, Indian Prime Minister Manmohan Singh formally apologized to the Sikh Nation for the genocide against the Sikhs in November 1984 in which over 20,000 Sikhs were killed in Delhi and surrounding areas while Sikh police were locked in their barracks and Indian radio and television called for more Sikh blood. This apology establishes the Indian government's responsibility for the genocide against the Sikh Nation. India must end its occupation of Khalistan, which is the root cause of this genocide. Sikhs are a sovereign nation and they are fighting for their freedom.

In September 1995, Indian police arrested human-rights activist Jaswant Singh Khalra following his report exposing the government's policy of mass cremation of Sikhs, in which over 50,000 Sikhs have been arrested, tortured, and murdered, then their bodies were declared unidentified and secretly cremated. He was murdered in police custody. His body was not given to his family.

"Only a sovereign, independent Khalistan will end the repression and lift the standard of living for the people of Punjab," said Dr. Gurmit Singh Aulakh, President of the Council of Khalistan. "Democracies don't commit genocide."

"The flame of freedom still burns bright in the hearts of Sikhs despite the deployment of over half a million Indian troops to crush it," Dr. Aulakh said. "As Professor Darshan Singh, a former Jathedar of the Akal Takht, said, 'If a Sikh is not a Khalistani, he is not a Sikh'," Dr. Aulakh noted. Last year, Punjab Chief Minister Amarinder Singh signed a bill cancelling the agreements that allowed the diversion of Punjabi water to non-riparian states. The bill asserted the sovereignty of Punjab. Sardar Atinder Pal Singh, a former Member of Parliament, held a seminar on Khalistan in Punjab. It was well attended and featured outstanding presentations, including one by Professor Gurtej Singh, IAS, Professor of Sikhism. There have been several recent marches through Punjab demanding the establishment of an independent Khalistan. "The Khalistan movement is on the rise and India is on the verge of disintegration," Dr. Aulakh said.

History shows that multinational states such as India are doomed to failure. Countries like India's longtime friend the Soviet Union, Yugoslavia, Czechoslovakia, and others prove this point. India is not one country; it is a polyglot like those countries. In Forbes magazine, Steve Forbes wrote that India is doomed to disintegrate like the Austro-Hungarian Empire. "India is not a homogeneous state," he wrote. "Neither was the Austro-Hungarian Empire. It attacked Serbia in the summer of 1914 in the hopes of destroying this irritating state after Serbia had committed a spectacular terrorist act against the Hapsburg monarchy. The empire ended up splintering and the Hapsburgs lost their throne." India is doomed to fall apart just as Austria-Hungary and the others did.

"The best way to honor the memory of General Narinder Singh is to continue to pray for and work for our God-given birthright of freedom," Dr. Aulakh said. "We must continue to press for our God-given birthright of freedom," he said. "Without political power religions cannot flourish and nations perish. India claims to be a democracy. It is time it recognized the right of self-determination for all people in South Asia."

***

Document

CONGRESSIONAL RECORD -- EXTENSIONS

Monday, October 17, 2005
109th Congress, 1st Session
151 Cong Rec E 2091

REFERENCE: Vol. 151, No. 131
SECTION: Extension of Remarks
TITLE: COUNCIL OF KHALISTAN CONVENTION VERY SUCCESSFUL

Speech of
HON. EDOLPHUS TOWNS
of New York
in the House of Representatives
Monday, October 17, 2005

Mr. TOWNS . Mr. Speaker, the Council of Khalistan, which leads the movement to liberate the Sikh homeland, Khalistan, from Indian occupation, held its annual convention in the Detroit area October 7 through October 9. It was very successful. Delegates came from around the country and from Canada to participate.

I recently made a statement about Prime Minister Manmohan Singh's apology to the Sikh Nation for the Delhi massacres of November 1984 in which over 20,000 Sikhs lost their lives. This established India's culpability for the violence and terror that swept Punjab and other parts of India at that time. That underlines the need for a sovereign Khalistan to put an end to these kinds of acts. Recently, an organization called ENSAAF published a report detailing the ongoing human rights violations committed by Indian security forces in recent-militancy related arrests. From June 2005 to August 2005, Indian police claim to have arrested several dozen individuals on charges that they were trying to "revive militancy" in Punjab. They have been held incommunicado and tortured, according to the report.

In June, 35 Sikhs were arrested and several were charged simply for making speeches in support of an independent Khalistan and raising the Sikh flag. Those arrested and charged include Simranjit Singh Mann, a former Member of Parliament, who is out on bail after making a speech in support of Khalistan. Is making a speech a crime in a democracy? Is raising a flag a crime in a democracy? How can India claim it is democratic when people are arrested for making speeches and raising a flag?

These recent incidents are the latest in a pattern of repression by the Indian government that demonstrates why a free and sovereign Khalistan is needed. The Council of Khalistan convention helped maintain and increase support for that goal.

We can help the people in Punjab and throughout South Asia live in freedom, Mr. Speaker. We can do so by withholding aid and trade from India until it respects human rights and by putting the Congress on record in support of self-determination for the Sikhs of Punjab, Khalistan, the Muslims of Kashmir, predominantly Christian Nagaland, and all the nations seeking freedom from India. It's time to stop using violence and settle these matters democratically.

Mr. Speaker, I would like to place the Council of Khalistan's press release on its convention into the Record at this time.

[From the Council of Khalistan, Oct. 12, 2005]
Council of Khalistan Annual Convention Very Successful

Washington, DC_Delegates came from Canada, New Jersey, Philadelphia, Memphis, Florida, Illinois, California, Washington, DC, and other locations to the Council of Khalistan's annual convention, which was held October 7-9, 2005 at the Sikh Gurdwara in Rochester Hills, Michigan. The convention was very well attended and successful. The delegates were enthusiastic in support of freedom for Khalistan, the Sikh homeland that declared its independence from India on October 7, 1987.

Resolutions were passed in support of a sovereign, independent Khalistan, in support of the Washington office, thanking the Sangat of Detroit, condolences for the victims of the earthquake in Kashmir, and other resolutions. Delegates spoke in support of independence for Khalistan and discussed the need to remain active on the grassroots level. They stressed the need for the active participation of Sikhs in this country and worldwide.

The Council of Khalistan has preserved the true history of the Sikh Nation since 1984 by documenting every major incident in the Congressional Record, internationalizing the Sikh struggle for independence, and exposing the Indian government's repression against the Sikhs and other minorities.

India has murdered over 250,000 Sikhs since 1984, according to figures compiled by the Punjab State Magistracy and human-rights groups and reported in the book The Politics of Genocide by Inderjeet Singh Jaijee. It has also killed more than 90.000 Kashmiri Muslims since 1988, over 300,000 Christians in Nagaland since 1947, and thousands of Christians and Muslims elsewhere in the country, as well as tens of thousands of Assamese, Bodos, Dalits ("Untouchables," the dark-skinned aboriginal people of South Asia), Manipuris, Tamils, and other minorities.

The Indian Supreme Court called the Indian government's murders of Sikhs "worse than a genocide." According to a report by the Movement

Against State Repression (MASR), 52,268 Sikhs are being held as political prisoners in India without charge or trial. Some have been in illegal custody since 1984! Amnesty International reported that tens of thousands of other minorities are also being held as political prisoners. We demand the immediate release of all these political prisoners.

Cases were registered against dozens of Sikhs for raising the Sikh flag at the Golden Temple on the anniversary of the Golden Temple attack in the presence of over 30,000 Sikhs. Warrants have been issued for their arrest. The flag of Khalistan was also raised on Republic Day, January 26. 35 Sikhs were arrested at that time. Some of them have been denied bail.

Recently, Indian Prime Minister Manmohan Singh formally apologized to the Sikh Nation for the genocide against the Sikhs in November 1984 in which over 20,000 Sikhs were killed in Deihl alone while Sikh police were locked in their barracks and Indian radio and television called for more Sikh blood. This apology establishes the Indian government's responsibility for the genocide against the Sikh Nation. India must end its occupation of Khalistan, which is the root cause of this genocide. Sikhs are a sovereign nation and they are fighting for their freedom.

Indian police arrested human-rights activist Jaswant Singh Khalra after he exposed their policy of mass cremation of Sikhs, in which over 50,000 Sikhs have been arrested, tortured, and murdered, then their bodies were declared unidentified and secretly cremated. He was murdered in police custody. His body was not given to his family.

"Only a sovereign, independent Khalistan will end the repression and lift the standard of living for the people of Punjab," said Dr. Gurmit Singh Aulakh, President of the Council of Khalistan. "Democracies don't commit genocide."

History shows that multinational states such as India are doomed to failure. Countries like Austria-Hungary, India's longtime friend the Soviet Union, Yugoslavia, Czechoslovakia, and others prove this point. India is not one country; it is a polyglot like those countries. Steve Forbes, writing in Forbes magazine, said that India is doomed to disintegrate like the Austro-Hungarian Empire. "India is not a homogeneous state," Forbes wrote. "Neither was the Austro-Hungarian Empire. It attacked Serbia in the summer of 1914 in the hopes of destroying this irritating state after Serbia had committed a spectacular terrorist act against the Hapsburg monarchy. The empire ended up splintering, and the Hapsburgs lost their throne." India is doomed to fall apart just as Austria-Hungary and the others did.

"We must continue to pray for and work for our God-given birthright of freedom," Dr. Aulakh said. "As Professor Darshan Singh, a former Jathedar of the Akal Takht, said, "If a Sikh is not a Khalistani, he is not a Sikh," Dr. Aulakh noted. "We must continue to press for our God-given birthright of freedom, he said, "Without political power, religions cannot flourish and nations perish. India claims to be a democracy. It is time it recognized the right of self-determination for all people in South Asia,"

***

Document

CONGRESSIONAL RECORD -- EXTENSIONS

Thursday, September 15, 2005
109th Congress, 1st Session
151 Cong Rec E 1866

REFERENCE: Vol. 151, No. 116
SECTION: Extension of Remarks
TITLE: INDIAN PRIME MINISTER APOLOGIZES TO SIKHS FOR
GENOCIDE OF 1984_INDIAN MUST FREE KHALISTAN AND ALL
OCCUPIED TERRITORIES

Speech of
HON. EDOLPHUS TOWNS
of New York
in the House of Representatives
Thursday, September 15, 2005

Mr. TOWNS . Mr. Speaker, recently the Prime Minister of India, Manmohan Singh, apologized to the Sikhs for the massacres of Sikhs that took place in November 1984. Over 20,000 Sikhs died in that massacre just in Delhi. Meanwhile, Sikh police officers were locked in their barracks and the state television and radio were encouraging more Sikh bloodshed.

This is a sad chapter in the history of India and it is appropriate that the Government has finally admitted its own culpability and apologized for this atrocity. These kinds of admissions are always welcome. But Prime Minister Singh's apology is 21 years too late and it is only a baby step in the direction of justice. And an apology for the military attack on the Golden Temple in June of that year is still not forthcoming.

Mr. Speaker, there are families of those who died in this massacre who have still never been compensated in any way. We know that no compensation can bring back their loved ones, but at least it can help make their lives better. India must compensate the victims' families if this apology is serious. It must also bring to justice the officials responsible for the massacre. These are necessary steps for the apology to be taken as anything more than mere empty words.

But there is something else that India must do as well. It must make proper restitution to the whole Sikh Nation for this massacre and its many other atrocities against the Sikhs.

How do you pay such a huge debt, Mr. Speaker? How do you pay back an entire nation for atrocities against it? On October 7, 1987, the Sikh Nation declared its independence, declaring the new country of Khalistan. Since then, India has continued to occupy Khalistan. Over half a million Indian troops still carry out this brutal occupation to this day. These troops must be withdrawn and India must recognize the sovereignty of a free and independent Khalistan. That is how it can compensate the Sikh Nation.

Now, Mr. Speaker, the Indian Government maintains that there is no support for Khalistan among the Sikhs in Punjab, despite large marches that have occurred as recently as June demanding Khalistan. In June, 35 Sikhs were charged with a crime. Their offense? They made some speeches and raised the Khalistani flag. To quote my friend Dr. Gurmit Singh Aulakh, president of the Council of Khalistan, "Is asking for freedom a crime in a democracy?"

So if India is democratic and there is no support for Khalistan, then why is the Indian Government afraid to have a vote on the matter? Why not simply have a vote and prove it? It is time for the United States to hold India's feet to the fire on its proclaimed democratic principles. We must stop our aid to India until it respects human rights and ceases activities such as the Delhi massacre, the arrests of activists for raising a flag, and the like. And we must demand self-determination for the people of Khalistan, Kashmir, Nagaland, and all the suppressed, captive nations of South Asia. In a democracy you cannot rule against the will of the people, and the essence of democracy is the right to self-determination. It is time to press India, the self-proclaimed "world's largest democracy," to do the right thing and let the people have their freedom.

Mr. Speaker, I would like to insert the Council of Khalistan's press release on Prime Minister Singh's apology into the Record at this time. Thank you.

Washington, DC, Sept. 14, 2005._Indian Prime Minister Manmohan Singh has formally apologized to the Sikh Nation for the genocide against the Sikhs in November 1984 in which over 20,000 Sikhs were killed in Delhi alone while Sikh police were locked in their barracks and Indian radio and television called for more Sikh blood.

"We appreciate the Prime Minister's apology," said Dr. Gurmit Singh Aulakh, President of the Council of Khalistan. "It is more than any other Indian leader has done, but it is too little, too late_21 years too late, in fact." The Council of Khalistan leads the struggle to liberate the Sikh homeland, Khalistan, which declared its independence from India on October 7, 1987. "We need to see if this apology is sincere or just another propaganda ploy by the Indian government." However, he noted that the Indian government's military attack on the Golden Temple, the center and seat of Sikhism, in June 1984 was more important to the Sikh Nation. "Where is the apology for that?," he asked.

"India must pay full and appropriate restitution to the families and bring the officials responsible to justice," Dr. Aulakh said. "But the most appropriate and important restitution that can be made to the Sikh Nation is to withdraw all Indian forces from Khalistan and allow it to enjoy its independence," he said. "Only then can the Sikh Nation live in peace, dignity, and freedom, secure in the knowledge that these kinds of incidents will not happen again," he said. "If India and Prime Minister Singh truly believe in freedom and democracy, they have a moral obliga-

tion to withdraw from Khalistan and all the nations they occupy, such as Kashmir, Nagaland, and others," he said.

Professor Darshan Singh, a former Jathedar of the Akal Takht, has said, "If a Sikh is not a Khalistani, he is not a Sikh." The Indian government has murdered over 250,000 Sikhs since 1984, more than 300,000 Christians in Nagaland since 1948, over 90,000 Muslims in Kashmir since 1988, and tens of thousands of Tamils, Assamese, Bodos, Manipuris, Dalits, and others. The Indian Supreme Court called the Indian government's murders of Sikhs "worse than a genocide." According the Movement Against State Repression (MASR), 52,268 Sikhs are being held as political prisoners in India without charge or trial.

"The flame of freedom still burns bright in the hearts of Sikhs despite the deployment of over half a million Indian troops to crush it," Dr. Aulakh said. "Last year, Punjab Chief Minister Amarinder Singh signed a bill cancelling the agreements that allowed the diversion of Punjabi water to non-riparian states. The bill asserted the sovereignty of Punjab. Sardar Atinder Pal Singh, another former Member of Parliament, held a seminar on Khalistan in Punjab. It was well attended and featured outstanding presentations, including one by Professor Gurtej Singh, IAS, Professor of Sikhism," he said. "There have been several marches through Punjab demanding the establishment of an independent Khalistan. India is on the verge of disintegration," he said.

Cases were registered against dozens of Sikhs for raising the Sikh flag at the Golden Temple on the anniversary of the Golden Temple attack in the presence of over 30,000 Sikhs. Warrants have been issued for their arrest. The flag of Khalistan was also raised on Republic Day, January 26. 35 Sikhs were arrested at that time. Some of them have been denied bail. Dr. Aulakh demanded that India release all the people arrested for hoisting the flag and drop all charges against all these individuals. "Is it a crime to demand freedom in a democracy?," he asked. "Is this the freedom of speech that is guaranteed under India's constitution?"

History shows that multinational states such as India are doomed to failure. The collapse of countries like Austria-Hungary, India's longtime friend the Soviet Union, Yugoslavia, Czechoslovakia, and others prove this point. India is a polyglot like those countries, thrown together for the convenience of the British colonialists. It has never been a single nation. It is doomed to break up as they did. Steve Forbes, writing in Forbes magazine, said that India is a multinational, multiethnic, multireligious, multicultural, multilinguistic state that is doomed to disintegrate like the Austro-Hungarian Empire. "India is not a homogeneous state," Forbes wrote. "Neither was the Austro-Hungarian Empire. It attacked Serbia in the summer of 1914 in the hopes of destroying this irritating state after Serbia had committed a spectacular terrorist act against the Hapsburg monarchy. The empire ended up splintering, and the Hapsburgs lost their throne." India is doomed to fall apart just as Austria-Hungary and the others did.

"We must continue to pray for and work for our God-given birthright of freedom," Dr. Aulakh said. "While this apology is a small first step, only

a free Khalistan will satisfy the Sikh Nation," he said. "We must continue to work until this goal is achieved."

***

Document

CONGRESSIONAL RECORD -- EXTENSIONS

Thursday, September 15, 2005
109th Congress, 1st Session
151 Cong Rec E 1869

REFERENCE: Vol. 151, No. 116
SECTION: Extension of Remarks
TITLE: COUNCIL OF KHALISTAN CONVENTION TO BE HELD OCTOBER 7 TO 9 IN DETROIT

Speech of
HON. EDOLPHUS TOWNS
of New York
in the House of Representatives
Thursday, September 15, 2005

Mr. TOWNS . Mr. Speaker, the Council of Khalistan will be holding its annual convention in Detroit next month. It will be held from October 7 through October 9. This is a very appropriate date because Khalistan declared its independence from India on October 7, 1987 and the Council of Khalistan was formed at that time to lead the struggle to liberate Khalistan, a struggle that continues to this day, 18 years later.

It is outrageous that this struggle has had to go on so long, but the Council of Khalistan has been tireless in keeping it going and keeping the flame of freedom for the Sikh nation burning. I salute them on their convention and I wish them success both with their convention and with their efforts to bring freedom to the Sikh people.

It is time for India to get out of Khalistan and allow the people there to live in freedom. Until then, Mr. Speaker, we should stop our aid and trade with India and demand self-determination for the people of Khalistan, for the Kashmiris, as India promised in 1948, for the people of Nagaland, and for all the people and nations of South Asia. That is the only way to bring peace and stability to that troubled region.

***

Document

CONGRESSIONAL RECORD -- EXTENSIONS

Wednesday, July 13, 2005
109th Congress, 1st Session
151 Cong Rec E 1478

REFERENCE: Vol. 151, No. 94
SECTION: Extension of Remarks
TITLE: SIKH FLAG RAISED IN CALIFORNIA

Speech of
HON. EDOLPHUS TOWNS
of New York
in the House of Representatives
Wednesday, July 13, 2005

Mr. TOWNS . Mr. Speaker, on July 3 in Turlock, California, the Sikh flag was raised at an event there. There were speeches from many distinguished Sikhs, including Dr. Gurmit Singh Aulakh, President of the Council of Khalistan, and many others. The event was organized by Dal Khalsa America, the American branch of a Sikh political party that is strongly in support of independence for Khalistan, the Sikh homeland. Leaders of Dal Khalsa have been arrested in India, along with other leaders, for raising the Khalistani flag there.

In all, dozens were charged last month on the 21st anniversary of India's military attack on the Golden Temple for daring to raise the flag of Khalistan and making speeches, even though these are not crimes in India. They are not crimes in any democratic country. Yet these charges follow the arrests of 35 Sikhs in January for hoisting the Sikh flag and making speeches on India's Republic Day.

These are just the latest acts in a pattern of repression that includes the killings of over 250,000 Sikhs since 1984, over 300,000 Christians in Nagaland, over 89,000 Muslims in Kashmir, tens of thousands more Christians and Muslims around the country, and tens of thousands of Assamese, Bodos, Dalits, Manipuris, Tamils, and other minorities. It seems that the more support for the freedom movement rises, the more brutal India's repression of it gets.

Self-determination is the essence of democracy. But instead of settling the issue of freedom democratically in a free and fair vote, India chooses to suppress the freedom movements with excessive and brutal force.

I am glad that we do not live in that kind of democracy, Mr. Speaker. Instead, we live in a country where you can say what you want, believe what you want, and raise a flag if you want. We must do what we can to help bring India to that kind of democracy, especially with Prime Minister Manmohan Singh coming for a visit soon.

Mr. Speaker, the time has come to stop our aid and trade with India and to put the Congress on record in support of self-determination for the people of Punjab, Khalistan, of Kashmir (as India promised in 1948), of predominantly-Christian Nagaland, and of the other states and nations seeking their freedom. It should start with the dropping of all charges against those arrested or charged for raising a flag and with the release of all political prisoners, and I urge President Bush to bring up these two issues when Prime Minister Singh is here. Only when these goals are achieved can India be welcomed into the family of democratic nations. Only then can these minorities live in freedom, peace, security, stability, dignity, and prosperity.

Mr. Speaker, I would like to place the Council of Khalistan's press release on the flag raising in California and its open letter on the charges against the Sikh activists who raised the flag into the Record at this time.

Khalistan Flag Hoisted in California, USA

Washington, D.C., July 12, 2005._At an event on July 3 in Turlock, California, Sardar Paramjit Singh Sekhon and Sardar Gagandeep Singh of Dal Khalsa America, invited Dr. Gurmit Singh Aulakh, President of the Council of Khalistan, to hoist the flag of Khalistan. The Council of Khalistan is the government pro tempore of Khalistan. It is leading the struggle for Khalistan's independence. Dal Khalsa has led several marches and other events in Punjab to promote independence for Khalistan, the Sikh homeland that declared its independence from India on October 7, 1987. The event was shown throughout India on an Indian television channel called Aaj Tak on July 6. Dr. Aulakh was interviewed by a California representative of Voice of America.

As soon as Dr. Aulakh raised the flag, slogans of "Khalistan Zindabad" ("Long live Khalistan") were raised. Speakers at the event spoke out strongly for a free and independent Khalistan. Speakers included Dr. Awatar Singh Sekhon from Canada, Dr. Aulakh, Sardar Sekhon, Sardar Ajit Singh Pannu, Dr. Ranbir Singh Sandhu from Tracy, California, Sardar Karj Singh Sandhu from Philadelphia, Dr. Paramjit Singh Ajrawat, Sardar Dharam Singh Bains of Philadelphia, and others.

"If anyone speaks out for freedom, the Indian government labels them terrorists," Dr. Aulakh said. "This is not going to work. Everyone knows the modus operandi of the Indian government." The Indian government has murdered over 250,000 Sikhs since 1984, more than 300,000 Christians in Nagaland since 1948, over 90,000 Muslims in Kashmir since 1988, and tens of thousands of Tamils, Assamese, Bodos, Manipuris, Dalits, and others. The Indian Supreme Court called the Indian government's murders of Sikhs "worse than a genocide."

According to a report by the Movement Against State Repression (MASR), 52,268 Sikhs are being held as political prisoners in India without charge or trial. Some have been in illegal custody since 1984! "These prisoners never committed any crime but peacefully speaking out for Sikh freedom," said Dr. Aulakh. "How can there be political prisoners in a democracy?" he asked. "We demand the release of all political prisoners," he said.

"As Professor Darshan Singh, a former Jathedar of the Akal Takht, said, 'If a Sikh is not a Khalistani, he is not a Sikh'," Dr. Aulakh noted. He added that the event in Turlock was in line with the strong sentiment for freedom in Punjab, Khalistan. "We must work hand-in-hand, the Sikh diaspora and our Sikh brothers and sisters in Punjab, Khalistan, until the glow of freedom shines on a free and sovereign Khalistan," he said. "I thank Sardar Sekhon for organizing this event."

"The flame of freedom still burns bright in the hearts of Sikhs despite the deployment of over half a million Indian troops to crush it," Dr. Aulakh said. "Last year, Punjab Chief Minister Amarinder Singh signed a bill canceling the agreements that allowed the diversion of Punjabi water to non-riparian states. The bill asserted the sovereignty of Punjab. Sardar Atinder Pal Singh, another former Member of Parliament, held a seminar on Khalistan in Punjab. It was well attended and featured outstanding presentations, including one by Professor Gurtej Singh, IAS, Professor of Sikhism," he said. "Dal Khalsa has held marches through Punjab demanding the establishment of an independent Khalistan."

On the Anniversary of the Indian government's military attack on the Golden Temple, the center and seat of Sikhism, last month, Dal Khalsa, the Khaisa Panchayat, the Shiromani Akali Dal (Amritsar), Damdami Taksal, the Sikh Student Federation (Bittu), and the Akal Federation marched through the streets of Amritsar demanding freedom for Khalistan. They carried posters of the demolished Golden Temple and distributed pamphlets on the life of Sant Jarnail Singh Bhindranwale, a Sikh leader who was murdered in the Golden Temple attack along with General Shabeg Singh, Bhai Amrik Singh, and others. Bhindranwale was a strong advocate of Sikh freedom. Dal Khalsa also raised the flag of Khalistan on Republic Day, January 26. 35 Sikhs were arrested at that time. Some of them have been denied bail. Cases were registered against dozens of Sikhs for raising the Sikh flag at the Golden Temple on the anniversary of the Golden Temple attack in the presence of over 30,000 Sikhs. Warrants have been issued for their arrest. Those charged include Dal Khalsa leaders such as Kanwarpal Singh Bittu, Sarabjit Singh Ghuman, Dr. Manjinder Singh Jandi, and others, as well as former Member of Parliament Simranjit Singh Mann.

History shows that multinational states such as India are doomed to failure. Countries like Austria-Hungary, India's longtime friend the Soviet Union, Yugoslavia, Czechoslovakia, and others prove this point. India is a polyglot like those countries, thrown together for the convenience of the British colonialists. It is doomed to break up as they did. Steve Forbes, writing in Forbes magazine, said that India is a multinational, multiethnic, multireligious, multicultural, multilinguistic state that is doomed to disintegrate like the Austro-Hungarian Empire.

"We must continue to pray for and work for our God-given birthright of freedom," Dr. Aulakh said. "Without political power, religions cannot flourish and nations perish."

- - - - - - - - -

**Council of Khalistan,
Washington, DC, July 12, 2005.**

Dear Khalsa Ji: Last month on the anniversary of India's brutal military attack on the Golden Temple and 125 other Gurdwaras throughout Punjab, dozens of Sikhs were charged by the Indian government. Warrants for their arrest were issued. Their crime was raising the flag of Khalistan in the presence of over 30,000 Sikhs. We salute them for this action and for their courage. Apparently, peacefully demonstrating in support of self-determination and freedom can get you arrested in India. Unfortunately, this is part of a pattern.

The flame of freedom continues to burn brightly in the heart of the Sikh Nation. No force can suppress it. On Republic Day, Sikh leaders raised the Sikh flag in Amritsar and made speeches in support of Khalistan. 35 Sikhs were arrested for raising the Sikh flag. Eleven of them continue to be held and they have been denied bail. I was invited to raise the flag on July 3 in Turlock, California, at an event organized by Dal Khalsa America. I would like to thank Sardar Paramjit Singh Sekhon and Sardar Gagandeep Singh of Dal Khalsa America, who invited me to hoist the flag of Khalistan. Speakers included Dr. Awatar Singh Sekhon from Canada, Dr. Aulakh, Sardar Sekhon, Sardar Ajit Singh Pannu, Dr. Ranbir Singh Sandhu from Tracy, California, Sardar Karj Singh Sandhu from Philadelphia, Dr. Paramjit Singh Ajrawat, Sardar Dharam Singh Bains of Philadelphia, and others. The event was shown throughout India on an Indian television channel called Aaj Tak on July 6. I was interviewed by a California representative of Voice of America. When I raised the flag, slogans of "Khalistan Zindabad" were raised.

In 1699, Guru Gobind Singh gave sovereignty to the Sikh Nation, giving the blessing "In grieb Sikhin ko deon Patshahi" ("I give sovereignty to the humble Sikhs.") Just two years after his departure from this earthly plane in 1708, the Sikhs established our own independent state in Punjab. Sikhs ruled Punjab from 1710 to 1716 and from 1765 to 1849. There was no such thing as India then.

Today we struggle to regain the sovereignty that Guru Gobind Singh bestowed upon us over 300 years ago. Yet the Jathedar of the Akal Takht, Joginder Singh Vedanti, was quoted as saying that "We don't want a separate territory." Does Jathedar Vedanti, like every other Sikh, pray "the Khalsa shall rule" every morning and evening? Has he forgotten our heritage of freedom? How can the spiritual leader of the Sikh religion deny the Sikh Nation's legitimate aspiration for freedom and sovereignty? Is he not stung by the words of one of his predecessors, former Akal Takht Jathedar Professor Darshan Singh, who said, "If a Sikh is not a Khalistani, he is not a Sikh"? Is Akal Takht occupied by a person who does not believe in Sikh values and Sikh aspirations?

Punjab's Chief Minister, Captain Amarinder Singh, was declared a hero of the Sikh Nation for asserting Punjab's sovereignty and preserving Punjab's natural resource, its river water, for the use of Punjab farmers by cancelling Punjab's water agreements. In so doing, Amarinder Singh and the Legislative Assembly explicitly declared the sovereignty of the state of Punjab. In December former Member of Parliament Simranjit Singh Mann again reverted to public support of Khalistan. He pledged that his party will lead a peaceful movement to liberate Khalistan. Obviously, Mr. Mann is aware of the rising support of our cause. Mann joins Sardar Atinder Pal Singh, Sardar D.S. Gill of the International Human Rights Organization, and other Sikh leaders in Punjab in supporting freedom for Khalistan openly. Jagjit Singh, President of Dal Khalsa, was quoted in the Deccan Herald as saying that "the Indian government can never suppress the movement. Sikh aspirations can only be met when they have a separate state." There is no other choice for the Sikh nation but a sovereign, independent Khalistan. Every Sikh leader must come out openly for Khalistan. We salute those Sikh leaders in Punjab who have done so.

Any organization that sincerely supports Khalistan deserves the support of the Sikh Nation. However, the Sikh Nation needs leadership that is honest, sincere, consistent, and dedicated to the cause of Sikh freedom. Leaders like Dr. Jagjit Singh Chohan, Harchand Singh Longowal, Didar Bains, Ganga Singh Dhillon, the Akali Dal leadership, and others who were complicit in the attack on the Golden Temple cannot be trusted by the Sikh Nation. The evidence against them is clear in Chakravyuh: Web of Indian Secularism. The Sikh Nation cannot believe that these leaders will not betray the cause of Khalistan, just as they betrayed the Sikh Nation in 1984. We must be careful If we are to continue to move the cause of freedom for Khalistan forward in 2005 as we did in 2004.

The Akali Dal conspired with the Indian government in 1984 to invade the Golden Temple to murder Sant Bhindranwale and 20,000 other Sikh during June 1984 in Punjab. Even the Pope spoke out strongly against this invasion and desecration of our most sacred shrine. How can these so-called Sikh leaders connive with the people who carried It out? If Sikhs will not even protect the sanctity of the Golden Temple, how can the Sikh Nation survive as a nation?

The Akali Dal has lost all its credibility. The Badal government was so corrupt openly and no Akali leader would come forward and tell Badal and his wife to stop this unparallelled corruption. If Jathedar Vedanti opposes freedom and sovereignty for the Sikh Nation, then he is not fit to sit in Akal Takht, in the seat of the Khalsa Panth. The Sikh Nation should have a Jathedar who is committed to restoring sovereignty that is our birthright and that Guru Gobind Singh granted.

Is this the freedom that Guru Gobind Singh bestowed upon us? Is this the "glow of freedom" that Nehru promised us when Master Tara Singh and the Sikh leaders of the time chose to take our share with India?

The Council of Khalistan has stood strongly and consistently for liberating our homeland, Khalistan, from Indian occupation. For over 19 years we have led this fight while others were trying to divert the resources and the attention of the Sikh Nation away from the issue of freedom in a sovereign, independent Khalistan. Khalistan is the only way that Sikhs will be able to live in freedom, peace, prosperity, and dignity. It is time to start a Shantmai Morcha to liberate Khalistan from Indian occupation.

The Akal Takht Sahib and Darbar Sahib are under the control of the Indian government, the same Indian government that has murdered more than a quarter of a million Sikhs in the past twenty years. The Jathedar of the Akal Takht and the head granthi of Darbar Sahib toe the line that the Indian government tells them. They are not appointed by the Khalsa Panth. Otherwise they would behave like a real Jathedar, Jathedar Gurdev Singh Kaunke, rather than like Indian government puppet Jathedar Aroor Singh, who gave a Siropa to General Dyer for the massacre of Sikhs and others at Jallianwala Bagh. These institutions will remain under the control of the Indian regime until we free the Sikh homeland, Punjab, Khalistan, from Indian occupation and oppression and sever our relations with the New Delhi government.

The Sikhs in Punjab have suffered enormous repression at the hands of the Indian regime in the last 25 years. Over 50,000 Sikh youth were picked up from their houses, tortured, murdered in police custody, then secretly cremated as "unidentified bodies." Their remains were never even given to their families! Another 52,268 are being held as political prisoners. Some have been in illegal custody since 1984! Over 250,000 have been murdered at the hands of the Indian regime. Even now, the capital of Punjab, Chandigarh, has not been handed over to Punjab, but remains a Union Territory. How can Sikhs have any freedom living under a government that would do these things?

Sikhs will never get any justice from Delhi. The leaders in Delhi are only interested in imposing Hindu sovereignty over all the minorities to advance their own careers and their own power. Ever since independence, India has mistreated the Sikh Nation, starting with Patel's memo labelling Sikhs "a criminal tribe." What a shame for Home Minister Patel and the Indian government to issue this memorandum when the Sikh Nation gave over 80 percent of the sacrifices to free India.

How can Sikhs continue to live in such a country? There is no place for Sikhs in supposedly secular, supposedly democratic India. Let us dedicate ourselves to living up to the blessing of Guru Gobind Singh. It is time to launch a Shantmai Morcha to liberate Khalistan. We must demand self-determination in a free and fair vote, the democratic way. It is time to shake ourselves loose from the yoke of Indian oppression and liberate our homeland, Khalistan, so that all Sikhs may live lives of prosperity, freedom, and dignity.

Sincerely,
Gurmit Singh Aulakh,
President.

***

Document

CONGRESSIONAL RECORD -- EXTENSIONS

Tuesday, June 21, 2005
109th Congress, 1st Session
151 Cong Rec E 1309

REFERENCE: Vol. 151, No. 83
SECTION: Extension of Remarks
TITLE: DEMAND FOR FREEDOM ALIVE IN PUNJAB, KHALISTAN

Speech of
HON. EDOLPHUS TOWNS
of New York
in the House of Representatives
Tuesday, June 21, 2005

Mr. TOWNS . Mr. Speaker, I rise today to take note of the demonstrations in Punjab, Khalistan that surrounded the 21st anniversary of the Indian government's attack on the Golden Temple. Groups such as Dal Khalsa and others marched through the streets of Amritsar, converging at the Golden Temple for a big rally, according to The Times of India. They carried posters of Sant Jarnail Singh Bhindranwale, a Sikh freedom leader killed in the Golden Temple attacks, as well as posters of the demolished Golden Temple.

As you know, the Indian government also attacked 125 other Gurdwaras_Sikh places of worship_at the same time. Over 20,000 Sikhs were killed. The Sikh holy book, the Guru Granth Sahib, was shot full of bullet holes. Sikh boys between the ages of 8 and 13 were shot on the premises.

Former Member of Parliament Simranjit Singh Mann said that the only way to assuage the wounds of the attack is by freeing Khalistan, the Sikh homeland. Another speaker said that the movement to free Khalistan is by peaceful means. Khalistan declared its independence from India in 1997. That is now eight years ago.

Police and intelligence operatives were surreptitiously watching this peaceful demonstration. Apparently, 21 years after the Golden Temple attack, the Sikhs' demand for freedom still frightens them.

India claims it is democratic, Mr. Speaker, yet it sends police to spy on a peaceful demonstration. In January, 35 Sikhs were arrested for raising the Sikh flag and making speeches. The Movement Against State Repression reports that over 52,000 Sikhs are political prisoners in "the world's largest democracy." More than a quarter of a million Sikhs have been murdered, according to figures compiled from the Punjab State Magistracy.

Sikhs are only one of India's targets. Other minorities such as Christians, Muslims, and others have also been subjected to tyrannical repression. More than 300,000 Christians have been killed in Nagaland, and thousands elsewhere in the country. Over 900,000 Kashmir Muslims, at least 2,000 to 5,000 Muslims in Gujarat, and thousands of other Muslims, have been victims of India's tyranny. And tens of thousands of people in Assam, Bodoland, Manipur, Tamil Nadu, and around the country, as well as countless Dalit "Untouchables" have been killed as well.

Mr. Speaker, this is unacceptable. We must take a stand for freedom for all, as the President committed us to doing in January. The time has come to stop all our aid and trade with India, to end our burgeoning military cooperation, and to demand the peaceful resolution of the situation in South Asia through a free and fair plebiscite for all the national groups there.

Mr. Speaker, I would like to put the Times of India article about the demonstration into the Record at this time.

[From the Times of India, Jun. 6, 2005]
Khalistan Demand Raised on Genocide Day
(By Yudhvir Rana)

Amritsar._The pent up secessionist emotions of Sikh radicals whipped up on the Genocide Day observed as Ardas Divas at Akal Takht on Monday, as a large number of Sikh youth including women brandishing naked swords raised slogans for Sikh's independent state Khalistan while passing pejorative remarks against SAD-Badal president Parkash Singh Badal and SGPC president Bibi Jagir Kaur for not coming up to the aspirations of Sikhs and addressing their problems.

The ferocity of slogans multiplied after Sikh radical leader Simranjit Singh Mann, president of SAD (Amritsar) announced that Sikhs's hurt feelings could only be assuaged when Sikhs independent state Khalistan comes into existence. He suggested that Khalistan could be created on the buffer zone between India and Pakistan.

Baba Harnam Singh, 15th chief of Damdami Taksal joined Simranjit Singh Mann with his arms wielding supporters and announced to observe the martyrdom day of Sant Jarnail Singh Bhinderanwalae at Taksal's headquarters at Gurdwara Gurdarshan Parkash, Chowk Mehta on June 12.

The radical activists including from Dal Khalsa, Dal Khalsa, SAD(A), Damdami Taksal, Sikh Students Federation (Bittu), Akal Federation jointly put up the board of Shaheedee Gallery at the gallery situated outside Akal Takht against the wishes of SGPC. A large number of Sikhs and converged at Akal Takht on the 21st anniversary of Operation Bluestar.

Posters of demolished Akal Takht, Sikh militant leaders and pamphlet on the life of Jarnail Singh Bhinderanwalae were distributed among Sikh sangat.

A large number of policemen in plain clothes and sleuths of various intelligence agencies were hovering around the Akal Takht and its surrounding. A police officer of DSP rank remained present among Sikh sangat sitting in front of Akal Takht during the ceremony.

Earlier Parkash Singh Badal and Bibi Jagir Kaur condemned congress government for rubbing salt to the wounds of Sikhs. About the postponement of foundation stone alying ceremony of Yadgara-e-Shaheedan, Badal said the foundation stone would be laid once its design was approved.

Justifying the demand of Khalistan, Jagjit Singh Chauhan, a Khalistan ideologue said that they would peruse their mission through peaceful democratic means.

Jathedar of Akal Tkaht, Giani Joginder Singh Vedanti presented siropas's to Ishar Singh, Mata Pritam Kaur son and wife of Jarnail Singh Bhinderanwalae and relatives of other martyrs. Earlier addressing the gathering he said it was unfortunate that even after 21 years of Operation Bluestar, the central government has not condemned the incident nor those responsible for the 1984 anti Sikh riots have been brought to books and Operation Bluestar was a black chapter in the history of Independent India. The Sikhs had laid down their lives under the aegis of Sant Jarnail Singh Bhinderanwalae to protect the sanctity of gurdhams.

Meanwhile Damdami Taksal presented photographs of Jarnail Singh, Amrik Singh, Shubeg Singh and Thara Singh to Jathedar of Akal Takht Giani Joginder Singh Vedanti for displaying them in the gallery. Vedanti however asked them to contemplate over their request. Meanwhile chief spokesperson of Damdami Taksal. Bhai Mohkam Singh said that they also performed ardas at the gallery's gate. He said panth would decide if there was no desirable reply from Jathedar.

On the other hand SAD(A) had demanded to display the photograph of Jarnail Singh Bhinderanwalae at central Sikh Museum, handing over of personal belongings of Bhinderanwale by his family, Taksal and Army to panth without any conditions, naming the road between Sri Guru Arjun Dev Niwas to Sri Hargobind Niwas on Sant Jarnail Singh Marg, setting up of a Sant Jarnail Singh Dharmik Vidya Kendar and beginning of Shaheed Bhai Amrik Singh Award for those schools helping to check apostism among Sikhs and General Shubeg Sigh Award to promote traditional sports.

***

Document

CONGRESSIONAL RECORD -- EXTENSIONS

Friday, May 13, 2005
109th Congress, 1st Session
151 Cong Rec E 975

REFERENCE: Vol. 151, No. 63
SECTION: Extension of Remarks
TITLE: NEW BOOK REVEALS VOICES OF SOUTH ASIA

Speech of
HON. EDOLPHUS TOWNS
of New York
in the House of Representatives
Thursday, May 12, 2005

Mr. TOWNS . Mr. Speaker, I have recently been given a copy of an interesting new book called Authentic Voices of South Asia, edited by retired Brigadier General Usman Khalid and published by the London Institute of South Asia. The book is an excellent discussion of India's hegemonic ambitions in South Asia and the drive for self-determination for all the peoples of the subcontinent. I recommend it to my colleagues as an excellent source of information about that difficult and troubled region.

The book includes essays on the situation in Punjab, Khalistan, in Kashmir, and in other troubled parts of the subcontinent. It extensively discusses India's ambition to be the overwhelming, hegemonic power in South Asia and control all the countries there and its disrespect for the sovereignty of its neighbors. It is dedicated to "250,000 Sikhs, 90,000 Muslim Kashmiri Martyrs and many more who have been killed in all parts of India, notably Assam, Maharashtra, and Gujarat by Hindu mobs or the Indian police and armed forces." This doesn't mention the fact that the Hindu mobs carry out their atrocities with the connivance of the Indian police and armed forces. For example, a policeman in Gujarat told an Indian newspaper that the massacre of 2,000 to 5,000 Muslims there was pre-planned by the Indian government and the police were told to stand aside, a remarkable parallel to the 1984 Delhi massacre of Sikhs, in which Sikh policemen were locked in their barracks.

In all, Mr. Speaker, over 250,000 Sikhs have been murdered by the Indian government, according to the Punjab State Magistracy, in addition to more than 300,000 Christians in Nagaland, over 90,000 Kashmiri Muslims, tens of thousands of Christians and Muslims throughout India, and tens of thousands of Assamese, Bodos, Dalits, Manipuris, Tamils, and others, as well as the minorities cited in the introduction to Authentic Voices of South Asia. In addition, according to the Movement Against State Repression, India holds over 52,000 Sikh political prisoners, some of whom have been in illegal detention without charge or trial since 1984. Amnesty International reports that tens of thousands of other minorities are also held as political prisoners. This is why this book is so urgently needed and so important.

The book includes essays by Dalit leader V.T. Rajshekar, Dr. Gurm Singh Aulakh, President of the Council of Khalistan, Dr. Awatar Singh Sekhon, Editor of the International Journal of Sikh Affairs, and many other leaders and scholars. Mr. Rajshekar writes that "the glitter of Brahminism lies in its imperial ambitions and its fascist agenda." Dr. Sekhon writes that only accepting the principle of national self-determination provides a basis for peace and stability in South Asia.

India agreed in 1948 to a plebiscite in Kashmir to determine its status. That plebiscite has never been held, even as India proudly proclaims itself "the world's largest democracy." Well, why not simply let the people of Kashmir, of Punjab, Khalistan, of Nagalim, and of all the other minority states and communities determine their status by means of a free and fair vote. Isn't that how democracies do business? It is time for the U.S. Congress to go on record demanding a tree and fair vote, demanding that India keep its promises and act like the democracy it claims to be. It is also time to stop American aid and trade with India until its "imperial ambitions and its fascist agenda" are abandoned and all people within its borders enjoy full civil liberties and human rights. Only then can India's claim of democratic principles be taken seriously.

Mr. Speaker, I would like to insert the Preface from Authentic Voices of South Asia into the Record at this time for the information of my colleagues and the American people.

Authentic Voices of South Asia
Preface

South Asia is the only major region in the world with unsettled frontiers. This is not because the states that emerged from the end of British colonial rule in the subcontinent have no 'principle' or 'agreement' to draw on for settling their disputes, it is because the largest country_India_has simply resiled on the agreements it made. The 'core' dispute in the area is over the future of the State of Jammu and Kashmir. India took the matter of its 'ownership' of the State to the UN Security Council which ordered a cease fire but rejected its claim; it upheld the UN Charter and secured an agreement of both India and Pakistan that the people would decide which country their state would join_India or Pakistan_in a UN supervised Plebiscite. India used the cease-fire to consolidate its military position and then went back on its agreement in 1953 to hold the Plebiscite on the specious grounds that Pakistan had signed a bilateral defence agreement with the US and introduced a 'foreign' element that India found unacceptable.

The root cause of all the problems in South Asia is India's self view as an 'imperial' power with a role to keep order in the region. India acts like the US did when it exercised control over South and Central America under the Monroe Doctrine or the Soviet Union exercised control over East Europe under the Brezhnev Doctrine. India does not recognise the sovereign equality of states of South Asia; it acts as if it operated a 'doctrine of limited sovereignty' of sorts in the region. India is resented and abhorred by all its neighbours for that reason. India became a 'strategic partner' of the Soviet Union during the Cold War and is now a 'strategic partner' of the US and Israel. It chose its 'partners' with only one consideration_who will recognise India as the 'primary power' in the region (a policeman in American parlance) and thus help keep a lid on the pressure cooker that India had turned South Asia into.

Pakistan is not the only victim of India's 'imperial' aspiration; the religious minorities and the 'low born' inside India suffer even more. India betrayed the Sikh who it promised to give their own 'sovereign state'. It betrayed the Untouchables by Poona Pact promising meaningless 'legal safeguards' in exchange for the effective 'political safeguard' of 'separate electorate' offered to them by the British Government. All the various tribal peoples all over India, who had been self governing under British rule, have been denied their separate identity and rights. The betrayal of India is matched by the ineptitude of Pakistan's leaders who neither understood the Indian mindset nor their own role as the champion of 'post imperialism' to uphold the right of 'national self-determination' in South Asia and as a 'nation state' with Islam as the principle of national solidarity.

Putting this book together was a huge task that could be done better if some of the constraints had been absent. Because it is so difficult to speak the truth and survive in South Asia, many of the Authentic Voices live in exile and those who live in India have to be careful. Being a soldier rather than scholar, my editing is not characterised by 'academic restraint' but by 'forthright clarity'. But I have not tried to harmonise style or substance; the differences of views between the various contributors exist, as they must. After all, these are the Authentic Voices of different I peoples. I am grateful to all the contributors, particularly to Syed Ali Geelani and Mr V.T. Rajshekar, who are under close watch in India, to have taken risks to address the people of South Asia and given them hope and direction._Brigadier (R) Usman Khalid.

***

Document

CONGRESSIONAL RECORD -- EXTENSIONS

Thursday, April 07, 2005
109th Congress, 1st Session
151 Cong Rec E 566

REFERENCE: Vol. 151, No. 39
SECTION: Extension of Remarks
TITLE: VISA DENIAL TO INDIAN OFFICIAL LEADS TO BURNING OF PEPSI PLANT

Speech of
HON. EDOLPHUS TOWNS
of New York
in the House of Representatives
Wednesday, April 6, 2005

Mr. TOWNS . Mr. Speaker, as you know, the United States government denied a visa to Narendra Modi, Chief Minister of Gujarat, due to the state government's complicity in the massacre of Muslims there and his insensitive statements about minorities. His visa was revoked under the law that prohibits those responsible for violations of religious freedom from getting visas. This was the right thing to do, and I salute those who made this decision.

According to the March 25 issue of India-West, the denial of a visa to Mr. Modi was met with attacks from the Indian government. Prime Minister Manmohan Singh, who, as a Sikh, is a member of a religious minority himself, complained in Parliament that "we do not believe it is appropriate . . . to make a subjective judgment question a constitutional authority in India." The Foreign Ministry said that the denial of Mr. Modi's visa "is uncalled for and displays lack of courtesy and sensitivity toward a constitutionally elected chief minister of a state of India." Of course, they completely neglected to mention Mr. Modi's lack of courtesy and sensitivity towards the 2,000 to 5,000 Muslims killed in the riots that his government helped organize. India's Human Rights Commission held Mt. Modi and his government responsible for the massacre.

The Indian government officially stated that the decision showed "a lack of courtesy and sensitivity" and that their "sovereignty" was violated by the decision. This is the standard argument of tyrants. It is the argument countries like Red China make when they are criticized.

On March 19 in New Delhi, India-West reported, fanatical Hindu nationalist fundamentalists affiliated with the militant organization Bajrang Dal rioted against the United States because Mr. Modi was denied his visa. They barged into a Pepsi-Cola warehouse, smashed bottles of Pepsi, and set fire to the building. The warehouse was partially burned. About a dozen workers fled. The rioters also ransacked a nearby Pepsi office. Another group protested the U.S. consulate in Bombay. They carried signs reading "Down With the United States." Some Bajrang Dal members tried to enter the visa application center in Ahmedabad. Modi himself said, "Let us pledge to work for such a day that an American would have to stand in line for entry into Gujarat." He accused the United States of trying to "impose its laws on other countries." He urged India to deny visas to American officials.

Mr. Speaker, this is just the latest chapter in India's ongoing repression of its minorities, which has been well documented in this House over the years, and its virulent hatred of America. Why do we spend our time, energy, and money supporting such a country?

The time has come to hold India's feet to the fire. Denying Mr. Modi a visa was simply a small first step, and a good one. We must do more. The time has come to stop our aid and trade with India until all people enjoy the full flower of human rights and to support self-determination for all the peoples and nations seeking their freedom through a free and fair plebiscite. The essence of democracy is the right to self-determination. As the world's oldest and strongest democracy, it is up to the United States to take fhese measures in support of freedom for all.

Mr. Speaker, I would like to place the India-West article of March 25 into the Record at this tIme.

[From the India-West, Mar. 25, 2005]
Pepsi Warehouse Burned in Visa Denial Uproar_Continued from
page A1

The riots were sparked by the burning of a train coach by Muslims in Godhra, killing 59 Hindu kar sevaks.

Modi was denied a diplomatic visa to travel to the United States and his existing tourist/business visa was revoked under the U.S. Immigration and Nationality Act that bars people responsible for violations of religious freedom from getting a visa.

Modi had been scheduled to address a gathering of Indian American groups and motel owners in New York, Florida and in New Jersey.

India slammed the decision, saying it showed a "lack of courtesy and sensitivity," and Prime Minister Manmohan Singh criticized the American decision in Parliament.

"The American government has been clearly informed . . . we do not believe that it is appropriate to use allegations or anything less than due legal process to make a subjective judgment to question a constitutional authority in India," Singh told the Rajya Sabha.

Responding to opposition leader Jaswant Singh's submission that the decision was unacceptable, Manmohan Singh said, "We agree that this is not a matter of partisan politics, but rather a matter of concern over a point of principle. Our prompt and firm response clearly shows our principled stand in this matter."

Earlier, Indian officials summoned Ambassador Mulford's deputy Robert Blake "to lodge a strong protest."

"This action . . . is uncalled for and displays lack of courtesy and sensitivity toward a constitutionally elected chief minister of a state of India," the Foreign Ministry said in a statement, expressing the government's "deep concern and regret."

The U.S. stood by its decision after a review sought by India. Mulford, who was out of town when the news broke March 18, said the U.S. decision was aimed at Modi alone, and not Gujaratis. He also denied it would affect ties with India.

In Washington, State Department spokesman Adam Ereli said the U.S. response was based on a finding by India's National Human Rights Commission that held Modi's government responsible for the 2002 Hindu-Muslim violence in the state, India's worst in a decade.

The decision led to widespread uproar in parts of Gujarat. A day after the decision, nearly 150 Bajrang Dal activists barged into the warehouse of U.S.-based PepsiCo in the Surat, smashed bottles and set fire to the place, said Dharmesh Joshi, a witness. The warehouse was partially burned.

A witness said about a dozen workers at the warehouse fled during the attack and firefighters doused the flames.

The protesters also ransacked a nearby PepsiCo office and demonstrated outside the American consulate in Mumbai. Some carried placards reading: "Down with the United States," "Boycott the U.S. goods and the Americans."

Up to 150 Bajrang Dal activists also tried to enter the U.S. visa application center in Ahmedabad but were turned back by police.

Modi called the U.S. decision "an insult to India and its Constitution." In a public address in Ahmedabad, he lashed out at the United States.

"A man from Gujarat was thrown out of a train in South Africa. This led to a movement that overthrew the British Empire," Modi thundered, in a reference to Mahatma Gandhi. "Let us pledge to work for such a day that an American would have to stand in line for entry into Gujarat," he added.

"The United States can't impose its laws on other countries. In the same way, India should deny visas to U.S. officials as a protest against Washington's policies in Iraq," Modi said.

"On what basis has the U.S. decided this?" Modi asked. "Where has the U.S. got its information from? The American government should know that every state in India is ruled by the Constitution and no one can violate that. No court has indicted the Gujarat government or the CM of complicity in the incidents that took place in the state."

If the Pakistani president and the Bangladesh prime minister could visit the U.S., two countries in which minorities have suffered, Modi said he could be admitted too.

***

Document

CONGRESSIONAL RECORD -- EXTENSIONS

Thursday, April 07, 2005
109th Congress, 1st Session
151 Cong Rec E 573

REFERENCE: Vol. 151, No. 39
SECTION: Extension of Remarks
TITLE: SIKHS ABOUT TO CELEBRATE VAISAKHI DAY

Speech of
HON. EDOLPHUS TOWNS
of New York
in the House of Representatives
Wednesday, April 6, 2005

Mr. TOWNS . Mr. Speaker, April 13, which is the birthday of Thomas Jefferson, author of the Declaration of Independence, is Vaisakhi Day for the Sikhs. I wish all the Sikhs around the world a happy Vaisakhi Day.

Vaisakhi Day is the anniversary of the day in 1699 when Guru Gobind Singh, the last of the ten Sikh Gurus, created the Khalsa Panth. At that time, he said, "I give sovereignty to the humble Sikhs." Yet over 300 years later, they still struggle for that sovereignty while they suffer under severe repression from "the world's largest democracy."

More than 250,000 Sikhs have been murdered at the hands of the Indian government, according to figures compiled by the Punjab State Magistracy. The Movement Against State Repression reports that 52,268 Sikhs are being held as political prisoners under the repressive TADA law. How can this happen in a democracy?

Sikhs have an opportunity this Vaisakhi Day to reclaim their sovereignty. In January, 35 Sikhs were arrested for simply raising the Sikh flag and making speeches in support of Khalistan, the Sikh homeland that declared its independence on October 7, 1987. Political leaders are coming out for Khalistan. All of India's efforts to suppress the Sikhs sovereignty movement have just given it new life.

What can we do to support this worthy cause? We should stop our aid and trade with India as long as it continues to kill ethnic minorities, hold political prisoners, and engage in other wholesale violations of the most basic human rights. We should go on record in support of self-determination in the form of a free and fair plebiscite on independence in Khalistan, in Kashmir, in Nagaland, and wherever the people are seeking freedom. These measures will help bring a new glow of freedom to all people in the subcontinent.

Mr. Speaker, at this time I would like to place the Council of Khalistan's Vaisakhi Day message into the Record for the information of my colleagues.

Vaisakhi Day Should Be Celebrated in Freedom

I would like to take this opportunity to wish you and your family and friends and all Sikhs a Happy Vaisakhi Day. As you know, Vaisakhi Day is the anniversary of the founding of the Khalsa. On Vaisakhi Day in 1699, Guru Gobind Singh baptized the Sikhs and required them to keep the five Ks. He made the Sikhs into saints and soldiers, giving the blessing "In grieb Sikhin ko deon Patshahi" ("I give sovereignty to the humble Sikhs.") Just two years after his departure from this earthly plane in 1708, the Sikhs established our own independent state in Punjab.

Today we struggle to regain the sovereignty that Guru Gobind Singh bestowed upon us over 300 years ago. Yet the Jathedar of the Akal Takht, Joginder Singh Vedanti, was quoted as saying that "We don't want a separate territory." Does Jathedar Vedanti, like every other Sikh, pray "Raj Kare Ga Khalsa" ("the Khalsa shall rule") every morning and evening? Has he forgotten our heritage of freedom? How can the spiritual leader of the Sikh religion deny the Sikh Nation's legitimate aspiration for freedom and sovereignty? Is he not stung by the words of one of his predecessors, former AkalTakht Jathedar Professor Darshan Singh, who said, "If a Sikh is not a Khalistani, he is not a Sikh"? Is Akal Takht occupied by a person who does not believe in Sikh values and Sikh apsirations?

The flame of freedom continues to burn brightly in the heart of the Sikh Nation. No force can suppress it. On Republic Day, Sikh leaders raised the Sikh flag in Amritsar and made speeches in support of Khalistan. 35 Sikhs were arrested for raising the Kesri Nishan. Eleven of them continue to be held and they have been denied bail. Is this the freedom that Guru Gobind Singh bestowed upon us? Is this the "glow of freedom" that Nehru promised us when Master Tara Singh and the Sikh leaders of the time chose to take our share with India?

Punjab's Chief Minister, Captain Amarinder Singh, was declared a hero of the Sikh Nation for asserting Punjab's sovereignty and preserving Punjab's natural resource, its river water, for the use of Punjab farmers by cancelling Punjab's water agreements. In so doing, Amarinder Singh and the Legislative Assembly explicitly declared the sovereignty of the state of Punjab. In December former Member of Parliament Simranjit Singh Mann again reverted to public support of Khalistan. He pledged that his party will lead a peaceful movement to liberate Khalistan. Obviously, Mr. Mann is aware of the rising support of our cause. Mann joins Sardar Atinder Pal Singh, Sardar D.S. Gill of the International Human Rights Organization, and other Sikh leaders in Punjab in supporting freedom for Khalistan openly. Jagjit Singh, President of Dal Khalsa, was quoted in the Deccan Herald as saying that "the Indian government can never suppress the movement. Sikh aspirations can only be met when they have a separate state." There is no other choice for the Sikh nation but a sovereign, independent Khalistan. Every Sikh leader must come out openly for Khalistan. We salute those Sikh leaders in Punjab who have done so.

Any organization that sincerely supports Khalistan deserves the support of the Sikh Nation. However, the Sikh Nation needs leadership that is honest, sincere, consistent, and dedicated to the cause of Sikh freedom. Leaders like Dr. Jagjit Singh Chohan, Harchand Singh Longowal, Didar Bains, Ganga Singh Dhillon, the Akali Dal leadership, and others who were complicit in the attack on the Golden Temple cannot be trusted by the Sikh Nation. The evidence against them is clear in Chakravyuh: Web of Indian Secularism. The Sikh Nation cannot believe that these leaders will not betray the cause of Khalistan, just as they betrayed the Sikh Nation in 1984. We must be careful if we are to continueto move the cause of freedom for Khalistan forward in 2005 as we did in 2004.

The Akali Dal conspired with the Indian government in 1984 to invade the Golden Temple to murder Sant Bhindranwale and 20,000 other Sikh during June 1984 in Punjab. Even the Pope spoke out strongly against this invasion and desecration of our most sacred shrine. How can these so-called Sikh leaders connive with the people who carried it out? If Sikhs will not even protect the sanctity of the Golden Temple, how can the Sikh Nation survive as a nation?

The Akali Dal has lost all its credibility. The Badal government was so corrupt openly and no Akali leader would come forward and tell Badal and his wife to stop this unparallelled corruption.

If Jathedar Vedanti opposes freedom and sovereignty for the Sikh Nation, then he is not fit to sit in Akal Takht, in the seat of the Khalsa Panth. The Sikh Nation should have a Jathedar who is committed to sovereignty.

The Council of Khalistan has stood strongly and consistently for liberating our homeland, Khalistan, from Indian occupation. For over 18 years we have led this fight while others were trying to divert the resources and the attention of the Sikh Nation away from the issue of freedom in a sovereign, independent Khalistan. Khalistan is the only way that Sikhs will be able to live in freedom, peace, prosperity, and dignity. It is time to start a Shantmai Morcha to liberate Khalistan from Indian occupation.

The Akal Takht Sahib and Darbar Sahib are under the control of the Indian government, the same Indian government that has murdered more than a quarter of a million Sikhs in the past twenty years. The Jathedar of the Akal Takht and the head granthi of Darbar Sahib toe the line that the Indian government tells them. They are not appointed by the Khalsa Panth. Otherwise they would behave like a real Jathedar, Jathedar Gurdev Singh Kaunke, rather than like Indian government puppet Jathedar Aroor Singh, who gave a Siropa to General Dyer for the massacre of Sikhs and others at Jallianwala Bagh. These institutions will remain under the control of the Indian regime until we free the Sikh homeland, Punjab, Khalistan, from Indian occupation and oppression and sever our relations with the New Delhi government.

The Sikhs in Punjab have suffered enormous repression at the hands of the Indian regime in the last 25 years. Over 50,000 Sikh youth were picked up from their houses, tortured, murdered in police custody, then secretly cremated as "unidentified bodies." Their remains were never even given to their families! Another 52,268 are being held as political prisoners. Some have been in illegal custody since 1984! Even now, the capital of Punjab, Chandigarh, has not been handed over to Punjab, but remains a Union Territory. How can Sikhs have any freedom living under a government that would do these things?

Sikhs will never get any justice from Delhi. The leaders in Delhi are only interested in imposing Hindu sovereignty over all the minorities to advance their own careers and their own power. Ever since independence, India has mistreated the Sikh Nation, starting with Patel's memo labelling Sikhs "a criminal tribe." What a shame for Home Minister Patel and the Indian government to issue this memorandum when the Sikh Nation gave over 80 percent of the sacrifices to free India.

How can Sikhs continue to live in such a country? There is no place for Sikhs in supposedly secular, supposedly democratic India. Let us make Viasakhi Day a day of freedom. Let us dedicate ourselves this Vaisakhi Day to living up to the blessing of Guru Gobind Singh. Let us take the occasion of Vaisakhi Day to begin to shake ourselves loose from the yoke of Indian oppression and liberate our homeland, Khalistan, so that all Sikhs may live lives of prosperity, freedom, and dignity.

***

Document

CONGRESSIONAL RECORD -- EXTENSIONS

Thursday, March 17, 2005
109th Congress, 1st Session
151 Cong Rec E 492

REFERENCE: Vol. 151, No. 33
SECTION: Extension of Remarks
TITLE: TWO SIKHS ACQUITTED IN AIR INDIA CASE

Speech of
HON. EDOLPHUS TOWNS
of New York
in the House of Representatives
Thursday, March 17, 2005

Mr. TOWNS . Mr. Speaker, I was pleased to learn that this past Wednesday, two Sikhs named Ajaib Singh Bagri and Ripudaman Singh Malik, who were accused of carrying out the 1985 Air India bombing, were acquitted. These Sikhs were found innocent because the witnesses against them were not believable.

The Indian government has maintained for 20 years that the Sikhs were responsible for the Air India disaster and has used it as an excuse to kill Sikhs and tighten the repression against them. Now it is clear that they were not responsible.

Why did India grant a loan of $2 million to the main financial backer of the organization that carried out the bombing? Why did Indian operatives approach Lal Singh, offering him "2 million dollars and settlement in a nice country" if he would offer false testimony against the two accused Sikhs? Why did the Consul General of India in Toronto call in a detailed description of the disaster just hours later when it took the Canadian investigators weeks to find that information? How did he know so much? Why was the Consul General later expelled?

His successor as Consul General was quoted as saying that Sikhs who support Khalistan, the independent Sikh homeland, are terrorists, but the movement for Sikh independence is led by the Council of Khalistan, which is committed to achieving an independent Khalistan by peaceful, democratic, nonviolent means.

The book Soft Target, which is the definitive account of the Air India case, quotes a Canadian Security Investigative Service investigator as saying, "If you really want to clear the incidents quickly, take vans down to the Indian High Commission and the consulates in Toronto and Vancouver, load up everybody and take them down for questioning. We know it and they know it that they are involved." And the acquittal of the Sikhs accused just provides further substantiation of India's guilt.

Mr. Speaker, this country must not support terrorism. We cannot support the people who bombed the Air India airliner and killed 329 innocent people, especially at a time when we are fighting terrorism around the world. It is time to cut off all our aid and trade with India and support freedom and self-determination for all the nations struggling for their independence in South Asia. That is the best way to establish peace, freedom, security, and dignity for all in that troubled region of the world.

I would like to insert the press release on the acquittal of these two Sikhs from the Council of Khalistan into the Record, Mr. Speaker. I believe it will clearly show who is responsible for this terrible act of terrorism.

Malik, Bagri Acquitted of All Charges in Air India Case
justice has been done despite pressure from indian regime

Washington, DC, March 16, 2005. Ripudaman Singh Malik and Ajaib Singh Bagri have been acquitted of all charges in the Air India bombing case, in a major rebuke to the Indian regime. Malik and Bagri were found not guilty today in the deaths of 329 people who perished when Air India Flight 182 was brought down by a bomb on June 23, 1985 in Canada's worst case of mass murder. Justice Ian Josephson delivered the verdicts this afternoon, saying he didn't believe many of the witnesses.

"Justice has been done for these Sikhs," said Dr. Gurmit Singh Aulakh, President of the Council of Khalistan, which leads the Sikh struggle for independence. "Despite the effort of the Indian government to blame these Sikhs for its own acts, they have been found innocent. This is a major setback for the Hindustani regime," he said. Canadian Member of Parliament wrote in 1989 that the Canadian government had spent $60 million on the case. "On behalf of over 600,000 Sikhs in Canada and the 25 million Sikhs worldwide, we would like to express our gratitude to Judge Josephson for doing the right thing and not caving in to the pressure of the Indian government," Dr. Aulakh said.

Air India flight 182 was blown up off Ireland in 1985. It was on its way from Toronto to Bombay. It was supposed to be blown up at the London airport when no passengers would be aboard, but due to delays it blew up over Ireland. The book Soft Target by Canadian journalists Zuhair Kashmeri of the Toronto Globe and Mail and Brian McAndrew of the Toronto Star exposed India's responsibility for this bombing. In the book, Kashmeri and McAndrew quoted a Canadian Security Investigative Service (CSIS) investigator as saying, "If you really want to clear the incidents quickly, take vans down to the Indian High Commission and the consulates in Toronto and Vancouver, load up everybody and take them down for questioning. We know it and they know it that they are involved."

The book shows that within hours after the flight was blown up, the Indian Consul General in Toronto, Surinder Malik (no relation to Ripudaman Singh Malik), called in a detailed description of the bombing and the names of those he said were involved, information that the Canadian government didn't discover until weeks later. Mr. Malik said to look on the passenger manifest for the name "L. Singh." This would turn out to be Lal Singh, who told the press that he was offered "two million dollars and settlement in a nice country" by the Indian regime to give false testimony in the case.

In his book Betrayal: The Spy Canada Abandoned, Member of Parliament David Kilgour wrote that Canadian-Polish double agent Ryszard Paszkowski was approached to join a plot to carry out a second bombing.

The people who approached Paszkowski were connected to the Indian government.

The main backer of the group that was supposedly behind the Air India bombing had received a $2 million loan from the State Bank of India just before the plane was attacked, according to Soft Target. The year after the bombing, three Indian consuls general were asked to leave the country. At the time of the bombing, the Congress Party needed the Sikhs as scapegoats to win votes on a law-and-order platform. The attack also served as justification for the government to shed more Sikh blood.

The Indian government has murdered over 250,000 Sikhs since 1984, more than 300,000 Christians since 1948, over 90,000 Muslims in Kashmir since 1988, and tens of thousands of Tamils, Assamese, Manipuris, Dalits, Bodos, and others. The Indian Supreme Court called the Indian government's murders of Sikhs "worse than a genocide." According to a report by the Movement Against State Repression (MASR), 52,268 Sikhs and tens of thousands of other minorities are being held as political prisoners in India without charge or trial. Some have been in illegal custody since 1984! We demand the immediate release of all these political prisoners.

The Sikh Nation declared its independence from India on October 7, 1987 and formed the Council of Khalistan at that time to lead the struggle for independence. When India became independent, Sikhs were equal partners in the transfer of power and were to receive their own state, but the weak and ignorant Sikh leaders of the time were tricked into staying with India on the promise that they would have "the glow of freedom" and no law affecting the Sikhs would pass without their consent. Sikhs ruled an independent and sovereign Punjab from 1710 to 1716 and again from 1765 to 1849 and were recognized by most of the countries of the world at that time. Sikhs do not accept the Indian constitution. No Sikh representative has ever signed it.

V.P. Singh, who was the Indian Consul General in Toronto when Soft Target came out, was quoted in the June 22, 1989 issue of the Washington Times, as saying that Sikhs who support Khalistan are terrorists. The Council of Khalistan, which leads the Sikh struggle to liberate Khalistan, openly repudiated militancy and has an 18-year record of working to free Khalistan by peaceful, democratic, nonviolent means.

Indian police arrested human-rights activist Jaswant Singh Khalra after he exposed their policy of mass cremation of Sikhs, in which over 50,000 Sikhs have been arrested, tortured, and murdered, then their bodies were declared unidentified and secretly cremated. Khalra was murdered in police custody. His body was not given to his family. No one has been brought to justice for the kidnapping and murder of Jaswant Singh Khalra. The police never released the body of former Jathedar of the Akal Takht Gurdev Singh Kaunke after SSP Swaran Singh Ghotna murdered him. He has never been tried for the Jathedar Kaunke murder. In 1994, the U.S. State Department reported that the Indian government had paid over 41,000 cash bounties for killing Sikhs.

Missionary Graham Staines was murdered along with his two sons, ages 8 and 10, by a mob of militant, fundamentalist Hindu nationalists who set fire to the jeep, surrounded it, and chanted "Victory to Hannuman," a Hindu god. None of the people involved has been tried. The persons who have murdered priests, raped nuns, and burned Christian churches have not been charged or tried. The murderers of 2,000 to 5,000 Muslims in Gujarat have never been brought to trial. An Indian newspaper reported that the police were ordered not to get involved in that massacre, a frightening parallel to the Delhi massacre of Sikhs in 1984.

India is not one country; it is a polyglot thrown together for the convenience of the British colonialists. It is doomed to break up as they did. Last year, the Punjab Legislative Assembly passed a bill cancelling the government's daylight robbery of Punjab river water. The Assembly explicitly stated the sovereignty of Punjab.

"The Indian regime stands exposed for the bloody tyranny that it is," said Dr. Aulakh. "This verdict is a major setback to their repressive drive for hegemony over all of South Asia," he said. "This is a victory not only for the Sikh Nation, but for freedom-loving people everywhere."

"I urge the international community to help us free Khalistan from Indian occupation," Dr. Aulakh said. "Freedom is the birthright of all people and nations," he said. "As Professor Darshan Singh, a former Jathedar of the Akal Takht, said, 'If a Sikh is not for Khalistan, he is not a Sikh'," Dr. Aulakh noted. "We must continue to press for freedom," he said. "Without political power, religions cannot flourish and nations perish. A sovereign Khalistan is essential for the survival of the Sikh religion and the Sikh Nation."

***

Document

CONGRESSIONAL RECORD -- EXTENSIONS

Tuesday, February 15, 2005
109th Congress, 1st Session
151 Cong Rec E 239

REFERENCE: Vol. 151, No. 16
SECTION: Extension of Remarks
TITLE: SIKH LEADER AGAIN SPEAKS OUT FOR FREEDOM FOR KHALISTAN

Speech of
HON. EDOLPHUS TOWNS
of New York
in the House of Representatives
Tuesday, February 15, 2005

Mr. TOWNS . Mr. Speaker, there are encouraging developments in the fight for freedom for minorities in India. It looks like the people of Nagaland are making progress in their negotiations with India to achieve autonomy. This is a potentially significant development that will begin, at long last, the unraveling of the web of Indian oppression. Can Kashmir and Khalistan be far behind?

To add to this, the fire of freedom continues to burn as brightly as ever in Punjab, Khalistan. On December 7, a Sikh leader named Simranjit Singh Mann, who is a former Member of India's Parliament and has held events right here in the Capitol and met many Members of Congress, again spoke out for independence for the Sikh homeland, Khalistan. Mr. Mann put his party, the Akali Dal, Amritsar, on record for independence. He pledged that he would lead a peaceful movement for independence, which he said was a dream of the Sikh people that "will be materialized one day." It looks like that day is getting closer.

The government of Punjab acted last year to cancel all water agreements with the other states in India, by which Punjab's water was being diverted to those other states. In so doing, they declared the sovereignty of the state of Punjab. Imagine that, Mr. Speaker. They are openly claiming their sovereignty. This is good to see.

Mr. Speaker, when India became independent, the Sikhs were supposed to get an independent state in Punjab. But the Indian leaders assured them they would have "the glow of freedom" there, so they stayed with India. Well, that "glow of freedom" has taken the lives of over 250,000 Sikhs as well as over 300,000 Christians in Nagaland, over 89,000 Kashmiri Muslims, and tens of thousands of other minority people. It has resulted in 52,268 Sikhs being held as political prisoners under a repressive law called TADA that expired in 1995. It is time for real freedom for the Sikhs, the Nagas, the Kashmiris, and all people in the subcontinent.

The essence of democracy is self-determination. If India wants to be treated as a democracy, it must allow self-determination and all other rights to all its citizens. We should not provide any money to India until it does. In 1948, India promised to hold a plebiscite to let the people of Kashmir decide their status. It's now 56 years later and they are still waiting. Similarly, the demand for self-determination in Khalistan, in Nagaland, and elsewhere has been met with nothing but violent resistance. Is that democracy, Mr. Speaker? Is that freedom?

The Tribune, a newspaper in Chandigarh, Punjab, carried excellent coverage of Mr. Mann's remarks in its December 8 issue. I would like to place that article in the Record at this time for the information of my colleagues.

[From the (Chandigarh, India) Tribune, Dec. 8, 2004]
Mann Reverts to Sovereign Punjab Theme

Ludhiana, Dec. 7._Shiromani Akali Dal (Amritsar) supremo Simranjit Singh Mann yesterday reverted to the theme of sovereign Punjab, declaring that his party would launch a peaceful movement to realise this dream. He said his party had never given up the demand for a separate and sovereign Punjab as the Sikhs' was a separate nationality, foundations of which had been laid down by Guru Gobind Singh himself.

Mr. Mann, who was here to preside over a meeting of the party officebearers at Gurdwara Akalgarh, said to ensure lasting peace in South Asia in the face of deep hostility between "Hindu civilisation (India) and Muslim civilisation (Pakistan)", it was in the interest of the people of the region to create a neutral and buffer sovereign state.

He maintained that the foundations for a separate sovereign Sikh state had been laid down by Guru Gobind Singh and Banda Singh Bahadur followed by Maharaja Ranjit Singh. This dream was furthered by "Sant Jarnail Singh Bhindranwale" and "would be materialised one day". He said since both Pakistan and India had nuclear weapons, it was necessary that some buffer state should be created so that the two countries did not come face to face with each other.

Mr. Mann refused to give the geographical outline of the "sovereign state" envisioned by him. He evaded an answer to a question whether it included the part of the state which is now with Pakistan.

Welcoming the close cooperation between the Pakistani Punjab and the Indian Punjab, Mr. Mann claimed it was he who had initiated this move by demanding way back in 1990 that the border between the two Punjabs should be opened up for the people to cross over.

To a question on the demand of the Dal Khalsa that ban on cow slaughter in Punjab should go, Mr. Mann said he or his organisation had nothing to do with that organisation (Dal Khalsa). At the same time, he said, he or his party would not like to hurt the sentiments of a majority of people as "Hindus held the cow to be sacred and their sentiments should be respected".

Mr. Mann also accused Shiromani Akali Dal leader Parkash Singh Badal of having connived with Hindu organisations in demolishing the Babri mosque. He alleged that Mr. Badal had sent a special jatha, led by Mr. Avtar Singh Hit, to Ayodhaya on December 6, 1992, to join the kar sevaks for demolishing the Babri mosque.

***

Document

CONGRESSIONAL RECORD -- EXTENSIONS

Tuesday, February 15, 2005
109th Congress, 1st Session
151 Cong Rec E 240

REFERENCE: Vol. 151, No. 16
SECTION: Extension of Remarks
TITLE: SIKHS ARRESTED FOR RAISING FLAG ARE DENIED BAIL

Speech of
HON. EDOLPHUS TOWNS
of New York
in the House of Representatives
Tuesday, February 15, 2005

Mr. TOWNS . Mr. Speaker, on January 26, India celebrated its Republic Day, the anniversary of the adoption of its constitution. On that day a group of Sikh activists raised the Sikh flag at a Gurdwara in the city of Amritsar in accordance with Sikh tradition. For this, complaints were issued against 35 Sikhs and 31 have been arrested.

Now eleven of them have had their bail denied, keeping them in detention. The Punjab and Haryana High Court has ruled that speaking out for Khalistan is not a crime, yet they are charged with "sedition" and "making inflammatory speeches" for raising a flag and speaking out for freedom for the Sikh homeland.

Mr. Speaker, what kind of democracy is this? The Movement Against State Repression (MASR) was already reporting that India held 52,268 political prisoners. These activists add 11 to that number.

This is just the latest illustration that exercising your freedom of speech can be a very dangerous thing in India if you are a minority. India has a pattern of repression. It has killed over 250,000 Sikhs since 1984, more than 300,000 Christians in Nagaland, over 90,000 Kashmiri Muslims, thousands of other Christians and Muslims throughout the country, and tens of thousands of Assamese, Bodos, Dalits (the aboriginal people of South Asia), Manipuris, Tamils, and others. The U.S. State Department reported in 1994 that the Indian government had paid over 41,000 cash bounties to police officers for killing Sikhs. One such bounty went to an officer who killed a three-year-old boy.

We must not just sit and watch while a country that proclaims itself "the world's largest democracy" tramples on the most basic of democratic freedoms, such as the freedom to speak out and to hold a peaceful demonstration. That is not the hallmark of a democracy. It is the hallmark of a police state.

The time has come to let India know that we are watching and to let them know that this is unacceptable.

There are steps that we can take to support the rights of all people in south Asia. It is time that we take these steps. They include cutting off our aid and trade with India and putting the Congress on record in support of self-determination for the Sikhs of Punjab, Khalistan, the Christian people of Nagaland, the Kashmiris, and all the people of South Asia who are seeking freedom. Only by exercising their right to self-determination, which is the essence of democracy, can the people there finally live in freedom, peace, and prosperity.

Mr. Speaker, I would like to place the Council of Khalistan's very informative press release on the denial of bail to these Sikh activists into the Record at this time.

[From Council of Khalistan]
Bail Denied for 11 Sikhs Arrested for Hoisting Sikh Flag in Amritsar_Is This Democracy, Freedom of Speech?

Eleven Sikhs who were arrested for raising the Sikh flag on Republic Day, January 26, have been denied bail. Thirty-five Sikhs were charged and 31 are being held. They raised the saffron flag of Khalsa Raj at Gurdwara Shaheed Ganj in Amritsar. They have been charged with sedition and "making inflammatory speeches." Khalsa Raj Party President Dr. Jagjit Singh Chohan said that they had raised the flag according to Sikh tradion.

Punjab Pradesh Congress Party President Hanspal said, "We will not allow them to raise their heads for Khalistan." Maninder Singh Bitta, President of the All-India Youth Congress, demanded that Dr. Chohan and others be deported to Pakistan, claiming they are Pakistani agents. Former Chief Minister Badal said, "We will not permit the militancy to raise its head again."

"How can India call itself democratic when it suppresses a basic right like freedom of speech?," said Dr. Gurmit Singh Aulakh, President of the Council of Khalistan, which leads the Sikh struggle for freedom. "The Punjab and Haryana High Court has already ruled in the case of the late Colonel Partap Singh that speaking in support of freedom for Khalistan is not a crime," Dr. Aulakh said. "How can these activists be arrested for something that is not a crime?"

The Indian government has murdered over 250,000 Sikhs since 1984, more than 300,000 Christians since 1948, over 90,000 Muslims in Kashmir since 1988, and tens of thousands of Tamils, Assamese, Manipuris, Dalits, Bodos, and others. The Indian Supreme Court called the Indian government's murders of Sikhs "worse than a genocide." According to a report by the Movement Against State Repression (MASR), 52,268 Sikhs and tens of thousands of other minorities are being held as political prisoners in India without charge or trial. Some have been in illegal custody since 1984! We demand the immediate release of all these political prisoners.

"The Sikh Nation is indebted to the leaders of Dal Khalsa who raised the Sikh flag, including Harcharan Singh Dhami, President, Kanwarpal Singh Bittu, General Secretary, Satnam Singh Paonta Sahib, and others," said Dr. Aulakh. "We praise Dr. Chohan for his remarks. But how can Sikhs like Badal, Hanspal, Bitta, and others call themselves Sikhs when they deny the Sikh aspirations for freedom? Clearly, they are doing the bidding of the Indian government, which controls them."

The Sikh Nation declared its independence from India on October 7, 1987 and formed the Council of Khalistan at that time to lead the struggle for independence. When India became independent, Sikhs were equal partners in the transfer of power and were to receive their own state, but the weak and ignorant Sikh leaders of the time were tricked into staying with India on the promise that they would have "the glow of freedom" and no law affecting the Sikhs would pass without their consent. Sikhs ruled an independent and sovereign Punjab from 1710 to 1716 and again from 1765 to 1849 and were recognized by most of the countries of the world at that time. Sikhs do not accept the Indian constitution. No Sikh representative has ever signed it.

Indian police arrested human-rights activist Jaswant Singh Khalra after he exposed their policy of mass cremation of Sikhs, in which over 50,000 Sikhs have been arrested, tortured, and murdered, then their bodies were declared unidentified and secretly cremated. Khalra was murdered in police custody. His body was not given to his family. No one has been brought to justice for the kidnapping and murder of Jaswant Singh Khalra. The police never released the body of former Jathedar of the Akal Takht Gurdev Singh Kaunke after SSP Swaran Singh Ghotna murdered him. He has never been tried for the Jathedar Kaunke murder. In 1994, the U.S. State Department reported that the Indian government had pad over 41,000 cash bounties for killing Sikhs.

India is not one country; it is a polyglot thrown together for the convenience of the British colonialists. It is doomed to break up as they did. Last year, the Punjab Legislative Assembly passed a bill cancelling the government's daylight robbery of Punjab river water. The Assembly explicitly stated the sovereignty of Punjab.

"I urge the international community to help us free Khalistan from Indian occupation," Dr. Aulakh said. "Freedom is the birthright of all people and nations," he said. "The arrest and denial of bail for these activists for raising the Sikh flag and making speeches shows that there is no freedom for Sikhs within India," he said. "As Professor Darshan Singh, a former Jathedar of the Akal Takht, said, 'If a Sikh is not for Khalistan, he is not a Sikh'," Dr. Aulakh noted. "We must continue to press for freedom," he said. "Without political power, religions cannot flourish and nations perish. A sovereign Khalistan is essential for the survival of the Sikh religion and the Sikh Nation."

***

Document

CONGRESSIONAL RECORD -- EXTENSIONS

Tuesday, February 01, 2005
109th Congress, 1st Session
151 Cong Rec E 127

REFERENCE: Vol. 151, No. 8
SECTION: Extension of Remarks
TITLE: SIKHS OBSERVE INDIA'S REPUBLIC DAY AS DAY OF BETRAYAL

HON. EDOLPHUS TOWNS
of New York
in the House of Representatives
Tuesday, February 1, 2005

Mr. TOWNS . Mr. Speaker, this past Wednesday, January 26, was India's Republic Day, the anniversary of the adoption of their constitution. It is a very important day in India's calendar. The Indian constitution is supposed to guarantee freedom for everyone and ensure everyone full human rights and democratic freedoms. However, in practice, it has not worked that way in the 58 years that India has been independent. I salute the ideals of the Indian constitution, but I cannot urge India strongly enough to start living up to them.

Independent India has been no picnic for the minorities of India. They have suffered severe repression. Sikhs, Christians, Muslims, and others have suffered greatly at the hands of democratic, secular India. That is why Sikhs in Washington, London, and even Amritsar protested on Republic Day. In Amritsar, the Sikh organization Dal Khalsa hoisted the Sikh flag and distributed flyers saying that the Indian flag "is not our flag" and the Indian constitution "is not our constitution." No Sikh representative has ever signed the Indian constitution.

Over a quarter of a million Sikh have been murdered at the hands of the Indian government, along with over 300,000 Christians in Nagaland and still more Christians elsewhere. Priests have been murdered throughout the country, nuns have been raped, churches have been burned, Christian schools and prayer halls have been vandalized. By now, the burning death of missionary Graham Staines and his two young sons and the beating of missionary Joseph Cooper are well known. In recent days, evangelist Benny Hinn had to travel under heavy security after being attacked and vandalized.

Over 90,000 Kashmiri Muslims have been murdered, along with thousands of Muslims in other parts of the country. Recently, according to the BBC, the Indian government finally admitted that Muslims in Gujarat did not set the train fire that led to the massacre of 5,000 of them, a massacre that a policeman told an Indian newspaper was planned in advance by the Indian government.

India forced Untouchables out of a refugee camp after the tsunami, according to Yahoo! News. The Washington Post reported that they were being given only the leftover food of Brahmins and India has refused all efforts by the international community to come and help them. Even though the very Indian constitution that Republic Day celebrates outlawed the caste system, it is alive and well to this day.

Mr. Speaker, these are just the latest examples of the repression of minorities that continues to occur while India celebrates its secular, democratic constitution. This is unacceptable. In the President's recent Inaugural Address, he spoke about extending freedom to all the world. India is one place where that effort needs to be carried out before the country, a multinational, polyglot empire like Austria-Hungary, the Soviet

Union, or Yugoslavia, falls apart. We must do whatever we can to ensure freedom and peace for all in the subcontinent.

The best things we can do are to stop our aid and trade with India until human rights are respected and the violent repression ceases and to put ourselves on record in support of a free and fair plebiscite in Punjab, Khalistan, in Kashmir (as promised in 1948), in Nagaland, and throughout the minority areas of the subcontinent.

Mr. Speaker, at this time I would like to place an article about Dal Khalsa's protest in Amritsar and a press release about the Council of Khalistan's protest here in Washington into the Record.

Council of Khalistan,
Washington, DC.
Sikhs Mark Indian Republic Day
by Protesting Genocide, Repression

Washington, DC, January 26, 2005._Sikhs from all over the East Coast came to Washington today to mark Indian Republic Day by protesting the genocide and repression against the Sikhs and other minorities. They raised slogans such as "India out of Khalistan" and carried signs such as "India: Democracy for Brahmins, Tyranny for Minorities." The demonstration was organized by the Council of Khalistan, which leads the struggle to establish a sovereign, independent Khalistan free from Indian occupation. On October 7, 1987, the Sikh Nation declared its independence from India, naming its new country Khalistan. The Council of Khalistan was established at that time to lead the peaceful, democratic, nonviolent movement to liberate Khalistan from Indian oppression. It is the government pro tempore of Khalistan, the Sikh homeland.

Republic Day is the anniversary of the adoption of India's constitution, which is supposed to ensure a secular, democratic government. But the Indian government has murdered over 250,000 Sikhs since 1984, more than 300,000 Christians since 1948, over 89,000 Muslims in Kashmir since 1988, and tens of thousands of Tamils, Assamese, Manipuris, Dalits, Bodos, and others. The Indian Supreme Court called the Indian government's murders of Sikhs "worse than a genocide." According to a report by the Movement Against State Repression (MASR), 52,268 Sikhs are being held as political prisoners in India without charge or trial. Some have been in illegal custody since 1984! Tens of thousands of other minorities are also being held as political prisoners, according to Amnesty International. We demand the immediate release of all these political prisoners.

Indian police arrested human-rights activist Jaswant Singh Khalra after he exposed their policy of mass cremation of Sikhs, in which over 50,000 Sikhs have been arrested, tortured, and murdered, then their bodies were declared unidentified and secretly cremated. Khalra was murdered in police custody. His body was not given to his family. No one has been brought to justice for the kidnapping and murder of Jaswant Singh Khalra. The police never released the body of former Jathedar of the

Akal Takht Gurdev Singh Kaunke after SSP Swaran Singh Ghotna murdered him. He has never been tried for the Jathedar Kaunke murder. In 1994, the U.S. State Department reported that the Indian government had paid over 41,000 cash bounties for killing Sikhs.

Missionary Graham Staines was murdered along with his two sons, ages 8 and 10, by a mob of militant, fundamentalist Hindu nationalists who set fire to the jeep, surrounded it, and chanted "Victory to Hannuman," a Hindu god. None of the people involved has been tried. The persons who have murdered priests, raped nuns, and burned Christian churches have not been charged or tried. The murderers of 2,000 to 5,000 Muslims in Gujarat have never been brought to trial. An Indian newspaper reported that the police were ordered not to get involved in that massacre, a frightening parallel to the Delhi massacre of Sikhs in 1984.

"Is Jaswant Singh Khalra celebrating? Is Jathedar Kaunke celebrating? Is Graham Staines celebrating?," Dr. Aulakh asked. "How can a democracy celebrate the kind of violent repression that claimed their lives?"

When India became Independent, Sikhs were equal partners in the transfer of power and were to receive their own state, but the weak and ignorant Sikh leaders of the time were tricked into staying with India on the promise that they would have "the glow of freedom" and no law affecting the Sikhs would pass without their consent. Sikhs ruled an independent and sovereign Punjab from 1710 to 1716 and again from 1765 to 1849 and were recognized by most of the countries of the world at that time. No Sikh representative has ever signed the Indian constitution.

History shows that multinational states such as India are doomed to failure. Countries like Austria-Hungary, India's longtime friend the Soviet Union, Yugoslavia, Czechoslovakia, and others prove this point. India is not one country; it is a polyglot like those countries, thrown together for the convenience of the British colonialists. It is doomed to break up as they did. Last year, the Punjab Legislative Assembly passed a bill annulling all water agreements with the Indian government, preventing the government's daylight robbery of Punjab river water. Punjab needs its river water for its crops. In the bill, the Assembly explicitly stated the sovereignty of Punjab. Political leaders in Punjab have again called for an Independent Khalistan.

"This shows that the drive for freedom is still alive in Punjab," Dr. Aulakh said. "It is clear that India does not accept Sikhs," said Dr. Aulakh. "The Indian government continues to persecute and kill our Sikh brethren," he said. "As Professor Darshan Singh, a former Jathedar of the Akal Takht, said, 'If a Sikh is not for Khalistan, he is not a Sikh'," Dr. Aulakh noted.

"We must continue to press for our God-given birthright of freedom," he said. "Without political power, religions cannot flourish and nations perish. A sovereign Khalistan is essential for the survival of the Sikh religion."

- - - - - - - - -

[From WebIndia123.com, Jan. 26, 2005]
Dal Khalsa Observe R-Day as "Betrayal Day" in Amritsar

Amritsar, January 26, 2005 (ANI). Leaders of Dal Khalsa on Wednesday gathered at Gurudwara Shahid Ganj, Amritsar to observe the Indian republic day as betrayal day.

The Dal Khalsa leaders, including president of Dal Khalsa Harcharn-jit Singh Dhami, Khalistan ideologue Jagjit Singh Chauhan, Satnam Singh Paunta Sahib, hijacker of Indian Airlines plan in 1981 performed a Ardaas for the freedom of the Sikh nation.

They hoisted the Khalsa flag of Maharaj Ranjit Singh's regime, which symbolises Sikh raj, and prayed for the freedom of the Sikh community as they took guard of honour and pledged to continue their struggle for a free Sikh nation.

Dal Khalsa leaders describe 26th January as "betrayal day" for the Sikhs as Indian leaders betrayed the Sikh nation and imposed the present Constitution on them.

They also believe that Sikhs have been massacred in Punjab, Delhi and elsewhere after the Blue Star Operation in 1984.

***

Document

CONGRESSIONAL RECORD -- EXTENSIONS

Tuesday, January 25, 2005
109th Congress, 1st Session
151 Cong Rec E 71

REFERENCE: Vol. 151, No. 5
SECTION: Extension of Remarks
TITLE: COUNCIL OF KHALISTAN ISSUES NEW YEAR'S MESSAGE, CALLS
FOR INDEPENDENCE FOR SIKH HOMELAND

Speech of
HON. EDOLPHUS TOWNS
of New York
in the House of Representatives
Tuesday, January 25, 2005

Mr. TOWNS . Mr. Speaker, recently the Council of Khalistan issued a new year's message to the Sikh Nation. It is worth reading. My colleagues and the people should find it very informative. In the letter, the Council of Khalistan called again for the liberation of Khalistan. They noted the progress that has been made towards that goal in 2004 and the rising support among the political leadership in Punjab. They commended those leaders who have moved the Sikh homeland closer to freedom and criticized those who have supported India's brutal occupation of Khalistan in which over 250,000 Sikhs have been murdered and over 52,000 held as political prisoners without charge or trial, illegally. Some have been held since 1984.

In addition, more than 89,000 Kashmiri Muslims, over 300,000 Christians in Nagaland, Muslims and Christians throughout India, and other minorities such as Assamese, Bodos, Dalits, Manipuris, Tamils, and others are also being treated to brutal oppression by the Indian government. According to Amnesty International, tens of thousands of these minorities are being held as political prisoners.

Freedom is the birthright of everyone and self-determination is the cornerstone and essence of democracy. Yet India, which proclaims itself democratic and secular, will not allow the free expression of the democratic will of the people of Khalistan, Kashmir, Nagaland, and the other areas seeking their freedom. Instead, it continues to hold them in subjugation by brutal force. India promised to hold a plebiscite on the status of Kashmir in 1948. It has never done so. Instead, it kills in massive numbers to hold onto its empire. But history tells us that multinational, polyglot empires such as India are doomed to fall apart.

America is a beacon of freedom for the world. That is why so many people come from around the world to America. How often America has sent its troops to fight for freedom. Sometimes we may have made errors in judgment or strategy, but the intent is always to promote freedom. Can we not at least take peaceful, moderate measures to promote freedom in South Asia?

Mr. Speaker, we must stand for freedom. We must do what we can. We should stop all aid to India, except direct aid to tsunami victims, until such time as all the political prisoners are released. We must stop the aid until democratic values prevail all through India and everyone within its borders can freely exercise his or her rights without fear of reprisals from the government. We must demand a free and fair plebiscite on the political status of Khalistan, Kashmir, Nagaland, and all those lands seeking their freedom from India. That will help bring freedom, peace, and stability to the subcontinent.

Mr. Speaker, I would like to place the Council of Khalistan's new year message into the Record at this time.

May Guru Bless the Khalsa Panth in 2005 With Freedom, Happiness, Unity, and Prosperity_Freedom Lies in the Heart of the Sikh Nation; No Force Can Suppress It

(By Dr. Gurmit Singh Aulakh)

Happy New Year to you and your family and the Khalsa Panth. May 2005 be your best year ever. I wish you health, joy, and prosperity in the new year.

The flame of freedom continues to burn brightly in the heart of the Sikh Nation. No force can suppress it. All the political leaders in Punjab are recognizing it. Punjab's Chief Minister, Captain Amarinder Singh, was declared a hero of the Sikh Nation for asserting Punjab's sovereignty and preserving Punjab's natural resource, its river water, for the use of Punjab farmers by cancelling Punjab's water agreements. As recently as December 7, former Member of Parliament Simranjit Singh Mann again reverted to public support of Khalistan. He pledged that his party will lead a peaceful movement to liberate Khalistan. Obviously, Mr. Mann is aware of the rising support of our cause. Mann joins Sardar Atinder Pal Singh, Sardar D.S. Gill of the International Human Rights Organization, and other Sikh leaders in Punjab in supporting freedom for Khalistan openly. Jagjit Singh, President of Dal Khalsa, was quoted in the Deccan Herald as saying that "the Indian government can never suppress the movement. Sikh aspirations can only be met when they have a separate state." There is no other choice for the Sikh nation but a sovereign, independent Khalistan. Every Sikh leader must come out openly for Khalistan. We salute those Sikh leaders in Punjab who have done so and urge more Sikh leaders to join the cause.

Any organization that sincerely supports Khalistan deserves the support of the Sikh Nation. However, the Sikh Nation needs leadership that is honest, sincere, consistent, and dedicated to the cause of Sikh freedom. Leaders like Dr. Jagjit Singh Chohan, Harchand Singh Longowal, Didar Bains, Ganga Singh Dhillon, the Akali Dal leadership, and others who were complicit in the attack on the Golden Temple cannot be trusted by the Sikh Nation. The evidence against them is clear in Chakravyuh: Web of Indian Secularism. The Sikh Nation cannot believe that these leaders will not betray the cause of Khalistan, just as they betrayed the Sikh Nation in 1984. We must be careful if we are to continue to move the cause of freedom for Khalistan forward in 2005 as we did in 2004.

The Akali Dal conspired with the Indian government in 1984 to invade the Golden Temple to murder Sant Bhindranwale and 20,000 other Sikhs during June 1984 in Punjab. If Sikhs will not even protect the sanctity of the Golden Temple, how can the Sikh Nation survive as a nation?

The Akali Dal has lost all its credibility. The Badal government was so corrupt openly and no Akali leader would come forward and tell Badal and his wife to stop this unparallelled corruption.

The Council of Khalistan has stood strongly and consistently for liberating our homeland, Khalistan, from Indian occupation. For over 18 years we have led this fight while others were trying to divert the resources and the attention of the Sikh Nation away from the issue of freedom in a sovereign, independent Khalistan. Yet Khalistan is the only way that Sikhs will be able to live in freedom, peace, prosperity, and dignity. It is time to start a Shantmai Morcha to liberate Khalistan from Indian occupation.

Never forget that the Akal Takht Sahib and Darbar Sahib are under the control of the Indian government, the same Indian government that has murdered over a quarter of a million Sikhs in the past twenty years. The Jathedar of the Akal Takht and the head granthi of Darbar Sahib toe the line that the Indian government tells them. They are not appointed by the Khalsa Panth. The SGPC, which appoints them, does not represent the Sikh Nation anymore. They have become the puppets of the Indian government and have lost credibility with the Sikh Nation. Otherwise they would behave like a real Jathedar, Jathedar Gurdev Singh Kaunke, rather than like Indian government puppet Jathedar Aroor Singh, who gave a Siropa to General Dyer for the massacre of Sikhs and others at Jalianawa Bagh. These institutions will remain under the control of the Indian regime until we free the Sikh homeland, Punjab, Khalistan, from Indian occupation and oppression and sever our relations with the New Delhi government.

The Sikhs in Punjab have suffered enormous repression at the hands of the Indian regime in the last 25 years. Over 50,000 Sikh youth were picked up from their houses, tortured, murdered in police custody, then secretly cremated as "unidentified bodies." Their remains were never even given to their families! More than a quarter of a million Sikhs have been murdered at the hands of the Indian government. Another 52,268 are being held as political prisoners. Some have been in illegal custody since 1984! Even now, the capital of Punjab, Chandigarh, has not been handed over to Punjab, but remains a Union Territory. How can Sikhs have any freedom living under a government that would do these things?

Sikhs will never get any justice from Delhi. The leaders in Delhi are only interested in imposing Hindu sovereignty over all the minorities to advance their own careers and their own power. Ever since independence, India has mistreated the Sikh Nation, starting with Patel's memo labelling Sikhs "a criminal tribe." What a shame for Home Minister Patel and the Indian government to issue this memorandum when the Sikh Nation gave over 80 percent of the sacrifices to free India.

How can Sikhs continue to live in such a country? There is no place for Sikhs in supposedly secular, supposedly democratic India. Let us work to make certain that 2005 is the Sikh Nation's most blessed year by making sure it is the year that we shake ourselves loose from the yoke of Indian oppression and liberate our homeland, Khalistan, so that all Sikhs may live lives of prosperity, freedom, and dignity.

***

Document

CONGRESSIONAL RECORD -- EXTENSIONS

Tuesday, January 04, 2005
109th Congress, 1st Session
151 Cong Rec E 25

REFERENCE: Vol. 151, No. 1
SECTION: Extension of Remarks
TITLE: FORMER MEMBER OF PARLIAMENT ENDORSES FREEDOM FOR
KHALISTAN_SOVEREIGNTY WILL END OPPRESSION

Speech of
HON. EDOLPHUS TOWNS
of New York
in the House of Representatives
Tuesday, January 4, 2005

Mr. TOWNS . Mr. Speaker, on December 8, the Tribune newspaper out of Chandigarh, Punjab reported that a former Member of Parliament, Simranjit Singh Mann, had endorsed sovereignty for the Sikh homeland, Khalistan. His endorsement is part of a rising tide that includes the Punjab government declaring its sovereignty when it ended its water agreements with the other states in India.

I note that Mr. Mann said that the Sikhs are a separate nation and promised to lead a movement to liberate Khalistan. I hope that he keeps his promise. My friend Dr. Gurmit Singh Aulakh, President of the Council of Khalistan and an invaluable resource for information about South Asian affairs, has been saying the same things for several years. It seems that India's oppression that killed a quarter of a million Sikhs and keeps more than 52,000 of them as political prisoners has failed to dampen the desire and enthusiasm of the Sikhs for their own sovereign, independent country. I salute Mr. Mann's position. It is important for leaders in Punjab to speak out strongly for Khalistan. We can help from here, but the effort must be won in Punjab, Khalistan itself.

Mr. Speaker, all peoples are entitled to live in freedom. The Sikhs of Punjab, Khalistan made their choice on October 7, 1987 when they declared their independence from India, calling their new country Khalistan. India, which proudly claims to be democratic, refuses even to hold a free and fair vote on the question, just as India has never kept its promise of 1948 to hold a plebiscite on the future of Kashmir. How can a country do these things and claim to be democratic? Self-determination is the essence of democracy.

A new Congress gives us a new opportunity to take a stand for freedom in South Asia and around the world. We should stop all U.S. aid to India until it allows full democratic rights and full human rights to all people living within its borders and we should strongly support a free and fair plebiscite in Punjab, Khalistan, in Nagaland, in Kashmir, and wherever people seek their freedom on the question of independence. By promoting such a plebiscite, we promote democracy and human rights for all people in that troubled region.

Mr. Speaker, I would like to insert the Council of Khalistan's press release on Mr. Mann's remarks into the Record at this time.

Mann Reverts To Supporting Khalistan

Washington, DC, December 10, 2004_Once again, former MP Simranjit Singh Mann, leader of the Shiromani Alkali Dal (Amritsar), has staked out a position in support of a sovereign, independent Khalistan. Speaking in Ludhiana on December 7 at a meeting of his party, Mann said that the SAD (Amritsar) would launch a peaceful movement to achieve a separate and sovereign Sikh state, according to the December 8 issue of The Tribune (Chandigarh.) Mann claimed that his party had never given up this position.

Mann reminded his party that Sikhs are a separate nationality. He said that the foundation for an independent Khalistan was laid by Guru Gobind Singh and furthered by Sant Jarnail Singh Bhindranwale and that this dream "will be materialized one day." Guru Gobind Singh gave sovereignty to the Sikh Nation ("In grieh Sikhin ko deon patshahi.") Sikhs are a separate nation. Sikhs ruled Punjab up to 1849 when the British conquered the subcontinent. Mann noted that it is in the interests of all the people in the region to have a buffer state between India and Pakistan to help ensure lasting peace in South Asia, given the deep hostility between "Hindu civilization and Muslim civilization."

Mann's remarks show that the desire for Khalistan remains strong in the Sikhs of Punjab, said Dr. Gurmit Singh Aulakh, President of the Council of Khalistan, which leads the Sikh struggle for independence. Dr. Aulakh also cited the actions taken by Chief Minister Amarinder Singh, such as declaring Punjab's sovereignty in stopping all water agreements between Punjab and other states, as moving toward this goal. On October 7, 1987, the Sikh Nation declared its independence from India, naming its new country Khalistan. The Council of Khalistan was established at that time to lead the peaceful, democratic, nonviolent movement to liberate Khalistan from Indian oppression.

History shows that multinational states such as India are doomed to failure. Countries like Austria-Hungary, India's longtime friend the Soviet Union, Yugoslavia, Czechoslovakia, and others prove this point. India is not one country; it is a polyglot like those countries, thrown together for the convenience of the British colonialists. It is doomed to break up as they did. Recently, the Punjab Legislative Assembly passed a bill annulling all water agreements with the Indian government, preventing the government's daylight robbery of Punjab river water. Punjab needs its river water for its crops. In the bill, the Assembly explicitly stated the sovereignty of Punjab.

The Indian government has murdered over 250,000 Sikhs since 1984, more than 300,000 Christians since 1948, over 89,000 Muslims in Kashmir since 1988, and tens of thousands of Tamils, Assamese, Manipuris, Dalits, and others. The Indian Supreme Court called the Indian government's murders of Sikhs "worse than a genocide."

Indian police arrested human-rights activist Jaswant Singh Khalra after he exposed their policy of mass cremation of Sikhs, in which over 50,000 Sikhs have been arrested, tortured, and murdered, then their bodies were declared unidentified and secretly cremated. He was murdered in police custody. His body was not given to his family.

The police never released the body of former Jathedar of the Akal Takht Gurdev Singh Kaunke after SSP Swaran Singh Ghotna murdered him. Ghotna has never been brought to trial for the Jathedar Kaunke murder. No one has been brought to justice for the kidnapping and murder of Jaswant Singh Khalra.

According to a report by the Movement Against State Repression (MASR), 52,268 Slikhs are being held as political prisoners in India without charge or trial. Some have been in illegal custody since 1984! Tens of thousands of other minorities are also being held as political prisoners, according to Amnesty International. We demand the immediate release of all these political prisoners.

"It is encouraging that Mr. Mann has comeback to demanding Khalistan," said Dr. Gurmit Singh Aulakh, President of the Council of Khalistan. "This is another step forward for the movement to liberate our homeland from Indian oppression."

"As Professor Darshan Singh, a former Jathedar of the Akal Takht, said, 'If a Sikh is not for Khalistan, he is not a Sikh'," Dr. Aulakh noted. "We must continue to press for our God-given birthright of freedom," he said. "Without political power, religions cannot flourish and nations perish. A sovereign Khalistan is essential for the survival of the Sikh religion."

***

Document

CONGRESSIONAL RECORD -- EXTENSIONS

Tuesday, December 07, 2004
108th Congress, 2nd Session
150 Cong Rec E 2186

REFERENCE: Vol. 150, No. 138
SECTION: Extension of Remarks
TITLE: SIKH-OWNED GAS STATION BURNED DOWN

Speech of
HON. DAN BURTON
of Indiana
in the House of Representatives
Tuesday, December 7, 2004

Mr. BURTON of Indiana . Mr. Speaker, in the early hours of Thanksgiving morning, two Sikh brothers, Sarabjit and Sukhjinder Singh, arrived for work at the gas station they owned, only to find it burned to the ground with racist graffiti scrawled all around the burning rubble.

I am glad to say that this sad incident was immediately reported to the local Chesterfield County police, to the FBI, and to the Civil Rights division of the U.S. Department of Justice, and all are now diligently working to make sure that whoever perpetrated this heinous crime is brought to justice.

It seems obvious from the graffiti left at the scene that whoever committed this crime intended to target Muslims not Sikhs proving that this unknown arsonist was not just a bigot, but an ignorant bigot. If they had been Muslims, this would still be a senseless and horrific crime, and one to be condemned in the strongest possible terms, because to attack innocent practitioners of any religion for the acts of a handful of misguided fanatics is inexcusable.

But these men were Sikhs. Sikhs are not Muslims; they are not Hindus. Sikhism is a noble independent religion that traces its roots back hundreds of years. It is not part of any other religion. Furthermore, Sikhs believe in one God and in equality for all_an ideal that forms one of the very pillars of our own society.

Swift prosecution and severe punishment of the perpetrators of this crime is the best way to combat this type of bigotry. I am sure every Member of this House joins me in urging the police, FBI, and Justice Department to promptly and thoroughly investigate this matter and bring the perpetrator or perpetrators of this crime to justice. I am sure all of my colleagues will also join me in extending our best wishes and prayers to Sarabjit Singh, Sukhjinder Singh, and their families during this traumatic time.

Mr. Speaker, I hope that one day_a day in the not too distant future_we will live in an America where this type of crime, born out of ignorance and fear, is forever a thing of the past.

***

Document

CONGRESSIONAL RECORD -- EXTENSIONS

Tuesday, December 07, 2004
108th Congress, 2nd Session
150 Cong Rec E 2192

REFERENCE: Vol. 150, No. 138
SECTION: Extension of Remarks
TITLE: GAS STATION BURNED OUTSIDE RICHMOND; CRIME MUST BE PROMPTLY AND FULLY PROSECUTED

Speech of
HON. EDOLPHUS TOWNS
of New York
in the House of Representatives
Tuesday, December 7, 2004

Mr. TOWNS . Mr. Speaker, I was disturbed to learn that on November 25, a gasoline station outside Richmond, Virginia was burned. It was owned by two Sikh brothers. From the graffiti that appeared on the charred remains, it appears that due to their turbans, the person who committed this horrible crime thought they were Muslims affiliated with Osama bin Laden.

It is important to note that whoever the victims of this brutal crime were, it is a terrible act that must be fully and quickly prosecuted. Blaming all Muslims for the terrorist acts of a few is unfair, bigoted, and intolerant. But it is interesting that the victims of this crime were not even members of the targeted group.

Sikhism is a distinct religion from any other, including Hinduism and Islam. It is monotheistic and believes in the equality of all, including equality for women. Our Sikh friends have made many contributions to this country as lawyers, doctors, engineers, farmers, computer specialists, and in many other fields. One Sikh, Dalip Singh Saund, was even a Member of this House from California, serving from 1959 to 1963. He was the first South Asian to be elected to Congress.

The President of the Council of Khalistan, Dr. Gurmit Singh Aulakh, has written to the Chief of Police in Chesterfield County asking for a swift investigation of this incident. He received a prompt response from the police chief stating that the incident is being fully investigated and those responsible will be caught and prosecuted.

It is unfortunate that incidents like this still occur in America. Three years after September 11, people are still attacking anyone they perceive as foreign. This must be stopped. This kind of hate crime does not advance America or its ideals; it only harms our national unity at a time when we are most in need of it.

Mr. Speaker, I would like to place Dr. Aulakh's letter into the Record.

Council of Khalistan,
Washington, DC, November 29, 2004.
Col. Carl R. Baker,
Chief of Police, Chesterfield County Police Department
Chesterfield, VA.

Dear Chief Baker: As you know, on November 24, a gas station owned by Sarabjit Singh and Sukhjinder Singh, two Sikhs, was set on fire. Graffiti, including "Go back to Bin Laden," "F*** Arab gas," and "Never Again Indian Monkey N*****," was sprayed on a dumpster behind the charred station.

This is clearly a hate crime and it is unacceptable. I urge you to prosecute this crime to the fullest possible extent. Do not let the people who perpetrated this crime think they can get away with it.

This would be an unacceptable crime if the owners of the stations were Muslims, as the perpetrators apparently thought they were, or members of any other group. But they are not. They are Sikhs. Sikhism is an independent, monotheistic, revealed religion that believes in the equality of all people, including gender equality. It is not part of either Islam or Hinduism. The perpetrator of this crime didn't even hit the target he intended to hit!

Sikhs are religiously, culturally, and linguistically distinct from any other people in the world. The Sikh Nation has declared its independence from India and is currently under Indian occupation. Sikhs are working to free our homeland, Khalistan.

The incident at the gas station is a setback for the American ideal of freedom for all people and those responsible must be fully and swiftly punished to protect these Sikh businessmen and protect the system of freedom under law.

I urge you to take all appropriate action to bring the criminals to justice.

Sincerely,
Dr. Gurmit Singh Aulakh,
President.

***

Document

CONGRESSIONAL RECORD -- EXTENSIONS

Friday, October 01, 2004
108th Congress, 2nd Session
150 Cong Rec E 1773

REFERENCE: Vol. 150, No. 122
SECTION: Extension of Remarks
TITLE: THE TIME HAS COME FOR INDIA TO LIVE UP TO DEMOCRATIC PRINCIPLES

Speech of
HON. EDOLPHUS TOWNS
of New York
in the House of Representatives
Thursday, September 30, 2004

Mr. TOWNS . Mr. Speaker, recently, Indian Prime Minister Dr. Manmohan Singh spoke to the General Assembly of the United Nations. He was met with protests from Sikhs, Muslims, and other protestors.

Although Dr. Singh is a fine economist, his speech masked the reality of life in India. He spoke out against terrorism but he failed to note that India has inflicted a reign of terror on its people while sponsoring terrorism in the Pakistani province of Sindh, according to the January 2, 2002 issue of the Washington Times. He spoke of cooperation against poverty, ignoring the fact that 40 percent of the people in his country live on less than $2 per day and farmers in Punjab are forced to accept prices for their crops that provide them with a less than subsistence wage, forcing them to go deeply in debt to stay alive. He spoke of eliminating weapons of mass destruction but India started the nuclear competition in South Asia. He spoke of democracy while basic human rights are being violated. Over 52,000 Sikhs and tens of thousands of other minorities languish in Indian prisons as political prisoners. India has killed over 250,000 Sikhs, over 89,000 Kashmiris, over 300,000

Christians in Nagaland, and tens of thousands of other minorities. Yet India continues to proclaim its democratic principles.

The irony is that India seeks a permanent seat on the United Nations Security Council. How can it be on the Security Council when it cannot live up to the most basic principles of freedom?

Mr. Speaker, it is time for the United States to take action. We must cut off our aid to India until it lets all people within its artificial borders be free. We must go on record in support of self-determination for the people of Kashmir, as India promised in 1948, and for all the other peoples seeking freedom, such as the Sikhs of Khalistan and the Christians of Nagaland, among others.

Mr. Speaker, the Council of Khalistan issued an excellent and informative press release on the protests against Dr. Singh. I am inserting it into the Record now for the information of my colleagues.

[From the Council of Khalistan, September 29, 2004

India Must Live by Principles of Democracy_Seeks UN Security Council Seat But Violates Principles It Proclaims

As Indian Prime Minister Manmohan Singh spoke to the United Nations General Assembly, Sikhs, Kashmiri Muslims, and other oppressed minorities of South Asia gathered at the United Nations Building in New York to protest his appearance. They demanded the immediate release of all political prisoners, the firing of Cabinet ministers who were involved in genocide against Sikhs, Muslims, Christians, and other minorities, and sovereignty for the peoples and nations of South Asia.

"If India seeks to be a permanent member of the Security Council, it must learn to practice the principles of democracy," said Dr. Gurmit Singh Aulakh, President of the Council of Khalistan, which leads the Sikh struggle for freedom. "In 1948, India demanded a free and fair plebiscite in Kashmir. That plebiscite has never been held," he said. "Similarly, India must grant self-determination to Khalistan, Nagaland, and the other countries seeking their independence," he said.

While Prime Minister Singh spoke of "a world in which a free people could together pursue a destiny of shared prosperity," the farmers of Punjab are forced to accept less than subsistence prices for their crops. Half the population of India lives below the international poverty line. Dr. Singh spoke of a global coalition against terrorism, but his government gives only lip service to the War on Terror. India sponsors cross-border terrorism in Sindh, according to the Washington Times of January 2, 2002. Although he spoke against the proliferation of weapons of mass destruction, it was India that began the nuclear competition in South Asia. Dr. Singh spoke of "democracy as an instrument for achieving both peace and prosperity," yet India denies the most basic of democratic freedoms to the Sikhs and other minorities living within its borders.

India has murdered over 250,000 Sikhs since 1984, according to figures compiled by the Punjab State Magistracy and human-rights groups and reported in the book The Politics of Genocide by Inderjeet Singh Jaijee. It has also killed more than 89,000 Kashmiri Muslims since 1988, over 300,000 Christians in Nagaland since 1947, and thousands of Christians and Muslims elsewhere in the country, as well as tens of thousands of Assamese, Bodos, Dalits ("Untouchables," the dark-skinned aboriginal people of South Asia), Manipuris, Tamils, and other minorities. The Indian Supreme Court called the Indian government's murders of Sikhs "worse than a genocide."

According to a report by the Movement Against State Repression (MASR), 52,268 Sikhs are being held as political prisoners in India without charge or trial. Some have been in illegal custody since 1984! Amnesty International reported that tens of thousands of other minorities are also being held as political prisoners. We demand the immediate release of all these political prisoners.

Recently, another church was burned in India. This is part of a pattern of violence against Christians that has been going on since Christmas 1998 with the approval of the Indian government. Nuns have been raped, priests have been murdered, prayer halls and schools have been vandalized. A Christian religious festival was broken up by police gunfire.

Indian police arrested human-rights activist Jaswant Singh Khalra after he exposed their policy of mass cremation of Sikhs, in which over 50,000 Sikhs have been arrested, tortured, and murdered, then their bodies were declared unidentified and secretly cremated. He was murdered in police custody. His body was not given to his family.

"Although Sikhs gave 80 percent of the sacrifices for India's independence, India has massacred Sikhs since achieving independence," said Dr. Gurmit Singh Aulakh, President of the Council of Khalistan. On October 7, 1987, the Sikh Nation declared its independence from India, naming its new country Khalistan.

"Only a sovereign, independent Khalistan will end the repression and lift the standard of living for the people of Punjab," Dr. Aulakh said. "Democracies don't commit genocide."

History shows that multinational states such as India are doomed to failure. Countries like Austria-Hungary, India's longtime friend the Soviet Union, Yugoslavia, Czechoslovakia, and others prove this point. India is not one country, it is a polyglot like those countries, thrown together for the convenience of the British colonialists. It is doomed to break up as they did. Recently, the Punjab Legislative Assembly passed a bill annulling all water agreements with the Indian government, preventing the government's daylight robbery of Punjab river water. Punjab needs its river water for its crops. In the bill, the Assembly explicitly stated the sovereignty of Punjab.

"As Professor Darshan Singh, a former Jathedar of the Akal Takht, said, 'if a Sikh is not a Khalistani, he is not a Sikh'," Dr. Aulakh noted. "We must continue to press for our God-given birthright of freedom," he said. "Without political power, religions cannot flourish and nations perish. India claims to be a democracy. It is time it recognized the right of self-determination for all people in South Asia."

***

Document

CONGRESSIONAL RECORD -- EXTENSIONS

Wednesday, September 15, 2004
108th Congress, 2nd Session
150 Cong Rec E 1628

REFERENCE: Vol. 150, No. 110
SECTION: Extension of Remarks
TITLE: SIKHS CELEBRATE 400TH ANNIVERSARY OF THEIR HOLY
SCRIPTURES

Speech of
HON. EDOLPHUS TOWNS
of New York
in the House of Representatives
Wednesday, September 15, 2004

Mr. TOWNS . Mr. Speaker, earlier this month Sikhs around the world celebrated the 400th anniversary of the first installation of their holy scriptures, known as the Guru Granth Sahib. The Guru Granth Sahib, written in the lifetimes of the 10 Sikh Gurus, contains the writings of the Sikh Gurus as revealed to them and some writings by other saints who share their basic philosophy. When the Indian military attacked the Golden Temple in Amritsar, Sikhism's holiest shrine, in June 1984, they shot bullet holes through the Guru Granth Sahib.

There was a major celebration of the anniversary in Amritsar, which was attended by the Indian President, Abdul Kalam; by the Prime Minister, Manmohan Singh; and by the Dalai Lama, the spiritual leader of Buddhism, among many others. Apparently, India was trying to maintain its false front of secularism. But the people of South Asia know better.

The Guru Granth Sahib established Sikhism as a monotheistic religion that believes in the equality of all people. Guru Gobind Singh, the last of the Sikh Gurus, who consecrated the Guru Granth Sahib, made independence a basic principle of the religion.

As you know, India continues to oppress the Sikhs. Over 250,000 Sikhs have been murdered at the hands of the Hindu militant Indian government. In addition, the Indian regime has murdered over 89,000 Muslims in Kashmir, over 300,000 Christians in Nagaland, and tens of thousands of other minorities. They are holding over 52,000 Sikhs as political prisoners, according to the Movement Against State Repression (MASR) and tens of thousands of other minorities, according to Amnesty International.

The only way to preserve basic human rights for minorities in India is to stop all aid and trade until India observes these basic liberties. And we should also go on record in support of self-determination for the Sikhs of Punjab, Khalistan, the Muslims of Kashmir, the Christians of

Nagaland, and the minority nations of South Asia. That will help bring freedom, prosperity, peace, and stability to this troubled region.

Mr. Speaker, I'd like to place the Council of Khalistan's press release on the celebration into the Record for the information of my colleagues.

400th Anniversary of Guru Granth Sahib

Washington, DC, Sept. 10, 2004._On September 1, Sikhs gathered in Anuitsar to observe the 400th anniversary of the first installation of the Granth Sahib, the Sikh holy scriptures, at Darbar Sahib, the holiest of Sikh shrines. Indian President Abdul Kalam, Prime Minister Manmohan Singh, and the Dalai Lama, the spiritual leader of Buddhism, attended the celebration. Sikhs remember that bullets pierced through the Guru Granth Sahib during Operation Bluestar, the Indian government's military attack on the Golden Temple in Amritsar, in 1984.

The Guru Granth Sahib was written by the Sikh Gurus as revealed to them by God. It was written at the time in which they lived. It also includes the writing of other saints of that time which fit the philosophy of the Sikh Gurus.

"This anniversary is a joyous occasion for the Sikh Nation as we celebrate the Sikh way of life as given to us by the Gurus," said Dr. Gurmit Singh Aulakh, President of the Council of Khalistan. The Council of Khalistan, the government pro tempore of the Sikh homeland, Khalistan, leads the struggle to liberate Khalistan, which declared its independence from India on October 7, 1987.

Sikhism is an independent, monotheistic religion that believes in the equality of the whole human race. The tenth and last Sikh Guru, Guru Gobind Singh, declared the blessing "In Grieb Sikhin Ko Deon Patshahi," conferring sovereignty on the Sikh Nation, which is culturally, linguistically, and religiously distinct from any other people in the world, including Hindu India. "We must honor the Guru by reclaiming our lost sovereignty," Dr. Aulakh said.

The Indian government has murdered over 250,000 Sikhs since 1984, more than 300,000 Christians in Nagaland since 1947, over 89,000 Muslims in Kashmir since 1988, and tens of thousands of Tamils, Assamese, Manipuris, Dalits, and others. Christians and Muslims have also been murdered in other parts of the country. The Indian Supreme Court called the Indian government's murders of Sikhs "worse than a genocide." According to a study by the Movement Against State Repression, 52,268 Sikhs are being held in illegal detention as political prisoners without charge or trial. Some of them have been held since 1984!

Christian missionary Joseph Cooper was expelled from India after a mob of militant Hindu nationalists allied with the Rashtriya Swayamsewak Sangh (RSS), a fundamentalist, pro-Fascist organization that is the parent organization of the BJP, beat him so severely he had to spend a week in the hospital. In 2002, 2,000 to 5,000 Muslims were murdered in Gujarat while police were ordered to stand aside, reminiscent of the 1984 Delhi massacres of Sikhs. Indian newspapers reported that the government planned the Gujarat massacre in advance.

India is not one country; it is a polyglot thrown together by the British for their administrative convenience. Sikhs ruled Punjab until 1849 when the British conquered the subcontinent. Sikhs were equal partners during the transfer of power from the British. The Muslim leader Jinnah got Pakistan, the Hindu leaders got India, but the Sikh leadership was fooled by the Hindu leadership promising that Sikhs would have "the glow of freedom" in Northwest India. The Sikhs took their share with India on that promise. For that mistake, Sikhs are suffering now. "As Professor Darshan Singh, a former Jathedar of the Akal Takht, said, 'If a Sikh is not for Khalistan, he is not a Sikh'," Dr. Aulakh noted.

"Democracies don't commit genocide," Dr. Aulakh said. *"Only in a free and sovereign Khalistan will the Sikh Nation prosper. In a democracy, the right to self-determination is the sine qua non and India should allow a plebiscite for the freedom of the Sikh Nation,"* he said.

"The Guru Granth Sahib is the reigning Guru of the Sikh Nation and reminds us of our heritage of freedom," Dr. Aulakh said. *"It is appropriate that it received a fitting celebration."*

***

Document

CONGRESSIONAL RECORD -- EXTENSIONS

Wednesday, September 15, 2004
108th Congress, 2nd Session
150 Cong Rec E 1632

REFERENCE: Vol. 150, No. 110
SECTION: Extension of Remarks
TITLE: INDIA SHOULD OPEN BORDER AT WAGAH FOR TRADE, TRAVEL

Speech of
HON. EDOLPHUS TOWNS
of New York
in the House of Representatives
Wednesday, September 15, 2004

Mr. TOWNS . Mr. Speaker, the Chief Minister of Punjab, Captain Amarinder Singh has called for an opening of the border between India and Pakistan at Wagah, about halfway between Amritsar, Punjab, and Lahore, Pakistan. Such an opening would help the farmers of Punjab to get higher prices for their produce than the less-than-subsistence prices the Indian government pays them. It would also make it much easier for Sikhs to make religious pilgrimages to the birthplace of the first Sikh Guru, Guru Nanak, in Nankana Sahib, which is also in Pakistan.

Chief Minister Singh is right. The border should be opened. This would be a significant step towards peace in the region. It would greatly reduce the need for India and Pakistan to expend exorbitant resources on their military rivalry. Instead, the cross-border contacts would strengthen the emerging relationship between the two countries.

Mr. Speaker, let me take this opportunity to call on both the governments of India and Pakistan to open this border. Let the people, money, and ideas flow freely.

By opening the border at Wagah, India would be able to begin to end its repression that has claimed the lives of over 250,000 Sikhs since 1984, over 300,000 Christians since 1976, over 89,000 Kashmiri Muslims since 1988, and tens of thousands of other minority people.

This repression must end if India is to be taken seriously as a member of the international community. We should cut off India's aid and trade until such time as it respects human rights. Opening the border at Wagah would be a first step. We should also go on record in support of all people in South Asia enjoying the basic democratic right to self determination.

Mr. Speaker, I am inserting the press release from the Council of Khalistan into the Record at this time.

[From the Council of Khalistan]
Open Wagah Border for Trade

Washington, DC, September 10, 2004._Dr. Gurmit Singh Aulakh, President of the Council of Khalistan, today endorsed the demand of Captain Amarinder Singh, Chief Minister of Punjab, to open the border at Wagah, about halfway between Amritsar and Lahore. This would allow direct trade between Punjab and Pakistan.

"The distance between Amritsar and Lahore is only about 35 miles, less than the distance between Washington and Baltimore in the United States," Dr. Aulakh said. "Why not allow trade between these neighbors?," he asked. "Chief Minister Amarinder Singh is to be praised for asking to open this border," said Dr. Aulakh. "His stand will help keep the fires of freedom lit in the Sikh Nation," he added. "This is more than all his Akali and Congress predecessors have done for the people of Punjab," Dr. Aulakh noted.

"We fully support opening this border," he said. "This is the wise thing for Punjab and the Sikh Nation," he added. "It is another step forward for the freedom and self-determination of the Sikh Nation. It will help secure the prosperity of the Sikhs in Punjab, Khalistan."

"Opening trade through the border at Wagah will bring peace in the subcontinent," said Dr. Aulakh. "This will enable the farmers of Punjab to get higher prices for their products and help Pakistan to overcome its shortages," he said. "If India truly cares about the well-being of the people, it must open the border at Wagah immediately" Dr. Aulakh also called for bus service across the border so that visitors can more easily visit the birthplace of Guru Nanak, the first Sikh Guru, at Nankana Sahib. "We are the same people. The same language is spoken on both sides of the border. Opening this border benefits everybody and it is much

better to open the border than to spend all this time and money constantly preparing for war," he said.

Khalistan is the independent Sikh homeland declared on October 7, 1987. It has been under Indian occupation since then. When India became independent, Sikhs were equal partners in the transfer of power and were to receive their own state, but the weak and ignorant Sikh leaders of the time were tricked into staying with India on the promise that they would have "the glow of freedom" and no law affecting the Sikhs would pass without their consent. Sikhs ruled an independent and sovereign Punjab from 1710 to 1716 and again from 1765 to 1849 and were recognized by most of the countries of the world at that time. No Sikh representative has ever signed the Indian constitution. The Council of Khalistan is the government pro tempore of Khalistan, the Sikh homeland.

"If India will not open this border, it is clear that there is no place for Sikhs in India," said Dr. Aulakh. "Sardar Atinder Pal Singh's question of 14 years ago is still the question facing the Sikh Nation: Why don't we liberate Khalistan? As Professor Darshan Singh, a former Jathedar, said, 'If a Sikh is not for Khalistan, he is not a Sikh'," Dr. Aulakh noted.

The Indian government has murdered over 250,000 Sikhs since 1984, more than 300,000 Christians since 1948, over 89,000 Muslims in Kashmir since 1988, and tens of thousands of Tamils, Assamese, Manipuris, Dalits (the aboriginal people of the subcontinent), and others. The Indian Supreme Court called the Indian government's murders of Sikhs "worse than a genocide." According to a report by the Movement Against State Repression (MASR), 52,268 Sikhs are being held as political prisoners in India without charge or trial. Some have been in illegal custody since 1984!

"We must move forward with the cause of Sikh freedom," Dr. Aulakh said. "Only in a free Khalistan will the Sikh Nation prosper and get justice," said Dr. Aulakh. "India should act like a democracy and allow a plebiscite on independence for Khalistan and all the nations of South Asia," Dr. Aulakh said. "We must free Khalistan now."

***

Document

CONGRESSIONAL RECORD -- EXTENSIONS

Wednesday, September 15, 2004
108th Congress, 2nd Session
150 Cong Rec E 1635

REFERENCE: Vol. 150, No. 110
SECTION: Extension of Remarks
TITLE: CONGRATULATING NEW PAKISTANI PRIME MINISTER
SHAUKAT AZIZ

Speech of
HON. EDOLPHUS TOWNS
of New York
in the House of Representatives
Wednesday, September 15, 2004

Mr. TOWNS . Mr. Speaker, Pakistan has installed a new Prime Minister, Shaukat Aziz. His installation was reported in the newspapers September 2. I would like to take this opportunity to congratulate Mr. Aziz on his new position.

Mr. Aziz takes the helm in Pakistan at a critical time for the people and nations of South Asia. I wish him well in his time as Prime Minister and I hope that he will dedicate himself to pursuing peace in the subcontinent.

The best way to achieve peace in South Asia, Mr. Speaker, is to work for self-determination for everyone in the region. Only by allowing everyone in the subcontinent to enjoy this cornerstone of democracy can all the peoples and nations live in peace, freedom, and prosperity.

I would also urge Mr. Aziz to work for a more open border so that Sikhs and Muslims, as well as members of other minorities, can trade and travel freely and raise their standard of living by doing so. This will be good for Pakistan and for India.

Mr. Speaker, the Council of Khalistan issued a press release congratulating Prime Minister Aziz, which I intend to insert into the Record.

Congratulations to Prime Minister Shaukat Aziz

Washington, D.C., September 10, 2004._Dr. Gurmit Singh Aulakh, President of the Council of Khalistan, today congratulated the new Prime Minister of Pakistan, Shaukat Aziz, on his ascension to the position.

"I would like to take this opportunity to congratulate Prime Minister Aziz and wish his government well," Dr. Aulakh said. "I hope that this will be a step forward for peace in South Asia," he said. "Prime Minister Aziz has done excellent work on Pakistan's finances," said Dr. Aulakh. "We are sure that he can bring that wisdom and expertise to all areas of life in his country," he added.

"Prime Minister Aziz must stand firm, as President Musharraf has done, in supporting the interests of freedom for the oppressed people in South Asia," said Dr. Aulakh. "We urge him to work to open the border, enhance trade in the border regions, establish peaceful relations, and assist the cause of freedom, not just in occupied Kashmir, but wherever people are struggling to be free," he added. "We look forward to easy passage to visit the birthplace of the first Sikh guru, Guru Nanak, in Nankana Sahib."

"Only when all people and nations in South Asia have freedom and self-determination can the subcontinent live in peace, prosperity, and dignity," said Dr. Aulakh. "Prime Minister Aziz has influence by virtue of his position," he said. "We urge him to use it for the benefit of the people

of Pakistan and all the people of the subcontinent by supporting freedom and self-determination."

The Council of Khalistan was constituted to lead the struggle to liberate Khalistan, the Sikh homeland which declared its independence on October 7, 1987. It is the government pro tempore of Khalistan. Khalistan has been under Indian occupation since then. India has sent over 500,000 troops to Punjab, Khalistan, and over 700,000 to neighboring Kashmir to suppress the independence movements there. Yet India is on the verge of collapse. As former Home Minister L.K. Advani said that "if Kashmir goes, India goes."

At the time of India's independence, Sikhs were equal partners in the transfer of power and were supposed to receive their own sovereign state, but the weak and ignorant Sikh leaders of the time were tricked into staying with India on the promise that they would have "the glow of freedom" and no law affecting the Sikhs would pass without their consent. That promise was broken immediately after independence was achieved.

Sikhs ruled an independent and sovereign Punjab from 1710 to 1716 and again from 1765 to 1849 and were recognized by most of the countries of the world at that time. No Sikh representative has ever signed the Indian constitution.

"Sardar Atinder Pal Singh's question of 14 years ago is still the question facing the Sikh Nation: Why don't we liberate Khalistan?," Dr. Aulakh said. "As Professor Darshan Singh, a former Jathedar, said, 'If a Sikh is not for Khalistan, he is not a Sikh'," he noted.

The Indian government has murdered over 250,000 Sikhs since 1984, more than 300,000 Christians since 1948, over 89,000 Muslims in Kashmir since 1988, and tens of thousands of Tamils, Assamese, Manipuris, Dalits (the aboriginal people of the subcontinent), and others. The Indian Supreme Court called the Indian government's murders of Sikhs "worse than a genocide." A report by the Movement Against State Repression (MASR) shows that India is holding 52,268 Sikhs as political prisoners without charge or trial. Some have been in illegal custody since 1984!

"We must move forward with the cause of Sikh freedom," Dr. Aulakh said. "Only in a free Khalistan will the Sikh Nation prosper and get justice," said Dr. Aulakh. "India should act like a democracy and allow a plebiscite on independence for Khalistan and all the nations of South Asia," Dr. Aulakh said. "We must free Khalistan now."

***

Document

CONGRESSIONAL RECORD -- EXTENSIONS

Thursday, July 15, 2004
108th Congress, 2nd Session
150 Cong Rec E 1375

REFERENCE: Vol. 150, No. 98
SECTION: Extension of Remarks
TITLE: PUNJAB GOVERNMENT CANCELS DEAL THAT ALLOWED
DIVERSION OF WATER TO OTHER STATES

Speech of
HON. EDOLPHUS TOWNS
of New York
in the House of Representatives
Wednesday, July 14, 2004

Mr. TOWNS . Mr. Speaker, the Legislative Assembly of Punjab recently annulled a longstanding agreement that allowed the diversion of water from Punjab to other states.

According to the Tribune of Chandigarh, whose article I will be inserting in the Record at the end of my remarks, the Legislative Assembly asserted the sovereignty of Punjab in doing so. The newspaper reports that the bill passed by the Legislative Assembly says that "as a sovereign authority [Punjab] considered it its duty to uphold the Constitution and the laws and to protect the interests of its inhabitants."

Apparently, all parties supported this measure. We congratulate them on taking this step forward to protect the interests of the people of Punjab. I urge them to continue claiming, promoting, and establishing the sovereignty of Punjab.

Mr. Speaker, we know that the people of Punjab have been severely oppressed by the tyrannical Indian government. Over a quarter of a million Sikhs have been killed since 1984, according to the Punjab State Magistracy. The Movement Against State Repression reports that 52,268 have been taken as political prisoners, held without charge or trial, some as long as 20 years. According to the Punjab Human Rights Commission, about 50,000 Sikhs have simply been made to disappear by being arrested, tortured, killed in police custody, declared "unidentified bodies," and secretly cremated, without their remains even being given back to their families.

Similar repression has been visited on Christians, Muslims, and other minorities. Yet India continues to say that it is the world's largest democracy.

If India is truly a democracy, it will allow the will of the people to be carried out in regards to the diversion of water. It will allow the people_Sikhs, Christians, Muslims, Assamese, Bodos, Dalits, Manipuris, Tamils, and everyone living under Indian rule_to enjoy the full range of human rights. And it will allow self-determination for these sovereign states.

Until that happens, Mr. Speaker, we should not provide any aid to India. And we should take a stand for self-determination, which is the cornerstone of democracy, by supporting a free and fair plebiscite on independence in Punjab, Khalistan, in Kashmir, in predominantly Christian Nagaland, and everywhere that people seek their freedom from Indian rule. The assertion of sovereignty by the Punjab Legislative

Assembly is a good first step. They should act to claim their sovereignty by severing their ties to India. We should take a stand by letting them know that when they do, we will be there with them.

Mr. Speaker, as I mentioned before, I would like to insert the Tribune article into the Record at this time.

Punjab Annuls All Water Pacts, Cong, Akalis Join Hands on Issue

Chandigarh, July 12_A special session of the Punjab Vidhan Sabha today unanimously passed the Punjab Termination of Agreements Bill, 2004, thereby "knocking down" the very basis on which the Supreme Court had passed its order on construction of SYL_Sutlej-Yamuna Link canal on June 4, last.

This Bill annuls the December 31, 1981, agreement between Punjab, Haryana and Rajasthan signed by the three Chief Ministers in the presence of the late Ms. Indira Gandhi and also all other agreements relating to the water of the rivers, Ravi and Beas. This, the Bill says, was done in "public interest". The annulment has come after 23 long years with two staunch political rivals, the Congress and the Akalis, joining hands to protect the state's riparian rights. Immediately after the Bill was passed, the Chief Minister, Capt. Amarinder Singh, accompanied by the Leader of the Opposition, Mr. Parkash Singh Badal, PPCC president, Mr. H.S. Hanspal, Ms. Rajinder Kaur Bhattal, Mr. Partap Singh Bajwa and a team of legal experts went to Raj Bhavan to meet the Governor, Justice O.P. Verma (retd.), to request him to give his assent to the Bill, as the dead-line for compliance with the Supreme Court order was July 15. The combined delegation spent an hour with the Governor. The Raj Bhavan sources said, "The Bill is being examined."

Capt. Amarinder Singh told TNS that he had not discussed the Bill with Ms. Sonia Gandhi. "Why involve her? When I go to Delhi, I shall brief her".

Presenting the Bill to the House, Capt. Amarinder Singh made an emotive speech giving facts, figures and background to the entire issue of sharing of river waters and steps taken in the recent past to protect and safeguard the interests of Punjab, particularly the farmers and save nine lakh acres going dry and barren, which would affect the livelihood of 1.5 million families.

The Bill says that Punjab was proud of its position in the Indian union, felt equal concern for its neighbours and as a sovereign authority also considered it its duty to uphold the constitution and the laws and to protect the interests of its inhabitants.

Under the 1981 agreement, flow series were changed from 1921-45 to 1921-60, which had the result of increasing the availability of Ravi-Beas waters from 15.85 MAF to 17.17 MAF. The allocation of water made to the states concerned under that Agreement was as under:

Haryana (non-riparian) 3.50 MAF, Rajasthan (non-riparian) 8.60 MAF, Delhi (non-riparian) 0.20 MAF, Punjab (riparian) 4.22 MAF and Jammu and Kashmir (riparian) 0.65 MAF. Under clause IV of this agreement, Punjab and Haryana withdrew their respective suits from the

Supreme Court. But the controversy rages on. The issue has become emotive.

Referring to the broad clauses of the proposed Bill, Capt. Amarinder Singh maintained that riparian and basin principles were ignored all along and allocation of the Ravi-Beas waters had always been affected by "ad hoc decisions and agreements, dictated by prevalent circumstances". Here was a typical case involving "emotive" issue of impending transfer of water from "deficit" Ravi-Beas basin to the "surplus" Yamuna basin.

Never any reliable and scientific study of hydrological, ecological and sociological impact of such large scale trans-basin diversion from Punjab to Haryana and Rajasthan had been undertaken. Besides this transfer, diversion was even contrary to the National Water Policy guidelines, he added.

Capt. Amarinder Singh pointed out, "Non-riparian and non-basin states of Haryana and Rajasthan are not only not entitled to any Ravi-Beas waters, even their current allocation and utilisation is totally disproportionate to the areas alleged to be falling in the Indus basin. Therefore, Punjab, as a good neighbour, has accepted such utilisations by Haryana and Rajasthan as 'uusages by sufferance' but not as a matter of any recognition of their rights".

He supported this hypothesis, when he posed the question, "Does Punjab have surplus water and do the claimants of our water a legal right to it? Then, he paused for effect, "The answer to this question is a resounding "no", and went on to give the following picture:

All three rivers, the Ravi, the Beas and the Sutlej, flow through the present Punjab and none through either Haryana or Rajasthan. No part of territories of these states fall within the basin areas of the Ravi and the Beas, although, according to unsubstantiated report of the Irrigation Commission, only 9,939 sq. kms. within Haryana fall in Indus basin, against 50,305 sq. kms. of Punjab.

Again, the present utilisation by Haryana was about 5.95 MAF, about 4.33 MAF from Sutlej and about 1.62 MAF from the Ravi-Beas water, through the existing systems. Also out of 17.17 MAF of "surplus" Ravi-Beas water, only 4.22 MAF was allocated to Punjab, a riparian state, against higher quantities to Haryana and Rajasthan. From the total surplus availability of 11.98 MAF of the Beas water, Punjab has been allocated 2.64 MAF.

Therefore, justifying the annulling of the December 31, 1981, agreement and all other agreements relating to the Ravi and the Beas, the Bill seeks to present the fact that ground realities have since undergone a sea change from that date and Punjab settlement of July 24, 1985, under the Rajiv-Longowal Agreement. Therefore, this had made the implementation of that 1981 agreement "onerous and injurious" to the public interest.

The availability of the Ravi-Beas water, 1717 MAF, as on December 31, 1981, has been reduced to 14.37 MAF, as per the flow series of 1981-2002. Haryana has been given 4.65 MA under the Yamuna agreement of May 12, 1994, which will be further augmented by the Sarda-Yamuna link. In the meanwhile, irrigation requirements have increased in

Punjab. "The Punjab settlement, except one para 9, relating to allocation of the Ravi-Seas water, has remained unimplemented in letter and spirit, to date.

"In these circumstances, the terms of 1981 agreement were 'onerous, unfair, un-reasonable and contrary to the interests of the inhabitants of the Ravi-Beas basin, who have law-full rights to utilise water of these rivers'. Is the Bill justified? Will it tantamount to contempt of the court? In his well prepared speech, Capt. Amarinder Singh has addressed such questions, as well.

Armed with the House resolution of June 15 that aims to protect the rights of Punjab, legal opinions and all-party resolution of June 12, the Chief Minister said.

"This mandate enables the government to find ways and means to protect the people from adverse consequences of the Supreme Court judgment of June 4. The state had been advised that the obligations arising from an agreement or the contract did not fetter the powers of the legislature to enact a law in public interest.

"We have been further advised that it is a well settled law that the legislature is competent to remove or take away the basis of judgment by law and thereby it does not encroach upon the exercise of the judicial power of the judiciary and the legislative action within its competence, do not commit a contempt of court. However, final decision in all these matters lies in the court, as any law enacted by this august House is subject to a judicial review".

When the Bill had been introduced, Mr. Parkash Singh Badal stood up to express the collective anguish of the opposition that on such an important item, involving the question of "life and death" had been treated lightly by the government and till noon today "we had no idea of what the agenda was all about nor we had received copy of the Bill or what it was all about".

Mr. Badal said the traditions and conventions of the House were being eroded, day-by-day. "It was also a disgrace that even the information inviting us to meet the Governor after the House had passed the resolution was sent by the Congress president, Mr. H.S. Hanspal, who was not involved in this in any which way. How can we discuss anything at such a short notice? We are against political confrontation and are available 24 hours for any thing related to the interests of the state and are willing to support the government".

Thereafter, the Speaker, Dr. Kewal Krishan said he had received a resolution sent by four Akali MLAs, Mr. Parkash Singh Badal, Capt. Kanwaljit Singh, Mr. Gurdev Singh Badal and Mr. Manpreet Singh Badal, for the consideration of the House.

Then, he ruled that since a comprehensive Bill was being presented, they could express their views while speaking on that. Mr. Manpreet Singh Badal and Capt. Kanwaljit Singh suggested that certain provisions, including Clause 78, in the Punjab Reorganisation Act, 1966, be also annulled. BJP's Tikshan Sud, said though a "belated step", the Bill was a welcome and offered full co-operation but rued that the Opposition be given due place and respect.

On this the Captain had stated in his reply that whatever steps were required to be taken to protect Punjab's interests would be taken in consultation with the legal experts. The speakers, including Mr. Bir Devinder Singh and Mr. Jeet Mohinder Singh spoke in the context of historical background, stressing time and again on the riparian principles. Mr. Bir Devinder Singh recalled how even the British Government had sought a certificate from Punjab that it will protect its own interests under the riparian rights while selling water to Rajasthan.

Mr. Bir Devinder Singh even cautioned to be prepared following the enactment of the Act, terminating 1981 and other agreements since new situation would develop. Mr. Jeet Mohinder Singh wondered if the Bill would stop the construction of SYL. He was for adding a new amendment in the form of a clause in the Eastern Punjab Canal and Drains Act, 1873 that permission of the state Assembly should be mandatory to dig or construct any canal that carries water beyond the boundaries of the state.

Rare Bonhomie in house

The discussion on the Bill was, however, not without the usual political punches and colour. There were moments when some ministers and opposition members took pot shots blaming either side for having failed Punjab and messed up the water issue. Some Opposition members said had such a Bill been brought forward 23 years ago, Punjab would have been spared the agony. Even the Bill says that in the wake of large-scale militancy, the Punjab settlement was reached, which however, had remained unimplemented in letter and spirit.

For once, the House was in a serious mood. There were no political skirmishes, though usual jibes were heard. The Governor's and Speaker's galleries were packed.

But it was the Captain's day all the way. Having worked overtime to get this Bill prepared, presented and passed by the House, he responded to the collective anguish of the opposition, expressed by Mr. Badal, with utmost humility and courtesy, acknowledging all what Mr. Badal had said. But then he point by point not only explained the unusual circumstances, including race against time, under which the Bill in as prepared and thus could not be circulated earlier, giving the members a chance to prepare themselves.

Capt. Amarinder Singh was apologetic and said so repeatedly taking the wind out of the sails of the Akalis. He showed faint starchiness in his voice, when he responded to some of the observations of Capt. Kanwaljit Singh, saying, "We are together here for an important task, not for rhetoric and emotive outbursts. We cannot allow Punjab to go back into the grip of violence".

Warming up, he concluded, "We will resort to all legal and constitutional means to seek justice. Already enough bloodshed has taken place. Even all the bodies have not been counted, so far. We shall fight to the end but within the parameters of laws, rules and the constitution. I will be willing to resign, if need be, for the sake of Punjab. The time is not for blame game. We have all made mistakes in the past. We are rectifying the same after 23 years. Come, lets join hands, close ranks. I appreciate the Opposition's cooperation".

***

Document

CONGRESSIONAL RECORD -- EXTENSIONS

Thursday, July 15, 2004
108th Congress, 2nd Session
150 Cong Rec E 1377

REFERENCE: Vol. 150, No. 98
SECTION: Extension of Remarks
TITLE: COUNCIL OF KHALISTAN WRITES TO UN HUMAN RIGHTS
COMMISSION TO EXPOSE REPRESSION OF MINORITIES IN INDIA

HON. EDOLPHUS TOWNS
of New York
in the House of Representatives
Wednesday, July 14, 2004

Mr. TOWNS . Mr. Speaker, recently Dr. Gurmit Singh Aulakh, President of the Council of Khalistan wrote to the United Nations Commission on Human Rights in Geneva to ask them to help keep the world aware of the repression of minorities, including Sikhs, Christians, Muslims, and others, in India.

The letter pointed out that over 250,000 Sikhs have been murdered by the Indian government, along with more than 300,000 Christians in Nagaland, over 88,000 Muslims in Kashmir, Muslims and Christians throughout India, and other minorities such as Dalits, the dark skinned aboriginal people of the subcontinent, Assamese, Bodos, Manipuris, Tamils, and others. Over 52,000 Sikhs and tens of thousands of other minorities are being held as political prisoners. The letter pointed out that the government has been involved in atrocities such as the massacre of Muslims in Gujarat and the massacre of Sikhs in Delhi and that it has not punished those who have carried out atrocities against Christians nor the killer of Jathedar Gurdev Singh Kaunke.

Such atrocities are unacceptable in any country, but especially in one that claims to be democratic. We must take a stand for freedom. It is time to stop our aid to India and go on record in support of self-determination for all the people seeking their freedom there.

Mr. Speaker, I would like to place Dr. Aulakh's letter to the Human Rights Commission into the Record at this time.

Council of Khalistan,
Washington, DC, July 13, 2004.
Madam Justice Louise Arbour,
High Commissioner, United Nations Commission on Human Rights

Plaise des Nations, Geneva, Switzerland.

Dear Justice Abrour: As the Chief Prosecutor for the International Court of Justice, you helped to bring the persons who committed massacres, genocide, and pogroms on the innocent people of Bosnia to justice. Your work for human rights around the world is well known and we salute you for it. It is because of that record that I am writing to you today about the plight of the Sikhs and other minorities in India. The plight of the Sikhs and other minorities in India is deplorable. India claims to be "the world's largest democracy" and claims that it is a secular country, but in practice it is not. As Narinder Singh, a spokesman for the Golden Temple, told America's National Public Radio, "The Indian government, all the time they boast that they are democratic, that they are secular, but they have nothing to do with a democracy, nothing to do with a secularism. They just kill Sikhs just to please the majority." Unfortunately, Sikhs are not the only victims of this brutality. Other minorities such as Christians, Muslims, even the Dalits (called "Untouchables") are persecuted in India.

The Indian government has murdered over 250,000 Sikhs since 1984, more than 300,000 Christians in Nagaland since 1947, over 88,000 Kashmiri Muslims since 1988. Christians and Muslims have been murdered in other parts of the country as well, along with tens of thousands of Assamese, Bodos, Dalits, Manipuri's, Tamils, and other minorities. According to the Movement Against State Repression (MASR), 52,268 Sikhs are being held as political prisoners under the repressive TADA law, which expired in 1995. Amnesty International reports that tens of thousands of other minorities are also being held as political prisoners. These prisoners are held without charge or trial in "the world's largest democracy," some of them since 1984! That is 20 years in illegal detention. Their whereabouts are unknown. They might have been killed while in police custody.

Sardar Jaswant Singh Khalra looked at the records of the cremation grounds at Patti, Tam Taran, and Durgiana Mandar and documented at least 6,018 secret cremations of young Sikh men ages 20-30. These young Sikhs were arrested by the police, tortured, murdered, then declared unidentified and secretly cremated. Their bodies were not even returned to their families. They have never officially been accounted for. The Punjab Human Rights Commission estimates that about 50,000 such secret cremations have occurred.

For exposing this horrendous atrocity, Sardar Khalra was abducted by the police on September 6, 1995 while he was washing his car, then murdered in police custody. The only witness to his kidnapping, Rajiv Singh Randhawa, has been repeatedly harassed by the police. Once he was arrested for trying to hand a petition to the then-British Home Minister, Jack Straw, in front of the Golden Temple in Amritsar.

Police SSP Swaran Singh Ghotna tortured and murdered Akal Takht Jathedar Gurdev Singh Kaunke and has never been punished for doing so. K.P.S. Gill, who was responsible for the murders of over 150,000 Sikhs in his time as Director General of Police, is still walking around scot-free. He was even involved in leading the Indian Olympic field hockey team. His trip to the Atlanta Olympics in 1996 was protested by the Sikh community in the United States, which is over half a million strong, but he was allowed to come to the Olympics on an Olympic Committee visa. Immediately after the Olympic hockey game, he was shipped back to Punjab as a threat to peace and an affront to the Sikh community. 50 members of the U.S. Congress from both parties wrote to the President protesting his appearance in the United States.

In addition to this, the Indian government attacked the Golden Temple in Amritsar, the center and seat of the Sikh religion, in June 1984, as well as 224 other Gurdwaras (Sikh places of worship) throughout Punjab. Sikh leaders Sant Jarnail Singh Bhindranwale, General Shabeg Singh, and others, as well as over 20,000 Sikhs were killed in these attacks. The Sikh holy scripture, the Guru Granth Sahib, written in the time of the Sikh Gurus, was shot full of bullet holes by the Indian Army. Over 100 young Sikh boys ages 8 to 13 were taken out into the courtyard and asked if they supported Khalistan, the independent Sikh state. When they answered with the Sikh religious incantation "Bole So Nihal" they were summarily shot to death.

Unfortunately, other minorities have also suffered greatly under the boot of Indian repression. In March 2002, 5,000 Muslims were killed in Gujarat while police were ordered to stand by and let the carnage happen, in an eerie parallel to the Delhi massacre of Sikhs in November 1984 in which Sikh police officers were locked in their barracks while the state-run television and radio called for more Sikh blood.

Christians have suffered under a wave of repression since Christmas 1998. An Australian missionary, Graham Staines, and his two young sons, ages 8 and 10, were burned to death while they slept in their jeep by a mob of Hindu militants connected with the Rashtriya Swayamsewak Sangh (RSS), an organization formed in support of the Fascists. The mob surrounded the burning jeep and chanted "Victory to Hannuman," a Hindu god. None of the mob has ever been brought to justice; instead the crime has been blamed on one scapegoat. Mr. Staines's widow was thrown out of the country after the incident. An American missionary, Joseph Cooper of Pennsylvania, was expelled from India after being beaten so severely that he had to spend a week in the hospital. None of the persons responsible for beating Mr. Cooper has been prosecuted. Churches have been burned, Christian schools and prayer halls have been attacked and vandalized, priests have been murdered, nuns have been raped, all with impunity. Police broke up a Christian religious festival with gunfire.

Amnesty International has not been allowed into Punjab since 1978. Even Castro's Cuba has allowed Amnesty into the country more recently. What is India hiding?

My organization, the Council of Khalistan, is leading the Sikh struggle for freedom and sovereignty. Working with the Congress of the United States, we have internationalized the struggle for freedom for the Sikhs and all the people of South Asia since the Council of Khalistan's inception on October 7, 1987, the day that the Sikh Nation declared its independence from India. We have worked to preserve the accurate history of the Sikhs and the repression of minorities by India by preserving the information in the Congressional Record. We continue to work for freedom for the Sikh Nation. Self-determination is the essence of democracy.

On behalf of the Sikh Nation, I am asking the Human Rights Commission to expose India's reign of terror to the international community. It is time for India to be held to account for its tyrannical rule covered by a veneer of democracy. Please do not let India hide behind a false claim of democracy and secularism. By shining the light on India's terroristic rule, you can help bring freedom and basic human rights to all the people of the subcontinent.

Thank you in advance for your attention to this situation and for helping the people of South Asia.

Sincerely,
Dr. Gurmit Singh Aulakh,
President, Council of Khalistan.

***

Document

CONGRESSIONAL RECORD -- EXTENSIONS

Wednesday, July 14, 2004
108th Congress, 2nd Session
150 Cong Rec E 1369

REFERENCE: Vol. 150, No. 97
SECTION: Extension of Remarks
TITLE: PUNJAB GOVERNMENT CANCELS DEAL THAT ALLOWED DIVERSION OF WATER TO OTHER STATES; LEGISLATURE ASSERTS SOVEREIGNTY

HON. EDOLPHUS TOWNS
of New York
in the House of Representatives
Tuesday, July 13, 2004

Mr. TOWNS . Mr. Speaker, the Legislative Assembly of Punjab recently annulled a longstanding agreement that allowed the diversion of water from Punjab to other states.

According to the Tribune of Chandigarh, whose article I will be inserting in the Record at the end of my remarks, the Legislative Assembly asserted the sovereignty of Punjab in doing so. The newspaper reports that the bill passed by the Legislative Assembly says that "as a sovereign authority [Punjab] considered it its duty to uphold the Constitution and the laws and to protect the interests of its inhabitants."

Apparently, all parties supported this measure. We congratulate them on taking this step forward to protect the interests of the people of Punjab. I urge them to continue claiming, promoting, and establishing the sovereignty of Punjab.

Mr. Speaker, we know that the people of Punjab have been severely oppressed by the tyrannical Indian government. Over a quarter of a million Sikhs have been killed since 1984, according to the Punjab State Magistracy. The Movement Against State Repression reports that 52,268 have been taken as political prisoners, held without charge or trial, some as long as 20 years. According to the Punjab Human Rights Commission, about 50,000 Sikhs have simply been made to disappear by being arrested, tortured, killed in police custody, declared "unidentified bodies," and secretly cremated, without their remains even being given back to their families.

Similar repression has been visited on Christians, Muslims, and other minorities. Yet India continues to say that it is the world's largest democracy.

If India is truly a democracy, it will allow the will of the people to be carried out in regards to the diversion of water. It will allow the people_Sikhs, Christians, Muslims, Assamese, Bodos, Dalits, Manipuris, Tamils, and everyone living under Indian rule_to enjoy the full range of human rights. And it will allow self-determination for these sovereign states.

Until that happens, Mr. Speaker, we should not provide any aid to India. And we should take a stand for self-determination, which is the cornerstone of democracy, by supporting a free and fair plebiscite on independence in Punjab, Khalistan, in Kashmir, in predominantly Christian Nagaland, and everywhere that people seek their freedom from Indian rule. The assertion of sovereignty by the Punjab Legislative Assembly is a good first step. They should act to claim their sovereignty by severing their ties to India. We should take a stand by letting them know that when they do, we will be there with them.

Mr. Speaker, as I mentioned before, I would like to insert the Tribune article into the Record.

[From the Tribune (Chandigarh), July 13, 2004]
Punjab Annuls All Water Pacts: Cong, Akalis Join Hands on Issue
(By P.P.S. Gill)

Chandigarh, July 12._A special session of the Punjab Vidhan Sabha today unanimously passed the Punjab Termination of Agreements Bill, 2004, thereby "knocking down" the very basis on which the Supreme Court had passed its order on construction of SYL_Sutlej-Yamuna Link canal on June 4, last. This Bill annuls the December 31, 1981, agreement between Punjab, Haryana and Rajasthan signed by the three Chief Ministers in the presence of the late Ms Indira Gandhi and also all other agreements relating to the water of the rivers, Ravi and Beas. This, the Bill says, was done in "public interest". The annulment has come after 23 long years with two staunch political rivals, the Congress and the Akalis, joining hands to protect the state's riparian rights. Immediately after the Bill was passed, the Chief Minister, Capt Amarinder Singh, accompanied by the Leader of the Opposition, Mr Parkash Singh Badal, PPCC president, Mr H.S. Hanspal, Ms Rajinder Kaur Bhattal, Mr Partap Singh Bajwa and a team of legal experts went to Raj Bhavan to meet the Governor, Justice O.P. Verma (retd.), to request him to give his assent to the Bill, as the dead-line for compliance with the Supreme Court order was July 15. The combined delegation spent an hour with the Governor. The Raj Bhavan sources said, "The Bill is being examined."

Capt Amarinder Singh told TNS that he had not discussed the Bill with Ms Sonia Gandhi. "Why involve her? When I go to Delhi, I shall brief her".

Presenting the Bill to the House, Capt. Amarinder Singh made an emotive speech giving facts, figures and background to the entire issue of sharing of river waters and steps taken in the recent past to protect and safeguard the interests of Punjab, particularly the farmers and save nine lakh acres going dry and barren, which would affect the livelihood of 1.5 million families.

The Bill says that Punjab was proud of its position in the Indian union, felt equal concern for its neighbours and as a sovereign authority also considered it its duty to uphold the constitution and the laws and to protect the interests of its inhabitants.

Under the 1981 agreement, flow series were changed from 1921-45 to 1921-60, which had the result of increasing the availability of Ravi-Beas waters from 15.85 MAF to 17.17 MAF. The allocation of water made to the states concerned under that Agreement was as under:

Haryana (non-riparian) 3.50 MAF, Rajasthan (non-riparian) 8.60 MAF, Delhi (non-riparian) 0.20 MAF, Punjab (riparian) 4.22 MAF and Jammu and Kashmir (riparian) 0.65 MAF. Under clause IV of this agreement, Punjab and Haryana withdrew their respective suits from the Supreme Court. But the controversy rages on. The issue has become emotive.

Referring to the broad clauses of the proposed Bill, Capt Amarinder Singh maintained that riparian and basin principles were ignored all along and allocation of the Ravi-Beas waters had always been affected by "ad hoc decisions and agreements, dictated by prevalent circumstances". Here was a typical case involving "emotive" issue of impending transfer of water from "deficit" Ravi-Beas basin to the "surplus" Yamuna basin.

Never any reliable and scientific study of hydrological, ecological and sociological impact of such large scale trans-basin diversion from Punjab to Haryana and Rajasthan had been undertaken. Besides this transfer, diversion was even contrary to the National Water Policy guidelines, he added.

Capt Amarinder Singh pointed out, "Non-riparian and non-basin states of Haryana and Rajasthan are not only not entitled to any Ravi-

Beas waters, even their current allocation and utilisation is totally disproportionate to the areas alleged to be falling in the Indus basin. Therefore, Punjab, as a good neighbour, has accepted such utilisations by Haryana and Rajasthan as 'usages by sufferance' but not as a matter of any recognition of their rights".

He supported this hypothesis, when he posed the question, "Does Punjab have surplus water and do the claimants of our water a legal right to it?" Then, he paused for effect, "The answer to this question is a resounding 'no'", and went on to give the following picture:

All three rivers, the Ravi, the Beas and the Sutlej, flow through the present Punjab and none through either Haryana or Rajasthan. No part of territories of these states fall within the basin areas of the Ravi and the Beas, although, according to un-substantiated report of the Irrigation Commission, only 9,939 sq. kms. within Haryana fall in Indus basin, against 50,305 sq. kms. of Punjab.

Again, the present utilisation by Haryana was about 5.95 MAF, about 4.33 MAF from Sutlej and about 1.62 MAF from the Ravi-Beas water, through the existing systems. Also out of 17.17 MAF of "surplus" Ravi-Beas water, only 4.22 MAF was allocated to Punjab, a riparian state, against higher quantities to Haryana and Rajasthan. From the total surplus availability of 11.98 MAF of the Beas water, Punjab has been allocated 2.64 MAF.

Therefore, justifying the annulling of the December 31, 1981, agreement and all other agreements relating to the Ravi and the Beas, the Bill seeks to present the fact that ground realities have since undergone a sea change from that date and Punjab settlement of July 24, 1985, under the Rajiv-Longowal Agreement. Therefore, this had made the implementation of that 1981 agreement "onerous and injurious" to the public interest.

The availability of the Ravi-Beas water, 1717 MAF, as on December 31, 1981, has been reduced to 14.37 MAF, as per the flow series of 1981-2002. Haryana has been given 4.65 MA under the Yamuna agreement of May 12, 1994, which will be further augmented by the Sarda-Yamuna link. In the meanwhile, irrigation requirements have increased in Punjab. "The Punjab settlement, except one para 9, relating to allocation of the Ravi-Beas water, has remained unimplemented in letter and spirit, to date."

In these circumstances, the terms of 1981 agreement were "onerous, unfair, un-reasonable and contrary to the interests of the inhabitants of the Ravi-Beas basin, who have law-full rights to utilise water of these rivers". Is the Bill justified? Will it tantamount to contempt of the court? In his well prepared speech, Capt. Amarinder Singh has addressed such questions, as well.

Armed with the House resolution of June 15 that aims to protect the rights of Punjab, legal opinions and all-party resolution of June 12, the Chief Minister said.

"This mandate enables the government to find ways and means to protect the people from adverse consequences of the Supreme Court judgment of June 4. The state had been advised that the obligations

arising from an agreement or the contract did not fetter the powers of the legislature to enact a law in public interest.

"We have been further advised that it is a well settled law that the legislature is competentremove or take away the basis of judgment by law and thereby it does not encroach upon the exercise of the judicial power of the judiciary and the legislative action within its competence, do not commit a contempt of court. However, final decision in all these matters lies in the court, as any law enacted by this august House is subject to a judicial review".

When the Bill had been introduced, Mr Parkash Singh Badal stood up to express the collective anguish of the opposition that on such an important item, involving the question of "life and death" had been treated lightly by the government and till noon today "we had no idea of what the agenda was all about nor we had received copy of the Bill or what it was all about".

Mr Badal said the traditions and conventions of the House were being eroded, day-by-day. "It was also a disgrace that even the information inviting us to meet the Governor after the House had passed the resolution was sent by the Congress president, Mr H S Hanspal, who was not involved in this in any which way. How can we discuss anything at such a short notice? We are against political confrontation and are available 24-hours for any thing related to the interests of the state and are willing to support the government".

Thereafter, the Speaker, Dr Kewal Krishan said he had received a resolution sent by four Akali MLAs, Mr Parkash Singh Badal, Capt. Kanwaljit Singh, Mr Gurdev Singh Badal and Mr Manpreet Singh Badal, for the consideration of the House.

Then, he ruled that since a comprehensive Bill was being presented, they could express their views while speaking on that. Mr Manpreet Singh Badal and Capt Kanwaljit Singh suggested that certain provisions, including Clause 78, in the Punjab Reorganisation Act, 1966, be also annulled. BJP's Tikshan Sud, said though a "belated step", the Bill was a welcome and offered full co-operation but rued that the Opposition be given due place and respect.

On this the Captain had stated in his reply that whatever steps were required to be taken to protect Punjab's interests would be taken in consultation with the legal experts.

The speakers, including Mr Bir Devinder Singh and Mr Jeet Mohinder Singh spoke in the context of historical background, stressing time and again on the riparian principles. Mr Bir Devinder Singh recalled how even the British Government had sought a certificate from Punjab that it will protect its own interests under the riparian rights while selling water to Rajasthan.

Mr Bir Devinder Singh even cautioned to be prepared following the enactment of the Act, terminating 1981 and other agreements since new situation would develop. Mr Jeet Mohinder Singh wondered if the Bill would stop the construction of SYL. He was for adding a new amendment in the form of a clause in the Eastern Punjab Canal and Drains Act,

1873 that permission of the state Assembly should be mandatory to dig or construct any canal that carries water beyond the boundaries of the state.

Rare bonhomie in House

The discussion on the Bill was, however, not without the usual political punches and colour. There were moments when some ministers and opposition members took pot shots blaming either side for having failed Punjab and messed up the water issue.

Some Opposition members said had such a Bill been brought forward 23 years ago, Punjab would have been spared the agony. Even the Bill says that in the wake of large-scale militancy, the Punjab settlement was reached, which however, had remained unimplemented in letter and spirit.

For once, the House was in a serious mood. There were no political skirmishes, though usual jibes were heard. The Governor's and Speaker's galleries were packed.

But it was the Captain's day all the way. Having worked overtime to get this Bill prepared, presented and passed by the House, he responded to the collective anguish of the opposition, expressed by Mr Badal, with utmost humility and courtesy, acknowledging all what Mr Badal had said. But then he point by point not only explained the unusual circumstances, including race against time, under which the Bill in as prepared and thus could not be circulated earlier, giving the members a chance to prepare themselves.

Capt. Amarinder Singh was apologetic and said so repeatedly taking the wind out of the sails of the Akalis. He showed faint starchiness in his voice, when he responded to some of the observations of Capt. Kanwaljit Singh, saying, "We are together here for an important task, not for rhetoric and emotive outbursts. We cannot allow Punjab to go back into the grip of violence".

Warming up, he concluded, "We will resort to all legal and constitutional means to seek justice. Already enough bloodshed has taken place. Even all the bodies have not been counted, so far. We shall fight to the end but within the parameters of laws, rules and the constitution. I will be willing to resign, if need be, for the sake of Punjab. The time is not for blame game. We have all made mistakes in the past. We are rectifying the same after 23 years. Come, lets join hands, close ranks. I appreciate the Opposition's co-operation".

***

Document

CONGRESSIONAL RECORD -- EXTENSIONS

Thursday, June 24, 2004
108th Congress, 2nd Session
150 Cong Rec E 1232

REFERENCE: Vol. 150, No. 89
SECTION: Extension of Remarks
TITLE: LEADER OF DELHI MASSACRE OF SIKHS COMING TO U.S. TO
MAKE A SPEECH

HON. DAN BURTON
of Indiana
in the House of Representatives
Wednesday, June 23, 2004

Mr. BURTON of Indiana . Mr. Speaker, on October 31, 1984, Indian Prime Minister Indira Gandhi was assassinated by her two Sikh body-guards after she ordered an attack upon the Golden Temple, which is the center and seat of the Sikh religion. In the aftermath of the assassination, thousands of Sikhs were killed in anti-Sikh riots. The massacre was by any definition a brutal atrocity, and one of the most prominent figures accused of helping to orchestrate the violence was Jagdish Tytler.

Now, Mr. Tytler, who led mobs of Hindus in killing Sikhs, some by burning them to death, and who saw to it that Sikh police were locked in their barracks and therefore unable to respond to the massacre, has been invited to speak at the convention of the American Association of Physicians of Indian Origin in San Diego, which begins on June 25th. As someone who has long championed the cause of freedom, democracy, and equal rights for the Sikh community and other oppressed minorities in that part of the world, I am deeply concerned about this man coming to the United States, and I would urge the American Association of Physicians of Indian Origin to reconsider their invitation to Mr. Tytler.

I am also deeply concerned to learn that Mr. Tytler has been given a position in the government of Prime Minister Manmohan Singh. Prime Minister Singh is a Sikh, and the Sikh community naturally had high hopes that Manmohan Singh's appointment to India's top job would bridge the gap between the Sikh and Hindu peoples. It is difficult to understand how this can be accomplished when Prime Minister Singh is willing to bring a person like Mr. Tytler into his government, as many Sikhs, including my good friend Dr. Gurmit Singh Aulakh, President of the Council of Khalistan, consider Mr. Tytler's presence in the govern-ment an affront to the Sikh people.

So long as people like Jagdish Tytler are in the India government, it draws into question whether India is truly willing to uphold the demo-cratic values that it preaches. In addition Mr. Speaker, it should also draw into question the wisdom of the hard-working taxpayers of this country supporting a government that rewards the Jagdish Tytler's of the world with power and authority.

***

Document

CONGRESSIONAL RECORD -- EXTENSIONS

Wednesday, June 23, 2004
108th Congress, 2nd Session
150 Cong Rec E 1216

REFERENCE: Vol. 150, No. 88
SECTION: Extension of Remarks
TITLE: CORRECTING PREVIOUS STATEMENT ON GOLDEN TEMPLE

HON. EDOLPHUS TOWNS
of New York
in the House of Representatives
Wednesday, June 23, 2004

Mr. TOWNS . Mr. Speaker, earlier this month I made a statement congratulating the Council of Khalistan on its commemoration of the twentieth anniversary of the massacre of Sikhs at the Golden Temple in June 1984. At that time, I intended to insert the Council of Khalistan's flyer into the Record. I even said that I was including it in the Record. Somehow, it did not get included. Therefore, I would like to place it in the Record at this time.

20th Anniversary of the Golden Temple Massacre, June 3-6, 1984
Sikhs must have freedom in sovereign homeland

"If the Indian government attacks the Golden Temple, it will lay the foundation stone of Khalistan."_Sant Jarnail Singh Bhindranwale.

From June 3 throughout 6, 1984, the Indian government brutally invaded the Golden Temple and 150 other Gurdwaras around Punjab. Over 20,000 people were killed in these attacks, including such Sikh leaders as Sant Jarnail Singh Bhindranwale, who was the strongest spokesman for Sikh rights and Sikh freedom. More than 100 young boys, ages 8 to 13, were taken outside into the courtyard and asked whether they supported Khalistan, the independent Sikh homeland. When they answered with the Sikh religious incantation "Bole So Nihal," they were summarily shot to death. The Guru Granth Sahib, the Sikh scripture, handwritten in the time of the ten Sikh Gurus, was shot full of bullet holes by the Indian military. Sant Bhindranwale warned that if the Indian government invaded the Golden Temple, it would "lay the foundation stone for Khalistan" and it did.

How can this happen in a democracy?

"The Indian government, all the time they boast that they are democratic, that they are secular. They have nothing to do with a democracy, nothing to do with a secularism. They just kill Sikhs to please the majori-

ty."_Narinder Singh, spokesman for the Golden Temple, on NPR August 1997.

U.S. Representative Dana Rohrabacher (R-Cal.) has said that for the minorities such as Sikhs and Kashmiris "India might as well be Nazi Germany."

A pattern of repression against the Sikh nation

Over 250,000 Sikhs murdered since 1984.

52,268 Sikh political prisoners, according to the Movement Against State Repression

More than 50,000 Sikhs disappeared in Indian government's secret cremations. Their remains have never been given to their families.

Indian government paid over 41,000 cash bounties to police to kill Sikhs

Gurnihal Singh Pirzada, a senior officer in the IAS, arrested after allegedly being seen at a meeting of gathering of Punjab "dissidents." Pirzada denies attending such a meeting, but points out that it would not be illegal if he did.

Jaswant Singh Khalra kidnapped by police and murdered in police custody after exposing Indian policy of arresting Sikhs, torturing them, murdering them, cremating the bodies, as "unidentified."

Gurdev Singh Kaunke, former Jathedar of the Akal Takht, highest Sikh religious leader, murdered by police official Swaran Singh Ghotna, who has never been punished.

The Indian newspaper Hitavada reported that the Indian government paid the late Governor of Punjab, Surendra Nath, the equivalent of $1.5 billion to foment and support covert state terrorist activity in Punjab and Kashmir.

This is the state of freedom in Punhap, Khalistan under Indian rule.

"The mere fact that they have the right to choose their oppressors does not mean they live in a democracy."_Rep. Edolphus Towns (D-NY).

THE REPRESSION CONTINUES WHILE INDIA PROCLAIMS ITS SECULARISM AND DEMOCRACY

Half a million Indian forces have been sent to Punjab, Khalistan to subdue the freedom movement there. Another 700,000 are deployed in Kashmir. They join with the police in carrying out the kinds of atrocities described above. India calls this "protecting its territorial integrity. "

In March 2000 in the village of Chithisinghpora, 35 Sikhs were massacred. Two studies of this massacre, one by the International Human Rights Organization, based in Ludhiana, and the other conducted jointly by the Punjab Human Rights Organization and the Movement Against State Repression, concluded that the massacre was the work of Indian forces, a conclusion supported by reporter Barry Bearak in the December 31, 2000 issue of the New York Times Magazine. In another village in Kashmir, Indian troops were caught red-handed trying to set fire to several Sikh houses and the local Gurdwara. Sikh and Muslim villagers joined together to stop this atrocity before it could be carried out

Sikhs ruled Punjab as an independent, secular country from 1765 to 1849. Sikhs have never accepted the Indian constitution. At the time of the transfer of power, Sikhs were equal partners who were to receive sovereignty along with Muslims and Hindus. When the Indian constitution was adopted in 1950, no Sikh representative signed it and no Sikh representative has signed it to this day.

On October 7, 1987, the Sikh Nation formally declared its independence from India, naming their new country Khalistan. Since then, Khalistan has been under illegal occupation by the Indian government and its forces.

"If a Sikh is not for Khalistan, he is not a Sikh."_Professor Darshan Singh, former Jathedar of the Akal Takht

Unfortunately, Sikhs are not the only victim of India's brutal tyranny.

India has murdered over 300,000 Christians in Nagaland since 1947, more than 85,000 Kashmiri Muslims since 1988, and tens of thousands of other minorities

Australian missionary Graham Staines and his two young sons were brutally murdered by being burned to death while they slept in their jeep by a mob of Hindu militants affiliated with the militant, pro-Fascist Rashtriya Swayamsewak Sangh (RSS) who chanted "Victory to Hannuman," a Hindu god.

An American missionary from Pennsylvania, Joseph Cooper, was expelled from the country after being so severely beaten by RSS goons that he had to spend a week in the hospital.

In January 2003, an American missionary and seven other individuals were attacked.

Christian schools and prayer halls have been attacked and destroyed.

A Christian religious festival was broken up by police gunfire.

In March 2002, between 2,000 and 5,000 Muslims were brutally murdered in Gujarat. India's National Human Rights Commission (NHRC), an official body, found evidence in the killings of premeditation by members of Hindu extremist groups and complicity by Gujarat state officials. A police officer confirmed to an Indian newspaper that the massacre was pre-planned by the government.

The most revered mosque in India, the Ayodhya mosque, was destroyed by Hindu mobs affiliated with the BJP and a Hindu Temple was built on the site.

The states of Gujarat, Tamil Nadu, and Orissa have all passed bills barring religious conversions.

DEMOCRACIES DON'T COMMIT GENOCIDE; SUPPORT SELF-DETERMINATION IN SOUTH ASIA

The right to self-determination is the essence of democracy. Please urge your representatives to support self-determination for Khalistan, Kashmir, Nagaland, and all the stations seeking their freedom. Demand a free and fair plebiscite on the question of independence and an end to foreign aid to India until human rights are respected.

***

Document

CONGRESSIONAL RECORD -- EXTENSIONS

Wednesday, June 23, 2004
108th Congress, 2nd Session
150 Cong Rec E 1218

REFERENCE: Vol. 150, No. 88
SECTION: Extension of Remarks
TITLE: UNITED STATES SHOULD NOT LET TYTLER ENTER COUNTRY

HON. EDOLPHUS TOWNS
of New York
in the House of Representatives
Wednesday, June 23, 2004

Mr. TOWNS . Mr. Speaker, I was disturbed to read that Jagdish Tytler, India's Minister of State for Non-Resident Indian Affairs, was coming to the United States to speak to the American Association of Physicians of Indian Origin. While there are many fine people of Indian origin, Jagdish Tytler is a person who is unfit to visit this country. He is the person most responsible for the genocide against Sikhs in Delhi in November 1984. To bring Jagdish Tytler to America is to give our implicit blessing to that massacre.

After the assassination of Indira Gandhi, Tytler and others organized bands of Hindus who grabbed Sikhs and burned them to death. He was one of the people responsible for getting the Sikh police locked in their barracks so that they could not intervene. Meanwhile, the state-run radio and TV screamed for more Sikh blood. In all, over 20,000 Sikhs were murdered.

Mr. Speaker, why is such a person being granted entry to the United States? And why is he in India's Cabinet? Unfortunately, rewarding people who carry out such activities is too common in India. We do not have to grant it our implicit approval.

As you know, over a quarter of a million Sikhs have been murdered at the hands of the Indian government since 1984. The Indian government has also killed more than 300,000 Christians in Nagaland, over 87,000 Muslims in Kashmir since 1988, and thousands upon thousands of other minorities as well. They continue to hold tens of thousands of political prisoners, according to Amnesty International. This includes over 52,000 Sikhs, some of whom have been held in illegal custody without charge or trial for 20 years. A democratic country should be embarrassed to have carried out acts like these, and I call on Prime Minister Singh to begin to rectify India's record by releasing the political prisoners and by removing Mr. Tytler and others involved in atrocities from his government. This will be a good first step towards restoring democracy for all the people.

America is the beacon of freedom. It is a country dedicated to the principles of freedom and equal rights. While we have not always been perfect in our efforts to follow these principles, they form the foundation of America. We embarrass ourselves and our principles by allowing the likes of Jagdish Tytler to come and make speeches in our country.

As long as people like Mr. Tytler are in the government, it is confirmation that there is no place for Sikhs and other minorities in India. Until it repudiates this and allows all people to exercise their full rights, we should provide no aid to India. And we should put ourselves on record in support of a free and fair vote on independence for the Sikh homeland, Khalistan, and for all the other nations seeking their freedom. And we should keep the leaders who practice brutality and commit atrocities out of our country.

***

Document

CONGRESSIONAL RECORD -- EXTENSIONS

Friday, June 18, 2004
108th Congress, 2nd Session
150 Cong Rec E 1153

REFERENCE: Vol. 150, No. 85
SECTION: Extension of Remarks
TITLE: TWENTIETH ANNIVERSARY OF GOLDEN TEMPLE ATTACK

HON. DAN BURTON
of Indiana
in the House of Representatives
Thursday, June 17, 2004

Mr. BURTON of Indiana . Mr. Speaker, this month marks the 20th anniversary of one of the most brutal attacks in history, the Indian government's military attack on the Golden Temple, which is the center and seat of the Sikh religion. Attacking the Golden Temple is the equivalent of attacking the Vatican or Mecca.

The Golden Temple was under siege from June 3 to June 6, 1984, under a Congress Party government led by Indira Gandhi, whose daughter-in-law Sonia Gandhi is now the President of the Congress Party and its floor leader in Parliament.

As you know, the supposedly secular Congress Party was recently swept back into power in India's elections. But for minorities, it doesn't really matter whether the Congress Party or the just-ousted Hindu nationalist Bharatiya Janata Party (BJP) is in power. Either way, the repression continues. Although there is a Sikh Prime Minister in India, he has no real power. He is at the mercy of Mrs. Gandhi. India continues to hold 52,268 Sikh political prisoners without charge, trial, or access to legal counsel, according to the Movement Against State Repression (MASR.) India has murdered over 250,000 Sikhs since June 1984. Another

50,000 have "disappeared." These are not the tactics of a democracy, Mr. Speaker. They are the tactics of a police state. What is India afraid of? Are they scared of a little free speech?

125 other Sikh Gurdwaras were also attacked at the same time. In all, over 20,000 Sikhs were murdered in this brutal attack, known as Operation Bluestar. These included major spokesmen for Sikh freedom such as Sant Jarnail Singh Bhindranwale, General Shabeg Singh, and others. The Sikh holy scriptures, the Guru Granth Sahib, written in the time that the ten Sikh Gurus lived, was shot full of bullet holes by the Indian forces. Young Sikh boys, ages 8 to 13, were taken out in the courtyard and asked whether they supported Khalistan, the independent Sikh state. When they answered with the Sikh religious incantation "Bole So Nihal," they were shot to death.

The Golden Temple attack made it clear that there is no place for Sikhs in supposedly secular and democratic India. As Bhindranwale himself said, "If India attacks the Golden Temple, it will lay the foundation stone for Khalistan." On October 7, 1987, Khalistan formally declared itself independent from India. India claims that there is no support for Khalistan. Then let them test the issue democratically at the ballot box by holding a free and fair plebiscite in Punjab, Khalistan on the subject of independence.

The Sikh Nation had sovereignty before, from 1710 to 1716 and from 1765 to 1849. No Sikh representative has ever signed India's constitution. The Sikhs have a heritage of freedom from their Gurus and they will be free again. Iraq is becoming a free country and will soon have a representative government. In the 21st century, you cannot suppress people for long. The people must determine their own fate. Only a free Khalistan will enable the Sikhs to live in peace, freedom, dignity, and prosperity. This cannot happen as long as their homeland is under Indian control.

If the Sikhs were the only victims of Indian repression, that would be bad enough. They are not. India has killed over 300,000 Christians in Nagaland since 1947. It has killed priests, raped nuns, attacked Christian schools, prayer halls, and festivals, expelled and killed missionaries, and carried out other atrocities against the Christian community. In short, it is not safe to be a Christian in India today. India has killed over 87,000 Muslims in Kashmir since 1988. Between 2,000 and 5,000 Muslims were massacred in Gujarat while the police were ordered to stand aside. Even India's own Human Rights Commission found evidence that the government pre-planned the Gujarat massacre. Amnesty International says that tens of thousands of minorities are being held as political prisoners.

This is unacceptable in any country, Mr. Speaker, especially a country that proclaims itself democratic. The Sikhs cannot forget or forgive the brutal Golden Temple attack. Neither can the other minorities forget the brutality that has been done to them. That is why America must act. Not one dollar of U.S. aid should be provided to India until basic human rights are respected. India can start by releasing all its political prisoners. We should also demand that India hold a free and fair plebiscite on the issue of independence for Khalistan, for Kashmir, for Nagaland, and for all the nations seeking their freedom. Multinational states like India are inherently unstable, as the examples of Austria-Hungary and the Soviet Union show. And the essence of democracy is the right to self-determination. It is time for the United States to take a stand for democracy, freedom, and stability.

Mr. Speaker, on June 5, the Council of Khalistan sponsored a demonstration to commemorate the Golden Temple attack. I would like to have the text of the Council of Khalistan's Press Release regarding this event placed into the Congressional Record following my statement.

[Press Release from the Council of Khalistan June 5, 2004]
Sikhs Commemorate 20th Anniversary of Golden Temple Attack

Washington, D.C._Sikhs from Philadelphia, Florida, New Jersey, Maryland, Virginia, and elsewhere on the East Coast came to Washington, D.C. to commemorate the twentieth anniversary of the Indian government's brutal military attack on the Golden Temple, the center and seat of the Sikh religion, and 125 other Sikh Gurdwaras throughout Punjab, in which over 20,000 Sikhs were murdered. They chanted slogans such as "India out of Khalistan", "Khalistan Zindabad", and others.

During the attack, young boys ages 8 to 13 were taken outside and asked if they supported Khalistan, the independent Sikh country. When they answered with the Sikh religious incantation "Bole So Nihal," they were shot. The Guru Granth Sahib, the Sikh holy scriptures, written in the time of the Sikh Gurus, were shot full of bullet holes and burned by the Indian forces.

The Golden Temple attack was a brutal chapter in India's repression of the Sikhs, according to Dr. Gurmit Singh Aulakh, President of the Council of Khalistan, the government pro tempore of Khalistan, which leads the struggle for Khalistan's independence. "This brutal attack clarified that there is no place in India for Sikhs," Dr. Aulakh said. On October 7, 1987, Khalistan declared its independence from India.

"Sant Bhindranwale said that attacking the Golden Temple would lay the foundation stone of Khalistan, and he was right," said Dr. Aulakh. "Instead of crushing the Sikh movement for Khalistan, as India intended, the attack strengthened it," he said. "Just last year, Sardar Atinder Pal Singh, a former Member of Parliament, held a seminar on Khalistan in Punjab. It was well attended and featured outstanding presentations, including one by Professor Gurtej Singh, IAS, Professor of Sikhism," said Dr. Aulakh. "The flame of freedom still burns bright in the hearts of Sikhs despite the deployment of over half a million Indian troops to crush it," he said. "Dal Khalsa, a Sikh political party, held marches through Punjab demanding the establishment of an independent Khalistan."

History shows that multinational states such as India are doomed to failure. Countries like Austria-Hungary, India's longtime friend the Soviet Union, Yugoslavia, Czechoslovakia, and others prove this point. India is not a single country; it is a polyglot like those countries, thrown together for the convenience of the British colonialists. It is doomed to break up as they did.

The Indian government has murdered over 250,000 Sikhs since 1984, more than 300,000 Christians since 1948, over 87,000 Muslims in Kashmir since 1988, and tens of thousands of Tamils, Assamese, Manipuris, Dalits, and others. The Indian Supreme Court called the Indian government's murders of Sikhs "worse than a genocide."

Indian police arrested human-rights activist Jaswant Singh Khalra after he exposed their policy of mass cremation of Sikhs, in which over 50,000 Sikhs have been arrested, tortured, and murdered, then their bodies were declared unidentified and secretly cremated. He was murdered in police custody. His body was not given to his family. The police never released the body of former Jathedar of the Akal Takht Gurdev Singh Kaunke after SSP Swaran Singh Ghotna murdered him. Ghotna has never been brought to trial for the Jathedar Kaunke murder. No one has been brought to justice for the kidnapping and murder of Jaswant Singh Khalra.

According to a report by the Movement Against State Repression (MASR), 52,268 Sikhs are being held as political prisoners in India without charge or trial. Some have been in illegal custody since 1984! "These prisoners never committed any crime but peacefully speaking out for Sikh freedom," said Dr. Aulakh. "What is a democracy doing holding political prisoners?," he asked. "This alone shows that for Sikhs and other minorities, there is no democracy, no freedom of speech."

"As Professor Darshan Singh, a former Jathedar of the Akal Takht, said, 'If a Sikh is not a Khalistani, he is not a Sikh'," Dr. Aulakh noted. "We must continue to pray for and work for our God-given birthright of freedom," he said. "Without political power, religions cannot flourish and nations perish."

***

Document

CONGRESSIONAL RECORD -- EXTENSIONS

Friday, June 18, 2004
108th Congress, 2nd Session
150 Cong Rec E 1155

REFERENCE: Vol. 150, No. 85
SECTION: Extension of Remarks
TITLE: COUNCIL OF KHALISTAN HONORS PRESIDENT REAGAN

HON. DAN BURTON
of Indiana
in the House of Representatives
Thursday, June 17, 2004

Mr. BURTON of Indiana . Mr. Speaker, all over America, people are honoring the memory of President Ronald Reagan, who passed away on

June 5th. Among those who have paid homage to President Reagan's legacy is the Council of Khalistan, led by my friend Dr. Gurmit Singh Aulakh. Dr. Aulakh wrote an excellent letter to President Bush offering condolences to the American people on President Reagan's passing. He took special note of President Reagan's vision and his efforts to extend freedom all over the world.

President Reagan referred to America as "the shining city on a hill," the bright hope for the entire world. It is our job to pick up that torch and continue to promote freedom wherever it is denied. A good start would be to work to extend freedom to all peoples and nations of South Asia. In India, there are 18 official languages. Over 300,000 Christians have been murdered in Nagaland, as well as more than a quarter of a million Sikhs, almost 88,000 Kashmiri Muslims, thousands of Muslims in other parts of the country, and tens of thousands of Assamese, Bodos, Dalits, Manipuris, Tamils, and other minorities. Over 52,000 Sikhs are being held as political prisoners, some as long as 20 years, without charge of trial. According to Amnesty International, tens of thousands of other minorities are also being held as political prisoners. A Sikh named Gurnihal Singh Pirzada was recently arrested for attending a meeting of "dissidents," a meeting he says he didn't attend, while noting that it would not have been illegal for him to have done so. This does not sound like freedom or democracy to me.

Mr. Speaker, we should give serious thought to reconsidering our aid to India until basic human rights are freely exercised by all, and we should support the very basic principle of democracy through a free and fair plebiscite on independence for the Sikhs of Punjab, Khalistan, for predominantly Christian Nagaland, for Kashmir, and for every nation seeking to free itself from the yoke of Indian oppression. That is the way to bring freedom, security, stability, dignity, and prosperity to one of the world's most troubled regions. Perhaps the best memorial we can give to President Reagan is to help the people of South Asia achieve their freedom, just as we did in so many other countries during his Administration.

I would like to have the text of Council of Khalistan's letter to President Bush placed into the Congressional Record following my statement.

Council of Khalistan
Washington, DC, June 15, 2004.
The Honorable George W. Bush,
President of the United States,
The White House
Washington, DC.

Dear President Bush: On behalf of over 500,000 Sikh Americans and the 25 million strong Sikh Nation, I would like to send our condolences to the people of the United States on the passing of President Ronald Reagan. Although his illness had already taken him from us in many ways, the finality of his death is still a cause for grief.

We appreciated your very classy remarks at President Reagan's state funeral, as well as those of your father, Lady Thatcher, and former Prime Minister Mulroney. All of you gave moving tributes to President Reagan that helped to inspire and uplift a grieving nation.

President Reagan was a great American leader. His rise from humble beginnings in Dixon, Illinois to becoming a sportscaster, a movie star, governor, and President inspires us all to continue trying to achieve the very highest and best that we can.

His Words, "Whatever else history may say about me when I'm gone, I hope it will record that I appealed to your best hopes, not your worst fears; to your confidence rather than your doubts. My dream is that you will travel the road ahead with liberty's lamp guiding your steps and opportunity's arm steadying your way" serve as an inspiration to Americans of all backgrounds today. That is exactly how he will be remembered.

President Reagan believed in the greatness of America and its people and in extending freedom throughout the world. His work in defeating the Soviet Union and in restoring the American economy marked the greatness of President Reagan and of the people of the country he so loved. We must continue to extend freedom in his memory.

One place where freedom needs to be extended is the Indian subcontinent. Today in India, the Indian government has murdered over 250,000 Sikhs since 1984, almost 88,000 Kashmiri Muslims since 1988, over 300,000 Christians in Nagaland, and tens of thousands of other minorities. More than 52,000 Sikhs as well as tens of thousands of other minorities are held as political prisoners without charge or trial, some since 1984. I hope that you will press India to support human rights and self-determination for these oppressed minorities. I am convinced that this would be a great follow-through to President Reagan's vision.

Once again, our condolences to the American people on the loss of President Reagan.

> *Sincerely,*
> *Dr. Gurmit Singh Aulakh,*
> *President, Council of Khalistan*

***

Document

CONGRESSIONAL RECORD -- EXTENSIONS

Friday, June 18, 2004
108th Congress, 2nd Session
150 Cong Rec E 1166

REFERENCE: Vol. 150, No. 85
SECTION: Extension of Remarks
TITLE: SIKHS REMEMBER 20TH ANNIVERSARY OF ATTACK ON
GOLDEN TEMPLE_FREEDOM FOR KHALISTAN WILL END THE
BRUTALITY

HON. EDOLPHUS TOWNS
of New York
in the House of Representatives
Thursday, June 17, 2004

Mr. TOWNS . Mr. Speaker, Sikhs observe the twentieth anniversary of India's brutal attack on the Golden Temple, the seat of their religion, this month. From June 3 to 6, 1984, the Indian military brutally attacked the Golden Temple and 125 other Sikh Gurdwaras all over Punjab. This brutal and devastating attack, carried out by the Indira Gandhi government, which was always proudly proclaiming its commitment to secularism, killed over 20,000 Sikhs.

This attack made it clear that even when the secular parties are in power, the minorities in India are not safe and they have no real rights, despite what is written in India's constitution. Whether the Hindu nationalist BJP is in power or the secularist Congress Party is in power, the policy of killing the Sikhs and other minorities in the futile effort to preserve what India considers its territorial integrity marches brutally on.

Among those killed in the Golden Temple attack were major Sikh leaders like Sant Jarnail Singh Bhindranwale, Bhai Arnrik Singh, General Shabeg Singh, and many others. The Guru Granth Sahib, the Sikh holy scriptures, were shot full of bullets from the guns of the Indian military. Sikh boys were taken outside and asked if they supported Khalistan. Then they were shot to death. Khalistan, of course, is the name of the independent Sikh homeland.

There is no place for Sikhs or other minorities such as Christians and Muslims in India despite its claims of secularism. On October 7, 1987, Khalistan formally declared its independence. If India is the democratic country it claims to be, why not simply decide the issue in a free and fair plebiscite in Punjab, Khalistan on the subject of independence? Isn't that the democratic way? I was under the impression that in democracies, things were decided by votes. The United States allows the people of Puerto Rico to vote on independence every few years. Canada has held democratic plebiscites on the status of Quebec. In 1947, India promised to settle the Kashmir issue by plebiscite, but it has never allowed that vote to be held. Why not simply put the question to a democratic vote? That is self-determination and self-determination is the essence of democracy.

The Sikh Nation was independent from 1765 to 1849. The Sikhs were supposed to receive sovereignty when India became independent. Although the Indian constitution was adopted in 1950, more than half a century ago, to this day no Sikh representative has ever signed it. How can India claim that it holds sovereignty over the Sikh Nation?

Unfortunately, the Sikhs are not the only victims of India's repressive tyranny. More than 300,000 Christians in Nagaland have been killed by the Indian government since 1947. They have seen priests murdered, nuns raped, schools, prayer halls, and festivals attacked_the government even shut down one festival with gunfire_missionaries murdered, beaten, and thrown out of the country, and so many other atrocities carried out against them. Almost 88,000 Kashmiri Muslims have fallen victim to India's brutal tyranny since 1988. Another 2,000 to 5,000 Muslims were massacred in Gujarat with the connivance of the government. And these are just a few of the atrocities committed against minorities by the Indian forces.

Mr. Speaker, we must do something to stop these atrocities. If real democracy and real freedom is going to come to all the people of South Asia, the United States must take a stand. It is good that a Sikh is now Prime Minister. He must know the feeling of India's brutality against his people. Therefore, I call on him to use his office to release all of India's political prisoners and bring the persons who carried out these atrocities to justice. We must stop our aid to India until it shows that it is willing to act like a democracy and protect human rights. We are setting up a democratic government in Iraq with a new President and a new Prime Minister. Isn't it time that real democracy finally came to India?

In addition, it is vital for the Congress to declare its support for a free and fair plebiscite on the issue of independence for Khalistan. There should also be similar plebiscites for Kashmir, Nagaland, and every other nation that seeks its freedom from Indian rule. India says there is no support for these freedom movements. Well, it is time for India to prove its point by holding a free vote on the matter. This is the only way for the people of South Asia to live in freedom, peace, democracy, and stability.

Mr. Speaker, there will be demonstrations around the world this weekend to commemorate the Golden Temple attack. The one in Washington will be led by the Council of Khalistan. I would like to insert their very informative flyer into the Record at this time.

***

Document

CONGRESSIONAL RECORD -- EXTENSIONS

Tuesday, June 01, 2004
108th Congress, 2nd Session
150 Cong Rec E 968

REFERENCE: Vol. 150, No. 74
SECTION: Extension of Remarks
TITLE: INDIA'S HUMAN RIGHTS VIOLATIONS IN PUNJAB, KASHMIR SUCCESSFULLY EXPOSED

Speech of
HON. EDOLPHUS TOWNS
of New York
in the House of Representatives
Tuesday, June 1, 2004

Mr. TOWNS . Mr. Speaker, on May 12, the Subcommittee on Human Rights and Wellness conducted a hearing into human-rights violations in Kashmir and in Punjab, Khalistan. It was a very successful hearing. Witnesses travelled from Kashmir and from out of state to testify.

Those testifying included The Honorable Michael Kozak, Principal Deputy Assistant Secretary of State, Bureau of Human Rights and Labor; The Honorable Donald Camp, Deputy Assistant Secretary of State, Bureau of South Asian Affairs; Mr. T. Kumar, Advocacy Director_Asia, Amnesty International; The Honorable Robert Giuda, Deputy Majority Leader of the New Hampshire House of Representatives and Chairman, Americans for Resolution of Kashmir; Dr. Ghulam Nabi Fai, Executive Director, Kashmiri American Council; Mrs. Attiya Inayatullah, a human-rights activist from Kashmir; Selig Harrison, Director of the Asia Program, Woodrow Wilson Center for International Policy; and Dr. Gurmit Singh Aulakh, President of the Council of Khalistan.

Many witnesses talked about the atrocities that have become every-day policy in India's minority states, such as Punjab, Khalistan and Kashmir. Witnesses testified to such atrocities as extrajudicial killings, including fake encounter killings, custodial deaths throughout the country, excessive use of force by security forces, youth sexually incapac-itated through torture, rapes, murders, burning villages, and others.

India claims to be democratic, but it is really a brutal tyranny, as these atrocities show. It has placed over 700,000 troops in Kashmir and another 500,000 in Punjab, Khalistan to suppress any opposition to its brutal rule. The Indian government has murdered over 250,000 Sikhs since 1984, more than 300,000 Christians since 1948, over 87,000 Mus-lims in Kashmir since 1988, and tens of thousands of Tamils, Assamese, Bodos, Manipuris, Dalits, and others.

Mr. Speaker, the United States of America, the beacon of freedom for the world, cannot just stand by and let these atrocities occur. We should stop aid to India until it respects human rights and we should put this Congress on record in support of self-determination for the Sikhs, Kashmiris, Nagas, and everyone who is seeking freedom from India's brutal rule.

Mr. Speaker, the Council of Khalistan issued an excellent, detailed, and informative press release on the hearing, which I would like to insert in the Record now.

Dr. Aulakh, Others Expose Indian Human Rights Violations at Con-gressional Hearing

Washington, DC, May 12, 2004._Dr. Gurmit Singh Aulakh, President of the Council of Khalistan, exposed Indian human rights violations against the Sikhs and other minorities at a Congressional hearing today entitled "Decades of Terror: Exploring Human Rights Abuses in Kashmir and the Disputed Territories." He gave a very emotional informative, strong statement. It was a very successful appearance.

"Repression is the official policy of supposedly secular and democratic India," said Dr. Aulakh. "The reality is that India is a Hindu theocracy, not the democracy it claims to be," he said. On October 7, 1987, the Sikh Nation declared its independence from India, naming its new country Khalistan. India's brutal occupation of Khalistan and other minority nations is now internationalized and brought to the attention of the world. On December 5, President Bush told Dr. Aulakh, "I am aware of the Sikh and Kashmiri problem." Dr. Aulakh made it clear to the committee that "freedom for all the minority nations of South Asia is the only way to end the repression and secure full human rights for everyone in that troubled region."

Dr. Aulakh testified that "An Army commander in Amritsar district threatened that he would murder the Sikh men, bring the women to the Army barracks, and 'produce a new generation of Sikhs.' Mr. Chairman, this is disgraceful and extremely insulting to the proud Sikhs. It is unbecoming of an army commander of a nation which claims to be the world's largest democracy." He blasted India's policy of Hindutva, the total Hinduization of every aspect of life in India. He noted that Amnesty International has not been allowed into Punjab since 1978. "Even Castro's Cuba has allowed Amnesty International into the country more recently," he said.

Subcommittee Chairman Representative Dan Burton (R-Indiana) opened the hearing with a statement. Congressman Burton said, "Just as the world is disgusted by the abuse of Iraqi prisoners by United States servicemen and women, we should be disgusted by the tactics that have been systematically employed by Indian military and paramilitary forces." He quoted the U.S. State Department report on India: "Significant human rights abuses included: Extrajudicial killings, including fake encounter killings, custodial deaths throughout the country, and excessive use of force by security forces." Chairman Burton noted "techniques like reprisal killings, burning down of whole villages, and summary executions." He said that "India's insistence on resolving a political problem by force has dragged it down into a campaign of essentially lawless state terrorism."

"We thank Chairman Burton for holding this important hearing," said Dr. Aulakh. "It has been helpful in showing the world the truth about India's claim to be a secular democracy. What India really is is one of the world's most brutal tyrannies," he said.

Other speakers included The Honorable Michael Kozak, Principal Deputy Assistant Secretary of State, Bureau of Democracy, Human Rights, and Labor; The Honorable Donald Camp, Deputy Assistant Secretary of State, Bureau of South Asian Affairs; Mr. T. Kumar, Advocacy Director_Asia, Amnesty International; The Honorable Bob Giuda, Chairman of Americans for Resolution of Kashmir and Deputy Majority Leader of the New Hampshire House of Representatives; Dr. Ghulam Nabi Fai, Executive Director of the Kashmiri American Council; Mrs. Attiya Inayatullah, a human-rights activist and aid worker; and Selig Harrison, Director of the Asia Program, Woodrow Wilson Center for International Policy. Sikhs from Maryland, Virginia, the District of Columbia, New Jersey, and Pennsylvania came to the hearing. Representatives of the Sikh Coalition were in attendance. Such Sikh youth leaders as Amardeep Singh Bhalla, Gurpreet Singh Dhillon, Mona Kaur Dhillon, and others, as well as Sikh activists Ranjit Singh, Gurbax Singh Dhillon, Karj Singh Sandhu, Kavneet Singh Pannu, and many others attended in an excellent show of Sikh strength.

The Indian government has murdered over 250,000 Sikhs since 1984, more than 300,000 Christians since 1948, over 87,000 Muslims in Kashmir since 1988, and tens of thousands of Tamils, Assamese, Bodos, Manipuris, Dalits, and others. The Indian Supreme Court called the Indian government's murders of Sikhs "worse than a genocide." Mrs. Inayatullah testified that in Kashmir, "Since 1989 and as of January 2004 the death toll stands at 87,648. The orphan count is 105,210, women ages 7-70 molested is a shameful 9,297 and another 21,286 reported widowed, with there being no record of the number of youth sexually incapacitated through torture and disabled for life." She said that "Buzz words like cross-border terrorism and fundamentalism will not cover India's guilt." Rep. Giuda noted that "Indian law immunizes its army and police from prosecution for actions committed under color of 'prevention of terrorism', enabling a hideous government-sanctioned repertoire of torture, rapes, murder, arson, and custodial killing. Pakistan allows U.N. observers and human-rights organizations unfettered access to Free Kashmir, while India denies access to substantial parts of IOK. One must ask, 'Why are no observers allowed? What is India hiding?'"

Mr. Kumar said that "torture, including rape, deaths in custody, extrajudicial killings, and 'disappearances' have been perpetrated by agents of the state with impunity." He said that "Most families of all backgrounds have experienced some form of loss_of livelihood, of a relative, or of the sense of security of life, liberty, and other fundamental human rights." Dr. Fai reported that "Killings in Kashmir have become so commonplace that they are reported like car accidents in the United States." He described rapes, torture, arbitrary arrests, and other activities. He noted that "freedom to speak, write, or organize around self-determination or criticism of the Indian government for millions of Kashmiris is chimerical." He noted that the Official Secrets Act gives the government authority to suppress criticism of its policies. He said that "India has authorized a police state reminiscent of the Gestapo."

Mr. Harrison stated that India has built "an inflated military force that has committed well-documented atrocities." Secretary Kozak said, "Our annual human-rights report documents our concern and gives examples of the abuses that take place all too frequently."

Dr. Aulakh testified that Indian police arrested human-rights activist Jaswant Singh Khalra after he exposed their policy of mass cremation of Sikhs, in which over 50,000 Sikhs have been arrested, tortured, and murdered, then their bodies were declared unidentified and secretly cremated. Khalra was murdered in police custody. His body was never given to his family. The police never released the body of former Jathedar of the Akal Takht Gurdev Singh Kaunke after SSP Swaran Singh Ghotna murdered him. Ghotna has not been brought to trial for the murder of Jathedar Kaunke. No one has been brought to justice for the kidnapping and murder of Jaswant Singh Khalra. According to a report by the Movement Against State Repression (MASR), 52,268 Sikhs are being held as political prisoners in India without charge or trial. Some have been in illegal custody since 1984! Amnesty International recently reported at least 100 current torture cases in Punjab. A Sikh leader named Gurnihal Singh Pirzada was arrested on charges that he attended a meeting with "dissidents." Although he denies attending the meeting, he said that it would not be illegal if he did.

Dr. Aulakh noted that history shows that multinational states such as India are doomed to failure. Countries like Austria-Hungary, India's longtime friend the Soviet Union, Yugoslavia, Czechoslovakia, and others prove this point. India is not one country; it is a polyglot like those countries, thrown together for the convenience of the British colonialists. It is doomed to break up as they did. India is ruled by Hindu theocrats whose agenda is "Hindu, Hindi, Hindutva, Hindu Rashtra," or total Hindu domination of every facet of Indian life. An Indian Cabinet minister said that everyone who lives in India must be a Hindu or subservient to Hindus.

"As Professor Darshan Singh, a former Jathedar of the Akal Takht, said, 'If a Sikh is not for Khalistan, he is not a Sikh'," Dr. Aulakh noted. "We must continue to press for our God-given birthright of freedom," he said. "Without political power, religions cannot flourish and nations perish."

***

Document

CONGRESSIONAL RECORD -- EXTENSIONS

Tuesday, June 01, 2004
108th Congress, 2nd Session
150 Cong Rec E 973

REFERENCE: Vol. 150, No. 74
SECTION: Extension of Remarks
TITLE: COUNCIL OF KHALISTAN CONGRATULATES INDIA'S NEW SIKH PRIME MINISTER

Speech of
HON. EDOLPHUS TOWNS
of New York
in the House of Representatives
Tuesday, June 1, 2004

Mr. TOWNS . Mr. Speaker, as you know, a Sikh, Dr. Manmohan Singh, has been named as the new Prime Minister of India. Dr. Singh is a former Finance Minister in the government of Narasimha Rao from 1991 to 1996. He is a very experienced Indian official.

I hope that this will be a step forward for good relations between the United States and India, Mr. Speaker. We all seek good relations. However, the support of India's Communists for the governing coalition makes me wonder if good relations are possible under this particular government.

Dr. Gurmit Singh Aulakh, President of the Council of Khalistan has sent a letter to Prime Minister Singh congratulating him on his new position. In the letter, Dr. Aulakh notes that it is good for the image of Sikhs worldwide that Dr. Manmohan Singh is now Prime Minister. He also notes that it was the RSS, parent organization of the ousted BJP, that assassinated Mohandas Gandhi and takes note of India's violent history, urging Prime Minister Singh to take strong measures to avoid repeating this history, such as releasing the political prisoners that India holds, punishing those responsible for atrocities, ending the taking of Punjabi water to nonriparian states without compensation, and other such policies I think we can all support. India will be a better place if Prime Minister Singh implements these policies.

According to the Movement Against State Repression (MASR), 52,268 Sikhs are being held as political prisoners. Amnesty International reports that tens of thousands of other minorities are also being held as political prisoners. A democracy should not hold political prisoners. I am sure all my colleagues will agree with me that all these political prisoners should be released immediately.

The letter also reminds Prime Minister Singh that while ending the BJP's policy of Hindutva_total Hinduization of every aspect of Indian life_will be welcome, it was the Congress Party under Dr. Singh's political patrons, the Gandhi family, that carried out the military attack on the Golden Temple, the center and seat of the Sikh religion and the massacre of Sikhs in Delhi and elsewhere in India. Dr. Aulakh urges Dr. Singh to make a complete break with these policies by punishing those responsible.

In 1987, the Sikhs declared themselves independent from India, naming their new country Khalistan. As Dr. Aulakh points out in his letter, allowing Khalistan, Kashmir, Nagaland, and the other nations seeking their freedom from India to be free is the best way to spare the subcontinent any more bloodshed.

I join in that call, Mr. Speaker. We should support a free and fair plebiscite on the question of independence for the minority nations of

South Asia. And until human rights are fully observed and a complete break is made with the bloody and repressive policies of the past, the United States should stop providing aid to India. These measures will encourage India to take the steps necessary to bring peace, freedom, prosperity, and dignity to everyone in the subcontinent.

Mr. Speaker, I would like to insert the Council of Khalistan's letter to Prime Minister Singh into the Record at this time.

Council of Khalistan,
Washington, DC, May 26, 2004.
The Hon. Dr. Manmohan Singh,
Prime Minister of India, Chanakyapouri, New Delhi, India.

Dear Prime Minister Singh: Congratulations on becoming Prime Minister of India. You have been entrusted with a significant responsibility.

We are very pleased to see a Sikh as Prime Minister. You have reached this high office because of your intelligence and hard work and your presence in this position gives the world a strong and positive impression of Sikhs. However, remember the way that the Gandhi family used Giani Zail Singh when he was President of India. He became the figurehead for their repression of the Sikhs. Unlike Zail Singh, you are in a position of real power. Sikhs around the world will be watching what you do and hoping that you will not allow yourself to be used in a similar manner.

As a Sikh, you are in a position to understand the problems of the Sikh Nation. The Movement Against State Repression (MASR) did a report that showed the government admitted to holding 52,268 Sikh political prisoners. They have been held without charge or trial, some for as long as 20 years! If you are truly committed to secularism, one of your first acts should be to release all political prisoners. If any have died in custody, their bodies should be released to their families. These are people who have committed no crime but opposition to the government. How can there be political prisoners in a democracy?

I urge you to restore to Punjab what is rightfully Punjab's. I call on you to restore the Punjabi-speaking areas that were removed from the state of Punjab to it. Punjab was meant to be a unified Sikh state and Indian governments of the past have pursued a deliberate policy of dividing, bankrupting, and weakening it to divide and weaken the Sikhs. As a Sikh and as Prime Minister, you are in a position to put a stop to this policy. You are also in a position to restore Punjab's water rights. For years, Punjab's water has been diverted to non-riparian states with no compensation to Punjab or to the people of Punjab. Please put an end to the diversion of Punjab's water to non-riparian states and when such diversion is necessary, please make certain that the Sikh farmers of Punjab get appropriate compensation for their water. This is only fair and right, and it is a policy that will earn you greater support among the Sikhs. All other states control their water resources.

We are also pleased that the BJP is out of power. Rahul Gandhi, MP, the son of Sonia and Rajiv Gandhi and a member of your party, pointed out that the RSS, which is the parent organization of the BJP, assassinated

Mahatma Gandhi. The RSS is a pro-Fascist organization and both Vajpayee and Advani are proud RSS members. The end of the policy of Hindutva will be a welcome development. Sikh support for the Congress Party is also a by-product of the corrupt Parkash Singh Badal regime in Punjab, the most corrupt government in Punjab's history. The Badal government even invented a new word for bribery: fee for service. However, it was a Congress government that attacked the Golden Temple and carried out the massacre of Sikhs in Delhi and throughout India.

As your own nephew pointed out, Sikhs can never forget the attack on the Golden Temple. Thus it is disturbing to read that you have said you intend to follow the policies of Rajiv Gandhi. His policy was the murder of at least 8,000 Sikhs in Delhi alone and over 20,000 throughout India. It is also disturbing that your party gave tickets to Jagdish Tytler and Sajjan Kumar, who are responsible for ordering the murders of thousands of Sikhs in Delhi, and that Tytler was appointed to your Cabinet. Tytler and Sajjan Kumar supplied gasoline for these murders and incited the crowd. These people belong in jail, not in the government.

I hope that you will not follow such undemocratic, anti-secularist, anti-Sikhs policies. Policies such as these have made it clear that there is no place for Sikhs in India. If you are truly committed to secularism, you cannot follow such brutal, repressive policies against Sikhs and other minorities. The brutal policies have brought about the murders of over 250,000 Sikhs since 1984, more than 87,000 Kashmiri Muslims since 1988, over 300,000 Christians in Nagaland, and tens of thousands of Assamese, Bodos, Dalits, Manipuris, and other minorities. The United States State Department exposed the fact that between 1992 and 1994, a Congress government paid out more than 41,000 cash bounties to police officers for killing Sikhs. One officer received a bonus for murdering a three-year-old boy, claiming the toddler was a "terrorist."

The time has come for India to make a clean break with its past by punishing those responsible for these actions, compensating the victims' families, and committing itself to preventing and punishing such acts in the future. This will show your commitment to secular, democratic government and not the theocratic repression of the country's past governments.

India is a very fractured country. Because of past history, no party is able to unify the people and command a majority of the support, so coalition governments are inevitable. Coalition governments are inherently unstable. For example, the support of India's three Communist parties for your coalition weakens your ability to pursue good relations with the United States and other Western countries, which could increase India's isolation from the world.

History also shows us that multinational countries are doomed to failure. Austria-Hungary, the Soviet Union, Czechoslovakia, and Yugoslavia are examples of this. India is a multinational state, not a single country, thrown together by British colonialists and with 18 official languages. How can such a country be held together except by massive repression and bloodshed? And the repression has simply created greater resentment of the central government, which also strengthens the support for the 17 independence movements throughout India. Either way, holding India together is a futile enterprise destined to fail.

Since India is a democracy, I urge you to solve this problem the democratic way. In 1947, India committed itself to a plebiscite on the status of Kashmir. The Sikhs also seek their freedom and sovereignty, as the Nagas and others also do. If India is truly the world's largest democracy, why not simply allow the people to decide their status by a free and fair vote. That is the way that you achieved power, by the people's votes. Why not let the people vote on this critical issue? The essence of democracy is the right of self-determination.

As a Sikh, you are aware that the Sikh Nation is a separate nation which was supposed to receive sovereignty at the time of India's independence. As you know, Sikhs ruled Punjab from 1710 to 1716 and from 1765 to 1849. No Sikh representative has signed the Indian Constitution to this day. Every day, Sikhs pray "Raj Kare Ga Khalsa," the Khalsa shall rule. As you know, the Sikh Nation declared its independence from India on October 7, 1987, calling their new country Khalistan. As former Jathedar of the Akal Takht Professor Darshan Singh has said, "If a Sikh is not a Khalistani, he is not a Sikh."

I know that you are a Sikh, Mr. Prime Minister. I can see your turban. I know that you are concerned about the future of the Sikh Nation. Therefore, I urge you to sit down with Sikh representatives and negotiate the boundaries of a sovereign, independent, free Khalistan. This is the best thing that you can do for the Sikh Nation, your own people, and it is the best way to ensure that India goes the way of Czechoslovakia, not that of Yugoslavia. Please spare India, Khalistan, and all the nations of South Asia any further bloodshed.

Congratulations again on your new position.

Sincerely,
Dr. Gurmit Singh Aulakh,
President, Council of Khalistan.

***

Document

CONGRESSIONAL RECORD -- EXTENSIONS

Wednesday, May 12, 2004
108th Congress, 2nd Session
150 Cong Rec E 828

REFERENCE: Vol. 150, No. 66
SECTION: Extension of Remarks
TITLE: ELECTIONS IN PUNJAB MAY 10_THIS IS AN OPPORTUNITY TO CLAIM FREEDOM

Speech of
HON. EDOLPHUS TOWNS
of New York
in the House of Representatives
Wednesday, May 12, 2004

Mr. TOWNS . Mr. Speaker, India is undergoing a cycle of elections. Unlike this country, India does not hold the elections on a single day but over a period of time. I guess it's difficult to hold elections on one day when you have a billion people.

Elections in Punjab have been scheduled for May 10. Recently, the Council of Khalistan put out an open letter to the people of Punjab urging them to use these elections to bring about independence for the Sikh homeland, Punjab, Khalistan.

It looks like the elections will result in a hung Parliament. The militantly Hindu nationalist Bharatiya Janata Party (BJP), which has been leading the government, seems to have lost some ground. A coalition government will need to be formed.

That brings substantial power to the regional parties in the various states and regions of the country. These parties could well control who runs the Indian government. The Council of Khalistan called on these regional parties to band together in a "freedom bloc" to unite for freedom and self-determination for all of the minorities of South Asia.

The open letter notes that both the BJP and the rival Congress Party are dangerous to the freedom of the Sikhs and other minorities, and the regional Akali Dal is in coalition with the BJP. The Akali leaders invited the Congress Party government of Indira Gandhi to invade the Golden Temple, the seat of the Sikh religion, and they surrendered quickly when the attack came.

This letter points out these and other reasons why it is important to use these elections as a springboard to achieve freedom for Khalistan and the other nations seeking to free themselves of Indian rule.

Mr. Speaker, we all know the brutality of India's suppression of these freedom movements. They have murdered over 250,000 Sikhs since 1984, over 85,000 Kashmiri Muslims, over 300,000 Christians in Nagaland, and tens of thousands of other minorities. Now, according to the Tribune of Chandigarh, the Indian government is demanding that the government of Punjab pay them back for the costs accrued in suppressing the Sikhs.

This is outrageous, Mr. Speaker. As the beacon of freedom, the United States must be strong against this kind of repression. We should stop all American aid to India until it stops the repression and allows all people within its borders to enjoy their most basic human rights fully. And we should put this Congress on record as supporting self-determination for the Sikhs of Khalistan, the Muslims of Kashmir, the Christians of Nagaland, and all the other people seeking freedom from India's brutal rule.

The right to self-determination is the essence of democracy, Mr. Speaker. The lack of self-determination and the repression show that

India's claim to be a democracy is fake. It is time for us to take a stand on behalf of freedom for all.

Mr. Speaker, I would like to insert the Council of Khalistan's open letter into the Record at this time.

Open Letter to the Sikh Nation, April 27, 2004.

Elections in Punjab have been set for May 10. Elections under the Indian Constitution will not free the Sikh Nation. Use this opportunity, however, to elect committed, hottest Sikhs who are committed to freeing Khalistan to Parliament.

These elections will certainly result in a hung Parliament. No party is capable of putting together the national majority needed to control Parliament on its own. A coalition government will be formed. The regional parties will be very important in deciding who will control the government. This gives the regional parties and the regions they represent enormous power. We must use this power to our benefit. It is time for the regional parties to form a "freedom bloc" to work together for freedom for Khalistan, Kashmir, Nagaland, and all the minority nations seeking their freedom from India's brutal rule. We agree with L.K. Advani when he said, "When Kashmir goes, India goes." By securing freedom for any of the captive nations of South Asia, we bring about freedom for all of us. Working together in a common, unified effort will hasten that day for everyone.

Congress and the BJP are both the enemies of the Sikh Nation. They both watch out for the interests of the Hindu majority at the expense of the Sikh Nation and other minorities. The BJP has murdered Muslims in Gujarat, in Kashmir, and elsewhere and Christians in Nagaland and throughout India. They have forcibly reconverted Christians back to Hinduism. They preach Hindutva (total Hindu control of the culture and society) and openly preach that if you live in India, you must either be Hindu or be subservient to Hinduism.

The Congress Party attacked the Golden Temple, the most sacred shrine of the Sikh Nation, 125 other Gurdwaras throughout Punjab. Over 20,000 Sikhs were murdered in those attacks, known as Operation Bluestar, including Sant Jamail Singh Bhindranwale, General Shabeg Singh, Bhai Amrik Singh, and over 100 Sikh religious students ages 8-13 who were taken out into the courtyard and shot. The BJP congratulated Indira Gandhi on the attack and said it should have been done earlier.

These attacks accelerated the Sikh independence movement and deep-ened the desire for independence in the hearts of Sikhs, a fire that burns brightly in the hearts of the Sikh Nation to this day. Sant Bhindranwale said that the attack on the Golden Temple would "lay the foundation stone of Khalistan" and he was right. Late in 2003, former Member of Parliament Atinder Pal Singh organized a seminar on Khalistan at Baba Makhan Shah Labana Hall, Sector 30, Chandigarh. This shows that the flame of freedom is still burning in the hearts of Sikhs. Sikhs can never forgive or forget the Indian government's military attack on the Golden Temple. It is time to take action to free our homeland.

The Badal Akalis are totally controlled by their coalition partners, the BJP. Chief Minister Captain Anarinder Singh is in bed with the Congress Party. He honored the former Chief Minister, Beant Singh, who is responsible for the mass murder of hundreds of thousands of Sildis and gave over 41,000 cash bounties to police officials for Killing Sikhs. Neither will protect the interests of the Sikh Nation. They have undermined Sikh character and Sikh values. Simply by joining the Congress Party, Captain Amarinder Singh is undermining Sikh values. Badal, Tobra, and Longowal said that India would have to get to the Golden Temple by rolling tanks over their dead bodies, then quickly surrendered. The Alkalis invited the Indian Army to the Golden Temple to murder Sant Bhindranwale, General Shabeg Singh, Bhai Amrik Singh, and so many other committed Sikhs.

Do not support Badal or the Alkalis. The Badal government was the most corrupt government in the history of Punjab. They sold jobs for a fixed fee. They came up with a new, dignified term for bribery: "fee for service." If you didn't pay the fee, you didn't get the service. Badal's wife was so experienced that she could pick up a bag of money and tell how much money was in it. Parkash Singh Badal was a disaster for Puniab and a disgrace to the Sikh Nation. Yet the Akali Dal continues to support Badal, even though he was prosecuted and jailed for his corruption. What has happened to the character of the present-day Alkalis? They are defaming the name of the pre-partition pious Akalis who suffered and sacrificed for the cause of the Khalsa Panth.

Not even a singe Akali protested the unprecedented corruption of Badal. According to India-West, the Punjab Vigilance Bureau carried out raids on Badal's properties for several months and filed a charge-sheet in a local court charging Mr. Badal with siphoning off Rs. 784 million, the equivalent of $17 million in U.S. money, during his five years as chief minister. The article says that Mr. Badal and his family hold assets of Rs. 4326 crores (nearly $1 billion), most of which are located outside India. Half the population of India lives below the international poverty line. About 40 percent live on less than $2 per day.

Lalit Mansingh, the outgoing Indian Ambassador to the United States, has said, "There is no India without Sikhs and no Sikhs without India." He is wrong. The Sikh Nation has survived perfectly fine without India. Before there was an India, Sikhs flourished. The Sikhs ruled Punjab as an independent country from 1710 to 1716 and again from 1765 to 1849. Sikhs stopped the invasion from the West, annexed Kashmir from the Afghans, and occupied Kabul for a short period.

Remember the words of Professor Darshan Singh, former Jathedar of the Akal Takht, during the celebration of Guru Nanak's birthday: "If a Sikh is not a Khalistani, he is not a Sikh." He was only reiterating the Guru's blessing, "In Grieb Sikhin Ko Deon Patshahi." The time to achieve our independence is now.

The opportunity these elections provide must be used to liberate our homeland, Khalistan, from Indian oppression. We must choose leaders who will work for freedom for the Sikh Nation. Remember, you get what you vote for. Always remember our heritage: Raj Kare Ga Khalsa; Khalsa Bagi Yan Badshah. Freedom for Khalistan is very close. Let us take this opportunity to make it happen.

> *Panth Da Sewadar,*
> *Dr. Gurmit Singh Aulakh,*
> *President, Council of Khalistan.*

***

Document

CONGRESSIONAL RECORD -- EXTENSIONS

Tuesday, April 20, 2004
108th Congress, 2nd Session
150 Cong Rec E 549

REFERENCE: Vol. 150, No. 51
SECTION: Extension of Remarks
TITLE: VAISAKHI DAY, SIKH HOLIDAY_USE OPPORTUNITY TO FREE KHALISTAN

Speech of
HON. EDOLPHUS TOWNS
of New York
in the House of Representatives
Tuesday, April 20, 2004

Mr. TOWNS . Mr. Speaker, April 13 is Vaisakhi Day, the anniversary of the founding of the Sikh Nation in 1699. The Sikhs love freedom as we do, Mr. Speaker. They have a long tradition of fighting oppression wherever it rears its ugly head and they have a history of self-rule.

I would like to take this opportunity to wish the Sikhs in America and the Sikhs around the world a happy Vaisakhi Day.

The Council of Khalistan, the organization that is leading the Sikh movement to liberate their homeland, Khalistan, recently published an open letter to the Sikhs, a Vaisakhi Day message. It urged the Sikhs to use the opportunity to liberate their homeland. The letter called upon them to remember the Sikh Nation's heritage of freedom.

The letter pointed out the suffering of the Sikhs at the hands of the Indian government. That repression has taken the lives of over 250,000 Sikhs in the last 20 years, in addition to over 50,000 Sikhs who were picked up, tortured, killed, and secretly cremated, declaring their bodies "unidentified." Another 52,000-plus are being held as political prisoners, according to the Movement Against State Repression, a Punjabi human-rights organization. In addition, India has killed more than 300,000

Christians in Nagaland, over 85,000 Kashmiri Muslims, and tens of thousands of Assamese, Bodos, Dalits, Manipuris, Tamils, and other minorities. Yet the U.S. taxpayer continues to be taxed to send foreign aid to this brutal country.

The letter calls on the Sikhs to take the opportunity of Vaisakhi to demand a free and independent Khalistan by means of slogans, by peaceful resistance, and by bringing forth new leadership. It takes note of the death of Gurcharan Singh Tohra, the President of the Shiromani Gurdwara Prabandhak Committee, and the political collapse of former Chief Minister Parkash Singh Badal to call for new leadership that supports freedom for Khalistan. It notes the seminar held on Khalistan last year, which shows that the desire for freedom remains strong in Punjab.

This letter makes a very strong case for a sovereign, independent Khalistan and it does a good job of exposing the brutal tyranny that India has inflicted on the Sikh Nation.

Mr. Speaker, how can we, as the bastion of freedom, sit idly by and close our eyes to this terror? The time has come to stop U.S. aid to India. This may be the most effective way that we can influence them to stop the repression of Sikhs, Christians, Muslims, and other minorities. And if India is the democratic state that it says it is, it should conduct a free and fair vote on the question of independence. This Congress should put itself on record urging India to do this as soon as possible. That is the democratic way to settle issues, and we should use our influence to help this occur.

Mr. Speaker, the letter from the Council of Khalistan is very informative. For the information of my colleagues and the public, I would like to insert it into the Record.

Council of Khalistan,
Washington, DC, April 6, 2004.
Vaisakhi Day Message to the Sikh Nation: Sikhs Will Celebrate
Vaisakhi Day April 13

Dear Khalsa Ji: On April 13, the Sikh Nation will celebrate Vaisakhi Day, observing the 305th anniversary of the day Guru Gobind Singh established the Khalsa Panth. The Guru granted sovereignty to the Sikh Nation, saying "In Grieb Silrhin Ko Deon Patshahi." We must remind ourselves of our heritage by raising slogans of "Khalistan Zindabad" and beginning a Shantmai Morcha to liberate our homeland, Khalistan. Every morning and evening we recite, "Raj Kare Ga Khalsa." Now is the time to act on it. Do we mean what we say every morning and evening?

The Sikhs in Punjab have suffered enormous repression at the hands of the Indian regime in the last 20 years. The Indian government has murdered over 250,000 Sikhs since 1984. In addition, over 50,000 Sikh youth were picked up from their houses, tortured, murdered in police custody, then secretly cremated as "unidentified bodies." Their remains were never even given to their families! Over 52,000 Sikhs sit in Indian jails as political prisoners without charge or trial, according to the

Movement Against State Repression (MASR.) Some of them have been in illegal custody for 20 years!

The Indian government forgot the Sikh tradition. Sikhs can never forgive or forget the Indian government's military attack on the Golden Temple and 125 other Gurdwaras throughout Punjab. Over 20,000 Sikhs were murdered in those attacks, known as Operation Bluestar, including Sant Janail Singh Bhindranwale, General Shabeg Singh, Bhai Amrik Singh, and over 100 Sikh religious students ages 8-13 who were taken out into the courtyard and shot. These attacks accelerated the Sikh independence movement and deepened the desire for independence in the hearts of Sikhs, a fire that burns brightly in the hearts of the Sikh Nation to this day. Sant Bhindranwale said that the attack on the Golden Temple would "lay the foundation stone of Khalistan" and he was right. Late in 2003, former Member of Parliament Atinder Pal Singh organized a seminar on Khalistan at Baba Makhan Shah Labana Hall, Sector 30, Chandigarh. This shows that the flame of freedom is still burning in the hearts of Sikhs. It is time to take action to free our homeland. Repression and genocide of this magnitude at the hands of the Indian government is unparalleled in the late part of the 20th century. India should be ashamed of the genocide it has committed against Sikhs, Christians, Muslims, and other minorities.

With the passing of Gurcharan Singh Tohra, new leadership must emerge at the Shiromani Gurdwara Prabandhak Committee (SGPC.) In addition, new political leadership must emerge with Prakash Singh Badal under indictment. Mr. Badal's time is not long either. He has had cancer already and he is an old man. This new leadership must be committed to the cause of freeing our Sikh homeland from the repression and brutality of the Indian government by reclaiming our lost sovereignty in a free and independent Khalistan.

Khalsa Ji, at this time of Vaisakhi, the whole Khalsa Panth must be energized to reestablish a sovereign, independent Khalsa Raj by freeing our homeland, Khalistan. It is time for Sikhs to look back at our history of persecution and suffering over the past 20 years. The Hindu government of India, whether run by the Congress Party or by the BJP, wants minorities either subservient to Hinduism or completely wiped out. The Indian government and its allies have tried to weaken the Sikh religion by saying that Sikhism is part of Hinduism. If that is true, why have they murdered so many Sikhs? Hindus practice idol worship; Sikhism is monotheistic, worshipping only one God. Hindus believe in the caste system; Sikhs believe in the equality of the whole human race. Remember the words of Guru Gobind Singh: "Recognize ye all the human race as one." In spite of the fact that the religions believe completely opposite things, Hindus desire to engulf Sikhism just as they did with Jainism and Buddhism in India. They think that Buddhism is part of Hinduism because Siddhartha Gautama, the Buddha, was born in India. Similarly, Guru Nanak was born Hindu, so they proclaim Sikhism to be part of Hinduism. Yet Guru Nanak said that he was "neither Hindu nor Muslim." Jesus was born Jewish. Does that mean that Christianity is merely part of Judaism?

On this auspicious occasion celebrating the birth of the Khalsa Panth, we must bring back our Khalsa spirit. We must remember our heritage and tradition of "Khalsa Bagi Yan Badshah" by committing ourselves to freeing our homeland, Punjab, Khalistan, from Indian occupation. We need a new Sikh political party which has a dedication to the interests of the Sikh Nation as its sole objective, to establish Khalsa Raj by liberating Khalistan, severing all political ties with India. If the BJP wants Hindu Raj, it cannot object to Khalsa Raj.

The Indian government wants to break the will of the Sikh Nation and enslave them forever, making Sikhism a part of Hinduism. This can only be stopped if we free Punjab from Delhi's control and reestablish a sovereign, independent country, as declared on October 7, 1987. We must recommit ourselves to freeing our homeland, Punjab, Khalistan. Raise slogans of "Khalsa Bagi Yan Badshah," "Raj Kare Ga Khalsa," "Khalistan Zindabad," and "India out of Khalistan." Use this Vaisakhi to launch a Shantmai Morcha to liberate Khalistan.

Last year's seminar on Khalistan shows that the flame of freedom still burns brightly in Punjab in spite of the Indian government's brutal repression. Perhaps this is why India is afraid to hold a free and fair vote on the subject of independence. The essence of democracy is the right to self-determination.

Remember the words of Professor Darshan Singh, former Jathedar of the Akal Takht, during the celebration of Guru Nanak's birthday: "If a Sikh is not a Khalistani, he is not a Sikh." He was only reiterating the Guru's blessing, "In Grieb Sikhin Ko Deon Patshahi." The time to achieve our independence is now.

Always remember our heritage: Raj Kare Ga Khalsa; Khalsa Bagi Yan Badshah. Freedom for Khalistan is very close.

Panth Da Sewadar,
Gurmit Singh Aulakh, President.

***

Document

CONGRESSIONAL RECORD -- EXTENSIONS

Tuesday, April 20, 2004
108th Congress, 2nd Session
150 Cong Rec E 552

REFERENCE: Vol. 150, No. 51
SECTION: Extension of Remarks
TITLE: GURCHARAN SINGH TOHRA, SIKH LEADER, DIES_LEFT LEGACY OF BETRAYAL

HON. EDOLPHUS TOWNS
of New York
in the House of Representatives
Tuesday, April 20, 2004

Mr. TOWNS . Mr. Speaker, I noticed in the April 3 issue of the Washington Post that Gurcharan Singh Tohra, a Sikh who led the Shiromani Gurdwara Prabandhak Committee (SGPC), the Sikhs' highest administrative body, which administers all the Sikh places of worship, called Gurdwaras, in Punjab, died April 1 in a hospital in New Delhi. He was 79 years old.

On behalf of my colleagues in the U.S. Congress, I would like to extend my sympathies to Mr. Tohra's family. In this time of loss for them, we all pray for them and for the departed. However, it is important to have the record reflect the actions that Mr. Tohra took against his own people.

The Council of Khalistan published a press release on April 6 which details the betrayal of the Sikhs by Mr. Tohra. It is excellent reading and I recommend it to my colleagues.

In that press release, the Council of Khalistan took note of Mr. Tohra's invitation to the Indian government to launch its military attack on the Golden Temple, the most sacred of Sikh shrines, in June 1984, in order to eliminate his political rival, Sant Jarnail Singh Bhindranwale, who was a strong advocate of an independent Sikh state, Khalistan. Sikhs will be commemorating this brutal attack on June 5 here in Washington. The Indian forces simultaneously attacked 125 Sikh Gurdwaras throughout Punjab and murdered over 20,000 Sikhs in these attacks alone. They shot bullet holes in the Sikh holy scriptures, the Guru Granth Sahib. They took young Sikh boys ages 8 through 13 out in the courtyard and shot them at point blank range. Meanwhile, Mr. Tohra, who had said that the tanks would have to roll over his body to get to the Temple, came out with his hands up. The Golden Temple complex is also the headquarters of the SGPC.

Mr. Tohra was also in a longstanding political alliance with the corrupt Parkash Singh Badal, who was thrown out of office after running the most corrupt government in Punjab's history_a regime so corrupt that the voters chose the Congress Party, which organized and carried out the Golden Temple attack, rather than re-elect Mr. Badal. Mr. Tohra also was an ally of the Indian government, first under the Congress Party and then under the current regime of the BJP. This is the same Indian government that has murdered over 250,000 Sikhs, Mr. Speaker. It is also holding over 52,000 Sikhs as political prisoners, some since the 1984 attacks!

With Mr. Tohra gone, new leaders must emerge. I call on my Sikh friends to make sure that these new leaders are strong supporters of freedom for the Sikhs of Punjab, Khalistan. And as the beacon of freedom, I urge the United States to take action to help liberate the Sikh Nation and all the nations seeking their freedom from India, including Kashmir, predominantly Christian Nagalim, and others.

The time has come to stop our aid to India until it respects the basic human rights of all people within its borders and to demand that India act like the democracy it says it is by holding a free and fair vote on the matter of independence for Khalistan, for Kashmir, for Nagalim, and for all the other nations seeking their freedom. This is the democratic way and self-determination is the essence of democracy. It is also the only way to prevent leaders in the mode of Gurcharan Singh Tohra from emerging again to connive with the Indian government to keep the Sikhs in slavery.

Mr. Speaker, I would like to place the Council of Khalistan's press release on Mr. Tohra into the Record at this time.

G.S. Tohra Passes Away at 79

Washington, DC, April 6, 2004._Gurcharan Singh Tohra, the long-time President of the Shiromani Gurdwara Prabandhak Committee (SGPC), which runs all the Gurdwaras (Sikh places of worship) in Punjab, died of a heart attack April 1 in New Delhi. He was 79 years old.

"We offer our sympathies and prayers to Mr. Tohra's family," said Dr. Gurmit Singh Aulakh, President of the Council of Khalistan, which leads the struggle for independence for the Sikh homeland, Khalistan, as declared on October 7, 1987. "We pray for them in their time of loss and may Guru bless this departed soul," he said. "However, it is better to leave a legacy of service and sacrifice rather than a legacy of betrayal as Tohra did," he said. "What Tohra did in life will remain a part of the history of the Sikh Nation. He will not be remembered as a friend of the Sikh Nation," Dr. Aulakh said.

Tohra connived with the Indian government prior to its invasion of the Golden Temple, the center and seat of the Sikh religion. The Golden Temple is the headquarters of the SGPC. He joined with Harchand Singh Longowal and others in inviting the Indian government to attack the Golden Temple to murder pro-Khalistani leaders Jarnail Singh Bhindranwale, General Shabeg Singh, and others, even while they were telling the Sikh Nation that Indian tanks would "have to roll over our dead bodies" to get to the Temple. From June 3 through June 6, 1984, the Indian government carried out Operation Bluestar, a military attack on the Golden Temple and over 125 other Sikh Temples throughout Punjab. More than 20,000 Sikhs were killed in Operation Bluestar. Longowal was assassinated by a patriotic Sikh for his betrayal of the Sikh Nation. "Sikhs can never forgive or forget the attack on the Golden Temple," said Dr. Aulakh. On Saturday, June 5, Sikhs will gather in Washington, D.C. to commemorate the twentieth anniversary of this brutal massacre and desecration.

The Indian government has murdered over 250,000 Sikhs since 1984, more than 300,000 Christians since 1948, over 85,000 Muslims in Kashmir since 1988, and tens of thousands of Tamils, Assamese, Manipuris, Dalits, and others. The Indian Supreme Court called the Indian government's murders of Sikhs "worse than a genocide." According to a study by the Movement Against State Repression (MASR), 52,268 Sikhs are being held in illegal detention as political prisoners without charge or trial. In September 1995, human-rights activist Jaswant Singh Khalra was kidnapped by police for publishing a study documenting that the Indian government secretly cremated thousands of Sikh youth by declaring them "unidentified bodies" after torturing and murdering them. He was murdered about six weeks later while in police custody. His body was never returned to his family. Police SSP Swaran Singh Ghotna murdered former Jathedar of the Akal Takht Gurdev Singh Kaunke.

Although Tohra was not corrupt like former Punjab Chief Minister Parkash Singh Badal, he maintained an alliance with Badal, even though he once said publicly that he would not even go near Badal's grave. The Badal regime was the most corrupt in Punjab's history. In 1993, Tohra urged Sikhs to "prepare for the long struggle" to liberate Khalistan, yet he maintained a political alliance with the Indian government, first with the Congress Party (which carried out the Golden Temple attack) and then with the militant Hindu nationalist Bharatiya Janata Party (BJP.) "It seems as if there were two Gurcharan Singh Tohras," Dr. Aulakh said.

India is not one country; it is a polyglot thrown together by the British for their administrative convenience. Sikhs ruled Punjab until 1849 when the British conquered the subcontinent. Sikhs were equal partners during the transfer of power from the British. The Muslim leader Jinnah got Pakistan, the Hindu leaders got India, but the Sikh leadership was fooled by the Hindu leadership into taking their share with India on the promise that Sikhs would have "the glow of freedom" in northwest India. For that mistake, Sikhs are suffering now. "As Professor Darshan Singh, a former Jathedar of the Akal Takht, said, 'If a Sikh is not for Khalistan, he is not a Sikh'," Dr. Aulakh noted. "Tohra worked with the Indian government in its most brutal efforts to suppress the Sikh Nation's effort to realize the Guru's blessing by reclaiming its sovereignty," he said.

"Democracies don't commit genocide," Dr. Aulakh said. "Only in a free and sovereign Khalistan will the Sikh Nation prosper. In a democracy, the right to self-determination is the sine qua non and if India is truly a democracy, it should accept the sovereignty of the Sikh Nation," he said.

***

Document

CONGRESSIONAL RECORD -- EXTENSIONS

Friday, March 26, 2004
108th Congress, 2nd Session
150 Cong Rec E 460

REFERENCE: Vol. 150, No. 40
SECTION: Extension of Remarks
TITLE: VAISAKHI DAY: GREETINGS TO THE SIKH NATION_COUNCIL
OF KHALISTAN ISSUES VAISAKHI MESSAGE TO SIKH NATION

HON. EDOLPHUS TOWNS
of New York
in the House of Representatives
Thursday, March 25, 2004

Mr. TOWNS . Mr. Speaker, next month the Sikhs will celebrate one of their most important holidays, Vaisakhi Day. On this day in 1699, Guru Gobind Singh constituted the Sikh Nation. He issued a blessing of sovereignty to the Sikhs, a blessing they are looking to reclaim.

Vaisakhi Day is one of the most important Sikh holidays and there are over 500,000 Sikhs in this country, so I would like to take this opportunity to wish them all a happy Vaisakhi Day. Hopefully, they will use the occasion to work for freedom for their people.

It is an interesting coincidence that Vaisakhi Day happens to fall on the birthday of Thomas Jefferson, author of our Declaration of Independence, who wrote: "We hold these truths to be self-evident: that all men are created equal; that they are endowed by their Creator with certain inalienable rights; that among these are life, liberty, and the pursuit of happiness; that to secure these rights, governments are instituted among men, deriving their just powers from the consent of the governed; that whenever any form of government becomes destructive of these ends, it is the right of the people to alter or abolish it and to institute new government, laying its foundations on such principles and organizing its powers in such form as to them shall seem most likely to effect their safety and happiness."

Mr. Speaker, the Indian government has done everything it can to destroy the safety and happiness of Sikhs, Christians, Muslims, and other minorities living within the country. Is it any wonder that all these groups are seeking their freedom from India's brutal rule?

India has murdered over a quarter of a million Sikhs in the past 20 years. It holds over 52,000 of them as political prisoners. More than 300,000 Christians in Nagaland have been murdered by the Indian government, and Christians seem to be targets everywhere else in India too. India has killed over 85,000 Kashmiri Muslims since 1988, and that doesn't count the thousands who have been killed in places like Gujarat.

Yet India continues to proclaim loudly that it is a democracy. As Jefferson noted, the central principle of a democratic state is "the consent of the governed." How can India claim to have the consent of the minorities it governs so brutally while killing tens of thousands of them? It doesn't make sense to me. The essence of democracy is the right to self-determination.

We must do what we can, Mr. Speaker, as a country dedicated to the principle of liberty. We should stop U.S. aid to India until it respects human rights and we should use whatever influence we can to get India to hold a free and fair plebiscite on the question of independence, under international observation.

The Council of Khalistan has issued a very informative letter in honor of Vaisakhi Day, which contains a lot of useful information about the occasion and the atrocities that have been committed by India against the Sikhs and others. Therefore, I would like to put it in the Record now, Mr. Speaker. Thank you.

Vaisakhi Day Message to the Sikh Nation:
(By Dr. Gurmit Sigh Aulakh)

In 1699 on Vaisakhi Day, 305 years ago, Guru Gobind Singh established the Khalsa Panth. The Guru granted sovereignty to the Sikh Nation, saying "In Grieb Sikhin Ko Deon Patshahi." It is this spirit instilled in the Sikh Nation by Guru Gobind Singh that led them to fight tyrants like lions until they defeated them. We always remember it by reciting every morning and evening, "Raj Kare Ga Khalsa." Now is the time to act on it. Do we mean what we say every morning and evening?

Punjab is the gateway to India. Many invaders have come from the West_the Moguls, the Afghans, and others_to conquer and established their rule in Delhi. Sikhs saw this unprecedented persecution at the hands of invaders and rulers. Banda Singh Bahadur established the first Khalsa Raj in Punjab in 1710, lasting until 1716. Then the Sikh missals again established their rule in the various regions of Punjab in 1765. Maharajah Ranjit Singh established Sikh Raj with Lahore as its capital in 1799, 100 years after the initiation of the Khalsa Panth. Sikhs ruled Punjab under Maharajah Ranjit Singh in the true Sikh tradition, the well being of everybody (Sarbat Da Bhalah). Hindus, Muslims, and Christians were all part of the Sikh government. The Sikh army included Hindus, Muslims, and Christians. A Christian, General Ventura, was in charge of the infantry. The period from 1799 to 1839, when Maharajah Ranjit Singh died, was the Golden Age of Punjab. The sovereign Sikh state of Punjab was recognized by China, Russia, and the European countries. It was the dominant power in South Asia at that time. Sikhs conquered Kashmir from Afghanistan in 1819, making it part of Punjab.

The British conquered us in 1849 with the help of their planted agents the Hindu Dogra brothers, Pahara Singh, etc., who connived with the British and betrayed the Sikh Nation. As a reward to the Dogra brothers for their betrayal, the British sold them Kashmir for Rs400,000. At the time of independence in 1947, the Sikh leadership was fooled into taking their share with India by the dishonest Hindu leaders Nehru and Gandhi, while the Muslims got their own sovereign country, Pakistan. Nehru and Gandhi promised that Sikhs would have the glow of freedom in Punjab, but instead we got unprecedented persecution at the hands of the Indian government. In June 1984 they attacked the Golden Temple and 127 other Gurdwaras throughout Punjab. Over 20,000 Sikhs were murdered in those attacks, known as Operation Bluestar, including Sant Jarnail Singh Bhindranwale, General Shabeg Singh, Bhai Amrik Singh, and over 100 Sikh religious students ages 8-13 who were taken out into the courtyard and shot. If Sikhs cannot protect the sanctity of the Golden Temple, then the Sikh Nation cannot survive as a nation.

The Golden Temple attacks set off a wave of repression and genocide that resulted in the murder of over 250,000 Sikhs at the hands of the

Indian government. Over 50,000 Sikh youth were picked up from their houses, tortured, murdered in police custody, then cremated by being declared "unidentified bodies." Their remains were never even given to their families! Over 52,000 Sikhs sit in Indian jails as political prisoners without charge or trial, many since 1984.

Repression and genocide of this magnitude at the hands of the Indian government is unparalleled in the late part of the 20th century. India should be ashamed of the genocide it has committed against Sikhs, Christians, Muslims, and other minorities. Khalsa Ji, at this time of Vaisakhi, the whole Khalsa Panth must be energized to reestablish a sovereign, independent Khalsa Raj by freeing our homeland, Khalistan.

India is not one nation. It is a polyglot empire thrown together under one roof for the administrative convenience of the British colonialists. It has 18 official languages. History shows that such countries are doomed to fall apart. India will collapse just like the Austro-Hungarian Empire, the Soviet Union, and other multinational states such as Yugoslavia and Czechoslovakia. The cracks are appearing and India is crumbling. The clock is ticking. The Kashmir issue has been internationalized. The United States is now involved in the issue. On December 5, President Bush told me "I am aware of the Sikh and Kashmiri problem." There will be a referendum in Kashmir under international supervision. Kashmir will either be independent or become part of Pakistan. It will not remain within India. As L.K. Advani predicted, "When Kashmir goes, India goes." This time we agree with Mr. Advani. Kashmir will go and India will disintegrate.

Khalsa Ji, bring back your Khalsa spirit. Look at Advani having a yatra of India and coming to Amritsar. Punjab belongs to the Khalsa Panth, not to India. He has no right to show Hindu dominance in Punjab. Shame on the Akali leaders like Badal, Tohra, and others who have joined hands with the BJP, which is the political arm of the RSS. We need a new Sikh political party which has a dedication to the interests of the Sikh Nation as its sole objective, to establish Khalsa Raj by liberating Khalistan, severing all political ties with India. If the BJP wants Hindu Raj, it cannot object to Khalsa Raj.

The Sikhs in Punjab have suffered enormous repression at the hands of the Indian regime in the last 20 years. The Indian government wants to break the will of the Sikh Nation and enslave them forever, making Sikhism a part of Hinduism. This can only be stopped if we free Punjab from Delhi's control and reestablish a sovereign, independent country, as declared on October 7, 1957. Then Punjab will be a member of the United Nations and we will have Ambassadors in almost 200 countries.

Khalsa Ji, remember that a free Khalistan will bring economic prosperity to Punjab farmers. They will be able to sell their produce internationally which will fetch them much higher prices than they are getting now from the Indian government. The Indian government fixes prices of produce so low that farmers get deeper and deeper in debt while they sell fertilizer, seeds, and insecticides to the farmers at artificially high prices. The Indian government has diverted Punjab river water to neighboring *states without any compensation to Punjab. Punjab farmers are forced to pump subsoil water for irrigation. This is expensive and brings salinity to soil, which lowers the crop production.*

Remember, 3 million (30 lakh) Sikhs live outside India. The outside Sikhs are free, prosperous, well educated, professional, and committed to establishing an independent, sovereign Khalistan. The Indian government does not have any control over the Sikh diaspora. Outside Sikhs have exposed the atrocities committed on the Sikhs by the Indian government. Outside Sikhs have also preserved the true history of the Sikhs since 1984 by documenting every incident in the U.S. Congressional Record while the Indian government tries to alter Sikh history. Outside Sikhs are committed to a continuing effort to free Khalistan. Remember the words of Professor Darshan Singh, former Jathedar of the Akal Takht, during the celebration of Guru Nanak's birthday: "If a Sikh is not a Khalistani, he is not a Sikh." He was only reiterating the Guru's blessing, "In Grieb Sikhin Ko Deon Patshahi." The time to achieve our independence is now.

Khalsa Ji, remain in Charhdi Kala. Always remember our heritage: Raj Kare Ga Khalsa; Khalsa Bagi Yan Badshah. Freedom for Khalistan is very close.

***

Document

CONGRESSIONAL RECORD -- EXTENSIONS

Friday, March 26, 2004
108th Congress, 2nd Session
150 Cong Rec E 462

REFERENCE: Vol. 150, No. 40
SECTION: Extension of Remarks
TITLE: 400TH ANNIVERSARY OF GURU GRANTH SAHIB, SIKH HOLY SCRIPTURES

HON. EDOLPHUS TOWNS
of New York
in the House of Representatives
Thursday, March 25, 2004

Mr. TOWNS. Mr. Speaker, on August 14, there will be a parade in Washington, DC to celebrate the 400th anniversary of the compilation of the Guru Granth Sahib, the holy scripture of the Sikh religion. It was the revelation of the Sikh Gurus and it is the basis for the Sikh religion and way of life.

In June 1984, during India's military assault on the Sikhs at their most sacred shrine, the Golden Temple in Amritsar, and 125 other Gurdwaras throughout Punjab, an original of the Guru Granth Sahib was riddled with bullet holes by Indian forces. This was a gratuitous insult to the Sikh people and a coordinated denigration of their religion. It made it clear to them that there is no place for them in supposedly democratic, supposedly secular India.

This will be a major celebration for the Sikh people, over half a million of whom live here in America. They are productive, committed citizens who contribute to every walk of American life and who share a commitment to bring the freedom they enjoy to their brothers and sisters back home in Punjab, Khalistan.

There was even a Sikh who served in Congress, Dalip Singh Saund.

In addition to the August 14 parade, there will also be a seminar here in Washington on June 5 to commemorate this momentous occasion.

Mr. Speaker, we are a diverse country. Our strength has always been the ability to preserve our individuality and diversity while creating a unified society. In that spirit, I would like to take this opportunity to honor the Sikhs of America and worldwide on the 400th anniversary of the Guru Granth Sahib.

Mr. Speaker, the Council of Khalistan published an excellent press release about the events that are coming up to celebrate this event, which I would like to place in the Record at this time.

400th Anniversary of Guru Granth Sahib_Remember Bullets Pierced Through Guru Granth Sahib in 1984 Reserve Saturday, August 14, 2004 for a Memorable Celebration, Parade in Washington, D.C.

Washington, D.C., March 24, 2004._On August 14, Sikh from around the East Coast will observe the 400th anniversary of the compilation of the Guru Granth Sahib, the Sikh holy scriptures. There will be a parade in Washington, D.C. to mark the occasion. The Guru Granth Sahib was dictated by the Sikh Gurus as revealed to them by God. It was written at the time in which they lived. It also includes the writing of other saints of that time which fit the philosophy of the Sikh Gurus.

In addition, there will be a seminar on Saturday, June 5 to celebrate the 400th anniversary of the Guru Granth Sahib sponsored by the International Conference on Sikh Studies along with Sikh Gurdwara and institutions of North America. Sikhs remember that bullets pierced through the Guru Granth Sahib during Operation Bluestar, the Indian government's military attack on the Golden Temple in Amritsar, in 1984.

"This parade and this anniversary will be a joyous occasion for the Sikh Nation as we celebrate the Sikh way of life as given to us by the Gurus," said Dr. Gurmit Singh Aulakh, President of the Council of Khalistan. Sikhism is an independent, monotheistic religion that believes in the equality of the whole human race. The tenth and last Sikh Guru, Guru Gobind Singh, declared the blessing "In Grieb Sikhin Ko Deon Patshahi," conferring sovereignty on the Sikh Nation, which is culturally, linguistically, and religiously distinct from any other people in the world, including Hindu India. "We must honor the Guru by reclaiming our lost sovereignty," Dr. Aulakh said

The Indian government has murdered over 250,000 Sikhs since 1984, more than 300,000 Christians since 1948, over 85,000 Muslims in Kashmir since 1988, and tens of thousands of Tamils, Assamese, Manipuris, Dalits, and others. The Indian Supreme Court called the Indian government's murders of Sikhs "worse than a genocide." According to a study by the Movement Against State Repression, 52,268 Sikhs are being held in illegal detention as political prisoners without charge or trial. Some of them have been held since 1984!

Christian missionary Joseph Cooper was expelled from India after a mob of militant Hindu nationalists allied with the Rashtriya Swayamsewak Sangh (RSS), a pro-Fascist organization that is the parent organization of the ruling BJP, beat him so severely he had to spend a week in the hospital. In 2002, 2,000 to 5,000 Muslims were murdered in Gujarat while police were ordered to stand aside, reminiscent of the 1984 Delhi massacres of Sikhs. Indian newspapers reported that the government planned the Gujarat massacre in advance.

India is not one country; it is a polyglot thrown together by the British for their administrative convenience. Sikhs ruled Punjab until 1849 when the British conquered the subcontinent. Sikhs were equal partners during the transfer of power from the British. The Muslim leader Jinnah got Pakistan, the Hindu leaders got India, but the Sikh leadership was fooled by the Hindu leadership promising that Sikhs would have "the glow of freedom" in Northwest India. The Sikhs took their share with India on that promise. For that mistake, Sikhs are suffering now. "As Professor Darshan Singh, a former Jathedar of the Akal Takht, said, "If a Sikh is not for Khalistan, he is not a Sikh'," Dr. Aulakh noted.

"Democracies don't commit genocide," Dr. Aulakh said. "Only in a free and sovereign Khalistan will the Sikh Nation prosper. In a democracy, the right to self-determination is the sine qua non and India should allow a plebiscite for the freedom of the Sikh Nation," he said. "The Guru Granth Sahib is the reigning Guru of the Sikh Nation and reminds us of our heritage and we must offer a fitting celebration," he said.

***

Document

CONGRESSIONAL RECORD -- EXTENSIONS

Wednesday, March 17, 2004
108th Congress, 2nd Session
150 Cong Rec E 393

REFERENCE: Vol. 150, No. 34
SECTION: Extension of Remarks
TITLE: ELECTIONS COMING IN PUNJAB OPPORTUNITY TO CLAIM FREEDOM

HON. EDOLPHUS TOWNS
of New York
in the House of Representatives
Wednesday, March 17, 2004

Mr. TOWNS . Mr. Speaker, elections have been scheduled in Punjab for May 10. They are part of India's national elections. The Sikhs in Punjab must seize this opportunity. Just changing the faces accomplishes nothing. Replacing one set of oppressors with another is not an exercise in democracy; it is merely proof of the need for independence from the tyranny that is the reality of daily life in Punjab.

The Council of Khalistan recently put out an open letter to the Sikhs in Punjab, Khalistan. They called for Sikhs to use these elections to elect officeholders who are committed to freeing the Sikh homeland, Khalistan.

Mr. Speaker, this is the only way to end the repression that has killed over 250,000 Sikhs since 1984, with more than 52,000 being held as political prisoners. Some of the prisoners are army officers who refused to participate in the brutal military attack on the seat of the Sikh religion, the Golden Temple, in 1984. Others are simply those who participated peacefully in the movement to liberate Khalistan.

India claims to be a democratic country. It also claims that there is no support for Khalistan. Why not simply hold a vote on the issue, the democratic way? Instead, this country that loudly proclaims that it is secular and democratic imposes the most brutal repression on the Sikhs and other minorities such as Christians in Nagaland and elsewhere, Muslims in Kas-hmir and throughout the country, Tamils, Dalit "Untouchables," Bodos, Assamese, Manipuris, and others.

I join with the Council of Khalistan in urging the Sikhs and all the minorities suffering under Indian oppression to vote for honest candidates committed to freedom for their people. This is the best thing that they can do to free themselves from this brutal tyranny.

We can help by stopping American aid to India until all people's basic human rights are respected and by declaring our support for a free and fair plebiscite on the question of independence. These measures will press India to begin living up to the democratic values that they so loudly proclaim.

I would like to place the Council of Khalistan's message to the Sikh Nation regarding the elections into the Record at this time.

Council of Khalistan,
Washington, DC, March 2, 2004.
Open Letter to the Sikh Nation
Punjab Elections Set for May 10 Opportunity for Sikh Nation to Claim Freedom

Choose honest leadership committed to Sikh Freedom_Don't miss this peaceful, democratic opportunity to liberate Khalistan
Dear Khalsa Ji: WAHEGURU JI KA KHALSA, WAHEGURU JI KI FATEH!

Elections in Punjab have been set for May 10. This is an opportunity for Sikhs to install honest, dedicated leadership. Choose only leaders who are committed to Khalsa Raj. Only when Khalistan is free can Sikhs live in prosperity, security, and dignity. Only when Khalistan is free of Indian occupation can Punjab's farmers get a fair price for their crops. Only when Khalistan is free will our water stop being diverted to nonriparian states. We must do everything that we can to free our homeland, Punjab, Khalistan, from Indian occupation. These elections provide an opportunity to reclaim our freedom democratically and peacefully.

The Guru granted sovereignty to the Sikh Nation, saying "In Grieb Silkhin Ko Deon Patshahi." The Sikh Nation must achieve its independence to fulfill the mandate of the Guru. We always remember it by reciting every morning and evening, "Raj Kare Ga Khalsa." Now is the time to act on it. Do we mean what we say every morning and evening? I urge Sikhs to unite and take action to liberate our homeland, Punjab, Khalistan.

Parkash Singh Badal disgraced the Sikh Nation by running the most corrupt government in Punjab's history. His government was so corrupt, they even came up with a new term for bribery: "fee for service." If you didn't pay the fee, you didn't get the service. The Badal family was so adept at receiving bribes that Mrs. Badal could tell how much money was in a bag just by picking it up! We are pleased that Chief Minister Amarinder Singh is prosecuting the Badal family for its corruption. Clearly, the Akalis do not merit the Sikh Nation's support.

Badal also broke his campaign promises of 1997. He promised to release all the political prisoners. Yet according to the Movement Against State Repression (MASR), the Indian regime admitted to holding 52,268 Sikhs as political prisoners. They are being held without charge or trial, some of them since 1984! How can a democratic state hold political prisoners? He promised to punish police officials who have committed atrocities against Sikhs since 1984. No such action was ever taken. Where is the punishment of Swaran Singh Ghotna, who murdered Jathedar Gurdev Singh Kaunke? Where is the punishment of the police officers who kidnapped and murdered Sardar Jaswant Singh Khalra? He promised to appoint a commission to study the human-rights violations against the Sikhs. Yet when such a commission was formed by concerned Sikhs, he used the power of government to shut it down and deny it a meeting place.

The Congress Party is no better. It is the party that invaded and desecrated the Golden Temple and 125 other Sikh Gurdwaras throughout Punjab in June 1984 to murder Sant Jarnail Singh Bhindranwale and 20,000 other Sikhs, including General Shabeg Singh, Bhai Amrik Singh, and over 100 Sikh religious students ages 8-13 who were taken out into the courtyard and shot. If Sikhs will not even protect the sanctity of the Golden Temple, how can the Sikh Nation survive as a nation? No conscientious Sikh can support the Congress Party. It is the enemy of the Sikh Nation.

Sikhs must speak for, work for, and vote for candidates committed to freeing our homeland, Punjab, Khalistan, from Indian occupation. Let us take this opportunity to put people in office who will work for Sikh freedom and will work to give the Sikh Nation a free and fair plebiscite on freedom for Khalistan.

Sarbjit Singh, the son of Sikh martyr Beant Singh, has been given a ticket in a reserved constituency in Bhatinda by the Akali Dal (Amritsar.) He deserves the support of Sikh voters, but Sikhs should not support Simranjit Singh Mann, who changes his colors on Khalistan almost daily. Mann is under the control of the Indian government, as shown by his letter to the Chief Justice of India, which is reprinted in the book Chakra-vyuh: Web of Indian Secularism, by Professor Gurtej Singh. Mann has been in Parliament for the past few years. What has he done to advance the cause of Sikh freedom? Has he even made a single speech on behalf of freeing our homeland?

We call on distinguished Sikh leaders such as Justice Ajit Singh Bains, General Narinder Singh, Professor Gurdarshan Singh Dhillon, Professor Gurtej Singh, former MP Atinder Pal Singh, and others to run themselves or find candidates who reflect their views. And we call on them to give a ticket to deserving, educated political prisoners. This will help to get the political prisoners freed and will help to put people in Parliament who are committed to Sikh freedom and sovereignty.

Remember the words of Professor Darshan Singh, former Jathedar of the Akal Takht: "If a Sikh is not a Khalistani, he is not a Sikh." The time to achieve our independence is now. India is not one country. It is a polyglot empire thrown together under one roof for the administrative conven-ience of the British colonialists. It has 18 official languages. History shows that such countries are doomed to fall apart. India will collapse just like the Austro-Hungarian Empire, the Soviet Union, and other multinational states such as Yugoslavia and Czechoslovakia.

The Indian government has murdered over 250,000 Sikhs since 1984, according to figures compiled by the Punjab State Magistracy and human rights groups and published in Inderjit Singh Jaijee's excellent book, The Politics of Genocide. India has killed over 300,000 Christians in Naga-land since 1947 and murdered priests, raped nuns, burned churches, and destroyed Christian schools and prayer halls. They expelled mission-ary Joseph Cooper from the country after militant Hindu nationalists beat him up so badly that he had to be in the hospital for a week. Missionary Graham Staines and his two young sons were burned to death while sleeping in their jeep by a mob of militant Hindus chanting "Victory to Hannuman," a Hindu god. Since they were allied with the pro-Fascist RSS, the parent organization of the ruling BJP, they were able to commit this atrocity with impunity. Muslims were massacred in Gujarat while the police were under orders to stand aside and let the massacre occur, a frightening parallel to the 1984 Delhi massacres of Sikhs. A policeman told an Indian newspaper that the Gujarat massacre was planned in advance by the government.

India is a fundamentalist Hindu theocracy, not secular or democratic at all. Remember what Narinder Singh, a spokesman for the Golden Temple, told America's National Public Radio in 1997: "The Indian government, they are always boasting that they are democratic, that they are secular. They have nothing to do with a secularism, nothing to do with a democracy. They just kill Sikhs just to please the majority." On December 5, President Bush told me "I am aware of the Sikh and Kashmiri problem."

Soon Kashmir will be free from Indian occupation. Now America is involved in it. As L.K. Advani predicted, "When Kashmir goes, India goes." We agree with him and we urge the Indian government to hold a free and fair plebiscite on the question of independence and to sit down with representatives of the Sikh Nation to negotiate the boundaries of a sovereign, independent Khalistan. Sikhs must use the upcoming elections to elect representatives who will make certain that India does that. Sikhs must claim their birthright by liberating Khalistan. Only by freeing Khalistan will we put an end to this corruption and restore control of Punjab and its assets to the people, to whom it rightfully belongs. A sovereign, independent Khalistan is a must for the survival of the Sikh Nation and will provide an optimal environment for the Sikh Nation to progress to its optimum potential politically, religiously, and economically. Let us take this opportunity to free Khalistan.

> *Panth Da Sewadar,*
> *Dr. Gurmit Singh Aulakh,*
> *President, Council of Khalistan.*

***

Document

CONGRESSIONAL RECORD -- EXTENSIONS

Wednesday, March 17, 2004
108th Congress, 2nd Session
150 Cong Rec E 396

REFERENCE: Vol. 150, No. 34
SECTION: Extension of Remarks
TITLE: SIKHS WILL CELEBRATE 400TH ANNIVERSARY OF THEIR HOLY SCRIPTURE

HON. EDOLPHUS TOWNS
of New York
in the House of Representatives
Wednesday, March 17, 2004

Mr. TOWNS . Mr. Speaker, the Sikhs will celebrate the 400th anniversary of the compilation of their holy scripture, the Guru Granth Sahib, this year. As you may know, there are over 500,000 Sikhs in the United States and about 25 million worldwide.

Observances will include a seminar on June 5 at George Washington University and a parade on August 14 here in Washington.

In June 1984, the Indian government launched a military attack on the Golden Temple in Amritsar, the center and seat of the Sikh religion, and 125 other Sikh Gurdwaras throughout Punjab in which over 20,000 Sikhs were murdered. Indian forces shot bullets through the Guru Granth Sahib, which was a major desecration and an insult to the Sikh people and the Sikh religion. They took over 100 young Sikh boys outside and shot them at point blank range.

Mr. Speaker, the Golden Temple attack made it clear to the Sikhs that there is no place for them in India's Hindu nationalist theocracy. It is against this background that they declared their independence on October 7, 1987, calling their country Khalistan.

The Golden Temple attack is unacceptable to all civilized people. We must work to ensure that human rights are respected in India and that nothing like the Golden Temple attack, the Gujarat massacre, or the campaign of violence against Christians occurs there again. We can help bring that about by stopping our aid to India until it learns to observe basic human rights.

We can also help by putting this Congress on record in support of a free and fair plebiscite in Punjab, Khalistan, in Kashmir, as India promised the United Nations in 1948, in primarily Christian Nagaland, and wherever the people are seeking independence. This is the democratic way to settle the issue and India claims to be a democracy, so why are they afraid of holding a free and fair vote?

Mr. Speaker, the Council of Khalistan has published a press release on the 400th anniversary of the Guni Granth Sahib and the 20th anniversary of the Golden Temple attack. It is very informative, so I would like to insert it into the Record at this time.

400th Anniversary of Guru Granth Sahib; 20th Anniversary of Golden Temple Attack

Washington, D.C., March 10, 2004._On June 5, Sikhs from around the East Coast will observe the 400th anniversary of the compilation of the Guru Granth Sahib, the Sikh holy scriptures. During India's June 1984 attack on the Golden Temple in Amritsar, the center and seat of the Sikh religion, the Guru Granth Sahib was pierced by Indian Army bullets. The Sikh Nation will never forget the desecration of the Guru Granth Sahib. Political power is essential for the survival of the Sikh Nation.

The Council of Khalistan, the organization leading the Sikh struggle for independence, will hold a demonstration Saturday, June 5, from 12:00 noon to 3:00 p.m. in front of the Indian Embassy at 21st and Massachusetts Ave. NW in Washington, D.C. It will commemorate the twentieth anniversary of the attack on the Golden Temple and 125 other Sikh Gurdwaras in Punjab, in which over 20,000 Sikhs were killed, including such major Sikh leaders as Sant Jarnail Singh Bhindranwale, General Shabeg Singh, Bhai Amrik Singh, and others who had taken refuge in the Darbar Sahib complex. The Indian army killed over 100 young religious students, ages 8 to 13. They were taken out into the courtyard and asked whether they supported Khalistan. When they answered "Bole So Nihal," they were shot.

"This attack, along with simultaneous attacks on 125 other Gurdwaras throughout Punjab, was the clearest sign that there is no place for Sikhs in India," said Dr. Gurmit Singh Aulakh, President of the Council of Khalistan. "It is a brutal, tyrannical, fundamentalist Hindu nationalist theocracy," he said. "Sant Bhindranwale said that if the Indian government invaded the Golden Temple, they would lay the foundation of Khalistan," Dr. Aulakh said. "He was right. The movement for Khalistan is strong in Punjab. Just last year, seminars were held on the subject. The fire of freedom burns bright in the hearts of Sikhs."

"The brutal attack on the Golden Temple and the 20-year wave of repression it set off must never be forgotten," Dr. Aulakh said. "Both the Congress Party and the Akalis are complicit in this criminal act against the Sikh Nation," he noted. . . . "India needs to be reminded that 20 years later, Sikhs have not forgiven nor forgotten this brutal atrocity. The younger generation must be reminded of this terrible atrocity."

In addition to the protest, there will be a seminar on Saturday, June 5 at George Washington University to celebrate the 400th anniversary of the compilation of the Guru Granth Sahib. It will be sponsored by the International Conference on Sikh Studies along with Sikh Gurdwaras and institutions of North America.

The Indian government has murdered over 250,000 Sikhs since 1984, more than 300,000 Christians since 1948, over 85,000 Muslims in Kashmir since 1988, and tens of thousands of Tamils, Assamese, Manipuris, Dalits, and others. The Indian Supreme Court called the Indian government's murders of Sikhs "worse than a genocide." According to a study by the Movement Against State Repression, 52,268 Sikhs are being held in illegal detention as political prisoners without charge or trial. Some of them have been held since 1984!

Christian missionary Joseph Cooper was expelled from India after a mob of militant Hindu nationalists allied with the Rashtriya Swayamsewarak Sangh (RSS), a pro-Fascist organization that is the parent organization of the ruling BJP, beat him so severely he had to spend a week in the hospital. In 2002, 2,000 to 5,000 Muslims were murdered in Gujarat while police were ordered to stand aside, reminiscent of the 1984 Delhi massacres of Sikhs. Indian newspapers reported that the government planned the Gujarat massacre in advance.

History shows that multinational states such as India are doomed to failure. Countries like Austria-Hungary, India's longtime friend the Soviet Union, Yugoslavia, Czechoslovakia, and others prove this point. India is not one country; it is a polyglot like those countries, thrown together by the British for their administrative convenience. Sikhs ruled Punjab until 1849 when the British conquered the subcontinent. Sikhs were equal partners during the transfer of power from the British. The Muslim leader Jinnah got Pakistan, the Hindu leaders got India, but the

Sikh leadership was fooled by the Hindu leadership promising that Sikhs would have "the glow of freedom" in Northwest India. The Sikhs took their share with India on that promise. For that mistake, Sikhs are suffering now. "As Professor Darshan Singh, a former Jathedar of the Akal Takht, said, 'If a Sikh is not for Khalistan, he is not a Sikh'," Dr. Aulakh noted.

"Democracies don't commit genocide," Dr. Aulakh said. *"Only in a free and sovereign Khalistan will the Sikh Nation prosper. In a democracy, the right to self-determination is the sine qua non and India should allow a plebiscite for the freedom of the Sikh Nation,"* he said. *"India should also allow self-determination in Christian Nagaland, Kashmir, Assam, and the other nations fighting for freedom. This is the only way to bring lasting peace to South Asia."*

***

Document

CONGRESSIONAL RECORD -- EXTENSIONS

Wednesday, March 17, 2004
108th Congress, 2nd Session
150 Cong Rec E 396

REFERENCE: Vol. 150, No. 34
SECTION: Extension of Remarks
TITLE: SIKHS CALL FOR AN APOLOGY FROM SENATOR KERRY

HON. DAN BURTON
of Indiana
in the House of Representatives
Wednesday, March 17, 2004

Mr. BURTON of Indiana . Mr. Speaker, on January 31, 2004 Democratic Presidential Candidate Senator John Kerry referred to "Sikhs in India" as an example of terrorists. As you know, I have been a supporter of freedom for all people in South Asia, including the Sikhs.

Dr. Gurmit Singh Aulakh, President of the Council of Khalistan is well known among my colleagues as an invaluable source of information on the situation in India and Kashmir. He and his organization are committed to freeing Khalistan, the Sikh homeland, by peaceful, democratic, and non-violent means. However, the Indian government portrays their actions as terrorism. I was saddened to see that Senator Kerry apparently agreed with this mischaracterization.

The Sikhs I have met are responsible citizens. They make important contributions to many facets of American life. Dalip Singh Saund, a Sikh, even proudly served in the Congress. Many Sikhs, including Dr. Aulakh, were quite offended by the statement made by Senator Kerry, and they have asked for an apology. I hope that the distinguished Senator from Massachusetts will do the right thing and retract his statement.

Mr. Speaker, I would like to have the Council of Khalistan's letter to Senator Kerry placed into the Congressional Record following my statement.

Council of Khalistan,
Washington, DC, February 11, 2004.
Senator John F. Kerry,
U.S. Senate, Washington, DC.

Dear Senator Kerry: I am writing to you today on behalf of half a million Sikh Americans and over 25 million Sikhs worldwide to say that your remarks equating Sikhs with terrorists were offensive to the Sikh community. While giving a speech in Oklahoma, you referred to "the Sikhs in India" as an example of terrorism.

Sikhism is an independent, monotheistic, revealed religion, not a part of any other religion. Sikhs are distinctive by our religion, language, and culture from any other people on Earth.

Sikhs ruled Punjab from 1710 to 1716 and again from 1765 to 1849. Sikhs, Hindus, Muslims, and Christians all participated in the government. Sikhs are a separate nation and people.

At the time of India's independence, three nations were to receive sovereign power: the Muslims, who got Pakistan, the Hindus, who got India, and the Sikhs. Sikhs took their share with India on the solemn promise that Sikhs would enjoy "the glow of freedom" in Punjab and no law affecting Sikh rights would be passed without our consent. Instead, almost as soon as the ink was dry on India's independence, Nehru sent out a directive describing Sikhs as "a criminal class" and ordering police to take extraordinary measures against us.

Since June 1984, India has murdered over 250,000 Sikhs, according to figures compiled by the Punjab State Magistracy and human rights groups and published in the book The Politics of Genocide by Inderjit Singh Jaijee. A report from the Movement Against State Repression (MASR) shows that India admitted to holding 52,268 Sikhs as political prisoners. Some have been in illegal custody since 1984! Tens of thousands of other minorities are also being held as political prisoners, according to Amnesty International. Indian forces carried out the March 2000 massacre in the village of Chithisinghpora, according to two independent investigations. Indian forces were caught red-handed trying to set fire to a Sikh Gurdwara and Sikh homes in a village in Kashmir. Sikh and Muslim villagers joined hands to stop them.

The book Soft Target, written by two Canadian journalists, Zuhair Kashmeri of the Toronto Globe and Mail and Brian McAndrew of the Toronto Star, shows conclusively that the Indian government blew up its own airliner in 1985, killing 329 innocent people, to blame it on the Sikhs and have an excuse for more repression.

Other minorities such as Christians and Muslims, among others, have also felt the lash of Indian repression. Over 300,000 Christians in Nagaland have been killed by the terrorist Indian regime. Nuns have been raped, priests have been murdered, churches have been burned, schools and prayer halls have been destroyed, all with impunity. A mob of militant Hindus affiliated with the parent organization of the ruling BJP murdered missionary Graham Staines and his two sons by burning them to death while they slept in their jeep, all the while chanting "Victory to Hannuman," a Hindu god. India threw missionary Joseph Cooper from Pennsylvania out of the country after he was beaten so severely that he had to spend a week in the hospital. A Christian religious festival on the theme "Jesus is the answer" was broken up by police gunfire.

Almost two year ago, Muslims were massacred in Gujarat while police were ordered to stand by and do nothing, according to Indian newspaper reports. One newspaper quoted a policeman as saying that the Indian government planned the massacre in advance. This is an eerie parallel to the 1984 massacre of Sikhs in Delhi, in which police were locked in their barracks while the state-run radio and television called for more Sikh blood.

An Indian Cabinet minister was quoted as saying that everyone who lives in India must either be a Hindu or be subservient to Hindus. This kind of religious fanaticism as state policy is dangerous and anti-democratic. We would not want it in America; why should we support it in India?

On October 7, 1987, Sikhs declared their independence from India, naming their new country Khalistan. We are committed to liberating Khalistan by peaceful, democratic, nonviolent means. History shows that multinational states such as Austria-Hungary, the Soviet Union, and India are doomed to fall apart. We intend to see that this happens peacefully, in the manner of Czechoslovakia, not violently like Yugoslavia. Yet simply supporting a sovereign, independent Khalistan is what India calls terrorism.

The 20,000 Sikhs who were murdered in the June 1984 attack on the Golden Temple and 37 other Sikh Gurdwaras throughout Punjab were not terrorists. They were seeking refuge from the Indian government's tyranny. Yet the Indian government insists on describing them as "terrorists," as if repeating it often enough will make it true.

Senator Kerry, we respectfully request that you apologize to the Sikh Nation and the Sikh community in the United States for your remark. I urge you to support measures to bring freedom to all the people of the subcontinent. Sikhs share the commitment to freedom you showed when you fought in Vietnam and in your service in public office. There was even a Sikh member of Congress in the late 1950s, Dalip Singh Saund of California. We look forward to working with you in the future to bring the blessings of liberty to everyone in the subcontinent.

If you would like any further information or would like to meet about these issues, please feel free to contact me.

Sincerely,
Dr. Gurmit Singh Aulakh,
President.

***

Document

CONGRESSIONAL RECORD -- EXTENSIONS

Tuesday, February 24, 2004
108th Congress, 2nd Session
150 Cong Rec E 198

REFERENCE: Vol. 150, No. 20
SECTION: Extension of Remarks
TITLE: INDIA DISSOLVES PARLIAMENT: ELECTIONS COMING;
MINORITY NATIONS SHOULD VOTE FOR FREEDOM

HON. EDOLPHUS TOWNS
of New York
in the House of Representatives
Tuesday, February 24, 2004

Mr. TOWNS . Mr. Speaker, I noticed the other day that India is dissolving its Parliament on February 6. They will be having new elections soon, perhaps as soon as March.

These elections, unlike ours, change faces, but don't seem to change policy. The repression of minorities continues no matter who wins. This repression has killed over 250,000 Sikhs since 1984, over 300,000 Christians in Nagaland since 1947, over 85,000 Kashmiri Muslims since 1988, and tens of thousands of other minorities. More than 52,000 Sikhs, as well as tens of thousands of other minorities, continue to be held as political prisoners. Yet India cites elections like the ones upcoming to show that it is a democracy.

That isn't very democratic for the minorities, is it, Mr. Speaker? As I have said before, the mere fact that they have the right to choose their oppressors doesn't mean they live in a democracy.

Dr. Gurmit Singh Aulakh, President of the Council of Khalistan, has issued an open letter to the Sikhs in Punjab on the elections urging the Sikhs in Punjab to reject all major parties and vote for candidates inclined to support the freedom of Khalistan, the Sikh homeland that declared its independence on October 7, 1987. That is the only way the Sikhs can survive. The Akali Dal is corrupt, he points out, and the Congress Party organized the June 1984 attack on the Golden Temple, the seat of Sikhism.

We can support this cause by stopping U.S. aid to India until human rights are fully observed for all people there and by declaring our support for a free and fair vote on the subject of independence for Khalistan, for Kashmir, for Nagalim, and for all the minority nations of South Asia.

Mr. Speaker, I would like to put the Council of Khalistan's open letter on the upcoming elections into the Record at this time.

Council of Khalistan,
Washington, DC, February 4, 2004.
Open Letter to the Khalsa Panth

Parliament Dissolved; Elections Coming Sikhs Must Stop Supporting Corrupt Badal, Who Diminished Image of Sikh Nation Only in a Free Khalistan Can Sikhs Prosper Akali Leadership Controlled by Indian Government

Dear Khalsa Panth: WAHEGURU JI KA KHALSA, WAHEGURU JI KI FATEH!

The Indian government has dissolved Parliament. New elections are coming, perhaps as soon as March. Elections under the Indian Constitution will not free the Sikh Nation. Use this opportunity, however, to elect committed, honest Sikhs who are committed to freeing Khalistan to Parliament. Do not support Badal or the Akalis. They are corrupt and have betrayed the Khalsa Panth. Not even a single Akali protested the unprecedented corruption of Badal. They have disgraced the name of the old Akalis who sacrificed their lives for the well being of the Sikh Nation.

The Guru gave sovereignty to the Sikh Nation. ("In Grieb Sikhin Ko Deon Patshahi.") The Sikh Nation must achieve it. We always remember it by reciting every morning and evening, "Raj Kare Ga Khalsa." Now is the time to act on it. Do we mean what we say every morning and evening?

The fire of freedom still burns strong and bright in the heart of the Sikh Nation. Last year Sikhs openly held seminars in Punjab on the subject of Khalistan. This is a very good sign and we salute the people who participated in these seminars. They are keeping the flame of freedom lit. Now I urge Sikhs to unite and take action to liberate our homeland, Punjab, Khalistan. It is time to start a Shantmai Morcha to liberate Khalistan from Indian occupation.

Never forget that the Akal Takht Sahib and Darbar Sahib are under the control of the Indian government, the same Indian government that has murdered over a quarter of a million Sikhs in the past twenty years. The Jathedar of the Akal Takht and the head granthi of Darbar Sahib toe the line that the Indian government tells them. They are not appointed by the Khalsa Panth. The SGPC, which appoints them, does not represent the Sikh Nation anymore. They have become the puppets of the Indian government and have lost credibility with the Sikh Nation. Otherwise they would behave like a real Jathedar, Jathedar Gurdev Singh Kaunke, rather than like Indian government puppet Jathedar Aroor Singh, who gave a Siropa to General Dyer for the massacre at Jalianawa Bagh. These institutions will remain under the control of the Indian regime until we free the Sikh homeland, Punjab, Khalistan, from Indian occupation and oppression and sever our relations with the New Delhi government.

Yet the Akali Dal continues to support Badal, even though he was prosecuted and jailed for his corruption. According to India-West, the Punjab Vigilance Bureau carried out raids on Badal's properties for several months and filed a charge-sheet in a local court charging Mr. Badal with siphoning off Rs. 784 million, the equivalent of $17 million in U.S. money, during his five years as chief minister. The article says that

Mr. Badal and his family hold assets of Rs. 43.26 billion (nearly $1 billion), most of which are located outside India. Half the population of India lives below the international poverty line. About 40 percent live on less than $2 per day.

The Badal government was the most corrupt one in Punjab's history. They sold jobs for a fixed fee. They came up with a new, dignified term for bribery: "fee for service." If you didn't pay the fee, you didn't get the service. The Chief Minister's wife was so experienced that she could pick up a bag of money and tell how much money was in it. Parkash Singh Badal was a disaster for Punjab and a disgrace to the Sikh Nation. How can the Akali Dal, which is supposed to represent the interests of the Sikh Nation, continue to support him?

Badal's corruption brought Punjab to bankruptcy. He was bankrupt morally and religiously as well as bankrupting Punjab financially. It is time for new leadership that shows the moral fabric a Sikh is supposed to have. Badal has destroyed the moral fabric of the Sikh religion. What happened to the concept of fairness and honesty?

The Akalis who protest Badal's prosecution are morally degenerate. They are destroying the moral fabric of Sikhism as a religion and a society. They should be ashamed of themselves. In addition to stealing from the people of Punjab, Mr. Badal worked against the cause of Sikh freedom. Badal was under the complete control of his masters in New Delhi, the militant, fundamentalist Hindu nationalist BJP. He has a long record of betraying the Sikh Nation.

The Akali Dal conspired with the Indian government in 1984 to invade the Golden Temple to murder Sant Bhindranwale and 20,000 other Sikh during June 1984 in Punjab. If Sikhs will not even protect the sanctity of the Golden Temple, how can the Sikh Nation survive as a nation?

The Akali Dal has lost all its credibility. The Badal government was so corrupt openly and no Akali leader would come forward and tell Badal and his wife to stop this unparalleled corruption. That is why the Akali Dal was defeated in the elections by the Congress Party. The Sikh Nation never can forgive or forget the attack on the Golden Temple. The Congress Party is the enemy of the Sikh Nation. Badal was so corrupt that the Sikhs had to vote for their enemy, the Congress Party, rather than Badal and his henchmen because there was no other party to vote for.

Because Sikhs are slaves in India, there is nobody to defend the Sikh interests internationally. Recently, an issue came up of the French banning the wearing of turbans in school. If Khalistan were free, the Sikh Nation could call the French Ambassador and tell him to stop this harassment of Sikhs. Our Ambassador to France would tell the French government the same thing: the turban is part of the Sikh religion and Sikhs should not be harassed.

Remember the words of Professor Darshan Singh, former Akal Takht Jathedar: "If a Sikh is not a Khalistani, he is not a Sikh." Sikhs should vote only for candidates who are prepared to do so. Otherwise, you are just voting to condemn your children and grandchildren to continued slavery under brutal Brahmin theocratic rule.

The time to achieve our independence is now. India is not one country. It has 18 official languages. Soon Kashmir will be free from Indian occupation. Now America is involved in it. As L.K. Advani predicted, "When Kashmir goes, India goes." We agree with him.

When I met President Bush on December 5, he personally told me, "I am aware of the Sikh and Kashmiri problem and we stopped India and Pakistan from going to nuclear war." The Sikh diaspora has a moral responsibility to help the Sikh Nation to achieve its sovereignty by freeing Khalistan from Indian occupation.

The time has come to liberate our homeland. It is the only way that we can prevent further degenerations of the Sikh Nation like the Badal regime. Sikhs must claim their birthright by liberating Khalistan. Only by freeing Khalistan will we put an end to this corruption and restore control of Punjab and its assets to the people, to whom it rightfully belongs. A free Khalistan is a must for the survival of the Sikh nation and will provide an optimal environment for the Sikh Nation to progress to its optimum potential politically, religiously, and economically.

> *Panth Da Sewadar,*
> *Dr. Gurmit Singh Aulakh,*
> *President, Council of Khalistan.*

***

Document

CONGRESSIONAL RECORD -- EXTENSIONS

Tuesday, February 24, 2004
108th Congress, 2nd Session
150 Cong Rec E 201

REFERENCE: Vol. 150, No. 20
SECTION: Extension of Remarks
TITLE: KERRY STATEMENT CALLING SIKHS TERRORISTS A MISTAKE

HON. EDOLPHUS TOWNS
of New York
in the House of Representatives
Tuesday, February 24, 2004

Mr. TOWNS . Mr. Speaker, as an American and a Democrat, it was not good news when I was informed by Dr. Gurmit Singh Aulakh, President of the Council of Khalistan, that Senator John Kerry, the frontrunner for my party's nomination for President, had made a speech in Oklahoma on January 31 in which he described the Sikhs as terrorists. This is a mistake on Senator Kerry's part and one I hope he will correct promptly.

I have been following South Asian affairs for some time now and I can tell you that Sikhs are committed to freedom. I have met members of the Sikh community here in the United States, which is half a million strong, and they are hardworking people who are dedicated to their families, their religion, America, and freedom for their Sikh brothers and sisters back home in Punjab, Khalistan.

The Indian government has been oppressing the Sikhs ever since independence. Shortly after India got its independence, the Indian government sent out a memo describing Sikhs as "a criminal class" and ordering police to take special measures to suppress them. This is shameful. Since 1984, India has murdered over 250,000 Sikhs, according to the Punjab State Magistracy and human-rights organizations. They hold over 52,000 political prisoners. Some have been in illegal custody without charge or trial for 20 years, Mr. Speaker. Two decades! Is that a democratic way to do things?

India's propaganda machine is working overtime to maintain this false picture of Sikhs as a "criminal class" devoted to terrorism. They have even hired two lobbying firms, expensive ones, to carry out this work. Unfortunately, it appears that they managed to misinform the Senator from Massachusetts on this matter. I am sure he will correct himself soon, and I urge him to do so.

In the meantime, Mr. Speaker, it is up to us to do what we can to press for democracy in the subcontinent. Cutting off India's aid would be a good start. This is one of the most effective ways to promote basic human rights for everyone in South Asia. Another very effective means would be to call on India to hold a free and fair vote on the question of independence, the democratic way. By doing this, we help bring the glow of freedom and the blessings of liberty to everyone in that troubled part of the world.

I also call on Senator Kerry to recognize the legitimate aspirations of the Sikhs and the others fighting to free themselves from the yoke of Indian oppression. That they are doing so by peaceful, democratic, nonviolent means shows that the Indian government's picture of them as terrorists is false. I await the Senator's correction.

Mr. Speaker, at this time I would like to add the Council of Khalistan's letter to Senator Kerry requesting a correction and repudiation of his statement to the Record so that people can see the real situation in South Asia.

Council of Khalistan,
Washington, DC, February 11, 2004.
Senator John F. Kerry,
U.S. Senate,
Washington, DC.

Dear Senator Kerry: I am writing to you today on behalf of half a million Sikh Americans and over 25 million Sikhs worldwide to say that your remarks equating Sikhs with terrorists were offensive to the Sikh commu-

nity. While giving a speech in Oklahoma, you referred to "the Sikhs in India" as an example of terrorism.

Sikhism is an independent, monotheistic, revealed religion, not a part of any other religion. Sikhs are distinctive by our religion, language, and culture from any other people on Earth.

Sikhs ruled Punjab from 1710 to 1716 and again from 1765 to 1849. Sikhs, Hindus, Muslims, and Christians all participated in the government. Sikhs are a separate nation and people.

At the time of India's independence, three nations were to receive sovereign power: the Muslims, who got Pakistan, the Hindus, who got India, and the Sikhs. Sikhs took their share with India on the solemn promise that Sikhs would enjoy "the glow of freedom" in Punjab and no law affecting Sikh rights would be passed without our consent. Instead, almost as soon as the ink was dry on India's independence, Nehru sent out a directive describing Sikhs as "a criminal class" and ordering police to take extraordinary measures against us.

Since June 1984, India has murdered over 250,000 Sikhs, according to figures compiled by the Punjab State Magistracy and human rights groups and published in the book The Politics of Genocide by Inderjit Singh Jaijee. A report from the Movement Against State Repression (MASR) shows that India admitted to holding 52,268 Sikhs as political prisoners. Some have been in illegal custody since 1984! Tens of thousands of other minorities are also being held as political prisoners, according to Amnesty International. Indian forces carried out the March 2000 massacre in the village of Chithisinghpora, according to two independent investigations. Indian forces were caught red-handed trying to set fire to a Sikh Gurdwara and Sikh homes in a village in Kashmir. Sikh and Muslim villagers joined hands to stop them.

The book Soft Target, written by two Canadian journalists, Zuhair Kashmeri of the Toronto Globe and Mail and Brian McAndrew of the Toronto Star, shows conclusively that the Indian government blew up its own airliner in 1985, killing 329 innocent people, to blame it on the Sikhs and have an excuse for more repression.

Other minorities such as Christians and Muslims, among others, have also felt the lash of Indian repression. Over 300,000 Christians in Nagaland have been killed by the terrorist Indian regime. Nuns have been raped, priests have been murdered, churches have been burned, schools and prayer halls have been destroyed, all with impunity. A mob of militant Hindus affiliated with the parent organization of the ruling BJP murdered missionary Graham Staines and his two sons by burning them to death while they slept in their jeep, all the while chanting "Victory to Hannuman," a Hindu god. India threw missionary Joseph Cooper from Pennsylvania out of the country after he was beaten so severely that he had to spend a week in the hospital. A Christian religious festival on the theme "Jesus is the answer" was broken up by police gunfire.

Almost two years ago, Muslims were massacred in Gujarat while police were ordered to stand by and do nothing, according to Indian newspaper reports. One newspaper quoted a policeman as saying that the

Indian government planned the massacre in advance. This is an eerie parallel to the 1984 massacre of Sikhs in Delhi, in which police were locked in their barracks while the state-run radio and television called for more Sikh blood.

An Indian Cabinet minister was quoted as saying that everyone who lives in India must either be a Hindu or be subservient to Hindus. This kind of religious fanaticism as state policy is dangerous and anti-democratic. We would not want it in America; why should we support it in India?

On October 7, 1987, Sikhs declared their independence from India, naming their new country Khalistan. We are committed to liberating Khalistan by peaceful, democratic, nonviolent means. History shows that multinational states such as Austria-Hungary, the Soviet Union, and India are doomed to fall apart. We intend to see that this happens peacefully, in the manner of Czechoslovakia, not violently like Yugoslavia. Yet simply supporting a sovereign, independent Khalistan is what India calls terrorism.

The 20,000 Sikhs who were murdered in the June 1984 attack on the Golden Temple and 37 other Sikh Gurdwaras throughout Punjab were not terrorists. They were seeking refuge from the Indian government's tyranny. Yet the Indian government insists on describing them as "terrorists," as if repeating it often enough will make it true.

Senator Kerry, we respectfully request that you apologize to the Sikh Nation and the Sikh community in the United States for your remark. I urge you to support measures to bring freedom to all the people of the subcontinent. Sikhs share the commitment to freedom you showed when you fought in Vietnam and in your service in public office. There was even a Sikh member of Congress in the late 1950s, Dalip Singh Saund of California. We look forward to working with you in the future to bring the blessings of liberty to everyone in the subcontinent.

If you would like any further information or would like to meet about these issues, please feel free to contact me.

> *Sincerely,*
> *Dr. Gurmit Singh Aulakh,*
> *President, Council of Khalistan.*

***

Document

CONGRESSIONAL RECORD -- EXTENSIONS

Tuesday, February 24, 2004
108th Congress, 2nd Session
150 Cong Rec E 203

REFERENCE: Vol. 150, No. 20
SECTION: Extension of Remarks
TITLE: SIKHS PROTEST INDIAN REPUBLIC DAY

HON. EDOLPHUS TOWNS
of New York
in the House of Representatives
Tuesday, February 24, 2004

Mr. TOWNS . Mr. Speaker, on January 26, India celebrated its Republic Day, the anniversary of the adoption of its Constitution. Now if it would only live by that constitution.

The Council of Khalistan organized a successful protest outside the Indian Embassy here in Washington. While India celebrated, minorities are being killed. India has murdered over 250,000 Sikhs since 1984, over 300,000 Christians in Nagaland, over 85,000 Kashmiri Muslims, and tens of thousands of other minorities. There are tens of thousands of political prisoners, according to Amnesty International. These include over 52,000 Sikhs, a study from the Movement Against State Repression showed. That doesn't sound like a republic to me.

People came to the protest from all over the East Coast. They chanted slogans like "Khalistan Zindabad," "Long live Khalistan," and many others. They educated the public about the repression of minorities in India while the attendees at the Ambassador's party celebrated India's freedom.

We salute India's freedom, but it is time that these benefits extended to everyone within its borders, not just the Brahmin elites and their friends. It is time for the repression to end and for the minorities to live in freedom too.

Mr. Speaker, this kind of repression is unacceptable in any country, but especially in one that proclaims itself democratic.

Perhaps they feel that this repression is necessary to hold the country together, since India is not a single nation but many nations thrown together under one banner, much like the Soviet Union or the Austro-Hungarian Empire. History shows that such nations cannot long survive.

Now I know you're wondering what America can do to help. We should uphold and support the principle of self-determination for all people. The right to self-determination is the cornerstone of democracy.

The time has come to end our aid to India so that all the people there can enjoy the glow of freedom. The best way to secure the blessings of liberty for everyone within India's artificial borders is to stop aiding the tyrants who oppress them with U.S. taxpayer dollars. The other thing that we must do, Mr. Speaker, perhaps equally important, is to take a stand for the essential right of self-determination by putting this Congress on record in support of a free and fair plebiscite with international monitoring on the question of independence for all the minority nations of the subcontinent. This will ensure them the opportunity to enjoy the full rights of free people.

Mr. Speaker, the Council of Khalistan issued an outstanding press release on its Republic Day protest. I would like to insert it into the Record at this time for the information of my colleagues and the public.

Council of Khalistan,
Washington, DC, January 26, 2004.
Sikhs Protest Indian Genocide on Republic Day
Demand Freedom for Sikh Nation of Khalistan. No Democracy for
Sikhs, Christians, Muslims, Others

Sikhs from around the East Coast demonstrated in Washington, D.C. today to protest the ongoing genocide against the Sikh Nation and other minorities by the Hindu fundamentalist, terrorist Government of India. They raised slogans of "Khalistan Zindabad", "India out of Khalistan," "2-4-6-8, India is a Fascist state," and other slogans.

India's Republic Day celebrates the day in 1950 when India adopted its Constitution. But what India calls "Republic Day" is Genocide Day for the minority peoples and nations of South Asia. The Indian government has murdered over 250,000 Sikhs since 1984, more than 300,000 Christians since 1948, over 85,000 Muslims in Kashmir since 1988, and tens of thousands of Tamils, Assamese, Manipuris, Dalits, and others. The Indian Supreme Court called the Indian government's murders of Sikhs "worse than a genocide." According to a study by the Movement Against State Repression, 52,268 Sikhs are being held in illegal detention as political prisoners without charge or trial. Some of them have been held since 1984!

"India is not a democracy for Sikhs, Muslims, Christians, and other minorities," said Dr. Gurmit Singh Aulakh, President of the Council of Khalistan, which leads the Sikh Nation's struggle for independence. "The rights guaranteed in the Indian constitution are not enjoyed by non-Hindus," he said. "While India celebrates, Sikhs and others are dying," he said. "Is that something to celebrate?"

Christian missionary Joseph Cooper was expelled from India after a mob of militant Hindu nationalists allied with the Rashtriya Swayamsewak Sangh (RSS), a pro-Fascist organization that is the parent organization of the ruling BJP, beat him so severely he had to spend a week in the hospital. In 2002, 2,000 to 5,000 Muslims were attacked in Gujarat while police were ordered to stand aside, reminiscent of the 1984 Delhi massacres of Sikhs. Indian newspapers reported that the government planned the Gujarat massacre in advance.

Indian police arrested human-rights activist Jaswant Singh Khalra after he exposed their policy of mass cremation of Sikhs, in which over 50,000 Sikhs have been arrested, tortured, and murdered, then their bodies were declared unidentified and secretly cremated. He was murdered in police custody. His body was not given to his family. The police never released the body of former Jathedar of the Akal Takht Gurdev Singh Kaunke after SSP Swaran Singh Ghotna murdered him. Ghotna has never been brought to trial for the Jathedar Kaunke murder. No one has been brought to justice for the kidnapping and murder of Jaswant Singh Khalra.

"It is good that American pressure has forced India and Pakistan to talk about Kashmir," said Dr. Aulakh. "But the atrocities still continue. Khalistan, Kashmir, and all the nations of South Asia have the right to self-determination," he said. "In a democracy, you cannot rule the people against their will." On October 7, 1987, the Sikh Nation declared its independence from India, naming its new country Khalistan. On December 5, Dr. Aulakh met President Bush. "I am aware of the Sikh and Kashmiri problem," President Bush told him.

History shows that multinational states such as India are doomed to failure. Countries like Austria-Hungary, India's longtime friend the Soviet Union, Yugoslavia, Czechoslovakia, and others prove this point. India is not one country; it is a polyglot like those countries, thrown together for the convenience of the British colonialists. It is doomed to break up as they did. India is ruled by Hindu theocrats whose agenda is "Hindu, Hindi, Hindutva, Hindu Rashtra," or total Hindu domination of every facet of Indian life. An Indian Cabinet minister said that everyone who lives in India must be a Hindu or subservient to Hindus.

Sikhs ruled Punjab until 1849 when the British conquered the subcontinent. Sikhs were equal partners during the transfer of power from the British. The Muslim leader Jinnah got Pakistan, the Hindu leaders got India, but the Sikh leadership was fooled by the Hindu leadership promising that Sikhs would have "the glow of freedom" in Northwest India. The Sikhs took their share with India on that promise.

"Democracies don't commit genocide," Dr. Aulakh said. "Only in a free and sovereign Khalistan will the Sikh Nation prosper. In a democracy, the right to self-determination is the sine qua non and India should allow a plebiscite for the freedom of the Sikh Nation," he said. "India should also allow self-determination in Christian Nagaland, Kashmir, Assam, and the other nations fighting for freedom to bring peace to South Asia."

"As Professor Darshan Singh, a former Jathedar of the Akal Takht, said, 'If a Sikh is not for Khalistan, he is not a Sikh'," Dr. Aulakh noted. "We must continue to press for our God-given birthright of freedom," he said. "Without political power, religions cannot flourish and nations perish."

***

Document

CONGRESSIONAL RECORD -- EXTENSIONS

Tuesday, February 24, 2004
108th Congress, 2nd Session
150 Cong Rec E 204

REFERENCE: Vol. 150, No. 20
SECTION: Extension of Remarks
TITLE: COUNCIL OF KHALISTAN URGES SIKH ORGANIZATIONS TO
TAKE STRONG STAND FOR FREEDOM

HON. EDOLPHUS TOWNS
of New York
in the House of Representatives
Tuesday, February 24, 2004

Mr. TOWNS . Mr. Speaker, recently, the French National Assembly enacted a law banning religious symbols such as "conspicuous crosses," yarmulkes, Muslim headscarves, and Sikh turbans from schools. Many religious organizations spoke out against it, including many Sikh organizations. Belgium is thinking about such a law also.

The Council of Khalistan wrote a letter on February 11 noting that none of the other Sikh organizations mentioned the persecution of Sikhs in India or their struggle for freedom in their communications about this law. Yet a free and sovereign Sikh homeland, Khalistan, would have put the Sikhs in a much stronger position to protest these discriminatory and unfair rules.

The letter, brought to me by Dr. Gurmit Singh Aulakh, the tireless fighter for freedom in South Asia, calls on Sikh organizations to stand up to the repression by working for freedom for the Sikh people.

In my years of public service, I have had the privilege of knowing many Sikhs. They are hardworking people and they are very supportive of the cause of freedom. Yet the Indian government's response is to step up the repression in the name of Hindutva_total Hindu domination of every facet of life in the subcontinent. An Indian Cabinet minister even said that everyone who lives in India must either be a Hindu or be subservient to Hindus.

Over a quarter of a million Sikhs have been killed by the Indian government in the last 20 years, Mr. Speaker. More than 52,000 are political prisoners. Even one political prisoner is unacceptable, Mr. Speaker. Even one government murder is unacceptable, especially when no one is punished for it and especially when the country where it happens proudly proclaims its commitment to democratic values.

Over 200 years ago, Americans fought to achieve our independence from an overbearing British monarchy. Today, the Sikhs fight for their freedom by peaceful means, which the Indian government falsely describes as terrorist. We are the beacon of hope for the freedom-loving people of the world, Mr. Speaker. We owe it to them and to ourselves to help them if we can.

One way to help is to stop aid to India as long as these egregious human rights violations continue. Everyone is entitled to live in peace and freedom, to go to work and enjoy life with the family and friends. Yet minorities in India are unable to do that because militant Hindus aligned with the RSS, the parent organization of the ruling party, and the government itself in many cases commit terrible acts of violence against

Christians, Sikhs, Muslims, Dalits, Assamese, Bodos, Tamils, Manipuris, and other minorities. This is unacceptable and the hardworking taxpayers of our country should not be called upon to support it.

Another measure that we can take is to declare our strong support for freedom through a free and fair plebiscite on independence where it is sought. India is a multinational state and history shows that such states do not survive. By helping to ensure that democracy is allowed to work for the cause of freedom and self-determination, we can make sure that whatever changes occur in the subcontinent happen peacefully.

Mr. Speaker, I don't mean to be long-winded, so I will stop here and place the Council of Khalistan's excellent open letter into the Record.

Council of Khalistan,
Washington, DC, February 11, 2004.
Open Letter to Sikh Organizations and Institutions:
An Appeal to the Khalsa Panth

Only in a free Khalistan can Sikhs prosper_Every Sikh must work to liberate Khalistan

Dear Khalsa Panth: Waheguru Ji Ka Khalsa, Waheguru Ji Ki Fateh!

Recently, France passed a law banning the wearing of turbans and other religious symbols such as yarmulkes, Muslim head scarves, and "conspicuous crosses" in schools. This is a major violation of religious rights. Belgium is considering a similar law. Sikhs must do whatever we can to protest this unfair, discriminatory action.

Because Sikhs are slaves in India, there is nobody to defend the Sikh interests internationally. Recently, an issue came up of the French banning the wearing of turbans in school. If Khalistan were free, the Sikh Nation could call the French Ambassador and tell him to stop this harassment of Sikhs. Our Ambassador to France would tell the French government the same thing: the turban is part of the Sikh religion and Sikhs should not be harassed.

When Khalistan is free, we will be in a much stronger position to fight such offenses against our religion. We will be able to exert influence that we cannot bring to bear now. This is just one more reason that the liberation of Khalistan is essential. Yet prominent Sikh organizations like the Sikh Council on Religion and Education (SCORE), SMART, the Sikh Coalition, and other organizations refuse to mention the oppression of the Sikhs by the Indian regime and the struggle to liberate Khalistan. They are more concerned about their positions than about the Sikh people. These organizations are heavily infiltrated and often controlled by operatives of the Indian government. We appreciate the British Sikh Federation, which continually promotes the cause of Sikh rights and freedom for Khalistan. These other organizations must promote the cause of Sikh freedom as well. Whenever they have the opportunity to communicate with the outside world, they should promote freedom and independence for Khalistan.

The Guru granted sovereignty to the Sikh Nation, saying "In Grieb Sikhin Ko Deon Patshahi." The Sikh Nation must achieve its independence to fulfill the mandate of the Guru. We always remember it by reciting every morning and evening, "Raj Kare Ga Khalsa." Now is the time to act on it. Do we mean what we say every morning and evening? I urge Sikhs to unite and take action to liberate our homeland, Punjab, Khalistan. It is time to start a Shantmai Morcha to liberate Khalistan from Indian occupation.

Never forget that the Akal Takht Sahib and Darbar Sahib are under the control of the Indian government, the same Indian government that has murdered over a quarter of a million Sikhs in the past twenty years. The Jathedar of the Akal Takht and the head granthi of Darbar Sahib toe the line that the Indian government tells them. They are not appointed by the Khalsa Panth. The SGPC also is controlled by the Indian government that has brutally murdered our people. These institutions will remain under the control of the Indian regime until we free the Sikh homeland, Punjab, Khalistan, from Indian occupation and oppression and sever our relations with the New Delhi government.

The Indian government invaded and desecrated the Golden Temple and 125 other Sikh Gurdwaras throughout Punjab to murder Sant Bhindranwale and 20,000 other Sikhs during June 1984 in Punjab. If Sikhs will not even protect the sanctity of the Golden Temple, how can the Sikh Nation survive as a nation?

The Indian government has murdered over 250,000 Sikhs since 1984, according to figures compiled by the Punjab State Magistracy and human rights groups. These figures were published in Inderjit Singh Jaijee's excellent book, The Politics of Genocide. According to the Movement Against State Repression (MASR), the Indian regime admitted to holding 52,268 Sikhs as political prisoners. They are being held without charge or trial, some of them since 1984!

How can a democratic state hold political prisoners? The regime has made over 50,000 Sikhs "disappear" by picking them up, torturing and murdering them, and then secretly cremating them, declaring them "unidentified." Their bodies are not given to their families. The bodies of Jathedar Gurdev Singh Kaunke and Sardar Jaswant Singh Khalra, who were murdered by the police, were never given to their families.

Other minorities also feel the lash of Indian repression. India has killed over 300,000 Christians in Nagaland since 1947 and murdered priests, raped nuns, burned churches, and destroyed Christian schools and prayer halls. They expelled missionary Joseph Cooper from the country after militant Hindu nationalists beat him up so badly that he had to be in the hospital for a week. Missionary Graham Staines and his two young sons were burned to death while sleeping in their jeep by a mob of militant Hindus chanting "Victory to Hannuman," a Hindu god. Since they were allied with the pro-Fascist RSS, the parent organization of the ruling BJP, they were able to commit this atrocity with impunity. Muslims were massacred in Gujarat while the police were under orders to stand aside and let the massacre occur, a frightening parallel to the 1984 Delhi massacres of Sikhs. A policeman told an Indian newspaper that the Gujarat massacre was planned in advance by the government.

This kind of treatment of its minorities only confirms the kind of country that India, is. It is a fundamentalist Hindu theocracy, not secular or democratic at all. Remember what Narinder Singh, a spokesman for the Golden Temple, told America's National Public Radio in 1997: "The Indian government, they are always boasting that they are democratic, that they are secular. They have nothing to do with a secularism, nothing to do with a democracy. They just kill Sikhs just to please the majority."

Remember the words of Professor Darshan Singh, former Jathedar of the Akal Takht: "If a Sikh is not a Khalistani, he is not a Sikh." The time to achieve our independence is now. India is not one country. It is a polyglot empire thrown together under one roof for the administrative convenience of the British colonialists. It has 18 official languages. History shows that such countries are doomed to fall apart. India will collapse just like the AustroHungarian Empire, the Soviet Union, and other multinational states.

Soon Kashmir will be free from Indian occupation. Now America is involved in it. As L.K. Advani predicted, "When Kashmir goes, India goes." We agree with him and we urge the Indian government to hold a free and fair plebiscite on the question of independence and to sit down with representatives of the Sikh Nation to negotiate the boundaries of a sovereign, independent Khalistan. We want to make sure that India's collapse happens peacefully like that of Czechoslovakia, not violently like the breakup of Yugoslavia. The essence of democracy is self-determination. It is time for India to act like the democracy it claims to be.

When I met President Bush on December 5, he personally told me, "I am aware of the Sikh and Kashmiri problem and we stopped India and Pakistan from going to nuclear war." The Sikh diaspora has a moral responsibility to help the Sikh Nation to achieve its sovereignty by freeing Khalistan from Indian occupation.

The time has come to liberate our homeland. Sikhs must claim their birthright by liberating Khalistan. Only by freeing Khalistan will we put an end to this corruption and restore control of Punjab and its assets to the people, to whom it rightfully belongs. A free Khalistan is a must for the survival of the Sikh nation and will provide an optimal environment for the Sikh Nation to progress to its optimum potential politically, religiously, and economically.

Panth Da Sewadar,
Dr. Gurmit Singh Aulakh,
President, Council of Khalistan.

***

Document

CONGRESSIONAL RECORD -- EXTENSIONS

Wednesday, January 21, 2004
108th Congress, 2nd Session
150 Cong Rec E 17

REFERENCE: Vol. 150, No. 2
SECTION: Extension of Remarks
TITLE: FRENCH BAN ON TURBANS IN SCHOOLS OPPOSED

Speech of
HON. EDOLPHUS TOWNS
STATE of New York
in the House of Representatives
DATE Wednesday, January 21, 2004

Mr. TOWNS . Mr. Speaker, the government of France has recently enacted a new policy prohibiting Sikh boys from wearing their turbans in school. They also prohibited Muslim girls from wearing the traditional head scarves in school.

This policy is a threat to religious expression in France. It limits the ability of religious minorities to express their religion in the way that they are supposed to express their religion.

Sikhs fought actively in both World Wars to help keep the French people free. They fought in their turbans in Africa and the Middle East in World War I and they fought in the liberation of France in World War II. Yet the French authorities see fit to deny them their full religious expression.

Recently, Dr. Gurmit Singh Aulakh, President of the Council of Khalistan, wrote an excellent letter to French President Jacques Chirac about this unreasonable policy. I am inserting it into the Record with the consent of the House and I urge my colleagues to read it.

Council of Khalistan,
Washington, DC
January 19, 2004.
Hon. Jacques Chirac,
President of France,
Champs Elysees

Paris, France
Dear President Chirac: I am writing to you today on behalf of the Sikh community of France and the 25 million strong Sikh Nation around the world.

Recently, France has made laws prohibiting Muslim schoolgirls from wearing head scarves and Sikh boys from wearing their turbans.

The turban is a Sikh religious symbol. Sikhs are not allowed to remove their turbans. They are a major symbol of our religion. The Sikh Gurus commanded us to wear the turban at all times over unshorn hair, which is a gift from God. The Sikh religion is a sovereign, independent, mono-theistic religion like Christianity. The Sikh religion requires every Sikh to wear five symbols. Unshorn hair is one of them.

As you know, Sikh soldiers wearing their turbans fought to defend France and defend its freedom during World War II. They also helped France and Britain to win World War I by fighting in Africa and the Middle East. We were proud to do so. Sikhs are commanded to fight against injustice wherever it appears. We believe in the freedom and equality of all people.

France is a secular, democratic republic. That implies a country that protects freedom of religious expression for all people. To force Sikhs to remove the turban is to destroy Sikhs' freedom of religious expression. That is neither secular, democratic, nor republican. It is simply the kind of system that Sikhs came to France and other countries to escape.

President Chirac, I encourage you to reconsider this ill-advised ban. Sikhs must be free to express our religion as fully as any other French-man.

Thank you for your time and attention.

Sincerely,
Dr. Gurmit Singh Aulakh.
President, Council of Khalistan.

***

Document

CONGRESSIONAL RECORD -- EXTENSIONS

Wednesday, January 21, 2004
108th Congress, 2nd Session
150 Cong Rec E 20

REFERENCE: Vol. 150, No. 2
SECTION: Extension of Remarks
TITLE: SEMINAR ON KHALISTAN HELD IN PUNJAB: STEP FORWARD FOR SIKH FREEDOM MOVEMENT

Speech of
HON. EDOLPHUS TOWNS
STATE of New York
in the House of Representatives
DATE Wednesday, January 21, 2004

Mr. TOWNS . Mr. Speaker, last month in Punjab, a seminar was held on the topic of Khalistan. Given the oppression that Sikhs have faced at the hands of the Indian government for attempting to secure their independence, this was a very courageous act. All of those who organized the event and who participated are to be commended for their courage. Freedom is the birthright of every people.

The seminar was organized by former Member of Parliament Atinder Pal Singh. Speakers included Professor Gurdarshan Singh Dhillon, who reportedly made an extremely strong argument for the Sikh Nation's right to self-determination.

The Indian government claims that there is no support for Sikh independence, Mr. Speaker, but this seminar and other events show otherwise. Perhaps this answers the obvious question: If India is a democracy and if there is no support for an independent Khalistan, then why not simply hold a free and fair plebiscite on the issue, as democratic countries do, and settle it once and for all? Wouldn't that be the fair and democratic way to take care of this issue?

America can support this just cause and we have a moral obligation to do so. We can stop our aid to India until all people there enjoy full freedom and we can officially call on India to hold a free and fair, democratic vote to determine the political future of the Sikhs of Khalistan and all the other minority nations seeking their freedom, such as predominantly Christian Nagaland and predominantly Muslim Kashmir.

The Council of Khalistan issued a press release on the Khalistan seminar, which I would like to put in the Record at this time to show that the cause of freedom is universal and that it still has strong support in Punjab, Khalistan.

Seminar on Khalistan Held in Punjab
Independence Movement Is Alive and Well in Punjab, Khalistan

Washington, D.C., December 17, 2003_Former Member of Parliament Atinder Pal Singh organized a seminar on Khalistan last month at Baba Makhan Shah Labana Hall, Sector 30, Chandigarh. Speakers included Professor Gurdarshan Singh Dhillon and others. Dr. Dhillon made a very strong argument for the right of the Sikh Nation to rule itself in a sovereign, independent Khalistan. General Narinder Singh was invited, but unable to attend. This seminar shows that the cause of Khalistan is alive and well in Punjab, despite the claims of the Indian government that there is no support for Khalistan and that only outside Sikhs are supporting independence.

"The outside Sikhs have an important role to play," said Dr. Gurmit Singh Aulakh, President of the Council of Khalistan. "They have exposed the human rights against the Sikhs to the international community and internationalized the cause of independence for Khalistan," he said. "They have also preserved Sikh history in the Congressional Record from 1984 to date, defeating the Indian government's attempts to alter it. However, it is the Sikhs in Punjab, Khalistan who are keeping the cause alive and liberating Khalistan," he said. "It is very good see this support for the cause of a sovereign, independent Khalistan," said Dr. Aulakh. On October 7, 1987, the Sikh Nation declared its independence from India, naming its new country Khalistan.

"We salute Sardar Atinder Pal Singh for organizing this important event and we salute all the presenters who presented their papers," Dr. Aulakh said. "They put the Indian government on notice that its effort to suppress the Sikh independence movement by force has failed and will continue to fail," he said.

"The mere fact that this seminar was conducted shows that there is a significant change in the repression in Punjab," Dr. Aulakh said. "It shows that people feel free to exercise their basic right of freedom of speech," he said. "This is a step forward for the liberation of the Sikh Nation. There is a new upsurge of support for the cause of Sikh freedom," Dr. Aulakh said. "The flame of freedom burns brightly in the hearts of the Sikh people, in Punjab, Khalistan and outside as well."

"Every day, Sikhs pray 'Raj Kare Ga Khalsa,' which means 'The Khalsa shall rule,' said Dr. Aulakh. "Sikhs must claim their birthright by liberating Khalistan. I hope that this seminar will be the forerunner to a Shantmai Morcha (peaceful agitation) to establish a sovereign, independent Khalistan, thus fulfilling the desires of the Sikh Nation for Raj Kare Ga Khalsa," he said. "Guru Gobind Singh gave sovereignty to the Sikh Nation and we must achieve it."

The Indian government has murdered over 250,000 Sikhs since 1984, more than 300,000 Christians since 1948, over 85,000 Muslims in Kashmir since 1988, and tens of thousands of Tamils, Assamese, Mampuris, Dalits, and others. The Indian Supreme Court called the Indian government's murders of Sikhs "worse than a genocide."

Indian police arrested human-rights activist Jaswant Singh Khalra after he exposed their policy of mass cremation of Sikhs, in which over 50,000 Sikhs have been arrested, tortured, and murdered, then their bodies were declared unidentified and secretly cremated. He was murdered in police custody. His body was not given to his family. The police never released the body of former Jathedar of the Akal Takht Sardar Gurdev Singh Kaunke after SSP Swaran Singh Ghotna murdered him. Ghotna has never been brought to trial for the Jathedar Kaunke murder. No one has been brought to justice for the kidnapping and murder of Jaswant Singh Khalra. According to a report by the Movement Against State Repression (MASR), 52,268 Sikhs are being held as political prisoners in India without charge or trial. Some have been in illegal custody since 1984!

"As Professor Darshan Singh, a former Jathedar of the Akal Takht, said, 'If a Sikh is not for Khalistan, he is not a Sikh',' Dr. Aulakh noted. "We must continue to press for our God-given birthright of freedom," he said. "Without political power, religions cannot flourish and nations perish."

***

Document

CONGRESSIONAL RECORD -- EXTENSIONS

Wednesday, January 21, 2004
108th Congress, 2nd Session
150 Cong Rec E 24

REFERENCE: Vol. 150, No. 2
SECTION: Extension of Remarks
TITLE: NEW YEAR'S WISHES FOR FREEDOM FOR THE SIKHS

Speech of
HON. EDOLPHUS TOWNS
STATE of New York
in the House of Representatives
Wednesday, January 21, 2004

Mr. TOWNS . Mr. Speaker, recently my friend Dr. Gurmit Singh Aulakh, the President of the Council of Khalistan, issued a New Year's message to the Sikhs. In it, he took note of the progress that has been made towards freedom for the Sikhs and other minority nations in South Asia. He also wrote that the effort to liberate the Sikh homeland, Khalistan, must continue.

As you may know, the Sikhs declared their independence from India on October 7, 1987. They named their country Khalistan. Since that time, tens of thousands of Sikhs have been murdered to suppress the Sikh freedom movement and tens of thousands more have been held as political prisoners.

Dr. Aulakh noted that seminars on Khalistan were held openly last year. He noted the ceremony honoring Sikh martyrs Satwant Singh, Beant Singh, and Kehar Singh. He wrote about recent initiatives by the Khalsa Panchayat to move the cause of freedom for the Sikhs forward.

Mr. Speaker, the right to self-determination is the cornerstone of democracy. It is time for the United States, founded on the principle of self-determination, to support self-determination for the Sikhs. We can do this by cutting off our aid to India until the Sikhs of Khalistan, the Muslims of Kashmir, the Christians of Nagaland, and all the minorities enjoy full rights and freedom and by putting the Congress on record in support of self-determination for Khalistan, Kashmir, Nagaland, and the other nations seeking their freedom in the form of a free and fair plebiscite on the question of independence.

Mr. Speaker, I would like to place Dr. Aulakh's letter into the Record at this time for the information of my colleagues.

New Year's Message to the Khalsa Panth

Washington, Jan. 19._Happy New Year to you and your family and the Khalsa Panth. May 2004 be your best year ever.

The Guru gave sovereignty to the Sikh Nation. ("In Grieb Sikhin Ko Deon Patshahi.") The Sikh Nation must achieve it. We always remember it by reciting every morning and evening, "Raj Kare Ga Khalsa." Now is the time to act on it. Do we mean what we say every morning and evening?

The fire of freedom still burns strong and bright in the heart of the Sikh Nation. 2003 was an encouraging year for the Sikh freedom struggle. Sikhs openly held seminars in Punjab on the subject of Khalistan. This is a very good sign and we salute the people who participated in these seminars. They are keeping the flame of freedom lit. Now I urge Sikhs to unite and take action to liberate our homeland, Punjab, Khalistan. It is time to start a Shantmai Morcha to liberate Khalistan from Indian occupation.

Never forget that the Akal Takht Sahib and Darbar Sahib are under the control of the Indian government, the same Indian government that has murdered over a quarter of a million Sikhs in the past twenty years. The Jathedar of the Akal Takht and the head granthi of Darbar Sahib toe the line that the Indian government tells them. They are not appointed by the Khalsa Panth. The SGPC, which appoints them, does not represent the Sikh Nation anymore. They have become the puppets of the Indian government and have lost credibility with the Sikh Nation. Otherwise they would behave like a real Jathedar, Jathedar Gurdev Singh Kaunke, rather than like Indian government puppet Jathedar Aroor Singh, who gave a Siropa to General Dyer for the massacre at Jalianawa Bagh. These institutions will remain under the control of the Indian regime until we free the Sikh homeland, Punjab, Khalistan, from Indian occupation and oppression and sever our relations with the New Delhi government.

The Sikh Nation is a nation of martyrs. It is encouraging that the SGPC and the Akal Takht honored the Sikh martyrs S. Satwant Singh, S. Beant Singh, and S. Kehar Singh. Recent initiatives by the Khalsa Panchayat to bring the Sikh tradition and glory to the Khalsa Panth are highly appreciated. This is a good start to establishing Khalsa Raj as the Akali movement in the 1920s freed the Sikh Gurdwaras from the Mahants who were puppets of the Indian government. Today, the Akali leaders are the new Mahants.

The Akali Dal conspired with the Indian government in 1984 to invade the Golden Temple to murder Sant Bhindranwale and 20,000 other Sikh during June 1984 in Punjab. If Sikhs will not even protect the sanctity of the Golden Temple, how can the Sikh Nation survive as a nation?

The Akali Dal has lost all its credibility. The Badal government was so corrupt openly and no Akali leader would come forward and tell Badal and his wife to stop this unparalelled corruption. That is why the Akali Dal was defeated in the elections by the Congress Party.

Chief Minister Amarinder Singh has done one good thing for which we must appreciate him. He is prosecuting Badal, his son, and his wife for their corruption during their five years in power, 1997-2002. How could a Chief Minister of modest means amass over Rs4300 crore? He should pay the taxes on this wealth and account to the Sikh Nation where he got it. This ill-gotten wealth should be confiscated.

Badal has destroyed the moral fabric of the Sikh religion. What happened to the concept of fairness and honesty? Because Sikhs are slaves in India, there is nobody to defend the Sikh interests internationally. Recently, an issue came up of the French banning the wearing of turbans in school. If Khalistan were free, the Sikh Nation could call the French Ambassador and tell him to stop this harassment of Sikhs. Our Ambassador to France would tell the French government the same thing: the turban is part of the Sikh religion and Sikhs should not be harassed.

When Sikhs ruled Punjab, a French general, General Ventura, commanded the Sikh artillery. He himself wore a beard and a turban. In World War II, the Sikh army wearing turbans helped to liberate France so that France could enjoy freedom.

Khalsa Ji, let's pray to Guru for freedom, unity, sovereignty, prosperity, and happiness for the Sikh Nation around the world and for everyone. The Khalsa Panth is determined to establish Khalsa Raj, as the events of this past year show.

India is not one country. It has 18 official languages. Soon Kashmir will be free from Indian occupation. Now America is involved in it. As L.K. Advani predicted, "When Kashmir goes, India goes." We agree with him.

When I met President Bush on December 5, he personally told me, "I am aware of the Sikh and Kashmiri problem and we stopped India and Pakistan from going to nuclear war." The Sikh diaspora has a moral responsibility to help the Sikh Nation to achieve its sovereignty by freeing Khalistan from Indian occupation.

As President of the Council of Khalistan, I wish everybody a 2004 that brings freedom, prosperity, and happiness to you and to the Khalsa Panth. A free Khalistan is a must for the survival of the Sikh nation and will provide an optimal environment for the Sikh Nation to progress to its optimum potential politically, religiously, and economically.

Panth Da Sewadar,
Dr. Gurmit Singh Aulakh,
President, Council of Khalistan.

***

Document

CONGRESSIONAL RECORD -- EXTENSIONS

Monday, October 20, 2003
108th Congress, 1st Session
149 Cong Rec E 2097

REFERENCE: Vol. 149, No. 147
SECTION: Extension of Remarks
TITLE: ANNUAL SIKH CONVENTION LAYS PLANS FOR EXPANDING
FREEDOM STRUGGLE

Speech of
HON. EDOLPHUS TOWNS
State of New York
in the House of Representatives
Monday, October 20, 2003

Mr. TOWNS . Mr. Speaker, the International Sikh Organization held its annual convention on the weekend of October 10-11-12, 2003, in Houston. The convention laid plans for the expansion of the movement to free Khalistan, the Sikh homeland that declared its independence on October 7, 1987.

The convention was attended by many delegates from all around the United States and Canada. They made plans to expand their office in Washington, which has been an invaluable resource to us here in Congress in getting out information about the oppression of the Sikhs and other minorities by the Indian government. This is good to see. The glow of freedom still burns brightly in the hearts of these Sikh leaders.

The delegates also congratulated Dr. Gurmit Singh Aulakh, President of the International Sikh Organization and the Council of Khalistan, for his tireless work in support of the interests of Sikhs in this country and the cause of freedom for Khalistan. I can say from my personal experience that Dr. Aulakh has worked for that cause with great dedication for several years and he has provided a lot of information to those of us in Congress who are interested in the cause of human rights and freedom in South Asia.

Mr. Speaker, I would simply like to take this opportunity to salute the International Sikh Organization on a very successful convention and wish it continued success in the future. We can support its efforts to bring freedom to the Sikh people, as well as the other captive nations of South Asia such as Nagaland, Kashmir, and others, by stopping American aid and trade with India until human rights are observed and by declaring our support for a fair plebiscite under international monitoring on the question of independence.

I would like to place the ISO's press release on its very successful convention into the Record at this time.

Annual Convention on Khalistan Very Successful_Plans To Strengthen Office Formulated

Washington, D.C., October 14, 2003_The annual convention of the International Sikh Organization on Khalistan was very successful. Delegates from all around the United States and Canada attended. The convention was held October 10-11-12 in Houston, Texas.

The convention recognized Dr. Gurmit Singh Aulakh, President of the International Sikh Organization and the Council of Khalistan, for his dedication, vision, persistence, and commitment to the cause of liberating Khalistan, the independent Sikh homeland declared on October 7, 1987. Since then, it has been under Indian occupation. When India became independent, Sikhs were equal partners in the transfer of power and were to receive their own state, but the weak and ignorant Sikh leaders of the time were tricked into staying with India on the promise that they would have "the glow of freedom" and no law affecting the Sikhs would pass without their consent. Sikhs ruled an independent and sovereign Punjab from 1710 to 1716and again from 1765 to 1849. No Sikh representative has ever signed the Indian constitution. The Council of Khalistan is the government pro tempore of Khalistan.

At the convention Dr. Bakshish Singh Sandhu of Pennsylvania and Sardar Harjinder Singh of New Jersey offered to spearhead the acquisition of a building in Washington, D.C. to house the International Sikh Organization's offices.

The delegates emphasized the need for an office in Washington to protect the interests of Sikhs in this country, as well as to work for freedom for Khalistan. An example of this need is the video recently removed from the State Department website entitled "Terrorism: A War Without Borders" which portrayed all Sikhs as terrorists. Because of the letter by U.S. Representatives Dan Burton (R-Ind.), Edolphus Towns (D-NY), and Wally Herger (R-Cal.), the State Department recently removed this video and its text from its website. The convention passed a resolution of appreciation of these Congressmen.

Other resolutions included one asking every Gurdwara to contribute $500 per month to the Washington office, one urging Sikhs not to support the various branches of the Akali Dal, which is under Indian government control, one calling for young Sikhs to step forward into leadership roles, and one demanding freedom for Khalistan.

History shows that multinational states such as India are doomed to failure. Countries like Austria-Hungary, India's longtime friend the Soviet Union, Yugoslavia, Czechoslovakia, and others prove this point. India is not one country; it is a polyglot like those countries, thrown together for the convenience of the British colonialists. It is doomed to break up as they did. India is ruled by Hindu theocrats whose agenda is "Hindu, Hindi, Hindutva, Hindu Rashtra," or total Hindu domination of every facet of Indian life. An Indian Cabinet minister said that everyone who lives in India must be a Hindu or subservient to Hindus.

"We thank everyone who attended this important convention," Dr. Aulakh said. "Their commitment, their ideas and their support are helpful as we move forward in our work to protect the interests of Sikhs in this country and to continue working for the liberation of Khalistan," he said. "We sincerely thank and appreciate the hospitality of the Management Committee of the Houston Gurdwara. Special thanks are due to the Council advisors of the Houston area."

The Indian government has murdered over 250,000 Sikhs since 1984, more than 200,000 Christians since 1948, over 85,000 Muslims in Kashmir since 1988, and tens of thousands of Tamils, Assamese, Manipuris, Dalits, and others. The Indian Supreme Court called the Indian government's murders of Sikhs "worse than a genocide."

Indian police arrested human-rights activist Jaswant Singh Khalra after he exposed their policy of mass cremation of Sikhs, in which over 50,000 Sikhs have been arrested, tortured, and murdered, then their bodies were declared unidentified and secretly cremated. He was murdered in police custody. His body was not given to his family. The police never released the body of former Jathedar of the Akal Takht Gurdev Singh Kaunke after SSP Swaran Singh Ghotna murdered him. Ghotna has never been brought to trial for the Jathedar Kaunke murder. No one has been brought to justice for the kidnapping and murder of Jaswant Singh Khalra. According to a report by the Movement Against State Repression (MASR), 52,268 Sikhs are being held as political prisoners in India without charge or trial. Some have been in illegal custody since 1984!

***

Document

CONGRESSIONAL RECORD -- EXTENSIONS

Friday, October 17, 2003
108th Congress, 1st Session
149 Cong Rec E 2079

REFERENCE: Vol. 149, No. 146
SECTION: Extension of Remarks
TITLE: ANNUAL SIKH CONVENTION LAYS PLANS FOR EXPANDING
STRUGGLE FOR FREEDOM

Speech of
HON. EDOLPHUS TOWNS
State of New York
in the House of Representatives
Friday, October 17, 2003

Mr. TOWNS . Mr. Speaker, the International Sikh Organization held its annual convention on the weekend of October 10-11-12, 2003 in Houston. The convention laid plans for the expansion of the movement to free Khalistan, the Sikh homeland that declared its independence on October 7, 1987.

The convention was attended by many delegates from all around the United States and Canada. They made plans to expand their office in Washington, which has been an invaluable resource to us here in Congress in getting out information about the oppression of the Sikhs and other minorities by the Indian government. This is good to see. The glow of freedom still burns brightly in the hearts of these Sikh leaders.

The delegates also congratulated Dr. Gurmit Singh Aulakh, President of the International Sikh Organization and the Council of Khalistan, for his tireless work in support of the interests of Sikhs in this country and the cause of freedom for Khalistan. I can say from my personal experience that Dr. Aulakh has worked for that cause with great dedication for several years and he has provided a lot of information to those of us in Congress who are interested in the cause of human rights and freedom in South Asia.

Mr. Speaker, I would simply like to take this opportunity to salute the International Sikh Organization on a very successful convention and wish it continued success in the future. We can support its efforts to bring freedom to the Sikh people, and other regions in South Asia by insisting that human rights are observed and by declaring our support for a free and fair plebiscite under international monitoring on the question of independence.

***

Document

CONGRESSIONAL RECORD -- EXTENSIONS

Wednesday, September 24, 2003
108th Congress, 1st Session
149 Cong Rec E 1876

REFERENCE: Vol. 149, No. 132
SECTION: Extension of Remarks
TITLE: MEMBERS OF CONGRESS WRITE TO STATE DEPARTMENT: WITHDRAW OFFENSIVE TERRORISM VIDEO

Speech of
HON. EDOLPHUS TOWNS
State of New York
in the House of Representatives
Wednesday, September 24, 2003

Mr. TOWNS . Mr. Speaker, I am proud to have co-sponsored with the gentleman from Indiana a recent letter to the State Department asking them to withdraw the offensive video "Terrorism: A War Without Borders," which characterized all Sikhs as terrorists. This is offensive and against America's principles. As a minority, I take special offense at this kind of characterization of any minority group.

While the video may have had some usefulness in reminding Americans what they can do to help combat the threat of terrorism, its stereotyping of Sikhs as terrorists is unacceptable.

Let me quote from the letter, Mr. Speaker: "This video should be corrected or withdrawn immediately. The United States government should not be in the business of spreading inaccurate information, especially when that information is offensive to a hard-working, honorable people and serves only to promote the interests of a foreign regime."

The Sikhs are hard-working people who have been involved in every aspect of American life. One Sikh American, Dalip Singh Saund, even served in the U.S. Congress. Back in the subcontinent, they are one of many national groups, along with predominantly Christian Nagas, Kashmiris, and others struggling for their sovereignty and independence from India, which is run by militant Hindu nationalists bent on imposing Hinduism on all aspects of Indian life. The Sikh leadership has committed to carrying out this struggle by peaceful, democratic, nonviolent means. Yet it is for seeking their freedom at all that India labels them "terrorists." In fact, shortly after India's independence Prime Minister Nehru issued a directive calling Sikhs a "criminal class" and ordering police to keep special track of them, despite the fact that the Sikhs, who were less than two percent of the population, gave the majority of the sacrifices in India's freedom struggle. I am very distressed to see the government of the United States repeating this offensive description.

That is why withdrawing this video is so important, Mr. Speaker. There were more than 300 cases of hate crimes or actions against Sikhs in the wake of September 11, 2001. For the United States to give support in an official production of the government to the characterization of all Sikhs as terrorists merely encourages more of this kind of hate against loyal, hard-working, honest Americans. It also unfairly supports the position of a repressive regime that has murdered over 250,000 Sikhs since the Golden Temple attack of June 1984, according to figures compiled by the Punjab State Magistracy and human rights groups, as well as over 200,000 Christians in Nagaland since 1947, over 85,000 Kashmiri Muslims since 1988, and tens of thousands of Assamese, Bodos, Dalits, Manipuris, Tamils, and others. It encourages a government that admits to holding 52,268 Sikh political prisoners and holds tens of thousands of other minorities as political prisoners as well, according to Amnesty International.

Mr. Speaker, we should not be endorsing the party line of such a repressive regime. Instead, we should be working to support freedom by stopping U.S. aid to India until all people there enjoy full and equal human rights and by supporting self-determination for the Sikhs of Khalistan, the Kashmiris, the Nagas, and everyone seeking freedom. That is the democratic way and it is the only way to bring real peace and freedom from terrorism to everyone in South Asia.

Mr. Speaker, I would like to place the letter from Members of Congress to Secretary Powell into the Record at this time for the information of my colleagues.

Congress of the United States,
Washington, DC
September 18, 2003.
Hon. Colin Powell,
Secretary of State,
Washington, DC.

Dear Secretary Powell: As Members of the United States Congress, we are very concerned about your Department's video, "War Without Borders." Your depiction of the Sikhs is discriminatory, unfair, and offensive.

The video is offensive to Sikhs around the world and to all people who support nondiscrimination and freedom. The video inaccurately broadly labels all of the world's 25 million Sikhs_500,000 of whom live in the United States_as terrorists. This is offensive and inaccurate.

The video's description of the June 1984 Indian military attack on the Golden Temple in Amritsar, the most sacred of Sikh shrines, misrepresents the circumstances of that unfortunate incident. Every terrorist act cited in the video is described as either the work of an individual or a group of a certain nationality or a group, such as Al Qaeda or the like, which honorably refrains from labelling an entire people as terrorists. Yet with the Sikhs it takes a different approach, referring to the terrorists merely as "Sikhs," thus implicitly creating the impression that all Sikhs are terrorists. But there were no terrorists in the Golden Temple complex. The book Chakravyuh: Web of Indian Secularism reprints letters showing conclusively that India planned this attack in order to kill Sant Jarnail Singh Bhindranwale and other Sikh leaders who spoke out for a sovereign Sikh state. Labelling all Sikhs who support an independent, sovereign Khalistan as terrorists is the propaganda line of the repressive Indian regime. We share your desire to have good relations with India, but good relations must not trump truth.

India is a repressive government. Over 250,000 Sikhs have been murdered by the Indian government since the Golden Temple attack, according to figures compiled by the Punjab State Magistracy and human rights groups and reported in The Politics of Genocide by Inderjit Singh Jaijee. According to a report by the Movement Against State Repression (MASR), the Indian government admits to holding 52,268 political prisoners under the brutal, repressive "Terrorist and Disruptive Activities Act" (TADA), which expired in 1995. In addition, India has murdered over 200,000 Christians in Nagaland since 1947, over 85,000 Kashmiri Muslims since 1988, and tens of thousands of Assamese, Bodos, Dalits, Manipuris, Tamils, and others. An Indian Cabinet minister said that everyone who lives in India must either be a Hindu or be subservient to Hinduism.

This video should be corrected or withdrawn immediately. The United States government should not be in the business of spreading inaccurate information, especially when that information is offensive to a hardworking, honorable people and serves only to promote the interests of a foreign regime.

Sincerely,
Dan Burton.
Ed Towns.
Wally Herger.

***

Document

CONGRESSIONAL RECORD -- EXTENSIONS

Wednesday, September 17, 2003
108th Congress, 1st Session
149 Cong Rec E 1837

REFERENCE: Vol. 149, No. 128
SECTION: Extension of Remarks
TITLE: STATE DEPARTMENT TERRORISM VIDEO OFFENSIVE, MUST BE
WITHDRAWN

Speech of
HON. EDOLPHUS TOWNS
State of New York
in the House of Representatives
Wednesday, September 17, 2003

Mr. TOWNS . Mr. Speaker, recently the State Department put out a video called "Terrorism: A War Without Borders" that is offensive. The video portrays all Sikhs as terrorists. This characterization is inaccurate. It is also offensive to any fair-minded person. How can the State Department portray an entire group as terrorists? Secretary Powell should order the immediate withdrawal of this offensive video. This kind of stereotyping is simply unacceptable.

There are more than half a million Sikhs in the United States. Are they all terrorists, Mr. Speaker? They are active in all phases of American life, from law to medicine to agriculture to information technology. These are people who contribute a lot to America's way of life. Many of them were attacked after September 11, yet they still believe in America.

To label all Sikhs terrorists demeans the Sikh people, their faith, and their national aspirations and culture. This is extremely unfair. Yet the video consistently labels Sikhs as "terrorists" while ignoring the brutal atrocities carried out against minorities by the Indian government. For example, the video's description of the attack on the Golden Temple in June 1984 simply refers to "Sikhs," thus condemning all Sikhs as members of a terrorist organization.

What the video ignores is that Sant Jarnail Singh Bhindranwale, General Shabeg Singh, and many other Sikh leaders took refuge in the Golden Temple to protect themselves from the atrocities that the Indian government was already carrying out. They had been threatened with violence for peacefully speaking out on behalf of the rights of their people.

Over 20,000 Sikhs were killed over that three-day period in June 1984 as the Indian government attacked the Golden Temple and 38 other Sikh Gurdwaras throughout Punjab to frighten the Sikhs and end their movement to free themselves. Instead, just as Bhindranwale predicted, they laid the foundations for an independent Sikh state called Khalistan, which finally declared its independence from India on October 7, 1987. Let me be among the first to congratulate the Sikhs on the upcoming anniversary of that event.

Mr. Speaker, we all seek good relations with India. But it is offensive and inappropriate to suppress atrocities and spread inaccurate propaganda to achieve this objective. Why is our government placing the derogatory label of terrorist on an entire people? This is not something the government of the United States, which was founded on tolerance, should be doing.

The State Department should immediately remove this from circulation immediately so that it can either be corrected or withdrawn. Fairness demands that we stop labelling entire peoples with derogatory characterizations like "terrorist."

Our government should stop American aid and trade with India until the Sikhs, the Nagas, the Kashmins and all the people of South Asia enjoy full freedom and democratic rights and we should strongly and actively support these peoples in their effort to have self-determination in free and independent states.

Mr. Speaker, I would like to insert the recent letter from International Sikh Organization to Secretary of State Powell about this video into the Record.

Guru Gobind Singh Ji, Tenth Master
Washington, DC, July 29, 2003.
Hon. Colin Powell
Secretary of State, Washington, DC.

Dear Secretary Powell: On behalf of the 25 million strong Sikh Nation and over 500,000 Sikhs in the United States, I am writing to express the outrage of the Sikh community at the new video "Terrorism: A War Without Borders." While Sikhs fully support the war against terrorism, your video inaccurately depicts Sikhs as terrorists.

The video is offensive to Sikhs around the world. It significantly misrepresents the Sikh faith and the Sikh culture. The video inaccurately uses the term "Sikh terrorist" to broadly label all of the world's 25 million Sikhs_500,000 of whom live in the United States_and condemns all people of the Sikh faith. This is offensive and inaccurate.

The video's description of the June 1984 Indian military attack on the Golden Temple in Amritsar, the most sacred of Sikh shrines, is completely bogus and entirely false. Every terrorist act cited in the video is described as either the work of an individual or a group of a certain nationality or a group with its own identity. But in the 1984 Attack on Darbar Sahib, the video refers to the terrorists as "Sikhs". It shows Sikhs, easily recognizable from their turbans and beards, with weapons in the Darbar Sahib complex along with some Indian soldiers. The fact is that there were no "terrorists" in Darbar Sahib. Sikh leaders, including Sant Jarnail Singh Bhindranwale and others, took refuge there to protect themselves from Indian government violence against Sikhs. Letters reprinted in the book Chakravyuh: Web of Indian Secularism *show conclusively that India pre-planned this attack in order to kill Bhindranwale and other Sikh leaders who spoke out peacefully for Sikh sovereignty. After the attack, Indira Gandhi said, "I have broken the back of the Sikh Nation by attacking the Golden Temple." If the sanctity of the Golden Temple cannot be protected, how can the Sikh Nation survive?*

Labelling all Sikhs who support an independent, sovereign Khalistan as terrorists is the propaganda line of the repressive Indian regime. I would expect better from the State Department, especially under your outstanding leadership, than to spout the cliches of Indian disinformation.

The segment on the Darbar Sahib attack states: "In an effort to establish an independent state, Sikh terrorists seized Darbar Sahib Shrine in Amritsar, India. Prime Minister Indira Gandhi ordered a military campaign to drive out the terrorists. Hundreds were killed." In fact, over 20,000 were murdered in the attack on Darbar Sahib and 38 other Sikh Gurdwaras throughout Punjab, which was known as Operation Bluestar. The aim of this operation was to wipe out the Sikh religion.

In actuality, it is the Indian government that is the terrorist organization. The Washington Times reported on January 2, 2002 that the Indian government is sponsoring cross-border terrorism in the Pakistani province of Sindh. India stationed troops on the border in Kashmir while Pakistani troops were helping American forces look for Al Qaeda operatives, forcing Pakistan to divert troops to that border and reducing the effectiveness of their help in the search for Al Qaeda. This was a de facto pro-terrorist action. It has provided heavy water to Iran and has done business with Iraq for many years. The Indian oil minister declared Iraq "a strategic partner."

In November 1994, the Indian newspaper Hitavada reported that India paid the late Governor of Punjab, Surendra Nath, about $1.5 billion to organize and support covert terrorist activities in Punjab and Kashmir. Two independent reports and an article in the New York Times magazine all showed that Indian forces were responsible for the massacre of 35 Sikhs in Chithisinghpora in March 2000 during President Clinton's visit. Indian forces were caught red-handed trying to set fire to a Gurdwara and some Sikh homes in a village in Kashmir. The book Soft Target conclusively shows that India blew up its own airliner, killing 329 innocent people, to blame the Sikhs. Why is the State Department trying to appease such a state?

In all, over 250,000 Sikhs have been murdered by the Indian government since the Golden Temple attack, according to figures compiled by the Punjab State Magistracy and human rights groups and reported in

The Politics of Genocide by Inderjit Singh Jaijee. According to a report by the Movement Against State Repression (MASR), the Indian government admits to holding 52,268 political prisoners under the brutal, repressive "Terrorist and Disruptive Activities Act" (TADA), which expired in 1995. Another 50,000 have been arrested, tortured, killed in custody, declared "unidentified," and secretly cremated. The man who exposed this secret cremation policy, Jaswant Singh Khalra, was kidnapped by the police and murdered while in police custody. His body was never handed over to his family.

India has murdered over 200,000 Christians in Nagaland since 1947, over 85,000 Kashmiri Muslims since 1988, and tens of thousands of Assamese, Bodos, Dalits, Manipuris, Tamils, and others. An Indian Cabinet minister said that everyone who lives in India must either be a Hindu or be subservient to Hinduism.

Since Christmas 1998, priests have been murdered, nuns have been raped, churches have been burned, Christian schools have been attacked. Missionary Graham Staines and his two sons, ages 8 and 10, were burned to death while sleeping in their jeep. Their killers chanted "Victory to Hannuman," a Hindu god. None of these people has been brought to justice. Missionary Joseph Cooper was deported back to Pennsylvania after Hindus attacked him so severely that he had to spend a week in the hospital. No action has been taken in these cases. Police broke up a Christian religious festival by opening fire on it. All over India, laws are being passed that ban conversion to any religion except Hinduism.

Newspaper reports show that the Indian government pre-planned the attack on Muslims in Gujarat last year in which 2,000 to 5,000 Muslims were killed, according to the Indian newspaper The Hindu. Police were ordered to stand aside and let the massacre happen, in a striking parallel to the 1984 Delhi massacre of Sikhs in which police were locked in their barracks while state-run television and radio called for more Sikh blood.

Secretary Powell, the State Department owes the Sikh Nation an apology. On behalf of the Sikh community in America and worldwide, I request an apology and correction from you for this offensive and inaccurate video. The video should be corrected or withdrawn. I thought that the United States of America was dedicated to the truth, not to spreading the disinformation of a terrorist regime.

I would like to meet with you about this at your earliest convenience. Please contact me at the above number to let me know when we can meet. Thank you for your time.

Sincerely,
Dr. Gurmit Singh Aulakh,
President, International Sikh Organization.

***

Document

CONGRESSIONAL RECORD -- EXTENSIONS

Tuesday, September 09, 2003
108th Congress, 1st Session
149 Cong Rec E 1739

REFERENCE: Vol. 149, No. 123
SECTION: Extension of Remarks
TITLE: SIKHS PROTEST ON INDIAN INDEPENDENCE DAY, DEMAND
FREEDOM

HON. EDOLPHUS TOWNS
State of New York
in the House of Representatives
Tuesday, September 9, 2003

Mr. TOWNS . Mr. Speaker, while we were in recess, India celebrated its Independence Day on August 15. I join my colleagues in congratulating India on 56 years of independence, but what is India really celebrating?

Indian Independence Day is certainly not a celebration for the minorities living under the boot of Indian repression. Is missionary Graham Staines, who was burned to death along with his two young sons while they slept in their jeep, celebrating? Is human-rights activist Jaswant Singh Khalra, who was murdered in police custody after exposing the Indian government's policy of mass cremations, celebrating? Is Gurdev Singh Kaunke, who was murdered by the Indian police official Swaran Singh Ghotna, celebrating? What about the priests who have been murdered, the nuns who have been raped, the Christians whose peaceful religious festival was broken up by police gunfire, or American missionary Joseph Cooper, who was thrown out of the country after being beaten so severely by Hindu nationalists that he had to spend a week in a hospital? Do you think they are celebrating Indian Independence Day? I seriously doubt it, Mr. Speaker.

India is a multinational state like the old Austro-Hungarian Empire or the Soviet Union. The record of history is that countries like that don't last. Eventually, they all break up. That makes India's 56 years of independence all the more remarkable, and perhaps it explains why India has to try to keep the country together by force.

This effort has claimed the lives of over a quarter of a million Sikhs, over 200,000 Christians in Nagaland, more than 85,000 Kashmiri Muslims as well as thousands of Muslims in Gujarat and other places around the country, and tens of thousands of Assamese, Bodos, Dalits, Manipuris, Tamils, and so many others. According to the Movement Against State Repression, India admitted to holding more than 52,000 Sikhs as political prisoners under TADA, a repressive law that expired in 1995. Some of these Sikhs have been in custody for almost 20 years without charge or trial. Even a Sikh Member of Parliament has recently had TADA charges brought to court against him. Amnesty International notes that tens of thousands of Christians, Muslims, and others are also being held as political prisoners, Mr. Speaker. Do you think they are celebrating India's independence?

Listen to what a spokesman for the Golden Temple, Narinder Singh, told National Public Radio on the fiftieth anniversary of Indian independence in 1997: "The Indian government, all the time they boast that they are secular, that they are democratic. They have nothing to do with a secularism, nothing to do with a democracy. They kill Sikhs just to please the majority." And Sikhs are unfortunately not the only ones. That is why Sikhs from the East Coast showed up to protest in front of the Indian Ambassador's residence, where an Independence Day celebration was being held. They demanded the basic democratic freedom of self-determination and freedom for the Sikh homeland, Khalistan, which declared itself independent on October 7, 1987.

Mr. Speaker, it is time for America to take a stand for freedom and democracy in South Asia. We must act now to cut off aid to India until it allows real democracy and freedom for the Sikhs, Christians, Dalits, Muslims, and other minorities. And we must put this Congress on record in full support of self determination for all the peoples and nations of South Asia in the form of a free and fair plebiscite on the question of independence. Self-determination is the cornerstone of democracy and India is not allowing self-determination for anyone but the upper-caste Brahmins. A free and fair plebiscite will allow everyone to have self-determination and allow this to happen peacefully. We must not allow militant Hindu fundamentalist theocrats to turn South Asia into another Yugoslavia, Mr. Speaker.

I would like to place the International Sikh Organization's press release on the Independence Day protest into the Record at this time.

Deceitful Indian Government Moves Independence Day Celebration To Avoid Sikh Demonstrators_ Are Victims of Indian Repression Celebrating?

Washington, D.C., August 15, 2003._The cowardly, deceitful Indian regime again moved its Independence Day celebration from the Indian Embassy in Washington, D.C. to the Ambassador's residence to avoid Sikhs who came from Pennsylvania, New Jersey, Maryland, and Virginia to protest Indian repression of Sikhs, Christians, Muslims, and other minorities and to demand an independent, sovereign Khalistan.

"This action shows the cowardice of the fundamentalist Hindu nationalists," said Dr. Gurmit Singh Aulakh, President of the Council of Khalistan. "They are afraid of a peaceful protest," Dr. Aulakh said. "That is not how democracies act," Dr. Aulakh said.

The protestors raised slogans like "India out of Khalistan", "Khalistan Zindabad", and others. They carried signs demanding the release of over 52,000 Sikh political prisoners in India as well as thousands of Christian, Muslim, and other political prisoners, denouncing India for its violent repression of minorities, pointing out India's long history of anti-

Americanism. and demanding freedom for Khalistan. Khalistan is the independent Sikh homeland declared on October 7, 1987. It has been under Indian occupation since then. When India became independent, Sikhs were equal partners in the transfer of power and were to receive their own state, but the weak and ignorant Sikh leaders of the time were tricked into staying with India on the promise that they would have "the glow of freedom" and no law affecting the Sikhs would pass without their consent. Sikhs ruled an independent and sovereign Punjab from 1710 to 1716 and again from 1765 to 1849 and were recognized by most of the countries of the world at that time. No Sikh representative has ever signed the Indian constitution. The Council of Khalistan is the government pro tempore of Khalistan, the Sikh homeland.

History shows that multinational states such as India are doomed to failure. Countries like Austria-Hungary, India's longtime friend the Soviet Union, Yugoslavia, Czechoslovakia, and others prove this point. India is not one country; it is a polyglot like those countries, thrown together for the convenience of the British colonialists. It is doomed to break up as they did. "We only hope that the breakup will be peaceful," said Dr. Aulakh, "and that the fundamentalist Hindu nationalists will not force a violent, bloody breakup like that of Yugoslavia." India is ruled by Hindu theocrats whose agenda is "Hindu, Hindi, Hindutva, Hindu Rashtra," or total Hindu domination of every facet of Indian life. An Indian Cabinet minister said that everyone who lives in India must be a Hindu or subservient to Hindus.

"It is clear that India does not accept Sikhs," said Dr. Aulakh. "The Indian government continues to persecute and kill our Sikh brethren," he said. "Sardar Atinder Pal Singh's question of 13 years ago is still the question facing the Sikh Nation: Why don't we liberate Khalistan? As Professor Darshan Singh, a former Jathedar, said, 'If a Sikh is not for Khalistan, he is not a Sikh'," Dr. Aulakh noted. An Indian newspaper reported on Tuesday that Sikhs in India had decided not to celebrate Indian Independence Day, but instead would hoist a black flag for the occasion. "This shows that the drive for freedom is still alive in Punjab," Dr. Aulakh said.

The Indian government has murdered over 250,000 Sikhs since 1984, more than 200,000 Christians since 1948, over 85,000 Muslims in Kashmir since 1988, and tens of thousands of Tamils, Assamese, Manipuris, Dalits (the aboriginal people of the subcontinent), and others. The Indian Supreme Court called the Indian government's murders of Sikhs "worse than a genocide."

"Is Jaswant Singh Khalra celebrating? Is Jathedar Kaunke celebrating? Is Graham Staines celebrating?," Dr. Aulakh asked. "How can a democracy celebrate the kind of violent repression that claimed their lives?"

Indian police arrested human-rights activist Jaswant Singh Khalra after he exposed their policy of mass cremation of Sikhs, in which over 50,000 Sikhs have been arrested, tortured, and murdered, then their bodies were declared unidentified and secretly cremated. He was mur-

dered in police custody. His body was not given to his family. The police never released the body of former Jathedar of the Akal Takht Gurdev Singh Kaunke after SSP Swaran Singh Ghotna murdered him. No one has been brought to justice for the Khalra kidnapping and murder. SSP Swaran Ghotna has never been brought to trial for the Kaunke murder. Yet according to a report by the Movement Against State Repression (MASR), 52,268 Sikhs are being held as political prisoners in India without charge or trial. Some have been in illegal custody since 1984!

Missionary Graham Staines was murdered along with his two sons, ages 8 and 10, by a mob of militant, fundamentalist Hindu nationalists who set fire to the jeep, surrounded it, and chanted "Victory to Hannuman," a Hindu god. None of the people involved has been tried. The persons who have murdered priests, raped nuns, and burned Christian churches have not been charged or tried. The murderers of 2,000 to 5,000 Muslims in Gujarat last year have never been brought to trial. An Indian newspaper reported that the police were ordered to stand aside in that massacre and not to get involved, a frightening parallel to the Delhi massacre of Sikhs in 1984.

"Only in a free Khalistan will the Sikh Nation prosper and get justice," said Dr. Aulakh. "India should act like a democracy and allow a plebiscite on independence for Khalistan and all the nations of South Asia," Dr. Aulakh said. "We must free Khalistan now."

***

Document

CONGRESSIONAL RECORD -- EXTENSIONS

Friday, July 18, 2003
108th Congress, 1st Session
149 Cong Rec E 1522

REFERENCE: Vol. 149, No. 107
SECTION: Extension of Remarks
TITLE: 19TH ANNIVERSARY OF THE INDIAN GOVERNMENT'S ATTACK
ON THE GOLDEN TEMPLE IN AMRISTAR

Speech of
HON. DAN BURTON
State of Indiana
in the House of Representatives
Thursday, July 17, 2003

Mr. BURTON of Indiana . Mr. Speaker, last month marked the nineteenth anniversary of the Indian government's attack on the Golden Temple in Amristar, the most sacred of Sikh shrines. The Indian government simultaneously attacked 38 other Sikh Temples, known as Gurdwaras, around India. It is reported that more than 20,000 Sikhs were killed in these attacks, which went by the name of Operation Bluestar.

The Sikh Nation has never forgotten this atrocity against them. These attacks laid the foundation of a sovereign, independent Sikh homeland, Khalistan, which was declared independent on October 7, 1987. Last month, they once again observed Khalistan Martyrs Day on June 7, marking the anniversary of the brutal attacks on the Golden Temple and the other Sikh Temples. Sikhs gathered in Washington, D.C. and protested outside the Indian Embassy. They chanted slogans and made speeches in support of freedom for the Sikh Nation.

Sikhs were equal partners in the transfer of power from the British and were supposed to have an independent state. Sikh leaders were promised that they would have "the glow of freedom" in India and no law would be passed affecting Sikhs without their consent. However, that is not the case. I would like to have the Council of Khalistan's press release on the Khalistan Martyrs Day events placed into the Congressional Record following my statement.

International Sikh Organization,
Washington, DC, June 7, 2003.
Sikhs Observe Khalistan Martyrs Day

Washington, D.C., June 7, 2003._It is a Sikh tradition and Sikh history that Sikhs never forgive or forget the attack on the Golden Temple, the Sikh Nation's holiest shrine. In that spirit, Sikhs from all over the East Coast gathered in Washington, D.C. today to observe Khalistan Martyrs Day. This is the anniversary of the Indian government's brutal military attack on the Golden Temple and 38 other Sikh Temples throughout Punjab, from June 3-6, 1984. More than 20,000 Sikhs were killed in those attacks, known as Operation Bluestar. These martyrs laid down their lives to lay the foundation for Khalistan. On October 7, 1987, the Sikh Nation declared its homeland, Khalistan, independent.

"We thank all the demonstrators who came to this important protest," said Dr. Gurmit Singh Aulakh, President of the Council of Khalistan. "These martyrs gave their lives so that the Sikh Nation could live in freedom," Dr. Aulakh said. "We salute them on Khalistan Martyrs' Day," he said. "As Sant Bhindranwale said, the Golden Temple attack laid the foundation of Khalistan."

Sikhs ruled Punjab until 1849 when the British conquered the subcontinent. Sikhs were equal partners during the transfer of power from the British. The Muslim leader Jinnah got Pakistan for his people, the Hindu leaders got India, but the Sikh leadership was fooled by the Hindu leadership promising that Sikhs would have "the glow of freedom" in Northwest India and the Sikhs took their share with India on that promise. No Sikh representative has ever signed the Indian constitution.

Former Senate Majority Leader George Mitchell (D-Me.) said, "The essence of democracy is the right to self-determination." The minority nations of South Asia need freedom. "Without political power nations perish. We must always remember these martyrs for their sacrifice," Dr.

Aulakh said. *"The best tribute to these martyrs would be the liberation of the Sikh homeland, Punjab, Khalistan, from the occupying Indian forces,"* he said. *"That must be the only objective,"* he said. *"We should use the opportunity presented by the situation in South Asia to liberate our homeland."*

The Golden Temple attack launched a campaign of genocide against the Sikhs that belies India's claims that it is a democracy. The Golden Temple attack made it clear that there is no place for Sikhs in India. Since 1984, India has engaged in a campaign of ethnic cleansing in which tens of thousands of Sikhs were murdered by the Indian police and security forces and secretly cremated after declaring them "unidentified." The Indian Supreme Court described this campaign as "worse than a genocide." General Narinder Singh has said, "Punjab is a police state." U.S. Congressman Dana Rohrabacher (R-Cal.) has said that for Sikhs, Kashmiri Muslims, and other minorities "India might as well be Nazi Germany."

According to a report by the Movement Against State Repression, India admitted that 52,268 Sikh political prisoners are rotting in Indian jails without charge or trial. Many have been in illegal custody since 1984. In February 2002, 42 Members of the U.S. Congress wrote to President Bush to get these Sikh political prisoners released. MASR report quotes the Punjab Civil Magistracy as writing "if we add up the figures of the last few years the number of innocent persons killed would run into lakhs [hundreds of thousands.]"

Indian security forces have murdered over 250,000 Sikhs since 1984, according to figures compiled by the Punjab State Magistracy and human-rights organizations. These figures were published in The Politics of Genocide by Inderjit Singh Jaijee. India has also killed over 200,000 Christians in Nagaland since 1947, over 80,000 Kashmiris since 1988, and tens of thousands of Tamils, Bodos, Dalits (the aboriginal people of the subcontinent labeled "Untouchables") as well as indigenous tribal peoples in Manipur, Assam and elsewhere. In March 2000, while former President Clinton was visiting India, the Indian government murdered 35 Sikhs in the village of Chithisinghpora, Kashmir and tried to blame the massacre on alleged militants. The Indian media reported that the police in Gujarat were ordered by the government to stand by and not to interfere with the massacre of Muslims there.

"Guru gave sovereignty to the Sikh Nation," Dr. Aulakh said. *"The Golden Temple massacre reminded us that if Sikhs are going to live with honor and dignity, we must have a free, sovereign, and independent Khalistan,"* he said.

***

Document

CONGRESSIONAL RECORD -- EXTENSIONS

Thursday, July 17, 2003
108th Congress, 1st Session
149 Cong Rec E 1494

REFERENCE: Vol. 149, No. 106
SECTION: Extension of Remarks
TITLE: FOR FREEDOM IN SOUTH ASIA

Speech of
HON. EDOLPHUS TOWNS
State of New York
in the House of Representatives
Wednesday, July 16, 2003

Mr. TOWNS . Mr. Speaker, I rise today to offer somewhat belated congratulations to the Sikh Nation on Vaisakhi Day, the anniversary of the creation of the Khalsa Panth, which occurred in April. This is a very important day in the Sikh calendar, the birthday of the Khalsa Panth.

The Khalsa Panth was created in a spirit of freedom, and this is reflected in their daily prayers in which they pray for the freedom of the Sikh Nation and the well being of all people. This freedom is an essential yearning of the human spirit and all people are entitled to freedom. Yet merely for trying to be free, the Sikhs have been oppressed by the Indian government, which has murdered more than 250,000 of them since 1984.

Against this backdrop, the Sikh Nation declared its independence on October 7, 1987, creating the new country of Khalistan. This was in a Sikh tradition of self-rule. From 1765 to 1849 Sikh ruled Punjab. They ran an inclusive government, with Hindus, Muslims, and others in high positions.

Now their dreams of freedom are being crushed by the force of 500,000 Indian troops while the Indian government tries to set up Hindutva_total Hindu domination of every aspect of the political, social, and cultural life of India, South Asia, and the people living there. One Indian Cabinet member was quoted as saying that everyone who lives in India must either be Hindu or be subservient to Hindus.

The Council of Khalistan, which leads the Sikh Nation's struggle to free its homeland, Khalistan, from Indian oppression, issued an excellent statement calling on Sikhs worldwide to use the occasion of the Sikh Nation's birthday to rededicate themselves to achieving freedom for the Sikhs in a sovereign, independent Khalistan. I would like to join in that call, Mr. Speaker. It is time to bring true freedom and democracy to South Asia. In addition, a free and sovereign Khalistan will be an American ally in the subcontinent.

We should declare our support for freedom for Khalistan and for all the other nations of South Asia that seek their freedom. And we should back this up by stopping aid to India until it learns the ways of democracy and self-determination for all peoples and nations. This is the most effective way that America, the bastion of freedom, can stand up for freedom for the oppressed peoples of South Asia.

Mr. Speaker, I would like to place the Council of Khalistan's open letter on Vaisakhi Day into the Record.

**Council of Khalistan,
Washington, DC, April 14, 2003.
Vaisakhi Message to the Sikh Nation**

Congratulations to the Khalsa Panth on Vaisakhi Day_In Grieb Sikhin Ko Deon Patshahi; Guru Gave Sovereignty to Sikh Nation, Sikh Nation Must Free Khalistan; Without Political Power, Nations Perish

Dear Khalsa Ji: WAHEGURU JIKAKHALSA, WAHEGURUJI KIATEH!

Happy Vaisakhi Day to you and your family, friends, and the Sangat. 304 years ago, Guru Gobind Singh Sahib established the Khalsa Panth, as desired by Almighty God. The Guru also gave sovereignty to the Sikh Nation. That is the reason that Sikhs always recite "Raj Kare Ga Khalsa."

Sikhs established a sovereign, independent Sikh state under the leadership of Banda Singh Bahadur from 1710 to 1716, then under the Sikh missals from 1765 until 1799 when Maharajah Ranjit Singh established Khalsa Raj in Punjab, which lasted until 1849 when the British conquered the subcontinent.

India is not a single nation. It is on the verge of disintegration. Multinational states like India historically have been doomed to disintegrate, as Austria-Hungary, the Soviet Union, Czechoslovakia, and Yugoslavia have shown us. The Sikh Nation must do its best to establish Khalsa Raj as soon as possible. The political situation in the world is very fluid today. The Kashmir problem must be resolved through self-determination, which is the essence of democracy. As soon as Kashmir goes, India will disintegrate, as L.K. Advani forecast.

Outside Sikhs have played and must continue to play an important role in the present struggle for an independent Khalistan. They have exposed Indian government violations of basic human rights of Sikhs and other minorities. They have internationalized the Sikh struggle for an independent Khalistan. They have also preserved Sikh history by documenting major events since 1984 in the Congressional Record.

Three million Sikhs live outside of India. They constitute a major political force in many democratic countries, including the United Kingdom, the United States, Canada, and others. I appeal to all Sikhs to get involved in the political process to preserve their interests in their home countries. Secure the help of political parties and officials to help free Khalistan and to preserve Sikh interests in your respective countries and also to help protect the Sikhs back in Punjab, Khalistan. Every Sikh must become a citizen of the country where he or she lives and become part of the political process. Only by beconung politically active will Sikhs be able to achieve our objectives of a free Khalistan and preserve our interests in our adopted countries.

The next generations of Sikhs are citizens of these adopted countries. They were born there and they are going to stay. They must play a very constructive role in the political, social, and economic life of thecountry. Make sure that our children are very well educated. There should not be any Sikh child, boy or girl, who does not have at least an undergraduate university degree. Make sure that your sons and your daughters are well educated. Make sure they get the best education that they can. Only by educating our women will we secure a better future for the Sikh Nation and for our coming generations.

Remember that the Sikh Nation must free our Sikh homeland, Punjab, Khalistan. Without political power nations perish. It is essential for the survival of the Sikh Nation.

Colonial rule was better for everyone in India except the Brahmins than Indian rule is. We have been victimized by repression, tyranny, discrimination, and other abuses of our basic, god-given rights. India has used genocide, murder, torture, rape, and everything in its arsenal to destroy the Sikh Nation. It has even blown up its own airliner to blame it on the Sikhs, as the book Soft Target, written by two Canadian journalists, proves beyond a doubt. They paid former Punjab governor Surendra Nath $1.5 billion to foment and support terrorism in Punjab and Kashmir.

The present Sikh leadership is dishonest, corrupt, and completely under Indian control. They are complicit in the crimes of the Indian regime. The book Chakravyuh: Web of Indian Secularism by Professor Gurtej Singh shows their complicity. They connived with the Indian government before the Golden Temple invasion to murder Sant Jarnail Singh Bhindranwale, General Shabeg Singh, and thousands of other good Sikhs who were working for Sikh freedom. The Indian government has murdered over 250,000 Sikhs since 1984. The death sentence given to Professor Devinder Pal Singh Bhullar based on a false confession is the latest example of India's effort to eliminate the Sikh religion and intimidate the Sikh Nation.

According to a report by the Movement Against State Repression (MASR), 52,268 Sikhs are being held as political prisoners in India without charge or trial. Some have been in illegal custody since 1984! Yet Chief Minister Amarinder Singh denies that there are any political prisoners at all. Have they murdered them all? The Indian regime paid over 41,000 cash bounties to police officers for killing Sikhs, according to a 1994 report from the U.S. State Department. Will the Indian government publish the names of those Sikhs who were murdered by those police officials to get rewards? On October 7, 1987, the Sikh Nation declared the independence of its homeland, Punjab, Khalistan. No Sikh representative has ever signed the Indian constitution.

The Sikh nation has awakened. I call on all Sikhs to support the Khalsa Panchayat. These good Sikhs forced Jathedar Manjit Singh of Kesgarh to resign. Now Jathedar Vedanti must resign along with him. Please help the Khalsa Panchayat in these efforts. And work to build a party that will lead a Shantmai Morcha to liberate our homeland, Khalistan, from

Indian occupation. Just as the Akalis took control from the Mahants of the last century, we must take control of our future from the new Mahants, the present Akali leadership and Indian-controlled Jathedars. We must liberate our homeland.

Only in a free Khalistan will the Sikh Nation prosper.-Only then will the Sikh Nation get justice. India must start acting like a democracy and allow self-determination in the form of a free and fair plebiscite on independence for Punjab, Khalistan and the other nations seeking their freedom from India. Let us join hands to secure our freedom, for future generations and ourselves.

> *Panth Da Sewadar,*
> *Dr. Gurmit Singh Aulakh,*
> *President, Council of Khalistan.*

***

Document

CONGRESSIONAL RECORD -- EXTENSIONS

Thursday, July 17, 2003
108th Congress, 1st Session
149 Cong Rec E 1497

REFERENCE: Vol. 149, No. 106
SECTION: Extension of Remarks
TITLE: NAGAS OPEN OFFICE IN D.C. TO FIGHT FOR FREEDOM

Speech of
HON. EDOLPHUS TOWNS
State of New York
in the House of Representatives
Wednesday, July 16, 2003

Mr. TOWNS . Mr. Speaker, as you know, there are many national groups fighting for their freedom from India. We have been following the struggles of the Sikhs to free their homeland of Khalistan for many years thanks to the tireless efforts of Dr. Gurmit Singh Aulakh, President of the Council of Khalistan. Now another of the minority nations that seeks freedom from India has opened an office to represent its interests in Washington, D.C. The people of Nagaland are now represented in a Washington office.

I am happy to see the Nagas open a Washington office. I would like to take this opportunity to congratulate them. Nagaland is predominantly Christian and the Nagas have suffered under Indian oppression for many years. India has murdered over 200,000 Nagas since 1947. They are a separate nation and people from predominantly Hindu India, but they are victims of India's ongoing efforts to establish fundamentalist Hindu hegemony over the entire subcontinent.

Nagaland is entitled to freedom. Freedom is the birthright of all peoples and nations. The essence of democracy is the right to self-determination and this right has been denied to the people of Nagaland just as it has been denied to the people of the Sikh homeland, Punjab, Khalistan, to the Kashmiri people, and to so many other nations living under the boot of Indian repression. It is time for India to start acting like the democracy it claims to be and settling these matters in a peaceful, democratic manner rather than trying to suppress the people and their natural ambitions by force.

The leaders of Nagaland have tried to establish their freedom peacefully through negotiations, but the Indian government has been unwilling to discuss independence with Nagaland. However, they finally recognized the Nagas as a separate people. This is the first step toward the independence of the Naga nation. Democratic India wishes to retain the right to continue repressing the minorities living under its rule.

That is why the opening of an office representing the freedom struggle of Nagaland is so important, Mr. Speaker. The Sikhs have had such an office for a long time, and the Kashmiris have also. The more information that can be put out about the brutal, repressive nature of the Indian government, the more success all of the movements for freedom will have. This will also be a significant boost for basic human rights throughout India, where Assamese, Bodos, Dalits (the dark-skinned aboriginal people of South Asia), Manipuris, Tamils, and so many others are being oppressed and killed for struggling for their freedom.

We can help in this effort. It is time to stop American aid to India until it respects basic human rights and to declare our support for the freedom of Nagaland, Khalistan, Kashmir, and all the oppressed nations of South Asia.

Mr. Speaker, I would like to insert a list of persecution of minorities in India into the Record at this time for the information of my colleagues.

Persecution of Minorities in India

Christians

- *Over 200,000 Christians in Nagaland have been murdered by the Indian government.*
- *Since Christmas 1998, Christians have been the favored target of Indian religious persecution.*
- *American missionary Joseph Cooper was expelled from India for preaching after he was beaten so severely he had to be hospitalized for a week.*
- *Gujarat, Tamil Nadu, and other states have recently passed laws banning conversion to any religion except Hinduism.*
- *Recently in Gujarat the government has been conducting a survey of Christians, asking how long they have been Christians, how long they have been in India, citizenship, and other intrusive questions.*

- *Hindu Nationalists associated with the parent organization of the ruling party have murdered several priests.*
- *Several nuns have been murdered.*
- *A nun named Sister Ruby was forced to drink her captors' urine.*
- *Hindu nationalists have burned churches.*
- *Christian schools and prayer halls have been attacked.*
- *Missionary Graham Staines and his two sons were burned to death while sleeping in their jeep by Hindu nationalists who chanted "Victory to Hannuman," a Hindu god.*
- *A Christian religious festival was broken up by police gunfire.*

Sikhs

- *Indian police have murdered over 250,000 Sikhs since 1984.*
- *52,268 Sikhs are rotting in Indian jails as political prisoners without charge or trial. Some have been there since 1984.*
- *The U.S. State Department reported that the Indian government paid over 41,000 cash bounties to police officers for killing Sikhs. One of these was awarded to a police officer who killed a three-year-old boy.*
- *In 1984, the Indian government attacked Sikhism's most sacred shrine, the Golden Temple, and 38 other Gurdwaras throughout Punjab, killing 20,000 Sikhs.*
- *Human-rights activist Jaswant Singh Khalra was killed in police custody after he exposed India's policy of secret cremations of Sikhs.*
- *Over 50,000 Sikhs have "disappeared" after they were picked up by the police. They were tortured, secretly cremated, then declared "unidentified bodies" and secretly cremated.*
- *The Indian government paid the late governor of Punjab, Surendra Nath, over $1.5 billion to generate and support terrorism in Punjab and Kashmir.*
- *Indian forces were caught red-handed trying to set fire to a Gurdwara and some Sikh homes in a village in Kashmir. Sikh and Muslim villagers overwhelmed them andstopped them.*
- *Indian forces carried out the March 2000 massacre of 35 Sikhs in Chithisinghpora, according to two independent studies.*
- *Over 20,000 Sikhs were murdered by the government in the Delhi massacres of Sikhs while police, on orders, stood by and did nothing.*
- *The Jathedar of the Akal Takht, Gurdev Singh Kaunke, was murdered by the police.*
- *The driver for Baba Charan Singh, a religious leader, was killed when his legs were tied to two jeeps that drove off in opposite directions.*

Muslims

- *2,000 to 5,000 Muslims were murdered in Gujarat last March.*

- *The police stood aside and let the murders happen. They had no orders to stop it.*
- *According to the Hindustan Times, the government pre-planned that massacre.*
- *Over 85,000 Muslims in Kashmir have been murdered by Indian forces.*
- *Hindu nationalists destroyed the most revered mosque in India, the Babri Mosque in Ayodhya, to build a Hindu Temple.*
- *India has not kept the promise it made in 1948 to hold a plebiscite on the future of Kashmir.*

Others

- *A Dalit girl was blinded by her teacher after she drank water from the community pitcher.*
- *A Dalit constable went into a Temple to take shelter on a rainy day and was stoned to death by the Brahmins in attendance.*

***

Document

CONGRESSIONAL RECORD -- EXTENSIONS

Wednesday, March 26, 2003
108th Congress, 1st Session
149 Cong Rec E 577

REFERENCE: Vol. 149, No. 49
SECTION: Extension of Remarks
TITLE: THE RIGHT TO SELF-DETERMINATION

Speech of
HON. DAN BURTON
State of Indiana
in the House of Representatives
Wednesday, March 26, 2003

Mr. BURTON of Indiana . Mr. Speaker, the right to self-determination is the essence of democracy. The lack of it is one reason that many of us here in Congress believe India falls short of a full-fledged democracy.

In January 1949, India promised the United Nations that it would allow self-determination in Kashmir through a free and fair vote. It is now 2003 and this plebiscite has still not been held. India refuses to allow the Sikhs of Punjab, Khalistan, predominantly Christian Nagaland, Muslim Kashmir, and the other nations seeking their freedom from India to exercise their right to self determination through a free and fair vote, the democratic way, despite their claim that there is no support for independence. If not, why not just hold a vote and get the issue behind you?

Instead of following the democratic principle of self-determination, India has tried to continue the subjugation of the Sikhs, Christians, Muslims, and other minorities through force. They have murdered over 250,000 Sikhs since 1984, over 200,000 Christians in Nagaland since 1947, over 85,000 Muslims in Kashmir since 1988, and tens of thousands of other minorities, including Assamese, Bodos, Dalits, Manipuris, and Tamils. A report from the Movement Against State Repression showed that India admitted to holding 52,268 Sikhs as political prisoners under the expired TADA law, one of the most repressive laws I know of. TADA expired in 1995. Some of these political prisoners have been held in illegal detention since 1984. According to Amnesty International, tens of thousands of other minorities, such as Christians, Muslims, and others, are also being held as political prisoners. How can a democratic country hold political prisoners? The State Department reported in 1994 that over 41,000 cash bounties were paid to police officers for killing Sikhs. They picked up human-rights activist Jaswant Singh Khalra after he exposed their practice of secret cremations and Mr. Khalra was killed in police custody. Independent investigations showed that the Indian government's forces carried out the massacre of 35 Sikhs in March 2000.

Recently, the All India Christian Council reported that the government is sending out agents to seek intrusive information about Christians, such as whether they are first-generation Christians and how long they have been in India. This is happening in a country where American missionary Joseph Cooper was severely beaten and had to spend a week in the hospital, then was thrown out of the country for the crime of preaching. Australian missionary Graham Staines and his two sons were burned to death while they slept in their jeep by militant Hindu nationalists chanting "Victory to Hannuman," a Hindu god. Priests have been murdered, nuns have been raped, churches have been burned, and schools and prayer halls have been violently attacked. A Christian festival was ended by police gunfire. Now two states, Gujarat and Tamil Nadu, have enacted laws prohibiting conversions to any religion except Hinduism. The survey of Christians is also occurring in Gujarat.

Gujarat is the state where at least 2,000 and up to 5,000 Muslims were murdered last year, according to Indian newspapers. The press also reported that the government planned the attacks in advance.

Mr. Speaker, the Council of Khalistan recently issued an open letter detailing these and other Indian government atrocities, repression, and violations of human rights. I urge everyone to read it. India has 18 official languages and it is not one nation. India must stop violating the human rights of minorities and instead follow democratic principles by allowing self-determination for all the minority nations that seek it. That is the only way to bring real freedom, peace, and stability to the region. Until then, the United States should stop its aid with India and Congress should put this country on record in support of self-determination.

I would like to place the Council of Khalistan's open letter into the Record at this time, Mr. Speaker. It will be very informative to my colleagues and the people of this country.

March 19, 2003.
Open Letter to the Sikh Nation: Khalsa Panchayat Represents Sikh Nation and Deserves Our Support; Akali Leadership and Jathedars Are Under Indian Government Control

We must liberate Khalistan now. This is the only way for the Sikh Nation to prosper, progress, and project the Sikh religion and the interest of the Sikh Nation. Nations and religions without political power disappear.

Our experience since 1947 has been very disappointing and repressive. Colonial rule was better for everyone in India except the Brahmins than Indian rule is. We have been victimized by repression, tyranny, discrimination, and other abuses of our basic, god-given rights. India has used genocide, murder, torture, rape, and everything in its arsenal to destroy the Sikh Nation. It has even blown up its own airliner to blame it on the Sikhs, as the book Soft Target, written by two Canadian journalists, proves beyond a doubt. They paid former Punjab governor Surendra Nath $1.5 billion to foment and support terrorism in Punjab and Kashmir.

The present Sikh leadership is dishonest, corrupt, and completely under Indian control. They are complicit in the crimes of the Indian regime. The book Chakravyuh: Web of Indian Secularism by Professor Gurtej Singh shows their complicity. What a shame that they connived with the Indian government before the Golden Temple invasion to murder Sant Jarnail Singh Bhindranwale, General Shabeg Singh, and thousands of other good Sikhs who were working for Sikh freedom. Over 20,000 Sikhs were murdered in the attack on the Golden Temple and 38 other Sikh Gurdwaras throughout Punjab, Khalistan in June 1984. Another 20,000 were killed in the November 1984 massacres in Delhi and other cities. Overall, the Indian government, which boasts about being "the world's largest democracy," has murdered over 250,000 Sikhs since 1984. The death sentence given to Professor Devinder Pal Singh Bhullar based on a false confession is the latest example of India's effort to eliminate the Sikh religion and intimidate the Sikh Nation.

Indian police arrested human-rights activist Jaswant Singh Khalra after he exposed their policy of mass cremation of Sikhs, in which over 50,000 Sikhs have been picked up, tortured, and killed, then their bodies are declared unidentified and secretly cremated. Then Mr. Khalra was murdered in police custody. His body was not given to his family. Rajiv Singh Randhawa, the only witness to the Khalra kidnapping tried to give a petition to Jack Straw, then the British Home Minister and now its Foreign Minister, outside the Golden Temple in Amritsar. For this, he was arrested and tortured.

Similarly, the police murdered former Jathedar of the Akal Takht Gurdev Singh Kaunke. His body was not handed over to his family. No one has been brought to justice for the Khalra kidnapping and murder.

The murderer of Akal Takht Jathedar Gurdev Singh Kaunke, SSP Swaran Ghotna, has never been brought to trial. Nor have those who carried out the massacre of 35 Sikhs in Chithisinghpora three years ago this month.

According to a report by the Movement Against State Repression (MASR), 52,268 Sikhs are being held as political prisoners in India without charge or trial. Some have been in illegal custody since 1984! Yet Chief Minister Amarinder Singh denies that there are any political prisoners at all. Have they murdered them all? Most of these political prisoners were taken into illegal custody under the Beant Singh regime, a Congress government. Can't Amarinder Singh find these records? Amarinder Singh should be commended for prosecuting corrupt government officials. Now he should keep his promise to prosecute Parkash Singh Badal and his family for their corruption during his tenure as Chief Minister. He sold government jobs for money. Services were only delivered after they received bribes. His wife Surinder Kaur is so experienced at this corrupt practice that she could tell the amount of money in a paper bag just by lifting it. What a shame for the Akali government! The Badal family has tarnished the pious Akali name of the first half of the last century. That Sikh leadership gave sacrifices for the glory of the Khalsa Panth.

The Indian regime paid over 41,000 cash bounties to police officers for killing Sikhs, according to a 1994 report from the U.S. State Department. One of these bounties was paid to a policeman who killed a three-year-old boy! In another case, a man brought suit because he had been listed as having been killed in one of these incidents but was actually alive. Who was murdered in his place?

The legs of the driver for Baba Charan Singh were tied to two jeeps which drove off in opposite directions and he was torn in half. An attorney in Ropar who defended Sikh youth was picked up along with his wife and his two-year-old son. They were made to "disappear" just like 50,000 other Sikhs. The Indian Supreme Court called the Indian government's murders of Sikhs "worse than a genocide." On October 7, 1987, the Sikh Nation declared the independence of its homeland, Punjab, Khalistan. No Sikh representative has ever signed the Indian constitution.

The Sikh nation has awakened. I call on all Sikhs to support the Khalsa Panchayat. These good Sikhs forced Jathedar Manjit Singh of Kesgarh to resign. Now Jathedar Vedanti must resign along with him. Please help the Khalsa Panchayat in these efforts. And work to build a party that will lead a Shantmai Morcha to liberate our homeland, Khalistan, from Indian occupation. Just as the Akalis took control from the Mahants of the last century, we must take control of our future from the new Mahants, the present Akali leadership and Indian-controlled Jathedars.

India is on the verge of disintegration. Khalistan will soon be free. Home Minister L.K. Advani said that if Kashmir goes, India goes. The Kashmir problem has been internationalized. The only way to solve the Kashmir problem is to have a referendum where the Kashmiri people can decide their own future. With self-determination, the Kashmiri people will either be independent or go with Pakistan. Either way, Kashmir is going to go. As soon as Kashmir goes, Khalistan will be independent within a year. We can achieve freedom much earlier if our leadership is not under Indian control and they are sincere and honest.

Only in a free Khalistan will the Sikh Nation prosper. Only then will the Sikh Nation get justice. India must start acting like a democracy and allow self-determination in the form of a free and fair plebiscite on independence for Punjab, Khalistan and the other nations seeking their freedom from India. Let us join hands to secure our freedom, for ourselves and future generations.

> *Sincerely,*
> *Dr. Gurmit Singh Aulakh,*
> *President, Council of Khalistan.*

***

Document

CONGRESSIONAL RECORD -- EXTENSIONS

Tuesday, March 25, 2003
108th Congress, 1st Session
149 Cong Rec E 571

REFERENCE: Vol. 149, No. 48
SECTION: Extension of Remarks
TITLE: APPRECIATING DR. GURMIT SINGH AULAKH FOR BRINGING PLIGHT OF SIKHS, OTHER MINORITIES TO INTERNATIONAL ATTENTION

Speech of
HON. EDOLPHUS TOWNS
State of New York
in the House of Representatives
Tuesday, March 25, 2003

Mr. TOWNS . Mr. Speaker, for 17 years, Dr. Gurmit Singh Aulakh has been serving the Sikhs in this country and worldwide, first as President of the International Sikh Organization, a post in which he still serves, and later as President of the Council of Khalistan, which came into being when Sikhs declared their independence from India on October 7, 1987. He has been a tireless worker for the rights of Sikhs and other minorities in India, such as Christians, Muslims, Dalits (the dark-skinned "Untouchables," the aboriginal people of South Asia), and others. Many of us in Congress have helped to expose the tyranny and terrorism that India has practiced against these groups and Dr. Aulakh has been a friend and an invaluable source of information to us.

Sikhs are a separate nation and they ruled Punjab from 1710 to 1716 and again from 1765 to 1849. They are working to reclaim their lost sovereignty. They face persecution and terror for doing so.

Dr. Aulakh's efforts and the support of those who back him have been crucial in bringing the Sikh struggle to the attention of the international community. He has worked with us in this House to the true and accurate history of the Sikh struggle and the struggles of other minorities in India. In these efforts he has been opposed by the Indian government, which has spent large amounts of money to counteract his efforts and spread disinformation. They even started a rumor on the Internet that he was dead. He has a tough job trying to achieve freedom for the Sikh Nation against the opposition of the Indian government.

Even in the U.S. Congress, the Indian government has formed the Indian Caucus, which has 139 members, to support India and deflect our attention away from the oppression and terror there. He has done a yeoman job in exposing the brutal oppression of the Indian government against the Sikh Nation which has killed over 250,000 Sikhs since 1984. Another 50,000 Sikhs were arrested by the police, tortured, murdered, and then declared "unidentified bodies" and secretly cremated. He has brought to the attention of Congress that even at present, 52,268 Sikh political prisoners are rotting in Indian jails as political prisoners, according to the Movement Against State Repression.

Dr. Aulakh has been tireless in promoting self-determination, which is the cornerstone of democracy. He has been a relentless advocate for the cause of Sikh freedom and the independence of their homeland, Punjab, Khalistan.

Like those of us in Congress, Dr. Aulakh knows and appreciates the privilege of service. Service is essential to the Sikh religion as it is to all religions.

Accordingly, Mr. Speaker, I would like to take this opportunity to salute Dr. Gurmit Singh Aulakh.

***

Document

CONGRESSIONAL RECORD -- EXTENSIONS

Tuesday, March 18, 2003
108th Congress, 1st Session
149 Cong Rec E 500

REFERENCE: Vol. 149, No. 43
SECTION: Extension of Remarks
TITLE: INDIAN POLICE COLLECTING DATA ON CHRISTIANS

HON. EDOLPHUS TOWNS
State of New York
in the House of Representatives
Tuesday, March 18, 2003

Mr. TOWNS . Mr. Speaker, I was disturbed to read an article in the Hindustan Times saying that Indian police are collecting data on Christians in Gujarat. Gujarat is the site of the massacres of Muslims last March in which 2,000 to 5,000 Muslims were killed. Hasn't Gujarat seen enough trouble?

According to the report, the All-India Christian Council submitted a memorandum to the state police chief detailing the survey. The police are seeking information on family sizes, job profiles, sources of funds, and even whether the person is a first-generation Christian and/or has converted. At least 25 Christian institutions have been questioned in just a few days. The article quotes Bishop Gregory of Rajkot as saying that he was asked "about the number of Christians and institutions here." Father Cedric Prakash of the United Christian Forum for Human Rights predicts that "this survey may be a buildup to the anticonversion bill."

India has already outlawed conversions to any religion but Hinduism in two states. Recently the ruling BJP has begun an effort to make that national.

This is outrageous, Mr. Speaker. It is a major violation of religious freedom, which is one of the main pillars of a democracy. Instead, India is again acting like a Hindu fundamentalist theocracy.

In 1997, a Christian festival on the theme "Jesus is the answer" ended when the police fired their guns at it to close it down after they received complaints that the festival was converting people. Missionary Graham Staines and his two sons, ages 8 and 10, were murdered while they slept in their jeep. The murderers surrounded the jeep and chanted "Victory to Hannuman, " according to contemporaneous news reports. None of these people has been held accountable. Now an American missionary, Joseph Cooper, has been expelled from India after being severely beaten by Hindu nationalists.

Since 1998, Christian priests have been murdered, nuns have been raped, churches have been burned as they were in the Old South during segregation, Christian schools and prayer halls have been violently attacked. Since India's independence in 1947, its forces have murdered over 200,000 Christians. They have also murdered over 250,000 Sikhs since 1984, over 85,000 Kashmiri Muslims since 1988, and tens of thousands of Dalits, Bodos, Assainese, Manipuris, Tamils, and other minorities. Many lowercaste Hindus are converting to Christianity and other religions and now the BJP is passing laws to prohibit this.

Mr. Speaker, these are the acts of a theocratic tyranny, not a real democracy. We must impose the sanctions appropriate for a violator of religious freedom. We must also stop our aid and trade with India until it begins to allow the exercise of basic human and religious rights. And we must support selfdetermination for all the people of South Asia as the best way to bring real freedom, peace, stability, and prosperity to that troubled region.

Mr. Speaker, I would like to place the Hindustan Times article into the Record at this time.

[From the Hindustan Times, Mar. 9, 2003]
Gujarat Christians Allege Survey of Families
(By Rathin Das)

Ahmedabad, March 8._The Gujarat Police have reportedly started a discreet survey of Christians in some parts of the state, seeking information on family sizes, job profiles and sources of foreign funds. The All-India Christian Council, which submitted a memorandum to the state police chief on Friday, is planning to move the High Court over the issue next week.

State Director General of Police K. Chakravarthy told the Hindustan Times that no statewide survey had been ordered. He added, however, that some information might have been sought from some people on the orders of district police chiefs.

A senior home department official echoed the state police chief. He told the Hindustan Times that no survey of Christians had been ordered. "It may be a survey about foreign funds and its use, but that is applicable for institutions of all communities," he said.

But despite official denials, community leaders alleged that policemen came calling at some houses in Ahmedabad, Sabarkantha, Banaskantha and Kutch districts over the past few days and asked about the antecedents and assets of Christian families.

Community leaders also said at least 25 Christian institutions and families had been questioned over the past few days. Police personnel who visited Christian institutions, they said, wanted information on the number of Christians in the area and other details, like the sources of their funds. Bishop Gregory of Rajkot, who was questioned by the police on Friday, said: "I was asked about the number of Christians and institutions here." The police also asked him to contact the nearest police station if he needed help, Bishop Gregory told this correspondent.

The police have also asked some Christians whether they converted voluntarily or under pressure, and whether they were first-generation Christians.

"This survey may be a build-up to the anti-conversion bill the government wants to introduce in the state assembly during this session," said Father Cedric Prakash of the United Christian Forum for Human Rights.

One church leader in Saurashtra was asked whether Christians would hold demonstrations if the anti-conversion bill is introduced in the assembly, sources said.

Individual Christians are scared to speak to the press as many of them are in government employment. In the wake of the attack on Christians and the burning of churches in the Dangs district around Christmas 1998, the state intelligence department had ordered a similar survey, but abandoned it after a petition was filed in the Gujarat High Court.

Minority report: July 1998_Copies of the New Testament burnt in a Rajkot school; Oct 1998_Christian congregation attacked in Vadodara; Dec 1998_Government threatens to stop grants to Christian schools; Dec 1998_Churches razed in Dangs district; Jan 1999_PM visits Dangs, calls for national debate on conversions; Feb 1999_Secret survey ordered, first of Christians, later of Muslims; Jan 2000_Government lifts ban on employees joining RSS.

***

Document

CONGRESSIONAL RECORD -- EXTENSIONS

Tuesday, March 18, 2003
108th Congress, 1st Session
149 Cong Rec E 501

REFERENCE: Vol. 149, No. 43
SECTION: Extension of Remarks
TITLE: SAVE THE LIFE OF DEVINDER PAL SINGH BHULLAR

HON. EDOLPHUS TOWNS
State of New York
in the House of Representatives
Tuesday, March 18, 2003

Mr. TOWNS . Mr. Speaker, Devinder Pal Singh Bhullar is about to be put to death in India for a crime even India admitted he didn't commit.

I thank my friend Dr. Gurmit Singh Aulakh, President of the Council of Khalistan, for bringing this shameful case to my attention. The Council of Khalistan put out a very informative press release on the case.

The chief judge of a three-judge panel from India's Supreme Court found Mr. Bhullar not guilty of the crime of which he was accused, involvement in a bombing. The judge ordered Mr. Bhullar's release. Instead, the Indian government tortured Mr. Bhullar until he signed a fake confession. Now they are trying to put him to death.

Unfortunately, this is just the latest episode in India's abuse of minorities, which has been well documented in Congress by many of my colleagues and me. This brutal atrocity against justice must be stopped.

The Bush Administration should demand Mr. Bhullar's release, or at least a new trial. In addition, they should impose sanctions on India, cut off its aid and trade, and put this Congress on record in support of self-determination for the Sikh Nation of Khalistan and the other 16 minority nations seeking their freedom from India. This should be done in the democratic way, through a free and fair plebiscite. It is time for India to start acting like a democracy, and it can start by sparing the life of Devinder Pal Singh Bhullar.

Mr. Speaker, I would like to enter the Council of Khalistan's press release on Bhullar into the Record at this time for the information of my colleagues and the public.

[Council of Khalistan_Press Release, Feb. 25, 2003]
Devinder Pal Singh Bhullar's Life Must Be Spared
Indian Constitution Only Protects Majority Hindus Minorities
Eliminated, Directly or by Courts

Washington, D.C._The impending execution of Devinder Pal Singh Bhullar shows that the Constitution of India only protects the majority Hindu population, according to Dr. Gurmit Singh Aulakh, President of the Council of Khalistan, which leads the Sikh struggle for independence from India. Dr. Aulakh called on the President of India to stop the execution. Bhullar was accused of a 1993 bomb blast near the Youth Congress office in Delhi in which 20 people were killed. Congress leader M.S. Bitta lost a leg in that attack.

The presiding Judge of a three-Judge bench in the Supreme Court of India found Professor Bhullar, a political activist, 'Not Guilty' and directed that he be released. However, Professor Bhullar was convicted based on a forced confession obtained through torture, which was retracted. On that basis India wants to impose capital punishment on Professor Bhullar. Sajjan Kumar and H.K.L. Bhagat, who personally incited the murder of thousands of Sikhs in Delhi, got off scot-free without any punishment. Even by Indian standards, this is an outrageous miscarriage of justice.

"The Bhullar case is merely the latest example of how India eliminates minorities," said Dr. Aulakh. Indian police arrested human-rights activist Jaswant Singh Khalra after he exposed their policy of mass cremation of Sikhs, in which over 50,000 Sikhs have been picked up, tortured, and killed, then their bodies are declared unidentified and secretly cremated. Then Mr. Khalra was murdered in police custody. His body was not given to his family. Similarly, the police murdered former Jathedar of the Akal Takht Gurdev Singh Kaunke. His body was not handed over to his family.

Last spring the Indian police stood aside under orders while militant Hindus murdered 2,000 to 5,000 Muslims in Gujarat. Australian missionary Graham Staines was murdered a few years ago by VHP activists. Staines and his two young sons were burned to death while they slept in their jeep. Their killers surrounded the jeep and chanted "Victory to Hannuman," a Hindu god. After the murder, Staines's widow, who was working with lepers, was expelled from India. No one is ever punished for these atrocities. Nuns have been raped, priests have been murdered, and Christian churches have been burned by the fanatic, fundamentalist Hindu nationalist militants.

"It is clear from these actions that India is not the democracy it claims to be," said Dr. Aulakh. "Instead it is a tyrannical Hindu theocracy where minorities die or disappear," he said. "There is a consistent

pattern of Indian government efforts to protect its tyrannical rule over the minorities of South Asia."

The Indian government has murdered over 250,000 Sikhs since 1984, more than 200,000 Christians since 1948, over 85,000 Muslims in Kashmir since 1988, and tens of thousands of Tamils, Assamese, Manipuris, Dalits (the aboriginal people of the subcontinent), and others. More than 52,000 Sikhs are being held as political prisoners. The Indian Supreme Court called the Indian government's murders of Sikhs "worse than a genocide." On October 7, 1987, the Sikh Nation declared the independence of its homeland, Punjab, Khalistan. No Sikh representative has ever signed the Indian constitution. The Council of Khalistan is the government pro tempore of Khalistan, the Sikh homeland. The Sikh Nation demands freedom for its homeland, Khalistan.

"Only in a free and sovereign Khalistan will the Sikh Nation prosper. In a democracy, the right to self-determination is the sinc qua non and India should allow a plebiscite for the freedom of the Sikh Nation and all the nations of South Asia," Dr. Aulakh said.

***

Document

CONGRESSIONAL RECORD -- EXTENSIONS

Thursday, March 13, 2003
108th Congress, 1st Session
149 Cong Rec E 474

REFERENCE: Vol. 149, No. 41
SECTION: Extension of Remarks
TITLE: SPARE THE LIFE OF DEVINDER PAL SINGH BHULLAR

HON. DAN BURTON
State of Indiana
in the House of Representatives
Thursday, March 13, 2003

Mr. BURTON of Indiana . Mr. Speaker, Devinder Singh Pal Bhullar faces the death penalty. He should be spared. His pending execution shows that the Indian constitution only protects the Hindu majority.

Bhullar was accused of being involved in a 1993 bombing near the offices of the Youth Congress in Delhi. 20 people were killed in that blast and Congress leader M.S. Bitta lost a leg.

This might be a justifiable sentence for such a crime except for a few small details. Mr. Bhullar was found "not guilty" by the presiding judge of a three-judge panel from India's Supreme Court. The judge directed that he be released. Apparently, that was not acceptable to the fundamentalist Hindu nationalist regime. So they tortured him to coerce him into signing a false confession which was subsequently retracted. Yet they are executing him on the basis of this forced confession.

This is offensive to anyone with a sense of justice. Mr. Speaker. This is not the way a democratic country does things. It is how criminal cases are handled in such models of democracy as Red China and Iraq. Meanwhile, Sajjan Kumar and H.K.L. Bhagat, the officials responsible for inciting the murders of thousands of Sikhs in Delhi, have never been brought to justice.

Unfortunately, this is typical of how India treats its minorities. Last year in Gujarat 2,000 to 5,000 Muslims were murdered by militant Hindu nationalists while police, under orders, stood by and did nothing. No one has been punished for this atrocity. Now police in Gujarat are demanding very intrusive information about Christians there. Meanwhile, two states have enacted laws prohibiting religious conversions_except to Hinduism, of course.

Police have murdered over a quarter of a million Sikhs, over 200,000 Christians in Nagaland, over 85,000 Muslims in Kashmir, and tens of thousands of Assamese, Bodos, Dalit "untouchables," Manipuris, Tamils, and other minorities. Indian forces were caught red-handed in a village in Kashmir trying to set fire to the Sikh Gurdwara and some homes there. Two studies have shown that Indian forces carried out the massacre of 35 Sikhs in Chithisinghpora three years ago this month.

Missionary Graham Staines and his two sons were murdered by being burned to death in their jeep while the killers surrounded the jeep and chanted "Victory to Hannuman." Missionary Joseph Cooper was severely beaten and had to spend a week in the hospital. Then he was expelled from the country for preaching. The widow of Mr. Staines was also expelled from India. Christian churches have been burned and schools and prayer halls have been violently attacked with impunity. There have been priests murdered and nuns raped.

In 1995, Indian police picked up human-rights activist Jaswant Singh Khalra did a study of cremation grounds in Punjab which showed that thousands of Sikhs have been picked up, tortured, murdered, then declared "unidentified" and secretly cremated. For his efforts, Khalra was picked up by the police and murdered while in police custody. More than 52,000 Sikhs sit in jail as political prisoners without charge or trial.

The time has come to stop our aid to India. We should also support the self-determination to which all peoples and nations are entitled. This is the only way to end atrocities such as these and to ensure peace, freedom, stability, and prosperity in South Asia.

Mr. Speaker, I would like to place the Council of Khalistan's outstanding press release on the Bhullar case into the Record.

Devinder Pal Singh Bhullar's Life Must Be Spared
Minorities eliminated, directly or by courts

Washington, DC, Feb. 25, 2003._The impending execution of Devinder Pal Singh Bhullar shows that the Constitution of India only protects the majority Hindu population, according to Dr. Gurmit Singh

Aulakh, President of the Council of Khalistan, which leads the Sikh struggle for independence from India. Dr. Aulakh called on the President of India to stop the execution. Bhullar was accused of a 1993 bomb blast near the Youth Congress office in Delhi in which 20 people were killed. Congress leader M.S. Bitta lost a leg in that attack.

The presiding Judge of a three-Judge bench in the Supreme Court of India found Professor Bhullar, a political activist, "Not Guilty" and directed that he be released. However, Professor Bhullar was convicted based on a forced confession obtained through torture, which was retracted. On that basis India wants to impose capital punishment on Professor Bhullar. Sajjan Kumar and H.K.L. Bhagat, who personally incited the murder of thousands of Sikhs in Delhi, go off scot-free without any punishment. Even by Indian standards, this is an outrageous miscarriage of justice.

"The Bhullar case is merely the latest example of how India eliminates minorities," said Dr. Aulakh. Indian police arrested human-rights activist Jaswant Singh Khalra after he exposed their policy of mass cremation of Sikhs, in which over 50,000 Sikhs have been picked up, tortured, and killed, then their bodies are declared unidentified and secretly cremated. Then Mr. Khalra was murdered in police custody. His body was not given to his family. Similarly, the police murdered former Jathedar of the Akal Takht Gurdev Singh Kaunke. His body was not handed over to his family.

Last spring the Indian police stood aside under orders while militant Hindus murdered 2,000 to 5,000 Muslims in Gujarat. Australian missionary Graham Staines was murdered a few years ago by VHP activists. Staines and his two young sons were burned to death while they slept in their jeep. Their killers surrounded the jeep and chanted "Victory to Hannuman," a Hindu god. After the murder, Staines' widow, who was working with lepers, was expelled from India. No one was ever punished for these atrocities. Nuns have been raped, priests have been murdered, and Christian churches have been burned by the fanatic, fundamentalist Hindu nationalist militants.

"It is clear from these actions that India is not the democracy it claims to be," said Dr. Aulakh. "Instead it is a tyrannical Hindu theocracy where minorities die or disappear," he said. "There is a consistent pattern of Indian government efforts to protect its tyrannical rule over the minorities of South Asia."

The Indian government has murdered over 250,000 Sikhs since 1984, more than 200,000 Christians since 1948, over 85,000 muslims in Kashmir since 1988, and tens of thousands of Tamils, Assamese, Manipuris, Dalits (the aboriginal people of the subcontinent), and others. More than 52,000 Sikhs are being held as political prisoners. The Indian Supreme Court called the Indian government's murders of Sikhs "worse than a genocide." On October 7, 1987, the Sikh Nation declared the independence of its homeland, Punjab, Khalistan. No Sikh representative has ever signed the Indian constitution. The Council of Khalistan is the government pro tempore of Khalistan, the Sikh homeland. The Sikh Nation demands freedom for its homeland, Khalistan.

"Only in a free and sovereign Khalistan will the Sikh Nation prosper. In a democracy, the right to self-determination is the sine qua non and India should allow a plebiscite for the freedom of the Sikh Nation and all the nations of South Asia," Dr. Aulakh said.

***

Document

CONGRESSIONAL RECORD -- EXTENSIONS

Thursday, February 27, 2003
108th Congress, 1st Session
149 Cong Rec E 334

REFERENCE: Vol. 149, No. 32
SECTION: Extension of Remarks
TITLE: CANADIAN PLEA IN AIR INDIA CASE COVERS UP GOVERNMENT INVOLVEMENT

HON. EDOLPHUS TOWNS
State of New York
in the House of Representatives
Thursday, February 27, 2003

Mr. TOWNS . Mr. Speaker, recently, the Canadian courts accepted a plea bargain from Inderjit Singh Reyat in a case related to the bombing of an Air India jet in 1985 that killed 329 people. The plea covers up the clear and strong evidence that the Indian government itself blew up the airplane.

The book Soft Target, written by Canadian journalists Zuhair Kashmeri of the Toronto Globe and Mail and Brian McAndrew of the Toronto Star, shows that the story agreed to by Mr. Reyat matches a story first suggested in 1985 by the Royal Canadian Mounted Police (RCMP). A Sikh named Lal Singh reported that he was offered "two million dollars and settlement in a nice country" for false testimony in the case. He turned down that offer. There are some questions about whether the evidence in Reyat's first trial was valid, according to the National Post.

Canadian Member of Parliament David Kilgour wrote a book called Betrayal: The Spy Canada Abandoned about a Polish-Canadian double agent who was approached by the Indian government to carry out a second bombing. Soft Target shows that the Indian Consul General in Toronto knew more than the RCMP and the Canadian Security Investigative Service (CSIS) in the early hours of the investigation. Why did his daughter and wife, a friend of his who was an auto dealer, and the director of North American operations for the Indian government all cancel their reservations on the doomed flight at the last minute, Mr. Speaker?

Even if the Indian government's story that a Sikh carried the bomb onto the plane is true, it implicates them. The person they have identified is associated with a Sikh activist named Dr. Jagjit Singh Chohan, who was identified in the book Chakravyuh: Web of Indian Secularism as someone who has been supported by the Indian government and has worked at its behest, including cooperating with them on the attack on the Golden Temple in Amritsar in June 1984. Thus, even the Indian government's own version of the story places the blame squarely on the Indian government.

Back on July 26, 1992, the, India Monitor reported the arrest in Bombay of a Sikh named Manjit Singh in connection with the Air India case. The RCMP, however, said it knew of no Manjit Singh and he was not a suspect. The Indian government has been desperately trying to pin its crime on the Sikhs for years.

The Council of Khalistan has issued an excellent press release on the Reyat case. I would like to place it in the Record at this time, Mr. Speaker.

Canadian Courts Cover Up Indian Complicity in Bombing
Reyat Plea Matches RCMP Story Suggested in 1985 Questioning

Washington, DC., Feb. 12, 2003._The recent plea bargain by Inderjit Singh Reyat in the 1985 Air India crash is the result of a concerted Indo-Canadian effort to cover up the Indian government's own responsibility for this atrocity that killed 329 innocent people, said Dr. Gurmit Singh Aulakh, President of the Council of Khalistan, which leads the Sikh Nation's struggle for independence.

The book Soft Target, written by respected Canadian journalists Zuhair Kashmeri of the Toronto Globe and Mail and Brian McAndrew of the Toronto Star, clearly established that the Indian government is responsible for the bombing. The book quotes an investigator from the Canadian Security Investigative Service (CSIS) who said, "If you really want to clear up the incidents quickly, take vans down to the Indian High Commission and the consulates in Toronto and Vancouver, load up everybody and take them down for questioning. We know it and they know it that they are involved."

Mere hours after the incident, while the CSIS and the Royal Canadian Mounted Police were still retrieving the passenger list stored in the Air India computer, Indian Consul General Surinder Malik called the Globe and Mail to tell them to look for an "L. Singh" on the passenger manifest. How could Malik have known this? "L. Singh" turned out to be a Sikh named Lal Singh. Lal Singh told an Indian newspaper that he was offered "$2 million and settlement in a nice country" to testify falsely against the three individuals that Canada has charged with the bombing, an offer he refused. Curiously, Consul General Malik knew more details about the case than the police did.

Malik had pulled his wife and daughter off the flight suddenly, claiming that his daughter had a paper to write for school. A Canadian auto dealer who was a friend of Malik's cancelled his reservation on the flight at the last minute, as well. So did Siddhartha Singh, head of North

American Affairs for external relations in New Delhi. In addition the sister-in-law of the head of the Canadian wing of Dal Khalsa cancelled her reservations. Dal Khalsa is a political party formed by Zail Singh, who was President of India when Indira Gandhi was Prime Minister. How did all these people affiliated with the Indian government come to cancel their reservations at the last minute?

The story told in court in connection with Inderjit Singh Reyat's plea bargain matches in significant detail the story pressed upon him at the time of his initial arrest in November 1985, which he denied. An RCMP agent named Glen Rockwell told Reyat that he could get off the hook if he said that others hatched the bombing plot and sought his assistance and that he didn't know what he was doing. Reyat replied "I didn't help killing those people. No way." He said that Talwinder Singh Parmar, who has since been murdered by the Indian police, wanted to send some kind of explosive device to India. These details match the "statement of facts" at Reyat's trial.

The Indian Consul General planted a story in the Globe and Mail claiming that Reyat was given a parcel to carry onto the flight by Jagdev Nijjar, whose brother was in the inner circle of Jagjit Singh Chohan, who claims to be a Khalistani leader, but who was exposed in the book Chakravyuh: Web of Indian Secularism by Professor Gurtej Singh IAS in letters showing that he connived with the Indian government in planning the attack on the Golden Temple in Amritsar. Chohan is also tied to Dal Khalsa. If the Indian government really believes that Chohan's followers were involved in the incident, then why wasn't Chohan arrested when he returned to India last year?

A Member of the Canadian Parliament, David Kilgour, confirms the Indian government's involvement. In his book Betrayal: The Spy That Canada Forgot, he writes about a Canadian-Polish double agent who was introduced to Indian government agents. They asked him to join in their plot to carry out a second bombing of an Air India jet, telling him that "the first one worked so well."

The evidence clearly continues to show that the Indian regime blew up its own airliner to damage the Sikh freedom movement," said Dr. Aulakh. "This is consistent with the pattern of Indian government efforts to protect its tyrannical rule over the minorities of South Asia"

The government of India has murdered over 250,000 Sikhs since 1984, more than 200,000 Christians since 1948, over 85,000 Muslims in Kashmir since 1988, and tens of thousands of Tamils, Assamese, Manipuris, Dalits (the aboriginal people of the subcontinent), and others. Last March, the Indian government murdered 2,000 to 5,000 Muslims in Gujarat, according to the newspaper The Hindu. Over 52,000 Sikhs are being held as political prisoners. The Indian Supreme Court called the Indian government murders of Sikhs "worse than a genocide." On October 7, 1987, the Sikh Nation declared the independence of its homeland, Punjab, Khalistan. No Sikh representative has ever signed the Indian constitution. The Sikh Nation demands freedom for its homeland, Khalistan.

"Only in a free and sovereign Khalistan will the Sikh Nation prosper. In a democracy, the right to self-determination is the sine qua non and India should allow a plebiscite for the freedom of the Sikh Nation and all the nations of South Asia," Dr. Aulakh said.

***

Document

CONGRESSIONAL RECORD -- EXTENSIONS

Friday, February 07, 2003
108th Congress, 1st Session
149 Cong Rec E 171

REFERENCE: Vol. 149, No. 23
SECTION: Extension of Remarks
TITLE: INDIA EXPELS MISSIONARY AFTER HE IS SEVERELY BEATEN BY HINDU RADICALS

HON. EDOLPHUS TOWNS
State of New York
in the House of Representatives
Friday, February 7, 2003

Mr. TOWNS . Mr. Speaker, I was outraged to learn that a Christian missionary, Joseph Cooper, an American, was recently expelled from India. You see, Mr. Cooper came to the Indian government's attention after its radical, violent Hindu nationalist allies beat him so badly that he spent a week in an Indian hospital. He was expelled from the country on leaving the hospital.

Mr. Cooper was expelled simply for preaching, in another demonstration of the religious intolerance that characterizes India's "secular democracy." India has also demonstrated its secularism and tolerance when states ruled by the ruling BJP, such as Gujarat and Tamil Nadu, enacted laws prohibiting anyone from changing his or her religion, unless the person is changing to Hinduism. A Cabinet minister said that everyone who lives in India must either be Hindu or be subservient to Hindus.

The expulsion of Mr. Cooper brings to mind the disturbing case of Graham Staines, an Australian missionary who was burned to death along with his two young sons while they slept in their jeep. After this murder, Mr. Staines's widow was also expelled from India. A mob set fire to the jeep and chanted "Victory to Hannuman," a Hindu god. Since Christmas 1998, nuns have been raped, priests have been murdered, churches have been burned, schools and prayer halls have been attacked, and other acts of violence against Christians have been committed. Over 200,000 Christians in predominantly Christian Nagaland have been murdered by the Indian government.

It would be bad enough if Christians were the only victims of this violent radicalism, Mr. Speaker, but they are not. Sikhs, Muslims, and other minorities are also being victimized and terrorized. More than 250,000 Sikhs have been murdered by the Indian government since 1984. Two reports have confirmed that Indian forces killed 35 Sikhs in the village of Chithisinghpora in March 2000. Indian forces were caught red-handed trying to burn down a Gurdwara (a Sikh place of worship) and some Sikh homes in a village in Kashmir. 52,268 Sikhs are being held as political prisoners, according to a report by the Movement Against State Repression (MASR.) Some of them have been in this illegal detention since 1984! I am proud to have been a signer and sponsor of a letter to President Bush last year asking him to help free these political prisoners. In addition to over 52,000 Sikhs, tens of thousands of other minorities are also being held as political prisoners, according to Amnesty International.

Between 2,000 and 5,000 Muslims were murdered in Gujarat last spring. According to Indian newspapers, the police were ordered to stand aside and do nothing to stop the massacre, in an eerie parallel to the 1984 Delhi massacre of Sikhs. The Indian press also reported that the Indian government planned the Gujarat massacre in advance. Over 85,000 Muslims have been murdered in Kashmir. In addition, tens of thousands of Assamese, Bodos, Dalits, Manipuris, Tamils, and other minorities have been killed by the Indian government.

Mr. Speaker, all of these acts have either been carried out by government forces or by radical Hindu nationalists who are part of the umbrella organization known as the RSS, which was formed in support of the Fascists. The ruling BJP is the political arm of the RSS. This is unacceptable. America must take a stand. We must work to stop these killings and attacks and to get all political prisoners freed. It is time to cut off our aid and trade with India and we should pass a resolution in support of self-determination for the Sikh homeland of Punjab, Khalistan, for Kashmir, Nagaland, and everyone else seeking freedom from radical Hindu repression. The essence of democracy is the right to self-determination. As the leader of the democratic world, we must hold India to these standards of true democracy. Only then will everyone in South Asia live in freedom, dignity, prosperity, and peace.

Mr. Speaker, I would like to place an article from The Hindu on Mr. Cooper into the Record at this time.

U.S. Missionary Attacked

Thiruvananthapuram, Jan. 14._A 60-year-old American national and Protestant missionary, Joseph Cooper, was grievously injured when he was attacked by a 10-member armed gang of suspected RSS activists near a gospel convention venue at the Koppam Harijan colony in the Kilimanoor police station limits near here late on Monday night.

Police said that seven other persons, including a preacher and his family accompanying Mr. Cooper, were also injured in the attack. Mr.

Cooper, hailing from New Castle in the U.S., sustained a deep cut on his right palm. He is under treatment at a private hospital here.

Mr. Cooper had come to Kilimanoor to speak at the Koppam Protestant Convention organised by the Puliyam Friends Bible Church. He and his fellow church members were waylaid by the armed gang while they were being escorted back to their vehicles from the convention venue at around 9:45 p.m., police said.

The assailants first exploded a cracker to create panic. They detained the missionary and other preachers for a few minutes before attacking them with short sticks, swords and crowbars.

Among those injured are the preacher Benson (37), his wife, Sali Benson, children Joy and Judith, Jayakumar and Mercy Christudas. Police said the attackers fled when other church members rushed to the rescue of Mr. Cooper. The injured were rushed to the Medical College Hospital.

In a statement to police, Mr. Benson alleged that the attack was carried out by local RSS workers led by an autorickshaw driver. Police have arrested Raju (34), a former Kilimanoor RSS functionary.

The Circle-Inspector (Kilimanoor), D. Rajagopal, said there was no history of communal discord at the Koppam Harijan colony where about 60 families lived. Some of the families practised both the Christian and Hindu faith.

When contacted, the SP (Rural), T.K. Vinod Kumar, said that police raids were on to arrest the rest of the accused. RSS and BJP workers, meanwhile, took out a march to the Kilimanoor police station demanding the release of those arrested. When contacted, the RSS Jilla saha karyavah, R. Santhosh, said that his organisation had nothing to do with the attack. He alleged that the speeches made by the U.S. missionary and other preachers at the convention were "communally inflammatory" and "insulting to practitioners of the Hindu faith"

***

Document

CONGRESSIONAL RECORD -- EXTENSIONS

Friday, February 07, 2003
108th Congress, 1st Session
149 Cong Rec E 172

REFERENCE: Vol. 149, No. 23
SECTION: Extension of Remarks
TITLE: SIKH LAWYER'S REFUSAL TO REMOVE TURBAN HELPS TO EXPAND CIVIL RIGHTS

HON. EDOLPHUS TOWNS
State of New York
in the House of Representatives
Friday, February 7, 2003

Mr. TOWNS . Mr. Speaker, on January 28, the New York Times ran an article about New Jersey lawyer Ravinder Singh Bhalla. Mr. Bhalla won a significant victory for civil rights when he got the rules changed regarding searches at our prisons.

Mr. Bhalla went to visit a client at the Metropolitan Detention Center in Brooklyn, where I am from. The guards would not let him in because he refused to remove his turban. Mr. Bhalla informed the guards that the turban is not a hat, but is a religious symbol required of all observant Sikhs. Mr. Bhalla is of the Sikhs faith. He cited his first amendment right to practice his religion and his fourth amendment protection against unreasonable searches, nothing that he had already passed through the metal detector. He also cited his client's sixth amendment right to see his lawyer, a right that could not be exercised unless Mr. Bhalla was allowed into the prison.

Mr. Bhalla took his case to the Federal District Court in Newark. Then on January 17, the Federal Bureau of Prisons changed the policy, saying that turbans, prayer shawls, yarmulkes, and other religious items do not have to be searched. I commend the Bureau of Prisons for this enlightened decision, and I commend Mr. Bhalla for taking a stand on principle. By doing so, he has raised awareness of the rights of the Sikhs in this country and made all Americans more conscious of civil rights for all members of our diverse society.

Sikhs have been subjected to attacks and violence in the wake of the horrible September 11 attacks. A Sikh gas station operator was murdered in his gas station in Arizona simply because he wore a turban. All in all, there have been over 300 attacks on Sikhs. These attacks stem mostly from ignorance coupled with Americans' legitimate anger at the events of September 11. Because Osama bin Laden wears a turban, some ignorant people assume that anyone who wears a turban is a terrorist and an enemy of this county. Nothing could be further from the truth, as Mr. Bhalla showed us. There are over 500,000 Sikhs in this country and they are proud Americans who contribute in all walks of life from law and medicine to farming. One Sikh American, Dalip Singh Saund, served two terms in the House in the late fifties and early sixties.

African-Americans have been through the civil rights struggle; in some ways we are still fighting it. As Mr. Bhalla says, Sikhs are going through many of the same things. By taking a stand for his rights, Mr. Bhalla has expanded Americans' awareness of Sikhs and expanded our tolerance as a society, something that benefits us all.

Mr. Speaker, I would like to place the New York Times article on Mr. Bhalla into the Record.

[From the New York Times, Jan. 28, 2003]
How One Man Took a Stand and Changed Federal Policy Toward

the Sikh Community
(By Ronald Smothers)

Newark, Jan. 27._When guards at Brooklyn's Metropolitan Detention Center demanded last September that a Newark lawyer let them search his turban before being admitted to visit a client, they may have not have known much about the traditions of his Sikh faith.

"To a Sikh, removing his turban in public is the same as a strip-search and as intrusive as asking a woman to remove her blouse," said the lawyer, Ravinder Singh Bhalla.

But Mr. Bhalla, 29, knew quite a bit about the traditions of American law. Born in New Jersey of immigrant parents and educated at the University of California, the London School of Economics and Tulane University Law School, he knew his rights and was not afraid to list them, one by one.

There was his First Amendment right to practice his religion, including the ritual public wearing of the head covering, he told the guards. Then he expounded on his Fourth Amendment right against unreasonable searches, since he had already passed through the metal detector without setting off alarms. Finally there was his client's Sixth Amendment right to the lawyer of his choice - a right that could be exercised only if Mr. Bhalla forfeited his own rights.

Mr. Bhalla refused to remove his turban, and the guards refused to let him in. But on Jan. 17, the federal Bureau of Prisons issued a clarification of its search policy, after Mr. Bhalla asserted all of these rights in Federal District Court here, before the Office of the Inspector General of the Department of Justice in Washington and, armed with letters of support from a host of Sikh groups, directly to the Bureau of Prisons hierarchy.

Dan Dunn, a spokesman for the bureau, said that religious garments like turbans, prayer shawls or yarmulkes need not be considered part of the routine searches of personal effects that prison guards must make of visitors. They could be searched, he said, if there is a "reasonable suspicion that the person is about to engage in or is engaging in criminal activity."

What Mr. Dunn described as a simple clarification of policy is being hailed as a milestone by Mr. Bhalla and others. They say that by treating searches of religious garments as distinct from other personal-effects searches and subjecting them to stricter requirements, the agency is recognizing their intrusiveness.

"This marks a significant improvement in agency policy," said Harpreet Singh, the director of the Sikh Coalition, an amalgam of groups representing the nation's estimated 500,000 Sikhs. The group was founded just after Sept. 11, 2001, when many Sikhs found themselves the objects of suspicion at airports and elsewhere.

Since the terror attacks, he said, his group has won concessions from the federal Department of Transportation on airport security searches of Sikhs, given the faith's prohibitions against removing turbans, as well as the requirement among the more devout that they carry a "kirpan," or dagger.

Under the department's revised procedures, turbans will not be searched unless there is a positive reading on a metal detector. For their part, Sikh groups have agreed that it is legitimate to require those carrying daggers to secure the items in their checked luggage.

"But the broader significance of all of this is that we are educating a broader range of people about Sikhs and our rights," Mr. Singh said.

Sikhism, a monotheistic religion, dates back to the 15th century in the Punjab region of what is now India. Its doctrine has evolved through a succession of prophets or gurus, and in an atmosphere of persecution by the larger numbers of Hindus and Muslims in South Asia. One of Sikhism's main requirements is that adherents not cut their hair, which is considered a visible testament to their connection with their creator, especially in times of persecution.

Mr. Bhalla said many people mistakenly believe that the Sikh turban is a hatlike garment molded in one piece. It is actually a long swath of cotton, 3 feet by more than 15 feet, which takes Mr. Bhalla 15 minutes each morning to fold and carefully wind onto his head.

In taking on Mr. Bhalla at the gates of the Metropolitan Detention Center, guards may have picked the wrong person, said Gerald Krovatin, a New Jersey criminal lawyer in whose firm Mr. Bhalla works. Mr. Krovatin said that last November his colleague was one of the founding members of the national Sikh Bar Association and the only one among the estimated 50 Sikh lawyers in the country who is a criminal litigator.

Perhaps the seminal moment for Mr. Bhalla came in a federal courtroom in Newark when he was just 13. He and his father were attending a hearing for two Sikh community leaders whom the United States attorney's office was trying to extradite to India as suspected terrorists.

Mr. Bhalla recalled that SWAT teams and snipers were stationed outside the court, and plainclothes agents shadowed his and his father's every step because the judge and the prosecutor had reported receiving death threats. It turned out that the prosecutor in the case was the one sending the death threats, apparently in an effort to heighten the sense of danger.

Mr. Bhalla said the incident taught him how "ridiculous" sterotyping and prejudice could be.

"Right now Sikhs are going through some of the same things that African-Americans went through, and like them we are learning the importance of having some political power and knowing how the system works," he said. "But we are just starting."

***

Document

CONGRESSIONAL RECORD -- EXTENSIONS

Friday, February 07, 2003
108th Congress, 1st Session
149 Cong Rec E 175

REFERENCE: Vol. 149, No. 23
SECTION: Extension of Remarks
TITLE: INDIAN GOVERNMENT HARASSES WEBSITE THAT EXPOSED
CORRUPTION

HON. EDOLPHUS TOWNS
State of New York
in the House of Representatives
Friday, February 7, 2003

Mr. TOWNS . Mr. Speaker, in 2000, the website www.tehelka.com exposed the fundamental corruption of the Indian government. They did a video expose showing high-ranking government officials, including the Defense Minister, as well as the President of the ruling BJP, taking bribes. At that time, it was recording 30 million hits a week. It was quite embarrassing for the Indian government.

On January 6, The Guardian reported that the Indian government has struck back at tehelka.com. It has harassed their contributors. It sent its agents to investigate tehelka, searching its offices and harassing its workers. The website has had to reduce the staff from 120 people to four. All the office furniture has been sold and the site is scraping for money. Clearly the government has set out to destroy tehelka.com, and it appears to be succeeding. Meanwhile, the corrupt officials they exposed are still in their posts.

This shows that India is intolerant of free speech and free journalism. It reminds me of the old joke; "You have every right to your own opinion as long as it agrees with mine." That's the state of free speech and the free press in India. Freedom of speech and freedom of the press are cornerstones of a democracy, along with the right to self-determination. The government campaign to shut down tehelka.com is another piece of evidence that India, despite its claims, is not a democracy but an authoritarian police state.

Mr. Speaker, why are U.S. taxpayers_your constituents and mine_being asked to pay taxes to support this kind of radical, fundamentalist tyranny? We should stop our aid to India until real freedom exists there, including the right of a free press, the right to freely practice any religion a person chooses without the threat of being killed by the government and without anti-conversion laws, and the right of all the peoples of the subcontinent to decide their futures in a free and fair vote. We should work for self-determination, which is a basic right, by promoting a plebiscite on the question of independence in Christian Nagaland, Muslim Kashmir, the Sikh homeland of Punjab, Khalistan, and wherever else it is sought. And we should demand the release of all political prisoners in India and an end to its sponsorship of cross-border terrorism. America is a free country. We seek freedom not just for ourselves, but for all people of the world. These measures will help secure the blessings of liberty to all the people of the world's most troubled region and allow them to enjoy the glow of freedom.

Mr. Speaker, I am inserting the Guardian article on the tehelka situation into the Record at this time.

[From the Guardian, Jan. 6, 2003]
Website Pays Price for Indian Bribery Expose
(By Luke Harding)

Tarun Tejpal is sitting amid the ruins of his office. There is not much left_a few dusty chairs, three computers and a forlorn air-conditioning unit. "We have sold virtually every thing. I've even flogged the air conditioner," he says dolefully.

Twenty months ago Tejpal, editor in chief of tehelka.com, an investigative website, was the most feted journalist in India. He had just broken one of the biggest stories in the country's history_an expose of corruption at the highest levels of government.

His reporters, posing as arms salesmen, had bribed their way into the home of the defence minister, George Fernandes, and handed over 3,000 to one of the minister's colleagues. The journalists found many other people prepared to take money_senior army officers, bureaucrats, even the president of the ruling Bharatiya Janata party, who was filmed shovelling the cash into his desk.

The scandal was deeply embarrassing for the BJP prime minister, Atal Bihari Vajpayee. Mr. Vajpayee sacked Mr. Fernandes and ordered a commission of inquiry.

The scandal promoted a mood of national catharsis, and congratulations poured in from ordinary Indians tired of official corruption. Tehelka, which had only been launched in June 2000, was receiving 30 million hits a week. But the glory did not last.

"I had expected a battle. But we had not anticipated its scale," Tejpal said yesterday. "The propaganda was started the next day."

Nearly two years later, he has been forced to lay off all but four of his 120 staff. He has got deeply into debt, sold the office furniture and scrounged money from friends. "They drop by for dinner and leave a cheque behind."

The website,which once boasted sites on news, literature, sport and erotica, is "virtually defunct". George Fernandes, meanwhile, is again the defence minister.

The saga is a depressing example of how the Kafkaesque weight of government can be used to crush those who challenge its methods.

In the aftermath of the scandal, the Hindu nationalist-led government "unleashed" the inland revenue, the enforcement directorate and the intelligence bureau, India's answer to M15, on Tehelka's office in suburban south Delhi.

They did not find anything. Frustrated, the officials started tearing apart the website's investors. Tehelka's financial backer, Shanker Sharma, was thrown in jail without charge. Detectives also held Aniruddha Bahal, the reporter who carried out the expose, and a colleague, Kumar Badal. Badal is still in prison.

"It got to the stage that I used to count the number of booze bottles in my house to make sure there wasn't one more than the legal quota," Tejpal recalls.

The government commission set up to investigate Operation West-End, Tehelka's sting, meanwhile, started behaving very strangely. "The commission didn't cross-examine a single person found guilty of corruption. It was astonishing," said Tejpal. Instead, it spentits days rubbishing Tehelka's journalistic methods.

The official campaign of vilification against the website has attracted protests from a few of India's prominent liberal commentators, such as the veteran diplomat Kuldip Nayar and the respected columnist Tavleen Singh. Tehelka's literary supporters, who include Salman Rushdie, Amitav Ghosh and VS Naipaul, Tejpal: Kafkaesque situation have also expressed their outrage. But in general, India's civil society has reacted with awkwardness and embarrassment to the website's plight.

"I read all of Franz Kafka when I was 19 and 20, but I only understand him now," Tejpal wrote in a recent essay in the magazine Seminar. "He accurately intuited that all power is essentially implacable and malign."

The treatment of the web-site's investors has scared away anybody else from pumping money into Tehelka. The company owes 620,000.

Mr. Vajpayee's rightwing government has bounced back from the scandal and is expected to win the next general election in 2004. Last month, it won a landslide victory in elections in the riot-hit western state of Gujarat after campaigning on a virtually fascist anti-Muslim platform.

The murky world of arms dealing goes on. Tony Blair and his ministers are still trying to persuade the Indian government to buy 77 British-made Hawk jet trainers, but the billion-pound deal remains mysteriously stuck over the price.

Tehelka's expose was not about "individuals", but about "systemic corruption", Tejpal insists. He admits that his sting operation would have gone down badly with any government, but says that the BJP's response was venomous.

"The degree of pettiness has been extraordinary. They have a crude understanding of power and a lot of that stems from the fact they are in power for the first time. Our struggle is emblematic of a wider issue: can media organizations be killed off when they criticize governments."

The gloomy answer appears to be yes.

Last night Balbir Punj, a leading BJP member of parliament, claimed the government had nothing to do with the website's collapse. "Just because you do a story exposing the government doesn't mean the gods make you immortal," he said. "Many other [internet] portals have closed down. The boom is over."

***

Document

CONGRESSIONAL RECORD -- EXTENSIONS

Wednesday, January 08, 2003
108th Congress, 1st Session
149 Cong Rec E 42

REFERENCE: Vol. 149, No. 2
SECTION: Extension of Remarks
TITLE: BAN ON CONVERSIONS IN INDIA SHOWS IT IS THEOCRACY,
NOT DEMOCRACY

HON. DAN BURTON
of Indiana
in the House of Representatives
Wednesday, January 8, 2003

Mr. BURTON of Indiana . Mr. Speaker, while we were in recess, a law was passed in the Indian state of Tamil Nadu by the Hindu fundamentalist government there that bans religious conversions to any religion but Hinduism. The Washington Times did an excellent report on this bill in its issue of November 11.

According to the article, the bill "penalizes those who convert to a religion other than Hinduism with imprisonment and a hefty fine." The ruling BJP and its coalition partners, as well as one of its sister organizations, the Vishwa Hindu Parishad (VHP), have endorsed this bill and called for similar bills to be passed all over the country.

The militant Hindu nationalists claim that people are being converted by force. However, as John Dayal, secretary-general of the All-India Christian Council in New Delhi, said, "In fact, the only inducements by fraud and fear are those being carried out by [Hindu organizations] in the tribal belt, where innocent tribals are being forced to become Hindus." A Cabinet members was quoted several months ago as saying that everyone who lives in India must be a Hindu or be subservient to Hindus. This is the reality of Indian democracy, Mr. Speaker.

India must start acting like a democracy. 52,268 Sikhs political prisoners and tens of thousands of other political prisoners being held in India must be released. Since 1984, over 250,000 Sikhs have been murdered by the Indian government. The Indian regime has also killed over 85,000 Kashmiri Muslims since 1988, over 200,000 Christians in Nagaland, and tens of thousands of other minorities, including Assamese, Bodos, Dalits, Manipuris, and Tamils, among others. Last spring, 2,000 to 5,000 Muslims were murdered in Gujarat with the connivance and support of the police. In November, the government of Pakistan issued 400 visas to Sikhs to come and celebrate the birthday of one of the Sikh Gurus, Guru Nanak. India only let 48 Sikhs to the celebration.

Why are American taxpayers being asked to support this theocratic regime? It is time to cut off our aid to India, and it is time to support the American principles of freedom, democracy, peace, and stability by openly and publicly supporting self-determination for all the peoples and nations of South Asia, such as Khalistan, Kashmir, Nagalim, and others, through a free and fair plebiscite. This will show India's commitment to being a true democracy rather than a Hindu theocracy.

Mr. Speaker, I would like to place the Washington Times article on the anti-conversion ordinance into the Record at this time for the information of my colleagues.

[From the Washington Times, Nov. 11, 2002]
Low-Caste Hindus Eye New Religions
(By Shaikh Azizur Rahman)

New Delhi._Low-caste Hindus in the southern Indian state of Tamil Nadu are threatening to embrace Christianity, Buddhism or Islam to protest a new law that outlaws religious conversion.

A bill passed into law by the state legislature last month penalizes those who convert to a religion other than Hinduism with imprisonment and a hefty fine.

While religious minorities in Tamil Nadu plan to challenge the law in court, many Hindus from so-called "untouchable castes," known as Dalits, are threatening to publicly defy the new law.

One group of Dalit Hindus in the state capital, Chennai, said that a group of 10,000 will convert to Buddhism on Dec. 6 if the law is not revoked.

Another group, known as the Dalit Panthers of India [DPI], pledged that 25,000 of its members would become Christians to protest what they called an "unjustified" decree.

"The upper class has been torturing the Dalits for centuries, and now, by passing the bill, the government has decided to shackle us in a society where we are denied even our basic democratic rights," said one Dalit activist, who identified himself by the Christian name Emmanuel.

On Oct. 31, Tamil Nadu became the first_but probably not the last_Indian state to outlaw religious conversions. Though the law targets conversions "by force, allurement or fraudulent means," opponents say the language offers the means to challenge all conversions to faiths other than Hinduism.

"Even if one changes one's religion of one's own free will, those involved in the conversion can be punished on the ground that it's a case of forced conversion," said M. Karunanidhi a former chief minister of Tamil Nadu.

The new law was welcomed by Hindu fundamentalists, who govern the nation in a coalition led by the Hindu nationalist Bharatiya Janata Party (BJP).

"The BJP is strongly of the view that this law is most necessary for the whole country. Lots of money is coming into the country from Islamic organizations to aid conversions," said BJP President M. Venkaih Naidu.

Ashok Singhal, leader of the World Hindu Council (VHP), hailed the law as a "timely and bold step" and he urged other states to pass similar laws.

The issue of religious conversion has long been a source of strife in India. While federal law allows Indians to change their faith, the ruling BJP makes no secret of its dislike to the practice, while its ruling part-ner_the VHP party_views conversions as betrayal.

Opponents of the new law warn it will only trigger an even larger exodus of Hindus to other faiths.

The Global Council of Indian Christians said it was "alarmed by the hurriedly promulgated ordinance," and called it "the most heinous violation of religious freedom aimed at targeting Christian missionaries engaged in poverty alleviation and spreading the light of education.

The All-Indian Christian People's Forum said that it went against the core of the Constitution. "This ordinance is uncalled for, unwarranted and smacks of a pro-Hindu ideological basis of the . . . government".

"The bill runs foul of Article 25 [25] of the Indian Constitution, which grants freedom of conscience and free profession, practice and propaga-tion of religion to every Indian citizen," the group said.

Dominic Emmanuel, director of New Delhi Catholic Archdiocese, called the measure, "an assault as much on civil rights as on human rights as on human dignity."

John Daya, secretary-general of the Christian Council in New Delhi, said: "In fact the only inducements by fraud and fear are those being carried out by [Hindu organizations] in the tribal belt, where innocent tribals are being forced to become Hindus."

Muslims, too, are concerned.

How can conversions be prevented if an individual is attracted to another religion because of his or her faith in it? Force is never used to convert one to Islam because it is against the basic tenets of [Islam]," said Maolana Siddikullah Chowdhury, general secretary of the Jamiat-e-Ulema party in Calcutta.

He added that low-caste Hindus converted to Islam simply to "escape discrimination and ill treatment" and not under any coercion.

***

Document

CONGRESSIONAL RECORD -- EXTENSIONS

Wednesday, January 08, 2003
108th Congress, 1st Session
149 Cong Rec E 45

REFERENCE: Vol. 149, No. 2
SECTION: Extension of Remarks
TITLE: HATE SUCCEEDS IN INDIA

HON. DAN BURTON
State of Indiana
in the House of Representatives
Wednesday, January 8, 2003

Mr. BURTON of Indiana . Mr. Speaker, there was an interesting article in the Washington Post on December 11. It shows that hate can be a winning platform in India.

The article focuses on Jeetubhai Waghela, a candidate of the ruling BJP in the recent elections. He was involved in the killings in Gujarat last year, according to Muslims there. Now he runs as a protector of Hindus and this platform of hatred gains votes for him.

The Indian government has oppressed minorities for many years. In 1984, almost 20 years ago, it invaded the Golden Temple in Amritsar, the most sacred of Sikh shrines. Since then, over 250,000 Sikhs have been murdered by the government, according to figures from the Punjab State Magistracy. 52,268 Sikhs are being held as political prisoners, according to a study from the Movement Against State Repression. These political prisoners should be released immediately.

The government was directly involved in the murders in Gujarat last year, according to published reports in India. It has killed over 85,000 Kashmiri Muslims as well as Muslims throughout the country. Over 200,000 Christians have been killed in Nagaland. Since Christmas 1998, priests have been murdered, nuns have been raped, churches have been burned, and Christian schools and prayer halls have been attacked. Missionary Graham Staines and his two young sons were burned to death while they slept in their Jeep. Police broke up a religious festival with gunfire. These acts have been carried out by government forces or by their Hindu nationalist allies with government connivance. Is this a democracy?

We can help stop hate in the subcontinent. We must cut off our aid to India and we must come out for a free and fair plebiscite on independence in Kashmir, as India promised in 1948, as well as in Khalistan, in Nagaland, and the other countries seeking their freedom from India. Self-determination is the right of all peoples and nations, Mr. Speaker. That was the principle on which America is founded. It must be the principle that we promote around the world.

Mr. Speaker, I would like to place the Washington Post article I referred to into the Record at this time.

[From the Washington Post, Dec. 11, 2002]
In Indian Election, Hate Is Part of Platform
(By Rama Lakshmi)

Ahmedabad, India_The candidate marched down the slum's narrow lanes, followed by men dancing to the sound of loud drums and spraying the streets with marigold petals. Hindu women paused from their chores of peeling garlic and doing laundry to offer garlands and blessings.

The cheerful scene, part of Jeetubhai Waghela's campaign for a seat in the state legislature, played out beneath a cloth banner that revealed a more ominous aspect of the coming election here in India's western state of Gujarat. The banner vows to avenge the killing of 58 Hindus during an attack on a train by Muslims last February, and as the supporters of Waghela, a member of the Hindu-nationalist Bharatiya Janata Party (BJP), pressed forward and choked the alleys, Muslim residents quickly hurried indoors.

"Here comes the lion," roared Waghela's men.

Nine months ago, as Gujarat was being riven by religious violence that followed the killing of the Hindus, Waghela stormed the same streets with a mob of Hindu men wearing orange bandanas and armed with swords, sticks and gasoline, according to witnesses and police records. Shouting angry slogans at Muslim residents, Waghela allegedly ordered the mob to loot and destroy their homes, leaving them homeless for months.

"For three days, Waghela and his men looted and burnt our homes. For eight months, we lived in relief camps because of him," said Nasir Khan, a complainant. "Now he tells Hindus he is their protector against us. Where do we run for cover if he gets elected?"

After a Muslim mob in the town of Godhra killed 58 Hindu train passengers in February, more than 1,000 people died, most of them Muslim, in weeks of arson and killing throughout Gujarat. Human rights groups have accused the BJP_the ruling party in Gujarat as well as in India's national government_of essentially ignoring the killings by its Hindu extremist allies.

As Gujarat prepares to elect a new state legislature on Thursday, many analysts are describing the vote as an important test of the secular foundations of India's religiously and ethnically diverse democracy.

In a state where only 9 percent of the population of 50 million is Muslim, the BJP is counting on sectarian passions to consolidate the Hindu vote. Throughout the state, BJP leaders have delivered fiery speeches against Muslims involved in the Feb. 27 attack and against Pakistan-aided Islamic militants killing Hindus in the revolt-wracked province of Jammu and Kashmir.

One such party stalwart is Waghela, who was arrested in connection with this year's riots on four charges, including murder and rioting. Jailed for 108 days and now free on bail, Waghela, 31, is back here in Gomtipur, a mixed working-class neighborhood in Ahmedabad, with folded hands, asking for votes for the BJP. He denies playing a role in the riots and insists he was framed.

Campaigning on a recent morning, Waghela identified a new target of hate for his Hindu voters. Climbing on a platform, he told them that a fancy new high-rise for Muslims is being planned adjacent to their homes, on the site of a closed textile mill. He warned them that they would not be safe any longer.

"You will be surrounded from all sides by Muslims," said Waghela, breathlessly flicking back his hair from his forehead. *"Don't let them gain power over you. Vote for me and I will stop that building plan."*

"Do you want the building here?" he said.

"No!" the crowd shouted back.

This election is critical to the political destiny of the BJP, which has suffered defeats in several state elections in the past two years. Gujarat is the last major state in which the party holds power, and critics fear that it could use a victory here as an endorsement of strident Hindu politics. The national coalition that the BJP leads in New Delhi under Prime Minister Atal Bihari Vajpayee will face the polls in 2004.

"In this election, the BJP is seeking a legitimization of violence that its members indulged in against the Muslims," said Achyut Yagnik, a political analyst and social worker in Gujarat. *"The results in Gujarat will determine whether they take this appeal of Hindutva [Hindu chauvinism] beyond Gujarat."*

The BJP's main challenger in Gujarat_and at the national level_is the Congress party, which attacks the BJP's Hindu fundamentalism for endangering the lives and rights of India's religious minorities. As a result, Gujarat's Muslims and Christians have rallied behind Congress, while many Hindu voters in Gujarat feel that Congress, headed at the national level by the Italian-born Sonia Gandhi, has an anti-Hindu slant and defends only the religious minorities.

Opinion polls show that it is likely to be a close contest between the BJP and Congress. Some secular analysts said that although Hindu voters may find the demagoguery of the BJP attractive, the social divisions inherent in the caste system may prevent Hindus from voting as a bloc.

The Muslims of Gujarat, on the other hand, appear to have decided to vote en masse for Congress. Yet many complained that Congress took their support for granted and often forgot them when attaining power. They will vote for Congress, they say, simply because they have no other choice.

Nowhere is this frustration felt more sharply than in Godhra, the epicenter of Gujarat's religious strife.

The BJP's candidate in Godhra, Haresh Bhatt, campaigns under banners of the burning train, distributes pictures of the dead Hindu passengers and describes the election as a *"religious war."* But the Congress candidate there, Rajendra Singh Patel, many Muslims said, was involved in burning the shops and homes of Muslims in March.

"We made two appeals to the Congress last month not to field Patel in the elections, but they still made him the candidate," said Mohammad Yusaf, 56, a clerk in the city government. *"But we are caught between a ditch and a well. To defeat the BJP, we will have to vote for Patel. But our heart is not in it."*

***

Document
CONGRESSIONAL RECORD -- EXTENSIONS

Friday, November 15, 2002
107th Congress, 2nd Session
148 Cong Rec E 2049

REFERENCE: Vol. 148, No. 148
SECTION: Extension of Remarks
TITLE: POLICE AGAIN ENTER GOLDEN TEMPLE COMPLEX

HON. DAN BURTON
of Indiana
in the House of Representatives
Thursday, November 14, 2002

Mr. BURTON of Indiana . Mr. Speaker, in June 1984, Indian forces invaded the Golden Temple, the most sacred Sikh shrine, and other Sikh Gurdwaras around Punjab, killing 20,000 people. As Sant Jarnail Singh Bhindranwale said, this helped lay the foundation of Khalistan, the Sikh homeland that declared its independence in 1987. Now the police have again invaded the Golden Temple complex on the pretext of searching the three buildings in the complex in connection with the upcoming elections for the Shiromani Gurdwara Prabandhak Committee (SGPC), which oversees all the Gurdwaras in India.

The police were accompanied by Indian political officials, including the Chemicals and Fertilizers Minister, Sukhdev Singh Dhindsa.

People of all religions and from all over the world have been welcomed to worship at the Golden Temple. Now even members of the SGPC may well be blocked from entering it. Some SGPC workers had a verbal altercation with two of the invading police officials, according to the Tribune newspaper out of Chandigarh. The article reports that SGPC members have already had to sneak into the Golden Temple complex.

Mr. Speaker, this is further proof that there is no religious freedom in "the world's largest democracy." India has already been added to our government's list of countries that violate religious freedom. Now sanctions should be implemented to help ensure real religious liberty in India.

This is just the latest chapter in a long history of repression of Sikhs by India. Over a quarter of a million Sikhs have been murdered since 1984. More than 52,000 are being held as political prisoners, according to a report by the Movement Against State Repression. Another 50,000 have simply been made to "disappear." The police picked up 50,000 Sikh youth, tortured them, murdered them, declared their bodies "unidentified" and secretly cremated them, and refused to hand the remains over to the families. Christians, Muslims, Dalits, and other minorities have seen similar atrocities committed against them, yet the world treats India as a respectable, democratic country.

Mr. Speaker, we must stop our aid to India now. We must declare our support for self-determination for the Sikhs of Khalistan, for predominantly Christian Nagaland, for Kashmir, and for everyone in South Asia. The cornerstone of democracy is the right to self-determination.

I would like to place the Tribune article on the police invasion of the Golden Temple complex into the Record at this time. I think my colleagues will find it very informative.

From the Tribune (Chandigarh), Nov. 11, 2002
Police Enters Golden Temple Complex
(By Prabhjot Singh)

Chandigarh, Nov. 10._Less than 24 hours before a five-member NDA team, led by union minister Sahib Singh Verma, could fly into the Holy City of Amritsar to oversee the conduct of next Tuesday's annual election to the SGPC executive committee, Punjab policemen in plain clothes entered the Golden Temple complex on the pretext of searching all three serais (inns) there.

Accompanying the team would be not only Union Chemicals and Fertilisers Minister, Sukhdev Singh Dhindsa, who is also a SAD General Secretary, but also 100-odd SGPC members owing allegiance to SAD chief Parkash Singh Badal.

Though preventive arrests continued throughout the state and Golden Temple complex was put under police siege with the deployment of hundreds of anti-riot policemen in anti-combat gear, some of the Akali leaders, including former Finance Minister Kanwaljit Singh managed to sneak into the sanctum sanctorum.

Talking to The Tribune over the telephone, Mr Sukhdev Singh Dhindsa said the names of four NDA observers_Mr Sahib Singh Verma, Mr Thomas (MP, Samata), Mrs D'Souza (MP, Samata), and Mrs Anita Arya (MP, BJP)_have already been cleared, the Union Civil Aviation Minister, Mr Shah Nawaz, is also expected to be a part of the special NDA team to oversee the SGPC elections. The observers and the SGPC members would take a chartered flight from New Delhi to Amritsar tomorrow afternoon.

Mr Dhindsa further said that on the basis of the complaint lodged by the Shiromani Akali Dal with the Union Home Minister yesterday, the Union Home Secretary today called Punjab Chief Secretary Y.S. Ratra on the telephone and expressed his "strong displeasure" over "politicalisation of the bureaucracy".

The Chief Secretary reportedly assured the Union Home Secretary that no SGPC member would be stopped from reaching the Golden Temple complex for attending the election meeting. Efforts would be made to facilitate those lodged in jails in one case or the other to attend and vote in the elections.

Meanwhile, reports indicate that so far the Punjab police has taken 1,222 Akali workers into custody. Of these 934 belong to Shiromani Akali Dal, 234 to Sarb Hind Shiromani Akali Dal, 50 to Shiromani Akali Dal (Amritsar) and one owes allegiance to Mr Ravi Inder Singh. The remaining three belong to the Mehta faction of the AISSF.

Of these, the maximum arrests of the Badal men were made in San-grur (73), followed by Majitha (64), Tarn Taran (60) and Patiala (62). Rashmi Talwar and Ashok Sethi in their reports from Amritsar said the police in a pre-dawn swoop entered the Golden Temple complex on the pretext of searching all three serais_Guru Nanak Niwas, Guru Hargod-bind Niwas and Mata Ganga Niwas.

When the police arrived to get the three serais vacated to ensure im-plementation of the orders, among those evicted were 50 schoolchildren in the age group of six to eight years from Lucknow. The police parties which were headed by Mr Jagdish Khera and Mr R.S. Ghuman, both DSPs, had a verbal altercation with the SGPC workers who resisted the attempts of the raiding party to get the serais vacated. Mr Harbant Singh and Mr Ajaib Singh, Secretary of the SGPC, and personal assistant to the SGPC chief, respectively, refused to budge holding that the orders were not specific to the SGPC and "devotees" could not be evicted from a religious complex.

The SGPC Chief, Prof Kirpal Singh Badungar, who had to rush to Amritsar from Bathinda, after the police entry into the complex, assailed the government action maintaining that it was a direct attack on the most sacred Sikh shrine and the Congress Government was bent upon disturbing communal peace and harmony.

The police officials managed to get computer printouts of the names and addresses of 2,000 devotees staying in the serais.

Hundreds of policemen in top anti-combat gear laid a siege to the Golden Temple complex. The mounted police has also been deployed around the complex.

Talking to The Tribune over the cellphone, Capt Kanwaljit Singh said that that action of the police in the morning and again in the evening of searching serais and evicting yatris was a serious "violation of the sanctity of the Golden Temple complex." The action of the government amounts to gross interference in the religious affairs of the Sikhs and could lead to serious complications besides disturbing communal harmo-ny and peace in the state."

He said a number of SGPC members and dal workers had already managed to sneak into the complex.

Professor Badungar told newsmen that in case the police entered Teja Singh Samundari Hall on the day of the election meeting, the repercus-sions would be "drastic".

He said the government was gripped by a "fear psychosis" and its nervousness was evident from the desperate steps it was taking. He maintained that the national and international media would be permit-ted to cover the executive committee elections as he disapproved on any NDA observers to oversee the elections. No other SGPC employee would be allowed inside the meeting hall.

The SGPC chief said that non-bailable warrants issued against for-mer SGPC chief Jagir Kaur by a Kapurthala court was an indication of the desperation of the state government.

Meanwhile, Mr. Sukhdev Singh Bhaur, General Secretary, SHSAD supported the orders issued by the District Magistrate but held that these orders should be applicable in case of "bad elements" and not the devotees.

The SHSAD was ready for a truce with Mr. Parkash Singh Badal provided he agreed to apologize at Akal Takht and accepted Bhai Ranjit Singh as Jathedar of Akal Takht. He claimed that 50 SGPC members were strongly behind the SHSAD.

Senior Akali leader and close aide of Mr. Parkash Singh Badal, Capt Kanwaljit Singh claimed that the SAD has formulated its secret strategy to bring all 120 SGPC members to Teja Singh Samundri Hall on November 12 to elect the President and the executive committee. Talking to newsmen this evening at Bhai Gurdas Hall after managing to enter the city in disguise. He said the reign of terror unleashed by the Amarinder Singh government on Akali leaders and workers were trampling upon their democratic rights.

Capt Kanwaljit Singh said Mr. Badal, along with all 120 members, would land at Rajasansi Airport tomorrow for the SGPC general house election meeting. Party leaders and workers would ensure that all SGPC members manage to enter the Golden Temple complex on that day.

He claimed that the ex-parte disqualification of SGPC members by the SGJC was likely to be set aside by the Punjab and Haryana High Court tomorrow.

Discounting the rumors of a patch-up between Mr. Badal and Mr. Tohra, Capt Kanwaljit Singh said there was no scope for any compromise. The Badal candidate would win hands down, he asserted.

The arrival of the Jathedar of Akal Takht, Giani Joginder Singh Vedanti, here this evening has raised speculation about an appeal being made by him for a patch-up between the two Akali stalwarts to avoid a confrontation even as the Congress Government has queered the pitch with heavy deployment of the police around the complex.

***

Document

CONGRESSIONAL RECORD -- EXTENSIONS

Tuesday, November 12, 2002
107th Congress, 2nd Session
148 Cong Rec E 1988

REFERENCE: Vol. 148, No. 145
SECTION: Extension of Remarks
TITLE: OPPOSITION PARTY MEMBERS BEING ARRESTED IN PUNJAB

HON. EDOLPHUS TOWNS
of New York
in the House of Representatives
Tuesday, November 12, 2002

Mr. TOWNS . Mr. Speaker, in Punjab, there are elections coming up for the SGPC, the organization that is in charge of all the Gurdwaras, or Sikh Temples, in India. According to the Times of India, members of the Shiromani Akali Dal, which used to run the state government until it lost the state elections to the Congress Party earlier this year, are being arrested in connection with these elections. Many members of the party are going into hiding.

The Akali government under the leadership of Parkash Badal was the most corrupt government in Punjab's history. They came up with a new term for bribery. They called it "fee for service." You didn't get the service unless you paid the fee. And they did nothing to get Sikh political prisoners released or to bring police officers who committed murder and other atrocities against the Sikhs to justice. I was proud to be one of the 42 Members of this House from both parties who signed a letter earlier this year asking President Bush to work for the release of these political prisoners.

We all support the prosecution of corrupt and brutal officials who were responsible for crimes against the people. However, those who committed these crimes should be brought to justice for these crimes. They and their followers should not be arrested merely for belonging to the Akali party.

A democracy does not arrest people for their political affiliations. A democracy does not hold political prisoners. Yet these things are happening today in India, which says that it is the "world's largest democracy." A report from the Movement Against State Repression showed that India admitted to holding 52,268 Sikhs as political prisoners. Some have been there since 1984. Tens of thousands of other minorities are also being held, according to Amnesty International.

More than 250,000 Sikhs have been murdered by the Indian government. It has also killed over 80,000 Kashmiri Muslims, over 200,000 Christians in Nagaland, and tens of thousands of other minorities as well. Priests have been killed, nuns have been raped, churches have been burned, prayer halls and schools have been attacked by members of the RSS, the pro-Fascist parent organization of the ruling BJP. Indian soldiers were caught red-handed trying to set fire to some Sikh homes and a Gurdwara in a village in Kashmir. The government has been implicated in the mass murders of Muslims in Gujarat this spring and in the March 2000 massacre of 35 Sikhs in Chithisinghpora. It is clear that the true face of India is not democratic at all, but it is a Hindu theocratic tyranny.

The political arrest of members of the opposition party underline the fact that India is not democratic. Therefore, it is not worthy of U.S. support. We should stop our aid to India and our trade with that corrupt, theocratic state. We should make a public declaration of support for self-determination for Punjab, Khalistan, for predominantly Christian Nagaland, for Kashmir, and for all the peoples and nations seeking their freedom from India. This is the best way to bring real freedom, peace, stability, and security to everyone in that troubled region.

Mr. Speaker, I would like to place the Times of India article into the Record at this time.

The Times of India, Nov. 12, 2002
Beards Were Tied Up, Blue Discarded
(By Ks Dhaliwal)

Jalandhar/Beas/Rayya._Gurcharan Singh Channi heard the knock on the door at 2.30 am of November 7. He guessed right. It was the early morning swoop. He slipped out of the back door. From then on till Monday he remained underground, travelling to Nadda Sahib, boldly giving interviews to various TV channels, moving on to Chandigarh, Ludhiana. Only on Monday he reached Harminder Sahib along with thousands of others who were on the run after the Punjab Police went into an overdrive to arrest SAD (Badal) leaders in view of the SGPC elections. Channi is the general secretary, Jalandhar urban unit, SAD (Badal). Many more like Channi reached Harminder Sahib on Monday in disguise. They hoodwinked the nakas en-route by rolling up their flowing beards, switching over from the traditional Akali blue turban to maroon, coffee colour and sky blue.

They even got past nakas adopting urban styles. Instead of the kurta pajama, they switched to trousers, shirts and neckties.

Hundreds of them were taken out of buses. At Nadkodar Chowk on Monday all bearded men were barred from boarding buses. Sucha Singh Langah tied up his beard to get into the Golden Temple. Sarwan Singh Phillaur, who was under house arrest, also managed to give police the slip.

Venturing out from Jalandhar many followed circuitous routes through link roads. One popular route used to reach Amritsar was from Jalandhar to Tanda, Hargobindpur Sahib, Mehta Chowk, Mattewal, Majitha bypass and then the Golden Temple. It took double the time as they traversed twice the distance.

Some went from Jalandhar to Kapurthala, Goindwal Sahib, Tarn Taran, Amritsar. Armarjit Singh took his wife and sister-in-law along posing at the nakes that the latter was sick and was being taken to the hospital.

Resham Singh Thiara, who contested the last assembly elections from Nawanshahr on an Akali Dal ticket, posed as a businessman from Delhi.

Buses entering Punjab on Monday were halted at over 40 nakas on way to Jalandhar. "It was only by evening that the nakas appeared to relent as news spread and probably the signal was beeped to relax the check after the government probably realised that it was having a damaging effect on the psyche of the people," said Thiara.

SAD members shout anti-government slogans at the Golden Temple Complex, on Monday.

***

Document

CONGRESSIONAL RECORD -- EXTENSIONS

Tuesday, November 12, 2002
107th Congress, 2nd Session
148 Cong Rec E 1992

REFERENCE: Vol. 148, No. 145
SECTION: Extension of Remarks
TITLE: MURDER OF 5 DALITS SHOWS THERE IS NO FREEDOM IN INDIA

HON. EDOLPHUS TOWNS
of New York
in the House of Representatives
Tuesday, November 12, 2002

Mr. TOWNS . Mr. Speaker, much has happened while we were in recess. In Dulena, India, five Dalits, the dark-skinned "Untouchables," the lowest caste in India's repressive caste system, were murdered because of a rumor that they had killed a cow. Cows are revered in Hinduism.

According to the Washington Post, family members stated that at least one of the Dalits was murdered by the police because the Dalits refused to pay them a bribe. The remainder were killed by upper-caste Hindus after the police planted a rumor that the Dalits had killed a cow.

To make this case even more offensive, charges have been filed against the five Dalit victims, but no charges have been filed against the police who were involved in these murders. In Hindu-dominated India, apparently the life of a cow is worth more than those of five humans. What kind of country protects cows but engages in the massive killing of minorities?

Dalits are converting in large numbers in order to escape from this oppression, prompting the BJP to pass laws in the states it controls banning anyone from converting to any religion other than Hindu.

Unfortunately, this is part of a long pattern of Indian tyranny against the Dalits. Tens of thousands of Dalits have been killed by the Indian government. In an incident several years ago, a Dalit constable went into a Hindu Temple on a rainy day and he was stoned to death. A little Dalit girl was blinded by her teacher when she drank water from the community pitcher. And Sikhs, Christians, Muslims, and other minorities have suffered from similar persecution. As you know, over 250,000 Sikhs have been murdered since 1984, over 80,000 Kashmiri Muslims have been killed since 1988, and over 200,000 Christians have been killed in Nagaland, in addition to tens of thousands of Assamese, Bodos, Manipuris, Tamils, and others.

Mr. Speaker, this is not the conduct of a democratic state. If America wants to live by its principles and help spread democracy, it must take action against this kind of repression. India has already been declared a country that violates religious freedom, which seems to be confirmed by these latest incidents. It is time to impose the sanctions that this status brings. We should also cut off our aid and trade with India until human rights are respected and declare our support for self-determination for all the peoples of South, because self-determination is the very essence of democracy. These measures will help bring real freedom, peace, prosperity, and stability to all the peoples and nations of the subcontinent.

Mr. Speaker, I would like to place the Council of Khalista's press release on the killing of these five Dalits into the Record at this time.

Council of Khalistan, Press Release, Oct. 29, 2002
5 Dalits Murdered on Rumor of Cow Killing

Fundamentalist Hindu Fascist Police Kill One Because They Did Not Get a Bribe, Then Incite Villagers to Murder Other Four_Life of a Cow Worth More Than 5 Human Lives in Hindu Theocracy

WASHINGTON, D.C., Oct. 29, 2002_Five Dalits, the dark-skinned "Untouchables," were murdered in Dulena, India, about an hour outside Delhi, on a rumor that they had killed a cow. According to a report in the Washington Post, family members stated that one of the Dalits was murdered by the police because the group refused to pay a bribe, then the upper-caste police planted the rumor that the Dalits had killed a cow to get the upper-caste village residents to kill the other four. Cows are revered in Hinduism. No charges have been filed against the killers, but charges have been filed against the five Dalits.

Dalits, also called "Untouchables," are the lowest casts in the Hindu social structure. Tens of thousands of Dalits have been murdered by the Indian government. Several years ago, a Dalit constable entered a Hundu Temple on a rainy day and was stoned to death by upper-casts Brahmins. A few years ago, a five-year-old Dalit girl was hit by her teacher and blinded for drinking water from the community water pitcher.

"This act of Indian tyranny shows that in India, the life a cow is worth more than the lives of five humans," said Dr. Gurmit Singh Aulakh, President of the Council of Khalistan. The Council of Khalistan, the government pro tempore of Khalistan, leads the peaceful, democratic, nonviolent movement to liberate Khalistan from Indian occupation and tyranny. "This shows that India is not a democracy but a Hindu theocracy in which the lives of lower castes are worthless," he said. "Are these the acts of a democratic country or a fundamentalist Hindu police state?," he asked. "The Sikh Nation sympathizes with the Dalits," he said. "Dalits and other minorities must resist India's racist tyranny."

Dalits have not been the only ones oppressed. All minorities have suffered under the boot of Indian repression. The Indian government has murdered over 250,000 Sikhs since 1984. Over 80,000 Kashmiri Muslims have been killed since 1988. More than 200,000 Christians have been killed since 1947, along with tens of thousands of Dalits, Tamils, Assamese, Bodos, Manipuris, and other minorities. In February 42 Members of Congress wrote to President Bush to get 52,268 Sikh political prisoners released from Indian prisons. Since Christman 1998, Chrisitans have felt the brunt of the attacks. Priests have been murdered, nuns have been raped, churches have been burned, Christian schools and prayer halls have been destroyed, and no one has been punished for these acts. Militant Hindu fundamentalists allied with the RSS, the pro-Fascist parent organization of the ruling BJP, burned missionary Graham Staines and his two young sons to death. Recently, fundamentalist Hindu fascists murdered about 5,000 Muslims in Gujarat with the connivance of the police.

"This pattern of oppression and tyranny helps to explain the existence of 17 freedom movements within India's artificial borders," Dr. Aulakh said. "We support the aspirations of the Dalits and all the minorities of South Asia. We must end India's tyranny and brutal violations of Sikh human rights and those of other minorities," he said. "The time has come to launch a Shantmai Morcha to liberate Khalistan from Indian occupation,"said Dr. Aulakh.

"Sikhs are a separate nation and ruled Punjab until 1849. No Sikh representative has signed the Indian constitution," Dr. Aulakh said. Sikhism is a sovereign, independent, monotheistic, divenely revealed religion that believes in the equality of the whole human race, including gender equality. Sikhs pray every day for the well being of the whole world. "The people of South Asia must have self-determination now," Dr. Aulakh said. "India is on the verge of disintegration," he said. "The Kashmir issue has been internationalized. America is now involved in South Asia. Self-determination in Kashmir is the only solution," he said. "In a democracy you cannot rule the people against their wishes. Khalistan will be free by 2008."

***

Document

CONGRESSIONAL RECORD -- EXTENSIONS

Thursday, October 17, 2002
107th Congress, 2nd Session
148 Cong Rec E 1877

REFERENCE: Vol. 148, No. 137
SECTION: Extension of Remarks
TITLE: MAIL CENSORSHIP IN INDIA BELIES ITS DEMOCRATIC CLAIMS

HON. DAN BURTON
of Indiana
in the House of Representatives
Wednesday, October 16, 2002

Mr. BURTON of Indiana . Mr. Speaker, I was disturbed to find out that mail sent by the Council of Khalistan has not been reaching India for the past two months. The "world's largest democracy" is once again violating democratic principles by practicing mail censorship. It is violating the fundamental freedom of the people within its borders by prohibiting them from receiving information relating to the violations of the human rights of Sikhs and the peaceful, democratic, nonviolent effort to liberate Khalistan from Indian control.

This is in clear contravention of democratic principles, but that is not surprising from India. It has never been a democracy for the minorities within its borders, but only for the Brahmin fanatics. General Narinder Singh, a respected Sikh leader in Punjab, has said that "Punjab is a police state."

A few years ago, the late journalist Sukhbir Singh Osan was subjected to censorship of his mail and harassment, including telephone calls from unidentified persons saying things like "It is dangerous to write against the government." All this happened because Mr. Osan ran the outstanding news website Burning Punjab, which featured news about government corruption, until he died earlier this year.

These actions prove that India is not a democracy. It is a theocratic Hindu fundamentalist tyranny, and a supporter of terrorism in Sindh and elsewhere, as well as internal terrorism. Accordingly, it should not be a country that receives U.S. aid, yet it is one of the largest recipients despite its anti-Americanism.

We should stop our aid to India until it allows basic human rights such as receiving mail without content control and we should support basic human rights like self-determination. Self-determination is the very foundation of democracy. We should put this Congress on record in support of self-determination for the people of Khalistan, Kashmir, Nagalim, and the other states seeking their freedom. This is the way to real freedom, peace, stability, and prosperity in South Asia.

Mr. Speaker, the Council of Khalistan has issued an excellent press release on this issue, which I would like to place in the Record at this time.

Mail Censorship in "World's Largest Democracy"
Mail From Council of Khalistan Is Not Being Allowed to Get to Addressees in India

Washington, D.C., October 8, 2002_Mail censorship is again being practiced in India, which bills itself as "the world's largest democracy." Mail from the Council of Khalistan to addresses in India has not been received in India for the last two months. The Council of Khalistan is the government pro tempore of Khalistan, the Sikh homeland that declared its independence on October 7, 1987. It has worked for 15 years to liberate Khalistan by peaceful, democratic, nonviolent means and has specifically rejected militancy. Dr. Gurmit Singh Aulakh, President of the Council of Khalistan, has talked to many people in Punjab who have not received any mail from the Council of Khalistan during the last two months. The Council has mailed two mailings to India in that time.

"This undemocratic action shows the true nature of India," said Dr. Aulakh. "Although it claims to be democratic, India has engaged in this kind of censorship before. It controls information and uses its control to whip up hatred and violence against Sikhs and other minorities," he said. "Is this what a democracy does, or is it what a tyranny does?," he said. "Why is a 'democracy'threatened by facts? Is this freedom of speech? These mailings included statements from the Congressional Record, press releases from the Council of Khalistan, and clippings from U.S. and international newspapers," he said.

A few years ago, similar mail censorship was imposed on the late Sukhbir Singh Osan, the journalist who founded the website Burning Punjab, which reported on Indian government corruption, tyranny, and human-rights violations against the Sikh Nation. Osan, who died of a heart attack early this year, also received a telephone call telling him that "it is dangerous to write against the government."

The Indian government controls both major Indian news services, Press Trust of India (PTI) and United News of India (UNI). India has used its control of media to generate violence against minorities. During the 1984 Delhi massacres of Sikhs, Indian media called for the shedding of more Sikh blood.

In February 42 Members of Congress wrote to President Bush to get 52,268 political prisoners released from Indian prisons. The Indian government has murdered over 250,000 Sikhs since 1984. Over 80,000 Kashmiri Muslims have been killed since 1988. More than 200,000 Christians have been killed since 1947, along with tens of thousands of Dalits, Tamils, Assamese, Bodos, Manipuris, and other minorities.

Since Christmas 1998, Christians have been subjected to a wave of oppression. According to the Indian Express of October 7, Hindu militants have forcibly reconverted Christians in Ajmer. Priests have been murdered, nuns have been raped, churches have been burned, Christian schools and prayer halls have been destroyed, and no one has been punished for these acts. Militant Hindu fundamentalists allied with the RSS, the pro-Fascist parent organization of the ruling BJP, burned missionary Graham Staines and his two young sons to death.

"Sikhs are a separate nation. We ruled Punjab until 1849. No Sikh representative has ever signed the Indian constitution," Dr. Aulakh said. "Nations that do not have political power perish," he said. "Remember the words of former Jathedar of the Akal Takht Professor Darshan Singh: 'If a Sikh is not a Khalistani, he is not a Sikh.'Support for Khalistan is picking up internationally. Last month, members of the British Parliament from both political parties supported the Sikh demand for an independent Khalistan. Many U.S. Congressmen are on record in support of an independent Khalistan."

"The censorship of the Council of Khalistan's mail shows that India is a fundamentalist majority Hindu theocracy and is a tyranny, not a democracy. It does not respect human rights for Sikhs, Christians, Muslims, or anyone but Brahmin extremists," Said Dr. Aulakh. "For the well being of the Sikh Nation, to prevent abuses like this from occurring

in the future, we must free Khalistan," he said. "I call on the Sikh leadership in Punjab to launch a Shantmai Morcha to liberate Khalistan from Indian occupation," said Dr. Aulakh. "I call on the Sikh leadership in Punjab to begin a Shantmai Morcha immediately. The people of South Asia must have self-determination now."

***

Document

CONGRESSIONAL RECORD -- EXTENSIONS

Tuesday, October 15, 2002
107th Congress, 2nd Session
148 Cong Rec E 1867

REFERENCE: Vol. 148, No. 135
SECTION: Extension of Remarks
TITLE: COUNCIL OF KHALISTAN MARKS 15 YEARS OF SERVICE

HON. DAN BURTON
of Indiana
in the House of Representatives
Tuesday, October 15, 2002

Mr. BURTON of Indiana . Mr. Speaker, this week the Council of Khalistan, which leads the fight to free the Sikhs from the repression of India, marked its fifteenth anniversary. It was founded on October 7, 1987, when the Sikh Nation declared its independence and named their new country Khalistan.

The repression that has been inflicted on the Sikhs and other minorities in India before and after that declaration is well documented. The Indian regime has murdered over 250,000 Sikhs since 1984, according to the book "The Politics of Genocide" by Inderjit Singh Jaijee. A report from the Movement Against State Repression notes that over 52,000 remain in Indian jails as political prisoners without charge or trial. Some of them have been held since 1984. Another 50,000 have simply been made to "disappear."

Sikhs are not the only ones. Christians, Muslims, Bodos, Assamese, Manipuris, and others have felt the brunt of Indian oppression, with tens of thousands of them losing their lives. That is why there are seventeen freedom movements in India. The Council of Khalistan, while it focuses on the Sikh struggle, has spoken out for freedom and an end to the repression for all these peoples and nations.

Mr. Speaker, I would just like to take the occasion to congratulate the Council of Khalistan on its 15 years of service.

***

Document

CONGRESSIONAL RECORD -- EXTENSIONS

Friday, October 11, 2002
107th Congress, 2nd Session
148 Cong Rec E 1859

REFERENCE: Vol. 148, No. 134
SECTION: Extension of Remarks
TITLE: TWO SIKH MEN DETAINED AFTER FLIGHT_RACIAL PROFILING
MUST BE STOPPED

HON. CYNTHIA A. McKINNEY
of Georgia
in the House of Representatives
Friday, October 11, 2002

Mrs. McKINNEY Mr. Speaker, I was disturbed to read that two Sikh men were detained after a flight simply for using the bathroom. This is ethnic profiling of the worst kind and it must be stopped.

Apparently, what happened was that the two men, Gurdeep Wander and Harinder Pal Singh, were flying to Las Vegas for a convention and they missed their connection. They were a bit late the next morning so they ran onto the plane. Apparently, this made the flight crew suspicious.

Then Mr. Singh, Mr. Wander, and another man, who was Hispanic, used the same bathroom on the plane. When Mr. Singh, the last of the three, went to use it, the flight attendant tried to convince him that it was locked and unavailable. She claimed that she had read that people could make bombs in the bathrooms by bringing the parts on separately. I wonder if three white people using the bathroom in quick succession would have made her think the same thing.

After the plane made an emergency landing, the two Sikh men and an Egyptian man were detained on the plane while police dogs surrounded it and sniffed for weapons. Then the Sikh men were arrested for interfering with a flight crew.

Mr. Speaker, the Secretary of Transportation must take appropriate action against this airline and its discriminatory employees. This kind of racial profiling cannot be allowed. I call on the Secretary of Transportation to take appropriate steps to end this racist practice and to make sure that the victims of this incident are fully compensated. We must make it clear that we will not tolerate racial profiling.

Mr. Speaker, the Council of Khalistan has written a letter to Secretary Mineta asking him to take appropriate action in response to this incident. I would like to place that letter into the Record now.

Council of Khalistan,
Washington, DC, October 8, 2002.
Hon. Norman Mineta
Secretary of Transportation,
Washington, DC.

Dear Secretary Mineta: I am writing to you to protest an incident of racial profiling against Sikhs that occurred on a Northwest Airlines flight on September 11. Gurdeep Wander and Haninder Pal Singh, two men of Sikh descent, were headed to a convention in Las Vegas on a Northwest Airlines flight after missing a previous connecting flight in Minneapolis.

Mr. Wander and Mr. Singh chose to fly on September 10 to avoid flying on the anniversary of the September 11 attacks. However, they missed their connecting flight so they had to stay overnight in Minneapolis. They were then placed on a flight on the morning of the September 11. Mr. Wander and Mr. Singh were late for their flight. They rushed on board the plane, which the flight attendant apparently regarded as suspicious. All that the two Sikh men carried was the shaving kits that they had been given by the airline. Their luggage had already been forwarded to Las Vegas. Would the flight attendants regard white men rushing onto the flight as suspicious? I don't think so.

The flight attendants' suspicion was apparently further aroused when right after Mr. Singh and Mr. Wander, a Hispanic man named Carlos Nieves rushed onto the plane.

Shortly before departure, Mr. Wander got out of his seat and got the shaving kit the airline had given him. He took it with him to the bathroom. When Mr. Wander had been in the bathroom a few minutes, a flight attendant asked him to sit down. He asked for a minute to finish up what he was doing. When Mr. Wander came out, Mr. Nieves went to use the bathroom. Mr. Singh was next to use it. The flight attendant tried to prevent Mr. Singh from using the restroom, claiming that it was locked. She later claimed that she had read that explosive devices could be assembled on the flight if separate individuals carried the components.

After the plane made an emergency landing in Fort Smith, Arkansas, Mr. Singh, Mr. Wander, and a Muslim from Egypt named Alaaeldin Abdelsalam were detained. The plane was surrounded by bomb-sniffing dogs and all the luggage was taken out of the plane.

Secretary Mineta, this is clearly racial profiling and it must not be allowed. I urge you to take appropriate corrective action to correct the abuse of Mr. Singh, Mr. Wander, Mr. Abdelsalam, and Mr. Nieves. I also respectfully request that you issue an urgent directive banning racial profiling on any U.S. flight. Since these airlines are regulated by your department and your department controls airport security, you must act to ensure that every passenger is treated equally and fairly. Please take appropriate action to correct this situation today. Thank you in advance for your help.

Sincerely,

Gurmit Singh Aulakh,
President.

***

Document

CONGRESSIONAL RECORD -- EXTENSIONS

Friday, October 11, 2002
107th Congress, 2nd Session
148 Cong Rec E 1865

REFERENCE: Vol. 148, No. 134
SECTION: Extension of Remarks
TITLE: CONGRATULATING THE COUNCIL OF KHALISTAN ON 15 YEARS
OF WORKING FOR FREEDOM

HON. CYNTHIA A. McKINNEY
of Georgia
in the House of Representatives
Friday, October 11, 2002

Ms. McKINNEY . Mr. Speaker, one of the things I have been proud of in my time in Congress is the opportunity I have had to help inform people about human rights and the struggle for freedom in the world. In that light, I would like to take this opportunity to note the fifteenth anniversary of the declaration of independence by the Sikh Nation of Khalistan which occurred on October 7, 1987, and the formation of the Council of Khalistan at that time.

The Council of Khalistan leads the Sikhs in their struggle to free themselves from repression, corruption, and tyranny imposed on them by India. It has always conducted that struggle in a peaceful, democratic, nonviolent way and has explicitly rejected militancy. I am proud to have been able to help the Council inform people about the Sikhs' struggle for freedom.

The President of the Council of Khalistan, Dr. Gurmit Singh Aulakh, has been tireless in fighting for freedom in the subcontinent. I am proud to know him. I wish everyone in Washington were so tireless, and I wish him success in his endeavors.

I would like to congratulate Dr. Aulakh and the Council of Khalistan on this occasion and I would like to wish them a successful convention this coming weekend in Philadelphia. Last year's convention was in my home town, Atlanta.

Mr. Speaker, I hope my colleagues will Join me in congratulating the Council of Khalistan on this important milestone.

***

Document

CONGRESSIONAL RECORD -- EXTENSIONS

Tuesday, October 08, 2002
107th Congress, 2nd Session
148 Cong Rec E 1796

REFERENCE: Vol. 148, No. 131
SECTION: Extension of Remarks
TITLE: STOP RACIAL PROFILING OF SIKHS

HON. EDOLPHUS TOWNS
of New York
in the House of Representatives
Tuesday, October 8, 2002

Mr. TOWNS . Mr. Speaker, racial profiling of Sikhs continues in our country a year after terrorists attacked New York and Washington. According to the September 20 issue of the New York Times, two Sikh men were arrested while trying to fly from New York to Las Vegas for an Exxon convention. Mr. Wander could be facing up to 20 years in prison, according to the article.

Gurdeep Wander and Harinder Pal Singh were headed to that convention on a Northwest Airlines flight after missing a previous connecting flight in Minneapolis. They were flying on the night of September 10 to avoid flying on the anniversary of the September 11 attacks, but had to fly on the morning of the 11th after being delayed. Apparently, it is now a crime to fly if your hair is long and your skin is dark.

Mr. Wander and Mr. Singh were late for their flight and ran on board. Right after them, a Hispanic man named Carlos Nieves rushed onto the plane. All that the two Sikh men carried was the shaving kits they had been given by the airline, because their luggage had already been forwarded to Las Vegas. The flight attendants said that they found three swarthy men rushing onto the plane suspicious. I can't help but wonder if they would have been suspicious of three white men rushing onto a plane.

Right before departure, Mr. Wander got out of his seat and got the shaving kit the airline had given him. He asked to use the restroom. After a few minutes, the flight attendant asked him to sit down and he asked for a minute to finish up. After Mr. Wander came out, Mr. Nieves went to the restroom, followed by Mr. Singh. The flight attendant tried to prevent Mr. Singh from using the restroom, claiming that explosive devices could be assembled if separate individuals carried the components. Because of Mr. Wander's, Mr. Nieves's, and Mr. Singh's skin color, she clearly assumed that they were doing so.

After the plane made an emergency landing in Arkansas, Mr. Singh, Mr. Wander, and an Egyptian man named Alaaeldin Abdelsalam were detained. All the luggage was taken out of the plane. Soon, the plane was surrounded by bomb-sniffing dogs.

It is clear that Northwest Airlines detained these individuals because of their darker skin color. This is racial profiling, and it is wrong. It must be ended. The Transportation Department must put out an order banning racial profiling. Otherwise, it will be dangerous for any minority to fly.

We must treat all passengers equally. No one should be detained for his or her skin color. It must be stopped now. I call on Northwest and all the airlines to end this racist practice and I hope that those who are victimized by this practice will get full recompense.

Mr. Speaker, I would like to place the New York Times article I referred to into the Record at this time.

From the New York Times, Sept. 20, 2002
Bound for Las Vegas, 2 Men Take a 9/11 Detour to Jail
(By Edward Wong)

Fort Smith, Ark., Sept. 19._The distance between a convention in Las Vegas and a brick jail here in the lush plains of western Arkansas proved far shorter than Gurdeep Wander and Harinder Singh ever could have imagined.

Mr. Wander and Mr. Singh, two gas station workers of Indian descent from New Jersey and Pennsylvania, boarded a Northwest Airlines flight on Sept. 10 from La Guardia Airport, bound for an Exxon convention. In one of the more Kafkaesque instances of air travel jitters, they landed in the county jail here on Sept. 11, and spent more than a week sleeping in orange jump suits between razor-wire fences. Today, Mr. Wander appeared in a federal courtroom and quietly listened as Judge Beverley Stites Jones said that she had found probable cause that he had intimidated a flight attendant.

A grand jury will probably decide next week whether to indict him in the crime, which carries up to 20 years in prison.

The story of how Mr. Wander and Mr. Singh, who was released on Wednesday, ended up here involves a missed plane connection, terrorism concerns, a surplus of facial hair and arguably poor judgment on the part of many people. Mr. Wander's lawyer, Matthew J. Ketcham, says his client is the victim of racial profiling and paranoia. Federal prosecutors argue that Mr. Wander scared a flight attendant when he refused to sit down, which resulted in the pilot's landing the Las Vegas-bound plane here.

Mr. Wander, who is a 48-year-old American citizen, and Mr. Singh, a 41-year-old citizen of India, made it a point to travel on Sept. 10 because they wanted to avoid flying on the anniversary of the Sept. 11 attacks, Mr. Ketcham said. Their plane arrived late in Minneapolis, and the two missed their connecting flight. The airline gave each a shaving kit, and they slept in a nearby hotel, Mr. Ketcham said.

They caught a flight the next morning, barely making a connection to Las Vegas through Memphis. They rushed on board, followed by a Hispanic man named Carlos Nieves. Mr. Wander and Mr. Singh carried only their shaving kits, because their luggage had been forwarded. The three men sat in different parts of the plane.

The sudden appearance of the men seemed suspicious to the three flight attendants, who asked burly passengers to keep an eye on them, said Deborah Summers, a flight attendant who testified here today. Right before takeoff, with the "fasten seatbelt" sign on, Mr. Wander left his seat at the rear to get his shaving kit from an overhead compartment. Ms. Summers said she noticed from his boarding pass that he had not taken his assigned seat next to Mr. Singh.

Mr. Ketcham said Mr. Wander just wanted to stretch out because he had had little sleep.

After the plane began ascending, and while the "fasten seatbelt" sign was still on, Mr. Wander asked Ms. Summers if he could use the restroom. She let him go. He stayed inside for 10 minutes, Ms. Summers said, prompting her to knock on the door. Mr. Wander opened the door, told her he needed to clean up and shut the door. She knocked again soon afterward. When he opened the door, he was shirtless and in the middle of shaving. The pilot urged her to check his razor, then told her to tell him to get out. After five exchanges, Mr. Wander sat down.

"He didn't refuse to leave," Mr. Ketcham said. "She only asked him explicitly twice to sit down and he asked for a minute to finish up."

Almost immediately, Mr. Nieves, who did not know the other two men, got up to use the same restroom. This was reported to the pilot, Capt. David McGuirk, who had ordered all passengers to stay in their seats. After Mr. Nieves left the restroom, Mr. Singh went to use it.

By now, Ms. Summers said, she was trying to lock the restroom. She had learned that "an explosive device can be assembled if separate individuals carry the components," an affidavit by an F.B.I. agent who questioned her said.

Ms. Summers tried to dissuade Mr. Singh from using the same restroom, saying it was broken. Mr. Singh insisted, because another one in the rear was occupied, said George Lucas, a lawyer for Mr. Singh. He used the other restroom, then sat down next to Mr. Wander.

While Mr. Singh was in the restroom, Captain McGuirk decided to make an emergency landing here. Soon, the plane was surrounded by police officers, fire trucks and bomb-sniffing dogs. The three men, along with a native of Egypt living in Louisiana named Alaaeldin M. Abdelsalam, were told to remain in their seats, Mr. Ketcham said. "It's no coincidence that these dark-skinned men were singled out," he said.

The plane's luggage was pulled out, and a dog raised an alert at Mr. Abdelsalam's bag, which was blown open with a water cannon. He was arrested, along with Mr. Wander and Mr. Singh. Mr. Nieves was released after questioning. Mr. Abdelsalam was released after he explained that he worked in an oil field and that his chemical-stained boots and hard hat were in his bag.

The authorities let Mr. Singh go on Wednesday after he agreed to pay a $500 civil penalty. As for Mr. Wander, Mr. Cromwell said the intimidation charge "is warranted." Mr. Wander was released today on a $25,000 bond.

Ms. Summers, prosecutors and Northwest Airlines said the flight crew's actions were based on the behavior of the men, not on their skin color.

Mr. Singh could not be reached for comment, and Mr. Wander did not make a public statement today. After his release, he piled into a car with family members to return to his home in Washington, N.J. Apparently, no one wanted to fly.

***

Document

CONGRESSIONAL RECORD -- EXTENSIONS

Thursday, October 03, 2002
107th Congress, 2nd Session
148 Cong Rec E 1738

REFERENCE: Vol. 148, No. 128
SECTION: Extension of Remarks
TITLE: INDIAN COMPANIES SELLING MILITARY MATERIALS TO IRAQ

HON. DAN BURTON
of Indiana
in the House of Representatives
Wednesday, October 2, 2002

Mr. BURTON of Indiana . Mr. Speaker, just as we are about to go to war with Iraq, supposedly democratic India is propping up that brutal dictatorship.

According to an article in the September 25 issue of the Times of India by Rashmee Z. Ahmed, Iraq possesses some of the deadliest weapons of mass destructions and missile infrastructures thanks to the illicit help of Indian companies. One such company, NEC Engineers Private Limited, has "extensive links in Iraq," according to the article. Although such transactions violate India's export control laws, they are apparently taking place with a wink and a nod from the Indian government. Earlier I exposed India's oil transactions with Iraq, which violates UN sanctions.

In spite of this, according to the September 18 issue of the Times of India, the United States and India are conducting joint naval exercises.

On January 2, the Washington Times exposed the fact that India is sponsoring cross-border terrorism in the province of Sindh in Pakistan. India's leading newsmagazine, India Today, reported that India created the Liberation Tigers of Tamil Eelam (LTTE), which the United States government calls a "terrorist organization." The U.S. State Department reported that the Indian government paid 41,000 cash bounties to police officers for killing Sikhs. According to the Indian newspaper Hitavada, the late governor of Punjab, Surendra Nath, received $1.5 billion from the Indian government to forment terrorism in Punjab and Kashmir. The book Soft Target shows that the Indian government blew up its own airliner in 1985 to blame Sikhs. This has been discussed many times.

If India is practicing and sponsoring terrorism and helping to build Saddam Hussein's war machine, why are we conducting joint naval exercises with India? Isn't this like conducting joint exercises with the enemy? I call on the Defense Department to call off these exercises.

Mr. Speaker, we can help bring freedom to South Asia and end India's flirtation with terrorist enemies of the United States. The time has come to impose sanctions on India, cut off its aid, and openly declare our support for self-determination for all the people of the subcontinent. This is the best way to help see to it that everyone in that troubled region can live in freedom, dignity, prosperity, stability, and peace.

I am inserting the articles from the Times of India into the Record.

[From the Times of India, Sept. 25, 2002]
Indian Firms Arming Iraq, Says UK
(By Rashmee Z. Ahmed)

London: Britain has alleged that Saddam Hussein's Iraq is able and willing to deploy some of its deadliest weapons of mass destruction in under one hour from the order being given and that it possesses missile infrastructure produced with the illicit help of Indian companies.

The British claims of Indian involvement are contained in a 55-page dossier controversially and uniquely published by Tony Blair on Tuesday on the basis of what he called "unprecedented and secret" intelligence information.

The dossier, received by largely skeptical political, press and public opinion here, tries to make a case for a Gulf War II-type operation to disarm Saddam and "regime change". Repeating US and UK claims that Baghdad continues to improve its missile capability, the dossier names names when it comes to alleged Indian support for Iraqi missile production.

The document, which only obliquely blames "Africa" for supplying uranium to Saddam's secret nuclear weapons programme, pinpoints India as part of the supply chain for banned propellant chemicals destined for ballistic missiles. One of these, ammonium perchlorate, the dossier says, was "illicitly" provided by an Indian company, NEC Engineers Private Limited, which had "extensive links in Iraq", particularly to its al-Mamoun missile production plant and Fallujah 2 chlorine plant.

Analysts added that in an intriguing insight, the dossier appeared to indicate that much of this had been known to New Delhi for some time.

"(The) Indian authorities recently suspended its (the company's) export license" after "an extensive investigation", the dossier says, "although other individuals and companies are still illicitly procuring for Iraq".

In what defense experts suggested was yet another indication of a host of "front companies" in India and elsewhere, the dossier further says the machine tools and raw materials supply chain crucially remains in place for Iraq's al-Samoud and longer-range missile systems.

Even as Iraq refuted the dossier's claims as "totally baseless" and a "Zionist campaign", Blair went before a heated emergency session of the British parliament to declare, "regime change would be a wonderful thing".

Blair's dossier, which precedes Washington's promised evidence on Iraq, was greeted by boredom and yawns among sections of the pundits and politicians, who said it crucially lacked the so-called killer fact.

Commentators said the dossier, which Blair described as primarily for the British people, may do little to persuade opinion further afield, notably India. India has long said that it is opposed to military intervention in Iraq and that "regime change" is an issue for the Iraqi people.

Indian diplomats react

Responding to the allegations in Blair's dossier, Navdeep Suri, spokesman for the Indian High Commission confirmed that the case against the company, NEC, had been charged and the matter was currently sub-judice.

He said, "such actions are in violation of India's export control laws and whenever such a violation comes to the government's attention, firm action is taken". He declined to comment on what he called "speculative statements" about "other (Indian) individuals and companies" continuing to procure illicit material for Iraq.

- - - - - - - - -

From the Hindustan Times, Sept. 23, 2002
Labour MP Stokes Khalistan fire in Britain
(By Sanjay Suri)

Wolverhampton, September 23._A senior ruling Labour Party MP has supported a demand for a separate Sikh state of Khalistan if the move is made "peacefully and democratically".

Rob Marris, Labur MP, expressed his support at a meeting organized by a pro-Khalistan group in a gurdwara in Wolverhampton Sunday.

At the same meeting a senior shadow minister of the Conservative Party expressed support for Sikhs in Britain to register themselves as Sikhs and not Indians.

Rob Marris, who is treasurer of the All Party Panjabis in Britain Parliamentary Group, expressed strong support for the Sikh Agenda that the Sikh Secretariat has produced. The agenda calls for Sikhs to be registered as separate from Indians in Britain, and calls for self-determination in Punjab.

Marris addressed specifically the demand for Khalistan raised at the meeting. "That is an issue dear to your hearts I can see by looking down the hall. Those in the Indian subcontinent, who peacefully and democratically push for self-determination for that part of the Indian subcontinent, their opinion for self-determination, their right for an independent Khalistan should not be suppressed."

The comment was followed by loud cries of Khalistan zindabad.

Marris said it would not be right for parties in Britain to decide whether there should be self-determination in that part of the subcontinent. "But it would be right for people to democratically and peacefully express their opinions."

A senior shadow minister of the Conservative Party declared at the meeting of Khalistanis Sunday that the Conservatives will give Sikhs the option to register as Sikhs and not Indians when the party comes to power.

The announcement follows backing to the Khalistanis' demand by two senior shadow ministers of the Conservative Party earlier. The developments at the meeting Sunday mark rapid strides the Khalistani group has made in Britain in recent weeks. There has been little evidence of support for the Khalistanis among Sikhs, but strong Conservative Party backing to this group pursuing what they call the "Sikh agenda" has given them new prominence.

The Sikh Secretariat, which organised the meeting in Wolverhampton, had said 10,000 would attend. Only a few hundred came, most of them brought in coachloads from London and Southampton.

Caroline Spelman, shadow cabinet minister for international development and women's affairs, told the meeting that the Sikhs are a distinctive group, "and yet we have very little idea how many Sikhs there are".

Spelman said: "At best that is discourteous, at worst it deprives you of proper monitoring of what your needs are."

She said it was "extraordinary" that an opportunity to find out had been missed in the 2001 census.

She said the Labour government should monitor Sikhs separately and "if they fail, then that will be a task for a Conservative administration to deliver on".

The move is politically loaded. It would give Sikhs the option to declare themselves Sikhs and not Indians. It would mean that the estimated 1.2 million Indian population in Britain could fall to about half of that on the records.

Marris supported the demand for separate listing of Sikhs in Britain. He said there would be many opportunities to do so before the 2011 census.

Amrik Singh Gill, who heads the group that called the meeting, said Khalistan "is the only way out" for Sikhs and that "we will get our own rule". Posters of separatist leader Bhindranwale lined the walls of the hall where the meeting was held.

***

Document

CONGRESSIONAL RECORD -- EXTENSIONS

Monday, September 30, 2002
107th Congress, 2nd Session
148 Cong Rec E 1705

REFERENCE: Vol. 148, No. 125
SECTION: Extension of Remarks
TITLE: SIKH AUTHOR AND SCHOLAR GURTEJ SINGH EXPOSES INDIAN TYRANNY

HON. CYNTHIA A. McKINNEY
of Georgia
in the House of Representatives
Monday, September 30, 2002

Ms. McKINNEY . Mr. Speaker, recently a seminar was held in New York on the oppression of minorities in Hindu nationalist India. One of the speakers was the Sikh scholar and author Gurtej Singh, Professor of Sikhism. He is also the author of the book Chakravyuh: Web of Indian Secularism.

Professor Gurtej Singh discussed the history of Sikh independence and the Sikh religion. He exposed the connivance of Sikh leaders of all parties with the Indian government. He discussed the efforts of the Hindu nationalists to absorb the Sikh religion.

Professor Gurtej Singh has been honored by the Shiromani Gudrwara Prabandhak Committee, which runs the Gurdwaras (Sikh Temples) in Punjab, Khalistan. He is a very well respected Sikh scholar.

The information he discussed underlies the need for the Sikhs in Punjab, Khalistan to work to achieve their freedom. Unfortunately, the Indian government has recently reaffirmed through its Ambassador to the U.S. that it will hold a plebiscite in Kashmir, as it promised in 1948, or in Punjab.

Since the United States was formed to be the bastion of freedom, we owe it to the people there to do what we can to support their freedom efforts. We should declare our support for a free and fair plebiscite in Punjab, Khalistan, in Kashmir, in primilarly Christian Nagaland, and elsewhere in the subcontinent where people are seeking freedom and independence. The democratic way is the best way to resolve issues. Until all people in India enjoy the full civil rights of democratic citizens, until human rights are respected, India should receive no American aid or trade. This is the best way that America can help bring freedom to that troubled region.

Mr. Speaker, the Council of Khalistan recently published a press release commending Professor Gurtej Singh for his work for human rights and his presentation at the New York panel. I would like to insert this press release into the Record at this time.

S. Gurtej Singh Exposes Indian Tyranny at Seminar

Washington, D.C., May 16, 2002._The Sikh Nation appreciates the contributions of S. Gurtej Singh IAS, who spoke at a seminar in New York last week. He exposed the genocide of the Indian government and the betrayal and corruption of the Akali Dal leadership in his book, Chakravyuh: Web of Indian Secularism, and in his speech he gave historical facts about the sovereign, independent Sikh state and the independence of the Sikh religion since its inception. He explained how the Hindu majority wants to assimilate the Sikh religion and establish a Hindu Rashtra. We recommend that everyone read his book.

"S. Gurtej Singh has done an excellent job of exposing the connivance of the Akali leaders, such as Badal, Tohra, and Mann, with the Indian government in its campaign of terror against the Sikh Nation," said Dr. Gurmit Singh Aulakh, President of the Council of Khalistan. "He is to be saluted," Dr. Aulakh said. "The Sikh Nation needs more good Sikhs like S. Gurtej Singh if it is ever to end the oppression." The Council of Khalistan is the government pro tempore of Khalistan, the Sikh homeland that declared its independence from India on October 7, 1987. The Council of Khalistan leads the Sikh Nation's struggle for independence.

"Gurtej Singh's presentation was excellent and he made a detailed presentation of the abuses and oppression of the Sikh Nation," Dr. Aulakh said. "The time has come to throw out the conniving Sikh leadership of the Akalis and Congress and unite behind committed, principled, pro-Sikh leaders who are committed to freedom," he said.

The Indian government has murdered over 250,000 Sikhs since 1984. Over 75,000 Kashmiri Muslims have been killed since 1988. More than 200,000 Christians have been killed since 1947, along with tens of thousands of Dalits, Tamils, Assamese, Bodos, Manipuris, and other minorities. Last month, police stood by as militant Hindus attacked Muslims in Gujarat. Over 5000 people died, according to the Indian newspaper The Hindu. The Indian government paid twice as much compensation to the families of Hindus who were killed as it paid to Muslims who were killed.

The U.S. State Department reported in 1994 that the Indian government paid out over 41,000 cash bounties to police officers for killing Sikhs. Since Christmas 1998, a wave of violence against Christians has seen priests murdered, nuns being raped, churches being burned, Christian schools and prayer halls destroyed, and no one has been punished for these acts. Militant Hindu fundamentalists allied with the pro-Fascist RSS, the parent organization of the ruling BJP, burned missionary Graham Staines and his two young sons to death.

"For the survival of the Sikh Nation, the time has come to launch a Shantmai Morcha (peaceful agitation) to liberate Khalistan from Indian occupation," Dr. Aulakh said. "I call on the Sikh leadership in Punjab to begin a Shantmai Morcha immediately. If they will not, the Sikh Nation should rid itself of them and support leaders who will do so," he said. "I also call on the United States government to support freedom for Khalistan and the other minority nations seeking their freedom from India,"

he said. *"Sikhs are a separate nation and ruled Punjab until 1849. No Sikh has signed the Indian constitution," Dr. Aulakh said.*

Sikhism is a sovereign, independent, monotheistic religion which believes in the equality of the whole human race, including gender equality. Sikhs pray every day for the well being of all humanity. The Sikh Nation was established as sovereign. Guru gave political power to the Sikh Nation. ("In Grieb Sikhan Ko Deon Patshahi.") "Freedom and self-determination are the birthright of all peoples and nations. The people of South Asia must have self-determination now," Dr. Aulakh said. "India is on the verge of disintegration," he said. "Khalistan will be free by 2008."

***

Document

CONGRESSIONAL RECORD -- EXTENSIONS

Monday, September 30, 2002
107th Congress, 2nd Session
148 Cong Rec E 1706

REFERENCE: Vol. 148, No. 125
SECTION: Extension of Remarks
TITLE: INDIA CANNOT GOVERN WITHOUT THE PEOPLE'S CONSENT

HON. CYNTHIA A. McKINNEY
of Georgia
in the House of Representatives
Monday, September 30, 2002

Ms. McKINNEY . Mr. Speaker, no government can govern without the consent of the governed. That is one of the founding principles of America.

Earlier this year, my friend Dr. Gurmit Singh Aulakh, President of the Council of Khalistan, issued a "New Year's Message to the Sikh Nation." In it, he noted that India is governing the Sikhs of Punjab, Khalistan, the Christians of Nagaland, the Muslims of Kashmir, and many other minority nations without their consent.

In the letter, the Council of Khalistan said that the elections earlier this year in Punjab won't have any effect in terms of freeing the people, but merely change the facts of the oppressors. The letter noted that in the likely event of a war between India and Pakistan, it will be the Sikhs and the Kashmiris who will be the primary victims. He called on Sikhs not to fight for India. He reminded us that no Sikh representative ever signed India's constitution. How can India's constitution be binding on the Sikhs when they have never been a party to it?

Dr. Aulakh wrote that India is not one country and is just a remnant of British colonialism. He wrote that its breakup is inevitable. On January 25, Indian Home Minister L.K. Advani admitted that when Kashmir leaves

India, India will unravel. That is why India is so scared of the 17 freedom movements within its borders. There is clear sentiment for freedom within India's borders, Mr. Speaker. We must do what we can to help that cause along.

What can America do to help the cause of freedom in South Asia? For one thing, we can try to keep India and Pakistan at peace. Unfortunately, there has already been firing across the Line of Control in Kashmir. We should use our diplomatic power to stop the fighting before it becomes all-out war. Both sides have nuclear weapons, Mr. Speaker, and the Pakistani government has been quite helpful to us in the war on terror, at least until India's military maneuvers forced them to divert troops to the Indian-Pakinstani border.

We should stop our aid to India to help stop the atrocities against Sikhs, Christians, Kashmiri Muslims, dark-skinned Dalit "untouchables," and others. We should also publicly declare our support for self-determination for Khalistan, Kashmir, Nagaland, and all the minority nations and peoples seeking their freedom from India.

Mr. Speaker, the Council of Khalistan's open letter is very informative. I think my colleagues will be very well informed by reading it. Therefore, I would like to place it in the Record now.

Council of Khalistan,
Washington, DC, January 3, 2002.

Khalsa Ji: Wahe Guru Ji Ka Khalsa, Wahe Guru Ji Ki Fateh!

Happy New Year to you and your family and friends. May 2002 be the best year you have ever had.

At the dawn of a new year, freedom for Khalistan is closer than ever. India is showing its instability. The Indian government is so desperate that it was caught red-handed murdering. Sikh girls in Kashmir. Just as it did in Chithisinghpora, the regime is committing terrorist acts to try to set minority nations against one another in pursuit of India's ongoing drive for hegemony in South Asia. On May 27, several Indian soldiers were caught red-handed trying to set fire to a Gurdwara and some Sikh homes in Kashmir. Sikh and Muslim residents of the village overwhelmed the troops and stopped them from carrying out this atrocity. Now India has set up another terrorist incident that has cost the lives of at least three Sikh girls.

India has massed large numbers of troops and warheads on the border. Unfortunately, the upcoming war will result in the deaths of many Sikhs, Kashmiris, and other minorities, exactly the result the Indian government wants. I urge Sikhs not to support India. Punjab and Kashmir will be the main battlegrounds. Sikhs will be killed in the upcoming war more than any other people will, as they have in every war in the past. It is Sikhs who will suffer the most, and that suffering would be made worse by shedding Sikh blood for the oppressors of the Sikh Nation. We do not have a choice of peace or war. The Sikh Nation has a right to choose peace, and that choice requires the independence of

Khalistan. To save Sikh lives, do not fight with the Hindu slavemasters. Instead, work to liberate Khalistan.

This is an ideal opportunity to begin a Shantmai Morcha and form a Khalsa Raj Party to achieve independence for Khalistan and to liberate the other countries seeking their freedom from Indian occupation. Take advantage of this opportunity. Fight to free Khalistan. Remember the words of former Akal Takht Jathedar Professor Darshan Singh: "If a Sikh is not Khalistani, he is not a Sikh." Self-determination is the right of all people and nations.

India is not one nation. It has 18 official languages. The Sikh Nation's sentiment for Khalistan is clear. Pro-Khalistan handbills were handed out at the Golden Temple on June 7 during the commemoration of Gallughara Divas and Sant Bhindranwale's martyrdom. Ajmer Singh Lakhowal, the head of the Bharat Kisan Union, has called for self-determination for the Sikhs. The flame of freedom burns bright in the hearts of the Sikhs.

India wants to wipe out minority nations so that they cannot ask for their freedom. To achieve that objective, the Indian government has murdered over 250,000 Sikhs since 1984, over 200,000 Christians in Nagaland since 1947, more than 75,000 Kashmiri Muslims since 1988, and tens of thousands of Dalits (dark-skinned "Untouchables," the aboriginal people of South Asia), Tamils, Bodos, Assamese, Manipuris, and others.

The Deccan Chronicle reported that the Indian government knew of the attack on Parliament, which killed 13 people, in advance and did nothing. The Indian army carried out the attack to provide a pretext for an attack on Pakistan and Kashmir. It hopes to use the killings of young Sikh girls to get Sikh to fight against Kashmiris.

India has a long record of terrorism. In November 1994, the Indian newspaper Hitavada reported that the Indian government paid the late governor of Punjab, Surendra Nath, approximately $1.5 billion to organize and support covert state terrorism in Punjab, Khalistan, and in Kashmir. The book Soft Target, written by two very respected journalists from the Toronto Star and the Toronto Globe and Mail, conclusively establishes that the Indian government blew up its own airliner in 1985, killing 329 innocent people. According to India Today, the Indian government created the Liberation Tigers of Tamil Eelam (LTTE) and put up LTTE leaders in New Delhi's finest hotel. According to journalist Justin Raimondo of www.antiwar.com, George Fernandes, now the Defense Minister, even raised funds for the LTTE. The LTTE were created to stoop a U.S. broadcast tower in Sri Lanka. The Indian government turned on the LTTE because the LTTE nows seeks an independent country for Tamils.

A report issued in April by the Movement Against State Repression (MASR) shows that India admitted that it held 52,268 political prisoners under the totalitarian "Terrorist and Disruptive Activities Act" (TADA), which expired in 1995. Persons arrested under TADA are routinely re-arrested upon their release. Cases were routinely registered against Sikh activists under TADA in states other than Punjab to give the police an excuse to continue holding them. The MASR report quotes the Punjab Civil Magistracy as writing "If we add up the figures of the last few years the number of innocent persons killed would run into lakhs [lsqb]hundreds of thousands.[rsqb]" As General Narinder Singh has said, "Punjab is a police state."

These Sikh political prisoners and the tens of thousands of other political prisoners held in India must be released immediately. Even before their release, the political prisoners should also be given the Khalsa Raj Party nomination for the seats in the Legislative Assembly, the SGPC, and when the parliamentary elections come up, for Parliament. The Sikh Nation will vote for these Sikh political prisoners, as they are the heroes of the Sikh Nation. No government can govern without the consent of the governed. The present Akali leadership of Badal, Tohra, Mann and others are the agents of the Indian government and are under their control. Do not trust them. Remember, Badal promised during the last election campaign that he would release Sikh political prisoners, punish guilty police officials who committed atrocities against the Sikh, and from a commission to investigate atrocities committed against the Sikhs since 1984.

In 1947, when India was divided, the cunning and deceitful Hindu leadership promised that Sikhs would have the glow of freedom in Punjab and that no law affecting Sikh rights would be passed without Sikh consent. As soon as the transfer of power had occurred and India was free, those promises were broken. Instead, India began its effort to wipe out the Sikh people, the Sikh Nation, and the Sikh religion. The Sikh Nation must regain its sovereignty to survive.

Sikh gave over 80 percent of the sacrifices to free India from the British. At that time, they were only 1.6 percent of the population. Sikhs are the ones who suffered the most after the freedom and partition of India. The Khalsa Panth can do it again to free itself from the slavery of Hindu India.

A free Khalistan will bring prosperity to the people of Punjab farmers will be able to sell their produce at high prices in the international market and buy cheaper fertilizers, insecticides, and seeds. Farm produce will not lie in the market for weeks without buyers as it did during the sale of the rice crop last year.

We must have a full, free, and fair plebiscite on the status of Khalistan and we must launch a Shantmai Morcha to liberate our homeland. Let us take this opportunity to bring freedom to our homeland and all the countries of South Asia.

Panth Da Sewadar,
Dr. Gurmit Singh Aulakh,
President, Council of Khalistan.

***

Document

CONGRESSIONAL RECORD -- EXTENSIONS

Monday, September 30, 2002
107th Congress, 2nd Session
148 Cong Rec E 1708

REFERENCE: Vol. 148, No. 125
SECTION: Extension of Remarks
TITLE: GUJARAT VIOLENCE A POGROM AGAINST MUSLIMS, NEWS
REPORT SAYS

HON. CYNTHIA A. McKINNEY.
of Georgia
in the House of Representatives
Monday, September 30, 2002

Ms. McKINNEY . Mr. Speaker, on June 4, an interesting article appeared at Islam Online, an Internet news site. It said that the People's Union for Democratic Rights (PUDR) had found that the recent violence in Gujarat in which, according to The Hindu newspaper, over 5,000 people were killed, was a planned pogrom designed to reduce Muslims to second-class citizens. Unfortunately, Muslim and other minorities such as Christians, Sikhs, and others are already second-class citizens in India.

The article says that the violence was well organized and planned long before the train attack in Godhra. It reports, that "the organizers of the carnage tapped on a seam of hatred, based on anti-Muslim propaganda which had been carefully cultivated over many years." It clearly points the finger at the Vishwa Hindu Parishad (VHP) and the Bajrang Dal, militant Hindu fundamentalists organizations inclined to violence which are under the umbrella of the militant, Hindu nationalist, pro-Fascist Rashtriya Swayamsewak Sangh (RSS), whose political wing is the BJP, the party that leads India's government. It was the RSS that published a booklet last year on how to implicate Christians and other religious minorities in fake criminal cases. It was the VHP that murdered missionary Graham Staines, yet has not been punished for it. In New York a couple of years ago, Prime Minister Atal Bihari Vajpayee told an audience proudly, "I will always be a Swayamsewak".

This reveals the reality of so-called democracy in India. It is a democracy for the Brahmins, but it is a tyranny for the minorities. We should stop our aid to India until they allow human rights and we should declare our support for self-determination for all the people living within its borders. Otherwise, I am afraid, violence will be even more a way of life in South Asia than it already is, and that would be a tragedy for all the people there. If we can do anything to prevent that, we should do so.

Mr. Speaker, I would like to add the Islam Online article to the Record at this time to give more detail on the pogrom in Gujarat.

Gujarat Pogrom Aimed at Reducing Muslims to Second Class Citizens

New Delhi, June 3 (IslamOnline)._The People's Union for Democratic Rights (PUDR), one of India's premiere human rights organizations, said in its report on the violence in Gujarat, "The whole intent of the pogrom has been to reduce Muslims to second class citizens in their own country."

The PUDR is a well-known independent human rights organization in India monitoring human rights violations against minorities and weaker sections of society.

The PUDR report "Maaro, Kaapo, Baaro: State, Society and Communalism in Gujarat" said that the organizers of the carnage tapped on a seam of hatred, based on anti-Muslim propaganda which had been carefully cultivated over many years.

The report said that the anti-Muslim carnage was planned well before the Godhra train tragedy. It says that the hate propaganda increased in the six months prior to February 2002.

The PUDR report says that the VHP (World Hindu Council) and its youth wing, the Bajrang Dal, organized trishul (tridents) distribution ceremonies in villages with Muslim populations. Speeches were made abusing and threatening Muslims during these ceremonies.

The report gives the instance of Pandarwada village where one of the worst massacres and sexual abuse cases took place. A meeting was held in this village about a fortnight before the attack.

The PUDR report provides detailed lists of people named as organizers and attackers.

Many of these are functionaries of the ruling party, BJP, the VHP and the Bajrang Dal.

The report gives a list of victims in some of the mass killings, which establishes that their numbers were higher than the ones the government admits.

The PUDR has accused the state government of abetting the anti-Muslim pogrom. "The fact that the Gujarat government supported the bandh (general strike) of February 28 and March 1 despite its experience of large-scale violence against Muslims after a similar bandh in 2000, is evidence of its complicity in the violence right from the start," it said.

The report also accuses the judiciary of not performing its duty. It illustrates as to how the criminal justice system in the state is complicit in the denial of justice to the riot victims. It corroborates the widely-reported fact that the police make a mockery of the investigative process. And that even courts have shown reluctance to do their duty.

The PUDR team visited 21 relief camps and 75 villages and towns where it spoke to government officials, members of traders' associations, the VHP, the Jamait-e-Ulema-e Hind and NGOs.

It has demanded the Narendra Modi government in Gujarat be dismissed and asked for an independent probe by the Central Bureau of Investigation into major incidents of communal violence, and expressed doubts over the Modi government's intentions to take action against the perpetrators of riots.

***

Document

CONGRESSIONAL RECORD -- EXTENSIONS

Monday, September 30, 2002
107th Congress, 2nd Session
148 Cong Rec E 1710

REFERENCE: Vol. 148, No. 125
SECTION: Extension of Remarks
TITLE: INDIANS BOAST OF SUCCESSFUL INTERVENTION IN U.S. ELECTION

HON. CYNTHIA A. McKINNEY
of Georgia
in the House of Representatives
Monday, September 30, 2002

Ms. McKINNEY . Mr. Speaker, as you know, I recently suffered a setback in my bid for reelection. I am beginning to get over the disappointment that I will no longer be able to serve the people of Georgia in the next Congress. I will miss serving.

However, there were some alarming things about the campaign to defeat me that I think my colleagues of both parties should look out for. I am not talking about the Republicans who crossed over to vote for my opponent, but the heavy involvement of Indians in the primary. I am one of the Members of Congress who has tried to get out the truth about South Asia, and I am proud of that. Earlier this year, I was one of 42 Members of Congress who wrote to President Bush to urge the release of Sikh and other political prisoners in India.

Apparently, this irritated the Indians because the newspaper article I am inserting in the Record along with this statement shows that they admitted that they invested heavily in the effort to defeat me. To my colleagues of both parties who have also been involved in the effort to expose India's brutal record, I say: Watch out; they are coming after you, too.

India has a record of illegal interference in U.S. elections. Former Ambassador S.S. Ray publicly urged the reelection of former Senator Larry Pressler and in opposition to now Senator Robert Torricelli. An Indian American immigration lawyer named Lalit Gadhia funneled money from the Indian Embassy to Congressional candidates, according to the Baltimore Sun. Most of the candidates were of my party, people I am proud to have had as my colleagues during my service in Congress. But it is still illegal and wrong for India to funnel Embassy money to these Members' campaigns.

Now I have become the latest political officeholder in India's cross hairs. I won't be the last unless their activities are exposed. Mr. Speaker, whether I am in office or not, I don't intend to let a foreign power determine the results of American elections if I can help it.

Mr. Speaker, I would like to insert the article showing Indian involvement in my primary into the Record to help expose their activities.

From The Times of India, Aug. 21, 2002
Indian-Americans Help Unseat US Lawmaker
(By Chidanand Rajghatta)

Washington._The headlines credit the Jewish lobby for the defeat of lawmaker Cynthia McKinney in the Congressional primaries on Tuesday. But a neophyte Indian-American activists group, which co-wrote the script for this unusual Georgia election that attracted nationwide attention, is happy with just the footnote that recorded their role.

They like to do it quietly. They are not as political or as established as the Jewish lobby.

Congresswoman McKinney outraged a lot of people with some bizarre remarks. Among her more provocative comments was her theory that President Bush purposely ignored warnings about 9/11 to help the U.S. arms industry. The comment angered not just the Jewish groups, but regular Americans as well.

The African American incumbent was not shy of expressing her opinion on the subcontinent either_mostly ill-informed repeats made at the behest of the Pakistani and Khalistani lobby, according to Indian-Americans.

A sample: The Indian government is responsible for terrorism against its own people. It engineered the massacre of bus passengers in Kashmir and the blowing up of a passenger airliner.

Community leaders said she recorded that kind of "unsubstantiated nonsense, usually peddled by disgruntled and discredited conspiracy theorists," in the Congressional Record.

But it was when she began talking about the imminent breakup of India because of its "17 different separatist movements" that the Indians of Georgia lost it for her and banded together.

One prominent activist sent out an e-mail to 3400 Indian-Americans in the area reporting her remarks (under the subject line_"Balkanisation of India_advocated by Rep. Cynthia McKinney") and urging them to work for her opponent, a local judge named Denise Majette.

Led by a prominent dotcommer in the area, they were soon holding fund-raisers for Majette, who like McKinney is also African-American. They chipped in with $20,000, although much larger sums came in later from Middle East groups_the Jews backing Majette and Arabs and Muslims supporting McKinney.

Indian-Americans contributed in other ways too. Several volunteers worked full weeks for Majette's campaign. She was invited as the chief guest for an Indian-American beauty pageant. A motel owner turned his electronic billboard next to the main highway into her campaign sign.

It was much after the Indian-American effort began that the Jewish lobby rolled into town. But the two sides joined hands for a phono-thon and pooled other resources for the campaign.

When the results came in on Tuesday, Majette had polled 58 per cent to McKinney's 42 per cent. The Indian bush telegraph_e-mail_was buzzing.

"Money is important. But volunteer and other efforts are equally important. Even more important is that we need to be on the radar screen of the candidate we are supporting. Ms. Denise Majette hopefully knows that we made a difference in her bid. Please keep in communication with her to further the relationship between IA (Indian Americans) and her," one prominent activist wrote. "The good news is that we offered our support before the poll numbers and Jewish money transpired. Thus, we got noticed," another group leader responded.

In keeping with the low-profile effort, none of them were eager to be identified.

The Indian embassy also quietly celebrated McKinney's loss, although, sticking to the principle of non-interference in local elections, it declined any comment. The embassy has been accused in the past of being a little too interested in the Congressional races.

Democrat Majette will now go up against the winner of the Republican primary for a seat in the Congress in the main elections due in November. But for now, Indians and Indian-Americans can breathe easy that they do not have to hear Cynthia McKinney's conspiracy theories in Congress.

***

Document

CONGRESSIONAL RECORD -- EXTENSIONS

Wednesday, September 25, 2002
107th Congress, 2nd Session
148 Cong Rec E 1645

REFERENCE: Vol. 148, No. 123
SECTION: Extension of Remarks
TITLE: REPRESSION OF MINORITIES CONTINUES IN INDIA_SIKHS, MUSLIMS, CHRISTIANS CONTINUE TO BE TARGETED

HON. DAN BURTON
of Indiana
in the House of Representatives
Tuesday, September 24, 2002

Mr. BURTON of Indiana . Mr. Speaker, I am distressed about two recent articles that show the continuing repression of minorities in India. One article appeared in The Hindu, an Indian newspaper. It said that over 5,000 Muslims were killed in the violence this spring in Gujarat. Then the Times of India reported that a group of Indian police officers fired on a group of peaceful Sikh protestors. These articles show that minorities such as Sikhs, Christians, Muslims, and others continue to suffer the worst kind of repression in "democratic" India.

In Gujarat, the police were quoted as saying that they were ordered to stand aside and let the Muslims be killed. This was strangely reminiscent of the 1984 massacre of Sikhs in Delhi. It is part of India's pattern of repression of its minorities. Now, it comes out that peaceful Sikh protestors who were simply holding a peaceful protest against what they see as desecration of their gurus and their scriptures were fired upon by Indian police. What kind of a democracy fires on peaceful protestors engaged in peaceful action?

Christians continue to be oppressed as well. Churches have been burned, prayer halls have been attacked, nuns have been raped, and priests have been murdered. Militant Hindu nationalists burned a missionary and his two young sons to death while they slept in their jeep. A few years ago, police fired on a Christian religious festival that was peacefully promoting the theme "Jesus Is the Answer."

Mr. Speaker, it is time to stop U.S. aid to India. It is time to declare our support for self-determination for the Sikhs of Khalistan, the Muslims of Kashmir, the Christians of Nagaland, and all the peoples demanding their freedom from India. We cannot just stand by and allow India's repression to go on with our support. Self-determination is everyone's birthright. Freedom is everyone's birthright. It is time for America to follow our principles and support it.

The Council of Khalistan issued an excellent press release on the police firing at the peaceful demonstrators. I would like to insert that into the Record at this time. In addition, I would like to place the article from The Hindu into the Record to show my colleagues the ongoing repression of minorities in supposedly democratic India.

Indian Police Fire at Peaceful Sikh Protestors
India again shows it is not a democracy

Washington, DC, August 5, 2002._The Times of India reported on August 1 that police in Malout fired on a crowd of peaceful protestors, injuring many of them. Several have been admitted to Civil Hospital, Malout. Eight protestors were arrested. The police used tear gas on the demonstrators. Two people suffered bullet wounds, according to the article.

The demonstrators were protesting against a so-called religious function organized by the Divya Jyoti Jagriti Sansthan which was aimed at undermining the Sikh religion and slandering the Sikh gurus, according to the Times of India.

"Like the attack on the Golden Temple, this incident shows that there is no place in India for Sikhs," said Dr. Gurmit Singh Aulakh, President of the Council of Khalistan. Khalistan is the Sikh homeland declared independent on October 7, 1987. "The Indian government is dedicated to

wiping out the Sikh religion," he said. "Nations that do not have political power perish. The only way to ensure that the Sikh religion can survive is to liberate Khalistan as soon as possible," he said.

"This attack shows that India is not a democracy, despite its pretensions," said Dr. Aulakh. "Democracies don't attack minorities and minority religions. Democracies don't commit genocide."

Indian security forces have murdered over 250,000 Sikhs since 1984, according to figures compiled by the Punjab State Magistracy and human-rights organizations. These figures were published in the book "The Politics of Genocide" by Inderjit Singh Jaijee. India has also killed over 200,000 Christians in Nagaland since 1947, over 80,000 Kashmiris since 1988, and tens of thousands of other minorities.

A report issued last year by the Movement Against State Repression (MASR) shows that India admitted that it held 52,268 political prisoners under the repressive "Terrorist and Disruptive Activities Act" (TADA) even though it expired in 1995. Many have been in illegal custody since 1984. There has been no list published of those who were acquitted under TADA and those who are still rotting in Indian jails. Additionally, according to Amnesty International, there are tens of thousands of other minorities being held as political prisoners. On February 28, 42 Members of the U.S. Congress from both parties wrote to President Bush to urge him to work for the release of Sikh political prisoners. The MASR report quotes the Punjab Civil Magistracy as writing "if we add up the figures of the last few years the number of innocent persons killed would run into lakhs [lsqb]hundreds of thousands.[rsqb]"

In November 1994, the Indian newspaper Hitavada reported that the Indian government paid the late governor of Punjab, Surendra Nath, $1.5 billion to organize and support covert terrorist activity in Punjab, Khalistan, and in neighboring Kashmir. The book "Soft Target", written by Canadian journalists Brian McAndrew and Zuhair Kashmeri, shows that the Indian government blew up its own airliner in 1985 to blame Sikhs and justify further repression. It quotes an agent of the Canadian Security Investigation Service (CSIS) as saying, "If you really want to clear up the incidents quickly, take vans down to the Indian High Commission and the consulates in Toronto and Vancouver. We know it and they know it that they are involved." On January 2, the Washington Times reported that India sponsors cross-border terrorism in the Pakistani province of Sindh.

Christians have been victims of a campaign of terror that has been going on since Christmas 1998. Churches have been burned, Christian schools and prayer halls have been attacked, nuns have been raped, and priests have been killed. Missionary Graham Staines and his two sons were burned alive while they slept in their jeep by militant Hindu members of the RSS, the parent organization of the ruling BJP. Earlier this year, over 5,000 Muslims were murdered by Hindus in Gujarat, according to The Hindu. These attacks were planned by the government, according to human-rights organizations, and news reports quoted a police officer as saying they had orders not to intervene to stop the violence.

"*India's efforts to eliminate the Sikh religion are doomed to fail,*" *Dr. Aulakh said.* "*This terrible act of police brutality shows that India is neither secular nor democratic, and it is time to launch a Shantmai Morcha to liberate our homeland, Khalistan, so that the Sikh Nation can finally enjoy the glow of freedom that was promised to us in 1947. Sovereignty is our birthright, and self-determination is the cornerstone of democracy. It is time for self-determination for all the peoples of South Asia.*"

- - - - - - - - -

From the Hindu, April 16, 2002
Gujarat Riot Toll Could Be Up to 5,000

Jaipur, April 15._Various social and political groups and human rights organizations, which held a public meeting here over the week-end to protest against the recent violence in Gujarat, demanded removal of the Narendra Modi Government and spoke out against the move to hold elections to the State Assembly prior to the return of normalcy.

The meeting addressed by K.S. Subramanyam, former Director-General of Police, Tripura; Magsaysay Award winner, Aruna Roy; noted economist, Prabhat Patnaik; Renuka Khanna, PUCL Activist from Baroda in Gujarat and others, asked for immediate steps to restore people's faith in the system in the riot-ravaged Gujarat.

Presenting the report of a delegation comprising prominent citizens who toured the affected areas of Gujarat, Mr. Subramanyam, who was a member of the delegation, said the police in Gujarat had extended a helping hand to the rioters on the instructions of the Chief Minister, Narendra Modi.

The official records speak of over 700 casualties in Gujarat riots but they had learnt that the number of those killed could be between 2,000 and 5,000, he observed. "*Senior administrative as well as police officers confided with us that in a meeting with the officials called on the eve of the VHP-announced bandh of February 28, Mr. Modi had asked them to honour Hindu sentiments*". *This directive made the officers passive spectators to what went on in Gujarat on the day of bandh and thereafter, Mr. Subramanyam said.*

He also said the delegation could see that the Godhra carnage itself was not the result of any pre-planned strategy but the outcome of a tussle between the Kar Sevaks in the train and the people living in the slum clusters near the railway station. Ms. Renuka Khanna said the police colluding with the rioters to wreak havoc with the lives and property of the minority community, would only lead to the birth of terrorism.

Ms. Aruna Roy said it was for villagers to preserve the pluralistic culture of India's rural areas and stop trouble-makers from disturbing the social fabric.

Prof. Patnaik traced the roots of the social and communal unrest to the growing unemployment and poverty in the wake of globalisation.

The meeting, which held the Gujarat Government, its police and administration fully responsible for the killings in that State, also found them guilty of discriminating against the victims and their families later, as well by denying them relief and compensation. By giving a clean chit to Mr. Modi, the National Democratic Alliance Government at the Centre too shared the guilt of the genocide in Gujarat, the meeting noted.

***

Document

CONGRESSIONAL RECORD -- EXTENSIONS

Thursday, September 19, 2002
107th Congress, 2nd Session
148 Cong Rec E 1620

REFERENCE: Vol. 148, No. 119
SECTION: Extension of Remarks
TITLE: "WE HAVE NO ORDERS TO SAVE YOU"

HON. EDOLPHUS TOWNS
of New York
in the House of Representatives
Thursday, September 19, 2002

Mr. TOWNS . Mr. Speaker, the organization Human Rights Watch has issued a report on the violence earlier this year in Gujarat, India, entitled "We Have No Orders To Save You." About 5,000 Muslims were killed in these riots, according to the newspaper "The Hindu." News reports quoted a police official as saying that he was ordered not to intervene to stop the violence and save lives. Another published report said that the government of India pre-planned these riots. The report from Human Rights Watch confirms this.

The riot was allegedly a response to the attack on a trainload of Hindus in Godhra. However, in the report, Human Rights Watch writes, "Human Rights Watch's findings, and those of numerous Indian human rights and civil liberties organizations, and most of the Indian press indicate that the attacks on Muslims throughout the state were planned, well in advance of the Godhra incident, and organized with extensive police participation and in close cooperation with officials of the Bharatiya Janata party (Indian Peoples Party, BJP) state government." The BJP, which is the political arm of the pro-Fascist Rashtriya Swayamsewak Sangh (RSS), also controls the central government in Delhi.

"The attacks on Muslims are part of a concerted campaign of Hindu nationalist organizations to promote and exploit communal tensions to further the BJP's rule," Human Rights Watch wrote, calling it "a movement that is supported at the local level by militant groups that operate with impunity and under the patronage of the state."

This report makes it clear that the Indian government supports terrorist groups that are murdering minorities all over India. India Today, India's largest newsmagazine, reported that the Indian government created the Liberation Tigers of Tamil Eelam (LTTE), which the U.S. government has labeled a "terrorist organization." It has supported cross-border terrorism in Sindh, a province of Pakistan, according to the Washington Times. The book "Soft Target" shows that India shot down its own airliner to blame the Sikhs. It paid out over 41,000 cash bounties to police officers for killing Sikhs. According to the "Hitavvada" newspaper, India paid the late governor of Punjab, Surendra Nath, $1.5 billion to foment terrorism in Punjab and Kashmir.

Unfortunately, this violence is all too reminiscent of previous incidents that took place before the BJP took power. In 1997, police gunfire broke up a Christian religious festival. And the violence in Gujarat was strangely reminiscent of the 1984 massacre of Sikhs in Delhi which cost 20,000 Sikhs their lives. It seems that in India, no matter who is in power, it is not safe to be a minority.

Mr. Speaker, we must act. America can't just sit and watch this terrorism and repression unfold. India has already been put on the watch list of countries that violate religious freedom. We must cut off aid and trade with India until human rights are enjoyed by all, and we must support self-determination for all peoples and nations in South Asia. Then perhaps there will no longer be need for reports like the one recently issued by Human Rights Watch. Instead, everyone in the subcontinent will be able to have real democracy, freedom, stability, prosperity, and peace.

***

Document

CONGRESSIONAL RECORD -- EXTENSIONS

Tuesday, September 17, 2002
107th Congress, 2nd Session
148 Cong Rec E 1589

REFERENCE: Vol. 148, No. 117
SECTION: Extension of Remarks
TITLE: IN MEMORY OF SEPTEMBER 11 AND ITS FORGOTTEN VICTIMS

HON. DAN BURTON
of Indiana
in the House of Representatives
Tuesday, September 17, 2002

Mr. BURTON of Indiana . Mr. Speaker, we are commemorating the terrible attack on America this past September 11. This was a terrible event in which about 3,000 people lost their lives. A year later, they are in our prayers.

Also in our prayers are the other victims - those who were subjected to violent, unfair attacks in the aftermath of September 11. One of these was Balbir Singh Sodhi, a gasoline station owner from Arizona. He was murdered at his gas station by someone who apparently mistook him for a follower of Osama bin Laden. His brother, Sukhpal Singh Sodhi, a cab driver in the San Francisco Bay area, was recently killed in his taxicab. I am sure that we would all like to extend our sympathies to the Sodhi family.

No one should be killed because of his religion. Even if Mr. Sodhi had been a Muslim and a follower of bin Laden that would not justify murdering him. But what makes this crime even more disturbing is that this perception was a mistake. Mr. Sodhi was a Sikh, not Muslim.

Sikhism is an independent, monotheistic, revealed religion that believes in the equality of all people, including gender equality. It is not part of either Hinduism or Islam, yet because of the turbans they wear, which are required by their religion, Sikhs are sometimes mistaken for Muslim followers of bin Laden.

The violence has mostly ended, but there are still some unrelated violent incidents. Unfortunately, Balbir Singh Sodhi's brother was also killed just a couple of months ago in his taxicab outside San Francisco. I call for an end to all these attacks and for full and prompt prosecution of all the people responsible.

Mr. Speaker, I would like to place the Council of Khalistan's recent press release on the anniversary of September 11 into the Record at this time.

In Memory of Those Killed in Last Year's Attack on United States
Sikhs Suffered the Most After the Attacks
Council of Khalistan Condemns Attacks,
Calls for End to Violence Against Minorities

Washington, D.C., September 11, 2002._Dr. Gurmit Singh Aulakh, President of the Council of Khalistan, today remembered the attacks on America a year ago that killed almost 3,000 Americans. He also condemned the violence against Sikh Americans and other minorities that broke out in the wake of the September 11 attacks.

"On behalf of the 21-million strong Sikh Nation and especially on behalf of more than 500,000 Sikh Americans, we remember with sadness and outrage the attacks on America a year ago and offer our prayers and sympathies on this sad anniversary to the people of the United States for

the terrible attack on the United States and for the loss of life it entails," Dr. Aulakh said. "We especially pray for the families of those who have departed."

"America must do what it can to eradicate terrorism from the world," Dr. Aulakh said. "We support all the efforts to do so and we must do our part as American citizens," he said. "This sad anniversary reminds us that we stand together as a nation. We must show unity on this occasion."

"We also condemn the violence against Sikhs and other minorities that took place last year after the September 11 attacks," Dr. Aulakh said. "Sikhs suffered the most in the post-September 11 violence," he said. "The very first victim of this violence was Balbir Singh Sodhi, a Sikh gasoline station owner from the Phoenix area," he noted. Recently, his brother was killed in his taxicab. All this violence must stop," Dr. Aulakh said.

"Nobody should be killed for his or her religion, whether Sikh, Muslim, Christian, Jewish, Hindu, or whatever religion one may follow," Dr. Aulakh said. "But it is important to note that Sikhs are not Muslims nor followers of bin Laden. We condemn bin Laden," he said. "Unfortunately, because of the turbans we are required to wear, many people mistake Sikhs for bin Laden followers," he said. "The Sikh religion is an independent, monotheistic, sovereign religion that believes in the equality of the whole human race, including gender equality," he said. "Daily we pray for the well being of the whole human race."

In the wake of the September 11 attacks, a couple of young Sikhs were attacked in Brooklyn. Sikh businesses have been stoned and cars have been burned. A Sikh boy was even shot in New York. Many Muslims and other minorities were also subjected to violent attacks.

"We hope that there will not be any more of these incidents in connection with the anniversary of the attacks. "Violence against innocent people of any religion or ethnicity is unacceptable," said Dr. Aulakh. "It must be condemned and the violence must be ended."

***

Document

CONGRESSIONAL RECORD -- EXTENSIONS

Tuesday, September 17, 2002
107th Congress, 2nd Session
148 Cong Rec E 1594

REFERENCE: Vol. 148, No. 117
SECTION: Extension of Remarks
TITLE: EXPRESSING THE SENSE OF CONGRESS ON THE ANNIVERSARY
OF TERRORIST ATTACKS LAUNCHED AGAINST THE UNITED STATES
ON SEPTEMBER 11, 2001

Speech of
HON. EDOLPHUS TOWNS
of New York
in the House of Representatives
Wednesday, September 11, 2002

Mr. TOWNS . Mr. Speaker, we are commemorating the terrible attack on America on September 11 last year. This was a terrible event in which about 3,000 people lost their lives. A year later, they are in our prayers.

Also in our prayers are the other victims_those who were subjected to violent, unfair attacks in the aftermath of September 11. One of these was Balbir Singh Sodhi, a gasoline station owner from Arizona. He was murdered at his gas station by someone who apparently mistook him for a follower of Osama bin Laden. His brother, Sukhpal Singh Sodhi, a cab driver in the San Francisco Bay area, was recently killed in his taxicab. I am sure that we would all like to extend our sympathies to the Sodhi family.

No one should be killed because of his religion. Even if Mr. Sodhi had been a Muslim and a follower of bin Laden, that would not justify murdering him. But what makes this crime even more disturbing is that this perception was a mistake. Mr. Sodhi was a Sikh, not Muslim.

Sikhism is an independent, monotheistic, revealed religion that believes in the equality of all people, including gender equality. It is not part of either Hinduism or Islam, yet because of the turbans they wear, which are required by their religion, Sikhs are sometimes mistaken for Muslim followers of bin Laden.

The violence has mostly ended, but there are still some unrelated violent incidents. Unfortunately, Balbir Singh Sodhi's brother was also killed just a couple of months ago in his taxicab outside San Francisco. I call for an end to all these attacks and for full and prompt prosecution of all the people responsible.

Mr. Speaker, I would like to place the Council of Khalistan's recent press release on the anniversary of September 11 into the Record at this time.

In Memory of Those Killed in Last Year's Attack on United States

Sikhs Suffered the Most After the Attacks; Council of Khalistan Condemns Attacks, Calls for End to Violence Against Minorities

Washington, D.C., September 11, 2002._Dr. Gurmit Singh Aulakh, President of the Council of Khalistan, today remembered the attacks on America a year ago that killed almost 3,000 Americans. He also condemned the violence against Sikh Americans and other minorities that broke out in the wake the September 11 attacks.

"On behalf of the 21-million strong Sikh Nation and especially on behalf of more than 500,000 Sikh Americans, we remember with sadness and outrage the attacks on America a year ago and offer our prayers and sympathies on this sad anniversary to the people of the United States for the terrible attack on the United States and for the loss of life it entails,"

Dr. Aulakh said. "We especially pray for the families of those who have departed."

"America must do what it can to eradicate terrorism from the world," Dr. Aulakh said. "We support all the efforts to do so and we must do our part as American citizens," he said. "This sad anniversary reminds us that we stand together as a nation. We must show unity on this occasion."

"We also condemn the violence against Sikhs and other minorities that took place last year after the September 11 attacks," Dr. Aulakh said. "Sikhs suffered the most in the post-September 11 violence," he said. "The very first victim of this violence was Balbir Singh Sodhi, a Sikh gasoline station owner from the Phoenix area," he noted. "Recently, his brother was killed in his taxicab. All this violence must stop," Dr. Aulakh said.

"Nobody should be killed for his or her religion, whether Sikh, Muslim, Christian, Jewish, Hindu, or whatever religion one may follow," Dr. Aulakh said. "But it is important to note that Sikhs are not Muslims nor followers of bin Laden. We condemn bin Laden," he said. "Unfortunately, because of the turbans we are required to wear, many people mistake Sikhs for bin Laden followers," he said. "The Sikh religion is an independent, monotheistic, sovereign religion that believes in the equality of the hole human race, including gender equality," he said. "Daily we pray for the well being of the whole human race."

In the wake of the September 11 attacks, a couple of young Sikhs were attacked in Brooklyn. Sikh businesses have been stoned and cars have been burned. A Sikh boy was even shot in New York. Many Muslims and other minorities were also subjected to violent attacks.

"We hope that there will not be any more of these incidents in connection with the anniversary of the attacks. "Violence against innocent people of any religion or ethnicity is unacceptable," said Dr. Aulakh. "It must be condemned and the violence must be ended."

***

Document

CONGRESSIONAL RECORD -- EXTENSIONS

Wednesday, September 11, 2002
107th Congress, 2nd Session
148 Cong Rec E 1550

REFERENCE: Vol. 148, No. 114
SECTION: Extension of Remarks
TITLE: INDIAN INTELLIGENCE PROMOTING TERRORISM IN U.S.,
WORLDWIDE_INFILTRATES ORGANIZATIONS, CREATES TERRORIST
INCIDENTS

HON. EDOLPHUS TOWNS
of New York
in the House of Representatives
Wednesday, September 11, 2002

Mr. TOWNS . Mr. Speaker, a recent intelligence report states that there are 25,000 agents of the Indian government's "Research and Analysis Wing" (RAW) outside India. While there is nothing wrong with legitimate intelligence work, RAW habitually infiltrates organizations of minority groups and creates terrorist incidents in order to discredit these groups.

The Indian government has recently been declared a violator of religious freedom by the United States government. On January 2, columnist Tony Blankley reported in the Washington Times that India is sponsoring cross-border terrorism in the Pakistani province of Sindh. This comes at a time when President Musharraf of Pakistan is actively helping us in the war against terrorism, at substantial risk to himself personally and politically.

The organizations Babbar Khalsa International (BKI) and the International Sikh Youth Federation (ISYF) have been identified by the U.S. government as "terrorist organizations." The ISYF has been banned in Canada. These organizations have been heavily infiltrated by the Indian government, to the point that they are government-controlled organizations. They have spawned other organizations designed to embarrass the Sikhs, especially those in the Khalistan freedom movement, and blame them for terrorism.

The Liberation Tigers of Tamil Eelam (LTTE) is another organization that our government has labelled "terrorist." Yet journalist Tavleen Singh of India Today, India's leading newsmagazine, reported that the Indian government itself created the LTTE and put up its leaders at the most upscale hotel in Delhi. If LTTE is a terrorist organization, then India created its terrorism.

In November 1994, the Indian newspaper Hitavada reported that the Indian government paid the governor of Punjab, the late Surendra Nath, the equivalent of $1.5 billion to foment terrorist activity in Punjab, Khalistan, and in neighboring Kashmir. In a country where half the population lives below the international poverty line, the supposedly democratic government could afford to lay out one and a half billion dollars to create state-sponsored terrorism. I'm sorry, Mr. Speaker, but I don't understand how that could happen in a democracy.

Also in 1994, our own State Department reported that the Indian government paid out more than 41,000 cash bounties to police officers for killing Sikhs. One of them killed a three-year-old boy and received a bounty for that! A report from the Human Rights Wing showed that at least 25,000 Sikhs were arrested, tortured, murdered, and cremated, then their bodies were declared "unidentified" and cremated. Two reports, one from the International Human Rights Organization (IHRO) and the other jointly issued by the Movement Against State Repression (MASR) and the Punjab Human Rights Organization (PHRO), showed that Indian forces carried out the massacre of 35 Sikhs in Chithisinghpora in Kashmir in March 2000.

In the excellent book Soft Target, journalists Brian McAndrew of the Toronto Star and Zuhair Kashmeri of the Toronto Globe and Mail prove that the Indian government itself carried out the bombing of an Air India airliner in 1985, killing 329 people, then blamed the Sikhs. There is too much good information in this book to quote here, but I would like to quote one statement from the Canadian State Investigative Service which appears in the book: "If you really want to clear the incidents quickly, take vans down to the Indian High Commission and the consulates in Toronto and Vancouver, load everybody up and take them down for questioning. We know it and they know it that they are involved."

Mr. Speaker, this ongoing pattern of terrorism against its neighbors and against the minority peoples living within its borders shows that India's claim to be a secular democracy and an opponent of terrorism is a lie.

India should be declared a terrorist state and subjected to appropriate penalties. These should include a cutoff of U.S. aid to India until the terrorism stops and human rights are fully enjoyed by all people within the country. And we should declare our support for the freedom movements seeking their freedom from India. By doing these things, we will advance the fight against terrorism in the world and help all people to enjoy the basic democratic right of self-determination.

As former Senate Majority Leader George Mitchell said, "the essence of democracy is the right to self-determination." It is time for real democracy in India rather than a continued campaign of terrorism.

***

Document

CONGRESSIONAL RECORD -- EXTENSIONS

Wednesday, September 11, 2002
107th Congress, 2nd Session
148 Cong Rec E 1552

REFERENCE: Vol. 148, No. 114
SECTION: Extension of Remarks
TITLE: RELEASE OVER 52,000 SIKH POLITICAL PRISONERS, STOP ITS REPRESSION AND TERRORISM

HON. EDOLPHUS TOWNS
of New York
in the House of Representatives
Wednesday, September 11, 2002

Mr. TOWNS . Mr. Speaker, on August 12, Indian Prime Minister Atal Bihari Vajpayee will meet with President Bush. The next day he will speak at the United Nations in New York. I am sure he will be preaching the principles of democracy and human rights, things that we all support. However, Mr. Vajpayee would have much more credibility on these issues if India lived by the principles it preaches.

Unfortunately, India is only a democracy for the upper-caste Brahmins. For minorities, it is a repressive state with little freedom. According to the Movement Against State Repression, India admitted to holding 52,268 political prisoners under the repressive, expired TADA law.

Recently, it was reported in the Hindu newspaper that the violence in Gujarat this spring killed over 5,000 Muslims. According to published reports, the government orchestrated the violence and ordered police not to stop it. This is typical of India's pattern of repression against minorities.

The Indian government has murdered over 250,000 Sikhs since 1984, over 200,000 Christians in Nagaland since 1947, more than 85,000 Kashmiri Muslims since 1988, and thousands of other minorities. Over 50,000 Sikhs have been made to "disappear." The Washington Times reported that India admitted that its forces committed the March 2000 massacre of 35 Sikhs in Chithisinghpora.

The former majority leader of the Senate, George Mitchell, has said that "the essence of democracy is the right to self-determination." Yet India has never kept its promise to the UN in 1948 that it would hold a plebiscite in Kashmir. India refuses to do the democratic thing and allow the people of Nagaland, Khalistan, and the other nations seeking their freedom from Indian rule. Multinational states like India, the Soviet Union, Austria-Hungary, and others are doomed to eventual collapse.

India is a practitioner of terrorism, as an excellent article by Tim Phares at NewsMax.com entitled "The Terrorism of the Indian Government" demonstrates. The Washington Times reported on January 2 that India sponsors cross-border terrorism in Sindh, a province of Pakistan. Journalist Tavleen Singh reported in India's leading news magazine, India Today, that India itself created the Liberation Tigers of Tamil Eelam (LTTE), which the U.S. government has called a "terrorist organization." It paid the late governor of Punjab, Surendra Nath, $1.5 billion to foment covert state terrorist activity in Kashmir and in Punjab, Khalistan, according to the Indian newspaper Hitavada. India has recently made deals to provide materials to Iraq. When we are fighting a war on terrorism, "the world's largest democracy" is practicing and supporting it.

Mr. Speaker, we must do something to stop these activities. I hope that President Bush and Secretary General Annan will press Mr. Vajpayee on the issues of political prisoners, violence against minorities, and terrorism. The U.S. government also has other actions at its disposal. It is time to impose sanctions on India and cut off its aid and trade. And the U.S. Congress should go on record in support of self-determination for Khalistan, Kashmir, Nagaland, and the other nations seeking their freedom in South Asia.

I would like to insert the article "The Terrorism of the Indian Government" into the Record at this time.

The Terrorism of the Indian Government
(By Tim Phares)

The South Asian subcontinent has been called the most dangerous place in the world, and events there over the past few months seem to confirm this description. While the danger of war seems to have passed for now, India and Pakistan remain on alert and both countries continued to point nuclear-capable missiles at each other. Unfortunately, tensions remain high as each side tries to gain an advantage over the other. Pakistan and minorities within India's borders charge that India is seeking hegemony in the South Asian subcontinent. Certainly is deployment of new missiles that can reach deep into Pakistan and its tests that began the nuclear escalation in the region suggest that this may be true.

At the recent Asian security conference in Kazakhstan, India refused to talk with the Pakistanis about Kashmir. In 1948, India promised to hold a plebiscite on the status of Kashmir, but it has never been held. Recently, the BBC reported that Iraq and India have signed an agreement to boost trade ties, especially in the oil sector. This comes at a time when the United States may be preparing to fight Iraq again. Unfortunately, this is consistent with India's pattern of behavior.

India now tries to create the impression that it supports the United States, but its long record says otherwise. The May 18, 1999, issue of the Indian Express reported that George Fernandes, the defense minister, organized and led a meeting with the ambassadors from Red China, Cuba, Russia, Yugoslavia, Libya and Iraq to discuss setting up a security alliance "to stop the U.S."

India had a long-term friendship with the former Soviet Union and supported its invasion of Afghanistan, yet it has shown little support for the United States in its war on terrorism. On Jan. 2, Tony Blankley wrote in the Washington Times that India is sponsoring cross-border terrorism in the Pakistani province of Sindh. Journalist Tavleen Singh has reported in India's leading news magazine, India Today, that the Indian government created the Liberation Tigers of Tamil Eelam (LTTE), which the U.S. government has identified as a "terrorist organization."

The government also has taken quiet, implicit control of two Sikh organizations, Babbar Khalsa International and the International Sikh Youth Federation, which the United States also has designated as "terrorist organizations."

India's implicit support for terrorist activity is consistent with its internal behavior. It has a record of repressing minorities that undermines its proclamation of democratic values.

The violence this spring in Gujarat, in which over 5,000 people were killed, according to The Hindu newspaper, has also heightened tensions. Muslims and other minorities charge that the violence was stirred up by the government to diminish Muslims in India.

In addition, the pro-Fascist Rashtriya Swayamsewak Sangh (RSS), the parent organization of the ruling BJP, has recently called for the majority-Muslim state of Kashmir to be divided into three states, despite India's 1948 pledge to the United Nations that it would let the people of Kashmir decide their fate in a plebiscite. The majority-Sikh state of Punjab, Khalistan, the predominantly Christian state of Nagaland, and several other states also have strong, active movements seeking their independence.

Human rights organizations report that more than 200,000 Christians in Nagaland have been killed by the Indian government. The book "The Politics of Genocide," by Inderjit Singh Jaijee, cites figures from the Punjab State Magistracy showing that over 50,000 Sikhs have been murdered by the Indian government since it invaded the Sikhs' holiest shrine, the Golden Temple, in June 1984.

In addition, according to a report by the Movement Against State Repression (MASR), the Indian government admitted to holding 52,268 Sikhs as political prisoners under the repressive, expired TADA law. According to Amnesty International, tens of thousands of other minorities are also being held.

In February, a bipartisan coalition of 42 members of the U.S. House of Representatives, led by Reps. Dan Burton, R-Ind., and Edolphus Towns, D-N.Y., wrote to President Bush urging him to work for the release of these political prisoners.

In 1994, the U.S. State Department reported that the Indian government paid out over 41,000 cash bounties to police officers for killing members of the Sikh minority. In the same year, the Indian newspaper Hitavada reported that the Indian government paid the late governor of Punjab, Surendra Nath, the equivalent of $1.5 billion to foment terrorist activity in Punjab and Kashmir. According to human rights groups, Indian forces have killed over 80,000 Muslims in Kashmir and thousands of other minorities, including Dalit "untouchables," Tamils and others.

MASR also co-sponsored with the Punjab Human Rights Organization an investigation of the March 2000 massacre of 35 Sikhs in Chithisinghpora. It concluded that Indian forces carried out the massacre. A separate investigation conducted by the International Human Rights Organization came to the same conclusion. Retired General Narinder Singh has said that "Punjab is a police state."

The book "Soft Target," written by Canadian journalists Zuhair Kashmeri of the Toronto Globe and Mail and Brian McAndrew of the Toronto Star, shows that India blew up its own airliner in 1985, killing 329 people, apparently in order to blame Sikhs for the atrocity and create a pretext for more violence against them. The book shows that the Indian consul general in Toronto pulled his daughter off the flight shortly before it was due to depart. An auto dealer who was a friend of the consul general also canceled his reservation at the last minute. Surinder Singh, director of North American Affairs for the External Affairs office in New Delhi, also canceled his reservation on that flight.

The consul general also called to finger a suspect in the case before the public knew that the bombing had taken place. The book quotes an agent of the Canadian State investigative Service (CSIS) as saying, "If you really want to clear the incidents quickly, take vans down to the Indian High Commission and the consulates in Toronto and Vancouver, load up everybody and take them down for questioning. We know it, and they know it, that they are involved."

In recent months, India has been added to the State Department's "watch list" of countries that violate religious freedom. Some members of Congress have called for sanctions against India and for an end to American aid. Some have also endorsed self-determination for the peoples seeking freedom from India through a plebiscite on independence. While these events seem unlikely to occur anytime soon, the Indian government has held negotiations with the freedom fighters in Nagaland. Home Minister L.K. Advani recently admitted that if Kashmir achieves freedom (which now seems more likely than ever), it will cause India to break apart. Some experts have predicted that within a decade, neither India nor Pakistan will exist in their current form.

The Indian subcontinent will continue to be a region that bears close attention by American policymakers.

***

Document

CONGRESSIONAL RECORD -- EXTENSIONS

Tuesday, September 10, 2002
107th Congress, 2nd Session
148 Cong Rec E 1535

REFERENCE: Vol. 148, No. 113
SECTION: Extension of Remarks
TITLE: INDIAN PRIME MINISTER TO SPEAK TO UNITED NATIONS: U.N.
SHOULD PRESS HIM ON HUMAN RIGHTS, TERRORISM

HON. DAN BURTON
of Indiana
in the House of Representatives
Tuesday, September 10, 2002

Mr. BURTON of Indiana . Mr. Speaker, on September 13, the Prime Minister of India, Atal Bihari Vajpayee, will speak to the United Nations in New York. There are several issues that should be brought up while Mr. Vajpayee is there.

I am sure that Prime Minister Vajpayee will denounce terrorism. India claims to be democratic, after all. But India continues to sponsor cross-border terrorism in the Pakistani province of Sindh, according to the Washington Times. It continues to engage in terrorist activity against the minorities within its own borders. Recently, India admitted that its troops were responsible for the massacre of 35 Sikhs in the village of Chithisinghpora in March 2000. The Council of Khalistan issued an excellent press release on this, which I will introduce later. In November 1994, the Indian newspaper Hitavada reported that the late governor of Punjab,

Surendra Nath, was paid $1.5 billion by the Indian government to foment terrorism in Punjab and Kashmir. The book Soft Target alleged that India blew up its own airliner in 1985 to blame Sikhs and justify further repression. These are just a few examples.

India continues to practice repression against its minorities. Its ongoing repression of Christians is well-documented. Recently, The Hindu reported that the death toll for this spring's violence in Gujarat is as high as 5,000. That is more people than were killed in the World Trade Center attack. The newspaper also reported that police officers were ordered not to intervene to stop the violence, in a scary echo of the Delhi massacre of Sikhs in 1984. Recently, in Malout, a peaceful demonstration of Sikh activists was fired upon by Indian police. In 1997, police gunfire broke up a Christian religious festival. The pattern continues.

America cannot and must not permit this to go unchallenged. When Prime Minister Vajpayee is in the country, he must be pressed on the issues of terrorism, democracy, and human rights. We should halt aid to India until it corrects these patterns of behavior, and we should support self-determination for all of the 17 freedom movements within India's borders. These measures will help to end terrorism in South Asia and promote real democracy and stability there. Mr. Speaker, I would like to place the Council of Khalistan's press release on India's admission that it was responsible for the Chithisinghpora massacre into the Record at this time.

Indian Government Admits Its Responsibility for Massacre in Chithisinghpora_Evidence a Fraud, Indian Soldiers Implicated

Washington, DC, Aug. 2, 2002._According to today's Washington Times, the Indian government has admitted that its forces were responsible for the massacre of 35 Sikhs in the village of Chithisinghpora, Kashmir on March 20, 2000. India finally admitted that the evidence it used to implicate alleged Kashmiri "militants" in the murders was faked.

This is a victory for Sikhs, including the Council of Khalistan, who have maintained that the Indian government is responsible for this atrocity. However, it is only after India's case against the alleged "militants" was exposed that it took responsibility.

The massacre was timed to occur at the time of former President Clinton's visit to India. Recent attacks on minorities also blamed on alleged "militants", took place just before Secretary of State Colin Powell visited. At the time of the Chithisinghpora massacre, Dr. Gurmit Singh Aulakh, President of the Council of Khalistan, strongly condemned the murders. "What motive would Kashmiri freedom fighters have to kill Sikhs? This would be especially stupid when President Clinton is visiting. The freedom movements in Kashmir, Khalistan, Nagaland, and throughout India need the support of the United States," he said. Khalistan is the Sikh homeland declared independent on October 7, 1987.

The massacres continued a pattern of repression and terrorism against minorities by the Indian government, which it attempts to blame on other minorities to divide and rule the minority peoples within its artificial borders. In November 1994, the Indian newspaper Hitavada reported that the Indian government paid the late governor of Punjab, Surendra Nath, $1.5 billion to organize and support covert terrorist activity in Punjab, Khalistan, and in neighboring Kashmir. The book Soft Target, written by Canadian journalists Brian McAndrew and Zuhair Kashmeri, shows that the Indian government blew up its own airliner in 1985 to blame Sikhs and justify further repression. It quotes an agent of the Canadian Security Investigation Service (CSIS) as saying, "If you really want to clear up the incidents quickly, take vans down to the Indian High Commission and the consulates in Toronto and Vancouver. We know it and they know it that they are involved." On January 2, the Washington Times reported that India sponsors cross-border terrorism in the Pakistani province of Sindh.

A report issued last year by the Movement Against State Repression (MASR) shows that India admitted that it held 51,268 political prisoners under the repressive "Terrorist and Disruptive Activities Act" (TADA) even though it expired in 1995. Many have been in illegal custody since 1984. There has been no list published of those who were acquitted under TADA and those who are still rotting in Indian jails. Additionally, according to Amnesty International, there are tens of thousands of other minorities being held as political prisoners. On February 28, 42 Members of the U.S. Congress from both parties wrote to President Bush to urge him to work for the release of Sikh political prisoners. The MASR report quotes the Punjab Civil Magistracy as writing "if we add up the figures of the last few years the number of innocent persons killed would run into lakhs (hundreds of thousands)."

Indian security forces have murdered over 250,000 Sikhs since 1984, according to figures compiled by the Punjab State Magistracy and human-rights organizations. These figures were published in the book The Politics of Genocide by Inderjit Singh Jaijee. India has also killed over 200,000 Christians in Nagaland since 1947, over 80,000 Kashmiris since 1988, and tens of thousands of other minorities. Christians have been victims of a campaign of terror that has been going on since Christmas 1998. Churches have been burned, Christian schools and prayer halls have been attacked, nuns have been raped, and priests have been killed. Missionary Graham Staines and his two sons were burned alive while they slept in their jeep by militant Hindu members of the RSS, the parent organization of the ruling BJP.

"It is good that India has finally admitted its responsibility for the massacre at Chithisinghpora," Dr. Aulakh said. "Now I urge the U.S. government to place sanctions on India as a country and practices and promotes terrorism. The Chithisinghpora massacre proves that India is not a democracy, but a repressive, terrorist state which murders it minorities."

***

Document

CONGRESSIONAL RECORD -- EXTENSIONS

Monday, July 29, 2002
107th Congress, 2nd Session
148 Cong Rec E 1417

REFERENCE: Vol. 148, No. 105
SECTION: Extension of Remarks
TITLE: INDIA SHOULD ACT LIKE A DEMOCRACY_SELF-
DETERMINATION FOR KASHMIR,KHALISTAN AND OTHER NATIONS
OF SOUTH ASIA

HON. DAN BURTON
of Indiana
in the House of Representatives
Friday, July 26, 2002

Mr. BURTON of Indiana . Mr. Speaker, India calls itself "the world's largest democracy" yet it does not act democratic. As you know, a report from the Movement Against State Repression shows that India admitted to holding 52,268 Sikhs as political prisoners. Fort-two Members of Congress from both parties wrote to President Bush to urge him to work for the release of these political prisoners. There are tens of thousands of other political prisoners also, according to Amnesty International, and they must also be released. Recently, the Council of Khalistan wrote to Secretary of State Colin Powell to urge him to work for the release of political prisoners.

India has killed over 250,000 Sikhs since 1984, over 80,000 Kashmiri Muslims since 1988, over 200,000 Christians in Nagaland since 1947, and tens of thousands of other minorities. Mr. Speaker, this is not acceptable, and it shows that using the term "democracy" to describe India may not be the best use of the term.

Recently, former Senator George Mitchell said "the essence of democracy is the right to self determination." I'm not in the habit of quoting Democrats, Mr. Speaker, but Senator Mitchell is right about this. In 1948, India promised the United Nations that it would allow the people of Kashmir to decide their future in a free and fair plebiscite. No such vote has ever been held. Instead, over 600,000 troops have been sent to Kashmir to suppress the legitimate aspirations of the people for freedom. Similarly, in Punjab, Khalistan, which declared its independence from India on October 7, 1987, over half a million troops have terrorized the population to destroy the Sikh Nation's freedom movement, even though the Sikhs were one of the parties to the agreement establishing the independence of India and were supposed to get their own state. Nagaland, which is predominantly Christian, has been trying to secure its freedom and India has reacted with similar terror. All in all, there are 17 freedom movements within India's artificial borders.

Mr. Speaker, it is time for all the people of South Asia to enjoy freedom. Until India allows the people to exercise their legitimate rights, we should stop all U.S. foreign aid to India. We also should formally declare our support for self-determination for Kashmir, Khalistan, Nagaland, and all the people and nations of South Asia. These measures will go a long way towards securing the blessings of freedom to all the people of the subcontinent.

***

Document

CONGRESSIONAL RECORD -- EXTENSIONS

Tuesday, July 16, 2002
107th Congress, 2nd Session
148 Cong Rec E 1275

REFERENCE: Vol. 148, No. 96
SECTION: Extension of Remarks
TITLE: SIKHS OBSERVE ANNIVERSARY OF GOLDEN TEMPLE ATTACK

HON. EDOLPHUS TOWNS
of New York
in the House of Representatives
Tuesday, July 16, 2002

Mr. TOWNS . Mr. Speaker, I would like to take this opportunity to note a historic occasion that is being observed this week. In addition to our observance of D-Day, the day that Allied troops landed in Europe to begin the attack on Nazi Germany, this week marks the anniversary of India's military attack on the Golden Temple in Amritsar and the brutal massacre of 20,000 Sikhs in June 1984. Recently, Sikhs from the East Coast gathered to commemorate this event in front of the Indian Embassy here in Washington. Similar events have been held or will be held in New York, London, and many other cities.

The Golden Temple attack was an attack on the seat of the Sikh religion. It forever put the lie to India's claim that it is secular and democratic. How can a democratic state launch a military attack on religious pilgrims gathered at the most sacred site of their religion? The Indian troops shot bullet holes through the Sikh holy scriptures, the Guru Granth Sahib, and took boys as young as eight years old out in the courtyard and shot them in cold blood. This set off a wave of repression against Sikhs that continues to this day.

Mr. Speaker, I would like to put the flyer from that event into the Record now. It contains a lot of important information about the Golden Temple attack that shows the tyranny just under the facade of Indian democracy.

Khalistan Martyrs Day, June 1, 2002
PROTESTING INDIAN GOVERNMENT DESECRATION OF THE GOLDEN TEMPLE AND MASSACRE OF SIKHS

Sikhs Demand Freedom for Sikh Nation of Khalistan. Remember the Victims of Indian Genocide. "If the Indian government attacks the Golden Temple, it will lay the foundation of Khalistan."_Sant Jarnail Singh Bhindranwale, Sikh martyr

Indian government genocide against the Sikh nation continues to this day. From June 3 to 6, 1984 the Indian Government launched a military attack on the Golden Temple in Amritsar, the holiest of Sikh shrines and seat of the Sikh religion. This is the equivalent of attacking the Vatican or Mecca. 38 other Gurdwaras throughout Punjab, Khalistan were simultaneously attacked. More than 20,000 Sikhs were killed in these attacks.

Desecration of the Temple included shooting bullets into the Guru Granth Sahib, the Sikh holy scripture, and destroying original Hukam Namas written by hand by the ten Sikh Gurus. Young Sikh boys ages 8 to 12 were taken outside and asked if they supported Khalistan, the independent Sikh homeland. When they responded "Bole So Nihal," a religious statement, they were shot to death in cold blood by the brutal Indian troops.

The Golden Temple attack launched an ongoing campaign of genocide against Sikhs by the Indian government that continues to this day. Punjab, Khalistan, the Sikh homeland, has been turned into a killing field. The Golden Temple attack made it clear that there is no place for Sikhs in India. "The essence of democracy is the right to self-determination."_Former Senate Majority Leader George Mitchell (D-Me.)

The Movement Against State Repression issued a report showing that India is holding at least 52,268 Sikh political prisoners, by their own admission, in illegal detention without charge or trial. Some of them have been held since 1984. Many prisoners continue to be held under the repressive, so-called "Terrorist and Disruptive Activities Act (TADA) even though it expired in 1995. According to the report, in many cases, the police would file TADA cases against the same individual in different states "to make it impossible for them to muster evidence in their favor." It was also common practice for police to re-arrest TADA prisoners who had been released, often without filing new charges.

"In November 1994," the report states, "42 employees of the Pilibhit district jail and PAC were found guilty of clubbing to death 6 Sikh prisoners and seriously wounding 22 others. They were TADA prisoners. Uttar Pradesh later admitted the presence of around 5000 Sikh TADA prisoners." Over 50,000 Sikhs have been made to disappear since 1984.

Sikhs in Punjab, Khalistan formally declared independence on October 7, 1987, to be achieved through the Sikh tradition of Shantmai Morcha, or peaceful resistance. Sikhs ruled Punjab from 1765 to 1849 and were to receive sovereignty at the time that the British quit India.

"When it comes to Kashmir and Punjab and Jammu, the Indian Government might as well not be a democracy. For people in those areas,

India might as well be Nazi Germany. "_U.S. Representative Dana Rohrabacher (R-Cal)

Only a terrorist state could commit atrocities of such magnitude.

While India seeks hegemony in South Asia, the atrocities continue. India has openly tested nuclear weapons and deployed them in Punjab, weapons that can be used in case of nuclear war with Pakistan. These warheads put the lives of Sikhs at risk for Hindu Nationalist hegemony over South Asia. The Indian government is run by the BJP, the militant Hindu nationalist party in India, and is unfriendly to the United States. In May 1999, the Indian Express reported that Indian Defense Minister George Fernandes led a meeting with representatives from Cuba, Russia, China, Libya, Iraq, and other countries to build a security alliance "to stop the U.S."

In March 42 Members of the U.S. Congress from both parties wrote to President Bush asking him to help free tens of thousands of political prisoners.

India voted with Cuba, China, and other repressive states to kill a U.S. resolution against human-rights violations in China.

India is a terrorist state. According to published reports in India, the government planned the massacre in Gujarat (which killed over 5,000 people) in advance and they ordered the police to stand by and not to interfere to stop the massacre. Last year, a group of Indian soldiers was caught red-handed trying to set fire to a Gurdwara and some Sikh homes in a village in Kashmir.

According to the Hitavada newspaper, India paid the late Governor of Punjab, Surendra Nath, $1.5 billion to organize and support covert state terrorism in Punjab and Kashmir.

Continuing Repression Against Sikhs

"The Indian government, all the time they boast that they're democratic, they're secular, but they have nothing to do with a democracy, they have nothing to do with a secularism. They try to crush Sikhs just to please the majority." Narinder Singh, a spokesman for the Golden Temple, Amritsar, Punjab, interviewed on National Public Radio, July 11, 1997.

Since 1984, India has engaged in a campaign of ethnic cleansing and murdered tens of thousands of Sikhs and secretly cremated them. The Indian Supreme Court described this campaign as "worse than a genocide."

The book Soft Target, written by two Canadian journalists, proves that India blew up its own airliner in 1985 to blame the Sikhs and justify more genocide. The Indian government paid over 41,000 cash bounties to police officers for killing Sikhs, according to the U.S. State Department.

Indian police tortured and murdered the religious leader of the Sikhs, Gurdev Singh Kaunke, Jathedar of the Akal Takht. No one has been punished for this atrocity and the Punjab government refused to release its own commission's report on the Kaunke murder.

Human-rights activist Jaswant Singh Khalra was kidnapped by the police on September 6, 1995, and murdered in police custody. His body was not given to his family. Rajiv Singh Randhawa, the only eyewitness to the police kidnapping of Jaswant Singh Khalra, was arrested in front of the Golden Temple in Amritsar Sikhism's holiest shrine, while delivering a petition to the British Home Minister asking Britain to intervene for human rights in Punjab.

In March 2000, 35 Sikhs were massacred in Chithisinghpora in Kashmir by the Indian government.

A Wave of Repression Against Christians

Since Christmas 1998, India has carried out a campaign of repression against Christians in which churches have been burned, priests have been murdered, nuns have been raped, and schools and prayer halls have been attacked. On January 17, 2001, Christian leaders in India thanked Sikhs for saving them from Indian government persecution. Members of the Bajrang Dal, part of the pro-Fascist Rashtriya Swayamsewak Sangh (RSS), the parent organization of the ruling BJP, burned missionary Graham Staines and his two young sons, ages 8 and 10, to death while they slept in their jeep. The RSS published a booklet last year on how to implicate Christians and other minorities in false criminal cases.

Democracies don't commit genocide. Support self-determination for the people of Khalistan.

***

Document

CONGRESSIONAL RECORD -- EXTENSIONS

Tuesday, July 16, 2002
107th Congress, 2nd Session
148 Cong Rec E 1277

REFERENCE: Vol. 148, No. 96
SECTION: Extension of Remarks
TITLE: INDIA'S HEGEMONIC AMBITIONS LEAD TO CRISIS IN SOUTH ASIA

HON. EDOLPHUS TOWNS
of New York
in the House of Representatives
Tuesday, July 16, 2002

Mr. TOWNS . Mr. Speaker, we are all hoping that war can be avoided in South Asia. A war there would take an enormous toll in human lives and in damage to land and the fragile economies of India and Pakistan. The biggest losers, clearly, would be the Islamic people of Kashmir and Sikhs of Punjab, Khalistan.

Unfortunately, some of the media accounts of this conflict have been very one-sided. You would think after reading a lot of the papers and watching a lot of TV news that India is absolutely blameless in this conflict. That is not true. As the Wall Street Journal pointed out on June 4, it is India's hegemonic ambitions, as much as anything, that have brought this crisis to a head.

Mr. Speaker, at the time that India was partitioned, the Hindu maharajah of Kashmir, despite a majority Muslim population, acceded to India. That accession has always been disputed and India promised the United Nations in 1948 that it would settle the issue with a free and fair plebiscite on Kashmir's status. As we all know, the plebiscite has never been held. Instead, India has tried to reinforce its rule there with over 700,000 troops. According to columnist Tony Blankley in the January 2, Washington Times, meanwhile, India supports cross-border terrorism in the Pakistani province of Sindh. Indian officials have said that everyone who lives in India must either be Hindu or subservient to Hindus, and they have called for the incorporation of Pakistan into "Akand Bharat" - Greater India.

In January, Home Minister L.K. Advani admitted that once Kashmir is free from India rule, it will bring about the breakup of India. India is a multinational state and history shows that such states always unravel eventually. We all hope that it won't take a war to do it. No one wants another Yugoslavia in South Asia, but there are 17 freedom movements within India. Unless India takes steps to resolve these issues peacefully and democratically, a violent solution becomes much more likely. As the former Majority Leader of the other chamber, Senator George Mitchell, said, "The essence of democracy is self-determination." It is true in the Middle East and it is true in South Asia.

The Sikh Nation in Punjab, Khalistan also seeks its freedom by peaceful, democratic, nonviolent means, as does predominantly Christian Nagaland, to name just a couple of examples. The Sikhs declared the independence of Khalistan on October 7, 1987. They ruled Punjab prior to the British conquest of the submcommittee and no Sikh representative has signed the Indian constitution.

India claims that these freedom movements have little or no support. Well, if that is true, and if India is "the world's largest democracy," as it claims, then why would it not hold a plebiscite on the stauts of Kashmir, of Nagaland, of Khalistan? Wouldn't that be the democratic way to resolve these issues without a violent solution?

Until that day comes, Mr. Speaker, we should support self-determination. We should declare our support for a plebiscite in Khalistan, in Kashmir, in Nagaland, and wherever they are seeking freedom. We should stop aid to India until all people in the subcontinent live in freedom and peace. These measures will help bring the glow of freedom to everyone in that troubled, dangerous region.

Mr. Speaker, I would like to place the Wall Street Journal article into the Record at this time.

From the Wall Street Journal
India's Kashmir Ambitions

Western worry over Kashmir has focused on Pakistan's willingness to control terrorists slipping over the border with India, and rightly so. But that shouldn't allow U.S. policy to overlook India's equal obligation to prevent a full-scale war from breaking out in Southwest Asia.

That obligation has come into focus with today's Asian security conference in Kazakstan. Indian Prime Minister Atal Bihari Vajpayee and President Pervez Musharraf of Pakistan will both be on hand, and everyone has been urging a bilateral meeting on the sidelines. But so far Mr. Vajpayee has ruled out any dialogue until Pakistan presents evidence that it is acting against the Kashmiri terrorist groups crossing the U.N. line of control to attack Indian targets.

This is shortsighted, not least for India, because it allows Mr. Musharraf to take the moral high ground by offering to talk "anywhere and at any level." On Saturday the Pakistani leader also went on CNN to offer an implied assurance that he wouldn't resort to nuclear weapons, as something no sane individual would do. This went some way toward matching India's no-first-use policy and could be considered a confidence-building measure, however hard it would be for any leader to stick to such a pledge were national survival at stake.

India's refusal even to talk also raises question about just what that regional powerhouse hopes to achieve out of this Kashmir crisis. If it really wants terrorists to be stopped, some cooperation with Pakistan would seem to be in order. We hope India isn't looking for a pretext to intervene militarily, on grounds that it knows that it would win (as it surely would) and that this would prevent the emergence of a moderate and modernizing Pakistan.

This question is one the mind of U.S. leaders who ask Indian officials what they think war would accomplish, only to get no clear answer. India is by far the dominant power in Southwest Asia, and it likes it that way. Some in India may fear Mr. Musharraf less because he has tolerated terrorists than because he has made a strategic choice to ally his country with the U.S. If he succeeds, Pakistan could become stronger as a regional competitor and a model for India's own Muslim population of 150 million.

The danger here is that if India uses Kashmir to humiliate Pakistan, Mr. Musharraf probably wouldn't survive, whether or not fighting escalates into full-scale war. That wouldn't do much to control terrorism, either in India or anywhere else. It would also send a terrible signal to Middle Eastern leaders about what happens when you join up with America. All of this is above and beyond the immediate damage to the cause of rounding up al Qaeda on the Afghan-Pak border, or of restoring security inside Afghanistan.

No one doubts that Mr. Musharraf has to be pressed to control Kashmiri militants, as President Bush has done with increasing vigor. The Pakistani ruler was the architect of an incursion into Indian-controlled

Kashmir at Kargil two years ago, and his military has provided ed mortar fire to cover people crossing the line of control.

But at least in the past couple of weeks that seems to have changed, as Pakistani security forces have begun restraining militants and breaking their communications links with terrorists already behind Indian lines. In any case, the line of control is so long and wild that no government can stop all incursions. More broadly, Mr. Musharraf has already taken more steps to reform Pakistani society than any recent government. U.S. officials say he has taken notable steps to clean up his intelligence service and that he has even begun to reform the madrassa schools that are the source of so much Islamic radicalism. (The problem is that Saudi Arabia hasn't stopped funding them.)

The Pakistani leader has done all this at considerable personal and strategic risk, and it is in the U.S. and (we would argue) Indian interests that he process continue and succeed. He deserves time to show he is not another Yasser Arafat, who has a 20-year record of duplicity.

As it works to defuse the Kashmir crisis, the U.S. has to press Mr. Musharraf to stop as many terror incursions into India as possible. But it also must work to dissuade India from using Kashmir as an excuse to humiliate Pakistan, a vital U.S. ally. The U.S. has a long-term interest in good relations with India, a sister democracy and Asian counterweight to China. But self-restraint over Kashmir is a test of how much India really wants that kind of U.S. relationship.

***

Document

CONGRESSIONAL RECORD -- EXTENSIONS

Thursday, July 11, 2002
107th Congress, 2nd Session
148 Cong Rec E 1240

REFERENCE: Vol. 148, No. 93
SECTION: Extension of Remarks
TITLE: INDIA AND IRAQ: "STRATEGIC PARTNERS" STRENGTHEN
TRADE TIES WITH OIL DEAL

HON. DAN BURTON
of Indiana
in the House of Representatives
Thursday, July 11, 2002

Mr. BURTON of Indiana . Mr. Speaker, India calls itself "the world's largest democracy" and it claims it is a partner in the fight against terrorism, yet it just signed an agreement to strengthen its trade ties with one of the nation's major sponsors of terrorism, Iraq. According to the

British Broadcasting Company (BBC), Amir Muhammad Rasheed, the Iraqi Oil Minister, called India a "strategic partner."

Under the agreement, India will provide medicine, wheat, rice, railway equipment, and turbines for electrical generators to Iraq. In addition, India, Iraq, and Algeria are in the final stages of an agreement to drill oil in the southern part of Iraq. Mr. Rasheed's counterpart, Indian Oil Minister Ram Naik, said that India opposes the sanctions on Iraq.

On May 18, 1999, the Indian Express reported that Indian Defense Minister George Fernandes organized and led a meeting with the Ambassadors from Iraq, Red China, Cuba, Russia, Serbia, and Libya to discuss setting up a security alliance "to stop the U.S." This demonstrates that many in India do not view America as an ally, but instead, view us as an enemy. Apparently, these people are even willing to support America's enemies.

The time has come for the United States to recognize the truth about India. India has a long way to go before it can be considered an American ally. It is a supporter of terrorist regimes and a practitioner of terrorism itself. It has already been placed on the State Department's watch list of violators of religious freedom. Now it is time to impose appropriate sanctions on India. We should immediately cut off all American aid to India, and we should declare our support for the self-determination movements in South Asia, such as those in Kashmir, in Punjab, Khalistan, and in Nagalim, among others. If India is going to support terrorism around the world, it is not worthy of the support of the hard-working, freedom-loving people of the United States.

Mr. Speaker, I would like to place the BBC report on the India-Iraq deal into the Record at this time for the information of my colleagues and the American people.

Iraq and India Ties Warmed by Oil Deals

Iraq and India have signed an agreement to boost trade ties, especially in the oil sector.

Indian Oil Minister Ram Naik told a press conference that the Indian oil firm Oil Natural Gas Corporation Limited (ONGC) would soon open offices in Baghdad.

Mr. Naik added, after meeting his Iraqi counterpart Amir Muhammed Rasheed, that "work was progressing" on an ONGC oil concession in southern Iraq.

Iraq has awarded Indian companies a number of contracts under the United Nations "oil-for food" programme, in return for India's diplomatic support.

The programme allows Iraq to bypass sanctions imposed for its 1990 invasion of Kuwait and use oil revenues to buy food and humanitarian goods.

The U.S. has classified Iraq as a member of the "axis of evil" while it has strengthened relations with India to prosecute the war in Afghanistan.

Strategic partner

After meeting with Iraqi President Saddam Hussein on Saturday, Mr. Naik said that India opposed the sanctions on Iraq, and called for them to be ended immediately.

Mr. Rasheed described India as a "strategic partner".

"We have entered new projects in railways, oil and gas, health and industry in addition to technical co-operation and this will give a boost to the economic relations of the two countries, which in consequence will be reflected on the volume of trade exchange," Mr. Rasheed said.

Under the agreement, India is to supply Iraq with medicine, wheat, rice railway equipment and turbines for electricity generations.

Mr. Rasheed said trade between Baghdad and New Delhi under an "oil-for-food" deal with the UN had reached $1.1 bn.

Expanding oil interests

Iraq, India and Algeria are "in the final state" of a deal to start exploring and drilling the Tuba oil field between Zubair and Rumaila in the south of the country.

"It is a consortium between Indian companies and the Algerian Sonatrach Company, and we hope to realize it by the end of summer," Mr. Rasheed was quoted as saying in the ruling Baath party's Al-Thawra newspaper.

The field was being developed by Iraq until the 1991 Gulf War, when storage facilities were destroyed.

ONGC is awaiting approval from its board to invest approximately $63m in Iraq.

India, which imports more than two-thirds of its crude oil requirement, has been seeking foreign sources as domestic output matures.

Last month it took over a concession in Sudan from Canadian oil company Talisman.

***

Document

CONGRESSIONAL RECORD -- EXTENSIONS

Tuesday, June 18, 2002
107th Congress, 2nd Session
148 Cong Rec E 1080

REFERENCE: Vol. 148, No. 81
SECTION: Extension of Remarks
TITLE: WAR CLOUDS GATHERING IN SOUTH ASIA

HON. DAN BURTON
of Indiana
in the House of Representatives
Tuesday, June 18, 2002

Mr. BURTON of Indiana . Mr. Speaker, the danger of war in South Asia concerns us all. Such a war would be useless, dangerous, and a disaster for Pakistan, India, the minorities of the subcontinent, and the world.

Many South Asia's watchers speculate that India needs a war to keep its multinational empire together and to divert attention away from its other internal problems. They have even speculated that India's collapse is not a fantasy, and that even L.K. Advani, the militant Hindu Home Minister of India, is worried about India's territorial integrity.

However, a war in South Asia could become the trigger that brings freedom to the minority nations such as the Sikh homeland of Khalistan, predominantly Christian Nagaland, Kashmir, and others, just as World War I brought independence to many nations living under the rule of the Austro-Hungarian Empire and the Ottoman Empire. The end of the Cold War brought freedom to many nations which had been living under Soviet rule, including Estonia, Latvia, Lithuania, and others. A war in South Asia could have a similar effect on the nations and peoples of the subcontinent.

The Council of Khalistan recently called on Sikh soldiers not to fight for India, but to fight to free their homeland, Khalistan. Given the oppression that has killed over 250,000 Sikhs since 1984 according to the Punjab State Magistracy, that continues to hold 52,268 political prisoners, which the Movement Against State Repression reported that the Indian government has admitted to, that has killed over 80,000 Muslims, over 200,000 Christians in Nagaland, thousands upon thousands of other minorities like Bodos, Dalit "Untouchables," Tamils, Assamese, Manipuri's, and others, why should any of these minorities fight for the Indian state?

The Council of Khalistan's recent Open Letter contains much more information on this. To help my colleagues and constituents stay fully informed about the sentiments of many Sikhs within India, I would like to put that open letter into the Record at this time.

Council of Khalistan,
Washington DC, May 21, 2002.
Open Letter to the Sikh Nation

Clouds of War Between India and Pakistan Gather; India Is on the Verge of Disintegration_Sikh Soldiers and Officers Should Not Fight for India But to Free Khalistan; Now Is the Perfect Time to Launch Shantmai Morcha to Liberate Khalistan

Dear Khalsa Ji: WAHE GURU JI KA KHALSA, WAHE GURU JI KI FATEH!

War clouds are gathering in South Asia. War between India and Pakistan looks imminent. It is expected to break out this fall. Troops have been gathering on the borders, and the recent killings in Kashmir provide the Indian government with an excuse to attack Pakistan. The killing of Abdul Ghanni Lone, a leader of the Kashmiri freedom movement, merely heightens the tensions.

Remember that the fanatic BJP leaders are on record that they want to make an "Akand Bharat" by defeating Pakistan and incorporating it into India. Their aggression in Kashmir is internationally known. They will not hold a plebiscite in Kashmir, as they promised to do in 1948. It is India that launched the nuclear arms race in South Asia and has nuclear weapons pointed at Pakistan. Despite the militant Hindu nationalist government's statement that they do not intend to attack Pakistan, it is clear that their drive for hegemony over all of South Asia continues.

If war breaks out, Sikh soldiers and officers should not fight for India. Instead, Sikhs should take this opportunity to reclaim our lost sovereignty and liberate our homeland, Punjab, Khalistan, from Indian occupation.

L.K. Advani has said that when Kashmir goes, India will fall apart, and he is right. We must take advantage of this situation to reclaim our lost sovereignty. Sovereignty is our birthright. The Guru gave sovereignty to the Khalsa Panth. ("In grieh Sikhin ko deon Patshahi.") Banda Singh Baliadur established the first Khalsa rule in Punjab from 1710 to 1716. Then there was a period of persecution of the Sikhs. Again Sikhs established a sovereign, independent rule from 1765 to 1849, when the British annexed the Sikh homeland, Punjab, into British India.

This is a wake-up call for the Sikh Nation. The massacre of Muslims in Gujarat is a testament to this. The fanatic Vishav Hindu Parishad (VHP) burned Christian missionary Graham Staines and his two young sons alive. They murdered priests, raped nuns, and burned churches. They are assimilating Christianity, Islam, and every other minority into Hinduism. The Sikh Nation must free itself from India to ensure its survival as a nation and to enjoy a prosperous future. Without political power, nations perish.

About 80 percent of the sacrifices during the fight to regain freedom from the British were Sikhs, even though Sikhs formed only 1.5 percent of the Indian population at the time. At the time of India's independence, Sikhs were equal signatories to the transfer of power from the British. The Sikh leadership should have gotten an independent country for the Sikhs at that time, but they were fooled by the Hindu leadership of Nehru and Gandhi so Sikhs took their share and joined India on the promise that they would have the glow of freedom.

We have seen this "glow of freedom" in the form of the attack on the Golden Temple in June 1984, when over 20,000 Sikhs were killed in Punjab in a single month. Sikhs can never forgive or forget the desecration of the Golden Temple. This is the history and tradition of the Sikh Nation.

The next massacre of Sikhs occurred after the assassination of Indira Gandhi in Delhi. There was a mass murder of Sikhs throughout India, including Delhi. The Sikhs were pulled out of trains and burned alive.

Sikh truck drivers were pulled out of their trucks. Hindu militants put tires around their necks and burned them to death. Sikh police officers were disarmed and confined to their barracks. This is very similar to what happened recently to the Muslims in Gujarat.

Human Rights Watch Asia has clearly stated that the Indian government orchestrated the recent genocide in Gujarat. Policemen stood and watched while Muslims were attacked and murdered. One policeman said that he was ordered not to stop the violence. This is the same modus operandi that the Indian government used in 1984 to burn the Sikhs alive and destroy their property. For the Sikh Nation to ensure their safety, we must free our homeland, Punjab, Khalistan, from Indian occupation. We pray every day "Raj Kare Ga Khalsa." We must do our best to realize our God-given right to be free.

The Indian government has murdered over 250,000 Sikhs since 1984. The U.S. State Department reported in 1994 that the Indian government paid out over 41,000 cash bounties to police officers for killing Sikhs. According to a report by the Movement Against State Repression MASR), the Indian government admitted that 52,268 are rotting in Indian jails under TADA, which expired in 1995. Many of them have been in illegal custody since Operation Bluestar in 1984. In February, 42 Members of the U.S. Congress from both political parties wrote to President Bush to get these political prisoners released. The U.S. government recently added India to its "watch list" of violators of religious freedom. It should impose sanctions to stop the oppression of Sikhs, Christians, Muslims, and others.

Jaswant Singh Khalra, who exposed the government killing of Sikhs in fake encounters, became a victim of the Indian police himself. He was kidnapped outside his house and murdered in police custody. Even Akal Takht Jathedar Sardar Gurdev Singh Kaunke was murdered by SSP Swaran Singh Ghotna and then his body was disposed of. The Badal government was forced to conduct an inquiry by three Punjab police officials under the leadership of DIG Tiwari into the killing of Jathedar Kaunke. As of today that report has not been made public.

The only solution is the formation of a Khalsa Raj Party under new, honest, dedicated, and committed leadership. Now is the time to do it. Let's not waste time and prolong the suffering and agony of the Sikh Nation. The only remedy is to sever our relationship with Delhi completely, declare independence from India and start a peaceful agitation to free the Sikh homeland, Punjab, Khalistan. The present Akali leadership of Badal, Tohra, Mann, and others are under Indian government control. Their betrayal of the Sikh Nation is well documented in the Book Chakravyuh: Web of Indian Secularism by S. Gurtej Singh.

Siklis are a sovereign, independent nation and ruled Punjab until 1849. The only way the Sikh Nation can protect itself from the Indian government's ongoing efforts to destroy the Sikh religion is to achieve independence for our homeland, Khalistan. Guru gave sovereignty to the Khalsa Panth. The new Sikh leadership must launch a Shantmai Morcha to liberate our homeland. The only way the Sikh Nation can prosper is to free the Sikh homeland, Punjab, Khalistan. The freedom of the Sikh

Nation will bring prosperity, stability, and peace to Punjab and to South Asia.

> *Panth Da Sewadar,*
> *Dr. Gurmit Singh Aulakh,*
> *President, Council of Khalistan.*

***

Document

CONGRESSIONAL RECORD -- EXTENSIONS

Thursday, June 13, 2002
107th Congress, 2nd Session
148 Cong Rec E 1032

REFERENCE: Vol. 148, No. 78
SECTION: Extension of Remarks
TITLE: IN MEMORY OF INDIA'S ATTACK ON A RELIGIOUS SHRINE

HON. DAN BURTON
of Indiana
in the House of Representatives
Wednesday, June 12, 2002

Mr. BURTON of Indiana . Mr. Speaker, as you may know, this week marked the anniversary of India's June 1984 attack on the Golden Temple in Amritsar, the seat of the Sikh religion. This is the equivalent of attacking the Vatican of Mecca.

In the attack, which also included attacks on 38 other Sikh Temples (known as Gurdwaras), more than 20,000 Sikhs were killed, including Sant Jarnail Singh Bhindranwale, a Sikh political leader. The Indian government hoped that by murdering Bhindranwale, it would end the Sikh Nation's aspirations for freedom, but as Bhindranwale himself said, the attack "laid the foundation of Khalistan," the independent Sikh homeland.

I would like to extend my sympathies to all Sikhs on this occasion and I would like to let them know that many of us grieve with them at this brutal atrocity committed against them.

The Council of Khalistan recently led a commemoration of the Golden Temple attack. I would like to place the report of that commemoration into the Record for the information of my colleagues.

Sikhs Observe Khalistan Martyrs Day_Sikhs Never Forgive or Forget Attack on Golden Temple
Golden Temple Attack Laid Foundation of Khalistan

Washington, D.C., June 1, 2002._It is a Sikh tradition and Sikh history that Sikhs never forgive or forget the attack on the Golden Temple, the

Sikh Nation's holiest shrine. In that spirit, Sikhs from all over the East Coast gathered in Washington, D.C. today to observe Khalistan Martyrs Day. This is the anniversary of the Indian government's brutal military attack on the Golden Temple and 38 other Sikh Temples through Punjab, from June 3-6, 1984. More than 20,000 Sikhs were killed in those attacks, known as Operation Bluestar. These martyrs laid down their lives to lay the foundation for Khalistan. On October 7, 1987, the Sikh Nation declared its homeland, Khalistan, independent.

"We thank all the demonstrators who came to this important protest," said Dr. Gurmit Singh Aulakh, President of the Council of Khalistan. "These martyrs gave their lives so that the Sikh Nation could live in freedom," Dr. Aulakh said. "We salute them on Khalistan Martyrs' Day," he said. "As Sant Bhindranwale said, the Golden Temple attack laid the foundation of Khalistan."

Sikhs ruled Punjab until 1849 when the British conquered the sub-continent. Sikhs were equal partners during the transfer of power from the British. The Muslim leader Jinnah got Pakistan for his people, the Hindu leaders got India, but the Sikh leadership was fooled by the Hindu leadership promising the Sikhs would have "the glow of freedom" in Northwest India and the Sikhs took their share with India on that promise. No Sikh representative has ever signed the Indian constitution.

Recently, former Senate Majority Leader George Mitchell (D-Me.) said, "The essence of democracy is the right to self-determination." The minority nations of South Asia need freedom. "Without political power nations perish. We must always remember these martyrs for their sacrifice," Dr. Aulakh said. "The best tribute to these martyrs would be the liberation of the Sikh homeland, Punjab, Khalistan, from the occupying forces," he said. "That must be the only objective," he said. "We should use the opportunity presented by the situation in South Asia to liberate our homeland."

The Golden Temple attack launched a campaign of genocide against the Sikhs that belies India's claims that it is a democracy. The Golden Temple attack made it clear that there is no place for Sikhs in India. Since 1984, India has engaged in a campaign of ethnic cleansing in which tens of thousands of Sikhs were murdered by the Indian police and security forces and secretly cremated after declaring them "unidentified." The Indian Supreme Court described this campaign as "worse than a genocide." General Narinder Singh has said, "Punjab is a police state." U.S. Congressman Dana Rohrabacher (R-Cal.) has said that for Sikhs, Kashmiri Muslims, and other minorities "India might as well be Nazi Germany."

According to a report last year by the Movement Against State Repression, India admitted that 52,268 Sikh political prisoners are rotting in Indian jails without charge or trial. Many have been in illegal custody since 1984. In February, 42 Members of the U.S. Congress wrote to President Bush to get these Sikh prisoners released. MASR report quotes the Punjab Civil Magistracy as writing "if we add up the figures of the last few years the number of innocent persons killed would run into lakhs hundreds of thousands. "

Indian security forces have murdered over 250,000 Sikhs since 1984, according to figures compiled by the Punjab State Magistracy and human-rights organizations. These figures were published in The Politics of Genocide by Inderjit Singh Jaijee. India has also killed over 200,000 Christians in Nagaland since 1947, over 80,000 Kashmiris since 1988, and tens of thousands of Tamils, Bodos, Dalits (the aboriginal people of the subcontinent labelled "Untouchables") as well as indigenous tribal peoples in Manipur, Assam and elsewhere. In March 2000, while former President Clinton was visiting India, the Indian government murdered 35 Sikhs in the village of Chithisinghpora, Kashmir and tried to blame the massacre on alleged militants. The Indian media reported that the police in Gujarat were ordered by the government to stand by and not to interfere with the massacre of Muslims there.

"Guru gave sovereignty to the Sikh Nation," Dr. Aulakh said. "The Golden Temple massacre reminded us that if Sikhs are going to live with honor and dignity, we must have a free, sovereign, independent Khalistan," he said.

***

Document

CONGRESSIONAL RECORD -- EXTENSIONS

Thursday, June 06, 2002
107th Congress, 2nd Session
148 Cong Rec E 974

REFERENCE: Vol. 148, No. 73
SECTION: Extension of Remarks
TITLE: IS INDIA AN ALLY OR A TERRORIST STATE?

HON. DAN BURTON
of Indiana
in the House of Representatives
Wednesday, June 5, 2002

Mr. BURTON of Indiana . Mr. Speaker, recently, the news website NewsMax.com ran a vary comprehensive article called "India: Allies or Instigators?" It details India's pattern of abuse against the Christians, Sikhs, Muslims, and other minorities, its anti-Americanism, and its support of terrorism against its neighbors.

The article shows that the Indian government has killed tens of thousands of Sikhs, Christians, Muslims, and other minorities; that it holds tens of thousands of political prisoners; and it is funding terrorism in Pakistan and created and supported the Liberation Tigers of Tamil Eelam (LTTE), an organization the U.S. government has called a "terrorist" organization. It shows India's domestic terrorism against Sikhs, Christians, Muslims, and all the other minority groups.

Reading this article should cause any fair-minded reader to ask whether or not India is a terrorist state seeking hegemony in South Asia and questions whether India is a country we should trust as an ally. The United States should work for freedom for all the people of the subcontinent. I was proud to be one of 42 Members of Congress from both parties who signed a letter urging President Bush to press for the release of Sikh and other political prisoners in India. The Administration should do that. But it should do more.

After reading this article, it is clearly time for the U.S. government to cut off its aid to India and to come out in support of self-determination for all the peoples and nations of South Asia. This is the best way to spread liberty, democracy, prosperity, and true stability to the subcontinent.

Mr. Speaker, I would like to place the article into the Record at this time. I urge my colleagues and all people interested in South Asian affairs to read it.

India: Allies or Instigators?
(By Tim Phares)

Trouble is brewing again in South Asia, as India and Pakistan move troops to their border. The recent violence in Gujarat, in which over 540 people have been killed, has merely heightened tensions.

It follows an attack by Muslims on a train full of Hindu activists headed for Ayodhya, where the BJP government in India is seeking to build a Hindu Temple on the site where the most revered mosque in India was destroyed by Hindu militants a few years ago. It was reported that the passengers were taunting the Muslims by chanting slogans about rebuilding the Temple.

Unfortunately, India, which proclaims itself "the world's largest democracy," has made moves that undermine America's war on terrorism. Indian military maneuvers have forced Pakistan to divert troops from the border with Afghanistan to the Line of Control in Kashmir, creating a potential opening for terrorists to escape.

On January 2, Tony Blankley wrote in the Washington Times that India is sponsoring cross-border terrorism in the Pakistani province of Sindh.

Journalist Tavleen Singh has reported in India's leading newsmagazine, India Today, that the Indian government created the Liberation Tigers of Tamil Eelam (LTTE), which the U.S. government has identified as a "terrorist organization."

According to Internet journalist Justin Raimondo, the Indian Defense Minister, George Fernandes, raised money and arms for the LTTE.

Pakistan and minorities within India's borders charge that India is seeking hegemony in the South Asian subcontinent. Certainly its deployment of new missiles that can reach deep into Pakistan and its tests that began the nuclear escalation in the region suggest that this may be true.

While India blames Pakistan for the attack on its Parliament, President Pervez Musharraf says he has evidence that the Indian government itself was responsible. No Indian soldiers were killed, just guards, workers, and other lower-caste people.

The book Soft Target, written by Canadian journalists Brian McAndrew of the Toronto Star and Zuhair Kashmeri of the Toronto Globe and Mail, shows that India blew up its own airliner in 1985, killing 329 people, apparently in order to blame Sikhs for the atrocity and create a pretext for more violence against them.

It shows that the Indian Consul General in Toronto pulled his daughter off the flight shortly before it was due to depart. An auto dealer who was a friend of the Consul General also cancelled his reservation at the last minute. Surinder Singh, director of North American Affairs for the External Affairs office in New Delhi, also cancelled his reservation on that flight. The Consul General also called to finger a suspect in the case before the public knew that the bombing had taken place. The book quotes an agent of the Canadian State Investigative Service (CSIS) as saying, "If you really want to clear the incidents quickly. take vans down to the Indian High Commission and the consulates in Toronto and Vancouver, load up everybody and take them down for questioning. We know it and they know it that they are involved."

India has a long record of Anti-Americanism. On May 18, 1999, The Indian Express reported that Mr. Fernandes, the Defense Minister, organized and led a meeting with the Ambassadors from Red China, Cuba, Russia, Yugoslavia, Libya, and Iraq to discuss setting up a security alliance "to stop the U.S."

India votes against the United States at the United Nations more often than any country except Cuba. It had a long term friendship with the former Soviet Union and supported its invasion of Afghanistan.

India's implicit support for terrorist activity is consistent with its internal behavior. It has a record of repression of minorities that undermines its proclamation of democratic values.

The ruling Bharatiya Janata Party (BJP), which leads a 23-party coalition, is a branch of the Rashtriya Swayamsewak Sangh (RSS), an organization founded in 1925 in support of the Fascists.

The governing ideology of the BJP and all the branches of the RSS is Hindutva, the subjugation of society, politics, and culture to Hinduism. Last year, a cabinet member said that everyone living in India must either be a Hindu or be subservient to Hinduism. And in New York in 2000, Prime Minister Atal Bihari Vajpayee said, "I will always be a Swayamsewak." This is the ideology behind the attacks on Christians, Sikhs, Muslims, and other minorities.

The target of choice these days seems to be Christians. Human-rights organizations report that more than 200,000 Christians in Negaland have been killed by the Indian government.

On February 17, the Associated Press reported an attack on the Catholic church on the outskirts of Bangalore in which several people were injured. The assailants threw stones at the church, then broke in, break-

ing furniture and smashing windows before attacking worshipers. the February 25 issue of the Washington Times reported another church attack in which 20 people were wounded.

In February, two church workers and a teenage boy were shot at while they prayed. The boy was injured. Two Christian missionaries were beaten with iron rods while they rode their bicycles home. A Christian cemetery in Port Blair was vandalized.

These attacks continue a pattern of oppression of Christians that has been going on heavily since Christmas 1998. Since then, members of the RSS have murdered priests, raped nuns, burned churches, and committed other atrocities with impunity.

The RSS published a booklet last year detailing how to file false criminal cases against Christians and other religious minorities. The RSS objects to the presence of missionaries in India.

The missionaries are having a good deal of success in converting members of the lower castes, especially Dalits, also known as "Untouchables." This removes the lower-caste people from the stratification of the caste system, which is essential to the Hindu religion and social structure.

RSS activists also burned a missionary and his two sons to death while they slept in their jeep. They surrounded the jeep and chanted "Victory to Hannuman," a Hindu god. Now the Indian authorities have found a single individual to blame and they are moving to throw the missionary's widow out of the country. In 1997, Indian police broke up a Christian religious festival with gunfire.

In 1994, the U.S. State Department reported that the Indian government paid out over 41,000 cash bounties to police officers for killing members of the Sikh minority. In the same year, the Indian newspaper Hitavada reported that the Indian government paid the late governor of Punjab, Surendra Nath, the equivalent of $1.5 billion to foment terrorist activity in Punjab and in Kashmir.

According to the book The Politics of Genocide, over 250,000 Sikhs have been killed by the Indian government's forces. According to human-rights groups, Indian forces have killed over 75,000 Muslims in Kashmir and thousands of other minorities, including Dalit "untouchables," Tamils, and other groups.

A report issued last year by the Movement Against State Repression (MASR) showed that India admitted to holding 52,268 political prisoners. Amnesty International reports that tens of thousands of other minorities are also being held as political prisoners.

These prisoners continue to be held under a law called the "Terrorist and Disruptive Activities Act" (TADA), which expired in 1995, It empowered the government to hold people virtually indefinitely for any offense or for no offense at all.

According to many reports, some of these political prisoners have been in custody for almost two decades. Amnesty International reported last year that tens of thousands of minorities are big held as political prisoners. On February 28, 42 Members of the U.S. Congress wrote to President Bush asking him to work for freedom for these political prisoners.

MASR also co-sponsored with the Punjab Human Rights Organization an Investigation of the March 2000 massacre of 35 Sikhs in Chithisinghpora. It concluded that Indian forces carried out the massacre. A separate investigation conducted by the International Human Rights Organization came to the same conclusion.

As Rep. Dana Rohrabacher (R-Cal.) said on the floor of Congress on August 2, 1999, "for the people in Kashmir and Punjab and Jammu, India might as well be Nazi Germany."

In the words of Narinder Singh, a spokesman for the Golden Temple, the seat of the Sikh religion, who was interviewed in August 1997 by National Public Radio, "The Indian government, all the time they boast that they are secular, that they are democratic. But they have nothing to do with a democracy, nothing to do with a secularism. They just kill Sikhs to please the majority."

In the March 4 issue of Forbes, Steve Forbes compared India to the Austro-Hungarian Empire, arguing that as a multinational State, India is inherently unstable. Prior to the British conquest of the subcontinent, there was no political entity called India. It was a series of princely states brought together by the British.

The Kashmiri people were promised a referendum on their status in 1948, but that vote has never been held. The Sikhs, who were supposed to receive independence, have never had any of their representatives sign the Indian constitution. Instead of respecting "the glow of freedom" that Nehru and Patel promised the Sikhs, the government declared them a "criminal class" as the ink was dry on the constitution. Currently, 17 freedom movements are going on within India's borders.

Some Members of Congress have called for sanctions against India and for an end to American aid. Some have also endorsed self-determination for the peoples seeking freedom from India through a plebiscite on independence. While these events seem unlikely to occur any time soon, the Indian government has held negotiations with the freedom fighters in predominantly Christian Nagaland. Home Minister L.K. Advani recently admitted that if Kashmir achieves freedom (which now seems more likely than ever), it will cause India to break apart.

Some experts have predicted that within a decade, neither India nor Pakistan will exist in the form we know them presently. The Indian subcontinent will continue to be a region that bears close attention by American policymakers.

***

Document

CONGRESSIONAL RECORD -- EXTENSIONS

Tuesday, May 14, 2002
107th Congress, 2nd Session
148 Cong Rec E 796

REFERENCE: Vol. 148, No. 61
SECTION: Extension of Remarks
TITLE: BBC EXPOSES MILITANT HINDU VHP

HON. DAN BURTON
of Indiana
in the House of Representatives
Tuesday, May 14, 2002

Mr. BURTON of Indiana . Mr. Speaker, the British Broadcasting Company recently ran an expose of the Vishwa Hindu Parishad (VHP), a fundamentalist, militant Hindu nationalist organization. The VHP is an organization, which operates under the umbrella of the pro-Facist Rashtriya Swayamsewak Sangh (RSS). The RSS is the parent organization of the ruling BJP.

The BBC notes that the VHP has promoted Hindu supremacy and has engaged in violent acts against minorities. These acts include the murder of missionary Graham Staines and his two young sons while they slept in their jeep.

The report states that the VHP, which it identifies as "a hardline Hindu outfit," rarely makes a "distinction between fellow (Muslim) citizens of the present and (Muslim marauders' of the past." It further reports that "the ambition of establishing a resurgent Hinduism by inculcating what some historians call a carefully constructed common Hindu spirit' is very much central to the VHP." Moreover, it exposes the VHP's support for a militant Hindus' project to build a Hindu Temple on the site of the most revered mosque in India, which was destroyed by the BJP.

Since the BJP is also part of the RSS umbrella, it is critical to help ensure the rights of minorities in India. Tens of thousands of Sikhs and other minorities have been held in illegal custody as political prisoners for many years. Tens of thousands of minorities have been killed by the Indian governments regardless of the political party in power. It is time to stop American aid to India and to support self-determination for all the people of South Asia in the form of a plebiscite on independence so that their rights are not subject to the whims of militant Hindu nationalists.

Mr. Speaker, I would like to place the text of the BBC report into the Record at this time.

The British Broadcasting Co., Mar. 8, 2002
Profile: The Vishwa Hindu Parishad
(By Rajyasri Rao)

The Vishwa Hindu Parishad (VHP) was founded in 1964 by a group of senior leaders from a hard-line Hindu organisation, the Rashtriya Swayamsevak Sangh (RSS), to give Hindus what they believed would be a clearly defined sense of religious identity and political purpose.

Hindu hardliners have grown more vocal

Its founders felt the need to present Hinduism in a rigorous though simplified form which would be comparable to most other world religions.

The superiority of other faiths was believed to stem from their being far less diffuse and more uniform than Hinduism.

But its critics call the VHP a hardline Hindu outfit with unmistakably close ties to its parent organisation, the extremist RSS, whose objective to Hinduise' the Indian nation, it shares.

Central to the RSS ideology has been the belief that real national unity and progress will come only when India is purged' of non-Hindus, or, when members of other communities subordinate themselves willingly' to Hindu superiority.'

Linked groups

The VHP has tended to tone down the rhetoric of Hindu supremacy and even make an occasional distinction between fellow (Muslim) citizens of the present and (Muslim) marauders' of the past.

But the ambition of establishing a resurgent Hinduism by inculcating what some historians call a carefully constructed common Hindu spirit' is very much central to the VHP.

The Temple project enjoys a lot of support

This is also something it shares with the Bharatiya Janata Party (BJP), which currently leads the Indian Government at the centre.

Earlier known as the Bharatiya Jana Sangh (BJS), the BJP was established in 1951 as a political wing of the RSS to counter rising public revulsion after the revered independence figure Mahatma Gandhi was assassinated by a former RSS member.

Some commentators say the party came close to obliteration in the 1960s with the Congress led by the charismatic and secular Jawaharlal Nehru, leaving little room for hardline communal politics.

But a political emergency announced by Nehru's daughter, Indira Gandhi, in 1975 enabled the BJS leaders, Atal Behari Vajpayee and LK Advani among them, to gain near stardom after serving brief prison sentences. Many women have joined the hardliners' campaign.

But it didn't really emerge as a political presence until the early 1980s.

A series of events in that decade including the mass conversion of lower-cast Hindus to Islam pushed the BJP's close affiliate, the VHP, to the forefront.

Historians say the VHP-led Hindu right considered the mass conversion of "dalits" or lower-caste Hindus to Islam to be an unforgivable insult.

The dalits, for centuries beholden to the upper castes, outraged Hindu hardliners by daring to convert at all, and moreover, convert to Islam.

The VHP saw this as a serious threat to its notion of Hinduism.

It proceeded to whip up Hindu support for a re-defined communal force, organising a series of religious meetings, cross-country marches and processions through the 1980s.

This phase coincided with the launch of an electoral strategy by the BJP to corner and hold on to the "Hindu" vote.

Temple controversy

Following the success of their campaign, senior VHP leaders announced at a religious meeting in 1984 their programme to "liberate" a site in Ayodhya from an ancient mosque to make way for a Temple to the Hindu god Ram.

Some moderate' Hindu leaders support the VHP

Analysts say this announcement heralded a turning point in the history of the Hindu nationalist movement.

The VHP has since then claimed that the site belongs rightfully to Hindu worshippers who believe that the mosque stood on the birthplace of the god, Lord Ram. Although the claim does not stand up to substantial archaeological or historical scrutiny, the VHP and BJP are seen to have made possible the creation of a shared Hindu symbol that cuts through most divisions in Hindu society.

***

Document

CONGRESSIONAL RECORD -- EXTENSIONS

Wednesday, May 08, 2002
107th Congress, 2nd Session
148 Cong Rec E 755

REFERENCE: Vol. 148, No. 57
SECTION: Extension of Remarks
TITLE: TYRANNICAL NEW LAW ALREADY BEING ABUSED

HON. EDOLPHUS TOWNS
of New York
in the House of Representatives
Wednesday, May 8, 2002

Mr. TOWNS . Mr. Speaker, I was saddened to read an article in the Times of India showing that India's repressive new "Prevention of Terrorism Ordinance" (POTO) is already being abused. The new law allows the police to hold someone without charges for up to 180 days, according to the Washington Post.

According to the article, a court granted bail to a POTO defendant named Abdul Ahmed Bhat and granted him bail of Rs 2,500. The judgment shows how the police are abusing POTO. The police filed two varying reports against Mr. Bhat, abusing the process to make certain that he stayed in police custody. The official police reports exonerates Mr. Bhat of the charges against him, while the investigating officer's report implicates him.

Unfortunately, this kind of abuse is typical of the Indian government. The Rashtriya Swayamsewak Sangh (RSS), a hardline, militant Hindu fundamentalist organization published a booklet on how to implicate Christians and other minorities in false criminal cases. The RSS is the parent organization of the ruling BJP, which sponsored and passed POTO.

Mr. Speaker, we must not support this kind of tyranny. We should end all our aid to India until it ends. We should also put ourselves on record in favor of self-determination for everyone in the subcontinent by means of a free and fair, democratic vote on independence for Khalistan, Kashmir, Nagaland, and the other nations seeking their freedom from India.

Mr. Speaker, I would like the permission of the House to insert the Times of India article into the Record for the information of my colleagues.

From the Times of India, Apr. 3, 2002
POTO Misused by Police in Bhat Case

Srinagar._Two varying police reports by the same investigating officer prompted the special court to grant bail to Abdul Ahmed Bhat on Monday. Bhat, a resident of Ahmad Nagar, was booked under the Prevention of Terrorism Ordinance (POTO) under FIR No 12/2002 at police station Soura.

The special court had granted bail to Bhat against a bond of Rs 25,000.

The judgment points a finger of suspicion at the police for misuse of the prevention of terrorism law_despite the Centre and the state government's assurance for its fair use to tackle terrorism across the country.

Announcing the judgment on Monday, special Judge M I Qureshi said: "After close and minute examination of the two police reports and case diary that the prima-facie case under Sections 3 and 21 of POTO is made out against the accused persons except Abdul Ahad Bhat."

The judgment further reveals that there were variations in the two police reports about the date of Bhat's arrest. Also, the police report exonerates Bhat from the implication of alleged offences, while the second report submitted before the court on March 14 by the investigating officer of his own, implicates him (Bhat) for the alleged offences.

***

Document

CONGRESSIONAL RECORD -- EXTENSIONS

Thursday, April 11, 2002
107th Congress, 2nd Session
148 Cong Rec E 502

REFERENCE: Vol. 148, No. 39
SECTION: Extension of Remarks
TITLE: IN SECULAR INDIA, HINDU LIVES WORTH TWICE AS MUCH AS
MUSLIM LIVES

HON. CYNTHIA A. McKINNEY
of Georgia
in the House of Representatives
Thursday, April 11, 2002

Ms. McKINNEY . Mr. Speaker, the government of India is compensating the families of those who lost their lives in the recent riots in Gujarat. While no amount of money makes up for the loss, this is a decent thing to do and I salute India for it.

However, Mr. Speaker, I was disturbed to find out that apparently in the world's largest secular democracy, a Hindu life is worth twice as much as a Muslim life. According to News India-Times, the Indian government is paying out 200,000 Rupees each to the families of Hindus who were killed, but just 100,000 Rupees to the family of each Muslim killed.

Mr. Speaker, I think it is offensive that a country that claims it is democratic thinks that the life of one person or group is twice as valuable as that of another person or group. What if our government declared white lives twice as valuable as black ones, or vice versa? Would that be tolerated?

The article also notes that during the riots, "Muslim establishments were targeted in an organized manner_even when they masqueraded under Hindu names and were run in Hindu majority areas." This seems to indicate the government's hand in the planning of the riots, an impression that is reinforced by the fact that the police stood by and let the carnage happen.

This is simply part of an ongoing Hindu nationalist campaign to wipe out religious minorities. It is unacceptable, Mr. Speaker, and America must help to put a stop to it. We should stop all aid to India until all people enjoy equal rights and we should demand a free and fair plebiscite in Kashmir, Khalistan, Nagaland, and the other nations seeking to get out from under India's brutal occupation. These steps will help bring real freedom, stability, and prosperity to the South Asian region.

Mr. Speaker, I would like to place the News India-Times article into the Record.

From the News India-Times March 29, 2002
Muslims suffer bias even after the riots

AHMEDABAD_The state government has been booking those responsible for the Godhra carnage under draconian Prevention of Terrorism Ordinance (POTO), while those who targeted Muslims and their business establishments in an organized manner in the state are being booked under the milder Criminal Procedure Code. POTO allows a person to be held without bail for 30 days.

Rights activists here contended that this was yet another example of the state government's bias against the Muslim community, and called for the scrapping of POTO.

Earlier, Chief Minister Narendra Modi's government had announced compensation of Rs. 200,000 ($4,166) for the victims of the Godhra tragedy, while the amount for those who died in the widespread retaliatory riots was fixed at half that amount, Rs. 100,000 ($2,083).

Rights activists as well as journalists covering the riots have noted how Muslim establishments were targeted in an organized manner_even when they masqueraded under Hindu names and were run in Hindu majority areas.

***

Document

CONGRESSIONAL RECORD -- EXTENSIONS

Wednesday, April 10, 2002
107th Congress, 2nd Session
148 Cong Rec E 479

REFERENCE: Vol. 148, No. 38
SECTION: Extension of Remarks
TITLE: VAISAKHI GREETINGS TO THE SIKH NATION

HON. DAN BURTON
of Indiana
in the House of Representatives
Wednesday, April 10, 2002

Mr. BURTON of Indiana . Mr. Speaker, this Saturday, April 13, is Vaisakhi, the birthday of the Sikhs. It marks the day on which the last of the Sikh gurus, Guru Gobind Singh, consecrated the Khalsa Panth. It is the Sikhs' most important holiday. I would like to take this opportunity to wish the Sikhs in America, In Khalistan, and around the world a happy Vaisakhi Day.

This important occasion is usually marked with parades and services in the Gurdwara. It should also be a time for the Sikh Nation to focus on freedom.

Sikhs have made many contributions to this country. They have been leaders in agriculture, law, medicine, and many other fields. One Sikh, Dr. Dalip Singh, a mathematics professor from California, served two terms in this House from 1959-63. He was the first person from the subcontinent to serve in Congress.

As is the regular practice, Dr. Gurmit Singh Aulakh, President of the Council of Khalistan, has issued a Vaisakhi Day greeting to the Sikh Nation. He urges the Sikhs to use this occasion to begin a peaceful movement to reclaim their lost sovereignty and freedom. I urge all my colleagues to read this outstanding letter.

The time has come for America to cut off its aid to India and to support a free and fair plebiscite on independence in Punjab, Khalistan, in Kashmir, in Christian Nagaland, and in the many nations seeking their freedom from India. These are the best measures to ensure freedom, peace, security, and prosperity in South Asia.

Vaisakhi Message to the Sikh Nation, Mar. 25, 2002.

Khalsa Ji: Wahe Guru Ji Ka Khalsa, Wahe Guru Ji Ki Fateh!

This is a time of celebration of our 303rd anniversary of the Khalsa Panth. It is also time to look back at our history. The Guru gave sovereignty to the Khalsa Panth. ("In grieb Sikhin ko deon Patshahi.") Banda Singh Bahadur established the first Khalsa rule in Punjab from 1710 to 1716. Then there was a period of persecution of the Sikhs. Again Sikhs established a sovereign, independent rule from 1765 to 1849, when the British annexed the Sikh homeland, Punjab, into British India.

To regain freedom from the British, Sikhs were on the front line of the fight. The Sikh Nation gave about 80 percent of the sacrifices during this freedom struggle when they formed only 1.5 percent of the Indian population. At the time of the independence of India, Sikhs were equal signatories to the transfer of power from the British. Muslim leader Mohammed Ali Jinnah was very wise and well educated and he did not trust the majority Hindu leadership. He got an independent Pakistan for the Muslims. The Sikh leadership should have gotten an independent country for the Sikhs at that time, but they were fooled by the Hindu leadership of Nehru and Gandhi so Sikhs took their share and joined India on the promise that they would have the glow of freedom in the northwest part of India.

Khalsa Ji, we have seen this "glow of freedom" in the form of the attack on the Golden Temple in June 1984, when over 20,000 Sikhs were killed in Punjab in a single month. The next massacre of Sikhs occurred after the assassination of Indira Gandhi in Delhi. There was a mass murder of Sikhs throughout India, including Delhi. The Sikhs were pulled out of trains and burned alive. Sikh truck drivers were pulled out of their trucks. Tires were put around their necks by Hindu militants and they were burned to death. In Punjab, this genocide continued under Beant Singh's government. Sikhs were arrested, tortured, and then cremated and their bodies were declared "unidentified."

Since 1984, over 250,000 Sikhs have been murdered. 52,268 are rotting in Indian jails under TADA, which expired in 1995. Many of them have be in illegal custody since Operation Bluestar in 1984. Only last month, 42 Members of the U.S. Congress wrote to President Bush to get these political prisoners released. Jaswant Singh Khalra, who exposed the government killing of Sikhs in fake encounters, became a victim of the Indian police himself. He was kidnapped outside his house and murdered in police custody. He documented 6,018 Sikhs who were secretly cremated by the government in three cremation grounds, Patti, Tarn Taran, and Durgiana Mandir. Subsequently, Punjab Human Rights Organization (PHRO) chairman Justice Ajit Singh Bains said that about 50,000 Sikhs were secretly cremated in this manner. Even Akal Takht Jathedar Gurdev Singh Kaunke was murdered by SSP Swaran Singh Ghotna and then his body was disposed of.

The Badal government was forced to conduct an inquiry into the killing of Jathedar Kaunke. It was done by three Punjab police officials under the leadership of DIG Tiwari. He submitted a report to the Badal government, which has not been made public as of today. How could a democratically elected Akali government hide the murder of the Akal Takht Jathedar by not releasing this report, which was conducted by its own order?

The Badal government was the most corrupt one in Punjab's history. They invented a new term for bribery: "fee for service." If you didn't pay the fee, you didn't get the service. There was a fixed amount of money for government jobs. Bags of money were received by Mrs. Badal in return for these jobs. The Punjab economy deteriorated under Badal and the Punjab government had its largest debt ever. It is bankrupt now. Badal made three promises to get elected. He promised to free the political prisoners, to punish the police officers who carried out atrocities against the Sikh Nation, and to appoint a commission to investigate atrocities. He did not keep any of them.

The Sikh leadership is completely under Indian government control, whether it is the Akali leadership of Badal, Tohra, Mann, and others or the Congress leadership of Punjab under Captain Amarinder Singh or former Chief Minister Mrs. Bhatthal. Changing parties and faces every election will not solve the problems of the Sikh Nation. Congress is no better than the Akalis and the Alkalis proved to be the worst enemies of the Sikh Nation. How could an Akali government keep 52,268 Sikhs in jail without charge or trial for the last 16 years? It is shameful and a black mark on the present Akali leadership. They have cashed in on the sacrifices and good will of the pre-independence Akali leadership.

Khalsa Ji, the only solution to this quagmire is the formation of a Khalsa Raj Party under new, honest, dedicated, and committed leadership. The time is now to do it. Let's not waste time and prolong the suffering and agony of the Sikh Nation under the present corrupt Akali leadership which is controlled by the Indian government and is determined to wipe out the Sikh Nation and the Sikh religion. The only remedy is to sever our relationship with Delhi completely, once and for all, and declare the independence from India and start a peaceful agitation to free the Sikh homeland, Punjab, Khalistan.

The victory of the Congress Party was a massive rejection of the Akalis, who were elected five years ago to reject the Congress Party. However, the Congress Party remains the enemy of the Sikh Nation. In the last two elections, the Sikh Nation has soundly rejected both parties. Neither supports the interests of the Sikh Nation; neither can be trusted by the Sikh Nation. The time has come to discard the present Akali leadership that has betrayed the Sikh Nation.

We must press for action against the police officials who carried out the police kidnapping and murder of human-rights activist Jaswant Singh Khalra. These would be good first steps for the Sikh leadership and for the new government in Punjab. But we must continue to pursue our ultimate goal of freeing the Sikh homeland, Punjab, Khalistan.

The Sikh Nation is sovereign and it must have its sovereign, independent country. Guru gave sovereignty to the Khalsa Panth. Remember "Raj Kare Ga Khalsa." Sikhs can never forgive or forget the desecration of the Golden Temple. This is the history and tradition of the Sikh Nation. The time has come to form a Khalsa Raj Party to liberate Khalistan. The new Sikh leadership must launch a Shantmai Morcha to liberate our homeland. The only way the Sikh Nation can prosper is to free the Sikh homeland, Punjab, Khalistan. The freedom of the Sikh Nation will bring prosperity, stability, and peace to Punjab and to South Asia.

Panth Da Sewadar,
Dr. Gurmit Singh Aulakh,
President, Council of Khalistan.

***

Document

CONGRESSIONAL RECORD -- EXTENSIONS

Tuesday, April 09, 2002
107th Congress, 2nd Session
148 Cong Rec E 457

REFERENCE: Vol. 148, No. 37
SECTION: Extension of Remarks
TITLE: HAPPY VAISAKHI DAY TO THE SIKH NATION

HON. EDOLPHUS TOWNS
of New York
in the House of Representatives
Tuesday, April 9, 2002

Mr. TOWNS . Mr. Speaker, on April 13, the Sikhs will be celebrating Vaisakhi Day, their most important holiday. I want to salute the Sikh Nation for its contributions to America and wish all the Sikh people a happy Vaisakhi Day.

Vaisakhi Day is the day when the Sikhs were formed by their guru into the Khalsa Panth. It is the anniversary of the founding of their order, and the Sikh Nation has been a very important contributor to every country in which Sikhs live. A Sikh named Dalip Singh Saund served in Congress in the late 1950s and early 1960s. Dr. Amarjit Singh Bhullar of Connecticut is an elected school board member. Sikhs have been very active and successful in this country in virtually every walk of life. They have also made important contributions to India, including giving about 80 percent of the sacrifices for India's independence. Yet India persecutes them. Over 250,000 Sikhs have been murdered by the Indian government since 1984, according to the book The Politics of Genocide. At least 50,000 were picked up, tortured, murdered, and then declared "unidentified" and their bodies were cremated. The Movement Against State Repression reports that India admitted to holding 52,268 Sikh political prisoners. Tens of thousands of Christians, Muslims, and other minorities are also being held. Our own State Department reported in 1994 that the Indian government paid more than 41,000 cash bounties to police officers for killing Sikhs. These are just a few examples of the oppression of the Sikhs by the Indian government. I could give a very long list, but I do not wish to take up too much of the House's time.

April 13 also happens to be the birthday of Thomas Jefferson, who wrote the Declaration of Independence. In that document he wrote that when a government becomes tyrannical, "it is the right of the people to alter or abolish it and institute new government, laying its foundation on such principles and organizing its powers in such form as to them shall seem most likely to effect their safety and happiness." That certainly applies to the Sikh Nation today, as well as Kashmir, primarily Christian Nagaland, and the other nations living under Indian occupation. It is time for them to claim their own.

America should support these nations' right to self-determination by stopping aid to India and by supporting a free and fair vote on independence. Then the people of South Asia can finally live in freedom and enjoy stability, prosperity, and peace. That is something we should all work for.

Dr. Gurmit Singh Aulakh, President of the Council of Khalistan, put out an excellent and informative statement for Vaisakhi Day. It really lays out the issues well. With the consent of the House, I would like to insert it into the Record at this time.

From the Council of Khalistan, March 25, 2002
Vaisakhi Message to the Sikh Nation
(By Dr. Gurmit Singh Aulakh)

This is a time of celebration of our 303rd anniversary of the Khalsa Panth. It is also time to look back at our history. The Guru gave sovereignty to the Khalsa Panth. ("In grieb Sikhin ko deon Patshahi.") Banda Singh Bahadur established the first Khalsa rule in Punjab from 1710 to 1716. Then there was a period of persecution of the Sikhs. Again Sikhs established a sovereign, independent rule from 1765 to 1849, when the British annexed the Sikh homeland, Punjab, into British India.

To regain freedom from the British, Sikhs were on the front line of the fight. The Sikh Nation gave about 80 percent of the sacrifices during this freedom struggle when they formed only 1.5 percent of the Indian population. At the time of the independence of India, Sikhs were equal signatories to the transfer of power from the British. Muslim leader Mohammed Ali Jinnah was very wise and well educated and he did not trust the majority Hindu leadership. He got an independent Pakistan for the Muslims. The Sikh leadership should have gotten an independent country for the Sikhs at that time, but they were fooled by the Hindu leadership of Nehru and Gandhi so Sikhs took their share and joined India on the promise that they would have the glow of freedom in the northwest part of India.

Khalsa Ji, we have seen this "glow of freedom" in the form of the at-tack on the Golden Temple in June 1984, when over 20,000 Sikhs were killed in Punjab in a single month. The next massacre of Sikhs occurred after the assassination of Indira Gandhi in Delhi. There was a mass murder of Sikhs throughout India, including Delhi. The Sikhs were pulled out of trains and burned alive. Sikh truck drivers were pulled out of their trucks. Tires were put around their necks by Hindu militants and they were burned to death. In Punjab, this genocide continued under Beant Singh's government. Sikhs were arrested, tortured, and then cremated and their bodies were declared "unidentified."

Since 1984, over 250,000 Sikhs have been murdered. 52,268 are rot-ting in Indian jails under TADA, which expired in 1995. Many of them have been in illegal custody since Operation Bluestar in 1984. Only last month, 42 Members of the U.S. Congress wrote to President Bush to get these political prisoners released. Jaswant Singh Khalra, who exposed the government killing of Sikhs in fake encounters, became a victim of the Indian police himself. He was kidnapped outside his house and murdered in police custody. He documented 6,018 Sikhs who were secretly cremated by the government in three cremation grounds, Patti, Tam Taran, and Durgiana Mandir. Subsequently, Punjab Human Rights Organization (PHRO) chairman Justice Ajit Singh Bains said that about 50,000 Sikhs were secretly cremated in this manner. Even Akal Takht Jathedar Sahib Gurdev Singh Kaunke was murdered by SSP Swaran Singh Ghotna and then his body was disposed of.

The Badal government was forced to conduct an inquiry into the kill-ing of Jathedar Kaunke. It was done by three Punjab police officials under the leadership of DIG Tiwari. He submitted a report to the Badal government, which has not been made public as of today. How could a democratically elected Akali government hide the murder of the Akal Takht Jathedar by not releasing this report, which was conducted by its own order?

The Badal government was the most corrupt one in Punjab's history. They invented a new term for bribery: "fee for service." If you didn't pay the fee, you didn't get the service. There was a fixed amount of money for government jobs. Bags of money were received by Mrs. Badal in return for these jobs. The Punjab economy deteriorated under Badal and the Punjab government its largest debt ever. It is bankrupt now. Badal made three promises to get elected. He promised to free the political prisoners, to punish the police officers who carried out atrocities against the Sikh Nation, and to appoint a commission to investigate atrocities. He did not keep any of them.

The Sikh leadership is completely under Indian government control, whether it is the Akali leadership of Badal, Tohra, Mann, and others or the Congress leadership of Punjab under Captain Amarinder Singh or former Chief Minister Mrs. Bhatthal. Changing parties and faces every election will not solve the problems of the Sikh Nation. Congress is no better than the Akalis and the Akalis proved to be the worst enemies of the Sikh Nation. How could an Akali government keep 52,268 Sikhs in jail without charge or trial for the last 16 years? It is shameful and a black mark on the present Akali leadership. They have cashed in on the sacrifices and good will of the pre-independence Akali leadership.

Khalsa Ji, the only solution to this quagmire is the formation of a Khalsa Raj Party under new, honest, dedicated, and committed leadership. The time is now to do it. Let's not waste time and prolong the suffering and agony of the Sikh Nation under the present corrupt Akali leadership which is controlled by the Indian government and is determined to wipe out the Sikh Nation and the Sikh religion. The only remedy is to sever our relationship with Delhi completely, once and for all, and declare the independence from India and start a peaceful agitation to free the Sikh homeland, Punjab, Khalistan.

The victory of the Congress Party was a massive rejection of the Akalis, who were elected five years ago to reject the Congress Party. However, the Congress Party remains the enemy of the Sikh Nation. In the last two elections, the Sikh Nation has soundly rejected both parties. Neither supports the interests of the Sikh Nation; neither can be trusted by the Sikh Nation. The time has come to discard the present Akali leadership that has betrayed the Sikh Nation.

We must press for action against the police officials who carried out the police kidnapping and murder of human-rights activist Jaswant Singh Khalra. These would be good first steps for the Sikh leadership and for the new government in Punjab. But we must continue to pursue our ultimate goal of freeing the Sikh homeland, Punjab, Khalistan.

The Sikh Nation is sovereign and it must have its sovereign, independent country. Guru gave sovereignty to the Khalsa Panth. Remember "Raj Kare Ga Khalsa." Sikhs can never forgive or forget the desecration of the Golden Temple. This is the history and tradition of the Sikh Nation. The time has come to form a Khalsa Raj Party to liberate Khalistan. The new Sikh leadership must launch a Shantmai Morcha to liberate our homeland. The only way the Sikh Nation can prosper is to free the Sikh homeland, Punjab, Khalistan. The freedom of the Sikh Nation will bring prosperity, stability, and peace to Punjab and to South Asia.

***

Document

CONGRESSIONAL RECORD -- EXTENSIONS

Thursday, March 21, 2002
107th Congress, 2nd Session
148 Cong Rec E 426

REFERENCE: Vol. 148, No. 34
SECTION: Extension of Remarks
TITLE: SIKH ACTIVIST DETAINED IN CANADA AND BRITAIN AT
BEHEST OF INDIAN GOVERNMENT

HON. DAN BURTON
of Indiana
in the House of Representatives
Wednesday, March 20, 2002

Mr. BURTON of Indiana . Mr. Speaker, Dr. Bhagwan Singh Sandhu, a leader of the Sikh Students Federation, was detained at the airports in Vancouver and in London last month, apparently at the behest of the Indian government. According to information I have received, Dr. Sandhu was detained overnight and interrogated by Canadian intelligence agents who were in constant contact with Indian officials in Delhi. According to Dr. Sandhu, he was told that he was a terrorist, yet no evidence to support this claim was produced by authorities in Canada. The same thing apparently happened to him on his arrival in London. All records of his interrogation were retained by the Indian regime.

Mr. Speaker, the Indian Government appears to be trying to capitalize on the world's heightened concerns about terrorism to harass innocent Sikhs beyond its own borders. In the case of Dr. Sandhu, it appears that India manipulated our friends in Canada and Great Britain so that they would detain Dr. Sandhu. The Council of Khalistan has issued an excellent press release on the detention of Dr. Sandhu. It is very informative. I would like to place it in the Record at this time.

From the Council of Khalistan, Mar. 11, 2002
Sikh Activist Arrested in Canada and England
at Behest of Indian Government
India Terrorizing Sikhs internationally

Washington, D.C., March 11, 2002._Dr. Bhagwan Singh Sandhu, a leader of the Sikh Student Federation, was arrested at the Vancouver airport on February 12 on the instructions of the Indian government. Canadian intelligence agents interrogated Dr. Sandhu while they were in constant touch with Indian intelligence in Delhi. They offered no evidence of any involvement by Dr. Sandhu in any terrorist activity in India or any other country. Yet he was labeled a terrorist by the Canadian intelligence operatives. They locked him in a cold, small cell with only a cement bench to lie down on. The following evening, February 13, he was put on a plane to London.

When Dr. Sandhu arrived in London, the British, acting at the behest of the Indian government arrested him. He was interrogated and searched, then held in jail overnight. He was then sent back to India. The Indian government kept all the papers related to his arrest and detention. When he arrived in India, he was arrested again. He had to get medical attention due to his injuries from his arrests. His letters of protests to the Canadian, British, and Indian authorities have gone unanswered.

"This arrest shows the true face of Indian secularism," said Dr. Gurmit Singh Aulakh, President of the Council of Khalistan, the organization that leads the Sikh Nation's struggle for independence. "These illegal arrests show that the Hindu nationalists will reach anywhere to destroy Sikhs and other minorities," he said. "They attacked the Golden Temple in 1984. They have attacked Christian churches, schools, and prayer halls. It has been an ongoing pattern of repression," he said.

"It is shameful that the Canadian and British governments have gone along with India's repression by illegally arresting and harassing Dr. Sandhu," said Dr. Aulakh. "Dr. Sandhu is a victim of India's tyrannical, fanatical drive to eliminate all minority populations in the service of rampaging Hindu cultural imperialism," he said. "It is clear that the agents at the airports in Vancouver and London were working at the behest of the brutal Indian government, perhaps at its direction since they were apparently in constant contact with Delhi."

The Indian government has murdered over 250,000 Sikhs since 1984. Over 75,000 Kashmiri Muslims have been killed since 1988. More than 200,000 Christians have been killed since 1947, along with tens of thousands of Dalits, Tamils, Assamese, Bodos, Manipuris, and other minorities. A report issued last year shows that 52,268 Sikh political prisoners are held in Indian jails, as well as tens of thousands of others. On February 28, 42 Members of the U.S. Congress wrote to President Bush, asking him to work to get these political prisoners freed. Since Christmas 1998, Christians have felt the brunt of the attacks. Priests have been murdered, nuns have been raped, churches have been burned, Christian schools and prayer halls have been destroyed, and no one has been punished for these acts. Militant Hindu fundamentalists allied with the RSS, the pro-Fascist parent organization of the ruling BJP, burned missionary Graham Staines and his two young sons to death.

Last year, a cabinet member said that everyone living in India must be a Hindu or be subservient to Hindus. In July 1997, Narinder Singh, a spokesman for the Golden Temple, told National Public Radio, "The Indian government, all the time they boast that they're democratic, they're secular, but they have nothing to do with a democracy, they have nothing to do with a secularism. They try to crush Sikhs just to please the majority."

"The only way to escape this government-supported violence and tyranny is for the Sikhs, Christians, Muslims, and other minorities to claim

their freedom from India," Dr. Aulakh said. "That is the only way to prevent the Hindu theocracy from wiping us out," he said. "We must launch a Shantmai Morcha (peaceful agitation) to liberate Khalistan," he said.

"Sikhs are a separate nation and ruled Punjab until 1849. No Sikh leader has signed the Indian constitution. The people of South Asia must have self-determination now," Dr. Aulakh said. "India is on the verge of disintegration, as Steve Forbes predicted in the current issue of Forbes magazine," he said. "Khalistan will be free by 2008."

***

Document

CONGRESSIONAL RECORD -- EXTENSIONS

Thursday, March 14, 2002
107th Congress, 2nd Session
148 Cong Rec E 364

REFERENCE: Vol. 148, No. 29
SECTION: Extension of Remarks
TITLE: EVIDENCE IN CHITHISINGPHORA FAKED, GOVERNMENT ADMITS

HON. DAN BURTON
of Indiana
in the House of Representatives
Thursday, March 14, 2002

Mr. BURTON of Indiana . Mr. Speaker, back in March 2000, just before former President Clinton visited India, 35 Sikhs were massacred in the village of Chithistinghpora in Kashmir. At the time, many people accused the Indian government of this atrocity while the Indian government laid the blame on Pakistani-sponsored militants. A study by the Movement Against State Repression (MASR) and the Punjab Human Rights Organization (PHRO) showed that the Indian government's own forces had killed these innocent Sikhs, a conclusion confirmed by a study from the international Human Rights Organization (IHRO) and by an article in the New York Times Magazine by Barry Bearak. Yet the Indian government maintained the fiction that Pakistanis carried out the massacre. They killed five young Kashmiris, claiming they were responsible, then were force to admit that they were not. Then five other Kashmiris were arrested and charged with the crime.

On March 8, Reuters news service reported that the chief minister of Kasmir, Farooq Abdullah, admitted that the evidence against these Kashmiris was faked. That's right, Mr. Speaker, the "world's largest democracy" faked evidence to falsely convict some Kashmiris of the massacre of these Sikhs in order to set these two minorities against each other. Fortunately, it has not worked. Last year, some Indian troops were caught red-handed trying to set fire to a Gurdwara and some Sikh homes in Kashmir and they were overwhelmed by Sikh and Muslim villagers.

Remember also, Mr. Speaker, that the ruling BJP is part of a militant Hindu nationalist organization the Rashtriya Swayamsewak Sangh (RSS), which published a booklet last year on how to implicate minorities in false criminal cases.

Given the government's admission of fraud in this case, how many other cases have they faked? They admit to holding 52,268 Sikhs as political prisoners, according to a MASR report. Amnesty International says that that tens of thousands of other minorities are also being held as political prisoners in "the world's largest democracy." How many cases have been faked against these prisoners?

Mr. Speaker, it is shameful that the evidence in the Chithistinghpora massacre was faked, and it is shameful that it needed to be. However, the people who carry out atrocities like this massacre are rarely if ever punished. Instead, the state either finds scapegoats like the five Kashmir-is it is currently holding or it does nothing. It has found a scapegoat in the killing of Graham Staines, even though every report at the time reported that a mob of people chanting Hindu slogans burned Mr. Staines and his two sons. No one has been punished in the murder of former Akal Takht Jathedar Gurdev Singh Kaunke or in the kidnapping and murder of Jaswant Singh Khalar, who was killed in police custody.

I call on the Indian government to punish those who tampered with the evidence in this case immediately. I also call on the United States to cut off aid with India until they allow people to enjoy basic human rights and a fair, impartial system of justice. We should also press for a free and fair plebiscite on independence for the people of Khalistan, Kashmir, Nagaland, and the other countries seeking their freedom. That is only way to protect their rights and end this kinf of abuse.

Kashmir Govt. Says Sikh Massacre Samples Faked
(By Ashok Pahalwan)

Jammu, India (Reuters)._The state government of Kashmir admitted on Friday that forensic samples taken in an attempt to confirm the guilt of five young men blamed for a Sikh massacre two years ago were faked. The killing of 36 Sikhs in remote Chitisingpora village in the violence-racked state of Jammu and Kashmir in March 2000 occurred hours before a visit by U.S. President Bill Clinton to India and drew strong condemnation from him. Indian newspapers have alleged that soon after the massacre security forces picked up five innocent youths, killed them in a stage-managed gun battle, burned their bodies and then claimed they were "foreign militants" responsible for the Sikhs' deaths. The bodies of the five youths were exhumed and forensic samples taken only after massive demonstrations in Kashmir by protesters. Kashmir state chief minister Farooq Abdullah told the legislature on Friday "it appears fake samples were sent" to laboratories and apologized for "the injustice done to the people for which I feel ashamed". "We strongly suggest those responsible for collecting and sending the samples had something to hide," he added, promising an investigation into the tampering. India had identified the five youths blamed for the Sikh killings as belonging to the militant separatist groups Lashkar-e-Taiba and Hizbul Mujahideen.

Both groups denied responsibility and, with Pakistan, blamed India for the massacre which they said was aimed at discrediting the Kashmiri independence cause during Clinton's visit. The laboratories to which the samples were sent to establish the youths' identity said they were mislabeled and showed serious discrepancies. Abdullah said a judge would lead the probe, which would take two months. He also said fresh test samples would be taken under the supervision of police and doctors. The Times of India, one of the newspapers which investigated reports that the samples had been falsified, accused the state in an editorial on Friday of a "brazen" cover-up. "From knowingly foisting the charge of terrorism on innocents to eliminating them in a fake encounter . . . (it) is an example of the worst kind of state high-handedness," it said in an editorial. More than 33,000 people have been killed since 1989 when Islamic guerrillas seeking either independence or union with neighboring Pakistan launched a revolt in Kashmir.

Human rights groups have frequently accused Indian security forces of abuses such as summary killings and torture. India has always denied systematic human rights abuses and said that any allegations are investigated and the guilty punished.

***

Document

CONGRESSIONAL RECORD -- EXTENSIONS

Tuesday, March 12, 2002
107th Congress, 2nd Session
148 Cong Rec E 324

REFERENCE: Vol. 148, No. 27
SECTION: Extension of Remarks
TITLE: ATTACKS ON MUSLIMS IN INDIA ARE A REPEAT OF 1984
ATTACKS ON SIKHS

HON. EDOLPHUS TOWNS
of New York
in the House of Representatives
Tuesday, March 12, 2002

Mr. TOWNS . Mr. Speaker, more than 540 people have recently died in violent attacks on Muslims in Gujarat, India while police stand by and do nothing. This violence is very disturbing and very reminiscent of the violence against Sikhs in Delhi in November 1984. At that time, police also stood by and did nothing. Sikh police were locked in their barracks and the state-run radio and television stations fanned the flames of the massacre. Even a former Member of Parliament was killed in the riots last week while police stood by, according to a report in the National Post.

When the government, through its police, stands by and lets these attacks unfold, it condones them. Unfortunately, this shows the real truth about India's claim that it is secular and democratic. In a secular, democratic country, the police do not allow minorities to be massacred. This is the act of a theocratic country that seeks to wipe out minorities. That is not the kind of country that America should be supporting.

We should stop providing aid to India while its minorities suffer from this kind of repression. We should not build up its economy with trade. And we should support the people and nations of South Asia in achieving freedom. Self-determination is the right of all people; let us support a free and fair plebiscite on the future of Khalistan, Kashmir, Nagaland, and the other countries seeking their freedom from India.

Mr. Speaker, the Council of Khalistan recently published a press release discussing the parallels between the current violence and the Delhi massacres of Sikhs.

Killing of Over 540 Muslims By Hindu Militants Parallels 1984 Massacre of Sikhs

Washington, D.C., March 5, 2002._The attacks on Muslims in Ahmedabad parallel the November 1984 massacre of Sikhs in Delhi, according to Dr. Gurmit Singh Aulakh, President of the Council of Khalistan, the government pro tempore of the Sikh homeland, Khalistan, which leads the struggle for the independence of Khalistan. "The police stood by then, too, and the police gave a nod to the violence," Dr. Aulakh said. "This is part of the overall plan of a Hindu fundamentalist regime that is determined to wipe out minorities," he said. More then 540 people have died during the last week in the current violence in Ahmedabad. "When 13 people were killed in the attack on the Indian Parliament, there was a lot of outrage, as there should be for the killing of any human being," Dr. Aulakh said. "Where is the outrage at the death of over 540 people in this massacre?" he asked.

"The true face of Indian secularism is exposed," Dr. Aulakh said. "They demolished a mosque the other day, they demolished the mosque in Ayodhya and they are proceeding with plans to build a Hindu Temple on the site," he said. "They attacked the Golden Temple in 1984. They have attacked Christian churches, schools, and prayer halls." In 2000, Indian troops were caught red-handed trying to set fire to Sikh homes in Kashmir. During the Delhi massacres in November 1984, Sikh police officers were locked in their barracks while more than 20,000 Sikhs were massacred and the state-run television and radio called for more Sikh blood. "It is too bad that atrocities like these are carried out with impunity," he said.

The Indian government has murdered over 250,000 Sikhs since 1984. Over 75,000 Kashmiri Muslims have been killed since 1988. More than 200,000 Christians have been killed since 1947, along with tens of thousands of Dalits, Tamils, Assamese, Bodos, Manipuris, and other minorities. A report issued last year shows that 52,268 Sikh political prisoners are held in Indian jails, as well as tens of thousands of others. Since Christmas 1998, Christians have felt the brunt of the attacks. Priests have been murdered, nuns have been raped, churches have been burned, Christian schools and prayer halls have been destroyed, and no one has been punished for these acts. Militant Hindu fundamentalists allied with the RSS, the pro-Fascist parent organization of the ruling BJP, burned missionary Graham Staines and his two young sons to death. Pakistan has requested the extradition of Home Minister L.K. Advani, who is wanted for the murder of Muhammad Ali Jinnah, the founder of Pakistan, 50 years ago.

Last year, a cabinet member said that everyone living in India must be a Hindu or be subservient to Hindus. In July 1997, Narinder Singh, a spokesman for the Golden Temple, told National Public Radio, "The Indian government, all the time they boast that they're democratic, they're secular, but they have nothing to do with a democracy, they have nothing to do with a secularism. They try to crush Sikhs just to please the majority."

The attacks in Ahmedabad reportedly came in retaliation for an attack on a railroad car full of Hindus on their way to Ayodyha to build a Temple on the site where the most revered mosque in India was destroyed several years ago. 58 Hindus were burned to death in that attack. For several days, train loads of Hindu extremists had passed through the village of Godha, where the train attack occurred, shouting provocative slogans about building a Temple.

"By standing by while this violence went on, the government condones it," Dr. Aulakh said. "The only way to escape this government-supported violence and tyranny is for the Sikhs, Christians, Muslims, and other minorities to claim their freedom from India," he said. "That is the only way to prevent the Hindu militant theocracy from wiping us out," he said. "Now is the time for a Shantmai Morcha (peaceful agitation) for the independence of Khalistan," he said. "Sikhs are a separate nation. Sikhs ruled Punjab until the British annexed Punjab in 1849. The people of South Asia must have self-determination now," he said. "India is on the verge of disintegration, as Steve Forbes predicted in the current issue of Forbes magazine," he said. "Khalistan will be free by 2008."

***

Document
CONGRESSIONAL RECORD -- EXTENSIONS

Tuesday, February 26, 2002
107th Congress, 2nd Session
148 Cong Rec E 194

REFERENCE: Vol. 148, No. 17
SECTION: Extension of Remarks
TITLE: ANOTHER CHURCH ATTACKED IN INDIA

HON. DAN BURTON
of Indiana
in the House of Representatives
Tuesday, February 26, 2002

Mr. BURTON of Indiana . Mr. Speaker, recently another Christian church was attacked in India. The Associated Press reported on February 17 that about 50 militant, extremist Hindu fundamentalists attacked a Catholic church on the outskirts of Bangalore. Unfortunately, this is just the latest incident in a longstanding campaign of repression against Christians and other religious minorities in India, which appears to be tacitly supported by the government. Last year, a cabinet member was quoted as saying that everyone who lives in India must either be a Hindu or be subservient to Hindus. This is part of the Hindutva ideology of the ruling BJP and its parent organization, the RSS, which was founded in support of the Fascists.

This latest incident seems to mirror with so many other actions perpetrated by Hindu militants under the umbrella of the RSS. They have murdered priests, raped nuns, and burned churches. They have attacked Christian schools and prayer halls. It was Hindu militants under the RSS umbrella who burned missionary Graham Staines and his two young sons to death while they slept in their jeep, all the while chanting "Victory to Hannuman," a Hindu god. India subsequently threw Mr. Staines's widow out of the country rather than let her continue his work providing health services for the downtrodden. The RSS itself published a booklet on how to file fake criminal cases against Christians and other religious minorities. Indian police used gunfire to break up a Christian religious festival. More than 200,000 Christians in Nagaland have been murdered by Indian forces. In the face of this pattern of repression, abuse, and tyranny, Prime Minister Vajpayee told an audience in New York, "I will always be a Swayamsewak," invoking the self-designation of RSS members.

Unfortunately, Mr. Speaker, the Indian government has done little to stop or prevent these acts of violence. If the abuse and repression of Christians were the only story, it would be bad enough, but it is not. Sikhs, Muslims, and other minorities have faced repression also. The Indian government has murdered over 250,000 Sikhs, over 75,000 Kashmiri Muslims, and many thousands of other minorities, including Tamils, Dalit "untouchables," Bodos, Assamese, Manipuris and others. According to the Movement Against State Repression, India admitted to holding 52,268 Sikhs as political prisoners, and we know the numbers the government admits to are generally low. Amnesty International reports that tens of thousands of other minorities are also being held as political prisoners.

To make it worse, Mr. Speaker, it was reported in the January 2 issue of the Washington Times that India is sponsoring cross-border terrorism in the province of Sindh to destabilize Pakistan, which has been a solid, strong ally in the war on terrorism. In addition, India's aggressive military maneuvers have forced Pakistan to shift troops away from the border with Afghanistan to the Indian border, possibly creating an escape for Taliban and Al Qaeda terrorists. In effect, India's actions are abetting the Al Qaeda terrorists.

In light of all this repression and terrorism America must make a strong stand. We must make it clear that such practices are unacceptable for countries that proclaim democratic principles and for countries that seek U.S. support. To do so, we should stop U.S. aid to India until these abuses are ended and we should publicly support the freedom movements within India's borders by calling for a free and fair plebiscite on the issue of Independence for Kashmir, Khalistan, predominantly Christian Nagaland, and the other nations seeking their freedom from India. These measures will help shine the light of freedom on everyone in South Asia.

Mr. Speaker, I would like to place the Associated Press article into the Record at this time.

From the Associated Press, Feb. 17, 2002
Police: Hindu Extremists Hit Church

Bangalore, India._About 50 Hindu hard-liners attacked a Roman Catholic church in southern India on Sunday and injured several worshipers, police said.

V.V. Bhaskar, the police chief in the city of Mysore, declined to say how many people were hurt in the attack, which happened on the outskirts of the city.

The assailants threw stones at the church before forcing their way inside, breaking furniture, smashing windows and attacking worshipers.

The men demanded the priest end what they said were efforts to convert local villagers, who are mainly Hindu, Bhaskar said.

Christians make up only a tiny fraction of India's 1 billion-plus population. About 80 percent are Hindus.

Some Hindu extremist groups have accused church officials of trying to attract poor Hindus with promises of money and jobs.

The worst attack against Christians in India took place in 1999, when an Australian missionary and his two children were burned alive by a mob.

***

Document

CONGRESSIONAL RECORD -- EXTENSIONS

Tuesday, February 26, 2002
107th Congress, 2nd Session
148 Cong Rec E 198

REFERENCE: Vol. 148, No. 17
SECTION: Extension of Remarks
TITLE: ARTICLE COMPARES INDIA TO AUSTRIA-HUNGARY: INDIA IS
HEADING FOR SIMILAR BREAKUP

HON. EDOLPHUS TOWNS
of New York
in the House of Representatives
Tuesday, February 26, 2002

Mr. TOWNS . Mr. Speaker, I would like to call the attention of my colleagues to an article by Steve Forbes in the March 4 issue of Forbes magazine called "India, Meet Austria-Hungary." In the article, Mr. Forbes compares present-day India to the old Austro-Hungarian Empire. Like Austria-Hungary, India is a multiethnic, multinational country. Such countries are unstable, as Mr. Forbes notes, and they face a similar peril.

The article notes that some leaders in India are "itching to go to war with Pakistan, even though Pakistan's President Pervez Musharraf has taken considerable political risks by moving against Pakistani-based-and-trained anti-India terrorist groups." At the same time, according to a January 2 article in the Washington Times, India continues to sponsor cross-border terrorism against Pakistan. The article notes that when the Austro-Hungarian monarchy attacked Serbia in 1914, it launched a war in which the Hapsburgs lost their empire. Today, several countries exist where the Austro-Hungarian Empire once was.

India is in similar circumstances. It should learn from the example of Austria-Hungary, the Soviet Union, and other multinational empires. It should realize that the breakup of such states is inevitable. The Soviet Union and Austria-Hungary had a stronger, more stable political structure and they fell apart because such multinational states cannot be held together. In fact, Indian Home Minister L.K. Advani recently said that if Kashmir gets its freedom, India will unravel.

Yet India continues its futile efforts to maintain its multinational state by force, in pursuit of Hindu hegemony. It continues to attack and kill Christians, Sikhs, Muslims, Dalits, and other minority groups. It continues to hold tens of thousands of political prisoners, something I find very odd for a democracy. Indian forces have killed more than 250,000 Sikhs, over 200,000 Christians in Nagaland, more than 75,000 Kashmiri Muslims, and many thousands of minorities of all kinds. This repressive policy will not work. Eventually, the force that broke up the Soviet Union and broke up the Austro-Hungarian Empire will break up India. I hope that this happens peacefully. With the war on terrorism ongoing, we do not need another violent trouble spot in the world.

America can encourage this process of nationalism and freedom in South Asia. We should press India for the release of all political prisoners. We should stop our aid and trade with India until they are released and the oppression of minorities ends. We should openly declare our support for self-determination for all peoples and nations in South Asia. By these measures we will help everyone in the subcontinent to live freely, prosperously, in dignity, stability, and peace.

Mr. Speaker, I would like to insert the Forbes article into the Record at this time.

From Forbes Magazine, Mar. 4, 2002
India, Meet Austria-Hungary
(By Steve Forbes)

Influential elements in India's government and military are still itching to go to war with Pakistan, even though Pakistan's President Pervez Musharraf has taken considerable political risks by moving against Pakistani-based-and-trained anti-India terrorist groups. Sure, Musharraf made a truculent speech condemning India's "occupation" of Kashmir, but that was rhetorical cover for cracking down on those groups. Washington should send New Delhi some history books for these hotheads; there is no human activity more prone to unintended consequences than warfare. As cooler heads in the Indian government well know, history is riddled with examples of parties that initiated hostilities in the belief that conflict would resolutely resolve outstanding issues.

Pericles of Athens thought he could deal with rival Sparta once and for all when he triggered the Peloponnesian War; instead his city-state was undermined and Greek civilization devastated. Similarly, Hannibal brilliantly attacked Rome; he ended up not only losing the conflict but also setting off a train of events that ultimately led to the total destruction of Carthage. Prussia smashed France in 1870, annexing critical French territory for security reasons, but that sowed the seeds for the First World War. At the end of World War I the victorious Allies thought they had dealt decisively with German military power. Israel crushed its Arab foes in 1967, but long-term peace did not follow.

India is not a homogeneous state. Neither was the Austro-Hungarian Empire. It attacked Serbia in the summer of 1914 in the hopes of destroying this irritating state after Serbia had committed a spectacular terrorist act against the Hapsburg monarchy. The empire ended up splintering, and the Hapsburgs lost their throne.

And on it goes.

Getting back to the present, do Indian war hawks believe China will stand idly by as India tried to reduce Pakistan to vassal-state status? Do they think Arab states and Iran won't fund Muslim guerrilla movements in Pakistan, as well as in India itself? Where does New Delhi think its oil comes from (about 70%, mainly from the Middle East)? Does India think the U.S. will stand by impotently if it starts a war that unleashes nuclear weapons?

In his second inaugural address, Abraham Lincoln summed up the unpredictable consequences of war, vis-a-vis America's Civil War: "Neither party expected for the war the magnitude or the duration which it has already attained. . . . Each looked for an easier triumph, and a result less fundamental and astounding."

DUTCH TREAT

While cracking down on anti-India terrorist groups operating in Pakistan, Islamabad can take the wind out of Indian war sails by turning over the arrested terrorists who carried out murderous acts in Kashmir and New Delhi. It can turn them over not to India_which would be political suicide domestically_but to The Hague for investigation and trial by an international tribunal. India's moral case would then evaporate.

***

Document

CONGRESSIONAL RECORD -- EXTENSIONS

Tuesday, February 26, 2002
107th Congress, 2nd Session
148 Cong Rec E 200

REFERENCE: Vol. 148, No. 17
SECTION: Extension of Remarks
TITLE: CHURCH ATTACKED BY HINDU MILITANTS_PERSECUTION OF CHRISTIANS IN INDIA CONTINUES

HON. MIKE PENCE
of Indiana
in the House of Representatives
Tuesday, February 26, 2002

Mr. PENCE . Mr. Speaker, the other day the Washington Times ran an excellent article on an attack on a church outside Mysore, India by the Bajrang Dal, a branch of the Rashtriya Swayamsewak Sangh (RSS), which is the parent organization of the ruling party, the BJP. The attack seriously wounded about 20 people, according to the article. Approximately 70 attackers wore the saffron headbands that symbolize the militant Hindu nationalists. They attacked while worship was going on.

This attack is part of what the Times called a "new spate of attacks." It also reports that in February, two church workers and a teen-age boy were shot while praying and the boy was injured; two Christian missionaries were beaten with rods while bicycling home; and a Christian cemetery in Port Blair was vandalized. Those are just incidents that have occurred this month. Unfortunately, they are part of a pattern that church leaders described as a "reign of terror."

Since Christmas 1998, a number of priests have been murdered in India, several nuns have been raped (with the enthusiastic endorsement of the Vishwa Hindu Parishad (VHP), another branch of the RSS), churches have been burned, missionary Graham Staines and his two young sons have been burned to death while sleeping in their jeep, Christian schools and prayer halls have been attacked, and numerous other acts of violence and/or hatred have taken place. In 1997, police opened fire on a Christian religious festival, putting an end to it.

Last year, a member of the Indian cabinet said that everyone who lives in India must either be a Hindu or be subservient to Hindus. It is clear, Mr. Speaker, that India intends to ram its Hindutva policy down the throats of everyone in the subcontinent.

Christians are not the only ones being oppressed by the militant Hindu regime in Delhi. Sikhs, Kashmiris, Dalits, and others have also been tyrannized in the name of Hindu nationalism. Just recently more Kashmiris have been made to disappear by the Indian government. A report by the Movement Against State Repression shows that India holds over 52,000 Sikh political prisoners and Amnesty International reports that there are tens of thousands of others. The government's forces have murdered more than a quarter of a million Sikhs, over 200,000 Christians in Nagaland, over 75,000 Kashmiri Muslims, and thousands upon thousands of people from the Dalit caste, as well as minorities such as Tamils, Assamese, Manipuris, Bodos, and others. How can India call itself a democracy when things like this go on with the support of the government? These are not the acts of a democracy.

It is important for America to speak out. I am speaking out today because religious and political freedoms are essential democratic values. America must bring its power to bear peacefully in support of true democracy and freedom in South Asia, and if our influence does not move the region toward real freedom, then we should be willing to use whatever other peaceful means we have at our disposal to end the violence and bring peace, freedom, and stability to all the peoples and nations there.

Mr. Speaker, I would like to place the Times article in the Record at this time.

From the Washington Times, Feb. 25, 2002
New Spate of Attacks Targets Christians
(By Julian West)

New Delhi._Violence against India's Christian minority has surged this year, with reports of at least one attack each week in what church leaders are calling a "reign of terror" spreading throughout the country.

In the most recent incident, about 70 men wearing saffron headbands_an emblem of the Hindu nationalist_attacked a church near Mysore, in South India, where children were attending a catechism class. The attack last week seriously wounded about 20 people.

In other incidents this month:

Two church workers and a teen-age boy were shot at while praying, and the boy was injured.

Two Christian missionaries were beaten with iron rods while bicycling home.

A Christian cemetery in Port Blair on the Andaman Islands was vandalized.

Four of the attacks were in Uttar Pradesh, the North Indian state where counting in local government elections ends today and where the Hindu nationalist Bharatiya Janata Party (BJP) fared poorly.

Much of the violence against Christians has taken place in states ruled by the BJP, but church leaders say that last year the number of incidents in states like Karnataka, which has a Congress party government, has risen alarmingly.

In the latest and most violent incident in the state, an angry mob wearing saffron headbands, carrying placards and shouting anti-Christian slogans descended on the Holy Family church in Hinkal, a suburb of Mysore, just after Mass last Sunday.

"The children were crying," said Father William, who was protected by his parishioners. "They could see their parents being beaten up, from the windows."

About 20 people were later taken to the hospital.

Describing the incident as unprecedented in a city whose roughly 30,000 Christians have previously had good relations with their Hindu neighbours. Father Nerona, a member of the Diocesan Council, said that he thought the attack had been provoked by a misunderstanding over a round of Christmas carols.

"They said the carols were converting people, but actually the carol singers only went to Catholic homes," he said. "We were terribly shocked. This has always been such a peaceful city."

The recent attacks follow what church leaders call "a false lull," occurring after the international outrage last year over the burning alive of Graham Staines, an Australian missionary, and his two small sons last year.

"Physically, many of the incidents are now less obvious," said John Dayal, secretary general of the All India Christian Council. "But there is a 24-hour reign of terror, which occasionally bursts into violence."

Last year the Indian government reported 240 incidents_including about 22 murders_in the year leading up to 2000, and almost every week newspapers carry an account of a ransacked church, an assaulted or murdered priest or a vandalized cemetery.

Many of the assailants are member of the Bajrang Dal, a militant Hindu nationalist organization linked to the BJP, which has carried out many of the most violent attacks on Christians in India.

Church leaders maintain, however, that all the attacks_whether they are carried out by the Bajrang Dal or its fellow Hindu nationalist organizations_have the tacit approval of the BJP government.

"The Bajrang Dal are ruffians, but someone must have told them what to do the previous night," said Mr. Dayal.

***

Document

CONGRESSIONAL RECORD -- EXTENSIONS

Tuesday, February 12, 2002
107th Congress, 2nd Session
148 Cong Rec E 133

REFERENCE: Vol. 148, No. 12
SECTION: Extension of Remarks
TITLE: INDIA: CANDIDATE FOR A TERRORIST STATE

HON. DAN BURTON
of Indiana
in the House of Representatives
Tuesday, February 12, 2002

Mr. BURTON of Indiana . Mr. Speaker, it is disappointing to note that India's actions of late have had the effect of undermining our war against terrorism. India's massive military buildup has forced Pakistan to pull troops away from the Afghan border, creating a potential opportunity for Taliban and Al Qaeda leaders to escape.

India claims that this act is in response to Pakistan's failure to turn over alleged terrorists to them, but Pakistan has been cracking down on terrorists and has jailed many of them so far. It will not turn over non-Indians to India, however. India also blames Pakistan for the attack on its parliament, even though India has a record of committing acts of terrorism in the guise of various minorities. Two independent investigations have proven that they did so in Chithisinghpora in March 2000, when they murdered 35 Sikhs. The book Soft Target asserts that the Indian government was responsible for shooting down an Air India airliner in 1985, killing 329 people. In addition, India created the militant Liberation Tigers of Tamil Eelam (LTTE), which our government has labeled a "terrorist organization," and put up its leaders in Delhi's finest hotel, according to India Today, India's leading newsmagazine. Internet journalist Justin Raimondo has reported that Defense Minister George Fernandes supplied money and arms to the LTTE. On January 2, columnist Tony Blankley, writing in the Washington Times, reported that the Indian government sponsors cross-border terrorism in the Pakistani province of Sindh.

The time has come for India to release its political prisoners. According to the Movement Against State Repression (MASR), India admitted to holding 52,268 Sikhs as political prisoners in "the world's largest democracy." In addition, according to Amnesty International, tens of thousands of other minorities are also being held in jail.

India has also been guilty of terrorism against the minorities within its own borders. The newspaper Hitavada reported on November 1994 that the Indian government paid $1.5 billion to the late governor of Punjab, Surendra Nath, to foment terrorist activity in Kashmir and Punjab, Khalistan.

If we are going to win the war on terrorism, we must eliminate it wherever it shows up. That includes countries that claim to be democratic. I call on the White House to urge India to end its support for terrorism. In addition, it is time to cut off U.S. aid to India and to declare our support for a free and fair plebiscite in Punjab, Khalistan, in Christian Nagaland, in Kashmir, and in the other minority nations under Indian occupation on the subject of independence.

Mr. Speaker, on January 7, the Council of Khalistan published a press release urging that India be declared a terrorist state. I would like to place it into the Record at this time.

Press Release from the Council of Khalistan, Jan. 7, 2002
Declare India a Terrorist Nation_It Sponsors
Domestic and International Terror
India Must Free Over 52,000 Sikh Political Prisoners

Washington, DC._"The time has come to declare India a terrorist nation," Dr. Gurmit Singh Aulakh, President of the Council of Khalistan, said today. The Council of Khalistan leads the Sikh Nation's struggle for independence and is the government pro tempore of Khalistan, the Sikh homeland, which declared its independence from India on October 7, 1987. "India pays lip service to the war on terrorism, but it is a terrorist nation itself," Dr. Aulakh said. "If America is committed to eradicating terrorism everywhere, that must include India, a major sponsor of international and domestic terrorism," Dr. Aulakh said.

Columnist Tony Blankley, writing in the Washington Times on January 2, wrote that India sponsors cross-border terrorism in the Pakistani province of Sindh. Internet journalist Justin Raimondo recently reported that Indian Defense Minister George Fernandes raised money for the militant Liberation Tigers of Tamil Eelam (LTTE), which the U.S. government has labelled as a "terrorist organization," and provided arms for them. Journalist Tavleen Singh, writing in India Today, India's premier newsmagazine, reported that the Indian government created the LTTE and put up its leaders in the finest hotel in Delhi.

The Deccan Chronicle reported on December 14 that the Indian government knew of the terrorist attack on its Parliament, which killed 13 people, in advance and that the government did nothing to stop it. No Members of Parliament were killed in the attack, but the victims were lower-caste people. This shows government involvement in the incident. India seeks to use this attack as a pretext for a war against Pakistan. Indian cabinet members have said that Pakistan should be incorporated into India. "Sikhs and Kashmiris will be the main victims of war," said

Dr. Aulakh. "This is part of India's design. India is putting the stability of the entire South Asian region at risk for its own hegemonic ambitions," he said.

"We condemn terrorism in all forms, wherever it comes from," he said. "It is time for India to release more than 52,000 Sikh political prisoners and the tens of thousands of other political prisoners and end its repression," Dr. Aulakh said . . . According to a report in May by the Movement Against State Repression, India admitted that 52,268 Sikh political prisoners are rotting in Indian jails without charge or trial. Many have been in illegal custody since 1984. "I call on the Sikh leadership in Punjab to stop making coalitions with the Indian government and work for freedom for the Sikhs and the other minority nations of South Asia," he said.

The book Soft Target, written by two respected Canadian journalists, shows that the Indian government blew up its own airliner in 1985 to provide a pretext for more repression against Sikhns. In November 1994, the newspaper Hitavada reported that the government paid the late governor of Punjab, Surendra Nath, $1.5 billion to generate terrorist activity in Punjab and Kashmir. The Indian government has murdered over 250,000 Sikhs since 1984. Over 75,000 Kashmiri Muslims have been killed since 1988. In May, Indian troops were caught red-handed trying to set fire to a Gurdwara (a Sikh Temple) and some Sikh houses in Kashmir. Two independent investigations have proven that the Indian government carried out the March 2000 massacre of 35 Sikhs in Chithisinghpora. In August 1999, U.S. Congressman Dana Rohrabacher said that for Sikhs, Kashmiri Muslims, and other minorities "India might as well be Nazi Germany."

India has also repressed Christians. More than 200,000 Christians have been killed since 1947. Priests have been murdered, nuns have been raped, churches have been burned. Christian schools and prayer halls have been destroyed, and no one has been punished for these acts. Militant Hindu fundamentalists allied with the RSS, the pro-Fascist parent organization of the ruling BJP, burned missionary Graham Staines and his two young sons to death. In 1997, police broke up a Christian religious festival by firing their weapons at it.

"Now is the time for Sikhs, Kashmiris, Nagas, and other nations to claim their freedom," he said. "Now is the time for a Shantmai Morcha (peaceful agitation) for the independence of Khalistan," he said. "If India is truly the democracy it claims, then it should allow a free and fair vote on this issue," Dr. Aulakh said. "Sikhs are a separate nation and ruled Punjab up to 1849 when the British annexed Punjab. The nations and peoples of South Asia must have self-determination now."

***

Document

CONGRESSIONAL RECORD -- EXTENSIONS

Tuesday, February 05, 2002
107th Congress, 2nd Session
148 Cong Rec E 79

REFERENCE: Vol. 148, No. 7
SECTION: Extension of Remarks
TITLE: REMEMBERING SUKHBIR SINGH OSAN

HON. DAN BURTON
of Indiana
in the House of Representatives
Tuesday, February 5, 2002

Mr. BURTON of Indiana . Mr. Speaker, I was saddened to hear of the passing of Khalistani journalist Sukhbir Singh Osan. He died of a heart attack on January 19, 2002. Mr. Osan was only 31 years of age.

Mr. Osan was a terrific reporter who exposed many scandals through his website, Burning Punjab. He reported many stories showing India's pattern of terrorism against its own people. In addition to running his website, he wrote for several Indian newspapers.

The Indian government had banned the viewing of Burning Punjab in Punjab and a few neighboring states. When that did not shut down the site, India brought a fake criminal case against Burning Punjab, falsely claiming it was a "newspaper" operating out of Punjab. These actions make it clear that Mr. Osan's reports were greatly disturbing to the Indian government.

Sukhbir Singh Osan was a courageous reporter, one of the few who would stand up to the Indian government. He will be greatly missed by the people whose interests he served, the Sikhs of Punjab, Khalistan, and by all the people who care about freedom in South Asia.

The Council of Khalistan put out an excellent press release on Mr. Osan's passing. I am placing it in the Record in his memory. In addition, I would also like to insert a February 1, 2002, article from PPA News regarding the killing of Kashmiris by Indian soldiers.

In Memory of S. Sukhbir Singh Osan
Longtime Journalist, Founder of Burning Punjab, Exposed Human Rights Violations, Reported on Freedom Struggle_Government Had Filed False Case Against Burning Punjab, Banned It

Washington, DC, January 21, 2002._Sukhbir Singh Osan, 31, journalist and founder of the website Burning Punjab (http://www.burningpunjab.com), died of a heart attack over the weekend. Sardar Osan also wrote for several Indian newspapers.

"The passing of Sardar Osan is a great loss for the Sikh Nation," said Dr. Gurmit Singh Aulakh, President of the Council of Khalistan. The

Council of Khalistan is the government pro tempore of Khalistan and leads the struggle to liberate the Sikh homeland, Khalistan, which declared its independence from India on October 7, 1987. "He was an excellent reporter and a stalwart Sikh who exposed the human-rights violations against the Sikhs by the Indian government and reported on the Sikh freedom struggle," he said. "His website, Burning Punjab, is one of the best sources available for news from Punjab, Khalistan." Osan was also a lawyer.

Recently, the Indian government filed a false case against Burning Punjab, falsely claiming it was a "newspaper." The Indian government had banned the viewing of Burning Punjab in Punjab and elsewhere in northwest India. A Deputy Inspector General was specifically assigned to "deal with" Sardar Osan. "I think the stress from that false case may have brought about his heart attack," said Dr. Aulakh.

"Sardar Osan was one of the leading voices in exposing the Indian government's repression of the Sikhs," Aulakh said. "He exposed phony Sikh leaders such as S.S. Mann, Dr. Jagjit Singh Chohan, Didar Singh Bains, and others. This was an extremely important service," said Dr. Aulakh.

According to a report in May by the Movement Against State Repression, India admitted that 52,268 Sikh political prisoners are rotting in Indian jails without charge or trial. Many have been in illegal custody since 1984. The Indian government has murdered over 250,000 Sikhs since 1984. Over 75,000 Kashmiri Muslins have been killed since 1988. In May, Indian troops were caught red-handed trying to set fire to a Gurdwara (a Sikh Temple) and some Sikh houses in Kashmir. Two independent investigations have proven that the Indian government carried out the March 2000 massacre of 35 Sikhs in Chithisinghpora. In August 1999, U.S. Congressman Dana Rohrabacher said that for Sikhs, Kashmiri Muslims, and other minorities "India might as well be Nazi Germany."

"The service Sardar Osan gave to the Sikh Nation was immense," said Dr. Aulakh. "He is one of the few people in Punjab who was not afraid to tell the truth. The Sikh Nation will miss him very much," Dr. Aulakh said. "On behalf of the Sikh diaspora, I would like to offer my condolences to Sardar Osan's family. I can only hope that Burning Punjab will be continued in his memory."

- - - - - - - - -

From the PPA News, Feb. 1, 2002
Indian Soldiers Kill 376 Kashmiris in January 2002, 107 Women, Children Among Killed in Police Custody

Islamabad (PPA)._The Indian army during its genocidal operations in the month of January 2002, killed 376 innocent citizens in held Kashmir including 107 killed in custody.

According to statistical data compiled by the Research Section of the Kashmir Media Service, those who fell victim to Indian army's brutalities included 246 men, 11 men and 12 kids.

During the month under review, 625 common people were tortured or critically injured by the Indian troops in the course of crackdowns upon villages, towns and cities. 630 people were arrested during the outgoing month without any valid charge against them while 139 houses and shops were arsoned by setting them on fire on using dynamite blasts.

Twenty-one persons had been kidnapped or reported missing. Relatives of these persons forcibly disappeared by the Indian army have no access to them and they are worried about their missing loved ones.

Molestation of women is one of the weapons being used by the Indian forces to terrorize people and 32 cases of gang rape and molestation were recorded during the month under review. Police and civilian authorities are reluctant to register complaints in this behalf and the victims are left to suffer their fate. The army personnel even threaten their victims of dire consequences if the matter was reported to the authorities.

***

Document

CONGRESSIONAL RECORD -- EXTENSIONS

Tuesday, February 05, 2002
107th Congress, 2nd Session
148 Cong Rec E 85

REFERENCE: Vol. 148, No. 7
SECTION: Extension of Remarks
TITLE: MORE INDIAN REPRESSION OF TRIBAL AND CHRISTIAN
MINORITIES

HON. EDOLPHUS TOWNS
of New York
in the House of Representatives
Tuesday, February 5, 2002

Mr. TOWNS . Mr. Speaker, I was disturbed to learn of more Indian repression of its tribal Christian minorities. According to a statement issued by the All India Christian Council, the Sangh Parivari, a wing of the pro-Fascist Rashtriya Swayamsewak Sangh (RSS), the parent organization of the ruling BJP, has been distributing weapons to Hindu militants in the tribal areas of Gujarat, Madhya Pradesh, and Rajasthan.

In recent months, according to the statement, it has distributed 350,000 trishuls to be used as weapons. It has set up new Temples in Madhya Pradesh. In the Hindu schools, the curriculum already rewrites history. The All India Christian Council calls the curriculum "outside the pale of any academic and public scrutiny" and says it "poisons young minds."

The statement calls this RSS plan "an effort to polarize and communalize the tribal society" in these and several other states. This is a well-established part of India's ongoing campaign to establish itself as the hegemonic power in South Asia.

Given these activities, it is time to strike a blow for freedom by suspending all American aid to India until it respects all human rights for all people and by supporting an internationally-monitored vote on independence for Christian Nagaland, for Punjab, Khalistan, for Kashmir (which it promised in 1948), and for all the other nations seeking their freedom. These are very moderate measures, Mr. Speaker, but they are measures that can go a long way to help promote real freedom and democracy in South Asia.

I would like to place the recent statement from the All India Christian Council into the Record for the information of my colleagues.

From the All India Christian Council, Jan. 17, 2002
Sangh Parivar Actions Communalising Adivasi Area

(The following is the text of the statement issued by Dr. Joseph D. Souza, President, and Dr. John Dayal, Secretary General, of the All India Christian Council on recent moves by the Sangh Parivar to aggravate the communal situation in the Adivasi tribal belt of North India.)

The All India Christian Council thanks Madhya Pradesh Chief minister Digvijay Singh and his government for taking effective steps to reassure the small Christian community in the Adivasi-majority district of Jhabua, which had seen much tension on the eve of the meeting organized today by the Rashtriya Swayamsewak Sangh wing Seva Bharati.

The All India Christian Council deputed its Gujarat unit secretary and well-known Human rights activist Mr. Samson Christian to Jhabua yesterday in solidarity with the Christians of the district, which was scene of the infamous mass rape of Catholic nuns three years ago. A vicious Hindutva communal rhetoric preceded the holding of the Sangh meeting, targeting Christians in the region. Much of the social educational and Medicare work in the Madhya Pradesh Tribal belt has been by Christian missions.

The Council has repeatedly expressed its deep apprehension at the activities of the Sangh Parivar in the contiguous tribal areas of Gujarat, Madhya Pradesh and Rajasthan. In recent months, more than 3.5 lakh trishuls machined as weapons and not as innocuous religious symbols, have been distributed in the Rajasthan area. In Madhya Pradesh, the Sangh has announced the setting up of 3.5 lakh Devals, or family Temples. These areas are already penetrated by Sangh's Shishu mandirs manned by RSS cadres. These schools follow a curricula and textual material, which is outside the pale of any academic and public scrutiny, blatantly rewrites history, and poisons young minds.

Taken together, these actions constitute a well thought out strategy to polarize and communalise the tribal society in the state of Madhya

Pradesh and also in the states of Gujarat, Rajasthan, Orissa, Jharkand and Chhatisgarh to serve the political agenda of the Sangh Parivar. The Adivasis have strongly objected to these efforts to obliterate their culture and their identity.

The Council has called upon the governments of the concerned states, as also on the Central government to ensure that this insidious conspiracy against the Adivasi identity is not allowed to succeed.

***

Document

CONGRESSIONAL RECORD -- EXTENSIONS

Tuesday, February 05, 2002
107th Congress, 2nd Session
148 Cong Rec E 88

REFERENCE: Vol. 148, No. 7
SECTION: Extension of Remarks
TITLE: INDIA MUST RELEASE SIKH POLITICAL PRISONERS

HON. EDOLPHUS TOWNS
of New York
in the House of Representatives
Tuesday, February 5, 2002

Mr. TOWNS . Mr. Speaker, many of my colleagues are strong supporters of India. They apparently believe India's claim that it is "the world's largest democracy." But why does a democracy have political prisoners?

According to a report last year by the Movement Against State Repression (MASR), the Indian government admitted to holding 52,268 Sikhs as political prisoners. Amnesty International has reported that tens of thousands of other minorities are also being held as political prisoners. These prisoners are being held without charge or trial, illegally. Some of them have been in illegal custody for many years, despite the provisions of the law. Many of the Sikh political prisoners have been in detention since 1984. That's 18 years, Mr. Speaker. Eighteen years! How can a democratic state justify this?

Now, all of us want good relations with India and with all nations, as the President said in his State of the Union speech. But we also want to support the cause of freedom for all the people in the world. That is one of the main reasons we are fighting terrorism. We should use our increasing ties to India to pressure them to release all their political prisoners. As the bastion of democracy, it is our duty to speak up for these oppressed minority people.

Leading activists like Jaswant Singh Khalra, former Jathedar Gurdev Singh Kaunke, and so many others have been killed by the Indian government after being made to disappear. Christians have suffered an ongoing wave of persecution, which many of us in this House have detailed repeatedly. It is time for the civilized world, under the leadership of the United States, to speak out strongly against this repression. But in addition, we must take prudent, peaceful, measured action to stop the repression of these minorities.

The Sikh leadership and the leadership of the other minorities should nominate the political prisoners for office as a way to help secure their release. This would make it much more difficult for India to continue holding them.

I might note that India has also been a practitioner of terrorism. It created the Liberation Tigers of Tamil Eelam (LTTE), a Tamil militant group that our government designates as "terrorist," and harbored its leaders in the most elegant hotel in Delhi. It has been reported that the Indian Defense Minister has raised money and supplied arms for the LTTE. It has also been reported that the Indian government sponsors terrorist activity in Sindh, a border province of Pakistan. As you know, Pakistan has been a strong supporter of our efforts in the war on terrorism until India's troop movements forced them to divide their effort and pull troops off the Afghan border to counter an impending threat from India.

In addition, India paid the late governor of Punjab a lot of money to generate terrorism in Punjab and Kashmir. Indian troops were caught trying to set fire to a Sikh Gurdwara. There are numerous other incidents, such as the Air India bombing, the Chithisinghpora massacre, and other incidents, where the evidence points strongly to the Indian government.

If India cannot behave like a civilized, democratic nation, it does not deserve to be treated like one. We should stop American aid to India until the political prisoners are released and the minorities can enjoy their full rights and liberties, and we should strongly urge India to hold a free and fair plebiscite in Kashmir, Khalistan, Nagaland, and all the nations seeking their freedom. Remember that India promised a plebiscite in Kashmir in 1948. I call on India to deliver on that promise. We should work with them to bring this about. That is the way that we can help secure the blessings of liberty for all the people of South Asia.

***

Document

CONGRESSIONAL RECORD -- EXTENSIONS

Thursday, December 20, 2001
107th Congress, 1st Session
147 Cong Rec E 2360

REFERENCE: Vol. 147, No. 1
SECTION: Extension of Remarks
TITLE: TERRORIST ATTACK ON INDIAN PARLIAMENT
CONDEMNED_ATTACK IS INEVITABLE CONSEQUENCE OF
REPRESSION IN INDIA

HON. EDOLPHUS TOWNS
of New York
in the House of Representatives
Wednesday, December 19, 2001

Mr. TOWNS . Mr. Speaker, I join with my colleagues and all decent people of the world in condemning the terrorist attack on the Indian Parliament. I extend my sympathies to the victims and their families. Terrorism is never acceptable. We are currently at war against terrorism, as we should be.

However, India is a country that has practiced terrorism against the peoples living within its borders. It has a pattern of terrorism. Remember that two government officials there were quoted last year as saying that Pakistan should be absorbed into India. It is clear that India seeks hegemony over all the peoples and nations of South Asia.

In May, Indian troops were overwhelmed by villagers, both Sikhs and Muslims, while they were trying to set fire to a Sikh Gurdwara and some Sikh houses in Kashmir. Independent investigations by the International Human Rights Organization and jointly by the Punjab Human Rights Organization and the Movement Against State Repression have conclusively shown that the Indian government carried out the massacre of 35 Sikhs in Chithisinghpora in March 2000 while former President Clinton was visiting India. Its police broke up a Christian religious festival with gunfire. According to the excellent book Soft Target, written by two respected Toronto reporters, the Indian government blew up its own airliner in 1985, killing 329 innocent people. According to a report in the Hitavada newspaper, India paid the late Governor of Punjab, Surendra Nath, $1.5 billion to create terrorism in Punjab, Khalistan and in Kashmir.

We must work to stop terrorism wherever it occurs. India's terrorism is no exception. We should stop our aid to India until it stops its repression of the Christians, Sikhs, Muslims, and other minorities, and we should declare our public support for self-determination for all the people of South Asia in the form of a free and fair plebiscite on the question of independence.

A report published this past May by the Movement Against State Repression showed that the Indian government admitted that 52,268 Sikh political prisoners are rotting in Indian jails without charge or trial. Many have been in illegal custody since 1984. The Indian government has murdered over 250,000 Sikhs since 1984, according to the Politics of Genocide by Inderjit Singh Jaijee. Over 75,000 Kashmiri Muslims and over 200,000 Christians have been killed.

Mr. Speaker, the Council of Khalistan has published an excellent press release on this attack. I would like to share it with my colleagues by inserting it into the Record now.

From the Council of Khalistan, Dec. 14, 2001
Council Of Khalistan Condemns All Terrorism_Terrorist Attack on Indian Parliament Is a Product of Indian Repression
(By Guru Gobind Singh Ji, Tenth Master)

India Must End Its Repression Instead of Blaming Paki-stan_Newspaper Says Indian Government Knew of Attack in Advance

Washington, DC_The Council of Khalistan today condemned the terrorist attack on the Indian Parliament, but called on the Indian government to join the fight against terrorism worldwide and to end its own terrorism against minorities.

"We condemn terrorism in all forms, wherever it comes from," said Dr. Gurmit Singh Aulakh, President of the Council of Khalistan, the government pro tempore of Khalistan, the Sikh homeland, which declared its independence from India on October 7, 1987. "We strongly condemn this terrorist action and we condemn the Indian government's terrorism that gave rise to this act," he said. "When you repress people long enough, they strike back. India's repression of minorities made this incident inevitable."

The Deccan Chronicle reported today that the Indian government knew of the attack in advance and did nothing to stop it. This shows government involvement in the incident. yet the Indian government has blamed Pakistan for the attacks. India will use this incident as an excuse for more repression of the minorities, such as the Sikhs of Khalistan, the Muslims of Kashmir, the Christians of Nagaland, and others.

"India must stop blaming Pakistan for everything that goes wrong in India and end its own terrorism against the Sikhs, Christians, Muslims, and other minorities," said Dr. Aulakh. "It is time for India to release more than 52,000 Sikh political prisoners and the tens of thousands of other political prisoners and end its repression," Dr. Aulakh said. The book "Soft Target," written by two Canadian journalists, proves that the Indian government blew up its own airliner in 1985 to generate more repression against Sikhs. In November 1994, the newspaper Hitavada reported that the government paid the late governor of Punjab, Surendra Nath, $1.5 billion to generate terrorist activity in Punjab and Kashmir.

"I salute Pakistani President Musharraf for risking his political life by supporting America and the world in its fight against terrorism. It is time for India to get on board," Dr. Aulakh said. "I call on India to join the fight against terrorism and I call on the Sikh leadership in Punjab to stop making coalitions with the Indian government and work for freedom for the Sikhs and the other minority nations of South Asia," he said. "There is a very good reason that there are 17 freedom movements within India's current borders."

The Indian government has murdered over 250,000 Sikhs since 1984. According to a report in May by the Movement Against State Repression,

India admitted that 52,268 Sikh political prisoners are rotting in Indian jails without charge or trial. Many have been in illegal custody since 1984. Over 200,000 Christians have been killed since 1947 and over 75,000 Kashmiri Muslims have been killed since 1988. The Indian Supreme Court described the situation in Punjab as "worse than a genocide." In May, Indian troops were caught red-handed trying to set fire to a Gurdwara (a Sikh Temple) and some Sikh houses in Kashmir. Two independent investigations have proven that the Indian government carried out the March 2000 massacre of 35 Sikhs in Chithisinghpora. U.S. Congressman Dana Rohrbacher has said that for Sikhs, Kashmiri Muslims, and other minorities "India might as well be Nazi Germany."

India has also repressed Christians. Two leaders of the ruling BJP said that everyone who lives in India must either be a Hindu or be subservient to Hinduism. Priests have been murdered, nuns have been raped, churches have been burned, Christian schools and prayer halls have been destroyed, and no one has been punished for these acts. Militant Hindu fundamentalists allied with the RSS, the pro-Fascist parent organization of the ruling BJP, burned missionary Graham Staines and his two young sons to death. In 1997, police broke up a Christian religious festival with gunfire.

"Nations that do not have political power vanish," Dr. Aulakh said. "Sikhs are a separate nation and ruled Punjab up to 1849 when the British annexed Punjab. The nations and people of South Asia must have self-determination now."

***

Document

CONGRESSIONAL RECORD -- EXTENSIONS

Thursday, December 20, 2001
107th Congress, 1st Session
147 Cong Rec E 2363

REFERENCE: Vol. 147, No. 1
SECTION: Extension of Remarks
TITLE: NEWSPAPER SAYS INDIAN GOVERNMENT KNEW OF
PARLIAMENT ATTACK

HON. DAN BURTON
of Indiana
in the House of Representatives
Wednesday, December 19, 2001

Mr. BURTON of Indiana . Mr. Speaker, the recent attack on India's Parliament by terrorists must be condemned. While there are many legitimate grievances against the Indian government, terrorism is never acceptable. Nevertheless, the Deccan Chronicle, an Indian newspaper, reported something very interesting about the recent attack. It reported that the Indian government knew about the attack in advance and did nothing. Thirteen people, including the terrorists, lost their lives as a result of the attack.

Mr. Speaker, India has a history of supporting terrorism and making it look like the work of others in order to condemn people who oppose the actions of the Indian government and to justify their own attacks on these targets. According to Soft Target, published in 1989 by two Canadian journalists, the Indian government blew up its own airliner in 1985, killing 329 innocent people, including some Americans, to create the impression of "Sikh terrorism" and enhance its repression of the Sikhs. In November 1994, the Hitavada newspaper reported that the Indian government paid Surendra Nath, who was then the governor of Punjab, the equivalent of $1.5 billion to generate and support terrorist activity in Kashmir and Punjab, Khalistan.

While I appreciate recent words of support from the Indian Government regarding America's war against terrorism, it is important that we do not forget some recent actions by the very same government. For example, in May 1999, the Indian Express reported that the Indian Defense Minister convened a meeting with the Ambassadors from Cuba, Communist China, Russia, Serbia, Libya, and Iraq_the latter two known terrorist nations and potential targets in the ongoing effort to eradicate terror_to set up a security alliance "to stop the U.S.".

It is also important to re-examine India's own human rights record in a number of areas. It has been reported that India represses its Christian minority. Specifically, it has been reported that nuns have been raped, priests have been murdered, and a missionary and his two sons were burned to death. The media reports that numerous churches have been burned. A few years ago, police gunfire closed a Christian religious festival. In addition, the pro-Fascist RSS, the parent organization of the ruling party, published a booklet detailing how to bring false criminal complaints against Christians and other minorities. Press reports indicate that Prime Minister Vajpayee promised a New York audience that he would "always be" remain a member this organization.

Since 1984, certain human rights organizations have reported that the Indian government has murdered over 250,000 Sikhs. Since 1947, over 200,000 Christians have been killed, and since 1988, over 75,000 Kashmiri Muslims have been killed. In addition, tens of thousands of other minorities, such as Dalit "untouchables," Tamils, Assamese, Manipuris, and others have been killed.

A May report issued by the Movement Against State Repression cited the Indian government's admission that 52,268 Sikh political prisoners are rotting in Indian jails without charge or trial. It further claims that many have been in illegal custody since 1984. Tens of thousands of other minorities are also being held as political prisoners in the country that proudly proclaims itself "the world's largest democracy."

Also in May, Indian troops set fire to Gurdwara (a Sikh Temple) and some Sikh homes in a village in Kashmir. Two independent investigations have shown that the Indian government carried out the massacre of 35

Sikhs in Chithisinghpora. These incidents are just the tip of the iceberg of Indian terror against its minorities and its neighbors.

Again, while I am grateful for recent words of support from the Indian Government regarding America's war against terrorists, the U.S. Government and the American public should not forget about these recent acts of repression. Democracies are not supposed to behave this way. If we are going to fight terrorism, then we must be consistent. There are actions we can take that will help influence India to end its reign of terror in South Asia. We must end our aid to India until they demonstrate a better regard on human rights. The hard-earned dollars of the American people should not be going to support countries that practice terrorism. We should also show our support for freedom rather than terrorism by supporting a free and fair plebiscite on the question of independence in Khalistan, Kashmir, Nagalim, and all the nations of South Asia that seek freedom from repressive occupation. Let us strike a blow for freedom, not terrorism.

Mr. Speaker, I would like to place the Deccan Chronicle article into the Record.

From the Deccan Chronicle, Dec. 14, 2001
Delhi Knew But Advani Slept

New Delhi, Dec. 13. Union Home Minister L K Advani had full intelligence information of a terrorist attack on Parliament.

Despite this, no measures were taken to tighten security in and around the Parliament House with the five terrorists driving in past two security parameters manner by the Delhi police and the CRPF, unchallenged.

In his first reaction to the terrorist attack, Advani claimed, "There has been no breach of security." He said there was "no intelligence lapse". He said on television that there could be no protection against fidayeen attacks maintaining that they even "had the temerity to attack Pentagon." The Home Minister said it was not possible to provide fool-proof security cover in a democracy "where everything was open." The Union Home Ministry has been flooded with intelligence information about a possible attack on Parliament by terrorists. The other two targets were identified as Rashtrapati Bhavan and the Prime Minister's residence.

Intelligence reports have also suggested the use of women suicide squads. These have also spoken of terrorists using State vehicles to launch the attack, similar to the modus operandi of the terrorist groups in Kashmir for over a decade now.

Despite this, the security agencies were not alerted. The terrorists used a white ambassador car with a red light, the symbol of government officialdom.

They were dressed Black Cat commandos, and were detected only after they got out of the car and displayed their weapons in full public view. Advani, who had been full of praise for the Delhi police, did not explain how the two security rings manned by the police outside Parliament were penetrated with such ease.

In fact defence minister George Fernandes stepped out of line by admitting before the cameras that the government had full information about a possible terrorist attack on Parliament.

He said, "We had intelligence information of this, we knew that the fidayeen could attack Parliament." Even so, the home minister claimed there had been no intelligence lapse while briefing reporters after the meeting of the Cabinet committee on security.

Najma Heptullah, who was in her room in Parliament when it was attacked, said, "The Home Minister knew of the Al Qaeda threat, he should have increased the security in Parliament."

She said she had herself asked for measures to be taken to beef up Parliament security. "There are all these people roaming around all over the building" but nothing had been done.

Interestingly Advani himself spoke of a threat to Parliament at a Border Security Force function a few days ago. Officials point out that despite the security threat little was done to take stock of the entire situation and work out a comprehensive strategy to deal with it.

"It was all in the realm of talk, we have always known that the terrorists have been using and would use the cover of the government-like vehicles and uniforms to penetrate our security layers, but obviously we were unable to get this across to our people," a senior official said.

***

Document

CONGRESSIONAL RECORD -- EXTENSIONS

Wednesday, November 28, 2001
107th Congress, 1st Session
147 Cong Rec E 2153

REFERENCE: Vol. 147, No. 162
SECTION: Extension of Remarks
TITLE: SIKHS MUST HAVE A FREE KHALISTAN, ALL OTHER RELIGIOUS
GROUPS HAVE THEIR OWN COUNTRIES, SIKHS ARE SEPARATE
RELIGION, CULTURE, LANGUAGE, AND PEOPLE

HON. EDOLPHUS TOWNS
of New York
in the House of Representatives
Wednesday, November 28, 2001

Mr. TOWNS . Mr. Speaker, all over the world, religious and ethnic groups have their own countries. There are numerous countries dominated by Christians and as we have recently been reminded, there are numerous Muslim countries as well. The Hindus rule India and a few other countries. There are a number of Buddhist countries. The Jewish people have Israel. Only the Sikhs do not have their own country.

Sikhs declared their independence from India on October 7, 1987, naming their country Khalistan. Unfortunately, Khalistan continues to live under a brutal occupation by India that has cost a quarter of a million Sikhs their lives since 1984. Earlier this year, the Movement Against State Repression issued a report showing that India is holding at least 52,268 Sikh political prisoners, by their own admission, in illegal detention without charge or trial. Some of them have been held since 1984. Former Member of Parliament Atinder Pal Singh noted that "there is no family in the 12,687 villages of Punjab of which one or the other Sikh member has not been killed by the police."

As I have previously said, "The mere fact that they have the right to choose their oppressors does not mean they live in a democracy." My colleague, the gentleman from California, Mr. Rohrabacher, has said that for Sikhs and Kashmiris, "India might as well be Nazi Germany." I cannot make a better statement of how brutal India's occupation of the Sikh homeland is. A new Indian law makes any act a "terrorist offense" to "threaten the unity or integrity of India." Under this law, anyone who peacefully advocates independence for Khalistan or any of the minority nations such as predominantly Christian Nagaland, Kashmir, or any other can be held as a "terrorist" for as long as it suits the Indian government to do so. This is not democracy, Mr. Speaker.

When India got its independence from Britain, Sikhs were one of the three nations that were to receive their own sovereign state. Muslims got Pakistan, Hindus got India. Sikh leaders stayed with India because Mr. Nehru and Mr. Gandhi promised them that they would enjoy "the glow of freedom" in Punjab and no law would pass affecting Sikhs without their consent. However, as soon as the ink was dry on the agreement for Indian independence, the Indian government put out a memo describing Sikhs as "a criminal class" and began the tyrannical harassment of the Sikhs. Accordingly, no Sikh representative has ever signed the constitution of India.

Sikhs ruled Punjab as an independent country from 1765 to 1849, when the British conquered the subcontinent. Punjab was recognized by most of the major countries at that time. Under Sikh rule, Punjab was a secular state in which Sikhs, Muslims, Hindus, and Christians all had a part in the government. The people prospered.

In June 1984, the Indian government attacked the Sikh religion's most sacred shrine, the Golden Temple in Amritsar, the Vatican or Mecca of the Sikhs. Sant Jarnail Singh Bhindranwale, a leader of the Sikh freedom movement had warned that "If the Indian government attacks the Golden Temple, it will lay the foundation of Khalistan." After the Golden Temple attack, the movement for an independent Sikh country, Khalistan, took on steam. As a result, India stepped up the repression. In the words of Narinder Singh, a spokesman for the Golden Temple who appeared on NPR in August 1997, "The Indian government, all the time they boast that they're democratic, they're secular, but they have nothing to do with a democracy, they have nothing to do with a secularism. They try to crush Sikhs just to please the majority."

Mr. Speaker, this is unacceptable. I must join Atinder Pal Singh, the former Member of Parliament in asking, "why can't the Khalistan, Sikhistan, or whatever name you might like to give it be formed for the Sikhs?"

India claims to be "the world's largest democracy." If that is so, then why can't India do the democratic thing and let the people of Khalistan and the peoples of all the minority nations have a free and fair plebiscite, with international monitoring, to decide the question of independence? Isn't that the democratic way? The United States does it for Puerto Rico, Canada does it for Quebec. Why can't "the world's largest democracy" do it for the people of Khalistan, Kashmir, Christian Nagaland, and all the other minority nations? Only when these nations are free will the repression of minorities in India end.

The U.S. Congress should go on record in support of self-determination for all the people of South Asia and we should stop American aid to India until the repression ends. The only answer is freedom. Let's do what we can to support it and expand it.

***

Document

CONGRESSIONAL RECORD -- EXTENSIONS

Wednesday, November 28, 2001
107th Congress, 1st Session

147 Cong Rec E 2155
REFERENCE: Vol. 147, No. 162
SECTION: Extension of Remarks
TITLE: IN MEMORY OF NAZAR SINGH FAGOORA

HON. EDOLPHUS TOWNS
of New York
in the House of Representatives
Wednesday, November 28, 2001

Mr. TOWNS . Mr. Speaker, recently Nazar Singh Fagoora, a Sikh leader from Fresno, California, passed away. December 3 would have been his 86th birthday. I was informed of his passing by Dr. Gurmit Singh Aulakh, President of the Council of Khalistan, to whom he was an advisor.

Nazar Singh Fagoora believed deeply in freedom for all people. He supported the struggle to free the Sikh homeland, Khalistan, with financial contributions and with his political support. In the Fresno Gurdwara, he would post letters from the Council of Khalistan on the bulletin board to inform his fellow Sikhs of what was going on back in Punjab, Khalistan, and to encourage them to get involved in the freedom movement.

Nazar Singh Fagoora was a committed, dedicated Sikh, and a staunch Khalistani. He led a simple life. He was active in many efforts to help his fellow Sikhs, whether by trying to help people in the local community or by his financial, moral, political, and personal support of the freedom movement. I know that his family, friends, and the members of his Gurdwara will greatly miss him. Let him serve to remind us all of what it is to be a good citizen. I know I speak for everyone here when I say let God bless him and his family.

Mr. Speaker, the Council of Khalistan issued a press release in Mr. Fagoora's memory. I would like to place that in the Record at this time.

Sikh Nation Mourns Passing of S. Nazar Singh Fagoora
Fresno Sikh Was Dedicated Servant of Khalsa Panth and All People

Washington, DC, November 20, 2001._The Sikh Nation is mourning the loss of Sardar Nazar Singh Fagoora, a dedicated Sikh leader from Fresno, California, who died at the age of 85. He was a dedicated servant of the Khalsa Panth, and he will be greatly missed.

"Sardar Nazar Singh was a great human being, a committed, dedicated Sikh, and a staunch Khalistani," said Dr. Gurmit Singh Aulakh, President of the Council of Khalistan, the organization leading the Sikh Nation's struggle for the independence of the Sikh homeland. Khalistan is the name of the independent Sikh homeland declared on October 7, 1987.

"Sardar Nazar Singh gave large amounts of money in support of the struggle to liberate Khalistan. He led a simple fulfilling life, according to the principles laid down by our Gurus," Dr. Aulakh said. "He was a true follower of Guru. He was a truly noble and dedicated Sikh," Dr. Aulakh said.

"Sardar Nazar Singh really served the Guru very well by serving the Khalsa Panth," Dr. Aulakh said. "He was active in many ways in efforts to help the Khalsa Panth, whether by trying to help people in the local Sangat or by his financial, moral, political, and personal support of the freedom movement," he said. "In the Fresno Gurdwara, he made sure every letter written by this office was posted on the walls of the Gurdwara as soon as it arrived. The Sangat would browse through those documents carefully," Dr. Aulakh said. "I know that I will miss his counsel and advice. I don't see anyone in this country who can fill the vacuum created by his departure," Dr. Aulakh said.

"Sardar Nazar Singh understood that Sikhs will continue to suffer oppression in India and will continue to be misunderstood in this country as long as we do not have our own country," said Dr. Autakh. "This kind of repression will continue as long as Khalistan continues to live under Indian occupation," he said. "Only in a sovereign, free Khalistan will Sikhs live with honor and dignity where the Sikh religion can flourish," he said. "Nations that do not have political power vanish."

The Indian government has murdered over 250,000 Sikhs since 1984. More than 52,000 Sikh political prisoners are rotting in Indian jails without charge or trial. Many have been in illegal custody since 1984. Over 200,000 Christians have been killed since 1947 and over 75,000

Kashmiri Muslims have been killed since 1988. The Indian Supreme Court described the situation in Punjab as "worse than a genocide." As General Narinder Singh has said, "Punjab is a police state." U.S. Congressman Dana Rohrabacher has said that for Sikhs, Kashmiri Muslims, and other minorities "India might as well be Nazi Germany."

"Sardar Nazar Singh will be greatly missed by his family and by all Sikhs who care about freedom and about the dignity of the Khalsa Panth," Dr. Aulakh said. "May Guru give peace to this departed, noble soul," Dr. Aulakh added.

***

Document

CONGRESSIONAL RECORD -- EXTENSIONS

Thursday, November 15, 2001
107th Congress, 1st Session
147 Cong Rec E 2103

REFERENCE: Vol. 147, No. 158
SECTION: Extension of Remarks
TITLE: INDIA ILLEGALLY DETAINS WIDOW OF HUMAN-RIGHTS
ACTIVIST

HON. DAN BURTON
of Indiana
in the House of Representatives
Thursday, November 15, 2001

Mr. BURTON of Indiana . Mr. Speaker, I was disturbed to read that the Indian government has once again put its utter contempt for basic human rights on public display. At a time when India is posturing as an ally in the fight against terrorism, it is commiting more terrorism against the minority peoples living within its own borders.

The Indian government is currently holding Mrs. Paramjit Kaur Khalra and six other Sikh human-rights activists in detention supposedly "to prevent disruption," or in other words to prevent them from carrying out peaceful political activities. Mrs. Khalra is the widow of Jaswant Singh Khalra, the late General Secretary of the Human Rights Wing, who exposed India's brutal policy of picking up young Sikhs, torturing them, killing them, then declaring their bodies "unidentified" and secretly cremating them. Mr. Khalra published a report showing that there had been at least 25,000 Sikhs victimized by this brutal policy. The Khalra Mission Committee, which Mrs. Khalra heads, in conjunction with other human-rights groups, has subsequently shown that the number is in excess of 50,000.

After Mr. Khalra published this report, he received a phone call from a police official saying, "We made 25,000 disappear. We can make one more disappear." On September 6, 1995, while he was washing his car, he was abducted by the police. One eyewitness who saw him while he was in custody said that he was severely tortured, to the point that he could barely eat. In late October 1995, Khalra was murdered in a police station. None of the police officials responsible for this heinous crime has ever been punished. All the Indian government has done is transfer them to other police stations, where they can find new victims to torture.

According to "The Politics of Genocide" by Inderjit Singh Jaijee, the Indian government has murdered over 250,000 Sikhs since 1984, over 200,000 Christians in Nagaland since 1947, over 75,000 Kashmiri Muslims since 1988, and thousands and thousands of Dalit "Untouchables," Tamils, Manipuris, Assamese, tribal people all in pursuit of "Hindutva"_a Hindu state, society, and culture. Last year, a government official was quoted as saying that everyone who lives in India must either be a Hindu or be subservient to Hindus. That is not democracy, Mr. Speaker. It is theocracy. It takes more than elections to make a democracy; it takes genuine respect for basic human freedoms.

I have serious misgivings about current U.S. plans to resume arms sales to India. We should very cautious in considering such an aid resumption, especially given India's terrible human-rights record. We should also support a free and fair plebiscite on independence in Khalistan, Kashmir, Christian Nagaland, and all the countries seeking their freedom from India. This is the best thing we can do for freedom, peace, prosperity, and stability in South Asia.

Mr. Speaker, I would like to place an article from Burning Punjab on the detention of Mrs. Khalra into the Record at this time.

From the Burning Punjab News, Nov. 2, 2001
Mrs. Khalra Held
(Our Correspondent)

Amritsar, November 2_The police today early morning arrested Mrs Paramijit Kaur Khalra of the Khalra Mission Committee to prevent disturbance of the peace in the state.

She reportedly was arrested at 4:30 a.m. hours before the arrival of the Prime Minister at 10 a.m. today reportedly from her residence here. The police also rounded-up six others, including Kirpal Singh Randhwa PHRO vice-president.

***

Document

CONGRESSIONAL RECORD -- EXTENSIONS

Thursday, November 15, 2001
107th Congress, 1st Session
147 Cong Rec E 2104

REFERENCE: Vol. 147, No. 158
SECTION: Extension of Remarks
TITLE: TURBAN IS RELIGIOUS SYMBOL; IT MUST NOT BE REMOVED

HON. EDOLPHUS TOWNS
of New York
in the House of Representatives
Thursday, November 15, 2001

Mr. TOWNS . Mr. Speaker, I was distressed to find out that another Sikh was forced to remove his turban at LaGuardia Airport in New York. I am from New York, as you know, and it particularly distresses me to learn that this occurred in my home city.

According to the website Rediff.com, Surjit Babra, president of a $100 million company called SkyLink, "was forced to remove his turban" at LaGuardia airport in New York, allegedly as part of a security inspection. Mr. Babra is a Canadian Sikh who was trying to board a flight back to Toronto. Previously, a sitting judge who is Sikh was forced to remove his turban at the same airport. We must clean up the security procedures at this airport.

Security guards asked Mr. Babra to remove his turban. Mr. Babra suggested that the guard use a hand-held scanner to scan his turban. The security guard wouldn't accept that and made him remove his turban immediately.

Mr. Speaker, the turban is a religious symbol. It is required by the Sikh religion. It is one of the five symbols every Sikh is required to carry on his person. Removing a Sikh's turban is an insult to him and to the Sikh faith.

Dr. Gurmit Singh Aulakh, President of the Council of Khalistan, who visits my office often, sports a bright saffron turban. It looks very impressive. He is a committed, practicing Sikh and he will not remove his turban in public under any circumstances. I am sure other Sikhs feel the same way. They should not be harassed by asking them to remove their turbans at routine security checks at the airport.

I agree with Gurbax Singh Malhi, a Sikh member of the Canadian Parliament, who said that "while understanding and sharing the terrible circumstances that have led to this point", the United States should "train and educate security personnel so that they will respect the right of people of the Sikh religion to wear turbans and not subject them to this undignified and unnecessary procedure".

I urge Transportation Secretary Mineta to order the FAA to stop the harassment of Sikhs and order that their turbans not be removed unless other security means show an absolute necessity to do so.

America is a land of freedom. Sikhs come here to escape from the repression they suffer in India. They have contributed to every aspect of American life. We even had one Sikh, Dalip Singh Saund, who served in this House in the early 60s. America must respect the religious freedom of Sikhs just as it respects the religious freedom of other faiths.

Mr. Speaker, I would like to place the Rediff.com article on the Babra case in the Record for the information of my colleagues.

From Rediff.com, Nov. 10, 2001
Canadian Sikh Forced To Remove Turban at LaGuardia
(By Ajit Jain)

Surjit Babra, president of the $100 million portfolio SkyLink, "was forced to remove his turban" at LaGuardia airport in New York, allegedly as part of a security inspection.

In a press release, Indo-Canadian Member of Parliament Gurbax Malbi, himself a turbaned Sikh, said that "while understanding and sharing the terrible circumstances that have led to this point", the United States should "train and educate security personnel so that they will respect the right of people of the Sikh religion to wear turbans and not subject them to this undignified and unnecessary procedure".

Rediff.com tried to reach Babra several times, but he wouldn't respond to telephone calls.

Businessman Garry Singh, a close friend of Babra, recounted that it was on Wednesday evening, when he was going through security before boarding his flight to Toronto at LaGuardia, that the incident took place.

Babra was asked to remove his turban by the security guard. The Sikh businessman suggested that the guard use a hand-held scanner to scan his turban. If he were still not satisfied, he would then remove his turban.

The security guard wouldn't accept that and made him remove his turban immediately.

Malbi said, "In Canada we have learned to respect religious symbols." The Royal Canadian Mounted Police has changed its rules to allow Sikhs to wear turbans on duty.

Barbra's SkyLink moves U.N. peacekeeping personnel and equipment to various countries in the world.

***

Document

CONGRESSIONAL RECORD -- EXTENSIONS

Thursday, November 08, 2001
107th Congress, 1st Session
147 Cong Rec E 2048

REFERENCE: Vol. 147, No. 154
SECTION: Extension of Remarks
TITLE: HUMAN-RIGHTS ACTIVIST DETAINED IN INDIA

HON. EDOLPHUS TOWNS
of New York
in the House of Representatives
Thursday, November 8, 2001

Mr. TOWNS . Mr. Speaker, the Indian government recently detained Mrs. Paramjit Kaur Khalra, widow of a human-rights activist and a human-rights activist in her own right, along with six other human-rights activists, including the Vice President of the Punjab Human rights Organization (PHRO), Kirpal Singh Randhawa. They were apparently arrested under TADA, the repressive "Terrorist and Disruptive Activities Act, " which expired in 1995. Now India has promulgated an even worse law, known as POTO, which would make advocating the breakup of India a "terrorist offense" and would allow the arrest of journalists for publishing information critical of the government. Is this the kind of law promulgated in a democratic and free society?

You may remember, Mr. Speaker, that the President of the PHRO, Judge Ajit Singh Bains, testified several years ago before the Human Rights Caucus of the House and was very impressive. After his testimony, you could have no doubt that Punjab under Indian rule is a very tyrannical state.

Mrs. Khalra is the widow of Jaswant Singh Khalra, who exposed the Indian government's policy of mass, secret cremations of Sikhs. This policy has been called "worse than a genocide" by the Punjab High Court. For exposing it, Mr. Khalra was kidnapped from his house in Amritsar in September 1995 and tortured to death. None of the police officers responsible has ever been punished. Now Mrs. Khalra's efforts to continue her husband's work have gotten her arrested. It is clear that she and the other human-rights activists were arrested to prevent their participation in political events and stop public protest. India still believes, after all the bloodshed, that it can intimidate the Sikhs and other minorities such as the Christians of Nagaland, the Muslims of Kashmir, and others into submission to Hindu supremacy.

It is not a good time to be a widow in India, Mr. Speaker. First the Indian government tried to expel the widow of missionary Graham Staines from the country, and now they are harassing Mrs. Khalra. This is Indian democracy in action, and it is not pretty.

There was one eyewitness to the kidnapping of Jaswant Singh Khalra, a man named Rajiv Singh Randhawa. Last year, he was arrested in front of the Golden Temple in Amritsar for trying to hand a petition to the British Home Minister. In light of repeated incidents like this, India should be embarrassed to proclaim itself "the world's largest democracy."

Mr. Speaker, the United States should not sit idly by and let these acts of repression go on without consequences. Our government must immediately press for the release of Mrs. Khalra and the 52,000-plus Sikh political prisoners currently being held without charge or trial in India, as well as the thousands of other political prisoners of other nationalities. All of them must be released. If they are not, I urge them to secure their release by running for political office from their jail cells.

In addition, America should stop its aid to India and support an internationally-supervised vote on the political status of Punjab, Khalistan, of Kashmir, of Nagalim, and of all the countries seeking their independence. Remember that India promised in 1948 to hold a plebiscite in Kashmir, a promise it has not kept. It is time for India to start acting like a democracy. This vote would be a good way to start.

Mr. Speaker, I have here an Urgent Action Request from the Canadian branch of the World Sikh Organization demanding the immediate release of Mrs. Khalra. It was brought to me by Dr. Gurmit Singh Aulakh, President of the Council of Khalistan. I would like to place it in the Record to show my colleagues the real workings of Indian democracy.

Urgent Action Request

Ottawa, November 3, 2001._The World Sikh Organization requests your immediate assistance to procure the release of Mrs. Laswant Singh Khalra and six other human rights activists and lawyers who were arrested by the Indian police on November 2, 2001. It is known that these individuals were arrested to prevent their participation in political events in Punjab, and to prevent public protest. Mrs. Khalra's husband, Jaswant Singh was the lead investigator who uncovered illegal cremation grounds maintained throughout Punjab by police. Mr. Khalra and Mr. Jaspal Singh Dhillon both leaders of the Human Rights Wing of the Shiromani Akali Dal were arrested, and presumably tortured by the very same Punjab Police they sought to prosecute. Mr. Khalra was tortured to death, and now Mrs. Khalra and six others have been arrested under a charge of "threat to the peace".

Soft-spoken and peaceful, Mr. and Mrs. Khalra visited with Canadian and American politicians, including Canadian Prime Minister Jean Chretien to apprize them of ongoing oppression in Punjab. Providing evidence of the disposal grounds for thousands of unidentified Sikhs murdered by Indian officials with the support of central government, Mrs. Khalra has been an outspoken activist since the murder of her husband. Nonetheless the central Indian government has been seeking general amnesty for the police officers involved in the cremation grounds and thousands of other illegal executions. Since the early nineteen eighties thousands of Sikhs have suffered illegal arrest, detention, torture, and murder at the hands of state and government officials. Arresting human rights activists like Mrs. Khalra and lawyers involved in important human rights cases, once again prevents public scrutiny of the realities of present day Punjab. Recently a professor by the name of Davinder Singh was prosecuted under the Terrorist and Disruptive Activities Act, an Act which was purportedly repealed in 1995. Despite the United Nations condemning India's laws, and evidence of coercion and torture of the accused for the purposes of extracting a confession, Mr. Singh has been sentenced to the death penalty. In India, the new Prevention of Terrorism Ordinance (POTO) seeks to fill the void created following the lapsing of TADA, and makes the TADA legislation look mild. POTO provides for suppression of information and therefore makes journalists subject to terrorism charges if they publish information unfavorable to the government. It makes the disclosure of information to police investigators mandatory with prison terms of up to three years for non compliance. Under the POTO citizens of Punjab will be forced to live in a police state that is even more brutal than the last two decades.

We need your urgent assistance to let the Indian government know that democratic nations will not tolerate such abuses of innocent citizens and such shameless violations of civilian rights from a Commonwealth partner. Please take every action possible to obtain the immediate release of Mrs. Khalra and six other lawyers, and to repeal the death penalty sentence against Davinder Singh. Your active and vocal response to these travesties of justice are imperative to the future of all civilians in India.

***

Document

CONGRESSIONAL RECORD -- EXTENSIONS

Wednesday, October 31, 2001
107th Congress, 1st Session
147 Cong Rec E 1973

REFERENCE: Vol. 147, No. 148
SECTION: Extension of Remarks
TITLE: INDIA FILES FAKE CRIMINAL CASE AGAINST BURNING PUNJAB
WEBSITE

HON. EDOLPHUS TOWNS
of New York
in the House of Representatives
Wednesday, October 31, 2001

Mr. TOWNS . Mr. Speaker, I was distressed to learn that the government of India, which calls itself "the world's largest demoncracy," has filed a criminal case against the website Burning Punjab, which reports news about the abuse of Sikhs in Punjab, Khalistan by the Indian government. The website can be found at http://www.burningpunjab.com/news.html

The government made the case fit under Indian law by falsely claiming that Burning Punjab is "a newspaper published from Chandigarh." There is no newspaper published, just online news, and Burning Punjab uses services in the United States and Britain to publish its news. The case was filed by the Deputy Inspector General of the terrorist Central Reserve Police Force. Previously, viewing Burning Punjab had been prohibited in several states in northwest India, including Punjab, Delhi, and Chandigarh. This is clearly a case filed to harass Burning Punjab for reporting news the government does not like. I'm sorry, Mr. Speaker, but I fail to see the difference between this action by "the world's largest democracy" and the repression of the press in the most tyrannical dictatorships of the world.

If this is how India treats those who expose its corruption and brutality, it is no democracy. We should support democracy in South Asia in the form of a free and fair plebiscite with international monitoring on the question of independence for Khalistan, Kashmir, Nagaland, and the other countries seeking their freedom from Indian. This will provide the opportunity for every one in the subcontinent to live in freedom, dignity, peace, and prosperity. That is the best way to promote stability in South Asia.

I would like to place an article from Burning Punjab on the complaint into the Record at this time.

Harassment Continues: Forged Criminal Case Filed Against "Burning Punjab"

Jalandhar_A forged criminal case against web site Burning Punjab' has been filed in the Court of Judicial Magistrate Mohinder Singh deputed in Jalandhar Courts. The case referred Burning Punjab News' on-line web news as a newspaper' published from Chandigarh, just to cover the Burning Punjab staff under India Penal Code. One Lashkar Singh has filed the case: DIG of Central Reserve Police Force (CRPF) of Indian Hindu Regime.

It is pertinent to mention that Burning Punjab web site is aired through European and American based servers and satellites. It's registered address is located in United Kingdom but with a motive to harass human rights activists working for Burning Punjab web site, Indian Police have now manipulated forge case against them by alleging that Burning Punjab News is a daily newspaper published from Chandigarh. Whereas no such newspaper' published from Chandigarh.

A formal representation has been sent to Chief Justice of Supreme Court and the High Court, urging them to take initiative and prevent abusing human right activists and also legal process of the land.

***

Document

CONGRESSIONAL RECORD -- EXTENSIONS

Wednesday, October 31, 2001
107th Congress, 1st Session
147 Cong Rec E 1975

REFERENCE: Vol. 147, No. 148
SECTION: Extension of Remarks
TITLE: NEW POTO LAW IN INDIA PERHAPS MOST REPRESSIVE EVER

HON. DAN BURTON
of Indiana
in the House of Representatives
Wednesday, October 31, 2001

Mr. BURTON of Indiana . Mr. Speaker, in 1995 the Indian law known as the "Terrorist and Disruptive Activities Act (TADA)" expired. It was one of the most repressive laws ever put on the books anywhere in the world. It allowed people to be picked up for any reason or no reason, held without charge or trial for an indefinite period, deprived them of the right to know of the charges against them or face their accusers. The law was widely abused. When a rare TADA defendant would get released, the police would immediately pick him up again and often would file TADA complaints in more than one jurisdiction to make it impossible to contest. Despite the fact that it expired over six years ago, the Movement Against State Repression reports that over 52,000 Sikhs are being held as political prisoners in India, most under TADA and many of them since 1984.

India took TADA off the books under intense political pressure but continued to enforce it. Now the country that likes to boast of being "the world's largest democracy" has taken advantage of the terrorist incident that occurred in September to promulgate a law called the Prevention of Terrorism Ordinance (POTO) that makes TADA look mild. Twenty three organizations have already been banned under POTO, including the International Sikh Youth Federation (ISYF), a group that has engaged in peaceful political protest for human rights and sometimes for independence for the Sikh homeland, Khalistan. This ban just goes to show that in the eyes of the Indian government, anyone who speaks up peacefully for freedom for for freedom is considered a "terrorist." Oddly, it also bans the Liberation Tigers of Tamil Eelam (LTTE), which India today reported was a creation of the Indian government and whose leaders, according to the article, were put up in Delhi's finest hotel.

In addition, POTO provides for suppression of information, and therefore makes journalists subject to terrorism charges if they publish information unfavorable to the government. It makes the furnishing of certain information to police investigators mandatory with a prison term of up to three years for failure to tell them what they want to hear and it allows for coerced confessions.

A respected retired Indian general, General Narindr Singh, said "Punjab is a police state." Under POTO, minorities in India will be forced to live in a police state, which is even more brutal than before. Unfortunately, the United States has been trying to strengthen its ties with India, which in the past, voted to throw the United States off the Human Rights Commission and to suppress a resolution critical of Red Chinese human-rights violations. India, a longtime Soviet ally, votes against the United States at the UN more often than any country except Cuba. According to the Indian Express, India's Defense Minister, led a meeting in 1999 with the Ambassadors of Red China, Cuba, Russia, Yugoslavia, Libya, and Iraq to set up a security alliance "to stop the U.S."

Mr. Speaker, why should a country with a long record of anti-Americanism be a recipient of U.S. aid? The obvious answer is that it should not. The hard-working, overtaxed people of this country should not be supporting this brutal, corrupt, and hostile country. We should stop all U.S. id to India, restore the sanctions previously in place against that country, and put the Congress on record in support of a free and fair plebiscite in Kashmir, in Punjab, Khalistan, in Christian Negaland, and everywhere that people are seeking their freedom from this brutal regime. It is our obligation to the principles that give birth to our great country.

Mr. Speaker, on October 26, the Tribune News Service in India ran an excellent article on the repressive new POTO law, which I would like to place in the Record at this time.

From the Tribune News Service, Oct. 26, 2001
Centre Bans 23 Terrorist Outfits

New Delhi, October 25_The Centre today justified the promulgation of the Prevention of Terrorism Ordinance (POTO) saying it is the first comprehensive legal salvo against terrorism with complete safeguards to check the menace speedily and effectively. Under the ordinance, 23 organizations have been banned. Briefing newspersons here, Union Home Secretary Kamal Pande said care had been taken to ensure that the 50-page, 61-clause ordinance avoided all pitfalls and criticisms that the erstwhile Terrorist and Disruptive Activities Prevention Act (TADA), which expired in 1995, had to face.

Justifying the promulgation of the ordinance, Mr. Pande said there was an upsurge in terrorist activities, intensification of cross-border terrorism and insurgent groups in different parts of the country and the existing criminal justice system was not designed to deal with the types of heinous crimes that had appeared in the country in the past 50 years.

The ordinance defines terrorist acts as those done by using weapons and explosive substances or other methods in a manner as to cause or likely to cause death or injuries to persons or loss or damage to property or disruption of essential supplies and services with intent to threaten the unity or integrity of India or to strike terror in any section of the people. It also has a comprehensive definition of terrorist organizations indulging in terrorist acts and provides for proscribing them under a set procedure.

A total of 23 organizations have been banned under the ordinance, which Mr. Pande said, would be placed before Parliament in the form of a Bill for approval soon.

"The ordinance, of course, will have to be passed through Parliament as it will be valid for a maximum period of six months . . . it will be placed before Parliament," he said.

Stating that all state governments and other departments concerned were consulted twice on the various provisions of the ordinance and their suggestions were taken note of and included wherever necessary before it was promulgated, Mr. Pande said "special features/safeguards have been built in to prevent the possibility of misuse of the special power given to investigating authorities also keeping in view the observations of the Supreme Court."

Asked about the mounting criticism over the clause pertaining to "disclosure of information", which is equally applicable to journalists, Mr. Pande said the clause was in line with the provisions pertaining to suppression of information already existing in CrPC and the IPC. Section 3(8) of the ordinance places responsibility on all persons to disclose information which the person knows or believes to be of material assistance in preventing any terrorist activity as soon as reasonably practicable to the police. However, exception has been provided in case of persons engaged as legal attorney of the accused who may have acquired such knowledge for the purpose of preparing the defense for the accused.

Section 14 provides a new provision which makes it obligatory to furnish information in respect of a terrorist offense. Failure to furnish the information called for or deliberately furnishing false information to investigating officer shall be punishable with imprisonment for a term which may extend to three years or fine or both. The investigating officer can call for such information only with prior approval in writing of an officer not below the rank of Superintendent of Police.

Mr. Pande said Section 32 provided for admissibility of confessions made to a police officer under certain conditions. But unlike TADA, the confession of an accused shall not be admissible as an evidence against a co-accused. Further such confessions had to be made before a police officer not lower in rank of a SP and had to be further recorded with a Chief Judicial Magistrate within 48 hours.

There is a provision to review the ban and a review committee headed by a sitting or retired judge of a high court will be constituted to hear such applications.

Financing of terrorism, possession of unauthorised arms, explosive substances or other lethal weapons capable of mass destruction and/or use in biological and chemical warfare have also been brought under the purview of this ordinance and the punishment could range from three years imprisonment to life imprisonment or fine or both and also death penalty.

Twenty-three organisations, including Deendar Anjuman, the Students Islamic Movement of India (SIMI) and some of the almost defunct outfits in Punjab have been branded as terrorist organisations in the ordinance.

The hurriedly promulgated ordinance lists the Babbar Khalsa International, the Khalistan Commando Force, the Khalistan Zindabad Force and the International Sikh Youth Federation among the list of terrorist outfits.

The ordinance has also branded almost all Kashmiri and North-East militant outfits and the Liberation Tigers of Tamil Eelam (LTTE) as terrorist organisations.

The outfits operating in Kashmir, which have been listed as terrorist organisations, are the Lashkar-e-Toiba/Pasban-e-Ahle Hadis, the Jaish-e-

Mohammed/Tahrik-e-Fuqran, the Harkat-ul-Jehad-e-Islami, the Hizb-ul-Mujahideen and the Jammu and Kashmir Islamic Front.

The North-East outfits which have been branded as terrorist organisations, under Chapter III of the ordinance which deals with the terrorist organisations, are the United Liberation Front of Assam (ULFA), the National Democratic Front of Bodoland (NDFB), the People's Liberation Army (PLA), the United National Liberation Front (UNLF), the People's Revolutionary Party of Kangleipak (PREPAK), the Kangleipak Communist Party (KCP), the Kanglei Yaol Kanba Lup (KYKL), the Manipur People's Liberation Front (MPLF), the All-Teipura Tiger Force and the National Liberation Front of Tripura. Meanwhile, the government will seek to replace three ordinances, including the controversial POTO in the forthcoming winter session of Parliament beginning on November 19.

The Union Cabinet, at its special meeting here today, decided not only on the dates of Parliament's winter session but also on seeking the passage of the three ordinances.

Briefing newspersons after the meeting, Parliamentary Affairs Minister Pramod Mahajan said the government was confident of getting the Opposition's support on POTO, despite some of the parties having extreme reservations on it. POTO seeks to fill the void created following the lapsing of TADA.

The minister was of the view that such a law was necessary in the prevailing conditions in the country and would help the government and the police in combating terrorism. He added that the Opposition was equally concerned about terrorism.

The minister said that two other ordinances, seeking to replace the ordinance on passport and the buy-back of shares would also come up for consideration during the session, which would have a total of 23 sittings.

The Bill seeking to replace the ordinance on passport would give the government, both the Centre and state, powers to suspend the passport or the travel documents of any citizen who it may suspect to be a terrorist. The ordinance signed by President K.R. Narayanan, came into force from October 23. It seeks to make amendments to the Indian Passport Act of 1967.

The ordinance on buy-back of shares was promulgated following a long-pending demand of the industry. It will enable companies to buy-back up to 10 percent of their equity every six months against the prevailing restriction of two years.

***

Document

CONGRESSIONAL RECORD -- EXTENSIONS

Tuesday, October 30, 2001
107th Congress, 1st Session
147 Cong Rec E 1960

REFERENCE: Vol. 147, No. 147
SECTION: Extension of Remarks
TITLE: SIKHS ASKED TO REMOVE TURBANS AT AIRPORT, TURBAN IS
RELIGIOUS SYMBOL AND MUST NOT BE REMOVED

HON. EDOLPHUS TOWNS
of New York
in the House of Representatives
Tuesday, October 30, 2001

Mr. TOWNS . Mr. Speaker, there have been more incidents in which
Sikh men were asked to remove their turbans at an airport. Dr. Gurmit
Singh Aulakh, President of the Council of Khalistan, has brought these to
my attention.

Satpal Singh Kohli was about to board a Southwest Airlines flight
from Albuquerque to Los Angeles when members of the ground crew
demanded that he remove his turban. He told the ground crew that his
Sikh religion required him to wear the turban and he could not remove
it. The ground crew insisted that he remove his turban. He needed to get
to Los Angeles to be with his ailing father. When the agents would not
budge, Mr. Kohli demanded to see their supervisor. He was told that if he
had a complaint, he should contact customer service.

The agents not only searched his turban in full view of other passengers, they searched his unshorn hair_required by his religion_as well. Mr.
Kohli said that "In my whole life I have never been humiliated like this."
The agents had only told him that they wanted to search his bag, not his
turban or hair. Yet they never checked his bag.

Last Saturday, Tejinder Singh Kahlon, a sitting judge in New York,
was asked to remove his turban at a New York airport. He refused. He
was not allowed to board his plane. He called the media to report his
harassment by the airport security personnel.

The turban is a symbol of the Sikh religion, to which Mr. Kohli and
Judge Kahlon belong. It is religiously mandated. They are required to
carry five symbols. Unshorn hair covered by a turban is one of these.
More than 99 percent of the people in this country who wear turbans are
Sikhs. Turbans should not be removed and searched.

Linda Rutherford, a spokeswoman for Southwest Airlines, admitted
that the incident had to do with "passenger profiling" and claimed that
the rules had to do either with what a passenger wears or what he looks
like, but she blamed the Federal Aviation Administration for these new
rules. If that is true, the FAA should be ashamed of themselves. They
have institutionalized racial profiling as a part of their antiterrorism
policy. If it is the airline's own policy, then decent Americans should
flood Southwest Airlines' headquarters with protests.

We must not allow racial, religious, or ethnic profiling. The airport
ground crews should be prohibited from stopping Sikh passengers and
searching their religiously-mandated turbans. This kind of discrimination
is never acceptable. I ask Attorney General Ashcroft and Secretary of

Transportation Mineta to look into this matter and stop this harassment of Sikh Americans immediately.

Mr. Speaker, I would like to place an India-West article on the Kohli incident into the Record for the information of my colleagues.

From India-West, Oct. 26, 2001
Sikh Asked to Hand Over Turban Before Boarding Plane
(By Viji Sundaram)

Satpal Singh Kohli was about to board a Southwest Airlines flight from Albuquerque, N.M., to Los Angeles Oct. 22, when ground crew at the security gate demanded that he hand over his turban to them before he enplaned. When Kohli protested, telling them that as a Sikh his religion forbade him from baring his head in public, the agents insisted that he do as he was told. Kohli said that they told him that he would have to fly minus his turban, which would be returned to him at the Los Angeles airport. Kohli said he told them that he had flown Southwest from Los Angeles to Albuquerque just two days earlier and "my turban wasn't an issue then." He also told them that he had to make that flight because his elderly father, who was home alone in Los Angeles, needed to be given medication and may even need to be hospitalized.

When Kohli realized he was getting nowhere with the agents, he asked to see their supervisor. He said he was told that if he had a complaint, he should call customer service, Kohli said in a e-mail he sent to India-West. The agents told him that if he wanted to make that flight, he would have to submit to a complete turban and hair search.

Because of his father's medical condition, Kohli said he reluctantly agreed, but requested that it be done in a private area, out of view of the other passengers. Kohli said the agents told him there was no private area and that the search would be done at the security area behind the counter.

He said an agent not only searched his turban thoroughly in full view of the other passengers and ground staff, she also searched his hair, before allowing him to board the plane.

"My sentiments were hurt," Kohli said. "In my whole life I have never been humiliated like this."

Kohli said that in pulling him over for a check, the agent had told him he needed to have his bag searched, not his turban or his hair. Yet, after searching his turban and hair, they waved him through, without checking his carry-on bag, according to Kohli, who works as a travel agent.

When he arrived in Los Angeles, Kohli said he went to Southwest's customer service center and told the two men there_the customer service supervisor and station manager_about what he had been put through. Both men, as well as the captain of the plane who happened to stop by, agreed that turban searches were not a part of the new security requirements, Kohli said. He said they apologized for what had happened.

Called for a comment, Linda Rutherford, a Southwest Airlines spokeswoman in its corporate headquarters in Dallas, Texas, told India-

West that following the Sept. 11 terrorist attacks on America, there has been some new Federal Aviation Administration-mandated procedures "regarding passenger profiling." She said she was not aware of the Kohli incident, but noted that "if a passenger had been flagged as a selectee, there would have been additional security checks." She said she was not sure if those additional checks are triggered by what a passenger wears or what he or she looks like.

"Certainly, it could be a bit awkward for passengers to have their personal belongings searched in front of other passengers," Rutherford acknowledged, adding: "It is certainly not our intent to embarrass our passengers." Manjit Singh, executive director of the Maryland-based Sikh Media Watch and Resource Task Force, told India-West that since the Sept. 11 attacks, his organization has received at least a dozen complaints similar to Kohli's. "We are very disturbed by what's happening," Singh said.

He said his group plans to meet with Norm Mineta, Secretary of Transportation, as well as with FAA officials to make them aware of what was happening. "A Sikh should never be forced to remove his turban," Singh said. "It's a religiously mandated headdress."

He said turban searches should only be done if the metal detector beeps. Security agents, he said, should first do an electronic check, then pat down the turban if they suspect something, and only as a last resort should they ask the passenger to remove his turban.

Since Sept. 11, Sikhs nationwide have become targets of hate crimes in the U.S., as people misidentify them as Taliban supporters because of their beards and turbans. A number of them have in recent weeks reportedly set aside their turbans and concealed their tresses under baseball caps.

***

Document

CONGRESSIONAL RECORD -- EXTENSIONS

Wednesday, October 17, 2001
107th Congress, 1st Session
147 Cong Rec E 1912

REFERENCE: Vol. 147, No. 140
SECTION: Extension of Remarks
TITLE: COUNCIL OF KHALISTAN HAS VERY SUCCESSFUL CONVENTION

HON. DAN BURTON
of Indiana
in the House of Representatives
Wednesday, October 17, 2001

Mr. BURTON of Indiana . Mr. Speaker, last weekend, October 6 and 7, the Council of Khalistan held its annual convention down in Atlanta. It was very successful. The organization laid out strategies for liberating the Sikh homeland, Khalistan, discussed the political situation there, worked on the concerns of Sikhs here in America, and passed several resolutions. I would like to take this opportunity to congratulate the Council of Khalistan on a successful convention.

Mr. Speaker, freeing Khalistan is an important effort to secure freedom for the Sikh people. America was founded on the principles of freedom and self-determination and these things are the birthright of all people. Yet the response of "democratic" India is to use force to suppress the natural yearning for freedom.

India is a land of massive human-rights violations. Secretary Powell is there now and we hope that he can maintain good relations with India and that no violence breaks out. But I also hope he will press the Indian government on its abysmal human-rights record and its record, until very recently, of anti-Americanism. It is holding over 52,000 Sikhs as political prisoners without charge or trial, according to a recent report by the Movement Against State Repression. Dr. Aulakh, the President of the Council of Khalistan, recently wrote to Secretary Powell urging him to seek the release of these political prisoners during his visit to India.

We should insist on full and active support for our anti-terrorist efforts. We should also insist that India begin to respect basic human rights. If they do not, we should maintain our sanctions on India and cut off its aid. And we should go on record for an end to the terrorism in South Asia by publicly supporting a free and fair plebiscite with international monitoring on the issue of freedom in Punjab, Khalistan, in Kashmir, in Christian Nagaland, and all the nations that seek their freedom. Only then can real security, freedom, and peace reign in South Asia.

Mr. Speaker, the Council of Khalistan has published a press release on its convention. I would like to place it in the Record.

Delegates Discuss Strategies to Liberate Khalistan, Pass Resolutions for Khalistan, Other Sikh Causes

Washington, DC, Oct. 9, 2001._The Council of Khalistan's annual international convention was held this past weekend in Atlanta, Georgia. It was very successful. A large number of delegates came from around the United States and Canada. The convention honored Khalistan Day, the anniversary of the declaration of independence by the Sikh homeland, Khalistan, which took place on October 7, 1987. The Council of Khalistan was constituted at that time to serve as the government pro tempore of Khalistan and lead its struggle for independence.

The convention mapped out strategy to bring about the liberation of Khalistan. There was much very inspired, energetic, and intelligent discussion of how to move the freedom struggle forward. Delegates also passed several resolutions, including resolutions demanding a free and fair plebiscite on independence in Khalistan and the other nations India occupies; demanding the release of Sikh and other political prisoners; to form a Khalsa Raj Party to liberate Khalistan; to let human-rights organizations into Punjab; condemning the attacks on Sikhs and other minorities since the September 11 terrorists acts at the World Trade Center and the Pentagon; condemning the attack on the United States; to raise money for the Washington office; to nominate Dr. Gurmit Singh Aulakh, President of the Council of Khalistan, for the Nobel Prize; naming Dr. Aulakh Khalistan Man of the Year; condemning Simranjit Singh Mann and Tarlochan Singh for their betrayal of the Sikh Nation and unwarranted attack on Dr. Aulakh; calling on Sikhs, Sikh leaders, and Gurdwaras to support the freedom struggle; and commending convention chairman Dr. Gulbarg Singh Basi and his wife, Rup Kaur Basi, for their hard work to make the convention successful. They decided that next year's convention will be held on Columbus Day weekend 2002 in Philadelphia.

Dr. Aulakh thanked all the delegates who came to the convention. "I am very impressed with the turnout," he said. "We have many people who took time out of their busy schedules to come here. They gave this weekend to the cause of Sikh freedom," he said. "Their efforts are noticed and appreciated."

"These are true Sikhs," Dr. Aulakh added. "The Sikh leadership in Punjab would do well to emulate the people at this convention. Remember In grieb Sikhin ko deon Patshahi' and Raj Kare Ga Khalsa,'" Dr. Aulakh said. "As Professor Darshan Singh said, If a Sikh is not a Khalistani, he is not a Sikh.' We must keep this in mind when we deal with corrupt leaders such as Badal, Tohra, Chohan, and others."

"This convention has been a significant step forward in the effort to reclaim the Sikh Nation's lost sovereignty," said Dr. Aulakh. "Only then will Sikhs live in freedom, dignity, peace, and prosperity," he said. "Everyone who came to this convention should be saluted for making the effort," he said. "I would like to thank the Atlanta Gurdwara for their input and their hospitality. Special thanks go to Dr. and Mrs. Basi for organizing the convention."

***

Document

CONGRESSIONAL RECORD -- EXTENSIONS

Tuesday, October 16, 2001
107th Congress, 1st Session
147 Cong Rec E 1901

REFERENCE: Vol. 147, No. 139
SECTION: Extension of Remarks
TITLE: INDIA FIRING ON KASHMIR OPPORTUNITY TO BRING
FREEDOM TO SOUTH ASIA

HON. EDOLPHUS TOWNS
of New York
in the House of Representatives
Tuesday, October 16, 2001

Mr. TOWNS . Mr. Speaker, last year when former President Clinton
visited India, 35 Sikhs were massacred in the village of Chithisinghpora.
Two independent investigations have shown that the Indian government
carried out this massacre. Now Secretary of State Powell is visiting India
and Indian troops are firing on Kashmir. I can't help but wonder why the
sudden outbreak. It seems odd these incidents occur when American
officials visit the country.

Mr. Speaker, this could be an opportunity for the people and nations
seeking freedom in South Asia. The Council of Khalistan has put out an
open letter saying that now is the ideal time for the people of Kashmir,
Khalistan, Nagaland, and the other minority nations of South Asia to
claim their freedom.

Clearly, India is taking advantage of the U.S. war on terrorism to advance its own hegemonic agenda. The fact that Sikhs, Kashmiri Muslims,
and other minorities are going to be casualties of this strategy is apparently of no importance to them. It's just another opportunity to take
down their enemy, Pakistan, which has been an active supporter and
participant in the U.S. antiterrorist coalition.

America was founded on the idea of freedom. It is that freedom that
the terrorists are trying to destroy. One of the best ways to fight the
terrorists is to help spread freedom to new corners of the world.

Mr. Speaker, the time has come to cut off U.S. aid to India in light of
its human-rights abuses and its opportunistic use of the antiterrorist
effort to promote its narrow interest. It is also time to put the U.S.
Congress on record in support of the freedom movements around South
Asia in the form of a free and fair plebiscite on their political status.
These measures will help spread freedom and undermine the efforts of
the terrorists to destroy our principles.

Mr. Speaker, I would like to place the Council of Khalistan's open
letter on the Indian attack on Kashmir into the Record for the information of my colleagues.

Indian Attack on Kashmir Provides Opportunity for Freedom; India Is Not One Nation

*Taking advantage of the U.S. war on terrorism to advance its own
agenda, India has begun shelling Azad (Free) Kashmir. This action
brings the war over Kashmir out into the open just as Secretary of State
Colin Powell is arriving in South Asia. Unfortunately, there will undoubt-*

edly be casualties, and most of them will be Kashmiris, Sikhs, and other minorities. The only party that benefits from this is the Indian government, which has murdered over 250,000 Sikhs since 1984, over 200,000 Christians in Nagaland since 1947, more than 75,000 Kashmiri Muslims since 1988, and tens of thousands of Dalits (dark-skinned "Untouchables," the aboriginal people of South Asia), Tamils, Bodos, Assamese, Manipuris, and others.

This act by India shows who America's real allies are, and which country is the real supporter of terrorism. Once again, India is claiming that it is going after terrorism, despite India's own record of terrorism.

In November 1994, the Indian newspaper Hitavada reported that the Indian government paid the late governor of Punjab, Surendra Nath, approximately $1.5 billion to organize and support covert state terrorism in Punjab Khalistan, and in Kashmir. The book Soft Target, written by journalists from the Toronto Star and the Toronto Globe and Mail, shows that the Indian government blew up its own airliner in 1985, killing 329 innocent people. According to India Today, the Indian government created the Liberation Tigers of Tamil Eelam (LTTE) and put up LTTE leaders in New Delhi's finest hotel. The LTTE were created to stop a U.S. broadcast tower in Sri Lanka. Then the Indian government turned on the LTTE because the LTTE seeks an independent country for Tamils.

The Indian government sentenced Devinder Singh Bhullar to death because he advocated Khalistan, yet Ribeiro, Ray, K.P.S. Gill, Swaran Singh Ghotna, and the other police and political officials who committed genocide against the Sikhs are not punished. In June a train carrying Sikh religious pilgrims was attacked by militant Hindu fundamentalists. On May 27, several Indian soldiers were caught red-handed trying to set fire to a Gurdwara and some Sikh homes in Kashmir. Sikh and Muslim residents of the village overwhelmed the troops and stopped them from carrying out this atrocity.

A report issued in April by the Movement Against State Repression (MASR) shows that India admitted that it held 52,268 political prisoners under the repressive "Terrorist and Disruptive Activities Act" (TADA). These Sikh political prisoners must be released immediately. These prisoners continue to be held under TADA even though it expired in 1995. Persons arrested under TADA are routinely re-arrested upon their release. Cases were routinely registered against Sikh activists under TADA in states other than Punjab to give the police an excuse to continue holding them. The MASR report quotes the Punjab Civil Magistracy as writing "if we add up the figures of the last few years the number of innocent persons killed would run into lakhs hundreds of thousands. " As General Narinder Singh has said, "Punjab is a police state." U.S. Congressman Dana Rohrabacher has said that for minorities like the Sikhs, the Muslims of Kashmir, and others, "India might as well be Nazi Germany."

It is not just Sikhs who are being targeted by Indian terrorism. In 1997, a Christian religious festival was broken up by police gunfire. Since Christmas 1998, Christians have been subjected to a reign of terror which has seen the murder of priests, the rape of nuns, the burning of churches, attacks on Christian schools and prayer halls, and other incidents carried out by supporters of the pro-Fascist Rashtriya Swayamsewak Sangh (RSS), the parent organization of the ruling BJP, which was formed in support of the Nazis. RSS activists also burned missionary Graham Staines and his two young sons, ages 8 and 10, to death while they slept in their jeeps. The killers gathered around the jeep chanting "Victory to Hannuman," a Hindu god. Prime Minister Atal Behari Vajpayee told an audience in New York last year, "I will always be a Swayamsewak."

India is also anti-American. According to the May 18, 1999 issue of the Indian Express, the Indian Defense Minister met with the Ambassadors from terrorist countries Iraq, Libya, and Cuba, as well as Red China, Russia, and Serbia, to set up a security alliance "to stop the U.S." India voted with the dictatorships to throw the United States off the UN Human Rights Commission. It votes against America at the United Nations more often than any country except Cuba. It voted to suppress a U.S.-sponsored resolution critical of China's human-rights violations. It was a strong Soviet ally.

This is an ideal opportunity to begin a Shantmai Morcha and form a Khalsa Raj party to achieve independence for Khalistan and to liberate the other countries seeking their freedom from Indian occupation. Remember the words of former Akal Takht Jathedar Professor Darshan Singh: "If a Sikh is not Khalistani, he is not a Sikh." Self-determination is the right of all people and nations.

Pro-Khalistan handbills were handed out at the Golden Temple on June 7 during the commemoration of Gallughara Divas and Sant Bhindranwale's martyrdom. Ajmer Singh Lakhowal, the head of the Bharat Kisan Union, has called for self-determination for the Sikhs. The flame of freedom bums bright in the hearts of the Sikhs.

When we liberate Khalistan, we will be more respected, appreciated, and understood by Americans and throughout the world. We must take this occasion to renew our commitment to free Khalistan. Every Sikh should put a bumper sticker on his or her car saying "INDIA FREE KHALISTAN." This sticker is available from this office

In 1947, when India was divided, the cunning and deceitful Hindu leadership promised that Sikhs would have the glow of freedom in Punjab and that no law affecting Sikh rights would be passed without Sikh consent. As soon as the transfer of power had occurred and India was free, those promises were broken. Instead, India began its effort to wipe out the Sikh people, the Sikh Nation, and the Sikh religion.

Sikhs gave over 80 percent of the sacrifices to free India from the British. At that time, they were only 1.6 percent of the population. Sikhs are the ones who suffered the most after the freedom and partition of India. Fifty percent of the Sikh population had to migrate from the Pakistan side of Punjab to the Indian side of Punjab. Sikhs were prosperous farmers in West Punjab. They lost their fertile farming land. When they were allotted lands in Indian Punjab, everyone got a cut between 25 and 95 percent of their acreage.

In a free Khalistan, there will be economic prosperity. The Punjab farmers will be able to sell their produce at high prices in the international market and buy cheaper fertilizers, insecticides, and seeds. Farm produce will not lie in the market for weeks without buyers as it did during the sale of the rice crop last year.

We must have a full, free, and fair plebiscite on the status of Khalistan and we must launch a Shantmai Morcha to liberate our homeland. India is not one nation. It has 18 official languages. Let us take this opportunity to bring freedom to our homeland and all the countries of South Asia.

***

Document

CONGRESSIONAL RECORD -- EXTENSIONS

Wednesday, October 03, 2001
107th Congress, 1st Session
147 Cong Rec E 1790

REFERENCE: Vol. 147, No. 131
SECTION: Extension of Remarks
TITLE: ATTACKS ON SIKHS SUBSIDING_STILL UNDER SIEGE IN INDIA

HON. EDOLPHUS TOWNS
of New York
in the House of Representatives
Wednesday, October 3, 2001

Mr. TOWNS . Mr. Speaker, I am glad that the attacks on Sikhs and other Americans in the wake of the September 11 attacks have subsided. While there are still some incidents, Sikhs, Muslims, and other Americans are safer now then they were a week or two ago. That is good news.

However, Sikhs continue to be under assault in India. The Indian government holds over 52,000 Sikhs as political prisoners. It has murdered over 250,000 Sikhs since 1984. A few months ago, Indian troops were caught red-handed trying to set fire to a Gurdwara (a Sikh Temple), but Sikh and Muslim villagers prevented them from carrying out this atrocity.

This is part of a long pattern of violation of the rights of Sikhs and other minorities by the Indian government. The attacks on Sikhs in America, which are terribly unfortunate and should be condemned by all, have been incidents carried out by individuals. That is a key difference. Much of the problem is that since the Sikhs don't have their own country, Americans and others don't know who they are. This is one more reason why a free Khalistan is essential.

Khalistan is the Sikh homeland which declared its independence from India on October 7, 1987. This week marks Khalistan's independence anniversary. It will also see the annual convention of the Council of Khalistan, the government pro tempore of Khalistan which leads its independence struggle.

Given India's apparent reluctance to cooperate with the United States in our war on terrorism, American support for a free Khalistan and for freedom for the Kashmiris, for predominantly Christian Nagaland, and for all the other nations seeking their freedom is more urgent than ever. We must do what we can to extend the glow of freedom all over the world. We can help that along by maintaining our sanctions on India, by cutting off our aid to India until human rights are respected, and by supporting an internationally-supervised plebiscite on the question of independence for all the nations of South Asia. Our war on terrorism is about preserving freedom. Let's not forget that freedom is universal.

***

Document

CONGRESSIONAL RECORD -- EXTENSIONS

Tuesday, October 02, 2001
107th Congress, 1st Session
147 Cong Rec E 1766

REFERENCE: Vol. 147, No. 130
SECTION: Extension of Remarks
TITLE: VIOLENCE AGAINST SIKHS EXPOSED_ATTACKS MUST STOP

HON. DAN BURTON
of Indiana
in the House of Representatives
Tuesday, October 2, 2001

Mr. BURTON of Indiana . Mr. Speaker, I spoke previously about the violence against Sikh Americans in the wake of the attacks on the World Trade Center and the Pentagon. I have said previously that these attacks must stop. Now efforts are underway to expose them through the media and to collect information to catalogue these incidents. I applaud those efforts.

Last weekend, a Sikh gasoline station owner in Mesa, Arizona, Balbir Singh Sodhi was shot to death at his gas station by someone, who apparently thought the gas station owner was a supporter of Osama bin Laden because of his turban and beard. It should be noted that 99.9 percent of the people who wear turbans and beards in this country are Sikhs.

Mr. Speaker, this kind of crime must be condemned. The Sodhi killing was just one of over one hundred incidents of harassment or violence against Sikhs. All of these crimes are catalogued on the internet at http://www.sikh.org/hatecrime for the information of the public.

This past Tuesday, September 18, the Council of Khalistan held a press conference to expose the violence against Sikh Americans. They called for an investigation by Attorney General Ashcroft. One of the Sikhs, who created the website I mentioned above, Amardeep Singh Bhalla, was there to announce it. The news conference was attended by reporters from IBN Radio, News Channel 8, and a Chicago TV station, WMAQ. News Channel 8 broadcast it in the evening of the 18th and IBN Radio broadcast it on the 19th.

The Council of Khalistan has put out a press release about the press conference. I would like to place this in the Record at this time for the information of my colleagues.

Dr. Aulakh, Sikh Leaders Condemn Murders of Sikhs and Others Sikhs Are Not Moslems - Ask Attorney General to Investigate

Washington, D.C., Sept. 18, 2001._Dr. Gurmit Singh Aulakh, President of the Council of Khalistan, today condemned the murders of Sikhs and other Americans in the wake of the World Trade Center attack. Dr. Aulakh an other Sikh leaders spoke at the National Press Club. The press conference was attended by reporters from NewsChannel 8, NBC, the Japanese newspaper Sankei Shimbun, India Globe, and others.

"I call on Attorney General John Ashcroft to look into this nationwide pattern of violence and I urge the victims these attacks to call their police departments and their local prosecutors," Dr. Aulakh said. "This is the best way I ensure that those who perpetrate this violence are appropriately punished."

"I condemn the violence against Muslim Americans and I condemn the attacks on Sikh Americans," Dr. Aulakh said. There have been over 100 acts of harassment or violence against Sikhs. Since the World Trade Center and Pentagon bombings on Tuesday, there has been a wave of violent incidents aimed at Sikhs and other individuals. Over the weekend, a Sikh gasoline station owner was murdered at his business in Mesa, Arizona. The Granthi of the Sri Guru Singh Sabha Gurdwara in Fairfax, Virginia was attacked while walking with his wife. Attackers threw a brick through the window of a local Sikh, Ranjit Singh of Fairfax, Virginia. They were in attendance at the press conference.

Another local Sikh, Sher Singh, was arrested by police in Rhode Island after the attack, but was released the next day. A couple of young Sikhs were attacked in Brooklyn, New York. Sikh businesses have been stoned and cars have been burned. An Egyptian Christian man was shot in San Gabriel, California. A Pakistani Muslim who owned a grocery store was shot in Dallas.

"Sikh Americans, Muslim Americans, Christian Americans, our neighbors and countrymen, are being harassed and acts of violence are being committed against them merely because of their religious or ethnic heritage," Dr. Aulakh said. "All Americans should join together to condemn these cowardly acts."

"What a group of terrorists did Tuesday was a terrible crime and an act of war against America, but it was done by group of individuals who

are no more typical of their religion than Timothy McVeigh is typical of Christianity," said Dr. Aulakh. "Members of minority religious communities are being targeted for violence, and this is unacceptable especially in America."

"Sikhism is an independent, divinely revealed, monotheistic religion with our own symbols and has no relation to other religions like Islam, Hinduism, Judaism, or Christianity, but we respect all religions" Dr. Aulakh said. He noted that Sikhism has its own symbols. "Among those symbols are a turban and beard. That does not make us supporters or associates of Osama bin Laden, yet we are being targeted for violence in the wake of the atrocities last Tuesday." I said.

Two young Sikh activists announced the creation of a website for information about hate crimes against Sikhs. It c 7Ean be found at http://www.sikh.org/hatecrime. They noted that "99.9 percent" of the people who wear turbans in America, are Sikhs.

"Let's not let America descend to the level of those who attacked it," Dr. Aulakh said.

***

Document

CONGRESSIONAL RECORD -- EXTENSIONS

Tuesday, October 02, 2001
107th Congress, 1st Session
147 Cong Rec E 1780

REFERENCE: Vol. 147, No. 130
SECTION: Extension of Remarks
TITLE: INDIAN GOVERNMENT BARS VIEWING OF BURNING PUNJAB

HON. DAN BURTON
of Indiana
in the House of Representatives
Tuesday, October 2, 2001

Mr. BURTON of Indiana . Mr. Speaker, for quite a while, people interested in South Asian issues have had a valuable resource in the website Burning Punjab, located at http://www.burningpunjab.com. This website has reported many stories about the Indian government's tyranny against Sikhs and other minorities. Now the Indian government has banned the viewing of Burning Punjab in the northwest part of India, where Punjab, the Sikh homeland, is. Punjab, of course, declared its independence on October 7, 1987, calling itself Khalistan. The website has been blocked in Punjab and in the state of Haryana, which has a substantial Sikh population, and Delhi.

Suppressing information is not the way that democratic countries do things. This ban shows that India is a deficient democracy. It has about as much freedom of the press as Communist China. Burning Punjab was founded on September 15, 1997. On March 29, 2000, the site's founder, Sukhbir Singh Osan, was reportedly threatened with murder, apparently by the Indian government. Are these the acts of a democracy?

The massive human-rights violations of the Indian government have been well documented. Over 250,000 Sikhs, more than 200,000 Christians, over 75,000 Kashmiri Muslims, and tens of thousands of Dalits and other minorities have been killed by the government. It holds over 52,000 Sikhs and tens of thousands of others as political prisoners with no charges and no trial. Some have been in custody for 17 years. There have been rapes of nuns, murders of priests, the burning death of a Christian missionary, attacks on Christian prayer halls, schools, and churches, on mosques, on the Golden Temple. A group of Indian soldiers were caught trying to burn down a Gurdwara (a Sikh Temple) but were stopped by villagers.

Why does a country like that receive U.S. aid? Do we support them so they can suppress the information their citizens need? Do we support them so they can maintain bloody repression against the minorities within their borders? We should stop all aid to India until basic human rights like the free flow of information are allowed for all citizens. Furthermore, we should put this Congress on record in support of self-determination for the people of Khalistan, Kashmir, Nagaland, and the 14 other countries seeking their freedom from India. This should take the form of an internationally-monitored, free and fair plebiscite on the question of independence. That is the democratic way and the way of major world powers. We owe it to the principles that gave birth to America to take these measures to promote the principles of freedom in South Asia and around the world.

Mr. Speaker, I would like to place the article on the banning of Burning Punjab into the Record at this time.

From Burning Punjab News, Sept. 23, 2001
Viewing Web Site "Burning Punjab" Banned in North India

New Delhi._The Indian Intelligence Agencies have banned the viewing of World Wide Web site Burning Punjab' (www.burningpunjab.com). The site was not accessible in Punjab, Haryana and Delhi for the past four days. It is reliably learnt that the Research Analysis Wing (RAW) of the Indian Hindu Regime ordered ban. The Burning Punjab' has now decided to change its IP identity and servers.

Here it is pertinent to mention that web site Burning Punjab' was launched on September 15, 1997 by a Chandigarh based journalist and lawyer, Sukhbir Singh Osan. The staff and manager of the site were threatened number of time by the Indian Police. On 29 March 2000, France based organization Reporters sans Frontier's (RSF) also objected to various restrictions imposed by the Indian Government on the staff and manager of the web site Burning Punjab' RSF General Secretary Robert Menard issued a letter to the Indian authorities opposing unwarranted censorship'.

It's worth mentioning that Burning Punjab' www.burningpunjab.com is an endeavor of IHRF. International Human Rights Forum (IHRF) is engaged in propagating the cause of Human Rights worldwide. Organization is taking special care for the welfare of state victims and is lending a helping hand to hapless and helpless to mitigate their sufferings. The activities of the IHRF have been appreciated by one and all irrespective of politico-religious affiliations. During the cult of violence in Punjab, Kashmir, Delhi, Assam, Bengal and elsewhere, the IHRF played a significant role in exposing inhuman & barbaric treatment and excesses committed by the State against the innocent & law abiding citizens.

About web site Burning Punjab: Burning Punjab is Punjab's first ever media site on Sikh Holocaust. It deals with the situation in East Punjab. Site contains news & views, political scenario, human rights values and holocaust of Sikhs. Sukhbir Singh Osan has created site. S.S.Osan is a Law Graduate from Punjab University, Chandigarh. He is a prolific writer and a born journalist. The International Human Rights Forum is operating this site.

***

Document

CONGRESSIONAL RECORD -- EXTENSIONS

Monday, September 24, 2001
107th Congress, 1st Session
147 Cong Rec E 1711

REFERENCE: Vol. 147, No. 125
SECTION: Extension of Remarks
TITLE: STOP THE VIOLENCE AGAINST SIKHS

HON. EDOLPHUS TOWNS
of New York
in the House of Representatives
Monday, September 24, 2001

Mr. TOWNS . Mr. Speaker, I was distressed to hear that on Saturday, September 15, a Sikh named Balbir Singh Sodhi, who owned a gas station in Mesa, Arizona, was murdered at his place of business. It appears that he was killed because of his turban and beard, which are required by the Sikh religion. Apparently, his killer thought that Mr. Sodhi was a follower of Osama bin Laden.

This was just one of well over 100 acts of harassment or violence against Sikhs in the week since the terrorist bombings of the Pentagon and the World Trade Center. A list of these acts can be found by visiting http://www.sikh.org/hatecrime.

This past Tuesday, just one week after the terrorists carried out their brutal acts, the Council of Khalistan held a press conference at the National Press Club to denounce these crimes against Sikhs and other minorities. Dr. Gurmit Singh Aulakh, the President of the Council of Khalistan, made some excellent remarks. He called on the Attorney General to investigate and called on the victims of these crimes to contact their local prosecutors and police. At this time, I would like to insert Dr. Aulakh's remarks into the Record so that we can all have a better understanding of this problem.

Remarks of Dr. Gurmit Singh Aulakh

Ladies and Gentlemen of the Media: Thank you for coming today. I want to talk to you about a very important issue. Then I will be open-for questions. Sikh Americans, Muslim Americans, Christian Americans, our neighbors and countrymen, are being harassed and acts of violence are being committed against them merely because of their religious or ethnic heritage. All Americans should join together to condemn these cowardly acts.

On behalf of the 2 1_million strong Sikh Nation and more than 500,000 Sikhs in the United States, I strongly condemn these acts of violence. I condemn the violence against Muslim Americans and I condemn the attacks on Sikh Americans. There have been over 100 acts of harassment or violence against Sikhs. A Sikh man was murdered in Mesa, Arizona, a suburb of Phoenix, over the weekend. Balbir Singh Sodhi, who owned a Chevron gasoline station, was shot to death at his business. Some time later, the same gunman shot a Lebanese gasoline station owner. We demand that the man who killed Balbir Singh Sodhi. be prosecuted and punished to the fullest extent of the law.

Attackers threw a brick through the window of a local Sikh, Ranjit Singh of Fairfax, Virginia. Another local Sikh, Sher Singh, was arrested by police in Rhode Island after the attack, but was released the next day. A couple of young Sikhs were attacked in Brooklyn, New York. Sikh businesses have been stoned and cars have been burned. An Egyptian Christian man was shot in San Gabriel, California. A Pakistani Muslim who owned a grocery store was shot in Dallas.

What a group of terrorists did Tuesday was a terrible crime and an act of war against America, but it was done by a group of individuals who are no more typical of their religion than Timothy McVeigh is typical of Christianity. Members of minority religious communities are being targeted for violence, and this is unacceptable, especially in America.

Sikhs are not Muslims. We are not Hindus. Like Hinduism, Christianity, Islam, and any other religion, we are an independent, monotheistic religion with our own symbols. Among those are a turban and beard. That does not make us followers or associates of Osama bin Laden, yet we are being targeted for violence in the wake of the atrocities last Tuesday.

We appreciate the support of Congressmen Dan Burton, Edolphus Towns, and all our other friends in the Congress who condemned the acts of violence against the Sikhs and other minorities. Their statements in the Congressional Record are available here.

I call on Attorney General John Ashcroft to look into this nationwide pattern of violence and I urge the victims of these attacks to call their police departments and their local prosecutors. This is the best way to ensure that those who perpetrate this violence are appropriately punished. Let's not let America descend to the level of those who attacked it.

***

Document

CONGRESSIONAL RECORD -- EXTENSIONS

Thursday, September 20, 2001
107th Congress, 1st Session
147 Cong Rec E 1679

REFERENCE: Vol. 147, No. 123
SECTION: Extension of Remarks
TITLE: SIKHS CONDEMN ATTACK ON UNITED STATES

HON. CYNTHIA A. McKINNEY
of Georgia
in the House of Representatives
Thursday, September 20, 2001

Ms. McKINNEY . Mr. Speaker, the Council of Khalistan has written a letter to President Bush condemning Tuesday's brutal terrorist attack on the United States. This terrible attack is an act of war against all Americans and the freedom-loving people of all the world. The Council has also issued an excellent press release on the matter.

In the letter, the Council's President, Dr. Gurmit Singh Aulakh, writes, "On behalf of the 21-million strong Sikh Nation and especially on behalf of more than 500,000 Sikh Americans, I would like to express our sadness and our sympathies to the people of the United States for the terrible attack on the United States yesterday and for the loss of life it entails."

Mr. Speaker, I would like to place this letter to President Bush and the Council of Khalistan's press release on the bombing into the Record.

Council of Khalistan,
Washington, DC
September 12, 2001.
Hon. George W. Bush
President of the United States,
The White House,
Washington, DC.

Dear Mr. President, On behalf of the 21-million strong Sikh Nation and especially on behalf of more than 500,000 Sikh Americans, I would like to express our sadness and our sympathies to the people of the United States for the terrible attack on the United States yesterday and for the loss of life it entails. This is a terrible tragedy and we know that you will take appropriate action. Like all Americans and all decent people everywhere, we condemn this brutal senseless attack.

The Sikh religion recognizes all humanity as our brothers and we pray for the well- being of all. Our prayers and our sympathies are with the people of the United States at this tragic time. We especially pray for the families of those who have departed. May God bring peace to these departed souls and to their families.

We support you and we pray for the people of America. God bless you and God bless America.

Sincerely,

> *Dr. Gurmit Singh Aulakh*
> *President, Council of Khalistan.*

- - - - - - - - -

Council of Khalistan Condemns Attack on United States
Urges Sikhs to Give Blood

WASHINGTON, DC._September 12, 2001_Dr. Gurmit Singh Aulakh, President of the Council of Khalistan, today condemned the brutal attack on the United States that occurred yesterday.

"On behalf of the 21-million strong Sikh Nation and especially on behalf of more than 500,000 Sikh Americans, I would like to express our sadness and our sympathies to the people of the United States for the terrible attack on the United States yesterday and for the loss of life it entails," Dr. Aulakh said.

"I urge Sikh Americans to give blood and to pray for the victims, for their families, and for all those who are helping our country and our communities in this time of need," Dr. Aulakh said. "We must do our part as American citizens," he said. "We stand together as a nation."

"Like all Americans and all decent people everywhere, we condemn this brutal and senseless attack. The Sikh religion recognizes all the human race as one and we pray for the well-being of all. Our prayers and our sympathies are with the people of the United States at this tragic time. We especially pray for the families of those who have departed."

"This tragic event happened in the most diverse city in the world," Dr. Aulakh said. "There is hardly a national or ethnic group that has not been touched directly by this tragedy. Our sympathies are extended to those who have been touched personally," he said. "Violence against innocent people of any religion or ethnicity is unacceptable. It must be ended."

Unfortunately, some people have engaged in violence against Sikhs in the wake of the bombings yesterday. A couple of young Sikhs were attacked in Brooklyn. Sikh businesses have been stoned and cars have been burned. A Sikh boy was even shot in New York.

"Today we all stand together as Americans, regardless of race, religion, or ethnicity," he said. "We must not accept terrorism. We must unite against this evil," he said. "We must work to bring all Americans together to defeat this brutal enemy."

***

Document

CONGRESSIONAL RECORD -- EXTENSIONS

Thursday, September 13, 2001
107th Congress, 1st Session
147 Cong Rec E 1641

REFERENCE: Vol. 147, No. 119
SECTION: Extension of Remarks
TITLE: INDISCRIMINATE ATTACKS ON SIKHS MUST STOP; SIKHISM IS VERY DIFFERENT FROM ISLAM

HON. DAN BURTON
of Indiana
in the House of Representatives
Thursday, September 13, 2001

Mr. BURTON of Indiana . Mr. Speaker, on Tuesday, a despicable terrorist attack was carried out on the United States of America. I am pleased to see how all of us, Republican and Democrat, liberal and conservative, are pulling together in support of our nation. That is inspiring and it shows the greatness of America.

At the same time, it is very unfortunate that some Americans have been made targets of violence simply because of the way they look and the way they dress. That is unacceptable. Despite the anger that we all share against those responsible for the terrorists attacks, we must not sink to their level and become a people who extract revenge indiscriminately.

It appears that there have been several attacks on Sikhs, largely in the New York area but elsewhere as well, including a beating of an elderly Sikh man with baseball bats. Apparently, some Sikhs are being singled out for attacks because their turbans and beards remind people of the terrorist chief Osama bin Laden. Other Sikhs are being mistaken for Muslims.

Attacking innocent American Muslims is wrong, and we should stand together in condemning attacks on them. However, it must be emphasized that Sikhs are not Muslims. Sikhism must not be mistaken for Islam, Hinduism, or any other religion. Every Sikh is required to wear a turban; it is part of the religion. Very few Muslims wear turbans. Osama bin Laden is one of the few Muslims who does. The style in which a turban is worn by a Sikh is quite different from the style that is worn by some Muslims. In addition, Sikhs can be identified by the kirpans (small ceremonial swords) that they carry and the bracelets they wear. These are two of the five things that identify a practicing Sikh. Tragically, some people, who are ignorant of Islam and Sikhism, have targeted innocent Sikh-Americans for violence. It must be made clear that Sikhs do not hold any ill will toward America. Sikhs from around the world have always looked toward the United States as a beacon of freedom to be emulated, not a nation to be destroyed.

Mr. Speaker, attacks against Sikhs must stop. I am calling for an end to this violence against Sikh Americans and anyone else of any faith who was not involved in the terrorist attack on our country. I call on our nation's leaders to speak our forcefully against these attacks. I also believe that it is the responsibility of the media to expose these attacks and denounce them. All Americans are justified in being very angry about what happened on September 11, but that does not justify acts of violence against innocent Americans.

***

Document

CONGRESSIONAL RECORD -- EXTENSIONS

Thursday, September 13, 2001
107th Congress, 1st Session
147 Cong Rec E 1644

REFERENCE: Vol. 147, No. 119
SECTION: Extension of Remarks
TITLE: SIKHS ARE NOT MUSLIMS

HON. EDOLPHUS TOWNS
of New York
in the House of Representatives
Thursday, September 13, 2001

Mr. TOWNS . Mr. Speaker, in general I have been proud of America's response to the attack on our country that took place Tuesday. There have been no threats against the embassies of countries that might be involved. There have been no riots while the police have been concentrated in one particular area. However, there is one disturbing element. A number of Sikhs have been attacked by ignorant people seeking to vent their anger at what happened. In New York, an old Sikh man was beaten with baseball bats. A couple of young Sikhs were attacked Wednesday afternoon in Brooklyn. Sikh businesses have been stoned and cars have been burned. Apparently, these Sikhs were targeted because of their turbans and beards, which are required by their religion.

It would be grossly unfair to attack Muslims, even though Mr. bin Laden, who appears to be the prime suspect, claims to be an adherent of the Muslim faith. I know many Muslims and they are good people who are not involved in this kind of activity in any way. Yet what makes these attacks even stranger is that Sikhs are not Muslims. They don't even wear a turban the same way. Sikhism is an independent religion. It is not part of Islam; it is not part of Hinduism. Sikhs are identified by five specific markers: uncut hair covered by a turban, a kirpan, or ceremonial sword, a bracelet, special underwear, and a special comb. These are distinct identifiers and are required by the Sikh religion.

I call on the media to report on the attacks on Sikhs and note the fact that they are not connected to the terrorist campaign in any way and have, in fact, condemned it. I urge the media to speak out against the attacks, and I urge President Bush to do the same. Let's not attack anyone for his or her religion or the way he or she looks. Those who do so are cut from the same cloth as Mr. bin Laden. In America, we do not accept that.

The Council of Khalistan, which is the organization representing Sikhs, has written a letter to the President and a press release strongly condemning the attack Tuesday. I would like to place them in the Record at this time for the information of my colleagues.

Council of Khalistan Condemns Attack on United States Urges Sikhs to Give Blood

Washington, D.C., September 12, 2001._Dr. Gurmit Singh Aulakh, President of the Council of Khalistan, today condemned the brutal attack on the United States that occurred yesterday.

"On behalf of the 21-million strong Sikh Nation and especially on behalf of more than 500,000 Sikh Americans, I would like to express our sadness and our sympathies to the people of the United States for the terrible attack on the United States yesterday and for the loss of life it entails," Dr. Aulakh said.

"I urge Sikh Americans to give blood and to pray for the victims, for their families, and for all those who are helping our country and our communities in this time of need," Dr. Aulakh said. "We must do our part as American citizens," he said. "We stand together as a nation."

"Like all Americans and all decent people everywhere, we condemn this brutal and senseless attack. The Sikh religion recognizes all the human race as one and we pray for the well-being of all. Our prayers and our sympathies are with the people of the United States at this tragic time. We especially pray for the families of those who have departed."

"This tragic event happened in the most diverse city in the world," Dr. Aulakh said. "There is hardly a national or ethnic group that has not been touched directly by this tragedy. Our sympathies are extended to those who have been touched personally," he said. "Violence against innocent people of any religion or ethnicity is unacceptable. It must be ended."

Unfortunately, some people have engaged in violence against Sikhs in the wake of the bombings yesterday. A couple of young Sikhs were attacked in Brooklyn. Sikh businesses have been stoned and cars have been burned. A Sikh boy was even shot in New York.

"Today we all stand together as Americans, regardless of race, religion, or ethnicity," he said. "We must not accept terrorism. We must unite against this evil," he said. "We must work to bring all Americans together to defeat this brutal enemy."

- - - - - - - - -

Council of Khalistan,
Washington, DC
September 12, 2001.
Hon. George W. Bush,
President of the United States
The White House
Washington, DC.

Dear Mr. President: On behalf of the 21-million strong Sikh Nation and especially on behalf of more than 500,000 Sikh Americans, I would like to express our sadness and our sympathies to the people of the United States for the terrible attack on the United States yesterday and for the loss of life it entails. This is a terrible tragedy and we know that you will take appropriate action. Like all Americans and all decent people everywhere, we condemn this brutal and senseless attack.

The Sikh religion recognizes all humanity as our brothers and we pray for the well-being of all. Our prayers and our sympathies are with the people of the United States at this tragic time. We especially pray for the families of those who have departed. May God bring peace to these departed souls and to their families.

We support you and we pray for the people of America. God bless you and God bless America.

Sincerely,
Dr. Gurmit Singh Aulakh,
President, Council of Khalistan.

***

Document

CONGRESSIONAL RECORD -- EXTENSIONS

Thursday, September 13, 2001
107th Congress, 1st Session
147 Cong Rec E 1646

REFERENCE: Vol. 147, No. 119
SECTION: Extension of Remarks
TITLE: INDIAN RACISM

HON. EDOLPHUS TOWNS
of New York
in the House of Representatives
Thursday, September 13, 2001

Mr. TOWNS . Mr. Speaker, last week I made a statement on the excellent discussion of India's racist caste system at the World Conference on Racism in Durban. At that time I intended to place three articles in the Record: an article from the National Post, a press release from the Council of Khalistan, and an article from the Information Times. Unfortunately, only the article from the National Post made it into the Record. Therefore, I would like to place the other two articles in the Record at this time for the information of my colleagues.

Council of Khalistan, Press Release
India Practices Worst Racism in the World
Laws Are On the Books Only; Human Rights Are Ignored - Self-Determination and Equality Are the Most Basic Human Rights

Washington, D.C., September 4, 2001_Dr. Gurmit Singh Aulakh, President of the Council of Khalistan, today praised the Dalit and Kashmiri activists who have brought the issue of India's human-rights violations to bear in Durban, site of the World Conference Against Racism. The Council of Khalistan, the government pro tempore of Khalistan, leads the democratic, nonviolent, peaceful struggle to liberate Khalistan, the Sikh homeland that declared its independence on October 7, 1987.

"India practices the worst racism in the form of the caste system," said Dr. Aulakh. "The caste system is very reminiscent of the segregation that prevailed in parts of America some years ago, except it is backed by a tyrannical abuse of human rights of Dalits (the black untouchables of India)," he said. "Is that the way of a democracy or the way of a totalitarian theocracy."

Dr. Aulakh noted that the Dalits, who are considered the lowest caste, are the most oppressed people in the world. He cited the fact that they are not allowed in the Temple. He took note of an incident a few years ago when a Dalit constable entered a Hindu Temple on a rainy day and was stoned to death by Brahmins. A Dalit girl drank water from a community pitcher and was blinded by her teacher. Dr. Aulakh noted that Dalits are the victims of the worst racism in the world, oppressed by high-caste Brahmins.

"Despite the laws abolishing caste, it remains a guiding principle for India's militant Hindu nationalist theocracy," Dr. Aulakh said. "And despite the laws requiring that anyone who is arrested must be charged within 48 hours, India continues to hold political prisoners for many years without charge or trial," he said. "One of the foundations of democracy is the rule of law. In practice, there is no rule of law in India, " he said.

More than 52,000 Sikh political prisoners are rotting in Indian jails without charge or trial. Many have been in illegal custody since 1984. Over 50,000 Sikhs have been arrested, tortured, and murdered by the Indian police and security forces, then declared "unidentified" and secretly cremated. Indian forces have murdered over 250,000 Sikhs since 1984, according to figures reported in the The Politics of Genocide by Inderjit Singh Jaijee.

In June, militant fundamentalist Hindu fanatics attacked a train carrying Sikh pilgrims and the Sikh holy scripture, the Guru Granth Sahib. The holy scriptures were burned and the pilgrims were stoned. In May, Indian troops were caught red-handed trying to set fire to a Gurdwara (a Sikh Temple) and some Sikh houses in Kashmir. In March 2000 during the visit of former President Clinton, the Indian government massacred 35 Sikhs in Chitihisinghpora. Two independent investigations have proven that the Indian government carried out this massacre.

Sikhs ruled Punjab until 1849 when the British forcibly annexed it into British India. No Sikh representative has ever signed the India constitution. India is not one country. It has 18 official languages. It is an empire of many countries thrown together by the British for their convenience. Like the former Soviet Union, it is destined to fall apart.

"The Durban conference must address racism and human-rights violations in India despite India's objections," said Dr. Aulakh. "Only continued international pressure for human rights, the rule of law, and sovereignty will end the racism in India and allow all the people of South Asia to live in freedom," he noted.

"If India is the democracy it claims to be, then why not hold a plebiscite on independence in Punjab, Khalistan and in the other nations seeking their freedom from India?" Dr. Aulakh asked. "The conference should declare its support for the Dalits and for the freedom movements in Khalistan, in Kashmir, in Nagaland, and elsewhere in South Asia," he said. "Democracies don't practice racism," he said. "Democracies don't commit genocide."

- - - - - - - - - -

INFORMATION TIMES, Sept. 1, 2001
INDIAN CASTE SYSTEM IS ALSO A MAJOR ISSUE IN DURBAN
UN Secretary-General Kofi Annan is Still a slave of His Masters
(By Chaliss McDonough)

Durban, South Africa, 31 August 2001 (VOA): The caste system in India has become a major issue at the U.N. World Conference Against Racism. The Indian Government did not want to discuss the issue, but they may not be able to avoid it.

Scores of protesters stand in a circle, drumming and chanting, outside the cricket stadium in downtown Durban. The drummers are from India, and they have come to insist that the caste system not be ignored at the UN World Conference Against Racism, Racial Discrimination, Xenophobia and Related Intolerance (31 August_7 2001).

They are handing out headbands and buttons demanding equal rights for those who belong to India's Dalit community, the so-called "lowest caste, untouchables."

This woman, who gave her name only as Vimele, explains there is still blatant discrimination against Dalit people in India. "Dalit people cannot enter the Temple," she says. "And if you go to a teashop, they have a separated tea shop."

Separate living areas, separate burial grounds and restrictions on their movements. Vimele says these are some of the hardships Dalits face every day.

Vimele came to Durban with the Tamil Nadu Women's Forum. She says Dalit women confront even more discrimination and harassment than men.

Officially, discrimination based on caste has already been banned in India. But another delegate from Tamil Nadu, Joseph Raj, notes that changing the laws has not changed the system.

"In the documents, Constitution and the law, they prohibited discrimination," he says. "But in practice it is there. We have mechanisms within our country, but it has failed to protect our rights."

Mr. Raj is pleased with the amount of popular support he and his colleagues are getting in Durban. He points to the large number of non-Indians roaming the conference grounds wearing headbands, jackets and buttons supporting their cause.

He and other campaigners want the Indian Government to address the issue at the U.N.-sponsored conference, which began Friday. And they want India to put an end to caste discrimination for good.

U.N. Secretary-General Kofi Annan briefly touched on the matter during the meeting of non-governmental organizations. He said delegates at the U.N. conference will need to address discrimination based on caste but he failed to use that word to describe it. He simply referred to discrimination based on origin or work, which is commonly seen as a euphemism for caste.

An activist pressed him further on the matter, but Mr. Annan did not respond. That prompted an angry outcry from some members of the audience.

Getting public support for the Dalits' cause in Durban may not translate into a solution for caste discrimination. But it seems clear that the activists have accomplished at least one of their goals. They have put the issue in the public eye on a global scale.

***

Document

CONGRESSIONAL RECORD -- EXTENSIONS

Thursday, September 06, 2001
107th Congress, 1st Session
147 Cong Rec E 1606

REFERENCE: Vol. 147, No. 115
SECTION: Extension of Remarks
TITLE: INDIAN RACISM EXPOSED AT RACISM
CONFERENCE_PRESENTATION MOVES CONFERENCE TO TEARS

HON. EDOLPHUS TOWNS
of New York
in the House of Representatives
Thursday, September 6, 2001

Mr. TOWNS . Mr. Speaker, at the World Conference on Racism in Durban, Dalit and Kashmiri activists showed up to exert pressure against India's racist caste system. The caste system, which discriminates against people merely because of the group into which they are born, is one of the most racist systems in the world.

The demonstrators handed out literature, buttons, and headbands demanding equal rights for all peoples. They have been chanting and drumming to force the caste system onto the agenda for the conference.

India argued for keeping casteism off the agenda in Durban, saying that there are laws against caste discrimination on the books. This is true, but unlike our civil rights laws, the anti-caste laws are never enforced and are routinely violated. Dalits are forced to use separate facilities, such as tea shops. Dalits are forced to endure separate living areas, separate burial grounds and restrictions on their movements. They cannot enter the Temple. A few years ago, a Dalit constable entered a Hindu Temple on a rainy day to seek refuge from the rain and he was stoned to death by the Brahmins in the Temple. In another incident, a Dalit girl was blinded by her teacher after she drank water from the community water pitcher. This kind of racism is unforgivable, especially in a country that calls itself a democracy.

According to a report in Canada's National Post, a Dalit woman named Murugesan Manimegalai spoke at the Durban conference. She told the story of how her husband, with a tenth-grade education, was elected Sarpanch of their village, the president of the village council, similar to the mayor. Almost immediately, they received death threats from the upper-castes. "We will see how the president functions without a head," said one note. After he had been in office six months he was followed home on the bus. A group of men surrounded the road and told everyone "except Dalits" to leave. Then they grabbed Mr. Manimegalai and stabbed him in the stomach. Despite his pleas not to kill the other Dalits, they chopped up the six other Dalits in front of him. Then they murdered Mr. Manimegalal, chopped off his head, and threw it in a well. Unfortunately, incidents like this are all too common in India.

I would like to take this opportunity to salute the protestors for their success in bringing India's racism to the world's attention. That is the first step towards ending it.

Mr. Speaker, India must learn that a democracy respects the basic human rights of all people, not just those in a position of power and privilege. It must transcend its Brahminocracy and bring real democracy to all the people. How can people continue to live in the facade of Indian democracy when they cannot enjoy even the most basic rights?

America can help this process along. We should maintain the existing sanctions on India. We should stop all aid to India until the full range of human rights can be enjoyed by all the people there, not just the Brahmins. We should declare our overt support for the 17 freedom movements currently operating within India's borders. We can do so by supporting a free and fair plebiscite, under international supervision, on the question of independence for Khalistan, Kashmir, Nagaland, and the other minority nations living under the boot of Indian oppression. Former President Carter might be a good person to head an international monitoring team.

The Council of Khalistan has issued a press release praising the demonstrators who are bringing the issue of Indian racism to the forefront. The Information Times has also run an excellent article on the demonstrations. I would like to place them both into the Record at this time for the information of my colleagues. In addition, I would like to insert the National Post article into the Record.

From the National Post, Sept. 6, 2001
UN Racism Conference Moved to Tears,
not Action_Race Victims Tell Stories
(By Corinna Schuler)

Durban, South Africa._In an oft-ignored chamber of the cavernous convention centre, the real victims of racism struggle to have their stories of suffering heard.

This is not one of the dozens of rooms where international negotiators spend days behind closed doors, locked in debate about where to place a comma or whether to spell "Holocaust" with a capital "H."

Here, persecuted people from every corner of the globe take their turn on stage between 1:30 p.m. and 3 p.m. every day to tell simple stories abut real suffering_the only forum at this massive United Nations gathering where the personal pain of discrimination is laid bare.

One day, the speaker was an escaped slave from Niger. The next, an aboriginal woman from Australia. Then, a migrant worker from Brazil.

Yesterday it was Murugesan Manimegalai's turn. The 29-year-old mother of four is a member of India's lowest caste, so impoverished she had never left the confines of her squalid settlement before boarding a plane this week for Durban. "I was very worried that it might fall," she confides with a shy smile. But she pushed her fear aside yesterday, took a deep breath and told the story of her husband's horrifying murder to a crowd of 200 human rights activists and a few journalists. By the time she was done, even the moderator was blinking back tears. "We are Dalits"_untouchables_began Ms. Manimegalai.

As one of India's 1.4 million lowest-caste people, she grew up in a seg-regated village_forbidden to draw water from the communal well or to attend the same Temple as upper-caste people.

Her husband had only a Grade 10 education, but became an elo-quent activist and was elected president of a village council. Members of the upper caste warned he would not last six months. "We will see how the president functions without a head," said one written death threat.

After six months in office, when Mr. Manimegalai took a trip into town, upper-caste people followed him home in a bus. A crowd of men blocked off the road, screaming wildly for everyone to run away_"except Dalits."

"They grabbed my husband by the shirt and stabbed him in the stom-ach. Even then, my husband pleaded with the dominant caste people not to kill the rest of the Dalits. They ignored him, and chopped the six others in front of his eyes." Ms. Manimegalai did not stop for a breath as the next words tumbled out. "Even after my husband's death, the anger, the bitterness, the caste-fanatic feeling did not subside."

"They cut off his head and threw it in a well nearby." Witnesses were too terrified to come forward and it was only after three years of protest that some of the attackers were finally jailed. "We strongly demand," Ms. Manimegalai concluded, "that the caste system in our country be abol-ished. We demand education for our children, job opportunities_and dignity." The roar of applause continued for a solid minute. When the diminutive Ms. Manimegalai stepped off the stage, a burly African woman grabbed her in a bear hug, sobbing. Ms. Manimegalai was overwhelmed as others waited in line to give a hug or shake her hand. Tears streamed down her face as she stood in the glare of the TV lights.

It was not the first time the Voices Forum has borne witness to such raw emotion. But many of the 1,100 journalists in Durban to cover the UN's World Conference Against Racism have been too preoccupied by arguments over Israel and demands for reparations for the colonial-era slave trade to take much note.

The armies of suited government officials working to write up a "his-toric" blueprint for fighting racism and intolerance were not present to hear Ms. Manimegalai's demands.

Many were in a room down the hall, arguing about whether words such as "descent" and "ethnic origin" should be included in the list of grounds for discrimination.

At the end of her speech, a moderator thanked Ms. Manimegalai and other presenters for having the courage to speak out. "You should never doubt raising your voice in this chamber," she said assuringly. "Never doubt the importance of doing that."

The sorry truth is that the powerful testimonies heard in the Voices Forum have little chance of being incorporated into the UN's final declaration on racism, or its program of action.

"Cast out Caste" posters have been plastered all across Durban and activists have handed out thousands of information brochures in an effort to highlight the injustice of the caste system in Hindu society. But India has fought all attempts to include any mention of caste, and neither the UN nor any government is pushing the point. The strongest language in the draft declaration comes in a single paragraph that refers to discrimination based on work or descent_and even those watered-down words seem set to be withdrawn. Likewise, Eastern European countries refuse to acknowledge the discrimination endured by the Roma, or gypsies, no matter how many emotional stories they have told in Durban this week.

The African slave girl who told her story moved an audience to tears, too.

Inside conference rooms, however, African government delegates are so engrossed in debate about the slave trade of centuries past there has been almost no talk of how people like 17-year-old Mariama Oumarou and 20,000 others in Niger could be spared the horror of slavery today.

Will this conference change Ms. Manimegalai's life? The document under such hot debate is not an international treaty or a UN resolution. In fact, it's not a legal document of any kind and_if agreement is reached here by tomorrow_countries are free to ignore it.

But, Ms. Manimegalai lives with the hope her presence here will help the suffering Dalits of India break free from their oppression. "I am destitute," she said. "My house is just a matchbox and I do not have enough money to care for my children. They are living with relatives.

"But when I saw the big crowd in the room today, I was not afraid. I was happy. At least I can tell the world our story. There are many people back home who are relying on me here."

***

Document

CONGRESSIONAL RECORD -- EXTENSIONS

Friday, August 03, 2001
107th Congress, 1st Session
147 Cong Rec E 1527

REFERENCE: Vol. 147, No. 112
SECTION: Extension of Remarks
TITLE: CONGRATULATIONS TO THE COUNCIL OF KHALISTAN FOR 15
YEARS OF SERVICE

HON. DAN BURTON
of Indiana
in the House of Representatives
Thursday, August 2, 2001

Mr. BURTON of Indiana . Mr. Speaker, I would like to take this opportunity to congratulate Dr. Gurmit Singh Aulakh and the Council of
Khalistan, who have completed 15 years of service to the Sikh community in this country and the people of the Sikh homeland, Khalistan.

For the past 15 years, Dr. Aulakh has been diligently walking the
halls of the U.S. Congress to tell us about the latest developments in
India and the massive violations of human rights that have been perpetrated against Sikhs, Christian, Muslims, and other minorities. We appreciate the work he has done and the information he has provided.

Dr. Aulakh's efforts have made a valuable contribution to the consideration of our policy towards India and South Asia. I appreciate his
efforts, and I congratulate him on 15 years of tireless efforts on behalf of
the oppressed.

***

Document

CONGRESSIONAL RECORD -- EXTENSIONS

Friday, August 03, 2001
107th Congress, 1st Session
147 Cong Rec E 1545

REFERENCE: Vol. 147, No. 112
SECTION: Extension of Remarks
TITLE: CONGRATULATING THE COUNCIL OF KHALISTAN ON 15 YEARS
OF SERVICE

HON. JOHN T. DOOLITTLE
of California
in the House of Representatives
Thursday, August 2, 2001

Mr. DOOLITTLE . Mr. Speaker, I rise today to congratulate Dr. Gurmit
Singh Aulakh, President of the Council of Khalistan, for 15 years of
service to the Sikhs, the people of South Asia and America.

Fifteen years ago Dr. Aulakh left a well-paying job to begin striving
day in and day out in an effort to draw attention to the plight of the
minorities of India. Since that time he has succeeded in raising aware-

ness of the treatment of Christians, Kashmiri Muslims, and other minorities in India and throughout the world. Dr. Aulakh has spoken out on behalf of these people; he has highlighted injustices, and in so doing, has raised the level of awareness of such issues throughout the United States.

On October 7, 1987, the Sikh homeland declared its independence from India. At that time, Dr. Aulakh was named to lead the struggle to regain the lost sovereignty of the Sikhs.

If it were not for Dr. Aulakh's tireless efforts, the human-rights conditions in India would go unexposed and unpunished. Because of his efforts, all of us in Congress are much better informed on these matters and we are more able to take appropriate action. Therefore, I would like to take this opportunity to congratulate Dr. Aulakh and the Council of Khalistan for their tireless efforts on behalf of freedom.

***

Document

CONGRESSIONAL RECORD -- EXTENSIONS

Thursday, August 02, 2001
107th Congress, 1st Session
147 Cong Rec E 1502

REFERENCE: Vol. 147, No. 111
SECTION: Extension of Remarks
TITLE: CONGRATULATIONS TO COUNCIL OF KHALISTAN

HON. EDOLPHUS TOWNS
of New York
in the House of Representatives
Wednesday, August 1, 2001

Mr. TOWNS . Mr. Speaker, the Council of Khalistan, led by my friend Dr. Gurmit Singh Aulakh, recently completed 15 years of service and I would like to take this opportunity to congratulate the Council of Khalistan. Dr. Aulakh is a well-known presence around here. He has been working these halls for 15 years, advocating the cause of freedom for the Sikhs of Punjab, Khalistan, who are being subjected to brutal tyranny by the Indian government.

The Sikhs and other minorities like the Christians, Muslims, Dalit "untouchables," and others have been killed by the tens of thousands, held as political prisoners in large numbers_over 52,000 Sikhs alone, according to a recent report from the Movement Against State Repression_and subjected to other atrocities like violent attacks on religious institutions like Christian churches and schools, the Golden Temple, and the Babri mosque, attempts to burn down a Gurdwara and some houses, the Staines murder. In the face of these atrocities democratic India does nothing.

It is because of the efforts of activists like Dr. Aulakh that these matters come to light. He is a major leader in the human-rights movement and the leader of the Sikh community. I salute him for his tireless efforts and submit the following articles.

Concern at New Threats to Religious Freedom

The following statement was issued in New Delhi and Hyderabad on Sunday, 29th July 2000 by All India Christian Council President Dr Joseph D'Souza and Secretary General John Dayal in the wake of reports of draconian changes in the Foreign Contributions regulation act, the Private members Bill in the Lok Sabha against freedom of faith, the incidence of Vishwa Hindu Parishad goons "arresting" Christian workers in Varanasi, the forcible "re-conversion" of Orissa Christians under the combined pressure of the VHP and the Orissa Police.

The All India Christian Council calls upon Civil Society, the national Human Rights Commission and fellow citizens to take united action to counter a series of recent incidents in several Indian states by Fundamentalist extremists of the Sangh Parivar, as well as by police forces acting at their behest, in which the civil rights of Christian individuals and groups have been violently attacked. The Council is deeply concerned that the central and state governments, instead of taking urgent steps to restore confidence among the terrorised minorities, have seemingly condoned such actions. The Centre is in fact, according to media reports, bringing forward legislation that will further and more seriously affect religious minorities in the country and their work, and injure Constitutional guarantees.

The Council has declared it will extend all legal assistance to the victims who have been terrorised, specially in the states of Orissa, Gujarat, Uttar Pradesh and Rajasthan.

The most ominous incident has taken place in Varanasi in the state of Uttar Pradesh, where the state government controlled by the Bharatiya Janata party has condoned military training with firearms provided to elements of the Sangh Parivar in recent months. In that city on 24th July 2001, a Christian religious worker was among five persons "detained" by self styled vigilantes of the Vishwa Hindu Parishad. The five men had come to the city to attend a meeting. The City Superintendent of Police, who had the five men released, admitted they were innocent of the charges of conversion levied against them. The police have however taken no action against the VHP goons who terrorised the Christian group.

VHP groups are also terrorising the inmates of an ashram in Kota district of Rajasthan which is home to over 1,500 destitute and orphaned young people from various parts of the country. Death threats have been made against Bishop M A Thomas and officials of the Ashram. Many other similar cases have been reported from other states.

In Orissa, ruled by a coalition in which the BJP is a partner, the police have looked on while Tribal Christians are being coerced into "reconverting" to Hinduism. The Police have evoked the infamous and ironically named Freedom of Religion Act selectively against the Chris-

tians but not against their tormentors. As the media has reported, 17 adult persons had some time ago become Christians, and had told the police they had done so of their own free will, without any duress or allurement. The police, acting at the behest of local religio-political goons, however, chose to prosecute them and registered cases against them. Emboldened by this, the local fundamentalist elements intimidated the Christians, organising social ostracisation against them. Reports suggest that the authorities tacitly supported the "reconversion." The council has deplored the blatant religious partisanship of the local police and civil administration.

It is quite clear that these elements are getting strengthened by the attitude of the Central government. The minority communities, specially Christians are alarmed, at the failure of the Central government to denounce a Private Members bill moved by one of their party members in the Lok Sabha, the lower house of Parliament, which seeks a ban on religious conversions, which in effect means a ban on freedom of faith. This bill evoked dark memories of a similar Hitlerian OP Tyagi Bill in the late Seventies which the government, of which the current Bharatiya Janata party was a part, had extended its support.

The council has also strongly criticised the government's reported plan to enact new laws to strangle foreign donations and grants to minority, specially Christian, institutions and organisations. The existing Foreign Contributions Act, FCRA, is already being used as a weapon by the BJP government to target Christian groups and to stifle all protest. We fear the proposed laws are being designed to entirely curtail the educational and public welfare work of the Christian church in India. Christian groups have been thoroughly investigated in the law two years and have been found innocent, and yet extremist groups as well as ruling political parties have persisted a hate campaign against us using disinformation, half truths and malicious lies.

We call upon Civil Society, the national Human Rights Commission and all fellow citizens to unite in fighting this erosion of civil liberties and constitutional guarantees.

Have You Done Enough???

The anti-Christian Bill is in the Parliament. This is a place where even very sensitive Bills have been passed by manipulations, ignorance and negligence. Pandemoniums are created to pass Bills by voice votes. Bills become Acts in a second as opposition stages a walkout.

Have you heard your representative opposing the Bill? Have you heard the Christian MP's forum responding? Have you read about the Bill in your newspaper? Have you heard any of the church leaders speaking out? Now the burden is upon you. Do you know that it is the Sikh leader Gurmit Singh Aulakh who dedicates all his energies to bring up the issue of Christian persecution before the American legislative bodies?

How many Indian Christians have you seen lobbying against the persecution of Christians at the UN organisations or the US Committees?

Do you know that it is dalits, atheists and even moslems who have taken up the issue of the present Bill which is bound to affect the Christians the most? Dr. Satinath Choudhry is one of the earliest to respond. The objections to the Bill have appeared before the secular and dalit E-fora even before the head of any Church has even taken note of the Bill. Fascism is here and now. The very rights of individuals are at stake. Have you done enough???

***

Document

CONGRESSIONAL RECORD -- EXTENSIONS

Tuesday, July 31, 2001
107th Congress, 1st Session
147 Cong Rec E 1477

REFERENCE: Vol. 147, No. 109
SECTION: Extension of Remarks
TITLE: INDIAN DUPLICITY EXPOSED; INDIA MUST LIVE UP TO DEMOCRATIC PRINCIPLES

HON. DAN BURTON
of Indiana
in the House of Representatives
Monday, July 30, 2001

Mr. BURTON of Indiana . Mr. Speaker, the duplicity of India is clearer after the collapse of its talks with Pakistan. Pakistani President Musharraf went home abruptly because India was not dealing in good faith. Although much discussion focused on the Kashmir issue, India's spokeswoman never even acknowledged that Kashmir was on the agenda. India refused to go along with three drafts of a joint statement approved by both leaders. Instead, India insisted on including its unfounded accusations that Pakistan is fomenting terrorism in Kashmir and other places that India controls.

India has a long record of supporting terrorism against the people within its borders. The most recent incident took place last month when Indian military troops tried to burn down a Gurdwara and some Sikh homes in Kashmir, but were stopped by Sikh and Muslim residents of the town. There are many other incidents. The massacre in Chithisinghpora is very well known by now. It's also well known that India paid out over 41,000 cash bounties to police officers for killing Sikhs. It's well known that India holds tens of thousands of political prisoners, Sikhs and other minorities, in illegal detention with no charges and no trial. Some of them have been held since 1984. Is this how a democratic state conducts its affairs?

It is India that introduced the specter of nuclear terrorism into South Asia with its nuclear tests. Can we blame Pakistan for responding? Although it claims that the nuclear weapons are to protect them from China, the majority of them are pointed at Pakistan. Unfortunately, if there is a war between India and Pakistan, it is the minority peoples in Punjab and Kashmir who will suffer the most and bear most of the cost.

The United States must become more engaged in the subcontinent. We should continue to encourage both India and Pakistan to reduce their nuclear stockpiles. However, we should not remove the sanctions against India for its introduction of nuclear weapons into this region. In addition, we should end all aid to India until the most basic human rights are respected and not violated. Finally, we should publicly declare support for a free and fair vote in Kashmir, as promised in 1948 and as President Musharraf was pushing for, and in Punjab, Khalistan, in Nagalim, and in all the 17 nations under Indian occupation where freedom movements are ongoing. Only by these means can we strengthen America's hand in South Asia, ensure that a violent breakup like that of Yugoslavia does not occur in the subcontinent, and let the glow of freedom shine for all the people of that troubled region.

***

Document

CONGRESSIONAL RECORD -- EXTENSIONS

Tuesday, July 24, 2001
107th Congress, 1st Session
147 Cong Rec E 1412

REFERENCE: Vol. 147, No. 104
SECTION: Extension of Remarks
TITLE: END OF INDIA-PAKISTAN TALKS SIGNALS INSTABILITY IN SOUTH ASIA

HON. CYNTHIA A. McKINNEY
of Georgia
in the House of Representatives
Tuesday, July 24, 2001

Ms. McKINNEY . Mr. Speaker, I was disappointed to see that the recent talks between Pakistan and India ended with no agreement due to India's intransigence. India wanted a statement that Pakistan was engaging in cross-border terrorism, when India itself is responsible for terrorism against its own people.

Last month, a group of Indian soldiers tried to burn down a Gurdwara and some Sikh houses near Srinagar in Kashmir. This terrorist act was prevented by the efforts of townspeople of both the Sikh and Muslim faiths. In March 2000, during former President Clinton's visit to India, the government killed 35 Sikhs in Chithisinghpora, according to two independent investigations. The book Soft Target shows that India blew up its own airliner in 1985. 329 innocent people died in that explosion. The newspaper Hitavada report that the Indian government paid an official to generate state terrorism in Kashmir and in Punjab, Khalistan. According to a 1994 State Department report, the Indian government paid more than 41,000 cash bounties to police officers to kill Sikhs.

Before the meeting, the Council of Khalistan wrote to President Musharraf. They noted that he and his government had been friendly to the Sikhs and their cause of freedom. They noted that in 1948 the Indian government promised the United Nations that it would hold a plebiscite so Kashmiris could decide their political status in a free and fair vote. This shouldn't be too hard for "the world's largest democracy" to do, but we are now more than halfway through 2001 and it hasn't been held yet. When does India plan to keep its promise?

In addition, the people of Khalistan, the Sikh homeland, declared their independence from India on October 7, 1987 and the people of primarily Christian Nagaland are actively seeking theirs. In all, there are 17 freedom movements in India. When will these people be allowed by "the world's largest democracy" to exercise their right to self-determination? Self-determination is the birthright of all people and nations.

Mr. Speaker, if America can do something to help bring democracy and freedom to South Asia, that is not only in our national interest, it is the right thing to do. Fortunately, there are measures we can take to help bring freedom, peace, and stability to that dangerous region. The time has come to stop providing American aid to India_remember, this is public money_until India begins to treat all its people fairly and ends the repression against the minorities. The other thing that we can do is strongly urge India to hold a plebiscite, not just in Kashmir as it promised in 1948, but in Khalistan, Nagalim, and everywhere else that people seek their freedom. This will help to defuse the tense situation in South Asia and enhance America's national security by bringing us new allies in the subcontinent.

Mr. Speaker, I would like to place the Council of Khalistan's letter to President Musharraf into the Record for the information of my colleagues.

Council of Khalistan,
Washington, DC
June 27, 2001.
Hon. General Pervez Musharraf,
President of Pakistan,
Islamabad, Pakistan.

Dear President Musharraf, On behalf of the Sikh Nation, I congratulatle you on becoming President of Pakistan. We hope and pray that this step will be useful for the people of Pakistan, the Sikhs, and the people of South Asia.

Soon you will be visiting India. We sincerely hope that your visit will go well and will be productive to the cause of peace and freedom in South Asia.

While you are in India, I urge you to visit the Golden Temple in Amritsar. The Sikhs who visited Nankana Sahib last fall were so well treated that we know you are a friend of the Sikh Nation. Your visit to the Golden Temple will enhance your friendship with the Sikh nation.

You are aware that India divided Pakistan through a war and created the nation of Bangladesh. You are also aware that India promised in 1948 to hold a plebiscite on the future of Kashimir. Fifty-three years later, that plebiscite has still not been held. The people of Punjab, Khalistan also seek their freedom, and General Javed Nasir has endorsed the achievement of Khalistan by peaceful means. In addition, there are freedom movements in Nagalim, Tamil Nadu, Assam, Manipur, and other nations under Indian occupation. Self-determination is the birthright of all peoples and nations. Support for the freedom movements within India's borders would also be in Pakistan's interest, as well as the interest of peace, freedom, and stability in South Asia. In addition, it would help to prevent another war between India and Pakistan.

India has murdered over 250,000 Sikh since 1984, more than 75,000 Kashmiri Muslims since 1988, over 200,000 Christians in Nagaland since 1947, and tens of thousands of Dalits, Tamils, Manipuris, Assamese, and others. It has admitted to holding over 52,000 Sikh political prisoners without charge or trial. Recently in Kashmir, Muslim and Sikh villagers caught a group of Indian soldiers trying to burn down a Gudwara and overpowered them. Is this the way of "the world's" largest democracy"? Add to this the fact that India started the nuclear arms race in South Asia with their nuclear tests. India is a destabilizing and repressive country seeking hegemony in the subcontinent.

President Musharraf, I urge you to support the freedom movements in Kashmir, Khalistan, Nagaland, and all the other nations seeking their freedom from India. I urge you to press the Indian government on this issue and urge them to hold a free and fair plebiscite on the question of independence, monitored by the international community. This would go a long way towards establishing stability, peace, and freedom in South Asia.

Sincerely
Dr. Gurmit Singh Aulakh,
President, Council of Khalistan.

***

Document

CONGRESSIONAL RECORD -- EXTENSIONS

Tuesday, July 24, 2001
107th Congress, 1st Session
147 Cong Rec E 1414

REFERENCE: Vol. 147, No. 104
SECTION: Extension of Remarks
TITLE: BREAKDOWN OF INDIA-PAKISTAN TALKS SHOWS INDIA'S
CONTEMPT FOR DEMOCRACY, PEACE

HON. EDOLPHUS TOWNS
of New York
in the House of Representatives
Tuesday, July 24, 2001

Mr. TOWNS . Mr. Speaker, I think we were all distressed by the breakdown of 7Ethe talks between India and Pakistan aimed at reducing tensions in South Asia, one of the most troubled areas in the world. The fact that the talks broke down increases the danger and the instability in that region.

It looks as if much of the blame for the breakdown goes squarely to the Indian government. As Dr. Gurmit Singh Aulakh, President of the Council of Khalistan, put it, "It is very clear that India does not want a peaceful solution to the Kashmir issue." India's Defense Ministry spokeswoman did not even mention Kashmir among the topics under discussion. Three drafts of a joint statement were vetoed by the Indian cabinet. As you know, the Indian government is run by the militant, Hindu nationalist BJP, a branch of the pro-Fascist Rashtriya Swayamsewak Sangh (RSS), which has said that everyone in India must be Hindu or be subservient to Hinduism. The RSS published a booklet last year showing how to implicate Christians and other religious minorities in false criminal cases.

India's human-rights violations have been well documented. It has killed over tens of thousands of Sikhs, Muslims, Christians, Dalits, and other minorities. It has burned churches, prayer halls, and Christian schools, destroyed the most revered Muslim mosque in India, and attacked the seat of Sikhism, the Golden Temple. It has killed priests and raped nuns. Indian troops were recently caught in a village in Kashmir trying to set fire to a Gurdwara and some Sikh homes. This atrocity was prevented by the joint action of Sikh and Muslim villagers. The Indian government killed 35 Sikhs in Chithisinghpora in March 2000. In 1997, Indian troops broke up a Christian religious festival with gunfire.

India admitted to holding over 52,000 Sikhs in illegal detention without charge or trial under the repressive TADA law, which expired in 1995, according to a recent report by the Movement Against State Repression. It was routine to rearrest people released under TADA and to file charges in more than one state simultaneously to deter prisoners from contesting the charges. Amnesty International notes that there are tens of thousands of Si 7Ekhs and others being held as political prisoners. Christians, Muslims, and other minorities are also held as political prisoners in large numbers. A few months ago, the Council of Khalistan called on the political prisoners to run for office from their jail cells. This might be the most effective action that the political prisoners and minority political leaders can take. I call upon President Bush to press India for the release of all political prisoners. Why are there political prisoners in a democracy?

India has murdered Christians, Sikhs, Dalits, Muslims, and other minorities by the tens of thousands. Should the United States be supporting such a country, especially when it tries to immunize its human-rights violations by proclaiming itself a democracy?

America is the bastion of freedom in the world. It is our mission to extend and expand liberty wherever and whenever we can. Accordingly, we should stop U.S. aid to India until we no longer have to stand up here denouncing its human-rights abuses and we should support the birthright of all people, the democratic right to self-determination. If India is truly a democracy, it should live up to its promise made 53 years ago to hold a plebiscite in Kashmir. If India genuinely believes in democratic values, it must hold plebiscites on the political future of Kashmir, of Nagaland, of Punjab, Khalistan, and of all the nations seeking their freedom from India. India is an inherently unstable country composed of many different nations whose breakup is inevitable. For the cause of peace, prosperity, stability, security, and freedom, we must do whatever we can to ensure that this occurs peacefully like the breakups of the Soviet Union and Czechoslovakia, not violently like that of Yugoslavia. Unfortunately, India seems to beheaded down the violent path. Let us work to help end the violence, repression, and terrorism and to ensure freedom and peace for all the peoples of that troubled region.

Mr. Speaker, I would like to insert the Council of Khalistan's press release about the breakdown of the India-Pakistan talks into the Record at this time.

Indian Arrogance Exposed During Musharraf-Vajpayee Summit Plebiscite in Kashmir, Punjab, and Other Nations Essential for Peace in South Asia

Washington, DC, July 17, 2001._Indian hypocrisy was exposed to the international community when they refused to mention the word Kashmir during the bilateral talks between Pakistani President Musharraf and Indian Prime Minister Vajpayee. The Indian Foreign Ministry's press spokeswoman, Niruparna Rao, did not even list Kashmir among the items discussed. Aides to President Musharraf said that three drafts of a joint statement had been approved by both sides but the Indian Cabinet vetoed them.

"It is very clear from these actions that India does not want any peaceful solution to the Kashmir issue," said Dr. Gurmit Singh Aulakh, President of the Council of Khatistan, which leads the Sikh struggle for

independence from India. "India must learn that 54 years of repression in Kashmir which resulted in the murder of over 75,000 Kashmiris and the expenditure of over $2 billion a year have not extinguished the flame of freedom which is burning in the hearts of the people of Kashmir," he said.

"India must keep its promise of a plebiscite in Kashmir, which it agreed to in 1948 in a United Nations resolution," Dr. Aulakh said. "India is morally wrong. If India is a democracy, why is it afraid of a vote?," he asked. "How can India justify its invasion annexation of Hyderabad, where the ruler was a Muslim and the majority population was Hindu, but by the same token in Kashmir population is Muslim and the ruler was Hindu and India sent the army to maintain its illegal occupation?," Dr. Aulakh asked.

India is not one country and it is not one nation. It is a multinational state put together by the British for administrative convenience. India is a vestige of colonialism. India has 18 official languages and there are 17 freedom movements within its borders. The fundamentalist Hindu ruling BJP government is on record that anyone living in India must either be a Hindu or subservient to the Hindus. This is not acceptable to the Sikh Christian, or Muslim minorities.

India has unleashed a reign of terror on the minorities. In 1984, the Indian government attacked the Golden Temple, the holiest shrine of the Sikh religion, and 38 other Gurdwaras and killed over 20,000 people during that attack throughout Punjab. India demolished the Babri mosque in Ayodhya, the most revered mosque in India, and it is planning to build a Hindu Temple on that site. Similarly, Christian churches, prayer halls, and schools have also been demolished. Christians have also seen the murder of priests, rape of nuns, the murder of a missionary and his two sons, ages 8 and 10, by burning them alive while they slept in their jeep and other atrocities. Now the government plans to expel his widow from the country.

Last month, Indian soldiers were caught red-handed attempting to burn down a Gurdwara and several Sikh homes in Kashmir. Sikh and Muslim townspeople overpowered the troops and prevented them from carrying out this atrocity. In March 2000, while former President Clinton was visiting India, the Indian government murdered 35 Sikhs in the village of Chithisinghpora in Kashmir and tried to blame the massacre on alleged militants. In November 1994 the Indian newspaper Hitavada reported that the Indian government paid the late governor of Punjab, Surendra Nath, $1.5 billion to organize and support covert state terrorism in Punjab and Kashmir.

Indian security forces have murdered over 250,000 Sikhs since 1984, according to figures compiled by the Punjab State Magistracy and human-rights organizations and published in The Politics of Genocide by Inderjit Singh Jaijee. Over 52,000 Sikh political prisoners are rotting in Indian jails without charge or trial. Many have been in illegal custody since 1984. Since 1984, India has engaged in a campaign of ethnic cleansing in which over 50,000 Sikhs have been murdered by the Indian police and security forces and secretly cremated. The Indian Supreme Court described this campaign as "worse than a genocide." General Narinder Singh has said, "Punjab is a police state." U.S. Congressman Dana Rohrabacher has said that for Sikhs, Kashmiri Muslims, and other minorities "India might as well be Nazi Germany."

"The people and nations of the subcontinent are entitled to freedom and self-determination," said Dr. Aulakh. "It is time for India to do the democratic thing and end the repression," he said. "It will help the Indian government and the people of India to give freedom to all the nations of South Asia," he said. "As soon as it happens, the South Asian nations can make a South Asian economic market parallel to the European Economic Community where the nations are independent but joined economically, which benefits every member," he s 7Eaid. "It will also include Pakistan, Bangladesh, Nepal, Sri Lanka, and others. This will reduce tensions and the nuclear threat in this dangerous region and will benefit all the people of South Asia," Dr. Aulakh said.

***

Document

CONGRESSIONAL RECORD -- EXTENSIONS

Wednesday, July 11, 2001
107th Congress, 1st Session
147 Cong Rec E 1297

REFERENCE: Vol. 147, No. 96
SECTION: Extension of Remarks
TITLE: INDIA, RUSSIA AGREE ON $10 BILLION IN DEFENSE
CONTRACTS

HON. DAN BURTON
of Indiana
in the House of Representatives
Tuesday, July 10, 2001

Mr. BURTON of Indiana . Mr. Speaker, on June 4, the Information Times reported that India and Russia have signed $10 billion worth of defense contracts. This is not good for American interests in the world or for the cause of freedom.

Much has been written lately about the Indian Government's desire to improve its relations with the United States. However, we must not forget that India just recently voted to oust the United States from the UN Human Rights Commission. It supported a Chinese bid to table our resolution condemning Chinese human-rights violations. In May 1999, according to the Indian Express, Defense Minister George Fernandes convened a meeting with the ambassadors to India from Cuba, Communist China, Libya, Yugoslavia, and Russia to construct a security alliance "to stop the U.S." India was an ally of the former Soviet Union and publicly supported its invasion of Afghanistan.

Mr. Speaker, America's national interests are best served by seeking new allies in south Asia. The best way to achieve that is to support the legitimate aspirations for freedom of the occupied and oppressed nations of South Asia such as Khalistan, Kashmir, Nagalim, and several others by means of a free and fair plebiscite under international supervision on the question of independence. Until India allows that democratic vote and permits all the minorities and every citizen to exercise their rights freely, we should cut off all aid to India. That should focus their attention on practicing democratic principles, not on grabbing every available military technology in pursuit of hegemony in South Asia. These are the best measures we can take to support the cause of freedom in the Indian subcontinent.

Mr. Speaker, I would like to place the Information Times article of June 4 into the Record.

India, Russia Sign About 10 Billion Dollars Defense Contracts

Russia, 4 June 2001 (VOA): India and Russia have signed defense contracts worth some $10 billion as the two countries seek to increase their military cooperation.

The signing came during a visit to Russia by Indian Foreign Minister Jaswant Singh.

Singh arrived in Moscow late Sunday for a series of meetings with Russian officials that will also focus on the United States' proposal for a national missile defense system.

Russia opposes the plan, while India has indicated it is open to the idea.

Among the agreements already concluded are major Indian purchases of Russian Su-30MKI fighter jets and T-90 tanks.

Russian Deputy Prime Minister Ilya Klebanov says the two countries will sign an agreement later this year to jointly develop a military transport aircraft and a next-generation fighter plane.

Klebanov says contracts for the sale of a Soviet-era aircraft carrier to India will be signed later this year.

India has traditionally been one of the largest customers for Russian weapons.

***

Document

CONGRESSIONAL RECORD -- EXTENSIONS

Wednesday, July 11, 2001
107th Congress, 1st Session
147 Cong Rec E 1313

REFERENCE: Vol. 147, No. 96
SECTION: Extension of Remarks
TITLE: INDIAN MINORITIES SEEKING THEIR OWN STATES

HON. EDOLPHUS TOWNS
of New York
in the House of Representatives
Wednesday, July 11, 2001

Mr. TOWNS . Mr. Speaker, I was interested in a Washington Post article on Sunday, July 8 which reported that all across India, minorities are demanding their own states. For example, the article reports that the Bodos, who live in the northeast part of India, are demanding a separate state of Bodoland.

This demand underlines the fact that India is not one country any more than the Soviet Union was. Much of India's instability can be traced to the fact that it is a multinational state thrown together by the British for their administrative convenience, a vestige of the colonial era. The Soviet experience showed how difficult it is to keep such a multinational state together.

Unfortunately, instead of listening to the demands of the people, India has responded by stepping up the oppression of its minorities. Instead of listening to the people, the Indian government has killed more than 250,000 Sikhs since 1984, over 75,000 Muslims in Kashmir since 1988, over 200,000 Christians in Nagaland since 1947, and tens of thousands of other minorities. India was caught by the Movement Against State Repression admitting that it held over 52,000 Sikh political prisoners under the so-called "Terrorist and Disruptive Activities Act," known as TADA, which is one of the most repressive laws in the world. TADA expired in 1995. India also holds political prisoners of other minorities, according to Amnesty International. In 1994 the State Department reported that the Indian government paid more than 41,000 cash bounties to police officers for killing Sikhs.

Recently in a village in Kashmir, Indian soldiers were caught red-handed in the act of trying to set fire to a Sikh Temple, known as a Gurdwara, and some Sikh homes. This appears to have been aimed at setting the Sikh and Muslim residents against each other. Village residents, both Sikh and Muslim, came out and intervened to stop the soldiers from carrying out this nefarious plan.

Unfortunately, this is only one recent chapter in an ongoing saga of repression of minorities and denial of basic human rights in "the world's largest democracy." In India, minorities have seen the destruction of the Muslims' most revered mosque to build a Hindu Temple, the burning death of a missionary and his two sons while they slept in their jeep followed by an effort to expel his widow from the country, church burnings, the murder of priests, the rape of nuns, attacks on schools and prayer halls, the massacre of 35 Sikhs in the village of Chithisinghpora, a recent attack on a train carrying Sikh religious pilgrims, troops attacking a crowd of religious pilgrims with lathis, police breaking up a religious festival with gunfire, and many other such intolerant acts.

In November 1994 the Indian newspaper Hitavada reported that the Indian government paid Surendra Nath, then the governor of Punjab, the equivalent of $1.5 billion to generate terrorist activity in Punjab and in Kashmir. In India, half the population lives below the international poverty line. About 40 percent lives on less than $2 per day. Yet they could find $1.5 billion to pay a government official to generate and support terrorism. We have programs in our government that don't cost $1.5 billion. This is not a small amount of money.

Mr. Speaker, India has been caught red-handed engaging in domestic terrorism against its minorities. This is why they are seeking their own states. This is why there are 17 freedom movements within India's artificial, colonial-era borders. The minorities are looking for any means of protection against the brutal Indian state.

America is the beacon of freedom, and as an old song from the 70s said, "you can't be a beacon if your light don't shine." We must do what we can to shine the light of freedom on all the people of south Asia. We can do this by maintaining the existing sanctions against India, by stopping our aid to India until it stops denying basic human rights that are the cornerstone of real democracies, and by supporting self-determination for the peoples of South Asia in the form of a free and fair plebiscite on their political status. By these measures, we can help bring freedom, security, stability, and prosperity to the subcontinent and bring America new allies and new influence in this dangerous region.

***

Document

CONGRESSIONAL RECORD -- EXTENSIONS

Friday, June 29, 2001
107th Congress, 1st Session
147 Cong Rec E 1274

REFERENCE: Vol. 147, No. 93
SECTION: Extension of Remarks
TITLE: SELF-DETERMINATION FOR SIKH HOMELAND DISCUSSED ON CAPITOL HILL

HON. CYNTHIA A. McKINNEY
of Georgia
in the House of Representatives
Thursday, June 28, 2001

Ms. McKINNEY . Mr. Speaker, on Friday, June 15, the Think Tank for National Self-Determination held a very informative meeting here on Capitol Hill in the Rayburn House Office Building. The featured speaker was Dr. Gurmit Singh Aulakh, President of the Council of Khalistan. He laid out very well the strong case for self-determination for the Sikhs of Punjab, Khalistan, and for the other nations of South Asia, such as predominantly Christian Nagaland and predominantly Muslim Kashmir.

During his speech, Dr. Aulakh noted that "self-determination is the birthright of all peoples and nations." He quoted Thomas Jefferson, who wrote in our own Declaration of Independence that when a government tramples on the basic rights of the people, "it is the right of the people to alter or abolish it." Jefferson also wrote, "Resistance to tyranny is obedience to God."

India certainly is that kind of government. It has killed over 200,000 Christians in Nagaland since 1947, more than 250,000 Sikhs since 1984, over 75,000 Kashmiri Muslims since 1988, and many thousands of other minorities, including people from Assam, Manipur, Tamil Nadu, and members of the Dalit caste, the dark-skinned "Untouchables," who are the aboriginal people of South Asia, among others. Currently, there are 17 freedom movements in India.

Just recently, a group of Indian soldiers was caught trying to set fire to a Gurdwara, a Sikh Temple, in Kashmir, and some houses. Local townspeople, both Sikh and Muslim, overwhelmed the soldiers and prevented them from committing this atrocity. Unfortunately, that is the reality of "the world's largest democracy."

Mr. Speaker, there are measures that America can take to prevent further atrocities and help the people of the subcontinent live in freedom. We should end our aid to the Indian government until it stops repressing the people and we should openly and publicly declare our support for self-determination for the people of Khalistan, Nagalim, Kashmir, and the other nations seeking their freedom in South Asia. This is the best way to help them. It supports the principles that gave birth to our country and it strengthens our security position in that region.

Mr. Speaker, I would like to insert Dr. Aulakh's speech into the Record for the information of my colleagues.

Remarks of Dr. Gurmit Singh Aulakh, President, Council of Khalistan

It is a pleasure to be back here with my friends at the Think Tank for National Self Determination. This is a very important organization and I am proud to support its work.

Self-determination is the birthright of all peoples and nations. Next month America will celebrate its independence. Thomas Jefferson, author of the American Declaration of Independence, wrote that when a government tramples on the people's rights, "it is the right of the people to alter or abolish it." He also wrote that "resistance to tyranny is obedience to God." Sikhs share that view. We are instructed by the Gurus to be vigilant against tyranny wherever it rears its ugly head. Guru Gobind Singh, the last of the Sikh Gurus, proclaimed the Sikh Nation sovereign. Every day we pray "Raj Kare Ga Khalsa," which means "the Khalsa shall rule."

Let me tell you a little about the history of Sikh national sovereignty. Sikhs established Khalsa Raj in 1710, lasting until 1716. In 1765, Sikh rule in Punjab was re-established, and it lasted until the British conquered the subcontinent in 1849. Under Maharajah Ranjit Singh, Hindus, Sikhs, and Muslims all served in the government. All people were treated equally and fairly. The Sikh state was extensive, at one point reaching all the way to Kabul.

At the time that the British quit India, three nations were supposed to get sovereignty. Jinnah got Pakistan for the Muslims on the basis of religion and the Hindus got India. India made a deal with the Hindu maharajah of Kashmir to keep the state within India despite a Muslim majority population, but at the same time it marched troops into Hyderabad to annex it to India by defeating the Muslim ruler, Nizam of Hyderabad. Hyderabad at the time had a majority Hindu population and a Muslim maharajah.

The third nation that was to receive sovereign power was the Sikh Nation. However, Nehru tricked the Sikh leadership of the time into taking their share with India on the promise that Sikhs would enjoy "the glow of freedom" in Punjab and no law affecting the rights of Sikhs would pass without Sikh consent. As soon as the ink dried, however, the Indian government broke those promises. They sent a memo to all officials declaring Sikhs "a criminal race" does that sound like a democracy or a totalitarian state in the Nazi/Communist mold?_and the repression of Sikhs began. No Sikh representative has ever signed the Indian constitution to this day.

In June 1984 the Indian government attacked the holiest of Sikh shrines, the Golden Temple in Amritsar. Ask yourself, what would you think if someone launched a military attack on the Vatican or Mecca? That is how Sikhs felt about the Golden Temple massacre and desecration. Seventeen years later, we have still not forgotten it, as the attendance at our recent protest shows.

Since that attack, the Indian government has murdered more than 250,000 Sikhs, according to figures published in The Politics of Genocide by human-rights leader Inderjit Singh Jaijee, convenor of the Movement Against State Repression. A new report from Jaijee's organization shows that India admitted that it held over 52,000 Sikhs as political prisoners without charge or trial under the expired "Terrorist and Disruptive Activities Act." Some of the political prisoners have been in illegal custody since 1984! In 1994, the U.S. State Department

Unfortunately, there is often no way to answer that question. Human rights activist Jaswant Singh Khalra exposed the fact that the Indian government picked up over 50,000 Sikhs, tortured them, killed them, then declared their bodies "unidentified" and cremated them. Just recently, more bodies were found in a river bank. For this, Mr. Khalra was arrested and killed in police custody. The only eyewitness to the Khalra kidnapping was arrested for trying to hand the British Home Secretary a petition asking Britain to get involved in helping to secure human rights for the Sikhs.

Two independent investigations showed that the Indian government killed 35 Sikhs last year in the village of Chithi Singhpora in Kashmir. Just last week, five Indian troops were overwhelmed by Sikh and Muslim residents of another village while they were trying to burn down the local Gurdwara and some Sikh homes. This is part of India's ongoing effort to set the minorities against each other. With 17 freedom movements within India's borders, the idea that the minorities might support each other scares the Indian government.

It is not just Sikhs who are being oppressed. While my main focus is on my own people, I am committed to freedom and human rights for all peoples and nations. There has been a wave of oppression of Christians since Christmas 1998. Members of the RSS, the pro-Fascist parent organization of the ruling BJP, murdered missionary Graham Staines and his two sons, ages 8 to 10, by burning them to death while they slept in their jeep. Nuns have been raped, priests have been killed, schools and prayer halls have been attacked. Last year, the RSS published a booklet on how to implicate Christians and other minorities in false criminal cases.

The BJP destroyed the Babri mosque in Ayodhya and still intends to build a Hindu Temple on the site. Leaders of the BJP have said that everyone who lives in India must be Hindu or must be subservient to Hinduism. They have called for the "Indianization" of non-Hindu religions.

Is that a democratic country? U.S. Congressman Edolphus Towns pointed out that "the mere fact that Sikhs have the right to choose their oppressors does not mean they live in a democracy." Congressman Dana Rohrabacher said that for the minorities "India might as well be Nazi Germany."

Sikh martyr Jarnail Singh Bhindranwale said that "If the Indian government attacks the Golden Temple, it will lay the foundation of Khalistan." He was right. On October 7, 1987, the Sikh Nation declared the independence of its homeland, Punjab, Khalistan. India claims that there is no support for Khalistan. It also claims to be democratic despite the atrocities. Then why not simply put the issue of independence to a independence to a vote, the democratic way? What are they afraid of?

Self-determination is the right of all people and nations. America should sanction India and stop its aid until all the people of South Asia are allowed to live in freedom.

Thank you for giving me this opportunity. I hope you will support freedom for Khalistan, Kashmir, Nagaland, and all the nations of South Asia.

***

Document

CONGRESSIONAL RECORD -- EXTENSIONS

Wednesday, June 27, 2001
107th Congress, 1st Session
147 Cong Rec E 1235

REFERENCE: Vol. 147, No. 91
SECTION: Extension of Remarks
TITLE: INDIAN GOVERNMENT FOUND RESPONSIBLE FOR BURNING
SIKH HOMES AND TEMPLE IN KASHMIR

HON. EDOLPHUS TOWNS
of New York
in the House of Representatives
Wednesday, June 27, 2001

Mr. TOWNS . Mr. Speaker, in March 2000 when President Clinton was visiting India, 35 Sikhs were murdered in cold blood in the village of Chithi Singhpora in Kashmir. Although the Indian government continues to blame alleged "Pakistani militants," two independent investigations, by the Movement Against State Repression and Punjab Human Rights Organization and the International Human Rights Organization based at Ludhiana, have proven that the Indian government was responsible for this atrocity.

Now it is clear that this was part of a pattern designed to pit Sikhs and Kashmiri Muslims against each other with the ultimate aim of destroying both the Sikh and Kashmiri freedom movements. The Kashmir Media Service reported on May 28 that five Indian soldiers were caught in Srinagar trying to set fire to a Sikh Temple and some Sikh homes. Sikh and Muslim villagers overpowered the troops as they were about to sprinkle gunpowder on Sikh houses and the Temple. The Border Security Forces rescued several other troops. The villagers even seized a military vehicle, which the army later had to come and reclaim.

At a subsequent protest rally, local leaders said that this incident was part of an Indian government plan to create communal riots. As such, it fits perfectly with the Chithi Singhpora massacre.

Mr. Speaker, India has been trying to commit atrocities in order to promote violence by minorities against each other. Now that the massive numbers of minorities, that the Indian government has murdered, have been exposed, the government is trying to get these same minority groups to kill each other. The plan to create more bloodshed is backfiring on the Indian government. Fortunately, the groups have joined together to oppose the government's plan.

Such a plan is an unacceptable abuse of power. As the leader for democracy in the world, we should take a stand against this government's actions, which target minority groups for violence and abuse.

Given these kinds of actions it makes it very difficult to advocate that this Administration should lift the sanctions against India. To ensure the survival and success of freedom in South Asia, our government should go on record strongly supporting self-determination for all the peoples and nations of South Asia in the form of a free and fair, internationally-monitored plebiscite. This is the best way to support democracy in all of South Asia and to create strong allies for America in that troubled region.

***

Document

CONGRESSIONAL RECORD -- EXTENSIONS

Tuesday, June 26, 2001
107th Congress, 1st Session
147 Cong Rec E 1215

REFERENCE: Vol. 147, No. 90
SECTION: Extension of Remarks
TITLE: INDIAN GOVERNMENT CAUGHT RED-HANDED TRYING TO BURN DOWN SIKH HOMES, GURDWARA IN KASHMIR

HON. EDOLPHUS TOWNS
of New York
in the House of Representatives
Tuesday, June 26, 2001

Mr. TOWNS . Mr. Speaker, in March 2000 when President Clinton was visiting India, 35 Sikhs were murdered in cold blood in the village of Chithi Singhpora in Kashmir. Although the Indian government continues to blame alleged "Pakistani militants," two independent investigations have proven that the Indian government was responsible for this atrocity.

Now it is clear that this was part of a pattern designed to pit Sikhs and Kashmiri Muslims against each other with the ultimate aim of destroying both the Sikh and Kashmiri freedom movements. The Kashmir Media Service reported on May 28 that five Indian soldiers were caught red-handed in Srinagar trying to set fire to a Gurdwara (a Sikh Temple) and some Sikh homes. The troops were overpowered by Sikh and Muslim villagers as they were about to sprinkle gunpowder on Sikh houses and the Gurdwara. Several other troops were rescued by the Border Security Forces. The villagers even seized a military vehicle, which the army later had to come and reclaim.

At a subsequent protest rally, local leaders said that this incident was part of an Indian government plan to create communal riots. As such, it fits perfectly with the Chithi Singhpora massacre.

Mr. Speaker, India has been caught red-handed trying to commit an atrocity to generate violence by minorities against each other. Now that the massive numbers of minorities the Indian government has murdered have been exposed, it is trying to get the minorities to kill each other. Instead they are banding together to stop the government's sinister plan.

The plan to create more bloodshed is backfiring on the Indian government.

Such a plan is a tyrannical, unacceptable abuse of power. As the superpower in the world and the leader of the forces of freedom, we must take a stand against this tyrannical, terrorist activity. First, President Bush should reconsider the idea of lifting the sanctions against India. Those sanctions should remain in place until the Indian government learns to respect basic human rights. Until then, the United States should provide no aid to India. And to ensure the survival and success of freedom in South Asia, we should go on record strongly supporting self-determination for all the peoples and nations of South Asia in the form of a free and fair, internationally-monitored plebiscite on the issue of independence for Khalistan, Kashmir, Nagalim, and all the nations seeking their freedom. This is the best way to let freedom reign in all of South Asia and to create strong allies for America in that troubled region.

Mr. Speaker, I would like to place the May 28 Kashmir News Service article on the Indian forces trying to burn the Gurdwara into the Record at this time for the information of my colleagues, especially those who defended India at the time of the Chithi Singhpora massacre.

From the Kashmir Media Service, May 28, 2001
Attempt to Set Ablaze Sikh Houses in IHK Foiled

Srinagar_Evil forces behind incidents like collective murder of Sikhs in Chatti Singhpora were publicly exposed when the people frustrated the Task Forces' designs to set ablaze Sikh houses and Gurdwara in Srinagar late Saturday night.

According to Kashmir Media Service, Muslims and Sikhs came out of their houses in full force and over powered five of the Indian troops who were about to sprinkle gun powder on Sikhs' houses and adjoining Gurdwara in Alucha Bagh locality with an intention to set them on fire.

The people also seized a military vehicle, the Task Force personnel were riding in. Twelve troops, however, succeeded to escape. Later, the Border Security Force personnel rescued the Task Force personnel. However, the captured vehicle was retained by the people from which, petrol, hand grenades and hundreds of tear gas shells were recovered.

Former APHC Chairman, Syed Ali Gilani led an APHC delegation, including Qazi Ahadullah and Abdul Khaliq Hanif, to the site of the incident. A protest procession was taken out in the locality. The protestors were addressed by Syed Ali Gilani, Ranjiet Singh Sodi, Sardar Bali, Qazi Ahadullah and Abdul Khaliq Hanif.

Syed Ali Gilani recalled the collective murder of Sikhs in Chatti Singhpora and said, now that India has invited Pakistan's Chief Executive General Musharraf for talks, this sinister plan had been hatched to vitiate the atmosphere by creating communal riots.

***

Document

CONGRESSIONAL RECORD -- EXTENSIONS

Wednesday, June 13, 2001
107th Congress, 1st Session
147 Cong Rec E 1083

REFERENCE: Vol. 147, No. 82
SECTION: Extension of Remarks
TITLE: INDIA PURSUES MISSILE DEFENSE IN IS DRIVE FOR
HEGEMONY

HON. DAN BURTON
of Indiana
in the House of Representatives
Wednesday, June 13, 2001

Mr. BURTON of Indiana . Mr. Speaker, on June 6, the French news agency, Agence France Presse, reported that Russia offered to provide an anti-missile system to India, which Indian "defense expert" Uday Bhaksur called a "desirable development." This offer comes from the same Russian government that has told us that we cannot build a missile defense system because of the ABM treaty. It is ironic that Russia is vigorously opposing our missile defense efforts while providing an anti-missile system to a country that has a longstanding tradition of opposing America on a variety of issues and in a variety of foreign policy forum.

For example, India, a country which supported the former Soviet Union's invasion of Afghanistan, recently voted with China to table a U.S. resolution at the United Nations against Chinese human-rights violations. India later voted to remove America from the U.N. Human Rights Commission. In fact, India votes against the United States at the U.N. more often than any country except Cuba. We should not forget that in May 1999, the Indian Express reported that Defense Minister George Fernandes convened and led a meeting with the Ambassadors from Red China, Cuba, Russia, Yugoslavia, Iraq, and Libya. According to this article, the aim of this meeting was to set up a security alliance "to stop the United States."

According to the Council of Khalistan, India has murdered over 250,000 Sikhs since June 1984 when it attacked the Golden Temple, the Sikh religion's holiest shrine. According to a recent report from the Movement Against State Repression, India admitted to holding over 52,000 Sikh political prisoners without charge or trial. Just recently, five Indian troops were overwhelmed when they were trying to set fire to a Gurdwara and some Sikh homes in Kashmir to set Sikhs and Muslims against each other. Both Sikh and Muslim residents of the village came out to stop the troops from burning down the houses and the Gurdwara. Two reports accuse the Indian government of killing 35 Sikhs in Chithi Singhpora in March 2000. By some calculations, India has also killed more than 75,000 Muslims in Kashmir. Other reports indicate that the

Indian government has killed tens of thousands of Dalit "untouchables," Assamese, Tamils, Manipuris, and other minorities.

Since Christmas 1998, India has pursued a policy of terror against Christians. A missionary named Graham Staines, who was running a program to help treat leprosy, was burned to death in his jeep, along with his two sons, ages eight to ten, while the killers surrounded the jeep and chanted "Victory to Hannuman," a Hindu god. This wave of terror has been characterized by church burnings, the murder of priests, the rape of nuns (supporters of the RSS, the parent organization of the ruling BJP described these murders as "patriotic"), attacks on prayer halls, and attacks on Christian schools. Reports indicate that over 200,000 Christians have been killed by the Indian government since 1947.

Mr. Speaker, America should not support this military provocation and human-rights abuse. We should stop all our aid to India until the human rights violations have ceased. We should also support the fundamental right of all peoples to self-determination. Whether it is the Sikhs of Khalistan, the Kashmiris in Indian-occupied Kashmir, or the people of Nagalim, all peoples and all nations should have the right to govern themselves. States which rule through the force of violence are destined to collapse. In the case of India, it is better that this happens peacefully like the Soviet breakup. We do not want another Yugoslavia in South Asia. And when all the people and nations of South Asia have achieved freedom, our help will bring us new allies in that troubled region.

Mr. Speaker, I would like to place the Agence France Presse article into the Record for the information of my colleagues.

From the Agence France Presse, June 6, 2001
Indian Expert Welcomes Russia's Anti-missile Offer

New Delhi, June 6 (AFP). Russia's offer to develop a national missile defence system for India is a "desirable development", an Indian defence expert said Wednesday.

"India should definitely says, We would like more details' It is a very desirable development," Institute of Defence Studies and Analysis deputy director Uday Bhaskar told AFP.

"This gives a sense of the direction that Indo-Russian strategic cooperation is likely to take," he added.

Russian Deputy Prime Minister Ilya Klebanov, who is holding talks with Indian Foreign Minister Jaswant Singh in Moscow, unexpectedly announced Wednesday that Russia would shortly make a full proposal on the system. Indian defence ministry officials in New Delhi declined to comment.

"The political intent now to pursue defence or even missile defences of deterrence is now becoming more palpable and evident," Bhaskar said.

U.S. Deputy Secretary of State Richard Armitage visited India last month to talk to leaders about the U.S. plan to build a missile defence shield, which India has partially supported.

Moscow has traditionally enjoyed warm ties with India, which is currently engaged in a nuclear arms race with arch-rival Pakistan.

However, Russia has expressed concern about India's initial warm response to the U.S. missile defense shield.

Bhaskar said India was correct to hold discussions with other world powers on the issue. "If India is talking to the Americans, then they should also talk to the others," Bhaskar said. Klebanov also said India and Russia would cooperate on the development "of the latest type of submarine". The two sides also agreed to jointly develop an II-214 military cargo plane.

***

Document

CONGRESSIONAL RECORD -- EXTENSIONS

Tuesday, June 12, 2001
107th Congress, 1st Session
147 Cong Rec E 1075

REFERENCE: Vol. 147, No. 81
SECTION: Extension of Remarks
TITLE: SIKHS REMEMBER ATTACK ON THE GOLDEN TEMPLE, THEIR MOST SACRED SHRINE

HON. EDOLPHUS TOWNS
of New York
in the House of Representatives
Tuesday, June 12, 2001

Mr. TOWNS . Mr. Speaker, in June 1984, the Indian government attacked the Golden Temple in Amritsar, the holiest shrine of the Sikh religion. Attacking the Golden Temple is the equivalent of attacking Mecca or the Vatican. It is a great affront to the Sikh Nation. As the Sikh martyr Jarnail Singh Bhindranwale, who was killed in the Golden Temple, said, "If the Indian government attacks the Golden Temple, it will lay the foundation of Khalistan," the name of the independent Sikh homeland which declared its independence on October 7, 1987.

This attack included the desecration of the Sikh holy scriptures, the Guru Granth Sahib, which they shot with bullets. Young Sikh boys were murdered. How can a democratic country commit this atrocity?

On June 2, Sikhs from around the East Coast demonstrated in protest of the Golden Temple massacre. Sikhs came from Philadelphia, Baltimore, Miami, and other places on the East Coast. They let it be known that the Sikhs still remember their martyrs and that the flame of freedom still burns in their hearts.

This launched a wave of violence which has killed over 250,000 Sikhs since 1984. In a new report, India is quoted as admitting that it held over 52,000 Sikh political prisoners without charge or trial. India has also killed more than 200,000 Christians in Nagaland and engaged in a wave of terror against them since Christmas 1998. Over 75,000 Kashmiri Muslims have died at the hands of the Indian government, as well as thousands of people from Assam, Manipur, and Tamil people, and Dalits (the dark-skinned "untouchables.")

America should not accept this kind of activity from a country that calls itself democratic. We should cut off aid to India until it allows full human rights for every citizen within its borders and we should support self-determination for all the peoples and nations of South Asia, such as the people of Khalistan, Kashmir, Nagalim, and others.

Mr. Speaker, I submit the Council of Khalistan's very informative press release on the June 2 demonstration into the Record.

Sikhs Observe Khalistan Martyrs Day
Indian Attack on Golden Temple Laid Foundation of Khalistan

Washington, D.C., June 2, 2001._Sikhs of the East Coast gathered in Washington, D.C. today to observe Khalistan Martyrs Day. This is the anniversary of the Indian government's brutal military attack on the Golden Temple, the Sikh Nation's holiest shrine, and 38 other Sikh Temples throughout Punjab. More than 20,000 Sikhs were killed in those attacks, known as Operation Bluestar. These martyrs laid down their lives to lay the foundation for Khalistan. On October 7, 1987, the Sikh Nation declared its homeland, Khalistan, independent.

"We thank all the demonstrators who came to this important protest," said Dr. Gurmit Singh Aulakh, President of the Council Khalistan. "We must remind the Indian government that Sikhs will never forget or forgive the Golden Temple desecration and the sacrifice the Sikh martyrs made for our freedom. These martyrs gave their lives so that the Sikh Nation could live in freedom," Dr. Aulakh said. "We salute them on Khalistan Martyrs' Day," he said. "As Sant Bhindranwale said, the Golden Temple attack laid the foundation of Khalistan."

The Golden Temple attack launched a campaign of genocide against the Sikhs that continues to this day. This genocide belies India's claims that it is a democracy. The Golden Temple attack made it clear that there is no place for Sikhs in India.

"Without political power nations perish. We must always remember these martyrs for their sacrifice," Dr. Aulakh said. "The best tribute to these martyrs would be the liberation of the Sikh homeland Punjab, Khalistan, from the occupying Indian forces," he said.

Over 50,000 Sikh political prisoners are rotting in Indian jails without charge or trial. Many have been in illegal custody since 1984. Since 1984, India has engaged in a campaign of ethnic cleansing in which thousands of Sikhs are murdered by Indian police and security forces and secretly cremated. The Indian Supreme Court described this campaign as "worse than a genocide." General Narinder Singh has said, "Punjab is a police state." U.S. Congressman Dana Rohrabacher has said that for Sikhs, Kashmiri Muslims, and other minorities "India might as well be Nazi Germany."

A report issued last month by the Movement Against State Repression (MASR) shows that India admitted that it held 52,268 political prisoners under the repressive "Terrorist and Disruptive Activities Act" (TADA). These prisoners continue to be held under TADA even though it expired in 1995. Persons arrested under TADA are routinely re-arrested upon their release. Cases were routinely registered against Sikh activists under TADA in states other than Punjab to give the police an excuse to continue holding them. The MASR report quotes the Punjab Civil Magistracy as writing "if we add up the figures of the last few years the number of innocent persons killed would run into lakhs hundreds of thousands. " There has been no list published of those who were acquitted under TADA.

In March 2000, while former President Clinton was visiting India, the Indian government murdered 35 Sikhs in the village of Chatti Singhpora in Kashmir and tried to blame the massacre on alleged militants. Indian security forces have murdered over 250,000 Sikhs since 1984, according to figures compiled by the Punjab State Magistracy and human-rights organizations. These figures were published in The Politics of Genocide by Inderjit Singh Jaijee. India has also killed over 200,000 Christians in Nagaland since 1947, over 75,000 Kashmiris since 1988, and tens of thousands of Untouchables as well as indigenous tribal peoples in Manipur, Assam and elsewhere.

The Indian government has also targeted Christians. They have been victims of a campaign of terror that has been going on since Christmas 1998. Churches have been burned, Christian schools and prayer halls have been attacked, nuns have raped, and priests have been killed. Missionary Graham Staines and his two sons were burned alive while they slept in their jeep by militant Hindu members of the RSS, the parent organization of the ruling BJP. Now his widow is being expelled from India.

"The Golden Temple massacre reminded us that if Sikhs are going to live with honor and dignity, we must have a free, sovereign, and independent Khalistan," Dr. Aulakh said.

***

Document

CONGRESSIONAL RECORD -- EXTENSIONS

Thursday, May 10, 2001
107th Congress, 1st Session
147 Cong Rec E 765

REFERENCE: Vol. 147, No. 64
SECTION: Extension of Remarks
TITLE: SIKH ACTIVIST MANN SHOULD APOLOGIZE FOR THREAT
ISSUED BY A LEADER OF HIS PARTY

HON. EDOLPHUS TOWNS
of New York
in the House of Representatives
Wednesday, May 9, 2001

Mr. TOWNS . Mr. Speaker, on Saturday, April 29, a number of Sikh leaders got together for Khalistan Day celebrations in Stockton, California. Overall, the event was very successful and it featured a number of outstanding speakers, including Dr. Gurmit Singh Aulakh, President of the Council of Khalistan, and Dr. Awatar Singh Sekhon, the Managing Editor of the International Journal of Sikh Affairs. Unfortunately, something that happened to Dr. Sekhon seriously marred this otherwise successful, celebratory event.

According to Burning Punjab, an online news service, a leading supporter of Member of Parliament Simranjit Singh Mann made a "death threat" against Dr. Sekhon after Dr. Sekhon strongly criticized Mr. Mann. Most of us in this House have been subjected to strong criticism but we have never threatened our critics nor would we permit our supporters to do so. That is not the democratic way.

Mr. Mann, a former member of the Punjab police who has become an Indian politician, has been silent on this event. If Mr. Mann wants to be taken seriously as a leader in a democratic state, he must condemn the threat that his supporter made and issue an apology on behalf of his party to Dr. Sekhon. Otherwise, people will see that there is no difference between Mr. Mann and other Indian politicians.

The Indian government's oppression of Sikhs, Christians, Muslims, and other religious minorities in India has been very well documented. Has that oppression now extended to an effort to suppress their critics in free countries like ours?

***

Document

CONGRESSIONAL RECORD -- EXTENSIONS

Thursday, May 10, 2001
107th Congress, 1st Session
147 Cong Rec E 773

REFERENCE: Vol. 147, No. 64
SECTION: Extension of Remarks
TITLE: FREEDOM FOR POLITICAL PRISONERS IN INDIA

HON. CYNTHIA A. McKINNEY
of Georgia
in the House of Representatives
Thursday, May 10, 2001

Ms. McKINNEY. Mr. Speaker, I was proud to be one of 19 signers of a letter sent last month to President Bush urging him to work to get political prisoners in India freed. We are Republicans and Democrats from across the political spectrum, but we understand that democracies don't hold political prisoners and countries that do are not friendly to democracy.

It is interesting that on the day after we sent our letter, a well-known Sikh human-rights organization called the Movement Against State Repression (MASR) issued a report exposing the continuing holding of political prisoners in India and the repressive laws under which they have been held, such as the very repressive "Terrorist and Disruptive Activities Act" (TADA), which expired in 1995. Despite this, many prisoners are still being held under TADA. According to the report, in many cases, the police would file TADA cases against the same individual in different states "to make it impossible for them to muster evidence in their favor," It was also common practice for police to re-arrest TADA prisoners who had been released, often without filing new charges.

MASR reports that the Indian government itself admitted in 1993 to 52,258 persons, detained under TADA. Of those, according to the report, "14,457 were in Punjab and 14,094 in Gujarat, a relatively peaceful state. Obviously there were a number of Sikh TADA prisoners held in Gujarat jails." Gujarat was only one state that the police would use to register secondary TADA cases against Sikhs. They would also register cases in Rajasthan, Madhya Pradesh, Uttar Pradesh, Haryana, and Delhi, among others.

"In November 1994," the report states, "42 employees of the Pilibhit district jail and PAC were found guilty of clubbing to death 6 Sikh prisoners and seriously wounding 22 others. They were TADA prisoners. Uttah Pradesh later admitted the presence of around 5000 Sikh TADA prisoners," the Movement Against State Repression wrote, "Another press report in 1993 mentioned beating of striking prisoners held in jail at Bharatpur, Rajasthan. Nearly 500 of these prisoners belonged to Punjab and were held under TADA," It was also in November 1994 that the Indian newspaper Hitavada reported that the Indian government paid the late Governor of Punjab, Surendra Nath, $1.5 billion to foment covert state-sponsored terrorist activity in Punjab and Kashmir.

According to the report, the Punjab Civil Magistracy wrote a memorandum to the Governor of Punjab in 1993 in which it said that "if we add up the figures of the last few years the number of innocent persons killed would add up to lakhs tens of thousands. " To this date, neither the central government nor the state government has revealed the list of people killed or those detained under TADA. In September 1995, the police kidnapped Jaswant Singh Khalra, a human-rights activist who exposed the government's policy of picking up innocent Sikhs, torturing them, murdering them, then cremating their bodies, declaring them "unidentified." The Jaijee report says that "thousands of Sikh young men have disappeared since 1984." According to General Narinder Singh, another human-rights leader, "Punjab is a police state."

The Movement Against State Repression is headed by Inderjit Singh Jaijee, a longtime human-rights activist who wrote the book The Politics of Genocide, which exposed the fact that the Indian government has killed over a quarter of a million Sikhs in the last 17 years. The government has also killed more than 200,000 Christians in Nagaland, over 70,000 Kashmiri Muslims, and many thousands of other minorities, including the Dalit "untouchables," the dark-skinned aboriginal natives of the subcontinent. Is this the behavior of a democracy?

If India is a democracy, as it claims, why does it need a Movement Against State Repression anyway?

According to Amnesty International, tens of thousands of Sikhs are being held in illegal detention in India without charge or trial. Some of them have been held since 1984. Many Christians, Muslims, and other minorities are also being held.

This is not an acceptable situation, Mr. Speaker. I am a minister's daughter. I understand the importance of religion and the need for religious tolerance. It is time to take action to protect the religious liberty of all the people of South Asia.

There are so many more details of this repression in the report that I do not have time to tell my colleagues about all of them. I would like to submit materials relating to this situation into the Record.

Like an Undeclared Emergency
(By G.S. Grewal)

Militancy in Punjab was not controlled by the extra-judicial killings or by the enforcement of harsh laws like TADA. It was contained, firstly, because the people in Punjab did not support it and secondly, by establishing democratic rule under the determined mass-based leader Sardar Beant Singh who had built a successful bridge between the people and the rulers.

Under the Terrorist and Disruptive Activities (Prevention) Act (TADA), not a single known militant had been convicted in Punjab. During Operation Black Thunder, more than 250 militants hiding in the Golden Temple complex were arrested and the whole scene was viewed by millions of people all over the world on television. They were booked under TADA. Within a few months, they had to be released from jail because of insufficient evidence. The prosecution made the request and the court discharged them. Mr. K.P.S. Gill was confronted with this episode at a Rotary Club (Mid town) meeting and he replied that the investigating agency had become corrupt. When he was asked how and why none of the persons discharged was alive, he preferred to duck the question.

The validity of TADA was challenged in the Supreme Court with the plea of the government in defence of TADA being that under abnormal circumstances, abnormal laws were necessary. This plea was accepted by the Court. The State counsel further argued that an undeclared war was going on with the active provocation of our neighbour. The situation could not be classified as a mere law and order or disturbance of public order. Activities of terrorists were such which could not be controlled by ordinary laws. So TADA had been framed to meet that special situation.

In actual practice, the TADA became notorious more for its abuse than for its legal use. The head of the police department assumed more powers than the Chief Secretary of the state. It became impossible to tame the DGP of that time. Even the Chief Minister time found himself helpless before the DGP who was more feared than respected. This was the era when many innocent people were illegally killed. Some because of suspicion, others because of greed and revenge. The CBI had discovered the dead bodies of thousands of people who were supposed to have been killed in fake encounters by the police.

At the insistence of the Supreme Court, the matter is being debated before the National Human Rights Commission, for the last many years but no decision has yet been taken. The era of terrorism in Punjab

Though the police was and is, by and large, a disciplined force, during militancy many of them lost their sense of commitment towards duty and were involved in making a quick buck.

Militancy not only affected the routine life of an average citizen, it also made the administration spineless. While some lawyers were killed, allegedly by the police because they defended militants, some district and session judges were attacked. Threats were issued to some High Court Judges and it was not too difficult to believe that the cause of justice had received a setback.

Since religious places remained the centre of militancy, the sanctity of those places was also damaged. It further facilitated the cause of those who wanted to exploit religion for political powers.

During the Emergency, the government gagged the press with some success. During militancy, the terrorists tried the same with partial success. Now, when there is neither militancy nor emergency the government wants to control the press by making a law which would compel the Press to disclose their sources, which they gather through their own resourcefulness. Nowhere in the free world are such conditions imposed on the Press.

When the Press is not free, even other institutions become weak. During the Emergency, fundamental rights were suspended and it created fear and havoc among those who wanted to be bold and fearless. Even the Judiciary ceased to protect people and started justifying the excesses of the Executive. In the case of ADM, Jabalpur, the Supreme Court held that even if a person was to be killed illegally by the state executive with malafide intentions, he had no right of life and could not seek protection from the courts. When the Emergency ended, many judges, who had constituted the bench, admitted that the judgement was wrong and the Janata Party Government had to pass the 44th Amendment to the Constitution to nullify the affect of the judgment.

If the proposed amendment in the new TADA was incorporated into the law of the land, it would operate as an undeclared emergency with its side-effects. In one sense, undeclared war is more dangerous than the declared one because it lasts much longer. Similarly, an undeclared emergency with lame freedom of the press would convert our enlightened, democratic free society to an ignorant and controlled system that the country could and should never accept.

- - - - - - - - -

June 3, 1997.

To: The Prime Minister of India, Mr. I.K. Gujral

Dear Prime Minister: The Movement Against State Repression is heartened to read Mr. K.P.S. Gill's open letter to you, published in The Tribune of June 1, 1997, and supports his demand for equality before the law for all persons, for prosecution of all persons, including police, as per the due process of law, and for a review of judicial, and administrative functioning in Punjab over the past 15 years.

Mr. Gill admits that security forces committed excesses during these years and pleads--not for immunity--but that they may be judged leniently in view of the circumstances. MASR has always advocated that justice be tempered by mercy. In the case of officers of the state accused of serious crimes it must be remembered that not only is the crime per se at issue, but there is an issue of public responsibility. All officers of the state, whether administrative, police or military, take an oath at the time of joining service to uphold the Constitution. This is a most sacred duty, making it all the more important for them to not only observe the law in letter and spirit in all their actions ... but to be seen to observe the law. When one sworn to uphold the law himself disregards it, the common citizen is all the more encouraged to hold the law in contempt.

The citizen does not exist for the state, rather the state exists for the citizen ... to provide protection to life and property, to provide opportunities for potential of every citizen may be realised and brought to productive use. This is the raison d'etre of the state. When officials of the state act in a way that betrays disrespect for human life they act against the very purpose of the state.

Mr. Gill asks for a special fund to be raised to pay for best legal defense of policemen brought to trial for excesses. There is reason to believe that the Punjab Police already gives policemen money to hire the best lawyers from its own secret fund. Is Mr. Gill in fact asking that this practice be brought into the open? In any case, the Constitution already empowers the courts to appoint lawyers at state expense for those who cannot afford them. However, "best lawyers" raises the issue of equality. If the state provides lawyers of great ability to the defendent while the complainant, having no such assistance, can only afford a weak lawyer, then where is equality before the law?

It may be remembered that the next of kin of the alleged militants suffered not only loss of their relatives but confiscation and destruction of property, with a result that they can ill afford litigation costs and in many cases have to depend on lawyers on "shared compensation" basis. This category of persons need state aid.

Aside from a commission to be set up to examine records of judicial processes, Mr. Gill demands a commission to identify all officers in all branches of the judiciary and administration who were guilty of gross dereliction of duty during this period. Mr. Gill goes on to urge that "these steps demand the active participation of the judiciary and the legislature". MASR appreciates this suggestion but cautions that while such commissions must be respected by the government, at the same time they must be independent and insulated from official pressures; their findings must be placed before the public. A situation in which the judiciary and legislature sits in judgement on themselves must be avoided. The interests of truth and justice demand independent commissions.

MASR points out that the past 15 years saw not only the malfeasance of individuals, it was also a period when institutions were subverted, with some services subjected to the dictation of others. The civil services ceased to control the police, rather the police controlled the civil services, including the state magistracy. Officers of the state medical service were made to give reports dictated by police. Even the office of governor came under Police domination to the extent that two governors were made to leave the state abruptly for demanding accountability from the police.

MASR sympathises with conscientious and upright officers of the Punjab Police who may feel that they have been unjustly maligned on account of the misdeeds of some of their colleagues. We also sympathise with the families of

It is certainly a terrible thing to be slandered. The entire Sikh community will vouch for this, as they have borne some of the most abhorrent epithets--"anti-national", "traitor", "terrorist", "religious fanatic"; the Sikh soldier has smarted under the label "questionable reliability". They have not only had to bear verbal insult, the Sikh community has been subjected to genocide on a terrible scale for the "crime" of demanding more powers for the state.

The Sikhs were made victims of politicians' power games. In "Policing the Police", (Indian Express, August, 1996) Shekhar Gupta asked "... who provided K.P.S. Gill and a select band of the most trusted Intelligence Bureau aces suitcases full of unaudited cash to buy militant loyalties, to build a whole army of cats? ... The Punjab crisis saw five prime ministers as many internal security ministers. Each one knew precisely what was going on. Some routinely boasted of how ruthlessly they were putting rebellion down. Why are they hiding now?"

In his letter, Gill says "the real question is whether a strategy of state terrorism was adopted by the police; and the answer is unequivocally in the negative." Was the strategy adopted at a higher level and simply passed on to the police for implementation? In "Dateline: Tarn Taran" (Pioneer, June 1, 1997) Ajaz Ashraf and Bindu quote Satya Pal Dang as *saying: "The clearance for fake encounters could have only been given by political leaders."*

Regarding Mr. Gill's apprehensions of "media trial" of accused policemen and hounding of the police in the press, MASR sees little evidence to support these misgivings. The press, both local and national, has given ample space to police versions both during the worst days of turmoil and now. Nearly two full columns of precious space have been spared for Mr. Gill's letter--surely that does not bespeak a biased press. No human rights group has ever had it's letter published in full, even if it were a short one.

Mr. Gill accuses the human rights movement of twisting facts. If we have erred in respect of any case we are sorry. Part of the problem is that we must rely on Mr. Gill for much of our information. For instance in his letter he writes: "Even in a case as fully documented as Operation Blackthunder, where the entire action was carried out in full view of the media, not a single conviction was pronounced." But earlier, addressing a Rotary Club (Midtown) meeting, Mr. Gill said: "that some people sympathetic to the militants had infiltrated into the prosecution agency of the police and, therefore, enough evidence could not be collected" and subsequently cases against all the persons accused in Operation Black Thunder had to be withdrawn. Mr. G.S. Grewal, Advocate General has accused Mr. Gill of twisting facts. Grewal says: "Those persons who were arrested during Operation Black Thunder were in fact put on trial. After a few months all were released at the insistence of the prosecution because of lack of evidence. It is another matter that, perhaps, none of them may be alive today. It will be too much to presume that they have died a natural death."

Mr. Gill also has no reason to disparage the human rights movement. Human rights are for all, including Mr. Gill and his policemen. Human rights stands for political and religious freedom, for the legal rights of common citizen of criminal offenses.

Mr. Prime Minister, a previous letter sent to you jointly by MASR, PHRO and PUCL Punjab Chapter, will be in your hands. This letter asked your support for our request to the Punjab Chief Minister Parkash Singh Badal for an independent census of human rights violations, including killings and disappearances during the 1984-1996 period. We had also enclosed the various assessments regarding disappearances and killings. We again ask for your help in implementing this census.

> *With regards,*
> *Yours sincerely,*
> *Inderjit Singh Jaijee,*
> *Convenor, Movement Against State Repression.*

- - - - - - - - -

From the Burning Punjab News, May 9, 2001
Bihar--Blast in Church, Christ Statue Damaged

Muzaffapur.--Cracker explosions by miscreants in a church here has caused partial damage to a statute of Christ sending shock waves among the Christian community in the Bihar town, official sources said. The unidentified miscreants burst three crackers one after another on Saturday evening in St. Francis Church which led to the ripping off of the head of a statute of child Christ seated on the lap of St. Joseph, the sources said. The miscreants also left behind pamphlets which said "Seva Ki Aar Mein Dharmantaran Band Karo (stop religious conversions in the garb of service)," "Isaiyon Bharat Choro (Christians leave India)" and "Poore Bharat Ko Hindu Rang Mein Rangna Hai (Hindus should prevail in entire India)." An FIR was lodged at the local police station by Father Julius Lazarus of the church. The top district and police officials remained tight-lipped over the incident, but said the investigation was on. A police contingent had also been posted at the church, they said. When contacted, State Director General of Police RR Prasad in Patna ruled out the possibility of the explosion being triggered by bombs and said the police were looking into the matter. Lazarus said the Christian community was terribly hurt by the incident and described it as "extremely serious." He felt that some religious institution was behind the incident, but refused to name anybody.

***

Document

CONGRESSIONAL RECORD -- EXTENSIONS

Tuesday, May 08, 2001
107th Congress, 1st Session
147 Cong Rec E 752

REFERENCE: Vol. 147, No. 62
SECTION: Extension of Remarks
TITLE: VAISAKHI DAY

HON. DAN BURTON
of Indiana
in the House of Representatives
Tuesday, May 8, 2001

Mr. BURTON of Indiana . Mr. Speaker, the Sikhs recently celebrated their important holiday of Vaisakhi Day. It is the 302nd birthday of the Sikh Nation. On Vaisakhi Day in 1699, Guru Gobind Singh, the last of the Sikh gurus, formed the Khalsa Panth. He blessed them with the blessing "Raj Kare Ga Khalsa," which means, "the Khalsa shall rule."

The Sikhs consider Vaisakhi a very important holiday. It is effectively the Sikh national holiday. As this Vaisakhi Day passed, however, the Sikh Nation still lives in slavery.

Sikhs ruled Punjab from 1765 to 1849. They ran a secular state with religious tolerance. Sikhs, Muslims, and Hindus participated in the government. When the British vacated the subcontinent, the Sikhs were to receive sovereign power, but they were taken in by the false promises of Nehru and Gandhi that they would have freedom in Punjab. No Sikh representative has ever signed the Indian constitution, and many Sikhs are demanding their independence, as declared on October 7, 1987. Although they seek this peacefully, India considers anyone who speaks out for a separate Sikh state, called Khalistan, to be a "terrorist." Instead, it is India that has used the tools of terrorism.

A new report from the Movement Against State Repression shows that the Indian government holds, by its own admission, at least 52,268 political prisoners under the illegal and expired "Terrorist and Disruptive Activities Act," called TADA. Both the Movement Against State Repression and Amnesty International have confirmed that tens of thousands of political prisoners are being held without charge or trial. Some of them have been in jail since 1984. According to The Politics of Genocide by respected human-rights worker Inderjit Singh Jaijee, the Indian government since 1984 has murdered over 250,000 Sikhs. They join thousands of Christians, Muslims, Dalits, and others who have been killed at the hands of the Indian government.

In the spirit of Vaisakhi, the U.S. Congress should support freedom for the Sikh Nation and the other nations of South Asia who are seeking their sovereignty and independence. We must support a free and fair plebiscite in Punjab, Khalistan, on the question of independence and also plebiscites for Kashmir, as India promised in 1948, for Nagalim, and for all the nations living under Indian occupation. We should also cut off American aid until India learns to respect its own laws and the basic human rights of all people. Let the Sikhs, celebration of Vaisakhi remind us that the freedom is the birthright of all peoples and nations.

Council of Khalistan,
Washington, DC, April 16, 2001.
Open Letter to the Sikh Nation:
Political Prisoners Should Run in Elections
Form Khalsa Raj Party, Start a Stantmai Morcha to Free Khalistan

Several reports, including a recent one from Amnesty International, confirm that tens of thousands of Sikh political prisoners are being held in illegal detention in India without charge or trial. Democracies do not hold political prisoners, yet tens of thousands of political prisoners are being held in "the world's largest democracy."

Recently, 19 Members of the U.S. Congress wrote to President Bush asking him to get involved in the effort to secure freedom for these political prisoners. These political prisoners are being held for peaceful activities in support of a sovereign, independent Khalistan and/or activities in support of human rights. Some of these political prisoners have been held since 1984. We must secure their freedom.

Sovereignty is essential to the survival of the Sikh Nation. As long as we live under Indian rule, these political prisoners will continue to be held and we will all continue to live as slaves. The only way that Sikhs can live in freedom is to liberate our homeland. Self-determination is the right of all peoples and nations.

We must tell the Indian government that we demand our freedom. In order to do so, the political prisoners should run for Parliament and for the Legislative Assembly under the banner of the Khalsa Raj Party. The primary plank of the Khalsa Raj Party should be freedom for Khalistan. The Khalsa Panth must be prepared to pay any price, whatever it may be, to free ourselves from the occupation of the Indian government.

We must have a full and fair plebiscite on the status of Khalistan and we must launch a Shantmai Morcha to liberate Khalistan. If the political prisoners run for office, Sikhs will have someone to vote for who is committed to freedom. None of the current parties will make any effort to liberate Khalistan.

If the political prisoners will not run for office from their jail cells, then their family members should be given the Khalsa Raj Party ticket in the elections. We must have a real choice that will allow us to demand our freedom. Only then can our ve make any difference. Let us vote for a free Khalistan, not just for a change of faces among the oppressors.

Guru Gobind Singh Sahib gave sovereignty to the Khalsa Panth. "In Grieb Sikhan Ko Deon Patshahi", that is "Khalsa shall rule and is sovereign." Guru gave the Sikh Nation sovereignty. Nations that do not have sovereignty perish. Nations that do not have political power vanish from the face of the Earth. Sikhs are instructed to remain free always. It is time to reclaim freedom that is our birthright. In a free Khalistan Sikhs will enjoy freedom and respect the world over. For the survival of Sikh Nation, we must regain our lost sovereignty. It is our duty as Sikhs.

The present Akali government and its leadership is corrupt to its bone. The Akalis are in alliance with the militant Hindu fundamentalist BJP, which has recently been rocked by a corruption scandal as well. They are agents of the Indian government. They take their orders from Delhi rulers. They lie to the Sikh Nation. We must discard them now and replace them with a new committed, honest, pro-Khalsa Panth leadership.

As instructed by the Guru, Banda Singh Bahadar established the first Khalsa Raj in 17 10 after the complete destruction of city of Sirhand where the two younger sons of Guru Sahib were beheaded after immobilizing them in a wall. Sikhs regained

In 1947, when India was divided, the cunning and deceitful Hindu leadership of Nehru and Gandhi promised that Sikhs would have the glow of freedom in Punjab and that no law affecting Sikh rights would be passed without Sikh consent. As soon as the transfer of power had occurred and India was free, those promises were broken. Instead, India began its effort to wipe out the Sikh people, the Sikh Nation, and the Sikh religion. The Home Ministry even sent a circular to the deputy commissioners of Punjab saying that Sikhs are "a criminal tribe" and should be carefully watched. Since independence, Sikhs have been persecuted, betrayed, robbed of their natural resources, and discriminated against. We must stand up against the oppressors and say enough is enough. We will no longer live under your oppressive regime.

Badal did not even fulfill the promises he made before the election. How can they call themselves an Akali government when more than 50,000 people have been tortured, murdered, declared unidentified, and cremated by the police? There is no accountability for them and no police official has been punished. How can they call themselves an Akali government when they have not punished Swaran Singh Ghotna, the murderer of Jathedar Gurdev Singh Kaunke, and the other police officers who kidnapped and murdered human-rights activist Jaswant Singh Khalra? With a Khalsa Raj Party and with the politicl prisoners elected, these people can be brought to justice.

In pursuit of its divide and rule strategy, the Indian government has murdered over 250,000 Sikhs in their effort to create fear psychosis and destroy the Sikh freedom movement. Tens of thousands of Sikh youth are being held as political prisoners without charge or trial. Recently, it has tried to set the Sikhs and the Kashmiri Muslims against each other by creating incidents between the communities. Over 20,000 people were murdered in Delhi alone after Indira Gandhi's assassination. So far, the perpetrators of these heinous crimes roam free in Delhi. The Khalsa Raj Party must demand accountability for the perpetrators of these atrocities.

After the Golden Temple attack in June 1984 by the Indian government it was clear to the Sikhs that the Indian government is determined to destroy Sikhism completely. The attack on the Golden Temple was conducted to crush the Sikh aspirations of Khalsa Raj. It doesn't matter whether Congress or the BJP runs the government. Former Indian Prime Minister Chandra Shekhar said that there is no difference between Congress and the BJP. He is right. The party label on the Hindu majority does not matter. Congress and BJP are equally anti-Sikh. Only a Khalsa Raj Party will work to break the cycle of tyranny and oppression.

Do you want to live as slaves and jeopardize the future of your children and your children's children, disobeying the Guru's order of Raj Kare Ga Khalsa, or do you want to free yourself from the slavery of the Indian government and enjoy the blessings and happiness of Guru by freeing Khalistan? Always remember that the Guru gave the Sikh Nation Charhdi Kala.

For the Charhdi Kala of the Khalsa Panth, let's join hands to form a Khalsa Raj Party to free our homeland, Khalistan. We pray and ask the blessing of the Guru to help us achieve the pious, God-given right to freedom for the Sikh Nation. The Khalsa Panth prays for the well being of the whole human race. We wish every human being in the world, including South Asia, well. We hope that the entire world will live in peace and freedom and let the Sikh Nation also flourish, prosper, and enjoy the glow of freedom in a free Khalistan.

Khalsa Ji, always remember "Khalsa Bagi Yan Badhshah" and "Raj Kare Ga Khalsa."

> *Sincerely,*
> *Dr. Gurmit Singh Aulakch,*
> *President Council of Khalistan.*

***

Document

CONGRESSIONAL RECORD -- EXTENSIONS

Tuesday, May 01, 2001
107th Congress, 1st Session
147 Cong Rec E 679

REFERENCE: Vol. 147, No. 57
SECTION: Extension of Remarks
TITLE: CONGRATULATIONS TO SIKH NATION ON VAISAKHI DAY

HON. EDOLPHUS TOWNS
of New York
in the House of Representatives
Tuesday, May 1, 2001

Mr. TOWNS . Mr. Speaker, April 13 was the anniversary of the founding of the Sikh Nation by Guru Gobind Singh, called Vaisakhi Day. It is the most important of Sikh holidays. I would like to take this opportunity to congratulate the Sikhs on Vaisakhi Day.

Sikhs have made many contributions to American life in fields ranging from agriculture to law to medicine. One Sikh, Dalip Singh Saund, even served in the House of Representatives, representing a California district in the late 50s to the early 1960s.

Sikhs are suffering from significant persecution in India. Since 1984, according to The Politics of Genocide by Inderjit Singh Jaijee, over 250,000 Sikhs have been killed by the Indian government. A new report from the Movement Against State Repression--an organization that should not be necessary in a democracy--confirms that tens of thousands of Sikh political prisoners are being held in illegal detention in India without charge or trial, some for as long as 17 years! This confirms what Amnesty International had previously reported. 19 of us from both parties sent a letter to the President last month urging him to get involved in freeing these political prisoners.

This is part of a pattern of repression against religious minorities that engulfs India. In India, there has been an ongoing campaign of terror against the Christian community since Christmas 1998, which many of us have discussed in the Record. It has included killing priests, burning churches, raping nuns, and burning a missionary and his two young sons to death in their jeep while they slept. Muslims have also been subjected to fierce religious oppression. It is time for India to live up to the standards of a democratic state.

The fact that Vaisakhi Day this year coincided with the Jewish celebration of Passover, which celebrates the escape from slavery, and the Christian celebration of Good Friday and Easter, celebrating the triumph of life over death, should underline the importance of freedom, life, and basic human rights for all people.

American is the hope of the world. It is the land of freedom. We must take a stand for freedom. It is time to stop American aid and trade with India until it respects basic human rights. Also, it is time to declare our support for self-determination for the people of Khalistan, Kashmir, Nagalim, and all the other nations seeking their freedom. This would be a great way to celebrate Vaisakhi and Easter, by doing our part to bring freedom to all the people and nations of the subcontinent.

I am including the Council of Khalistan's press release on Vaisakhi Day in the Record for the information of my colleagues.

A Time for Freedom

Washington, D.C., April 9, 2001--Citing the words of Guru Gobind Singh, who said "Recognize ye all the human race as one," Dr. Gurmit Singh Aulakh, President of the Council of Khalistan, extends Happy Vaisakhi Day wishes to the Sikh Nation, Happy Easter wishes to the Christian community, and Happy Passover wishes to the Jewish community. "It is interesting that these celebrations and the birthday of Thomas Jefferson, author of the American Declaration of Independence, all come together at this time," Dr. Aulakh said. The Council of Khalistan is the organization leading the Sikh Nation's struggle for freedom for its homeland, Khalistan.

Vaisakhi Day, which marks the formation of the Khalsa Panth by guru Gobind Singh in 1699, falls on April 13, which is also Mr. Jeferson's birthday. This year, April 13 is also Good Friday in the Christian calendar. April 15 is Easter. The Jewish holiday of Passover started this past weekend and runs for eight days, concluding this coming weekend.

Passover celebrates the Jewish people's escape from slavery in Egypt. Good Friday is the observance of Jesus's death on the cross, followed on Sunday by the Resurrection. It celebrates not only the resurrection of Jesus, but also the triumph of life over death and the resurrection of spirit in every person.

"The coming-together of these important occasions is a time to celebrate freedom," said Dr. Aulakh. "As the Jewish community celebrates the escape of their ancestors from slavery in Egypt, let us rededicate our efforts to the cause of freedom for the Sikh Nation," he said. "As Thomas Jefferson wrote, when a government becomes destructive of the inalienable rights of any people, 'it is the right of the people to alter or abolish it.' Guru instructed the Sikh Nation to oppose tyranny wherever it is found. Let us step up the struggle against the tyranny that engulfs our own people," he said. "As Christians celebrate the triumph of life, let us devote ourselves to protecting the life of our Sikh brothers and sisters and the

Sikh Nation by liberating our homeland, Khalistan, from Indian occupation."

Dr. Aulakh called on the Sikhs in Punjab, Khalistan to observe Vaisakhi as a day of prayer and introspection, not working or doing business with the Indian government, but taking a day to go to the Gurdwara and celebrate the lives of the Gurus and remember their words. He also urged them to pray for freedom for the Sikh Nation and also for every other people in the world.

"India is not a democracy for Sikhs, Muslims, Christians, and other minorities," said Dr. Aulakh. "Congressman Rohrabacher was right when he said that for minorities 'India might as well be Nazi Germany.' " Police witnesses have confirmed that the police tortured and murdered the former Jathedar of the Akal Takht, Gurdev Singh Kaunke, and human-rights activist Jaswant Singh Khalra.

Sikhs ruled Punjab up to 1849 when the British conquered the subcontinent. Sikhs were equal partners during the transfer of power from the British. The Muslim leader Jinnah got Pakistan for his people, the Hindu leaders got India, but the Sikh leadership was fooled by the Hindu leadership promising that Sikh would have "the glow of freedom" in Northwest India and the Sikhs took their share with India. Sikhism was not even recognized in the Indian constitution as a separate religion, while Islam, Buddhism, Hinduism, etc., were recognized. Discrimination against the Sikh Nation took place in every sphere. After the Golden Temple attack, the Sikh Nation stepped up its struggle to achieve its God-given right to the free. Tens of thousands of Sikh political prisoners are rotting in Indian jails without charge or trial. On October 7, 1987, the Sikh Nation declared the independence of its homeland, Punjab, Khalistan. No Sikh representative has ever signed the Indian constitution. The Sikh Nation demands freedom for Khalistan.

The government of India has murdered over 250,000 Sikhs since 1984, more than 200,000 Christians since 1947, over 70,000 Muslims in Kashmir since 1988, and tens of thousands of Tamils, Assamese, Manipurls, Daltis (the aboriginal people of the subcontinent), and others. The Indian Supreme Court called the Indian government's murders of Sikhs "worse than a genocide." Government-allied Hindu militants have murdered priests, and raped nuns. Hindu radicals, members of the Bajrang Dal, burned missionary Graham Stewart Staines and his two sons, ages 10 and 8, to death while they surrounded the victims and chanted "Victory to Hannuman," a Hindu god.

"Democracies don't commit genocide," Dr. Aulakh said. "India should stop the repression and allow a plebiscite on the future status of Kashmir, Nagaland, and Khalistan," he said. "Only freedom will bring peace and justice in South Asia."

***

Document

CONGRESSIONAL RECORD -- EXTENSIONS

Thursday, March 29, 2001
107th Congress, 1st Session
147 Cong Rec E 499

REFERENCE: Vol. 147, No. 44
SECTION: Extension of Remarks
TITLE: CORRUPTION SCANDAL ENGULFS INDIAN GOVERNMENT

HON. DAN BURTON
of Indiana
in the House of Representatives
Thursday, March 29, 2001

Mr. BURTON of Indiana . Mr. Speaker, the world has been shocked by the recent news stories about a corruption scandal that has engulfed the Indian government. Already, the president of the ruling BJP and the Defense Minister have been forced to resign after they were caught taking bribes from two internet news reporters posing as arms dealers in regard to a fake defense contract. The opposition is calling for the government to resign.

The resignation of Defense Minister George Fernandes is no loss for friends of democracy. Mr. Fernandes is the man who led a meeting in 1999 with the Ambassadors from China, Cuba, Russia, Libya, Serbia, and Iraq aimed at putting together a security alliance "to stop the U.S." This meeting was reported in the May 18, 1999 issue of the Indian Express.

Those of us who have been following Indian and South Asian issues are not surprised. The Indian Government has demonstrated many times before how deeply it is infected with corruption. In India, people have come up with a new word for bribery. They call it "fee for service." It has become necessary to pay a fee to get government workers of any kind to deliver the services that they are mandated to provide. In November 1994, the newspaper Hitavada reported that the Indian government paid Surendra Nath, the late governor of Punjab, $1.5 billion to generate terrorist activity in Punjab, Khalistan, and in Kashmir as well. This is in a country where half the population lives below the international poverty line. Forty-two percent of the people live on less than a dollar a day and another forty-two percent live on less than $2 per day.

In India, corruption is endemic as is tyranny against minorities. Christians, Muslims, Sikhs, and others have been subjected to violence, tyranny, and massive human-rights violations for many years. Christian churches have been burned. Priests have been killed, nuns have been raped, and many other atrocities have been committed with impunity. Muslims have been killed in massive numbers and the ruling party has destroyed mosques. The Indian government has killed Sikhs. Religious pilgrims have been attacked with lathis and tear gas. This is just a recent sample of the atrocities against minorities in India.

Mr. Speaker, India is a significant recipient of American aid. Why should the taxpayers of this country pay taxes to support the corruption and tyranny of the Indian Government? There is, however, something that America, as the world's only superpower, can do about it. America can stop sending aid to India and support self-determination for the people of Khalistan, Kashmir, and Nagalim. Let us take these steps to free the people of the subcontinent from corruption and brutality.

Mr. Speaker, I insert into the Record an article from the current issue of The Economist about the latest Indian Government bribery scandal. I commend it to all my congressional colleagues who care about spending our foreign aid dollars wisely.

From The Economist, Mar. 24, 2001
India's Corruption Blues

Though it may well survive the latest corruption scandal, the authority of the leading party in the government is badly dented

Fatalism is ever present in India, and the government in Delhi seems to be hoping that a popular belief in the inevitability of corruption will help it survive the biggest scandal of recent times. That hope seems well founded. But whether the government will regain the authority it needs to pursue its two main initiatives--economic reform and peace in Kashmir-- is much more doubtful.

The uproar over the release of videotapes last week showing top politicians and officials taking bribes from two Internet news reporters posing as arms dealers has reached a noisy impasse. The defence minister, George Fernandes, has resigned, though he remains "covener" of the 18-party ruling National Democratic Alliance. The NDA has lost one member, the Trinamul Congress party of West Bengal, but remains sure enough of its majority to dare the opposition to bring a no-confidence vote in Parliament. The opposition, equally sure of its minority, has declined. Instead, it has blocked parliamentary proceedings for a week, relenting long enough only to allow money to be voted for the state to continue functioning.

Both sides have converted an occasion for shame into one for self-righteousness. Sonia Gandhi, leader of a suddenly alert Congress party, vowed at its plenary meeting in Bangalore to "wage every war" to "ensure that this country is liberated from the shackles of this corrupt, shameful and communal government". But she herself was wounded when her own personal assistant came under investigation in a separate scandal. The prime minister, Atal Bihari Vajpayee, has blended penitence with defensiveness. He has promised a judicial probe into the allegations, and a clean-up. But, in a television address on March 16th, Mr. Vajpayee reserved the word "criminal" to describe the hurling of allegations, not the behaviour alleged.

It is true that tehelka.com, the enterprising website that armed its reporters with cash and spy cameras, used surreptitious means to persuade a variety of officials, generals and politicians to accept a total of 1.1m rupees (about $24,000) in bribes and gifts. It is also true that some of the *most serious allegations made against Mr. Fernandes and Brajesh Mishra, the prime minister's top aide, among others, are unsubstantiated gossip. But they have concentrated discussion on how many more heads will roll and when.*

The real import of the tapes is the evidence they give that corruption is the norm, not the exception, at every level of public life. This does not surprise Indians, who are expected to bribe everyone, starting with traffic policemen. India is beset by what some call a crisis of governance, which compromises nearly every public service, from defence to the distribution of subsidised food to the generation of electricity. Tehelka.com has simply rubbed Indians' faces in it.

Politicians, in honest moments, admit this, Kapil Sibal, a prominent member of Congress, says "the system is thoroughly corrupt." Pramod Mahajan, the minister of information technology and a member of Mr. Vajpayee's Bhraratiya Janata Party (BJP), thinks the voters face a choice "not between good and bad. It is between bad and worse."

With turpitude so common, removing one group of parties from power would not solve the problem. Given a chance to fight political corruption, Parliament usually ducks it. It now wants to shear the Central Vigilance Commission, the main body implementing anti-corruption law, of its role overseeing investigations of politicians.

The problem begins, says N. Vittal, the central vigilance commissioner, with the 40% of the economy that is unaccounted for. Indian democracy runs on this murky money. The total cost of a campaign for a parliamentary election has been estimated at 20 billion rupees (around $430m), which is often paid for by undeclared donations of the sort proffered by tehelka.com. Reformers such as Mr. Vittal want such donations to be declared and made tax deductible. Some also want the Election Commission to give the voters information about candidates' criminal backgrounds, as Delhi's High Court has directed. But that reform may also be stopped: the government has appealed against the decision. No one in power seems to back the promised cleaning.

Mr. Vajpayee's immediate concern is the fate of his closet advisers, widely resented for accumulating power in the prime minister's office at the expense of other ministries. On March 19th, Mr. Mishra and N.K. Singh, his top economic adviser, called a press conference to defend themselves against claims that they had improperly influenced decisions on deals in telecoms, power and, in Mr. Mishra's case, defence equipment. Pressure for their dismissal, form some of Mr. Vajpayee's best friends, is mounting. A fiercely right-wing ally of the BJP, the Shiv Sena, is calling for their heads. And although the Rashtriya Swayamsevak Sangh (Association of National Volunteers), ideological big brother to the BJP, has withdrawn its calls for their removal, it has done so only for fear of destablishing the government.

The departure of Mr. Mishra and Mr. Singh would probably blunt the government's drive for economic reform. Even if they stay, Mr. Vajpayee will have trouble enacting the most controversial but valuable elements of the reforms announced along with the budget last month. These include privatisation and making labour law more flexible. The labour reform requires the approval of Parliament's upper house, where the government lacks a majority. The crisis may also strengthen the home ministry, thought to be more reluctant than the prime minister's advisers to make gestures to separatists in Kashmir. If Mr. Vajpayee survives the tehelka scandal, he may begin to ask himself what, exactly, he is in power for.

***

Document

CONGRESSIONAL RECORD -- EXTENSIONS

Thursday, March 08, 2001
107th Congress, 1st Session
147 Cong Rec E 319

REFERENCE: Vol. 147, No. 30
SECTION: Extension of Remarks
TITLE: ARMY RESERVE OFFICER NOT ALLOWED TO WEAR RELIGIOUS SYMBOL

HON. EDOLPHUS TOWNS
of New York
in the House of Representatives
Thursday, March 8, 2001

Mr. TOWNS . Mr. Speaker, Dr. Trilok Singh Puniani is a member of the Army Reserve who is being denied the right to wear the symbol of his religion. Dr. Puniani is a Sikh and is required by his religion to wear his turban. It is one of the five symbols of Sikhism. Dr. Gurmit Singh Aulakh, President of the Council of Khalistan, has written to the President on Dr. Puniani's behalf.

Dr. Puniani joined the Army reserve in 1999. There had been a exemption granted that permitted the wearing of a turban while in uniform and there are three Sikhs who have achieved the rank of Colonel who wear their turbans. However, new regulations adopted in July 1999, just a month before Dr. Puniani joined the Army Reserve, denied this exemption for those who joined the service after 1984.

Mr. Speaker, the turban is not a hat. It is a religious symbol like the cross or the star of David. It should be afforded the same treatment.

One concern about this regulation is that it might discourage Sikhs and other minorities from joining the military services of the United States. Our armed services need manpower. We should not be discouraging anyone from joining. These minority Americans are important to our country and to the Army.

Canada and Britain have significant numbers of Sikhs in their military. They both allow these Sikhs to wear their turbans. Why can't we?

Whatever your religious beliefs, the military should treat you equally. This is about civil rights and equal treatment. We cannot give a preference to any religion, but we also cannot discriminate against any religion. I strongly urge the Secretary of Defense to restore the exemption so that the religious expression of Dr. Puniani and others will be respected.

I insert Dr. Puniani's complaint and Dr. Aulakh's letter to the President into the Record.

Council of Khalistan,
1901 Pennsylvania Ave. NW, Suite 802
Washington, DC
February 20, 2001
Hon. George W. Bush,
President of the United States,
The White House,
Washington, DC.

Dear Mr. President: Today I received by email a letter from Dr. Trilok Singh Puniani, who is a practicing physician and a member of the Army Reserve. He wrote to me about the regulation of July 1999 denying Sikhs who joined the military after 1984 the ability to wear their turbans.

The turban is a symbol of the Sikh religion. A practicing Sikh is symbolized by five symbols, one of which is uncut hair covered by a turban. In view of this, Dr. Puniani writes that "this new regulation will deprive the opportunity of joining the US Armed Forces of many aspiring Sikhs who have tremendous potential to serve the country." I agree with him. This would be a loss for America and for its armed forces.

Today there are over half a million Sikh citizens in the United States. They would be deprived of the opportunity to serve their country, the United States of America.

Not to allow Sikhs in the military to practice their Sikh religion is discriminatory and bad for morale. Sikhs fought valiantly in World Wars I and II along with the Allied forces in Europe and Africa. They suffered heavy casualties. The Sikh soldiers wore their turbans. Belgium erected a special monument to the Sikh forces in Ypres.

The British and Canadian forces encourage Sikhs to maintain their Sikh appearance. I respectfully urge you to follow their lead and order the armed forces of the United States to allow Sikhs to practice their religion. By so doing, you would raise the morale and effectiveness of the armed forces. America allows freedom of religion and the armed forces would be the best place to put it into practice.

Thank you for your attention to this problem. God bless you and God bless America.

Sincerely,
Dr. Gurmit Singh Aulakh,
President, Council of Khalistan.

Enclosure: Email from Dr. Puniani.
Received by email, February 20, 2001
Re Denial of Sikh attire in the U.S. Army.

Respected Dr. Aulakh, I would like to bring to your attention that I am in the U.S. Army Reserve since Aug. 1999. According to army regulation there was a provision to an exception for religious accommodation to wear turban while in the uniform. However, with new regulation published in July 1999 retroactive as of 1984, the request for religious accommodation will not be entertained, with exception of Sikhs who joined the U.S. Army prior to 1984.

To my knowledge, there are three other turbaned Sikhs in the US Army in the rank of Colonels. I am not sure about their date of commission. Those of us who joined the army after 1984 may have to separate honorably.

My concern is that this new regulation will deprive the opportunity of joining the US Armed Forces of many aspiring Sikhs who have tremendous potential to serve the country. America is the champion of democracy and we are being discriminated. I believe as physicians and in other fields we are a valuable asset to the US Army.

The Sikh soldiers are well respected in the British and Canadian Royal Armed Forces and encouraged to maintain their Sikh appearance. Why this discrimination in the US?

I think that this matter be brought to the attention of the Senators and the Congress in Washington for us Sikhs to be part and parcel of this nation and allowed to serve the country with pride.

I am also writing to my local congressman and the unit commanders of the US Army Reserve.

I am looking forward to seeing you in person when you visit us in Fresno. I will be happy to provide you with more information if needed.

Wish you all the best and a long life.

> *Trilok S. Puniani,*
> *Fresno, CA.*

***

Document

CONGRESSIONAL RECORD -- EXTENSIONS

Wednesday, March 07, 2001
107th Congress, 1st Session
147 Cong Rec E 298

REFERENCE: Vol. 147, No. 29
SECTION: Extension of Remarks
TITLE: CHRISTIAN PRIESTS ABDUCTED AND BEATEN IN INDIA

HON. DAN BURTON
of Indiana
in the House of Representatives
Wednesday, March 7, 2001

Mr. BURTON of Indiana . Mr. Speaker, I was distressed to recently hear that two priests were abducted and beaten in India. On January 4, according to a report in India-West, the priests, known as Simon and David, were abducted from the village of Zer in Rajasthan and taken to the neighboring state of Gujarat, where they were beaten.

Unfortunately, this is just the latest in a series of attacks on Christians in the so-called "world's largest democracy" which has been going on since Christmas of 1998. It follows the murders of other priests, the rape of nuns, church burnings, attacks on Christian schools and prayer halls, the burning deaths of missionary Graham Staines and his two sons while they slept in their jeep by Hindu militants chanting "Victory to Hannuman (a Hindu god)," and other incidents.

After one incident that involved the rape of nuns, the VHP, which is part of the pro-Fascist RSS (the parent organization of the ruling BJP, hailed the rapists as "patriotic youth" and denounced the nuns as "antinational elements." BJP leaders have said openly that everyone who lives in India must either be Hindu or be subservient to Hinduism. It has even been reported that the RSS has published a booklet on how to implicate Christians and other religious minorities, such as Sikhs and Muslims, in false criminal cases. The Indian government has killed more than 200,000 Christians in Nagaland. This pattern of religious tyranny and terrorism is apparently what India considers religious freedom.

It is not just Christians who have suffered from this kind of persecution, of course, but it seems to be their turn to be the featured victims. Sikhs, Muslims, and others have also been persecuted at the hands of the Indian government. Over 250,000 Sikhs have been murdered by the Indian government. Two independent investigations have shown that the massacre of 35 Sikhs in the village of Chithi Singhpora was carried out by the Indian government. The evidence also seems to show that the Indian government is responsible for the recent massacre of Sikhs in Kashmir. In November, 3,200 Sikhs, who were trying to get to Nankana Sahib in Pakistan on a religious pilgrimage, were attacked by 6,000 police with heavy sticks called lathis and tear gas. only 800 of these Sikhs made it to the celebration of the birthday of Guru Nanak.

It is the BJP that destroyed the Babri mosque and still seek to build a Hindu Temple on the site. Now BJP officials have been quoted as calling for the "Indianization" of Islam, according to Newsroom Online. The Indian government has killed over 70,000 Muslims in Kashmir since 1988. In addition, Dalits (the "black untouchables"), Tamils, Manipuris, Assamese, and others have seen tens of thousands of their people killed at the hands of the Indian government.

Mr. Speaker, in light of this ongoing pattern of state terrorism against the peoples living within its borders, it is appropriate for America, as the leader of the world, to do what we can to protect these people and expand freedom to every corner of the subcontinent. The best way to do this is to stop American aid to India and to support self-determination for all the peoples and nations of the subcontinent.

Mr. Speaker, I insert into the Record an India-West report regarding the beating of these two priests. I commend it to all my congressional colleagues who care about human rights.

From India-West, Jan. 12, 2001
Two Christian Priests Abducted and Beaten

JAIPUR (Reuters)--Two Christian priests were recovering in hospital Jan. 5 after being abducted and beaten in a tribal village in western India, police said.

They said the priests, identified only as Simon and David, were abducted from Zer, a village in Rajasthan's Udaipur district, Jan. 4 and forcibly taken to the neighboring state of Gujarat where they were beaten.

Anand Shukla, an Udaipur police chief, told Reuters the two abductors had been identified. One was a Zer villager and the other a resident of Gujarat.

The priests suffered minor injuries and were admitted to a hospital in Bijaynagar in Gujarat, Shukla said.

No motive was given for the attack, but Gujarat has in the past been the scene of violent attacks on Christians, who make up about two percent of India's billion-strong population. Right-wing Hindu organizations have been blamed for the attacks.

Hindu leaders deny the charge. They say forced religious conversions by Christian missionaries are responsible for unrest in tribal areas.

***

Document

CONGRESSIONAL RECORD -- EXTENSIONS

Tuesday, February 27, 2001
107th Congress, 1st Session
147 Cong Rec E 225

REFERENCE: Vol. 147, No. 24
SECTION: Extension of Remarks
TITLE: EVEN OUTSIDE INDIA, SIKHS CONTINUE TO BE HARASSED BY THE INDIAN GOVERNMENT AND ITS ALLIES

HON. EDOLPHUS TOWNS
of New York
in the House of Representatives
Tuesday, February 27, 2001

Mr. TOWNS . Mr. Speaker, a disturbing case of Indian harassment against the Sikhs recently came to my attention. Dr. Harjinder Singh

Dilgeer is a Sikh who serves as co-editor of the International Journal of Sikh Affairs. Dr. Dilgeer is a Norwegian citizen.

Dr. Dilgeer went to India a few years ago to work for the Shiromani Gurdwara Prabandhak Committee (SGPC). When new leaders achieved power in the SGPC, Dr. Dilgeer lost his job. He decided to move his family back to Norway.

On January 1, Dr. Dilgeer and his wife and two sons went to the New Delhi airport. The Indian immigration authorities at the airport detained the Dilgeer family because Dr. Dilgeer was on the Indian government's blacklist. An immigration official took Mrs. Dilgeer and the Dilgeer's two sons into another room. He accused them of not being related to Dr. Dilgeer and he threatened them.

After about an hour, Dr. Dilgeer demanded to speak to the Norwegian Ambassador and to a Member of Parliament who is a friend of his. At that point, the Dilgeers were allowed to board their flight. They arrived at the gate with just two minutes to go.

The Dilgeers' flight to Moscow, where they were to meet a connecting flight back to Norway, missed the connection, so the Dilgeers had to stay in Moscow. They were supposed to be put up in a hotel, but when the Russian immigration authorities checked their passports, they detained Dr. Dilgeer and his family at the airport because Dr. Dilgeer was labelled an "International Terrorist." They said they were acting on information received from Indian immigration authorities. The Dilgeers spend the night sleeping on the airport floor while Dr. Dilgeer is in a Russian lock-up.

Russia is India's long-time ally. India supported the Soviet invasion of Afghanistan and has a friendship treaty with the Soviet Union. Russia was one of the countries whose Ambassador attended a meeting led by Indian Defense Minister George Fernandes to discuss setting up a security alliance "to stop the U.S." The Indian government used its influence with its old ally to harass a Sikh simply for leaving the country.

This is typical of Indian tyranny. The Indian government 250,000 Sikhs since 1984, more than 200,000 Christians in Nagaland since 1947, over 70,000 Muslims in Kashmir since 1988, and tens of thousands of Dalits, Assamese, Tamils, Manipuris, and others. Two independent investigations confirmed that the Indian government massacred 35 Sikhs in the village of Chithi Singhpora in March and evidence suggests that the government was responsible for the murders of six Sikhs last month. The book Soft Target shows that the Indian government shot down its own airliner in 1985, killing 329 people, to damage the Sikhs. Christians have been subject to a wave of violence and oppression since Christmas 1998. This repression has included church burnings, raping nuns, murdering priests, and the burning to death of a missionary and his 8- and 10-year old sons. The Hitavada newspaper reported in 1994 that the Indian government paid the late governor of Punjab, Surendra Nath, to foment covert terrorist activity in Punjab, Khalistan, and in Kashmir. These are just some examples of India's ongoing tyranny against minorities.

Mr. Speaker, this is not acceptable conduct from any country, especially one that claims to be "the world's largest democracy." Yet despite a pattern of tyranny India remains one of the largest recipients of U.S. aid. That aid should be ended and Congress should go on record in support of self-determination for the people of Khalistan, Kashmir, Nagalim, and the other minorities seeking their freedom from India. That is the best way to ensure freedom for all the people in South Asia.

I would like to place in the Record a report on the Dilgeer incident by Dr. Awatar Singh Sekhon, editor of the International Journal of Sikh Affairs. It is very informative about India's repressive treatment of minorities.

From the International Journal of Sikh Affairs
Torture, Threats and Inhumane Treatment by Indian Immigration Personnel at the Indira Gandhi International Airport, on 1st January, 2001 and by the Russian Immigration Personnel, Moscow (International) Airport, Moscow, Russia
(By Dr. Awatar Singh Sekhon, Editor)

No. of Victims: Four (Husband and wife and Two sons) (a) First Names of victims: (Dr.) Harjinder and Mrs. Harjinder Middle Name: Singh, Mrs. Dilgeer & Singhs (Two sons).

Dr. Harjinder Singh Dilgeer is an authority on the Sikh faith, Sikh history and Sikh culture. Dr. Dilgeer is the founder and Editor in Chief of The Sikhs: Present and Present An International Journal of Sikh Affairs Dr. Dilgeer is the Editor in Chief (on leave) of the International Journal of Sikh Affairs ISSN 1481-5435.

(b) Family Name: Dilgeer (Author of the article, "Delhi Airport Te Sikhan Naal Salook" meaning "Delhi Airport Authorities' Treatment To the Sikhs": Sant Sipahi (International), Punjabi monthly, published from AMRITSAR, PUNJAB, February 2001, Volume 55 (issue No 2), p. 34-35.

(c) E-mail/address: Sant Sipahi C/-<santsipahi@hotmail.com>

(d) Country: formerly of PUNJAB, India (C/-<santsipahi.hotmail.com>

(e) Persons involved: Family of the Victims (Total 4 persons of a family).

(f) Details of incident: Dr. Harjinder Singh Dilgeer, Mrs. Dilgeer and their two sons arrived at the Delhi airport on 1st January, 2001, to go back to his country, Norway. His connecting flight was via Moscow. After checking in, Dr. Dilgeer and family went to the Immigration counter. The immigration authorities detained the family as his name was in their computer (Black listed). One of the immigration personnel told his colleague that he (they) is going out of country and let him/them go. However, the checking continued and they were asked to sit on a bench. In the meantime, another personnel came. He took away their passports (Dr. Dilgeer and Mrs. Dilgeer; their sons travelled on the mother's passport). This immigration personnel asked Mrs. Dilgeer and her sons that you have to prove that you are Dr. Dilgeer's wife and his sons. In the meantime another personnel named Chohan (Chauhan) came. He behaved rudely. Dr. dilgeer told him that "I am not an Indian citizen and

you behave like a gentleman." This Chohan fellow took Mrs. Dilgeer and their sons along and asked them (mother and sons) and threatened them that "you have no relationship with Dr. Dilgeer." Dr. Dilgeer and you (three) are not related. The immigration personnel threatened them and applied psychological pressure during the interrogation. One hour had gone/passed. Then Dr. Dilgeer demanded from the personnel that "he would like to speak to the Ambassador of Norway, Delhi, on phone. Also he would like to speak to one of his friend who is a Member of Parliament of India. After his demand, the immigration personnel changed his behavior and "stamped their passports." Dr. Dilgeer and family arrived just "two" minutes before closing the aircraft's door.

Treatment at Moscow Airport

The flight from Delhi missed connection to their flight to Norway. The Russian Immigration personnel checked their passport in order to provide them Hotel until the next available flight to Norway. Dr. Dilgeer was told that you cannot stay in a hotel and you will have to stay at the airport, because you are an "International Terrorist." Their terminology of the International Terrorist was based on the "Terrorists' List provided by the Government of India." The Moscow Immigration authorities kept him (Dr. Dilgeer) in a lock up under their custody. Dr. Dilgeer's family spent the night at the airport and slept on the floor.

This has been the treatment, threats and slandering the Sikhs by the Indian immigration personnel at the Delhi international airport and by the Russian airport authorities of the Moscow airport. India, as everybody knows it, is the best partner (political) bed fellow of Russia in the world affairs.

The writer, Dr. Awatar Singh Sekhon (Machaki), Managing Editor and Acting Editor in Chief of the International Journal of Sikh Affairs ISSN 1481-5435, requests the Amnesty International, UN High Commission for Human Rights and other agencies to consider Dr. Dilgeer and his family's case based on the serious violations of their human rights, violations of the rights as international passengers and defaming Dr. Dilgeer as International terrorist by the Russian immigration authorities, based on the information provided to them by the world's "terrorist" administration. India is known to the peace-loving countries of the world as "the largest democracy, India." Democracies do not harass and kill innocent citizens and torture them indiscriminately.

***

Document
CONGRESSIONAL RECORD -- EXTENSIONS

Thursday, February 08, 2001
107th Congress, 1st Session
147 Cong Rec E 145

REFERENCE: Vol. 147, No. 18
SECTION: Extension of Remarks
TITLE: TERRORIST INDIAN POLICE MURDER SIKHS, KASHMIRI
RICKSHAW DRIVER

HON. DAN BURTON
of Indiana
in the House of Representatives
Thursday, February 8, 2001

Mr. BURTON of Indiana . Mr. Speaker, recently a Kashmiri rickshaw driver was killed by Sikh police officers. In retaliation, five Sikhs were killed, and later, a sixth Sikh was murdered at a peaceful protest rally. These killings are tragic, and I know every member of the U.S. House of Representatives condemns these murders.

I have recently met with representatives of several minority groups from within India who claim that these murders are part of the Indian government's deliberate strategy of setting minorities against each other for the purpose of keeping them within India and under the boot of Indian tyranny. According to these representatives, the Indian police have been recruiting members of the Black Cats, a notorious criminal terrorist gang in India, into the police force. They are apparently handing out these plum positions in the police force as a reward for the "good work" the Black Cats have done for the government. Tragically, this "good work" consists mainly of killing Sikhs and other minorities. It is these Black Cats, often dressed as police, who often carry out these minority-targeted murders.

Dr. Gurmit Singh Aulakh, President of the Council of Khalistan, has put out a press release condemning these murders. He points out that the killings serve no one's interest but that of the Indian government. "When these things happen, just as in Chithi Singhpora, you have to ask the question: Who benefits?," Dr. Aulakh said. According to him, "In all these cases, the answer is the same: the Indian government. Neither the Sikh Nation nor the Kashmiris benefit in any way from the murders of Sikhs or Kashmiris." He noted that there were some threats to destroy a Muslim mosque in retaliation for the murders. It is the Indian government that has a record of attacking, desecrating, and destroying Christian, Sikh, and Muslim religious places. Dr. Aulakh urged both communities to keep their cool and not to be sucked into the Indian government's strategy. "The Indian government has shown its disregard for basic human rights," said Dr. Aulakh.

Mr. Speaker, the hard-working American taxpayers should not be taxed to support this kind of a government. American principles of freedom require that we help these people. We should stop all aid to India until it stops repressing its minorities and we should put the Congress on record demanding a free and fair plebiscite in Punjab, Khalistan, in Kashmir, in predominantly Christian Nagaland, and anywhere else where people seek their freedom from India. These actions will go a long way towards bringing freedom to the subcontinent. I urge this Congress and President Bush to act now in support of freedom.

Mr. Speaker, I submit the following press release from the Council of Khalistan's about this terrible incident; into the Record. I urge all my colleagues to read it carefully. It is very revealing about the true nature of Indian "democracy."

Sikhs Condemn Killings in Kashmir, Appeal to Both Communities to Exercise Restraint--Do Not Become Part of the Indian Government's Divide and Rule Strategy--India Should Free Kashmir and Khalistan Instead of Murdering People

Washington, D.C., February 6, 2001--The Council of Khalistan today condemned this week's killings of five Sikhs and the murder of a Muslim scooter driver by Indian Sikh security force personnel in Kashmir. "These killings are reprehensible," said Dr. Gurmit Singh Aulakh, President of the Council of Khalistan, which leads the Sikh Nation's struggle for independence. "Neither Sikhs nor Muslims nor any other people should be killed because of who they are," he said. "These killings only advance the Indian government's divide and rule strategy," he said. "I urge both the Sikh community and the Muslim community not to get worked up and commit more violence against each other," said Dr. Aulakh.

"When these things happen, just as in Chithi Singhpora, you have to ask the question: Who benefits?," Dr. Aulakh said. "In all these cases, the answer is the same: the Indian government. Neither the Sikh Nation nor the Kashmiris benefit in any way from the murders of Sikhs or Kashmiris."

Members of the violent Black Cats commandos have been recruited into the police due to their "good work"--killing Sikhs and other minorities. These Indian agents have infiltrated Sikh organizations and Muslim organizations. "They were the ones who threatened to destroy a mosque in retaliation for the killings," Dr. Aulakh noted. "No Sikh would ever destroy anyone's religious places. But the theocratic Hindu militant government of India has a record of doing so," he said. He noted that the BJP destroyed the Babri mosque and still plans to build a Hindu Temple on the spot. A mosque in Kashmir was also destroyed. Hindu militants affiliated with the RSS, the parent organization of the ruling BJP, have burned Christian churches. The Indian government attacked the Golden Temple and 38 other Sikh Gurdwaras in Punjab in June 1984.

Tens of thousands of Sikh political prisoners are rotting in Indian jails without charge or trial. India is in gross violation of international law. The government of India has murdered over 250,000 Sikhs since 1984, more than 200,000 Christians since 1947, over 70,000 Muslims in Kashmir since 1988, and tens of thousands of Tamils, Assamese, Manipuris, Dalits (the aboriginal people of the subcontinent), and others. The Indian Supreme Court called the Indian government's murders of Sikhs "worse than a genocide." Government-allied Hindu militants have murdered priests, and raped nuns. The Vishwa Hindu Parishad (VHP) described the rapists as "patriotic youth" and called the nuns "Nantina-

tional elements." Hindu radicals, members of the Bajrang Dal, burned missionary Graham Stewart Staines and his two sons, ages 10 and 8, to death while they surrounded the victims and chanted "Victory to Hannuman," a Hindu god.

"India is not a democracy for Sikhs, Muslims, Christians, and other minorities," said Dr. Aulakh. The rights guaranteed in the Indian constitution are not enjoyed by non-Hindus, he said. "Congressman Rohrabacher was right when he said that for minorities 'India might as well be Nazi Germany." Police witnesses have confirmed that the police tortured and murdered the former Jathedar of the Akal Takht, Gurdev Singh Kaunke, and human-rights activist Jaswant Singh Khalra.

Sikhs ruled Punjab up to 1849 when the British conquered the subcontinent. Sikhs were equal partners during the transfer of power from the British. The Muslim leader Jinnah got Pakistan for his people, the Hindu leaders got India, but the Sikh leadership was fooled by the Hindu leadership promising that Sikhs would have "the glow of freedom" in Northwest India and the Sikhs took their share with India on that promise.

Sikhism was not even recognized in the Indian constitution as a separate religion, while Islam, Buddhism, Hinduism, etc. were recognized. Discrimination against the Sikh Nation took place in every sphere. After the Golden Temple attack, the Sikh Nation stepped up its struggle to achieve its God-given right to be free. On October 7, 1987, the Sikh Nation declared the independence of its homeland, Punjab, Khalistan. No Sikh representative has ever signed the Indian constitution. The Sikh Nation demands freedom for its homeland, Khalistan.

"Democracies don't commit genocide," Dr. Aulakh said. "In a democracy, the right to self-determination is the sine qua non and India should allow a plebiscite in Kashmir and Punjab, Khalistan," he said. "Only freedom will bring peace and justice in South Asia."

***

Document

CONGRESSIONAL RECORD -- EXTENSIONS

Thursday, February 08, 2001
107th Congress, 1st Session
147 Cong Rec E 147

REFERENCE: Vol. 147, No. 18
SECTION: Extension of Remarks
TITLE: SIKHS, MUSLIMS MURDERED IN KASHMIR

HON. EDOLPHUS TOWNS
of New York
in the House of Representatives
Thursday, February 8, 2001

Mr. TOWNS . Mr. Speaker, I was disturbed when I read that more violence is taking place in Indian-controlled Kashmir. Some Sikh policemen murdered a Muslim rickshaw driver after he demanded that they pay their fare. In retaliation, five Sikhs were killed by a Muslim gunman. Then one more was killed while participating in a protest march. Now the Indian government has imposed a curfew in Jammu and Kashmir.

Recently, the Indian government has been recruiting members of the terrorist, vigilante commandos called the Black Cats into the police. This is apparently a reward for doing a good job of killing Sikhs and other minorities. The police who carried out the rickshaw murder are former Black Cats. It is an open secret that the former Black Cats have infiltrated Sikh and Kashmiri organizations for the purpose of setting them against each other.

As in the case of last March's massacre of 35 Sikhs at Chithi Singhpora, the relevant question that must be asked is who benefits? Mr. Speaker, neither the Sikhs nor the Muslims benefit from these killings. The only beneficiary is the theocratic, fundamentalist Hindu nationalist government of India and its divide-and-rule strategy. This looks like a clear effort to set the Sikhs and the Kashmiri freedom fighters against each other to keep both movements weak, divided, and unable to liberate their people. Sikhs have not usually been targets of the violence in Kashmir. These murders and the tragedy at Chithi Singhpora are the only recent incidents involving Sikhs. They are outside the usual pattern.

In addition, some of the participants in the protest threatened to harm a mosque. The Sikhs have not harmed any religious places, but the Indian government has a pattern of it. They invaded the Sikhs' holiest shrine, the Golden Temple, and 38 other Gurdwaras in 1984. The BJP destroyed the Babri mosque to put a Hindu Temple where it sat. Since Christmas 1998, Christian churches and prayer halls have been attacked and burned. All of these acts have been carried out by the Indian government or by persons associated with the RSS, which is the parent organization of the BJP, the party that leads the coalition government. BJP officials have said that anyone living in India must either be a Hindu or be subservient to Hindus.

These murders have been condemned by the Kashmiri freedom fighters and by the Council of Khalistan, which leads the Sikh freedom movement. No organization has come forth to take responsibility for the killings, another parallel to the massacre at Chithi Singhpora.

Mr. Speaker, one doesn't have to look very hard to find the hand of the Indian government on these terrible killings. This appears to be part of the Indian government's pattern of terrorism and repression against Sikhs, Muslims, Christians, and other minorities. In that light, this Congress should cut off American aid to India until the repression ends and human rights are restored and we should support a free and fair plebiscite to decide democratically the future of Khalistan, Kashmir, Nagalim, and all the countries seeking their freedom from India. That is how to let the glow of freedom shine all over South Asia.

Mr. Speaker, I would like to submit an article from Reuters News Service on the Kashmir murders into the Record.

From the Reuters News Service, Feb. 5, 2001
Kashmir Capitals Put Under Curfew After Killings

Jammu, India, Feb. 4 (Reuters).--Indian authorities imposed curfews on the two capitals of troubled Jammu and Kashmir state on Sunday after gunmen shot dead six Sikhs and wounded five others.

Srinagar, the state's summer capital, was brought under a curfew from Sunday following the killing of the Sikhs in the city's Mahjoor Nagar area the day before.

Similar measures were announced in the winter capital Jammu. "An indefinite curfew has been imposed in Jammu city from Monday in view of the heightening tension following the killing of the Sikhs," Deputy Commissioner of Police R.K. Goel said.

He said the curfew was imposed after Sikh groups had called for a general strike on Monday. A group of Sikhs threw stones at shops and cars and blocked traffic in Jammu on Sunday to protest against the killings.

A police official said in Srinagar that security had been tightened in Sikh areas of Kashmir, the only Indian state with a Muslim majority.

Separatist rebellion broke out in the Himalayan region in 1990, among Islamic groups seeking either independence or union with neighbouring Pakistan.

Authorities say more than 30,000 people have died in the conflict since.

The Sikh minority, who make up 300,000 of the state's eight million people, have usually been spared violence, which pits Islamic rebels against government forces, Hindus and pro-Indian Muslims.

No group claimed responsibility for Saturday's gun attack on the group of Sikhs. Last March, 35 Sikhs were shot dead by unidentified gunmen as U.S. President Bill Clinton visited India.

KASHMIRI SEPARATISTS CONDEMN KILLINGS

Several Kashmiri separatist groups expressed grief over the latest killings and said they were aimed at harming their struggle for freedom from Indian rule.

"We appeal to the Kashmiri Sikhs not to leave the (Kashmir) Valley and foil the designs of those who want to malign our freedom struggle," Abdul Majid Dar, chief commander of the guerrilla group Hizbul Mujahideen, said in a statement. Kashmir's main separatist alliance, All Parties Hurriyat (Freedom) Conference, condemned the killings, a spokesman of the alliance said.

The attack on Sikhs came a day after Indian Prime Minister Atal Behari Vajpayee and Pakistan's General Pervez Musharraf held their first talks in more than a year, prompted by the devastating earthquake in Western India.

In New Delhi, Bangaru Laxman, president of the ruling Bharatiya Janata Party, said the killings were a desperate attempt by militant groups to sabotage Vajpayee's peace initiative.

India recently extended a unilateral ceasefire which began last November 28 in Kashmir. Most militant Muslim groups rejected it and vowed to press on with their fight.

"The terrorist organisations must understand that the Indian government has the necessary will and the capabilities to completely crush the evil designs of the terrorist," Laxman said.

"Therefore, the government's peace initiatives need not be misunderstood as government's weakness."

Vajpayee is sending a three-member team to Srinagar on Monday to investigate the incident.

***

Document

CONGRESSIONAL RECORD -- EXTENSIONS

Wednesday, January 31, 2001
107th Congress, 1st Session
147 Cong Rec E 82

REFERENCE: Vol. 147, No. 13
SECTION: Extension of Remarks
TITLE: NEW YORK TIMES: INDIA CLEARLY RESPONSIBLE FOR CHITHI SINGHPORA MASSACRE

HON. EDOLPHUS TOWNS
of New York
in the House of Representatives
Wednesday, January 31, 2001

Mr. TOWNS . Mr. Speaker, on December 31, the New York Times Magazine ran a good article on the massacre of 35 Sikhs that took place in Chithi Singhpora in March while President Clinton was visiting India. The article makes it clear that "Everyone knows who did it" and that the responsibility rests squarely on the Indian government. The Times writer, Barry Bearak, the newspaper's bureau chief in New Delhi, wrote that "Among the careful preparations for the historic occasion were a painstaking cleanup around the Taj Mahal, a reconnoitering for wild tigers he might glimpse on a V.I.P. safari and the murder of 35 Sikh villagers in a place called Chittisinghpora."

I will not place the entire article into the Record, Mr. Speaker, be-cause it is very long, but I recommend it to my colleagues. Bearak interviewed several people who were witnesses to the massacre or who lost family members. It is very clear from his interviews that the Indian government is responsible. This confirms the findings of two independ-ent investigations, one by the International Human Rights Organization, which is based in Ludhiana, and another jointly conducted by the Movement Against State Repression and the Punjab Human Rights Organization.

This is typical of the Indian government. The Indian newspaper Hitavada reported in November 1994 that the Indian government paid the late Governor of Punjab, Surendra Nath, $1.5 billion to organize terrorist activities in Punjab and Kashmir. The book "Soft Target", written by two Canadian journalists, proved that the Indian government shot down its own airliner in 1985, killing 329 innocent people, to create an image of Sikhs as terrorists.

The article noted that the killers were dressed in the regulation uni-form of the Indian Army. Some had their faces painted in celebration of the Hindu holiday of Holi. They rounded up 37 Sikhs, one of whom escaped and one of whom survived. The other 35 were murdered in cold blood. They called out the parting phrase "Jai mata di," a Hindu phrase in praise of a Hindu goddess.

Clearly the Indian government was trying to create a bad image of the Kashmiri freedom fighters for the President's visit. It looks like President Clinton was right when he called the region "the most danger-ous place in the world."

Bearak came to Chithi Singhpora in the company of a businessman, who is an associate of a fellow reporter. "So you want to know the truth?" the businessman said to Bearak. "Don't you know the truth can get these people killed?" The Indian government had killed five Muslims, claiming they were Pakistanis responsible for the massacre, but at least one village resident said that he recognized the remains of one of his relatives. One of the men killed was a man of 60. The Indian government has subse-quently admitted that the so-called "militants" they killed were in fact innocent. Now they have made another arrest in the case. This is also equally dubious. The 18-year-old that they arrested was "intensively interrogated," according to the article, which usually means torture.

At the close of the article, Bearak writes that "Everyone knows about this crime. The Indian Army did it." The evidence makes it clear that this is true. Why should such a country receive any support from the U.S. government? Let us stop our aid to this terrorist regime and let us openly support self-determination for Punjab, Khalistan, for Kashmir, and for all the nations of South Asia.

***

Document

CONGRESSIONAL RECORD -- EXTENSIONS

Tuesday, January 30, 2001
107th Congress, 1st Session
147 Cong Rec E 65

REFERENCE: Vol. 147, No. 12
SECTION: Extension of Remarks
TITLE: CHRISTIANS THANKS SIKH IN INDIA: DR. GURMIT SINGH
AULAKH COMMENDED

HON. DAN BURTON
of Indiana
in the House of Representatives
Tuesday, January 30, 2001

Mr. BURTON of Indiana . Mr. Speaker, on January 17 a group of Christians in India known as the Persecuted Church of India issued a statement commending the protection that Sikhs have provided to Christians in India from Indian government persecution.

Father Dominic Immanuel appeared on Star News to thank the Sikhs community for protecting Christians from Indian government persecution. As you know, the Christians in India have undergone a wave of violence and terror by militant Hindu nationalists associated with the pro-Fascist RSS, the parent organization of the ruling BJP. This violence has taken the form of church burnings, rape of nuns, murders of priests, and attacks on Christian schools and prayer halls. Graham Staines and his two little boys were burned to death in their jeep while they slept. Earlier, in 1997, police broke up a Christian religious festival with gunfire. No one has ever been punished for these activities. Instead, there have been Indian officials who have been quoted as saying that everyone who lives in India must either be a Hindu or be subservient to Hinduism. Last year RSS leader Kuppa Halli Sitharamaiya called for a ban on foreign churches.

Interestingly, the article mentions Dr. Gurmit Singh Aulakh, the President of the Council of Khalistan, for his lobbying efforts here on Capitol Hill. The Sikhs and Christians are suffering from the same kind of terror. More than 250,000 Sikhs have been murdered by the Indian government since 1984, according to Inderjit Singh Jaijee's "The Politics of Genocide". The Indian government has also killed more than 200,000 Christians in Nagaland. According to Amnesty international, there are about 50,000 Sikhs held in Indian jails as political prisoners without charge or trial. In November, Indian police with heavy sticks called lathis attacked 3,200 Sikh religious pilgrims at a railroad station on the Indian-Pakistani border. These pilgrims were attempting to get to Nankana Sahib in Pakistan to celebrate the birthday of the first Sikh guru, Guru Nanak. Only 800 managed to get to the celebration. In July, police arrested Rajiv Singh Randhawa, the only witness to the September 1995 kidnapping of human-rights activist Jaswant Singh Khalra, while he was trying to give a petition to the British Home Minister in front of the Golden Temple, the holiest Sikh shrine that the Indian government brutally attacked in June 1984. Mr. Khalra was killed in police custody about six weeks after he was kidnapped. More than five years later, no one has been punished. Now the Indian police are harassing the only witness. In March, according to the findings of two independent investigations, the Indian government murdered 35 Sikhs in the village of Chithi Singhpora.

In addition to its persecution of Christians, Sikhs, and other minorities, India has worked aggressively to thwart several U.S. foreign policy goals around the world. Not only does it vote against the United States at the United Nations more often than any country except Cuba, but in 1999 the Indian Defense Minister led a meeting with the Ambassadors from Iraq, Cuba, Libya, Russia, Serbia, and China in which the parties discussed setting up a security alliance "to stop the U.S."

We should stop U.S. aid to India until the oppression of Christians, Sikhs, Muslims, and other minorities ends and human rights are observed. We must also put the United States on record in support for the freedom movements in Khalistan, Nagalim, Kashmir, and the other nations seeking their freedom from India, through a free and fair plebiscite. That is the democratic way and the way that world powers do things. These measures will help bring peace, freedom, stability, prosperity and dignity to all the people of the subcontinent.

Mr. Speaker, I would like to submit a statement issued by the Persecuted Church of India that discusses the efforts that Sikhs have made on behalf of India's Christian community. I commend this statement to anyone who would like to better understand the plight of minorities in India.

Persecuted Church of India--January 17, 2001-- the Sikhs rush to protect the christians

A few days ago when the attacks against the Christian missionaries in Rajasthan took place, Fr Dominic Immanual went on record on Star News to acknowledge the protection that the Sikh community was providing to the persecuted Christians of Haryana and elsewhere. That was a belated recognition to the much maligned Sikh minorities. We had earlier reported the incidents wherein the nuns were protected by the Sikhs at the time of attacks. However almost all the cases have gone unreported. Fr Dominic did great justice to the Sikhs when he underlined incidents in rural Haryana where the helpless Christians had none to help but the Sikhs during the attacks by the Hindu fascists. He quoted the incidents in Panipat, Sonepat and Gannore where the Christians have been saved by the Sikhs, many a time risking their own lives as the Hindu terrorists struck. The recognition is too little for the community whose plight was ignored by the Christians as they too had been under the influence of the Hindu nationalist lies against the Sikhs. THE LEGACY OF SADHOO SUNDER SINGH

Sadhu Sunder Singh was one of the greatest Christian missionaries India has known. Punjab, more particularly the districts like Ludhiana has a considerable concentration of Christians. The Sikhs themselves have been victims of Hindu majoritarinism and ethnic cleansing. A vast number of their youth had been annihilated in the anti-Sikh riots and fake encounters. Thousands of innocent Sikh youth are persecuted in jails as undertrials. The anti-Sikh crackdown saw the flight of thousands of Sikhs abroad. When the recent wave of anti-Christian persecution started, at least one Christian bishop recognized the injustice done to the Sikh minority by the Christians. Bishop Philipose Mar Chsysostem, the Mar Thoma Metropolitan, wrote that it was due to our apathy during the earliest atrocities against other (minorities) that this danger has befallen us. The community which we did injustice to has now become our saviors. In fact Gurmeet Singh Aulakh, the Sikh leader in the U.S. was one of the first persons to lobby against the Christian persecution in the U.S. Congress by the Hindu fundamentalists.

THE ANTI-SIKH MOVEMENT

One of the reasons for the insurrection in Punjab was the attempt by the Hinduists to brand Sikhism as a part (or panth) of Hinduism. The RSS went on to call the Sikhs "Kesadhari Hindus". History says that the no Sikh participated in the drafting of the Constitution, and as they were away, the Hindu nationalists branded them as "Hindus". The governments finally accepted the independent identity of the Sikhs apart from the Hindus. Recently the Hindu majoritarians revived the old tension by once again branding the Sikhs as part of Hinduism. The Sikhs are idol-haters and do not liked to be linked to it's worship forms. The Sikh community warned with one voice that any attempt by the Hinduists to carry the Guru Granth Sahib to the Temples will be met with stiff resistance. The tension in Punjab has increased manyfold due to the upsurge in the activities of RSS, VHP and the Bajrang Dal. There are reports of the raising of a Bajrang Dal army of 30,000 cadres from Punjab. As per an article that appeared in the Hindu, the Bajrang Dal is giving fierce arms training to their cadre. They have the blessings of the rulers of Delhi. The formation of the new organization Rashtriya Sikh Sangatana (RSS) by the Rashtriya Swayamsevak Sangh (RSS) have angered the Sikhs and this has once again brought most Sikhs to a single platform. The majoritarian ambitions of the Hindutva forces in Punjab are sure to lead to doom.

Conclusion

At this instance we can only pray for peace in Punjab. We pray that good sense prevails with the majoritarians and they do not do anything harmful to the interests of the nation. We also thank the valiant but unsung Sikh heros and heroines who have and are risking their own lives to save the defenseless Christians in Haryana, Punjab and elsewhere from the atrocities of the Hindu organizations.

***

Document

CONGRESSIONAL RECORD -- EXTENSIONS

Thursday, December 14, 2000
106th Congress, 2nd Session
146 Cong Rec E 2183

REFERENCE: Vol. 146, No. 154
TITLE: INDIAN POLICE TRY TO STOP SIKHS FROM VISITING
RELIGIOUS SHRINE IN PAKISTAN--SIKHS REALIZE NEED FOR
INDEPENDENT KHALISTAN

HON. EDOLPHUS TOWNS
of New York
in the House of Representatives
Thursday, December 14, 2000

Mr. TOWNS. Mr. Speaker, many of us have spoken to the House about the oppression of Sikhs and other minorities in India. I am distressed to have to report yet another incident.

Last month, thousands of Sikhs gathered from around the world to celebrate the birthday of the first Sikh guru, Guru Nankana Sahib, in his birthplace, Nankana Sahib, which is in present-day Pakistan. My good friend Dr. Gurmit Singh Aulakh, President of the Council of Khalistan, was among those in attendance. The government of Pakistan had issued 3,200 visas for Sikhs from Punjab to come across the border and visit Nankana Sahib for this very important religious occasion. At the Attari, railroad station on the border between India and Pakistan, a group of 6,000 police with sticks called lathis charged the 3,200 Sikhs. They sprayed them with tear gas. Only 800, one-fourth of the number granted visas, were allowed to go to Nankana Sahib. Three- fourths were prevented from attending this religious event.

Now, Mr. Speaker, this is purely a religious event. There was no politics involved. It was an observance of a religious occasion at a religious shrine, not a rally against the government of India. There was no good reason to prevent these Sikhs from attending this religious event except to intimidate them and create a climate of fear because of their religion. Freedom of religion is one of the essential freedoms of a democratic state, yet this action makes it clear again that religious freedom does not exist in India. It may exist in theory, it may be written in Indian law, but in actual fact there is no religious freedom for Sikhs, Christians, Muslims, and other minorities. In practice, the real policy of the militant Hindu nationalist Indian government, no matter who is charge, is to create a Hindu state and wipe out all other religious expressions. As former Prime Minister Chandra Shekhar pointed out, there is no difference between the ruling BJP and the opposition Congress Party. The effect for religious minorities is the same.

Since 1984, according to Inderjit Singh Jaijee's The Politics of Genocide, over 250,000 Sikhs have been murdered in India. India has killed more than 200,000 Christians in Nagaland since 1947, over 70,000 Kashmiri Muslims since 1988, and tens of thousands of other minorities. There is only one way to put an end to the killing and the oppression, as the Sikhs who were attacked at the Attari station can tell you. It is to allow the people of Khalistan, the people of Kashmir, the people of Nagalim, and all the nations of South Asia to live in freedom.

Mr. Speaker, it is time to tell the truth about India. Despite its pretense of democracy, it is a theocratic Hindu state where human rights for minorities are a matter of personal whim and political expediency. Such a country must be declared a violator of basic religious rights, with all the penalties that entails. It must be declared a terrorist nation, as 21 of us wrote to President Clinton earlier this year, and a hostile country, as 17 of us wrote in another letter. Given this abysmal record the United States must stop its aid to India and demand a free and fair plebiscite in Punjab, Khalistan, in Kashmir, in Nagaland, and throughout India to decide the future of these Indian-held states in a democratic way. These measures will help to ensure that the glow of freedom can finally shine on all the people of South Asia.

I would like to submit the Council of Khalistan's open letter on this incident into the Record at this time. It is very informative, and I urge everyone to read it.

Council of Khalistan,
Washington, DC, December 7, 2000.
Police Harass Sikh Pilgrims to Discourage Them
From Visiting Nankana Sahib

There Is No Place for Sikhs in Indian "Democracy"--Professor Darshan Singh Said at Nankana Sahib, "If a Sikh Is Not a Khalistani, He Is Not a Sikh"

Khalsa Ji: Last month, it was my privilege to attend the 531ˢᵗ birthday celebration of Guru Nanak Sahib. I would like

to thank everyone involved for their hospitality. However,

some Sikh pilgrims from Punjab who tried to attend this important religious event were not so cordially treated. A majority of the Sikhs were stopped at the Attari railway station on the border by 6000 police with lathis. 3200 pilgrims were beaten by the police and tear gas was used. Only 800 were allowed to visit Nankana Sahib. It was very clear to the Sikhs that the Indian government does not want Sikhs to visit Guru Nanak's birthplace. These Sikhs from Punjab realize that they need a free and independent Khalistan so that no one can ever again stop them from participating in the birthday celebration of Guru Nanak in Nankana Sahib.

This harassment of Sikhs shows us again that we need a sovereign, independent Khalistan to visit our holy shrines, to protect our rights, our security, and our dignity. Under Indian rule, Sikhs are not even allowed to visit Guru Nanak's birthplace to celebrate his birthday. Sikhs are slaves under Indian rule. As long as India continues to occupy our homeland, our slavery will continue. There is only one solution: a sovereign, free, and independent Khalistan. Only in a free Khalistan can Sikhs live in freedom, dignity, prosperity, and peace. Without political power, nations perish. Professor Darshan Singh Ragi, former Jathedar of the Akal Takht, said, "If a Sikh is not a Khalistani, he is not a Sikh." We must reclaim our lost sovereignty. If the BJP wants Hindu Raj, then why does it object to Khalsa Raj?

The Sikh Nation is sovereign and ruled Punjab up to 1849 when the British took over. Punjab was recognized by most of the world's major powers at that time. It was a truly democratic, truly secular state, rule of the Punjabis, by the Punjabis, for the Punjabis. Maharajah Ranjit Singh had Muslims and Hindus in his cabinet and among his generals. Under his rule, religious shrines of all religions were built, with his support. This is the kind of state that India claims to be, but is not. Behind the pretense of secular democracy, India is a Hindu theocratic state that oppresses Sikhs, Christians, Muslims, and others.

The Sikhs outside India are Khalistanis. They are the ones who will free Khalistan. The present Akali leadership is under Indian government control. India will only allow Akali leaders to come out of India if they toe the line of the Indian government. These Akali leaders are not welcome in foreign countries.

None of the political parties will lead Punjab, Khalistan to freedom. The Shiromani Akali Dal, under the leadership of Chief Minister Badal, is in political coalition with the militant Hindu nationalist Bharatiya Janata Party (BJP), which is part of the RSS, an organization founded in support of Fascism. Badal has not even kept the modest promises that he made to get elected: to free the political prisoners and to hold police officers responsible for their actions in the genocide against the Sikh Nation. Gurcharan Singh Tohra, leader of the All-India Akali Dal, worked with the Indian government prior to the attack on the Golden Temple and surrendered to the Indian forces when they came into the Sikh Nation's holiest shrine. Simranjit Singh Mann was elected to Parliament with the support of Badal after promising not to mention Khalistan. At the Sikh Day Parade in New York, Mann would not join in when the crowd chanted "Khalistan Zinbabad." Even U.S. Congressman Major Owens joined in. Yet Mann would not do so. This revealed his true colors. In 1989, he wrote to the Chief Justice of India pledging his support for India's constitution and territorial integrity.

The Congress Party is no better. It is the party that conducted the invasion and desecration of the Golden Temple. Recently, former Prime Minister Chandra Shekhar said that there is no difference between the BJP and Congress, and he is right.

India's genocide against the Sikh Nation highlights the problem the Sikh Nation faces without our own raj. The Indian government continues its effort to try to wipe the Sikh religion out of existence. A free Khalistan is essential for the survival of the Sikh Nation.

There are still 50,000 Sikhs rotting in Indian jails without charge or trial. Yet the Sikh leaders have remained silent. According The Politics of Genocide by Inderjit Singh Jaijee, over 250,000 Sikhs have been murdered at the hands of the Indian government according to the Punjab State Magistracy, yet the Sikh leadership remains silent. Why can't they start a Shantmai Morcha to free the Sikh political prisoners?

The massacre of 35 Sikhs in Chithi Singhpora shows that without sovereignty, the Indian oppression of the Sikh Nation will continue. Two exhaustive investigations have proven that the Indian government is responsible for this massacre. Now the Indian government has even admitted that the alleged militants they killed were innocent. This atrocity underlines the need for a sovereign, independent Khalistan. The Indian government has demonstrated that it can conduct massacres of Sikhs whenever and wherever it wants. The Khalsa Panth must answer this wake-up call and free Khalistan.

Punjab is a police state. None of the political parties will bring us Khalistan. If we do not show courage and liberate Khalistan, the coming generations of Sikhs will also live in slavery. They will not forgive us if we do not liberate our homeland.

In Panjab, they will not procure your rice crop. Farmers are forced to buy fertilizer at extremely high prices; then the government buys up all their produce at artificially low prices to keep the farmers poor even though Panjab, with just two percent of the population, produces over 60 percent of India's wheat and rice reserves. The farmers of Punjab should not have to live that way. In a free Khalistan, we can sell our produce anywhere in the world to maximize our profit. We will not have to have our water diverted to non-riparian states. Free Khalistan will bring economic prosperity for the farmers of Punjab in particular and other Punjabis in general. Indian rule only means economic deprivation and slavery.

India claims that it is a democracy, but there is more to democracy than elections. Democracies don't commit genocide. If India is a democracy, then why won't it allow the people of Punjab, Khalistan, Kashmir, and the other minority nations it occupies to vote on their political status in a free and fair plebiscite?

India is very unstable. India is on the verge of disintegration. It will disintegrate by the year 2010. Kashmir is going to be free from Indian control soon. As soon as Kashmir is free, Khalistan will follow it. The only way to escape Indian slavery is to liberate Khalistan. New Sikh leadership must emerge to free the Sikh Nation. They should demand self-determination. They should raise the slogan "India Quit Khalistan" and start Shantmai Morcha until we achieve freedom. We have now seen how the India government controls Sikh institutions and the entire Sikh leadership in Punjab.

Unless the Sikh Nation brings back the Sikh spirit and fight for truth and justice as practiced by Guru Nanak, the Khalsa Panth will not prosper. Remember Guru required the Khalsa to remove evil. Only in a free Khalistan will Sikhs be able to live as required by the Guru. Only in a free Khalistan can the Sikh religion flourish. Only then can the Sikh Nation finally enjoy the glow of freedom that is our birthright. Let us join hands to accomplish our goal of a free Khalistan by 2010.

Khalsa Ji, the responsibility is ours. We must start a Khalsa Raj Party and begin a Shantmai Morcha to liberate Khalistan. We must stop supporting leaders who are under the control of the brutal Indian government. We must remember our heritage, "Khalsa Bagi Yan Bad-shah." Let us commit ourselves to liberate Khalistan and control our own destiny so that the Sikh Nation can flourish and prosper. Support only those new leaders who are honest, dedicated, fearless, and committed to freedom for Khalistan. Any other course is support for keeping the Khalsa Panth in slavery.

> *Sincerely,*
> *Dr. Gurmit Singh Aulakh,*
> *President,*
> *Council of Khalistan.*

***

Document

CONGRESSIONAL RECORD -- EXTENSIONS

Tuesday, October 31, 2000
106th Congress, 2nd Session
146 Cong Rec E 2044

REFERENCE: Vol. 146, No. 141
TITLE: REAL CULPRIT IN AIR INDIA BOMBING IS INDIAN GOVERNMENT

HON. EDOLPHUS TOWNS
of New York
in the House of Representatives
Tuesday, October 31, 2000

Mr. TOWNS. Mr. Speaker, we are all pleased that the Canadian government has maintained an active investigation of the Air India bombing in 1985 that killed 329 people. Terrorism is always unacceptable, and all decent people condemn it.

Thus, I read with interest this past weekend that Canada had arrested two Sikhs, Ripudaman Singh Malik and Ajaib Singh Bagri, for this bombing. Unfortunately, I believe that these two individuals are being scapegoated. The book Soft Target, written by journalists Brian McAndrew of the Toronto Star and Zuhair Kashmeri of the Tornoto Globe and Mail, shows that the Indian government itself carried out this atrocity.

According to McAndrew and Kashmeri, the Indian Consul General in Toronto, Mr. Surinder Malik, pulled his wife and daughter off the flight shortly before it took off. A friend of the Consul General who was a car dealer in Toronto also cancelled his reservation. An Indian government official named Siddhartha Singh was also scheduled on the doomed flight and cancelled. Surinder Malik called the Canadian authorities about the crime before it was reported publicly that it had occurred to try to point them to a Sikh he claimed was on the passenger list. The pilot of the flight was a Sikh.

It looks like the Royal Canadian Mounted Police, who made the two arrests this weekend, were not open to the evidence that the Indian government was responsible, even though Canada's other investigate agency, the Canadian State Investigative Service, tried to warn them. Soft Target quotes a CSIS agent as saying. "If you really want to clear the incident quickly, take vans down to the Indian High Commission and the consulates in Toronto and Vancouver, load up everybody and take them down for questioning. We know it and they knew it that they are involved."

Clearly, the objective was to damage the Sikh freedom movement and raise the spectre of "Sikh terrorism" to justify another of India's campaigns of violence against the Sikhs.

Mr. Speaker, this is unfortunately not the only case of Indian state terrorim. The repression of Christians, which has taken the form of burning churches, murdering priets, raping nuns, burning a missionary and his two young sons to death, and other atrocities, is well known. In November 1994, the Indian newspaper The Hitavada reported that the late Governor of Punjab, Surendra Nath, was paid over $1.5 billion by the Indian government to foment state terrorism in Punjab and Kashmir. In March, during President Clinton's visit to India, the government murdered 35 Sikhs in the village of Chithi Singhpora, Kashmir. Two independent investigations and an Amnesty International report have confirmed the government's responsibility.

Between 1993 and 1994, 50,000 Sikhs were made to disappear by Indian forces. More than 250,000 Sikhs have been murdered since 1984. Over 200,000 Christians have been killed since 1947 and over 70,000 Kashmiri Muslims have been killed since 1988, as well as tens of thousands of Dalit "untouchables," Assamese, Manipuris, Tamils, and others. As you know, Mr. Speaker, 21 of us wrote a letter in June calling for India to be declared a terrorist state. These are some reasons why we said that.

Mr. Speaker, India should be declared a terrorist nation and subjected to the penalties that status brings. We should cut off our aid to India until it respects human rights. And Mr. Speaker, the only way that Sikhs, Christians, Muslims, and other minorities will ever escape Indian tyranny is through the democractic right of self- determination. We should go on record in support of an internationally- supervised plebiscite in Punjab, Khalistan, in Nagalim, in Kashmir, and wherever people in South Asia are seeking their freedom from this terrorist government, to resolve their status the democratic way, by the vote. Democratic states don't practice repression and genocide, they decide issues by voting. Is India a democracy or not?

The Council of Khalistan has issued a press release on these arrests. I would like to insert it into the Record for the information of the American people.

Canadian Government Arrests Innocent Sikhs
Evidence shows Indian Government planned, executed Bombing of
Air India Flight 182 - Punish the Real Culprits, Not the Scapegoats

WASHINGTON, D.C., October 31, 2000--Despite strong evidence that the Indian government carried out the bombing of Air India Flight 182 in 1985, killing 329 people, the Royal Canadian Mounted Police (RCMP) arrested two Sikhs, Ripudaman Singh Malik and Ajaib Singh Bhagri, in the bombing. Flight 182 was piloted by a Sikh.

"The RCMP has never even considered the evidence that this bombing was an Indian government operation," said Dr. Gurmit Singh Aulakh, President of the Council of Khalistan, the government pro tempore of Khalistan, the Sikh homeland that declared its independence from India on October 7, 1987. He noted that the book Soft Target, written by two Canadian journalists, proves that the Indian government carried out the bombing. This finding is confirmed by Canadian Member of Parliament David Kilgour in his book Betrayed: The Spy That Canada Forgot. According to Kilgour, a Canadian-Polish double agent was recruited by terrorists working with the Indian government to help carry out a second bombing. The agent declined and reported what had happened.

According to Soft Target, the Candian State Investigative Service (CSIS) was so convinced of the Indian government's involvement that at a meeting of the task force on the Air India bombing, one CSIS agent said, "If you really want to clear the incident quickly, take vans down to the Indian High Commission and the consulates in Toronto and Vancouver, load up everybody and take them down for questioning. We know it and they know it that they are involved."

According to Soft Target, Surinder Malik, the Indian Consul General in Toronto, pulled his wife and daughter off the flight suddenly, claiming that his daughter had to do some examinations for school. A Toronto car dealer who was a friend of the Consul General also canceled his reservation on Flight 182. Siddhartha Singh, head of North American affairs for external relations in New Delhi, who was visiting Indian officials in Canada, also suddenly cancelled his reservation. The book reports that Consul General Malik called the police about the bombing to alert them to an "L. Singh" who was allegedly on the passenger manifest even before the incident became public knowledge. Malik was one of several Indian diplomats Canada later asked to have removed from the country after CSIS unearthed evidence of an Indian spy network. CSIS agents believe that Vice Consul Davinder Singh Ahluwalia laid the groundwork for the bombing. He was transferred in 1985.

"India has practiced this kind of terrorism both inside and outside Punjab, Khalistan, for a long time," Dr. Aulakh said. He noted that in March, during President Clinton's visit to India, the Indian government murdered 35 Sikhs in the village of Chithi Singhpora, Kashmir. Two *independent investigations and an Amnesty International report have confirmed the government's responsibility. In November 1994, the Indian newspaper Hitavada reported that the Indian government paid the late Governor of Punjab, Surendra Nath, about $1.5 billion to organize and support covert state terrorism in Punjab, Khalistan and in Kashmir. The Indian Supreme Court described the situation in Punjab as "worse than a genocide."*

About 50,000 Sikhs languish in Indian prisons as political prisoners without charge or trial. Between 1993 and 1994, 50,000 Sikhs were made to disappear by Indian forces. More than 250,000 Sikhs have been murdered since 1984. Over 200,000 Christians have been killed since 1947 and over 70,000 Kashmiri Muslims have been killed since 1988, as well as tens of thousands of Dalit "untouchables," Assamese, Manipuris, Tamils, and others. "Democracies don't commit genocide," Dr. Aulakh said.

On June 21 Members of the U.S. Congress wrote to President Clinton urging him to declare India a terrorist state because of the repression against Christians, such as burning churches, murdering priests, raping nuns, and other atrocities. "We must not let the Indian government's terrorist apparatus repress the minorities and derail our just struggle for independence by labeling them terrorists," Dr. Aulakh said. "The time has come for the Sikh Nation to begin a Shantmai Morcha to liberate Khalistan."

***

Document

CONGRESSIONAL RECORD -- EXTENSIONS

Friday, October 27, 2000
106th Congress, 2nd Session
146 Cong Rec E 1962

REFERENCE: Vol. 146, No. 137
TITLE: CONGRATULATIONS TO THE COUNCIL OF KHALISTAN

HON. JOHN T. DOOLITTLE
of California
in the House of Representatives
Thursday, October 26, 2000

Mr. DOOLITTLE. Mr. Speaker, earlier this month, the Council of Khalistan held its international convention in Fort Lauderdale, Florida. The Council of Khalistan leads the peaceful struggle to liberate the Sikh homeland, Punjab, Khalistan. I would like to congratulate the Council on a very successful convention.

Delegates came from all around the United States, Canada, and even as far away as Great Britain. They engaged in extensive discussion of plans to liberate Khalistan, and they passed resolutions for independence, human rights, and self-determination. The convention opened on October 7, which is the anniversary of Khalistan's declaration of independence from India.

Dr. Gurmit Singh Aulakh, who is the President of the Council of Khalistan, has been a tireless advocate for his people and has made himself a well-known presence in the halls of Congress by his persistence over the last thirteen years or so. He also fights for human rights of Christians, Muslims, and anyone else who is being oppressed by India. His tireless efforts have helped to keep this issue alive, and I salute him for this work. His struggle merits our support.

Mr. Speaker, I submit the Council of Khalistan's press release on its convention for the Record.

Council of Khalistan, Press Release, Oct. 10, 2000 Council International Convention Very Successful--Delegates Very Enthusiastic and Upbeat Free Khalistan Essential for Survival of Sikh Nation

Washington, D.C., October 10, 2000--The annual convention of the Council of Khalistan, held this weekend in Fort Lauderdale, Florida, was very successful. Delegates came from all over the United States, Canada, and the United Kingdom. The delegates were very enthusiastic and their spirit was very upbeat (charhdi kala). They expressed appreciation for the work of the Council of Khalistan, the government pro tempore of Khalistan, the Sikh homeland that was declared independent on October 7, 1987.

Very candid discussion was held concerning the Sikh Nation and its struggle for independence. The delegates agreed that the liberation of Khalistan is essential for the survival of the Sikh Nation. The delegates agreed to contribute one (1) percent of their annual incomes to the Washington office and to ask others to do the same.

Delegates passed resolutions calling for the liberation of the Sikh homeland, Khalistan, through a Shantmai Morcha (peaceful agitation), for self-determination, demanding the release of political prisoners in Punjab, calling for the formation of a Khalsa Raj Party in Punjab, condemning the Sikh Youth of America for inviting Simranjit Singh Mann to their convention, and many others. The delegates decided that next year's convention will be held on Columbus Day weekend, 2001, in Atlanta, Georgia.

Dr. Gurmit Singh Aulakh, President of the Council of Khalistan, expressed satisfaction at the success of the convention. "I would like to thank everyone who helped to make this convention so successful," he said, "especially the Fort Lauderdale Gurdwara and Sardar Manmohan Singh Randhawa, who took all the reservations and helped to organize the convention. The success of this convention and the fact that people came from great distances to be there send a strong message to the Indian government that Sikhs demand an independent, sovereign Khalistan," he said.

Other resolutions that were passed at the conventions included resolutions demanding that human-rights groups be allowed to operate in Punjab, where they have not been allowed since 1978, nominating Dr. Aulakh for the Nobel Peace Prize, naming Dr. Aulakh Khalistan Man of the Year 2000, calling on all Gurdwaras to support the freedom struggle, demanding leaders with vision, appreciating the Council of Khalistan, to raise money for the Council's office, and urging Sikhs and youth to get involved in the political process. A committee was formed to find new leadership if anything should happen to Dr. Aulakh and also support and advise the Council of Khalistan in its effort to expedite the liberation of Khalistan.

"It is appropriate that the convention opened on the anniversary of Khalistan's declaration of independence," Dr. Aulakh said. He noted that Sikhs ruled Punjab until 1849 when the British forcibly annexed it into British India. No Sikh representative has ever signed the Indian constitution.

Thousands of Sikhs languish in prisons without charge or trial, according to Amnesty International. Between 1993 and 1994, 50,000 Sikhs were made to disappear by Indian forces. More than 250,000 Sikhs have been killed since 1984. Over 200,000 Christians have been killed since 1947 and over 70,000 Kashmiri Muslims have been killed since 1988. In March, during President Clinton's visit to India, the Indian government murdered 35 Sikhs in the village of Chithi Singhpora, Kashmir. Two independent investigations and an Amnesty International report have confirmed the government's responsibility. The Indian Supreme Court described the situation in Punjab as "worse than a genocide."

"India is on the verge of disintegration," said Dr. Aulakh. "Kashmir is going to be free. Khalistan will also be free during this decade, by the grace of Guru. Guru gave sovereignty to the Sikh Nation," he said. "This convention was a step forward in that effort."

***

Document

CONGRESSIONAL RECORD -- EXTENSIONS

Thursday, October 26, 2000
106th Congress, 2nd Session
146 Cong Rec E 1952

REFERENCE: Vol. 146, No. 136
TITLE: A VISION OF HINDU INDIA

HON. JOHN T. DOOLITTLE
of California
in the House of Representatives
Thursday, October 26, 2000

Mr. DOOLITTLE. Mr. Speaker, I noticed two recent articles that underline the religious tyranny in India. One was in the New York Times and the other was in the Washington Times. Together, they show that for minorities, the promise of Indian secularism and religious freedom is a mirage.

The RSS, a militant Hindu nationalist organization, wants to ban foreign churches from India. It wants to reconvert everybody who converted from Hinduism to any other religion, such as Christianity or Islam. The RSS published a booklet encouraging people to file false criminal cases against Christians and members of other minority religions. They are moving ahead with plans to build a Hindu Temple on the site of a very revered mosque. Is this how they practice secularism and religious tolerance in India?

The ruling BJP is under the umbrella of the RSS. In fact, Prime Minister Vajpayee just about a month ago told an audience that he will "always" be a part of the RSS. Shiv Sena, a militant coalition partner of the BJP, is also part of the RSS.

Since Christmas 1998, Christians have been subjected to church burnings, attacks on Christian schools and prayer halls, nuns being raped, priests being murdered, the burning murder of a missionary and his two little sons, and so many other atrocities that I have lost trace of them. Two independent investigations show that 35 Sikhs were massacred in Chithi Singhpora while the President was visiting in March. Now these disturbing articles have come to light. How far will this pattern of religious hostility go on before we do something to stop it?

We should declare India a violator of religious rights. In light of that, we should cut U.S. aid to India. Why should the American taxpayer be forced to pay taxes to support a government that engages in such policies? We should also put ourselves on record in support of self-determination for Khalistan, Kashmir, Nagalim, and the other minority nations living under Indian rule. It is our responsibility to do what we can to support freedom.

Mr. Speaker, I submit the following New York Times article into the Record for the information of my colleagues and the American people.

A Camp Meeting Celebrates the Vision of a Hindu India
By Celia W. Dugger

AGRA, India, Oct. 15--Dust rose in dervishes across the dun-colored parade ground here, swirling around the legs of almost 60,000 uniformed men and boys from more than 7,000 villages. Those foot soldiers in the quest for a Hindu nation stood in ruler-straight lines that stretched as far as the eye could see.

They had come to a three-day camp to celebrate the 75th anniversary of the Rashtriya Swayamservak Sangh, or the National Volunteers Association. It is a powerful disciplined and, some believe, dangerously divisive organization that has given rise to a raft of affiliated groups, including the Bharatiya Janata party that now leads India's coalition government.

After an hour of toe touches, deep knee bends and push-ups, the volunteers sat cross-legged in the dirt and lay down their long bamboo staffs to listen raptly to their leader, K.S. Sudarashan. He inspired them with a vision of India as an ancient and tolerant Hindu nation, but warned that the country was threatened from within by Christian churches that he described as foreign dominated and funded.

Although Christians have lived in India for 2,000 years and make up only 2 percent of its one billion people, he raised the specter of Christian conversions diminishing the dominance of Hindus and leading to secessionist movements. He criticized Christian and Muslim Indians who have refused, in his eyes, to embrace their Hindu heritage. He called on Christians to sever links with "foreign" churches and set up a Church of India. And he condemned Roman Catholic missionaries who believe that only their path leads to salvation.

"How can we allow such people to work here?" he asked from his podium high above the ground. A larger-than-life likeness of the Hindu god Krishna loomed behind him.

Fifty-three years after India gained its independence from British rule, Mr. Sudarshan's movement is still agitating for a redefinition of the

In contrast, the Hindu nationalist ideology defines India as a Hindu nation whose people share a common geography, culture and ancestry. In this view, Muslims and Christians were converted from Hinduism and need to be reintegrated into the Hindu mainstream--a theme first sounded in the 1920's and articulated by Mr. Sudarshan today.

After the closing ceremony, thousands of volunteers, all dressed in paramilitary-style khaki shorts, white shirts and black caps, rushed from their rigid grid on the field toward the dignitaries sitting on red velvet couches in the blazing sun. A group of them surrounded Home Minister Lal Krishna Advani, who started in the R.S.S., moved to the Bharatiya Janata party, and is now believed to be in line to inherit the mantle of leadership from Prime Minister Atal Behari Vajpayee, who joined the R.S.S. back in the 1940's.

As orders blared from a tower of loudspeakers, Mr. Advani joined the rows of men in making the movement's salute (hand held stiffly across the chest, palm down) on the count of one, lowering his head on two and dropping his arm on three.

His presence here was another tantalizing clue in one of the country's favorite parlor games: Are the R.S.S. and the B.J.P.--the political party that is part of the Sangh Parivar, or R.S.S. family--hand in glove or at each other's throats?

The answer seems to be a little of both. There is a natural tension between them, Mr. Sudarshan's movement, which is striving to build a Hindu nation from the grass roots up, is purist in its ideology. The ruling party, which is striving for political power, has set aside many of its Hindu nationalist planks to win the support of regional parties with secular outlooks. It is no longer pushing for the construction of a Hindu Temple on the site of a demolished 16th-century mosque in Ayodhya, for example.

But the movement and the governing party also need each other. The party relies on the movement's vast network of committed volunteers at election time. And the movement enjoys a measure of political influence because of its close ties to the party.

"The relationship is a bit like that between the Christian Coalition and the Republican Party," said Ashutosh Varshney, a political scientist at Notre Dame and an expert on India.

More than half a million boys and men attend the daily meetings of the R.S.S. in 45,000 local branches all over India. The group's appeal is part Boy Scouts, part crusaders. Many become volunteers for the daily physical exercise, sports and camaraderie, but were later fired by the association's idea of nationhood.

The camp here in Agra was an organization feat, subdivided into many smaller neighborhoods where sanitation, roads, electricity and cooking facilities had all been installed by the association.

At 4:30 this morning, a bugle woke the swayamsevaks, or volunteers, while a full moon still dangled over the grounds. By 6 a.m., as dawn broke and a pinkish-orange orb of sun rose, they had lined up for exercise drills. Afterward, they sang a song calling on the volunteers to awaken to threats from India's enemies and traitors. The high-pitched voices of young boys cut through the low hum of the men's singing.

Many of those here were new recruits. Rajkumar Gupta, 13, could explain little of the group's ideology. He studies in a school run by an affiliate of the association. He and the 160 students in the school had come with their teachers "because the school told us to."

Abhinay Kumar Sharma, 15, was attending his second camp and he had learned some of the association's thinking. "The Sangh is here to fight social evils, for example, conversions to Christianity," he said. "This is a Hindu nation and conversions are divisive and this will lead to the division of the country."

Lal Singh, a 65-year-old farmer, echoed the same theme, saying: "Conversion is wrong. This is against our culture. And in these other religions, this sense of humanity and service to man is not there, while it is in our religion."

Yashpal Singh Nayak, 26, a traveling perfume salesman, worried that extended families are breaking down into nuclear families and that women are leaving their faces unveiled in front of elders and males. "If it continues like this," he said, "it will be a serious threat to Indian culture."

***

Document

CONGRESSIONAL RECORD -- EXTENSIONS

Wednesday, October 25, 2000
106th Congress, 2nd Session
146 Cong Rec E 1903

REFERENCE: Vol. 146, No. 135
TITLE: INDIAN GOVERNMENT INFILTRATING ORGANIZATIONS TO PROMOTE THE SPECTRE OF "TERRORISM" IN PUNJAB

HON. EDOLPHUS TOWNS
of New York
in the House of Representatives
Tuesday, October 24, 2000

Mr. TOWNS. Mr. Speaker, it has recently come to light that the police in Punjab have been planting RDX explosives on members of the Babbar Khalsa organization in Punjab and then killing them in encounters, claiming that they are importing the explosives from Pakistan.

The Indian government is known to have infiltrated the organization's top levels. They used their agents within this and other organizations to carry out the bombing of their own Air India airliner off Canada in 1985, which killed 329 innocent people.

In November 1994, the Hitavada, an Indian newspaper, reported that the Indian government paid $1.5 billion to the late Governor of Punjab, a man named Surendra Nath, to foment terrorist activity in Punjab and Kashmir. In March, according to two extensive investigations, the Indian government murdered 35 Sikhs in the village of Chithi Singhpora. Between 1993 and 1994, 50,000 Sikhs "disappeared" at the hands of

Indian forces. According to Amnesty International, there are thousands of political prisoners being held without charge or trial. Human-rights activists say that there are 50,000 Sikh political prisoners alone. The Akali Dal government in Punjab promised to get these political prisoners released, buy they have made no move to do so.

Mr. Speaker, it is clear who the real terrorists are. As the defenders of freedom and democracy, America must declare India a terrorist state and cut off its aid until the terrorism and human- rights violations end. We should also declare our support for protecting the rights of Sikhs, Christians, Muslims, and other minorities by supporting self-determination for their homelands in the form of a free and fair plebi-scite on their political status, with international supervision to make sure that neither side tries to corrupt the vote.

Mr. Speaker, the Council of Khalistan has issued a press release on the Indian government's effort to revive the spectre of "terrorism" in Punjab by planting RDX explosives on Sikh activitists. I encourage all my colleagues to read this informative press release, and I would like to insert it into the Record at this time.

Babbar Khalsa Members Being Killed for RDX--Planting Explosive Is Modus Operandi of Indian Intelligence Indian Government Has Infiltrated Sikh Organizations

Washington, D.C., October 24, 2000.--Punjab Police have been killing members of Babbar Khalsa in encounters in Punjab, claiming that they are bringing RDX explosives in from Pakistan. Planting RDX explosives is the modus operandi of the Indian government. A few years ago, they planted RDX in the car of an American businessman who was visiting Punjab and Pakistan to visit relatives and religious shrines.

"The Indian government has infiltrated the top levels of Babbar Khalsa," said Dr. Gurmit Singh Aulakh, President of the Council of Khalistan, the government pro tempore of Khalistan, the Sikh homeland that declared its independence from India on October 7, 1987. He noted that the book "Soft Target," written by two Canadian journalists, proves that the Indian government carried out the 1985 bombing of an Air India jetliner that killed 329 people. They used their agents within Babbar Khalsa in that operation, he charged.

"There is no terrorism in Punjab except the terrorism of the Indian government," Dr. Aulakh said. He noted that in March, during President Clinton's visit to India, the Indian government murdered 35 Sikhs in the village of Chithi Singhpora, Kashmir. Two independent investigations and an Amnesty International report have confirmed the government's responsibility. In November 1994, the Indian newspaper Hitavada reported that the Indian government paid the late Governor of Punjab, Surendra Nath, about $1.5 billion to organize and support covert state terrorism in Punjab, Khalistan and in Kashmir. The Indian Supreme Court described the situation in Punjab as "worse than a genocide."

About 50,000 Sikhs languish in Indian prisons as political prisoners without charge or trial. Between 1993 and 1994, 50,000 Sikhs were made to disappear by Indian forces. More than 250,000 Sikhs have been murdered since 1984. Over 200,000 Christians have been killed since 1947 and over 70,000 Kashmiri Muslims have been killed since 1988, as well as tens of thousands of Dalit "untouchables," Assamese, Manipuris, Tamils, and others.

"There are many good people in Babbar Khalsa who just want freedom for our homeland, Khalistan," Dr. Aulakh said, "but they are being used by Indian intelligence and its agents within Babbar Khalsa to revive the myth of Sikh terrorism and undermine the Sikh struggle for freedom. The infiltration goes to the highest levels," he said. "I call on Babbar Khalsa members to make sure that they are not used by Indian infiltrators. I call on them to unite with the Council of Khalistan in the peaceful, democratic, nonviolent movement to liberate Khalistan," he said.

"India is on the verge of disintegration," said Dr. Aulakh. "Kashmir is going to be free. Khalistan will also be free during this decade, by the grace of Guru. Guru gave sovereignty to the Sikh Nation," he said. "It is time for a unified effort to liberate Khalistan. We need to support the leadership which is sincere, capable, committed, and dedicated to the liberation of Khalistan," he said. "The Council of Khalistan has led the struggle for the last 15 years and has the above mentioned qualities. We must unite behind the Council of Khalistan, form a Khalsa Paj Party in Punjab, Khalistan, and begin a Shantmai Morcha to liberate Khalistan."

***

Document

CONGRESSIONAL RECORD -- EXTENSIONS

Wednesday, October 25, 2000
106th Congress, 2nd Session
146 Cong Rec E 1937

REFERENCE: Vol. 146, No. 135
TITLE: INDIA PRACTICING STATE TERRORISM IN PUNJAB AND KASHMIR

HON. DAN BURTON
of Indiana
in the House of Representatives
Wednesday, October 25, 2000

Mr. BURTON of Indiana. Mr. Speaker, there have been several disturbing reports lately coming out of India on its human rights violations in Punjab, Kashmir, and elsewhere. These reports demonstrate that India is still heavily involved in terrorism.

On September 16, 2000, Indian author Pankaj Mishra wrote an article in the New York Times about how India has lost its way in terms of democracy and human rights. He wrote that "the Hindu nationalists remain attached to a stern 19th century idea of nationalism, which dilutes traditional social and cultural diversity and replaces it with one people, one culture and one language." This is a climate of intolerance that no government, especially one claiming to be "democratic," should be promoting. He noted that the Indian government "has used brute force in Punjab, the northeastern states, and now Kashmir to suppress disaffected minorities."

This "preference for force over democracy," as Mishra calls, it is also explained in material published by the Human Rights Network in New York. It cites the tens of thousands of Sikhs who are being held as political prisoners in "the world's largest democracy," as well as the massacre of 35 Sikhs in Chithi Singhpora, Kashmir, during the President's visit to India in March. The organization also documents the government's arrest of human-rights activist Rajiv Singh Randhawa, who was the only eyewitness to the police kidnapping of Jaswant Singh Khalra, and other incidents. Khalra, the General Secretary of the Human Rights Wing, was subsequently murdered while in police custody. The police picked up Mr. Randhawa in June of 2000 when he tried to give British Home Minister Jack Straw a petition on human rights.

The Indian government has murdered over 250,000 Sikhs since 1984, according to the Politics of Genocide by Inderjit Sigh Jaijee. More than 200,000 Christians in Nagaland, over 70,000 Muslims in Kashmir, and tens of thousands of other minority people are also being killed at the hands of the Indian government. The U.S. Commission on International Religious Freedom has cited India for "denial of religious freedom to her people."

It is incumbent upon the United States as the moral and democratic leaders of the world to do whatever we can to spread freedom to every corner of the world. We must impose penalties on India for its violations of religious freedom, as the law demands. We should declare India a terrorist state, as 21 Members of this House urged the President to do in a letter earlier this year. We should stop most foreign aid to India until everyone within its borders enjoys the basic human rights that define a democratic country. And we should urge India to hold free and fair plebiscites under international monitoring in Punjab, in Kashmir, in Nagaland, and wherever there is a freedom movement to determine the political future of these states in the democratic way. Canada has held periodic votes in Quebec on its political status. In America, we have done the same for Puerto Rico. When will India follow the lead of the real democracies in the world and allow people to decide their own future by the democratic means of voting.

All of this information and more can be found in the report of the Human Rights Network, the Mishra article in the New York Times, and an open letter to Indian Prime Minister Vajpayee from the National Association of Asian Indian Christians in the USA. I submit these documents into the Record.

From the Human Rights Network, Sept./Oct. 2000
India's Brute Force in Punjab, Kashmir & Northeastern States

Mr. Pankaj Mishra's article in the New York Times (9/16/ 2000) is refreshing in its boldness and articulate in its contents and style. It is also a wake up call for India's ruling regime under Prime Minister Atal Bihari Vajpayee. It underscores the fact that during the last two decades the central government... has used brute force in Punjab, the northeastern states, and now in Kashmir to suppress disaffected minorities.' He warns that "the preference for force over dialogue could end up undermining India's fragile

democracy." This is in complete contrast with the Prime Minister's

sermons on peace and harmony, both at the United Nations Millennium Summit as well as in Washington, D.C. We would like to remind the Prime Minister that his claim of rosy picture in the so- called democratic and secular India masks the painful truth, and draw his attention to the following:

1. Tens of thousands of Sikh prisoners of conscience--men and women--are languishing in Indian jails without a charge or a fair trial. Many have been in illegal custody since 1984.

2. Most independent observers and human rights organizations have blamed the Government sponsored militant groups for the mass murder of the Sikhs in Kashmir (India) during President Clinton's visit in March, 2000. In the absence of an independent investigation by the UN Human Rights Commission, the Sikh nation holds the Indian Government, under Prime Minister Vajpayee, responsible for this barbarian act of mass murder of the Sikhs.

3. Indian security forces have murdered over 250,000 Sikhs since 1984, according to figures compiled by the Punjab State Magistracy and human rights organizations. These figures were published in The Politics of Genocide, by Inderjir Jaijee, a highly respected human rights advocate.

4. The Government of India is silent about the Interim Report on Enforced Disappearances, Arbitrary Executions and Secret Cremations in Punjab (August 1999), prepared under the leadership of an eminent human rights champion, Mr. Ram Narayan Kumar.

5. The Government is also silent about the kidnapping and murder of Mr. Jaswant Singh Khalra in police custody. Mr. Khalra was reported to have compiled a list of several thousand Sikhs, who were secretly cremated as "unidentified bodies," by Taran Taran (Punjab) police (US Department of State Report, January 1998). In a recent press release (9/7/ 00) Amnesty International has reported the arrest of Mr. R.S. Randhawa, a key eyewitness in the case of Mr. Khalra. The Amnesty has called upon the international community to intervene on behalf of Mr. Randhawa and against suppression of "evidence in this case."

6. In a letter to President Bill Clinton (9/12/00), seventeen Congressmen have pointed out that besides the mass murder of the Sikhs, "India has also killed more than 200,000 Christians in Nagaland since 1947, over 70,000 Kashmiri Muslims since 1988, and tens of thousands of Dalits, Assamese, Tamils, and others." In an open letter to Prime Minister

Vajpayee (NYT 9/8/00), Asian Indian Christians have expressed their "deep concerns regarding the persecution of Christians in India by extremist groups. Priests, missionaries and church workers have been murdered, nuns and other women assaulted, churches and schools bombed and burned, cemeteries desecrated, Christian institutions harassed and intimidated." The US Commission on International Religious Freedom has recommended that India be closely monitored for "denial of religious freedom to her people."

7. Some high profiled and officially blessed emissaries have been negotiating the nature of "ransom" for the release of Mr. Raj Kumar, a renowned movie actor, who has been kidnapped by a notorious bandit Mr. Veerappan in South India. The "ransom" includes, inter alia, the demand by the bandit to release more than 100 of his associates from Indian jails. The officials agreed to comply with the "ransom" demands until the Supreme Court intervened to delay the official duplicity.

8. In complete contrast with the "ransom" negotiations with a bandit, the Government has spent hundreds and thousands of dollars to provide unreliable and tainted evidence against young Sikhs, like Sardars Sukhminder Singh (Sukhi) and Ranjit Singh (Kuki)--who have been advocating the creation of an environment in Punjab where the aspirations of the Sikh nation can find full expression. India's intelligence agencies have hounded Sukhminder and Ranjt around the world and then dragged them to India's torture chambers through a decade-long and expensive extradition proceeding in the U.S.

9. Instead of offering an apology to the people of Punjab (for state terrorism and crime of genocide committed by India's paramilitary forces over the last two decades), and initiating the process of restitution, the Indian Government continues pouring salt on the wounds of the people of Punjab, through a policy of deception and distortion.

10. RSS, the parent organization of the ruling BJP, in a secret memorandum to its local units, has recently outlined a master plan for ethnic cleansing in India by wiping out all the minorities--through water and food poisoning, rape, orchestrated conflicts, riots, mass killing and disposal of bodies, etc.--whether they are Christians, Sikhs, Muslims, Dalits, Budhhists, and others. This "final solution," is reminiscent of Nazi genocide of the Jews and other minorities during WW II. It is no wonder that the Indian Government is silent on this very serious issue of national and international concern.

11. The 1985 agreement regarding the rehabilitation of the Sikh soldiers, who had protested, as a matter of deep faith and conscience, against the Indian Army's brutal attack on the Golden Temple Complex and almost forty other Sikh shrines, has not been honored. Many of these soldiers are living in poverty. The families of those, who have died during the attack are living under appalling conditions.

12. India's nuclear arsenal hovers over Punjab and escalating conflict between India and Pakistan over Kashmir endangers the very survival of Punjab.

13. The water from Punjab's rivers is still being diverted to other states, without the consent of Punjab and without a fair compensation to Punjab. Since the Punjabi farmers are forced to rely more and more on tube-wells (a more expensive alternative), the water level in Punjab is sinking lower and lower, seriously endangering its agricultural economy. Punjab's farmers, who have ushered in the green revolution, are still being robbed of their hard earned income, through the Government's arbitrary procurement policy. Many of them are committing suicide because of increasing bankruptcies-- the byproduct of official arrogance and discrimination, and

14. Finally, the Sikh nation is still yearning for "freedom, justice, and peace," as enshrined in the Universal Declaration of Human Rights, and is aspiring for self-determination in accordance with Articles 1 and 55 of the UN Charter. We would like to realize this quest for self- determination within the framework of a regional commonwealth of free nations (like the European Union). This South Asian Commonwealth, consisting of India, Pakistan, Punjab, Kashmir, Nagaland, Bangladesh, Sri Lanka, the Tamil Homeland, Nepal, and others, can usher in a new era of freedom, justice and peace for all in the subcontinent. By the same token, it can liberate the entire region from this lethal armament race and constant fear of mutual annihilation through a nuclear holocaust. The resources, worth billions of dollars, saved through the elimination of the weapons of mass murder, can be utilized for meeting the basic needs of the people of South Asia--like education, housing, health, food, drinking water, social welfare, and employment.

- - - - - - - - -

From the New York Times, Sept. 16, 2000
Yearning To Be Great, India Loses Its
(By Pankaj Mishra)

New Delhi--In the last two years, the Indian government, dominated by the Hindu nationalist party, Bharatiya Janata, has tried to establish an exalted position in the world for India. It has conducted nuclear tests, lobbied hard for a permanent seat on the United Nations Security Council and played up the West's high demand for India's skilled information-technology workers. Atal Behari Vajpayee, the Indian prime minister, who met with President Clinton in Washington and addressed the Congress this week, hopes to achieve, among other things, an American endorse-ment of India's claim to superpower status.

For all these aspirations to 21st century greatness, however, the Hindu nationalists remain attached to a stern 19th-century idea of nationalism, which dilutes traditional social and cultural diversity and replaces it with one people, one culture and one language.

The intolerant climate can be seen in the growing incidents of vio-lence against minorities, particularly Christian missionaries, the steady takeover of government research institutions by Hindu ideologues and the introduction of Hindu-oriented syllabuses in schools and universities.

In neighboring Pakistan, which was created as a homeland for Muslims in 1947, a similar attempt at building a monolithic national identity, through Islam, has produced disastrous results.

Since Islam has failed to bind the country's many ethnic and linguistic minorities, the job of holding the country together has fallen to the Pakistani army. It has tried to pacify the minorities through brutal, and sometimes counterproductive, methods. For instance, in 1971, the terrorized Bengali Muslim population of East Pakistan seceded to form, with India's assistance, the new nation of Bangladesh.

Despite that loss, the power of the Pakistani army grew and grew. Ruled by a military dictator, Pakistan became the overeager host, in 1979, of the C.I.A's proxy war against the Soviet Union in Afghanistan. The arms received from the United States and Saudi Arabia found their way to the black market. Civil war broke out as competing Islamic outfits fought each other with their deadly new weapons. And a flourishing drug trade led to an estimated five million Pakistanis becoming heroin addicts.

In the last 20 years, drug smugglers, Islamic fundamentalists and army intelligence officers have come to dominate Pakistan's political life. Jihad, now exported to the disputed territory of Kashmir and the Central Asian republics, is the semi-official creed of many in the ruling elite. Pakistan is now even further away from being a multi- ethnic democracy.

India looks more stable, but its political culture has changed drastically in the last two decades. The central government as distrustful of federal autonomy as Pakistan's ruling elite, has used brute force in Punjab, the northeastern states, and now in Kashmir to suppress disaffected minorities.

In the process, India's awkward but worthy experiment with secular democracy has been replaced by a vague, but aggressive ideology of a unitary Hindu nationalism.

The new upper-caste Hindu middle class, created by India's freshly globalized economy, includes this nationalism's most fervent supporters. It greeted India's nuclear tests in 1998 euphorically.

But this middle class is also apolitical and a bit unsure of itself. Its preoccupations are best reflected in the revamped news media, which now focus more on fashion
designers and beauty queens than on the dark realities of a
poor and violent country.

Popular patriotism brings temporary clarity to the confused self-image of the new middle class and helps veil some of the government's more questionable actions. For instance, in Kashmir, the government's failure to accommodate the aspirations of the mostly Muslim population led to a popular armed uprising against Indian rule.

The Hindu nationalists describe the uprising as an attack on the very idea of India and have diverted an enormous amount of national energy and resources--including some 400,000 soldiers--toward fighting the insurgents and their Pakistani supporters.

Since the invisible majority of India's billion-strong population--its destitute masses--couldn't care less about Kashmir, it is the affluent

Hindu middle class that enforces the domestic consensus on the subject. It blames Pakistan for everything, ignoring the harshness of Indian rule and the near-total collapse of civil liberties in Kashmir.

Supporters of Hindu nationalism assume that a country with a strong military can absorb any amount of conflict and anomie within its borders. But the preference for force over dialogue could end up under-mining India's fragile democracy and growing economy--just as the excessive reliance on military solutions to political problems has blighted Pakistan.

- - - - - - - - -

From the New York Times, Sept. 8, 2000
An Open Letter to the Hon. Atal Behari Vajpayee,
Prime Minister of India

The President, Officers, the Governing Council and the members of the National Association of Asian Indian Christians in the U.S.A. Inc. (NAAIC USA) are extremely pleased that you are here on an official visit to the U.S. and will be meeting with President Clinton and the high dignitaries of this country. We warmly welcome you and extend our best wishes to you for productive deliberations and consultations which we hope would strengthen the relationship between the people of India and the United States.

We are also taking this opportunity to express our deep concerns regarding the persecution of Christians in India by extremist groups. Priests, missionaries and church workers have been murdered, nuns and other women assaulted, churches and schools bombed and burned, cemeteries desecrated, and Christian institutions harassed and intimidated. There have been scores of incidents involving extortions, illegal and preventive detention, tortures, custodial deaths, anti- conversion laws that would make genuine conversions illegal. All these have created an atmosphere for Christians in many parts of India to live in fear; these are increasing unabated. This situation is antithetical to the declared ideals of the Republic of India and the provisions of its Constitution. Anti-Christian crusade and "hate campaigns" being waged through pamphlets, posters, and newspapers, lead to more violence. The pattern and intensity of these attacks and provocative comments by leaders close to the Government and the ruling Coalition show that attacks are organized efforts to intimidate a peace-loving minority community in India.

It is appalling to note that your Government is still in the denial mode by labeling these attacks as isolated incidents' and even as the work of some "foreign hands."

These attacks and the inability to control the growing violence of self-proclaimed Hindu nationalists against Christians have simply tarnished India's image as a secular nation. They have created a feeling of absence of rule of law in India and apprehension as to whether the Indian democracy is teetering towards a theocratic state. The U.S. Commission on International Religious Freedom has recommended that India be closely monitored for "denial of religious Freedom to her people." Even the U.S. Congressional Record cites a number of these attacks on Christians and depicts them as indicative of the depth of religious intolerance in India. These acts are atrocious also because of the well-acknowledged loyalty and commitment of Indian Christian community to the welfare of India demonstrated through participation in the independence struggle, in the established of schools and institutions of health care and patriotic sacrifices of thousands of Christians.

Your visit now provides a fitting opportunity for the Government of India to assure the world and the U.S. that India will continue its constitutional commitment as a secular state to protect the interests of all people, including the religious minorities, and uphold the constitutional freedom to "profess, practice and propagate" one's religious faith. We urge you to set forth the steps so far taken by the Government to bring the culprits, both individuals and organizations, to justice. It is imperative that you explain to the international community steps taken by the Government to protect the Christian community of India. We ask that the Government of India make every effort to put an end to the atrocities committed against Christians in the great land of India. May your leadership be strengthened through such decisive actions. We pray to God to help you in such efforts.

> *Respectfully,*
> *The National Association of Asian Indian Christians in the USA, Inc., P.O. Box 279, Martinsville, NJ 08836.*

***

Document

CONGRESSIONAL RECORD -- EXTENSIONS

Thursday, October 19, 2000
106th Congress, 2nd Session
146 Cong Rec E 1846

REFERENCE: Vol. 146, No. 132
TITLE: INDIAN GOVERNMENT SHOULD STOP ITS STATE TERRORISM

HON. EDOLPHUS TOWNS
of New York
in the House of Representatives
Wednesday, October 18, 2000

Mr. TOWNS. Mr. Speaker, on September 27, a letter from the Council of Khalistan was published in the Washington Times. It details the propaganda spread by the Indian government to discredit its opponents.

That propaganda is necessary for the Indian government to cover up the atrocities and state terrorism against Christians, Sikhs, and other minorities. Former Indian cabinet minister R.L. Bhatia admitted in 1995 that the Indian government is spending "large sums of money" to spread this propaganda and influence affairs in the United States.

Earlier this month, militant Hindu fundamentalists attacked the home of a priest. They beat him and his neighbor. The neighbor was beaten so badly that he died. Unfortunately, this kind of thing is not unusual. It is just the latest in a series of atrocities carried out by organizations under the umbrella of the Rashtriya Swayamsewak Sangh (RSS), the parent organization of the ruling BJP. While Prime Minister Vajpayee was in New York during his recent visit to the U.S., he said, "I will always be a Swayamsewak."

Last week, former Prime Minister Chandra Shekhar said that there is no difference between the ruling BJP and the supposedly secular Congress Party. Unfortunately, from the point of view of the minorities in India, it is true. There is no difference. Whoever is in power, the repression continues. India has murdered over 250,000 Sikhs since 1984, over 200,000 Christians in Nagaland since 1947, over 70,000 Kashmiri Muslims since 1988, and tens of thousands of Dalit "untouchables" and other minorities. Thousands of Sikhs and other minorities are in illegal detention without charge or trial simply because they are opposed to the government, or because they are members of a minority.

Mr. Speaker, it is time for India to stop its state terrorism against the minorities within its borders. We must stop American aid to India and declare our support for self-determination for the people of Khalistan, Kashmir, Nagalim, and the other nations seeking their freedom, in the form of a free and fair democratic plebiscite. These measures are the only ones we can take that will help to bring real freedom and democracy to the people of South Asia.

I would like to submit the Council of Khalistan's letter into the Record for the information of my colleagues.

From The Washington Times, Wed. Sept. 27, 2000
No Militants in the Council of Khalistan

Manpreet Singh Nibber's Sept. 16 letter, "India human rights criticism from unreliable source?" is so full of disinformation that he must be fronting for the Indian Embassy in its effort to confuse the American people.

Mr. Nibber, who is a member of the Punjab Welfare Council of the USA, does not address any of the facts we brought up in our last letter. Instead, he spreads Indian disinformation about the Council of Khalistan and its origins. He knows there are no "militants" involved in the council. We consistently support the liberation of Khalistan, the Sikh homeland that declared its independence from India on Oct. 7, 1987, by democratic, nonviolent means through the Sikh tradition of "Shantmai morcha," or peaceful agitation.

The Indian Embassy has interfered in American elections, calling for the re-election of former Sen. Larry Pressler and attempting to damage the re-election campaign of Sen. Robert Torricelli. A few years ago, the Indian Embassy was caught giving illegal campaign donations to members of

Congress through an immigration lawyer named Lalit Gadhia, who pleaded guilty to the scheme in federal court.

There are many other Gadhias throughout this country. Former Indian cabinet minister R.L. Bhatia admitted in a 1995 news conference that the Indian government is spending "large sums of money" through the embassy to influence American politics. But what is that money defending?

On Sept. 8, militant Hindus attacked the home of a priest and beat the priest and his servant. The servant was so severely beaten that he died of the injuries. On Aug. 25, news stories reported that militant Hindu nationalists kidnapped and tortured a priest in Gujarat, then paraded him naked through town. This attack was part of a wave of terror against Christians since Christmas 1998.

Incidents have included the murder of priests, the rape of nuns and the burning to death of a missionary and his two sons in their van by members of the Rashtriya Swayamsevak Sangh (RSS), the parent organization of the ruling Bharatiya Janata Party. Schools and prayer halls have been attacked and destroyed. The individuals who raped the nuns were described by the Vishwa Hindu Parishad, a militant organization within the RSS, as "patriotic youth." The RSS was founded in support of fascism.

In March, 35 Sikhs were murdered in the village of Chithi Singhpora in Kashmir. Two extensive independent investigations, one conducted by the Movement Against State Repression and the Punjab Human Rights Organization and another conducted by the Ludhiana-based International Human Rights Organization, proved that the Indian government was responsible for this massacre.

The Indian government has murdered more than 250,000 Sikhs since 1984, according to figures published in Inderjit Singh Jaijee's "The Politics of Genocide." India also has killed more than 200,000 Christians in Nagaland since 1947, more than 70,000 Kashmiri Muslims since 1988 and tens of thousands of other minorities. Amnesty International reports that thousands of political prisoners are being held without charge or trial in "the world's largest democracy."

India is hostile to the United States. It votes against America at the United Nations more often than any country except Cuba.

In May 1999, the Indian Express reported that Indian Defense Minister George Fernandes led a meeting with Cuba, China, Iraq, Serbia, Russia and Libya to construct a security alliance "to stop the U.S."

India openly supported the Soviet Union's invasion of Afghanistan. Its nuclear weapons test started the nuclear arms race in South Asia. It refuses to allow the Sikhs, Kashmiris, Christians and other minority nations seeking their freedom to decide their political future in a free and fair vote, the democratic way.

America must not accept this kind of brutality and tyranny from a government that claims to be democratic. We must cut off aid and trade to India and support a free and fair plebiscite to ensure human rights *and self-determination for Khalistan, Christian Nagalim, Kashmir and all the minority nations and peoples living under Indian rule.*

***

Document

CONGRESSIONAL RECORD -- EXTENSIONS

Wednesday, September 27, 2000
106th Congress, 2nd Session
146 Cong Rec E 1604

REFERENCE: Vol. 146, No. 117
TITLE: AMNESTY INTERNATIONAL DENOUNCES ARREST OF WITNESS
TO POLICE KIDNAPPING OF HUMAN RIGHTS ACTIVIST JASWANT
SINGH KHALRA

HON. EDOLPHUS TOWNS
of New York
in the House of Representatives
Tuesday, September 26, 2000

Mr. TOWNS. Mr. Speaker, police tyranny in Punjab has reared its ugly head again. Rajiv Singh has been arrested in Amritsar on false charges of robbery and murder. At the time of his arrest, Mr. Randhawa was attempting to hand a petition to Jack Straw, the Home Secretary of the United Kingdom, in front of the holiest shrine of Sikhism, the Golden Temple, which was invaded and desecrated by the Indian military in June 1984. The petition asked for intervention of the British government in the matter of human rights in Punjab.

Mr. Randhawa was arrested once before on false charges. He has been a target of police harassment since he saw the Punjab police kidnap Mr. Khalra, who was General Secretary of the Human Rights Wing (SAD). Mr. Khalra was subsequently murdered in police custody and no one has ever been charged or otherwise held responsible in the Khalra case. In that light, there is reason to believe that Mr. Randhawa's life and his safety may be in danger.

September 6 was the fifth anniversary of the Khalra kidnapping. Mr. Khalra conducted an investigation which proved that the Indian government had kidnapped, tortured, and murdered thousands of Sikhs, then declared their bodies "unidentified" and cremated them. No one has been held accountable for these atrocities either.

This is merely the latest action by the police against anyone who speaks up for human rights in Punjab, Khalistan. It is clear from this action that General Narinder Singh, a human-rights leader in Punjab, was right when he said that "Punjab is a police state."

Amnesty International has issued a press release and an Urgent Action bulletin denouncing the lawless actions of the police. I will be introducing them at the end of my statement, and I urge my colleagues to read these chilling documents.

Mr. Speaker, the Indian Prime Minister is visiting the United States to meet with the President and address Congress. Our government must press Prime Minister Vajpayee on the Randhawa case, on human-rights violations, on self-determination, on the release of political prisoners, on nuclear proliferation, and on the Indian government's efforts to construct a security alliance "to stop the U.S.," as the Indian Express reported last year. If the responses are not satisfactory, then we must take action to ensure freedom in South Asia. This Congress should put itself on record in support of a free and fair plebiscite in Punjab, Khalistan, in Kashmir, in Nagalim, and everywhere that the people are seeking freedom. We must maintain our sanctions on India and cut off its aid. And we should declare India a terrorist state.

Mr. Speaker, I submit the Amnesty International press release and Urgent Action bulletin that I mentioned before into the Record for the information of my colleagues.

From Amnesty International, Sept. 6, 2000
Urgent Action

A key witness in the trial of police officers accused of abducting a human rights activist has been arrested by Punjab police. Amnesty International fears this is an attempt to prevent him testifying, and is extremely concerned for his safety in police custody.

Rajiv Singh was arrested as he attempted to hand a petition to UK Home Secretary Jack Straw in Amritsar, Punjab, on 5 September. The petition reportedly called on the UK government to persuade the Indian authorities to take action over human rights violations in Punjab.

He was held overnight and brought before a magistrate the next day and reportedly charged with the murder of two people who were killed in a bank robbery in Amritsar. He was remanded in police custody until 8 September.

This is the third time that Rajiv Singh has been arrested by Punjab police and charged with serious offences. Earlier this year the Punjab Human Rights Commission ruled that police had "concocted" previous charges to persuade him not to testify against them. He had been accused in July 1998 of setting up an organization to fight for a separate Sikh state of Khalistan, called Tigers of Sikh Land. The Commission recommended that the police officers involved should face criminal charges and that there should be further investigations. Rajiv Singh was awarded compensation for being illegally detained.

Today is the fifth anniversary of the "disappearance" of human rights activist Jaswant Singh Khalra, who unearthed evidence that Punjab police had illegally cremated the bodies of hundreds of people who had been arrested and then "disappeared". A number of Punjab police are now on trial for his abduction, and Rajiv Singh is a key eyewitness in the case.

RECOMMENDED ACTION: Please send telegrams/telexes/faxes/ express/airmail letters in English or your own language: expressing grave concern about the arrest and detention of Rajiv Singh on 5 September in Amritsar; expressing concern that since the Punjab police have unlawfully detained and charged Rajiv Singh before, to try to prevent him from testifying in the case of Jaswant Singh Khalra, the current charges against him may be false, and that he is at grave risk of further harassment or torture in police custody; calling for an immediate review of the charges against him by a judicial body; and calling for commitments from the authorities in Punjab to ensure that he will not be ill- treated in custody.

APPEALS TO: Mr. Prakash Singh Badal, Chief Minister of Punjab, Office of the Chief Minister, Chandigarh, Punjab, India.

Salutation: Dear Chief Minister Fax: +91 172 740936 Telegrams: Chief Minister, Punjab, India Mr. S. Sarabjit Singh, Director General of Police, Office of the Director General, Police Headquarters, Punjab, India.

Saluation: Dear Director General Telegrams: Director General of Police, Punjab, India COPIES TO: Mr. L.K. Advani, Minister of Home Affairs, Ministry of Home Affairs, North Block, New Delhi 110 001, India.

Salutation: Dear Minister Fax +91 11 301 5750 and to diplomatic representatives of India accredited to your country.

PLEASE SEND APPEALS IMMEDIATELY. Check with the International Secretariat, or your section office, if sending appeals after 18 October 2000.

(Amnesty International Press Release Sept. 7, 2000)
India: Arrest of Witness Points to Continuing Police Harassment

A key eyewitness to the "disappearance" of a human rights activist has been arrested in Amritsar, India. Rajiv Singh Randhawa was attempting to hand a petition to UK Home Secretary Jack Straw in front of the Golden Temple when the arrest took place on 5 September. Amnesty International today expressed serious concern for his safety while in police custody.

The petition called on the UK government to intervene with the Indian government on the matter of human rights violations in Punjab.

Rajiv Singh Randhawa has since been charged with robbery and murder as well as offences under the Arms Act in connection with a robbery at a bank in Amritsar in which two people were killed. The magistrate remanded him to police custody until 8 September. Amnesty International has appealed to the authorities in Punjab for assurances that he will not be subjected to torture or ill-treatment while in police custody.

"This case highlights the continuing lawlessness of sections of the police in Punjab. Amnesty International is seriously concerned that these charges against Rajiv Singh Randhawa, like other charges brought in the past, are merely a means of harassing and intimidating him," the organization said.

Rajiv Singh Randhawa is a key eyewitness in the case of the "disappearance" of human rights activist Jaswant Singh Khalra. Yesterday, 6 September, was the fifth anniversary of the "disappearance" of Khalra who unearthed evidence that hundreds of bodies of individuals who had "disappeared" after arrest in the 1980s and early 1990s had been illegally cremated by Punjab police. Amnesty International has learned that a hearing in the case was scheduled for 21 September at which evidence, including that of Rajiv Singh, was due to be recorded.

This is the third time that Rajiv Singh Randhawa has been arrested by Punjab police and charged with serious offenses. On the last occasion, he was accused of setting up an organization to fight for a separate Sikh state of Khalistan, the Tigers of Sikh land. In July this year the Punjab Human Rights Commission ruled that those charges against Rajiv Singh were "concocted" by police as a means of dissuading him from giving evidence against police in the Khalra case. The Commission recommended that criminal cases be registered against the police officers and further investigations carried out. Rajiv Singh was awarded compensation for his illegal detention.

Amnesty International believes that the failure by the state to systematically investigate a pattern of grave human rights violations in Punjab during the 1980s and early 1990s has led to a climate of impunity within the police force and continuing illegal actions of police in the state. Attempts by human rights organizations in the state to seek justice for victims of human rights violations have been met with harassment, intimidation and official obstruction to redress.

"The silencing of Rajiv Singh Randhawa in front of a foreign dignitary shows how desperate sections of the Punjab police are to suppress evidence in this case. We call on the international community to intervene in this case," Amnesty International said.

***

Document

CONGRESSIONAL RECORD -- EXTENSIONS

Tuesday, September 19, 2000
106th Congress, 2nd Session
146 Cong Rec E 1531

REFERENCE: Vol. 146, No. 111
TITLE: REACTION TO INDIAN PRIME MINISTER

HON. DAN BURTON
of Indiana
in the House of Representatives
Tuesday, September 19, 2000

Mr. BURTON of Indiana. Mr. Speaker, last week the Indian Prime Minister spoke in this very chamber to a joint session of Congress. In addition, he will meet with several American leaders, including President Clinton and perhaps both major-party Presidential candidates. When he meets with these leaders, they must bring up the issue of human rights and self-determination.

India claims to be a democracy, but in truth there is no democracy in India. It is a militant Hindu fundamentalist state. Christians, Sikhs, Muslims, Dalits, and other minorities suffer severe oppression and atrocities at the hands of Hindu fundamentalists.

Just last month, a priest in India was kidnapped, tortured, and paraded through town naked by militant Hindu nationalists. The Indian government has refused to register a complaint against the kidnappers. This is the latest act in a campaign of terror against Christians that has been going on since Christmas of 1998. This campaign has seen the murders of priests, 5 of which were beheaded; rape of nuns, Hindu militants burning a missionary and his two sons to death in their van, the destruction of schools and prayer halls, and other anti-Christian atrocities. Most of these activities have been carried out by allies of the government or people affiliated with organizations under the umbrella of the RSS, the parent organization of the ruling BJP, which was founded in support of Fascism.

And its not just Christians, where more than 200,000 have been murdered in Nagaland since 1947, who are in danger in India. Over 250,000 Sikhs have been murdered since 1984, and well over 70,000 Kashmiri Muslims since 1988, as well as tens of thousands of other minorities by Indian security forces. We cannot accept this kind of brutality and tyranny from a government that claims to be democratic.

Last year, India denied the U.N. Special Rapporteurs on torture and extrajudicial killings permission to visit the country. And since the 1970's, Amnesty International & other human rights groups have been barred from areas in India. Even Cuba allows Amnesty in! In 1999 Human Rights Watch issued their annual report that noted, "Despite government claims that normalcy' has returned to Kashmir, Indian troops in the state continue to carry out summary executions, disappearances, rape and torture". (Human Rights Watch Report; India: Human Rights Abuses Fuel Conflict, July 1, 1999.)

And, while the Prime Minister talks today about a strong relationship with the U.S., just last year his Defense Minister led a meeting with Cuba, China, Iraq, Serbia, Russia, and Libya to construct a security alliance. The Indian Express quoted the Defense Minister in explaining that this security alliance was intended "to stop the U.S."

India is not a country to be trusted. India introduced the nuclear arms race to South Asia, it supported the Soviet invasion of Afghanistan and it votes against us in the United Nations. Its time that India clean up its human rights violations and ends its anti- Americanism. And, let Kashmir determine its own fate as it was promised nearly 50 years ago to by offering a referendum for self-determination. If it is a democracy, it should let its own people vote on their future.

Mr. Speaker, a bipartisan group of 17 Members of Congress, including myself, have written a letter to President Clinton urging him to press the Prime Minister on issues of self-determination for Khalistan, human rights, and release of political prisoners. I'd like to submit a copy of the letter into the Record, as well as a press release from the Council of Khalistan that sheds more light on the issue.

Washington, DC, September 12, 2000.
Hon. Bill Clinton,
President of the United States,
The White House, Washington, DC.

Dear Mr. President: Indian Prime Minister Atal Bihari VaJpayee will be visiting you from September 13 to September 17. It is important that you press him on the issue of the persecution of Christians, Sikhs, Muslims, and other minorities by the Indian government.

Press Trust of India reported on August 25 that a Christian priest in Gujarat was kidnapped, tortured, and paraded through town naked. This attack was not an isolated incident. Since Christmas 1998, priests have been murdered, nuns have been raped, a missionary and his two sons were burned to death in their van by members of the RSS, which is the parent organization of the ruling BJP, schools and prayer halls have been attacked and destroyed. Yet the Indian government refuses to take any action against the people who perpetrate these atrocities.

During your trip to India, 35 Sikhs were murdered in the village of Chithi Singhpora, Kashmir. The Ludhiana-based International Human Rights Organization investigated this and separately the Movement Against State Repression and the Punjab Human Rights Organization conducted an investigation. Both of these investigations have proven that the Indian government carried out this massacre. The Indian government has admitted that the five Muslims they killed on the claim that they were responsible for the massacre were innocent. Now they have arrested two more people, claiming that they were responsible for this massacre. Yet despite the fact that so-called "militant" groups almost always claim responsibility for incidents they are responsible for, nobody has emerged to claim responsibility for the killings in Chithi Singhpora.

The Politics of Genocide by Indejit Singh Jaijee reports that the Indian government has murdered more than 250,000 Sikhs since 1984. These figures were derived from figures put out by the Punjab State Magistracy. India has also killed more than 200,000 Christians in Nagaland since 1947, over 70,000 Kashmiri Muslims since 1988, and tens of thousands of Dalits, Assamese, Tamils, Manipuris, and others. According to Amnesty International, there are thousands of political prisoners being held in illegal detention without charge or trial in "the world's largest democracy."

India is a hostile country. Last year the Indian Defense Minister led a meeting with Cuba, China, Iraq, Serbia, Russia, and Libya to construct a security alliance "to stop the U.S." India openly supported the Soviet invasion of Afghanistan. It tested five nuclear warheads, beginning the nuclear arms race to South Asia. And it refuses to allow the Sikhs, Kashmiris, Christians, and other minority nations and peoples decide their own political future in a free and fair vote, as democratic countries do. America has repeatedly granted this opportunity to Puerto Rico and Canada has permitted Quebec to do so. Why can't the "world's largest democracy" settle these issues the democratic way?

America is the bastion of freedom for the world. We cannot accept this kind of brutality and tyranny from a government that claims to be democratic. We call on you to press Prime Minister Vajpayee on the issues of human rights and self- determination for Khanistan, Christian Nagalim, Kashmir, and all the minority nations and peoples living under Indian rule.

> *Sincerely, Edolphus Towns, Donald M. Payne, Wally Herger, Lincoln Diaz-Balart, Cynthia McKinney, Dan Burton, James Traficant, John T. Doolittle, James Rogan, James Oberstar, Peter King, Roscoe Bartlett, Randy "Duke" Cunningham, Eni F.H. Faleomavaega, Philip M. Crane, Ileana Ros-Lehtinen, George P. Radanovich.*

- - - - - - - - -

Press Release Council of Khalistan
U.S. Congress: India Is a "Hostile Country"
Letter Urges President to Press Indian Prime Minister on Self-Determination for Khalistan, Human Rights, Release of Political Prisoners

Washington, D.C., September 13, 2000--A bipartisan group of 17 Members of the U.S. Congress have written a letter to President Clinton urging him to press Indian Prime Minister Atal Bihari Vajpayee, who arrives for a state visit today, on issues of self-determination for Khalistan, human rights, andrelease of political prisoners. The letter called India "a hostile country."

"We call on you to press Prime Minister Vajpayee on the issues of human rights and self-determination for Khalistan, Christian Nagalim, Kashmir, and all the minority nations and peoples living under Indian rule," the Members of Congress wrote. The Members noted the recent incident in which a priest in Gujarat was kidnapped, tortured, and dragged naked through the streets. This incident is part of a pattern of repression against Christians that has been going on since Christmas 1998, they noted. They also took note of the massacre of 35 Sikhs in Chithi Singhpora during the President's visit to India in March, which

two independent investigations have proven was carried out by the Indian government. They wrote about the murders of over 250,000 Sikhs since 1984, over 70,000 Muslims since 1988, more than 200,000 Christians in Nagaland since 1947, and tens of thousands of other minorities by the Indian government. "We cannot accept this kind of brutality and tyranny from a government that claims to be democratic," they wrote.

They also wrote, "India is a hostile country. Last year the Indian Defense Minister led a meeting with Cuba, China, Iraq, Serbia, Russia, and Libya to construct a security alliance to stop the U.S.," they noted. They also wrote that India introduced the nuclear arms race to South Asia and that it supported the Soviet invasion of Afghanistan.

The lead sponsor of the letter was Representative Edolphus Towns (D-NY). Other co-signers include Representative Wally Herger (R-Cal.); Representative Donald M. Payne (D-NJ); Representative Lincoln Diaz-Balart (R-Fla.); Representative Cynthia McKinney (D-Ga.); Representative Roscoe Bartlett (R- Md.); Representative Dan Burton (R-Ind.), chairman of the Government Reform and Oversight Committee; Representative Randy (Duke) Cunningham (R-Cal.); Representative James Traficant (D-Ohio); Representative Eni F.H. Faleomavaega (D- American Samoa); Representative John T. Doolittle (R-Cal.); Representative Philip M. Crane (R-Ill.); Representative James Rogan (R-Cal.); Representative Ileana Ros-Lehtinen (R-Fla.); Representative James Oberstar (D-Minn.); Representative George P. Radanovich (R-Cal.); and Representative Peter King (R-NY).

Indian security forces have murdered over 250,000 Sikhs since 1984, according to figures compiled by the Punjab State Magistracy and human-rights organizations. These figures were published in The Politics of Genocide by Inderjit Singh Jaijee. About 50,000 Sikh political prisoners are rotting in Indian jails without charge or trial. Many have been in illegal custody since 1984. India is in gross violation of international law. Since 1984, India has engaged in a campaign of ethnic cleansing in which about 50,000 Sikhs were murdered by the police and secretly cremated, according to Justice Ajit Singh Bains, chairman of the Punjab Human Rights Organization, in an interview broadcast on "Ankhila Punjab" radio in Toronto, Canada. The Indian Supreme Court described this campaign as "worse than a genocide."

"On behalf of half a million Sikhs in the United States, I would like to thank Congressman Towns and every Member who signed this letter," said Dr. Gurmit Singh Aulakh, President of the Council of Khalistan, the government pro tempore of Khalistan, the Sikh homeland that declared its independence from India on October 7, 1987. "We thank our friends in both parties for their support for freedom in South Asia. This letter can help focus the attention of the United States and India on the important democratic values of self- determination and human rights," he said. "The willingness of these Members of Congress to call India a hostile country also advances freedom in South Asia by helping to frustrate India's drive for hegemony in the region," he said. He predicted that "the breakup of India draws closer every day and Khalistan will be free in this decade."

***

Document

CONGRESSIONAL RECORD -- EXTENSIONS

Wednesday, September 6, 2000
106th Congress, 2nd Session
146 Cong Rec E 1403

REFERENCE: Vol. 146, No. 102
TITLE: PRESIDENT MUST PRESS VAJPAYEE ON HUMAN RIGHTS AND
SELF-DETERMINATION

HON. EDOLPHUS TOWNS
of New York
in the House of Representatives
Wednesday, September 6, 2000

Mr. TOWNS. Mr. Speaker, next week Indian Prime Minister Atal Bihari Vajpayee is coming to visit the United States. He will meet with several American leaders, including President Clinton and perhaps both major-party Presidential candidates. When he meets with these leaders, they must bring up the issue of human rights and self-determination.

India claims to be a democracy, but in truth there is no democracy in India. It is a militant Hindu fundamentalist state. Christians,,Sikhs, Muslims, Dalits, and other minorities suffer severe oppression and atrocities at the hands of Hindu fundamentalists.

Just last month, a priest in Gujarat was kidnapped, tortured, and paraded through town naked by militant Hindu nationalists. The Indian government has refused to register a complaint against the kidnappers. This is the latest act in a campaign of terror against Christians that has been going on since Christmas 1998. This campaign has seen the murders of priests, rape of nuns, Hindu militants burning a missionary and his two sons to death in their van, the destruction of schools and prayer halls, and other anti-Christian atrocities. Most of these activities have been carried out by allies of the government or people affiliated with organizations under the umbrella of the RSS, the parent organization of the ruling BJP, which was founded in support of Fascism.

Recently, Bal Thackeray, the leader of Shiv Sena, a coalition partner of the ruling BJP, threatened to engulf the country in violence if he is held responsible for his part in hundreds of murders in 1992. In India, democracy apparently requires making coalitions with killers.

The Christians are not the only minority that is being oppressed. When President Clinton visited India in March, 35 Sikhs were massacred in the village of Chithi Singhpora in Kashmir. The Indian government killed five Muslims, claiming that they were the individuals responsible for the killings. Later they were forced to admit that these Muslims were innocent. Now the Indian government has arrested two more people on the claim that they are responsible for the massacre. Yet two independent investigations have clearly established that the Indian government itself was responsible for the massacre. How can a democratic nation justify these actions?

The Sikhs have declared their independence from India, forming the new country of Khalistan in 1987. The people of Kashmir were promised a plebiscite on their future in 1948, and India promised the United Nations that this referendum would be held as well. The people of predominantly Christian Nagalim seek their independence. There are several other freedom movements within India's borders. It seems to this Member that the best, fairest, and most democratic way to settle these issues is to conduct a free and fair plebiscite on the question of independence in these minority nations.

In addition to our legitimate nuclear-proliferation concerns, it is important that as the world's only superpower, our leaders press the government of India to live up to the democratic standards they proclaim by allowing all people within their borders to enjoy basic human rights and self-determination. If they do not do so, we should cut off U.S. aid to India and put this Congress on record with a resolution in support of human rights, self-determination, and nuclear nonproliferation for all the people of South Asia.

***

Document

CONGRESSIONAL RECORD -- EXTENSIONS

Thursday, July 27, 2000
106th Congress, 2nd Session
146 Cong Rec E 1329

REFERENCE: Vol. 146, No. 100
TITLE: DECLARE INDIA A TERRORIST NATION

HON. JOHN T. DOOLITTLE
of California
in the House of Representatives
Wednesday, July 26, 2000

Mr. DOOLITTLE. Mr. Speaker, recently 20 of us wrote to the President urging him to declare India a terrorist nation. India has done a lot to deserve this designation.

In the letter, we expressed our concern about the massacre of 35 innocent Sikhs in Chithi Singhpora, which took place while the President was visiting India in March. Two independent investigations have now confirmed that the Indian Government carried out this atrocity.

After the massacre, the government killed five Kashmiri Muslims, declaring them militants who were responsible for the massacre. Now they have admitted that the Muslims they killed were innocent. When will they admit their role in the massacre itself?

Until the minority peoples and nations of India enjoy freedom, there can be no stability in the subcontinent. It becomes increasingly clear every day that they cannot enjoy that freedom within Hindu India. America can also help to bring freedom to South Asia by cutting off our aid to India and by openly supporting self-determination for the people of the Sikh homeland of Punjab, Khalistan, the predominantly Muslim Kashmir, Christian Nagalim, and the other nations seeking their freedom from India.

Mr. Speaker, I am submitting the letter to the President into the Record for the information of my colleagues. It describes the situation in India in much more detail than I can possibly go into here.

Congress of the United States,
Washington, DC, June 15, 2000.
Hon. Bill Clinton, President of the United States
The White House, Washington, DC.

Dear Mr. President: While you were visiting India, 35 innocent Sikhs were massacred in the village of Chatti Singhpora in Kashmir. In recent days it has been reported that the Indian government admitted that the five Kashmiri Muslims it killed as "militants" responsible for the massacre were innocent. The Punjab Human Rights Organization and the Movement Against State Repression recently issued a report showing that the government's counterinsurgency forces, under the command of RAW, the Indian intelligence agency, carried out this massacre. An intensive investigation by the International Human Rights Organization also concluded that the Indian government carried out the massacre. Indian Home Minister L.K. Advani identified the Chatti Singhpora massacre as one of three recent events that have helped strengthen India's standing in world opinion. He implicitly admits that India benefitted from this atrocity.

If India can admit that the Muslims it killed are innocent, when will it admit its own responsibility for the Chatti Singhpora massacre? This is a terrible atrocity and the United States must condernn it in the strongest possible terms. America must take action to make it clear that these actions are unacceptable.

India has also committed similar acts of terrorism against its Christian population. Recently, six Christian missionaries were beaten by militant Hindu fundamentalists while distributing Bibles and religious tracts as part of a gospel campaign called "Love Ahmedabad." They were beaten so savagely that one of them may lose his arms and legs. In Indore, St. Paul's Church was attacked. These acts are part of a campaign of terror against Christians that has been in full swing since Christmas 1998. Whether one is a Sikh, a Muslim, a Christian, or a member of another minority, there is no religious freedom in India, despite its claim that it is democratic. The essence of democracy is respect for the rights of all people. Our government should work to help bring real democracy to South Asia.

Mr. President, it is time that America takes a stance against these terrorist atrocities by the Indian government. We urge you to add India to the list of terrorist nations. It is also time to stop aid to India until it observes human rights. And we should put America on record in support of self-determination for all the peoples and nations living under India's brutal rule. These are the most effective steps to bring freedom, prosperity, peace, and stability to South Asia.

Sincerely,
Donald M. Payne, M.C. and others.

***

Document

CONGRESSIONAL RECORD -- EXTENSIONS

Thursday, July 27, 2000
106th Congress, 2nd Session
146 Cong Rec E 1329

REFERENCE: Vol. 146, No. 100
TITLE: DECLARE INDIA A TERRORIST COUNTRY

HON. EDOLPHUS TOWNS
of New York
in the House of Representatives
Wednesday, July 26, 2000

Mr. TOWNS. Mr. Speaker, a group of 21 of us wrote to President Clinton last month asking him to declare India a terrorist country due to its terror campaign against Christians and other minorities. Since Christmas of 1998, there has been a wave of terrorist attacks against Christians, Christian churches, and Christian institutions throughout India.

No one is ever held accountable for these actions. In fact, Bal Thackeray, leader of Shiv Sena, recently threatened to engulf the entire country in violence if he is held accountable for his part in the 1992 murders of thousands of people in Bombay. Mr. Thackeray's party, Shiv Sena, is a coalition partner of the ruling BJP and both parties are member organizations of the Rashtriya Swayamsewak Sangh (RSS), a Fascist organization with a program of "Hindu, Hindi, Hindutva, Hindu Rashtra"--in other words, Hindu rule. BJP leaders have been quoted as saying that everyone who lives in India must be Hindu or must be subservient to Hindus. Is this democracy or theocracy?

Recently, a group of four missionaries were beaten by Hindu nationalists for their religious work. They were peacefully distributing religious literature and Bibles. Now one of them may lose his arms and legs. A Catholic priest who came under attack from militant Hindus recently was saved when his landlady, a Hindu, poured boiling oil on the Hindu mob that was attacking him. There have been so many incidents. After the recent murder of another priest, the only eyewitness was picked up by a police official who was under suspension. The witness was hanged in his jail cell. The Indian government ruled that he hung himself, but it seems to be a murder by the police.

Hindus chanting "Victory to Hannuman" burned Graham Stuart Staines, an Australian missionary, and his 8 and 10 year old sons to death as they slept in their jeep. Nuns have been raped, priests have been murdered, churches have been burned and schools have been destroyed. All of these acts, and more, have been done at the hands of militant Hindu nationalists allied with the RSS. No one has been punished for any of these atrocities.

Mr. Speaker, Christians are not the only ones. The Indian government massacred 35 Sikhs in Kashmir during President Clinton's visit to India, then tried to blame Kashmiri "militants." Two extensive investigations have confirmed the Indian government's responsibility.

These latest victims join over 200,000 Christians, more than a quarter of a million Sikhs, over 70,000 Kashmiri Muslims, and tens of thousands of other minorities who have been killed in the Indian government's genocide. Tens of thousands of Sikhs are held without charge or trial, as political prisoners in "the world's largest democracy." Well, if India is really a democracy, it must allow all the peoples and nations under its rule, including the Christians of Nagaland, the Sikhs of Khalistan, the Muslims of Kashmir, and the others, to enjoy self-determination and freedom.

Given its past and present conduct, India must be declared a terrorist country and we should stop giving American taxpayers' money to the Indian government until its religious terrorism and its killing of minorities end and all the peoples and nations of South Asia live in freedom.

Mr. Speaker, I would like to insert our letter to President Clinton into the Record, and I hope my colleagues will read it. It will be very informative.

**Congress of the United States,
Washington, DC, June 15, 2000.
Hon. Bill Clinton, President of the United States,
The White House, Washington, DC.**

Dear Mr. President: We are deeply concerned by the ongoing repression of Christians in India. A wave of violence against Christians and that has been going on since Christmas 1998 has intensified recently.

On May 21, a prayer meeting of a Christian women's group was bombed. An investigation by the All India Christian Conference shows that the Sangh Parivar, a branch of the Fascist RSS, the parent organization of the ruling BJP, carried out the bombing, which injured 30, four of them very seriously.

Also in May, six Christian missionaries who were distributing Bibles and religious literature were beaten by militant Hindu fundamentalists.

One of them may lose his arms and legs due to the savage beating. On April 21 in Agra, a group of Hindu militants affiliated with the Bajrang Dal attacked a Christian group and burned Biblical literature. The Bajrang Dal is a wing of the RSS. In Haryana, three nuns were run down by a motor scooter while they were on their way to Easter services. The RSS recently published a booklet on how to implicate Christians and other minorities in false criminal cases, the Hindustan Times reported.

Missionary Graham Staines was burned to death along with his sons, who were 8 years old and 10 years old, while they were asleep in their jeep. The killers chanted "Victory to Hannuman." Hannuman is a Hindu god with the face of a monkey. Hindu nationalists have murdered at least four priests, raped four nuns and kidnapped another, whom they forced to drink her own bodily fluids. More than 200,000 Christians in predominantly Christian Nagaland have been killed by the Indian government. No one is punished for any of these acts.

India has also committed similar acts of terrorism against its Sikh and Muslim minorities, among others. It has killed over 250,000 Sikhs. In March, the government massacred 35 Sikhs.in the village of Chatti Singhpora. According to the State Department, between 1991 and 1993, India paid out more than 41,000 cash bounties to police officers for killing Sikhs. India has killed more than 70,000 Kashmiri Muslims and destroyed the most revered mosque in Kashmir. Tens of thousands of Sikhs, Kashmiris, Christians, and others are being held as political prisoners.

Mr. President, America cannot just watch these atrocities happen. We call on you to declare India a terrorist nation. We further urge an end to U.S. aid to India until human rights are enjoyed by all people there. And we ask the United States to support self-determination for all the peoples and nations of the subcontinent. Let the light of freedom shine everywhere in South Asia.

Sincerely,
Edolphus Towns, M.C., and 20 others.

***

Document

CONGRESSIONAL RECORD -- EXTENSIONS

Thursday, July 27, 2000
106th Congress, 2nd Session
146 Cong Rec E 1331

REFERENCE: Vol. 146, No. 100
TITLE: CHRISTIAN PERSECUTION IN INDIA

HON. EDOLPHUS TOWNS
of New York
in the House of Representatives
Wednesday, July 26, 2000

Mr. TOWNS. Mr. Speaker, I recently joined with 20 of our colleagues in a letter to President Clinton urging him to declare India a terrorist state because of its repression of Christians Sikhs, and other minorities. Today in India, Christians, Sikhs, Muslims, and others are being subjected to a reign of terror at the hands of the Indian government. Since Christmas Day 1998, there has been a wave of persecution and terrorism against Christians in India. Churches have been burned, Christian schools and prayer halls have been attacked, nuns have been raped, and priests have been killed.

Earlier this month, two more churches were bombed in the Indian state of Karnataka, according to a report from Newsroom.org. These attacks came just a month after a Catholic church was bombed in Bangalore. This is a frightening reminder of the resistance to civil rights in the South of the 1950s.

Late last month, a Hindu woman poured boiling oil on a group of militant Hindu nationalists who were attacking her tenant, a Catholic priest. Four Christian missionaries were beaten last month, one so severely that he may lose his arms and legs. These missionaries were beaten for distributing Christian religious literature and Bibles. The RSS, a Fascist organization that is the parent organization of the ruling BJP, has published a booklet on how to implicate Christians in false criminal cases. On Easter, a group of nuns on their way to Easter services were run down by Hindu fundamentalists riding motor scooters. In March, a Sikh family saved some nuns whose convent was attacked by Hindu fundamentalists.

Last month, a women's prayer meeting was bombed by militant Hindu fundamentalists. In April, fundamentalist Hindus attacked a Christian group and burned biblical literature. These are, unfortunately, just the latest incidents in a pattern of oppression of Christians.

The pattern has been long term. Last fall, Hindu fundamentalists aligned with the ruling BJP abducted a nun named Sister Ruby and forced her to drink their urine. Hindus chanting "Victory to Hannuman," a Hindu god, burned missionary Graham Staines to death along with his 8- year-old and 10-year-old sons, while they slept in their jeep. The violence has been carried out by the RSS and other allies and supporters of the BJP government in India and no one ever seems to be punished for these acts.

Sikhs and Muslims have also been targeted, and we should take note of that. In March, while President Clinton was visiting India, 35 Sikhs were murdered in the village of Chithi Singhpora. Two independent investigations have shown that the Indian government carried out this massacre. This, too, is part of a pattern of genocide.

India's campaign of terror against minorities is clearly designed to wipe out the minorities. It is time to declare India a terrorist state and it is time to cut off American aid to India to help strengthen the hand of human rights there. And we should support self-determination for all the minority nations seeking their freedom from India. The predominantly Christian nation of Nagalim, which India holds, is about to begin talks with the Indian government on their political status. I hope that these talks will be the beginning of freedom not just for the people of Naga-land but for all the minority peoples and nations of South Asia.

Strong action must be taken. We should cut off India's aid until human rights are respected. We should demand self-determination for the people of Khalistan, Kashmir, Nagalim, and the other minority nations under Indian rule in the form of a free and fair plebiscite on the question of independence. That is the way democratic nations do it. Is India the democracy it claims to be or not?

I would like to place the Newsroom article of July 10 into the Record for the information of my colleagues. I urge my colleagues to take a look at it.

Two Churches Hit With Bomb Attacks in India

July 10, 2000 (Newsroom)--Bomb blasts damaged two churches in India's southern Karnataka state over the weekend as Christians across the nation staged marches and rallies to protest sectarian violence.

Early on Saturday a low-intensity bomb exploded at the doors of a Protestant church in Hubli, about 270 miles north of the state capital, Bangalore. Police the blast occurred between 4 a.m. and 4:30 a.m. at St. John's Lutheran Church in Hubli's Keshavapura area, which has a 15,000-strong Christian population. The explosion damaged the church's steel gates and its belfry, but no injuries were reported, police said.

On Sunday an explosion left a small crater and shattered windows in the St. Peter and Paul Church in Bangalore.

The attack in Hubli came exactly one month after a bomb blast shook a Roman Catholic church in Wadi in the north Karnataka town of Gulbarga. Three other bomb attacks on churches occurred on June 8, in the coastal town of Goa and the southern state of Andhra Pradesh. Police say that the attack on Saturday is similar to the June 8 blasts, which are still under investigation.

The federal government blames sympathizers of the Pakistan intelligence agency ISI (Inter Service Intelligence) and claims the neighboring nation is out to destabilize India and drive a wedge between Christians and Hindus.

Church leaders allege, however, that right-wing Hindu groups are behind a series of attacks against India's 23 million Christians, and may be responsible for the latest church bombings. Christians believe many of the Hindu groups are closely connected to near the Hindu nationalist Bharatiya Janata Party (BJP), which leads the federal government's ruling coalition. A number of marginalized social groups have been victims of radical Hindus who go unpunished by the regime, said Sajan George, national convenor of the Global Council of Indian Christians. "It becomes clear from these attacks that whether it is Christians, Muslims, or

Dalits, the attacks never end; they are part of the continuing spiral built into the sectarian ideology, out to justify acts of blatant violence and denial of fundamental rights to life, equality before the law, freedom of religion, and freedom of expression," George said after the Hubli church bombing.

In the BJP-ruled northern state of Uttar Pradesh a Roman Catholic priest was murdered last month as he slept in the town of Mathura, near the Taj Mahal. One of the key witnesses to the murder, a cook called Ekka, died mysteriously under police custody.

Bangalore was one, of several state capitals where Christians marched on Saturday in remembrance of victims of religious persecution and in protest of continuing violence. At a rally in Hyderabad on Sunday the president of the All India Christian Council, Joseph D'Souza, read a list of demands to which a crowd of some 100,000 expressed agreement by raising their hands. The demands included state protection for church property and arrest and prosecution of all who openly engage in hate campaigns against Christians.

The Deccan Herald of Bangalore reported Monday that city police had been directed by the Congress Party-led Karnataka government to step up security churches and other places of worship.

***

Document

CONGRESSIONAL RECORD -- EXTENSIONS

Thursday, July 27, 2000
106th Congress, 2nd Session
146 Cong Rec E 1347

REFERENCE: Vol. 146, No. 100
TITLE: INDIA COALITION PARTNER THREATENS TO ENGULF
COUNTRY IN VIOLENCE

HON. JOHN T. DOOLITTLE
of California
in the House of Representatives
Wednesday, July 26, 2000

Mr. DOOLITTLE. Mr. Speaker, last week, Bal Thackeray, founder and head of Shiv Sena, threatened to engulf India in violence if he is held accountable for his part in thousands of deaths in 1992.

Shiv Sena is a coalition partner of the ruling BJP. Shiv Sena has been assigned responsibility for the bombing of the Ayodhya mosque in Uttar Pradesh.

How could a democratic country accept a violent, intolerant person like this into the government? It is bad enough that the allies of the government commit atrocities and no one is ever held to account. Now a coalition partner says that he will engulf the country in violence. This shows that violence and intolerance are the prevailing way to life in India. Minorities are suffering from the intolerance of militant Hindu fundamentalists.

A wave of violence against Christians has swept India since Christmas 1998. The most recent incident was the bombing of two churches in the state of Karnataka. The violence against Christians has been so severe that they appealed to the international community for help. Churches have been burned and now bombed. There have been attacks on prayer halls, Christian schools, and other Christian institutions. Militant Hindu nationalists burned missionary Graham Staines and his two young boys to death in their jeep while they were sleeping.

These atrocities show the truth about India. If it is "the world's largest democracy," how can it allow atrocities like this to keep occurring with nobody being held responsible? As the world's only superpower and the bastion of freedom for the world, we should take action. We should stop aid to India until all people within its borders enjoy human rights. And we should put the Congress on record in support of self-determination for the people of Khalistan, Kashmir, Nagalim, and all the countries seeking their freedom from India.

I submit the article on Mr. Thackeray into the Record, Mr. Speaker. I hope everyone will read it.

From the New York Times International, July 17, 2000
Protests by Hindu Group Raise Fear in India

BOMBAY, July 16 (Reuters)--Much of Bombay was shut down today by fear and protests over the possible prosecution of a militant Hindu leader in connection with riots that left more than 2,000 people dead in 1992.

Supporters of Bal Thackeray, the leader of the Hindu nationalist party Shiv Sena, took to the Streets Saturday after the Maharashtra State government decided to let the police prosecute him in the countrywide rioting. That violence, directed mainly at India's Muslim minority, erupted after the destruction of a mosque in the town of Ayodhaya, and Shiv Sena got most of the blame.

Police officials said no action had been taken to arrest Mr. Thackeray. but many shops closed and people stayed indoors here and in other parts of the state as Shiv Sena supporters pelted buses with stones and blocked commuter train services.

Today Mr. Thackeray appealed for calm, but on Saturday he was quoted as saying, "Not only Maharashtra but the entire country will burn" as a result of the decision, which he called "an incitement to communal riots."

***

Document

CONGRESSIONAL RECORD -- EXTENSIONS

Thursday, July 27, 2000
106th Congress, 2nd Session
146 Cong Rec E 1379

REFERENCE: Vol. 146, No. 100
TITLE: KASHMIRI LEADER RAISES AUTONOMY ISSUE--OTHER STATE
LEADERS FOLLOW HIS LEAD

HON. DAN BURTON
of Indiana
in the House of Representatives
Thursday, July 27, 2000

Mr. BURTON of Indiana. Mr. Speaker, the Chief Minister of Kashmir, Farooq Abdullah, recently called for greater autonomy for the state of Kashmir. However, Abdullah is closely allied with India's ruling BJP, and the BJP government firmly rejected the demand. Other state leaders like Gurcharan Singh Tohra and Simrangid Singh Mann asked Chief Badal to pass a similar measure in the Punjab Assembly.

Under India's constitution, Kashmir was supposed to have a special status, but India has systematically chipped away at it. How would Chief Minister Abdullah make sure that they do not do so under his autonomy plan? The Indian government has imposed President's Rule on Punjab nine times. How would Punjabi leaders ensure that it would not happen again if Punjab has autonomy?

When India forcibly and illegally occupied Kashmir, they promised that there would be a plebiscite on Kashmir's status. That promise has not been kept. The Sikhs in Punjab were promised "the glow of freedom" in Punjab. That promise, too, has been broken. India proclaims its democratic principles loudly, but fails to live up to them when the time comes.

Mr. Speaker, the book The Politics of Genocide by Iderjit Singh Jaijee reports that the Indian government has murdered over 250,000 Sikhs since 1984, over 70,000 Kashmiri Muslims, more than 200,000 Christians in Nagalim, and thousands of others. According to Amnesty International, thousands of innocent civilians are being held as political prisoners. Christmas of 1998 unleashed a waive of violence against Christians that has resulted in church burnings and bombings, the murders of priests and missionaries, and other atrocities. Just recently, two extensive, independent studies concluded that the Indian government killed 35 Sikhs in Chithi Singhpora. Amnesty International has also said that India is responsible. How is autonomy going to prevent these things from happening?

America should support self-determination for all the peoples and nations of South Asia. We should act against the atrocities by cutting off American aid against India until basic human rights are enjoyed by all people within its borders. We should declare India a terrorist nation. And we should declare our support for self-determination in South Asia by calling for a free and fair plebiscite on the question of independence. Not autonomy, but independence. That is the only solution, the only way to bring true freedom to all the peoples and nations of South Asia. If India is truly a democracy, why can't it allow the people of Kashmir to have the plebiscite fifty-two years ago? Why can't it allow the people of Khalistan, Nagalim, and the other nations seeking their freedom to vote on their status the democratic way? Is that too much to ask of democracy?

***

Document

CONGRESSIONAL RECORD -- EXTENSIONS

Thursday, July 13, 2000
106th Congress, 2nd Session
146 Cong Rec E 1219

REFERENCE: Vol. 146, No. 90
TITLE: ATROCITIES AGAINST CHRISTIANS IN INDIA

HON. EDOLPHUS TOWNS
of New York
in the House of Representatives
Wednesday, July 12, 2000

Mr. TOWNS. Mr. Speaker, recently a list was published of atrocities against Christians in India from January to May of this year. It listed 38 specific incidents just in a period of five months. This should indicate the depth of India's religious terrorism against Christians.

On July 8 and 9, two more churches were bombed. The pattern of Indian terrorism against its minorities continues.

It is not just the Christians who are being attacked. In March, the Indian government massacred 35 Sikhs in the village of Chithi Singhpora. This was confirmed by two separate investigations. Some of our colleagues may deny it, but the evidence is clear. This, too, is part of the Indian government's pattern of repression.

This pattern of repression and terrorism must be stopped. The U.S. Congress must take strong action. We should cut off aid to India until this terrorism stops. India should be declared a terrorist nation, as 21 of us recently urged the President to do. And Congress should support self-determination for the people of Khalistan, Kashmir, Nagaland, and all the minority nations seeking their freedom from India. Self-determination is the cornerstone of democracy.

Mr. Speaker, I submit the atrocity list I mentioned earlier into the Record for the information of my colleagues.

ATTACKS ON CHRISTIANS (JANUARY-MAY 2000)
Sources: the Indian Currents, 21 May, 2000

S. No. Date	Place/State	Description
1 January	Philliaur, Punjab	Sts. Peter and Paul Church robbed.
2 January	Philliaur, Punjab	St. Joseph's Convent robbed.
3 Jan. 3	Gajapati, Orissa.	17, Dalit Christian house torched, 12 killed.
4 Jan. 9	Panipat, Haryana	Fr. Vikas of St. Mary's Church attacked.
5 Feb. 4	Rajgarh, MP	Hostel forced to closed down
6 Feb. 20	Pudiyattuvil	Statues of Mary destroy.
7 Feb. 2	Sevit, Gujarat	Protestant Church damaged.
8 March 6	Mysore, Karnataka	BD threatens Bishop Roy to install Hindu statue in Churches.
9 March 8	Basara, Panipat	Isa Mata Church Haryana. attacked.
10 March 12	Panipat, Haryana	St. Mary's Church attacked.
11 March 12	Suryanagar. UP	Media Computer Centre robbed.
12 March 17	Changanacherry,	St. Berchman's College Kerala, Chapel desecrated, robbed.
13 March 31	Agra UP	Police lock up two priests without charge.
14 March 31	Bulandshaher, UP	Nirmala School
15 March 31	Dasna, Masuri,	UP Fr. S. George, Christ Vihar School attacked robbed.
16 April 3	Panaji, Goa	Priest and 21 Catholics wounded by police.
17 April 5	Barwatoli, Bihar	5 Oraon Catholic tribals kidnapped, 2 killed.
18 April 6	Mathura, UP	Sacred Heart School Principal Sr. Maria Pereira attacked.
19 April 7	Belatanr, Giridih	Holy Cross Convent Bihar. watchman shot dead.
20 April 9	Bettiah, Bihar	Jesuit Social Centre stoned.
21 April 10	Mathura Cantt, UP	Fr. Joseph Dabre, St. Dominic School attacked.
22 April 11	Kosikalan, Fr. K.K.	Thomas and Haryana. maid beaten up, house looted.
23 April 11	Kosikalan Haryana	St. Teresa's School looted, Srs. Mary and Gloria beaten.
24 April 14	Khagaria Bihar	50 Christians in Charismatic prayer attacked.
25 April 15	Timerpur, Bijnor	Convent, three UP. Catholic homes attacked.

26 April 16	Babupet, Chanda	Maharashtra Convent tabernacle robbed.
27 April 21	Agra, UP	Bajrang Dal attack 14 neo Christians.
28 April 22	Rajabari, Assam	Priest and 2 brothers seriously beaten in Church robbery.
29 April 22	Rewari, Haryana	Two nuns attacked, hit by scooter.
30 May 3	Paricha	Jhansi, Chapel desecrated, UP. nuns attacked, robbed.
31 May 3	Dangs, Gujarat	13 Evangelist arrested for holding prayer.
32 May 4	Patna, Bihar	St. Xavier's School principal Fr. A.B. Peter Sj accused of sodomy.
33 May 5	Anabha, Gujarat	8 Protestant missionaries attacked with swords, Bibles burnt.
34 May 5	Bhojpur, Bihar	Mary's statue smashed.
35 May	Uchhal Taluka	Rev. Jhalam Singh Gujarat. attacked, Church damaged.
36 May 9	Nashik	Protestant Shelter Maharashtra. School for Tribal girls attacked.
37 May 11	Indore, MP	Fire bomb thrown at Dialogue Centre, 3 churches attacked.
38 May 11	Anekal, Karnataka	Anthony Selva, Jesuit student stabbed.

***

Document

CONGRESSIONAL RECORD -- EXTENSIONS

Tuesday, July 11, 2000
106th Congress, 2nd Session
146 Cong Rec E 1208

REFERENCE: Vol. 146, No. 88
TITLE: DECLARE INDIA A TERRORIST STATE

HON. EDOLPHUS TOWNS
of New York
in the House of Representatives
Tuesday, July 11, 2000

Mr. TOWNS. Mr. Speaker, on June 28, the Washington Times published an excellent letter from our friend Dr. Gurmit Singh Aulakh, President of the Council of Khalistan, calling for strong action to end religious persecution in India.

The letter cited the recent incident in which a Hindu woman poured boiling oil on militant Hindu fundamentalists who were attacking her tenant, a Catholic priest. The Hindu nationalists who carried out this attack are allies of the ruling BJP. It also refers to several other incidents, including the recent savage beating of some Christian missionaries, one so severely that he might lose his arms and legs.

The letter also made reference to a letter send by 21 members of this House in which we asked the President to declare India a terrorist state because of its reign of terror against Christians which has been going in full force since Christmas 1998, as well as its oppression of Sikhs, Muslims, and other minorities. Unfortunately, Mr. Speaker, it is not safe to be a minority in India.

India should be declared a terrorist state, its aid should be stopped, and the Sikhs of Khalistan, the Muslims of Kashmir, the Christians of Nagaland, and the other minorities of the subcontinent should enjoy self-determination. It is the responsibility of the Congress to speak out in support of these things.

I submit Dr. Aulakh's letter to the Washington Times for the Record.

From the Washington Times, June 28, 2000
Oppression of Christians Continues in India
(By Gurmit Singh Aulakh)

We commend the Hindu woman who poured boiling oil on militant Hindu fundamentalists who were attacking her tenant, a Catholic priest ("Hindu woman protects Christian priest," World, June 25). This is an act of religious tolerance, which is very rare in India these days.

Last week, a bipartisan group of 21 members of the U.S. Congress wrote to President Clinton asking him to declare India a terrorist state because of its oppression of Christians and religious minorities. They took note of the pattern of violence against Christians that has been going on since Christmas 1998.

Last month, four Christian missionaries who were distributing Bibles and religious pamphlets were beaten severely by militant Hindu funda-mentalists. The beating was so severe that one of the victims may lose his arms and legs. In April, Hindu fundamentalists affiliated with the Rashtriya Swayamsevak Sangh, a pro-fascist organization that is the parent organization of the ruling Bharatiya Janta Party (BJP), attacked a Christian group and burned biblical literature. In March, a Sikh family saved a group of nuns whose convent had come under attack from Hindu fundamentalists. On Easter, a group of nuns who were going to Easter services were run down by Hindu fundamentalists on motor scooters.

Churches have been burned, prayer halls and Christian schools have been destroyed, nuns have been raped, and priests have been murdered by the militant Hindu nationalists advocating "Hindutva," a Hindu culture, society and nation. Hindu fundamentalists chanting "Victory to hannuman," a Hindu god, burned missionary Graham Staines and his two sons, ages 8 and 10, to death while they slept in their Jeep. The Indian government, led by the Hindu nationalist BJP, has not taken action to punish the persons responsible for any of these atrocities.

Christians are the primary targets of the militant Hindu nationalists, but they are not the only ones who are suffering. In March, 35 Sikhs were murdered in the village of Chithi Singhpora in Kashmir. India promptly blamed Kashmiri "militants" and killed five Kashmiris, claiming that they were responsible. However, two independent investigations have established clearly that the Indian government's counterinsurgency forces carried out this massacre. India has since admitted that the five Kashmir- is the government killed were innocent.

The Sikhs who were murdered in Chithi Singhpora join more than 250,000 Sikhs who have been murdered by the Indian government, according to "The Politics of Genocide," by Inderjit Singh Jaijee. In addition, the Indian government has killed more than 200,000 Christians in Nagaland, more than 70,000 Kashmiri Muslims and tens of thousands of Assamese, Manipuris, Tamils, Dalits (the dark-skinned "untouchables," the aboriginal people of South Asia) and others. Tens of thousands of Sikhs are rotting in Indian jails as political prisoners without charge or trial.

This is nothing less than a campaign of terror designed to wipe out minority peoples and nations from the Indian subcontinent and achieve hegemony in South Asia. The United States should declare India a terrorist state because of these ongoing atrocities. It also should cut off American aid and trade to India and openly declare its support for self- determination for the minority peoples and nations of South Asia through an internationally supervised plebiscite on the question of independence. If India wants to be seen as a democratic nation and a major world power, it will stop its reign of terror against its minorities and allow them to exercise their democratic rights. Until then, America must hold India's feet to the fire.

***

Document

CONGRESSIONAL RECORD -- EXTENSIONS

Wednesday, June 28, 2000
106th Congress, 2nd Session
146 Cong Rec E 1131

REFERENCE: Vol. 146, No. 84
TITLE: CATHOLIC PRIEST MURDERED IN INDIA

HON. DAN BURTON
of Indiana
in the House of Representatives
Tuesday, June 27, 2000

Mr. BURTON of Indiana. Mr. Speaker, a publication entitled the Burning Punjab reported recently that another priest was murdered in India on Tuesday, June 6, 2000 by militant Hindu fundamentalist extremists. He was murdered in his mission near Mathura in the state of Uttar Pradesh. The priest, Brother George, was a 35-year-old member of the Borivili order.

According to reports, the killers locked up Brother George's servant, broke into his room, and beat him to death. The assailants quickly escaped following the brutal attack. Because the crime seems to form a pattern with a previous incident in which a priest and two nuns were beaten in their rooms in Kosi Kalan, many people are beginning to believe that this act was the work of Hindu nationalist militants associated with a branch of the RSS, the parent organization of the ruling BJP. Several Christian organizations in India, including the All-India Catholic Union, the United Christian Forum of Human Rights, and the All-India Christian Council, have lodged strong protests about the incident with the government. They also condemned the attempt by the National Human Rights Commission to minimize two violent incidents against Christians in April. Unless the National Human Rights Commission begins taking these incidents seriously, it unfortunately will be regarded as a puppet for the government.

Mr. Speaker, just recently I informed my colleagues that many people already believe that the March massacre of 35 Sikhs at Chatti Singhpora was the responsibility of government forces. In fact, two separate investigations have already implicated Indian government counterinsurgency forces in that brutal massacre.

If we discover that these recent crimes have been committed by this group of BJP militants or government forces, India will have much explaining to do to this Congress. In fact, they should be held accountable for all their senseless actions. For years, I have been providing this Congress with reports that the Indian government has murdered over 250,000 Sikhs since 1984; 200,000 Christians in Nagaland since 1947; more than 65,000 Kashmiri Muslims since 1988; and tens of thousands of Assamese, Manipuris, Tamils, and Dalits.

As a result, I still believe we should cut off U.S. development aid to India until it respects the hurpan rights of its people. Also, if we are looking for terrorism in South Asia, why are we completely ignoring India? Finally, we should openly support self-determination for the people of Christian Nagaland, of Khalistan, of Kashmir, and all the other nations seeking their freedom from India.

We must make it clear that oppression in India must end and all people in South Asia must enjoy freedom. This pattern of oppression of Christians, Sikhs, Muslims, and other minorities is not going to end until America, the only superpower in the world, takes a strong stand and makes it clear to India that these actions are not acceptable, especially in a country that claims to be democratic.

I am placing the article from Burning Punjab into the Record.

From the Burning Punjab News, June 7, 2000
Catholic Priest Murdered in His Mission Home

New Delhi--A Catholic priest was murdered in his mission home near Mathura in Uttar Pradesh last night, All-India Catholic Union (AICU) alleged here. Quoting information from Archbishop of Agra Diocese Vincent Concessao, AICU said in a statement that "brother George, a 35-year-old member of the Borivili order, was found battered to death in Nevada in the Adviki post area on the Mathura bypass." The Union also alleged that though there were no indications about the motives, the crime seemed to follow the pattern of violence at Kosi Kalan earlier this year in which a priest and two nuns were assaulted and their rooms ransacked. "Early information said some persons, still to be identified, entered the house, locked up the servant, and then entered George's room. They beat him up till he was dead and then escaped in the night," the statement said. Besides AICU, other church and human rights groups, including the United Christian Forum for Human Rights and the All-India Christian Council, lodged strong protests with the Government on the violence. The church groups also condemned the alleged attempt by the National Commission for Minorities, which sent a team to Mathura and Agra in April to probe the attacks on Christians, to "trivialise" the violence in its report.

***

Document

CONGRESSIONAL RECORD -- EXTENSIONS

Tuesday, June 20, 2000
106th Congress, 2nd Session
146 Cong Rec E 1055

REFERENCE: Vol. 146, No. 78
TITLE: CHRISTIANS IN INDIA SEEK INTERNATIONAL HELP

HON. JOHN T. DOOLITTLE
of California
in the House of Representatives
Tuesday, June 20, 2000

Mr. DOOLITTLE. Mr. Speaker, Newsroom.org, a website devoted to religious news from around the world, reported on June 15 that Christian leaders in India have appealed for help from abroad.

The Christian leaders of India, including the United Forum of Catholics and Protestants of West Begal, wrote to the Secretary General of the

United Nations complaining that the Indian government and police have ignored the wave of terror against Christians since Christmas 1998. They have also requested help from Amnesty International in stopping these atrocities.

"We are scared," said Herod Malik, the leader of the United Forum. "We have to go to international organizations because we have no faith in the Indian government." Just a few days ago Hindu nationalist militants murdered a priest and placed five bombs in four churches. Some Christians who were peacefully distributing Bibles and Christian religious literature were savagely beaten, one so badly that he may lose his arms and legs. These are just the most recent incidents.

Unfortunately, Mr. Speaker, it is not just Christians who are suffering atrocities and persecution. Sikhs, Muslims, Dalits, and others are oppressed in a similar fashion, although Christians seem to be the primary targets at the moment.

We can help these people to live in freedom and in the assurance that their rights will finally be respected. If Indian promotes terror against its religious and ethnic minorities, it is not a country that the United States should be supporting. Cutting off its aid is one message it would understand loudly and clearly. We should also declare our support for self-determination through an internationally- supervised plebiscite on the future of political status of Christian Nagaland, of the Sikh homeland, Khalistan, Kashmir, and other nations of Indian. Remember that the people of Kashmir were promised a plebiscite in 1948 and it has never been held. It is time for the United States and the international community to hold India's feet to the fire.

Mr. Speaker, I submit the Newsroom.com article of June 15 into the Record for the information of my colleagues.

From Newsroom.com, June 15, 2000
Christians in India seek help from abroad

A wave of church bombings and murders of clergy has prompted Christian leaders in India to appeal for international help, according to Ccatholic World News. The United Forum of Catholics and Protestants of West Bengal claimed Tuesday that the Indian government and police have ignored their pleas and have insisted the attacks are random crimes.

The Christian leaders said they have written to the secretary general of the United Nations and also are appealing to the human rights group Amnesty International. "We are scared. We have to go to international organizations because we have no faith in the Indian government," said Herod Malik, the head of the United Forum.

The leaders said that unless international groups pressure the Indian government to protect Christians from Hindu fundamentalists, the "atrocities will increase."

Bombs exploded in four churches in the southern Indian states of Andhra Pradesh, Karnataka, and Goa on June 8, injuring at least one person. The blasts occurred the day after a Roman Catholic priest was murdered in the Mathura district of Uttar Pradesh in northern India.

The nation's governing Bharatiya Janata Party (BJP) blamed the four church bombings on Pakistani intelligence "out to give Hindu organizations a bad name." Opposition parties, however, assert that the bombings are the work of the Sangh Parivar, the extended family of Hindu organizations.

Prime Minister Atal Behari Vajpayee promised a delegation of Christian leaders on Monday that his government would investigate the incidents fully.

Christians charge that the Hindu nationlist Rashtriya Swayamsevak Sangh (RSS), considered the ideological parent of the BJP, have engaged in a campaign against Christians since the BJP came to power two years ago. The New Delhi-based United Christian Forum for Human Rights says that in the past year it has documented 120 attacks by Hindu fundamentalists against Christian individuals, churches, and schools.

Indian government officials deny having any influence on the aggression. CWN said a senior interior ministry official, speaking on condition of anonymity, insisted the Christian community had nothing to fear and the government was taking steps to prevent such attacks.

***

Document

CONGRESSIONAL RECORD -- EXTENSIONS

Thursday, June 15, 2000
106th Congress, 2nd Session
146 Cong Rec E 1023

REFERENCE: Vol. 146, No. 75
TITLE: RULE OF LAW DETERIORATING IN INDIA

HON. EDOLPHUS TOWNS
of New York
in the House of Representatives
Thursday, June 15, 2000

Mr. TOWNS. Mr. Speaker, Newsroom.org reported on June 6 that a group of human rights and religious freedom activists in India issued a written statement saying that political leaders have failed to guarantee the rule of law for religious minorities. This is significant, Mr. Speaker, because these are Indians saying this. The statement follows a similar one from the All-India Christian Council (AICC). The AICC said that it "holds the government responsible for the lack of safety of Christians in various parts of India."

The recent statement was signed by Hasan Mansur, head of the Karnataka unit of the People's Union for Civil Liberties; Ruth Manorama of the National Alliance of Women's Organizations; Sister Dolores Rego, who represents 10,000 Catholic nuns in India; and H. Hanumanthappa, former chairman of the National Commission for Scheduled Castes and Scheduled Tribes, among others.

The statement said that the Indian government is "incapable of guaranteeing the rule of law for protecting the right to life and security of peace-loving citizens" and "has become so anarchic as to have derailed democracy." Indian human rights activists are saying that there is effectively no democracy in India.

There have been several recent incidents. Just within the past few days a priest was murdered and five churches were bombed. A group of Christians was savagely beaten while distributing religious literature and Bibles. These are just the latest incidents of violence against Christians, a reign of terror that has been going on since Christmas 1998. In March, the Indian government murdered 35 Sikhs while President Clinton was visiting India. Remember that these Indian human rights leaders hold the government responsible for all these incidents. They were carried out by militant Hindu nationalists under the umbrella of the RSS, the parent organization of the BJP, the political party that rules India.

The Indian government has murdered over 250,000 Sikhs, according to the Politics of Genocide by Inderjit Singh Jaijee of the Movement Against State Repression. And why does a democracy need a Movement Against State Repression? India has also killed more than 20,000 Christians in Nagaland, more than 70,000 Kashmiri Muslims, and tens of thousands of Dalits, Assamese, Manipuris, Tamils, and others. It is holding about 50,000 Sikhs as political prisoners without charge or trial, as well as thousands of others.

It offends me that our government continues to funnel aid to a government that has such a complete disregard for basic human rights. We should immediately cut off American aid to India until everyone there enjoys the liberties that we expect from democratic states. India should be declared a terrorist state. And we should put the Congress on record in support of self-determination for the people of Khalistan, Kashmir, Nagaland, and all the other nations seeking their freedom. That is what we can do to ensure freedom and the rule of law in the troubled South Asian subcontinent.

Mr. Speaker, I submit the Newsroom Article of June 6 into the Record.

Indian Human Rights Activists Chastise Politicians for Deteriorating Rule of Law

Delhi, India, 6 June 2000 (Newsroom)--Prominent Indian advocates of human rights and religious freedom accused political leaders in a written statement of failing to guarantee the rule of law for social and religious minorities and appealed to the government to uphold the rule of law and India's constitutional democracy.

The All Indian Christian Council last week had issued a similar statement expressing concern "about the unabated violence against Christians" taking place in the state of Gujarat and elsewhere. The council said it *"holds the central government responsible for the lack of safety of Christians in various parts of India."*

Among the signatories of last month's statement were Hasan Mansur, a Muslim intellectual who also heads the Karnataka unit of the People's Union of Civil Liberties, a well-known civil rights group; Ruth Manorama of the National Alliance for Women's Organizations; Sister Dolores Rego, who represents 10,000 Catholic nuns in India; and H. Hanumanthappa, former chairman of the National Commission for Scheduled Castes and Scheduled Tribes.

Indians are *"deeply disturbed about the virulent, premediated, and recurrent attacks on persons and institutions of the social, cultural, and religious minority communities being carried out in recent months by the Sangh Parivar (various Hindu groups) in different parts of the country,"* the advocates said. *"The unending spate of propaganda unleashed against these communities is a matter of rave concern to us. We are very much distressed about the dubious manner in which the political leaders at the helm of affairs in this country today have been responding to such methodically orchestrated malicious behavior of these communal outfits."*

Government at the national and state levels is so disorganized that it is *"incapable of guaranteeing the rule of law for protecting the right to life and security of peace-loving citizens."* It *"has become so anarchic as to have derailed democracy that was built up very assiduously during the past 50 years,"* the group charged.

The statement comes amid continuing attacks against Christians and Muslims, as well as Dalits, the lowest group in India's caste system. Dalits typically perform the most menial tasks in Indian society and are shunned by members of upper castes.

The rights advocates expressed their shock at recent attacks on Christians and members of the so-called *"untouchable"* community in India. They took particular note of the murders of seven Dalits who were burned to death by members of the dominant castes in Kambalapalli village in the south Indian state of Karnataka on March 11. Eleven Dalits died in the same way last month in the north Indian state of Bihar.

"We are dismayed at the direction in which the nation is moving," the statement said: *"... Social, cultural and religious minorities are the constant targets of these atrocious attacks. Recurrence of such assaults has become the order of the day. Inaction, or the lethargic response, to say the least, of the law-enforcing machinery is the maximum that the citizens are (acculturated) to expect from the governance system."*

The Christian Council was especially critical of what it called *"the whitewashing of communal incidents by the minority Commission"* and apathy on the part of the Delhi government in putting a stop to the violence. *"These are not criminal attacks, but planned, deliberate attacks on the Christian community by the elements of the Sangh Parivar,"* the council said. *"The culture of impunity that has been perpetuated is now getting out of control."*

***

Document

CONGRESSIONAL RECORD -- EXTENSIONS

Friday, June 9, 2000
106th Congress, 2nd Session
146 Cong Rec E 919

REFERENCE: Vol. 146, No. 71
TITLE: RSS BOMBS CHRISTIAN WOMEN'S PRAYER MEETING

HON. EDOLPHUS TOWNS
of New York
in the House of Representatives
Wednesday, June 7, 2000

Mr. TOWNS. Mr. Speaker, on May 31 Newsroom.org reported that a May 21 bomb blast that injured 30 Christians during a prayer meeting was apparently carried out by the RSS, the pro-Fascist, militant Hindu fundamentalist organization that is the parent organization of the BJP, the party that leads India's government.

According to the Newsroom report, which was brought to me by the President of the Council of Khalistan, Dr. Gurmit Singh Aulakh, the bomb exploded during a meeting of the Women's Club, a Christian group. An extensive investigation by the All-India Christian Conference showed that the Sangh Parivar, a branch of the RSS, was responsible for the incident despite police claims that it came about as a result of strife within the Christian community. The Catholic Bishops' Conference has written to the Indian government demanding action.

This bombing is the latest in a string of violent attacks on Christians and other religious minorities. According to the article, "the community is being threatened with anonymous letters and telephone calls ordering citizens to stop Christian prayers." Anti- Christian slogans have been painted on walls all over town.

In the light of incidents like this against Christians, Sikhs, Muslims, and other minorities, the United States must act. Our aid to India, one of the largest recipients of American aid, must be stopped until all people's rights are respected. India should be declared a terrorist state and punished accordingly. Congress should call for a free and fair plebiscite under international supervision to allow the Christians, Sikhs, and other minority nations under Indian rule to enjoy self-determination, as a democracy should.

I would like to place the article from Newsroom into the Record. I urge my colleagues to read it and see the reality of religious freedom in India.

Christians in India claim Bombing Is Part of Hate Campaign

NEW DELHI, India, 30 May 2000 (Newsroom)--A bomb blast that injured 30 people in the coastal state of Andhra Pradesh last week was part of a campaign of hate by Hindu extremists, leaders of a Christian organization claim.

The blast at a prayer meeting in the Women's Club at Machilipatnam on May 24 was not the result of strife within the community as police first said, according to a team assembled by the All India Christian Council (AICC). The AICC has presented its report to Andhra Pradesh, Chief Minister Nara Chandrababu Naidu, who said in a press release that he has directed police to review the investigation.

"We have already written to Prime Minister Atal Behari Vajpayee about this," Father Dominic of the Catholic Bishop's Conference of India (CBCI) said. "With the report we hope the government will take it seriously."

The incident follows a series of attacks against Christian institutions, priests, and nuns in the states of Uttar Pradesh, Haryana, and Madhya Pradesh.

The AICC team--composed of an advocate, a pastor, and a community representative--said it found disturbing elements of a deliberate hate campaign by the Sangh Parivar, the extended family of the Rashtriya Swayamsevak Sangh (RSS), a Hindu nationalist organization that is the ideological parent of India's governing Bharatiya Janata Party. Provocative statements and signs have been painted on the walls in the town, the AICC said.

The community is being threatened with anonymous letters and telephone calls ordering citizens to stop Christian prayers in the schools or face dire consequences, according to the AICC.

Police previously attributed the bombing to rivalry between two local pastors. After interviewing Christians belonging to both congregations, the AICC concluded that police were incorrect. Local police have since said that senior officers who made the earlier statements did so in haste.

"Going by the facts, evidence, and circumstances, in our opinion the cause of the blast is a handiwork of fundamentalists who conspired and executed a meticulous precision blast without leaving any evidence to the site," the AICC report said. The bomb was not an "ordinary (crude) one but it appears to be either a time bomb or a remote bomb," according to the report.

***

Document

CONGRESSIONAL RECORD -- EXTENSIONS

Friday, June 9, 2000
106th Congress, 2nd Session
146 Cong Rec E 921

REFERENCE: Vol. 146, No. 71
TITLE: FREEDOM FOR THE SIKHS OF KHALISTAN

HON. EDOLPHUS TOWNS
of New York
in the House of Representatives
Wednesday, June 7, 2000

Mr. TOWNS. Mr. Speaker, the Council of Khalistan recently issued an open letter about the deplorable situation in Punjab, the Sikh homeland which declared its independence on October 7, 1987, as Khalistan.

The Sikhs are under attack from a militant Hindu organization called the RSS. The RSS was formed during World War II in support of the Fascists. It is the parent organization of the ruling BJP and many other organizations also come under its umbrella. Its agenda is to promote fundamentalist Hindu nationalism. Two members of the ruling BJP, which is a part of the RSS, were quoted in the newspapers as saying that everyone who lives in India should be Hindu or subservient to Hinduism.

Now the RSS is trying to form a satellite organization called the Rashtriya Sikh Sangat which is designed to subsume Sikhs under Hinduism and wipe out their religion. Since the ruling party is part of the RSS, it is implicitly part of this effort to eliminate the Sikh religion. As people who believe in freedom of religion, this assault on anyone's freedom of religion ought to concern all of us.

The recent massacre of 35 Sikhs in Chatti Singhpora is just another chapter in this campaign. Two recent investigations have proven that the Indian government was responsible for that massacre. There are still 50,000 Sikhs political prisoners rotting in Indian jails without charge or trial. The Indian government has murdered over 250,000 Sikhs. Punjab is a police state. The only way to end this campaign against the Sikhs is to support self-determination and freedom for Punjab, Khalistan.

Mr. Speaker, there are measures the United States can take to promote freedom for Khalistan and throughout South Asia. I urge the President to declare India a terrorist nation. We can cut off American aid and trade to India until all people there enjoy their basic human rights. And in accord with American principles, we must declare our support for self-determination for the people of Khalistan, the people of Kashmir, the people of Nagaland, and the other peoples and nations of South Asia. This can be achieved by allowing the people to vote in a free and fair plebiscite under international supervision on the question of independence. Such a plebiscite is similar to the periodic votes in Puerto Rico and Quebec on their political futures. This is how democratic nations do it and it is how great powers do it. If India wants to be taken seriously as a member of the family of democratic nations, it must allow self-determination and human rights for all peoples and nations within its artificial borders.

Mr. Speaker, I would like to place the Council of Khalistan's open letter on the situation in Punjab into the Record.

Council of Khalistan,
Washington, DC, May 12, 2000.
A Sovereign Khalistan Is the Only Solution
All Sikh Institutions and Present Leadership in Punjab Are Under
Government Control

Khalsa Ji: The militant Hindu fundamentalists of the RSS are now attacking the Sikh Nation. They are trying to insinuate themselves into the Sikh Nation by forming the "Rashtriya Sikh Sangat." They are trying to bring Sikhs under the Hindu umbrella by any means necessary. The Sikh Nation must stay alert and fight back against these efforts.

The only way to stop these efforts is political power. Without political power, nations perish. If we cannot reclaim our lost sovereignty, the RSS will succeed in its efforts to wipe out the Sikh Nation and the Sikh religion. Every day, we pray "Raj Kare Ga Khalsa." Do we mean it? A true Sikh cannot lie to Guru. If we mean what we say, we must do everything we can to establish Khalsa Raj.

The turmoil of the Akal Takht and the SGPC, and the other problems of the Sikh Nation are the result of the fact that we have lost the sovereignty that the Guru gave us. These problems have come about because the entire Sikh leadership and the Sikh institutions in Punjab are under Indian government control. We can only solve these problems by liberating our homeland, Khalistan.

Why are there still 50,000 Sikhs rotting in Indian jails without charge or trial? Why have the Sikh leaders in Punjab been silent about the murders of over 250,000 Sikhs at the hands of the Indian government? There is an Akali government and there are other Akali parties like Mann's Akali Dal. Why can't they start a Shantmai Morcha to free those political prisoners? Why can't they demand that Amnesty International be allowed into Punjab to conduct an independent human-rights investigation?

The government previously sent Professor Manjit Singh to destroy the Khalistan movement abroad. Now it has sent Simranjit Singh Mann. No Sikh leader who speaks for Khalistan will be allowed to leave the country and come here. There is moral degeneration of the Sikh character due to the lack of political power.

Four years ago, the Sikh leadership passed the Amritsar Declaration. It said that if India did not grant Punjab complete autonomy within six months, they would start a peaceful agitation for Khalistan. Four years later, Mann still supports the Amritsar Declaration. He still says that there should be a federation with India controlling defense, foreign affairs, and finances. These are the things that define your political status. The other Sikh leaders in Punjab have backed away from even that position. On February 12 at the celebration of Sant Bhindranwale's birthday, Mann opposed the speakers who spoke for Khalistan, saying that they spoke only for themselves and that Bhindranwale supported secularism.

The proposal for a federated India still keeps Hindustan in control. That is why Mann made it. At the Sikh Day parade, U.S. Congressman Major Owens raised slogans of "Khalistan Zindabad," yet Mann would not even use the word Khalistan. He has long posed as a Khalistani. Even last year at the 300th anniversary celebration, he raised slogans of "Khalistan Zindabad" but now he has changed his stand. He, too, is clearly under government control. There is only one solution: a sovereign, free, and independent Khalistan, as declared on October 7, 1987. Only in a free Khalistan can Sikhs live in freedom, dignity, prosperity, and peace.

The Sikh Nation will not achieve its legitimate aspirations with any of the current political parties in Punjab. None of these parties will bring us a free Khalistan. Whether the Akalis, Congress, or the Akali Dal Mann is elected, elections under the Indian constitution will not free Khalistan and they will not end the slavery of the Sikh Nation and the corruption in the Punjab government. Badal made three promises to get elected: that he would release all political prisoners, that he would punish guilty police officers, and that he would appoint a commission to look into the excesses by the Indian government against the Sikh Nation. He could not even keep these modest promises. Instead, he put the heat on the People's Commission and shut it down.

The massacre of 35 Sikhs in Chatti Singhpora shows that without sovereignty, the Indian oppression of the Sikh Nation will continue. An investigation by the Ludhiana-based International Human Rights Organization, led by D.S. Gill, showed that the Indian government was responsible for the massacre. A recent report by the Justice Ajit Singh Bains, chairman of the Punjab Human Rights Organization, Sardar Inderjit Singh Jaijee, convenor of the Movement Against State Repression, and General Kartar Singh Gill, also found that the government counter-insurgency forces were responsible. This atrocity underlines the need for a sovereign, independent Khalistan.

Punjab is a police state. None of the political parties will bring us Khalistan. The Sikh Nation needs new leadership and a new party that are committed to liberating Khalistan. We need a Khalsa Raj Party. The Khalsa Raj Party should be committed to self-determination. It should demand freedom for Khalistan and any peaceful, democratic, nonviolent means should be used to achieve this goal, whether it is a plebiscite or any other democratic means.

The only way to escape Indian slavery is to liberate Khalistan. New Sikh leadership emerge to free the Sikh Nation. They should raise the slogan "India Quit Khalistan" and start a Shantmai Morcha until we achieve freedom. We have now seen how the Indian government controls Sikh institutions and the entire Sikh leadership in Punjab.

Unless the Sikh Nation brings back the Sikh spirit and fight for truth and justice, the Khalsa Panth will not prosper. Remember the Guru Ka Bag Morcha and the Jaito Morcha. We did it then and we can do it now. Only in a free Khalistan can the Sikh religion flourish. Only in a free Khalistan will Sikhs be able to live in freedom and dignity. Only then can the Sikh Nation finally enjoy the glow of freedom that was promised to us so many years ago.

Khalsa Ji, the onus is on us. The time is now. We must start a Khalsa Raj Party and begin a Shantmai Morcha to liberate Khalistan. We must reclaim our lost sovereignty. New, young leadership which has dedication and the spirit of sacrifice must emerge. Support only these new leaders who are honest, dedicated, fearless, and committed to freedom for Khalistan. India is on the verge of disintegration. Kashmir is going to be free from Indian control. Let us make use of this opportunity to free Khalistan.

> *Sincerely,*
> *Dr. Gurmit Singh Aulakh, President, Council of Khalistan.*

***

Document

CONGRESSIONAL RECORD -- EXTENSIONS

Thursday, May 11, 2000
106th Congress, 2nd Session
146 Cong Rec E 720

REFERENCE: Vol. 146, No. 58
TITLE: MORE ANTI-CHRISTIAN ACTIVITIES IN INDIA

HON. JOHN T. DOOLITTLE
of California
in the House of Representatives
Thursday, May 11, 2000

Mr. DOOLITTLE. Mr. Speaker, I was distressed to read some recent articles showing that the repression of Christians in India continues. The RSS, the parent organization of the ruling BJP, has apparently published a booklet on how to besmirch Christians.

According to an article in the May 5 issue of India Abroad, the RSS has published a booklet on how to implicate Christians and other minorities in false criminal cases. It cites a Hindustan Times report that says the booklet, entitled "Save Hindus--Attacks and Laws," contains "guidelines for framing charges, false as well as genuine, against minorities." The booklet has been in circulation for three months, according to the article.

If India cannot learn religious tolerance, it is not deserving of the support of the free countries of the world. It is time to declare India a violator of religious liberty and other human rights until the situation improves. India should allow Amnesty International into Punjab and other troubled states to conduct an independent human-rights investigation. This has not happened since 1978. What is "the world's largest democracy" hiding? India should also hold a free and fair plebiscite on the question of independence for Khalistan, Kashmir, Nagaland, and the other states seeking their freedom from India.

I would like to introduce the article from India Abroad that I mentioned earlier into the Record for the information of the House and the public.

From India Abroad, May 12, 2000
Attack on Christians

New Delhi--A group of Christians who were distributing copies of the Bible and other evangelical literature in Vivekanandnagar, Ahmedabad, were reportedly attacked by activists of the right-wing Bajrang Dal on May 5.

The Christians were attacked with lathis (canes) and sharp- edged weapons, the reports said, adding that three persons were injured in the incident.

Samson C. Christian, executive member of the All India Christian Council, alleged that the attack was pre-planned as the Bajrang Dal was aware that members of the Operation Mobilization Association of Christians (OMAC) had been preaching in the area.

In a related development, reports stated that the Sangh Parivar, comprising Rashtriya Swayamsevak Sangh, the ideological parent of the Bharatiya Janata Party (BJP), and its affiliate organizations, have brought out a booklet in Gujarat, containing guidelines on how to implicate minorities in court cases, The Hindustan Times reported.

The 12-page booklet, titled "Hinduno Bachao--akraman ane kayedo" (Save Hindus--attacks and laws), contains guidelines for framing charges, false as well as genuine, against minorities under existing laws, the report said, adding that the booklet has been in circulation for the past three months.

***

Document

CONGRESSIONAL RECORD -- EXTENSIONS

Wednesday, May 10, 2000
106th Congress, 2nd Session
146 Cong Rec E 698

REFERENCE: Vol. 146, No. 57
TITLE: NEW REPORT SHOWS INDIAN GOVERNMENT IS TO BLAME
FOR MASSACRE OF 35 SIKHS IN CHATTI SINGHPORA

HON. EDOLPHUS TOWNS
of New York
in the House of Representatives
Wednesday, May 10, 2000

Mr. TOWNS. Mr. Speaker, recently two human-rights groups in Punjab, the Punjab Human Rights Organization and the Movement Against

State Repression, published a report on the massacre of 35 Sikhs in the village of Chatti Singhpora, Kashmir, this past March. Despite the Indian government's efforts to blame Pakistan and alleged Kashmiri "militants" for the massacre, an effort the Indian government reinforced by killing five innocent Kashmiris, the report clearly and unambiguously places the blame where it belongs--on the Indian government.

"It is our considered opinion," the report says, "that Pakistan has nothing to gain by ordering militants/mercenaries to massacre Sikhs in the Kashmir valley. Pakistan had steered clear of this kind of act during 10-15 years of militancy in J&K," the group wrote. "J&K militants too had nothing to gain from such an incident. Indian leaders however gained substantial mileage from this incident as a spate of international sympathy was forthcoming," the investigative team wrote. They noted that India's Home Minister, L.K. Advani, "was quoted as saying that three events brought a turn around in international opinion in India's favor. He mentioned Kargil, the hijacking of the Indian airliner, and the Chatti Singhpora incident."

According to the report, the people in the village of Chatti Singhpora "did not believe that militants had any hand in this incident." The report notes that "as a rule foreign mercenaries visit a village once and do not come back again. So these men cannot be militants. Also real militants do not part with their weapons even for a minute." The killers wore military uniforms and chanted "Jai Mata Di; Jai Hind," a Hindu nationalist slogan. The report notes that the Sikhs and Kashmiri Muslims have very good relations. Both the Chief Minister of Kashmir, Farooq Abdullah, and Mr. Advani had warned villagers against supporting "militants."

The authors of the report conclude that the Indian government's counterinsurgency forces, which are run by the Indian intelligence service, RAW, are responsible for the massacre of Chatti Singhpora.

Unfortunately, the Indian government is suppressing this information, and their friends in the democratic countries of the world are protecting them. There must be a full, fair, independent, and complete investigation and the people responsible for this terrible atrocity must be prosecuted. However, Parliamentary Affairs Minister Pramod Mahajan admitted that "security forces would not be punished for the killings of civilians. It would demoralize the troops who are fighting insurgency in different states." This is a very revealing statement by an official of the Indian government. Perhaps this is why an allegedly democratic country needs a "Movement Against State Repression."

America is the beacon of freedom. America must not allow an allegedly democratic country to continue these activities. We must do what we can to help bring freedom to the people of South Asia. It is time to stop our aid to India until it lets the people within its borders enjoy the human rights to which all people are entitled. We should stop supporting India's anti-Americanism. And we should declare our support for an internationally-supervised, free and fair plebiscite in Punjab, Khalistan on the question of independence. We should also support similar plebiscites in Kashmir, in Christian Nagaland, and throughout India. This is the way to bring real freedom, peace, prosperity, and stability to South Asia. It will also gain us new allies in that troubled region.

Mr. Speaker, I wish I could put this excellent report into the Record, but it is too long. I would like to place the summary sections of observations and recommendations into the Record, for the information of my colleagues. I urge my colleagues, especially those who are supporters of India, to read these sections carefully.

Visit to Chithi Singhpora
Observations

3.1. Team Observations

The facts narrated above clearly indicate that the visitors of Chithi Singhpora were not members of the security forces. Dress, language, careless handling of weapons and behaviour in general discounts the security forces. That they were militants, can also be safely ruled out because it is general knowledge that militants guard their weapons most carefully and would not visit a location repeatedly knowing that an RR post is located 3-4 kms away. The finger therefore points towards the so-called Counter Insurgents/Renegades (Surrendered militants). The description of the villagers, in fact, corroborates this assessment.

The fact that the RR Unit was located close to Chithi Singhpora and the statement of Principal Ranji Singh and teacher Niranjan Singh clearly indicated that the security forces know fully well about the identity of the visitors to Chithi Singhpora and did nothing about it.

The statements of various individuals in Anantnag/Srinagar tallies with what the villagers narrated to the team. One man Karamjit Singh spoke a different language. He stressed in his statement that the killers were militants. Secondly his various actions indicate that he has an inkling that some force had come to kill on March 20, 2000 evening. His escape was miraculous in spite of his being addressed directly by the so called CO not to go home. He still escaped. In our opinion Karamjit appears to have been in some contact with the security forces. His migration to Jammu and his nervousness during the teams meeting with him clearly point to this.

The State Chief Minister, Farooq Abdulla had asked for a Judicial enquiry into the Chithi Singhpora killings by a Supreme Court Judge. (Press Statement is attached as Annexture II). Instead, the Centre has ordered a judicial enquiry by Justice Pandhian into the Pathribal killings of five civilians and police firing at Brakpora. The Chithi Singhpora killings are to be probed by the Additional Judicial Magistrate only. This clearly indicates that the truth behind this Chithi Singhpora incident is not being allowed to surface.

All efforts should be made to normalise the situation and bring the Sikhs back into the mainstream in the State.

The team feels that Law and Order being a state subject, the handling and allotment of tasks to the Counter-Insurgency Force was done by the state authorities under the aegis of the Director General of Police. Events as they unfolded clearly indicate that this force was misutilised for criminal acts outside the parameters of law. Here we have support from the publication Amnesty International (Embargoed for February 22, 1999). An extract from the same (Page 26, Column 2) is reproduced here.

"... Only three months earlier, Chief Minister Dr. Farooq Abdullah was quoted as saying that the Jammu and Kashmir state police and the Punjab police had achieved excellence in fighting terrorism and they could be trusted in the proxy war-like situation facing the state. The referrnce to Punjab police was no chance remark as the Director General of Police appointed in February 1997 has served for many years in counter-insurgency operations in Punjab where high levels of human rights violations had been reported. The Jammu and Kashmir state police have shown a disturbing disregard for the rule of law in their expanding counter- insurgency operations, leading to increasing allegations of arbitrary arrests, torture, killings and disappearance' perpetrated by police officers themselves and reports of their connivance in abuses committed by other agencies such as the renegades. It is also shown in the way police have obstructed victims' and victims' families' access to redress."

We feel that a Central Agency directed this operation without the knowledge of the State Chief Minister and his Cabinet. This, therefore, is an act that needs to be condemned and a high level probe ordered to punish the guilty.

The Sikh soldiers have been used disproportionately in Nagaland, Assam, Sri Lanka and all along in Kashmir. This tends to endanger the amity existing between the minority and local majority community. This has special reference to the good relations existing between the majority Kashmiri Muslims and the minority Kashmiri Sikhs in J&K.

It is our considered opinion that Pakistan had nothing a gain by ordering militants/mercenaries to massacre Sikhs in the Kashmir valley. Pakistan had stressed clear of this kind of act during the past 10-15 years of military in J&K.

J&K militants too had nothing a gain from such an incident. Indian leaders however gained substantial mileage from the incident as a spate of international sympathy was forthcoming. In fact President Clinton was joined by a number of others in decrying terrorism and killing of civilians in Kashmir. Union Home Minister Advani

Recommendations

4.1. Team Recommendations

The Chithi Singhpora killings resulted in a major tragedy for the Sikh community in J&K. It was a traumatic event which had national and international ramifications. The killers have yet to be identified by the state and national authorities. It is therefore, very vital to discount various rumours and conjectures making the rounds. The team recommends that:

i. The Chithi Singhpora killings be investigated by the United Nations Human Rights Commission as these killings are symptomatic of killings that have taken place in various parts of India during counter-insurgency operations. Once the culprits are identified they should be dealt with speedily in accordance with the law.

ii. Compensation to be given to the victims of the killings at Chithi Singhpora.

Pathribal, Brakpora and other related incidents should be Rupees 10 Lakhs as recommended to be given to victims of custodial killings by the Indian NHRC along with allied benefits.

iii. In spite of assistance by the majority Kashmiri Muslims and security measures taken by the centre and state government, some Sikh families still feel insecure and desire to migrate. In case they do so they should be provided with adequate facilities at least equal to that provided to the migrating Kashmiri Pandits and their families.

iv. The Chithi Singhpora killings put a question mark on the employment of surrendered militants as a viable counter- insurgency force. This force consists of individuals who have changed loyalties for material benefits. Their misuse of arms and exploitation of the situation for personal gain has been highlighted by the media repeatedly. We strongly recommend that this force be disbanded forthwith. Surrendered militants should be absorbed into mainstream of civil life rather than be employed in the counter-insurgency role.

> *Dated: April 29, 2000.*
> *Signed, Ajit Singh Bains, Justice (Retd). Inderjit Singh Jaijee Kartar Singh Gill, Lt. Gen. (Retd).*

***

Document

CONGRESSIONAL RECORD -- EXTENSIONS

Tuesday, May 2, 2000
106th Congress, 2nd Session
146 Cong Rec E 612

REFERENCE: Vol. 146, No. 52
TITLE: END RELIGIOUS PERSECUTION IN INDIA

HON. EDOLPHUS TOWNS
of New York
in the House of Representatives
Tuesday, May 2, 2000

Mr. TOWNS. Mr. Speaker, the persecution of Christians and other religious minorities in India continues. Now even an ally of the ruling party has spoken out against it.

Newsroom, a website devoted to religious news, reported that the Trinamool Congress, a party in coalition with the ruling BJP, demanded the banning of Bajrang Dal, a militant Hindu nationalist organization. The Bajrang Dal is affiliated with the Vishwa Hindu Parishad (VHP), which in turn is part of the RSS, a Fascist organization that is the parent organization of the BJP.

Dara Singh, the person India has arrested in connection with the murder of missionary Graham Staines and his two young sons, has been linked to the Bajrang Dal. Christians have been subjected to three attacks in Uttar Pradesh in two weeks. On Good Friday, members of the Bajrang Dal attacked members of the House of Worship, a Christian church in Agra. Uttar Pradesh also has a law prohibiting Muslims from building new mosques or converting any building into a mosque without government permission. In the state of Orissa, religious conversions are banned without government permission.

In Haryana on April 22, three nuns were attacked by a Hindu fundamentalist. One, Sister Anandi, remains in Holy Family Hospital in serious condition. No one has been arrested for this crime.

The militant Hindu fundamentalists who carried out these acts are allies of the Indian government. The government itself has killed over 200,000 Christians in Nagaland, over a quarter of a million Sikhs, more than 65,000 Kashmiri Muslims since 1988, and tens of thousands of others. It holds tens of thousands of political prisoners without charge or trial. Some of them have been held for over 15 years. This is unacceptable.

America is the bastion of freedom in the world. It is our responsibility to do what we can to ensure freedom for all people. We should cut off India's aid until it learns to respect human rights. The government must stop killing religious and ethnic minorities. It must also punish strongly those who kill and do other acts of violence in the government's behalf. Amnesty International, which has not been allowed to enter India to investigate human rights abuses since 1978, must be allowed to come into the country. Until then, no American money should go to India.

We should also put this Congress on record in support of democracy in South Asia by calling for a free and fair plebiscite, under international supervision, to decide the political future of Khalistan, Kashmir, Nagaland, and all the other nations occupied by India. These steps are the best way to bring freedom to all the people of South Asia.

Mr. Speaker, I would like to submit the Newsroom article into the Record. I urge my colleagues to read it.

Bajrang Dal Ban Sought After Pre-Easter
Attacks on Christians in India

New Delhi, 25 April 2000 (Newsroom)--Allies of the Bharatiya Janata Party (BJP), which leads India's coalition government, this week demanded that the BJP ban a militant group of Hindu nationalists and dismiss the BJP-led Uttar Pradesh state government in the wake of recent attacks against Christians.

The call by the Trinamool Congress, an ally in the BJP-led National Democratic Alliance headed by Prime Minister Atal Bihari Vajpayee, to ban the Bajrang Dal and dismiss Uttar Pradesh Chief Minister Ram Prakash Gupta and his government stunned BJP leaders.

Leaders from the Trinamool Congress and from the opposition Congress and Samajwadi parties blasted the BJP for failing to control the Hindu nationalist group that many blame for the spate of violent incidents directed toward religious minorities in the last two years.

The Bajrang Dal, a militant Hindu organization affilated with the Vishwa Hindu Parishad (World Hindu Council) and linked to several attacks on Christians, believes it has a duty to promote the Hindu religion and Hindutva--Hinduness-- in India. Dara Singh, who is accused of masterminding the murders of Australian missionary Graham Staines and his two sons last year, has been linked to the Bajrang Dal, although the group denies he is a member.

Sudip Bandopadhyay of the Trinamul Congress and Yerram Naidu, Tulugu Desam party leader, demanded that security be provided to Christians and other religious minorities wherever possible, especially in states like Uttar Pradesh where there have been three violent attacks against Christians in the last two weeks.

Madhavrao Scindia, deputy leader of the Congress Party in the Lok Sabha (the lower house of Parliament), said the government should put a stop to incidents like those reported in Uttar Pradesh and Haryana this month. He demanded a response from Home Affairs Minister Lal Kishen Advani, who is considered a friend of most of India's Hindu nationlist groups and is the second most powerful man in India after Vajpayee. "Groups close to the BJP must be reined in as they are vitiating communal peace," Scindia said.

Opposition Samajwadi party leader Mulayam Singh Yadav, who once headed the defense ministry, said that militant Hindu groups pose a greater danger than the actions of religious minorities. "Majority communalism poses a greater danger compared to minority communalism," he said. Members of the Hindu group Shiv Sena tried to heckle him while he addressed members of Parliament.

During a two-day BJP national executive meeting in the Uttar Pradesh town of Lucknow, Vajpayee chastised Uttar Pradesh Chief Minister Ram Prakash Gupta over his state's handling of attacks on Christian missionaries in Mathura. Vajpayee reportedly said the state should have dispatched police to assess the situation and instill confidence among the Christian community. He also asked the state government to explain its position on the controversial religious places bill, which prohibits Muslims from building mosques or converting an existing building into a mosque without government permission.

Bajrang Dal national coordinator Surendra Kumar Jain said last month that his group was fighting to construct a Temple for Ram in Ayodhya in Uttar Pradesh. The extremist group also once demanded that the federal government declare Pakistan an enemy state.

Referring to the attacks against Christians, Jain said that "missionaries consider Hindus a soft target. Even the words soft target' were used in the missionary literature. However, now the Hindus have woken up. We are no more a soft target for their unholy activities. We appreciate missionary services, but only when the object is service and not conversion."

Monday's confrontation in parliament followed three attacks against Christians in Uttar Pradesh in the last two weeks. Members of the House of Worship, one of India's fastest- growing church groups headquartered in the southern state of Hyderabad, were attacked by suspected Bajrang Dal activists on the outskirts of Agra, site of the Taj Mahal, police said. The Good Friday attack on the 14-member preaching team from Hyderabad in the BJP-ruled state came a week after a Catholic priest and three nuns were attacked in a school. It was the seventh attack reported in the state in less than 100 days.

The Bajrang Dal complained to state police that the Hyderabad group was trying to convert villagers by offering them money, a charge church authorities deny. In a counter complaint the victims reported that a mob of 20 to 30 people attacked the van in which they were traveling and tried to burn the vehicle. The group returned to Hyderabad where the main church, Hebron Church, is located. The church, also known as the Indigenous Society of Churches in India, is one of the fastest growing in the country with mainly new converts as members. It was founded by a Punjabi Sikh agricultural engineer, Bakht Singh, in the 1920s. Bakht Singh is 99.

Three Catholic nuns on their way to attend midnight Mass in Rewari in neighboring Haryana state were attacked Saturday night by a man riding a scooter. It was the third attack on Christians reported in the past three months in this wheat- rich state. One nun, Sister Anandi, remains in Holy Family Hospital in serious condition. The other two nuns suffered minor injuries. Police so far have made no arrests.

John Dayal, convener of the United Christian Forum for Human Rights, said in a prepared statement that "this attack was part of the series of ongoing attacks on Christians and their institutions."

***

Document

CONGRESSIONAL RECORD -- EXTENSIONS

Tuesday, April 4, 2000
106th Congress, 2nd Session
146 Cong Rec E 483

REFERENCE: Vol. 146, No. 40
TITLE: 35 SIKHS MURDERED IN INDIAN-CONTROLLED KASHMIR

HON. DAN BURTON
of Indiana
in the House of Representatives
Tuesday, April 4, 2000

Mr. BURTON of Indiana. Mr. Speaker, on the evening of Monday, March 20, 2000, in a Sikh village located in the Indian-controlled side of Kashmir, several armed men roused Sikh villagers from their homes, lined up 35 of the men, and shot them to death. According to Associated Press (AP) reports, witnesses said the gunmen entered the village about 7 p.m., dressed in what appeared to be Indian army uniforms. They knocked on doors, forced the adult men to come out with their identity cards, lined them up in two groups and opened fire.

There has been much speculation about who is responsible for these gruesome murders. India claimed that Kashmiri militants were responsible for the massacre, and accused neighboring Pakistan of supporting the rebels. On the eve of President Clinton's visit to India, and considering Pakistan's current situation, it is difficult for me to believe that Pakistan would take this sort of a risk to their relationship with the United States.

That is why I am inserting into the Record a press release from Dr. Gurmit Singh Aulakh, President of the Council of Khalistan. Dr. Aulakh, who has conducted a peaceful, democratic, nonviolent effort for a free and sovereign Khalistan, suggests that this, as the AP reported, may be the handiwork of the Indian government.

Mr. Speaker, the Indian government has murdered over 250,000 Sikhs since 1984; 200,000 Christians in Nagaland since 1947; more than 65,000 Kashmiri Muslims since 1988; and tens of thousands of Assamese, Manipuris, Tamils, and Dalits. With a track record like that, I certainly believe that Dr. Aulakh's assertion merits a closer look.

Indian Government Murders 35 Sikhs
RAW Agents Pose as Kashmiri Militants--Continues Pattern of Pitting Minorities Against Each Other

Washington, DC, March 21--Thirty-five (35) Sikhs were murdered in Kashmir today by agents of the Indian government's Research and Analysis Wing (RAW) posing as Kashmiri militants. There are over 700,000 Indian troops stationed in Kashmir, yet the murderers disap-

peared without detection. The murders were carried out during President Clinton's visit to South Asia.

Dr. Gurmit Singh Aulakh, President of the Council of Khalistan, strongly condemned the murders. "These murders are evil, cowardly, and stupid acts designed to pit one community against another and prop up India's image for the President's visit," Dr. Aulakh said. "Whoever carried out these brutal acts, they are cowards," he said. "They may escape justice in this world, but they will face the justice of God. That will be worse for them."

"Sikhs and Kashmiris are allies in the struggle for freedom," said Dr. Aulakh.

"What motive would Kashmiri freedom fighters have to kill Sikhs? This would be especially stupid when President Clinton is visiting. The freedom movements in Kashmir, Khalistan, Nagaland, and throughout India need the support of the United States," he said. Khalistan is the Sikh homeland declared independent on October 7, 1987.

The murders continue a pattern of divide-and-rule terrorism by the Indian government. The government has recently tried to blame Sikhs for the murder of Christian missionary Graham Staines by arresting a Hindu man who uses the alias Dara Singh. Every Sikh male uses Singh in his name. Yet it was reported at the time of the Staines murder that he and his two sons were burned to death in their jeep by a mob chanting "Victory to Hannuman," a Hindu god. That mob was affiliated with the Fascist RSS, the parent organization of the ruling BJP. In November 1994, the Hitavada reported that the Indian government paid the late Governor of Punjab, Surendra Nath, $1.5 billion to organize and support covert state terrorism in Punjab, Khalistan, and in Kashmir. The book "Soft Target", written by two respected Canadian journalists, proved that the Indian government blew up its own airliner in 1985, killing 329 people, to blame the incident on the Sikhs and provide an excuse for more repression and bloodshed. This is a well-established modus operandi of RAW.

The Indian government has murdered over 250,000 Sikhs since 1984, according to figures compiled by the Punjab State Magistracy and human-rights organizations. The figures were published in "The Politics of Genocide" by Inderjit Singh Jaijee. The government has also killed over 200,000 Christians in Nagaland since 1947, more than 65,000 Kashmiri Muslims since 1988, and tens of thousands of Assamese, Manipuris, Tamils, Dalits, and others. The U.S. State Department reported that the Indian government paid more than 41,000 cash bounties to police to murder Sikhs. Amnesty International recently reported that there are thousands of political prisoners, including prisoners to conscience, held in Indian jails without charge or trial. Some Sikh political prisoners have been in this illegal detention since 1984.

"This shows that there is no freedom for minorities in India," Dr. Aulakh said. "For minorities, India is no democracy," he said. "As U.S. Congressman Dana Rohrabacher said, for the minorities India might as well be Nazi Germany.' "

"I urge President Clinton and Ambassador Richard Celeste to confront India on these brutal murders, as well as the recent harassment of journalist Sukhbir Singh Osan, getting Sikh and other political prisoners released, and the ongoing, massive, and brutal human-rights violations against Sikhs and other minorities," Dr. Aulakh said. "If the United States wants to see an end to these incidents, it should support self-determination for Khalistan, Kashmir, Nagaland, and all the other nations seeking their freedom from India," Dr. Aulakh said. "Only a free Khalistan will end India's corruption, tyranny and genocide against the Sikh Nation," he said. "India is on the verge of disintegration. The Sikh leadership should immediately begin a "Shantmai Morcha" to liberate our homeland, Khalistan."

- - - - - - - - -

From the Washington Post, Mar. 21, 2000
Near Clinton's India Visit, Violence Flares in Kashmir
(By Pamela Constable)

Srinagar, India March 20.--While their government and most of their countrymen are hoping President Clinton will play down the sensitive topic of Kashmir during his visit to India this week, people in this depressed, wintry city at the political heart of the disputed, violence-torn region are praying for just the opposite.

Today, in the worst single attack on civilians in a decade of guerrilla war, unidentified gunmen massacred 35 Sikh men in the Kashmiri village of Chati Singhpura Mattan, wire services reported. Security officials had feared that armed Pakistan-based insurgents, who have stepped up attacks here in recent months, might stage a dramatic attack during Clinton's stay in India.

Clinton condemned the attack in Kashmir. "On behalf of the president and all Americans let me express our outrage at the attack on a village in Kashmir last night," White House spokesman Joe Lockhart told reporters in New Delhi.

Many Kashmiris believe that only a world leader of Clinton's stature can put pressure on Indian officials to start meaningful negotiations with Pakistan over the mountainous, predominantly Muslim border region where separatist sentiment is strong, guerrilla violence is rapidly rising and Indian troops patrol with an iron fist.

"If Mr. Clinton can make a difference in places like Chechnya and Bosnia, why not in Kashmir?" said Shah Khan, 22, who sells shirts and pants in the teeming alleys of Lal Chowk bazaar. "We are happy because at least his visit will bring some attention to our problems, but we wish he would come to Kashmir and see for himself. Then we would all tell him one thing; we want freedom."

But this message is highly unlikely to reach Clinton's ears or the Indian capital this week. On Sunday, about 50 Kashmiri independence activists were arrested and jailed as they tried to board buses that would take them to New Delhi for a protest rally near Parliament, where Clinton is scheduled to speak Wednesday.

In a brief interview in jail today, the group's leader, Shabir Shah, 44, said they had been tear-gassed and dragged into police vans as they prepared to leave. He said the group, which seeks Kashmiri independence from India, had planned to stage a peaceful rally and a symbolic hunger strike.

"President Clinton says he wants to help ease tensions in the region, and he will be talking with India and Pakistan, but we wanted to tell him that it is futile until we Kashmiris are taken into account," Shah said.

Kashmir, which is divided between India and Pakistan, has been the major source of friction between the two neighbors and nuclear powers for a generation. Since the early 1990s, the Indian-occupied part has been the site of a violent conflict between anti-India insurgent groups and Indian security forces, which has cost tens of thousands of lives. Last summer, a 10-week border conflict in the Kargil mountains left hundreds dead.

Today's attack on the Sikhs seemed to represent an especially grue-some escalation of violence and attempt at ethnic cleansing in the Kashmir Valley, where Muslims dominate the population and the insurgency has become increasingly directed by Islamic groups based in Pakistan. The victims were separated from their families by unidentified gunmen who entered their village after dark and shot them.

In the past, Kashmiri insurgent groups have concentrated on military targets and have denounced terrorism against civilians. But in recent weeks, there have been a half-dozen attacks on Hindu truck drivers and on scattered villages of Kashmiri Pandits, or local Hindus, many of whom were violently driven from the region years ago. Now Sikhs, who have lived peaceably in northern Kashmir for years, appear to have become their latest target.

Clinton, who has called Kashmir "the most dangerous place in the world," has repeatedly expressed interest in helping to defuse the tensions and to nudge India and Pakistan back toward dialogue. But Indian authorities are adamantly opposed to any foreign intervention in the dispute, and have declared they will not resume talks with Pakistan until it stops arming and training Kashmiri insurgents.

In interviews over the weekend, some Srinagar residents said they were skeptical that Clinton's talks with Indian leaders could make any difference. They said the United States was too concerned with bigger issues, such as trade and nuclear non-proliferation, to let Kashmir become an irritant to improving relations. "Clinton is coming as a guest, so he won't want to embarrass his hosts. What he says in America about Kashmir may not be what he says here," said Masood Ahmed, 30, another shopkeeper in Lal Chowk. "He already knows that thousands of people have been killed in Kashmir, but he is only coming to see the Taj Mahal."

- - - - - - - - -

From the New York Times, Mar. 21, 2000
35 Massacred In Sikh Town In Kashmir

Srinagar, India, Tuesday, March 21 (AP).--Gunmen rounded up and killed 35 Sikh villagers in the disputed state of Kashmir, the police said today as President Clinton began a visit to India.

The massacre on Monday night was the first major attack on the small Sikh community in Kashmir since separatist Muslims started their insurgency 10 years ago. Sikhs are considered a neutral minority, but Indian officials had warned earlier of violence by Muslim militants hoping to draw attention to Kashmir during Mr. Clinton's visit.

Both India and Pakistan claim the Himalayan territory and have fought two wars over it.

The gunmen were not immediately identified and no group claimed responsibility for the attack, the police said.

Mr. Clinton arrived in New Delhi, 400 miles to the south, on Monday evening after a visit to Bangladesh. He has said that reducing tensions between India and Pakistan is one of his objectives of the trip.

Many Kashmiris were hoping that the president's visit would lead to a breakthrough in the long deadlock on the region's future.

Mr. Clinton's spokesman, Joe Lockhart, expressed outrage over the killings, saying in a statement that "our most profound sympathies go out to the victims of this brutal massacre."

The attackers entered the village of Chati Singhpura Mattan after dark and forced the residents from their homes, police officials said.

The assailants separated the men from the women, announcing that they were conducting a "crackdown," Indian security forces operate similarly when searching a neighborhood for militants that they suspect may be hiding there. The gunmen then opened fire on the men, killing 35 of them. One man was critically wounded.

Sikhs have lived mostly undisturbed in the Kashmir Valley, the only area in predominantly Hindu India with a Muslim majority. Many run the trucking companies that supply the valley.

In the last six months, attacks by the militants have focused on army bases and patrols rather than random terrorism, and have shown a higher degree of training and expertise, senior army officers have said. They said about 3,500 militants were in Kashmir, and many of them had infiltrated the cease-fire line from Pakistan, with the help of the Pakistan army. Pakistan denies giving active aid to the militants.

The area of the Sikh village is about 42 miles from Srinagar, Kashmir's summer capital, and is controlled by armed Kashmiri groups that abandoned separatism and were recruited by the Indian army as a counterinsurgency auxiliary force.

***

Document

CONGRESSIONAL RECORD -- EXTENSIONS

Thursday, March 23, 2000
106th Congress, 2nd Session
146 Cong Rec E 401

REFERENCE: Vol. 146, No. 34
TITLE: EXPRESSION OF SORROW FOR THE VICTIMS OF THE
MASSACRE IN THE VILLAGE OF CHATI SINGHPORA

HON. DAVID E. BONIOR
of Michigan
Thursday, March 23, 2000

Mr. BONIOR. Mr. Speaker, I rise today to express my profound sorrow at the horrific massacre of 35 Sikh men in the Kashmiri village of Chati Singhpora.

Today in Chati Singhpora, 35 families are mourning the loss of their fathers, their brothers and their sons. These men are victims of an inhumane war, suffering an unspeakable death before the eyes of their loved ones. The assassins who inflicted this punishment upon the families of Chati Singhpora are unknown. Regardless of their nationality and religion, they have covered this Kashmiri village with the blood of their victims and have taken 35 innocent men from the arms of their loving families.

Hundreds of villages like Chanti Singhpora are trapped, guilty only of unfortunate geography. I call upon all people to end the slaughter of innocents, to halt the violence which has divided Kashmir, and to search for common ground upon which a just and lasting peace may be erected. No more families should know such horror. I ask all of my colleagues here today to pledge themselves to peace in Kashmir, and to stop at nothing until the bloodshed has ended.

***

Document

CONGRESSIONAL RECORD -- EXTENSIONS

Tuesday, March 21, 2000
106th Congress, 2nd Session
146 Cong Rec E 368

REFERENCE: Vol. 146, No. 32
TITLE: INDIAN GOVERNMENT MURDERS 35 SIKHS: U.S. MUST TAKE
ACTION AGAINST THIS ATROCITY

HON. EDOLPHUS TOWNS
of New York
in the House of Representatives
Tuesday, March 21, 2000

Mr. TOWNS. Mr. Speaker, like everyone in this House, I was shocked and saddened to hear of the brutal murders of 35 Sikhs in Kashmir. The loss of life is a tragedy. I am sure that my colleagues will join me in expressing our sympathies to the victims' families.

Although the news media reported that "Kashmiri militants" were responsible for this incident, the latest information shows that India's Research and Analysis Wing carried out this brutal and cowardly atrocity.

There are over 700,000 Indian troops in Kashmir. How could the persons responsible for these crimes simply disappear without being detected? What motive would the Kashmiris have to kill Sikhs, who are their allies in the struggle for freedom? When these incidents occur, Mr. Speaker, one must ask who benefits from them. The only beneficiary is the Indian government, which again divides the minorities, setting them against each other to continue their divide-and-rule strategy.

India's pattern of terrorism is well known. It recently tried to blame the Sikhs for the murder of Christian missionary Graham Staines by arresting a Hindu man who calls himself Dara Singh despite the fact that Staines and his family were murdered by Hindu extremists allied with the ruling party. According to the Hitavada newspaper, the Indian government paid the late Governor of Punjab, Surendra Nath, to foment terrorist activities in Punjab and Kashmir to generate more repression and set minorities against each other.

In this country, if someone tried to create violence between, say, African Americans and Hispanics, that person would be rejected and likely arrested. In India, this is government policy.

It is also disturbing that this atrocity occurs just after President Clinton lifted the sanctions imposed on India after its nuclear tests. In light of these murders, those sanctions should be reimposed and India should be declared a terrorist state. Here in Congress, we should cut off U.S. aid to India and we should declare our support for the freedom movements in Khalistan, Kashmir, Nagaland, and throughout India. We must do these things to promote freedom for the people of South Asia and the world.

Mr. Speaker, Burning Punjab published the names of the victims of this massacre and the Council of Khalistan published an excellent press release on the incident. I would like to introduce these items into the Record to honor the memory of the victims and inform my colleagues and the people.

Indian Government Murders 35 Sikhs
RAW Agents Pose as Kashmiri Militants--Continues Pattern of Pitting Minorities Against Each Other

Washington, DC, March 21.--Thirty-five (35) Sikhs were murdered in Kashmir today by agents of the Indian government's Research and

Analysis Wing (RAW) posing as Kashmiri militants. There are over 700,000 Indian troops stationed in Kashmir, yet the murderers disappeared without detection. The murders were carried out during President Clinton's visit to South Asia.

Dr. Gurmit Singh Aulakh, President of the Council of Khalistan, strongly condemned the murders. "These murders are evil, cowardly, and stupid acts designed to pit one community against another and prop up India's image for the President's visit," Dr. Aulakh said. "Whoever carried out these brutal acts, they are cowards," he said. "They may escape justice in this world, but they will face the justice of God. That will be worse for them."

"Sikhs and Kashmiris are allies in the struggle for freedom," said Dr. Aulakh. "What motive would Kashmiri freedom fighters have to kill Sikhs? This would be especially stupid when President Clinton is visiting. The freedom movements in Kashmir, Khalistan, Nagaland, and throughout India need the support of the United States," he said. Khalistan is the Sikh homeland declared independent on October 7, 1987.

The murders continue a pattern of divide-and-rule terrorism by the Indian government. The government has recently tried to blame Sikhs for the murder of Christian missionary Graham Staines by arresting a Hindu man who uses the alias Dara Singh. Every Sikh male uses Singh in his name. Yet it was reported at the time of the Staines murder that he and his two sons were burned to death in their jeep by a mob chanting "Victory to Hannuman," a Hindu god. That mob was affiliated with the Fascist RSS, the parent organization of the ruling BJP. In November 1994, The Hitavada reported that the Indian government paid the late Governor of Punjab, Surendra Nath, $1.5 billion to organize and support covert state terrorism in Punjab, Khalistan, and in Kashmir. The book "Soft Target," written by two respected Canadian journalists, proved that the Indian government blew up its own airliner in 1985, killing 329 people, to blame the incident on the Sikhs and provide an excuse for more repression and bloodshed. This is a well-established modus operandi of RAW.

The Indian government has murdered over 250,000 Sikhs since 1984, according to figures compiled by the Punjab State Magistracy and human-rights organizations. The figures were published in "The Politics of Genocide" by Inderjit Singh Jaijee. The government has also killed over 200,000 Christians in Nagaland since 1947, more than 65,000 Kashmiri Muslims since 1988, and tens of thousands of Assamese, Manipuris, Tamils, Dalits, and others. The U.S. State Department reported that the Indian government paid more than 41,000 cash bounties to police to murder Sikhs. Amnesty International recently reported that there are thousands of political prisoners, including prisoners of conscience, held in Indian jails without charge or trial. Some Sikh political prisoners have been in this illegal detention since 1984.

"This shows that there is no freedom for minorities in India," Dr. Aulakh said. "For minorities, India is no democracy," he said. "As U.S.

Congressman Dana Rohrabacher said, for the minorities India might as well be Nazi Germany.' "

"I urge President Clinton and Ambassador Richard Celeste to confront India on these brutal murders, as well as the recent harassment of journalist Sukhbir Singh Osan, getting Sikh and other political prisoners released, and the ongoing, massive, and brutal human-rights violations against Sikhs and other minorities," Dr. Aulakh said. "If the United States wants to see an end to these incidents, it should support self-determination for Khalistan, Kashmir, Nagaland, and all the other nations seeking their freedom from India," Dr. Aulakh said. "Only a free Khalistan will end India's corruption, tyranny and genocide against the Sikh Nation," he said. "India is on the verge of disintegration. The Sikh leadership should immediately begin a Shantmai Morcha to liberate our homeland, Khalistan."

- - - - - - - - -

From the Burning Punjab News, Mar. 21, 2000
Massacred Sikhs identified

Srinagar.--The 35 Sikhs massacred at Chatti- Singpora in south Kashmir late last night by unknown armed persons have been identified. Following is the list of people killed by militants: Rajinder Singh (42), Karnail Singh (35), Rajan Singh (40), Naranjan Singh (50), Gurdeep Singh (25), Ajeetpal Singh (22), Joginder Singh (26), Gurbax Singh (35), Uttam Singh (30), Surjit Singh (22), Majit Singh (30), Devinder Singh (18), Rajinder Singh (35), Reshpal Singh (40), Gurmeek Singh (35), Sukha Singh (53), Ravi Singh (38), Jangbhadur Singh (36), Rajdeep Singh (18), Naseeb Singh (50), Kulbeer Singh (20), Darban Singh (28), Deader Singh (50), Gurmeet Singh (22), Ujal Singh (28), Charan Singh (50), Sartaj Singh (30), Rajnath Singh (45), Faqir Singh (65), Karnail Singh (45), Sheetal Singh (66), Ravinder Singh (22), Jagdesh Singh (25), Sagir Singh (60), and Sartaj Singh (26). One Devinder Kaur died of heart attack following the massacre.

***

Document
CONGRESSIONAL RECORD -- EXTENSIONS

Tuesday, March 21, 2000
106th Congress, 2nd Session
146 Cong Rec E 370

REFERENCE: Vol. 146, No. 32
TITLE: NEW MASSACRE OF SIKHS IN INDIA

HON. DANA ROHRABACHER
of California
in the House of Representatives
Tuesday, March 21, 2000

Mr. ROHRABACHER. Mr. Speaker, today, as President Clinton began a visit to India, a new act of political violence occurred in Kashmir, as 35 Sikh villagers were rounded up and killed by gunmen. The New York Times reports in the enclosed article that this was the first major attack on the small Sikh community in Kashmir since an insurgency by Kashmiri Muslims against Indian rule began 10 years ago. Sikhs had previously lived peacefully in the only predominantly Muslim area of India. It should be noted that in India, government security forces have been implicated by international human rights organizations in the murders, disappearances and torture of thousands of Sikhs.

The village of Chati Singhpura Mattan, 42 miles from Srinagar, is controlled by Kashmiri groups that abandoned the rebellion and were recruited by the Indian army as a counterinsurgency militia force. The Indian government has blamed Islamic radicals controlled by Pakistan for this heinous crime. However, the Indian government's control of this specific area has caused many Sikhs in the United States to believe that the gunmen were agents of the Indian government's Research and Intelligence Wing RAW posing as Kashmiri militants. There are more than 700,000 Indian security forces stationed in Kashmir, which has been called the most militarized area of this planet.

A fair and impartial investigation by international monitors is necessary to resolve this case and other acts of brutality committed in Kashmir. I have repeatedly advocated that fair elections, free of violence, that would permit the people of Kashmir to determine their own destiny is the best means to end this conflict. In addition, a peaceful resolution of the Kashmir issue would have a significant impact in easing the conflict between India and Pakistan.

From the New York Times, Mar. 21, 2000
35 Massacred In Sikh Town In Kashmir

Srinagar, India, Tuesday, March 21 (AP)--Gunmen rounded up and killed 35 Sikh villagers in the disputed state of Kashmir, the police said today as President Clinton began a visit to India.

The massacre on Monday night was the first major attack on the small Sikh community in Kashmir since separatist Muslims started their insurgency 10 years ago. Sikhs are considered a neutral minority, but Indian officials had warned earlier of violence by Muslim militants hoping to draw attention to kashmir during Mr. Clinton's visit.

Both India and Pakistan claim the Himalayan territory and have fought two wars over it.

The gunmen were not immediately Mr. Clinton arrived in New Delhi, 400 miles to the south, on Monday evening after a visit to Bangladesh. He has said that reducing tensions between India and Pakistan is one of his objective of the trip.

Many Kashmiris were hoping that the president's visit would lead to a breakthrough in the long deadlock on the region's future.

Mr. Clinton's spokesman, Joe Lockhart, expressed outrage over the killings, saying in a statement that "out most profound sympathies go out to the victims of this brutal massacre."

The attackers entered the village of Chati Singhpura Mattan after dark and forced the residents from their homes, police officials said.

The assailants separated the men from the women, announcing that they were conducting a "crackdown." Indian security forces operate similarly when searching a neighborhood for militants that they suspect may be hiding there. The gunmen then opened fire on the men, killing 35 of them. One man was critically wounded.

Sikhs have lived mostly undisturbed in the Kashmir Valley, the only area in predominantly Hindu India with a Muslim majority. Many run the trucking companies that supply the valley.

In the last six months, attacks by the militants have focused on army bases and patrols rather than random terrorism, and have shown a higher degree of training and expertise, senior army officers have said. They said about 3,500 militants were in Kashmir, and many of them had infiltrated the cease-fire line from Pakistan, with the help of the Pakistan army. Pakistan denies giving active aid to the militants.

The area of the Sikh village is about 42 miles from Srinagar, Kashmir's summer capital, and is controlled by armed Kashmiri groups that abandoned separatism and were recruited by the Indian army as a counterinsurgency auxiliary force.

- - - - - - - - -

From the Washington Post, Mar. 21, 2000
Near Clinton's India Visit, Violence Flares in Kashmir
(By Pamela Constable)

Srinagar, India, March 20--While their government and most of their countrymen are hoping President Clinton will play down the sensitive topic of Kashmir during his visit to India this week, people in this depressed, wintry city at the political heart of the disputed, violence-torn region are praying for just the opposite.

Today, in the worst single attack on civilians in a decade of guerrilla war, unidentified gunmen massacred 35 Sikh men in the Kashmiri village of Chati Singhpura Mattan, wire services reported. Security officials had feared that armed Pakistan-based insurgents, who have stepped up attacks here in recent months, might stage a dramatic attack during Clinton's stay in India.

Clinton condemned the attack in Kashmir. "On behalf of the president and all Americans let me express our outrage at the attack on a village in Kashmir last night," White House spokesman Joe Lockhart told reporters in New Delhi.

Many Kashmiris believe that only a world leader of Clinton's stature can put pressure on Indian officials to start meaningful negotiations with Pakistan over the mountainous, predominantly Muslim border region where separatist sentiment is strong, guerrilla violence is rapidly rising and

"If Mr. Clinton can make a difference in places like Chechnya and Bosnia, why not in Kashmir?" said Shah Khan, 22, who sells shirts and pants in the teeming alleys of Lal Chowk bazaar. "We are happy because at least his visit will bring some attention to our problems, but we wish he would come to Kashmir and see for himself. Then we would all tell him one thing: we want freedom."

But this message is highly unlikely to reach Clinton's ears or the Indian capital this week. On Sunday, about 50 Kashmiri independence activists were arrested and jailed as they tried to board buses that would take them to New Delhi for a protest rally near Parliament, where Clinton is scheduled to speak Wednesday.

In a brief interview in jail today, the group's leader Shabir Shah, 44, said they had been tear-gassed and dragged into police vans as they prepared to leave. He said the group, which seeks Kashmiri independence from India, had planned to stage a peaceful rally and a symbolic hunger strike.

"President Clinton says he wants to help ease tensions in the region, and he will be talking with India and Pakistan, but we wanted to tell him that it is futile until we Kashmiris are taken into account," Shah said.

Kashmir, which is divided between India and Pakistan, has been the major source of friction between the two neighbors and nuclear powers for a generation. Since the early 1990s, the Indian-occupied part has been the site of a violent conflict between anti-India insurgent groups and Indian security forces, which has cost tens of thousands of lives. Last summer, a 10-week border conflict in the Kargil mountains left hundreds dead.

Today's attack on the Sikhs seemed to represent an especially gruesome escalation of violence and attempt at ethnic cleansing in the Kashmir Valley, where Muslims dominate the population and the insurgency has become increasingly directed by Islamic groups based in Pakistan. The victims were separated from their families by unidentified gunmen who entered their village after dark and shot them.

In the past, Kashmiri insurgent groups have concentrated on military targets and have denounced terrorism against civilians. But in recent weeks, there have been a half-dozen attacks on Hindu truck drivers and on scattered villages of Kashmiri Pandits, or local Hindus, many of whom were violently driven from the region years ago. Now Sikhs, who have lived peaceably in northern Kashmir for years, appear to have become their latest target.

Clinton, who had called Kashmir "the most dangerous place in the world," has repeatedly expressed interest in helping to defuse the tensions and to nudge India and Pakistan back toward dialogue. But Indian authorities are adamantly opposed to any foreign intervention in the dispute, and have declared they will not resume talks with Pakistan until it stops arming and training Kashmiri insurgents.

In interviews over the weekend, some Srinagar residents said they were skeptical that Clinton's talks with Indian leaders could make any difference. They said the United States was too concerned with bigger issues, such as trade and nuclear nonproliferation, to let Kashmir become an irritant to improving relations.

"Clinton is coming as a guest, so he won't want to embarrass his hosts. What he says in America about Kashmir may not be what he says here," said Masood Ahmed, 30, another shopkeeper in Lal Chowk. "He already knows that thousands of people have been killed in Kashmir, but he is only coming to see the Taj Mahal."

***

Document

CONGRESSIONAL RECORD -- EXTENSIONS

Thursday, March 16, 2000
106th Congress, 2nd Session
146 Cong Rec E 334

REFERENCE: Vol. 146, No. 30
TITLE: NUNS ATTACKED IN INDIA, SAVED BY SIKH FAMILY

HON. EDOLPHUS TOWNS
of New York
in the House of Representatives
Thursday, March 16, 2000

Mr. TOWNS. Mr. Speaker, the wave of violence against Christians by Hindu fundamentalists continues. Since Christmas 1998, churches have been burned, priests have been murdered, nuns have been raped, and Christian schools and prayer halls have been destroyed. The government of Orissa now requires anyone who wishes to change religions to get a permit from the government. Sikhs and Muslims have previously been subjected to similar tyranny.

These attacks have been carried out by Hindu fundamentalists who belong to a branch of the RSS, an openly Fascist umbrella organization that includes the ruling Bharatiya Janata Party under its umbrella.

In the most recent incident, a gang of RSS militants attacked the Convent of Our Lady of Grace in Panipat. Previously, a priest from the same complex had been murdered. This is the fourth attack on the church in Panipat, according to The Deccan Herald.

Fortunately, when the militant Hindus attacked the convent, the nuns screamed and the alarm went off, attracting the attention of the Sikh family next door. They got their gun and came over to the complex, where the RSS mob attacked the rescuers using steel rods and guns. One of the attackers was captured.

Unfortunately, this incident shows us again that there is no religious freedom in India. Hindu nationalist mobs associated with the ruling party have free rein to commit these acts of violence against the religious minorities and they rarely get any punishment from the government. Instead, the government uses these incidents to try to set one religious group against the other so that they can continue their brutal, intolerant, tyrannical rule. In the murder of missionary Graham Staines, which was carried out by Hindu militants chanting "Victory to Hannuman," a Hindu god, the government arrested a man who uses the alias Dara Singh in order to blame the Sikhs.

This kind of intolerance is unacceptable. As the lone superpower and the beacon of freedom in the world, the United States must act to bring freedom to all the people of South Asia. While President Clinton visits India, it is crucial that he bring up the issues of political prisoners, religious freedom, and self-determination.

There are also things we can do here in Congress. We should stop all American aid to India until these basic human rights are respected and we should declare our support for an internationally-supervised plebiscite on independence for Punjab, Khalistan, for Kashmir, for Nagaland, and for the other nations seeking to free themselves from India's brutal, corrupt rule. We must be prepared to take responsible measures to extend freedom to all the people of the world.

From the Deccan Chronicle, Mar. 14, 2000
Sikh Family Saves Nuns From Bawaria Attack

New Delhi: A Sikh family saved the lives of five nuns who were attacked by a group of over ten armed men in the wee hours of the morning on 11 March, in Panipat. Putting their own safety at risk the male members of the family attacked the intruders armed with guns and steel rods who had entered the church where the Franciscan nuns were staying.

Answering to the alarm call of the nuns, the Sikh men immediately came to their rescue. The incident happened in Panipat in the convent of Our Lady of Grace. The Sikh family who have been staying in the Joti Nagar area next to the convent for over a decade, hearing the cries of the nuns and the alarm calls of the chowkidar, rushed to their help.

Armed with their licensed country made gun attacked the men. In the ensuing chaos the assailants attacked the Sikhs with steel rods and fired two rounds of gun shots. One of the Sikhs managed to nab one of the men, who in his desperation to escape bit him. Meanwhile the other gang members started firing from behind the church forcing the Sikhs to shoot back and attack them.

The nabbed man has been identified as Kala and belongs to the Bawaria caste. The gang is believed to be involved in the earlier attacks on the church. This is the fourth such attack in the past three months on the church in the Sonepath- Panipat Samalkha region.

The superior of the convent, Sr Vandana said, "We are very grateful to them for helping us, even though they could have been killed in the process. We will always remember them in our prayers."

Earlier a priest living in the same compound was attacked by unknown men a few weeks ago. As a result, two police guards were posted outside the church compound which houses a church, and quarters for the priest and nuns.

The police removed the guards from duty and within two days of this the church was attacked again. Recalling the incident Sr Vandana said, "Though convent houses six nuns, one of them was not present at the time of the incident. The men scaled the compound wall, broke opened the main wooden entrance of the convent and then tried to break in the door of the dormitories where the five nuns were sleeping. The shocked and panic struck nun rushed into the smaller rooms and bathroom, where they locked themselves. The men later broke open an almirah." The Sonepat-Panipat Samalkha region had reported spate of violence which included attack on a priest who narrowly escaped and threatened several nuns. The area also witnessed four cases of dacoity.

Earlier two cases of dacoity had taken place in Samalkha and Panipat within three days of each other. In Samalkha in the early hours of March 9, 2000, gang of ten men raided and looted the Ish Mata Church and made off with Rs 60,000 kept for refurbishing the church. Fr Azeem Raj of the church escaped by locking himself in the bathroom. On 1 January Fr Vikas of Panipat Church was serious injured and his skull and limbs fractured when he was attacked by a gang of armed men. This incident took place in the same compound where the nuns were attacked.

The district collector of the Panipat, Sandeep Garag said, thanked the Sikhs for the help and has advised that the guards be posted back to the church and more arms be sanctioned.

***

Document

CONGRESSIONAL RECORD -- EXTENSIONS

Thursday, March 9, 2000
106th Congress, 2nd Session
146 Cong Rec E 280

REFERENCE: Vol. 146, No. 26
TITLE: INDIA'S RELIGIOUS TYRANNY GOES ON

HON. EDOLPHUS TOWNS
of New York
in the House of Representatives
Thursday, March 9, 2000

Mr. TOWNS. Mr. Speaker, I was distressed to read an article in the Washington Times of February 25 datelined Calcutta reporting that the government of India's state of Orissa is now requiring anyone converting to Christianity to get a government permit. This policy has been met with protests in front of government offices in Calcutta, because it is just the latest chapter in the ongoing religious tyranny in India.

As you know, thousands of Sikhs languish in Indian jails without charge and without trial. These Sikhs are political prisoners in "the world's largest democracy." Many of them have been in prison illegally since the Indian government attacked the Sikhs' holiest shrine, the Golden Temple in Amritsar, in June 1984. That is coming up on 16 years now!

The BJP, which runs the central government, destroyed the most revered mosque in India, the mosque at Ayodhya, intending to put a Hindu Temple on the site. Hindus affiliated with the BJP's parent organization, the RSS, burned a Christian missionary and his two sons, ages 8 and 10, to death in their jeep while they slept. The mob surrounded the family's jeep and chanted "Victory to Hannuman," a Hindu god. RSS-affiliated Hindu extremists have burned down Christian churches, schools, and prayer halls. They have murdered priests and raped nuns. In 1997, the police broke up a Christian religious festival with gunfire.

The Indian government has sent over 700,000 troops to Kashmir and half a million to Punjab, Khalistan, to suppress the freedom of the Muslim and Sikh populations there. It has killed tens of thousands of Christians, Sikhs, Muslims, Assamese, Manipuris, Dalits, and others.

President Clinton will soon be going to India. While he is there, one important thing that he should do is to press the Indian government on the subject of human rights. If we do not support the human rights of all the people of South Asia, who will?

I call on the President to raise these issues in the strongest terms. Also, we should cut off aid to India until it observes the basic standards of human rights for all and we should support freedom for the people of South Asia by going on record in support for self- determination for the people of Punjab, Khalistan, Kashmir, Nagaland, and the other nations of South Asia that now live under occupation.

Mr. Speaker, I would like to submit the Times article into the Record.

From the Washington Times, Feb. 25, 2000
Christians in India Protest Bias' Order

Calcutta--Hundreds of Christians converged on a government office yesterday to protest what they said was a discriminatory order by the Orissa state government on religious conversions.

The protesters said the order, which requires people who are convert-ing to Christianity to apply to a local official and get police clearance, violates the Indian Constitution.

The protesters belong to the Bangiya Christiya Pariseba, or United Forum of Catholics and Protestants. They delivered a statement to the Orissa government through its local office in Calcutta.

***

Document

CONGRESSIONAL RECORD -- EXTENSIONS

Tuesday, February 29, 2000
106th Congress, 2nd Session
146 Cong Rec E 195

REFERENCE: Vol. 146, No. 20
TITLE: INDIA TRIES TO FALSELY IMPLICATE SIKHS IN MURDER OF
CHRISTIAN MISSIONARY BY USING ALIAS "SINGH"

HON. JOHN T. DOOLITTLE
of California
in the House of Representatives
Tuesday, February 29, 2000

Mr. DOOLITTLE. Mr. Speaker, the Tribune newspaper of India re-ported on February 9 that the Indian government has identified the killer of Christian missionary Graham Staines as Dara Singh, but his real name is Rabinder Kumar Paul. The use of "Singh" is a smear against the Sikhs designed to create the impression that Sikhs were somehow responsible for the Staines murder and put the Christians against the Sikhs, promot-ing India's divide-and-rule strategy against minorities.

The facts do not support this. Staines, an Australian missionary, and his two young sons were burned to death in their jeep. They were surrounded by a mob of militant Hindus affiliated with the RSS, which is the parent organization of the ruling BJP. These fundamentalist Hindus chanted "Victory to Hannuman," a Hindu god, while the Staines family's jeep burned. Yet India wants to create the impression that one person was responsible for this brutal murder and that he is a Sikh.

Mr. Speaker, I am offended by this open manipulation of both Chris-tians and Sikhs. Apparently, India is concerned about the support that leaders of the freedom movements of South Asia have showed for each other. So they have resorted to this divisive strategy to preserve their empire.

The time has come for America, the beacon of freedom, to take strong measures to stop India from pursuing this campaign to turn one minority against another. First, we must cut off our aid to India. We must recognize its violations of religious liberty and impose appropriate sanctions. Then we must declare our support for free and fair plebiscites, under international supervision, on the question of independence for Punjab, Khalistan, for Kashmir, and for Nagaland.

Pitting one group against the other to maintain a corrupt,brutal tyranny is not a democratic or a moral way to behave.

***

Document

CONGRESSIONAL RECORD -- EXTENSIONS

Wednesday, February 16, 2000
106th Congress, 2nd Session
146 Cong Rec E 156

REFERENCE: Vol. 146, No. 15
TITLE: S.S. OSAN, DELHI MASSACRE VICTIM, DENIED JUSTICE BY INDIA

HON. EDOLPHUS TOWNS
of New York
in the House of Representatives
Wednesday, February 16, 2000

Mr. TOWNS. Mr. Speaker, I rise today with yet another example of how India violates the basic human rights of its minorities and ignores the rule of law.

Sukhbir Singh Osan is a journalist in Punjab. He has exposed many scandals and acts of tyranny on the part of the Indian government and the government of Punjab. His family suffered losses in the 1984 massacre in Delhi, which were organized by government-inspired mobs while the Sikh police were locked in their barracks and the state-run TV and radio called for more Sikh blood. He has now filed suit for his rights as a 1984 riot victim.

Sukhbir Singh Osan earned an LL.B. degree from Punjab University seven years ago but it is being withheld from him because he has exposed corruption and brutality. For his aggressive reporting, the Indian government has damaged his career in an arbitrary and vindictive manner.

Mr. Osan's situation proves that in "democratic" India the law is subservient to the wishes of those in power. The people in power routinely violate the law for their own benefit. How can a country be a democracy when the government routinely subverts the rule of law?

It is clear from the treatment of Mr. Osan and from so many other incidents involving the abuse of Sikhs, Christians, Muslims, and other minorities that the only way these minorities will secure their freedom to live in peace, dignity, and security is by achieving their freedom from

India. In this light, it is appropriate for the United States to take action to protect the rights of the minority peoples of the subcontinent.

If India cannot observe the rule of law even for a victim of the 1984 Delhi massacres, then why should it receive any aid from the American taxpayers? We should stop that aid, subject India to the sanctions that their terrorist rule deserves, and throw the full weight of the U.S. Congress behind a free and fair, internationally-supervised plebiscite to decide the question of independence for Khalistan, Kashmir, Nagaland, and the other nations of South Asia.

Until these things are done, there will continue to be others mistreated like Sukhbir Singh Osan, and worse. America is the beacon of freedom. How can we accept this?

Mr. Speaker, I submit the Burning Punjab article on Mr. Osan's plight into the Record for the information of my colleagues.

From the Burning Punjab News
Riots Ruined Family, Judiciary His Life

Chandigarh--Sukhbir Singh Osan in a Civil Writ petition No. 14940 of 1999 filed in the Punjab & Haryana High Court has pleaded that--"he became a November 84 riot victim' neither by his own act nor by birth since he was just 14 years old when riots took place. He further pleaded that the failure of the executive and the law & order situation and also the failure of various provisions incorporated in the Indian Constitution, after the assassination of the then Indian Premier Indira Gandhi was the reason which placed him under the category of Sikh Migrant Family & Riot affected person". The petition has been fixed for hearing on November 15, 1999 before the Chief Justice Arun B. Saharia and Mr. Justice Swatantar Kumar. Osan has demanded justice' in this petition.

"Punishing those who were responsible for riots in November, 1984 and to grant certain concessions to the victims of these riots are two different things?", Sukhbir Singh Osan has questioned the division bench of the High Court. The petition elaborates, how a riot victim in Sukhbir Singh Osan was harassed, his career was ruined in an arbitrary and vindictive manner and that too right under the nose of judiciary shows that justice in India is not a virtue which transcends all barriers. It also proves that law never bends before justice on the land of Sri Guru Nanak Dev, Sri Guru Teg Bahadar and Sri Guru Gobind Singh.

Why Sukhbir Singh Osan's result/degree of LL.B. course is being withheld by the Panjab University for the past about seven years is a apathetic story because he in the capacity of a journalist tried to expose corruption, high-handedness and other irregularities at different levels in the University affairs through his dispatches in a leading daily during 1991.

Narrating chronology of his ordeal' Sukhbir Singh Osan in a writ petition filed by him "in-person" in the Punjab and Haryana High Court has said that in August, 1990 he was granted admission in LL.B. course under the Riot affected (November, 1984) category in the Department of Laws, Panjab University, Chandigarh. Being a journalist he in good faith published certain news items pertaining to nefarious activities including corruption, high-handedness, moral turpitude and other irregularities at different levels in the university affairs. Smitten by a news-item, Sukhbir Singh was asked by Dr. R.K. Bangia, Prof. & Chairman, Department of Laws in a written communication on May 29, 1991 to furnish some authentic proof as evidence of the facts as stated by you" in the news-item "Teen Hazaar Mein Uttirne Karva Date Hain Kanoon Ki Pariksha" otherwise strict action would be taken against him. On September 30, 1991 in an arbitrary and illegal manner his admission was cancelled when he was studying in the 3rd semester of the LL.B. course, since Dr. J.M. Jairath, Dr. R.K. Bangia and Dr. R.S. Grewal were got annoyed due to news reports filed by S.S. Osan. Sukhbir Singh Osan approached the Punjab & Haryana High Court against the Panjab University, but the High Court relegate him for his remedy to Civil Court. The Civil Court of Chandigarh after four years of hectic activities of examining evidence and witnesses termed the admission of Sukhbir Singh Osan as genuine and according to law. The judge in his 27 page order also declared Sukhbir Singh Osan as November 84 riot victim'. It was perhaps the first ever case in the history of India and Indian judiciary, that a riot victim was asked to prove that he is a November 1984 Riot affected person' and Sukhbir Singh Osan has proved the same in the civil court. Here it is pertinent to mention that Sukhbir Singh Osan along with his family migrated from Madhya Pradesh to Punjab in the year 1985 after November 1984 anti-Sikh riot which broke through out India after the assassination of the then Indian premier Indira Gandhi. Such was the agony of Sukhbir Singh Osan that he has to recall all those days, which his family has suffered during 1984.

The miserable plight of Sukhbir Singh Osan proves that in India law and judiciary are not meant for those who obey them but are subservient to those who outrage the modesty of the very concept of law & justice and that too, in connivance of those who are considered to be the custodian of law & justice. Will the law of India be able to punish those who have ruined the life of Sukhbir Singh Osan? Whither Indian Judiciary?

***

Document

CONGRESSIONAL RECORD -- EXTENSIONS

Wednesday, February 2, 2000
106th Congress, 2nd Session
146 Cong Rec E 60

REFERENCE: Vol. 146, No. 7
TITLE: SIKH BURNS SELF TO DEATH TO PROTEST POLICE BRUTALITY IN INDIA

HON. JOHN T. DOOLITTLE
of California
in the House of Representatives
Wednesday, February 2, 2000

Mr. DOOLITTLE. Mr. Speaker, I was distressed to hear that Mandeep Pal Singh Sodhi, a 27-year-old Sikh man, burned himself to death in front of the Uttar Pradesh Legislative Assembly building. His self-immolation was reported in the Hindustan Times on January 11. He was protesting police brutality against his family. Mandeep Pal Singh Sodhi's brothers were detained and brutalized by police. Their mother was promised an inquiry, but nothing happened.

Recently, the Committee for Coordination on Disappearances in Punjab, led by Hindu human rights activist Ram Narayan Kumar, issued a preliminary report that included the names and addresses of 838 Sikhs who were picked up, tortured, murdered, and secretly disposed of by the police. According to figures compiled by the Punjab State Magistracy and by human rights groups, the Indian government has killed over a quarter of a million Sikhs since 1984.

It is not just Sikhs who have suffered this kind of oppression. The Indian government has victimized Christians, Muslims, Dalits, and others. Groups associated with the ruling BJP have burned down Christian churches and prayer halls. Allies of the government have murdered nuns, priests, and missionaries.

The self-immolation of Mandeep Pal Singh Sodhi should serve as a wake-up call to the country that proudly proclaims itself "the world's largest democracy." It should serve as a call to India to begin living up to the democratic principles that it proclaims. India must stop this police brutality and release its political prisoners. It must hold a free and fair internationally-supervised plebiscite on the issue of independence in Khalistan, Kashmir, Nagaland, and wherever else people within India are struggling for freedom. Until then, the U.S. should stop its aid to India and encourage it to act like the democratic country it claims to be.

Mr. Speaker, I would like to submit the Hindustan Times article into the Record.

From the Hindustan Times, Jan. 11, 2000
Self immolation in front of UP Assembly
(By Bhupendra Pandey)

Lucknow, January 10--Motorists, pedestrians and policemen watched in shock as a young man, allegedly because of police harassment, immolated himself on the busy road opposite the Vidhan Sabha on Monday afternoon.

The 27-year-old youth, identified as Mandeep Pal Singh Sodhi, a resident of Krishna Nagar, suffered 70 per cent burns and died on way to hospital.

Later, the police inspector posted at Krishna Nagar was sent to the police lines for illegally detaining the deceased's brother and harassing his family members. Chief Minister Ram Prakash Gupta has announced a financial assistance of Rs 1 lakh to the dependents of the victim. The District Magistrate of Lucknow has directed the ADM, City, to probe the incident.

According to eyewitnesses, Mandeep got off a bus near the Royal Hotel intersection and doused himself with kerosene. Then, he went towards the Assembly and set himself on fire and started running. Soon, he was transformed into a ball of fire.

After he collapsed and lay writhing on the road, three policemen tried feebly to rescue him. Others also joined them, but by then Mandeep had already suffered excessive burns.

Thereafter, he was taken to the nearby Shyama Prasad Mukherjee Hospital from where he was referred to the KGMC. But he succumbed to burn injuries on the way.

Initially, policemen were unable to identify the youth but later found a slip of paper tucked in his shoes. According to it, Mandeep ran a small chemists shop outside a private nursing home in Krishna Nagar.

Meanwhile, Mandeep's mother, Mrs. Manpreet Kaur, has accused the police of forcing her son to commit suicide. "Fed up with police harassment, my son committed suicide," she said.

According to her, her husband, Surendra Pal Singh, who died five years ago, ran a flourishing transport business. But it ran into tough times after his death. She said that her tale of woes began a year ago when the SO of Sarojini Nagar raided her house and detained her two sons, Yashpal and Inderpal, without specifying the charges. Later, they were booked in a case of a motorcycle theft. In March last year, the two were again booked in a case of another motorcycle theft and jailed. The two brothers were also booked under the Gangster Act.

Mrs. Kaur said that she had earlier met then Chief Minister Kalyan Singh and also the Circle Officer of Sarojini Nagar. She had been assured of an inquiry into the matter. But nothing happened. In fact, Yashpal was picked again on Saturday night in connection with a recent case of motorcycle theft in Krishna Nagar.

Today, Mrs. Kaur decided to complain to the District Magistrate and despite Mandeep's request to her to stay at home, she left for the DM's office. Soon after Mandeep too boarded a bus for the Vidhan Sabha.

Mrs. Kaur learnt about her son's immolation in the afternoon when she came home after meeting the DM. Yashpal was released by the police following the DM's intervention.

***

Document

CONGRESSIONAL RECORD -- EXTENSIONS

Tuesday, February 1, 2000
106th Congress, 2nd Session
146 Cong Rec E 50

REFERENCE: Vol. 146, No. 6
TITLE: INDIA SHOULD BE DECLARED A TERRORIST STATE

HON. EDOLPHUS TOWNS
of New York
in the House of Representatives
Tuesday, February 1, 2000

Mr. TOWNS. Mr. Speaker, the time has come to declare India a terrorist state. India is one of the leading practitioners of terrorism in the world, but they get away with it by cloaking it under a mask of democracy. India practices terrorism internally against its minorities and externally against its neighbors.

The Coordination Committee on Disappearances in Punjab identified 838 victims of India's mass cremation policy in a preliminary report last year. It published their names and addresses. These young Sikhs were abducted by the police, tortured, and murdered, then the police disposed of their bodies. This policy amounts to nothing less than terrorism against the Sikhs of Punjab, Khalistan.

Tens of thousands of Sikh political prisoners continue to rot in Indian jails without trial. They are not the only ones. After an Indian airliner was hijacked in November, India agreed to release several prisoners. According to the Los Angeles Times, India violated international law by holding these prisoners without charge or trial.

On December 20, according to Reuters News Service (as reported in India West), Pakistani police arrested a man who confessed that he was an Indian agent and that he planted bombs that killed 9 people. Clearly, this is a terrorist act sponsored by the Indian government.

The book Soft Target, written by two Canadian journalists, proved that India blew up its own airliner in 1985, killing 329 people. In 1991, the Indian intelligence service, RAW, masterminded a hijacking of an Indian plane. These acts give us reason to suspect that India's hand may have been behind the recent Air India hijacking.

In November 1994, the Hitavada, a well respected newspaper in India, reported that the Indian government paid Surendra Nath, the late governor of Punjab, one and a half billion dollars to foment terrorism in Punjab, Khalistan and in Kashmir. Can anyone deny that a country which would do this is a terrorist nation?

The Indian government intelligence wing, RAW, supported the militant Liberation Tigers of Tamil Eelam to gain control of the port of Trincomelli. India Today magazine reported that the leader of the LTTE was entertained by the Indian government in one of Delhi's best hotels. Later, India turned against the LTTE and invaded Sri Lanka to crush the LTTE freedom movement. The Indian government has blood on its hands.

The Indian government has murdered minorities in massive numbers. Over 250,000 Sikhs since 1984, over 200,000 Christians in Nagaland since 1947, more than 65,000 Kashmiri Muslims since 1988, and tens of thousands of Assamese, Manipuris, Tamils, Dalits, and others have been murdered by the government of India. The State Department reported in 1994 that the government of India paid more than 41,000 cash bounties to police officers for murdering Sikhs.

Hindu militants allied with the government have burned down Christian churches and prayers halls, murdered priests, and raped nuns. Hindus affiliated with the Vishwa Hindu Parishad surrounded the jeep of missionary Graham Staines and his two sons, ages 8 and 10, and burned them to death. The VHP is part of the same umbrella organization as the ruling BJP. In 1997, police broke up a Christian religious festival with gunfire.

Last year, Indian Defense Minister George Fernandes organized and led a meeting with the Ambassadors from Cuba, Red China, Russia, Iraq, and Libya aimed at creating a security alliance "to stop the U.S." India supported the Soviet invasion of Afghanistan and votes against American interests consistently. The time has come to take strong measures against India's brutality and terrorism by declaring India a terrorist nation.

Mr. Speaker, recently the Council of Khalistan issued a news release on Indian state terrorism. I would like to place it into the Record for the information of my colleagues.

From the Council of Khalistan, Washington, DC, Jan. 13, 2000
U.S. Should Declare India a Terrorist State

Washington, D.C., January 13, 2000.--Dr. Gurmit Singh Aulakh, President of the Council of Khalistan, called on the United States government to declare India a terrorist state. "India is one of the leading sponsors of terrorism in the world," he said.

Earlier this week, Mandeep Singh Sodhi, a 27-year-old Sikh in Uttar Pradesh burned himself to death to protest police abuses against his family. The Los Angeles Times reported that India violated international law by holding the prisoners who were released without charge or trial. There are tens of thousands of Sikh political prisoners rotting in Indian jails without trial. On December 20, according to Reuters News Service and India West, Pakistani police arrested a man who confessed to being an Indian agent and to planting bombs that killed 9 people.

Responding to some recent reports, Dr. Aulakh said that he "would not put it past" the Indian government to organize the
hijacking themselves to justify a new wave of terror in Kashmir.
"They have created incidents to promote terror in Punjab, Khalistan,
Assam, Nagaland, Tamil Nadu, and other places within their artificial borders." he said.

The book Soft Target, written by two Canadian journalists, proved that India blew up its own airliner in 1985, killing 329 people, to blame the Sikhs. In 1994, the Hitavada, a well respected Indian newspaper, reported that the Indian government paid the late governor of Punjab, Surendra Nath, $1.5 billion to organize and support covert state terrorism in Punjab, Khalistan and in Kashmir.

The Indian government intelligence wing, RAW, infiltrated the militant Liberation Tigers of Tamil Eelam (LTTE) and supported the LTTE to gain control of the port of Trincomelli. When the Sri Lankan government agreed to give India control of the port, India turned against the LTTE and invaded Sri Lanka to crush the LTTE freedom movement. The Indian army suffered heavy losses at the hands of the LTTE freedom fighters and withdrew from Sri Lanka. Rajiv Gandhi, the ex-Prime Minister of India under whose government this took place, was blown up by a female Tamil freedom fighter.

The Indian government has murdered over 250,000 Sikhs since 1984. They have also killed over 200,000 Christians in Nagaland since 1947, more than 65,000 Kashmiri Muslims since 1988, and tens of thousands of Assamese, Manipuris, Tamils, Dalits, and others. "Only a terrorist state could commit atrocities of this magnitude," said Dr. Aulakh.

The U.S. State Department reported that the Indian government paid more than 41,000 cash bounties to police to murder Sikhs. One of these bounties was collected by police officers who killed a three-year-old boy, his father, and his uncle "Would you call this democracy or terrorism?," Dr. Aulakh asked.

Government-allied Hindu militants have burned down Christian churches and prayer halls, murdered priests, and raped nuns. The Vishwa Hindu Parishad, which is affiliated with the parent organization of the ruling BJP, described the rapists as "patriotic youth" and called the nuns "antinational elements." Hindus affiliated with the VHP surrounded the jeep of missionary Graham Staines and his two sons, ages 8 and 10, poured gasoline on it, set it on fire, and surrounded it, chanting "Victory to Lord Ram." In 1997, police broke up a Christian religious festival with gunfire. "Only a terrorist government could allow these kinds of atrocities," Dr. Aulakh pointed out.

Last year, Indian Defense Minister George Fernandes led a meeting with the Ambassadors from Cuba, Red China, Russia, Iraq, and Libya aimed at constructing a security alliance "to stop the U.S." "How could India form an alliance against the world's oldest democracy and then ask for help?," Dr. Aulakh asked. "Based on these and other pieces of India's pattern of terrorism, the time has come for Indian to be declared a terrorist state," Dr. Aulakh said.

***

Document

CONGRESSIONAL RECORD -- EXTENSIONS

Friday, November 19, 1999
106th Congress, 1st Session
145 Cong Rec E 2487

REFERENCE: Vol. 145, No. 165
TITLE: CHRISTIAN FAMILY HACKED TO DEATH--RELIGIOUS
PERSECUTION CONTINUES IN INDIA--AMERICA MUST SUPPORT
FREEDOM FOR KHALISTAN

HON. DAN BURTON
of Indiana
in the House of Representatives
Thursday, November 18, 1999

Mr. BURTON of Indiana. Mr. Speaker, the Indian Express reported on November 12, 1999 that a Christian family was hacked to death in Jamshedpur. The attackers stormed the house of 35 year-old Santan Kerai, dragging Mr. Kerai, his wife, their two year-old child, and a relative out of the house to murder them. Finally, the mutilated bodies of the Kerai family "were found on a football field about 100 yards from their house," according to the article. The newspaper does not identify the assailants, but the attack is part of the ongoing pattern of repression of Christians in India today.

I have been deeply concerned about recent reports of Hindu activists raping and terrorizing nuns. A nun named Sister Ruby was abducted by Hindu fundamentalists, who stripped her naked and forced her to drink their bodily fluids. They threatened to rape her if she refused.

Earlier this year, Australian missionary Graham Staines and his two young sons were burned alive by members of the Bajrang Dal, which is the youth arm of the openly Fascist organization called Rashteria Swayamsewak Sangh (RSS). The ruling BJP, which leads India's 24-party governing coalition, is the political arm of the RSS.

Since Christmas Day of 1998, Hindu fundamentalists have burned down Christian churches, prayer halls, and schools. Four priests have been murdered, some of them beheaded.

Christians have not been the only target of persecution in India. Sikhs and Muslims are routinely beaten, tortured, and murdered by these radical groups or even Indian security forces.

Mr. Speaker, India is neither secular, nor is it democratic. It is clear that there is no place for religious, linguistic, or ethnic minorities in India. So, it is no wonder that there are seventeen freedom movements in India.

I call on the President to press the Government of India on the issues of human rights and self-determination when he visits the subcontinent next year. If the United States will not speak out for freedom in the world, who will? If we don't press these issues today, when will we? We must do whatever we can to bring freedom to all the people of India.

Mr. Speaker, I would like to place the Indian Express article into the Record.

From the Indian Express, Nov. 12, 1999
Christian Family Hacked to Death

Jamshedpur--Four members of a tribal Christian family have been hacked to death by some unidentified people at Peteripa village of west Singhbhum district.

Police said some people had stormed the house of one Santan Kerai (35) at midnight on Wednesday.

The assailant pulled him, his wife and their two-year old child besides one female relative out of the house and killed them with sharp weapons.

The mutilated bodies of Santan, his wife and the child were found on a football ground, about 100 meter away from their house. PTI report.

***

Document

CONGRESSIONAL RECORD -- EXTENSIONS

Wednesday, November 17, 1999
106th Congress, 1st Session
145 Cong Rec E 2423

REFERENCE: Vol. 145, No. 163
TITLE: INDIA PROTESTS POPE'S VISIT

HON. DAN BURTON
of Indiana
in the House of Representatives
Tuesday, November 16, 1999

Mr. BURTON of Indiana. Mr. Speaker, I was disturbed to learn of the organized protests against Pope John Paul II in anticipation of his recent visit to India. In fact, many would tell you that there was more reason to worry about his safety on this trip than when he traveled to communist Poland under martial law. Although the Pope left the country safely, I cannot forget the ghastly image printed by the media of Hindu activists burning an effigy of Pope John Paul II in New Delhi before his visit.

Mr. Speaker, these protests were led by a violent faction of Hindu fundamentalists that are closely aligned with the Hindu nationalist government. They have carried out a wave of brutal attacks on Christians within the past year. Since Christmas Day of 1998, they have burned down Christian churches, prayer halls, and schools. Also, four priests have been murdered, and earlier this year Australian missionary Graham Staines and his two young sons were burned alive.

How much more of this must we witness? Already 200,000 Christians, 250,000 Sikhs, 65,000 Muslims, and tens of thousands of others have fallen at the hands of either the Indian government or those closely related to the government since the subcontinent's independence a half-century ago.

Mr. Speaker, I submit the articles from India Abroad and the New York Post into the Record regarding this disturbing issue.

From the New York Post, Oct. 28, 1999
Pope's Passage to India May Be Most Perilous Yet
(By Rod Dreher)

Will Pope John Paul II be safe in India? There is more reason to worry for the pontiff's welfare as he visits the world's largest democracy next week than there was when he went to communist Poland under marital law.

That's because a small but violent faction of Hindu fundamentalists aligned with the Hindu nationalist government have been conducting an organized campaign against the pope as part of a concerted effort to demonize and persecute the country's tiny Christian minority.

The government promises to protect the Holy Father from coalition fanatics. But while John Paul can rely on state security, his Catholic followers and Protestant brethren remain at the mercy of Hindu brownshirts.

These thugs have carried out vicious attacks on Christians since a coalition led by the hard-line Bharatiya Janata Party (BJP) came to power two years ago.

Freedom House, the Washington-based human-rights organization, says there have been more recorded incidents of violence against India's Christian minority in the past year than in the previous half-century.

The most shocking incident took place in January, when Hindu thugs burned alive Australian missionary Graham Staines and his two little boys. That was far from an isolated incident.

In 1998, the Catholic Bishop's Conference in India reported 108 cases of beatings, stonings, church burnings, looting of religious schools and institutions, and other attacks on Catholics and evangelicals.

It has been just as bad this year. Just last month, a Catholic priest working in the same territory as the Staines family was murdered while saying Mass for converts, his heart pierced by a poison-tipped arrow.

Why the attacks? Hindu nationalist leaders, particularly those associated with the BJP-allied World Hindu Congress (VHP), claim Christians are on "conversion overdrive."

This is preposterous. Despite being present in India for almost 2,000 years, and educating hundreds of millions of Indian children, Christianity claims the allegiance of less than 3 percent of the country's people.

Even in Orissa state, site of the worst anti-Christian violence, fewer than 500 conversions occur each year.

Still, Hindu nationalists continue to make wild-eyed assertions, such as VHP leader Mohan Joshi's recent statement that missionary homes run by Mother Teresa's order were "nothing but conversion centers."

Not true, but if it were, so what?

We know perfectly well what would have become of the diseased and the destitute had Mother Teresa's nuns not rescued them from the street: They would have been left to die in the gutter, condemned by a culture that decrees these lowborn souls deserve their fate.

"What has the VHP done to better the life of the low castes? The answer is nothing," says Freedom House investigator Joseph Assad.

"When I was in India, I talked to one Christian who was forcibly re-converted to Hinduism. He told me when no one cared for us, Christians came and gave us food, gave us shelter and gave us medicine."

An Indian Protestant activist who lives in New Jersey told me BJP rule has meant open season on followers of Christ.

"The last two years have been unprecedented," the man says.

"They have burned churches down, raped nuns, killed people. We complain to the government, but they look the other way."

The Hindu militants certainly do not represent the sentiments of all Hindus. But these thugs have the tacit support and protection of the ruling BJP. Indeed, the BJP Web site condemns "Semitic monotheism"--Judaism, Christianity and Islam--for "bringing intolerance to India."

This is what is known to professional propagandists as the Big Lie. No wonder Hindu hard-liners confidently pillage Christian communities.

How many more Hindu-led atrocities will Christians and others suffer before Prime Minister Atal Behari Vajpayee calls off the nationalist dogs?

Will it take a physical assault on the Holy Father for the world to wake up to the kind of place Gandhi's great nation has become.

- - - - - - - - -

From India Abroad, Oct. 29, 1999
Protest March Launched Against the Pope's Visit
(By Frederick Noronha)

Panaji, Goa.--Hindu right-wing groups flagged off a Goa-to- Delhi protest march on Oct. 21 that could fuel the controversy surrounding Pope John Paul II's visit to India, scheduled for early November.

The campaigners are protesting what they call large-scale conversions to Christianity in India and want the Pope to say that all religions are equal.

The protest march, which is scheduled to end in Delhi around the time of the Pope's visit, is being called a "Dharma Jagran Abhiyan." It was flagged off from Divar, an island off Old Goa, once a center for Catholic evangelization.

"This awareness march is for people of all religions. Christians are brothers of the same blood," said Subhash Velingkar, one of the organizers of the march.

Velingkar lashed out at the English language media for voicing concern that the march could ignite anti-Christian feelings.

At the same time, however, Velingkar condemned religious conversions saying that they changed "not just the religion of people, but also their culture and traditions."

He criticized Delhi Archbishop Alan de Lastic for "sending an SOS message to the Vatican" complaining about the situation in India. "Why should people from India complain to the Vatican?" he asked.

Velingkar reiterated the demand voiced by the Vishwa Hindu Parishad (VHP), the right-wing affiliate of the Bharatiya Janata Party (BJP) which leads the coalition government at the Center, that the Pope should make an admission in his public address at Delhi that all the religions are the same and all lead to salvation.

The VHP last week once again welcomed the Pope's visit, stating that it was not against Christianity, but was opposed to "Churchainity."

A VHP affiliate, the Sanskriti Raksha Manch, has already demanded an apology from the Pope for the atrocities committed during Inquisition in Portuguese-ruled Goa in the 16th century.

From Goa, the march passes through Belgaum, Nipani, Mumbai, Kolhapur and Nashik in Karnataka and Maharashtra, before entering Gujarat, Rajasthan and Madhya Pradesh and then onward to Delhi, covering the 1,300-mile route in about a fortnight. It will reach Delhi by the time of the Pope's visit on Nov. 5.

Newspaper reports quoted Manohar Parrikar, the BJP Leader of the Opposition in the Goa Assembly, as saying that his party was neither opposing nor supporting the march.

He said the movement's leadership was not under the control of the BJP and while individual members of the party were free to join it, the party could not be held responsible for any untoward incident arising from the march.

***

Document

CONGRESSIONAL RECORD -- EXTENSIONS

Tuesday, November 16, 1999
106th Congress, 1st Session
145 Cong Rec E 2389

REFERENCE: Vol. 145, No. 162
TITLE: CHRISTIAN GATHERING ATTACKED BY BJP-INSPIRED MOB--NO RELIGIOUS FREEDOM IN INDIA

HON. EDOLPHUS TOWNS
of New York
in the House of Representatives
Tuesday, November 16, 1999

Mr. TOWNS. Mr. Speaker, I was very distressed to see that the Indian rulers are fomenting religious violence again. According to the November 14 issue of The Times of India, "a group of about 40 persons attacked a Christian gathering outside an Independent Church (neither Catholic nor Protestant) in West Delhi's Khyala area on Saturday evening the 13th. " The newspaper reported that the attack, which injured 12 people, was "masterminded" by suspected Bharatiya Janata Party (BJP) activists,' according to the police."

The BJP is the party that advocates "Hindu, Hindi, Hindutva, Hindu Rashtra," which translates as "Hindu religion, Hindi language, Hindu culture, Hindu rule." A BJP spokesman said that everyone in India should either be Hindu or be subservient to Hinduism. Now, these statements might be insignificant except for the fact that the BJP heads India's governing coalition.

So far no one has been arrested in connection with this attack. According to the article, the Christians were conducting an open-air Bible reading in a tent when the tent was stormed by the Hindu militants. The attackers shouted anti-Christian slogans while they tore and burned Christian pamphlets with religious speakers.

Mr. Speaker, it is shameful that the party ruling "the world's largest democracy" condones and indeed organizes these kinds of attacks on people who are simply practicing their religion. But it is part of a pattern of repression which has been going on for quite some time. In 1997, police broke up a Christian festival with gunfire merely because they were presenting the theme that "Jesus is the Answer" and people were allegedly converting.

Just a little while ago, a nun was picked up, stripped naked, and threatened by her captors that they would rape her if she did not drink their body wastes. Sister Ruby was frightened by these threats because four nuns have been raped in 1998 and four priests were killed.

A BJP affiliate called the Bajrang Dal, a sister organization in the Fascist RSS, organized and carried out the murder by burning of missionary Graham Staines and his two sons who were just 8 and 10 years old. The killers chanted "Victory to Lord Ram" while they carried out this grisly murder. They surrounded the jeep where Staines and his sons slept and prevented anyone from helping the family.

There has also been a wave of violence against churches, prayer halls, and Christian schools since Christmas. But it is not just the Christians who are being persecuted.

In Kashmir, the BJP and its allies destroyed the most revered mosque in the state. In Punjab, Khalistan, the Sikh homeland, the Indian government continues to hold thousands of political prisoners and continues to carry out rapes, extrajudicial killings, and other offenses against their basic human rights.

Mr. Speaker, America is the beacon of freedom. We must do whatever we can to bring freedom to everyone. When President Clinton visits India, I urge him to bring up the issues of human rights for the Sikhs, Christians, Muslims, and all the other minorities living under Indian rule. It is time to tell India that they must respect human rights or we will stop their aid from the United States. We should also put the U.S. congress on record for self-determination by calling for a free and fair plebiscite on independence for Khalistan, Kashmir, Nagaland, and all the other countries now under India's artificial rule. It is only by taking these measures that we can spread the blessings of freedom throughout South Asia.

Mr. Speaker, I submit the article from The Times of India into the Record for the information of my colleagues.

From the Times of India, Nov. 14, 1999
Mob Attacks Christian Gathering

New Delhi.--In the first incident of its kind in Delhi, a group of about 40 persons attacked a Christian gathering outside an Independent Church (meaning neither Catholic nor Protestant) in west Delhi's Khyala area on Saturday evening. At least 12 persons were injured in the attack, allegedly masterminded by "suspected Bhartiya Janata Party activists," according to the police.

Though four persons--Radhey Shyam Gupta, Kapila, Charan and Ashok Sharma--have been named in the police FIR, no arrests have been made so far.

Area sources said the incident took place at about 8:30 pm in the C-block of a JJ colony in Khyala, near Tilak Nagar, where the group (including some women) stormed a tent where a group of Christians were conducting an open air Bible reading session. A small of group of Christians live in the colony.

Sources said the attackers raised anti-Christians slogans, tore and burnt pamphlets with religious scriptures. A couple of Bibles and a Holy Cross were also reportedly damaged in the attack. The group then had a scuffle with scores of people present in the tent which led to the injuries, the sources said. Senior Delhi Police officers confirmed the attack but denied any Bible was torn or burnt by the mob. They also denied that a Holy Cross was damaged. "Initial investigations have revealed that the mob, which may have had some BJP activists, disrupted the Bible reading session and then attacked the gathering. But all the injuries sustained in the attack are minor," joint police commissioner (southern range) Amod Kanth said.

He also said the attackers tore and burnt several pamphlets which contained passages in praise of Jesus. "But I have personally spoken to the pastor who was conducting the proceedings and he has denied any cross being damaged or Bible being burnt by the attackers," Mr. Kanth added.

Local sources said the Bible reading sessions were being conducted at this Independent church for several years, and as a continuation, a pastor, Father S. John had arrived in the area on Friday from Hosangipur in southwest Delhi.

Mr. Kanth also said the police had established that the attackers did not belong to the Tilak Nagar area and had come from some other areas. "It was clearly an unprovoked attack and all of them would be arrested," Mr. Kanth said.

He said the police had registered a case of rioting and of disturbing religious assembly in this connection but no arrests had been made so far. Officers said the west district police had rushed in reinforcements in the Khyala area to prevent any "further untoward" incidents, even though there was no tension in the area.

***

Document

CONGRESSIONAL RECORD -- EXTENSIONS

Tuesday, November 16, 1999
106th Congress, 1st Session
145 Cong Rec E 2396

REFERENCE: Vol. 145, No. 162
TITLE: THE WORLD MUST NOT FORGET SIKH POLITICAL PRISONERS
IN INDIA

HON. EDOLPHUS TOWNS
of New York
in the House of Representatives
Tuesday, November 16, 1999

Mr. TOWNS. Mr. Speaker, India frequently boasts about its democratic institutions, so the world pays little attention to the abuses of human rights that go on there. Yet it has recently come out that there are thousands of political prisoners being held in "the world's largest democracy."

These political prisoners are being held in illegal detention for their political opinions. Some have been held without charge or trial for 15 years. One known case is an 80-year-old man. Yes, India is holding an 80-year-old man in illegal detention for his political opinions.

What have these Sikhs done? They have spoken out for freedom for their people and an end to the violence against their people. They have spoken out against the repression and tyranny that have killed 250,000 Sikhs since 1984. In India, this is apparently a crime.

Other minority nations have also seen substantial numbers of their members taken as political prisoners by the democratic government of India. In addition, the Indian government has murdered over 200,000 Christians in Nagaland since 1947. Tens of thousands of people in Manipur, Assam, Tamil Nadu, and other areas have also died at the hands of the Indian government.

Mr. Speaker, why should the people of the United States support a government like this? The answer is that they shouldn't. Yet India remains one of the largest recipients of U.S. aid. That aid should be ended, Mr. Speaker. Perhaps then India will understand that it must respect human rights.

We should also make clear our strong support for the movement of self-determination for the minority peoples and nations of South Asia, such as the Sikh homeland of Punjab, Khalistan; the heavily-Muslim Kashmir; and Christian-majority Nagaland. Only by conducting a free and fair vote can real freedom come to the peoples and nations of South Asia.

I call on the President to press these important issues when he visits India next year. This is the only way to bring real stability, peace, freedom, and dignity to South Asia.

***

Document

CONGRESSIONAL RECORD -- EXTENSIONS

Friday, November 5, 1999
106th Congress, 1st Session
145 Cong Rec E 2278

REFERENCE: Vol. 145, No. 155
TITLE: COUNCIL OF KHALISTAN LETTER IN NEW YORK POST ALLEGES
RELIGIOUS PERSECUTION IN INDIA

HON. JOHN T. DOOLITTLE
of California
in the House of Representatives
Thursday, November 4, 1999

Mr. DOOLITTLE. Mr. Speaker, I would like to call the attention of my colleagues to a letter that appeared on Wednesday, November 3, 1999, in the New York Post by Dr. Gurmit Singh Aulakh, President of the Council of Khalistan. It reveals the religious persecution in India.

Christians have been actively persecuted in India in recent months, a pattern carried out on Sikhs, Muslims, and others.

I urge all my colleagues to read the attached letter, which I am placing in the Record.

From the New York Post, Nov. 3, 1999
Religious Persecution in India

Thank you, Rod Dreher, for an excellent article ("Pope's passage to India may be most perilous yet," Oct. 28) exposing the "Hindu brownshirts" who run India.

The religious persecution of Christians has reached unparalled proportions, as Dreher aptly points out. But it is not just Christians who have suffered severe religious persecution. India has killed over 200,000 Christians, over 250,000 Sikhs, more than 65,000 Muslims and tens of thousands of Assamese, Manipuris, Tamils, Dalits and others since its independence. Thousands of minorities, especially Sikhs, remain in Indian jails as political prisoners without charge or trial.

The Western world must not accept this pattern of religious tyranny. Dr. Gurmit Singh Aulakh, Council of Khalistan, Washington D.C. (via e-mail).

***

Document

CONGRESSIONAL RECORD -- EXTENSIONS

Friday, November 5, 1999
106th Congress, 1st Session
145 Cong Rec E 2282

REFERENCE: Vol. 145, No. 155
TITLE: ARTICLE EXPOSES HINDU FUNDAMENTALISTS' REPRESSION OF
CHRISTIANS; WILL THE POPE BE SAFE IN INDIA?

HON. EDOLPHUS TOWNS
of New York
in the House of Representatives
Thursday, November 4, 1999

Mr. TOWNS. Mr. Speaker, on October 28, the New York Post ran an excellent article by Rod Dreher exposing the tyranny of what he called "Hindu brownshirts" who run India. He notes that the Pope is heading to India soon and wonders if the Pope and his entourage will be safe in the face of this religious violence.

Dreher wrote that "a small but violent faction of Hindu fundamentalists aligned with the Hindu nationalist government have been conducting an organized campaign against the Pope as part of a concerted effort to demonize and persecute the country's tiny Christian minority."

In the article, Dreher states that there were 108 cases of beatings, stonings, church burnings, looting of religious schools, and other attacks on Christians. Freedom House, a widely respected human-rights monitoring organization, reports that there have been more incidents of violence against Indian Christians in the past year than in the previous 50 years, even though Christians make up just 3 percent of India's population.

Missionary Graham Staines and his two young sons were burned to death in their Jeeps by a Hindu mob affiliated with the ruling party. The Hindu militants surrounded the jeep and chanted "Victory to Lord Ram." Last month, Hindu fundamentalists kidnapped a nun named Sister Ruby and forced her to drink their body fluids. These are only two of so many incidents that I have lost count.

There have been cases of forcible reconversion to Hinduism along with the violent incidents against Christians and Christian institutions. Many of us have been standing here discussing this, yet it continues to go on in a country that continues to proclaim itself democratic.

It is not just the Christians. The persecution of Sikhs and Muslims has been well documented in this body time and time again. India has killed over 200,000 Christians since independence, and it has also murdered over 250,000 Sikhs, more than 65,000 Muslims, and tens of thousands of others. The highest shrines of India's Sikh and Muslim communities have been attacked by the Indian government.

It is clear that there is no religious freedom in "democratic" India. How can we be upset about China's persecution of Falun Gong and turn our heads when India practices oppression on Christians, Sikhs, Muslims, and others?

It is our responsibility as the leader of the Free World to help ensure freedom for everyone on the planet. We must subject India to the same penalties we impose on any other country that violates religious freedom. We should stop our aid to India until it respects basic human rights, including religious freedom. We should put the Congress on record in support of self-determination for all the minority nations that India is victimizing. Finally, I call on President Clinton to stress these human rights and self determination issues when he visits India early next year.

Mr. Speaker, I would like to put Mr. Dreher's article into the Record for the information of my colleagues.

Pope's Passage to India May Be Most Perilous Yet
From the New York Post, Oct. 28, 1999
(By Fred Dreher)

Will Pope John Paul II be safe in India? There is more reason to worry for the pontiff's welfare as he visits the world's largest democracy next week than there was when he went to communist Poland under martial law.

That's because a small but violent faction of Hindu fundamentalists aligned with the Hindu nationalist government have been conducting an organized campaign against the pope as part of a concerted effort to demonize and persecute the country's tiny Christian minority.

The government promises to protect the Holy Father from coalition fanatics. But while John Paul can rely on state security, his Catholic followers and Protestant brethren remain at the mercy of Hindu brownshirts.

These thugs have carried out vicious attacks on Christians since a coalition led by the hard-line Bharatiya Janata Party (BJP) came to power two years ago.

Freedom House, the Washington-based human-rights organization, says there have been more recorded incidents of violence against India's Christian minority in the past year than in the previous half-century.

The most shocking incident took place in January, when Hindu thugs burned alive Australian missionary Graham Staines and his two little boys. That was far from a isolated incident.

In 1998, the Catholic Bishop's Conference in India reported 108 cases of beatings, stonings, church burnings, looting of religious schools and institutions, and other attacks on Catholics and evangelicals.

It has been just as bad this year. Just last month, a Catholic priest working in the same territory as the Staines family was murdered while saying Mass for converts, his heart pierced by a poison-tipped arrow.

Why the attacks? Hindu nationalist leaders, particularly those associated with the BJP-allied World Hindu Congress (VHP), claim Christians are on "conversion overdrive."

This is preposterous. Despite being present in India for almost 2,000 years, and educating hundreds of millions of Indian children, Christianity claims the allegiance of less than 3 percent of the country's people.

Even in Orissa state, site of the worst anti-Christian violence, fewer than 500 conversions occur each year.

Still, Hindu nationalists continue to make wild-eyed assertions, such as VHP leader Mohan Joshi's recent statement that missionary homes run by Mother Teresa's order were "nothing but conversion centers."

Not true, but if it were, so what? We know perfectly well what would have become of the diseased and the destitute had Mother Teresa's nuns not rescued them from the street: They would have been left to die in the gutter condemned by a culture that decrees these lowborn souls deserve their fate.

"What has the VHP done to better the life of the low castes? The answer is nothing," says Freedom House investigator Joseph Assad.

"When I was in India, I talked to one Christian who was forcibly reconverted to Hinduism. He told me when no one cared for us, Christians came and gave us food, gave us shelter and gave us medicine."

An Indian Protestant activist who lives in New Jersey told me BJP rule has meant open season on followers of Christ.

"The last two years have been unprecedented," the man says. "They have burned chuches down, raped nuns, killed people. We complain to the government, but they look the other way."

The Hindu militants certainly do not represent the sentiments of all Hindus. But these thugs have the tacit support and protection of the ruling BJP. Indeed, the BJP Web site condemns "Semitic monotheism"-- Judaism, Christianity and Islam--for "bringing intolerance to India."

This is what is known to professional propagandists as the Big Lie. No wonder Hindu hard-liners confidently pillage Christian communities.

How many more Hindu-led atrocities will Christians and others suffer before Prime Minister Atal Behari Vajpayee calls off the nationalist dogs?

Will it take a physical assault on the Holy Father for the world to wake up to the kind of place Gandhi's great nation has become.

***

Document

CONGRESSIONAL RECORD -- EXTENSIONS

Wednesday, November 3, 1999
106th Congress, 1st Session
145 Cong Rec E 2247

REFERENCE: Vol. 145, No. 153
TITLE: BURNING POPE IN EFFIGY SHOWS INDIA'S RELIGIOUS INTOLERANCE

HON. JOHN T. DOOLITTLE
of California
in the House of Representatives
Tuesday, November 2, 1999

Mr. DOOLITTLE. Mr. Speaker, I rise today to condemn the recent act of burning the Pope in effigy by a Hindu fundamentalist group in India. My friend Dr. Gurmit Singh Aulakh, President of the Council of Khalistan, brought this disgraceful act to my attention. It was reported in India Abroad.

An organizer of the march criticized the Delhi Archbishop for contacting the Pope about religious persecution in India. The Pope is visiting India soon and the Hindu militants demand that the Pope declare all religions the same.

This follows the rapes of four nuns in India by individuals described by the Vishwa Hindu Parishad as "patriotic youth." Hindu fundamentalists have murdered four priests. Hindu fundamentalists also killed Australian missionary Graham Staines and his two little boys by surrounding their Jeep and setting it on fire. They have burned churches, prayer halls, and Christian schools.

Sikhs, Muslims, and others have also suffered from similar treatment. They, too, have seen their religious shrines desecrated and attacked and religious leaders kidnapped, tortured, and murdered by the Indian authorities and their Hindu fundamentalist allies. These are people who espouse total Hindu domination of every facet of life in India. In this light, is it any wonder that so many of the minorities in India's multinational empire, such as Christian Nagaland, the Sikhs of Punjab, Khalistan, the Kashmiri Muslims, and so many others seek independence from India?

It is time for Congress to encourage freedom for people of the subcontinent. I submit the Council of Khalistan's press release on the burning of the Pope's effigy into the Record.

Hindu Activists Burn Effigy of Pope,
March to Protest Christian Activity
There is No Religious Freedom in India

Washington, D.C., October 28, 1999.--Fundamentalist Hindu militants burned an effigy of Pope John Paul II on October 22 during a Goa-to-Delhi march to protest Christian religious activity in India, according to a report in the October 29 issue of India Abroad. The Vishwa Hindu Parishad (VHP), a branch of the Rashteriya Swayamsewak Sangh (RSS), a pro- Fascist, Hindu fundamentalist organization organized the march. The ruling BJP, which leads the 24-party governing coalition in India, is the political arm of the RSS.

Marchers are protesting large-scale conversions by Christians, according to the article. They are demanding that the Pope proclaim all religions equal during his visit to India next month.

Subhash Velingkar, an organizer of the march, condemned religious conversions. In the eyes of many Hindu activists, all conversions from Hinduism are forced" conversions. Velingkar attacked the Archbishop of Delhi, Alain de Lastic, for communicating with the Vatican about the persecution of Christians in India. "Why should people from India complain to the Vatican?," he demanded.

Recently a nun named Sister Ruby was abducted by militant Hindus and forced to drink their urine on the threat of being raped. Four other nuns were raped last year. The VHP called the nuns "antinational elements" and described the rapists as "patriotic youth." Another priest was recently murdered in India, joining four other priests who were murdered last year.

Christians have been subjected to a wave of violence since Christmas Day. Churches have been burned and schools and prayer halls have been destroyed. Missionary Graham Staines and his two sons, ages 8 and 10, were burned to death while they slept in their van by a mob of Hindus who surrounded the jeep and chanted "Victory to Lord Ram."

"We strongly condemn this march and the burning in effigy of the Pope," said Dr. Gurmit Singh Aulakh, President of the Council of Khalistan, the organization leading the Sikh Nation's struggle for independence from India. "The ordeal that the Christians are enduring is reminiscent of what the Sikhs, Muslims, and other religious minorities in India go through," he said. "There is no religious freedom in India," he said. "The VHp openly proclaimed that anybody living in India should be a Hindu or subservient to the Hindus."

March organizer Velingkar said, "Christians are brothers of the same blood." Dr. Aulakh dismissed that statement. "The Hindu fundamentalists say the same things about Sikhs being brothers of Hindus," he said. "If that is the case, then why do they continue to murder Sikhs, Christians, Muslims, and others in large numbers?"

India has murdered over 250,000 Sikhs since 1984, over 200,000 Christians in Nagaland since 1988, more than 65,000 Muslims in Kashmir since 1988, and tens of thousands of Assamese, Manipuris, Tamils, Dalits, and others. It continues to hold tens of thousands of members of these groups as political prisoners without charge or trial, according to a report by Amnesty International. Thousands have been illegally detained for as long as 15 years.

"Clearly there is no place for religious minorities in democratic, secular India," said Dr. Aulakh. "This only makes the case for freedom for all the minority nations of South Asia stronger," he said. "I call on President Clinton and the Pope to bring up the issues of religious freedom and self-determination on their visits to India," he said.

***

Document

CONGRESSIONAL RECORD -- EXTENSIONS

Thursday, October 14, 1999
106th Congress, 1st Session
145 Cong Rec E 2107

REFERENCE: Vol. 145, No. 139
TITLE: SENATE SHOULD PASS RELIGIOUS LIBERTY PROTECTION ACT

HON. EDOLPHUS TOWNS
of New York
in the House of Representatives
Thursday, October 14, 1999

Mr. TOWNS. Mr. Speaker, recently, this House passed H.R. 1691, the Religious Liberty Protection Act. The bill is currently in committee in the Senate and I would like to take this opportunity to urge our colleagues in the other house to pass this bill as soon as possible.

America is a secular democracy, a country where the religious rights of every citizen are protected by the Constitution. In many other countries, including some that call themselves secular and democratic, people do not enjoy these freedoms. We must do whatever we can to protect religious freedom for every American.

The Sikh religion requires Sikhs to have five symbols known as the "five Ks." The five Ks are unshorn hair (Kes), a comb (Kanga), a bracelet (Kara), a kind of shorts (Kachha), and a ceremonial sword (Kirpan). These are required by the religion.

In a recent incident in Mentor, Ohio, outside Cleveland, a 69-year-old Sikh named Gurbachan Singh Bhatia was involved in a minor traffic accident. When the police arrived at the scene, a policeman saw Mr. Bhatia's kirpan (ceremonial sword). He was arrested for carrying a concealed weapon. The case is scheduled to be heard in December. In a case in Cincinnati involving similar circumstances, the judge, the Honorable Mark Painter wrote, "To be a Sikh is to wear a kirpan--it is that simple. It is a religious symbol and in no way a weapon."

Dr. Gurmit Singh Aulakh, President of the Council of Khalistan, has been working to get the Religious Liberty Protection Act to protect the rights of Mr. Bhatia and all religious people of all faiths in America. No person should be harassed for his religious faith. He has written to Senator Hatch, who chairs the Judiciary Committee over there, and all members of the committee in support of this bill.

I call on the local authorities in Mentor to drop all charges against Mr. Bhatia and I also call on my colleagues over in the Senate to pass H.R. 1691, the Religious Liberty Protection Act.

I submit Dr. Aulakh's letter to Senator Hatch into the Record for the information of my colleagues.

Council of Khalistan,
Washington, DC
October 7, 1999.
Hon. Orrin Hatch,
Chairman, Senate Judiciary Committee

Washington, DC.

Subject: Request to Expedite Passage of H.R. 1691 to Protect Freedom

Dear Senator Hatch: On behalf of over 500,000 Sikhs, I am writing to you in support of H.R. 1691, the Religious Liberty Protection Act.

The Council of Khalistan represents the interests of the Sikh Nation in this country and worldwide. It was constituted by the Panthic Committee to represent the Sikh struggle for freedom. We have worked for the last 12 years in pursuit of this objective.

It is vitally important that the Religious Liberty Protection Act be reported out of committee and passed as soon as possible.

Charan Singh Kalsi of New Jersey was fired by the New York Transit Authority. The Transit Authority tried to force him to wear a hard hat instead of his turban, which he is required to wear as a symbol of his Sikh religion.

When a Sikh is baptized, he or she is required to have five symbols called the five Ks. They are unshorn hair (Kes), a comb (Kanga), a bracelet (Kara), a kind of shorts (Kachha), and a ceremonial sword (Kirpan). These are required by the religion.

Recently in Mentor, Ohio, Gurbachan Singh Bhatia, a 69- year-old Sikh, was involved in a minor traffic accident. The police were called to the scene of the accident. When the policeman saw Mr. Bhatia's kirpan (ceremonial sword), he was arrested for carrying a concealed weapon. He is currently scheduled to go to trial in December. In a similar case in Cincinnati, Judge Mark Painter wrote, "To be a Sikh is to wear a kirpan-- it is that simple. It is a religious symbol and in no way a weapon."

Mr. Bhatia and Mr. Kalsi are exercising their freedom of religion. The U.S. Constitution guarantees religious freedom to everyone. The Religious Liberty Protection Act will protect individuals like Gurbachan Singh Bhatia and Charan Singh Kalsi from being prosecuted and denied jobs for exercising their religious freedom. That is why this bill is so important.

On behalf of the Sikhs in America, I urge you to report the Religious Liberty Protection Act out so that it can be passed and become law as soon as possible.

Sincerely,
Dr. Gurmit Singh Aulakh, President, Council of Khalistan.

***

Document

CONGRESSIONAL RECORD -- EXTENSIONS

Thursday, October 14, 1999
106th Congress, 1st Session
145 Cong Rec E 2109

REFERENCE: Vol. 145, No. 139
TITLE: KHALISTAN LEADER DR. AULAKH TO BE NOMINATED FOR
NOBEL PRIZE

HON. JOHN T. DOOLITTLE
of California
in the House of Representatives
Thursday, October 14, 1999

Mr. DOOLITTLE. Mr. Speaker, at the recent convention of the Council of Khalistan, held October 9 and 10 in New York, the delegates passed a resolution to nominate Dr. Gurmit Singh Aulakh, President of the Council of Khalistan, for the Nobel Peace Prize. I believe that he would be an excellent candidate.

Dr. Aulakh's organization leads the struggle to liberate Khalistan, the Sikh homeland, from Indian occupation. It is committed to peaceful action to achieve that goal. While the Indian government continues to murder, kidnap, and torture Sikhs, Dr. Aulakh has been a clear and strong voice for freedom.

Dr. Aulakh would be an excellent recipient of the Nobel Peace Prize. I urge the Nobel Prize committee to act favorably on his impending nomination.

Mr. Speaker, I will place the Council of Khalistan's resolution nominating Dr. Aulakh for the Nobel Prize into the Record.

Resolution Recommending Dr. Gurmit Singh Aulakh for the Nobel Peace Prize Passed at the Convention of the Council of Khalistan October 9-10, 1999, Richmond Hill, N.Y.

Whereas Dr. Gurmit Singh Aulakh, President of the Council of Khalistan, has worked tirelessly to liberate the Sikh homeland, Khalistan;

Whereas Dr. Aulakh is committed to promoting a Shantmai Morcha, or peaceful agitation, to liberate Khalistan, as well as free and fair plebiscite;

Whereas Dr. Aulakh and the Council of Khalistan have consistently rejected militancy as a means of liberating Khalistan;

Whereas Dr. Aulakh's efforts have helped to expose Indian genocide against the Sikhs, Christians, Muslims, Dalits, and others; and

Whereas he has worked with the U.S. Congress, the American media, the United Nations, and the Unrepresented Nations and Peoples Organization to promote the peaceful, democratic, nonviolent movement for Sikh freedom;

Therefore be it Resolved by the delegates of this convention to the Council of Khalistan:

That we recommend Dr. Gurmit Singh Aulakh for the Nobel Peace Prize; and

That his name should be submitted to the Nobel Prize Committee at the first opportunity.

***

Document

CONGRESSIONAL RECORD -- EXTENSIONS

Wednesday, October 13, 1999
106th Congress, 1st Session
145 Cong Rec E 2090

REFERENCE: Vol. 145, No. 138
TITLE: DR. AULAKH NAMED KHALISTAN MAN OF THE YEAR

HON. EDOLPHUS TOWNS
of New York
in the House of Representatives
Wednesday, October 13, 1999

Mr. TOWNS. Mr. Speaker, I was pleased to note that the annual convention of the Council of Khalistan named Dr. Gurmit Singh Aulakh, President of the Council of Khalistan, as Khalistan Man of the Year.

Dr. Aulakh is well known to us here on Capitol Hill. He has been a tireless advocate for freedom for the Sikhs. He has consistently worked to expose the brutal human-rights violations committed against the Sikhs by the Indian government. He has worked with us here in Congress to preserve the true history of the Sikhs which the Indian government is trying to alter.

Dr. Aulakh has also worked for the rights of Sikhs in this country. He provided information to support asylum requests. He has supported Charan Singh Kalsi, the Sikhs who was fired by the New York Transit Authority because he refused to remove his turban for a hard hat. He is actively working to get the authorities in Mentor, OH, outside Cleveland, to drop concealed weapons charges against Gurbachan Singh Bhatia for carrying his kirpan, a ceremonial sword required by the Sikh religion.

For all of these reasons and more, Dr. Aulakh deserves the support of all Sikhs and richly deserves the title of Khalistan Man of the Year.

I submit the resolution designating Dr. Aulakh Khalistan Man of the Year into the Record for the information of my colleagues.

Resolution Designating Dr. Aulakh Khalistan's Man of the Year for 1999 Passed at the Convention of the Council of Khalistan, October 9-10, 1999, Richmond Hill, NY

Whereas the struggle for a free Khalistan is the most important issue facing the Sikh Nation;

Whereas Dr. Gurmit Singh Aulakh and the Council of Khalistan have been working tirelessly for this goal for eleven years;

Whereas Dr. Aulakh has been very successful in internationalizing the Sikh freedom struggle, in bringing the genocide against the Sikhs and other minorities to the attention of Congress and the media, in giving speeches, raising funds, and otherwise creating a political and social climate that brings Sikh freedom closer to fulfillment;

Therefore be it resolved by the delegates of this convention:

That Dr. Gurmit Singh Aulakh, President of the Council of Khalistan, is hereby designated as Khalistan's Man of the Year for 1999.

***

Document

CONGRESSIONAL RECORD -- EXTENSIONS

Wednesday, October 13, 1999
106th Congress, 1st Session
145 Cong Rec E 2090

REFERENCE: Vol. 145, No. 138
TITLE: WORLD SHOULD SUPPORT SIKH FREEDOM

HON. JOHN T. DOOLITTLE
of California
in the House of Representatives
Wednesday, October 13, 1999

Mr. DOOLITTLE. Mr. Speaker, when I picked up my Washington Times on October 7, I was pleased to see a letter from Dr. Gurmit Singh Aulakh, whom many of us know well.

Dr. Aulakh, who is the President of the Council of Khalistan, wrote about the Sikh independence struggle. He noted that Sikhs are "culturally, religiously, and linguistically distinct from Hindu India" and that they ruled Punjab independently for many years before the British conquered the subcontinent.

Dr. Aulakh's letter asked why India, which prides itself on being democratic, doesn't hold a plebiscite in Punjab, Khalistan on the question of independence. That is the democratic way to do things. But India appears to care more about achieving hegemony in South Asia than it does about the democratic principles it proclaims.

It is interesting that this letter ran on the 12th anniversary of the day the Sikh nation declared the independence of the Sikh homeland, Punjab, naming their new country Khalistan.

The recent elections in India underline the instability of India's multiethnic state. India has 18 official languages and Christians, Sikhs, Muslims, and others suffer from religious persecution. Many experts predict that India will soon break up.

America and the world should support the freedom movements in Khalistan, Kashmir, Nagaland, Assam, and the other nations seeking their freedom from India. We should cut American aid to India until it learns to respect human rights and we should work for an internationally-supervised plebiscite in Punjab, Khalistan, in Kashmir, in Nagaland, and in all the other areas seeking independence, on the question of their future political status.

Mr. Speaker, I insert Dr. Aulakh's letter into the Record. I hope that my colleagues will read it.

From the Washington Times, Oct. 7, 1999
Sikh Independence Deserves International Support
(By Gurmit Singh Aulakh)

We appreciate Arnold Beichman's mention of the Sikh struggle for an independent Khalistan ("Crossing the mini- state frontier," Commentary, Sept. 23). Sikhs are culturally, linguistically and religiously distinct from Hindu India, and we have a history of self-rule in Punjab. Sikhs are a separate nation.

Sikhs drove foreign invaders out of the subcontinent in the 18th century. Banda Singh Bahadar established Khalsa rule in Punjab in 1710. The Sikh rule lasted until 1716. Sikh rule was re-established in 1765, lasting until the British conquest of 1849. Sikh rule extended to Kabul and was considered one of the powers in South Asia. Since then, the Sikh nation has been struggling to regain its sovereignty.

No Sikh has ever signed the Indian constitution. On Oct. 7, 1987, the Sikh nation declared its independence, forming the separate nation of Khalistan. Our effort to liberate Khalistan is peaceful, democratic and nonviolent, but our declaration of independence is irrevocable and nonnegotiable.

India claims that the struggle for independence is over. If that is the case, why doesn't "the world's largest democracy" hold a plebiscite in Punjab to decide the question of independence the democratic way?

India is not one country. It is an empire of many countries that was thrown together by the British for their administrative convenience. Like the former Soviet Union, it is destined to fall apart.

In the June 17, 1994, issue of Strategic Investment, Jack Wheeler of the Freedom Research Foundation predicted that within 10 years, India "will cease to exist as we know it ." Stanley Wolpert, a professor at the University of California in Los Angeles who wrote a biography on the late Indian Prime Minister Jawaharlal Nehru, predicted on CNN that both India and Pakistan will soon break up.

Sikhs oppose tyranny wherever it rears its head. Consequently, we support freedom for the people of Kashmir, Nagaland and other countries seeking their freedom.

The world helped East Timor achieve its freedom. The world helped Kosovo achieve its freedom. It is time for the free nations of the world to cut off aid to India and support an internationally supervised plebiscite to help the people of Khalistan, Kashmir, Nagaland and all nations of South Asia to achieve their freedom.

***

Document

CONGRESSIONAL RECORD -- EXTENSIONS

Wednesday, October 6, 1999
106th Congress, 1st Session
145 Cong Rec E 2033

REFERENCE: Vol. 145, No. 134
TITLE: INDIAN HUMAN RIGHTS ACTIVISTS ISSUE NEW REPORT ON
ENFORCED DISAPPEARANCES, ARBITRARY EXECUTIONS, AND SECRET
CREMATIONS IN INDIA

HON. DAN BURTON
of Indiana
in the House of Representatives
Tuesday, October 5, 1999

Mr. BURTON of Indiana. Mr. Speaker, the Committee for Coordination on Disappearances in Punjab recently issued a new report on enforced disappearances, arbitrary executions, and secret cremations of Sikhs in Punjab. It documents the names and addresses of 838 victims of this tyrannical policy. The report is both shocking and distressing.

The Committee is an umbrella organization of 18 human rights organizations under the leadership of Hindu human rights activist Ram Narayan Kumar. The report discusses "illegal abductions and secret cremations of dead bodies." In fact, the Indian Supreme Court has itself described this policy as "worse than a genocide."

The report includes direct testimony from members of the victims' families, other witnesses, and details of these brutal cases. The human rights community has stated that over 50,000 Sikhs have "disappeared" at the hands of the Indian government in the early nineties. How can any country, especially one that claims to be the "world's largest democracy," get away with so many killings, abductions and other atrocities? Will the Indian government prosecute the officials of its security forces who are responsible for these acts? Will the Indian government compensate the victims and their families?

If America can compensate the Japanese victims of the internment camps during World War II, why can't India compensate the families whose husbands, sons, wives, or daughters have been murdered? Murder is a lot more serious than internment, and these acts are much more recent.

The Council of Kahlistan recently issued a press release on the Committees's report. I am placing that release in the Congressional Record for the information of my colleagues.

New Report Exposes Enforced Disappearances, Arbitrary Executions, Secret Cremations of Sikhs by Indian Government Identifies Victims of Genocide by Name

Washington, D.C., September 15, 1999--The Committee for Coordination on Disappearances in Punjab, led by Hindu human- rights activist Ram Narayan Kumar, has issued an interim report entitled "Enforced Disappearances, Arbitrary Executions, and Secret Cremations" which exposes secret mass cremations of Sikhs by the Indian government.

The report contains a 21-page list of 838 victims who were identified by name and address. This is a very preliminary report. Three of India's most respected human rights group issued a joint letter in 1997 stating that between 1992 and 1994, 50,000 Sikhs were made to disappear by Indian forces. They were arrested, tortured, and murdered by police, then their bodies were declared "unidentified" and cremated. The Indian Supreme Court described the situation as "worse than a genocide."

More than 250,000 Sikhs have been killed since 1984. Over 200,000 Christians have been killed since 1947 and over 65,000 Kashmiri Muslims have been killed since 1988. Thousands more languish in prisons without charge or trial, according to Amnesty International. Last month, 29 Members of the U.S. Congress wrote to the Prime Minister of India demanding the release of these political prisoners.

The report makes reference to the police kidnapping and murder of human-rights activist Jaswant Singh Khalra in 1995. Khalra "released some official documents which established that the security agencies in Punjab had been secretly cremating thousands of dead bodies labelled as unidentified," the report noted. "Khalra suggested the most of these cremations were of people who had earlier been picked up in the state on suspicion of separatist sympathies," according to the report.

"In September 1995, it was Khalra's turn to disappear; he was kidnapped from his Armristar home by officers of the Punjab police." In October 1995, the police murdered Mr. Khalra. Despite an order of the Supreme Court, none of the police officers involved has been brought to justice. The report also cited an official inquiry's findings of "flagrant violation of human rights on a mass scale."

"This report shows that for Sikhs there are no human rights in India," said Dr. Gurmit Singh Aulakh, President of the Council of Khalistan. "The genocide by the Indian Government shows Sikhs that there is no religious tolerance in India and India will never allow Sikhs or other religious minorities to exercise their religious or political rights," he said.

"If India is the democracy it claims to be, then why not simply hold a plebiscite on independence in Punjab, Khalistan? Dr. Aulakh asked. "Instead of doing the democratic thing and allowing the people of Punjab, Khalistan, of Kashmir, of Christian Nagaland to vote on their political status, as America has repeatedly allowed Puerto Rico to do and Canada has allowed Quebec to do, the Indians try to crush the freedom movements by killing massive numbers of people in these minority nations," he said. "Democracies don't commit genocide."

***

Document

CONGRESSIONAL RECORD -- EXTENSIONS

Friday, October 1, 1999
106th Congress, 1st Session
145 Cong Rec E 2007

REFERENCE: Vol. 145, No. 131
TITLE: POLICE STILL KILLING SIKHS IN PUNJAB

HON. LINCOLN DIAZ-BALART
of Florida
in the House of Representatives
Thursday, September 30, 1999

Mr. DIAZ-BALART. Mr. Speaker, on September 22, Burning Punjab reported that Devinder Singh, a young Sikh, died in police custody at the Ropar police station on September 18. A witness said that third- degree methods were used to extract "false information" from him. His brother and two associates said that he died of injuries inflicted by the police. The two associates were unable to walk due to injuries from torture.

About a week earlier, another young Sikh was killed by the police in the Sarhali police station. On August 16, Lakhbir Singh Lakha was tortured to death in police custody at police post, Chohla Sahib. Mr. Inder Singh, father of the deceased said they had to wait for the body as his son had died 48 hours earlier. Gurpreet, a 17 1/2 -year-old Sikh girl, was abducted and raped repeatedly by the son of a Punjab Akali minister and his brother-in-law. Another Catholic priest was murdered in Orissa by allies of the governing party.

The Indian government says that there are no more human-rights violations occurring in Punjab, yet incidents like these keep coming to light.

These terrible incidents are just part of a pattern that has seen the Indian forces allegedly murder over 250,000 Sikhs since 1984, as well as more than 200,000 Christians in Nagaland since 1948, over 65,000 Muslims in Kashmir since 1988, and thousands of other minorities such as Tamils, Manipuris, Dalit "untouchables," and Assamese people.

I thank Dr. Gurmit Singh Aulakh, President of the Council of Khalistan, for bringing these terrible incidents to my attention. These incidents show that for minorities like the Sikhs and others, there is no security in India. That is why the Sikhs of Khalistan, the Muslims of Kashmir, the Christians of Nagaland, and others seek their independence.

I call on my colleagues to support an internationally-supervised plebiscite in Punjab on the question of independence. These people should be given the same opportunity that citizens of Puerto Rico and Quebec have received--the chance to decide their political future and status in a democratic vote.

Many believe that the breakup of India is inevitable. Since India now has nuclear weapons, the democratic countries of the world, led by the United States, must work to make sure that if this happens, it happens peacefully like in Czechoslovakia (now the Czech Republic and Slovakia), not violently like in Yugoslavia. We can prevent another Yugoslavia type crisis from breaking out in South Asia by encouraging the democratic process in the subcontinent. Let us take this stand and help ensure democracy and stability throughout the region.

***

Document

CONGRESSIONAL RECORD -- EXTENSIONS

Monday, September 27, 1999
106th Congress, 1st Session
145 Cong Rec E 1972

REFERENCE: Vol. 145, No. 127
TITLE: HINDUS ABDUCT, ABUSE NUN IN INDIA

HON. JOHN T. DOOLITTLE
of California
in the House of Representatives
Monday, September 27, 1999

Mr. DOOLITTLE. Mr. Speaker, I was distressed to read an article from the Indian Express of September 24 which reported that a nun was abducted in the Indian state of Bihar. This is the state where a priest was beheaded last year. Will the religious violence in India never stop?

I thank Dr. Gurmit Singh Aulakh, President of the Council of Khalistan, for bringing this terrible event to my attention.

Sister Ruby of the Congregation of the Sisters of the Immaculate Heart of Mary was abducted September 20 after being forced into a rickshaw in the village of Chapra. The kidnappers threatened to rape her. The two men accused Sister Ruby of trying to convert Hindus and they threatened to "teach all Christians a lesson."

This is unfortunately typical. Christians were subjected to a wave of church burnings, as well as attacks on prayer halls and schools earlier this year. Another priest was murdered last week. Missionary Graham Staines and his two sons, ages 8 and 10, were burned to death while they slept in their Jeep by a Hindu fundamentalist mob. Last year four nuns were raped and four priests were murdered. In 1997, police broke up a Christian festival with gunfire.

These incidents are related to religious conversions by members of the lower castes. To the Hindu militants, all conversions are forced conversions.

But it is not just the Christians who have suffered from this kind of religious persecution. Many of my colleagues and I have detailed the religious repression of Sikhs and Muslims by the Indian government and its agents and allies. Sikhs continue to be murdered for their religion and their Golden Temple remains under surveillance by plainclothes police officers fifteen years after the Indian government's attack on the Sikh Nation's holiest shrine. Muslims have seen their most revered mosque in India destroyed and many of their adherents killed.

We should support the right of the minority peoples of Khalistan, Kashmir, and Nagaland to a free and fair vote on independence from India.

Mr. Speaker, I insert the Indian Express report on the abduction of Sister Ruby into the Record.

From the Indian Express, Sept. 24, 1999
Nun Kidnapped, Stripped in Bihar; Bishops Protest
(By Arun Srivastava)

Patna.--A nun was kidnapped, tied up and stripped in Chapra on September 20.

The nun, belonging to the congregation of the Sisters of the Immaculate Heart (better known as Pondicherry Blue Sisters), was forcefully taken in an autorickshaw by two unidentified men on Monday morning to a secluded spot. Her hands were tied behind her back, she was stripped and was forced to drink their urine.

The nun, who hails from Pondicherry, came to Bihar recently and does not know the dialect. She is an inmate of the St. Joseph's Convent in Khalpura Inchapra which is involved in working with the poorest of the poor.

She had left her convent around 9 in the morning for Gandhi Chowk from where she took an autorickshaw for the local post office. There were two men in the autorickshaw.

When she realised that she was being taken through an unfamiliar route, she asked to be dropped off. They did not stop the vehicle and one of them took out a knife, threatened to kill her and accused her of converting people.

He asked her why she and others were still in Chapra and why they have not left for south India. He told her that Christians would be taught a lesson once the elections were over.

According to the Bishop of Bettiah, who in a statement narrated the whole incident, the nun was dragged out of the vehicle, her hands tied and then she was stripped. The two men urinated in a bottle and threatened to rape her when she refused to drink.

Later she was given back her clothes and warned not to contact anyone on the phone. One of the attackers followed to make sure that she did as told. Director General of Police A R Jacob said: "I have been briefed by the Bishop of Patna about the incident." He added: "Right now, I am unable to say anything about the incident. But I am seriously looking into it. I can assure that no one will be spared."

Jacob has assigned IG A K Gupta and the SP of Chapra to "personally investigate the matter." He has also sent to Chapra a senior woman officer who knows Tamil to investigate the incident.

The DGP said the FIR was filed only today as the local police station refused to register the case yesterday because the petition was in English. He is also looking into the delay in registering the case. The Bishop of Bettiah, Rev Victor Henry Thakur, visited the convent. The Archbishop Benedict J Osta and the Bishop of Bettiah have strongly condemned the outrageous attack and have demanded a thorough probe.

They stated that the Christians will not be frightened by such threats and will continue to serve the poor and the distressed more zealously.

Allen R Johannes, press secretary of the Diocese of Bettiah, said the ugly and inhuman act has shocked the entire Christian community in North Bihar and is creating an atmosphere of fear and panic among the Christian minority as the news spreads over the state.

***

Document

CONGRESSIONAL RECORD -- EXTENSIONS

Friday, September 24, 1999
106th Congress, 1st Session
145 Cong Rec E 1953

REFERENCE: Vol. 145, No. 126
TITLE: RECOGNIZING THE 300TH ANNIVERSARY CELEBRATION OF
KHALSA PANTH'S BIRTH

HON. GEORGE RADANOVICH
of California
in the House of Representatives
Friday, September 24, 1999

Mr. RADANOVICH. Mr. Speaker, I rise today to recognize Khalsa Panth's 300th birth anniversary. Khalsa Panth was born April 13, 1699 and is a figure of the Sikh community.

The purpose of founding the Khalsa was to spread righteousness and to uproot the repression and injustice; to create love and harmony amongst humankind and to end evil hatred. Khalsa stands for gender equality; to instill self-confidence; to live a humble life with self-respect and serve the society as its honorable Sant Sipahi.

The guidelines to the Sikh religion are as follows: Sikh's must have honest earnings, worship only one god, and share with the needy. They may only perform Sikh religious ceremonies and should meditate on God's name everyday. Sikh's must not commit any one of the four misdeeds: cutting or shaving of the hair, drinking alcohol, using any intoxicant, and using adultery. Sikh's must give service to the religious congregation without expecting anything in return. They must not worship idols, graves and mortals. Sikh's must always be ready to defend the weak and fight for justice and freedom.

There are five symbols that have both practical and spiritual meaning for the Sikh's. Unshorn hair means moral and spiritual strength. A wooden comb is to keep the hair neat and tidy. The Sikh must always wear a turban and women must keep their heads covered with traditional heading or a turban. An Iron bracelet reminds a Sikh that he must keep himself away from bad deeds. Special tailored shorts remind a Sikh that he is not to indulge in adultery. A sword on the person of an Amritdhardi Sikh represents freedom. Last is political sovereignty. This reminds a Sikh of his duty to stand for truth, justice and righteousness.

Mr. Speaker, I rise today to recognize the Khalsa Panth's 300th birth anniversary. I urge my colleagues to join me in wishing the Sikh community many more years of continued success and happiness.

***

Document

CONGRESSIONAL RECORD -- EXTENSIONS

Thursday, September 23, 1999
106th Congress, 1st Session
145 Cong Rec E 1946

REFERENCE: Vol. 145, No. 125
TITLE: SIKHS SHOULD NOT BE HARASSED FOR CARRYING A
RELIGIOUS SYMBOL, THE KIRPAN

HON. EDOLPHUS TOWNS
of New York
in the House of Representatives
Thursday, September 23, 1999

Mr. TOWNS. Mr. Speaker, America is a country where everyone enjoys religious freedom. There are about 500,000 Sikhs in this country and they have every right to practice their religion in this country. Sikhs have contributed to America in many walks of life, from agriculture to medicine to law, among others. Sikhs participated in World War I and World War II, and a Sikh even served as a Member of Congress in the 1960s. His name was Dalip Singh Saund and he was from California.

When a Sikh is baptized, he or she is required to have five symbols called the five Ks. They are unshorn hair (Kes), a comb (Kanga), a tracelet (Kara), a kind of shorts (Kachha), and a ceremonial sword (Kirpan). Sometimes law enforcement officers in this country consider a Kirpan a concealed weapon and arrest the Sikh carrying a Kirpan.

Earlier this week, Gurbachan Singh Bhatia, a 69-year-old Sikh, was arrested in the suburbs of Cleveland for carrying a concealed weapon. He is to appear at a pretrial hearing on October 4. I hope that the case against Mr. Bhatia will be dismissed.

A similar case happened in Cincinnati in 1996. The First Ohio District Court of Appeals overturned a municipal court conviction of a Sikh man for carrying a concealed weapon. Judge Mark Painter of that court wrote that "to be a Skih is to wear a kirpan--it is that simple. It is a religious symbol and in no way a weapon."

Like Christianity, the Sikh religion is a monotheistic, divinely revealed and independent religion which believes in the equality of the whole human race, including gender equality. They pray, work hard to earn an honest living, and share their earnings with the needy.

I know many Sikhs in my district who are baptized and carry this symbol Kirpan. I would not like any of my constituents to be harassed for practicing their religion. We must educate our law-enforcement agencies regarding this religious symbol of the Sikhs.

Our Constitution grants religious freedom to all. We want Sikh Americans to practice their religion without any interference, even if we have to pass special legislation allowing the Sikhs to carry Kirpans.

I would like to put the Detroit News article on the Bhatia case into the Record.

From the Detroit News, Sept. 23, 1999
Can a Weapon Be a Religious Icon?

Mentor, Ohio--When he was baptized a Sikh in India, Gurbachan Singh Bhatia, now 69, vowed to always wear a kirpan, a 6-inch knife symbolizing his willingness to defend the faith.

But during investigation of a minor traffic mishap in this Cleveland suburb, Bhatia was arrested for carrying a concealed weapon. At the time, he was returning home from a religious ceremony blessing the new home of a Sikh family.

Police Chief Richard Amiott said his officers acted properly in enforcing the law banning concealed weapons. "How can you describe for me the difference between a ceremonial knife and any knife?" he asked.

Bhatia must appear for a pretrial hearing Oct. 4. If convicted, he could face up to six months in jail and a $1,000 fine. But Ron Graham, city prosecutor, said he may be willing to drop the charges if the Sikh *priest can demonstrate that he is required by his religion to carry the kirpan.*

Although state law does not allow for exceptions, Graham said, "We don't want to prosecute anyone for exercising religious freedom."

In a similar case in Cincinnati in 1996, the 1st Ohio District Court of Appeals overturned a municipal court conviction of a Sikh man for carrying a concealed weapon.

"To be a Sikh is to wear a kirpan--it is that simple. It is a religious symbol and in no way a weapon," Judge Mark Painter wrote.

***

Document

CONGRESSIONAL RECORD -- EXTENSIONS

Wednesday, September 22, 1999
106th Congress, 1st Session
145 Cong Rec E 1932

REFERENCE: Vol. 145, No. 124
TITLE: U.S. CONGRESSIONAL LETTER CALLS FOR RELEASE OF
POLITICAL PRISONERS IN INDIA

HON. JOHN T. DOOLITTLE
of California
in the House of Representatives
Wednesday, September 22, 1999

Mr. DOOLITTLE. Mr. Speaker, last month several of my colleagues and I sent a letter to Indian Prime Minister Atal Bihari Vajpayee calling for the release of political prisoners in India. So far we have received no response.

According to Amnesty International, thousands of political prisoners are being held in illegal detention without charge or trial. Several Sikh political prisoners wrote a letter from the Nabha Security jail on the Sikh Nation's 300th anniversary in which they urged Sikhs to get involved in getting them released. Some of these Sikh political prisoners have been held since 1984. Fifteen years in illegal detention without charge or trials is the tactic of a police state, not of the democracy India claims to be.

Our letter reminds the Indian leader that if India is going to proclaim its democratic principles, it should release all political prisoners and bring the police who have committed atrocities against the Sikhs to justice. If it does not, we should be ready to take appropriate action to deprive India of the privileges that accrue to democratic and friendly countries.

If India continues to oppress its minorities and hold thousands of political prisoners without charge of trial, America should stop aid and trade to the repressive Indian regime. In addition, we should support self-determination for all the nations and peoples of South Asia. This is the way to ensure that all the people and nations of South Asia may live in freedom.

Mr. Speaker, I would like to place the Congressional letter to Prime Minister Vajpayee into the Record.

Washington, DC,
July 30, 1999.
Hon. Atal Bihari Vajpayee,
Prime Minister of India, Chanakyapuri, New Delhi, India.

Dear Mr. Prime Minister: We are very disturbed by a recent Amnesty International report that thousands of political prisoners are being held in Indian prisons without charge or trial. In a democracy, there should not be political prisoners.

In addition, a group of political prisoners held at Nabha Security Jail wrote to the Sikhs earlier this year asking for help in getting them released. There are thousands of Sikh political prisoners being held in India. Some Sikh political prisoners have been held since 1984 without charge or trial. How can a country that proclaims its support for democratic principles continue to hold political prisoners?

Human-rights activist Jaswant Singh Khalra wrote a report showing that tens of thousands of Sikhs were abducted, tortured, murdered, and declared "unidentified," then their bodies were cremated. After Mr. Khalra published this report, he was kidnapped by the police and they killed him six weeks later, according to a witness. The police responsible for this act have never been punished, despite a court order. Neither has Swaran Singh Ghotna, the police officer responsible for the torture and murder of Akal Takht Jathedar Gurdev Singh Kaunke, who was torn in half.

Mr. Khalra's findings were confirmed by a recently-issued report from the Committee for Coordination on Disappearances in Punjab, which issued an "interim report" that identifies at least 838 cases of arbitrary execution and secret cremation. These are not the acts of a democratic country.

As members of the United States Congress, we will be watching with interest the actions that you take. If these kinds of acts continue, we will be forced to consider cutting off American aid and trade to India. We expect a democratic state like India to live up to the principles of democracy and the rule of law.

> *Sincerely, Edolphus Towns, Dan Burton, William Jefferson, Roscoe Bartlett, John T. Doolittle, Jack Metcalf, Sam Farr, George Radanovich, Eni Faleomavaega, Bobby L. Rush, James Traficant, Wally Herger, Gary Condit, Lincoln Diaz-Balart, Peter King, J.C. Watts, Donald Payne, Cynthia McKinney, Brian P. Bilbray, Major R. Owens, Bernard Sanders, Richard Pombo, Albert R. Wynn, Carlos Romero-Barcelo, James Rogan, Duke Cunningham, Ileana Ros-Lehtinen, David McIntosh, Collin C. Peterson.*

***

Document

CONGRESSIONAL RECORD -- EXTENSIONS

Tuesday, September 21, 1999
106th Congress, 1st Session
145 Cong Rec E 1905

REFERENCE: Vol. 145, No. 122
TITLE: ANOTHER PRIEST MURDERED IN INDIA

HON. JOHN T. DOOLITTLE
of California
in the House of Representatives
Tuesday, September 21, 1999

Mr. DOOLITTLE. Mr. Speaker, another Christian missionary has been murdered in India, according to recent press reports. According to India West, the priest, whose name was Aruldoss, was killed on September 2 with poison arrows by a Hindu mob in the village of Jambani in the state of Orissa.

This is the same region where Graham Staines, an Australian missionary, and his 8-year-old and 10-year-old sons were set on fire and murdered by a Hindu mob allied with the ruling party while they were sleeping in their van. The mob surrounded the van and kept anyone from getting to the Staines family, chanting "Victory to Lord Ram" while the Staines family was burning to death. Now the government has designated a single individual in the mob to take the fall in order to protect the government's allies.

Apparently, Aruldoss has been involved in conversions of Hindus to Christianity. According to the Hindu fundamentalists who run the government and their allies, virtually all conversions are called "forced" conversions. One of the ministers in the Orissa government, Ajit Tripathy, claimed that Christians were causing all the trouble by "trying to separate families after converting tribals and others, which is leading to social tensions." This kind of religious intolerance and excuse for mob violence has no place in a country that proudly labels itself "the world's largest democracy."

Authorities have said that the mob was angry about the observance of a religious festival. While the Hindus in the region were celebrating the festival of Nuakhai, the local Christians were holding a festival of their own. Remember that in 1997, a Christian festival was broken up by police gunfire.

There is a disturbing pattern of religious intolerance in India, not only towards Christians, but towards Muslims and Sikhs as well. None of these groups can enjoy full religious or political rights, and they are among the 17 freedom movements within India. The Indian government's response to these efforts to achieve freedom is bloodshed. Thousands are being held in Indian jails as political prisoners without charge or trial. Some have been there for 15 years.

I would like to submit the India West article on this event into the Record to inform my colleagues about the kind of country that India really is.

Orissa Priest Murdered, Linked to Conversions

Bhubaneshwar--Unidentified assailants killed a Christian missionary with poisoned arrows in a remote village in Orissa, a senior government official said Sept. 2.

"Preliminary reports say that a Christian... was attacked and killed by poisoned arrows last night," Orissa state chief secretary Sahadeva Sahoo told Reuters by telephone.

Police said Sept. 3 that an incident linked to the religious conversions of Hindus may have led to the murder of a Christian priest in a remote eastern Indian village this week.

"Local issues seem to have led to the killing," Pradeep Kapoor, police chief of Mayurbhanj district in Orissa, told Reuters. He was speaking by telephone from Karanjia town near the village where the priest, identified only as Aruldoss, was killed Sept. 2.

"It was a dispute over the observing of some festival," Sahoo said, without giving details.

"It is a very remote, inaccessible jungle area. Information is not coming easily. Even the ministers couldn't go there because helicopters cannot land within 5 km (3 miles) of the jungle area," Sahoo said.

Assailants shooting bows and arrows killed the missionary in Jambani, a hamlet of only 12 families in Mayurbhanj district.

Christian groups and Prime Minister Atal Behari Vajpayee have condemned the killing, which took place in the region where an Australian missionary, Graham Staines, and his two young sons were burnt to death in January as they slept in their jeep.

"There was a dispute over the celebration of Nuakhai, a Hindu festival. The (Christian) converts separately held the festival which might have angered the nearby villagers," Kapoor said.

"Several people have been rounded up for interrogation but no one has been arrested so far," he said.

Sahoo said earlier that two people had been arrested but gave no details.

Ajit Tripathy, the Orissa home secretary, said priests were causing tension in the area.

"Catholic priests are trying to separate the families after converting tribals and others, which is leading to social tension," Tripathy said.

Mayurbhanj district chief R. Balakrishnan said 10 of the 12 families in the hamlet had been converted recently by the slain missionary.

Christian missionaries had ignored warnings by authorities after the killing of Staines not to visit remote villages without informing them, he said.

Staines also worked in the districts of Mayurbhanj and Keonjhar.

An inquiry into Staines' murder blamed a lone religious fanatic wanted by police. It exonerated a Hindu group considered close to Vajpayee's ruling Hindu nationalist Bharatiya Janat. Party to which fingers of suspicion were initially pointed.

Hindu activists accuse Christian missionaries of using coercion or economic incentives to force religious conversions in remote tribal areas of India. Christian missionaries deny the charge.

Meanwhile, the Election Commission Sept. 5 rejected the Orissa government's proposal to shift general of police Dilip Mohapatra in the wake of his reported controversial remarks on the killing of the priest.

Chief Election Commissioner M.S. Gill told PTI: "We are in the midst of elections which will end by October 10. Therefore, the commission desires that Mohapatra, who is a key functionary, be not be shifted till October 10."

Gill made it clear that the Orissa chief secretary, home secretary and the DGP should under no circumstances be disturbed in any manner till the conclusion of the poll process.

The state government had sought the commission's permission to transfer and revert Mohapatra to the rank of additional DGP for his reported remarks linking Catholic priest Aruldoss's killing to "forced conversions."

Chief Minister Giridhar Gamang faced an angry outburst from church leaders Sept. 4, who demanded immediate suspension of home secretary Ajit Kumar Tripathy as well over his reported statement that Catholic priests were trying to split families through conversions.

Gamang had gone to attend the funeral of the slain priest at Balasore.

***

Document

CONGRESSIONAL RECORD -- EXTENSIONS

Wednesday, July 21, 1999
106th Congress, 1st Session
145 Cong Rec E 1616

REFERENCE: Vol. 145, No. 104
TITLE: AMERICA SHOULD SUPPORT KASHMIRI, SIKH, NAGA FREEDOM
STRUGGLES

HON. JOHN T. DOOLITTLE
of California
in the House of Representatives
Wednesday, July 21, 1999

Mr. DOOLITTLE. Mr. Speaker, the world watches carefully the situation in Kashmir, where the Indian military attacked the Kashmiri freedom fighters to shut down the seventeen freedom movements within its borders. The effort did not go well for India, despite its claims of victory. An Indian military spokesman admitted that Indian troops were "dying like dogs."

The Sikhs in Punjab, Khalistan have been very concerned that this war will spread to their homeland, where they are also seeking self-determination. One of India's strategies for keeping the freedom movements from succeeding is to set the minority nations against each other. In pursuit of this divide-and-rule strategy, they have sent Sikh soldiers to fight the Kashmiris, as they have done in Nagaland. The Christians in Nagaland have been fighting for their freedom for the last 52 years.

The Council of Khalistan wrote an open letter to the Sikh soldiers and officers. They called on the soldiers and officers to stop "dying like dogs" for the Indian government. The letter asked Sikh soldiers if they would rather die as Sikh martyrs or mercenaries for Indian oppression. It urged them to stop shooting at their fellow freedom fighters in Kashmir and join the movement to free Khalistan.

The reasons why Khalistan and the other nations of South Asia should enjoy their freedom have been outlined by many of us in the past, and they have not changed. Amnesty International reports that thousands of political prisoners are being held without charge or trial. Some of them have been in illegal custody for 15 years.

If India is democratic and if there is no support for the freedom movements, as India claims, then why not let the peoples of the subcontinent vote on their political status? America should support self-determination for all the nations and peoples. We should declare our support for the freedom movements and the right of self- determination and stop aid to the repressive Indian regime.

***

Document

CONGRESSIONAL RECORD -- EXTENSIONS

Tuesday, July 20, 1999
106th Congress, 1st Session
145 Cong Rec E 1600

REFERENCE: Vol. 145, No. 103
TITLE: OPEN LETTER FROM COUNCIL OF KHALISTAN CALLS ON SIKHS
TO STOP SUPPORTING INDIAN TYRANNY

HON. EDOLPHUS TOWNS
of New York
in the House of Representatives
Tuesday, July 20, 1999

Mr. TOWNS. Mr. Speaker, the conflict in Kashmir has been in the news a lot lately. The conflict stemmed from an attack on the Kashmiri freedom fighters in Kargil. While it looks as if the conflict may be receding, there is still fighting. The Sikhs in Punjab are afraid that it will spread to Punjab, Khalistan. The fighting will continue as long as India uses force to suppress the freedom movements of South Asia.

While the fighting was at its height, the Council of Khalistan, which leads the Sikh freedom struggle, issued an open letter on the situation. The letter told Sikh troops that if they died for India, they would die as mercenaries, but if they died for Sikh freedom, they would die as martyrs. It urged them to go home and join the struggle to liberate Khalistan.

In the letter, the Council of Khalistan pointed out that an Indian colonel said that the troops were "dying like dogs" and that 60 percent of the soldiers killed were Sikhs. This is typical of India's strategy to keep the minority nations of South Asia within their artificial borders. They send draftees from one minority to kill another. They don't put Hindu lives at risk. "Are you willing to die for a country that practices a policy of mass cremations against our Sikh brothers and sisters, a policy the Indian Supreme Court called, worse than a genocide'?," said the letter.

It is essential that we help bring real peace to South Asia. Both India and Pakistan have nuclear weapons, and we must do what we can to prevent these weapons from being used. So far, American involvement in the situation has been mainly to lean on Pakistan to bring an end to the conflict. But it is only India that can end the conflict. Only when India stops its efforts to repress the freedom movements can the conflict in South Asia end.

India is anti-American and has tried to organize a security alliance against the United States, and in May the Foreign Minister organized and led a meeting with Cuba, China, Russia, Serbia, Iraq, and Libya "to stop the U.S." Amnesty International reported that thousands of political prisoners remain in illegal detention without charge or trial. Some have been there for 15 years. India has murdered over 250,000 Sikhs since 1984 in its quest for "Hindutva." It has also killed tens of thousands of Christians in Nagaland, Muslims in Kashmir, Dalits, and other peoples in this pursuit. Sooner or later, India is doomed to break up. I only hope that it does so peacefully. We must not allow another Yugoslavia to emerge in South Asia, where nuclear weapons are present.

Mr. Speaker, the time has come for our country to support freedom for all the people of South Asia. If India cannot learn to respect basic human rights as we do in this country, then it should not receive any aid or trade from the United States. It is time for the Congress to put itself on record in support of the freedom movements in Khalistan, Kashmir, Christian Nagaland, and the other nations of South Asia.

Mr. Speaker, I would like to put the Council of Khalistan's open letter on Kashmir into the Record for the information of my colleagues.

Council of Khalistan,
Washington, DC, June 16, 1999.
Open Letter to the Sikh Soldiers and Officers
Stop "Dying Like Dogs" for the Indian Oppressors
Will You Be a Martyr or a Mercenary?
Join the Freedom Movement to Liberate Khalistan

Khalsa Ji: The Indian attack on the Kashmiri freedom fighters at Kargil again shows the reality of Hindutva. You see the death of your fellow Sikhs on a daily basis. About 60 percent of the casualties are Sikhs. When India wants to suppress a freedom movement, they send other minorities to do the dirty work, pitting minorities against each other. Hindustan will just use you and discard you. Do not let yourself be a mercenary for this divide-and-rule strategy by the Indian tyrants.

India is losing this war. Casualties are mounting. An Indian colonel admitted that the troops are "dying like dogs." A corporal is quoted as saying. "Even in war we don't have such senseless casualties." All these deaths are very tragic, but it is especially sad when Sikh soldiers give their lives for the oppressor. If a Sikh soldier must die, at least die for the Khalsa Panth. If you die for the Khalsa Panth, you will be a martyr. If you die for India, you are just a mercenary.

What are you dying for? Are you willing to die for a country that has murdered over 250,000 of our Sikh brothers and sisters since 1984? Are you willing to die for a country that desecrated the Golden Temple, shot bullet holes through the Guru Granth Sahib? Are you willing to die for a country that practices a policy of mass cremations against our Sikh brothers and sisters, a policy the Indian Supreme Court called "worse than a genocide"?

If you are dying anyway, come home and die for our homeland like the martyrs who were murdered in the Golden Temple attack. It is better to promote the freedom and glory of the Khalsa Panth than to promote Hindutva and the "territorial integrity" of India. When human-rights are being violated on such a massive scale, "territorial integrity" is not an issue.

The political creed of India is "Hindu, Hindui, Hindutva, Hindu Rashtra." As the former Speaker of the Lok Sabha, Balram Jakhar, said, "If we have to kill a million Sikhs to preserve our territorial integrity, so be it." When India wants to protect its artificial borders, it is Sikhs who get killed. When we seek freedom, it is Sikhs who get killed. How can Sikhs put their lives on the line for a country like that?

You are all aware of the plight of Sikhs back home in Punjab. The Indian government has bribed Sikh policemen with cash and promotions to murder their Sikh brothers and sisters. The U.S. State Department reported that between 1992 and 1994 the Indian government paid over 41,000 cash bounties to policemen for killing Sikhs. One policeman collected a bounty for murdering a three-year-old boy. Why should Sikhs give their lives for that?

Are you aware that in 37 border villages back in Punjab, the people have evacuated because they are afraid that his war on the Kashmiri freedom fighters will expand to Punjab? As the people of Kosovo fled from their homes in fear of the Serbian government's brutality, the people of Punjab, Khalistan--your family, friends, and neighbors--are fleeing their homes in fear of the brutal Indian government. There has been a new deployment of troops to Punjab, raising fears that India will launch an attack on Pakistan from the Sialkot sector. If that happens, more Sikhs will lose their lives.

Every day in Ardas, Sikhs pray "Raj Kare Ga Khalsa," the Khalsa shall rule. Our heritage is "Khalsa Bagi Yan Badshah," the Khalsa rules or it is in rebellion. Our Gurus teach us to oppose tyranny wherever it rears its ugly head. How can Sikhs say that and then go fight for a country that denies our Sikh brothers and sisters the most basic human rights?

India's political situation is unstable and it is losing this bloody war. In desperation, it has resorted to using chemical weapons. This is a shame on India. It shows the Indian government's complete disregard for the lives of Sikhs, Muslims, and other minorities. However, the instability provides an opportunity to liberate Khalistan.

Recently, a group of Sikhs living in Pakistan called for a common front with our Kashmiri brothers to liberate both Khalistan and Kashmir. They said that now is the ideal time for such an effort. They are right. Let us make common cause with the Kashmiri freedom fighters and liberate our countries together.

Sikhs remember their martyrs and we also remember our enemies. Sikhs ended the regime of the tyrant Indira Gandhi. A brave Sikh named Delawar Singh ended the tyranny of Beant Singh. Would you rather be remembered as a brave Sikh martyr like Delawar Singh or as a traitor like K.P.S. Gill?

I call on Sikhs in the Indian armed forces, whether officers or soldiers, to stop shooting at the Kashmiri freedom fighters and join the Sikh freedom movement. Stop "dying like dogs" for the theocratic Indian state. These Kashmiri freedom fighters have the same as the goal of the Sikh Nation: to live in freedom, peace, prosperity, and dignity.

Now is the time to join the Sikh freedom movement and liberate Khalistan. You are trained soldiers. The Khalsa Panth needs your services. You will be remembered as the liberators of Khalistan. Remember Gen. Shabeg Singh who gave his life defending the sanctity of Darbar Sahib and the honor of the Sikh Nation. We must free Khalistan. Nations don't survive without political power. This is the opportune time for us. We must not let this opportunity pass. Panth Da Sewadar,

Dr. Gurmit Singh Aulakh, President.

***

Document

CONGRESSIONAL RECORD -- EXTENSIONS

Thursday, July 1, 1999
106th Congress, 1st Session
145 Cong Rec E 1471

REFERENCE: Vol. 145, No. 96
TITLE: SIKH LEADER'S LETTER EXPOSES CONFLICT IN KASHMIR

HON. JOHN T. DOOLITTLE
of California
in the House of Representatives
Thursday, July 1, 1999

Mr. DOOLITTLE. Mr. Speaker, India has recently undertaken a military effort to eliminate the freedom movement in Kashmir. Supporters of freedom for all the nations of South Asia, especially neighboring Punjab, Khalistan, are concerned that if this conflict spreads, it could be a threat to other nations inside India's borders.

Recently, Dr. Gurmit Singh Aulakh, President of the Council of Khalistan, wrote a letter to the Washington Times which I am sure will be of interest to my colleagues. He pointed out that the air attacks are really an attack on the Kashmiri freedom fighters. "India has not yet learned that people struggling for freedom cannot be suppressed by force forever," he wrote.

Dr. Aulakh wrote that "the reason for these conflicts is the denial of self-determination by the country that proclaims itself the world's largest democracy.' " This is the cause not only of the conflict in Kargil, but many of the political problems in South Asia. India spends its money to build nuclear weapons and forcibly maintain its unstable, polyglot country while half its people live below the international poverty line. To make it worse, India convened a meeting last month with China, Cuba, Serbia, and other enemies of our country "to stop the U.S." Why are the overstressed taxpayers of America supporting this kind of government?

Only when free and fair plebiscites on independence are held in those regions that are seeking their freedom can India legitimately claim that it is a democratic power. India promised the people of Kashmir a plebiscite in 1948. It promised the Sikhs of Punjab, Khalistan, that they would have autonomy. India claims it is democratic and that there is no support for independence in these places or in Nagaland or any of the other lands it occupies. Then why not simply have a vote?

The conflict at Kargil shows that India is unstable. It is falling apart in front of our eyes. We should get on the right side of history and support the freedom movements by cutting off aid to India and by calling for free and fair plebiscites for those seeking freedom.

I insert the Council of Khalistan's letter into the Record.

The Washington Times,
June 8, 1999.

India's recent air attacks on Kashmir are really a war on the Kashmiri freedom movement. Everything India has tried to put down the freedom movement has failed, so now it has resorted to an air war against the Kashmiris. Sikhs are concerned that neighboring Punjab or Khalistan could be next.

This war is designed to suppress the freedom fighters in Kashmir. India has not yet learned that people struggling for freedom cannot be suppressed by force forever. This is why more than 500,000 Indian soldiers are stationed in Kashmir. Another 500,000 are stationed in Punjab to suppress the movement to free Khalistan. India has already lost two Russian-made MiG fighters and two helicopter gunships.

To suppress the freedom struggle, the Indian government has killed more than 250,000 Sikhs since 1984, more than 200,000 Christians in Nagaland since 1948, more than 60,000 Muslims in Kashmir since 1988 and tens of thousands of others.

The reason for these conflicts is the denial of self- determination by the country that proclaims itself "the world's largest democracy." America periodically conducts democratic votes on the status of Puerto Rico, with independence as an option. Canada does the same for Quebec, and Great Britain recently allowed Scotland and Wales to elect their own parliaments, moving them one step closer to a vote on independence. If self-determination is good enough for them, why shouldn't the Sikhs of Khalistan, the Muslims of Kashmir, the Christians of Nagaland and others seeking their freedom from India enjoy the same rights?

The United States, Canada and Great Britain are major world powers. Not only is a free and fair plebiscite the democratic way to settle these issues, it is how great powers conduct themselves. India claims that there is no support for Khalistan. Then why not hold a free and fair vote? If India wants to be a world power and if it claims that it is democratic, then it should allow the people of Khalistan, Kashmir, Nagaland and the others seeking their freedom to hold a plebiscite under international supervision on the question of independence so that this issue can be settled in a free and fair vote.

The war against the people of Kashmir shows the inherent weakness of the Indian government. Now is the best time for the people and nations of South Asia to claim their freedom. America can support this by cutting off aid to India until it lets people live in freedom and by declaring its open support for the freedom movements of South Asia.

Gurmit Singh Aulakh, President, Council of Khalistan.

***

Document

CONGRESSIONAL RECORD -- EXTENSIONS

Thursday, July 1, 1999
106th Congress, 1st Session
145 Cong Rec E 1474

REFERENCE: Vol. 145, No. 96
TITLE: SIKH JOURNALIST'S MAIL IS BEING INTERCEPTED

HON. JOHN T. DOOLITTLE
of California
in the House of Representatives
Thursday, July 1, 1999

Mr. DOOLITTLE. Mr. Speaker, it has come to my attention that journalist Sukhbir Singh Osan, proprietor of Burning Punjab and a writer for several Indian newspapers, is once again being harassed by the Indian government. After he came to North America to cover the big Sikh marches in Washington, New York, and Toronto and made a speech in the United Kingdom on the human rights situation in India, he was grilled for 45 minutes by Indian intelligence officers. Now, Indian postal authorities are intercepting his mail.

In a letter to the Chief Postmaster of Chandigarh, which was brought to my attention by Dr. Gurmit Singh Aulakh, President of the Council of Khalistan, Mr. Osan noted that postal officials were handling his mail over to police constables. Several important documents were found lying on the desk of a Deputy Inspector General of Police. Mr. Osan, who is a law graduate as well as a journalist, pointed out that this action violates the Indian constitution and violates a ruling by the Indian Supreme Court in 1995.

This is not the first time Mr. Osan has run afoul of the Indian state. His mail has been diverted before and he has received telephone threats for his reporting on corruption and human rights violations.

Here is Indian democracy in action. If you criticize the government, your mail is seized, the government grills you, and you are threatened. In spite of all this, Mr. Osan goes on providing information about the situation in Punjab, Khalistan on his website and in his articles. His courage deserves our respect.

This abuse of Mr. Osan's rights is just the latest Indian violation of the basic liberties of Sikhs in Punjab, Khalistan. In light of this pattern of tyranny, America should help bring liberty to the people living under Indian rule.

Let us use our influence constructively to bring freedom, peace, and stability to this troubled region before it turns into another Kosovo. If that happens, it could pose a serious danger to the entire world, given India and Pakistan's possession of nuclear weapons and India's alleged use of chemical weapons in the Kargil conflict. We must act now to keep this from happening.

***

Document

CONGRESSIONAL RECORD -- EXTENSIONS

Wednesday, June 30, 1999
106th Congress, 1st Session
145 Cong Rec E 1450

REFERENCE: Vol. 145, No. 95
TITLE: INDIA CELEBRATES NUKES AND DEMONSTRATES
INTOLERANCE

HON. JOHN T. DOOLITTLE
of California
in the House of Representatives
Wednesday, June 30, 1999

Mr. DOOLITTLE. Mr. Speaker, while our attention has been grabbed by Kosovo and China, the situation in India has dropped off our radar screen. While we weren't looking, India has been very busy.

The Indian election campaign began with the ruling party celebrating the anniversary of its nuclear weapons tests last year. These weapons were built out of India's development budget, as the people's health and education continue to decline and the population outside of the Brahmin caste lives in abject poverty.

Meanwhile, the Indian Defense Minister held a meeting looking to find ways to "stop the U.S.," which he called "vulgarly arrogant." Remember that we provide millions of dollars each year to help India pay its bills. How "vulgarly arrogant." of us! Other countries whose representatives attended this meeting included Serbia, China, Cuba, Russia, Libya, and Iraq.

Mr. Speaker, we are talking about a country in which there is little respect for religious freedom. On May 20, the government placed the Jathedar of the Akal Takht, Bhai Ranjit Singh, under house arrest. Since Christmas, there has been a wave of violence against Christians. A missionary has been burned to death along with his two young sons, nuns have been raped, priests have been murdered, and Christian churches, prayer halls, and schools have been burned to the ground by allies of the Indian government.

As if all that weren't enough, we have received word that Indian intelligence officers interrogated a journalist named Sikhbir Singh Osan for 45 minutes. For him to have been grilled and harassed by police would have been bad enough, but he was harassed by intelligence officers after he returned from the U.S., Canada, and the U.K., where he covered the recent Sikh 300th anniversary marches and gave a speech on the persecution of Christians.

The government of India is intolerant and anti-American. They do not allow freedom of religion or, apparently, of the press. I am proud to have joined several of my colleagues of both parties in co-sponsoring a resolution that calls for a free and fair plebiscite in Punjab, Khalistan on the question of independence. Freedom is America's mission. By taking steps against the anti-American government of India, we can help promote and extend the blessings of liberty to another corner of the world. We must get started.

***

Document

CONGRESSIONAL RECORD -- EXTENSIONS

Tuesday, June 29, 1999
106th Congress, 1st Session
145 Cong Rec E 1419

REFERENCE: Vol. 145, No. 94
TITLE: AMNESTY INTERNATIONAL REPORTS INDIA DETAINING
THOUSANDS OF POLITICAL PRISONERS WITHOUT CHARGE

HON. GARY A. CONDIT
of California
in the House of Representatives
Tuesday, June 29, 1999

Mr. CONDIT. Mr. Speaker, the June 25 issue of Indian Abroad reports that Amnesty International issued a report in which it said that India is holding thousands of political prisoners without charge or trial. Amnesty International's report was issued on June 16.

The article said that "torture and ill-treatment continued to be widespread and hundreds of people were reported to have died in custody." Amnesty International reported that "conditions in many prisons amounted to cruel, inhuman, or degrading treatment." It reported that "disappearances" continue to occur and hundreds of extrajudicial killings were reported. In other words, nothing has changed.

Mr. Speaker, do these sound like the actions of a democracy? Indian claims to be "the world's largest democracy" even while it continues these repressive, tyrannical policies. This report shows that India is not democratic. It is merely the tyranny of the majority exercised on the minorities. That is why there are 17 freedom movements within its borders.

This comes at a time when India is engaged in combat to wipe out the freedom fighters in Kashmir, a conflict in which it has fired shells containing chemical weapons. India brought nuclear weapons to South Asia; now it is introducing chemical weapons.

America was founded on the principle of liberty. We must act to help bring the blessings of liberty to the people of South Asia. We can begin by declaring our support for national self-determination in Kashmir,

Khalistan, Nagaland, and the other nations occupied by India. I am proud to have sponsored a resolution in the last Congress calling for an internationally-supervised plebiscite in Punjab, Khalistan on the question of independence. We should also cut off American aid to this government as long as it practices the kind of tyranny that Amnesty International reported, and we should impose reasonable economic sanctions. It is our responsibility to defend freedom wherever we can.

Mr. Speaker, I would like to introduce the India Abroad article into the Record for the information of my colleagues. I urge my colleagues to read it.

From the India Abroad June 25, 1999
Human Rights: Amnesty says thousands are detained without trial
(From News Dispatches)

LONDON--Thousands of political prisoners, including prisoners of conscience, were detained without charge or trial in India, Amnesty International said in its annual report, released on June 16.

Torture and ill-treatment continued to be widespread, and hundreds of people were reported to have died in custody, the London-based human rights oganization added.

"Conditions in many prisons amounted to cruel, inhuman or degrading treatment," it said, adding that "disappearances" also continued and hundreds of extrajudicial executions were reported. At least 35 people were sentenced to death but no executions were reported, the report said.

The London-based human rights watchdog said armed groups were also to blame. These groups committed grave human rights abuses including torture, hostage-taking and killing of civilians, it said.

Overall, the report lamented that 1998, which marked the 50th anniversary of the Universal Declaration of Human Rights, was marred by a worldwide catalogue of abuses.

But Amnesty secretary general Pierre Sane also pointed to two landmark events - the establishment of a permanent International Criminal Court and the arrest in October of former Chilean President Augusto Pinochet--which could help make human rights violators answerable.

Amnesty also singled out the United States as the only country known to have executed juvenile offenders in 1998.

***

Document

CONGRESSIONAL RECORD -- EXTENSIONS

Thursday, June 17, 1999
106th Congress, 1st Session
145 Cong Rec E 1317

REFERENCE: Vol. 145, No. 86
TITLE: INDIA IS USING CHEMICAL WEAPONS IN KASHMIR; U.S.
SHOULD STOP ITS PRO-INDIA TILT

HON. EDOLPHUS TOWNS
of New York
in the House of Representatives
Thursday, June 17, 1999

Mr. TOWNS. Mr. Speaker, I was disturbed to find out that India has been using chemical weapons in its war against the freedom fighters of Kashmir. Reuters, CNN, the BBC, the Associated Press, and others have all reported that India fired chemical weapons shells into Pakistan. Remember that India's nuclear tests last year started the nuclear arms race in South Asia, which is very destabilizing to our ally Pakistan, to India, the subcontinent, and the world.

In recent days, there have been news reports of a mass exodus from border villages in Punjab, the homeland of the Sikhs. According to at least one report, 70 percent of the population of these villages has fled. These Sikhs are apparently afraid that India's war on the freedom fighters will spread to Punjab. There are good reasons to believe this. India sent a new deployment of troops to Punjab, Khalistan. These troops are on top of the half-million troops who were already stationed in Punjab to suppress the Sikh freedom movement.

Mr. Speaker, this situation is entirely India's responsibility. India that started the conflict in Kargil to wipe out the freedom movement in Kashmir and scare the other freedom movements into submitting to Indian rule. India introduced nuclear weapons to South Asia last year and introduced chemical weapons into this conflict. These are weapons of mass destruction, Mr. Speaker. Indian has brought these weapons of mass destruction to South Asia. Why do we still give aid from American tax dollars to India?

Recently an Indian colonel admitted that Indian soldiers are "dying like dogs." India is losing this war in Kargil, while it loudly proclaims victory. As India's desperation increases, the situations gets more dangerous. It is feared that India will use its new deployment in Punjab, Khalistan to invade Pakistan in an attempt to cut off the Kashmiris' supply lines.

Mr. Speaker, we all salute the President for his attempt to keep the fighting from escalating, but there seems to be a pro-India tilt to our effort and to our policy in the region. Yet India denies self- determination and other basic human rights to the Kashmiris, the Sikhs of Khalistan, the Christians of Nagaland, and the other occupied nations of South Asia. When basic human rights are denied, we have an obligation to help people reclaim their rights. We should be working for peace, freedom, and self-determination. We should not be aligned with India, which remains one of the world's worst human-rights violators.

Let this Congress do whatever we can to support democracy, self-determination, peace, and stability in the subcontinent. We should impose sanctions on India, cut off American aid to India, and pass a resolution stating our support for a free and fair plebiscite under international supervision in Punjab, Khalistan, in Kashmir, in Nagaland, and everywhere else that the people seek their freedom. I am proud to have co-sponsored such a resolution in the last Congress. This is the right time to take these measures when they will have the greatest effect. Let us take these measures to support freedom.

Mr. Speaker, I would like to insert the Council of Khalistan's press release on India's chemical weapons use into the Record.

India Using Chemical Weapons in Its War Against Kashmiri Freedom Fighters; Now Is the Time to Free Khalistan

Washington, DC, June 14--Dr. Gurmit Singh Aulakh, President of the Council of Khalistan, today condemned India for using chemical weapons in its war against the Kashmiri freedom fighters at Kargil. Reuters, BBC, CNN, Associated Press, and other news sources have reported that India fired chemical weapons shells into Pakistan. The Pakistani Foreign Minister said that his country had found Indian chemical shells that were fired across the border.

Dr. Aulakh condemned "this irresponsible and dangerous action. India is using these weapons despite being a signatory to the Chemical Weapons Convention," he noted. "So far these weapons have only caused skin irritations, shortness of breath, and other minor health problems," he said, "but the potential dangers are frightening."

"Remember that India started this war to suppress the Kashmiri freedom movement," Dr. Aulakh said. He took note of an India Today report that the war is costing India 15 core (150 million) rupees each day. "Apparently, no amount of blood or money is too great for the Indian government," he said.

"America took action against Iraq for using chemical weapons in its war against Kuwait," he pointed out. "Why does America continue to support India with aid and trade?," he asked. "The United Nations should impose strong sanctions on India for this brutal act," he added.

"The news that India is using chemical weapons is very disturbing, not only to the people of Kashmir but to the people of Punjab, Khalistan," he said. "India, the country which started the nuclear arms race in South Asia, is now using weapons of mass destruction," he said. According to Kashmiri leaders, India also used chemical weapons against them in 1994.

"This terrorist act shows India's desperation to keep its artificial borders intact," Dr. Aulakh said. "India is losing this war," he said. "One Indian Army colonel admitted that Indian troops are dying like dogs.' I call on Sikh soldiers not to fire on Kashmiri freedom fighters," he said. "I urge Sikh soldiers to join the Sikh freedom movement and liberate Khalistan."

"I cannot help but think that these attacks are related to the massive evacuations of 37 villages along the border in Punjab," he said. "It is not

the Pakistanis the villagers are afraid of," he said, "it is expansion of India's terrorist war into Punjab, Khalistan."

"In war, people get killed, and that is unfortunate," Dr. Aulakh said. "Countries that are moral and democratic do not deliberately kill civilians," he said. The Indian government has murdered over 250,000 Sikhs since 1984. India has also murdered over 200,000 Christians in Nagaland since 1947, more than 60,000 Muslims in Kashmir since 1988, and tens of thousands of Assamese, Manipuris, Dalits ("black untouchables"), Tamils, and others.

"Freedom struggles don't go away," he said. "Just as India cannot suppress Kashmir's freedom struggle with weapons of mass destruction, the freedom struggle in Khalistan will go on until Khalistan is free," he said. "Now is the moment for the Sikh Nation to liberate Khalistan with the help of the Sikh soldiers. It is time to rebel. Khalsa Bagi Yan Badshah."

***

Document

CONGRESSIONAL RECORD -- EXTENSIONS

Wednesday, June 16, 1999
106th Congress, 1st Session
145 Cong Rec E 1281

REFERENCE: Vol. 145, No. 85
TITLE: INDIAN COLONEL: TROOPS "DYING LIKE DOGS"

HON. EDOLPHUS TOWNS
of New York
in the House of Representatives
Wednesday, June 16, 1999

Mr. TOWNS. Mr. Speaker, all of us have been following with alarm the Indian attack on the Kashmiri freedom fighters at Kargil and Dras. India has been losing many of its troops in this desperate effort to crush the freedom movements within its borders. Casualties are mounting. The soldiers they sent to discharge this dirty war are demoralized. According to the Associated Press, an Indian colonel said that Indian troops "are dying like dogs." A corporal is quoted as saying "Even in war we don't have such senseless casualties."

Unfortunately, Mr. Speaker, most of these troops are Sikhs and other minorities sent to die for India's effort to suppress the freedom of all the minorities. These Sikh troops should not be fighting for India; they should be working to free their own country.

Now there has been a new deployment of troops in Punjab. A mass exodus from villages in Punjab is underway because the villagers are justifiably afraid that India's war against the freedom movements will spread to their homeland.

India reportedly also used chemical weapons in this conflict, despite being a signatory to the Chemical Weapons Convention. India has a record of escalating the situation with regard to weapons of mass destructions. India began the nuclear arms race in South Asia by conducting underground nuclear tests.

There are steps that we can take to make sure that this conflict does not spread and that all the peoples and nations of South Asia are allowed to live in freedom. We should impose strict sanctions on India, the aggressor in this conflict. We should stop providing American aid to India and we should support a free and fair vote on national self- determination not only in Kashmir, Punjab (Khalistan), Nagaland, and the other countries held by India.

I thank my friend Dr. Gurmit Singh Aulakh for bringing this situation to my attention, and I urge India to allow the basic human right of national self-determination to all the people of South Asia.

Mr. Speaker, I place the Associated Press article on the conflict in the Record.

"We are dying like dogs," said one Indian Army colonel *Black Mood Hovers Over Kashmir* *(By Hema Shukla)*

DRASS, Kashmir--June 11, 1999 (AP): On the eve of talks aimed at ending a month of fighting in Kashmir, a black mood is
settling over Indian army camps on the front line. Casualties are mounting. Troops are ill-equipped for high-altitude fighting. The task, they say, is close to suicidal.

Since early May, the army has mobilized its largest fighting force in nearly 30 years against what India says are infiltrators from Pakistan who have occupied mountain peaks on India's side of the 1972 cease-fire line in disputed Kashmir.

On Saturday, Pakistan will send its foreign minister to New Delhi to discuss whether the fighting can be ended. India says that regardless of the talks it will persist until the last intruder is killed or flees back to Pakistan.

In daily briefings in New Delhi, military spokesmen report the fighters are being driven back. Indian airstrikes are punishing them, peaks are being recovered, the "enemy" is taking casualties in the hundreds. India's official casualty rate on Friday stood at about 70 dead and 200 wounded. The story on the front is much different.

In the fading evening light in a forward artillery camp, at checkpoints along a road under steady artillery bombardment, in bunkers where men shelter from showers of shrapnel, soldiers and junior officers grimly tell stories of death and defeat on the mountains. No one can say how many have died, but no one believes the official toll.

Amid the gloom, however, the Indian troops show a gritty determination to fight and a conviction that the opposing forces must be evicted at all costs. "We have a job to do and we will do the best we can," said one officer. "We will do our duty."

India says the guerrillas in Kashmir are mostly Pakistani soldiers, a charge Islamabad denies.

On Friday, India produced what it said were transcripts of telephone conversations between two Pakistani generals that proved Pakistan was involved in the fighting. In a transcript from May 26, army chief Pervez Musharraf tells another general that Prime Minister Nawaz Sharif was concerned the fighting could escalate into a full-scale war.

"We gave the suggestion that there was no such fear," Musharraf said he told Sharif, according to the transcript. "Whenever you want, we can regulate it."

Pakistan called the transcripts false. "This can't be given any credence or weight," Pakistan army spokesman Brig. Rashid Quereshi said.

As officials traded charges, heavy fighting continued in Kashmir. The guerrillas are entrenched on the mountain peaks defending their positions against soldiers scaling steep slopes, constantly exposed to gunfire and rocket-propelled grenades. "We are dying like dogs," said one colonel. Recapturing the peaks, said another officer, is "almost a suicide mission." None of the officers could be quoted by name, and senior officers who earlier briefed journalists on condition of anonymity have been ordered not to speak.

"This is worse than war. Even in war we don't have such senseless casualties," said M. Singh, a corporal and a veteran of India's campaign in Sri Lanka in the 1980s. Some of the casualties are from "friendly fire," either from Indian artillery or aerial bombing meant to provide cover to the advancing troops, officers said. The risk increased after the air force began high-altitude bombing to stay out of range of shoulder-fired anti-aircraft missiles. Indian troops wade through chest-high snow. The wind is so strong soldiers must be tied to each other with rope so they don't get blown over a cliff. Their opponents can pick them off with rifles or simply send boulders cascading down the mountain on top of them. One major said his unit was returning down the mountain when it came under withering fire from above. The soldiers dove into the icy water of a Himalayan river to escape.

Some forward units are living on one meal a day, the soldiers said. Mess camps in the rear cook puris--deep fried flat bread--but by the time it is delivered to the front it is frozen and can barely be chewed. The only drinking water is melted snow. There is no chance to pitch tents on the slopes. The men sleep in the open.

Few troops have had time to adjust to altitudes of 14,000 feet or more, where the air is thin and every exertion, every upward step, leaves strong men gasping.

Despite the difficulties, the tremendous pressure to recapture the peaks continues.

***

Document

CONGRESSIONAL RECORD -- EXTENSIONS

Tuesday, May 25, 1999
106th Congress, 1st Session
145 Cong Rec E 1076

REFERENCE: Vol. 145, No. 76
TITLE: INDIA'S ANTI-AMERICANISM REVEALED AS DEFENSE MINISTER
ATTACKS AMERICA

HON. LINCOLN DIAZ-BALART
of Florida
in the House of Representatives
Tuesday, May 25, 1999

Mr. DIAZ-BALART. Mr. Speaker, I was disturbed to hear that the Defense Minister of India, George Fernandes, led a meeting of some of the world's most repressive regimes at which they agreed that their main goal was to "stop the United States," according to the Indian Express. Fernandes himself called the United States "vulgarly arrogant." This should offend anyone who cares about this country.

Countries represented at this meeting, according to the newspaper, were Communist China--which has been stealing American nuclear secrets and pouring illegal money into our political campaigns, Libya, Russia, Serbia--the country we are currently fighting, Saddam Hussein's Iraq, and Castro's Cuba. Now, Mr. Speaker, I know a bit about Cuba. Castro's dictatorship in Cuba is one of the most brutal in the world. It has killed and tortured thousands of its opponents.

By now, we all know the stories of how the Indian government has killed tens of thousands of Christians, Sikhs, Muslims, Dalit untouchables, and others. Just in recent months, I am informed that an Australian missionary named Graham Staines and his two young sons were burned to death in their Jeep by a militant theocratic Hindu Nationalist gang affiliated with the RSS, which is also, I am told, the parent organization of the ruling BJP. I am informed that there are 17 freedom movements in India and the ongoing political instability there may be bringing India's breakup close. We should support the peaceful struggle for freedom throughout India.

India destablized South Asia with its nuclear weapons' tests. It was a close ally of the Soviet Union and supported the invasion of Afghanistan. I am told that it has the most anti-American voting record of any country in the United Nations with the exception of Cuba. Why does a government like that continue to receive aid from the United States?

Mr. Speaker, the time has come to stop supporting governments that actively work against us. We should cut off all American aid to India and declare our support for the freedom movements through democratic plebiscites. These are important steps to extend the hand of freedom to the people of South Asia.

***

Document

CONGRESSIONAL RECORD -- EXTENSIONS

Thursday, May 20, 1999
106th Congress, 1st Session
145 Cong Rec E 1050

REFERENCE: Vol. 145, No. 74
TITLE: SIKH JOURNALIST GRILLED BY INDIAN INTELLIGENCE
OFFICERS--THERE IS NO FREEDOM OF THE PRESS IN INDIA

HON. EDOLPHUS TOWNS
of New York
in the House of Representatives
Thursday, May 20, 1999

Mr. TOWNS. Mr. Speaker, India claims that it is democratic, but one of the cornerstones of democracy is freedom of the press. A recent event shows us again that there is no freedom of the press in India.

On May 11, Sukhbir Singh Osan, a journalist who has written for many papers in India and runs the website Burning Punjab, was interrogated by Indian intelligence officers for 45 minutes after he returned from a trip to the United States, Canada, and Great Britain. He came to cover the big Sikh marches in Washington, New York, and Toronto and to deliver a speech on the persecution of Christians that has been going on since Christmas Day.

Apparently, this coverage upset the Indian oligarchy. The intelligence officers who came to Mr. Osan's house said that they had "specific instructions from Delhi."

Mr. Osan has been targeted by the Indian government before. He was denied a degree he earned. His telephone has been bugged and he has received threats. He is not the only one. Reporters who exposed government abuses have received telephone threats. One reporter was told that "it is dangerous to report against the government." That was under a Congress Party government. The government controls the television and radio as well as Press Trust of India (PTI) and United News of India (UNI). How can you have a democracy if the government controls the media and tries to intimidate reporters who report news that they don't want to come out?

I thank my friend Dr. Gurmit Singh Aulakh, President of the Council of Khalistan, for bringing this story to my attention. His office issued an excellent press release on the grilling of Mr. Osan, which I believe will be very informative to my colleagues.

How can the United States continue to support a country that claims to be democratic but does not allow freedom of the press, kills tens of thousands over their religious beliefs, joins with the world's most notorious tyrants at the United Nations against the U.S., celebrates the anniversary of its nuclear explosion, routinely violates basic human rights, and will not even allow a simple vote on the political future of the minority nations seeking their freedom? Why should such a country be a major recipient of American aid and trade? We should stop our aid to India until it respects basic human rights and we should publicly declare our support for the 17 freedom movements within India's borders.

I place the Council of Khalistan's press release on the grilling of Mr. Osan into the Record.

Journalist Grilled by Indian Intelligence Officers
There is No Freedom of the Press in India

Washington, D.C., May 12--Sikh journalist Sukhbir Singh Osan, who runs the website Burning Punjab, was interrogated by Indian intelligence officers after returning from a trip to the United States, Canada, and Great Britain, where he covered the Sikh 300th anniversary marches in Washington, New York, and Toronto and made a speech on "Recent Attacks on the Christian Community in India."

Intelligence officers grilled Mr. Osan at his home yesterday for over 45 minutes. They claimed that "we have specific instructions from Delhi." Mr. Osan stated that this action is "true to their anti-Sikh stance."

Mr. Osan has previously had his telephone bugged by the Indian government. He was denied a degree he earned because he has exposed corruption, atrocities, and acts of terrorism by the Indian government. He has received anonymous telephone threats.

"The interrogation of Sukhbir Singh Osan shows that there is no freedom of the press in India," said Dr. Gurmit Singh Aulakh, President of the Council of Khalistan. "Both Press Trust of India (PTI) and United News of India (UNI) are completely controlled by the Indian government," Dr. Aulakh stated. Noting that Mr. Osan has met lawmakers in both the U.S. and Canada, Dr. Aulakh said that "any more harassment of Mr. Osan will cause India big trouble."

"Reporters who put out information contrary to the government line are often threatened and harassed as Mr. Osan was yesterday," he said. "Reporters who have exposed government corruption and brutality have received anonymous telephone calls telling them that it is dangerous to report against the government,' " Dr. Aulakh said.

Mr. Aulakh urged the United States government to stop supporting the government of India. "India has joined with China, Russia, Cuba, and Libya in action against the U.S. at the United Nations," he noted. "India tried to build a security alliance against the United States. It recently celebrated the anniversary of its nuclear explosion and reiterated its refusal to sign the Comprehensive Test Ban Treaty. India is a major human-rights violator. Amnesty International has not been allowed into the country since 1978," he pointed out. "Yet it remains one of the top recipients of U.S. aid."

The Indian government has murdered more than 250,000 Sikhs since 1984, over 200,000 Christians in Nagaland since 1988, more than 60,000 Muslims in Kashmir since 1988, and tens of thousands of As-

samese, Manipuris, Tamils, Dalit *"untouchables,"* and others. Tens of thousands of Sikhs languish in Indian jails without charge or trial, some since 1984.

"Why should the American taxpayers be forced to support a country where there is no religious freedom, no freedom of the press, and no human rights for minorities?" he asked. *"Why should America support a country that is so vehemently anti-American?"* he said. *"The time has come for America to defend freedom in South Asia by defending Mr. Osan and other journalists, by cutting off aid to India, and by supporting the 17 freedom movements within India's artificial borders,"* Dr. Aulakh said.

***

Document

CONGRESSIONAL RECORD -- EXTENSIONS

Thursday, May 20, 1999
106th Congress, 1st Session
145 Cong Rec E 1052

REFERENCE: Vol. 145, No. 74
TITLE: INDIAN INTELLIGENCE INTERROGATES REPORTER AFTER VISIT TO AMERICA

HON. JOHN T. DOOLITTLE
of California
in the House of Representatives
Thursday, May 20, 1999

Mr. DOOLITTLE. Mr. Speaker, India has once again shown true nature of its democracy by grilling a reporter who visited the United States. Journalist Sukhbir Singh Osan has exposed the corruption and the atrocities of the Indian government in newspapers and through his website, Burning Punjab. He visited the United States, Canada, and Great Britain to cover the Sikh 300th anniversary marches and speak on human rights. He met with my colleague from Indiana, Mr. Burton, and with a minister in the Canadian government. Their pictures appear on his website.

Mr. Osan returned to his home in Chandigarh before Indian intelligence officers showed up at his house to interrogate him for 45 minutes, claiming they were acting on instructions from the central government in New Delhi. This is not the first time the Indian government has gone after Mr. Osan. He has received anonymous threats and has been denied a law degree that he worked hard to earn because he had written news stories that the Indian government didn't like.

Dr. Gurmit Singh Aulakh, President of the Council of Khalistan, brought this to my attention. I understand that Dr. Aulakh has notified the Committee to Protect Journalists in New York of Mr. Osan's mistreatment.

What happened to Mr. Osan is not just an isolated incident. Other reporters have been threatened for reporting stories critical of the Indian government. Clearly, there is no press freedom in India despite its loud and frequent boasts that it is "the world's largest democracy."

Does a democratic country harass reporters for covering stories that the government doesn't like? Would a democratic country incite 17 freedom movements within its borders? India is a democracy only for the Brahmin ruling class. It is also anti-American, working with such models of democracy as China, Libya, and Cuba to undermine U.S. foreign policy. It approached China and Russia trying to build a triangular "security alliance" against America.

We should treat India as we do other violators of religious freedom. That will help to end the kind of abuse that Mr. Osan and his fellow Sikhs suffer and bring real freedom to all the nations and peoples living within India's Borders.

I am placing the Burning Punjab story on Mr. Osan's harassment into the Record for the information of my colleagues.

Intelligence Agencies Grill Sukhbir Singh Osan

Chandigarh.--True to their anti-Sikh stance, the Indian Intelligence Agencies have again started harassment of innocents. Punjab based journalist, Sukhbir Singh Osan, who recently visited Unites States, Canada and United Kingdom for the purpose of participating in a human right convention to read a paper on the subject "Recent attacks on Christian community in India" and covering the 300 year celebrations of the Khalsa community was grilled by the intelligence sleuths for more than forty-five minutes at his residence on May 11. When Mr. Osan asked the DSP Intelligence Bureau as to why he was questioning him about his visits abroad, the said DSP replied, "Delhi wants to know all about it." When again asked whether there were any written instructions, he replied that "we have specific instructions from Delhi". However, nothing in writing was given to Mr. Osan.

***

Document

CONGRESSIONAL RECORD -- EXTENSIONS

Wednesday, May 19, 1999
106th Congress, 1st Session
145 Cong Rec E 1031

REFERENCE: Vol. 145, No. 73
TITLE: INDIAN DEFENSE MINISTER'S STATEMENT SHOWS THAT INDIA IS ANTI-AMERICAN

HON. EDOLPHUS TOWNS
of New York
in the House of Representatives
Wednesday, May 19, 1999

Mr. TOWNS. Mr. Speaker, we knew that India was a repressive tyranny. Now they have shown us how anti-American they are. I was offended by an article in the May 18 issue of the Indian Express, which Dr. Gurmit Singh Aulakh, President of the Council of Khalistan, shared with me. In the article, the Indian Defense Minister, a man named George Fernandes, describes the United States as "vulgarly arrogant" and accused the United States and NATO of "aggression against Yugoslavia."

The meeting he was addressing, which was called by India, was also attended by representatives from China, Cuba, Yugoslavia, Russia, Libya, and Iraq, which leads me to wonder where the North Koreans were. They belong in this motley collection of America-bashers as much as any of these other countries.

The article says that everyone at the meeting agreed that "We have to stop the U.S. It started with Iraq, now Yugoslavia. We don't know who's next." The Russian Ambassador asked "India and China to join us in stopping U.S. attempts to dominate the world."

I would like to remind my colleagues that India is one of the largest recipients of American foreign aid. Does this sound to you like a country we should be supporting with the tax dollars of the American people? It doesn't sound like that kind of country to me.

Remember that it was India that started the nuclear arms race in South Asia by setting off five nuclear devices. It is India that refuses to sign the Comprehensive Test Ban Treaty. India has attacked Pakistan twice and invaded Sri Lanka once.

Whether or not one agrees with President Clinton's policy in Kosovo, we went there to stop the "ethnic cleansing" of the Kosovars by the Serbian government. Yet we have averted our glance from a similar campaign throughout India, a situation the Indian Supreme Court described as "worse than a genocide." This ethnic cleansing has taken the lives of over 250,000 Sikhs since 1984, over 200,000 Christians in Nagaland since 1947, over 60,000 Muslims in Kashmir since 1988, and thousands upon thousands of Dalits, Assamese, Manipuris, Tamils, and other minority peoples. India claims that it is democratic, but there is not democracy for these and other minorities. Currently, there are 17 independence movements in the nations under Indian control. Now India is joining with some of the world's most tyrannical police states in a joint effort to "stop the U.S." Not only that, but the so-called "world's largest democracy" organized the meeting.

We must stop funneling American money to countries that are repressive and are conspiring with our enemies against this country. We should place stringent economic sanctions on India to stop the repression and the anti-American activities, and we should apply every kind of peaceful pressure that we can to secure for the minority peoples and nations of South Asia the right to determine their own futures democratically in a free and fair vote, not by the force of Indian bayonets. This is our duty to the people of the world. We must begin today.

I would like my colleagues to read the Indian Express article, which is alarming, so I would like to submit it for the Record.

George Leads Envoys in Bashing A Vulgarly Arrogant US

New Delhi, May 17: Yugoslavia, Iraq, Cuba, Libya, Russia, China-- and India. That these countries produce the world's finest boxers probably had something to do with a session of US-bashing inside stuffy, old Sapru House in Delhi today. And also that each one of them have had a diplomatic disagreement with the US some time or the other. Defence Minister George Fernandes' Samata Party had organised the meeting "to denounce the US-led NATO's aggression on Yugoslavia". Fernandes, typically led from the front against a "much stronger and a vulgarly arrogant United States" since the days of the Vietnam war. Envoys from the other six countries to India added a long list of adjectives in the same vein.

"We have to stop the US," agreed everyone, "It started with Iraq, now Yugoslavia. We don't know who's next." In their anxiety, and in their furious speeches, there were subtle messages being put across. Like Yugoslav Ambassador Cedomir Strbac's statement that Belgrade was ready to "guarantee all Kosovars substantial autonomy" in accordance with international standards.

"But only if NATO stops its air strikes and a political dialogue is initiated in accordance with Gandhinan principles. We are ready to accept a solution which respects our freedom, sovereignty and territorial integrity," he said.

Others said the Cold War may be over, and the USSR may have disintegrated, but watch out for a new world order. "They (the US) are showing Russia and others what they can do. We want India and China to join us in stopping US attempts to dominate the world. The equation is: To be, or not to be," said Russian Ambassador Albert S. Tchernshyev.

"The forthcoming 21st century should not witness a unipolar world," added China's political counsellor Liu Jenfeng, venting China's anger over NATO's bombing the Chinese embassy in Belgrade which left three dead and 20 injured.

The ambassadors from Cuba, Libya and Iraq narrated their stories to express support for "Yugoslavia's resilience". "How can they pretend to solve a conflict by using destructive weapons themselves. For 38 years, they have held us to ransom with embargos," said Cuban Ambassador Olga Chamero Trias. "We have been called terrorists and law-breakers all these years. Now who is breaking the law?" said Libyan Ambassador Nuri Al-Fituri El-Madani. "People in Kosovo are becoming refugees because they are fleeing from the bombing, not because there is ethnic cleansing. We in Iraq know what it means to live in the middle of bombs exploding all around," said Iraqi ambassador Salah Al- Mukhtar.

George Fernandes agreed, and summarised. He said the US has run away from all norms set by the United Nations. "The UN hardly has a say these days, America merely wished its way to doing what it's doing. Therefore, we (referring to Russia, China, India, Libya, Cuba, Iraq and Libya) who represent more than half the world's population must get together to stop the US-led NATO hegemony."

He pointed out that the new doctrine adopted by NATO on its 50th anniversary on April 23, when Yugoslav towns were being bombed, made it clear that the military alliance was free to attack any sovereign country if it "thought that country was doing or was likely to do anything against the interests of any NATO country". Fernandes added: "That the United States is the author of this doctrine does not need to be emphasised here."

At the end of it all, inside the stuffy, old auditorium, an emotional Yugoslav ambassador Strbac stood up and said "Jai Hind".

***

Document

CONGRESSIONAL RECORD -- EXTENSIONS

Wednesday, April 14, 1999
106th Congress, 1st Session
145 Cong Rec E 649

REFERENCE: Vol. 145, No. 51
TITLE: SIKHS OBSERVE 300TH BAISAKHI BY MARCHING FOR
FREEDOM

HON. JOHN T. DOOLITTLE
of California
in the House of Representatives
Wednesday, April 14, 1999

Mr. DOOLITTLE. Mr. Speaker, I would like to take this opportunity to join some of my colleagues in wishing a happy 300th Baisakhi Day to the Sikh Nation. The contributions that Sikhs have made to American life have been significant. They have added to almost every walk of American life.

On April 10, the Sikhs marched in celebration of the 300th Baisakhi anniversary of the day of the last of the 10 Gurus, Guru Gobind Singh, initiated the Khalsa Panth. I understand that it was a glorious event for the Sikh nation, and I would like to congratulate the Sikhs of America and my friend Dr. Gurmit Singh Aulakh, who was the march coordinator, on its success.

I understand that the parade looked like a sea of saffron (the Sikh color of freedom) as it moved from the Lincoln Memorial to the Capitol and that the grounds outside here on the West Front were filled with over 40,000 enthusiastic Sikhs. It must have been something to see!

It is appropriate that the march began at the memorial to Abraham Lincoln, issuer of the Emancipation Proclamation. The Sikh Nation struggles for their freedom, as instructed by the Sikh Gurus. Sikhs are instructed to oppose tyranny wherever it occurs.

The Sikhs are a proud people, and justifiably so. They are a people dedicated to living a holy life, working hard, sharing with those in need, and to the equality of all people and freedom for everyone. Unfortunately, in their own homeland, Sikhs do not enjoy freedom. They have been subjected to tyranny. The Indian Government has also oppressed other minorities, such as Christians, Muslims, and Dalits (the so-called "untouchables"). Yet India proudly proclaims itself a democracy.

We cannot make India behave like a truly democratic country, but we can apply pressure by withholding aid and by publicly declaring our support for a democratic vote in Punjab, Khalistan, and other Indian states on the subject of self-determination. If India is truly democratic, this is the way it should settle these issues.

The Governors of New Jersey and Texas have declared the "Year of the Khalsa." Numerous Members of Congress from both parties have saluted the Sikhs on this historic anniversary. The new Mayor of Washington, D.C. sent congratulatory remarks. As Sikhs move into their fourth century, they should celebrate their next anniversary in freedom in their own sovereign, independent country. Let us honor their history and their struggle by supporting their effort to be free.

I would like to add Mayor Williams' letter of congratulations to the Record.

Congratulations, Council of Khalistan--"Recognize Ye All The Human Race As One" 300th Anniversary, April 10, 1999

As Mayor of the District of Columbia, it is my distinct pleasure to extend warm greetings and congratulations to the members, guest and friends of the Council of Khalistan as you celebrate your 300th Anniversary of the initiation of the Khalsa Panth.

This is a significant milestone in the history of the Sikh Nation as you celebrate this Vaisaakhee Day. Sikhism is the youngest of the world's religion, and it is humility and service to mankind that are regarded as most important. Religion plays an important role in our daily lives, and you are to be commended for your efforts to provide spiritual enhancement to your membership, service to the community and commitment to the principles of peace, progress, dignity, integrity, human rights and justice for all.

On behalf of the residents of the District of Columbia, thank you for making a difference in our lives and best wishes in your quest for holy fulfillment. Anthony A. Williams,
Mayor, District of Columbia.

***

Document

CONGRESSIONAL RECORD -- EXTENSIONS

Tuesday, April 13, 1999
106th Congress, 1st Session
145 Cong Rec E 621

REFERENCE: Vol. 145, No. 50
TITLE: SIKHS MARCH TO CELEBRATE 300TH BAISAKHI DAY

HON. EDOLPHUS TOWNS
of New York
in the House of Representatives
Tuesday, April 13, 1999

Mr. TOWNS. Mr. Speaker, on Saturday, April 10, the Sikhs of the United States marched to celebrate the 300th anniversary of the initiation of the Khalsa Panth. The march, which was led by Dr. Gurmit Singh Aulakh and the Council of Khalistan, was a celebration of all the Sikhs in this country. Similar celebrations have been held or are being held in other countries. This was a major milestone for the Sikh Nation. I congratulate the Khalsa Panth (Sikh Nation) on their auspicious 300th Baisakhi Day.

The Sikhs received congratulations from several of my colleagues including our own Minority Whip, and also from the Mayor of Washington, DC, Anthony Williams. I note that the Governors of Texas and New Jersey have also proclaimed "the Year of the Khalsa." It is good to see such bipartisan support for the Sikhs, who are being subjected to brutal atrocities and repression in India. Justice Ajit Singh Bains, Chairman of the Punjab Human Rights Organization, and General Narinder Singh from Punjab, Khalistan, spoke to the event. Their remarks were very well received, from what I am told.

I wish I could have joined my Sikh friends at this march, but I was not able to do so. I would like to take this opportunity to congratulate them on this important anniversary. I look forward to greeting many of them at the upcoming Vaisakhi Day parade in New York.

This anniversary has attracted worldwide attention. The Washington Post and many other important media outlets covered this event. At this march, the Sikhs of America raised their voices loudly for freedom.

The heritage of the Sikh Nation is freedom. They ruled Punjab from 1765 to 1849. It was noted at the march that the last of the Sikh Gurus, Guru Gobind Singh, gave them a sense of national identity 300 years ago. It was pointed out that every day the Sikhs pray that they shall again rule their homeland, Punjab, Khalistan.

Sikhs are a separate people, both religiously and culturally. They are not a part of Hindu India. No Sikh representative has ever signed the Indian constitution.

Many of us in this House, from both parties, have been calling for an end to American aid to India until it respects basic human rights and for a free and fair vote on the political status of Punjab, as well as notes on the status of Kashmir, Nagaland, and all the nations living under Indian rule. This auspicious anniversary would be a good time to renew that call and renew our efforts to bring freedom, peace, and prosperity to all the people of South Asia.

I insert the Washington Post article in the Record.

From the Washington Post, Apr. 11, 1999
Sikhs Parade and Pray for Separate Nation
(By Caryle Murphy)

Chanting praises to their greatest guru and walking behind a giant model of their Golden Temple, several thousand Sikhs marched down Constitution Avenue yesterday to celebrate the 300th anniversary of their religion's most sacred event, the creation of the first community of Sikh believers.

Five bearded Sikh priests bearing long daggers and dressed in saffron-hued turbans, led the colorful Khalsa March '99 from the Lincoln Memorial to the Capitol. A float carried the Sikh scripture, Granth, which was covered by a silver canopy decorated with flowers.

The march, which drew many of the Washington area's 7,000 Sikhs and others from across the country, was mainly to honor Sikhism.

"I came to celebrate our religion and what it's given to humanity," said Permeil Dass, 24, of Cleveland, who works in a community computer center.

"Our religion is very modern," she added, noting that it opposes inequality between human beings, the worship of idols and use of intoxicants.

But yesterday's day-long event was as much political as religious, with speakers at a pre-parade rally calling for an independent Sikh nation--to be named Khalistan--in the northwest Indian state of Punjab, home of the Sikh religion. The Indian government opposes a separate Sikh state in Punjab.

"In the Sikh religion, religion and politics are inseparable," said Gurmit Singh Aulakh, head of the District-based Council of Khalistan, one of the groups sponsoring yesterday's event. "We are aware that without political power no religion can flourish."

Among the banners carried in the parade were ones that said, "To Save Sikhism, Sikhs Want-Khalistan" and "A Sikh Nation, On the Move."

In an interview, San Diego resident Harinder Singh indicated that nationalism, as much as religious devotion, had brought him to yesterday's event.

"This is the least we can do to have some political voice around the world," the 36-year-old software engineer said. The message he hoped to deliver, he added, was that "sooner or later Khalistan is going to happen."

On Friday, the Indian Embassy's Deputy Chief of Mission T.P. Sreenivasan, said celebrations of the Sikh religion are "something we heartily support."

As for political demands voiced at the parade, Sreenivasan added: "This is a free country. But that is not the purpose of the march."

In a 1984 crackdown on Sikh militants, Indian police raided their Golden Temple at Amritsar. In retaliation, Sikh bodyguards killed Indian Prime Minister Indira Gandhi five months later.

Yesterday's event, which Aulakh estimated drew 25,000 Sikhs, commemorated the day in 1699 when the 10th and greatest Sikh teacher, Guru Gobind Singh, initiated Khalsa Panth, the "Brotherhood of the Pure."

Khalsa Panth is the community of those who commit themselves to the tenets of Sikhism. In creating Khalsa Panth, Gobind broadened authority within the religion and took the final step, Sikhs believe, in the centuries-long establishment of their religion, which began in the 1400s with the first Sikh teacher, Guru Nanak.

Before yesterday's march, the Sikhs gathered in front of the Lincoln Memorial, where many waved small U.S. flags and saffron-colored flags with the blue Sikh symbol of Khalsa. On state, musicians played Sikh songs on the harmonium and drums called "tabla."

Dressed in long, flowing tunics with matching pantaloons, women wound their way up a red carpet to kneel and kiss their holy scripture, dropping offerings of a dollar or two. Later, all stood in place with hands folded and heads bowed for a communal prayer. Then it was time to march.

***

Document

CONGRESSIONAL RECORD -- EXTENSIONS

Tuesday, April 13, 1999
106th Congress, 1st Session
145 Cong Rec E 623

REFERENCE: Vol. 145, No. 50
TITLE: CONGRATULATING THE SIKH NATION ON ITS 300th BAISAKHI
DAY SELF-DETERMINATION FOR THE SIKHS

HON. GARY A. CONDIT
of California
in the House of Representatives
Tuesday, April 13, 1999

Mr. CONDIT. Mr. Speaker, on April 14, the Sikh Nation will celebrate its 300th Baisakhi Day. This is a major milestone for the Sikhs of America and the world, and I would like to take this opportunity to congratulate them on this occasion.

More than 40,000 Sikhs came to Washington, D.C. this past weekend to celebrate with a march organized by Dr. Gurmit Singh Aulakh, President of the Council of Khalistan, who is a friend of many of ours. The march was a huge success, and I would like to congratulate Dr. Aulakh and everyone who was involved in this very successful event. Through their hard work one of the largest groups that Washington has seen in a long time showed up to celebrate the Sikh heritage and declare the need for a free and independent Khalistan.

There are about 500,000 Sikhs in the United States. They are part of a vibrant 22-million strong Sikh community around the world. They have added to America in many different fields of endeavor. Here the Sikhs live in freedom and prosperity. Yet in their homeland, Punjab, Khalistan, they suffer under the brutal tyranny of the Indian government. Under this brutal policy, the Indian government has murdered more than 250,000 Sikhs since 1984. Thousands more are held in Indian jails, most without charge or trial.

Sikhism is an independent, monotheistic, revealed religion. It is not part of any other religion, though it does have some beliefs that are also held by other religions. Like Christians and Muslims, Sikhs have been victims of the Hindu extremists who dominate Indian life. Like Christians and Muslims, Sikhs are religiously and culturally distinct from Hindu India.

The Sikhs have a heritage of self-rule. They ruled Punjab independently from 1765 to 1849. No representative of the Sikh people has ever signed the constitution of India, 51 years after India became independent. In October 1987, Khalistan declared itself independent from India, much as we declared our own independence in 1776. They created the Council of Khalistan, headed by Dr. Gurmit Singh Aulakh, to serve as the government pro tempore and lead the peaceful struggle for independence.

What we know as India never existed before the British created it. Prior to the British conquest of South Asia, the region had many countries which ruled themselves. Just as the Soviet Union's multiethnic empire collapsed, so must India's. It is inevitable. Given India's nuclear weapons and missile development, the world must remain alert to make certain that South Asia does not become another Balkan Peninsula full of Bosnias and Kosovos. The best way to do that is to work for peaceful solutions to the region's ethnic and religious violence.

In previous Congresses, I have sponsored a resolution calling for a free and fair plebiscite under international supervision to achieve a peaceful solution to the issue of independence for Khalistan. I urge the same also for Kashmir, where it was promised by India in 1947, for Nagaland, and for all the states and regions where there are independence movements. This is the democratic way to settle these issues, and India claims to be a democracy. Let the world see Indian democracy in action by scheduling these plebiscites now. If it is good enough for the people of Puerto Rico and Quebec, it is good enough for the people of Khalistan, Kashmir, Nagaland, and the rest of South Asia.

In addition to calling for a plebiscite, we should end U.S. aid to India until basic human rights can be freely exercised by all people under India's rule and we should declare India a violator of religious liberty for the killings of Christians, Muslims, Sikhs, and others, then impose the sanctions that this status brings. If the situation changes, the sanctions can and should be lifted.

Congratulations again to the Sikhs on their 300th anniversary. May this occasion mark not just an anniversary, but a new birth of freedom in South Asia.

***

Document

CONGRESSIONAL RECORD -- EXTENSIONS

Tuesday, April 13, 1999
106th Congress, 1st Session
145 Cong Rec E 626

REFERENCE: Vol. 145, No. 50
TITLE: SIKH MARCH FOR BAISAKHI SUPPORTS FREE KHALISTAN

HON. DAN BURTON
of Indiana
in the House of Representatives
Tuesday, April 13, 1999

Mr. BURTON of Indiana. Mr. Speaker, it was my pleasure to attend the Khalsa March this past Saturday. The March celebrated the 300th anniversary of the Sikh Nation. Over 40,000 people from all over America attended this special event. I thank my friend Dr. Gurmit Singh Aulakh, President of the Council of Khalistan, for inviting me to this auspicious occasion.

There are 22 million Sikhs in the world and nearly 500,000 here in the United States. They have enriched American life in almost every walk of life, including law, farming, medicine and many other. I was interested in learning that a Sikh named Dalip Singh Saund even served in the U.S. Congress. I would like to take this opportunity to salute their contributions to this country.

Mr. Speaker, the March was truly a success. There was a tremendous amount of excitement in the air, as they celebrated their heritage of freedom and showed their support for regaining their lost sovereignty in an independent homeland they call Khalistan. Their struggle against the oppression that the Indian government inflicts on them should be supported by every American and by those who support freedom around the globe.

Mr. Speaker, the Council of Khalistan has issued a press release about the March. I would like to place this press release into the Record for the information of my colleagues.

From the Council of Khalistan, April 12, 1999
Khalsa March Very Successful--Over 40,000 Sikhs Come to Washington, DC to Celebrate 300th Anniversary of Khalsa Panth

Washington, DC, April 12.--Over 40,000 Sikhs, more than twice as many as expected, came to Washington, D.C. on Saturday, April 10 to participate in Khalsa March 1999, celebrating the 300th anniversary of the day that Guru Gobind Singh baptized the Sikh Nation. It was the first time that so many Sikh gathered in the Nation's Capital. A sea of saffron turbans and scarves could be seen around the Reflecting Pool. There are 22 million Sikhs world wide and about 500,000 here in the United States.

The mood of attendees was jubilant and excited as they celebrated the Sikh heritage. The celebration began in front of the Lincoln Memorial, which is a symbol of freedom, and the participants marched to the U.S. Capitol. The stage displayed pictures of Guru Gobind Singh Baptizing the Panj Pyaras (the Five Beloved Ones), depictions of Gurdwara Kesgarh Sahib, the birthplace of the Sikh Nation, the Golden Temple in Amritsar, the holiest Sikh shrine, other major events in Sikh history, and banners with slogans like "Indian Free Khalistan", "Long Live Khalistan", etc.

"Guru Gobind Singh gave the Sikh Nation a heritage of freedom," said Dr. Gurmit Singh Aulakh, the coordinator of the march. "Today we had a joyous celebration of that heritage," he said. "Now we must dedicate ourselves to freeing our homeland, Khalistan."

Participants in the march celebrated with family and friends and raised slogans. They carried banners that said "India Free Khalistan," "Long Live Khalistan," and "Raj Karega Khalsa." There was a float bearing a replica of the Golden Temple in Amritsar, the holiest of Sikh shrines, and another promoting "Khalistan--the Sikh Nation on the Move.

Speakers included dignitaries from Punjab, Khalistan like Justice Ajit Singh Bains, chairman of the Punjab Human Rights Organization (PHRO), and retired General Narinder Singh, as well as U.S. Congress Dan Burton (R-Ind.), Dr. Walter Landry, Executive Director of the Think-Tank for National Self- Determination, representatives of Sikh women and youth, and others.

Justice Bains discussed the genocide and human-rights violations that the Indian government has committed against the Sikh Nation since 1984. He said that there is no rule of law in Punjab. He pointed out the Indian government's policy of mass cremations of Sikhs, which the Indian supreme Court called "worse then a genocide."

General Narinder Singh spoke of the sovereignty of the Sikh Nation. He noted that Guru Gobind Singh gave the Sikh Nation sovereignty and that this sovereignty is part of the Khalsa birthright. He said that there is no reason why the Khalsa Panth should not have sovereignty.

Congressman Burton offered his continued support for the Sikh cause. He spoke against the Indian government's atrocities against Sikhs,

Christians, Muslims, and other minorities. He urged that the United States stop supporting the Indian government. He said that Sikhs should have their freedom and that the United States should support it. Many other Members of Congress sent their greetings, including House Minority Leader David Bonior (D-Mich.), Congressman Nick Rahall (D-WV), and others.

Mayor Anthony Williams of Washington, D.C. sent a message of congratulations. He wrote, "It is my distinct pleasure to extend warm greetings and congratulations to the members, guests and friends of the Council of Khalistan as you celebrate your 300th anniversary of the initiation of the Khalsa Panth. This is a significant milestone in the history of the world's religions as you celebrate Vaisaakhee Day." Mayor Williams added that "you are to be congratulated for your efforts to provide spiritual enhancement to the principles of peace, prosperity, dignity, integrity, human rights and justice for all."

Dr. Paramjit Singh Ajrawat, the Secretary of the march and Master of Ceremonies at the Lincoln Memorial, reminded the audience that Guru Gobind Singh created the Khalsa and recognized the whole human race as equal, including gender equality. He noted that Abraham Lincoln also worked to end slavery.

Attendees passed resolutions to reiterate their support for a free Khalistan, the Sikh homeland that was declared independent on October 7, 1987; to honor Sikh martyrs; to ask the Indian government to release the tens of thousands of Sikh political prisoners it is holding; and to demand that the Akal Takht, the seat of the Sikh religion, be freed from the Badal government, asking the Khalsa Panth to boycott and oppose the Badal government; asking the Khalsa Panth to boycott and oppose the Badal government; and to declare there full support for Jathedar Bhai Ranjit Singh as the genuine Jathedar of the Akal Takht.

"Sikhs are religiously, culturally, and linguistically distinct from Hindu India or any other nation," said Dr. Aulakh. "On this once-in-a-lifetime, milestone anniversary, let us dedicate ourselves to reclaiming our lost sovereignty," he said.

"Nations and religions that do not have political power do not survive," Dr. Aulakh said. "Under Indian rule, the Sikhs are the victims of genocide," he said.

Since 1984, the Indian government has murdered more than 250,000 Sikhs. Tens of thousands more languish in Indian jails without charge or trial. Some of the have been there since 1984. India has also murdered than 200,000 Christians in Nagaland since 1947, over 60,000 Muslims in Kashmir since 1988, and tens of thousands of Assamese, Manipuris, Tamils, Dalits ("black untouchables," the aboriginal people of the subcontinent), and others.

"The atrocities clearly show that for Sikhs, India is not a democracy," Said Dr. Aulakh. "Every day we pray Raj Kare Ga Khalsa,' the Khalsa shall rule," he said. "It is time to keep our promise to the Guru, live up to our heritage, and unite to liberate Khalistan," he said.

***

Document

CONGRESSIONAL RECORD -- EXTENSIONS

Wednesday, March 24, 1999
106th Congress, 1st Session
145 Cong Rec E 544

REFERENCE: Vol. 145, No. 47
TITLE: SIKHS WILL CELEBRATE 300TH ANNIVERSARY--AMERICA
SHOULD SUPPORT SIKH FREEDOM

HON. EDOLPHUS TOWNS
of New York
in the House of Representatives
Wednesday, March 24, 1999

Mr. TOWNS. Mr. Speaker, this April marks a very significant occasion, the 300th anniversary of the Sikh Nation. The occasion will be celebrated with a big march in Washington, with prayers, and in many other ways. Let us join with the Sikhs on this auspicious occasion and pray that they will soon enjoy the same freedom in their homeland, Punjab, Khalistan, that we enjoy here in America.

I would like to congratulate the Sikh Nation on this major milestone, which was brought to my attention by Dr. Gurmit Singh Aulakh, President of the Council of Khalistan. Many of us have been made aware of the brutal oppression of the Sikhs by the Indian government due to Dr. Aulakh's tireless efforts. I am pleased to note that Dr. Aulakh's office is organizing the march.

There are half of a million Sikhs in the United States. They have added to the richness of American life in many aspects of life and work. They have been productive, proud, law-abiding Americans. The Sikhs came to this country to enjoy the freedom that has made America the great country that it is. On this very special occasion for he Sikh Nation, let us honor those fine Americans by taking steps to help their Sikh brothers and sisters in Punjab, Khalistan enjoy the same freedom. That is the best way to prevent another Bosnia or Kosovo in South Asia.

Make no mistake, Mr. Speaker, there is no freedom for Sikhs, Christians, Muslims, Dalits, or other minorities in India today. The Indian government continues to practice a brutal oppression that has taken tens of thousands of Sikh, Christian, Muslim, and other human lives. Yet this brutal country continues to be among the top five recipients of U.S. aid.

Why are we using tax dollars to support this repressive government? Even with our budget surplus, this is a bad use of taxpayers' money. We should cut off this aid and declare our support for self-determination in the Indian subcontinent. The Sikhs of Khalistan, the Muslims of Kashmir, the Christians of Nagaland, and others seek only to decide their futures in the democratic way, by voting. As the beacon of freedom in the world, it is our moral duty to support this struggle for freedom. Let us take the occasion of the Sikh Nation's 300th anniversary to commit ourselves to full support for freedom for all people, starting with these few simple measures.

***

Document

CONGRESSIONAL RECORD -- EXTENSIONS

Wednesday, March 24, 1999
106th Congress, 1st Session
145 Cong Rec E 548

REFERENCE: Vol. 145, No. 47
TITLE: CHRISTIAN VILLAGE BURNED BY HINDUS--WAVE OF SECULAR
VIOLENCE GOES BACK TO CHRISTMAS DAY

HON. EDOLPHUS TOWNS
of New York
in the House of Representatives
Wednesday, March 24, 1999

Mr. TOWNS. Mr. Speaker, I was very distressed to see an article in the March 19 issue of the New York Times reporting that in the village of Ranaloi in India, a mob chanting "Victory to Lord Ram" burned down 157 of 250 homes of Christians. I thank my good friend Dr. Gurmit Singh Aulakh for calling my attention to this atrocity, which unfortunately is not an isolated incident but part of a wave of anti-Christian violence that began on Christmas Day.

Since Christmas, several Christian churches, prayer halls, and religious missions were destroyed by Hindu extremists affiliated with the Bajrang Dal, a part of the VHP, a militant Hindu organization that belongs to the same family of organizations as the ruling BJP. The VHP also praised the Hindus who raped four nuns, calling them "patriotic youth" and denouncing the nuns as "antinational elements." In January a missionary and his two very young sons were burned to death in their jeep by a gang of Hindus chanting "Victory to Hannuman," then another nun was raped. In early February the bodies of two more Christians have been found in the state of Orissa. At least four priests have been murdered. In 1997, police broke up a Christian religious festival with gunfire. A country that engages in such practices should be declared a religious oppressor and perhaps a terrorist state.

This latest incident took place during the period of Lent, leading up to Easter. With Easter coming in April, followed soon after by the 300th anniversary of the Sikh Nation, we may now have the best opportunity to raise the consciousness of the world to the religious tyranny that exists just under the veneer of Indian democracy.

Although India has democratic elections, for Christians, Sikhs, Muslims, Dalits, and so many others, there is no democracy. No matter who they elect, the result is more killing and more oppression. Is this true democracy? As I have said before, this is not democracy, It is merely the opportunity to choose one's oppressors.

The only solution is freedom for all the people of South Asia. As the world's only superpower and the beacon of freedom for the world, the United States must do whatever it can to extend the blessings of liberty to all people living under tyrannical, intolerant leaders, even if they claim to be democratic. We should stop funding this repressive government with American aid, impose economic sanctions as we did against the apartheid regime in South Africa, and go on record urging India to allow a plebiscite--a free, democratic vote--in Punjab, Khalistan, in Kashmir, in Christian Nagaland, and throughout their polyglot state to decide the future political status of these regions. This is the only way to end the genocide, settle the differences, and finally bring lasting peace to this troubled tinderbox known as South Asia.

Freedom is not only America's founding principle, it is our mission. Let us carry that mission to the deserving peoples and nations of the subcontinent. We look forward to the day when the glow of freedom shines on all the people of South Asia and the world.

From The New York Times, Mar. 19, 1999
157 Homes Burned in Religious Clash in India
(By Celia W. Dugger)

Bhubaneswar, India, March 18.--Less than two months after a Hindu mob killed a Christian missionary from Australia and his two young sons here in the eastern state of Orissa, Hindus and Christians clashed in a village this week, and 157 of the 250 Christian homes were burned down, state officials say.

The officials said they presumed that Hindus set the fires on Tuesday, but have no solid evidence. Christian villagers interviewed by television reporters blamed Hindus, who they said shouted "Victory to Lord Ram," a Hindu god, as they set the fires. Thirteen people were wounded, three by gunfire, and the police have arrested more than 40 people, officials said.

The tensions in the village--Ranaloi, in southern Orissa-- developed after someone painted a trident, symbol of the Hindu god Shiva, over a Christian cross on a boulder about a mile outside the village.

The violence is part of a growing number of attacks on Christians in India in the last year. Church officials and opposition political parties say the problem has worsened since the Hindu nationalist Bharatiya Janata Party became the head of a national coalition Government a year ago. Party leaders say they oppose the violence.

It is not clear who was responsible for the violence in Orissa, which is governed by the Congress Party. The state's Chief Minister, J.B. Patnaik, resigned after the killing of the missionary, Graham Staines, and his sons, Timothy, 10, and Philip, 6.

D.P. Wadhwa, the Indian Supreme Court Justice who was named by the Government to head an inquiry into the Staines killings, harshly criticized the central Government for failing to provide resources to investigate. The commission of inquiry, which was set up six weeks ago, is due to issue its findings in two weeks but has yet to field a team of independent investigators or to be given functional offices to work from.

The state police blamed a mob that they said was led by a man from the Bajrang Dal, a Hindu nationalist youth group that belongs to the same family of Hindu nationalist organizations as the Bharatiya Janata Party.

Leaders of the Bajrang Dal denied involvement, and said the violence was a backlash against what they called the Christians' deceitful efforts to convert impoverished, illiterate Indians.

***

Document

CONGRESSIONAL RECORD -- EXTENSIONS

Thursday, March 18, 1999
106th Congress, 1st Session
145 Cong Rec E 495

REFERENCE: Vol. 145, No. 43
TITLE: HAPPY 300TH ANNIVERSARY TO THE SIKH NATION

HON. JOHN T. DOOLITTLE
of California
in the House of Representatives
Thursday, March 18, 1999

Mr. DOOLITTLE. Mr. Speaker, Dr. Gurmit Singh Aulakh, President of the Council of Khalistan, has brought it to my attention that on April 13, the Sikhs will be celebrating their 300th anniversary. Sikhs have been significant contributors to America in several sectors of life, but their anniversary is significant for another reason. The Sikh Nation is currently one of several nations struggling to reclaim its freedom from Hindu India.

It is an interesting coincidence that April 13, the Sikhs' anniversary, is also the birthday of Thomas Jefferson, the author of our Declaration of Independence. This symmetry of events highlights the Sikh Nation's desire to be free. It is time that the Sikhs enjoy the freedom that we enjoy here in America.

In the Declaration of Independence, Jefferson wrote that all people "are endowed by their Creator with certain unalienable rights; that among these are life, liberty, and the pursuit of happiness; that whenever any form of government becomes destructive of these ends, it is the right of the people to alter or abolish it." In India, the government allows

70,000 Sikh political prisoners to rot in jail without charge or trial, some since 1984. They should be released on or before April 13 as a goodwill gesture. Instead, I fear that even more Sikhs will be endangered as "democratic, secular" India tries to maintain what it calls its "territorial integrity."

In the spirit of Jefferson, let the 300th anniversary of the Sikh Nation be an occasion to do whatever we can to support the Sikhs and the other nations of South Asia in their struggle to live in the glow of freedom. By stopping U.S. aid to India (which is one of the top five recipient countries) until human rights are universally respected, by declaring our support for self-determination through a free and fair plebiscite, and by imposing the same sanctions on India that we would impose on any other religious oppressor, we can share the blessings of liberty with the people of South Asia. This is the best thing that we can do to celebrate this important occasion with the Sikh Nation.

***

Document

CONGRESSIONAL RECORD -- EXTENSIONS

Wednesday, March 17, 1999
106th Congress, 1st Session
145 Cong Rec E 473

REFERENCE: Vol. 145, No. 42
TITLE: CONGRESSMAN RECEIVES LETTER FROM CHRISTIANS OF NAGALAND: AMERICA SHOULD SUPPORT SELF-DETERMINATION IN SOUTH ASIA

HON. EDOLPHUS TOWNS
of New York
in the House of Representatives
Wednesday, March 17, 1999

Mr. TOWNS. Mr. Speaker, Dr. Gurmit Singh Aulakh, President of the Council of Khalistan, recently delivered to me a letter from the government-in-exile of Nagaland praising my previous statement of February 11 on the oppression of Christians in India. The letter also calls for self-determination for all the nations of South Asia.

In the letter, the Prime Minister of Nagaland quotes Secretary of State Albright as a supporter of self-determination. On February 24, the Washington Post quoted the Secretary of State as saying, "ethnic groups demanding independence should be allowed to have their own nations." Currently, there are 17 freedom movements within India's borders. Yet the government of India refuses even to allow the Sikhs of Khalistan, the Christians of Nagaland, the Muslims of Kashmir, and the people of the other nations they occupy to decide this issue in a free and fair vote, the way that democratic countries decide these things. Instead, they have resorted to state terrorism against the people in these occupied nations.

Recently, there has been a wave of violence against Christians in India. Christians are merely the target of the moment. Sikhs, Muslims, Daltis (dark-skinned aboriginal people), and others have been subjected to similar violence.

Numerous Christian churches and other religious facilities have been destroyed since Christmas by Hindu extremists affiliated with the ruling BJP. A missionary and his two young sons were burned to death. Nuns have been raped. Priests have been murdered. A Christian religious festival was broken up by gunfire. Is this Indian secularism?

The Indian government has killed more than 200,000 Christians since 1947 and the Christians of Nagaland, in the eastern part of India, are involved in one of 17 freedom movements within India's borders. India has murdered more than 250,000 Sikhs since 1984 and over 60,000 Muslims in Kashmir since 1988, as well as many thousands of other people.

The holiest shrine in the Sikh religion, the Golden Temple in Amritsar, was attacked by the Indian government. Gurdev Singh Kaunke, who was serving as Jathedar of the Akal Takht, the highest Sikh religious official, was killed in police custody by being torn in half. The police disposed of his body. He had been tortured before the Indian government decided to kill him. The very highly revered Babri mosque was destroyed by Hindu militants.

Next month marks two occasions, falling on the same day, that should bring these issues into focus: the 300th anniversary of the Sikh Nation and the birthday of Thomas Jefferson. It is an ironic coincidence that these anniversaries fall at the same time.

Thomas Jefferson was one of the leading voices for American independence and wrote the Declaration of Independence, which sets out the philosophical basis for the freedom that we built into our Constitution and that we enjoy today. In light of this religious oppression and the statements of Secretary Albright and others, I urge the Congress to take strong measures in support of self-determination in South Asia. We should put ourselves on record in support of a free and fair plebiscite in Punjab, Khalistan, in Kashmir, in Nagaland, and everywhere that people are demanding the right to determine their own future. We should impose the sanctions appropriate under the law for countries that practice religious oppression and violence. We should strongly urge the President to declare India a terrorist state. Finally, we should cut off U.S. aid to India until it begins to behave like a democracy and respects basic human rights, including the right to self-determination.

Mr. Speaker, I would like to place the letter from the Prime Minister of Nagaland in the Record.

Prime Minister (Ato-Kilonser),
Government of the People's Republic of Nagaland
March 12, 1999.

Hon. Edolphus Towns,
House of Representatives,
Washington, DC.
(Through our good friend Dr. Gurmit Singh Aulakh,
President, Council of Khalistan, 1901 Pennsylvania Ave. NW,
Suite 802, Washington, DC 20006)

Respected Sir: Dr. Gurmit Singh Aulakh sent us the proceedings and debates of the 106th Congress (First Session) dated Washington 11 February 1999. We have gone through your presentation, Hindu Nationalist Continue To Attack Christians in "Secular" India, with much appreciation and love.

In the light of the assertion of the truth made by U.S. Secretary of State Madeleine Albright "that ethnic groups demanding independence should be allowed to have their own nations" (as told to the Washington Post in Paris on 24 February 1999), your statement that "we should openly declare U.S. support for self-determination for all the peoples of the subcontinent. By these measures we can help bring religious freedom and basic human rights to Christians, Sikhs, Muslims, and everyone else in South Asia" makes a lot of sense. Indeed, this is what the Indian-suppressed peoples have been wishing for all these years.

That, Sir, the principled stand you and other policy-makers of the U.S. have taken in this all-important matter has inspired many nationalities and ethnic groups that continue to languish in the merciless world of religious persecution and political suppression. Kindly accept the heartfelt gratitude of the Naga people.

Even as the Naga people pray with renewed hearts for their suffering brothers and sisters belonging to the Christian, Dalit, Muslim and Sikh communities, it is our request that you presevere in your fight for the rights of these oppressed nations and peoples to freedom and justice. May God bless you richly in your endeavor.

Respectfully yours, Th. Muivah.

***

Document

CONGRESSIONAL RECORD -- EXTENSIONS

Tuesday, March 2, 1999
106th Congress, 1st Session
145 Cong Rec E 313

REFERENCE: Vol. 145, No. 32
TITLE: CHRISTIANS ATTACKED IN INDIA

HON. JOHN T. DOOLITTLE
of California
in the House of Representatives
Tuesday, March 2, 1999

Mr. DOOLITTLE. Mr. Speaker, James Madison, the primary author of the U.S. Constitution, warned about "the tyranny of the majority." The modern state of India is an example of what Madison warned us about. Between Christmas and New Year, several Christian churches, prayer halls, and missionary schools were attacked by extremist Hindu mobs affiliated with the parent organization of India's ruling Bharatiya Janata Party (BJP).

The Washington Post reported on January 1 that ten such attacks occurred the week between Christmas and New Year's Day. Six people were injured in one of these attacks. The Vishwa Hindu Parishad (VHP), or World Hindu Council, appears to be responsible for the attacks. The BJP is the political wing of the VHP.

The Hindu militants are apparently upset that Christians are converting low-caste Hindus. Their frustration does not justify acts of violence.

Christian activists report that there were more than 60 recorded cases of church and Bible-burning, rape, and other attacks in 1998 alone, including the recent rape of four nuns. The VHP called the rapists "patriotic youth."

In 1997 and 1998, four priests were murdered. In the fall of 1997, a Christian festival was stopped when the police opened fire. Clearly, there is a pattern here. However, Christians are not the only victims of India's tyrannical "democracy."

Muslims have seen their most revered mosques destroyed; Sikhs have seen their most sacred shrine, the Golden Temple in Amritsar, attacked and remain under occupation by plainclothes police. Their spiritual leader, the Jathedar of the Akal Takht, Gurdev Singh Kaunke, was tortured and killed in police custody. Although there is a witness to this murder, no action has been taken against those responsible. Is this the secular democracy that India is so proud of?

The United States is the beacon of freedom to the world. As such, we cannot sit idly by and watch India trample on the religious freedom of its minorities. We should put this Congress on record in support of peaceful, democratic freedom movements in South Asia and throughout the world.

The United States recently allowed Puerto Rico to vote on its status; our Canadian neighbors held a similar referendum in Quebec. When do the Sikhs of Khalistan, the Muslims of Kashmir, and the other peoples living under Indian rule get their chance to exercise this basic democratic right? Will we support democratic freedom for the people of South Asia, or will we look away while the tyranny of the majority continues to suppress fundamental rights like freedom of religion?

***

Document

CONGRESSIONAL RECORD -- EXTENSIONS

Thursday, February 11, 1999
106th Congress, 1st Session
145 Cong Rec E 212

REFERENCE: Vol. 145, No. 25
TITLE: HINDU NATIONALISTS CONTINUE TO ATTACK CHRISTIANS IN
"SECULAR" INDIA

HON. EDOLPHUS TOWNS
of New York
in the House of Representatives
Thursday, February 11, 1999

Mr. TOWNS. Mr. Speaker, I was disturbed by recent reports that there has been renewed violence against Christians in India. First a missionary and his two very young sons were burned to death in their jeep, then another nun was raped. Now the bodies of two more Christians have been found in the state of Orissa. Hindu nationalism is on an out- of-control rampage in India!

The Sunday, February 7 issue of the Washington Times reported that the Archbishop of New Delhi, Alan de Lastic, blamed "mercenaries" for these hate crimes. He called on the government to take strong action to stop these things from occurring. These "mercenaries" are associated with organizations like the Vishwa Hindu Parishad (VHP), a militant Hindu organization that comes under the militant, extremist Rashtria Swayamsevak Sangh (RSS). The Bharatiya Janata Party (BJP), the party that leads the governing coalition, is also part of the RSS.

Several Christian churches, prayer halls, and religious missions were destroyed in the last couple of months by Hindu extremists affiliated with the VHP. How can the Indian government be expected to take strong action against the perpetrators of these vicious acts when the perpetrators are part of their own political network?

The violence forced many Christian congregations to cancel New Year's celebrations for fear of offending the Hindu militants, which could lead to further violence. Is this the secularism that India boasts about? Clearly, there is no religious freedom for these Christians in India.

Unfortunately, these are just the latest incidents of violence against Christians in India. Four nuns were raped last year by a Hindu gang. The VHP described the rapists as "patriotic youth" and called the nuns "antinational elements." To be Christian in secular India is to be an antinational element! At least three priests were killed in 1997 and 1998, and in 1997 police opened fire on a Christian festival that was promoting the theme "Jesus is the Answer."

Apparently, the Hindu Nationalists are afraid that the Dalits, or "Un-touchables", the aboriginal people of South Asia who are at the bottom of the caste structure, are switching to other religions, primarily Christianity, thus improving their status. This undermines the caste structure which is the foundation of the Hindu social structure.

The Indian government has killed more than 200,000 Christians since 1947 and the Christians of Nagaland, in the eastern part of India, are involved in one of 17 freedom movements within India's borders. But the Christians are not the only ones oppressed for their religion.

India has murdered more than 250,000 Sikhs since 1984 and over 60,000 Muslims in Kashmir since 1988, as well as many thousands of other people. The holiest shrine in the Sikh religion, the Golden Temple in Amritsar, is still under occupation by plainclothes police, some 14 years after India's brutal military attack on the Golden Temple. The previous Jathedar of the Akal Takht, Gurdev Singh Kaunke, was killed in police custody by being torn in half. The police disposed of his body. He had been tortured before the Indian government decided to kill him.

The Babri mosque, the most sacred Muslim shrine in the state of Uttar Pradesh, was destroyed by the Hindu militants who advocate building a Hindu Temple on the site. Yet India proudly boasts that it is a religiously tolerant, secular democracy.

This kind of religious oppression does not deserve American support. We should take tough measures to ensure that India learns to respect basic human rights. All U.S. aid to India should be cut off and we should openly declare U.S. support for self-determination for all the peoples of the subcontinent. By these measures we can help bring religious freedom and basic human rights to Christians, Sikhs, Muslims, and everyone else in South Asia.

Mr. Speaker, I submit an article on the archbishop's statement from the February 7 Washington Times into the Record.

From the Washington Times, February 7, 1999
Mercenaries Blamed for Attacks in India

New Delhi--A prominent Catholic archbishop yesterday blamed "mercenaries" for a spate of attacks on Christians here and blamed the Indian government or tardy action against the perpetrators.

New Delhi Archbishop Alan de Lastic, in a scathing attack on national and state governments, called for justice for the growing number of Christian victims of murder, rape and battery in India.

A nun was raped Wednesday night in the eastern state of Orissa where Australian missionary Graham Staines and his two young sons were burnt to death in their car by a Hindu mob on January 22.

The rape and the Staines' murders followed a spate of anti- Christian violence in the western state of Gujarat over Christmas.

Radical Hindu groups linked to Prime Minister Atal Behari Vajyapee's ruling BJP party have been blamed for inciting the attacks.

***

Document

CONGRESSIONAL RECORD -- EXTENSIONS

Wednesday, January 20, 1999
106th Congress, 1st Session
145 Cong Rec E 77

REFERENCE: Vol. 145, No. 9
TITLE: SIKH LEADER WRITES ON REPRESSION OF CHRISTIANS

HON. EDOLPHUS TOWNS
of New York
in the House of Representatives
Tuesday, January 19, 1999

Mr. TOWNS. Mr. Speaker, as you know, there has been a recent wave of attacks by Hindu Nationalists on Christian churches, prayer halls, and schools. This has followed the killings of priests, the raping of four nuns by a Hindu mob described by the Hindu Nationalist VHP as "patriotic youth." Just this week, more churches have been attacked. No action has been taken to stop the religious violence. This situation has made it clear to the world that India's claims of democracy and secularism are fraudulent.

In this light, it was encouraging to see a letter in the January 18 issue of the Washington Times by Dr. Gurmit Singh Aulakh, President of the council of Khalistan, that addresses this issue. We all know Dr. Aulakh to be a tough and fair advocate of independence for the Sikhs in Khalistan, who have also come under the tyranny of Indian "secularism." I would recommend to my colleagues that they read Dr. Aulakh's letter. It will give them a lot of information on the reality of religious repression in India. As Dr. Aulakh wrote, "These attacks show that religious freedom in India is a myth."

Christians, Sikhs, and Muslims have suffered at the hands of India's ruling elite. As the letter shows, they are all being murdered by the Indian government. That government has paid more than 41,000 cash bounties to police officers for killing Sikhs. Meanwhile, Amnesty International and other independent human-rights monitors have been kept out of India since 1978, even longer than Communist Cuba has kept them out.

A country that kills its minorities for their ethnic or religious identity is not a fit recipient of American support. As the only superpower and the leader of the world, we have a duty to do whatever we can to support the cause of freedom in South Asia.

We should cut off American aid and trade to India until human rights, including religious liberty, are secure and regularly practiced. We should declare India a violator of religious freedom and impose the sanctions appropriate to that status. And to ensure the safety of religious and political freedom in South Asia, we should declare our support for the 17 freedom movements within India's borders. We can start by calling for full self-determination for the Sikhs of Khalistan, the Muslims of Kashmir, and the Christians of Nagaland. These steps will help bring the people of South Asia the kind of freedom that we in America enjoy.

Mr. Speaker, I would like to introduce Dr. Aulakh's letter in the January 18 Washington Times into the Record.

From the Washington Times, Jan. 18, 1999
India Continues to Restrict Religious Freedom
(By Gurmit Singh Aulakh)

Thank you for your editorial ("Mother Teresa's children," Jan. 10) exposing more than 90 attacks on Christians since the Bharatiya Janata Party (BJP) came to power last year. These attacks show that religious freedom in India is a myth.

Just when we thought the recent wave of attacks on Christians in India was over, your editorial exposed the burning of two more churches by Hindu mobs affiliated with the Vishwa Hindu Parishad, part of the Rashtriya Swayamsevak Sangh, a militant Hindu nationalist organization that is also the parent organization of the ruling (BJP).

It is not just Christians who have suffered from persecution and violence in the hands of the Indian government. Sikhs and Muslims, among others, have been victimized as well. In August 1997, Narinder Singh, a spokesman for the Golden Temple in Amritsar, the center and seat of the Sikh religion, told National Public Radio: "The Indian government, all the time they boast that they're democratic, they're secular, but they have nothing to do with a democracy, they have nothing to do with secularism. They try to crush Sikhs just to please the majority."

The Indian government has killed more than 200,000 Christians since 1947. It has also murdered more than 250,000 Sikhs since 1984, over 60,000 Muslims in Kashmir since 1988 and tens of thousands of other religious and ethnic minorities. The most revered mosque in India has been destroyed to build a Hindu Temple. Police murdered the highest Sikh spiritual and religious leader, Akal Takht Jathedar Gurdev Singh Kaunke, and human rights activist Jaswant Singh Khalra. There are police witnesses to both of these crimes. The U.S. State Department reported that between 1992 and 1994 the Indian government paid more than 41,000 cash bounties to police for killing Sikhs. Plainclothes police continue to occupy the Golden Temple. There have been more than 200 reported atrocities against Sikhs since the Akali/Dal/BJP government took power in March 1997.

It is not just the BJP that has practiced religious tyranny in pursuit of a Hindu theocracy in India. Many of these incidents came under the rule of the Congress Party. No matter who is in power, the minorities in India suffer from severe oppression. The only solution is to support self-determination for the peoples and nations of South Asia, so they can live in freedom, peace, prosperity and security.

India is not a single country; it is a polyglot empire that was thrown together by the British for their political convenience. Its breakup is inevitable. As the world's only superpower, the United States has a responsibility to make sure this process is peaceful, as it was for the Soviet Union and Czechoslovakia. Otherwise, a Bosnia will be created in South Asia.

Thank you for exposing the true nature of India's "secular democracy." Exposing these brutal practices will help bring true freedom to South Asia.

***

Document

CONGRESSIONAL RECORD -- EXTENSIONS

Thursday, January 7, 1999
106th Congress, 1st Session
145 Cong Rec E 57

REFERENCE: Vol. 145, No. 2
TITLE: HINDU NATIONALISTS DESTROY CHRISTIAN CHURCHES IN "SECULAR" INDIA

HON. EDOLPHUS TOWNS
of New York
in the House of Representatives
Wednesday, January 6, 1999

Mr. TOWNS. Mr. Speaker, I was disturbed by recent reports that several Christian churches, prayer halls, and religious missions have recently been destroyed by Hindu extremists affiliated with the Vishwa Hindu Parishad (VHP), a militant Hindu organization. The Bharatiya Janata Party (BJP), the party that leads the governing coalition, is also part of the VHP.

The violence forced many Christian congregations to cancel New Year's celebrations for fear of offending the Hindu militants, which could lead to further violence. Is this the secularism that India boasts about? Clearly, there is no religious freedom for these Christians in India.

Unfortunately, these are just the latest incidents of violence against Christians in India. Four nuns were raped last year by a Hindu gang. The VHP described the rapists as "patriotic youth" and called the nuns "antinational elements." To be Christian in secular India is to be an antinational element! At least three priests were killed in 1997 and 1998, and in 1997 police opened fire on a Christian festival that was promoting the theme "Jesus is the Answer."

Apparently, the Hindu Nationalists are afraid that the Dalits, or "Untouchables", the aboriginal people of South Asia who are at the bottom of the caste structure, are switching to other religions, primarily Christianity, thus improving their status. This undermines the caste structure which is the foundation of the Hindu social structure.

The Indian government has killed more than 200,000 Christians since 1947 and the Christians of Nagaland, in the eastern part of India, are involved in one of 17 freedom movements within India's borders. But the Christians are not the only ones oppressed for their religion.

India has murdered more than 250,000 Sikhs since 1984 and over 60,000 Muslims in Kashmir since 1988, as well as many thousands of other people. The holest shrine in the Sikh religion, the Golden Temple in Amritsar, is still under occupation by plainclothes police, some 14 years after India's brutal military attack on the Golden Temple. The previous Jathedar of the Akal Takht, Gurdev Singh Kaunke, was killed in police custody by being torn in half. The police disposed of his body. He had been tortured before the Indian government decided to kill him.

The Babri mosque, the most sacred Muslim shrine in the state of Uttar Pradesh, was destroyed by the Hindu militants who advocate building a Hindu Temple on the site. Yet India proudly boasts that it is a religiously tolerant, secular democracy.

This kind of religious oppression does not deserve American support. We should take tough measures to ensure that India learns to respect basic human rights. All U.S. aid to India should be cut off and we should openly declare U.S. support for self-determination for all the peoples of the subcontinent. By these measures we can help bring religious freedom and basic human rights to Christians, Sikhs, Muslims, and everyone else in South Asia.

Mr. Speaker, I would like to introduce Press reports on the attacks on Christian religious institutions into the Record.

From the Washington Post, January 3, 1999
Hindus Blamed for Attacks on Christians

New Delhi.--India's main opposition Congress party said a wave of attacks on Christians appeared to be a campaign by Hindu right-wing groups to whip up conflict.

Police detained 45 Hindus Friday in connection with torching a Catholic prayer hall by mobs Wednesday. Four nuns and two priests were injured in the 10th reported attack against Christians since Christmas.

No one has claimed responsibility for the attacks in the western state of Gujarat, but Congress and Christian activists blame Hindu right-wing activists, including the Vishwa Hindu Parishad--World Hindu Council-- and its affiliate, Bajrang Dal. Christians make up 2.3 percent of the 960 million people in politically secular India. More than 80 percent of the population are Hindus.

- - - - - - - - -

From the Washington Post, December 31, 1998
Indian Christians Cancel New Year Services

Mulchand, Indian.--Christian congregations in western India are canceling New Year prayer services this year, fearful of provoking more violence from radical Hindus who already have destroyed a dozen churches. The violence has put the governing Bharatiya Janata Party (BJP) in the awkward position of needing to protect India's Christian minority from groups affiliated with the Hindu nationalist party. Since Friday, mobs armed with axes, iron bars, hammers and stones have attacked 18 churches, prayer halls or Christian schools.

***

Dr. Gurmit S. Aulakh with President Ronald Reagan

Dr. Gurmit S. Aulakh with President George W. Bush (Sr)

To Gurmit
Best Wishes

Dr. Gurmit S. Aulakh with President George W. Bush (Jr.)

Dr. Gurmit S. Aulakh with President George W. Bush (Sr) and First Lady Barbara Bush

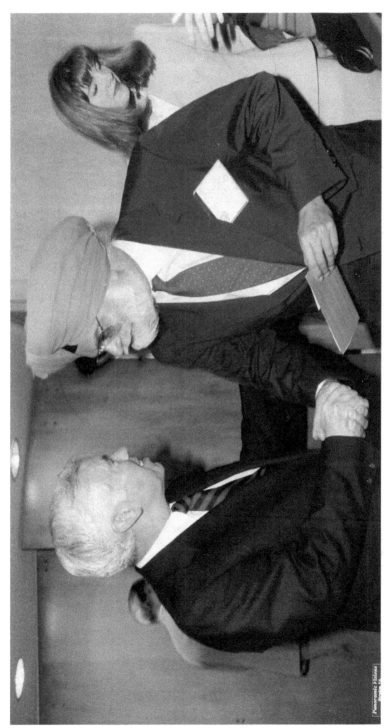

Dr. Gurmit S. Aulakh with Senator Richard Lugar

Dr. Gurmit S. Aulakh with CEO of Forbes, Inc., Steve Forbes

Dr. Gurmit S. Aulakh with Vice President Dan Quayle

To Gurmit Singh Aulakh With best wishes,

Ronald Reagan

Dr. Manohar Singh Grewal, President Ronal Reagan, Dr. Gurmit S. Aulakh

THE WHITE HOUSE

WASHINGTON

January 9, 1987

Dear Dr. Aulakh:

Thank you so very much for remembering me. Your thoughtful expression of concern is a great source of comfort and strength, and you were kind to have taken the time to drop me a line. It makes all the difference in the world to know that people like you are keeping me in their thoughts and prayers.

With my appreciation and warm best wishes,

Sincerely,

Ronald Reagan

Dr. Gurmit S. Aulakh
Post Office Box 10575
Rockville, Maryland 20850

*Letter of Appreciation by President Ronald Reagan
to Dr. Gurmit Singh Aulakh*

INDEX

printed in PRC

CPSIA information can be obtained
at www.ICGtesting.com
Printed in the USA
LVHW05s1135280418
575245LV00021B/338/P